Praise for *Handbook of Health Social Work, Second Edition*

"The major strength is the organization and comprehensive content of the book. This is a book that can serve as a reference book in any social worker's library, regardless of whether they are practicing in a health-care setting. There are no other books on this topic that are as comprehensive in scope as the *Handbook of Health Social Work, Second Edition*."

> **—Deborah Collinsworth, LAPSW, NSW-C,**
> **Director of Nephrology Social Work Services,**
> **Dialysis Clinics, Inc., West Tennessee**

"I'm quite impressed by the comprehensive nature of this revision. It's the enduring kind of text that serves an immediate purpose for social work instruction while also providing a reference for future practice. This is a book that you'll want to keep on your shelf."

> **—Kevin Lindamood,**
> **Vice President for External Affairs at Health Care for the Homeless,**
> **Adjunct Professor of Health Policy at the University of Maryland SSW**

"Sarah Gehlert and Teri Browne have thoughtfully covered the topics. The readers of this book will be empowered to deal with the daily challenges. It's simple but far reaching, a rich knowledge bank of social workers' interventions, and will benefit even policy makers in planning strategies to improve patients' quality of life."

> **—Sujata Mohan Rajapurkar, PhD,**
> **Medical Social Worker and Transplant Coordinator,**
> **Muljibhai Patel Urological Hospital, Gujarat, India**

"The book's strengths include the high quality of writing and the expertise of its contributors. It covers the field of health social work in significant depth and is sure to leave readers well informed."

> **—Mary Sormanti, PhD, MSW,**
> **Associate Professor of Professional Practice,**
> **Columbia University School of Social Work**

"Quite simply, this is the definitive volume for Health and Social Work. The first edition was well-executed, well-written, and comprehensive. In this second edition, Gehlert and Browne and their expert contributors have confidently managed to keep pace with current theory and empirical research across a wide range of subject matter that will be of interest to practitioners, educators, and researchers."

> **—Michael Vaughn, PhD,**
> **Assistant Professor, School of Social Work,**
> **School of Public Health,**
> **and Department of Public Policy Studies, Saint Louis University**

HANDBOOK OF HEALTH SOCIAL WORK

SECOND EDITION

Edited by

SARAH GEHLERT and
TERI BROWNE

WILEY
John Wiley & Sons, Inc.

Published by John Wiley & Sons, Inc., Hoboken, New Jersey.
Published simultaneously in Canada.

For general information on our other products and services, please contact our Customer Care Department within the U.S. at (800) 762-2974, outside the United States at (317) 572-3993 or fax (317) 572-4002.

Wiley also publishes its books in a variety of electronic formats. Some content that appears in print may not be available in electronic books. For more information about Wiley products, visit our Web site at www.wiley.com.

Library of Congress Cataloging-in-Publication Data:

Handbook of health social work / edited by Sarah Gehlert and Teri Browne. — 2nd ed.
    p. cm.
   Includes bibliographical references and index.
   ISBNs 978-0-470-64365-5; 978-1-118-11589-3; 978-1-118-11591-6; 978-118-11590-9
   1. Medical social work—Handbooks, manuals, etc.   I. Gehlert, Sarah, 1948-   II. Browne, Teri.
  HV687.A2H36 2012
  362.1'0425—dc22

                                                     2011010997

Printed in the United States of America

10 9 8 7 6 5 4 3 2

Contents

Foreword

It is both an exciting and a challenging time to be a social worker in the field of health. A diversity of roles is available for social workers. Areas of practice and opportunities for inter- and transdisciplinary collaborations are unprecedented in the history of the profession. Social workers along with other professionals are on the cutting edge of new health-relevant programs and practices, with social workers frequently in top leadership roles in these efforts. To note just a very few examples, social workers are providing genetic counseling and mental health treatment, coordinating hospice and palliative care, working with communities to develop better access to cancer care and clinical trials, advocating for and writing improved health-relevant policies, developing health programs and practices, and conducting research that provides an evidence base for effective practice in social work and other professions.

A number of events and trends have come to bear on this blossoming of social work in health. The Patient Protection and Affordable Care Act of 2010 (PPACA), itself the result of decades of advocacy and study on the part of many, including social workers, will radically change the context in which health care is delivered in the United States. This change will require profound and unsurpassed expertise in complex systems and their relationships to users of health care that is the domain of social workers. Effective implementation of the PPACA will require social work expertise at all levels, from front-line practitioner to policy maker and executive.

The evidence-based practice movement in social work and other health professions also has been integral to the rising importance of social work in health. From first-level, or T1, translation of research findings to cultural and community tailoring and dissemination and diffusion, social work has a principal role to play in getting health knowledge and knowledge-based practice to the populations that most can use it. Indeed, social work has been and will continue to be a key source of research producing such knowledge. As the profession is focused on improving people's well-being through practice that targets interrelationships among systems and people, social work research is of great consequence for knowledge production on which to base health-care reform and other efforts to improve health care in the United States. Thanks to the concerted and strategic efforts of academic social work and professional social work organizations, health social work research is growing and beginning to flourish.

The growth of the social determinants perspective on health has fostered a crucial place for social work in health. As a profession, social work has long understood the importance of multiple life dimensions and experiences as they affect human well-being across the life cycle and has built its practice on such a perspective. As other health professions catch up in this area, social work's contributions can be very influential in helping to prevent reinvention of the wheel in both health care and disease prevention.

I have noted just a few of the phenomena leading to social work's rich contributions to health and great potential for even more. As a postdoctoral fellow in applied anthropology, I once worked in a hospital setting on a geriatric consult team. Repeatedly I went to social work staff for information and advice. Indeed, my team (which included physicians, a nurse, and a pharmacologist) held to the mantra of "go ask a social worker, they know everything!" The breadth and depth of social work expertise in health is reflected in and supported by the material in the current work.

This volume is a crucial addition to the libraries of seasoned practitioners as well as an essential foundation for fledgling social workers ready to enter health as a practice and research area. Both editors are respected leaders in the field of health and social work with an abundance of experience, knowledge, and passion for their work. They have brought together a multiplicity of impressive contributors, all authorities in their respective areas, who share their knowledge and wisdom. The *Handbook*'s contributors address multiple theoretical foundations, models, issues, and dilemmas for the social worker in health.

Included are descriptions of skill sets and other expertise needed for direct practice clinicians, community workers, planners, policy makers, researchers, advocates, and administrators. The volume covers practice and research areas ranging from chronic disorders to infectious disease, from physical to mental disorders, and all the gray areas in between.

However, the book is not simply a how-to manual. Rather, it assesses the current state of the field while suggesting important new directions and developments for the future of social work in health. The ideas in this volume suggest that, perhaps, there is some truth to the sentiment that "social workers know everything." Certainly they know a great deal about working to improve health and about what will be needed in the future to improve the nation's health. At a time of great change in the United States in regard to facilitating the production of better health for populations and individuals, any social worker engaged in this area would be well advised to have this outstanding resource at hand.

Suzanne Heurtin-Roberts
Bethesda, Maryland

Acknowledgments

The preparation of the second edition of this *Handbook* involved the efforts of a number of people. First and foremost was Jerrod Liveoak, a very talented young man who again helped us organize and edit the *Handbook.* We could not have done it without his assistance. Rachel Livsey and Kara Borbely of John Wiley & Sons' behavioral science division were supportive throughout the process. We join them in mourning the loss of Lisa Gebo, a gifted member of the John Wiley & Sons team who worked with us on the first edition and lost her life to breast cancer on June 14, 2010. We also would like to thank these colleagues who reviewed the book and provided valuable feedback: Gary Rosenberg, Mount Sinai School of Medicine; Mary Sormanti, Columbia University; Judy Howe, Mount Sinai School of Medicine; Kevin Lindamood, University of Maryland; Deborah Collinsworth, Union University; and Michael Vaughn, St. Louis University. The 36 contributors to the *Handbook,* some of whom were friends and others known to us only by reputation prior to the collaboration, worked hard and were patient with this revision. Finally, we would like to thank our spouses, Roy Wilson and Lyle Browne, who were always willing to listen to our ideas and to provide feedback and support.

List of Contributors

Terry Altilio, MSW, ACSW
Beth Israel Medical Center
New York, New York

Wendy Auslander, PhD
Washington University
St. Louis, Missouri

Shantha Balaswamy, PhD
Ohio State University
Columbus, Ohio

Rose A. Bartone, MSW, LCSW-R
New York Medical College
Valhalla, New York

Candyce S. Berger, PhD
Stony Brook University
Stony Brook, New York

David S. Bimbi, PhD
LaGuardia Community College
Long Island City, New York

Penny B. Block, PhD
Block Center for Integrative Cancer Care
Evanston, Illinois

Sarah E. Bollinger, MSW, LCSW
Washington University
St. Louis, Missouri

Rebecca Brashler, MSW, LCSW
Rehabilitation Institute of Chicago
Chicago, Illinois

Teri Browne, PhD
University of South Carolina
Columbia, South Carolina

Yvette Colón, PhD, ACSW, BCD
American Pain Foundation
Baltimore, Maryland

Julie S. Darnell, PhD
University of Illinois at Chicago
Chicago, Illinois

Sadhna Diwan, PhD
San Jose State University
San Jose, California

Malitta Engstrom, PhD
University of Chicago
Chicago, Illinois

Iris Cohen Fineberg, PhD
Lancaster University
Lancaster, United Kingdom

Stacey Freedenthal, PhD
University of Denver
Denver, Colorado

Les Gallo-Silver, MSW, ACSW, CSW-R
LaGuardia Community College
Long Island City, New York

Daniel S. Gardner, PhD
New York University
New York, New York

Sarah Gehlert, PhD
Washington University
St. Louis, Missouri

Susan Hedlund, MSW, LCSW
Hospice of Washington County
Portland, Oregon

Suzanne Heurtin-Roberts, PhD, MSW
United States Department of Health and
    Human Services
Bethesda, Maryland

J. Aaron Hipp, PhD
Washington University
St. Louis, Missouri

Edward F. Lawlor, PhD
Washington University
St. Louis, Missouri

Sang E. Lee, PhD
San Jose State University
San Jose, California

Colleen A. Mahoney, PhD
University of Wisconsin
Madison, Wisconsin

Jeanne C. Marsh, PhD
University of Chicago
Chicago, Illinois

Christopher Masi, MD, PhD
University of Chicago
Chicago, Illinois

Shirley Otis-Green, MSW, ACSW, LCSW
City of Hope National Medical Center
Duarte, California

Kate Reed, MPH, ScM
National Coalition for Health Professional
    Education in Genetics
Lutherville, Maryland

John S. Rolland, MD
Chicago Center for Family Health
Chicago, Illinois

Marjorie R. Sable, DrPH
University of Missouri
Columbia, Missouri

Deborah R. Schild, PhD
Public Health Social Worker
Ann Arbor, Michigan

Jared Sparks, PhD
Ozark Guidance
Springdale, Arkansas

Nancy Boyd Webb, DSW, LICSW, RPT-S
Fordham University (retired)
New York, New York

Allison Werner-Lin, PhD
New York University
New York, New York

Terry A. Wolfer, PhD
University of South Carolina
Columbia, South Carolina

Introduction

In a faculty meeting a few years ago, a colleague from another profession referred to the "lower-level skills" of social workers in health care. She distinguished these skills from the "higher-level skills" of social workers in mental health settings. I addressed her comment by citing the broad array of information that social workers in health care must possess and be able to access quickly in order to assess client situations and devise optimal plans in the limited time available to them in health-care settings. I characterized the process as highly challenging, requiring skills at least as well developed as those of social workers in other arenas. This exchange between my colleague and me made me realize two things. First of all, health social work is not well understood by those working in other subfields of social work and other disciplines. Second, it would behoove health social work scholars to better define and represent the subfield.

As health care becomes increasingly more complex, social workers have much to know. We have yet to fully understand what the Patient Protection and Affordable Care Act that was enacted in March 2010 means for the health of the nation or what it means for social work practice and research. We do know that current federal approaches to addressing complicated health conditions like HIV/AIDS and cancer argue strongly for simultaneous attention to factors operating at the social, psychological, and biological levels (see, e.g., Warnecke et al., 2008). As members of health-care teams that take these approaches, social

workers must possess sufficient knowledge at the social, psychological, and biological levels to converse productively with other team members and to work in concert with them constructively. In addition, to be effective, social workers must be aware of how these factors operate with individuals, families, groups, communities, and societies. This awareness is best accomplished by engaging community stakeholders at many levels in research.

The *Handbook of Health Social Work* was developed to prepare students to work in the current health-care environment in which providers from a number of disciplines work more closely together than was ever the case in the past. Health care in the United States has moved from being multidisciplinary to being interdisciplinary, with the ultimate goal of being transdisciplinary. In multidisciplinary environments, professionals from different disciplines work on the same projects but speak their own languages, view health care through their own disciplinary lens, and often share knowledge with one another after the fact. Interdisciplinary teams interact more closely, but each discipline continues to operate within its own boundaries. Because an interdisciplinary approach almost never provides a broad enough view of health-care conditions to capture their inherent complexities, transdisciplinary teamwork has become the exemplar. Here health-care professionals work so closely together that they must develop a shared language and pool the best of their separate disciplinary theories. Absent this new, more interdependent approach, the team is reminiscent of the old cartoon of a roomful of blindfolded people touching different parts of an elephant, with each describing the beast based only on the part that she is touching. One might base his description on the trunk, another on the ears, and a third on the tail. To address complex health conditions like HIV/AIDS effectively, we must recognize the elephant in the room.

In 2009, my coeditor, Teri Browne, and I were asked by John Wiley & Sons if we would be interested in revising the *Handbook*. A good deal has changed on both the national and international fronts in the 4 years since the first edition was published. The mapping of the human genome in 2004 continues to change how we view and approach the treatment of disease. Our ability to treat some disorders has increased markedly. Over the four years between the first and second editions, increasing numbers of people lost their health-care coverage. Although health-care reform holds the potential to ensure that citizens have coverage, this is not true for those who are undocumented immigrants, and exactly how reform will impact the nation's steadily increasing health disparities remains a question.

These changes will continue, and require a great deal of flexibility on the part of health social workers. As was the case with the first edition of the *Handbook of Health Social Work,* the second edition considers social workers in health care to be active problem solvers who must draw from a variety of germane bodies of information to address the issues and problems faced by individuals, families, groups, communities, and societies. We believe that this approach allows flexibility and thus positions health social workers to deal optimally with a changing health-care environment. The authors and layout of the second edition reflect this approach. Learning exercises at the end of each chapter are designed to stimulate discussion and help readers process the information provided and consider it analytically. The book's chapters are sandwiched between a foreword by Suzanne Heurtin-Roberts and an afterword by Candyce Berger, both of whom

have broken ground as social work leaders in health-care practice and research and done much to raise the profile of the profession.

The book is divided into three sections. Part I, Foundations of Social Work in Health Care, provides information that we consider basic and central to the operations of social workers in health care. In Chapter 1, "Conceptual Underpinnings of Social Work in Health Care," Sarah Gehlert again discusses the principles that underlie the development of social work in health care and follows its course through time to discover any changes in principles and activities that may have occurred. Chapter 2, "Social Work Roles and Health-Care Settings," by Teri Browne, carefully outlines the wide array of roles performed by social workers in health-care settings today. After providing a framework for ethical decision making, Chapter 3, "Ethics and Social Work in Health Care," by Jared Sparks, again considers some key issues confronting social workers in health care in a variety of arenas, from practice with individuals to policy development. All three chapters take into account the unique challenges facing health care in the United States.

Public health social work recently was named as one of the top 50 professions by *U.S. News & World Report*, and training programs that combine the two continue to grow. Because of this, and because social work has for a long time played an integral role in the public health of the United States and other parts of the world, Chapter 4, titled "Public Health and Social Work," is an essential component of the *Handbook*, to orient readers to the public health perspective. J. Aaron Hipp, a community psychologist who works in a school of public health, joined health social workers Marjorie R. Sable and Deborah R. Schild in revising the chapter. The chapter introduces readers to the concepts of primary, secondary, and tertiary health care and considers health from a wider lens than is often used, including global patterns of health and disease. Chapter 5, "Health Policy and Social Work," written by Julie S. Darnell and Edward F. Lawlor, is almost totally revised from the first edition. It presents basic information on the interplay among clinical, administrative, and policy issues in health care. Although it is beyond the scope of this book to cover all possible health policies and considerations, an overview of the most pertinent policies and issues is provided. The authors address the likely sequelae of health care reform. Chapter 6, "Theories of Health Behavior," by Sarah Gehlert and Sarah E. Bollinger, outlines five key theories and methods that can help guide social work practice and research in health care. Empirical evidence for their use in certain situations is provided.

Part II is titled Health Social Work Practice: A Spectrum of Critical Considerations. Although cases and questions confronted by social workers in health care vary widely, certain critical issues should always be considered. The eight chapters in this part represent critical issues that should be considered in approaching cases or pursuing the answers to health-care questions, even though in time they may not prove to be germane to those cases or questions. Failing to consider issues such as religion, sexuality, or substance use may lead to incomplete understandings of cases or consideration of health-care questions. It was only after considering health beliefs, for instance, that Matsunaga and colleagues (1996) were able to understand why native Hawaiian women did not participate in breast cancer screening despite their high rates of breast cancer.

Because individuals and families do not operate independently but rather as parts of communities, an overview of the relationships between health and community factors is included in Part II. In Chapter 7, "Community and Health," Christopher Masi again reviews significant evidence-based data and provides information about how knowledge about community factors can be accessed and included in social work activities in health care. The complex interplay of physical and mental health is addressed in Chapter 8, "Physical and Mental Health: Interactions, Assessment, and Interventions." The chapter, again prepared by Malitta Engstrom, carefully outlines how to assess for mental health concerns and reviews a variety of interventions. In Chapter 9,

"Social Work Practice and Disability Issues," Rebecca Brashler again carefully frames social work practice with individuals and groups with disabilities and provides suggestions for practice. Because communication is central to the effective provision of heath care as it changes through time, the revised chapter titled "Communication in Health Care" is included as Chapter 10 in Part II of this *Handbook*. The chapter provides a basic framework for understanding the dynamics of health-care communication; reviews interventions for improving communication; considers the effect of culture, gender, race, and other salient factors on patient and provider communication; and provides guidelines for the use of interpreters. It also addresses the dynamics of health-care teams and social workers' positions on teams.

In Chapter 11, "Religion, Spirituality, Health, and Social Work," author Terry A. Wolfer, who is new to the *Handbook*, reviews the ways in which religion and spirituality affect health and individual and group responses to health care. Ways of incorporating religious and spiritual considerations into practice and policy are reviewed. Complementary and alternative treatments are reviewed in Chapter 12, "Developing a Shared Understanding: When Medical Patients Use Complementary and Alternative Approaches." Author Penny B. Block provides information on the extent of alternative and complementary treatments in the United States and reasons for their use. She reviews a number of treatments and their histories and addresses the importance for social workers of being familiar with complementary and alternative techniques. Chapter 13, "Families, Health, and Illness," again written by John S. Rolland, presents a framework for understanding the interplay between family structure and dynamics and health and addresses its implications for social work practice and policy in health care. Chapter 14, "Human Sexual Health," addresses the relationship between sexuality and health and discusses ways to incorporate sexual and other intimate considerations into practice and policy. Authors Les Gallo-Silver and David S. Bimbi make the point that sexual and other intimate issues are more likely to be faced by social workers in health care than in other areas of practice.

Part III, Health Social Work: Selected Areas of Practice, contains nine chapters by social workers with extensive practice and academic experience. Selecting the areas to include was difficult, and the list is not meant to be exhaustive. Our aim was to present a range of examples of good social work practice in sufficient detail to provide a reasonable overview of social work practice in health care. The second edition of the *Handbook* includes a new chapter devoted to health social work practice with young patients: Chapter 15, "Social Work With Children and Adolescents With Medical Conditions," by seasoned authors Nancy Boyd Webb and Rose A. Bartone. Chapter 16, "Social Work With Older Adults in Health-Care Settings," outlines the issues central to practice with older adults and the challenges faced by social workers. Sang E. Lee joins Sadhna Diwan and Shantha Balaswamy as an author of the revised chapter. Because substance use is widespread today and can negatively affect health and response to treatment, it is important that social workers consider the topic in practice and policy. The revised Chapter 17, titled "Substance Use Problems in Health Social Work Practice," again written by Malitta Engstrom, Colleen A. Mahoney, and Jeanne C. Marsh, carefully outlines the importance of considering substance use and abuse and provides guidelines for incorporation into practice and policy.

After providing background on end-stage renal disease and its psychosocial sequelae, in Chapter 18, "Nephrology Social Work," Teri Browne reviews evidence-based social work interventions, policies and programs, and resources and organizations available to nephrology social workers. In Chapter 19, "Oncology Social Work," Daniel S. Gardner joins Allison Werner-Lin as an author in the revised chapter. The chapter reviews psychosocial issues faced by patients with cancer and their families. Practice considerations are outlined and suggestions for interventions provided.

Issues of chronic illness are addressed by Wendy Auslander and Stacey Freedenthal in the revised and retitled Chapter 20, "Adher-

ence and Mental Health Issues in Chronic Disease: Diabetes, Heart Disease, and HIV/AIDS." Chronic conditions present a number of unique challenges to social workers, such as how to improve adherence to treatment recommendations. The authors outline these challenges and make suggestions for practice. Chapter 21, "Social Work and Genetics," has been revised in light of myriad advances in our understanding of genetics and health that have occurred in the last several years. Kate Reed, from the National Coalition for Health Professional Education in Genetics, joins Allison Werner-Lin as an author of the chapter, which considers the role of social workers in helping patients and families learn and make decisions about genetic testing and cope with its results.

The management of pain in acute and chronic illness increasingly has become the domain of social workers in health care. Chapter 22, "Pain Management and Palliative Care," orients readers to the effect of pain on behavior and functioning and reviews roles for social workers in pain management and palliative care teams. Terry Altilio, Shirley Otis-Green, Susan Hedlund, and Iris Cohen Fineberg are authors of the chapter. Finally, Chapter 23, "End-of-Life Care," again by Yvette Colón, discusses how social workers can assist patients and families in dealing with these end-of-life issues effectively.

Our aim in preparing the *Handbook of Health Social Work* has been to provide a source of information that would help social workers to be active problem solvers rather than followers of routines and existing protocols. The book enables social work students to learn the foundations of practice and policy in health care (Part I), critical considerations in implementing practice and policy (Part II), and the ways in which social work is practiced in a number of arenas and with a number of health conditions (Part III).

We hope that the book will continue to be useful in professional education, allowing those already in practice to learn about issues such as pain management and alternative and complementary medicine that they might not have been exposed to while in school or had the opportunity to learn after graduation. It also is a valuable source of information on evidence-based practice in a variety of areas of health care.

Social workers in health care today face a number of challenges, some new and some that have always been with the profession. We hope that readers will use the 23 chapters of the *Handbook of Health Social Work* as a set of tools to help them better address the health-care needs of the individuals, families, groups, communities, and societies with whom they work.

Sarah Gehlert
St. Louis, Missouri

Teri Browne
Columbia, South Carolina

REFERENCES

Matsunaga, D. S., Enos, R., Gotay, C. C., Banner, R. O., DeCambra, H., Hammond, O. W.,...Tsark, J. (1996). Participatory research in a native Hawaiian community: The Wai'anae Cancer Research Project. *Cancer, 78,* 1582–1586.

Warnecke, R. B., Oh, A., Breen, N., Gehlert, S., Lurie, N., Rebbeck, T.,...Patmios, G. (2008). Approaching health disparities from a population perspective: The NIH Centers for Population Health and Health Disparities. *American Journal of Public Health, 98,* 1608–1615.

PART I

Foundations of Social Work in Health Care

1

Conceptual Underpinnings of Social Work in Health Care

SARAH GEHLERT

The writing of the first edition of this text co-incided with the centennial of the hiring of the first medical social worker in the United States, Garnet Pelton, who began working at Massachusetts General Hospital in 1905. The writing of the second edition five years later comes at another key point for health social work, namely the passage of the Patient Protection and Affordable Care Act in March 2010, which will radically increase health insurance coverage for U.S. citizens over the next decade. It seems an appropriate time to consider the history of social work in health care and to assess the degree to which the vision of its founders has been met in its first 100 years. Ida Cannon (1952), the second social worker hired at Massachusetts General Hospital, whose tenure lasted for 40 years, wrote: "[B]asically, social work, wherever and whenever practiced at its best, is a constantly changing activity, gradually building up guiding principles from accumulated knowledge yet changing in techniques. Attitudes change, too, in response to shifting social philosophies" (p. 9). How, if at all, have the guiding principles of social work in health care changed over the century?

This chapter focuses on the development of the profession from its roots in the 19th century to the present. This longitudinal examination of the profession's principles and activities should allow for a more complete and accurate view of the progression of principles through time than could have been achieved by sampling at points in time determined by historical events, such as the enactment of major health-care policies.

Chapter Objectives

- Discuss the historical underpinnings of the founding of the first hospital social work department in the United States.
- Describe the forces and personalities responsible for the establishment of the first hospital social work department in the United States.
- Determine how the guiding principles of social work in health care have changed from the time of the founding of the first hospital social work department to the present time.
- Determine how the techniques and approaches of social work in health care have changed from the time of the founding of the first hospital social work department to the present time.

Frequent references to other chapters in this book capture the current conceptual framework of social work in health care.

HISTORICAL FOUNDATION OF SOCIAL WORK IN HEALTH CARE

Social work in health care owes it origins to changes in (a) the demographics of the U.S. population during the 19th and early 20th centuries; (b) attitudes about how the sick should be treated, including where treatment should occur; and (c) attitudes toward the role of social and psychological factors in health. These three closely related phenomena set the stage for the emergence of the field of social work in health care.

A number of events that began in the mid-1800s led to massive numbers of people immigrating to the United States. In all, 35 to 40 million Europeans immigrated between 1820 and 1924. The Gold Rush, which began in California in 1849, and the Homestead Act of 1862 added to the attractiveness of immigration (Rosenberg, 1967).

About 5.5 million Germans immigrated to the United States between 1816 and 1914 for economic and political reasons. Over 800,000 arrived in the 7-year period between 1866 and 1873, during the rule of Otto von Bismarck. The Potato Famine in Ireland in the 1840s resulted in the immigration of 2 million people during that decade and almost a million more in the next decade. Between 1820 and 1990, over 5 million Italians immigrated to the United States, mostly for economic reasons, with peak years between 1901 and 1920. A major influx of Polish immigrants occurred between 1870 and 1913. Those arriving prior to 1890 came largely for economic reasons; those after came largely for economic and political reasons. Polish immigration peaked again in 1921, a year in which over half a million Polish immigrants arrived in the United States. Two million Jews left Russia and Eastern European countries between 1880 and 1913 and traveled to the United States.

The United States struggled to adapt to the challenge of immigration. The Ellis Island Immigration Station opened in 1892 to process the large number of immigrants entering the country. By 1907, over 1 million people per year were passing through Ellis Island. The massive waves of immigration presented new health-care challenges, especially in the northeastern cities, where most of the new arrivals settled. Rosenberg (1967) wrote that 723,587 persons resided in New York City in 1865, 90% on the southern half of Manhattan Island alone. Over two thirds of the city's population at the time lived in tenements. Accidents were common, sanitation was primitive, and food supplies were in poor condition by the time they reached the city. One in 5 infants in

New York City died prior to their first birthday, compared to 1 in 6 in London (Rosenberg, 1967). Adding to the challenge, the vast majority of immigrants had very limited or no English language skills and lived in poverty. Immigrants brought with them a wide range of health-care beliefs and practices that differed from those predominant in the United States at the time.

In the late 1600s and early 1700s, people who were sick were cared for at home. A few hastily erected structures were built to house persons with contagious diseases during epidemics (O'Conner, 1976, p. 62). These structures operated in larger cities and were first seen before the Revolutionary War. As the U.S. population grew, communities developed almshouses to care for people who were physically or mentally ill, aged and ill, orphaned, or vagrant. Unlike the structures erected during epidemics, almshouses were built to operate continuously. The first almshouse, which was founded in 1713 in Philadelphia by William Penn, was open only to Quakers. A second almshouse was opened to the public in Philadelphia in 1728 with monies obtained from the Provincial Assembly by the Philadelphia Overseers of the Poor. Other large cities followed, with New York opening the Poor House of the City of New York (later named Bellevue Hospital) in 1736 and New Orleans opening Saint John's Hospital in 1737 (Commission on Hospital Care, 1947). Although called a hospital, Saint John's was classified as an almshouse because it primarily served people living in poverty who had nowhere else to go.

By the mid-1700s, people who became ill in almshouses were separated from other inhabitants. At first they were housed on separate floors, in separate departments, or in other buildings of the almshouse. When these units increased in size, they branched off to form public hospitals independent of almshouses. Hospitals eventually became popular among persons of means, who for the first time preferred to be treated for illness by specialists outside the home and were willing to pay for the service.

A number of voluntary hospitals were established between 1751 and 1840 with various combinations of public and private funds and patients' fees (O'Conner, 1976). The first voluntary hospital was founded in Philadelphia in 1751 with subscriptions gathered by Benjamin Franklin and Dr. Thomas Bond and funds from the Provincial General Assembly of Philadelphia. The New York Hospital began admitting patients in 1791 and the Massachusetts General Hospital in 1821. In 1817, the Quakers opened the first mental hospital, which began admitting anyone needing care for mental illness in 1834.

A third type of medical establishment, the dispensary, began to appear in the late 1700s. Dispensaries were independent of hospitals and financed by bequests and voluntary subscriptions. Their original purpose was to dispense medications to ambulatory patients. In time, however, dispensaries hired physicians to visit patients in their homes. The first four dispensaries were established in Philadelphia in 1786 (exclusively for Quakers), New York in 1795, Boston in 1796, and Baltimore in 1801.

19th-Century Efforts Toward Public Health Reform

The last half of the 19th century saw efforts to reform hospitals and dispensaries, many of which were led by women physicians. Dr. Elizabeth Blackwell, unable to find employment in hospitals because of her gender, established a dispensary for women and children in New York's East Side in 1853. The East Side had seen a massive influx of immigrants from Europe and was becoming increasingly crowded. Blackwell's dispensary provided home visits and by 1857 had secured a few hospital beds for its patients. The dispensary, which later became the New York Infirmary for Women and Children, provided home visits to 334 African American and White American patients in 1865 (Cannon, 1952). The following year, Dr. Rebecca Cole, an African American physician, was hired as a "sanitary visitor." When visiting families, Cole discussed topics

such as hygiene and how to select and cook food and addressed issues of education and employment. In 1890, Mrs. Robert Hoe provided funds to the New York Infirmary for Women and Children to employ a full-time home visitor to work under the direction of Dr. Annie Daniels. Daniels kept records of family size, income, and living expenses in the manner of social workers of the time, such as Jane Addams, who founded Hull House in Chicago in 1889.

The first medical resident to work with Dr. Blackwell in New York, Marie Zakrzewska, moved to Boston and in 1859 became the first professor of obstetrics and gynecology at the New England Female Medical College. Dr. Zakrzewska established a dispensary and 10-bed ward in Boston in 1862, the New England Hospital for Women and Children. It was the first hospital in Boston and the second in the United States (after the New York Dispensary for Women and Children) to be run by women physicians and surgeons. As had the New York Dispensary for Women and Children, the New England Hospital for Women and Children featured home visiting, with increased attention to social conditions. For many years, home visits were part of the education of nurses and physicians in training.

In 1890, Dr. Henry Dwight Chapin, a pediatrician who lectured at the New York Postgraduate Hospital and the Women's Medical College of the New York Infirmary for Women and Children, established a program in which volunteers visited the homes of ill children to report on conditions and to ensure that medical instructions had been understood and implemented. In 1894, he appointed a woman physician to do the job but soon replaced her with a nurse. Chapin's efforts led to a foster-care home for ill and convalescing children whose parents were unable to care for them adequately (Romanofsky, 1976). He founded the Speedwell Society in 1902 to encourage foster care. The Speedwell Society would have ties to the social work departments later established in New York hospitals.

A close partnership between the Johns Hopkins Hospital and Baltimore's Charity Organization Society at the turn of the 20th century served as a breeding ground for ideas about how to merge social work and medicine. Four people involved in these discussions were instrumental to the establishment of formal social work services in hospitals. Mary Richmond, Mary Wilcox Glenn, Jeffrey Brackett, and Dr. John Glenn, who became the director of the Russell Sage Foundation, were actively involved in the application of social work to medicine.

Hospital Almoners in London

The first social worker, called a hospital almoner, was hired by the Royal Free Hospital in London in 1895. This occurred when the Royal Free Hospital came together with the London Charity Organization Society through Charles Loch. Loch was a very religious man who had served in the Secretarial Department of the Royal College of Surgeons for three years. He was appointed secretary of the London Charity Organization in 1875 and brought with him a strong interest in the social aspects of health. While a member of the Medical Committee of the Charity Organization Society, Loch addressed a growing concern that patients might be misrepresenting their situations to receive free care. In 1874, the Royal Free Hospital asked the Charity Organization Society to screen patients to determine how many were indeed poor. They found only 36% to be truly eligible for services. Loch thought that individuals requesting care should be screened by "a competent person of education and refinement who could consider the position and circumstances of the patients" (Cannon, 1952, p. 13). Loch fought for many years to have an almoner appointed. He addressed the Provident Medical Association in 1885 and was called to testify before a committee of the House of Lords in 1891. In 1895, Mary Stewart was hired to be the first social almoner at the Royal Free Hospital. Prior to assuming the position, Stewart had worked for many years for the London Charity Organization Society. She was stationed at its entrance because her principal function at the hospital was to review applications for admission to the hospital's dispensary and accept those that were deemed suitable for care. Her secondary duties were to refer patients for services and determine who should be served at dispensaries (Cannon, 1952).

Stewart was given 3 months of initial funding by the London Charity Organization Society. Although by all accounts her work was considered productive, the Charity Organization Society refused to renew her contract until the Royal Free Hospital agreed to pay at least part of her salary. Ultimately, two of the hospital's physicians agreed to pay half of Stewart's salary for a year, and the Charity Organization Society covered the other half. From that point on, social almoners were part of hospitals in England. By 1905, seven other hospitals had hired almoners.

In 1906, the Hospital Almoners' Council (later the Institute of Hospital Almoners) took over the training of almoners. The Institute for Hospital Almoners was responsible for the expansion of the almoner's repertoire to include functions such as prevention of illness. The first years of its operation saw the development of classes for prospective fathers, a hostel for young women with socially transmitted diseases, and other programs (Cannon, 1952).

First Social Service Department in the United States

Garnet Pelton began work as a social worker in the dispensary of the Massachusetts General Hospital 10 years after Mary Stewart was first hired to work at the Royal Free Hospital in London. Ida Cannon, who replaced Pelton after she became ill six months into her tenure and who held the position for 40 years, described "a special bond of fellowship between the English almoners and the medical social workers of our country" (Cannon, 1952, p. 20). She also described her own 1907 visit with Anne Cummins, an almoner at London's St. Thomas Hospital.

Garnet Pelton, Ida Cannon, and Dr. Richard Cabot were central to the establishment of the social work department at Massachusetts General Hospital. Relatively little has been written about Pelton or her short tenure at the hospital. Cannon (1952) briefly described Pelton's nurse's training at Massachusetts General Hospital and her contribution to the Denison House Settlement. While at the settlement, she brought Syrian immigrants from her South End Boston neighborhood to the hospital for treatment. Pelton was hired by Cabot to work at Massachusetts General Hospital and began on October 2, 1905. She worked from a desk located in a corner of the corridor of the outpatient clinic at Massachusetts General Hospital and resigned after six months when she developed tuberculosis. The poor received treatment for tuberculosis in the outpatient department because they could not afford sanitarium treatment. There is some question about whether Pelton contracted tuberculosis through her work in the outpatient department. At any rate, Cabot arranged for her treatment at Saranac Lake, New York, and later at Asheville, North Carolina.

Pelton was succeeded by Ida Cannon, who published two books and several reports on medical social work and about whom a fair amount of biographical information is available. Cannon was born in Milwaukee into a family of means. She was trained as a nurse at the City and County Hospital of St. Paul and worked as a nurse for 2 years. She then studied sociology at the University of Minnesota, where she heard a lecture by Jane Addams and became interested in social work. She worked as a visiting nurse for the St. Paul Associated Charities for three years prior to enrolling in Simmons College of Social Work. Cannon met Richard Cabot through her older brother, a Harvard-educated physiologist, as Cabot was organizing social services at Massachusetts Hospital. She was hired to replace Pelton in 1906, began working full time after graduating from Simmons College in 1907, and was named the first chief of the Social Service Department in 1914. She retired from Massachusetts General Hospital in 1945.

Dr. Richard Cabot was an especially prolific writer and has himself been the subject of scholarship over the years (see, e.g., Dodds, 1993; O'Brien, 1985). Cabot was a Harvard-educated physician who had a great deal to do with the establishment of social work and other helping professions in U.S. hospitals. He was active professionally from the 1890s through most of the 1930s, a time when professions were being defined (see, e.g., Flexner, 1910) and medicine was the standard for what it meant to be professional.

Cabot's paternal grandfather, Samuel (1784 to 1863), made his fortune in trading after first going to sea at 19 years of age. Samuel Cabot married Eliza Perkins, daughter of Boston's most successful trader, and eventually took over his father-in-law's firm. He is described as a practical man who believed primarily in action and hard work and favored commerce over culture (Evison, 1995).

Cabot's father, James (1821 to 1903), studied philosophy in Europe, trained as a lawyer, taught philosophy at Harvard, and was a biographer and friend of Ralph Waldo Emerson. He considered himself a transcendentalist, holding that, "the transcendental included whatever lay beyond the stock notions and traditional beliefs to which adherence was expected because they were accepted by sensible persons" (Cabot, 1887, p. 249). The transcendentalists questioned much of the commercialism of their parents' generation and were particularly critical of slavery. The Civil War, which began when James Elliott Cabot was 40 years old, was waged in part due to the sentiments of this generation. Cabot's mother, Elizabeth, bore most of the responsibility of raising the couple's seven sons and shared with her husband the transcendentalist's questioning of stock notions and traditional beliefs. Elizabeth Cabot said of women: "[I]t seems to me that very few of us have enough mental occupation. We ought to have some intellectual life apart from the problems of education and housekeeping or even the interests of society" (Cabot, 1869, p. 45). O'Brien describes Elizabeth Cabot as "warmly maternal and deeply religious" and "tirelessly philanthropic" (O'Brien, 1985, p. 536).

The Civil War demoralized the nation and spawned a new conservatism and materialism. The publication of *The Origin of the Species* by

Charles Darwin in 1859 (1936), which brought an appreciation of the scientific method, and growing concern about the number of immigrants arriving in the country added to a shift to realism from the idealism of James Elliott Cabot's generation. In the wave of social Darwinism that ensued, charity was seen as naive and potentially harmful to its recipients. It was into this posttranscendentalist atmosphere that Richard Cabot was born in 1868.

The tension between his generation and that of his parents shaped Richard Cabot's vision. He took a radical centrist position based in philosophical pragmatism, taking two opposing views, and helped to locate a middle ground between them. Rather than considering either side as right or wrong, he held that a greater truth could emerge through creating a dialogue between the two sides. Throughout his career, Cabot saw himself as an interpreter or translator, able to find the middle ground between extremes.

Cabot first studied philosophy at Harvard and then switched to medicine. He rejected philosophers who observed rather than acted and for that reason was drawn to the philosophy of John Dewey. Evison (1995), a Cabot biographer, writes: "[A]ction drew him; Jane Addams and Teddy Roosevelt appealed to him because they did something" (p. 30). Cabot held that knowledge was gained through problem solving, even when hypotheses were not supported. Like Addams before him, he believed that people can learn from failure.

Cabot's senior thesis used epidemiologic methods to examine the efficacy of Christian Science healing (Dodds, 1993). By the time he had completed medical school in 1892, the germ theory of the 1870s and 1880s had taken hold, and the roles of technology and laboratory analysis had gained in salience. Cabot initially followed the trend by completing postgraduate training in laboratory research and a Dalton Research Fellowship in hematology. He turned down an appointment as the first bacteriologist at Massachusetts General Hospital and in 1898, four years after completing his fellowship, accepted a much less prestigious appointment in the outpatient department.

Patients were treated in the outpatient department at Massachusetts General Hospital rather than in the wards when their cases were considered uninteresting or hopeless (Evison, 1995). Because no treatment existed for conditions such as tuberculosis, typhus, and diabetes, patients with these conditions usually were treated in the outpatient department, especially if they were poor. Medicines prescribed were largely analgesic. (Antibiotics were not developed until the 1940s.) Many patients were immigrants who presented with language barriers and infectious diseases such as typhus. Adding to the bleakness of the situation was the depression of 1893, the worst that had been experienced to that date.

Cabot described the speed with which physicians saw patients when he first arrived in the outpatient department: Referred to by some physicians as "running off the clinic" (Evison, 1995, p. 183), a physician pulled a bell to signal a patient to enter the room. The physician would shout his questions while the patient was still moving and have a prescription written by the time the patient arrived at his desk. He would then pull the bell for the next patient.

Cabot began to see that social and mental problems often underlaid physical problems and that purely physical afflictions were rare (Cabot, 1915). He held that it was not possible to restore patients to health without considering what he called the nonsomatic factors, such as living conditions. He described one case in this way:

> One morning as I was working in the outpatient department, I had a series of knotty human problems come before me...that morning I happened to wake to the fact that the series of people that came to me had pretty much wasted their time. I had first of all to deal with a case of diabetes. That is a disease in which medicine can accomplish practically nothing, but in which diet can accomplish a great deal. We had worked out very minutely a diet that should be given such patients. We had it printed upon slips which were made up in pads so that we could tear off a slip from one of these pads and give the patient the best

that was known about diabetes in short compass. I remember tearing off a slip from this pad and handing it to the patient, feeling satisfaction that we had all these ready so that the patient need not remember anything....The woman to whom it had been given did not seem satisfied. I asked her what was the matter....She looked it over and among the things that she could eat she saw asparagus, Brussels sprouts, and one or two other things, and she called my attention to the fact that there was no possibility of her buying these things. We had, in other words, asked her to do things that she could by no possibility do. (Cabot, 1911, pp. 308–309)

Cabot's exposure to social work came first from his relationship with Jane Addams. In 1887, he took a course at Harvard entitled "Ethical Theories and Social Reform" from Francis Greenwood Peabody. Many who took the course went on to work for the Boston Children's Aid Society, as did Cabot when he became a director there in 1896. It was there that he was exposed to the case conference approach.

Cabot viewed the relationship between medicine and social work from his radical centrist perspective. He thought that each profession possessed the element that the other most needed. For medicine, this was empiricism, and for social work, it was breadth. Cabot thought physicians' enthusiastic acceptance of empiricism had made them far too narrow in scope, ignoring social and psychological factors in health. Social workers possessed the breadth that physicians lacked but relied too heavily on good intentions. They needed to become more scientific and systematic to ensure that their methods were effective and to develop a theoretical base for their work. Each profession could gain from association with the other.

Cabot set about reforming the treatment process in the outpatient clinic. He hired Garnet Pelton to fulfill three functions: (1) to critique while helping to socialize medicine, (2) to act as a translator between the physician and patient and family, and (3) to provide information on social and mental factors. Cabot described the critical role by saying

[S]he will not be there primarily as a critic, but nevertheless she will be far better than the average critic because she will be part of the institution and will be criticism from the inside, which I think is always the most valuable kind. (Cabot, 1912, pp. 51–52)

Pelton kept records of every case, which were used for instruction and to identify trends that would be published in regular reports. Prior to Pelton, no records of patient visits to the outpatient department were kept at Massachusetts Hospital.

Cabot viewed social workers as translators of medical information to patients and families in a way that they could understand. He said,

[T]he social worker...can reassure patients as to the kind of things that are being done and are going to be done with them. There is no one else who explains; there is no other person in the hospital whose chief business is to explain things. (Cabot, 1912, p. 50)

Cabot also saw social workers as translators of information about patients and families to physicians. Social work's role in providing social and psychological information to physicians is described in a quote from Ida Cannon:

While she must have an understanding of the patient's physical condition, the physical condition is only one aspect of the patient to which she must take account. As the physician sees the disease organ not isolated but as possibly affecting the whole body, so the hospital social worker sees the patient not merely as an isolated, unfortunate person occupying a hospital bed, but as a member belonging to a family or community group that is altered because of his ill health. Physician and nurse seek to strengthen the general physical state of the patient so that he can combat his disease. The social worker seeks to remove those obstacles, either in the patient's surroundings or in his mental attitude, that interfere with successful treatment, thus freeing the patient to aid in his own recovery. (Cannon, 1923, pp. 14–15)

Cabot thought that social work could best fulfill this role because nurses had "lost their claim to be a profession by allowing themselves to become mere implementers of doctor's orders" (Evison, 1995, p. 220). He defined social work's expertise as diagnosis and "treatment of character in difficulties," which he saw as encompassing expertise in mental health.

The hospital did not initially support Pelton's hiring, so Cabot paid her salary with his own funds. To convince the hospital's superintendent, Frederic Washburn, that Pelton was a good addition, Cabot set about documenting that her hiring was cost effective. He calculated that the hospital had spent $120 on a baby with gastrointestinal problems whose mother brought her to the hospital on four occasions over a short period of time because the family was unable to provide the nutrients prescribed for her. Cabot did not want administrators to view social work's primary role as preventing misuse of hospital services but instead to save money by helping to make treatment more effective. He viewed medical social workers as distinct from hospital almoners.

Ida Cannon took over for Garnet Pelton in 1906 when Pelton went to Saranac Lake, New York, to receive treatment for pulmonary tuberculosis. Cannon was named the first chief of social work in 1914. She shared status with the chief of surgery and the chief of medicine. Cannon developed training programs for social workers at Massachusetts General Hospital, including medical education. Cannon hired Harriett Bartlett to be the first educational director in the Social Work Department. Other programs begun during her tenure included a low-cost lunch counter for patients and staff; a committee to investigate the social correlates of tuberculosis, which produced the first comprehensive analysis of tuberculosis in the United States; interdisciplinary medical rounds with social workers; and clay modeling classes for psychiatric patients. Cannon and Cabot together developed systems for evaluating the effectiveness of social work interventions and included this information in medical records.

Cannon did not take the same radical views of hospital social work that were espoused by Pelton and Cabot, with whom she clashed often during their first years of working together. Cannon thought social workers should accommodate hospital mechanisms rather than being critics or reformers of medicine, as Cabot had advocated. Nevertheless, the two worked together until Cabot accepted a commission of major in the Medical Reserve Corps in 1917 during World War I. He returned to the outpatient department of Massachusetts General Hospital in 1918, but he then left to chair Harvard's Department of Social Ethics in 1919. Shortly before he left the hospital, its board of directors voted to make the Social Service Department a permanent part of the hospital and to cover the full cost of its functioning. Prior to that, Cabot had covered the cost of up to 13 social workers with his personal funds.

Ida Cannon was named director of the new Social Work Department in 1919. By the time she retired from Massachusetts General Hospital in 1945, the hospital employed 31 social workers. Several former social workers at Massachusetts General Hospital went on to direct departments in other hospitals, such as Mary Antoinette Cannon (the University Hospital of Philadelphia) and Ruth T. Boretti (Strong Memorial Hospital of the University of Rochester School of Medicine and Dentistry).

GROWTH OF HOSPITAL SOCIAL WORK DEPARTMENTS

In 1961, Bartlett described the course of social work in health care as spiraling, "in which periods of uncertainty and fluidity alternated with those of clarity and control" (p. 15). She said that in its first 30 years, growth was linear as social work spread from one hospital to another. Methods were simple because social work in hospitals "almost alone carried the responsibility for bringing the social viewpoint into the hospital."

The success achieved at Massachusetts General Hospital eventually drew the attention of the American Hospital Association and the American Medical Association. Johns Hopkins

Hospital hired Helen B. Pendleton, who had worked with the Charity Organization Society as its first social worker in 1907. As had been the case with Garnet Pelton at Massachusetts General Hospital, Pendleton remained on the job for only a few months. The position remained vacant for four months, then she was replaced by a graduate nurse. At Johns Hopkins, social workers initially were housed in a room that was also used for storing surgical supplies. They were not allowed on the wards, which were controlled by nurses (Nacman, 1990). Social workers, however, controlled access to medical records by physicians and nurses and had to approve all free medical care and prescriptions for medicine that was to last longer than one week (Brogen, 1964). The department prospered, as had the department at Massachusetts General Hospital, and by 1931 had a staff of 31.

Garnet Pelton completed a survey of social service in hospitals in the United States in 1911 at the behest of John M. Glenn, the first director of the Russell Sage Foundation and a strong proponent of social work in health care. She was able to locate 44 social service departments in 14 cities, 17 of which were in New York City alone. These departments provided a range of services, all focused on the provision of assistance to the patient (Cannon, 1952).

New York City, which housed nearly 40% of the country's hospital social service departments, organized the field's first conference in 1912, which was called the New York Conference on Hospital Social Work. The conference was held regularly between 1912 and 1933. A quarterly report entitled *Hospital Social Service* documented conference findings and highlighted the progress of various hospital social service departments.

By 1913, 200 U.S. hospitals had social workers. Ruth Emerson, who left Massachusetts General Hospital in 1918, established the social service department at the University of Chicago. Edith M. Baker, who left Massachusetts General Hospital in 1923, established the social service department at Washington University in St. Louis.

PROFESSIONALIZATION OF THE FIELD

The first training course in medical social work was held in 1912. Cannon (1932) wrote that the growth of such courses was slow and lacked coordination until 1918, when the American Association of Hospital Social Workers was established in Kansas City. The association, which employed an educational secretary, had a twofold purpose: to foster and coordinate the training of social workers in hospitals and to enhance communication between schools of social work and practitioners. Although the American Association of Hospital Social Workers was the first national organization of social workers in health care, it was preceded by local organizations in St. Louis, Boston, Philadelphia, Milwaukee, and New York. Mary A. Stites, the author of *History of the American Association of Medical Social Workers* (1955) says that prior to the establishment of the American Association of Hospital Social Workers, medical social workers in health care for some time had congregated at meetings of the National Conference of Social Work (formally called the National Conference of Charities and Corrections). The burning question at the first meeting of the American Association of Hospital Social Workers in 1918 was whether the group should orient more closely with social work or medicine. Eight of the 30 women who signed the association's first constitution were graduate nurses.

The American Association of Hospital Social Workers published a study of 1,000 cases from 60 hospital social work departments in 1928. According to the report:

> The social worker's major contributions to medical care, gauged by frequency of performance, are: (1) the securing of information to enable an adequate understanding of the general health problem of the patient; (2) interpretation of the patient's health problem to himself, his family and community welfare agencies; and (3) the mobilizing of measures for the relief of the patient and his associates. Briefly then, the basic practices of hospital

social work exhibited in the study under consideration can be described as discovery of the relevant social factors in the health problems of particular patients and influencing these factors in such ways as to further the patient's medical care. (p. 28)

This description does not differ appreciably from the way that hospital social work was conceptualized by Cannon and Cabot at Massachusetts General Hospital.

A survey of schools of social work published in 1929 (Cannon, 1932) listed 10 schools that offered formal courses in medical social work and 18 that were in the process of planning medical social work curriculum:

1. Washington University
2. University of Chicago
3. New York School of Social Work
4. Tulane University
5. University of Indiana
6. University of Missouri
7. Simmons College
8. Western Reserve University
9. Pennsylvania School of Social and Health Work
10. National Catholic School of Social Work

In all, medical social work was considered to be graduate-level work. A second survey that year was sent to social service department heads in hospitals asking them to query their workers about their training and experience. Of the 596 respondents, 70% had taken at least one course in general social work, and 48% of those had received a diploma or certificate between 1899 and 1930. Interestingly, 38% of respondents had completed at least one course in nursing, and 86% of those had received a certificate or diploma in nursing. The survey listed six activities of medical social workers:

1. Medical social case management
2. Securing data
3. Health teaching
4. Follow-up
5. Adjustment of rates

6. Medical extension of transfer to convalescent home, public health agency, or medical institution

In 1954, the year before the American Association of Medical Social Workers merged with six other specialty organizations to form the National Association of Social Workers, 2,500 people attended its annual meeting. The American Association of Medical Social Workers was the largest of all social work membership organizations. The current major specialty organization for social workers in health care on the national level, the Society for Leadership in Health Care, boasts 700 members (Society for Social Work Leadership in Health Care, 2011, January 2). This organization, which changed its name from the Society for Social Work Administrators in Health Care in the 1990s and is affiliated with the American Hospital Association, was founded in 1965. Other current national organizations include the American Network of Home Health Care Social Workers, the Association of Oncology Social Work, the Council of Nephrology Social Workers, the National Association of Perinatal Social Workers, and the Society for Transplant Social Workers.

DEFINING *MEDICAL SOCIAL WORK*

By 1934, the American Association of Medical Social Workers (the American Association of Hospital Social Workers changed its name that year) published a report prepared by Harriet Bartlett. The report defined medical social work as a specific form of social case work that focuses on the relationship between disease and social maladjustment. Bartlett wrote, "[I]t is an important part of the social worker's function to concern herself with the social problems arising directly out of the nature of the medical treatment. In this way, she facilitates and extends the medical treatment" (p. 99). Emphasis was placed on surmounting social impediments to health, "providing some occupation or experience for the person jolted out of his regular plan of life by chronic disease, to offset what he has lost and to make him feel that he has still a useful place in the world" (p. 99).

The 1934 report highlighted a series of problems as requiring particular attention. They were: (a) the integration of psychological concepts, defined in part as needing to know more about human motivation in general and in relation to illness; (b) problems of functional and mental disease, specifically the need to integrate the study of the organism with that of the personality; and (c) problems of methods of thinking, which had to do with balancing the study of personality with a consideration of the person in his social situation.

This competition for attention between personality and social environment gained salience with the advent of psychiatry and psychoanalysis in the United States. Although popular in Europe in the 1880s and 1890s, mental treatment in hospitals did not take hold in the United States at first. Courses in psychotherapy began appearing in medical schools in 1907, and Freud made his first tour of the United States two years later.

The emergence of psychiatry and psychoanalysis into medicine had two major effects on social work in health care. First, psychiatry's emergence into medicine is tied to the appearance of other professionals in hospitals, such as psychologists and social scientists. Their presence meant that the social and mental domains of health were no longer exclusive to social work and that medical social work for the first time had significant competition for a role in health care.

A second effect of psychiatry's emergence into medicine was the impact of psychoanalytic theory on how social workers in health care approached cases, namely, from a more person-centered perspective. The confusion between a focus on personality and on social environment remained after psychiatric social work separated from medical social work. The separation often is attributed to 1919, when Smith College developed a course for psychiatric aides attached to the U.S. Army during World War I (Grinker, MacGregor, Selan,

Klein, & Kohrman, 1961), although the Psychiatric Social Service Department was not established at Massachusetts General Hospital until 1930. Mary Jarrett (1919), the associate director of the Smith College Training School for Social Work, argued for a more psychiatric approach to case work in her address to the Conference of Social Work in 1919:

> One by-product of the psychiatric point of view in social case work is worth consideration in these days of overworked social workers, that is, the greater ease in work that it gives the social worker. The strain of dealing with unknown quantities is perhaps the greatest cause of fatigue in our work.... More exact knowledge of personalities with which we are dealing not only saves the worker worry and strain but also releases energy which can be applied to treatment.... Another result is that impatience is almost entirely eliminated. No time is wasted upon annoyance or indignation with the uncooperative housewife, the persistent liar, the repeatedly delinquent girl....I know of social workers who looked with suspicion upon the careful preliminary study of personality, because they feared that all the worker's interest might go into the analysis, and that treatment might be neglected. I believe that fear has been something of a bugaboo in social work. (p. 592)

The implication of Jarrett's address is that a focus on personality allows the social worker to get at the client's problem with ease, thus saving time for treatment.

Another possible source of social work's attraction to psychoanalytic theory was Abraham Flexner's 1915 address to the National Conference of Charities and Corrections, in which he said that social work was not a profession. Flexner defined professions as: (a) involving essentially intellectual operations, (b) having large individual responsibility, (c) deriving their raw material from science and learning, (d) working up their material to a practical and definite end, (e) possessing educationally communicable techniques, (f) tending to self-organization, and (g) becoming increasingly altruistic in motivation. He said that although social work had a professional spirit, it failed to meet all of the criteria for a profession because its members did not have a great deal of individual responsibility and lacked a written body of knowledge and educationally communicable techniques. Flexner's address had a profound effect on the field. Some social workers viewed medicine as a model profession and an intrapersonal approach as more professional than one focused on social and environmental factors.

Nacman (1990) notes that, by the 1940s, psychosocial information was increasingly being used by medical social workers to make medical diagnoses and treatment plans. This was in contrast to its use, in Ida Cannon's words, "to remove those obstacles, either in the patient's surroundings or in his mental attitude, that interfere with successful treatment, thus freeing the patient to aid in his own recovery" (1923, pp. 14–15). The work of Helen Harris Perlman countered the tendency to use information primarily to make medical diagnoses and plans by emphasizing social science concepts over psychoanalytic ones and refocusing on society and environment. A focus on environment was reinforced in the 1950s by the community mental health and public health movements (see Chapter 4 of this text) and the civil rights movement of the 1960s.

SOCIAL WORK IN HEALTH CARE: BEYOND THE HOSPITAL

After World War II and the passage of the Social Security Act, social work in health care began to branch out from its hospital base. Social work programs were established in the U.S. Army and Navy and the Veterans Administration. The advent in the mid-1960s of Medicare and Medicaid, and titles XVIII and XIX of the Social Security Act, provided coverage for people who might otherwise not have been treated. These two programs further increased the need for social work services.

The number of social workers in health care increased with the variety of work settings. Between 1960 and 1970, the number of social workers in health care nearly doubled (Bracht, 1974). By 1971, social workers were employed in a wide range of settings. A Medicare report from that year reported 11,576 social workers in 6,935 participating hospitals, 2,759 in 4,829 extended-care facilities, and 316 social workers in 2,410 home health agencies (U.S. Department of Health, Education, and Welfare, 1976). Social workers also could be found in state and local health departments and in federal agencies, such as the Department of Defense. Social workers entered new health-care arenas, such as preventive and emergency services. Techniques were added to the social work repertoire to address these new settings and arenas. Interventions appeared based on behavior, cognitive, family systems, crisis, and group work theories. Because health costs were growing at an alarming rate, the federal government began to institute measures to control costs. In 1967, utilization review measures were enacted that required Medicare providers to demonstrate that care was necessary and that its costs were reasonable. In 1972, Congress enacted the Peer Standards Review Act, which required the peer review of medical billing to ensure that services had been utilized appropriately.

Neither utilization review nor peer standards review proved as effective as was hoped. Another attempt to control costs took its cues from a long history of prepaid health-care arrangements provided to workers around the country, the first of which was a rural farmers' cooperative in Elk City, Oklahoma, in 1929. The best known of these arrangements was the Kaiser Permanente Health Plan. In 1973, the Health Maintenance Organization (HMO) Act was passed by the Nixon administration. The act authorized $375 million in federal grants to develop HMOs. Initially, employers saw HMOs as a less expensive way of providing insurance to their employees. In recent years, state governments have used managed care in their Medicaid programs. By 1993, 70% of Americans with health insurance were enrolled in some form of managed care.

Cornelius (1994) distills the perils of managed care for social workers by saying that

> the social worker becomes an agent of managed care and agrees to serve the public within the corporate guidelines and not necessarily according to the assessed needs of the client.... If the social worker practices outside the protocols,... the client is denied coverage and the social worker is denied reimbursement; money becomes the carrot and the stick. (p. 52)

Another major cost containment effort had a profound effect on hospital care. The prospective payment system, based on a set of 500 diagnostic-related groups (DRGs), each with its own specific payment rate, was instituted in 1983 to replace traditional retrospective reimbursement for hospital care. The rates were developed based on the nature of the illness, accepted treatment procedures, whether the hospital was a teaching facility, local wage scales, and the hospital's location (Reamer, 1985, p. 86). This standardization was intended to provide an incentive for hospitals to become more efficient.

Under DRGs, patients entered the hospital sicker and left sooner (Dobrof, 1991). This impacted hospital social work services in two major ways:

1. Hospitalization was seen as a failure of the system, and every effort was made to avoid it; thus, those who were admitted were quite ill.
2. Because hospitals were paid a specified rate, it was in their best interests to keep stays as short as possible. Because patients entered more ill and stayed for a shorter time, less comprehensive care could be provided in hospitals.

Although there is debate about the extent to which social workers were cut from hospitals (see, e.g., Coulton, 1988), many social work forces in hospitals were downsized or reconfigured during this period. Some were merged with other departments, others self-governed, and, in other cases, social workers and other professionals were organized by service rather than by department.

It is clear that hospital social workers found less opportunity to spend time with patients because patients were there for less time, and much of the social worker's time was taken by helping to prepare sicker patients and their families for recuperation at home or in other facilities, such as extended-care facilities. Dobrof (1991) describes "hospital-based social workers confronting larger caseloads of sicker patients with increased need for home care services or placement in nursing homes" (p. 44).

Both HMOs and DRGs affected how social workers in health care practiced. HMOs restricted social workers' ability to practice based on their own assessment of needs. DRGs limited the time that social workers in hospitals had to work with patients and forced an emphasis on discharge planning. This limited social workers' ability to perform in the manner outlined by its founders, such as Bartlett, "to concern herself with the social problems arising directly out of the nature of medical treatment" (1934, p. 99), or Cannon, "to remove those obstacles... that interfere with successful treatment" (1923, pp. 14–15).

New techniques have been developed in response to time limits on treatment. Task-centered case work (Reid & Epstein, 1972) emphasizes the goals of treatment, and a number of brief treatment techniques have been developed (see, e.g., Mailick, 1990). Social workers have helped to adapt intervention theories for use in health settings, such as stress inoculation from cognitive theory (see, e.g., Blythe & Erdahl, 1986).

Claiborne and Vandenburgh (2001) define a new role for social workers as disease managers. As patients live longer with disease conditions or survive conditions once considered fatal, such as cancer, issues of quality of life arise. Survivors of cancer, previously expecting to die, need assistance with learning how to live. Those with long-term health conditions, such as rheumatoid arthritis, require guidance on how to live a full life with their condition. As a rule, disease management entails "a team of professionals that integrates and coordinates care across an array of services to maintain optimal patient functioning and quality of life" (Claiborne & Vandenburgh, 2001, p. 220). These teams often operate across facilities. Claiborne and Vandenburgh see social workers as key members of disease management teams due to their ability to work across health systems and managed care settings. Chapters 8 and 20 of this text discuss mental health issues in chronic illness.

The Patient Protection and Affordable Care Act (PPACA), which was enacted in March 2010, represents a radical change in how healthcare services are constructed and delivered. Although its course and impact are yet to be seen, Darnell and Lawlor (in Chapter 5 of this text) argue that the PPACA will change the landscape of health social work practice for the foreseeable future and heighten its importance, for a number of reasons. Although the PPACA includes provisions to extend insurance coverage, for example, it falls short of universal coverage. Darnell and Lawlor estimate that 23 million people will remain uninsured in 2019, including undocumented immigrants, who except for emergency situations are excluded from Medicaid coverage. Health social workers will be important advocates for those who remain uninsured. Also, despite improved affordability of insurance coverage, the coordination of care will remain a challenge (Gorin, Gehlert, & Washington, 2010). Health social workers will play a crucial role in connecting patients to appropriate services and maintaining the safety net for those who do not qualify for services.

CHANGES IN TECHNIQUE AND APPROACH THROUGH TIME

The settings in which social work is practiced in health care have changed through time. From 1905 until 1930, medical social workers practiced almost entirely in hospitals. Harriet Bartlett (1957) described the course of change during that period as linear, with the number of social service departments increasing steadily and their claim to the social and

mental domains largely unchallenged by other disciplines. With the advent of psychotherapy, however, professionals such as psychologists and other social scientists began to work in hospitals, and for the first time social workers had to compete for roles.

The period of linear growth was followed by an expansion into previously unimagined settings. Federally imposed cost containment, beginning in the late 1960s, posed challenges to social workers in health care and forced a great deal of flexibility and creativity. In some respects, competition with other disciplines that social work experienced in its most recent 70 years in health care, and its failure to define a niche that was exclusively its own since that time (see, e.g., Lister, 1980), prepared social workers to remain viable in a changing healthcare environment. They have adapted well to these changing environments.

How do the visions of Ida Cannon and Richard Cabot hold in the current health environment in which social workers practice? At a time when the changing demographics pose problems of communication in health care, Cabot's idea of social worker as translator or interpreter seems modern and as salient today as it was in 1905. In 2000, 1 in 10 U.S. residents, over 28.4 million people, was born outside the country (Lollock, 2001). These figures do not include an estimated 10.9 million undocumented immigrants (Camarota & Jensenius, 2009).

The current 10% of U.S. residents who were born outside the country compares to a high of 15% between 1890 and 1910, the years during which Mary Stewart was hired in London and Garnet Pelton and Ida Cannon were hired in Boston. The percentage born outside the country in 2000 is higher than it was for the decades that immediately preceded 2000. According to U.S. Census Bureau records, 7% of the population was born outside the United States in the 1950s, 5% in the 1970s, and 8% in the 1990s (Lollock, 2001).

As outlined in Chapter 10 of this text, communication is the key to the provision of effective health care. Clinical encounters are more problematic when providers and patients are from different racial or ethnic groups or different socioeconomic statuses. A report by the Institute of Medicine (2002) implicated physician behavior in health disparities in the United States, and researchers (see, e.g., Johnson, Roter, Powe, & Cooper, 2004) have noted different communication patterns among White American physicians when they are dealing with African American versus White American patients. It is unlikely, however, that these biases are limited to physicians. Although empirical studies to date have centered on the behavior of physicians as the time that providers are able to spend with patients decreases, the opportunity for mental shortcuts that can lead to bias increases (Burgess, Fu, & von Ryn, 1990). Clearly, the translator or interpreter role first defined by Richard Cabot in 1905 remains important in health care today. Likewise, the idea that social workers are in the best position among professionals in health care to interpret information from patients and families to providers and to interpret and explain information from providers to patients and families holds true.

Cannon's dictum that the social worker see the patient "as a member belonging to a family or community group that is altered because of his ill health" (1923, p. 15) also seems germane to the current challenge of disease management. Cannon was writing at a time prior to the development of treatment advances, such as antibiotics, chemotherapy, and radiation therapy, when patients did not live for long periods of time with chronic health conditions. Her words seem even more salient today when a growing number of patients face living with chronic conditions.

Cabot's belief that social workers should become more scientific and systematic was evidenced with the advent of research in social work in the late 1960s and early 1970s. He and Cannon would be heartened by the success of evidence-based practice and the active incorporation of research in social work practice in health care. Social workers with health-care backgrounds now head research teams and serve as program directors and other key positions at the National Institutes of Health and other federal agencies.

Although they initially disagreed about the role of social workers as critics or agents of socialization within hospitals, both Cabot and Cannon doubtless would be impressed by the growing number of social workers who serve as administrators of hospitals and health-care agencies and institutions across the United States.

Ida Cannon's statement that social work, when practiced at its best, "is a constantly changing activity, gradually building up guiding principles from accumulated knowledge yet changing in techniques" (1923, p. 9), still holds true. Social work in health care has been through a great deal in 100 years and has weathered seemingly insurmountable challenges through time. As noted by Darnell and Lawlor in Chapter 5 of this text, health social workers now face a role as policy implementors and advocates for the health-care delivery systems changes that come from the 2010 Patient Protection and Affordable Care Act. Despite these never-ending challenges, however, the guiding principles of social work in health care remain in force and are as strong today as they were in 1905.

SUGGESTED LEARNING EXERCISES

Learning Exercise 1.1

The people involved in establishing the first Social Service Department at Massachusetts General Hospital (Ida Cannon, Garnet Pelton, and Richard Cabot) were all White Americans and came from families without financial difficulties. Cabot was from a very privileged background. Cannon's father was a railroad administrator in Minnesota. That Pelton was able to obtain nurses' training at the turn of the century suggests that she had means. The subsequent century of social work's involvement in health care has seen the inclusion of many people from a number of racial, ethnic, and socioeconomic backgrounds. In small groups, indicate how you think the diverse nature of the health social work today might influence the professions' ability to advocate for the 23 million people whom Darnell and Lawlor (see Chapter 5 of this text) estimate will remain uninsured in 2019, despite the passage of the 2010 Patient Protection and Affordable Care Act.

Learning Exercise 1.2

The first hospital almoner in England (Mary Stewart) and the first hospital social worker in the United States (Garnet Pelton) were women whose hiring was championed by men with influence in medicine (Charles Loch and Richard Cabot). Who should be credited for the development of social work in health care? To what extent do you think that the development of social work in health care is attributable to the vision of Loch and Cabot? Were Loch and Cabot necessary catalysts for the development of social work in hospitals rather than its pioneers? In other words, to what extent to you think that the vision and actions of women like Pelton and Cannon contributed to the development of health social work? What does this all say about gender roles and relationships in the United States and within the profession of social work?

Learning Exercise 1.3

Despite improvements in our ability to treat serious disease and improvements in the affordability of health insurance, health disparities by race, ethnicity, and socioeconomic status in the United States have continued to rise. Do you think that the enactment of the Patient Protection and Affordability Act will (1) decrease health disparities or (2) do you think that, while it will decrease the number of people who are at risk for adverse health outcomes, it will widen the gap between those who do and do not have access to adequate and appropriate health care, and thus increase disparities? Divide into two groups and develop arguments for each position. How might health social work help to ameliorate health disparities in the United States?

REFERENCES

American Association of Hospital Social Workers. (1928). *Medical social case records submitted in the 1927 case competition of the American Association of Hospital Social Workers.* Chicago, IL: University of Chicago Press.

Bartlett, H. M. (1934). *Medical social work: A study of current aims and methods in medical social case work.* Chicago, IL: American Association of Medical Social Workers.

Bartlett, H. M. (1957). *Fifty years of social work in the medical setting: Past significance/future outlook.* New York, NY: National Association of Social Workers.

Bartlett, H. M. (1961). *Analyzing social work practice.* Silver Spring, MD: National Association of Social Workers.

Blythe, B. J., & Erdahl, J. C. (1986). Using stress inoculation to prepare a patient for open-heart surgery. *Health & Social Work, 11,* 265–274.

Bracht, N. (1974). Health care: The largest human service system. *Social Work, 19,* 532–542.

Brogen, M. S. (1964). Johns Hopkins Hospital Department of Social Service, 1907–1931. *Social Service Review, 38,* 88–98.

Burgess, D. J., Fu, S. S., & von Ryn, M. (1990). Why do providers contribute to disparities and what can be done about it? *Journal of General Internal Medicine, 19,* 1154–1159.

Cabot, E. D. (1869, December 8). *Letters of Elizabeth Cabot, Boston: Vol. 2. From Mrs. Twistleton's death to the beginning of her son Edward's illness, 1862 to 1885.* Retrieved from http://ocp.hul.harvard.edu/ww

Cabot, J. E. (1887). *A memoir of Ralph Waldo Emerson.* Boston, MA: Houghton Mifflin.

Cabot, R. C. (1911). Social service work in hospitals. *Chicago Medical Recorder, 33,* 307–321.

Cabot, R. C. (1912). Humanizing the hospitals. In S. Breckenridge (Ed.), *The child in the city* (pp. 41–52). Chicago, IL: Chicago School of Civics and Philanthropy.

Cabot, R. C. (1915). *Social service and the art of healing.* New York, NY: Moffat, Yard and Company.

Camarota, S. A, & Jensenius, K. (2009). *A shifting tide: Recent trends in the illegal immigrant population.* Retrieved from Center for Immigration Studies Web site: http://www.cis.org/IllegalImmigration ShiftingTide

Cannon, I. M. (1923). *Social work in hospitals: A contribution to progressive medicine.* New York, NY: Russell Sage.

Cannon, I. M. (1932). Report on the subcommittee on medical social service. In White House Conference on Child Health and Protection (Eds.), *Hospitals and child care: Section 1. Medical service* (pp. 131–272). New York, NY: Century.

Cannon, I. M. (1952). *On the social frontier of medicine.* Cambridge, MA: Harvard University Press.

Claiborne, N., & Vandenburgh, H. (2001). Social workers' role in disease management. *Health & Social Work, 26,* 217–225.

Commission on Hospital Care. (1947). *Hospital care in the United States.* New York, NY: Commonwealth Fund.

Cornelius, D. S. (1994). Managed care and social work: Constructing a context and a response. *Social Work in Health Care, 20,* 47–63.

Coulton, C. (1988). Prospective payment requires increased attention to quality of post hospital care. *Social Work in Health Care, 13,* 19–30.

Darwin, C. (1936). *The origin of species by means of natural selection: Or, the preservation of favored races in the struggle for life and the descent of man and selection in relation to sex.* New York, NY: Modern Library. (Originally published 1859)

Dobrof, J. (1991). DRGs and the social workers role in discharge planning. *Social Work in Health Care, 16,* 37–54.

Dodds, T. A. (1993). Richard Cabot: Medical reformer during the Progressive Era (1890–1920). *Annals of Internal Medicine, 119,* 417–422.

Evison, I. S. (1995). *Pragmatism and idealism in the professions: The case of Richard Clarke Cabot, 1869–1935* (Unpublished doctoral dissertation). University of Chicago, IL.

Flexner, A. (1910). *Medical education in the United States and Canada: A report to the Carnegie Foundation for the Advancement of Teaching.* New York, NY: Carnegie Foundation for the Advancement of Teaching.

Flexner, A. (1915). *Is social work a profession?* Paper presented at the meeting of the National Conference of Charities and Corrections, Baltimore, MD.

Gorin, S. H., Gehlert, S. J., & Washington, T. A. (2010). Health care reform and health disparities: Implications for social workers. *Health & Social Work, 35*(4), 243–247.

Grinker, R. MacGregor, H., Selan, K., Klein, A., & Kohrman, J. (1961). Early years of psychiatric social work. *Social Service Review, 35,* 111–126.

Institute of Medicine. (2002). *Unequal treatment: What healthcare providers need to know about racial and ethnic disparities in health care.* Washington, DC: National Academy Press.

Jarrett, M. C. (1919). *The psychiatric thread running through all social case work. Proceedings of the National Conference of Social Work.* Chicago, IL: University of Chicago Press.

Johnson, R. L., Roter, D., Powe, N. R., & Cooper, L. A. (2004). Patient race/ethnicity and quality of patient-physician communication during medical visits. *American Journal of Public Health, 94,* 2084–2090.

Lister, L. (1980). Role expectations of social workers and other health professionals. *Health & Social Work, 5,* 41–49.

Lollock, L. (2001). *The foreign born population of the United States: March 2000. Current Population Reports* (pp. 20–534). Washington, DC: U.S. Census Bureau.

Mailick, M. D. (1990). Short-term treatment of depression in physically-ill hospital patients. In K. W. Davidson & S. S. Clarke (Eds.), *Social work in health care: Handbook for practice* (pp. 401–413). New York, NY: Haworth Press.

Nacman, M. (1990). Social work in health settings: A historical review. In K. W. Davidson & S. S. Clarke (Eds.), *Social work in health care: Handbook for practice* (pp. 7–37). New York, NY: Haworth Press.

O'Brien, L. (1985). "A bold plunge into the sea of values": The career of Dr. Richard Cabot. *New England Quarterly, 58,* 533–553.

O'Conner, R. (1976). American hospitals: The first 200 years. *Journal of the American Hospital Association, 50,* 62–72.

Reamer, F. G. (1985). Facing up to the challenge of DRGs. *Health & Social Work, 10,* 85–94.

Reid, W. J., & Epstein, L. (1972). *Task-centered casework.* New York, NY: Columbia University Press.

Romanofsky, P. (1976). Infant mortality: Dr. Henry Dwight Chapin and the Speedwell Society 1890–1920. *Journal of the Medical Society of New Jersey, 73,* 33–38.

Rosenberg, C. E. (1967). The practice of medicine in New York a century ago. *Bulletin of the History of Medicine, 41,* 223–253.

Society for Social Work Leadership in Health Care. (2011, January 2). About SSWLHC. Retrieved from http://www.sswlhc.org/

Stites, M. A. (1955). *History of the American Association of Medical Social Workers.* Washington, DC: American Association of Medical Social Workers.

U.S. Department of Health, Education, and Welfare. (1976). *Medicare, 1971: Participating providers.* Office of Research and Statistics (Social Security Administration Publication No. SSA 76-11706). Washington, DC: U.S. Government Printing Office.

2

Social Work Roles and Health-Care Settings

TERI BROWNE

Necessarily, the role of health social workers through time has changed to accommodate federal, state, and local policy changes; trends in health and disease; and the changing roles of other health-care professionals. As discussed in Chapter 1, however, the basic function of social work remains, and social workers' roles today reflect their responsibility for treating the whole person by taking a biopsychosocial approach to outreach, assessment, intervention, and care.

Health social workers operate in a variety of environments and assume numerous roles in the design, delivery, and evaluation of care. Social workers facilitate linkages across organizational systems and professions to improve health care for both individuals and populations. This occurs in myriad settings, in a number of different ways, and with various levels of transdisciplinary collaboration. Health social workers need to be aware of these factors to most effectively provide services to individuals and communities.

Chapter Objectives
- Describe a biopsychosocial approach to health care and the professionals who deliver it.

- Define the role of the social worker on the health-care team.
- Outline the tasks of health social workers related to the delivery and design of health care.
- Discuss professional issues and challenges related to teamwork and recommendations for effective collaboration.

SOCIAL WORK'S BIOPSYCHOSOCIAL APPROACH TO HEALTH CARE

Increasingly, the recommended approach for health-care service delivery today is biopsychosocial. Proposed by Engel in 1977, the biopsychosocial model addresses the biological, social, environmental, psychological, and behavioral aspects of illness. This model expands the traditional medical model of health care that focuses primarily on the biological causes of disease. The biopsychosocial model considers the nonmedical determinants of disease in collaboration with the purely biological components. For example, a biopsychosocial model of health service takes into account patients' ability to purchase recommended medicine for diabetes when creating a treatment plan for patients rather than focusing only on laboratory results and physical status, as a medical-model approach would do. Lindau, Laumann, Levinson, and Waite's (2003) interactive biopsychosocial model expands Engel's model to include general health status

Note: The author would like to thank her University of South Carolina College of Social Work research assistants, Sonya Davis-Kennedy, Lesley Jacobs, Olivia Jones, Derrick Jordan, Cassidy Shaver, Valerie Stiling, Felix Weston, and Jennifer Worthington, for reviewing this chapter and making suggestions for added content.

rather than illness alone and consideration of the important role of social networks and cultural contexts in health. For the purposes of this chapter, the term *biopsychosocial* is used to indicate an approach to health service delivery that addresses the psychological and social aspects of health and treatment that includes behavioral and environmental factors.

Intervention that considers biopsychosocial issues related to health requires the use of a transdisciplinary team of professionals to address medical problems and concerns in a variety of settings. In addition to social workers, professionals may include physicians, physician assistants, and residents; nurses and nurse practitioners; dietitians; psychologists; patient care technicians; nurse and home health aides; physical, occupational, and speech therapists; administrators; chaplains; and pharmacists. Individual patients and members of their social support network are also increasingly recognized as critically important members of transdisciplinary teams (McWilliam, 2009).

Limits of the Medical Approach: Psychosocial Issues Related to Health

Before the introduction of Engel's biopsychosocial model, Nason and Delbanco (1976) recommended that providers of medical services attend to patients' psychosocial issues and advocated for the inclusion of social workers on health-care teams. Health social workers directly address the social, behavioral, and emotional concerns of individuals and their social support network as well as develop and administer policies and programs and conduct research that are attuned to the psychosocial needs of individuals.

On an individual level, people may not be able to understand illness and recommended treatment because of developmental disabilities; low literacy levels; or language, hearing, or vision barriers. Many medical conditions and treatments are very complex, and social workers may be required to explain these issues to patients and their families. Socioeconomic disadvantage can greatly impact a patient's ability to receive medical care. If she lacks adequate health insurance, transportation to medical appointments, prescription coverage, or money to buy nutritional supplements and special dietary products, her health may be compromised. Patients may need myriad services from a number of agencies, such as meal delivery, homemaker services, or physical therapy. Arranging and coordinating community services can be confusing or overwhelming for patients, especially for those with additional social, psychological, or medical burdens. Environmental factors also directly impact individuals' social functioning and health status (see Chapters 4 and 7 for models of how environmental factors influence health and functioning).

Emotional problems can be caused by and result from health problems (see Chapter 8). After a major medical procedure such as open heart surgery, a patient's anxiety may increase (Ben-Zur, Rappaport, Ammar, & Uretzky, 2000). Among people with cardiovascular disease, untreated depression has been found to increase the risk of a heart attack (Monster, Johnsen, Olsen, McLaughlin, & Sorenson, 2004). A person who is depressed may be less motivated to follow up with medical appointments. If he is not coping well with his diagnosis and treatment regimen, he may do less well physically (Livneh, 2000). Effective coping, enhanced self-efficacy, and optimism have been associated with enhanced quality of life in people with chronic illnesses (Rose, Fliege, Hildebrandt, Schirop, & Klapp, 2002).

Patients' social support networks can influence their health status significantly. As discussed in Chapter 13, families can provide important support and assistance during times of health crisis, or they can represent barriers to optimal care. For example, the husband of a breast cancer patient who does not support the doctor's recommendation for a double mastectomy may confound and even further harm the patient's health status by causing her to become reluctant to have the necessary surgery. Family structure and the availability of social support impacts the health of patients across their life course (Thompson, Auslander, & White, 2001).

Conversely, illness may exacerbate existing psychosocial problems; for example, a woman in a troubled marriage who becomes ill may lose her primary social support when her partner leaves because he cannot cope with the stress of her illness and its treatment. This may leave her with no transportation to medical appointments in addition to coping with issues related to role adjustment and loss, both of which can negatively impact her health.

If a child has supportive family members to help him with the challenges of medical problems and hospitalizations, he will likely fare better than a child who does not. Likewise, a woman recovering from heart surgery who has neighbors or family to help with household chores and child care may recuperate better and be more likely to attend weekly cardiac rehabilitation appointments than someone who has no help. Psychosocial issues like these, which occur outside hospitals and doctors' offices, greatly influence individuals' abilities to maintain their health.

Many individuals who seek medical care also have what Rehr (1982) refers to as "social illnesses and problems." These illnesses and problems are psychosocial rather than biological in nature, such as child or elder abuse, violence (including sexual assault and family violence), substance use, other harmful behaviors such as "cutting" or bulimia, and suicide attempts. All are factors that require social work attention and intervention to improve biopsychosocial status and, consequentially, health status. For example, Sormanti and Shibusawa (2008) found that 5.5% of women ages 50 to 64 years seen at emergency departments and primary care clinics were victims of intimate partner violence. This and other findings suggest a need for social workers in medical settings to intervene with patients who are burdened with these "social illnesses and problems" in addition to medical illnesses.

The current health-care environment in the United States (see Chapter 5) emphasizes cost containment through shorter hospital stays, briefer medical interventions, and the provision of fewer comprehensive services with fewer personnel. For example, decades ago,

individuals may have spent a number of weeks in a hospital recuperating from hip replacement or liver transplant surgery. Many surgical procedures that were once done on an inpatient basis are now performed in outpatient, same-day facilities. Lengthy hospital stays are now the exception rather than the rule because of fixed reimbursement for medical procedures, and an individual who has a hip replaced or receives a liver transplant may be discharged from the hospital a few days after her surgery.

The trend toward shorter hospital stays and greater reliance on outpatient care may exacerbate patient psychosocial problems. Bateman and Whitaker (2002) assert that social workers are needed in medical settings to address increased home care needs in part because they can provide discharge planning that links patients to necessary home health services. The authors also suggest that social workers should play a greater role in primary care settings, addressing medical issues on a preventive level to decrease morbidity and the need for hospitalization. (See Box 2.1.)

Related to an emphasis on medical cost containment is an increase in community health programs. Aimed at preventing illness or health issues, programs that confront issues such as prenatal care and cancer screening employ social workers in their orchestration and day-to-day functioning.

Health Settings and the Social Worker's Place Within Them

Direct health services are provided in various settings and include public and private hospitals, outpatient clinics, neighborhood health centers, ambulatory surgery centers, physician's offices, mobile care units, skilled nursing facilities, military settings, correctional facilities, schools, and health maintenance organizations. Care may be provided in centers devoted to specific diseases, such as kidney failure (dialysis centers), cancer (chemotherapy clinics), and human immunodeficiency virus (HIV)/acquired immunodeficiency syndrome (AIDS) (community health clinics), or in multipurpose organizations that address

Box 2.1 Health Social Work Profile

Mildred Williamson, MSW, PhD, is the director of programs and research for the Ambulatory and Community Health Network of the Cook County Bureau of Health Services in Chicago, IL. In this capacity, she creates health programs based on the community's needs. She previously was the administrator of the Woodlawn Health Center in Chicago and the Women and Children HIV Program at the Cook County Hospital. Williamson is a recipient of many local, state, federal, and private foundation grants for health research. She has served as a member of the Centers for Disease Control and Prevention's Advisory Council on HIV/AIDS Prevention and Care and is on the boards of directors of two Chicago HIV-related organizations: Vision House and the Families' and Children's AIDS Network. Williamson currently serves on the board of the AIDS Alliance for Children, Youth, and Families, a national organization of HIV family- and youth-centered care providers, advocates, and consumers that she helped found in 1994. She served as president of the organization's board from 1997 to 2001.

numerous health issues. For example, Rock and Cooper (2000) describe possible social work activities in a primary care clinic. These activities include patient assessment; screening and treatment for alcoholism, depression, and anxiety; case management; cognitive-behavioral therapy to improve patient self-management of the treatment regimes; and bereavement counseling.

Other practice settings might specifically treat acute medical needs (including outpatient services or services provided on an ad hoc basis) or chronic medical needs where patients are admitted and receive services for a period of time. Indirect health services, such as program and policy planning and health programming, may be overseen by professionals working on transdisciplinary teams via

local, state, and federal agencies; community organizations; government offices; or schools and research institutions. Health is considered across the life course in micro- and macrolevel settings, from prenatal and infant care to older adult and end-of-life care.

Health is a critical practice area for all social workers, both on clinical levels and macro levels, and social workers play an important role in each of these care settings. *U.S. News & World Report* (2010) ranked medical and public health social work as one of their 50 best careers of 2011. In 2010, 22% of all social workers were employed as medical and public health social workers, and it is projected that between 2008 and 2018 the number of health social workers in the United States will increase by 22% (U.S. Department of Labor, 2010).

Regulatory standards for social work in health care vary by state in the United States, with each state having a different set of licensing rules for social workers. Health organizations also differ in how they recommend and regulate the inclusion of social workers on health-care teams. As noted in Chapter 1, social workers have been involved in medical settings for over a century and are essential to the implementation of biopsychosocial models of health service delivery.

Empirical evidence indicates that approaches to health care that include social workers and nurses in addition to physicians result in better patient outcomes than approaches involving physicians alone; such evidence also suggests that social worker and nurse interventions are less costly. For example, Sommers, Marton, Barbaccia, and Randolph (2000) conducted an experimental research study on the effectiveness of an interdisciplinary team model in the provision of primary care. In this study, the intervention group received care from a primary care physician, registered nurse, and social worker while the control group received care from the primary care physician alone. The researchers found that the group cared for by the multidisciplinary team experienced significantly lower rates of hospitalization and hospital readmission, fewer follow-up physician visits, and increased participation in social activities. They estimated that the interdisciplinary approach saved at least $90 per patient (including the cost of the additional personnel), not including the savings from fewer physician visits.

Additional research supports the notion that social work services are needed by patients in health-care settings. McGuire, Bikson, and Blue-Howells (2005) distributed self-administered surveys to 684 patients receiving primary care services at four Veterans Affairs clinics. These surveys were completed anonymously and offered to every patient seen at the clinics during data collection. They measured patients' psychosocial needs such as financial assistance, housing, and counseling. Almost two-thirds of patients reported experiencing psychosocial barriers. Sixty-three percent reported financial problems, and 62% reported personal stress. More than one third (38%) of the patients had problems such as unemployment, poor transportation, and relationship issues. About a quarter of the patients were homeless (28%) or needed home health care (21%). Only 15% of those surveyed reported experiencing no psychosocial barriers to following primary care recommendations, and most of the patients (74%) had more than one social problem.

SOCIAL WORKER'S ROLE ON HEALTH TEAMS

Social workers are essential to the delivery and design of optimal health care. Social workers contribute via direct clinical contact with patients and their families as well as through roles in macrolevel settings. They work on health teams comprised of direct patient-care professionals and as administrators overseeing program planning and implementation. Health social work tasks are congruent with the goals of the profession of social work and include helping clients problem solve and cope with life stressors; linking individuals with resources, services, and opportunities;

promoting effective and humane service systems; and developing and improving social policy (Gambrill, 1997).

Hands-On Practice: Social Workers as Part of Health-Care Delivery

A wide variety of health social work tasks exist in direct patient-care settings. These include interventions with patients and members of their social support networks, collaborations with members of transdisciplinary teams, coordination of services within the community and entitlement agencies, advocacy with governmental bodies for patient needs, and supervision or administration in health facilities. Activities of the health social worker in direct patient-care settings include careful assessment of patient situations and the design and implementation of interventions.

Health Social Work Assessment

Social workers conduct an evaluation of the strengths and needs of individuals and members of their social support network as part of a social work assessment to identify assets and potential barriers to care. These efforts are specific to practice settings and influenced by organizational or regulatory requirements and the type of services offered by the organization. For example, a hospital may have a standard social work assessment tool used in all departments. Oncology social workers may use a standardized tool that is specific to the needs of cancer patients, whereas rehabilitation social workers likely will use a different type of assessment tool. Such assessment tools are not limited to disease, and social workers also help health-care teams assess psychological and social issues, such as domestic violence (Danis, 2003) and socioeconomic barriers to the attainment of quality health care, among other issues.

Health Social Work Intervention

Based on a careful assessment of needs, social workers provide assistance and develop and implement interventions to address identified needs. This process may include explaining

Box 2.2 Health Social Work Profile

Kay Ammon, MSW, LCSW, QSW, is a
social worker in the intensive care nursery
at Santa Clara Valley Medical Center in
San Jose, CA. Working with critically ill
infants and their families, Ammon orients
families to the nursery, which is highly
technical and can be overwhelming, and
discusses its policies and procedures.
Ammon provides emotional support, grief
counseling, coping with guilt and anxiety,
end-of-life care and information, referral,
and linkages to resources for ill children
and their families. As a Spanish-speaking
health-care provider working with many
Hispanic families, she considers herself a
"key link" between families and the health-
care team. She translates sophisticated
medical communications for patients'
families and coordinates family care
conferences. She helps families understand
complex medical terminology and
discharge recommendations.

social functioning of individuals (Dhooper,
1994). Health social workers use their clinical skills to help patients and their families
cope with illness and treatment recommendations. Many diagnoses, such as amyotrophic
lateral sclerosis (ALS; also called Lou Gch-
rig's disease), are very difficult for patients to
accept. ALS is a progressive neuromuscular
disease that is very debilitating and ultimately
fatal. A person given an ALS diagnosis may
be depressed, angry, and fearful. A health social worker is trained to provide counseling
to assist the patient cope with his diagnosis,
provide grief counseling for the losses that he
will experience as a result of his disease, and
encourage him to follow up with medical care
to maximize his quality of life.

In addition, recommended treatment regimens can be difficult for patients to follow.
A teenage boy diagnosed with diabetes may
find that the need to test his blood glucose levels several times a day, self-administer insulin shots while at school, and avoid sugar is
very cumbersome. He may choose to not follow medical advice because it conflicts with
his preferred lifestyle. A health social worker
can help him by empathizing with the intrusiveness of the diabetic treatment regime, providing supportive counseling, and helping him
find ways to cope with the difficult aspects
of his treatment regimen. She also may collaborate with the school nurse to explore the
possibility of the boy testing his blood glucose
level and self-administering insulin in her office. This would afford him greater privacy
than if he were to use a public space. Another
lifestyle intervention might include the social
worker discussing with the boy's parents the
types of food or refreshments served at home
or at parties to ensure that these foods conform to his diet. Some children and adolescents face stigma or misunderstanding about
their illness from their peers and classmates,
and in this case the social worker might offer
a class presentation to educate the patient's
peers about his disease and dispel any myths
or misinformation about diabetes that they
may possess, making them more familiar with
the disease and demystifying the boy's unique

the disease and its treatment to patients in a
manner that is sensitive to their literacy levels;
developmental stages; and language, visual,
or hearing barriers. Facilitating communication between providers and patients is a key
health social work role further discussed in
Chapter 10. (See Box 2.2.)

Social workers are familiar with the eligibility requirements of local and federal entitlement programs and can help patients and their
families access and learn more about these resources. Social workers are the health professionals who possess "the knowledge necessary
to assess social services needs [and] to secure
and coordinate community-based services"
(Berkman, 1996, p. 545). Health social workers can help patients gain needed resources by
providing case management services that refer
and link patients and their families to services
and other resources.

Furthermore, health social work has a
dual focus of enhancing social institutions'
responses to human needs and enhancing the

diet requirements and need for insulin injections during the school day.

For older adults, social workers in health care are able to provide couples and family counseling. A couple grieving over the death of their newborn daughter may see the hospital social worker for grief counseling. The social worker may work with an entire family to discuss their adjustment after a father's leg amputation. Likewise, interventions related to end-of-life care often require family conferences and intervention using a range of theory- and evidence-based intervention strategies. Health social workers often run support groups for patients and their families to provide education and support on a variety of health issues.

Health social workers may see patients referred by other professionals. Patients may be referred because of psychosocial issues that represent a barrier to effective treatment. For example, a hospital social worker may not see all patients who come to the emergency room but will be called to assess and provide services to victims of sexual assault or family violence or refer these victims to appropriate services. A social worker employed in a primary care setting may be asked to work only with patients and families who have identified psychosocial needs, such as problems coping with vision loss that preclude follow-up with recommended referrals or a lack of insurance to pay for needed medications. Likewise, a social worker employed by a hospital emergency department may be asked to work with a patient who comes to the department frequently for what essentially are primary-care needs. The referral might be to assess barriers to receiving and using preventive care and refer the patient for community services.

Conversely, some social workers see every patient who passes through their particular setting. For instance, transplant social workers evaluate the psychosocial issues that affect every patient in need of a transplant. The goal of the evaluation is to help the team decide if the patient should be accepted into the program. The social worker addresses the psychosocial issues that might interfere with a successful transplant and that must be resolved before a patient is scheduled for transplant surgery. Case management services are provided by social workers to patients while they are being worked up for transplant. Such services include referrals for community resources, financial counseling, and family and caregiver preparation and education for their posttransplant caregiving roles.

A common phenomenon in health social work practice is having patients, their families, and community members actively participate on health teams or act as advisors to programs and research. Underlying this trend is the idea that patients have a voice equal to that of professionals in their health-care planning and health research. The Center for Interdisciplinary Health Disparities Research at the University of Chicago, led by Sarah Gehlert, PhD, MSW, is part of a multisite federal program to develop centers for the study of population health and health disparities. Each project includes community members as stakeholders along with scientific investigators with specialties in the biological, social, and psychological aspects of health. Gehlert's team conducted 49 intensive focus groups with 503 community residents to determine community beliefs, concerns, and attitudes about breast cancer and its treatment. Social workers in clinical, administrative, and research roles are instrumental in helping health-care teams incorporate community members and consumers in planning and serve as advocates for them throughout the process.

On a health-care team or in an administrative role, social workers ensure that the social context of health is addressed in patient care and program planning. Miller and Rehr (1983) refer to social workers in health care as mediators between the health-care system and consumers. This work also involves advocating at the systems level for improvements in the delivery of care.

Social Work as Part of the Design of Health Care

The profession of social work has a dual focus on enhancing the social functioning of individuals and the responses of social institutions to human needs (Dhooper, 1994). A wide variety of health social work tasks exist in nondirect patient-care settings, such as community, university-based, and government agencies. These tasks might include public health social work, policy development, program planning, community education and screening, or research. In these macrolevel settings, social workers collaborate with other professionals and with policy makers, elected officials, and university faculty, administrators, and community members.

Health social workers design and implement community health programs and initiatives. For example, a social worker may work on a team that is planning a program to improve prenatal care. The social worker must then ensure that psychosocial barriers to prenatal care, such as a lack of child care at a prenatal clinic, are addressed as part of the initiative. Social workers also may provide education to individuals, groups, and communities on different health issues. Health social workers are involved in preventive services, such as health screening and immunizations. They can help identify individuals in need of services and providing linkages to such services via outreach programs. (See Box 2.3.)

At an even broader level, many social workers are involved in research that directly and indirectly influences policy, community and public health, and clinical practice. Routinely health social workers perform quality assurance and outcome measurement on the services they provide to track psychosocial issues and the impact of social work intervention on alleviating these issues. Social workers also perform research at the community or university level with individuals and communities, or as it relates to health-care issues in general.

For example, Caroline Jennette, MSW, is a social work research specialist at the University of North Carolina Kidney Center. The mission of the Kidney Center is to reduce the burden of chronic kidney disease through research, clinical care, and community outreach. Jennette maintains a variety of roles in her position, including study coordination,

---

Box 2.3 Health Social Work Profile

Rose Popovich, MSW, LCSW, is the 2001 recipient of the Ida M. Cannon Award for Distinguished Leadership from the Society for Social Work Leadership in Health Care. She is the executive director of the performance improvement program for Community Health Network in Indianapolis, IN. The network consists of five acute care hospitals, outpatient surgery centers, a home care agency, a rehabilitation center, integrated physician services, a family medicine residency, outpatient clinics in schools, wellness services for employers, as well as other services. Her team applies the methodologies of performance improvement to a variety of issues confronting the system from throughput to electronic order entry, patient falls, frequent emergency room patient visitors, physician credentialing processes—anything and everything, both administrative and clinical. Popovich says that her social work background is essential to the creation of the community health program she oversees in that it helps her to better understand the needs of the population served. Her social work background also was essential to understand and assess customer needs, helping teams define their goals and metrics and facilitating the change process.

---

community education, and conducting research on health policy and state policy diffusion. She also acts as the legislative liaison for the Kidney Center and keeps her colleagues current on policy issues affecting the nephrology community and patient access to care. Jennette coordinates a large research registry of patients with glomerular disease and ensures that investigators abide by the rules governing ethical practice of research with human subjects. She is a member of the American Society of Nephrology's *KidneyNews* editorial board, of which she is a regular contributor of policy articles. A typical day for Jennette may include consulting with an investigator on a research project, scanning for policies in sessions pertaining to kidney disease, editing patient education materials, going over informed consent with a participant for inclusion in a research registry, and working on an independent research project.

Social workers have an active voice in large funding organizations such as the National Institutes of Health (NIH) and make sure that psychosocially relevant research is conducted. Many social work scholars have received funding from the NIH for health research, and social work research has been made a priority at NIH. In 2003, NIH created a social work research working group to promote NIH-funded social work research (see http://obssr.od.nih.gov/pdf/SWR_Report .pdf for more details). Since then, several NIH institutes have promoted social work research funding and conducted an NIH summer training course on topics of interest to social workers and others (such as genetics and community-based participatory research). Organizations such as the Society for Social Work Research and the Social Work Policy Institute provide information and resources for social workers who are interested in health research.

SURVEY OF SOCIAL WORK PROFESSIONALS

Social workers' roles are diverse and aspire to achieve total patient health as well as to provide community and public service to bring about positive health status on a larger scale. Social workers entering the field today have innumerable opportunities to affect the quality of individual patients' lives, the health of myriad communities, and the field in general. To illustrate the many and varied responsibilities and opportunities with which social workers are faced as they prepare to enter the field today, consider actual professionals currently contributing to the field.

Case Management and Patient Advocacy

In her former role as a hospital social worker at MedCenter One Health Systems in Bismarck, ND, Jennifer Schlinger, MSW, LCSW, primarily worked in the rehabilitation department, collaborating daily with physicians, physical and occupational therapists, dietitians, nurses, and other professionals. Although most of her patients were adults, she occasionally worked with pediatric patients and provided services to all individuals who were admitted to the rehabilitation department. Patient stays are limited to 6 weeks while patients receive medical treatment and are assisted with recuperation surgery or medical crises. Schlinger performed case management activities on a daily basis, helping patients plan their discharge and arrange follow-up care. This was particularly challenging for patients living in rural areas of the state in which no local home health or other health-care services are available. Schlinger spent a great deal of time advocating for patients, especially those on Medicaid who are burdened with an annual 30-day limit for rehabilitation services. Schlinger helped patients obtain entitlements, access community resources, and create and nurture social support systems. She acted as a liaison between patients and the medical team as well as community organizations. Schlinger currently works as a civilian social worker/case manager with the North Dakota Army National Guard. She works with soldiers to ensure that they are medically ready to deploy and meet retention standards. She serves as a liaison between the soldier and the state medical detachment physicians and the soldier's unit.

Health social workers also may serve as supervisors in their practice settings by providing clinical supervision, or they may hold a position as a liaison between the department of social work and the administration of the agency or organization for which they work.

Sharon Mass, PhD, MSW, is the director of case management and palliative care at Cedars-Sinai Medical Center in Los Angeles. In this position she oversees a cross-disciplinary group of over 120 staff members (50 social workers, 35 nurse case managers, 8 home care coordinators, 3 physicians, 2 advanced practice nurses, 6 administrative support staff, and other per diem staff). She is president-elect of the American Case Management Association, an organization of 3,000 nurses and social workers who provide case management in acute-care hospital settings. She is a founding member of the board of directors of the American Case Management Association. Mass has published in the areas of case management and end-of-life care. She is an adjunct professor at the School of Social Work at the University of Southern California and has received many awards for her work in social work in health care. Mass attends daily administrative and medical staff meetings about health-care delivery in which she advocates for patients from the social work and case management services departments. She provides supervision for social work licensure and guides social workers' professional development at the hospital. She also is active in committees on patients' rights and is a member of the institutional review board.

Assessment of Need: The First Step of Care

Some social workers in health care see all patients in the clinical settings in which they work. Jeff Harder, MSW, LICSW, is a transplant social worker at the University of Washington Medical Center in Seattle. In his work with the kidney and pancreas transplant program, Harder conducts psychosocial evaluations on all patients referred for a kidney or pancreas transplant. Harder assists patients and their caregivers with finding needed resources, such as local housing for follow-up outpatient care after transplant, if necessary. He provides counseling, education on what to expect after a transplant, and discharge planning. Harder assists patients and their families with coping, information, referrals, assessment of further needs, and vocational rehabilitation. He continues to assist patients who previously received transplants when they lose insurance

coverage or have questions about returning to work.

Needs-Based Care: Assisting the Client in Need

Some health social workers see only those patients in their health-care setting who require their services. In addition, other health social workers may work on a freelance basis. For example, Mary Raymer, MSW, ACSW, is a psychiatric social worker and licensed marriage and family therapist who has worked with terminally ill patients and their families for 25 years. An early hospice leader, she was the social work section leader for the National Hospice and Palliative Care Organization and is one of the originators of the Social Work End-of-Life Education Project. She has her own private practice and specializes in complicated grief reactions, stress, and terminal illness. The majority of her practice involves counseling individuals and families who are coping with grief.

Public Health Social Work

Marvin R. Hutchinson, MSW, LISWAP, CP, is the recently retired director of public health social work for the South Carolina Department of Health. He participated regularly in legislative, policy, and program meetings (ensuring a psychosocial emphasis to the proceedings) and oversaw the public health social work program. His staff included regional public health social work directors and state program public health social work consultants with whom he worked to develop new initiatives for more than 225 master's-level public health social workers. These social workers are employed in clinical, community, and management positions across the state in programs such as maternal health, child health, family planning, tuberculosis treatment, school health, children's rehabilitative services, AIDS, and home health services. Hutchinson taught at the College of Social Work of the University of South Carolina. He directed violence and suicide prevention initiatives and oversaw the MSW/master's in public health internship program. He presented workshops and papers to interagency staff as well as to audiences at state, regional, national, and international conferences. In addition, Hutchinson serves on national-level committees (representing the Association of State and Territorial Public Health Social Workers, the National Council on Aging, the Public Health Foundation, and the National Association of Social Workers) and legislative committees regarding issues such as school health, violence, systems, and integration. He received recognition from the Surgeon General for public health services and is the 2005 South Carolina NASW Social Worker of the Year.

Multilevel Intervention: Diversifying Responsibility

Social workers can intervene both on an individual and a systems level in health care. Patricia Ann Gibson, MSW, ACSW, is director of the Comprehensive Epilepsy Program at the Wake Forest University School of Medicine in North Carolina. She is involved in numerous organizations, including the American Epilepsy Society, the Epilepsy Foundation, the International Bureau of Epilepsy, and International Epilepsy Congress. Gibson also is on the professional advisory board of the National Tuberous Sclerosis Alliance and has authored numerous publications for patients and professionals. In 1976, she developed and continues to run a nationwide telephone information line for epilepsy. She speaks with patients and their families about their concerns. After learning of parents' inability to afford their children's medicine, she spent 8 years developing an epilepsy medication fund for the state of North Carolina and supplements this fund with a variety of fundraising efforts (including a chili cook-off, yard sales, and offering snacks at her office for donations). Gibson sees patients for education as well as individual, family, and group counseling. Much of her time is spent speaking and conducting workshops, conferences, and symposia. These include education on epilepsy for primary and secondary schools, parents, physicians, nurses, medical

students, hospitals, and community organizations. She also organizes several national conferences, such as Advances in the Management of Epilepsy, the Pediatric Neurology Symposium, and the International Conference on Epilepsy Care. In these trainings, she presents a transdisciplinary approach to the treatment of epilepsy.

John Q. Gowan, MSW, is the coordinator of consumer relations and community development for the End-Stage Renal Disease (ESRD) Network 7 of Florida and is another example of a health social worker involved in direct patient- and community-level service. A major part of his job is organizing and presenting workshops for dialysis unit staff members about challenging patient situations and increasing staff sensitivity to patient needs. At the ESRD Network, Gowan also provides assistance to renal patients and their families, assists with rehabilitation promotion for ESRD patients, and facilitates the state's Patient Advisory Committee, which addresses dialysis patient concerns and encourages patient involvement in their care.

Administration and Social Work in the Design of Health Care

Social workers play an important role in the design of health-care delivery through administrative roles in clinical settings, overseeing both social workers and other professionals. Polly Jones, MSW, MSM, LCSW, CPHQ, is the director of clinical excellence for Ascension Health in Burlington, IN. She is responsible for the coordination of accreditation activities for the more than 70 Ascension hospitals, including educational initiatives, individual consultations, and quality improvement activities, and for facilitating the Joint Commission on Accreditation of Health Care Organizations system survey each year. She also oversees programming and projects for all of the hospitals. In these capacities, she advocates for the social work profession by encouraging social work involvement in activities, programs, and teams at a local level. On a daily basis, she travels to different hospitals across the country to work with transdisciplinary teams on various projects. As a project manager, she facilitates team interaction and promotes improved patient outcomes. She reports that her social work training is invaluable as it relates to knowledge of group dynamics, change theory, and how systems work. Jones frequently publishes and speaks about various topics related to health social work and was the 2005 president of the Society of Social Work Leadership in Healthcare. As president of this organization, she networked with social work leaders across the country to provide education, advocacy, and other support to social workers in myriad health-care settings.

Filling the Health-Care Void: Social Work's Myriad Responsibilities

Social workers sometimes have health-care–specific responsibilities. Others, however, are responsible for a variety of roles within the setting in which they work. Douglas Kirk, MSSW, LCSW, for example, is the program director for mental health intensive case management at the Veterans Hospital in Madison, WI. He works with veterans at the hospital who require intensive mental health case management. In describing his various tasks in this role, Kirk stated:

> On any one day, I might be in with a client in a medical examination for hepatitis, helping both the physician understand the patient (not all doctors have patience for the mentally ill) and the patient to understand the doctor. I might then be on the phone with the district attorney [DA] advocating for probation rather than jail, helping the DA understand that jail may be counterproductive for this mentally ill person or explaining to the group home how to care for the edema in this man's legs. Later that day, I might be showing someone else how to operate a washing machine and observing him to see if the recent increase in medication has resulted in any side effects. While doing the wash, we might discuss how to cope with his voices. Afterward, we may rework his budget to reflect his wish to have more money for fun

on the weekends. Later that day, I might be meeting with the family of a patient who are trying their best but instead are enabling the patient to be stuck and not move forward. I help them see that their son has skills and strengths and is more than his mental illness. I might take that patient to the store to teach him how to shop more independently and eat more nutritiously. Earlier I cleaned diarrhea off the floor for a dehydrated person who lives alone, hugged another who is having a particularly lonely day, and spent time with a very psychotic person who has exercised his right to decline medication but is suffering as a result. (personal communication, March 25, 2005)

In treating each individual case, Kirk is faced with an unusual collection of responsibilities that fall under his area of expertise as a health social worker. In this role, he must work multilaterally in order to provide the best care for his patients, addressing microlevel needs for one patient and macrolevel issues in order to ensure that another is treated appropriately and in his or her best interest.

Dawn Romano, MSW, LMSW, LCSW, is a clinical social work supervisor at Children's Mercy Hospitals and Clinics in Kansas City, MO. She is another example of a social worker who performs a multitude of tasks. Her daily clinical responsibilities include crisis intervention, child abuse and neglect assessment, and trauma counseling to patients and families. As a supervisor, she oversees the hospital's social workers, providing child abuse orientation and clinical supervision. She serves on a variety of committees, including the trauma and domestic violence committees. The majority of her work centers on child abuse and neglect assessments, and she meets with children and families to complete psychosocial assessments for child abuse and neglect. Working closely with her team, she completes hotline reports and works with the child protection services agencies to assess the immediate safety of children. She advises law enforcement officials on the reporting and investigation of child abuse and neglect, provides support and education to families, and connects families to community support services. She provides case management services and is a part of the trauma and hospital emergency response teams. She is the social worker representative on a team including a chaplain and nursing supervisor that provides crisis intervention, education, emotional support, and grief counseling to families whose children have been injured in motor vehicle accidents, shootings, drownings, falls, suicides, and other tragedies.

COLLABORATING WITH OTHER PROFESSIONALS

In the various health settings described, social workers are called on to collaborate with other health-care professionals. Social workers may work on teams that are multidisciplinary (each professional works autonomously with little interaction), interdisciplinary (professionals interact with one another to provide services but maintain clear professional boundaries dictated by distinct terminology and interventive preferences), or, ideally, transdisciplinary (close collaboration among the professionals, including sharing a common language and approach to programming and intervention planning).

The level of collaboration within a team is specific to individual health settings and their norms and practices. At one end of the spectrum, collaborating with other professionals might occur indirectly. For example, physicians may read social work notes in a patient's chart yet never discuss the patient's care directly with the social worker. Social workers may be employed at health settings on a per diem or consultant basis and not be active members of teams. At the other extreme, professionals may work directly with one another on a daily basis, confer frequently about patient issues, visit patients as a team, and make all care planning decisions based on group meetings and group feedback, with all members having an equal voice in the process.

Challenges to Professional Collaboration

Professional collaboration can be challenging in a health setting. Even if the team interacts frequently, professionals may not have equal voices in the care planning process, professional roles may not be clear, and professional perspectives and ethics may clash. The execution of team collaboration varies significantly. At care planning meetings, the social worker may be a passive observer and not encouraged to participate unless necessary. Alternatively, social workers may organize and run such meetings.

Workplace change represents a significant challenge to health social workers. Health-care provision increasingly is focused on reducing costs and decreasing hospital stays. Professional departments, including counseling services and community education, have been reduced in size or eliminated (Sulman, Savage, & Way, 2001). Another challenge to health social work is the co-opting by other professions of tasks that historically have fallen under the rubric of social work. This is notably true in case management, with nurses and other professionals performing case management activities. Hospital social work departments are being replaced by nurse-led case management departments, and nursing professionals increasingly are supervising health social workers (Alveo, 2001; Globerman, White, & McDonald, 2003). In a study of discharge planners, Holliman, Dziegielewski, and Teare (2003) found that nurse case managers are paid more than social work case managers. The authors found that private hospitals were more likely to hire nurses as discharge planners, although federal and state hospitals were more likely to hire social workers as discharge planners.

Collaboration may be hampered by ambiguity of roles and tasks, and different disciplines may not understand one another's lexicon and procedures. Health professionals have unique training, education, and perspectives toward practice. Physicians, nurses, and social workers (along with the other members of the transdisciplinary team) view and frame patient problems and their solutions to those problems through separate lenses. Carlton (1984) wrote: "[S]ocial work is a profession whose purpose, logic, and underlying rationale differ from those of other professions" (p. xiii). Rolland (1994) asserts:

> Clinicians from different disciplines bring their own assets and liabilities to the interaction of family and illness and disability. Physicians and nurses have a surplus of technical medical information. They can have trouble seeing the psychosocial forest through the technological lens they need to use to help the patient medically. And if they can switch lenses, often they have trouble deciding which trees in the medical forest are psychosocially important. They may have difficulty taking the 1,001 facts about diabetes and distilling from them the essence of the psychosocial meaning of the disorder. (pp. 20–21)

Social workers are both trained and ethically obligated to advocate for their patients. This may lead to interprofessional strain because other professionals may be annoyed by patient and family behavior that does not fit neatly with the policies and procedures of health-care agencies or institutions. Physicians and nurses may get frustrated with the parents of an infant in an intensive care nursery who visit only late at night. They may view the parents as negligent because they do not spend the entire day with the ill child and awaken the baby when they do visit. While empathizing with the staff's need to cope with visitation beyond the "normal" visiting hours, the social worker can inform the team about the parents' work schedules that preclude daytime visits. The social worker also can advocate for these parents, pointing out that despite working during the day, the parents visit every day, spending several hours with the infant, and are indeed very devoted parents. Social work advocacy also can play a role when issues arise regarding nontraditional families. In situations in which the medical team does not view a same-sex partner as legitimate, social workers can advocate for inclusion of such partners in care planning.

Health Social Work Recommendations

Many recommendations can be made to maximize health team collaboration. Professional differences in health settings can be reframed as assets rather than liabilities. A biopsychosocial model of health requires the perspectives of a number of professionals to most effectively deliver health services. In terms of training transdisciplinary health professionals, Headrick and Khaleel (2008) suggest that students should be offered a curriculum that integrates theory and practice content from each discipline and that students should have interprofessional learning and training opportunities. An example of a transdisciplinary education model is the Institute for Healthcare Improvement's Open School, which offers students from social work, medicine, nursing, pharmacy, physical therapy, public health, dentistry, and other schools transdisciplinary learning opportunities online and at chapter meetings across the country (see www.ihi.org/ihi for more details).

Cowles (2003, p. 21) lists specific objectives that are essential to maximal team collaboration:

- Role clarity and flexibility
- Mutual respect and trust
- Consensus on group norms, values, commitment, and purpose
- An egalitarian attitude; a sense of equal importance
- A sense of group bond and interdependence rather than autonomy
- Open communication and sharing
- Flexible leadership and decision making; shared power
- Flexible membership composition based on case needs
- A stable core membership
- A sense of both group and professional identity
- Ability to negotiate and reach consensus
- Goal focus and goal clarity
- Record keeping of meetings

- Attention to both the task and maintenance functions of the team
- A systems perspective

Health social workers need to remember that clients do not normally present to the health-care system for social work services specifically; rather, they present with medical needs that have psychosocial components. As such, it is the social worker's responsibility to be familiar with the biological aspects of the biopsychosocial care model. Social workers should enhance their understanding of medical issues and terminology so that they are knowledgeable when talking to patients and their families and can participate fully on health-care teams.

Bronstein (2003) suggests a model of transdisciplinary collaboration grounded in the frameworks of collaboration theory, role theory, and ecological systems theory. Bronstein's model proposes that transdisciplinary teams should include interdependence of the individual team members, newly created professional activities, flexibility, collective ownership of goals, and process reflection. In this model, *interdependence* refers to frequent communication, interaction, and mutual respect among team members. Newly created professional activities represent collaborative opportunities that take advantage of team members' individual expertise to achieve team outcomes that would be difficult to accomplish if team members worked alone.

Health social workers can support and reinforce other team members' roles rather than engage in turf wars and provide staff education on psychosocial issues to other team members (Nason & Delbanco, 1976). Globerman, White, Mullings, and Davies (2003) recommend that social workers minimize role conflict with other members of the health team by proactively defining and promoting their unique roles and tasks, continuously updating their knowledge base related to the relevant practice area, and acknowledging the expertise of other professionals. They also advise that social workers evaluate and track the impact of their services. Doing this allows social

workers to identify areas in which they specialize, establish a niche on the team, and show the effectiveness of their unique contribution to health care. Social workers should play an active role on quality assurance or continuous quality improvement committees.

As Kayser, Hansen, and Groves (1995) state:

> [T]o obtain resources and the commitment from hospital administrations to provide comprehensive services, social work departments need to continually collect the data that substantiates that they are the professionals best trained for such responsibilities and can deliver the services in the most cost-effective manner. (p. 498)

This is particularly true in the era of managed care, for which medical spending is limited and cost containment is mandated by health organizations (Segal, 2002). If social workers can show that they reduce medical costs by reducing hospital stays, increasing patient satisfaction and quality of life, and reducing morbidity and mortality, they can maintain their presence in health organizations. Social workers also need to equip themselves with the skills to intervene effectively with patients on a short-term or ad hoc basis.

Simmons (1989) reviewed the fiscal advantage of social work services in health-care settings and noted that social workers conserve institutional resources in several ways. They link patients with insurance and resources and thus increase reimbursement, reduce hospital stays through effective discharge planning and linkages to outpatient resources, increase service provision through outreach and program planning and mediating conflicts between patients and providers, enhance revenue through the creation of new programs and services, and improve the productivity of the medical team by participating in employee assistance programs that support team members.

Health social workers also must advocate for themselves as active members of health teams. Lee (2002) and Globerman (1999) recommend that health social workers create literature that informs other professionals and consumers about the role of health social workers, provide team training about the social work activities and roles, provide evidence of the effectiveness of social work services, and be visible parts of health settings by volunteering to be part of task forces and committees. Social workers must document their interventions with patients and their families. Brief, quickly completed forms may suffice to achieve this aim if social workers are burdened by large caseloads and time constraints.

Changes in health-care delivery and organizational constraints affect all members of the health team. Just as they help clients cope with illness, its treatment, and the changes that illness entails, social workers can use those skills to help the health-care team adapt to hospital and program restructuring (Globerman, 1999). Social workers can provide professional support to their colleagues when they face challenging patient situations, such as when patients die (Roberts, 1989). These efforts allow health social workers to help minimize role conflict with other team members as well as demonstrate that social work is effective.

TREATING THE WHOLE PERSON: SOCIAL WORK'S PRIMARY ROLE

Health social workers fill various roles, work in myriad settings, and perform a broad collection of tasks on the clinical and administrative levels. Social work fulfills a critical function in the biopsychosocial approach to health care. As Romano (1981) wrote:

> [S]ocial work occupies a unique position in that it has its feet in health and mental health, its hands in the social sciences, its viscera in clinical intervention skills, and its head and heart in a commitment to the issues of the quality of life of disabled persons in society. (p. 15)

Although fiscal, organizational, and professional challenges exist in providing health services that fully incorporate the biological, social, and psychological determinants

of health, social work is a vital component to health teams to explain and significantly affect the complex pathways through which variables at different levels influence health (Keefler, Duder, & Lechman, 2001).

SUGGESTED LEARNING EXERCISES

Learning Exercise 2.1

As a group, compile a list of questions to ask a health social worker based on what you learned in this chapter. You may want to ask about the social worker's role or roles, tasks, and ethical challenges as well as if the social worker is part of an transdisciplinary health-care team. Find a health social worker in your community and arrange an individual interview, using the list of questions your group creates for this exercise. Be sure that your group interviews social workers working in a variety of health-care settings, including those who work with individuals and families and those who work on a community level or in a research institution. Either by an oral presentation or a written synopsis, report back to the group the information that you obtain.

Learning Exercise 2.2

Using the profiles of health social workers throughout this chapter and information that your group gathers from the interviews in Exercise 2.1, compare and contrast the different roles in health-care settings. What is it exactly that health social workers do? How are the roles in different settings similar? How are they different? What types of transdisciplinary teams and ethical challenges do different social workers encounter? What are the differences and similarities between clinical health social workers and those who work in an administrative or policy-level capacity?

Learning Exercise 2.3

Using information from this chapter and the interviews from Learning Exercise 2.1, discuss the differences between social workers and the other members of the health-care team. What are some fundamental differences? What does social work uniquely bring to the care of patients? What are differences in the codes of ethics of different professions? How can these differences manifest themselves in health settings at various levels? What are some examples of professional challenges or clashes? How can social workers collaborate most effectively with other professionals on a team-, agency-, and policy-level setting? How might you as a health social worker make a case for why social work, social services, case management, or patient education is your domain and not that of another discipline? (You also may incorporate content from Chapter 1 and social work history course(s) in answering these questions.)

Learning Exercise 2.4

Richard is a 38-year-old, married African American male who previously was diagnosed with type 1 diabetes. Recently, Richard was diagnosed with kidney failure. He is married with three children, ages 5, 10, and 12, and just started a job as an electrician. Richard is an only child and has limited social support network members. Although his wife is an active member of a Baptist church, Richard does not consider himself to be religious and does not attend church services with his family. He is the sole income provider for his family. Because Richard is in a probationary period for his new job, he will not qualify for employee group health insurance for two more months and thus cannot miss a day of work without risking termination. Richard's health problems and new job have caused him a significant amount of stress and increased marital discord. This is exacerbated by long work days and frequent overtime work. Richard's acute kidney failure condition has progressed to the point at which he will have to start dialysis, and he has been referred to a kidney transplant program for an evaluation by the transdisciplinary team that includes a transplant social worker. The team will interview Richard and determine if he is a candidate for a kidney transplant.

As mentioned in this chapter, psychosocial barriers can impact whether a patient will be considered for a transplant. Considering the biopsychosocial approach, identify factors that the transplant social worker may consider when assessing Richard. If possible, role-play a screening assessment of Richard with another member of your group. (This can be done by several dyads of group members.) Discuss as a group what items should be included in this social work assessment and why. Should the social worker recommend that Richard receive a kidney transplant, based on his biopsychosocial assessment? What are the benefits of a transdisciplinary approach in the kidney transplant center?

Learning Exercise 2.5

Using information from this and other chapters in this book, pick a setting that may employ a health social worker. Create a brochure or handout for clients or customers of that setting that describes the role of the social worker in that organization. Be sure to include information about the different services and tasks that the social worker is responsible for in that setting.

SUGGESTED RESOURCES

The National Association of Social Work (www.socialworkers.org) has numerous resources for health social work, including a health specialty practice section, social work summits that include health social work organizations, continuing education modules (available online) regarding social work and various health-care settings (such as oncology and end of life), and social work clinical indicators for various health settings.

Additional Resources for Social Workers
American Case Management Association— www.acmaweb.org

The goal of the American Case Management Association is to provide the highest quality professional developmental services such as mentoring, resource information, educational forums, and new opportunities for networking.

American Lung Association—www.lungusa.org

The American Lung Association is the leading organization working to save lives by preventing lung disease and improving lung health through education, advocacy, and research. The main goals of the organization are to stop tobacco use and tobacco-related lung disease, improve the air we breathe, and reduce the burden of lung disease on patients and their families.

American Network of Home Health Care Social Workers—www.homehealthsocialwork.org

This network is a professional association organized for the benefit of social workers in health-care settings. Its Web site has an abundance of resources related to health-care issues.

American Public Health Association—www.apha.org

The American Public Health Association is made up of and represents a diverse group of health professionals and others who are concerned about their health or the health of their communities. The association aims to protect families and communities from preventable, serious health threats and to ensure accessible education within the community regarding health services and disease prevention.

Association of Oncology Social Work—www.aosw.org

The Association of Oncology Social Work (AOSW) is a not-for-profit organization geared toward improving the psychosocial services of clients with cancer and their families. AOSW strives to improve services through education, advocacy, networking, research, and resource development.

Association of Pediatric Oncology Social Workers—www.aposw.org

The mission of the Association of Pediatric Oncology Social Workers is to enhance pediatric psychosocial oncology care through clinical social work practice, advocacy, research, education, and program development. Some of their goals include advocating for both national and international policies that will improve the lives of children with cancer and their families as well as promote the ethical standards of social workers working in pediatric oncology.

Association of State and Territorial Public Health Social Workers—www.astho.org

The Association of State and Territorial Public Health Social Workers is a not-for-profit organization that represents the public health agencies of the United States, U.S. territories, the District of Columbia, and its own public health employees. The agency's main focus is to create and influence sound public health policies as well as ensure excellence in state-based public health practice.

Council of Nephrology Social Work—www.kidney.org/professionals/CNSW/index.cfm

The Council of Nephrology Social Work works within the National Kidney Foundation as a professional membership council while also networking with other agencies, the government, and private groups. Its purpose is to aid patients and their families with the various psychosocial stressors of kidney disease and to support federal regulations governing standards of nephrology social work practice.

Council on Social Work Education—www.cswe.org

The Council on Social Work Education is a partnership of educational and professional institutions, social welfare agencies, and individual members. It is the only recognized accrediting agency for social work education in the country.

Epilepsy Foundation—www.epilepsyfoundation.org

The Epilepsy Foundation is a voluntary agency dedicated solely to the welfare of patients and their families with epilepsy. The agency strives to ensure that people with seizures are able to engage in all life experiences, to improve how people with epilepsy are viewed within society, and to promote research.

National Association of Children's Hospitals and Related Institutions—www.childrenshospitals.net

The National Association of Children's Hospitals and Related Institutions is a not-for-profit agency made up of children's hospitals, large pediatric units in medical centers, and related health systems. This agency is a voice for health-care systems and ensures children's access to services and hospitals' ability to provide services that are needed by children.

National Association of Perinatal Social Workers—www.napsw.org

This organization provides support and a forum to communicate for perinatal social workers and the unique situations in which they work, sharing knowledge as well as ensuring excellence in social work practice regarding families and individuals during pregnancy and the first year of life.

National Hospice and Palliative Care Organization—www.nhpco.org

This organization is dedicated to enhancing end-of-life care and expanding access to hospice care with the goal of profoundly improving quality of life for people dying in the United States and their families.

National Multiple Sclerosis Society—www.nationalmssociety.org

The National Multiple Sclerosis Society helps individuals throughout the nation fight the challenges associated with living with multiple sclerosis (MS). The society funds research to prevent, treat, and cure MS and provides advocacy and education for communities as well as services for individuals and their families dealing with MS.

Social Work Policy Institute—www.socialworkpolicy.org

The Social Work Policy Institute is a think tank created under the National Association of Social Workers (NASW). Their main ideals are to strengthen social work's voice in public policy, to educate policy makers through the collection and disbursement on the effectiveness of social work, and to create a forum to discuss issues in health care and social service delivery.

Society for Social Work Leadership in Health Care—www.sswlhc.org

This organization is committed to promoting the universal availability, accessibility, coordination, and effectiveness of health care in regard to the psychosocial components of health and illness.

Society for Transplant Social Workers—www.transplantsocialworker.org/index.cfm

This organization is dedicated to promoting and ensuring ethical social work practice and encourage research and publication on psychosocial issues related to transplants.

Veterans Health Administration—www1.va.gov/health

The Veterans Health Administration serves the needs of U.S. veterans by providing primary care, specialized care, and related medical and social support services.

INTERNATIONAL SOCIAL WORK ORGANIZATIONS

International Federation of Social Workers—www.ifsw.org

The International Federation of Social Workers is a worldwide organization striving for social justice, human rights, and social development through the growth of social workers, ethical practices, and the international cooperation and communication of social workers and their professional organizations.

The countries listed have Web sites for their national social work organizations.

Asian and Pacific Association for Social Work Education—www.apaswe.info

Australian Association of Social Workers—www.aasw.asn.au

Austria—www.sozialarbeit.at

Brazilian Congress of Social Workers—www.cfess.org.br/_ingles/home.php

British Association of Social Workers—www.basw.co.uk

Canadian Association of Social Workers—www.casw-acts.ca

Danish Association of Social Workers—www.socialrdg.dk

Finland Union of Professional Social Workers—www.talentia.fi

France Association of Social Workers—www.anas.fr

Ghana Association of Social Workers—www.gasow.org

Hellenic Association of Social Workers—www.skle.gr

Hong Kong Social Workers Association—www.hkswa.org.hk/chi

Icelandic Association of Social Workers—www.felagsradgjof.is

India: National Association of Professional Social Workers in India—www.napswionline.org

Irish Association of Social Workers—www.iasw.ie

Israel Association of Social Workers—www.socialwork.org.il

Italy—www.assnas.it

Japanese Association of Psychiatric Social Workers—www.japsw.or.jp

Japanese Association of Social Workers—www.jasw.jp

Korea Association of Social Workers—www.welfare.net/site/global/globalEng.jsp

Kyrgyz Republic: Association of Social Workers of the Kyrgyz Republic—http://asw.gratis.kg

Luxembourg—www.anasig.lu

New Zealand: Aotearoa New Zealand Association of Social Workers—http://anzasw.org.nz

Portugal—www.apross.pt

Romanian Association for the Promotion of Social Work—www.fnasr.ro

Singapore Association of Social Workers—www.sasw.org.sg

Spain—www.cgtrabajosocial.es

Sri Lanka Association of Professional Social Workers—www.slapsw.org/index.html

Sweden—www.akademssr.se

Swedish Union of Local Government Officers—www.sktf.se/Default.aspx

Switzerland—www.avenirsocial.ch

Social Workers' Association of Thailand—www.nontapum.com

Uruguay—www.adasu.org/menu.htm

REFERENCES

Alveo, G. (2001). Change in social work service in the VA system. *Continuum, 21*(1), 8–14.

Bateman, N., & Whitaker, T. (2002). The employment outlook for social workers. *National Association of Social Workers Intersections in Practice, 1,* 7–9.

Ben-Zur, H., Rappaport, B., Ammar, R., & Uretzky, G. (2000). Coping strategies, life style changes, and pessimism after open-heart surgery. *Health & Social Work, 25*(3), 201–209.

Berkman, B. (1996). The emerging health-care world: Implications for social work practice and education. *Social Work, 41*(5), 541–551.

Bronstein, L. (2003). A model for interdisciplinary collaboration. *Social Work, 48*(3), 297–306.

Carlton, T. O. (1984). *Clinical social work in health settings.* New York, NY: Springer.

Cowles, L. A. (2003). *Social work in the health field: A care perspective.* Binghamton, NY: Haworth Press.

Danis, F. S. (2003). The criminalization of domestic violence: What social workers need to know. *Social Work, 48*(3), 237–246.

Dhooper, S. (1994). *Social work and transplantation of human organs.* Westport, CT: Praeger.

Engel, G. L. (1977). The need for a new medical model: A challenge for biomedicine. *Science, 196*(4286), 129–136.

Gambrill, E. D. (1997). *Social work practice: A critical thinker's guide.* New York, NY: Oxford University Press.

Globerman, J. (1999). Hospital restructuring: Positioning social work to manage change. *Social Work in Health Care, 28*(4), 13–30.

Globerman, J., White, J., & McDonald, G. (2003). Social work in restructuring hospitals: Program management five years later. *Health & Social Work, 27*(4), 274–283.

Globerman, J., White, J. J., Mullings, D., & Davies, J. M. (2003). Thriving in program management environments: The case of social work in hospitals. *Social Work in Health Care, 38*(2), 1–18.

Headrick, L. A., & Khaleel, N. I. (2008). Getting it right: Educating professionals to work together in improving health and health care. *Journal of Interprofessional Care, 22*(4), 364–374.

Holliman, D., Dziegielewski, S. F., & Teare, R. (2003). Differences and similiarites between social work and nurse discharge planners. *Health & Social Work, 28*(4), 224–231.

Kayser, K., Hansen, P., & Groves, A. (1995). Evaluating social work practice in a medical setting: How do we meet the challenges of a rapidly changing system? *Research on Social Work Practice, 5*(4), 485–500.

Keefler, J., Duder, S., & Lechman, C. (2001). Predicting length of stay in an acute care hospital: The role of psychosocial problems. *Social Work in Health Care, 33*(2), 1–16.

Lee, J. S. (2002). Social work services in home health care: Challenges for the new prospective payment system era. *Social Work in Health Care, 35*(3), 23–36.

Lindau, S. T., Laumann, E. O., Levinson, W., & Waite, L. J. (2003). Synthesis of scientific disciplines in pursuit of health: The interactive biopsychosocial model. *Perspectives in Biology and Medicine, 46*(3, Suppl.), S74–S86.

Livneh, H. (2000). Psychosocial adaptation to cancer: The role of coping strategies. *Journal of Rehabilitation, 66*(2), 40–49.

McGuire, J., Bikson, K., & Blue-Howells, J. (2005). How many social workers are needed in primary care? A patient-based needs assessment example. *Health & Social Work, 30*(4), 305–313.

McWilliam, W. (2009). Patients, persons or partners? Involving those with chronic disease in their care. *Chronic Illness, 5*(4), 277–292.

Miller, M. S., & Rehr, H. (1983). *Social work issues in health care.* Englewood Cliffs, NJ: Prentice-Hall.

Monster, T. B., Johnsen, S. P., Olsen, M. L., McLaughlin, J. K., & Sorenson, H. T. (2004). Antidepressants and risk of first-time hospitalization of myocardial infarction: A population-based case-control study. *American Journal of Medicine, 117,* 732–737.

Nason, F., & Delbanco, T. (1976). Soft services: A major, cost-effective component of primary medical care. *Social Work in Health Care, 1*(3), 297–308.

Rehr, H. (1982). Social work and medicine at Mount Sinai: Then and now. In H. Rehr (Ed.), *Milestones in social work and medicine* (pp. 2–59). New York, NY: Prodist.

Roberts, C. S. (1989). Conflicting professional values in social work and medicine. *Health & Social Work, 14,* 211–218.

Rock, B. D., & Cooper, M. (2000). Social work in primary care. *Social Work in Health Care, 31*(1), 1–17.

Rolland, J. S. (1994). Families, illness, and disability: An integrative treatment model. New York, NY: Basic Books.

Romano, M. (1981). Social worker's role in rehabilitation: A review of the literature. In J. Brown, B. Kirlin, & S. Watt (Eds.), *Rehabilitation services and the social work role: Challenge for change* (pp. 13–21). Baltimore, MD: Lippincott Williams & Wilkins.

Rose, M., Fliege, H., Hildebrandt, M., Schirop, T., & Klapp, B. F. (2002). The network of psychological variables in patients with diabetes and their importance for quality of life and metabolic control. *Diabetes Care, 25*(1), 35–42.

Segal, S. P. (2002). Introduction: Pt. 3. *Social Work in Health Care, 35*(1/2), 351–358.

Simmons, W. J. (1989). Benefits of social work in hospitals. In B. S. Vourlekis & C. G. Leukefeld (Eds.), *Making our case: A resource book of selected materials for social workers in health care* (pp. 36–39). Silver Spring, MD: National Association of Social Workers.

Sommers, L. S., Marton, K. I., Barbaccia, J. C., & Randolph, J. (2000). Physician, nurse, and social worker collaboration in primary care for chronically ill seniors. *Archives of Internal Medicine, 160*(12), 1825–1833.

Sulman, J., Savage, D., & Way, S. (2001). Retooling social work practice for high volume, short stay. *Social Work in Health Care, 34*(3/4), 315–332.

Sormanti, M., & Shibusawa, T. (2008). Intimate partner violence among midlife and older women: A descriptive analysis of women seeking medical services. *Health & Social Work, 33*(1), 33–41.

Thompson, S. J., Auslander, W. F., & White, N. H. (2001). Influence of family structure on health among youths with diabetes. *Health & Social Work, 26*(1), 7–14.

U.S. Department of Labor. (2010). Occupational outlook handbook 2010–2011 Edition: Social Workers. Retrieved from www.bls.gov/oco/pdf/ocos060.pdf.

U.S. News & World Report. (2010). The 50 best careers of 2011. Retrieved from http://money.usnews.com/money/careers/articles/2010/12/06/the-50-best-careers-of-2011.html.

3

Ethics and Social Work in Health Care

JARED SPARKS

If this is the best of all possible worlds, what are the others like?

—*Voltaire, 1759*

When confronted with the harsh reality of illness and suffering that existed in the 18th century, the French author and philosopher Voltaire expressed his feelings of incredulity that such conditions were tolerated. Even now, as the tools of science and technology have advanced society's understanding of biology and the human condition, humankind continues to feel a sense of astonishment and vulnerability in the face of unresolved modern health-care issues and ethical dilemmas.

Today lives are increasingly influenced by human invention even prior to conception through genetic counseling and intervention. As a person progresses through each developmental stage of life, choices must be made regarding available health options. These can be especially difficult at the end of life.

The purpose of this chapter is to facilitate discussion and understanding of health social work ethics in a changing health-care environment. Toward this end, some of the philosophical foundations of ethics are reviewed and the history of social work ethics is discussed, as are decision making, theoretical frameworks, and other special topics.

Chapter Objectives
- Discuss the development of social work ethics, medical ethics, and bioethics within a historical and cultural context.

- Define ethical terminology and theory as these relate to the social work code of ethics.
- Outline decision-making models and theoretical applications as they relate to social work ethics in health care.
- Discuss particular ethical issues related to dual relationships, managed care, and research ethics.
- Outline ethical challenges in the 21st century and beyond.

OVERVIEW OF ETHICAL ISSUES IN SOCIAL WORK

Within each chapter of this book and the concomitant practice areas in social work reside compelling ethical issues and questions. Social workers play an important role in addressing these issues and answering these questions. In health social work, practitioners inform patients of their treatment and discharge options, advocate for patients within a transdisciplinary team, serve on ethics committees, and shape policy. These experiences provide a unique and valuable opportunity to gain both a micro- and macro-level perspective of health social work ethics. The ability to articulate a position clearly and effect change depends on understanding the ethical issues involved. Today more than at any time in history social workers must have a working knowledge of ethical dilemmas in health care and how health social work ethics may be employed to address these dilemmas.

Social workers and other health-care professionals may prefer to think of themselves discretely as completely homogeneous groups, each profession holding a unique value system and set of beliefs. All social workers may have an idea of what health social work ethics constitute and suggest. In reality, however, not everyone shares the same concept of exactly what that may be. The 18th-century French author Diderot described an appreciation of differences in understanding from person to person in his work *D'Alembert's Dream.*

For the obvious reason that no two of us are exactly alike, we never understand exactly and are never exactly understood. There is always an element of "more or less"—our speech falls short of the real sensation or overshoots it. We realize how much variety there is in people's opinions, and "there is a thousand times more that we don't notice and fortunately cannot notice" (Diderot, 1769/1976, p. 222).

Diderot reveals some unease in considering the possibility of understanding exactly how someone else experiences or interprets a certain phenomenon. It does seem fortunate that individuals experience life differently. In the study of health social work ethics, consensus may be reached fairly easily. That will not always be the case, and care should be taken to respect different opinions.

Throughout the course of a career, most social workers encounter situations for which no completely desirable solutions can be found, because each alternative has its own set of undesirable outcomes. Proctor, Morrow-Howell, and Lott (1993) further define *ethical dilemmas* as situations "when a social worker cannot adhere to professional values or when adhering to one ethic requires behaving counter to another" (p. 166).

Reamer (1987, pp. 801–809) identified eight areas of importance when considering ethical dilemmas in social work: (1) confidentiality and privileged communication; (2) truthfulness; (3) paternalism and self-determination; (4) laws, policies, and regulation; (5) whistle-blowing; (6) distributing limited resources; (7) personal and professional values; and (8) ethical decision making. Some of these topics are discussed throughout this chapter.

In contemplating ethical dilemmas, the point of ethical discourse is not necessarily to arrive at an immutably "right" solution. Value lies in thoughtful review and discussion. Through the process of ethics discourse, a more complete understanding may be reached, and alternative courses of action may appear; if not, there may be at the very least an appreciation that whatever decision was reached was the result of informed and thoughtful consideration rather than the singular expressed preference of a party involved in the patient's care.

Ethics codes provide some direct guidance for practice. Lowenberg and Dolgoff (1996) identified four other purposes of codes of ethics:

1. Protect the public.
2. Protect the profession. (Self-regulation is a hallmark of a profession and ideally more effective than governmental involvement.)
3. Prevent internal strife.
4. Protect practitioners from lawsuits. (The rationale for why a specific course of action was taken provides some defense against lawsuits.)

Before we discuss individual cases in which some of the purposes of codes of ethics may be made clear, we review the philosophic foundation of social work ethics. This review should not be considered comprehensive. You are encouraged to read on your own in this area to develop a more complete understanding and to prepare yourself to use the code of ethics in your social work practice.

ETHICS TERMINOLOGY AND THEORY

Most social workers do not have formal training in philosophy as it relates to ethics. Separate classes in professional ethics seldom are present in a social work curriculum. In practice, many social workers will find that their state social work boards require ongoing ethics education as a condition of licensure. Formal training and continuing education help develop ethical thought and practice in the profession. However, regardless of how little or how much of an ethics background social workers have, when in practice, they frequently engage in ethical discourse.

A basic understanding of terminology helps clarify thought and decision making in ethics. The National Association of Social Work (NASW) code of ethics provides some useful content. In an effort to supplement this content, special attention is paid in this chapter to vocabulary in the form of definition and distinction. Words like *values*, *morals*, and even *ethics* often are used interchangeably, yet their distinctions are important to social work practice.

Values

A discussion of values is fundamental to the study of professional ethics. Although they have specific meaning as they relate to social work ethics, values exist in personal, professional, and societal contexts. Confusion may arise from explanations of this notion because a multitude of definitions for the term *values* exists depending on the branch of philosophy or social theorist making reference to it. Furthermore, the term *values* has been co-opted by a variety of political influences, each claiming to have a more correct grasp of what values are. Nonetheless, through all this contention, values have specific and significant meaning in a code of ethics.

The word *value* is derived from the Latin word *valere,* which means "be worthy, be strong" (Angeles, 1992). The *Harper Collins Dictionary of Philosophy* defines *value* as "worth; the quality of a thing that makes it desirable, desired, useful, or an object of interest," as well as "of excellence; that which is esteemed, prized or regarded highly, or as a good." As value relates to human behavior, Rokeach (1973) provided this definition: "an enduring belief that a specific mode or end

state of existence is personally or socially preferable to an opposite or converse mode or end state of existence" (p. 23). Values serve as ideals of what is right. Within professions, values constitute what is unique and good that sets one profession apart from others.

As a profession, social work holds these core values: service, social justice, dignity and worth of the person, importance of human relationships, integrity, and competence (NASW, 2000). According to Reamer (1995), "Social work is among the most value-based of all professions" (p. 3).

Before attempting to identify, understand, and comment on ethical dilemmas, health social workers should examine their personal values. Each person has personal values that have been shaped by family, friends, culture, and prior life experiences. These personal values influence how dilemmas are viewed and whether a practitioner accepts the profession's core values. Understanding differences in individual value bases has special relevance as practitioners interact with patients operating from value positions different from their own. Hodge (2003) underscored this in an article providing data to suggest that the values of master's level social workers "were more to the left of working and middle class clients" (p. 107).

Morals

Morals is a term derived from the Latin word *moralis,* meaning custom, manners, or character. Morals have been defined as consisting of "principles or rules of conduct which define standards for right behavior" (Lowenberg & Dolgoff, 1996, p. 22). Morals encompass widely accepted notions of right and wrong. Although morals are not necessarily outlined in the NASW Code of Ethics, they do shape how social workers develop professional and personal values.

Laws

Laws also has been defined in different ways. Some definitions point to concerns with protection from abuses of power by authorities as well as individuals. Other definitions refer more to social control and welfare, and still others emphasize more consideration of social justice.

Laws, ethics, and values all have unique meanings. Simply passing legislation does not change individuals' deep-seated beliefs and ideas regarding a particular issue. For example, passing laws proscribing assisted suicide will not change people's personal perspectives. Simply attending to the law does not protect social workers from behaving in a professionally unethical way. When laws are passed that are unjust, social workers have an obligation to work through the courts to address social injustice. For example, NASW is active in addressing legislation affecting health-care issues such as prescription drug coverage.

Principles and Standards

Principles in a code of ethics may be thought of as a stage in the formation of values. In their own right, principles can serve as an ideal, of sorts. Principles inform social work practice (Reamer, 1995) and offer a reference point for the development of even more specific standards. Standards in a code of ethics specifically outline how social workers should conduct themselves.

Ethics

Ethics is a term derived from the Greek word ethos, which means a person's character or disposition (Angeles, 1992). There are several ways of defining ethics. For the purposes of this chapter, ethics will be divided into three branches: metaethics, normative ethics, and applied ethics.

Metaethics

Metaethics asks the questions "What does something really mean?" or "What does it really mean to be 'good' or 'bad'?" The term metaethics refers to the study of the "methods, language, logical structure, and reasoning used to arrive at and justify moral decisions and knowledge" (Angeles, 1992, p. 183).

Normative Ethics

In contrast to metaethics, normative ethics is concerned with identification of the morals, values, principles, or standards that might be relevant in addressing a dilemma. In developing a normative ethical response to such a situation, several values and principles might be relevant. The NASW 2000 Code of Ethics wisely reflects that there are situations in which values, standards, and principles conflict. In these situations, two reasonable and informed practitioners may disagree on what constitutes an ethical response to a clinical situation.

Applied Ethics

Applied ethics is a third branch of ethics and is concerned with the application of normative ethics (a relevant set of morals, values, principles, and standards) to specific situations. This would be the stage at which decisions actually are made. Social workers should consider if the ethical standard regarding legal obligations supersedes the principles of autonomy and self-determination or if they feel that they should act to have the law changed.

Ethics can be defined within each of the three contexts—metaethics, normative ethics, and applied ethics. That is, ethics can be considered: (a) a branch of philosophy interested in value-based reasoning and human conduct; (b) a framework of morals, values, principles, and standards; or (c) the actual decision-making process derived from that specific framework. As it relates to social work in health care, Joseph and Conrad (1989) provide a definition of ethical behavior as "social workers' professional behaviors in relation to biomedical ethical choices" (p. 23). The next section provides a discussion of ethical issues related to a topic that health social workers may encounter related to end-of-life care.

End-of-Life Care

The right-to-die debate resurfaced in 2005 with the case of Terri Schiavo, whose husband had her feeding tube and hydration removed against her parents' wishes. This case provides an example of just how divisive ethical dilemmas can become. Schiavo's case was not the first to capture national attention. Two other women, Karen Quinlan and Nancy Cruzan, similarly faced the court's involvement in their right-to-die cases. Both women suffered brain damage and never regained consciousness to the point that they were able to verbalize their wishes. Karen Quinlan's breathing tube ultimately was removed, but she lived another 10 years. Nancy Cruzan's parents won a lengthy court battle to have her feeding and hydration stopped. Cruzan died two weeks after her feeding tube was removed. Both Quinlan and Cruzan died in the 1980s. Amid even more controversy, Schiavo died on March 31, 2005, 13 days after her feeding tube was removed. These cases all reflect fundamental moral, ethical, and religious differences in this country. They also point to a strong need for health social workers to be attentive to their patients' wishes and advocate for completing advance directive documents specifying such wishes.

When responding to challenging situations such as the ones just described, the practitioner should first examine his or her own values as they relate to the wishes of the patient. A social worker's values may differ from the patient's and interfere with the ability to engage in a meaningful discussion. In a study of 110 hospice social workers, Csikai (2004) found that among the least discussed issues in hospice care were those of euthanasia and thoughts of suicide by a patient even though 34% of the social workers had been approached by their patients about assisted death. Under no circumstance should the social worker fail to address the patient's concerns. In situations in which a social worker's values conflict with those of a patient, it may be necessary to refer the patient to a colleague.

One of the first responses to a patient who is requesting to die should be a careful screening for depression and a review of any other possible health treatment modalities. It may be that after careful consideration and review of options the patient will still wish to die. However, it also may be that he would like reassurance from his family that he will be cared for and

will not be a burden or abandoned (Csikai, 1999). The patient also might be concerned about what options his life could hold. After these issues are addressed adequately, the patient might not continue to wish for euthanasia or assisted death.

Metaethics may be relevant in situations in which social workers believe that suicide is wrong. Questions considered in metaethical analysis include why it is wrong and if it is wrong in all situations. The definition of suicide influences any subsequent conversation. Metaethics would be involved in understanding whether suicide is wrong in the case of a suffering patient. Metaethics also would be concerned with questions about what suicide is. Is it suicide when it is physician assisted—that is, a doctor gives a competent patient the medications or other means to end his life? Is suicide somehow different from active voluntary euthanasia when a physician injects a competent patient who requests a lethal amount of an opiate-based painkiller? Is forgoing recommended medical treatment suicide?

In contrast to metaethics, normative ethics is concerned with the identification of the morals, values, principles, or standards that might be relevant in addressing a dilemma. A normative ethics dilemma may be whether one should support assisted death or euthanasia. Normative ethics also is concerned with assembling a framework out of those identified morals, values, principles, and standards that could be used in contemplating a specific instance of assisted death or euthanasia.

From a medical standpoint, the principles of beneficence and nonmalfeasance apply. The principle of beneficence basically instructs the practitioners to "do good." The principle of nonmalfeasance instructs the practitioner to "do no harm." From the social work code, the value in question could be dignity and worth of the person. The principles of autonomy and self-determination also seem to have bearing. However, the ethical standard of commitment to clients takes into account that social workers may have legal obligations falling into the realm of standards that would preclude facilitating euthanasia or assisted death. Also relevant would be evaluating whether patient autonomy supersedes preserving life in such a case.

A variety of broad philosophical theories exists within an ethics code to inform and influence decision making. Both social work and medicine have been influenced by a number of philosophies over the years. Modern medicine as a profession owes more to the positivist model than does social work. *Positivism* is the notion that reality exists, is based on fixed laws, and is thus understandable (Guba, 1990). Science in this framework is the mechanism by which we can determine what constitutes this reality and ultimately manipulate it in our interest. This thought came about during the Enlightenment period in the late 17th and throughout the 18th centuries, when the world was being viewed more in the context of a clockwork universe that was ultimately understandable and subject to our control (Spurlin, 1984).

At times health social work may be seen as a profession struggling to emulate the positivistic approaches that have led medicine to its present status in society. However, it would be difficult to argue that social work has not paid heed to a constructivist model. In contrast to a clockwork universe, *constructivism* proposes that society is not "a system, a mechanism, or an organism" (Parton, 2003, p. 5) but rather a symbolic construct relying on collaboration between the observer and observed, together creating a novel and fluid meaning.

As it relates to social work in health care, constructivism asks that a practitioner step outside the imposed work environments (in thought) and engage his patient on her own terms in order to develop a more thorough understanding of the patient, what she is experiencing, and what she would desire. The social work injunction to "start where the patient is" and not where the social worker is or where the social worker wants the patient to be would be a step in the right direction toward constructivism. Social workers may better provide relevant services if they understand the meaning imposed by a patient on her disease and the available treatments.

BASIC NORMATIVE THEORIES

Some ethics theories are more concerned with outcomes of actions. Others are more concerned with identifying principles, standards, and rules that can guide behavior before any action is taken. Hence, most normative ethical theory falls into the category of deontological or teleontological.

Deontological and Teleontological Theories

Deontological theory places primacy on the ethical value, standard, or principle in determining the correct action without consideration of the outcome. For example, with the principle of confidentiality, deontological theory would dictate that a social worker should under no circumstances violate the principle.

Teleontological theory is more concerned with the outcome of a particular action than with values, principles, or standards. The word *teleontological* comes from the Greek word *telos,* which means "end or goal" (Angeles, 1992, p. 369). For example, a teleontological consideration of confidentiality would be more concerned with what would happen if this confidentiality were violated.

Deontology and teleontology often clash, as do the values, principles, and standards of an ethical code. One example of this is the 1976 case of *Tarasoff v. Board of Regents of the University of California* (Kagle & Kopels, 1994). In this case, a patient informed his psychologist at the University of California that he was having homicidal ideations with Tatiana Tarasoff as the target. The patient even went so far as to inform his psychologist of his plans. The psychologist contacted the campus police, who detained the patient for a brief time and later released him with a warning not to go near Tarasoff.

Later, the psychologist's supervisors told him to destroy his case notes surrounding this incident, which by law is illegal and by the NASW standards would be a clear violation of the principles surrounding client records, deception, and fraud. Several months later, the patient murdered Tatiana. Tarasoff's parents ultimately successfully sued the university. The California Supreme Court indicated that the university had a duty to protect, which superseded the patient's privacy and confidentiality.

This controversy falls within the realm of "duty to protect" or "duty to warn." The deontological consideration in this case would be to attend to the ethical standard of confidentiality regardless of the outcome. This consideration obviously falls apart when the outcome seems much more harmful than the violation of confidentiality, as was affirmed by the court. A teleontological consideration to protect the intended victim ultimately may have more of a positive benefit in the sense that a life is saved.

In addition to framing ethical dilemmas via teleontological and deontological perspectives, other concepts such as utilitarianism, Kantian ethics, ethics of care, and virtue ethics can be applied in health social work.

Utilitarianism

Utilitarianism was strongly influenced by British philosophers Jeremy Bentham and John Stuart Mills. This theory is premised on the principle of utility. Utility is the doctrine that a person ought to do that which brings about the greatest happiness to the greatest number of people or to the community as a whole. The determination of right or wrong is teleontological in utilitarianism.

Utilitarianism has two main divisions: act and rule. *Act utilitarianism* focuses exclusively on the outcome. A classic example would be the experiments conducted by the Nazis during World War II. This "research" violated a host of ethical considerations and resulted in the torture and death of many. The question an act utilitarian might pose would be: "Could the research have some utility in providing usable data?" The act utilitarian might insist that the data be made available to provide insight into certain human conditions, treatments, or diseases because there might be value in these data.

Rule utilitarianism, however, defers to established standards within an ethical framework to make the decision of what produces the most good. Research ethics has informed consent as a cornerstone for its foundation. This was clearly violated by the Nazi experiments. With regard to these experiments, a rule utilitarian would suggest that the use of these data might generate more harm than good by setting a precedent for using data obtained unethically.

Ethics of Duty (Kantian Ethics)

In contrast to most utilitarian thought, especially act utilitarianism, stands ethics of duty. This concept was espoused by the German philosopher Immanuel Kant, who felt that the outcome of an act was not relevant to determining whether it was right or wrong. Kant believed that actions were right only if they were consistent with a particular standard, fitting within a categorical imperative. One way of determining what a categorical imperative was would be to pose the question "Would everyone benefit if everyone participated in a particular act?"

Kant believed that there were basically two types of duties: perfect and imperfect. *Perfect duties* are duties of omission, or clear duties of things one should not do, such as steal, lie, or kill. These duties are primarily "black and white" in terms of conduct. *Imperfect duties* are not as clearly defined. They are duties of commission, such as be a good person. These duties are more difficult to identify because they are difficult to clearly extrapolate in every instance.

Ethics of Care

Gilligan's (1982) study of morality and purported differences in male and female moral reasoning brought Kant's arguments to a new audience. She believed that there were differences, but they were not necessarily indicative of moral superiority. Gilligan held that females attended more to the ethics of care than the ethics of rights and justice. The ethics of care dictates that a more constructivist approach might be taken in speaking to patients and their families. Carse (1991) identified seven applications of care ethics in health settings:

1. A shift from principle-ism and institutional rules and emphasis on a more responsive relationship with the patient
2. An emphasis on self-awareness as a part of understanding others
3. Placing value on ethical discourse and not focusing exclusively on outcomes
4. A review of gender-based differences in health care
5. An emphasis on the nature and dynamics of relationships as particularly important in ethical deliberation
6. Acknowledgment of the reality of *moral ambivalence*
7. Consideration of what traits or virtues one should develop to further competence in ethical decision making.

Virtue Ethics

Virtue is a translation of the Greek word *arete*, which means "excellence" (Lacey, 1996). Both ethics of care and virtue ethics have been referred to as "theories without principles" because they do not arise from specific principles (Munson, 2000). Although the ethics of care theory may use principles during application, virtue ethics may rely on principles even less. *Virtue ethics* refers to the positive attributes of a particular type of person. Carse (1991) considered virtue ethics valuable in the sense that contemplating a virtue may result in a better-developed sense of professional self as it relates to others.

Virtue ethics may be problematic. For instance, ideas about what attributes a virtuous doctor must possess may vary from person to person. They might include patience, empathy, and intelligence. It may be more difficult to come up with an agreed-on definition of what attributes a virtuous social worker might have, especially as it relates to particular practice areas, even within health social work. For example, a hospital-based social worker in a case management department might be perceived

as virtuous because she is able to contain costs by discharging patients quickly. Another hospital-based social worker may be perceived as virtuous because he advocates for longer hospitalizations for his psychiatric patients.

DEVELOPMENT OF MEDICAL ETHICS, SOCIAL WORK ETHICS, AND BIOETHICS

Medical Ethics

If anyone conceal more than a single lunatic without a license, he becomes liable to a penalty of five hundred pounds.

—Percival, 1803

Western medical ethics can be traced to 477 BCE and the Oath of Hippocrates. However, Thomas Percival's 1803 code of ethics will serve as the starting point of this review. Although the language and perspective of this code may seem antiquated, as evidenced in the preceding passage, it intimates modern dilemmas. For example, licensing and credentialing of health-care institutions and practitioners continue to be relevant today.

Percival was a physician in England during the late 18th and early 19th centuries. In addition to being a physician, he was a writer of morality stories for the middle class. People sought his help resolving disputes at the local Manchester Hospital. He was also familiar with larger societal forces causing unrest in England, namely the introduction of spinning mills, the English slave trade, and treatment of the poor (Baker, Porter, & Porter, 1993). Much of his awareness of larger societal concerns can be seen in his 243-page *Medical Ethics* (Percival, 1803), which was progressive and thorough. Unfortunately, the publication has been criticized as more involved with professional etiquette than professional ethics. This criticism seems to miss the mark because topics covered are cogent even by today's standards and include abortion, rape, medical malpractice, and the purpose of charity. To be fair, the codes of both medicine and social work have components of trade etiquette as well as more value-based considerations. Percival's code eventually appeared in America in the early 1800s in a much abridged version of the original and influenced the American Medical Association's (AMA) first code of ethics in 1847.

Social Work Ethics

Abraham Flexner (1915) may have provided some impetus for the field of social work developing a unique code of ethics by posing the question of whether social work was, in fact, a profession. Flexner was one of the most influential figures of his day in medical education, and he imposed many changes in how education was conceptualized and delivered (Bonner, 2002). Flexner also commented on the profession of social work in his 1915 article, "Is Social Work a Profession?" published by the New York School of Philanthropy. In this article, he outlined the necessary criteria for a profession. According to Flexner, social work had not yet met all the criteria of a profession, but he posited that in some ways it was closer to doing so than law and medicine. One of the most important requirements of a profession, according to Flexner (1915), was that it should have "spirit" or values:

> In so far as accepted professions are prosecuted at a mercenary or selfish level, law and medicine are no better than trades.…In the long run, the first, main and indispensable criterion of a profession will be the possession of a professional spirit, and that test social work may, if with will, fully satisfy. (p. 24)

The social work community began a conversation about ethics shortly after Flexner's report. Reamer (1998) identified four distinct periods of development for the social work code of ethics: the morality period, the values period, the ethical theory and decision-making period, and the ethical standards and risk management period (p. 488).

The morality period for social work occurred in the late 19th century and lasted until the 1950s. Individuals receiving care from social workers often were viewed as defective in some way. In the early 20th century, social workers began to attend more to social justice concerns. External influences of society, such as poverty, disease, and educational opportunities, were appreciated. The settlement house movement reflected this concern with attempts to provide newcomers to the United States with some basic skills and understanding of how to better integrate into their new country.

Mary Richmond has been credited with drafting an early social work code of ethics in the 1920s (Reamer, 1987). This was during what was likely the beginning of the end of the morality period. During this time, articles were written on the need for social work ethics, and in 1923, the American Association for Organizing Family Social Work (AAOFSW) began work on a code of ethics (Lowenberg & Dolgoff, 1996). The American Association of Social Workers adopted a formal code of ethics in 1947, 100 years after the AMA's code was adopted (Reamer, 1999). AAOFSW merged with others to form the National Association of Social Workers (NASW) in 1955. NASW published its first code of ethics in 1960, consisting of a set of 15 "I" statements, such as "I respect the privacy of the people I serve." Shortly after the interest in settlement houses declined, social work focused more on developing a domain-specific knowledge base and area of practice that would set it apart from other professions. In the 1940s and 1950s, social work moved into the values period (lasting until the 1980s), during which there continued to be a shift away from focusing on the client's morality to identifying ethical standards and guidelines.

In social work, the 1980s ushered in the ethical theory and decision-making period. In both the medical and social work communities, this period was largely influenced by conferences and center and commission work in developing a normative ethical response to bioethical dilemmas. Lowenberg and Dolgoff (1996) and Reamer (1995) wrote about the importance of ethical theory and decision-making models in resolving health-care and social justice issues.

Malpractice concerns as well as the introduction of managed care also helped direct ethics in this period.

Social work ethics is now in a period of ethical standards and risk management, according to Reamer (1998). The 1990s through the beginning of the 21st century have seen a number of increasingly public scandals. Companies have been caught engaging in ethically unsound accounting practices that have impacted thousands. The Catholic Church has been beset as inappropriate sexual relationships have been made public. Also, as a consequence of some new homeland security initiatives, concern regarding confidentiality and privacy has increased. Social work has a role in treating and advocating for the victims of abuses by powerful organizations. Clearly understanding the ethical principles involved allows practitioners to more easily identify and address misconduct.

At the time of publication of this book, over 20 countries have developed codes of ethics for social work to address challenges at multiple levels of practice. For example, torture and terrorism, both increasingly a part of our global awareness, are mentioned specifically in the principles of the 2004 International Federation of Social Work Code of Ethics (www .ifsw.org/f38000032.html).

Recent abuses of power by large corporations, institutions, and the government suggest an ongoing need to set clearer standards for social work practice in more ethically unambiguous situations, such as when social workers enter into dual relationships with patients. Because standards for behavior in ethically challenging situations may prove elusive, social workers need to continue to update their knowledge base and learn decision-making skills that will protect their clients against harm and themselves against litigation. As a consequence of a litigious society and challenging practice environments, many social work ethics experts agree that all social workers should purchase malpractice insurance. The touchstone for guiding practice, however, remains the latest code of ethics. The revised 1999 NASW Code of Ethics clearly articulates

social work's mission and values base. This code is the best developed and refined to date and reflects an increasing sophistication in social work theory and practice.

Bioethics

During the late 1940s and early 1950s, there were significant advances in medical technology (Jonsen, 1998). In 1949, the polio vaccine was discovered. In 1950, antihypertensive medications were discovered. In 1952, antipsychotic medications for the treatment of schizophrenia were developed. Medical ethics at that time echoed a sense of accomplishment and security that the profession was respected. In what may have been medicine's self-satisfaction, thoughtful review and analysis of ethical dilemmas may not have seemed necessary.

This self-assuredness waned in the 1960s as biotechnology ushered in unforeseen difficulties. Albert Jonsen (1998) traces the birth of bioethics to the point in time at which technology made hemodialysis available on a chronic basis with the development of the Scribner shunt, which allowed for external access to the bloodstream. This marked the first time that a terminal illness—end-stage renal disease—moved from 100% fatal to 100% treatable by mechanical means. The ethics relevance of this was the subsequent development of dialysis selection committees. These committees had to make decisions regarding what nonmedical criteria should be used in determining who lives and who dies, which called into question individual social worth and what this constitutes. On the social front, the 1960s and 1970s were a period of growth in awareness and activism. The Nixon administration's Watergate scandal and the unpopular Vietnam War together brought ethics and social justice concerns to the public consciousness. Biotechnological realities and consequent real-life dilemmas presented the public with seemingly impossible ethical situations.

The 1960s also bore witness to conferences in the United States and other countries that addressed bioethical issues. These conferences acknowledged and reviewed dilemmas in areas such as genetics, eugenics, and transplantation. In addition to dialysis, heart transplantation became a feasible intervention. The discussion at the conferences ultimately resulted in the generation of scholarly papers on ethics. As these collections began to develop and several bioethics centers appeared to house these collections, further bioethical conversations developed. Some of these centers were the Hastings Center, the Kennedy Institute of Ethics at Georgetown, and the Society for Health and Human Values.

As bioethics centers were developing, the bioethical conversation moved to the realm of government. The Mondale Hearings of 1968, for example, raised important questions about end-of-life issues, behavior control, and experimentation with human participants. Ultimately the hearings gave birth to the National Bioethics Commission that exists today. The 2003 Commission was made up of 17 individuals appointed by the president. These individuals include scientists, doctors, ethicists, social scientists, lawyers, and theologians. The purpose of this committee is to advise the president and help shape policy.

As discussed in the research ethics section that follows, the Tuskegee story first appeared in the media in July 1972. Peter Bruxton, who had training as a social worker, was essential in exposing this story. He learned of the study from colleagues after he was hired to work with patients who had venereal disease. He attempted to work within the system to intervene by contacting superiors. Ultimately he became a "whistle-blower" and went to the press in 1972 to expose the study (Jones, 1981). Partly in response to the public outrage, the Commission for the Protection of Human Subjects of Biomedical and Behavioral Research was established in 1974. As its name suggests, the commission's imperative was to develop guidelines for protecting participants in research. This commission was one of the first governmental bodies to consider ethics and develop recommendations for policy and legislation. The Commission for the Protection of Human Subjects of Biomedical and Behavioral Research consisted of 12 individuals

from science, law, ethics, and the public. Its mandate was to publish guidelines for medical research, an example of which is the 1975 *Recommendations on Research with the Fetus* (National Commission for the Protection of Human Subjects of Biomedical and Behavioral Research, 1975). Several other important documents followed: the 1976 report *Research Involving Prisoners* (National Commission for the Protection of Human Subjects of Biomedical and Behavioral Research, 1976) and in 1979 the *Report and Recommendations on Institutional Review Boards* (National Commission for the Protection of Human Subjects of Biomedical and Behavioral Research, 1979). Finally in 1979, the National Commission issued the Belmont report in an effort to fulfill its mandate to identify basic ethical principles that could guide research. Albert Jonsen, who served on the commission, later wrote:

> As a commissioner I participated in the formulation of that [Belmont] Report. Today, I am skeptical of its status as serious ethical analysis. I suspect that it is in effect a product of American Moralism prompted by the desire of congressmen and of the public to see the chaotic world of biomedical research reduced to order by clear and unambiguous principle. (Jonsen, 1991, p. 125)

His commentary on the commission he was part of foreshadows the difficulty to find clear guidelines in right-to-die cases. Following the Belmont Report, the President's Commission for the Study of Ethical Problems in Medicine and Biomedical and Behavioral Research was established in 1979. This commission had a broader mandate than the National Commission for the Protection of Human Subjects. It addressed topics such as how death should be defined. One of the important documents to come out of this commission was *Deciding to Forego Life-Sustaining Treatment,* which suggested that a competent patient should have priority over others in decision making (President's Commission for the Study of Ethical Problems in Medicine and Biomedical and Behavioral Research, 1983). Before disbanding in 1983, the commission recommended that ethics committees should have a role in dilemmas involving life-or-death care and reviewed the concept of durable power of attorney. These committees are appointed to fulfill a specific mandate and are appointed for a specific period of time.

The Los Alamos National Laboratory, Lawrence Livermore National Laboratory, and Department of Energy Laboratories began producing DNA clone libraries of single chromosomes in 1983, marking the beginning of a process that ultimately would result in the mapping of the human genome. The Human Genome Project began in 1990, and by April 2003, the human genome had been mapped.

The National Bioethics Advisory Commission (1996–2001) and the President's Council on Bioethics (2001–2009) have both had to address the implications of human genome research. In addition to the governmental oversight in the form of commissions, the Human Genome Project also developed its own ethics program. This is the world's largest bioethics program, and it is a model for other programs throughout the world. Beginning in 2010, President Obama directed the Presidential Commission for the Study of Bioethical Issues to examine issues surrounding biosynthetic technology. This technology goes beyond the genetic manipulation of existing systems and proposes to create new systems entirely, namely those not found in nature.

DECISION-MAKING MODELS

Social workers routinely make key decisions in a variety of settings. One of the most visible settings for social work decision making is on health-care policy and ethics committees. Social work presence may have changed somewhat with the advent of managed care, but organizations historically have felt that social work input is essential (Mulvey, 1997). As these decisions become more transparent and subject to scrutiny, it becomes increasingly important to make them in an orderly and informed fashion.

This is in contrast to what Goldmeier (1984, p. 46) believes was in the recent past a "tendency to resolve ethical dilemmas on a case-by-case basis without systematic grounding in ethical principles."

Developing a sound ethical decision can be a daunting task, and currently a variety of models exist to help guide decision making. These models assume various geometric shapes—some square, some triangular, some two-dimensional, others three-dimensional. It is not the appearance of the model, however, that is important. Rather, it is the number of elements and complexity of ties that is important. Sound decision making involves consideration of a variety of factors and variables and not necessarily in a formulaic or linear fashion. For an informed decision to be made, the practitioner must be aware of many factors, such as:

- Personal values and collegial, institutional, and societal influences
- Ethical theory and decision-making models
- Social work theory, research, and practice standards
- Social work ethical codes, as well as other professional codes
- Relevant agency policy
- Federal and state laws and other regulations
- Impact on patients and, in some cases, impact on practitioner (as in whistle-blowing)

Identifying and attending to all of these factors is challenging. For example, Mattison (2000) reflects that identifying specifically what social work practice standards are may be somewhat difficult because a standard of practice often is not well defined. Also, most social workers in health care do not work in isolation. Rather, they are part of larger transdisciplinary teams. In considering institutional influences, the relationships with and perspectives of others on the health-care team have a significant impact on the contribution social workers have in ethical decision making (Landau, 2000).

After the social worker has developed understanding of the dilemma, he or she should first look to the social work code of ethics to identify values, principles, and standards that may be relevant in resolving the problem. In addition to the areas identified previously, there should be an added effort to identify sources of feedback. These may be colleagues, agency committees, local state boards of social work examiners, professional social work organizations including NASW, or legal counsel.

Models of decision making often share components. They may differ at times in some fundamental areas, such as how principles are ordered hierarchically. In this sense, models may represent different schools of thought in much the same way that models of treatment in health care vary and treatment theories differ from one another. Netting, Kettner, and McMurtry (1993), Murdach (1995), Lowenberg and Dolgoff (1996), Jonsen, Seigler, and Winslade (1997), and Mattison (2000), all review different models and decision-making approaches relevant to health social work practice.

According to Netting and colleagues (1993, pp. 411–412), the steps to decision making are:

1. Recognize the problem.
2. Investigate the variables.
3. Get feedback from others.
4. Appraise the values that apply to the dilemma.
5. Evaluate the dilemma.
6. Identify and think about possible alternatives.
7. Weigh the pros and cons of each alternative.
8. Make your decision.

Part of the difficulty in completing the last task in the list, actually making the decision, is weighing one principle against another or even rank-ordering a series of principles (such as freedom over well-being). Reamer (1990) proposes comparing principles to one another and deciding which one is more important. For example, "an individual's right to freedom takes precedence over his or her own right to well-being" (Reamer, 1990,

p. 63). In the case of a patient's decision to continue to engage in self-destructive behaviors, however, this ordering would allow a person with alcoholism to continue to drink. In considering other principles, Reamer does make provision for an attempt at intervention to determine "voluntariness and informed choice" as well as preventing harm to others (p. 63). However, in this example, the ontological considerations of freedom supersede the teleontological considerations, such as impact on family, friends, and work as well as long-term health consequences, such as cirrhosis. In other words, protecting individual freedom may be seen as a more important principle than forcing someone to live a healthy lifestyle.

Lowenberg and Dolgoff (1996, p. 414) propose a rank-ordering of principles from which an individual should be able to:

• Exist with basic needs.
• Receive treatment that is fair and equal.
• Have free choice and freedom.
• Have injury that is minimal or nonexistent.
• Cultivate a good quality of life.
• Secure privacy and confidentiality.
• Understand the truth.
• Receive available information.

SPECIAL TOPICS RELATED TO HEALTH SOCIAL WORK ETHICS

Dual Relationship

Dual relationship continues to be an area of challenges for many social workers. *Dual relationship* in health social work practice may be loosely defined as a type of violation of the practitioner and patient relationship. Injunctions against dual relationships in health care have been in evidence since the time of Hippocrates. "Whatever houses I may visit, I will come for the benefit of the sick, remaining free of all intentional injustice, of all mischief and in particular of sexual relations with both female and male persons, be they free or slaves" (Hippocratic Oath, 400 BCE).

In a 2009 study, Boland-Prom surveyed 27 state social work regulatory boards and examined 874 complaints that resulted in actions. The most frequently occurring complaint concerned inappropriate dual relationships. After another examination of NASW code violations, Strom-Gottfried (2000) found most to be boundary violations in dual relationships. The most frequently occurring violations were sexual relationships and nonsexual dual relationships.

Current definitions of dual relationships are varied. Craig (1991) describes them as "ambiguous relationships in which the goals and boundaries are tailored to meet the needs of the counselor" (p. 49). Hill and Mamalakis (2001) define dual relationships as "any concurrent or sequential relationship between a therapist and client that is distinct from the therapeutic relationship" (p. 200).

Early work on the topic of dual relationships focused on absolute contraindications in dual relationships, such as a practitioner having sex with a client. However, a variety of nonsexual dual relationships exist. Recently the paradigm has shifted to consideration of when dual relationships are appropriate. Reamer (2003) has divided dual relationships into those that are boundary crossings and those that are boundary violations.

Boundary crossings may not be inappropriate in all cases but remain controversial. One example might be a hospital social worker serving on a fundraising board with a current or former patient. The appropriateness of this situation greatly depends on the social worker's ability to make appropriate judgments in what could potentially become an ethically compromising environment. Some would caution social workers to avoid these potentially dangerous and libelous situations completely.

We could argue, however, that failing to collaborate with the patient would result in more harm than good for him. Health social workers may be cautioned not to engage in dual relationships with patients no matter what the situation. This certainly seems an outdated and perhaps alarmist position that might place patients at greater risk if it jeopardized potential collaborations between social workers and patients. Threatening the ability to collaborate on boards or planning committees, for example, might mean that social workers and patients would not engage in dialogues to establish the needs of end-stage renal patients.

How would one go about ordering principles and standards in this instance? Does the "slippery slope" argument have the final say in whether to proscribe potentially beneficial interactions? The slippery slope metaphor is a very prominent argument in the field of ethics. It is also called the "thin edge of the wedge" or "wedge" argument (Pence, 2004, p. 111). According to Pence, these arguments are most prominent at the beginning of end-of-life ethical dilemmas. Although colloquial in common parlance, the term does speak to some important considerations, such as conceptual or empirical trajectories. Would allowing dual relationships to occur in this area result in an ongoing reduction of standards in more clearly defined inappropriate relationships (conceptual)? Is there something about human nature that ultimately will take advantage of these situations (empirical)?

Lazarus (1994) would respond by saying that "one of the worst professional violations is that of permitting current risk management principles to take precedence over humane interventions" (p. 260). This is not a new idea. Miller and Rollnick (1991) and Carl Rogers (1959) all support the idea that relationships account for much of the changes that occur in treatment. Current literature echoes this sentiment by providing evidence to support a relationship between the quality of rapport between provider and client and outcome. These "clinical encounters and relationships may even be perceived by clients as more like 'friendships'" (Green et al., 2008, p. 9).

The careful consideration of the appropriateness of potential dual relationships is especially relevant to rural social workers who may encounter multiple dual relationships. In response to the misleading information provided by continuing education providers, the author of this chapter contacted by phone the Louisiana State Board of Social Work Examiners, NASW, and the Council of Nephrology Social Workers for input. In addition, the NASW Code of Ethics was consulted for guidance. No board expressly prohibited all dual relationships. However, it was suggested by the state board that guidelines be developed to address this issue.

Boundary violations, alternatively, are clearly inappropriate. These involve "exploitative, manipulative, deceptive, or coercive" actions (Reamer, 2003, p. 122). The 2000 NASW Code of Ethics proscribes social workers' engagement "in dual or multiple relationships with clients or former clients in which there is a great risk of exploitation or potential harm to the client" (Standard 1.06).

Clear dangers are inherent in the example of a social worker serving on a board or committee with a patient. If the social worker was not sensitive to the dynamics of the situation, the board role could devolve, and several untoward outcomes could be possible. For instance, the relationship could devolve into a more collegial or friendship-type relationship (and even possibly a sexual relationship), or the patient might feel he has more access to the social worker and attempt to use this time to address more clinical concerns. This access to the health-care provider beyond the provider-patient relationship may become increasingly problematic as social workers are responsible for more and more patients with less time to provide clinical services.

The issue of confidentiality could pose a problem if the social worker was not careful. For example, one scenario that conceivably could cause problems might be if the patient was sick and other board members asked the social worker about specifics of his illness. The social worker could abuse power in the relationship to stifle the patient's voice on the board or in the patient's health-care environment. Furthermore, the social worker and patient could manipulate decisions and available resources for economic or other gain.

Another potential danger is possible serving on boards with patients. In applying utilitarianism to this example, it becomes apparent that both courses of action may be defensible. Act utilitarian thought and care ethics may dictate that the potential benefits take precedence over the risks. Rule utilitarianism or Kantian ethics might suggest that more harm would be done to the profession if these rules were not maintained.

Arguments for considering dual relationships in light of the service provided also may be relevant. For example, Hardinia (2004) points out that direct clinical social work practice is substantively different from community social work. With this in mind, some would argue that collaboration takes on more of an ethical imperative in community work than it does in clinical work. Does this hold true for social work in health care? Strom-Gottfried (2003) provides data to suggest that private practitioners have a higher rate of ethical violations than do social workers in agencies. This was measured by reviewing 894 of 901 ethics complaints filed with NASW for the time period 1986 to 1997. More work should be undertaken to determine why this is the case, because the study questions how the data were gathered. One possible explanation would be that there is more oversight and thus fewer opportunities for violation in agency settings, such as hospital social work, compared with private practice. Another explanation might be that the nature of the client-social worker relationship is different in nonpsychotherapeutic settings and therefore lends itself less easily to abuse.

When inappropriate dual relationships do occur, they may have less to do with the nature of the relationship and more with intrapsychic features of the practitioner. Schoener (1995) suggests that clinicians who engage in sexual or other inappropriate relationships with clients may have underlying mood or personality disorders. In addition, Simon (1999) identified the egregious occurrence of impairment (as may occur in substance use) and incompetence as possible triggers of inappropriate dual relationships.

Managed Care and Whistle-Blowing

As discussed in Chapter 5 of this book, managed care has changed the dynamics of health-care provision in the United States dramatically. Neuman (2000) describes the new environment as one with decreased reimbursement for health-care providers, decentralization of services, a decrease in staff credentialing and expertise, and the emergence of standards of care. These conditions increase the possibility that ethical violations will occur.

Possible abuses that might occur more frequently in a managed care environment include the exaggeration of patient symptoms in order to ensure or increase reimbursement. This exaggeration may be well intentioned from the practitioner's perspective. It may assume the form of changing diagnoses from an adjustment disorder to a more severe psychiatric illness in order to secure or extend needed treatment in a psychiatric hospital. Employees may be encouraged to seek treatment from in-network providers. These providers, especially in health care, also may be the patient's colleagues, vendors, or own clients. This places an employee in a potential dual relationship with the provider.

Historically managed care has threatened informed consent through facilities' use of nondisclosure, or gag, clauses. These gag clauses prevented social workers or other practitioners from discussing the limits of services available as mandated by third-party payers or of discussing other available options beyond those offered by a particular managed care organization (Strom-Gottfried, 1998). Social work, specifically through NASW, was one of the first professions to address specifically the ethics involved in informed consent as it relates to nondisclosure clauses.

Confidentiality also may be more threatened in a health-care environment that relies on outsourcing services. The availability of electronic data and transfer of data from one facility to another may pose an ethical risk. However, this may be more a function of technology than managed care specifically. With the vast amount of data available electronically, this information has become a target of computer hackers and other criminals. There have been recent cases where criminals have accessed personal credit information of tens of thousands of individuals. It is not inconceivable for this to happen to personal health information. Personal health information in the wrong hands could affect a person's employment potential, finances, and interpersonal relationships.

Practitioners in managed care and other health-care environments may witness unethical practices. One decision is whether to inform authorities of these practices. *Whistle-blowing* refers to the act of notifying authorities of harmful deviation from standards of care or unethical practices within an organization. From a micro-level perspective, this may take the form of notifying superiors of a colleague's malpractice in terms of violations of the NASW Code of Ethics, law, or agency policies. From a macro-level perspective, this may involve a practitioner notifying people outside the agency of problems within the agency. Although the best policy generally is to follow a chain of command within an agency, this may not provide the appropriate results. For example, retaliation is a real concern in a corporate work environment.

If the identified problem is with the policies made by the management, and these have been brought to the attention of the management with no effect, it may be necessary to pursue other options outside the company. For example, in the past, whistle-blowers have accessed local media and the American Civil Liberties Union. However, Reamer (1999, p. 162) recommends that, before notifying authorities within or outside an agency of ethical violations, a practitioner should take time to consider the:

- Severity of harm and misconduct involved
- Quality of evidence of wrongdoing
- Effect of the decision on colleagues and agency
- Viability of alternative courses of action

It may be important to realize that no agency is perfect, and employees cannot be functional if they whistle-blow every time they encounter a problem. If a social worker comes across a problem with a colleague or an agency, there should be an effort to directly address the colleague or follow the chain of command. Careful documentation of the event and the efforts taken by the social worker to resolve the problem should be made.

The NASW Code of Ethics includes several references to situations in which reporting violations might be appropriate. However, lock-step or formulaic responses to this type of dilemma, as in all other ethical dilemmas, may prove incomplete. Decision making during the reporting process should be made in a reflective and orderly fashion, and documented. For any claim to be taken seriously, documentation must be provided. Documentation also serves to protect the social worker, especially if a court becomes involved.

Consideration should be made to what effect any accusations by the reporter might have. The accusations could ruin the reputation of a coworker or undermine the mission of an agency. As a consequence, clients could be harmed if there is an interruption or end to services. Finally, great care should be taken to consider other options. There are some governmental guidelines protecting people who report possible wrongdoing, but they are placed at great risk from the beginning. This may result in damage to their reputation. Still, when it is clear that there is harm to others, all reasonable efforts should be taken to remedy the situation.

SOCIAL WORK RESEARCH ETHICS

The ethics of social science are situation ethics.

—*Humphreys, 1975, p. 170*

This quote from Humphreys can be seen as morally ambiguous. Fortunately, safeguards exist today that protect ethical analysis from devolving into an argument used to justify a desired protocol (Lacey, 1996). For example, all universities and health-care facilities should have their own institutional review boards (IRBs) that provide some safeguard against potentially harmful research and ensure that research does not exploit human participants. IRBs ensure that there is informed consent, confidentiality consideration, policies regarding data storage, and other safeguards.

Unfortunately, problems occur even with these safeguards in place. While conducting research, social workers may deviate from ethical practice for a variety of reasons. One of the most seductive motives may be that the researcher believes the benefit from the results or knowledge accrued by bending rules for research on human subjects or other deviations from research protocols outweigh any harm done to participants. Deviations from ethically sound research, regardless of how seemingly innocuous or, conversely, compelling, can have serious consequences to the researcher, participants, and society at large. Within the realm of research, the areas of most importance are:

- Voluntary participation or consent
- No harm to participants or nonmalfeasance
- Anonymity and confidentiality
- Deception
- Analysis and reporting
- Justice and beneficence

Many people trace the development of research ethics to the Nuremburg Code. Following World War II, in 1946, the United States, France, the United Kingdom, and Russia participated in an eight-month trial in which 16 German physicians were convicted of crimes against humanity. These physicians had participated in research on prisoners without their consent, often inflicting great pain and death. Some of this wartime research in Nazi Germany involved shooting prisoners to study wounds and purposefully injecting prisoners with live viruses to study disease.

The Nuremberg Code was developed in response to these violations. Attention to voluntary consent was at the center of the Code

(*Trials of War Criminals Before the Nuremberg Military Tribunals Under Control Council Law 10,* 1950). In all, the Nuremberg Code identified 10 principles designed to protect research participants. This was a great step forward in research ethics, but its principles have not always been followed. In a sense, the publication of the Nuremberg Code marks the beginning of a cyclical phenomenon in which a crisis involving research occurs, a response is made in the form of legislation addressing the crisis, and the conditions preceding the crisis eventually reappear.

The United States was not immune from this phenomenon. In 1929, the U.S. Public Health Service with the local departments of health of Mississippi, Tennessee, Georgia, Alabama, North Carolina, and Virginia were involved in what is called the Tuskegee Study, the aim of which was to control syphilis. In 1932, syphilis treatment was withheld from approximately 400 African American men in Macon County, GA. The fact that African American men were used exclusively was reflective of the racist attitudes of the time. The ensuing study spanned some 40 years, despite the fact that penicillin became available to treat syphilis in the 1940s (Jones, 1981). The study was made public in the 1970s as an example of misuse of research on human subjects. In 1997, President Clinton made a formal public apology to the surviving participants of the study, and in 1999, the National Center for Bioethics and Health Care was established at Tuskegee University. Recently, Susan Reverby uncovered additional information about syphilis experiments that were sponsored by the U.S. government (McNeil, 2010).

In 2010, Secretary of State Hillary Rodham Clinton and Health and Human Services Secretary Kathleen Sebelius made a public apology to the government of Guatemala related to the actions of the U.S. Public Health Service from 1946 to 1948. Seven hundred Guatemalan prisoners were purposefully infected with syphilis using prostitutes, direct exposure to the virus, and spinal injection.

A common theme in both the Nazi atrocities and the Tuskegee and Guatemalan studies is the use of vulnerable populations, which often consist of the disenfranchised, minorities, and women. In all these cases, one of the primary violations of research ethics was in the lack of voluntary participation. The Guatemalan prisoners were a vulnerable population by virtue of being incarcerated. By today's standards, prisoners are considered a vulnerable population and require full IRB deliberation before any study is sanctioned. Many of the Guatemalan prisoners also had mental illnesses.

Informed consent also may be related to privacy concerns as outlined in the discussion of Henrietta Lacks (see Box 3.1). Cells labeled with her name were disseminated throughout the world without her understanding that she was providing tissue for research.

Millgram's obedience study provides another example of violation of the "no harm to participants" principle (Miller, 1986). Millgram conducted this study in the early 1960s. He was researching the phenomenon of obedience. For this study, he recruited participants via a newspaper advertisement. He then instructed the participants to assume the role of a teacher who would inflict punishment through an electric shock to a learner. An actor assumed the role of the learner and had an electrode strapped to his arm. The teacher was instructed to give the learner a shock with each incorrect response. The teacher was then instructed to increase the voltage incrementally. The actor would respond to each shock.

Disturbingly, the teachers continued to administer the shocks even when the voltage meter indicated that the shocks registered in the dangerous and severe range. Throughout this experiment, the teachers appeared to suffer psychological trauma while administering the shocks, yet they continued to follow Millgram's commands. A common criticism of Millgram is that he relied on the ends to justify the means, or attended to only teleontological considerations. This experiment did reveal valuable information. It has been viewed by some as shedding light on why people were able to commit violent acts while under the direction of an authority, such as in Nazi Germany. However, his study still is considered

Box 3.1 Henrietta Lacks and the First Immortal Cell Line

As health-care professionals, we often assume that we have a good understanding of the ethical issues revolving around informed consent, especially as it relates to medical procedures and research. Is that always the case? Are you aware of what happens to your blood or tissue when it is drawn or biopsied for diagnostic purposes? You might be surprised. General consent forms, in addition to consent for the tests, often contain a brief provision for saving a sample for research. Over the years, this and other collection consents have resulted in the storage of tissue from over 307 million samples from 178 million people (Eiseman & Haga, 1999) in the United States alone.

In her 2010 book *The Immortal Life of Henrietta Lacks*, Rebecca Skloot brings awareness to the issues revolving around informed consent and stored tissue samples by focusing her attention on the woman who generated the first immortal cell line. Henrietta Lacks was an African American woman who, at age 30, was diagnosed with an especially aggressive form of cervical cancer. She was treated at Johns Hopkins in 1951. In April of that year, after she signed a basic consent form that did not mention donating a sample, tissue was scraped from her cervix and sent to the hospital lab. The radium procedure used to treat her was then administered. She died that October. Since then, Lack's cells have been used all over the world in research ranging from Parkinson's disease to the flu, and they continue to be used today.

Enough of her cells have been grown to weigh "50 million metric tons...wrap around the earth at least three times, spanning more than 350 million feet" (Skloot, 2010, p. 2). They are commonly referred to as HeLa cells. In 2000, around the time of the first cloning of a mammal, Christine Borland, a Scottish artist, drew from this Lack's legacy by displaying a microscope examining HeLa cells and the magnified image of those cells. The work was titled *HeLa HOT* to reflect the "hot topic" of genetic research and was part of a larger exhibit commenting on the ambiguities and sometimes dehumanizing impact of genetic research.

The Health Insurance Portability and Accountability Act of 1996 would no longer allow the name of the donor of a tissue sample to be widely known. It does little to mitigate the effects of HeLa research and notoriety on Lack's family, a family who has benefited little from the immense amount of money generated by discoveries made using the HeLa cell line.

---

an egregious violation of research ethics for a variety of reasons, including the possible long-term psychological trauma to the participants.

Project Camelot was an attempt by the U.S. government in the 1950s to investigate how governments were overthrown and re-formed in Latin America (Horowitz, 1967). The underlying intent was to gain information that would allow some control over how governments in volatile political climates developed. This type of research has clear problems. Although this example may come from macro-level practice, it serves to illuminate the misuse of research in politics. This type of research immediately calls into question justice and beneficence. It also speaks to a clouded purpose of the research. The danger that health social workers should remember from this is that the true nature of research is not always apparent. Health social workers involved in their own and institutional research endeavors are wise to reflect carefully on the previously discussed research considerations. Many social workers, especially those working in teaching hospitals, either will be approached to participate in research or will have patients who are in research studies. Learning the funding source and the premise behind the research will help social workers assess its value to the patients and better inform them.

ETHICAL CHALLENGES IN THE 21ST CENTURY

As is apparent in some of the examples in this chapter, ethical challenges evolve in ways that at once demand and escape satisfying solutions. In the 21st century and beyond, ethical dialogue is inexorably tied to science. Health social work has an obligation to provide a voice to individuals and to existing culture as sciences provide an ever broadening array of ethically ambiguous choices. Health social workers providing direct care to patients, serving on ethics committees, shaping policy, and acting in the legislative arena must all have the ability to redirect attention to ethical and interpersonal considerations. From a micro-level to a macro-level perspective, this will be challenging because new health-care dilemmas have profound societal meaning.

Compelling health dilemmas have the potential to draw reasonable discourse and action away from the issue at hand. These dilemmas may be used as rallying cries for agendas far removed from the welfare of the patient. An inadequate and depersonalizing health-care industry further threatens ethical care in this country. Health social workers can effect change, however. By remaining grounded in an understanding of the profession's mission, values, and ethics, health social workers have the ability to avoid losing focus. With a clear sense of purpose, health social workers can help redirect health care to an ethical best fit with patients.

SUGGESTED LEARNING EXERCISES

Learning Exercise 3.1

Heather recently completed the requirements for her social work license. She was hired by a hospital's psychosocial rehabilitation center as its program coordinator. This program provides services to patients with a serious mental illness (SMI). With her social work license, Heather can now provide individual and group therapy and bill third-party payers,

such as Medicare and Medicaid. She also can supervise paraprofessionals who provide psychosocial rehabilitation day services to patients. These services are defined by her state Medicaid manual but encompass a broad array of needs, including social-skill development and community integration. One of Heather's new roles is to plan, supervise, and sign off on all of these services as the mental health professional. This is appropriate and required by Medicaid.

Within her first week, Heather learns that the most popular rehabilitation day program is taking clients to a casino. Usually two to four paraprofessionals accompany the clients to the casino. Clients spend the day there, and some gamble. They interact with community members, eat, and often see a show. The point of the program as it was explained to Heather was to promote social skills in a natural environment. As a new MSW graduate, Heather remembers that community-based social learning is essential for the SMI population. Clients who have cognitive deficits from a mental illness have a better chance of learning skills in a natural setting. This all makes perfect sense to Heather, but something about this whole situation bothers her.

What should Heather be concerned about, if anything? If Medicaid only considers active interventions as billable services, is it ethical to bill Medicaid to take clients to a casino? How should she go about finding some direction in this situation? What can Heather do in this situation?

Learning Exercise 3.2

Sam was a transplant candidate at liver transplant center where you are employed. His liver disease is due to hepatitis C virus and polysubstance dependence. About a year ago, Sam was denied a transplant because of medical contraindications and ongoing alcohol abuse. He was advised to lose weight and stop drinking before he would be reconsidered for transplant. Sam is well known regionally for his art and poetry, but he is best known for his charisma and over-the-top lifestyle. Several employees at the liver transplant center are fond of him. Sam brings paintings to the center every month or so, and the staff hang them in the waiting room.

Sam's health continues to deteriorate, but he tells everyone that he just knows that he will get a transplant soon. Sam's family and fans take some comfort in this information. As a social worker on this transplant team, your role has been to conduct a psychosocial evaluation and provide education and counseling. When it was clear that he was not going to engage in treatment with you or at your center, you made attempts to refer Sam elsewhere for counseling and then hospice care. He refused both. Multiple relational and ethical issues are involved in this scenario. What is the implicit message or messages that Sam is sending by gifting his paintings to the center? What is the message the office manager is sending back to Sam by accepting them? How is this impacting his care? More important, what is your role in his care now?

Learning Exercise 3.3

Kimberly has been a very effective spokesperson working as a social worker for a local hospice. She also is known for her good therapeutic work with patients. A local producer has heard lots of positive things about the hospice and has approached Kimberly with the idea of a documentary series to increase public awareness and support. They would film in the hospice and interview friends and family members in the community. This would all be tastefully done with the informed consent of patients and families.

Kimberly is familiar with this type of media. She has seen similar reality shows with prisoners, pregnant teens, hoarding, substance dependence and abuse, and mental disorders. There is even a local broadcast of drug court. Sometimes licensed therapists, including social workers, take part in these shows, and the actual treatment is recorded and broadcast. Kimberly realizes that this presents privacy issues but decides that, with a thorough review of the potential risks and benefits in the consent process, the clients can make informed decisions. She also thinks it is inappropriate and infantilizing to assume that people make these choices for themselves. She also believes that there will be broader benefits to society.

Even though reality shows have become the norm, they present numerous ethical challenges. In this example, what are the risks and benefits to the clients? Is a documentary on hospice any different from broadcasting a local drug court? How would the informed consent be impacted if the drug court participants were given the choice of prison or televised drug court? Are prisoners and people with serious mental illnesses vulnerable populations that warrant special consideration in the consenting process for television broadcasts? Is special consideration for informed consent just an issue for research? How does incentivizing participation by offering to pay for treatment impact the informed consent process?

SUGGESTED RESOURCES

The Genome Project—http://genomics.energy
.gov/
    This is a gateway site for the project.
The Hastings Center—www.thehasting
scenter.org
    The center is a nonpartisan research institution dedicated in part to bioethics.
Human Genome Project Information Ethical Legal and Social Issues—www.ornl
.gov/sci/techresources/Human_Genome/
elsi/elsi.shtml
International Federation of Social Workers Ethics in Social Work Statement of Principles—www.ifsw.org/p38000324.html
    This site includes links to approximately 20 countries with national codes of social work ethics.
National Association of Social Workers Office of Ethics and Professional Review—
www.socialworkers.org/nasw/ethics/
default.asp
National Institutes of Health Bioethics resources and links—http://bioethics
.od.nih.gov

Presidential Commission for the Study of Bioethical Issues—www.bioethics.gov

The Rand Corporation—www.rand.org/ This not-for-profit organization conducts research in numerous areas including health and health care.

Tuskegee University National Center for Bioethics in Research & Health Care— www.tuskegee.edu/Global/category .asp?C=35026&nav=menu200_14

REFERENCES

Angeles, P. (1992). *The Harper Collins dictionary of philosophy* (2nd ed.). New York, NY: HarperCollins.

Baker, R., Porter, R., & Porter, D. (Eds.). (1993). *The codification of medical morality* (Vols. 1–2). Boston, MA: Kluwer Academic.

Boland-Prom, K. (2009). Results from a national study of social workers sanctioned by state licensing boards. *Social Work, 54*(4), 351–360.

Bonner, T. (2002). *Iconoclast: Abraham Flexner and a life in learning.* Baltimore, MD: Johns Hopkins University Press.

Carse, A. (1991). The voice of care: Implications for bioethical education. *Journal of Medicine and Philosophy, 16,* 5–28.

Craig, J. (1991). Preventing dual relationships in pastoral counseling. *Counseling and Values, 36,* 49–54.

Csikai, E. (1999). Euthanasia and assisted suicide: Issues for social work practice. *Journal of Gerontological Social Work, 31*(3/4), 49–63.

Csikai, E. (2004). Social workers' participation in the resolution of ethical dilemmas in hospice care. *Health & Social Work, 29*(1), 67–76.

Diderot, D. (1976). *Rameau's Nephew and D'Alembert's Dream.* New York, NY: Penguin. (Original work published 1769.)

Eiseman, E., & Haga, S. (1999). Handbook of human tissue sources: A national resource of human tissue samples [Electronic version]. Rand Corporation. Retrieved from www.rand.org/pubs/monograph_reports/MR954.

Flexner, A. (1915). Is social work a profession? *Studies in Social Work, 4,* 1–24.

Gilligan, C. (1982). *In a different voice.* Cambridge, MA: Harvard University Press.

Goldmeier, J. (1984). Ethical styles and ethical decisions in health settings. *Social Work in Health Care, 10*(1), 45–60.

Green C., Polen, M., Janoff, S., Castelton, D., Wisdom, J., Vuckovic, N.,...Oken, S. L.(2008). Understanding how clinician-patient relationships and relational continuity of care affect recovery from serious mental illness: STARS study results. *Psychiatric Rehabilitation Journal, 32*(1), 9–22.

Guba, E. (1990). *The paradigm dialogue.* Newbury Park, CA: Sage.

Hardinia, D. (2004). Guidelines for ethical practice in community organization. *Social Work, 49*(4), 595–604.

Hill, M., & Mamalakis, P. (2001). Family therapists and religious communities: Negotiating dual relationships. *Family Relations, 50,* 199–208.

Hodge, D. (2003). Value differences between social workers and members of the working and middle classes. *Social Work, 48*(1), 107–119.

Horowitz, I. (1967). *The rise and fall of project Camelot.* Cambridge, MA: Massachusetts Institute of Technology.

Humphreys, L. (1975). *Tearoom trade: Impersonal sex in public places.* Hawthorne, NY: Aldine Transaction.

Jones, J. (1981). *Bad blood: The Tuskegee syphilis experiment.* New York, NY: Free Press.

Jonsen, A. (1991). American moralism and the origin of bioethics in the United States. *Journal of Medicine and Philosophy, 16,* 113–130.

Jonsen, A. (1998). *The birth of bioethics.* Oxford, UK: Oxford University Press.

Jonsen, A., Seigler, M., & Winslade, W. (1997). *Clinical ethics* (5th ed.). New York, NY: McGraw-Hill.

Joseph, M., & Conrad, A. (1989). Social work influence on interdisciplinary ethical decision making in health care settings. *Health & Social Work, 2,* 22–30.

Kagle, J., & Kopels, S. (1994). Confidentiality after *Tarasoff. Health & Social Work, 19*(3), 217–222.

Lacey, H. (1996). Philosophy of science and ethics. *Ethics, 2*(2), 111–120.

Landau, R. (2000). Ethical dilemmas in general hospitals: Social workers' contribution to ethical decision making. *Social Work in Health Care, 32*(2), 75–92.

Lazarus, A. (1994). How certain boundaries and ethics diminish therapeutic effectiveness. *Ethics and Behavior, 4,* 255–261.

Lowenberg, F., & Dolgoff, R. (1996). *Ethical decisions for social work practice* (5th ed.). Itasca, IL: Peacock Press.

Mattison, M. (2000). Ethical decision making: The person in the process. *Social Work, 45*(3), 201–212.

Miller, A. (1986). *The obedience experiments: A case study of controversy in social science.* New York, NY: Praeger.

Miller, W., & Rollnick, S. (1991). *Motivational interviewing: preparing people to change addictive behavior.* New York, NY: Guilford Press.

Mulvey, B. (1997). Synopsis of a practical guide: Guidelines for ethics committees. *Journal of Florida Medical Association, 84*(8), 506–509.

Munson, R. (2000). *Intervention and reflection: Basic issues in medical ethics* (6th ed.). Belmont, CA: Wadsworth/Thompson Learning.

Murdach, A. (1995). Decision making situations in health care. *Health & Social Work, 20*(3), 187–191.

National Association of Social Workers. (2000). *Code of ethics of the National Association of Social Workers.* Washington, DC: NASW Press.

National Commission for the Protection of Human Subjects of Biomedical and Behavioral Research. (1975). *Report and recommendations: Research on the fetus.* Washington, DC: U.S. Department of Health, Education, and Welfare.

National Commission for the Protection of Human Subjects of Biomedical and Behavioral Research. (1976). *Report and recommendations: Research involving prisoners.* Washington, DC: U.S. Government Printing Office.

National Commission for the Protection of Human Subjects of Biomedical and Behavioral Research. (1979). *Report and Recommendations on Institutional Review Boards.* Washington, DC: U.S. Government Printing Office.

Netting, F., Kettner, P., & McMurty, S. (1993). *Social work macro practice* (3rd ed.). Needham Heights, MA: Allyn & Bacon.

Neuman, K. (2000). Understanding organizational re-engineering in health care. *Social Work in Health Care, 31*(1), 19–33.

Parton, N. (2003). Rethinking professional practice: The contributions of social constructionism and the feminist ethics of care. *British Journal of Social Work, 33*(1), 1–16.

Pence, G. (2004). *Classic cases in medical ethics* (4th ed.). New York, NY: McGraw-Hill.

Percival, T. (1803). *Medical ethics.* Manchester, UK: S. Russel

President's Commission for the Study of Ethical Problems in Medicine and Biomedical and Behavioral Research. (1983). *Deciding to forego life-sustaining treatment.* Washington, DC: U.S. Government Printing Office.

Proctor, E., Morrow-Howell, N., & Lott, C. (1993). Classification and correlates of ethical dilemmas in hospital social work. *Social Work, 38*(2), 166–176.

Reamer, F. (1987). Values and ethics. In *Encyclopedia of social work* (18th ed., pp. 801–809). Silver Spring, MD: National Association of Social Workers.

Reamer, F. (1990). *Ethical dilemmas in social service* (3rd ed.). New York, NY: Columbia University Press.

Reamer, F. (1995). *Social work values and ethics.* New York, NY: Columbia University Press.

Reamer, F. (1998). The evolution of social work ethics. *Social Work, 43*(6), 488–497.

Reamer, F. (1999). *Social work values and ethics* (2nd ed.). New York, NY: Columbia University Press.

Reamer, F. (2003). Boundary issues in social work: Managing dual relationships. *Social Work, 48*(1), 121–133.

Rogers, C. (1959). A theory of therapy, personality, and interpersonal relationships as developed in client centered framework. In S. Koch (Ed.), *Psychology: the study of a science*: *Vol. 3. Formulations of the person and the social context* (pp. 184–256). New York, NY: McGraw-Hill.

Rokeach, M. (1973). *The nature of human values.* New York, NY: Free Press.

Schoener, G. (1995). Assessment of professionals who have engaged in boundary violations. *Psychiatric Annals, 25,* 95–99.

Simon, R. (1999). The natural history of therapist sexual misconduct identification and prevention. *Forensic Psychiatry, 22,* 31–47.

Skloot, R. (2010). *The immortal life of Henrietta Lacks.* New York, NY: Crown.

Spurlin, P. (1984). *The French enlightenment in America.* Athens, GA: University of Georgia Press.

Strom-Gottfried, K. (1998). Informed consent meets managed care. *Health & Social Work, 23*(1), 25–33.

Strom-Gottfried, K. (2000). Ensuring ethical practice: An examination of NASW code violations, 1986–1997. *Social Work, 45*(3), 251–261.

Strom-Gottfried, K. (2003). Understanding adjudication: Origins, targets, and outcomes of ethics complaints. *Social Work, 48*(1), 85–94.

Trials of War Criminal Before the Nuremberg Military Tribunals Under Control Council Law 10 (1950). Superintendent of Documents. Washington, DC: U.S. Government Printing Office.

Voltaire, F. (1759). *Candide* (Rev. ed., 2003; L. Walsh, trans.). New York, NY: Barnes & Noble Classics.

4

Public Health and Social Work

MARJORIE R. SABLE, DEBORAH R. SCHILD, AND J. AARON HIPP

In his seminal 1920 piece "The Untilled Fields of Public Health," Charles-Edward Amory Winslow, professor of public health at the Yale School of Medicine from 1915 to 1945, defined public health as:

> the science and the art of preventing disease, prolonging life, and promoting physical health and efficiency through organized community efforts for the sanitation of the environment, the control of community infections, the education of the individual in principles of personal hygiene, the organization of medical and nursing services for the early diagnosis and preventive treatment of disease, and the development of the social machinery which will ensure to every individual in the community a standard of living adequate for the maintenance of health. (Institute of Medicine [IOM], 1988, p. 39)

The core functions of public health agencies at all levels of government are assessment, policy development, and assurance (IOM, 1988; Schneider, 2000). *Assessment* refers to the regular collection, analysis, and sharing of information about health conditions, risks, and resources in a community. *Policy development* uses assessment data to develop local and state health and social welfare policies and to direct resources toward those policies. *Assurance* focuses on the availability of necessary health services throughout the community. It includes maintaining the ability of both public health agencies and private providers to manage day-to-day operations as well as the capacity to respond to critical situations and emergencies.

Public health is a field of practice with a specific orientation and framework for the various professionals who work within the public health arena. The professionals include both clinical practitioners, such as clinical social workers, nurses, health educators, occupational health and safety professionals, and physicians and nonclinical professionals, such as epidemiologists, administrators, and policy makers.

Social workers are well prepared to work within public health and with other public health professionals because they share many of the same values, theories, and practice methods. Shared values include a commitment to enhance social, economic, and environmental justice and a focus on eliminating disparities between and among various populations. Furthermore, social work and public health interventions primarily focus on oppressed, vulnerable, and at-risk groups (Wilkinson, Rounds, & Copeland, 2002). Theoretical approaches to develop interventions are, in social work, the ecological approach of person in environment (Germain, 1984; Germain & Gitterman, 1980; Kondrat, 2008) and, in public health, social epidemiology (Berkman & Kawachi, 2000; Oakes & Kaufman, 2006). Each is unique, but both rely on an understanding of how social systems relate to health status.

Social workers who work in public health serve as members of transdisciplinary teams, share many of the same skills as their colleagues, and participate in public health interventions. The unique approach that public health social workers bring to public health practice is grounded in social work theory, especially the person-in-environment approach to practice. The practice methods particular to social workers—family centered, community based, culturally competent, coordinated care—have been integrated into public health practice and adopted by various other providers of public health services (Bishop & Arango, 1997).

This chapter explores public health social work first by examining its history and then by exploring its intersection with social work practice, current practices, research, and future directions.

Chapter Objectives
- Review the history of public health social work and introduce Healthy People 2020, the U.S. national public health goals and objectives.
- Discuss shared values and common approaches in public health and social work practice.
- Describe levels of practice and components of prevention.
- Review public health interventions for health promotion and disease prevention.
- Identify emerging issues for public health social work practice and research.

HISTORY OF PUBLIC HEALTH SOCIAL WORK

An early public health intervention in the United States was an immunization campaign to prevent smallpox (World Health Organization [WHO], 1998). Public health interventions occurred before the modern era, but the combination of increasing sophistication in the medical sciences and the efforts of social reformers helped establish modern public health. The roots of the modern institution of public health in the United States are almost indistinguishable from the roots of social work itself. Social reformers established settlement houses, proposed legislation, and succeeded in establishing programs that had far-reaching impacts on the health status of Americans.

The efforts of early social reformers led to the development of settlement houses and eventually to the establishment of the Children's Bureau in the U.S. Department of Health and Human Services (DHHS) (Gordon, 1994). The Children's Bureau campaign to investigate and

reduce infant mortality provided the impetus for the passage of the Maternity and Infancy Protection Act, also known as the Sheppard-Towner Act of 1921 (Margolis, Cole, & Kotch, 2005). The Sheppard-Towner Act was the precursor to Title V of the Social Security Act of 1935, which established the role of the federal government in providing and regulating maternal and child health services, crippled children's services, and child welfare services (Gordon, 1994; Margolis et al., 2005). Title V, also referred to as the Maternal and Child Health Services Block Grant, is administered by the Maternal and Child Health Bureau (MCHB) in DHHS. More information about the history and programs of Title V can be found on the MCHB Web site (http://mchb.hrsa.gov).

Although public health social work had its roots in maternal and child health, the practice of public health social work has expanded into a number of areas (see Box 4.1). These include participation in transdisciplinary teams working on such issues as pandemic influenza, physical activity and obesity, tobacco cessation, human trafficking, and disaster preparedness for both natural and man-made disasters.

Settlement Houses and Social Reform Movements

In the late 1890s, residents of settlement houses worked to improve the health of the

---

Box 4.1 Brief Definition of Public Health Social Work

A public health social worker is a graduate-prepared social worker whose primary practice fulfills core public health functions within a public or private agency. Although it includes all of the 10 essential public health functions, public health social work practice focuses on interventions to strengthen communities, families, and individuals to promote health, well-being, and functioning and minimize disability and institutionalization.

Source: Adapted from *Public Health Social Work Standards and Competencies* (2005).

communities in which they lived. For example, Jane Addams, a cofounder of Hull House in Chicago, ran for and was elected to be the public sanitarian in her ward. She worked to establish rubbish removal, clean water, and sewage management. At Hull House and at the Henry Street Settlement in New York, founded by Lillian Wald (1887–1940), residents taught hygiene and other health-promoting behaviors to the community (Gordon, 1994). These social reform movements, which provided one of the foundations for the social work profession, served to inspire areas within public health such as community health, public health nursing, occupational health, and environmental health.

One resident of Addams' Hull House was Alice Hamilton, a professor at the Woman's Medical School of Northwestern University. While a professor of pathology and living at the Hull House, Hamilton became interested in the working conditions and occupational exposures of low-income residents. Her work

in industrial hygiene led to the creation of the Occupational Disease Commission of Illinois and her position as the first female professor at Harvard University. Hamilton was a pioneer in the emerging field of toxicology.

Healthy People 2020

Beginning in 1980 and continuing through each subsequent decade, DHHS has developed successive sets of national health promotion and disease prevention goals and objectives, the most recent of which is Healthy People 2020. The goals of Healthy People 2020 are to (a) eliminate preventable disease, disability, injury, and premature death; (b) achieve health equity, eliminate disparities, and improve the health of all groups; (c) create social and physical environments that promote good health for all; and (d) promote healthy development and healthy behaviors across every stage of the life cycle (Healthy People 2020, n.d. a). Figure 4.1 displays the Action Model

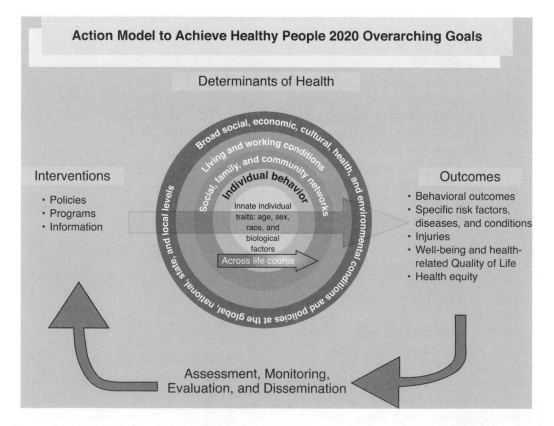

Figure 4.1   Action Model to Achieve Healthy People 2020 Overarching Goals (Healthy People 2020, n.d. a.).

to Achieve Healthy People 2020 Overarching Goals (Healthy People 2020, Phase I Report). The objectives for meeting these goals are divided into a broad spectrum of 38 topic areas. These objectives can be accessed through the Healthy People 2020 (n.d. b) home page (www.healthypeople.gov/hp2020).

The goals and objectives of Healthy People 2020 are guidelines for policy and prevention strategies. Many if not most of the topic areas and their objectives are arenas in which public health social workers practice and provide unique expertise to the development and implementation of public health prevention policies and programs.

Although it is widely accepted that social factors are major determinants of health, the current Healthy People 2020 initiative has only proposed social determinants of health as an objective area. As of this writing, anyone can create an online profile and propose a social determinant of health objective. Without set objectives, social objectives to reduce the number of children in poverty, reduce the number of children who go to bed hungry, and decrease the number of people who are unemployed are missing from the nation's public health objectives, yet all are recognized as social determinants of health care. Examples of current social determinant–associated objectives are provided in Box 4.2. As the primary providers of psychosocial interventions, public health social workers should take the lead in advocating for inclusion of social objectives in subsequent versions of Healthy People.

Box 4.2 Example Healthy People 2020 Objectives Associated With Social Determinants of Health

Access to Health Services
- Increase the proportion of people with health insurance.
- Reduce the proportion of individuals who experience difficulties or delays in obtaining necessary medical care, dental care, or prescription medicines.

Adolescent Health
- Increase educational achievement of adolescents and young adults.
- Increase the percentage of adolescents who are connected to a parent or other positive adult caregiver.

Early and Middle Childhood
- Decrease the percentage of children who have poor-quality sleep.
- Increase the proportion of children who are ready for school in all five domains of healthy development.

Educational and Community-Based Programs
- Increase high school completion.
- Increase the proportion of elementary, middle, and senior high schools that provide comprehensive school health education to prevent health problems in these areas: unintentional injury; violence; suicide; tobacco use and addiction; alcohol or other drug use; unintended pregnancy, human immunodeficiency virus (HIV)/acquired immunodeficiency syndrome (AIDS), and sexually transmitted disease infection; unhealthy dietary patterns; and inadequate physical activity.

Environmental Health
- Reduce the proportion of occupied housing units that have moderate or severe structural problems.
- Increase the proportion of the population in the U.S.–Mexico border region that has adequate drinking water and sanitation facilities.

Family Planning
- Increase the proportion of females at risk of unintended pregnancy who used contraception at most recent sexual intercourse.
- Increase the proportion of adolescents who received formal instruction on reproductive health topics before they were 18 years old.

INTERSECTION OF SOCIAL WORK AND PUBLIC HEALTH

As discussed in the introduction to this chapter, public health provides a specific orientation and framework for the various professionals who practice within the public health arena. Public health social workers fill many different positions, including: case managers; health educators; program planners and evaluators; grant writers; administrators and program directors at the federal, regional, state, and local levels; and executive directors of not-for-profit agencies. Social workers now work in a variety of areas that once would have been considered the purview of public health, such as wellness, obesity prevention, physical activity, and smoking cessation (Curry et al., 2007; Lawrence, Hazlett, & Hightower, 2010; Leung et al., 2007; Thomas, Supiano, Chasco, McGowan, & Beer, 2009) The public health arena has expanded to define issues important to social work, such as domestic violence and sexual assault, as significant public health problems (Kimerling et al., 2010; Saftlas et al., 2010; Silverman et al., 2010).

Beginning in 1996, a group of public health social workers convened to develop a useful definition of public health social work. They debated whether public health social workers are defined by training, job, or a combination of both. What, they asked, are the common attributes of the person and the job? The debate led to a brief and a longer definition and a philosophy for public health social work. The definitions, philosophy, and model practice standards and core competencies can be found online at http://oce.sph.unc.edu/cetac/phswcompetencies_may05.pdf

Social work practice in public health differs from clinical social work practice in two distinct ways:

1. Public health social work practice emphasizes health promotion, protection from environmental harms, and disease prevention.
2. Public health social work practice targets populations rather than individuals and groups (Watkins, 1985).

Social workers bring to public health practice skills, such as community assessment, and social work values, such as the promotion of social justice, a focus on the most vulnerable populations, recognition for the need of cultural competence, and sensitivity to race and ethnicity. For example, public health social workers understand the need to tailor interventions to specific populations. Interventions developed for White, middle-class populations may not be effective with lower-income, minority populations.

The need for tailoring interventions to specific populations has been supported by several researchers (Chin, Walters, Cook, & Huang, 2007; Green & Glasgow, 2006; Klesges, Dzewaltowski, & Glasgow, 2008). Chin and colleagues noted that few interventions work at the population level (are generalizable) and that interventions must be culturally tailored to work with each social, cultural, or racial/ethnic group. Green and Glasgow developed review criteria to assess the external validity and potential generalizability of interventions. Elements of the criteria include descriptions of representativeness of participants and settings, extent of program adaptation and implementation of intervention content, and maintenance of intervention effects and long-term sustainability of programs. Klesges and colleagues applied the Green and Glasgow model to review the external validity of childhood obesity prevention studies. They found that there remains a need for researchers to include external validity measures in their studies. They specifically identify three main criteria: "(1) representativeness of participants at the child, setting, and staff levels; (2) robustness of intervention effects across different subgroups, delivery staff, and conditions; and (3) replicability of results across settings and under different contexts" (Klesges et al., 2008, p. 222).

Epidemiology and the Determinants of Health

The foundation of public health research is epidemiology, the study of the distribution and determinants of disease in populations. Public health uses evidence-based interventions—those that are developed and verified through research—to control and prevent epidemics and disease outbreaks.

A focus of epidemiological studies has been to examine the determinants of health and well-being. As stated in Healthy People 2020:

> [H]ealth determinants are the range of personal, social, economic, and environmental factors that determine the health status of individuals or populations. They are embedded in our social and physical environments. Social determinants include family, community, income, education, sex, race/ethnicity, geographic location, and access to health care, among others. Determinants in the physical environments include our natural and built environments. (n.d. a)

Lung cancer is a useful example to demonstrate the interactions of health determinants. Biologically, lung cancer is caused by a manifestation of malignant cells. Some individuals may have a genetic predisposition to developing cancer, but other, nonbiologic causes of lung cancer exist. The most important additional determinant of lung cancer is the behavior of an individual. Cigarette smoking is the leading cause of lung cancer and is associated with 87% of cases (National Cancer Institute [NCI], n.d). Secondhand smoke, or passive smoking, is an example of a physical environmental cause of lung cancer. Bars where smoking is accepted and where people often socialize are another physical environment that leads to lung cancer. Although not as powerful a factor in the development of lung cancer as smoking, exposures to indoor and outdoor airborne toxins, such as ash, dust, asbestos, and particulate matter, represent another cause.

These latter correlates with lung cancer also are associated with social determinants of health. In developing nations, it is common for women to cook over open stoves, using wood- or dung-fueled fires. The women and their young children have direct exposure three times per day, as meals are prepared. Likewise,

asbestos has been linked causally to mesothelioma, a specific type of lung cancer. Asbestos is any of several silicate minerals mined for their flame-retardant and insulating properties. Many people in developed nations have been exposed during building renovations involving old insulation. Asbestos has been linked to some of the lung conditions currently being experienced by first responders to the World Trade Center on September 11, 2001. In developing nations, the mining of these silicate minerals continues, usually by impoverished workers using little or no airway protection.

Lung cancer rates, like those of many diseases, vary by race and socioeconomic status (SES). In the United States, lung cancer rates in the African American community are higher for both males and females compared with the White American community (NCI, 2010). The rate ratios for both men and women were higher among those with less than a high school education than for those with a college education (3.01 and 2.02, respectively), and incidence rates were 1.7 times higher among those with incomes below $12,500 than for those with incomes above $50,000 (Clegg et al., 2009). A number of social factors promote smoking. When smoking is acceptable in one's peer group, the social environment promotes that activity (Lakon, Hipp, & Timberlake, 2010). An example of a social factor is the placement of bright and colorful cigarette advertisements at children's eye level in stores, thus enticing the next generation to become smokers (Haviland & Sember, 2004). Public health efforts were effective in eliminating the use of marketing strategies directed at children, such as cartoons in advertising (Schooler, Feighery, & Flora, 1996).

Two overarching determinants of health are the macrolevel issues of policies and interventions and access to quality health care. Public health policies address health promotion and disease prevention. Some prevention policies to discourage tobacco use include smoke-free buildings and federal, state, and local laws that prohibit tobacco use where people work, especially in airplanes and restaurants. In addition to reducing smoking behavior, these types of restrictions also are designed to protect employees from constant exposure to secondhand smoke.

Access to care is especially important because the later that cancer is diagnosed, the worse its prognosis. Access to diagnosis and treatment is limited not only by lack of health insurance but also by other social and environmental factors. Although the passage of the Patient Protection and Affordable Care Act (PPACA) in March 2010 requires that everyone have insurance by 2014, it does little to address other issues of access to care (Kaiser Family Foundation, 2010). System and institutional barriers limit access to health care especially for lower-income and minority families (Dai, 2010). System barriers include inadequate capacity to serve the populations, and institutional barriers include problems in the organization and delivery of care. Some system factors for lower-income people are the limited numbers of health-care providers serving inner cities and rural areas and limited safety-net clinics for those who lack insurance. Clinic hours held only during the workday are an institutional barrier. Another institutional barrier is the lack of accommodation to communication needs of non-English speakers. Research on disparities in access to health care based on race, ethnicity, and language for those who are insured has shown that Spanish speakers are less likely to get health care than their English-speaking peers. These findings are consistent for physician visits, mental health services, mammograms, and influenza vaccinations (Fiscella, Franks, Doescher, & Saver, 2002; Weech-Maldonado et al., 2003). Many facilities have few interpreters, and providers sometimes rely on family members, often children, to translate.

COMMON VALUES

Two values shared by social work and public health are the elimination of health disparities and the promotion of social, economic, and environmental justice. Health disparities exist between and among populations defined by race or ethnicity, gender and gender identification, SES, education, employment or insurance status, disability status, and geography. Disparities also are found in screening, incidence, mortality, survivorship, and treatment (Gehlert, Mininger, Sohmer, & Berg, 2008).

Elimination of Health Disparities

At the request of Congress in 1999, IOM convened a panel of experts to examine the extent to which racial and ethnic minority health disparities are attributable to disparities in health-care services. Their report, *Unequal Treatment,* found a consistent body of research demonstrating minority disparities in health care. Minorities were less likely than White American patients to receive appropriate care for heart disease, such as cardiac medications and bypass surgery, but more likely to receive less desirable medical procedures, such as lower limb amputations for diabetes (Smedley, Stith, & Nelson, 2003). Keefe (2010) discusses racial and ethnic health-care disparities in seven health categories or conditions from a public health social work perspective: heart disease and stroke; cancer; HIV/AIDS; respiratory diseases; diabetes; maternal, infant, and child health; and mental health and mental disorders. For further information on social inequalities and health, please see the Public Broadcasting Series *Unnatural Causes* (www .pbs.org/unnaturalcauses/index.htm).

The overall health of an individual and the population is determined by a wide array of factors—from broad social economic, cultural, health, and environmental factors to individual behaviors. Interventions such as policies, programs, and health interventions work across the life course and the social-individual environments to influence outcomes. Urie Bronfenbrenner's ecological systems theory (1979), a precursor to both person-in-environment and social epidemiology, outlines the influence of systems from the individual level (micro) to the cultural level (macro) with the inclusion of life course (chronosystem).

In addition to health inequalities related to race and ethnicity, it has long been known that health disparities are related to SES; the lower a person's SES, the more likely that person is to have poor health. Recent research by Stringhini and colleagues (2010) found that health behaviors can account for some but not all of the SES effect. However, poor health behaviors related to diet, physical activity, and alcohol consumption are thought to be partially related to environmental stressors, which may be aggravated by low SES (Dunn, 2010). Health inequalities also are place based, as outlined in reference to access to care. Spatial influence also is captured in proximity and access to healthy environments, not just places of care. Mitchell and Popham (2008) found income-associated health inequalities in England but report that proximity to green spaces (i.e., parks) moderates this association. The incidence rate ratio of all-cause mortality and circulatory disease, on average, decreased the closer one lived to green space. This decrease was slight for those of high income but was quite steep for those in the lower quartile of income (see Figure 4.2).

Racially based health disparities are particularly apparent when examining three important maternal and child health status indicators: infant mortality (IM), low birth weight (LBW), and maternal mortality. IM is one of the leading indicators used to measure a country's health. Although the overall U.S. rate of IM dropped to 6.75 per 1,000 live births in 2007, this rate is still short of the Healthy People 2010 objective of reducing IM to 4.5 per 1,000 (Xu, Kochanek, Murphy, & Tejada-Vera, 2010). The 2008 IM rate places the United States 33rd among nations monitored by the United Nations Populations Division (United Nations

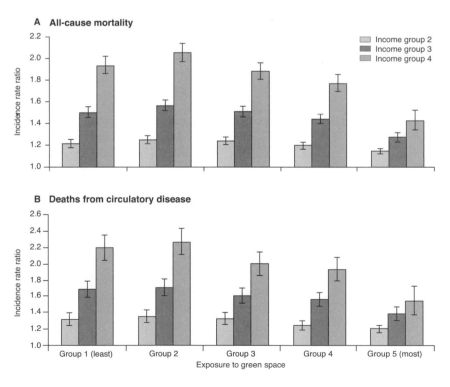

Figure 4.2   Exposure to Green Space Mediates the Effect of Income on All-Cause and Circulatory Disease Mortality

Source: From Mitchell and Popham (2008).

Department of Economic and Social Affairs, Population Division, 2007). The IM rate was 2.4 times greater in African American than in White American infants in 2007 (Mathews & MacDorman, 2010). LBW—the second leading cause of IM—rose to 8.3% in 2007, the highest level reported in the United States for four decades. LBW rates for non-Hispanic African Americans was 14.0%, nearly double the rate for non-Hispanic White Americans (7.3%) in 2006 (Martin et al., 2009). Maternal mortality for African American women was 26.5 per 100,000 live births, 2.7 times greater than the rate for White women (10.0 per 100,000) (Xu et al., 2010).

Place-based health disparities are also prevalent and often are tied to racial and socioeconomic status. Food deserts—neighborhoods with limited access to healthy food—have been identified in many low-income communities of color across the United States (Walker, Keane, & Burke, 2010). Disparities have been identified in the proximity and access to parks and natural open space for recreation, psychological restoration, and social health (Floyd, Taylor, & Whitt-Glover, 2009; Hartig, 2008). Place also is tied to inequalities in the prevalence and maintenance of chronic diseases including diabetes (Schootman et al., 2010), cancer (Freedman, Grafova, & Rogowski, 2011), HIV/AIDS and cardiovascular diseases (Nazmi, Diez Roux, Ranjit, Seeman, & Jenny, 2010).

Recognizing the vast health inequities across the world, WHO established the Commission on Social Determinants of Health (CSDH) in 2005. CSDH finds that health disparities are a matter of social justice and are created not only by policy but also by unequal distributions of power and wealth. In their final report, CSDH offers three principles of action to close the gaps in health:

> 1) Improve the conditions of daily life—the circumstances in which people are born, grow, live, work, and age. 2) Tackle the inequitable distribution of power, money, and resources—the structural drivers of those conditions of daily life—globally, nationally, and locally. 3) Measure the problem, evaluate

action, expand the knowledge base, develop a workforce that is trained in the social determinants of health, and raise public awareness about the social determinants of health. (CSDH, 2008, p. 2)

Promotion of Social, Economic, and Environmental Justice

Some current U.S. policies and inaccessibility to quality health services lead to social, economic, and environmental injustice. Social, economic, and environmental inequalities are determinants of disparities in health status. Thus, social work and public health both aim to promote changes that will lead to a more just society.

Social and physical environments that exist in poor neighborhoods, such as those in the inner city, contribute to adverse health outcomes. For example, the lack of job opportunities creates a situation in which a neighborhood may tolerate sales of illegal drugs in order to bring in sufficient income to support families. Drug sales in a community lead to addiction and its sequelae, such as illegal activities that lead to violent behavior, morbidity, and mortality.

A number of social factors, including the ubiquitous stressors of prejudice and poverty, also can lead to poor health status. Krieger (2003, 2005) has been conducting research on racism and health status for many years. She characterizes racism as one of the key factors in establishing health status and identifies five pathways through which racism can harm health. These include: (1) economic and social deprivation; (2) exposure to toxins; (3) socially inflicted trauma; (4) targeted marketing of products harmful to health, such as alcohol, tobacco, and illicit drugs; and (5) inadequate or degrading medical care. In various studies, Krieger and her colleagues have shown the effects of perceived racism on differences in LBW and IM rates between African American and White American women (Mustillo et al., 2004) and how racism plays into police violence (Cooper, Moore, Gruskin, & Krieger, 2004). Other groups, such as minority religions and those with different gender expression and identification (i.e., the lesbian, gay, bisexual, and transgendered [LGBT] community), also are oppressed and particularly vulnerable to system and institutional barriers to primary and secondary care.

Social epidemiology has been used as a tool to explain disparities within racial and ethnic groups. A study among middle-class African American women in Chicago found that birth outcomes were better for those living in predominantly African American census tracks compared with those living in racially mixed areas. The researchers concluded that "the positive effects of a better socioeconomic context may be countered for minority women by the adverse effects of racism or racial stigma" (Pickett, Collins, Masi, & Wilkinson, 2005, p. 2229).

Another example of a socially created health condition is obesity. The National Nutrition and Health Survey (NHANES) tracks the rates of overweight, obese, and extremely obese (measured using Body Mass Index [BMI], calculated as the ratio of kilograms/meter^2) in American

adults (Ogden & Carroll, 2010b). The prevalence of overweight (BMI = 25.0–29.9) in adults 20 years and older has remained stable at about 34% since 1960. The prevalence of obesity (BMI ≥ 30) and extreme obesity (BMI ≥ 40) have more than doubled during the same time frame. In the 1960 to 1962 National Health Study, 13.4% of adults were obese; in the 2007–2008 NHANES, 34.3% were. Extreme obesity has risen in prevalence from 0.9% in 1960–1962 to 6% in 2007–2008.

Disparities in the prevalence of obesity occur by race/ethnicity and gender (Ogden & Carroll, 2010b). In the 2007–2008 NHANES, prevalence was highest for non-Hispanic Black women (49.6%) and Hispanic women (45.1%) and lowest for non-Hispanic White men (31.9%). Clusters of obesity also is revealed geographically. The American South, especially the deep South and southern Appalachia, have the highest rates of adult obesity. Although the rates have increased over the past 20 years, the distribution of obesity remains mostly the same (see Figure 4.3).

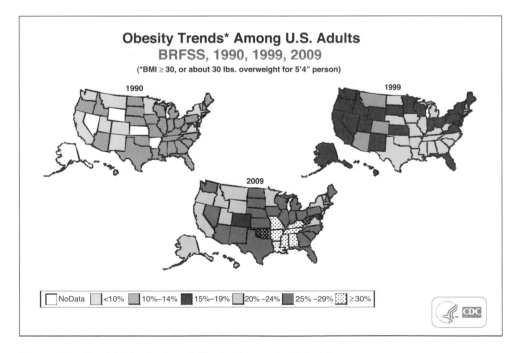

Figure 4.3   Spatial Distribution of Obesity Across the United States

Source: Adapted from Centers for Disease Control and Prevention (2010). Data for figure was derived from Behavioral Risk Factor Surveillance System, CDC.

Childhood obesity is a special concern of U.S. first lady Michelle Obama. (Obesity in children is defined as BMI greater than or equal to sex- and age-specific 95th percentile from the 2000 CDC growth charts [Ogden & Carroll, 2010a].) NHANES has measured obesity in three age groups of children since the 1970s. The 1971–1974 NHANES reported the prevalence of obesity in children ages 2 to 5 years to be 5.0%; in children 6 to 11 years, 4.0%; and in children 12 to 19 years, 6.1%. The prevalence in the 2007–2008 NHANES doubled for the youngest children (10.4%), grew nearly five times for children 6 to 11 years old (19.6%), and tripled for children 12 to 19 years old (18.1%). Similar to adults, adolescents (12–19 years old) exhibit inequalities in the distribution of obesity by race, ethnicity, and gender. The prevalence of obesity among non-Hispanic African American girls and Mexican American boys are highest (29.2% and 26.8%, respectively). The prevalence is lowest among non-Hispanic White girls (14.5%) and boys (16.7%) (Ogden & Carroll, 2010a).

Larger restaurant portions, fast food, and lack of exercise are some causes for the increased size of Americans. Busy work schedules limit parents' time to prepare healthy meals, leaving them to rely on high-fat cafeteria offerings for lunch (Eliadis, 2006). Time is spent on video games or watching television rather than on exercise. Cecil-Karb and Grogan-Kaylor (2009) studied the effects of parents' perceptions of neighborhood safety on children's BMI. They found a significant association between perceptions of poor neighborhood safety and BMI. This association was mediated by television watching. Another factor associated with increased time indoors is the suburbanization and driving culture throughout most of the United States. Many social and policy practices and decisions enacted in the first half of the 20th century have led to the urban–suburban dichotomy witnessed today in many cities.

As automobiles became more ubiquitous and vehicle traffic increased in city centers, the number of pedestrian–vehicle accidents increased along with other sequelae. Families began moving to the suburbs so that children would have more room to play outdoors, away from city traffic (Frank, Engelke, & Schmid, 2003). At the same time, the practice of redlining became acceptable. Redlining is the process by which lending institutions (generally for home mortgages) demarcate areas of cities to raise and lower interest rates and discriminate in loan dealings based on characteristics such as ethnicity or income (Gee, 2008). Over decades, such processes drained the city-center tax base and left downtowns with low-income, predominately minority residents while the suburbs became majority Caucasian and middle income. The residents leaving urban centers for the suburbs took with them their tax base. Cities were left with limited financial resources to support schools, parks, and public services. In turn, more people moved away from urban centers, creating a phenomenon that is only now being halted.

However, 70 years removed from the beginning of this exodus, families in the suburbs are suffering from a lack of physical activity. Suburban families now are forced to commute many miles by automobile for long periods, restricting active transportation, such as walking or bicycle riding. Time spent in the car is not replaced with play or physical activity when families return home. Meanwhile, downtowns across the United States are making efforts to revitalize with walkability as a core principle of regeneration. Cities are passing Complete Streets bills and ordinances that require streets to be multipurpose, including mixed-income residences, commercial space, and retail. The infrastructure of streets also is changing, with better-designed crosswalks and bike lanes and wider sidewalks (Frank et al., 2003).

Public health social workers can contribute to the development of public policies, such as making neighborhoods safe and inviting, by helping to determine the social and economic forces that encourage overweight and obesity. As cities work to reclaim their downtowns, many are turning to trendy loft districts to attract middle-income, and blue-collar workers. Unfortunately, this process is more akin to gentrification than mixed-income development. Wealthy developers are purchasing inexpensive buildings and developing a former low-income area for middle- to high-income residents with little consideration for the current residents. Low-income residents are forced to relocate, often away from social service providers proximate to their old neighborhoods. Cities usually benefit financially from gentrification because of the increase in tax base and "clean" downtown neighborhoods. However, the process continues to segregate along racial and socioeconomic lines (for more, see Slater, 2006).

Public health social workers have successfully advocated changes in public policy to improve the health status indicators in the population, particularly for the disadvantaged, such as the Medicaid expansions under the Omnibus Budget Reconciliation Act of 1989. This and the expanded State Children's Health Insurance Program (SCHIP), established as an optional program for states in 1997, are examples of policies that promote social and economic justice. In February 2009, the SCHIP program was reauthorized, and as of June 30, 2010, all states and territories and the District of Columbia had implemented SCHIP (Centers for Medicare and Medicaid Services, 2010).

Changing the distribution of financial resources and promoting socially just actions would reduce the disparities in health status of vulnerable populations (McGinnis, William-Russo, & Knickman, 2002). Unfortunately, these attempts have not all been successful. The Medicaid expansion policies of the 1980s, which were intended to reduce health disparities by increasing access to care for low-income pregnant women, failed to reduce the disparity in birth outcomes between African American and White American women (Martin et al., 2009; Mathews & MacDorman, 2010; Xu et al., 2010).

The social work profession is strongly in favor of the need to achieve economic justice. The Delegate Assembly of the National Association of Social Workers (NASW) meets every three years to develop and publish the public and professional policy statements for the association. A prominent policy position that has been included and updated by NASW is for the development of public policies that promote economic justice. NASW (2009) continues to advocate on the issues of poverty and access to health care for all. To achieve a socially and economically just society will require changes in American social values, but it is a worthy goal of both public health and social work.

COMMON METHODOLOGIES FOR PRACTICE

Sound social work and public health interventions and policy are evidence based. To arrive at evidence-based practices, both fields rely on strong research and evaluation of programs and policies. One common approach used by social work and public health is the community assessment. Public health also uses social epidemiology for program planning and evaluation. Epidemiological methods used in public health also could be used by social workers in developing interventions at all levels of practice. Another tool is a geographic information system (GIS), a software-based tool used in social work and public health practice and research to map spatial correlations, discriminations, and to identify areas of need.

Mussolino (2005) analyzed the NHANES I to provide evidence of a prospective association between depression and hip fracture. Interventions that target depression in elderly people theoretically may impact the contribution of hip fracture to morbidity and mortality. This is an example of how public health social work intervention might improve a public health outcome. Another example is based on data collected from the National Hospital Ambulatory Medical Care Survey, which established the home as the predominant location of injury for U.S. children. The researchers recommend interventions targeting the home environment to reduce the morbidity and mortality from unintentional injury in U.S. children (Phelan, Khoury, Kalkwarf, & Lanphear, 2005).

Community Assessment

Community assessment is a method of identifying the strengths and weaknesses in a defined community. Members of the community are involved in designing, implementing, and analyzing the information gathered from assessments. Other assessments are initiated by public authorities in response to legal mandate and may or may not involve community members. In either case, the assessments help to define problems and gaps in services so that the community and professionals can advocate for improvements to existing programs and for new policies and programs.

Comprehensive community assessments use various methods to obtain data for analysis. These methods include community surveys, health impact assessments (see Box 4.3), interviews with community leaders, and town hall meetings. Data collection may be from vital records of births and deaths, hospital discharge information, and other data from public health and social service agencies.

Because of their training, social workers are well prepared to conduct community assessments. Public health social workers contribute to public health assessments and in doing so provide insights regarding the social context of health and disease. Public health social workers collaborate with other public health professionals to apply social understanding to interventions that are developed in response to community assessment (Wilkinson et al., 2002). For example, they participate in child death review teams to provide the person-in-environment perspective. Community assessment is also crucial to the development of culturally competent social marketing strategies. A study that explored factors linking at-risk African Americans with health-promotion programs found that, contrary to common perception, the use of the African American church and the use of a high-profile person to deliver a message actually may be counterproductive to efforts to motivate people to use health prevention programs (Icard, Bourjolly, & Siddiqui, 2003). This finding is an example of how research should guide evidence-based practice.

Box 4.3 Health Impact Assessments

Health impact assessments (HIA) were first established in Europe in the late 1990s. The National Health Service of the United Kingdom defines an HIA as a

> developing approach that can help to identify and consider the potential—or actual—health impacts of a proposal on a population. Its primary output is a set of evidence-based recommendations geared to informing the decision-making process. These recommendations aim to highlight practical ways to enhance the positive aspects of a proposal, and to remove or minimise any negative impacts on health, wellbeing and health inequalities that may arise or exist. (Taylor & Quigley, 2002, p. 2)

Colleagues of the authors recently completed an HIA in St. Louis, MO. The core team consisted of two researchers from the school of medicine, one from the design and visual arts school, three from social work, and one from public health, in addition to one community partner. The steering committee consisted of eight stakeholders from the local community, either residents or local practitioners from schools, religious organizations, municipalities, or nongovernmental organizations. Finally, there were groups of consultants, students, community surveyors, and an advisory team, most of whom were associated with social work and/or public health. The team worked together to identify a series of recommendations offered to a redevelopment effort in a low-income community of color.

Social Epidemiology

Social epidemiology—the study of the impact of social factors on the distribution of health and illness in a population—examines the role of social variables on other known and accepted biological and behavioral factors that shape the health status of a community (Oakes

& Kaufman, 2006). Social epidemiology is a research method that uses mostly quantitative data to identify social determinants of health and health outcomes. For example, Lynch and Kaplan (2000) have conducted numerous studies to better understand the impact of socioeconomic position on health. Using the findings from their and others' studies, they have developed a theoretical model to explain these effects. This model uses a life-course perspective and takes into account a broad range of conditions and statuses, and it discusses the variation in measures of socioeconomic position. This variation demonstrates the challenges of conducting social epidemiologic studies. For example, Krieger and her colleagues have studied the effects of racism on health (Krieger, 2005; Krieger, Chen, Waterman, Rehkopf, & Subramanian, 2003). To do so, they had to develop a measure of perceived racism, which, although used by others, still is not universally accepted because the experience of racial discrimination can be thought of as subjective, and thus the measure might not work the same way in all settings. Others have examined race and health of children and found important associations (Flores, Olson, & Tomany-Korman, 2005).

Some social epidemiologists use qualitative as well as quantitative data. An example is the Fetal and Infant Mortality Review (FIMR), sponsored and monitored by MCHB (Hutchins, Grason, & Handler, 2004; Koontz, Buckley, & Ruderman, 2004). FIMRs are conducted at the community level after a fetal or infant death that cannot be attributed to a medical cause—for example, sudden infant death syndrome (SIDS). The purpose of an FIMR is to gather medical and social information that can be used to enhance the health and well-being of women, infants, and families. That information then can be used to improve community resources and service delivery systems to reduce additional fetal and infant deaths. FIMRs are conducted by examining medical care data, autopsies, and assessments, often completed by social workers, of the social environment of the pregnant woman and the infant. Attention is given to housing, number of adults and children in the household, and other

family resources. The data are reviewed by transdisciplinary technical advisory committees that, in addition to physicians and nurses, may include clinical social workers and community volunteers. Public health social workers contribute to these reviews by interpreting the social contexts in which deaths occur.

Geographic Information Systems

GISs allow for the spatial analysis of distributions, trends, services, clusters, and so on. Through a system of data management and software, a person can utilize a GIS to map information on scales from a neighborhood to worldwide. These skills are taught to students in many universities. For example, in a joint social work and public health course at Washington University in St. Louis that is built around a community-based teaching model, students work with community agencies in need of spatial analysis. Past analyses have included market research to analyze where donations most often come from and where agencies might better market their organizations to obtain additional donations and funds. Two recent projects mapped neighborhood assets, crimes, and empty lots to identify the best locales for service expansion. Another project mapped the percentage of students receiving free and reduced-price lunches across a city against the location of summertime meal providers and local soup kitchens (see Figure 4.4). This project allowed the agency to identify communities within the city that have a high proportion of children who receive free and reduced-priced lunch who also live in areas with limited access to summertime and weekend food services. This spatial analysis identified neighborhoods for the expansion of food provisions.

Community assessment, social epidemiology, and GISs are tools that clearly identify the social and physical environmental factors in the determination of health status and discrimination in a community. With the information gleaned from using these methods, public health social workers and other public health professionals can work together toward the goal of improving the quality of life of the public.

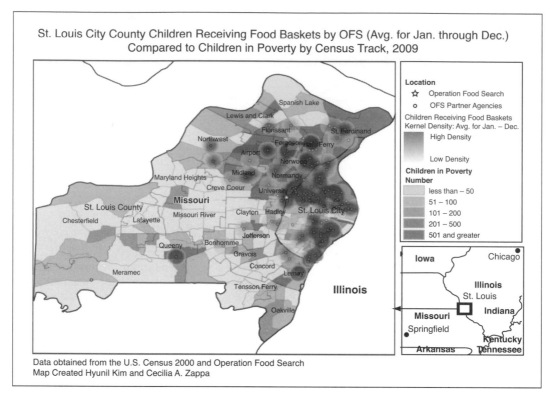

Figure 4.4 GIS Map Showing the Number of Children Living in Poverty per Census Track and the Number of Children Receiving Food Baskets From Community-Based Agencies

Source: Reproduced courtesy of Operation Food Search, St. Louis, MO, and MSW students Hyunil Kim and Cecilia Zappa.

LEVELS OF PRACTICE AND COMPONENTS OF PREVENTION

At the micro, or direct-practice, level, public health social workers implement public health interventions using clinical social work skills or provide social work services as part of a larger public health program. At the mezzo, or indirect-practice level, public health social workers develop, implement, and administer public health programs. At the macro level, public health social workers contribute their knowledge of psychosocial and cultural issues to the development of public health interventions. They also are involved in surveillance and evaluation of programs that serve low-income and vulnerable populations. Public health social workers are engaged in the policy-making arena in conjunction with other public health professionals.

Much of public health practice takes place at the macro level. Social work and public health

administrators at the macro level of practice use community-based assessments to develop interventions. Public health practitioners may use nonclinical social work interventions, such as job programs and health-care reform, to change the social environment. Public health practitioners, including public health social workers, conduct theoretical and intervention research in order to advance a shared commitment to evidence-based practice.

Components of Prevention

Disease prevention is divided into three levels: primary, secondary, and tertiary (Schneider, 2000). Primary prevention is intended to protect us from injury and disease. Examples include the Back-to-Sleep national campaign for the prevention of SIDS, immunizations against childhood and other diseases, and automobile restraints and airbags. Another primary prevention is the imposition of large taxes on tobacco to limit its use by increasing the cost of cigarettes and other tobacco products.

Secondary prevention is the early diagnosis and treatment of disease and seeks to reverse or retard a disease process from progressing. Examples are Pap smears, mammograms, and prostate-specific antigen tests to identify malignant or premalignant states and intervene to effect a cure or slow the progression of the illness.

Tertiary prevention includes those actions taken to minimize the effects of a disease and prevent further disability. Periodic eye exams to detect and treat diabetic retinopathy are a type of tertiary prevention because they prevent disability deriving from diabetes although they do not treat the primary disease.

TYPES OF PUBLIC HEALTH SOCIAL WORK INTERVENTIONS

The intersection of the three levels of social work practice with the three levels of prevention is displayed in Figure 4.5. The public health crisis of HIV is used to illustrate public health

social work interventions within the familiar framework of micro, mezzo, and macro levels of practice and components of prevention.

Primary Prevention of HIV at the Micro, Mezzo, and Macro Levels

The roles of public health social workers in the primary prevention of HIV at the micro level include condom distribution in clinics, counseling women living with HIV about their health and family planning, and participating in needle exchange programs. At the mezzo level, public health social workers administer community-based programs for safe needle exchange and condom distribution. Needle exchange has been a controversial primary prevention intervention for HIV, and public health social workers who advocate for federal, state, and local policy to permit this intervention are working at the macro level.

Secondary Prevention of HIV at the Micro, Mezzo, and Macro Levels

Outreach and early intervention services are particularly important to meet the needs of

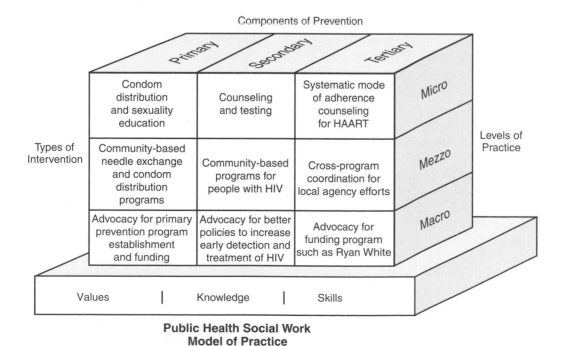

Figure 4.5   Components of Prevention and Levels of Practice

people living with HIV who are not receiving care. Many public health social workers work in hospitals, local health departments, and community-based programs that provide counseling and testing for HIV. The Positive Start program in Missouri provides an interface between the community HIV/AIDS agency and the Department of Corrections. It targets inmates living with HIV who are scheduled to be released (personal communication, Cale Mitchell, executive director, Rain Central Missouri, July 20, 2010). This mezzo program creates a connection to clients by providing referrals for case management after release and educates them about prevention when they rejoin society. Public health social workers who fight discriminatory policies targeting people with HIV, such as in employment and housing, are working at the macro level.

Tertiary Prevention of HIV at the Micro, Mezzo, and Macro Levels

Examples of tertiary prevention at the micro level include direct-service case management for medical services, securing resources to enhance health outcomes (supportive services such as housing and food vouchers), and making referrals and providing payment assistance for visits to infectious disease specialists or HIV-focused physicians. Mezzo-level public health social workers administer programs that help people living with HIV obtain and maintain stable and high-quality housing, for example. Public health social workers operating in the research and policy arenas to advance improved programs for people living with HIV are working at the macro level for tertiary prevention.

PUBLIC HEALTH SOCIAL WORK PRACTICE TODAY

Public health social work practice today is a growing field. There are social workers working in public health at all levels of practice and with all components of prevention. The practice settings for public health social workers

reflect the partnership between public health and social work.

Practice Settings

Public health social workers do not practice in isolation. Their practice, often on transdisciplinary teams, takes place in host settings that are usually public but also may be private. Public settings include federal public health agencies as well as state and local health departments. At all three levels of government, public health social workers work in various policy-making and program positions. In addition, public health social work practice is primarily at the population level. For example, public health social workers work side by side with public health environmental specialists to ensure that safe housing is available to a community of elders. They work with public health nurses, physicians, and epidemiologists to develop, implement, and evaluate programs that serve all ages in the population. They coordinate home visiting programs targeting pregnant women at high risk for poor birth outcomes.

Federal-level public health social workers work in national and regional offices. They create and administer regulations for policy implementation and manage and provide oversight for grants, such as the MCHB grant and Special Projects of Regional and National Significance and other federal grants. Some public health social workers provide training, and others conduct and use research to inform evidence-based interventions. Federal public health social workers act as liaisons to state programs funded by block grants.

Public health social workers are found in a variety of state-administered, federally funded programs, such as the Title V Children with Special Health Care Needs program. They work as the intermediaries between state and local health departments and other public health agencies in managing federal pass-through dollars. Public health social workers provide management oversight for the programs and train managers to comply with federal mandates. Public health social workers at the federal and state levels also provide expert testimony and advocate for public health programs when Congress and state legislatures develop policy and budgets that will affect the public's health.

Local health departments are the workhorses within the public health system, and programs generally associated with these agencies are the maternal and child health programs (family planning, prenatal care, well-child care, immunizations), disease surveillance and treatment programs (tuberculosis control, sexually transmitted infections, West Nile virus, pandemic influenza such as H1N1), and environmental protection programs (restaurant inspection, vermin control, air quality, milk safety, veterinary-borne disease). In addition, vital statistics (birth and death certificates) often are housed within local health departments.

At the local level, in public health departments as well as in private nonprofit agencies, public health social workers develop and implement programs and provide direct service. Some examples of direct practice are case management for specific populations, home visiting, immigrant health services, HIV/AIDS counseling and testing, outreach to elderly people for blood pressure screening and other health services, and family planning and other reproductive health care. Public health social workers also work in community and migrant primary care centers.

Private settings in which public health social workers are employed usually are located in not-for-profit agencies, such as Planned Parenthood, domestic violence shelters, AIDS organizations, and established agencies, such as the YMCA/YWCA. Public health social work practice in private settings usually does not differ from practice in the public sector. Private agencies often are created to provide services that are limited or prohibited by government regulations, such as counseling clients about abortion. Some programs that operate in the private sector are supported by public funds and must comply with government regulations that apply to the services they provide. Although the practice settings remain standard, the areas of concern for public health social workers shift as social and economic conditions change and as diseases emerge.

Both public and private development agencies offer another example of practice settings for public health social work. The U.S. Agency for International Development (USAID; www.usaid.gov) is a federal government agency that "supports long-term and equitable economic growth and advances U.S. foreign policy objectives by supporting economic growth, agriculture, and trade; global health; and democracy, conflict prevention, and humanitarian assistance." Both for-profit (e.g., Development Alternatives, Inc.) and not-for-profit (e.g., Hope International, Response To Intervention, Center for Agricultural Bioscience International) private agencies also work in international development to advance social, economic, and environmental justice.

PREPARING TO BE A PUBLIC HEALTH SOCIAL WORKER

There are various ways to prepare to be a public health social worker. Although many public health social workers do not have formal public health education or public health degrees, in applicants for these positions, employers look for sound social work knowledge as it relates to public health practice. Typically public health social workers are trained on the job and learn through continuing education and participation in regional and national meetings of public health social workers. The annual meetings of the American Public Health Association (APHA) and the Association of State and Territorial Public Health Social Workers (ASTPHSW) are examples of learning and networking opportunities for public health social workers.

Increasingly, social work students who plan on practicing in public health enroll in one of the existing dual or joint master's in social work/master's in public health (MSW/MPH) programs. These programs are growing in size and number. Courses completed in one degree fulfill requirements in the second, allowing students to meet all requirements with a reduced credit load. In some schools, practica and internships also are identified that meet the practice requirements of both social work and public health, affording the student experience in interdisciplinary or transdisciplinary work. Each university and each of the schools of social work and public health has unique programs and admissions processes.

For social work master's students who are considering public health practice but are not at a school where a dual-degree program is offered, there are many other ways to prepare. Some schools offer social work concentrations in pertinent areas, such as health, mental health, and gerontology, which may include some public health content. If there is a public health school, department, or program at the university or college, students can take courses in that program as electives. If there is no public health program, there may be one at a nearby institution. Faculty members with public health training can supervise independent study. Students can work with field placement offices to find a practicum experience in a public health agency. Students are welcomed at public health social work meetings and events, often at reduced rates.

Certain areas of knowledge and resources are particularly valuable. At the federal level, the primary agency related to public health social work practice is DHHS. Key agencies in DHHS are the Health Resources Services Administration (HRSA), the National Institutes of Health, the Centers for Disease Control and Prevention, the Administration of Children Youth and Families, and the Substance Abuse and Mental Health Services Administration. MCHB and the Office of the Surgeon General are located within HRSA. Each of these agencies publishes documents and reports with essential information about public health. They also sponsor research to develop new knowledge and test interventions related to the public's health. Two other important federal programs within the Department of Agriculture are Women, Infants, and Children and the Supplemental Nutrition Assistance Program (SNAP; formerly the Food Stamp Program).

The federal, state, and local public health programs all relate to one another, usually in regard to the flow of funds. How federal regulations affect state health departments and how state and local health departments interact is critical knowledge for public health social workers.

As professionals, public health social workers are expected to keep current with changes in the field. Important resources for public health social workers are, as mentioned, APHA (including the Social Work section) and ASTPHSW. Furthermore, there are numerous texts, federal publications (such as Healthy People 2020 and *Morbidity and Mortality Weekly Report*), and journals that will help inform public health social workers. Some of the important journals are the *American Journal of Public Health*, *Health & Social Work, Social Work in Health Care*, *Social Work in Public Health*, *Maternal and Child Health Journal*, *Public Health Reports*, and *Health Affairs*.

EMERGING ISSUES FOR PUBLIC HEALTH SOCIAL WORK

Global Issues of Disaster Preparedness, Terrorism, Climate Change, Oppression, and Social Justice

Terrorism, disasters, war, disease, climate change, and social justice will shape the focus of much public health social work practice during the coming years. The attacks on the World Trade Center and the Pentagon on September 11, 2001, stimulated awareness among Americans of both the reality of domestic terrorism and the plights of oppressed people in other parts of the world. The domestic terrorism threat increasingly is an area of practice for public health social workers who are active members of disaster preparedness and response teams (see Box 4.4).

Box 4.4 Disaster Preparedness and Response Teams: New Orleans Rebuilding

In fall 2005, the city of New Orleans suffered a trifecta of disasters: the winds and rain of Hurricane Katrina, the failure of the protective levee system, and the pressures of another storm, Hurricane Rita. The loss of life, home, and livelihood was unprecedented in American history, and images from the disasters exposed the harsh realities of poverty and vulnerability endemic in urban America.

With skills in population-focused intervention, perspective of social systems, and knowledge of individual assessments of well-being, public health social workers have played critical roles in the rebuilding and recovery of New Orleans and its citizenry. Looking back at the disasters for lessons and improvements, public health social workers have assisted in developing disaster plans and coordination agreements at civic, community, and agency levels. This assistance includes the creation of services that are sensitive to the unique needs of the city's most vulnerable groups in regard to transportation and shelter provisions. In addition to these activities focused on equipping the community for future challenges, public health social workers are active in recovery and resilience as communities work to repair the social fabric torn away by the trauma and struggle associated with loss and displacement. Public health social workers participate in recovery and rebuilding in diverse roles, including:

- Assisting in civic engagement activities that reflect on the lessons of the disaster and give voice to the displaced
- Advocating for homeowners and workers to be protected from environmental exposures during cleanup
- Coordinating safe housing and resources for those returning home
- Addressing needs within social service systems as population numbers and composition changes
- Supporting the development of community clinics and facilitating primary health-care providers for residents

The many roles of public health social workers in New Orleans illustrate the demand for professionals with these skills and the valuable contributions they can make.

Source: Courtesy of Holly Scheib, PhD, MSW, MPH, Director of International Programming, Tulane School of Social Work, New Orleans, LA.

Disaster Preparedness and Response

Public health social workers have increasingly played a role in disaster preparedness and response. Disasters are "emergencies of a severity and magnitude resulting in deaths, injuries, illness, and/or property damage that cannot be effectively managed by the application of routine procedures or resources" (Landesman, 2005, p. 1). Rounds and colleagues describe three types of disasters: natural, technological, and complex (Rounds, Caye, Ross-Sheriff, Bailey, & Anderson, 2005; Rounds, Caye, Walsh, Vaughn, & Anderson, 2008). Natural disasters include acts of nature, such as floods, hurricanes, tornados, volcanic eruptions, earthquakes, and landslides. Some technological disasters are machinery or equipment malfunctions, including factory explosions, nuclear power plant failures, chemical spills, and airplane failures. Examples of complex disasters are catastrophic events of intentional human strategy, including acts of terrorism and war. Emerging diseases, such as pandemic influenza, also can constitute disasters requiring public health social work intervention.

Hurricane Katrina and the ensuing flood in New Orleans (August 2005) represent both a natural and technological disaster. The hurricane itself was disastrous in areas such as Biloxi, MS, yet produced minimal damage in New Orleans. The lack of infrastructure and failure to repair a levee there, however, resulted in massive flooding in the Ninth Ward, a lower-income, mostly African American section of the city. Inadequate disaster planning for flooding exemplifies how disasters can disproportionately affect oppressed populations, because people without cars have limited ability to evacuate. The aftereffects of hurricanes and flooding include dislocation, separation from families, lack of medical and mental health care, and disruption of education for children. Similarly, the British Petroleum oil spill of 2010 not only led to ecological disaster but produced physical, mental, and economic health consequences for many of the residents of the Gulf Coast affected by Hurricane Katrina.

Public health social workers have developed detailed practice guidelines and educational training modules for disaster preparedness, reaction, and response. Landesman's 2005 text, *Public Health Management of Disasters: The Practice Guide* (2nd ed.), provides a broad overview of types of disasters and the role of public health in agency and community planning, assessment, and response. For example, in her chapter on mental health strategies, she reviews the psychological and emotional impact of disasters, such as posttraumatic stress disorder, and provides strategies for response. Landesman identifies three public health roles:

1. Help restore the psychological and social functioning of individuals and the community.
2. Reduce the occurrence and severity of adverse mental health outcomes due to exposure and technological disasters through prevention, assessment, and response.
3. Help speed recovery and prevent long-term problems by providing information about normal reactions to disaster-related stress and how to handle these reactions.

Disaster Preparedness for Public Health Social Workers is a two-part online educational training module. Part I focuses on natural disasters (Rounds et al., 2005), and Part II focuses on bioterrorism (Rounds et al., 2008).

Terrorism and Climate Change

In their 2009 article "Psychology in an Age of Ecological Crisis," Stokols and colleagues outline the myriad ecological changes humans currently face. The authors discuss global threats to personal and societal well-being, including terrorism and climate change. There is a disconnect and latent fear between the two seemingly unrelated challenges. A feeling of helplessness has led some terror researchers to coin the term *pretraumatic stress syndrome* (Sinclair & LoCicero, 2010) and to study helplessness depression (Berry, Bowen, & Kjellstrom, 2010).

According to environmental psychology, "people ideally strive to achieve optimal environments or those that maximize the fulfillment of their needs and the accomplishment of their goals and plans" (Stokols et al., 2009, p. 187). In other words, humans strive for optimal environments for our own well-being. Achieving such environments becomes extraordinarily difficult when environments are harmed or people are constantly afraid of the threat of such harm. Public health social workers are uniquely positioned to meet the challenges delineated by Stokols and colleagues.

New conceptualizations of human response to ecological, social, and technological change are needed, particularly those that

- Address the links between local and global events.
- Encompass collective as well as individual efforts to cope with impending threats.
- Incorporate an extended rather than narrow time perspective.

GLOBAL ISSUES OF OPPRESSION AND SOCIAL JUSTICE

Oppression

Internationally, particularly in West Asia and the Middle East, the health of women and children has been highly compromised by war, isolation due to religious rules, and political policies of western governments. Growing numbers of public health social workers will be needed as members of international teams to improve the health of refugees and residents in foreign nations. Foci of their work will be in the maternal and child health arena to improve women's overall and reproductive health, psychological capacity to deal with posttraumatic stress disorder, and prevent and protect communities from the effects of poverty and the aftermath of war and terrorism.

In the United States, HIV/AIDS is now being treated as a chronic disease. The ability of the United States and other industrialized nations to achieve this state is due to the wealth that supports provision of antiretroviral drugs to people living with HIV. In developing countries, expensive drugs are beyond the reach not only of HIV/AIDS populations but also of governments with very limited monetary resources.

In sub-Saharan Africa, the epidemic of HIV/AIDS affects up to 25% of the population in some countries. Social and economic consequences of the disease can be addressed by public health social workers. In response to the President's Emergency Plan for AIDS Relief (PEPFAR), which was proposed in 2003, Congress enacted the U.S. Leadership Against HIV/AIDS, Tuberculosis, and Malaria Act of 2003 (PL 108–25). PEPFAR was reauthorized on July 30, 2008. The new act (H.R. 5501, the Tom Lantos and Henry J. Hyde United States Global Leadership against HIV/AIDS, Tuberculosis, and Malaria Reauthorization Act of 2008) was signed into law, authorizing up to $48 billion over the following five years to combat global HIV/AIDS, tuberculosis, and malaria. The three goals of PEPFAR are to: (1) support treatment for 2 million HIV-infected individuals; (2) support prevention of 7 million infections; and (3) support care for 10 million infected and affected by HIV/AIDS, including orphans and vulnerable children (U.S. President's Emergency Plan for AIDS Relief, n.d.). Interventions to meet these three goals are within the scope of public health social work practice. U.S. social workers can

participate on international transdisciplinary teams to address these goals.

Another issue of oppression at global and national levels is human trafficking (see Box 4.5). Human trafficking has been described as a form of modern-day slavery. Although largely hidden, it is widespread throughout the United States. Trafficking can take the form of forced prostitution; forced labor situations such as domestic servants, nannies, sweatshop workers, janitors, restaurant workers, migrant farm workers, fishery workers, hotel or tourist industry workers, and beggars (U.S. Department of Health and Human Services [US DHHS], 2008a).

According to United Nations Office on Drugs and Crime (UNODC), the United States is one of the highest "countries of destination" for human trafficking victims globally (UNODC, 2006), with estimates of 18,000 to 20,000 human beings trafficked into and through the United States every year (US DHHS, 2008b). Although the exact number of people affected globally is unknown, the United Nations (2009/2010) estimates that some 2.5 million people throughout the world at any given time are the victims of human trafficking.

Public health social workers on the frontline can play supportive roles by helping to identify victims and by providing after-care services, such as rehabilitation and reintegration (Hokenstad, 2010; Salett, 2006). These might include services in housing, health care, addictions treatment, immigration, food, income, employment, and legal services. Social workers also can play a preventive role by educating potential victims, educating law enforcement personnel about the issue, and advocating for the protection of this vulnerable population. Community partnerships and support networks are critical for addressing and overcoming the social exclusion of these victims (Hokenstad, 2010; Salett, 2006).

An example of such a partnership is the Central Missouri Stop Human Trafficking Coalition, a multisector coalition made up of members of the community and representatives from different organizations, including

Box 4.5 Human Trafficking

Three cases on identifying human trafficking from the Family Violence Prevention Fund (2007) are presented in this box. As you read each case, ask yourself: Is this trafficking? If so, what is it for (sex or labor or both)? Here are some trafficking red-flag questions to ask about potential trafficking victims:

- How did they get here?
- What happened once they got here?
- Was there fraud or coercion?
- What were their real or perceived choices?
- Who is in control?
- Can they leave?
- Are they or their families threatened (real or perceived)?
- Who has their documents or other things that matter to them?

Joyce, a woman from the Philippines, attended a dance school that is sponsored by the Philippine government for overseas workers. She has received her "certification" and signed up with a broker to be an entertainer in Seattle. Upon her arrival, she learned that her debt for "school and transport into the United States" is $4,000. To ensure that she pays off the broker, she is required to stay at a home that the broker owns. She owes $500 per month in rent to live there and is not allowed to leave alone. She also is required to dance at the broker's club, where she is paid $100 a week; her rent and food is deducted from this amount. Her debt keeps mounting, and she feels she will never be able to pay it back. She is told that she could earn more money at the club by performing sexual acts with customers. She does not have any immigration documents. She agrees to work performing sexual acts at the club to "pay back her debt" to her employer and to send money home to her family.

Nadia was interested in coming to the United States and thought she could go to school as well as work and make money to support her family back home. She was approached by a prominent businessman in her community and told that he could get her into the United States to work. The businessman ran a mail-order bride business. He placed Nadia's picture in his catalog and explained to Nadia that she could come to the United States, marry an American, and have all her dreams come true. Tom has picked Nadia out of a catalog to possibly be his wife. Tom gets a fiancée visa for Nadia and brings her into the United States. After she gets here, Nadia is too busy taking care of the house and Tom's children from a previous marriage to go to school. Nadia works 16 hours a day to keep the house clean and Tom and the kids fed. Tom has Nadia's visa in his safe deposit box.

Carlos lived in Mexico and wanted to come to the United States to work. He paid a coyote (smuggler) to be brought into the country. Once he crossed the border, he was taken to a safe house where a contractor picked him up with others staying there and transported him to an apple farm in Washington State where he was to work. Carlos was told that the cost of being smuggled into the United States and transported to the farm was $2,500. After he arrived at the farm, Carlos understood that he could not leave and that he would be beaten if he attempted to do so. Carlos was paid for his work, but rent and food costs were subtracted. Carlos was moved to other farms throughout the West Coast depending on the season. He never felt he could leave the farms where he lived.

Source: Adapted from the Family Violence Prevention Fund, 2007.

social service providers, local and federal law enforcement, faith-based organizations, students, educators, health-care providers, and others. Its goal is to eradicate trafficking and provide supports for individuals through activities such as

- Building a collaborative network of health and social service providers, law enforcement agencies, and nongovernmental organizations that can provide direct services for victims of human trafficking
- Providing training for professionals in health care, social service, and law enforcement agencies regarding identifying and appropriately responding to victims of human trafficking
- Conducting community awareness and education events about the issue of human trafficking; raising funds for incidental victim needs that cannot be provided by existing social service or health-care agencies
- Providing assistance to community groups, service providers, educators, and governmental agencies who request information, training, or other assistance regarding human trafficking

Although the coalition does not provide direct services, the network established through its partnering agencies also can assist with investigation and protection, temporary emergency shelter, counseling and trauma therapy, and immigration consulting (personal communication, Deborah Hume, University of Missouri Masters in Public Health Program, August 12, 2010).

Social Justice

Access to Health Care

Since the passage of the PPACA of 2010, there is the potential that universal access (via reforms in health insurance) to health care may be achieved in 2014. Until universal access to health care is achieved in the United States, public health social workers will remain active in efforts to bring comprehensive,

high-quality, and affordable health care to all. Social workers must help to define comprehensive care as including primary and secondary prevention as well as psychosocial health assessments and interventions. Furthermore, public health social workers can continue to advocate for public policies that contribute to the improvement the nation's health, for example, through antipoverty programs, jobs programs, environmental health programs, and education.

Under our current health-care delivery system, the poor and elderly people will continue to rely on publicly financed programs: Medicaid, SCHIP, and Medicare. Public health social workers will be involved in the evaluation of these programs to propose and advocate for changes that reflect the social work values of social and economic justice.

SCHIP and Medicaid cover children ages 0 to 21 years. Other than pregnant women and certain low-income and groups with disabilities, people between the ages of 21 and 65 have no access to publicly funded health insurance. When the PPACA is fully implemented, the state-based exchanges will provide an opportunity for these groups to obtain affordable health insurance (Kaiser Family Foundation, 2010).

Local and global environmental justice is an important component of social justice (see Box 4.6). In Robert Bullard's seminal book, *Dumping in Dixie: Race, Class, and Environmental Quality* (1990), the author outlines the important connections among social justice, the civil rights movement, and environmentalism. Bullard uses examples from across the United States, especially the South, of companies that locate waste and polluting facilities disproportionately in low-income and/or minority communities. The U.S. Environmental Protection Agency (U.S. EPA; 2010) defines *environmental justice* as the "fair treatment and meaningful involvement of all people regardless of race, color, national origin, or income with respect to the development, implementation, and enforcement of environmental laws, regulations, and policies" (www .epa.gov/environmentaljustice/).

Box 4.6 Public Health Social Work and the Benefit Model

It is easy for social work and public health students, professionals, and researchers to focus on deficit models, but one also can work and research from a benefit model. Health promotion and nature contact is one area in particular. Natural public open space is receiving growing attention as a salutogenic resource for psychological, physical, and social health. Natural environments elicit improvements in mood and concentration, outpace entertainment and built urban environments in perceived psychological and attention restoration quality, increase social interactions and social capital, and correlate with self-reported health. Proximity and access to open space is reported to decrease blood pressure and increase walking and physical activity levels.

Restorative environments are places that afford visitors the opportunity to recover from stress and otherwise renew personal adaptive resources needed to meet the demands of everyday life, such as the ability to focus attention. In our daily lives, each of us uses a variety of psychological and physical facilities. As demands on these facilities compound across a time frame, need for psychological and physical restoration increases. If restoration does not occur, fatigue may become symptomatic.

During the 1970s and 1980s, Yi-Fu Tuan and E. O. Wilson described human evolutionary and innate response to geographic, topographic (Tuan), and biologic (Wilson) environmental attributes. Roger Ulrich followed with reported expedited recovery time in hospital patients with a natural view out their window and articulated the psychophysiological stress recovery theory. In the late 1980s, Rachel and Stephen Kaplan introduced the term *restorative environments* and the Attention Restoration Theory (ART)—that to be restored, we must be away from the stressor and be fascinated by our new environment, and the environment have sufficient scope and compatibility to our needs. More recently, the quality of life and psychosocial benefits of parks and open space have been highlighted. These studies have led to increased restorative environment research. This is an opportune time for public health social workers to help in translating the research to practice via "prescriptions" for clients to experience outdoor and natural settings.

A broad range of environmental justice issues and champions exist within the United States. In the Bronx in New York City, Majora Carter won a 2009 MacArthur "genius grant" fellowship for her work as founder and director of Sustainable South Bronx. The organization worked to keep a solid waste management plant out of the community and has expanded parks, bike paths, and healthy food options throughout the community. In Los Angeles, numerous efforts support low-income minorities, especially those living near the Port of Los Angeles. Residents living near the port are disparately exposed to diesel fumes from ships entering the port and transfer trucks and trains carrying goods from the port. Half a dozen oil refineries also are located there. The ZIP code around the port has a population of over 50,000 residents: 85% are Hispanic; 6% are over the age of 25 who have college degree; and 27% live below the federal poverty line. Organizations like Communities for a Better Environment are working to advance policies such as restricting idling times of transfer trucks, better notification about refinery flare events, and expanding public transportation for area residents.

Globally, electronic waste, or e-waste, has become a significant issue. Developed and developing countries dispose of billions of electronic devices per year. In 2005, the EPA estimated that over 300 million electronic devices were removed from homes in the United States alone, representing approximately 2 million tons of e-waste (U.S. EPA, 2008). Electronic devices, including cell phones, MP3 players, laptops, and televisions, are produced with metals such as lead, silver, zinc, and mercury, all of which can leach into groundwater when disposed of improperly (Lincoln, Ogunseitan, Shapiro, & Saphores, 2007). Because properly disposing of or recycling e-waste is costly, much of it is shipped to developing nations where workers dismantle e-waste in poor working conditions for only a few dollars per day. The workers are directly exposed to the heavy metals within the electronics, and their families and communities are exposed to the waste through local waterways and the burning of remaining equipment (Nnorom & Osibanjo, 2008).

Mental Health Services

The first Surgeon General's Report on Mental Health was issued in 1999 (U.S. DHHS, 1999). This report is important, as is emphasized in Chapter 8 in this volume, because it acknowledges the association between mental and physical health. It describes the toll of mental illness on the population and states that mental health programs in the United States are founded on a public health population-based model. Furthermore, the report highlights the issue of disparities in treatment based on culture, race, gender, and financial access. Finally, the report identifies stigma associated with mental illness as a major obstacle. In suggesting courses of action to the public health and medical communities, the Surgeon General's Report mentions facilitating entry into the mental health system. In recognition of the links between mind and body, the report identifies primary care providers as one route of entry to mental health services.

Clinical social workers deliver more mental health care than do any other professionals. Public health social workers have the potential to develop and contribute to population-level interventions to address the concerns cited in the Surgeon General's Report, such as alleviation of stigma and of barriers to care and disparities in diagnosis and treatment.

Research

Evidence-based interventions and sound public policy result from well-planned and executed research. As more public health social workers become involved in research, such as that described in this chapter, the importance of including social, behavioral, and environmental factors as determinants of health will become more apparent.

Public health social workers are increasingly engaged in community-based participatory research (CBPR). *CBPR* is defined by the Agency for Healthcare Research and Quality (AHRQ) as "a collaborative process involving researchers and community representatives; it engages community members, employs local knowledge in the understanding of health problems and the design of interventions, and invests community members in the processes and products of research" (2010, p. 1). CBPR is especially useful in populations that often are reluctant to engage in conventional research (minority, low income, rural, and central city) because of their use in previous, sometimes unethical, studies (e.g. Tuskegee study.)

Three additional factors support the use of participatory research to improve the health of disadvantaged communities.

> First, local community knowledge increases our understanding of the complex interactions among economic, social, and behavioral factors that contribute to disparities and, therefore, should inform the design of interventions aimed at reducing these disparities. In addition, there is a gap between the knowledge produced in research and practiced in these communities. Finally, members of these communities are increasingly reluctant to participate in research and are organizing to monitor and/or prevent such activities. (AHRQ, 2010, p. 1)

Examples of CBPR include projects aimed at: increasing the availability of high-quality food in inner-city neighborhoods; the environmental factors that contribute to childhood asthma; and the relationships among SES, physical environment, and heart disease (AHRQ, 2010, p. 1).

Another path to ameliorating health disparities is clinical and translational science (CTS). The emergence of CTS has many implications for public health social work research and interventions. The goal of translational science is to translate basic research findings into clinical practice and population-based interventions (Brekke, Ell, & Palinkas, 2007; Ruth & Sisco, 2008). Clinical and translational science is framed in at least four translational phases. *T1* refers to first knowledge developed through laboratory bench research; *T2* refers to taking this bench research to the bedside for clinical trials; *T3* is applying these findings in clinical practice; and *T4* involves applications of knowledge at the community and population level (Kon, 2008; Tufts CTSI, 2010). Social workers are critical to the success of the T3 and T4 phases through their individual clinical practices and by developing and implementing community-level interventions. CTS is transdisciplinary in nature. Professionals in CTS range from bench scientists, to clinical providers, to population-based workers. Social workers work at both the clinical and societal levels (Gehlert et al., 2010).

The direction from T1 to T4 CTS (bottom-up research) assumes that laboratory bench science is the beginning of studying health disparities. Gehlert and colleagues (2008; Gehlert, Mininger, & Cipriano-Steffens, 2011) suggest that rather than bottom-up research, studies of health disparities should examine the impacts of social and environmental factors on behavioral and hereditary components of health outcomes (top down). This approach examines the influence of upstream (T3 and T4) determinants, such as social environment, SES, and discrimination, on individual behavior, health status, and disease. If we know the effects of upstream determinants and how they vary by population, we are better positioned to develop T4 interventions (Gehlert et al., 2008).

Gehlert and colleagues (2008) conducted studies of African American women newly diagnosed with breast cancer using the top-down approach. They examined various upstream determinants, such as neighborhood environments, social isolation, depression, and perceived loneliness. They found significant associations among these factors to demonstrate a pathway from the community effects to inside the nucleus of the cell. Social environments create isolation and depression. These emotional states alter the stress-hormone response. When stress-hormone receptors are activated, farther downstream biochemical pathways known to increase tumor cell survival are activated. This research demonstrates the important contributions that social workers can make to the transdisciplinary team, both in understanding health determinants and in developing appropriate societal interventions to ameliorate downstream effects on the biological level.

Public health social work involvement in clinical and translational research that assesses psychosocial determinants can lead to more comprehensive and culturally competent interventions to address public health problems. Emerging areas for CTS research may include disparities in obesity and tobacco use. For example, the biological effects are well known, but associations with upstream factors warrant further study to establish population-based interventions (Gehlert et al., 2008).

Additional emerging research methods at the nexus of social work and public health include GIS, system dynamics, and social network analysis. GIS was discussed earlier as a practice method, but it is also very much a research method (see Figure 4.4). Social work and public health both use GIS. As outlined by Hillier (2007), GIS strengthens social work by (a) continuing and improving social surveys, (b) providing a geographic framework for the study and understanding of human behavior, (c) spatially locating needs and assets within a community, (d) mapping and improving the delivery of social services, and (e) emphasizing social justice through the empowerment of disenfranchised communities. The benefits of GIS to public health mirror those of social work by (a) strengthening epidemiological methods, (b) providing a geographic framework for the study of human disease and health, (c) spatially locating needs and assets within a community, (d) mapping and improving the delivery of public health interventions and programs, and (e) highlighting disproportionate exposures to environmental agents (environmental justice).

Most of today's public health social work challenges are complex and dynamic in terms of understanding and working toward improvements and eventual prevention. For example, how does posttraumatic stress disorder affect soldiers returning from the Iraq or Afghanistan wars? Potential negative effects are associated with psychological, physical, and social health. Friends and families may provide support or may be a source of additional stress. System dynamics (SD) is a methodological approach that assists in understanding complex systems over time. SD uses a system of internal and external feedback loops, flows, and outputs (see Figure 4.6). SD computer software allows researchers to set and change feedback loops, stocks, and flows and to run models to determine potential reactions and outcomes. Delayed effects and time series can be built in as well. Specific to public health social work, SD allows for the modeling of

individual, community, and organizational assets, needs, vulnerabilities, preventive efforts, responses, complications, and potential outcomes. Most important to SD are the feedback loops within and between these categories. For additional information, see Homer and Hirsch (2006) and Hirsch, Levine, and Miller (2007).

Social network analysis (SNA) uses a series of nodes and ties to build a three-dimensional structure of social networks. Nodes can be individuals, organizations, or policies, and ties are the connections between nodes (see Figure 4.7). SNA allows for the understanding of how and why certain ties are made and how information is or is not shared across ties and between nodes.

Christakis and Fowler (2007), in a prominent SNA article published in the *New England Journal of Medicine*, reviewed over 12,000 individuals who participated in the Framingham Heart Study to determine whether obesity is "contagious." The authors found that an individual's chance of becoming obese increased by 57% if the person had an obese friend, and 40% if the person had an obese sibling. Spousal

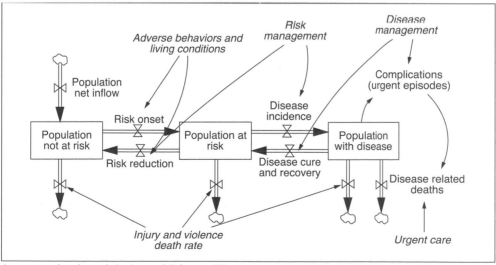

As an example, adverse behaviors and living conditions can result in individuals within the population not at risk to become at risk while improvements in behaviors and living conditions can have the effect of moving individuals from at risk to not at risk.

Figure 4.6 System Dynamics Example Showing the Population as Not at Risk, at Risk, or With Disease

Source: Homer, Hirsch, and Milstein, 2007.

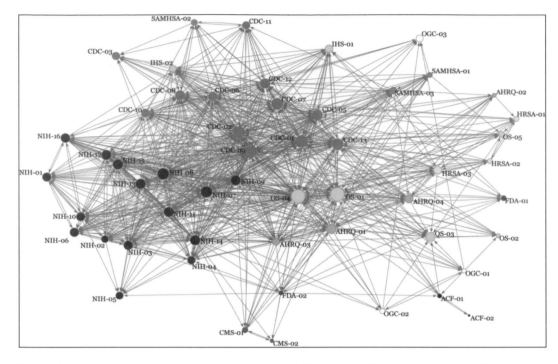

Figure 4.7 Network of Relationships Among Individuals Working on Tobacco Control at the Department of Health and Human Services

Source: Adapted from Leischow et al., 2010.

influence was slightly less strong, although still significant, at 37%. Lakon and colleagues (2010) used SNA to show that both individual and neighborhood ties (multilevel modeling) affected the smoking behaviors of teenagers. Luke and colleagues (Leischow et al., 2010; Luke & Harris, 2007) describe network-and organization-level SNA. Tobacco control and efforts to reduce the numbers of cigarette smokers require a coordinated effort. Luke and Harris use SNA to show the coordination and lack thereof between agencies under the guidance of DHHS. Repeat surveys and gaps in services across government agencies can greatly reduce efficiency in preventive efforts.

IMPACT OF PUBLIC HEALTH SOCIAL WORK

This chapter addressed only a sample of the issues, practice settings, and interventions encountered by public health social workers. Other issues that public health social workers address include: services for immigrants and refugees; health care for men and women not related to reproduction; and inner-city and rural concerns, such as safety, crowding, and social and physical isolation, all of which impact the ability of these populations to achieve the maximum potential health status.

Although medical social workers work with patients and their families to adapt to sudden and severe illness or trauma, public health social workers operate at the population level promoting primary prevention interventions to address the causes of these health problems. Public health social workers contribute their expertise grounded in the person-in-environment orientation (Kondrat, 2008) to incorporate responses to behavioral, social, and physical environmental determinants of health in public health interventions.

The problems will change over time, but well-prepared public health social workers will be ready to take on new challenges. The new generation of public health social workers will carry on the traditions of the founders of social work who created settlement houses and worked to improve environmental conditions, develop economic reforms, and protect children, all of which contributed to the improvement of the public's health. Their work laid the foundation of federal programs for children and families and gave direction for the future of our profession.

SUGGESTED LEARNING EXERCISES

Learning Exercise 4.1

The purpose of this exercise is to apply your understanding of the determinants of health to a public health problem and discuss the role of public health social work in addressing the problem.

Your class will be divided into small groups and each assigned one of 38 focus areas from Healthy People 2020 (found on the Healthy People Web site) at one class session. Between classes, your homework assignment is to gather data about the area and prepare a fact sheet for your classmates. In the next class session, each group will meet to identify determinants of the health problem in the various domains identified in Figure 4.1 and how they interact.

After identifying the determinants, your group will explore the roles of public health social workers in promoting health and preventing the public health problem and then present your understanding to the class. The presentation must identify issues of diversity and disparities in the distribution, treatment, and prognosis of the illness at the core of the problem. In addition, you should be prepared to present on issues of social and economic justice associated with the health concern.

Learning Exercise 4.2

Review the cases in Box 4.5. Discuss whether you would classify these cases as human trafficking. Discuss ways in which a transdisciplinary team can address the issues identified in these cases. What would be the public health social worker in each c___.

Learning Exercise 4.3

The purpose of this exercise is to explore primary, secondary, and tertiary levels of prevention that can be applied to an intervention for a public health problem.

In this activity, you will be assigned to play a role on a committee that has gathered to address a public health problem in your community. The professionals on the committee, in addition to a public health social worker, may include a physician; an epidemiologist; a public health nurse; and/or a public official, such as a prosecuting attorney, a city council member, or a law enforcement officer. The committee will meet and use data that were provided to you by your instructor to collaborate in the design of interventions at the three levels of prevention and then to decide which intervention will best serve the community.

Possible topics:

- Perinatal substance abuse
- Teen pregnancy
- Sudden increase in the number of syphilis cases
- Motor vehicle accidents involving adolescents and alcohol
- Rise in suicide rate
- Rise in childhood obesity
- Asthma in a minority population
- Domestic violence
- Human trafficking
- Dental caries

Learning Exercise 4.4

In this chapter, we discussed three emerging methods at the nexus of social work and public health: geographic information systems, system dynamics, and social network analysis. These methods rely on mapping, feedback loops, and social ties, respectively. We also outlined community-based participatory research (CBPR), in which researchers and community partners work in collaboration to overcome public health social work challenges. For this exercise, think of a way that CBPR can be utilized to map, develop system feedback loops, and determine social ties. What practice and research questions would you answer using this mixed methodology?

APPENDIX 4.1: GLOSSARY

Assessment   Collection, analysis, and sharing of data about health conditions, risks, and resources in a community.

Assurance   Monitoring the availability of health services in a community.

Epidemiology   Study of distribution and determinants of disease in populations.

Evidence-based practice   Interventions that are based on theory that is supported by empirical research.

Fetal and Infant Mortality Review (FIMR)   Review conducted to gather medical and social information after a fetal or infant death.

Healthy People 2020   Public health goals and objectives for the United States as set by the U.S. Department of Health and Human Services.

Infant mortality (IM)   Death prior to an infant's first birthday; one of the leading indicators used worldwide to measure a country's health.

Low birth weight (LBW)   Weight of less than 2,500 grams, or about 5.5 pounds, at birth; a cause of infant mortality and, thus, one of the leading indicators used worldwide to measure a country's health.

Policy development   Use of assessment data to develop local and state health and social welfare policies and to direct resources toward those policies.

Population-based intervention   Intervention focused on health promotion/disease prevention in populations rather than on the treatment of individuals.

Prevention, primary   Promotion of health and prevention of disease or trauma before it occurs.

Prevention, secondary   Early diagnosis and treatment of disease.

Prevention, tertiary   Action taken to minimize the effects of a disease and prevent further disability.

Social epidemiology   Study of the impact of social factors on the distribution of health and illness in a population.

Title V of the Social Security Act of 1935   Provides for maternal and child health programs that are delivered by states through a block grant mechanism; Title V programs are administered by the Maternal and Child Health Bureau of the Health Services and Resources Administration (HRSA) of the U.S. Department of Health and Human Services.

APPENDIX 4.2: PUBLIC HEALTH SOCIAL WORK STANDARDS AND COMPETENCIES

Public health social workers address health from a broad perspective that includes physical, social, emotional, and spiritual well-being throughout the continuum of the life cycle. They address health issues by identifying and implementing strategies and interventions that address pivotal times of transition from one phase of individual development to another. Public health social work ensures the competency of its practice to address the issues of public health effectively through a core body of knowledge, philosophy, code of ethics, and standards.

Public health social work employs a range of strategies to implement essential public health functions in a measurable fashion as specified in the Public Health Social Work Standards and Competencies (2005). These are available online at http://oce.sph.unc.edu/cetac/phswcompetencies_may05.pdf/.

REFERENCES

Agency for Healthcare Research and Quality. (2010). *Community-based participatory research*. Retrieved from www.ahrq.gov/about/cpcr/cbpr/cbpr1.htm

Berkman, L. F., & Kawachi, I. (Eds.). (2000). *Social epidemiology*. New York, NY: Oxford University Press.

Berry, H., Bowen, K., & Kjellstrom, T. (2010). Climate change and mental health: A causal pathways framework. *International Journal of Public Health, 55*(2), 123–132.

Bishop, K. K., & Arango, P. (1997). Creating the context: Family-centered, community-based, culturally-sensitive partnerships. In K. K. Bishop, M. S. Taylor, & P. Arango (Eds.), *Partnerships at work: Lessons learned from programs and practices of families, professionals and communities* (pp. 11–15). Burlington: University of Vermont, Department of Social Work.

Brekke, J. S., Ell, K., & Palinkas, L. A. (2007). Translational science at the National Institute of Mental Health: Can social work take its rightful place? *Research on Social Work Practice, 17*, 123–133.

Bronfenbrenner, U. (1979). *The Ecology of Human Development: Experiments by Nature and Design*. Cambridge, MA: Harvard University Press.

Bullard, R. D. 1990. *Dumping in Dixie: Race, class, and environmental quality*. Boulder, CO: Westview.

Cecil-Karb, R., & Grogan-Kaylor, A. (2009). Childhood body mass index in community context: Neighborhood safety, television viewing, and growth trajectories of BMI. *Health & Social Work, 34*, 169–177.

Centers for Disease Control and Prevention. (2010). Obesity trends among U.S. adults. Retrieved from www.cdc.gov/obesity/data/trends.html

Centers for Medicare and Medicaid Services. (2010). Low cost health insurance for families & children. Overview. Retrieved from www.cms.gov/LowCostHealthInsFamChild

Chin, M. H., Walters, A. E., Cook, S. C., & Huang, E. S. (2007). Interventions to reduce racial and ethnic disparities in health care. *Medical Care Research Review, 64*(5; Suppl.), 7S–28S.

Christakis, N. A., & Fowler, J. H. (2007). The spread of obesity in a large social network over 32 years. *New England Journal of Medicine, 357*(4), 370–379.

Clegg, L. X., Reichman, M. E., Miller, B. A., Hankey, B. F., Singh, G. K., Lin, Y. D.,…Edwards, B. K. (2009). Impact of socioeconomic status on cancer incidence and stage at diagnosis: Selected findings from the surveillance, epidemiology, and end results: National Longitudinal Mortality Study. *Cancer Causes Control, 20*(4), 417–435.

Commission on Social Determinants of Health. (2008). *Closing the gap in a generation: Final Report of the Commission on Social Determinants of Health. Geneva, World Health Organization*.

Retrieved from http://whqlibdoc.who.int/publications/2008/9789241563703_eng.pdf

Cooper, H., Moore, L., Gruskin, S., & Krieger, N. (2004). Characterizing perceived police violence: Implications for public health. *American Journal of Public Health, 94*, 1109–1118.

Curry, S. J., Emery, S., Sporer, A. K., Mermelstein, R., Flay, B. R., Berbaum, M.,…Wells, H. (2007). A national survey of tobacco cessation programs for youths. *American Journal of Public Health, 97*, 171–177.

Dai, D. (2010). Black residential segregation, disparities in spatial access to health care facilities, and late-stage breast cancer diagnosis in metropolitan Detroit. *Health & Place, 16*(5), 1038–1052.

Dunn, J. R. (2010). Health behavior vs. the stress of low socioeconomic status and health outcomes. *JAMA, 303*, 1199–1200.

Eliadis, E. E. (2006). The role of social work in the childhood obesity epidemic. *Social Work, 51*, 86–88.

Family Violence Prevention Fund. (2007). *Collaborating to help trafficking survivors: Emerging issues and practice pointers*. San Francisco, CA: Author.

Fiscella, K., Franks, P., Doescher, M. P., & Saver, B. G. (2002). Disparities in health care by race, ethnicity, and language among the insured: Findings from a national sample. In T. A. LaVeist (Ed.), *Race, ethnicity, and health: A public health reader* (pp. 198–209). San Francisco, CA: Jossey-Bass.

Flores, G., Olson, L., & Tomany-Korman, S. C. (2005). Racial and ethnic disparities in early childhood health and health care. *Pediatrics, 115e*, 183–193.

Floyd, M. F., Taylor, W. C., & Whitt-Glover, M. (2009). Measurement of park and recreation environments that support physical activity in low-income communities of color: Highlights of challenges and recommendations. *American Journal of Preventive Medicine, 36*(4), S156–S160.

Frank, L., Engelke, P., & Schmid, T. (2003). *Health and community design: The impact of the built environment on physical activity*. Washington, DC: Island Press.

Freedman, V. A., Grafova, I. B., & Rogowski, J. (2011). Neighborhoods and chronic disease onset in later life. *American Journal of Public Health. 101*(1), 79–86.

Gee, G. C. (2008). A multilevel analysis of the relationship between institutional and individual racial discrimination and health status. *American Journal of Public Health, 98*(Suppl. 1), S48–S56.

Gehlert, S., Mininger, C., & Cipriano-Steffens, T. M. (2011). Placing biology in breast cancer research. In D. Takeuchi (Ed.), *Expanding the boundaries of place*. New York, NY: Springer.

Gehlert, S., Mininger, C., Sohmer, D., & Berg, K. (2008). (Not so) gently down the stream: Choosing targets to ameliorate health disparities. *Health & Social Work, 33*, 163–167.

Gehlert, S., Murray, A., Sohmer, D., McClintock, M., Conzen, S., & Olopade, O. (2010). The importance of transdisciplinary collaborations for understanding and resolving health disparities. *Social Work in Public Health, 25,* 408–422.

Gehlert, S., Sohmer, D., Sacks, T., Mininger, C., McClintock, M., & Olopade, O. (2008). Targeting health disparities: A model linking upstream determinants to downstream interventions. *Health Affairs, 27,* 339–349.

Germain, C. B. (1984). *Social work practice in health care: An ecological perspective.* New York, NY: Free Press.

Germain, C., & Gitterman, A. (1980). *The life model of social work practice.* New York, NY: Columbia University Press.

Gordon, L. (1994). *Pitied but not entitled: Single mothers and the history of welfare.* New York, NY: Free Press.

Green, L. W., & Glasgow, R. E. (2006). Evaluating the relevance, generalization, and applicability of research. Issues in external validation and translation methodology. *Evaluation and the Health Professions, 29,* 126–153.

Hartig, T. (2008). Green space, psychological restoration, and health inequality. *Lancet, 372,* 1614–1615.

Haviland, L., & Sember, R. (2004). [Cover description]. *American Journal of Public Health, 94,* 163.

Healthy People 2020. (n.d. a). *Phase I report. Recommendations for the framework and format of Healthy People 2020.* Retrieved from www.healthypeople.gov/HP2020/advisory/PhaseI/PhaseI.pdf

Healthy People 2020. (n.d. b). Home page. Retrieved from www.healthypeople.gov/Default.htm

Hillier, A. E. (2007). Why social work needs mapping. *Journal of Social Work Education, 43*(2), 205–221.

Hirsch, G. B., Levine, R., & Miller, R. (2007). Using system dynamics modeling to understand the impact of social change initiatives. *American Journal of Community Psychology, 39*(3), 239–253.

Hokenstad, M. S. (2010). *Human trafficking brief.* 2010 Joint World Conference on Social Work and Social Development. International Council on Social Welfare. Retrieved from www.icsw.org/doc/2010 _JointWorldConf_Agenda_ICSW_HumanTrafficking .pdf

Homer, J. B., & Hirsch, G. B. (2006). Systems dynamics modeling for public health: Background and opportunities. *American Journal of Public Health, 96*(3), 452–458.

Homer, J., Hirsch, G., & Milstein. B. (2007). Chronic illness in a complex health economy: The perils and promises of downstream and upstream reforms. *System Dynamics Review, 23*(2/3), 313–343.

Hutchins, E., Grason, H., & Handler, A. (2004). FIMR and other mortality reviews public health tools for strengthening maternal and child health systems in communities: Where do we need to go next? *Maternal and Child Health Journal, 8,* 259–268.

Icard, L. D., Bourjolly, J. N., & Siddiqui, N. (2003). Designing social marketing strategies to increase African Americans' access to health promotion programs. *Health & Social Work, 28,* 214–223.

Institute of Medicine Committee for the Study of the Future of Public Health. (1988). *The future of public health.* Washington, DC: National Academy Press.

Kaiser Family Foundation. (2010). *Summary of the new health reform law. Focus on Health Reform.* Retrieved from www.kff. org/healthreform/upload/8061.pdf

Keefe, R. H. (2010). Health disparities: A primer for public health social workers. *Social Work in Public Health, 25,* 237–257.

Kimerling, R., Street, A. E., Pavao, J., Smith, M. W., Cronkite, R. C., Holmes, T. H., & Frayne, S. M. (2010). Military-related sexual trauma among Veterans Health Administration patients returning from Afghanistan and Iraq. *American Journal of Public Health, 100,* 1409–1412.

Klesges, L. M., Dzewaltowski, D. A., & Glasgow, R. E. (2008). Review of external validity reporting in childhood obesity prevention research. *American Journal of Preventive Medicine, 38,* 216–223.

Koontz, A. M., Buckley, K. A., & Ruderman, M. (2004). The evolution of fetal and infant mortality review as a public health strategy. *Maternal and Child Health Journal, 8,* 195–203.

Kon, A. A. (2008). The Clinical and Translational Science Award (CTSA) Consortium and the translational research model. *American Journal of Bioethics, 8,* 1–3.

Kondrat, M. E. (2008). Person-in-environment. In T. Mizrahi & L. E. Davis (Eds.), *Encyclopedia of Social Work* (20th ed., vol. 3, pp. 348–354). New York, NY: Oxford University Press.

Krieger, N. (2003). Does racism harm health? Did child abuse exist before 1962? On explicit questions, critical science, and current controversies: An ecosocial perspective. *American Journal of Public Health, 93,* 194–199.

Krieger, N. (2005). Race, genetics, and health disparities. Stormy weather: Race, gene expression, and the science of health disparities. *American Journal of Public Health, 95,* 2155–2160.

Krieger, N., Chen, J. T., Waterman, P. D., Rehkopf, D. H., & Subramanian, S. V. (2003). Race/ethnicity, gender, and monitoring socioeconomic gradients in health: A comparison of area-based socioeconomic measures—The Public Health Disparities Geocoding Project. *American Journal of Public Health, 93,* 1655–1671.

Lakon, C. M., Hipp, J. R., & Timberlake, D. S. (2010). The social context of adolescent smoking: A systems perspective. *American Journal of Public Health, 100*(7), 1218–1228.

Landesman, L. Y. (2005). *Public health management of disasters: The practice guide* (2nd ed.). Washington, DC: American Public Health Association.

Lawrence, S., Hazlett, R., & Hightower, P. (2010). Understanding and acting on the growing childhood and adolescent weight crisis: A role for social work. *Health & Social Work, 35* 147–153.

Leischow S., Luke D. A., Mueller N. B., Harris J. K., Ponder P., Marcus S., & Clark P. (2010). Mapping U.S. government tobacco control leadership: Networked for success? *Nicotine & Tobacco Research, 12*(9), 888–894.

Leung, G. M., Chan, S. S. C., Johnston, J. M., Chan, S. K. K., Woo, P. P. S., Chi, I., & Lam, T-H. (2007). Effectiveness of an elderly smoking cessation counseling training program for social workers. *CHEST, 131,* 1157–1165.

Lincoln, J. D., Ogunseitan, O. A., Shapiro, A. A., & Saphores, J.-D. M. (2007). Leaching assessments of hazardous materials in cellular telephones. *Environmental Science & Technology, 41*(7), 2572–2578.

Luke, D. A., & Harris, J. K. (2007). Network analysis in public health: History, methods, and applications. *Annual Review of Public Health, 28*(1), 69–93.

Lynch, J., & Kaplan, G. (2000). Socioeconomic position. In L. F. Berkman & I. Kawachi (Eds.), *Social epidemiology* (pp. 13–35). New York, NY: Oxford University Press.

Margolis, L. H., Cole, G. P., & Kotch, J. B. (2005). Historical foundations of maternal and child health. In J. B. Kotch (Ed.), *Maternal and child health: Programs, problems and policy in public health* (2nd ed., pp. 23–55). Gaithersburg, MD: Aspen.

Martin, J. A., Hamilton, B. E., Sutton, P. D., Ventura, S. J., Menacker, F., Kirmeyer, S.,…Mathews, T. J. (2009). Births: Final data for 2006. *National Vital Statistics Reports, 57*(7). Retrieved from www.cdc.gov/nchs/data/nvsr57/nvsr57_07.pdf

Mathews, T. J., & MacDorman, M. F. (2010). Infant mortality statistics from the 2006 period linked birth/infant death data set. *National Vital Statistics Reports, 58*(17), 1–32.

McGinnis, J. M., Williams-Russo, P., & Knickman, J. R. (2002). The case for more active policy attention to health promotion. *Health Affairs, 21,* 78–93.

Mitchell, R., & Popham, F. (2008). Effect of exposure to natural environment on health inequalities: an observational population study. *Lancet, 372,* 1655–1660.

Mussolino, M. E. (2005). Depression and hip fracture risk: The NHANES I epidemiologic follow-up study. *Public Health Reports, 120*(1), 71–75.

Mustillo, S., Krieger, N., Gunderson, E. P., Sidney, S., McCreath, H., & Kiefe, C. I. (2004). Self-reported experiences of racial discrimination and Black-White differences in preterm and low-birthweight deliveries: The CARDIA Study. *American Journal of Public Health, 94,* 2125–2131.

National Association of Social Workers. (2009). *Social work speaks* (10th ed.). Washington, DC: Author.

National Cancer Institute. (2010). *A snapshot of lung cancer.* Retrieved from www.cancer.gov/aboutnci/servingpeople/snapshots/lung.pdf

National Cancer Institute. (n.d.). *SEER Cancer Statistics Review, 1995–2007.* Retrieved from http://seer.cancer.gov/csr/1975_2007/results_merged/topic_mor_trends.pdf

Nazmi, A., Diez Roux, A., Ranjit, N., Seeman, T. E., & Jenny, N. S. (2010). Cross-sectional and longitudinal associations of neighborhood characteristics with inflammatory markers: Findings from the Multi-Ethnic Study of Atherosclerosis. *Health & Place, 16*(6), 1104–1112.

Nnorom, I. C., & Osibanjo, O. (2008). Overview of electronic waste (e-waste) management practices and legislations, and their poor applications in the developing countries. *Resources, Conservation and Recycling, 52*(6), 843–858.

Oakes, J. M., & Kaufman, J. S. (2006). Introduction: Advancing methods in social epidemiology. In J. M. Oakes & J. S. Kaufman (Eds.), *Methods in social epidemiology* (pp. 3–20). San Francisco, CA: Jossey-Bass.

Ogden, C. L., & Carroll, M. (June 2010a). *Prevalence of obesity in children and adolescents: United States, trends 1963–1965 through 2007–2008.* National Center for Health Statistics. Retrieved from www.cdc.gov/nchs/data/hestat/obesity_child_07_08/obesity_child_07_08.pdf

Ogden, C. L., & Carroll, M. (June 2010b). *Prevalence of overweight, obesity and extreme obesity among adults: United States, trends 1976–1980 through 2007–2008.* National Center for Health Statistics. Retrieved from www.cdc.gov/NCHS/data/hestat/obesity_adult_07_08/obesity_adult_07_08.pdf

Phelan, K. J., Khoury, J., Kalkwarf, H., & Lanphear, B. (2005). Residential injuries in United States children and adolescents. *Public Health Reports, 120*(1), 63–70.

Pickett, K. E., Collins, J. W., Masi, C. M., & Wilkinson, R. G. (2005). The effects of racial density and income incongruity on pregnancy outcomes. *Social Science & Medicine, 60,* 2229–2238.

President's emergency plan for AIDS relief. (n.d.). Retrieved from http://southafrica.usembassy.gov/wwwhaids.html

Public Health Social Work Standards and Competencies. (2005). Retrieved from http://oce.sph.unc.edu/cetac/phswcompetencies_may05.pdf

Rounds, K., Caye, J., Ross-Sheriff, T., Bailey, D., & Anderson, J. (2005). *Disaster preparedness planning for public health social workers. Part I: Natural Disasters.* Produced by the MCH Public Health Social Work Leadership Training Program & The Behavioral Healthcare Resource Program, Jordan Institute for Families, School of Social Work, University of North Carolina at Chapel Hill. Retrieved from http://behavioralhealthcareinstitute.org/kathleen2/index.htm

Rounds, K., Caye, J., Walsh, T., Vaughn, J., & Anderson, J. (2008). *Disaster preparedness planning for public health social workers. Part II: Bioterrorism.* Produced by the MCH Public Health Social Work Leadership Training Program & The Behavioral Healthcare Resource Program, Jordan Institute for Families, School of Social Work, and the NC Center for Disaster Preparedness, Institute of Public Health, University of North Carolina at Chapel Hill. Retrieved from http://behavioralhealthcareinstitute.org/kathleenB/index.htm

Ruth, B. J., & Sisco, S. (2008). Public health. In T. Mizrahi & L. E. Davis (Eds.), *Encyclopedia of social work* (20th ed., vol. 3, pp. 476–483). New York, NY: Oxford University Press.

Saftlas, A. F., Wallis, A. B., Shochet, T., Harland, K. K., Dickey, P., & Peek-Asa, C. (2010). Prevalence of intimate partner violence among an abortion population. *American Journal of Public Health, 100,* 1412–1415.

Salett, E. (2006). *Human trafficking and modern day slavery.* National Association of Social Workers Practice Update. Washington, DC: NASW Office of Human Rights and International Affairs.

Schneider, M.-J. (2000). *Introduction to public health.* Gaithersburg, MD: Aspen.

Schooler, C., Feighery, E., & Flora, J. A. (1996). Seventh graders' self-reported exposure to cigarette marketing and its relationship to their smoking behavior. *American Journal of Public Health, 86,* 1216–1221.

Schootman, M., Andresen, E., Wolinsky, F., Miller, J. P., Yan, Y., & Miller, D. (2010). Neighborhood conditions, diabetes, and risk of lower-body functional limitations among middle-aged African Americans: A cohort study. *BMC Public Health, 10*(1), 283.

Silverman, J. G., Decker, M. R., McCauley, H. L., Gupta, J., Miller, E., Raj, A., & Goldberg, A. B. (2010). Male perpetration of intimate partner violence and involvement in abortions and abortion-related conflict. *American Journal of Public Health, 100,* 1415–1417.

Sinclair, S. J., & LoCicero, A. (2010). Assessing the ongoing psychological impact of terrorism. In L. Baer & M. A. Blais (Eds.), *Handbook of clinical rating scales and assessment in psychiatry and mental health* (pp. 271–285). New York, NY: Humana Press.

Slater, T. (2006). The eviction of critical perspectives from gentrification research. *International Journal of Urban and Regional Research, 30*(4), 737–757.

Smedley, B. D., Stith, A. Y., & Nelson, A. R. (Eds.). (2003). *Unequal treatment: Confronting racial and ethnic disparities in health care.* Washington, DC: Institute of Medicine, Committee on Understanding and Eliminating Racial and Ethnic Disparities in Health Care.

Stokols, D., Runnerstrum, M. G., Misra, S., & Hipp, J. A. (2009). Psychology in an age of ecological crisis: From personal angst to collective action. *American Psychologist, 64*(3), 181–193.

Stringhini, S., Sabia, S., Shipley, M., Brunner, E., Nabi, H., Kivimaki, M., & Singh-Manoux, A. (2010). Association of socioeconomic position with health behaviors and mortality. *JAMA, 303,* 1159–1166.

Taylor, L., & Quigley, R. (2002). *Health Impact Assessment: A review of reviews.* London, UK: Health Development Agency.

Thomas, L. A., Supiano, K. P., Chasco, E. E., McGowan, J., & Beer, M. C. (2009). Smoking cessation for seniors: A program that works. *Clinical Gerontologist, 21,* 118–125.

Tufts CTSI. (2010). What is translational science? Retrieved from www.tuftsctsi. org/About-Us/What-is-Translational-Science.aspx?c=129239448128972191

United Nations Department of Economic and Social Affairs, Population Division (2007). World population prospects: The 2006 revision, highlights, Working Paper No. ESA/P/WP. 202. Retrieved from www.un .org/esa/population/publications/wpp2006/WPP2006 _Highlights_rev.pdf

United Nations Office on Drugs and Crime (2006). Trafficking in persons: Global patterns. Vienna, Austria: Author. Retrieved from www.unodc.org/documents/ human-trafficking/HT-globalpatterns-en.pdf

U.S. Department of Health and Human Services. (1999). *Mental health: A report of the surgeon general— Executive summary.* Rockville, MD: Author.

U.S. Department of Health and Human Services. (2008a). *Identifying and interacting with victims of human trafficking. DHHS: Administration for Children & Families, Campaign to Rescue and Restore Victims of Human Trafficking.* Retrieved from www.acf.hhs .gov/trafficking/campaign_kits/tool_kit_health/identify _victims.html

U.S. Department of Health and Human Services. (2008b). *Look beneath the surface: Role of law enforcement officers in identifying and helping victims of human trafficking* (PowerPoint presentation). Washington, DC: DHHS Administration for Children & Families, Campaign to Rescue and Restore Victims of Human Trafficking. Retrieved from www.acf.hhs.gov/ trafficking/campaign_kits/index.html

U.S. Environmental Protection Agency. (2008). *Fact sheet: Management of electronic waste in the United States.* Washington, DC: Author.

U.S. Environmental Protection Agency. (2010). Environmental justice. Retrieved from www.epa.gov/ environmentaljustice/

United States President's Emergency Plan for AIDS Relief. (n.d.) About PEPFAR. Retrieved from www .pepfar.gov/about/index.htm

Walker, R. E., Keane, C. R., & Burke, J. G. (2010). Disparities and access to healthy food in the United States: A review of food desserts literature. *Health & Place, 16*(5), 876–884. doi: 10.1016/j .healthplace.2010.04

Watkins, E. L. (1985, June). The conceptual base for public health social work. In A. Gitterman, R. B. Black, & F. Stein (Eds.), *Public health social work in maternal and child health: A forward plan* (pp. 17–33). Proceedings of the Working Conference of the Public Health Social Work Advisory Committee for the Bureau of

Health Care Delivery and Assistance, Rockville, MD: Division of Maternal and Child Health.

Weech-Maldonado, R., Morales, L. S., Elliott, M., Spritzer, K., Marshall, G., & Hays, R. D. (2003). Race/ethnicity, language, and patients' assessments of care in Medicaid managed care. *Health Services Research 38*, 789–808.

Wilkinson, D. S., Rounds, K. A., & Copeland, V. C. (2002). Infusing public health content into foundation and advanced social work courses. *Journal of Teaching in Social Work, 22*(3/4), 139–154.

World Health Organization. (1998). *Smallpox eradication: A global first.* Retrieved from www.who.int/archives/who50/en/smallpox.htm.

Xu, J. Q., Kochanek, K. D., Murphy, S. L., Tejada-Vera, B. (2010). Deaths: Final data for 2007. *National Vital Statistics Reports Web Release, 58*(19). Hyattsville, MD: National Center for Health Statistics. Retrieved from www.cdc.gov/NCHS/data/nvsr/nvsr58/nvsr58_19.pdf

5

Health Policy and Social Work

JULIE S. DARNELL AND EDWARD F. LAWLOR

Health policy refers to actions taken by government or the private sector to achieve a specific health-care goal. One such action is the Patient Protection and Affordable Care Act (PPACA), enacted in March 2010, which changed the landscape for health and social work practice for the foreseeable future. As it is implemented over the next 10 years, the legislation will significantly increase health insurance coverage and reset the philosophy, organization, and financing of care. The challenge for social workers in this environment is to know both the fundamentals of the current health-care systems and the changes resulting from the new law and their trajectory.

As practitioners in various settings, social workers assist clients in obtaining and navigating federal and state health programs with complex eligibility rules and application procedures, directly provide publicly supported health services, and disseminate information to individuals and groups about numerous aspects of health care. As advocates for poor, disadvantaged, and disenfranchised individuals and families, social workers act to influence health policies and legislation that enhance the welfare of at-risk and vulnerable populations and improve existing health-care delivery systems. As policy makers working in local, state, or federal agencies, social workers formulate health policies and administer health programs. These roles—far from being made obsolete by health reform—take on heightened importance in the reformed environment. The success of health reform will depend on its provisions remaining intact, the newly insured gaining access to insurance coverage, and people's ability to obtain needed

health-care services, regardless of their insurance status. For social workers to be effective in the new post–health-care-reform era, they must possess a thorough understanding of the law, which first requires a strong command of the broader health-care policy environment that the law amends.

This chapter provides an overall framework for understanding health policy that is essential to successful direct practice, advocacy, and policy making. The framework includes exposure to the key overall concerns of health policy—access, costs, quality, and accountability—as well as an introduction in the key organizational, finance, and payment structures in health care. We then provide an introduction to the structure and key issues in Medicare, Medicaid, and the State Children's Health Insurance Program (SCHIP), the three main public insurance programs. We highlight the implications of health reform for future policy and practice. Due to space considerations, we focus on federal health policy actions. For readers who are interested in state health policy issues, some additional resources are listed at the end of this chapter. With this background, we review the history of comprehensive health reform and its ultimate passage in 2010. Finally, the chapter raises a set of policy issues and provides a number of key resources for ongoing involvement for social workers interested in understanding and influencing health policy.

Chapter Objectives
- Provide a framework—access, cost, quality, accountability—for assessing all health policy initiatives.

- Describe the basic organization, financing, and payment structures of health care.
- Describe the key components of Medicare, Medicaid, and SCHIP.
- Briefly describe the history and content of health-care reform.
- Identify key long-term health policy issues and professional roles for social workers.

FRAMEWORK FOR UNDERSTANDING HEALTH POLICY

Anyone wishing to understand the U.S. health system is immediately confronted by a dichotomy: Massive amounts of spending occur against a backdrop of resource scarcity. Although the U.S. health-care system represents one of the largest economies in the world in its own right, health policy exists in a context of relative scarcity of resources. This is evident in much of the public debate: Although the country spends over $2.5 trillion on health services, it is a truism in public discourse that we are not "spending enough" on mental health, research, Medicaid nursing home reimbursement, and other worthy causes. Because medical knowledge and technology are constantly producing fantastic new possibilities for intervention and treatment, the overarching challenge of health policy is to allocate resources toward care that is effective and cost worthy.

In this environment of tremendous spending and resource scarcity, clinicians, managers, and policy makers face four general problems of health policy: access, costs, quality, and accountability.

Access refers to the "actual use of personal health services and everything that facilitates or impedes their use" (Andersen & Davidson, 2001, p. 3). Measures of access provide signals of the fairness or social justice of health systems, indicators of its efficiency or effectiveness, and important signposts for policy attention. Access is not just health insurance coverage but includes all of the practical and even cultural determinants—such as transportation and cultural competence of providers—

that influence whether individuals are able to obtain needed services in a timely fashion.

Costs of health care represent the opportunities forgone in the national economy as a result of devoting resources to health care. Resources allocated to health services mean that they are not available for their best alternative use, whether that consists of wages and salary, investments in things such as education or plant and equipment, or for other forms of consumption. In the United States, we are concerned not only about the level of health-care costs—such as per-capita spending, or the share of gross domestic product—but also the rate of growth of health-care expenditures. The problem of cost containment is endemic in health care and the preoccupation of employers who share in the costs of insurance, governments who finance public programs, and individuals who bear significant out-of-pocket costs for medical expenses such as prescription drug coverage.

Quality of health care can refer to structural, process, or outcome dimensions of health-care delivery. Structural dimensions of health-care quality include the facilities, technology, workforce, and other observable "inputs" into care. In the early history of accreditation of health-care organizations, for example, surveyors focused on life safety and hygienic aspects of providers as the most salient measures of quality. As health-care organizations became more sophisticated and standardized, quality improvement focuses on processes of care and, more recently, on outcomes (Lawlor & Raube, 1995).

Accountability of health care refers to the assurance that health care is clinically effective, prudently delivered, and serving the best interests of patients and payers. Examples of accountability measures in health policy include recent efforts to provide a patients' bill of rights, the administrative efforts to reduce fraud and abuse, legal efforts to reform medical malpractice litigation, and quality measures to promote better outcomes and process in hospitals (Chassin et al., 2010).

Virtually all health policy endeavors can be understood as responding to access, cost, quality, or accountability concerns in health care. Efforts to change insurance coverage are motivated largely by access concerns; efforts to increase the cost sharing (such as copayments and deductibles) are driven by cost containment concerns; efforts to reduce medical errors in hospitals are a form of quality initiative; and legislation to reform medical malpractice is a form of accountability change in the health system.

HEALTH SERVICES ORGANIZATION

The American approach to health-care delivery is an especially complicated mixture of public, nonprofit, and for-profit entities. To conceptualize all of the moving parts, it is helpful to separate out the organizations, finance and payment, and regulatory components of the system. In its organization, the health-care system is a complicated web of government, nonprofit, and for-profit organizations that interact in a mix of public and private relationships.

Government is responsible for a significant portion of health-care finance (appropriating and distributing money, primarily through taxes, that goes into the system); regulating access, cost, and quality; and actually producing health services in hospitals, clinics, prisons, and other settings.

The nonprofit sector in health care is extremely varied and includes: organizations such as BlueCross BlueShield; academic centers that carry out research and train physicians, nurses, social workers, and other personnel; foundations that fund research and health services; and nonprofit hospitals and clinics that provide health-care services directly.

The for-profit (otherwise known as the proprietary or investor-owned) sector has varying emphasis in the system, depending on the industry or sector. The pharmaceutical industry is almost entirely for-profit, the nursing home industry is roughly 66% for-profit, and the hospital industry is only 14% for-profit.

To understand health-care politics and policy, it is important to recognize that, taken together, these sectors add up to a large industry: from pharmaceutical manufacturers, to suppliers of medical devices and durable goods, to architects, to ambulances, to consultants, to social workers. All of these actors are both politically and economically invested in health policy. Social workers need to appreciate that in addition to access and quality of clinical care—the usual priority of professionals working in the system—health care is a political economy in its own right. Its power and vested interests add up to a $2.5 trillion industry. This power was most visibly on display when health reform legislation was being debated and when interests such as the pharmaceutical industry, the insurance industry, or hospitals see their control and markets being threatened. However, this political economy is an ongoing force in health care, affecting the politics and decisions at every level of policy making, from local planning, to federal payment policy for hospitals and physicians.

Finance and Payment

Social workers, whether in clinical, policy, management, or advocacy roles, need to understand the relationship of finance, payment systems, providers, and actual provision of health services. Table 5.1 illustrates the basic elements of this framework for understanding the flow of dollars through the health system. Financing arrangements gather up dollars through taxes in the public sector or insurance premiums in the private sector. These dollars are then paid out in various payment systems that carry their own incentives for cost savings, preventive care, or other policy goals. For example, Diagnosis Related Groups (DRGs) are the payment method that Medicare uses to reimburse hospitals for inpatient care. In payment systems, the dollars typically flow to particular provider types, whether they are ambulances, physicians, hospitals, health maintenance organizations (HMOs), or any of the hundreds of other provider types. Finally, payments that go to particular providers are calibrated for each individual service. For example, physicians often are paid on the

Table 5.1   Examples of Finance, Payment, Provider, Service Relationships

Finance	Payment Systems	Providers	Service
Payroll tax	Diagnosis-related groups	Hospitals	All inpatient expenses
Employer/employee premiums	Capitation	Managed care organization	All covered health services, including prescription drugs
Federal and state (Medicaid) tax revenues	Fee for service	Physicians	Office visits
Out-of-pocket expenditures	Fee for service	Dentist	Procedure

basis of a fee schedule that sets the specific amount based on cost, risk, or other criteria for payment.

Finance

Health services are financed via a complicated patchwork of out-of-pocket expenditures, employer and employee payments to insurers and other private intermediaries, and tax revenues that flow to public programs and public providers, such as the Veterans Administration or county public hospitals.

Tax revenues flow into the health-care system through a number of routes. The most important sources of public funds for health services are payroll tax contributions and general revenue receipts for Medicare. Payroll tax contributions are deposited in a Medicare Part A Trust Fund for Hospital Insurance. General revenue contributions are combined with premiums (75% general revenues, 25% Part B premiums) to finance physicians' services, home health, and other nonhospital expenses in Medicare. A combination of federal and state tax revenues finance Medicaid. The exact contribution of federal and state sources varies from state to state depending on a formula but averages about 50/50.

The federal government finances a variety of other health services and programs through appropriations in the federal budget. Examples include veterans' services, payments to Federally Qualified Health Centers (under the Health Resources and Services Administration), HIV and AIDS services (under the

Centers for Disease Control and Prevention), and Indian Health Services (under the Bureau of Indian Affairs). States fund a variety of health programs and providers as well as provide a significant amount of direct health services through state hospitals, state schools, and departments of correction. Cities and counties are responsible for funding a variety of health services ranging from school health to public hospitals and clinics.

A considerable amount of health care is provided without obvious sources of payment, either as charity care (provided as in-kind services) or by writing off bad debt. The most interesting form of unfunded health care is free care provided by individual providers, such as physicians who provide care in their offices without payment, or organizations, such as free clinics. This care, officially known as uncompensated or charity care, is a significant although often unaccounted for component of the health system. For some providers, such as inner-city teaching hospitals, charity care can be a significant proportion of overall care and must be supported by subsidies, fundraising, or other sources.

Monies that are paid by employers and employees to health insurance plans, usually in the form of premiums for health coverage, account for about 36% of all health-care revenues. Indeed, 60% of Americans receive health insurance through their employers (DeNavas-Walt, Proctor, & Mills, 2004). Employees are charged amounts that may reflect characteristics of their group (either their demographics or their cost and experience in using health services), the generosity of coverage, and the degree to which their employer wishes to distribute the burden differently among higher- or lower-compensated employees. Thus, the premiums that individuals pay for health insurance coverage vary widely across firms, occupations, and geography. Small firms with an expensive record of health-care costs and little ability or desire to subsidize coverage can face prohibitively high costs of coverage for workers.

Out-of-pocket expenditures usually are given to providers in the form of copayments or deductibles. Copayments require individuals to share in the costs of a service, such as a physician visit or a prescription drug order, in order to make the user sensitive to the price or cost of that service. Deductibles also create a kind of price sensitivity to the use of health services and typically apply to the first dollars of service use, such as the first day or days of a hospitalization. A large body of economic research, most notably the RAND Health Insurance Experiments, documents the reductions in the costs and use of care when patients are charged even small copayments or deductibles (Newhouse & the Insurance Experiment Group, 1993).

These kinds of financial disincentives to use health services can discourage needed or appropriate care. The rise of "consumer-directed health care" has been accompanied by an increase in the use of copayments, deductibles, limits, and other features of health insurance coverage that are designed to reduce costs and force patients to be prudent users of services. At the extreme, new plan types known as Medical Savings Accounts (MSAs) combine high deductibles, catastrophic coverage, and favorable tax treatment to encourage consumers to make very calculated choices about their use of medical resources. Because consumers may get to keep and roll over any savings that may accrue when they do not spend out-of-pocket dollars for health services, policy makers believe they will be much more careful and prudent about decisions to use resources. Critics of the MSAs worry that relatively healthy enrollees will select these plans, leaving other insurance pools with sicker and more costly enrollees and, ultimately, much higher premiums.

Payment

In general, payment systems can be designed as prospective or retrospective, cost based or risk based. A prospective payment system establishes the amount to be paid *in advance*, leaving the provider to assume the financial risk if a patient costs more than the predetermined amount. A cost-based system attempts to reimburse providers for the actual resource use in an episode of care. The disadvantage of cost-based systems is that they fail to provide incentives for providers to be efficient; when they began, cost-based systems such as in Medicare came to be known as "blank check Medicare." Risk-based systems push the costs (or risks) of health services back to providers, and this gives them powerful incentives to be efficient.

The most famous prospective payment system, and the one most consequential for social workers, is the Medicare Prospective Payment System (PPS), originally introduced in 1983. The unit of payment for the Medicare PPS was the diagnosis-related group, defined by the codes from the ninth edition of the *International Statistical Classification of Diseases and Related Health Problems* applied to the patient's condition or diagnosis at discharge. Hospitals were paid a fixed, prospectively determined amount based on the resource intensity of a particular diagnosis. This fixed prospective payment is a powerful example of a risk-based system. For example, a hip fracture would be classified into a particular DRG category, "DRG 210 hip and femur procedure except major joint, without comorbidities or complications." The hospital would be paid a fixed amount based on the DRG weight for that case, which has a mean length of stay of 4.5 days.

In general, if the hospital treated the patient quickly and at low cost, it could retain the margin it earned on this episode of care; if the patient had a long and costly hospital stay, the hospital could lose considerable money on that particular patient. The theory of this payment system is that, with large numbers of patients, the winners and losers would net out, resulting in a small operating margin for the hospital. The incentives in this system are for hospitals to treat patients quickly and efficiently.

For social workers, the introduction of PPS resulted in a tremendous emphasis on discharge planning because quick and effective discharge was the key to reduced lengths of stay, especially reductions in what hospital managers termed "administratively necessary days," the time it took to find an appropriate subacute setting, such as a skilled nursing facility to provide the next incidence of care for the patient. Because of the economic importance of discharge planning, this activity became the dominant task and even a professional identity for hospital social workers. In many hospitals, hospital social workers became discharge planners.

Prospective payment systems can take many forms. Typically, managed care organizations pay providers for taking care of persons for a year-long term (thus the expression *per person per year*), for bundles or packages of services (such as for a package of cardiac care services: preoperative, surgical, postoperative), or for treating certain diagnoses.

Retrospective payment systems, as the term suggests, pay for services after they have been delivered, on the basis of either costs or a fee schedule. The principal difference from prospective systems is that in retrospective systems, the risk for more or less costly cases is shifted away from the provider. Until the mid-1980s, the widespread use of retrospective cost-based payment systems, sometimes referred to as "blank check medicine," was implicated in rapidly increasing health-care costs. Providers had no incentives to limit costs; rather, the more costly services they provided, the more they were paid.

Managed care organizations typically rely on versions of risk-based payment systems that force the insurer or provider to assume some degree of financial risk or responsibility for the costs of covering enrollees. HMOs

were based on a model of prepaid health care, known as capitation, in which plans were paid a single payment per person per year (known as a capitation payment), irrespective of the illnesses or cost experience of that individual enrollee. The theory of these payments was that through the laws of large numbers, variations in the costs of illness experience of enrollees would smooth out. If the capitation payment was close to the average costs of covering this population, the managed care provider would have a strong incentive to control costs. Critics of these models charged that HMOs engaged in selection behavior, picking the healthiest enrollees for their plans, or engaged in treatment practices that restricted needed services or disadvantaged vulnerable patients.

As experience with and criticism of particular payment systems build, inevitably there are movements to refine and improve such systems. Examples of refinement would include the adoption of so-called partial capitation models (that attempt to blend fairness with the incentive effects of capitation), the extension of outlier payments in DRGs (to take account of extremely costly cases), and the application of sophisticated payment models to new provider types (such as the adoption of prospective payment in long-term specialty hospitals). As these payment systems become more fine-tuned, the overall complexity of the system escalates.

KEY FEDERAL HEALTH PROGRAMS: MEDICARE, MEDICAID, AND SCHIP

Social workers in the field of health care undoubtedly will encounter Medicare and Medicaid, two federal health insurance programs enacted into law in 1965. Together, Medicare and Medicaid cover 1 in 3 Americans, or 107 million beneficiaries. The newest public insurance program, the State Children's Health Insurance Program, enacted in 1997, covered 5 million children in 2009 (Smith, Roberts, et al. 2010). Medicare, Medicaid, and SCHIP account for over one third of national health spending and three fourths of all public spending—costing 770 billion in 2007 (Centers for Medicare and Medicaid Services [CMS], 2010).

In an era of increasingly complex and changing rules in federal health programs, knowledge about federal health policies and expertise in eligibility have become requisite skills for social workers to effectively connect clients with available resources and advocate for improvements in programs. Social workers are poised to help clients overcome persistent barriers to coverage that result from lack of knowledge or misinformation about public health programs.

Medicare

Medicare is a federal health insurance program that covered 47 million people in 2010, of whom 37.5 million are people age 65 and older and 8 million are people under age 65 with disabilities (Kaiser Family Foundation, 2010). Medicare's history is rich and consequential—eligibility, payment systems, public support, and the model of acute care delivery that guides most of Medicare's coverage are the products of overt political choices over its history (Lawlor, 2003). Medicare has four parts: A, B, C, and D.

Part A covers inpatient hospital, skilled nursing facility, hospice, and some home health-care services. People who are eligible to receive Social Security payments receive Part A automatically when they reach age 65. It is financed primarily by a mandatory 1.45% payroll tax paid by employees and matched by employers. In 2010, beneficiaries admitted to a hospital paid a $1,100 deductible for the first 60 days; thereafter, beneficiaries paid additional amounts per day for an inpatient stay.

Part B covers services offered by physicians and other providers (including clinical social workers); outpatient hospital services; some home health care; laboratory tests, X-rays, and other radiology services; physical and occupational therapy and speech pathology services; and medical equipment and supplies for home use. Part B is voluntary,

although 93% of people eligible for Part A elect Part B coverage (CMS, 2004h). Part B is financed by beneficiary premiums, which are set by law at 25% of the cost of Part B benefits, and general revenues from the U.S. Treasury. In 2010, the monthly premium for Part B coverage was $110.50. Beneficiaries also are required to meet an annual Part B deductible ($155 in 2010) and pay 20% coinsurance for most Part B services.

Added as part of the Balanced Budget Act of 1997, Part C (originally called Medicare+Choice and later renamed Medicare Advantage) provides beneficiaries the option to enroll in managed care plans. Medicare Advantage plans enrolled 11 million beneficiaries in 2010 (CMS, 2010), despite three decades of effort and expectations that the Medicare enrollment in managed care would dominate the program (CMS, 2004e; Lawlor, 2003).

Added under the Medicare Prescription Drug, Improvement, and Modernization Act of 2003, Part D provides a voluntary prescription drug benefit. Part D is financed jointly by a beneficiary premium (25.5%) and general revenues (74.5%) from the U.S. Treasury. Low-income beneficiaries receive additional subsidies for coverage. Part D has had rapid uptake, now covering 28 million beneficiaries and accounting for 11% of Medicare benefit expenditures. A controversial element of Part D coverage, addressed in the 2010 PPACA, was a gap in prescription drug coverage, known as the donut hole.

Medicare beneficiaries can elect to participate in Part D prescription drug coverage by paying a premium. Once on the plan, beneficiaries must pay the first $310 of drug expenses (the deductible) before any coverage is provided. After the deductible is met, Medicare will pay 75% up to the point at which a beneficiary has incurred $2,831 of drug expenses. Over the next $3,609 of drug expenses—the so-called donut hole—Medicare Part D provides no additional coverage. When a beneficiary has incurred $6,440 of prescription drug expenses, catastrophic coverage kicks in, covering 95% of any additional expenses. Provisions in the PPACA will reduce this out-of-pocket burden in the donut hole gradually, covering different proportions of brand name and generic expenses, until the law is fully phased in by 2020.

Although most Medicare beneficiaries are elderly people, Medicare essentially does not pay for the cost of long-term care. Medicaid, discussed next, is the major public program that pays for long-term care in a nursing home.

PPACA made a number of substantial changes in Medicare financing, coverage, and payment policy (Kaiser Family Foundation, 2010). A number of provider payments, especially payments for Medicare Advantage Plans, were reduced over time to limit overall Medicare cost growth. Overall, the package of Medicare spending cuts, taking account of additional spending in the law, is expected to reduce Medicare expenditures by a net of $428 billion between 2010 and 2019. A number of changes in the payroll tax financing, employer tax deductions, premium levels, and fees on prescription drug providers also will increase financing for Medicare over time. The PPACA also establishes a variety of innovations in delivery systems for beneficiaries, increased prevention services, reductions in fraud and abuse, and an independent advisory board for the program.

Medicaid

Medicaid is a means-tested health insurance entitlement program financed jointly by the federal government and the states. The program is a substantial player in the overall U.S. health-care system, accounting for approximately 16% of all health-care spending. (Medicaid is an especially large player in long-term care, accounting for 41% of all nursing home spending.) Medicaid covers nearly 60 million people, of whom 29 million are low-income children, 15 million are low-income adults, 8 million are elderly people, and 9 million are disabled people. Among those covered, Medicaid provides long-term care assistance to over 1 million nursing home residents and 2.8 million community-based residents (Kaiser Family Foundation, 2010).

Within broad federal guidelines, states establish their own eligibility criteria, determine the scope of covered services, establish payment rates, and administer the program. Consequently, the Medicaid program varies widely across states. Federal Medicaid law requires that states cover individuals who fall within certain categories, including people who meet the requirements of the Aid to Families with Dependent Children (AFDC). Although the Personal Responsibility and Work Opportunity Reconciliation Act of 1996 (PRWORA) replaced the open-ended entitlement to cash assistance, AFDC, with time-limited Temporary Assistance for Needy Families (TANF), states are not required to provide Medicaid coverage to TANF recipients. Only people who would have been eligible for AFDC under the AFDC requirements in effect on July 16, 1996, are guaranteed Medicaid coverage: pregnant women and children under age 6 with family income at or below 133% of the federal poverty level; children under age 19 who were born on or after September 30, 1983, and have family income at or below the federal poverty level; Supplemental Security Income (SSI) recipients in most states; recipients of adoption or foster care assistance under Title IV; and certain low-income Medicare beneficiaries. States have the option to extend coverage to groups beyond federal minimum standards.

Starting in 2014, PPACA expands Medicaid coverage to all individuals and families with incomes below 133% of the poverty line. Children in families with incomes below 133% of the poverty line who formerly were covered by SCHIP would then transition to Medicaid coverage. The effect of this coverage rule will vary tremendously from state to state; states that have had relatively low eligibility levels will experience dramatic increases in Medicaid coverage. All together, it is estimated that the Medicaid provisions in PPACA will increase coverage in the program by 15.9 million people (Holahan & Headen, Kaiser Commission on Medicaid and the Uninsured, 2010). These 16 million represent half of the 32 million people who are anticipated to become newly insured under health reform.

Federal Medicaid law also requires that states provide certain basic services, including inpatient and outpatient hospital services; physician, midwife, and nurse practitioner services; family planning services and supplies; prenatal care; vaccines for children; early and periodic screening; diagnosis and treatment (EPSDT) for children under age 21; laboratory and X-ray services; rural health clinic services; federally qualified health center services; home health care; and nursing home care. States have the option to expand the scope of services to provide certain optional services, such as prescription drugs, transportation services, optometrist services and eyeglasses, prosthetic devices, home and community-based care, and rehabilitation and physical therapy services.

Medicaid enrollment in managed care plans has increased steadily over the past decade, now accounting for 71% of all enrollees receiving health-care coverage. Medicaid-managed care programs have been the source of both innovation and controversy, especially in states with high penetration of managed care. The most innovative Medicaid-managed care programs have developed care management programs, creative outreach to assure timely and preventive care, quality standards, and increased reliance on evidence-based medicine. The latest generation of Medicaid innovation has been the development of medical home models that establish a continuing primary care point of service and coverage, increased patient education, and coordination of care across multiple health providers and social services (Rosenthal et al., 2010). The controversy over Medicaid-managed care has arisen where: predatory or exploitive marketing practices have occurred; service delivery systems or availability of physicians have been inadequate, either in certain places or for particular vulnerable populations; or quality of care has been poor.

Medicaid expenditures are spent disproportionately on elderly and disabled people. Although elderly and disabled people comprised 25% of the beneficiaries in 2007, they consumed 77% of Medicaid spending. As in other health insurance pools, a relatively

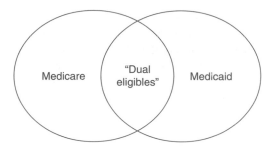

Figure 5.1

small proportion of Medicaid participants account for a large share of spending: In 2004, 5% of enrollees accounted for more than half of all spending. Moreover, more than 40% of all Medicaid spending is attributable to people who receive both Medicare and Medicaid, known as dual eligibles (see Figure 5.1; Kaiser Commission on Medicaid and the Uninsured, 2004). Dual eligibles may receive full Medicaid benefits plus assistance with Medicare cost sharing or may receive only assistance with paying Medicare premium and copayments. Dual eligibles are arguably among the most vulnerable Medicare beneficiaries, because they are poorer, sicker, and more likely to be members of a minority group than other Medicare beneficiaries. They experience higher rates of chronic disease, are more likely to suffer from mental disorders and Alzheimer's disease, are more likely to receive assistance with instrumental activities of daily living, and are more likely to be unable to walk without assistance than other Medicare beneficiaries (Kasper, Elias, & Lyons, 2004). Because of their multiple, complex needs, dual eligibles require services and supports that often fall outside Medicare's scope of services.

Medicare beneficiaries who are dually eligible for Medicaid often do not know about Medicaid or do not think they are eligible for it. It is estimated that between 41.5% and 47.9% of Medicare beneficiaries who are eligible for payment of cost-sharing expenses under the so-called Medicare buy-in program are not receiving assistance (Families USA Foundation,

1998). Social workers who advise clients about available programs can play a crucial role in remedying this problem (Ozminkowski, Aizer, & Smith, 1997). By informing clients about the Medicare buy-in options, social workers can help their eligible Medicare clients save thousands of dollars per year.

Social workers also routinely work with populations who are ineligible for public programs. Notably, because Medicaid historically has relied on categorical eligibility, nearly half of the poor have not qualified for Medicaid. As described, this fact will change in 2014 (or sooner at state option), when all nonelderly adults under 133% of the poverty level will qualify for Medicaid. Until then, nondisabled adults without children and poor parents in states with eligibility below the federal poverty level will continue to be ineligible for Medicaid. In addition, neither Medicare nor Medicaid pays for health services received by undocumented immigrants, with the exception of labor and delivery, which is covered by Medicaid. Moreover, legal immigrants' access to Medicaid was restricted as a result of changes adopted in the PRWORA. Before PRWORA, Medicaid eligibility was the same for citizens and noncitizens. PRWORA imposed a five-year ban on Medicaid eligibility for new legal immigrants entering the United States after August 1996. Furthermore, PRWORA required the inclusion of the income of an immigrant's sponsors in determining an immigrant's eligibility for Medicaid, effectively excluding many immigrants from Medicaid (Kaiser Commission on Medicaid and the Uninsured, 2003). The PPACA does not change legal and illegal immigrants' eligibility for Medicaid. Numerous studies (Capps et al., 2002; Fix & Zimmerman, 1998; Maloy, Darnell, Kenney, & Cyprien, 2000) have cited fear of deportation and confusion about eligibility as barriers to enrollment of eligible immigrants into Medicaid. During this time of transition to full implementation of health reform, social workers will have an important role to play in educating their clients about the changes in Medicaid eligibility, assessing their clients' eligibility for Medicaid, and encouraging those who are eligible to enroll in the program. The failure of immigration reform and legislation restoring immigrants' access to public benefits suggest a policy advocacy area where social workers can become involved.

State Children's Health Insurance Program

The State Children's Health Insurance Program is a federally funded and state-administered health insurance program for children up to 200% (or higher) of the federal poverty level. (States that already had extended coverage to children to levels at, near, or above 200% of poverty when the new law was enacted could further extend coverage up to 50 percentage points above whatever limits were in place in March 1997.) States that elect to participate in the program are entitled to higher federal contributions for every state dollar spent on child health programs. In designing their child health programs, states have the option to extend Medicaid coverage, create a separate program, or fashion some combination of the two. Unlike Medicaid, SCHIP is not an open-ended entitlement but a capped entitlement; states, not children, are entitled to assistance (Rosenbaum, Johnson, Sonosky, Markus, & DeGraw, 1998). Moreover, the law caps federal financial contributions to states at an annual aggregate level. Nearly $40 billion in federal funds were made available to states between 1998 and 2007 with an average allocation of $4 billion per year (Dubay, Hill, & Kenney, 2002). SCHIP originated in the Balanced Budget Act of 1997 and was reauthorized through 2013 under the Children's Health Insurance Program Reauthorization Act of 2009 (CHIPRA). When the CHIPRA reauthorization expires, the PPACA will extend authorization to 2015 but also requires states to hold the line on eligibility rules as of March 2010, when the law was enacted. PPACA also expands the funding available to states through an increase in the federal match rate.

All states (and the District of Columbia [DC]) participate in the SCHIP program. Of these, 12 states (including DC) expanded their existing Medicaid programs, 18 states created new state child health programs, and 21 states adopted some combination (CMS, 2004g). States that choose to implement a separate child health program have the flexibility to adopt more limited benefit packages than the state's Medicaid program, impose cost sharing at significantly higher levels than in Medicaid, and cap enrollment.

In this environment of dramatic change for Medicaid and SCHIP, social workers can help individuals and organizations make the transition by educating clients about their coverage options and the requirements to maintain coverage. Indeed, social workers employed in hospitals, ambulatory clinics, schools, and social service agencies have been conducting application assistance and outreach since SCHIP's enactment.

The combination of health reform and state fiscal crises present an interesting challenge for the maintenance or increase of Medicaid and SCHIP coverage until 2014 (Kaiser Commission on Medicaid and the Uninsured, August 2010). The recession simultaneously reduced state revenues and increased state social service and health-care demands. Stimulus support under the American Recovery and Reinvestment Act provided fiscal relief to states in 2010. Under reform, states have significant responsibilities to upgrade information technology, create coordination between new health insurance exchanges and Medicaid, and pilot numerous delivery system reforms and long-term care innovations. This interim period before health reform is fully implemented will produce an interesting contest between the federal government seeking to maintain states' level of effort and Medicaid coverage and the states facing dramatic fiscal crises brought on by the recession.

HEALTH-CARE REFORM: HISTORY AND CULMINATION

Enactment of the PPACA was the culmination of almost a century of political struggle and incremental steps toward universal coverage and access. A brief historical review of such failed efforts is instructive, because it points to the differences in approaches and raises issues that are likely to be revisited again.

Support for national health insurance dates back nearly a century. President Theodore Roosevelt, in his unsuccessful reelection bid against Woodrow Wilson in 1912, endorsed health insurance for all Americans (Davis, 2001; Kronenfeld & NetLibrary, 2002; Starr, 1982). The first national health insurance reform model bill was proposed in 1915 by the American Association for Labor Legislation (AALL), a group of social progressives. The AALL's model bill provided medical coverage to lower-paid workers and their dependents. It was financed by a tax on wages paid by employees, employers, and the states. Its eventual defeat is attributed to opposition from special interests (physicians, labor, and business) and America's entry into World War I (Starr, 1982).

At this point, the movement for universal health insurance stalled. Notably, President Franklin Roosevelt omitted national health insurance in his proposed Social Security bill because of concern that opposition would jeopardize the entire proposal (Kronenfeld & NetLibrary, 2002). Momentum for universal health insurance coverage did not emerge again until the 1940s. Introduced in 1943 in the U.S. Congress by Senators Robert Wagner and James Murray and Representative John Dingell, the Wagner-Murray-Dingell bill was the first congressionally sponsored bill to provide mandatory national health insurance. The bill sought to provide physician and hospital care to employees and retirees under the Social Security system. It included an employer mandate system of finance in which employers and employees contributed to a national trust fund that reimbursed providers (Bodenheimer & Grumbach, 2002; Starr, 1982). Amid opposition from organized medicine, Congress never voted on the bill (American Historical Association, n.d.). In 1945, President Truman endorsed a similar bill, becoming the first president to send a national health insurance bill to Congress. Physicians and other health-care interests opposed the health-care bill and federal agencies opposed the plan or bestowed only lukewarm support (Starr, 1982). Ultimately, only one component of the bill, the Hospital Survey and Construction Act (known as the Hill-Burton Act), was signed into law.

Despite the defeat of the Wagner-Murray-Dingell bill, it set the stage some 20 years later for the enactment of Medicare in 1965 (discussed in detail earlier). In an era in which fewer than 15% of the elderly population had health insurance, Congress adopted the Wagner-Murray-Dingell approach but restricted it to people age 65 and older. As with the original Wagner-Murray-Dingell bill, insurance is compulsory and is financed (in part) by a payroll tax. A companion program, Medicaid (also described earlier), enacted in 1965, adopted a very different model, with coverage provided only to certain groups of low-income people and financed by general federal and state taxes (Bodenheimer & Grumbach, 2002).

In 1970, Senator Edward Kennedy and Representative Martha Griffiths introduced a universal health insurance plan that went farther than either the AALL legislation or the Wagner-Murray-Dingell bill. A single-payer plan, the Kennedy-Griffiths proposal provided a national health insurance system administered by the federal government. It was financed by employment taxes (payroll and self-employment) and by general tax revenues. Like its predecessors, the bill could not overcome opposition from organized interests (Bodenheimer & Grumbach, 2002).

As an alternative to the Kennedy-Griffiths bill, President Nixon proposed a national health insurance plan that was administered privately (not by the government). His proposal imposed an employer mandate for those with 25 or more employees (Bodenheimer & Grumbach, 2002; Davis, 2001) and proposed public plans that would replace and improve on Medicare and Medicaid (Davis, 2001). With its focus on the private sector, the Nixon proposal marked a clear departure from earlier proposals that relied on government financing (Bodenheimer & Grumbach, 2002). Its defeat is attributed to lack of public will (Bodenheimer & Grumbach, 2002) and political scandal (Plissner, 2001).

President Carter supported a comprehensive program of national health insurance during his successful bid for the presidency, but skyrocketing inflation rates detracted attention from national health reform (Kronenfeld & NetLibrary, 2002).

A congressionally mandated commission, the Bipartisan Commission on Comprehensive Health Care (called the Pepper Commission after its first chairman, Congressman Claude Pepper, who served until his death), in 1990 recommended a pay-or-play approach to employer coverage. Interest in comprehensive health reform legislation accelerated following the commission's recommendations (Mueller, 1993). Senator Mitchell later adopted the pay-or-play model in bipartisan legislation (Davis, 2001). The legislation required employers to either provide a health plan for their employees or pay into a state insurance fund. A comparison of these major types of health-care reform approaches is found in Table 5.2.

President Bill Clinton pushed strongly for comprehensive health-care reform in what culminated as the Health Security Act legislation introduced in Congress in 1993. The legislation assured universal coverage through an "individual mandate," which required citizens and legal residents to purchase standardized comprehensive insurance coverage through a regional alliance, a state-established intermediary that contracted with health insurance plans. The legislation created an "employer mandate"; universal coverage was financed principally by mandatory contributions from employers (roughly 80%). Emphasizing individual responsibility, the legislation also required contributions from employees (roughly 20%). (Persons who were not in the workforce were entitled to income-related subsidies to purchase coverage through the alliance.) Federal subsidies supplemented contributions made by many firms and individuals. The Medicare program remained in place and was expanded to include prescription drug coverage. Medicaid coverage was supplanted by the alliance plans, with the exception of nonacute care for cash-assistance recipients who enrolled in health plans through the alliance but

Table 5.2   Comparison of Major Types of Health Care Reform Approaches

Type of Reform	Mandatory/Voluntary	Brief Description
Single payer	Mandatory	Single government-run insurance organization collects health-care fees and reimburses providers.
Employer mandate	Mandatory	Employers are required to contribute to the cost of health-care coverage for employees and dependents.
Vouchers/tax credits	Voluntary	Individuals purchase health insurance with the assistance of government subsidies.
Medical savings accounts	Voluntary	Individuals save money in tax-exempt accounts that they can use to pay medical expenses.
Individual mandate	Mandatory	Employees are required to purchase insurance.

retained Medicaid coverage (Fuchs & Merlis, 1993).

The defeat of the Clinton plan in 1994 is attributable to numerous factors. Commentators ascribe failure to the political process and, in particular, to misguided leadership (Johnson & Broder, 1996), political naivete (Brown, 1996), failure of public deliberation (Heclo, 1995), a narrow base of presidential political support (Heclo, 1995), insufficient attention to timing (Hamburg & Ballin, 1995; Johnson & Broder, 1996), failure to sell the plan to the public (Blendon, Brodie, & Benson, 1995), opposition from special interests that had a stake in the status quo (Judis, 1995; Oberlander, 2003), and the structure of U.S. political institutions (Oberlander, 2003). Its defeat also is attributed to the size and complexity of the legislation itself (Johnson & Broder, 1996; Starr, 1995) and to antistatist values (Jimenez, 1997; Johnson & Broder, 1996; Oberlander, 2003; Skocpol, 1995).

The specifics of the Obama Health Plan grew out of a set of campaign commitments, a political strategy, and a variety of compromises necessary to reconcile House and Senate differences. A complex and bipartisan reform in the State of Massachusetts in 2006 set the stage for a proposal that built on a requirement for private health insurance coverage, with a variety of subsidies and Medicaid expansions to cover low- and moderate-income populations. The Massachusetts experiment had demonstrated that it was possible to

assuage the many concerns of providers, advocates, and insurers in implementing reform and, by 2009, only 2.7% of the population were uninsured.

The political strategy that Obama pursued deliberately did not replicate the process of the Clinton plan. The administration provided relatively little guidance in the early phases of policy development, instead relying on congressional process and committees to negotiate the key provisions. Further, the administration worked to bring the various special interest groups "inside the tent" in the negotiations, to try to avoid the fierce opposition to reform that had been engendered by the Clinton approach. At crucial political moments in the evolution of the Obama plan, the Pharmaceutical Manufacturers Association (PhRMA), the insurance industry, hospitals, doctors, and other key special interests, and stakeholders publicly and visibly supported the reform. In each case, however, serious concessions and compromises had been made to win their support. Critics on the left suggested that the emerging legislation did not represent a significant and bold transformation of the system—such as a single-payer approach. Critics on the right argued that the proposed legislation, especially its mandate for individual coverage, represented a major incursion into individual liberties and structurally a major takeover of health services by the government.

After a surprising Republican Senate victory in Massachusetts (ironically an election to fill the seat of long-term reform champion Edward (Ted) Kennedy), the political calculus of health-care reform shifted still again in 2010. Through a complicated set of legislative maneuvers, the House version of the legislation was adopted without change by the Senate (avoiding the need to go through Conference Committee and renegotiate with the House), and further changes were adopted in the context of a subsequent large-scale budget reconciliation bill, the Health Care and Education Reconciliation Act of 2010.

KEY FEATURES OF HEALTH REFORM

In addition to changes in Medicare and Medicaid just described, PPACA makes significant changes in overall insurance coverage and regulation, affordability, quality, long-term care coverage, workforce development, and health promotion and prevention.

Under the new law, most individuals will be required to demonstrate health insurance provided through their employer, Medicaid, SCHIP, or Medicare, or to purchase health-care coverage through newly formed health insurance exchanges. (Individuals subject to the mandate and who do not have insurance coverage will be required to pay a penalty based on their income.) Larger employers with more than 50 employees must provide coverage for their workforce or pay an assessment that is calibrated to the number of employees participating in the publicly available options.

Individuals and families with incomes below 133% of the poverty line will be covered by Medicaid. Individuals and families with incomes between 133% and 400% of the poverty line and who do not receive coverage from their employers or public programs are eligible for premium subsidies to make coverage affordable. These premium subsidies will be applied to insurance coverage available through new state health insurance exchanges, which will function like marketplaces where individuals and families can purchase standardized health insurance plans. Low-income individuals are also eligible for cost-sharing subsidies.

The new law contains numerous provisions to regulate insurance coverage and protect consumers. These provisions protect individuals with preexisting conditions, regulate the rates and underwriting practices that determine eligibility and premiums, require certain forms of information and customer service (such as call centers), and control marketing practices.

Although the new law emphasizes primary care delivery as an important solution to the costs, access, quality, and accountability problems in health care, it is well known that there are huge shortages in primary care physicians, nurses, and allied health professionals, including social workers. PPACA allocates an additional $11 billion to the federal health center program over the next five years. These new monies are in addition to the annual discretionary funding ($2.2 billion in 2010). PPACA also increases reimbursement for primary care "evaluation and management" services, provides additional funding and regulates slots for primary care training, and provides additional loan forgiveness and incentives for physicians to practice primary care in underserved areas. PPACA also provides extensive funding and incentives to increase the pipeline of nurses who will enter primary care, including provisions to support nurse-managed primary care clinics.

Numerous provisions of the new law are directed at encouraging prevention and health promotion. Some of these provisions, such as reimbursement for preventive visits in Medicare, encourage more health promotion in the health-care delivery system. Some provisions are directed at increasing wellness programs sponsored by employers. Still a third arm of the legislation funds public health programming for obesity, infectious diseases, and other preventable conditions in community settings.

Long-term care coverage will be provided to participants who sign up for voluntary insurance under the Community Living Assistance Services and Supports program. Although many of the details of this program are yet to be determined, individuals will be eligible to contribute to a plan that provides a certain dollar coverage for in-home or community-based long-term care expenses. After contributing through payroll deductions for at least five years (the "vesting" period), individuals will be eligible for up to $50 per day for the social and long-term care supports necessary to keep them in the community. The law also makes numerous Medicaid changes designed to encourage more community-based long-term care options, making it easier for states to innovate in home and community-based services as well as provide incentives and coverage for attendants and other community-based supports for beneficiaries who are aged and disabled.

POLICY ISSUES FOR SOCIAL WORK

The PPACA shifts the orientation of health insurance and health policy to a more preventive and primary care mode. Now enacted, the law shifts much of the implementation challenge to the states. States will have responsibility to implement health exchanges and restructure their delivery systems to respond to significant new low- and middle-income populations who now have insurance coverage. This new model will put particular stressors on the delivery systems that exist in medically underserved areas (with already existing shortages of providers) as well as rural areas. Social workers can play important roles as policy implementors and advocates as these delivery system changes take place. It will be important to work collaboratively with primary care, nursing, public health, and social service organizations and providers in shaping the delivery systems required for successful implementation of reform.

In addition to the financing and delivery system issues that surround Medicare, Medicaid, and national health reform, social work has particular interests in the alleviation of health disparities, the future of the so-called health safety net, as well as the revitalization and replenishment of social work professional roles in health care.

Uninsured

The PPACA shifts attention away from the uninsured, who will no longer be in the policy spotlight. The individual mandate to purchase insurance is a key provision in PPACA, but it is essential to recognize that the PPACA falls short of achieving universal insurance. At full implementation in 2019, it is estimated that 23 million people will be uninsured. The pool of uninsured will be composed of individuals who are excluded from coverage expansions, those who opt out of coverage, and those who are left without coverage although they are eligible. This number represents 8% of the total U.S. nonelderly residents, when including those residing unlawfully; excluding the undocumented, the uninsured share is 5% of all nonelderly residents. Until 2019, the number of nonelderly people who are uninsured is predicted to hover around 50 million through 2013 and then is expected to decrease to 31 million in 2014, the year when a number of coverage expansions take effect. After 2014, the number of uninsured continues to decline but never falls below 20 million.

People who remain uninsured will fall into two categories: exempt from the penalty and not exempt. Several groups of people are exempt from the penalty associated with failing to purchase health insurance coverage. These include: undocumented immigrants, individuals who are unable to find affordable health insurance coverage (i.e., health insurance premium exceeds 8% of income), individuals who claim a (yet undefined) hardship exemption, people who are without health insurance coverage for less than three months, people whose gross income is below the threshold for filing a federal income tax return, members of American Indian/Alaska Native tribes, members of recognized religious groups that embrace teachings opposed to the acceptance of the benefits of insurance, and incarcerated individuals.

The Congressional Budget Office (CBO) has estimated that of the approximately 21 million people who are projected to be uninsured in 2016, approximately 4 million will pay a penalty for failing to purchase insurance coverage (CBO, 2010). Of these 3.9 million, 1 million uninsured individuals who pay the penalty have low incomes; specifically, 400,000 people are estimated to have income below the poverty line and 600,000 are estimated to have income between 100% and 200% of the poverty line. An additional 1.5 million uninsured individuals who pay the penalty have moderate incomes between 200% to 300% of the poverty line (.8 million) or between 300% to 400% of the poverty line (.7 million). The majority of uninsured who are subject to the penalty are projected to have incomes of 400% or more (2.4 million).

The CBO estimates do not include a complete itemization of the 23 million uninsured. But it is known that the largest share of the uninsured will be undocumented immigrants. Undocumented people are prohibited from purchasing insurance through the new exchanges and are ineligible for Medicaid coverage except for emergency medical services. People who are in the country unlawfully may be covered by an employer-sponsored health plan or purchase insurance from companies offering their products outside of the state-based insurance exchanges. They are estimated to number 8 million and to account for about one third of the uninsured in 2019.

The next largest group of uninsured will be individuals who are eligible for—but do not enroll in—Medicaid. Although the new law extends coverage to individuals who are under age 65 and have income up to 133% of the poverty level, it is well documented that not all eligible individuals actually obtain Medicaid coverage. There is considerable state variation in the rate of participation in Medicaid among eligible individuals. The General Accountability Office (GAO) has documented that between 56% and 64% of eligible nonelderly adults enroll (GAO, 2005).

The phenomenon of eligible people not enrolling in public programs is not new. A previous study (Holahan, Cook, & Dubay, 2007) estimated that a quarter of the uninsured in 2004 were eligible for public programs but not enrolled in them. Davidoff, Garrett, and Yemane (2001) conducted a study of Medicaid-eligible adults who are not enrolled and found that, compared with Medicaid enrollees, Medicaid-eligible-but-not-enrolled individuals are less likely to have chronic illnesses and are in better overall health. Despite their better health, however, Medicaid-eligible-but-not-enrolled adults still face substantial access barriers and, as a result, use fewer services. Compared with their Medicaid beneficiary counterparts, Medicaid-eligible-but-not-enrolled adults are more likely to be older, married, White or Hispanic, an immigrant, working full time, and have incomes between 50% and 100% of the poverty line (Davidoff et al., 2001). It is important for social workers to understand who has fallen through the Medicaid cracks in the past, because adults who share these characteristics also might be susceptible to failing to enroll in Medicaid in the post–health reform era.

Because of its 2006 adoption of comprehensive health reform legislation, Massachusetts foreshadows likely successes and failures that the country may experience as it rolls out a similar plan. The people who remain uninsured in Massachusetts are: male, young (age 18–26), and single; Hispanic; a noncitizen; and an adult with limited English proficiency or living in a household in which there is an adult unable to speak English; an adult who lacks a high school education; below 150% of the poverty line; and residing in a metropolitan area (Long, Phader, & Lynch, 2010). Further, it is reported that 42% of the uninsured adults in Massachusetts have income below 150% of the poverty line, an amount that makes them eligible for a full premium subsidy (Long et al., 2010). Thus, while affordability will be one important factor in predicting participation in health insurance coverage, it is by no means the only important factor. Cultural characteristics and language, such as inability to communicate well in English, low literacy, and noncitizenship, appear to make people especially vulnerable to being uninsured. As social workers routinely help people apply for public benefits and for subsidized coverage through the state-based exchanges, it will be important for them to target outreach and enrollment assistance to these at-risk populations.

Health Disparities

Wide disparities in access, costs, quality, and outcomes exist across groups in their healthcare use, quality, and outcomes. The most visible examples have been differences in infant mortality, low birth weight, and adverse birth outcomes by race. African Americans experience infant mortality rates double those of White Americans. This differential has been stubbornly consistent, even as infant mortality rates have dropped precipitously over the past four decades. Prostate cancer rates are 60% higher for African American men as compared to White American men. African Americans experience significantly higher rates (and higher death rates) from cardiovascular disease and stroke, diabetes, and HIV/AIDS as well as other major categories of disease and mortality. Other ethnic and racial groups also exhibit high rates of morbidity and mortality that are apparently not well addressed by the public health or health delivery system. For example, obesity and diabetes present at high rates in the American Indian/Alaskan Native population, the Mexican American population, and the Pacific Islander/Asian American population.

Racial and ethnic disparities have long been known to health services researchers and policy makers but more recently have become a matter of significant policy concern. A major impetus for national policy attention to racial and ethnic disparities was the Institute of Medicine (IOM) report, *Unequal Treatment: Confronting Racial and Ethnic Disparities in Healthcare* (Smedley, Stith, Nelson, & U.S. Institute of Medicine, Committee on Understanding and Eliminating Racial and Ethnic Disparities in Health Care, 2002). The IOM report documented significant differences in use and quality of health services—test, sophistication of treatment, and so on—even when insurance and income were controlled. The report was controversial, because it identified

discrimination in medical practice as a significant factor over and above the traditional access factors and operation of the delivery system. More specifically, the report focused on stereotyping and prejudice by clinical providers, whether conscious or unconscious.

The federal government, as well as numerous health foundations, has identified racial and ethnic disparities as a major initiative for funding, clinical and services attention, and research. Congress now requires an annual report, prepared by the Agency for Healthcare Research and Quality on issues in addressing disparities across a variety of vulnerable groups: the low-income population, racial and ethnic minorities, women, children, elderly people, and individuals with special or chronic health-care needs. The issues are complex and involve interactions among underlying social circumstances, health behaviors, and health services delivery.

Health-Care Safety Net

Because so many individuals and families have experienced access problems due to financial and nonfinancial barriers, the delivery of care by public and nonprofit organizations that provide care for free or on the basis of ability to pay is a critical issue (Smedley et al., 2002). These so-called safety net providers include public hospitals and clinics, federally qualified health centers (FQHCs), specialty providers (such as reproductive health centers), and free clinics that rely principally on volunteer contributions. Significant amounts of care also are provided by hospitals, physicians, and clinics in the form of free or subsidized care. Particular services, such as emergency room care or burn care, are provided disproportionately to uninsured patients because of poverty, shortcomings of the primary or public health systems, or regulatory requirements.

Historically, these providers have relied heavily on: grants from federal, state, and local sources; Medicaid and FQHC reimbursements; and private philanthropy. In the short run, before health reform is phased in, these sources are under stress in most states, and none has been able to keep up with the real costs of delivering health services. In the longer run, many urban centers will need to address planning, governance, and coordination of the safety net providers as health reform is implemented. The PPACA provides substantial new funding for community health centers—$11 billion over five years—with the expectation that these critical pieces of the safety net will implement some of the vision of community-based primary care as well as respond to the needs of uncovered individuals, such as undocumented workers, through the transition of reform.

Rural safety net providers have faced even greater challenges as the combined effects of technology growth, difficulties in recruiting and retaining physicians and allied health personnel, and payment policies have conspired against the efforts of rural areas to maintain small hospitals and access to primary care (Ormond, Wallin, & Goldenson, 2000). It is difficult to achieve the efficiencies and technologies of care demanded in modern medicine with the relatively small number of patients who, by definition, are present in rural hospitals and clinics. Doctors looking for colleagues, wanting to refer to specialists, or looking for access to sophisticated equipment or facilities naturally will practice in more urban settings. The fact that many rural areas have disproportionately high numbers of uninsured and low-income residents means that providers face a kind of triple jeopardy: a poor payer environment, disadvantaged and often high-risk patients, and high unit costs.

Both Medicare and Medicaid have promoted policies to support rural providers and physicians, and providers have endeavored to respond with mergers, affiliations, and the use of new technologies, such as telemedicine. The plight of the rural safety net, however, continues to be a major area of policy concern.

Patient-Centered Medical Home

Although it originated in 1967 as a strategy to care for children with special care needs, in recent years the medical home concept has evolved into a broadly accepted and widely tested model to deliver high-quality primary care for anyone. Although there is no standard definition of a *medical home*, most concur that its essential components are a personal primary care physician, enhanced access to care, care coordination, team-based care, a whole-person orientation, and a focus on quality and safety.

The patient-centered medical home model has been tested in a variety of ways and settings. Dozens of public and private demonstration programs exist, of which the American Academy of Pediatrics, one of the physician specialty groups responsible for the model's creation, maintains a listing (www.medicalhomeinfo.org). The model also has received widespread acceptance. The National Committee on Quality Assurance has developed three levels of Medical Home recognition for health-care practices. The American Medical Association House of Delegates adopted the "Joint Principles of the Patient-Centered Medical Home," which were developed by four physician specialty groups. The new health reform law authorizes continued experimentation with the medical home model. Specifically, the PPACA authorizes states to implement a "Health Home" for Medicaid enrollees with chronic conditions or serious mental health conditions. The PPACA also specifies the patient-centered medical home as one of the models to test for "high-need" beneficiaries under the newly created Center for Medicare and Medicaid Innovation within the CMS.

Social workers' expertise in connecting clients to appropriate services and resources makes them especially well suited to play a role in care coordination activities. With training and experience in case management, social workers are adept at each of the care management processes: identifying needs and developing, implementing, and evaluating the care plan. Arguably, care coordination is one of the most important components of a medical home because it can reduce costs and improve quality of care (McAllister, Presler, & Cooley, 2007). Nevertheless, some evidence suggests that a majority of practices have not adopted care coordination activities (Goldberg & Kuzel, 2009). This finding suggests a need for social workers to underscore the importance of care coordination activities and to step in to provide this service.

The profession of social work draws on theories of human behavior and social systems in order to change and improve the lives of people and society. Embracing the person-in-environment perspective, social workers have special insight into the medical home whole-person orientation. When considering the whole person, social workers consider the client's physical, emotional, and spiritual attributes in the context of each of her surroundings—her family, community, and society. As health-care practices begin to implement medical home models, social workers can bring to the table much understanding about the whole person and can help to ensure that this component of the model is fully realized and adopted. Social workers also have at their disposal a client-centered, field-tested tool, the aptly named person-in-environment system, for classifying problems. This system is intended to yield a better understanding of the problems that clients are experiencing so that more effective interventions can be designed.

Social Work Professional Role

Virtually absent from the policy discussions of health reform or more narrow considerations of state Medicaid policy or urban health-care delivery is the role of social work as a profession in the health-care system. Professional roles for social workers have changed dramatically in recent years, in part as a result of policy changes. The implementation of the Medicare Prospective Payment System, for example, fundamentally changed the responsibilities for medical social workers to an emphasis on discharge planning. The priority for hospitals was to shorten lengths of inpatient stays. With that priority, an emphasis emerged to find placements and make arrangements for expedited discharge. Social workers,

with knowledge of community resources, ability to work with families, and interdisciplinary orientation, became the default solution to this institutional need. Unfortunately, the status of medical social work and the breadth of responsibilities that medical social workers enjoyed in hospitals devolved as social work increasingly became identified simply with "discharge planning."

With the aging of the population, the growing primacy of chronic conditions such as diabetes and asthma, and the shift to new forms of community health-care delivery, the social work profession has the opportunity to define and advocate for new roles in practice. Efforts under way by the National Institute of Health's National Cancer Institute, CMS, the Health Resources and Services Administration, the American Cancer Society, and other local hospitals and clinics to use "patient navigation" to assist families and vulnerable patients in negotiating clinical, service, and social aspects of cancer care and chronic disease treatment represent important areas for role definition (or loss of role definition) for social work in health care (Darnell, 2007). Key to reinvigorating the social work professional role in health services delivery will be advocacy in policy: making sure that criteria, payment, and management designate social work as the professional provider of choice.

As advocates and proponents of social justice, social workers also have a role in arguing for sound and compassionate policy responses to disparities in and lack of access to health care. At a state level, social workers have been an important voice and source of analysis for Medicaid and SCHIP coverage and reimbursement policy. At a local level, especially in the absence of universal coverage, social workers play an important policy and political role in the maintenance of the so-called health-care safety net: public and nonprofit providers that serve low income, uninsured, or underinsured patients. At each of these levels of advocacy, substantive knowledge of programs and policy is essential. One source of political capital that social workers bring to legislative, administrative, and regulatory decisions is their expertise in the workings of programs such as Medicare and Medicaid as well as their understanding of the real-life effects of these programs on vulnerable populations and communities.

CONCLUSION

Health policy in the United States attempts to address systemic problems of access, costs, quality, and accountability. With the enactment of PPACA, the dominant policy concerns about the system will shift from access to costs and quality. Although the architects of health reform assert that it will lead to substantial overall cost controls (Orszag & Emanuel, 2010), others believe that the legislation did not deal with the fundamental drivers of cost, such as escalating technology, delivery system discipline, and insurance. Looked at more carefully, the problem of costs is not simply the level of health-care costs in the United States but rather a concern about the value or benefit that these services produce. As the government and private payers for health care have attempted to gain control over health-care expenditures, more and more policy attention has been paid to ensuring the quality and accountability of the system. Health policy will be increasingly preoccupied with outcomes, information, and incentives for quality care.

The key policy levers for affecting the size and scope of health services are financing arrangements (such as taxes and insurance premiums), payment arrangements (such as DRGs or managed care capitation payments), and information sources about quality and efficiency of services.

Although access cost, quality, and accountability concerns are the primary issues for policy analysis and reform, all legislative and regulatory actions in the health system take place within the context of huge political and economic interests. The recent history of reform was dominated by large interests, such as the insurance and pharmaceutical industries, shaping public perceptions and congressional behavior.

The next phase of reform shifts to the states, where the implementation of health exchanges, Medicaid and SCHIP coverage, delivery system reforms, health prevention and promotion, and workforce development will determine the ultimate success of PPACA. The largest transition will be the movement of uninsured and underinsured populations to a coverage model where they will be expected to select and participate in traditional insurance or Medicaid coverage and will be steered toward mainstream providers and services. Supporting and advocating for vulnerable populations during this transition will be a key role for social workers.

The two large policy arenas for social work in health care will continue to be the Medicare and Medicaid programs. In Medicare, the addition of prescription drug coverage and the evolution to more competitive and "consumer-driven" approaches to health plan choice and coverage will be important frontiers for social work advocacy and practice. Medicaid is facing threats to coverage and financing, particularly during the transition to reform in 2014, when eligibility for Medicaid shifts to 133% of the poverty line across the country. During this interim period, states face a kind of policy scissors: On one side, their economic downturn is straining resources and forcing cuts in programs, while on the other side, the ramp-up of reform is creating expectations and requirements for maintenance and expansion of coverage. The vigilance and advocacy of social workers will be especially important during this transitional period.

Social workers will need to be savvy about these health policy changes in their own practice, in professional roles that attempt to formulate or implement health policy, and in promoting broader advocacy for health-care reform. The implementation of health reform, rapidly escalating costs, the aging of the population, and increasing pressures to control public spending will continue to place health care at the top of the national policy agenda, providing important opportunities for social workers to exercise their vital professional, advocacy, and leadership roles.

SUGGESTED LEARNING EXERCISES

Learning Exercise 5.1

Identify the eligibility criteria for Medicaid for a low-income person with a disability in your state. Is the person eligible for other health insurance coverage besides Medicare? Under what circumstances would the individual be dually eligible for Medicare and Medicaid? What other programs would you explore? What prescription drug coverage is available to this individual? What safety net providers are available to provide health-care coverage? What gaps in service do you anticipate?

Learning Exercise 5.2

Propose a new professional role for social workers motivated by health reform. Provide a one-paragraph job description of this role. How would you advocate the benefits and rationale of this role to senior policy leadership at the CMS? How would you propose this role be financed and reimbursed? How would this role relate to that of other professionals—physicians, health-care administrators, nurses, and so on—in the health system?

Learning Exercise 5.3

Identify the single most compelling policy problem for social workers to address in health care. Is it disparities in access or outcomes? Is it the cultural competence of providers? Is it the erosion of Medicaid coverage in states? What strategies and approaches would you propose for social work to influence the path of health policy formulation?

SUGGESTED RESOURCES

More detailed presentations of program data, policy analysis, and eligibility rules can be found in government documents, foundation reports, Web resources, and journals. Social workers with ongoing interests in health policy should familiarize themselves with the overall government program structure and resource commitment to health services. The most comprehensive guide to government entitlement programs (especially Medicare and Medicaid), the Green Book, is published periodically by the U.S. House Ways and Means Committee and is also available on the Web at www.gpoaccess.gov/wmprints/green/index.html

Social workers interested in gaining a deeper understanding of Medicare and Medicaid should be familiar with the federal program's documents, especially "Medicare and You," available through the CMS at www.cms.gov

Ongoing policy issues in Medicare and Medicaid as well as specific topics in minority health, HIV/AIDS, and access for the uninsured are thoroughly covered by the Kaiser Family Foundation and its extensive Web resources. More information can be found at www.kff.org

Key journals with which social workers interested in health policy should be familiar include *Health Affairs*, *Health Care Financing Review*, and *Social Work and Health*.

A comprehensive glossary of health-care terminology has been published as the 2004 edition of *AcademyHealth Glossary of Terms Commonly Used in Health Care*, and can be found at www.academyhealth.org

APPENDIX 5.1: TIMELINE OF KEY FEDERAL HEALTH POLICY ACTIONS SINCE THE NEW DEAL

2000s

- 2010   Patient Protection and Affordable Care Act, the Health Care & Education Reconciliation Act.
- 2003   Medicare Prescription Drug Improvement and Modernization Act of 2003.
- 2001   Federal health centers program expanded under presidential initiative.
- 2000   Breast and Cervical Cancer Prevention and Treatment Act of 2000 permitted states to provide Medicaid to certain women diagnosed with breast or cervical

cancer, regardless of their income or resources.

1990s

1999 Ticket to Work and Work Incentives Improvement Act of 1999 expanded the availability of Medicare and Medicaid for certain disabled beneficiaries who return to work.

1997 Balanced Budget Act of 1997 established the State Children's Health Insurance Program (SCHIP) and created the MedicareChoice program.

1996 Health Insurance Portability and Accountability Act (HIPAA); Personal Responsibility and Work Opportunity Reconciliation Act of 1996; Mental Health Parity Act of 1996.

1994 Clinton health plan defeated.

1993 Health Security Act (Clinton Health Reform Plan) introduced in Congress; Family and Medical Leave Act of 1993.

1990 Americans with Disabilities Act (ADA); Ryan White Comprehensive AIDS Resources Emergency Act.

1980s

1989 Omnibus Budget Reconciliation Act of 1989; Medicare Catastrophic Coverage Act repealed.

1988 Medicare Catastrophic Coverage Act of 1988 provided coverage for catastrophic illness and prescription drugs.

1987 Omnibus Budget Reconciliation Act of 1987 expanded Medicaid eligibility for pregnant women and children and established the resource-based relative value scale for reimbursing physicians under Medicare; Stewart B. McKinney Homeless Assistance Act.

1986 Omnibus Budget Reconciliation Act of 1986; Omnibus Health Act.

1985 Emergency Deficit Reduction and Balanced Budget Act; Consolidated Omnibus Budget Reconciliation Act.

1984 Deficit Reduction Act of 1984 (DEFRA) required states to extend Medicaid coverage to children born after September 30, 1983, up to age 5

in families meeting Aid to Families with Dependent Children (AFDC) standards; Child Abuse Amendments established treatment and reporting guidelines for severely disabled newborns.

1983 Social Security Amendments established the Medicare prospective payment system (PPS), including the Diagnosis Related Groups (DRGs) scale for reimbursing inpatient services for Medicare and Medicaid patients.

1982 Tax Equity and Fiscal Responsibility Act of 1982 (TEFRA).

1981 Omnibus Budget Reconciliation Act of 1981.

1980 Omnibus Budget Reconciliation Act of 1980.

1970s

1979 Surgeon General report, Healthy People, laid foundation for national prevention agenda.

1977 Departments of Labor and Health, Education, and Welfare Appropriations Act for FY 1977 created the Hyde Amendment, which prohibited federal Medicaid payments for abortions, with certain exceptions.

1973 Health Maintenance Organization (HMO) Act.

1972 Social Security Amendments of 1972 established the Supplemental Security Income (SSI) program, created Professional Standards Review Organizations (PSROs), extended Medicaid eligibility to certain people with disabilities receiving SSI, and extended Medicare eligibility to people with end-stage renal disease (ESRD); National School Lunch and Child Nutrition Amendments established the Women, Infants, and Children (WIC) program.

1960s

1967 Social Security Amendments of 1967 enacted the Early and Periodic Screening Diagnosis and Treatment (EPSDT) benefit under Medicaid; Mental Health Amendments of 1967.

1965   Social Security Amendments of 1965 created Medicare and Medicaid.

1960   Social Security Amendments of 1960.

1950s

1950   National Science Foundation Act of 1950.

1940s

1946   Hospital Survey and Construction Act (Hill-Burton Act) provided federal grants and loans to build hospitals; National Mental Health Act.

1944   Public Health Service Act of 1944.

1943   Emergency Maternal and Infant Care Program provided maternity care and infants for wives and children of service members.

1930s

1935   Social Security Act of 1935 passed including Title V, Maternal and Child Health.

Sources: Adapted from *Healthcare Reform in America: A Reference Handbook*, by J. J. Kronenfeld and M. R. Kronenfeld, 2004, Santa Barbara, CA: ABC-CLIO; Appendix 1: Medicaid Legislative History—1965–2000, by Henry J. Kaiser Family Foundation, n.d., retrieved from http://www.kff.org/medicaid/loader.cfm?url=/commonspot/security/getfile.cfm&PageID=14255; *Breast and Cervical Cancer Prevention and Treatment*, by Centers for Medicare and Medicaid Services, 2004a, retrieved from http://www.cms.hhs.gov/bccpt/default.asp; CMS History Page Quiz, by Centers for Medicare and Medicaid Services, 2004b, retrieved from http://www.cms.hhs.gov/about/history/quiz/answers.asp; The Mental Health Parity Act, by Centers for Medicare and Medicaid Services, 2004f, from http://www.cms.hhs.gov/hipaa/hipaa1/content/mhpa.asp/.

REFERENCES

American Historical Association. (n.d.). *Has a national health program been put before Congress?* Retrieved from http://www.historians.org/Projects/GIroundtable/Health/Health4htm

Andersen, R. M., & Davidson, P. L. (2001). Improving access to care in America: Individual and contextual indicators. In R. M. Andersen, T. H. Rice, & F. Kominski (Eds.), *Changing the U.S. health care system: Key issues in health services policy and management* (pp. 3–30). San Francisco, CA: Jossey-Bass.

Blendon, R. J., Brodie, M., & Benson, J. (1995). What happened to Americans' support for the Clinton health plan? *Health Affairs, 14*(2), 7–23.

Bodenheimer, T., & Grumbach, K. (2002). *Understanding health policy: A clinical approach* (3rd ed.). New York, NY: Lange Medical Books/McGraw-Hill.

Brown, L. D. (1996). The politics of Medicare and health reform, then and now. *Health Care Financing Review, 18*(2), 163–168.

Capps, R., Ku, L., Fix, M. E., Furgiuele, C., Passel, J. S., Ranchand, R.,…Perez-Lopez, D. (2002). *How are immigrants faring after welfare reform? Preliminary evidence from Los Angeles and New York City final report.* Washington, DC: Urban Institute.

Centers for Medicare and Medicaid Services. (2004b). *CMS history page quiz.* Retrieved from http://www.cms.hhs.gov/about/history/quiz/answers.asp

Centers for Medicare and Medicaid Services. (2004e). *Medicare: A brief summary.* Retrieved from http://www.cms.hhs.gov/publication/overview-medicare-medicaid/default3.asp

Centers for Medicare and Medicaid Services. (2004g). *State children's health insurance program: Plan activity as of October 5, 2004.* Retrieved from http://63.241.27.79/schip/chip-map.pdf

Centers for Medicare and Medicaid Services. (2004h). *Trends by state by quarter report.* Retrieved from http://www.cms.hhs.gov/healthplans/statistics/trends/default.asp

Centers for Medicare and Medicaid Services. (2010). *Brief summaries of Medicare and Medicaid.* Retrieved from https://www.cms.gov/MedicareProgramRatesStats/downloads/MedicareMedicaidSummaries2010.pdf

Chassin, M. R., Leob, J. M., Schmaltz, S. P., & Wachter, R. M. (2010). Accountability measures—Using measurement to promote quality improvement. *New England Journal of Medicine, 363*(7), 683–688.

Congressional Budget Office (CBO). (2010). *Payments of penalties for being uninsured under the patient protection and affordable care Act.* Retrieved from: http://www.cbo.gov/ftpdocs/113xx/doc11379/Individual_Mandate_Penalties-04-30.pdf

Darnell, J.S. (2007). Patient navigation: a call to action. *Social Work, 52*(1), 81–84.

Davidoff, A. J., Garrett, B., & Yemane, A. (2001). *Medicaid-eligible adults who are not enrolled: Who are they and do they get the care they need?* Retrieved from http://www.urban.org/publications/310378.html

Davis, K. (2001). *Universal coverage in the United States: Lessons from experience of the twentieth century.* New York, NY: Commonwealth Fund.

DeNavas-Walt, C., Proctor, B. D., & Mills, R. J. (2004). *Income, poverty, and health insurance coverage in the United States, 2003*. Washington, DC: U.S. Census Bureau.

Dubay, L., Hill, I., & Kenney, G. (2002). *Five things everyone should know about SCHIP*. Washington, DC: Urban Institute.

Families USA Foundation. (1998). *Shortchanged: Billions withheld from Medicare beneficiaries*. Washington, DC: Families USA Foundation.

Fix, M. E., & Zimmerman, W. (1998). *Refusing a helping hand*. Washington, DC: Urban Institute.

Fuchs, B. C., & Merlis, M. (1993). *Health care reform: President Clinton's Health Security Act*. Washington, DC: Congressional Research Service, Library of Congress.

General Accountability Office. (2005). *Medicaid: States' efforts to maximize federal reimbursements highlight need for improved federal oversight*. Retrieved from http://www.gao.gov/products/GAO-05-836T

Goldberg, D. G., & Kuzel, A. J. (2009). Elements of the patient-centered medical home in family practices in Virginia. *Annals of Family Medicine, 7*, 301–308.

Hamburg, R. S., & Ballin, S. D. (1995). Politics of the demise of healthcare reform. *Circulation, 91*(1), 8–9.

Heclo, H. (1995). The Clinton health plan: Historical perspective. *Health Affairs, 14*(1), 86–98,

Henry J. Kaiser Family Foundation. (n.d.). *Appendix 1: Medicaid legislative history—1965–2000*. Retrieved from www.kff.org/medicaid/loader.cfm?url=/commonspot/security/getfile.cfm&PageID=14255

Holahan, J., Cook, A., & Dubay, L. (2007). *Characteristics of the uninsured: Who is eligible for public coverage and who needs help affording coverage?* Washington DC: The Kaiser Commission on Medicaid and the Uninsured.

Holahan, J., Headen, I., & Kaiser Commission on Medicaid and the Uninsured. (2010). *Medicaid coverage and spending in health reform: National and state-by-state results for adults at or below 133% FPL*. Retrieved from http://www.kff.org/healthreform/upload/Medicaid-Coverage-and-Spending-in-Health-Reform-National-and-State-By-State-Results-for-Adults-at-or-Below-133-FPL.pdf

Jimenez, M.A. (1997, March). Concepts of health and national health care policy: A view from American history. *Social Service Review*, 34–50.

Johnson, H. B., & Broder, D. S. (1996). *The system: The American way of politics at the breaking point* (1st ed.). Boston, MA: Little, Brown.

Judis, J.B. (1995). Abandoned surgery: Business and the failure of health care reform. *American Prospect, 21*, 65–74.

Kaiser Commission on Medicaid and the Uninsured. (2003). *Immigrants' health care coverage and access*. Washington, DC: Author.

Kaiser Commission on Medicaid and the Uninsured. (2004). *The Medicaid program at a glance*. Washington, DC: Author.

Kaiser Commission on Medicaid and the Uninsured. (August 2010). *State Medicaid Agencies prepare for health care reform while continuing to face challenges from the recession*. Washington, DC: Author.

Kaiser Family Foundation. (2010). *Medicare Chartbook: 2010*. Retrieved from http://www.kff.org/medicare/8103.cfm

Kasper, J., Elias, R., & Lyons, B. (2004). *Dual eligibles: Medicaid's role in filling Medicare's gaps*. Washington, DC: Kaiser Commission on Medicaid and the Uninsured.

Kronenfeld, J. J., & NetLibrary Inc. (2002). *Health care policy issues and trends*. Retrieved from http://www.netLibrary.com/urlapi.asp?action=summary&v=1&bookid=85899

Lawlor, E. F. (2003). *Redesigning the Medicare contract: Politics, markets, and agency*. Chicago, IL: University of Chicago Press.

Lawlor, E. F., & Raube, K. (1995). Social interventions and outcomes in medical effectiveness research. *Social Service Review, 69*(3), 383–404.

Long, S. K., Phadera, L., & Lynch, V. (2010). *Massachusetts health reform in 2008: Who are the remaining uninsured adults?* Retrieved from http://www.rwjf.org/files/research/67248.MassReform2008UninsuredBrief.pdf

Maloy, K. A., Darnell, J., Kenney, K. A., & Cyprien, S. (2000). *Effects of the 1996 welfare and immigration reform laws on the ability and willingness of immigrants to access Medicaid and health care services* (Vol. 1). Washington, DC: Center for Health Services Research and Policy, The George Washington University School of Public Health and Health Services.

McAllister, J. W., Presler, E., & Cooley W. C. (2007). Practice-based care coordination: A medical home essential. *Pediatrics, 120*(3), 723–33.

Mueller, K. J. (1993). *Health care policy in the United States*. Lincoln: University of Nebraska Press.

Newhouse, J. P., & the Insurance Experiment Group. (1993). *Free for all? Lessons from the Rand Health Insurance experiments*. Cambridge, MA: Harvard University Press.

Oberlander, J. (2003). The politics of health reform: Why do bad things happen to good plans? *Health Affairs, 22*(5), W391–W404.

Ormond, B. A., Wallin, S., & Goldenson, S. M. (2000). *Supporting the rural health care safety net*. Washington, DC: Urban Institute.

Orszag, P. R., & Emanuel, E. J. (2010). Health care reform and cost control. *New England Journal of Medicine, 363*, 601–603.

Ozminkowski, R. J., Aizer, A., & Smith, G. (1997). The value and use of the qualified Medicare beneficiary program: Early evidence from Tennessee. *Health & Social Work, 22*(1), 12–19.

Plissner, M. (2001). *A health-care bill fantasy*. Retrieved from http://www.slate.com/id/1007796

Rosenbaum, S., Johnson, K., Sonosky, C., Markus, A., & DeGraw, C. (1998). The children's hour: The State Children's Health Insurance Program. *Health Affairs*, *17*(1), 75–89.

Rosenthal, M. B., Beckman, H. B., Forrest, D. D., Huang, E. S., Landon, B. E., & Lewis, S. (2010). Will the patient-centered medical home improve efficiency and reduce costs of care? A measurement and research agenda. *Medical Care Research & Review*, *67*(4), 476–484.

Skocpol, T. (1995). The rise and resounding demise of the Clinton plan. *Health Affairs*, *14*(1), 66–85.

Smedley, B. D., Stith, A. Y., Nelson, A. R., & U.S. Institute of Medicine, Committee on Understanding and Eliminating Racial and Ethnic Disparities in Health Care. (2002). *Unequal treatment: Confronting racial and ethnic disparities in health care*. Washington, DC: National Academy Press.

Smith, V., Roberts, D., Marks, C., & Rousseau, D. (2010). *CHIP enrollment: June 2008 data snapshot*. Washington, DC: Kaiser Commission on Medicaid and the Uninsured.

Starr, P. (1982). *The social transformation of American medicine*. New York, NY: Basic Books.

Starr, P. (1995). What went wrong with health reform. *American Prospect*, *20*, 20–31.

6

Theories of Health Behavior

SARAH GEHLERT AND SARAH E. BOLLINGER

Theories of health behavior have the potential to order the panoply of constructs with which health social workers are faced and provide a conceptual framework that assists in understanding why people behave as they do in terms of their health. These theories provide direction for the helping process and structure for research. They allow us to unite practice and research by providing a shared language for discussing clinical realities.

A review of the 15 health social work model syllabi selected in 1999 by jury in conjunction with the Council on Social Work Education (Copeland, Jackson, Jarman-Rohde, Rosen, & Stone, 1999) revealed a paucity of items related directly to health behavior theory. This is indeed the case, although leading social work textbooks for years have emphasized the importance of theory in social work practice and research. Hepworth, Rooney, Rooney, Strom-Gottfried, and Larsen (2010), for example, believe that social work theory is essential both in understanding clients' situations and in providing appropriate interventions. The authors write, "[T]hroughout our professional history, social workers have drawn selectively on theories to help understand circumstances and guide intervention" (p. 18). It is clear that theory is integral to myriad aspects of the social work profession, which only serves to underscore the unsettling lack of health behavior theory available through social work curriculum.

We could say that social workers in health care make ample use of theory, if our definition of *practice theory* were limited exclusively to orienting theories, such as cognitive, behavioral, group, or family systems. Social work interventions are based on orienting theories, most of which come from the field of psychology.

Sheafor and Horejsi (2006) say that "most practice theories are rooted in one or more orienting theories" and give the example of "psychosocial therapy, which is based primarily on psychodynamic theory and ego psychology" (p. 51). Social workers in health care have used orienting theories amply and creatively, such as in the adaptation of cognitive and behavioral theories to produce stress inoculation (Blythe & Erdahl, 1986), a technique for preparing patients for difficult medical procedures.

This chapter argues, however, for a different category of theories that are equally important to practice: theories of health behavior. Although orienting theories and theories of health behavior are related, they differ in two ways.

1. Orienting theories can be seen as narrower than theories of health behavior because they focus on the origin and treatment of human problems rather than the full constellation of human behavior. Theories of health behavior are germane to all behaviors, not just those that are problematic. They might be used to consider why people protect their health through exercise and regular physician visits, for example.

2. Theories of health behavior, while considering all types of behavior, restrict themselves to the arena of health. Orienting theories, however, are concerned with problematic behavior in many areas, including health, education, employment, and marriage.

This chapter contends that adding theories of health behavior to our definition of practice theory provides valuable tools for social work practice and research in health care. After a brief discussion of the uses of theory in social work, a select group of theories of health behavior are introduced and reviewed. Each is discussed in terms of its past uses in health practice and research, its strengths and limitations, and empirical evidence of its ability to explain health behavior.

Chapter Objectives

- Define theory in general and theories of health behavior in particular.
- Distinguish theories of health behavior from orienting theories.
- Discuss ways in which theories of health behavior could be used to advance social work practice in health care.
- Discuss ways in which theories of health behavior could be used to advance social work research in health care.
- Describe the Health Belief Model, its limitations, and the empirical evidence for its use.
- Describe the Theory of Reasoned Action, its limitations, and the empirical evidence for its use.
- Describe how the Theory of Planned Action extends the Theory of Reasoned Action and the empirical evidence for its use.
- Describe the Social Action Theory, its limitations, and the empirical evidence for its use.
- Describe the Behavioral Model of Health Services Use, its limitations, and the empirical evidence for its use.
- Distinguish among the five theories in terms of their limitations and empirical evidence available for their use.
- Describe the Transtheoretical Model and how it might contribute to social work practice and research.

USE OF THEORY IN SOCIAL WORK PRACTICE AND RESEARCH

Kerlinger (1986) defines the word *theory* as "a set of interrelated constructs, definitions, and propositions that present a systematic view

of phenomena by specifying relations among variables, with the purpose of explaining and predicting the phenomena" (p. 9). He defines the word *constructs* as concepts that have been "deliberately and consciously invented for a special scientific purpose" (p. 27). Constructs such as well-being, self-esteem, and aggression are widely used in social work. By virtue of their ability to propose relationships among constructs, theories provide order in what otherwise might be an overwhelming confusion of abstract ideas. This order is especially important in social work, in which abstract, less perceptible constructs, such as aggression and self-esteem, are considered instead of the discrete, directly measurable subjects of inquiry of the natural sciences (e.g., molecular weight, temperature). Theory helps to order the array of constructs with which social workers are faced, providing a conceptual framework that assists in understanding client problems and, in doing so, provides directions for proceeding with the helping process.

Theory not only provides order for what is going on with any one client situation or with clients of the same social worker but also allows us to compare across practice situations and settings. In this way, we gain a shared understanding of the dynamics of certain constellations of behavior within the field. In addition, theory allows us to unite the arenas of research and practice by providing a shared language for discussing clinical realities.

Understanding how constructs relate to one another in the present allows us to predict how they are likely to operate in the future and, thus, to plan interventions. Glanz, Rimer, and Viswanath (2008) write, "A health educator without theory is like a mechanic or a technician, whereas the professional who understands theory and research comprehends the 'why' and can design and craft well-tailored interventions" (pp. 25–26). The knowledge that a certain action, covert or overt, likely will lead to another action makes it possible to intervene to promote behaviors that will have desired outcomes and decrease the likelihood of undesired outcomes. If we know, for instance, that people who understand their risk for acquiring a disease will be more likely to engage in preventive behaviors, interventions can be developed to focus on conveying risk.

Theories and skills are natural partners in social work practice. As the time allotted to assess and treat client problems decreases, tools that facilitate assessment and the development of effective treatment approaches increase in value. Theory represents the accumulation of knowledge about human behavior that is necessary to inform our use of skills. Relying on theories to help construct interventions increases the likelihood that they will be successful. If successful interventions are implemented as soon as possible after problems are noted, the hopelessness that results from multiple treatment failures can be avoided.

An example of how theory provides guidance for practice comes from an empirical study of adults with epilepsy. Adults with epilepsy experience high rates of psychosocial problems, such as a suicide rate 5 times higher than that of the population as a whole for all types of seizures combined and 25 times higher for seizures that originate in the temporal limbic system of the brain (Hauser & Hesdorffer, 1990; Robertson, 1997). In attempting to understand the etiology of these psychosocial problems so that effective interventions could be designed and implemented, Gehlert (1994, 1996) hypothesized that some people with epilepsy generalized their lack of physical control, as represented by epileptic seizures, to the social realm, causing them to have very low expectations that any of their behavioral efforts would result in foreseeable outcomes. The basis for this hypothesis was that repeated disruptions in the action-to-outcome sequence, such as when a young girl wants to succeed in school yet cannot because her parents are unable to provide her with clothing and books, led to a learned helpless state accompanied by high rates of depression and other psychosocial problems. Attribution theory (Abramson, Seligman, & Teasdale, 1978; Kelley, 1967; Weiner, 1985), which predicts depression for people who attribute negative events in their lives, such as not being able to get or keep a job, to their own doing, and positive events, such as being given a compliment, to outside influences (e.g., other people, fate, luck), was helpful in making sense of how constructs such as seizure control and psychosocial problems fit together.

Although not a theory of health behavior per se attribution theory (Abramson et al., 1978; Heider, 1958; Kelley, 1967) has been used widely to explain behavior. The theory holds that people, when faced with a world over which they have little control, attempt to impose control by offering explanations or causes for what happens to them. Illness is an example of a situation over which people have little control, and therefore it elicits causal explanations.

Abramson and colleagues (1978) speak of three dimensions of causal attributions: (1) internality versus externality, or whether the cause is due to the person or to other persons or circumstances; (2) globality versus specificity, or whether the same explanations are used for a variety of factors or are specific to one or a few factors; and (3) stability versus instability, which has to do with whether a factor is long lasting or transient. Pessimistic attributional style is said to occur when people make stable, global, internal attributions for bad events.

Attributions, the dimensions of which are measured using either the Attributional Style Questionnaire (Peterson et al., 1982) or the Content Analysis of Verbatim Explanations technique (Peterson, Bettes, & Seligman, 1985), are useful in explaining health behavior. Peterson, Seligman, and Vaillant (1988) divided 99 graduates of the 1942 to 1944 classes of Harvard University into those with optimistic and pessimistic attributional styles and followed their physical health at 5-year intervals for 30 years. They found pessimistic attributional style to predict poor health at ages 45 to 60 years, even when controlling for mental and physical health at age 25 years. The authors proposed that people with pessimistic attributional styles might tend to become passive in the face of illness, be less able to solve problems, and have fewer supportive social networks to buffer against stress. Negative attributional style has been associated with eating disorders in women (Morrison, Waller, & Lawson, 2006) and poorer outcomes among people with multiple sclerosis (Kneebone & Dunmore, 2004).

In the example of epilepsy, understanding how a key cognitive component of learned helplessness, termed *negative attributional style*, developed in people with epilepsy helped to determine both a point and a target of intervention. For example, people with epilepsy are faced with multiple messages from others that they are not as efficacious as other people. Even the most benign actions of others, such as assistance during a seizure, convey subtle messages of ineffectiveness and lack of control that, when internalized over the years by people with epilepsy, lead to negative attributional style. A small-group intervention in which individuals with epilepsy are helped to identify when negative thoughts are likely to occur, stop the thoughts, and substitute more realistic appraisals has proved effective in decreasing negative attributional style and depression (Gehlert, 1995).

THEORETICAL APPROACHES BASED ON RATIONAL CHOICE

The first theories of health behavior to be considered hold that human behavior stems from rational, logical thought processes. People make health choices largely based on consideration of the costs and benefits of various actions. The two major versions are the Health Belief Model and the Theory of Reasoned Action. The Theory of Planned Behavior (Ajzen, 1991; Ajzen & Madden, 1986) is an extension of the Theory of Reasoned Action and not a theory in itself.

Health Belief Model

The Health Belief Model (Hochbaum, 1958; Rosenstock, 1960, 1966, 1974) was developed originally to explain why people failed to participate in health screening for tuberculosis despite accommodations such as mobile vans that came into their neighborhoods. The model posits two major components of health behavior: threat and outcome expectations (see Table 6.1). *Threat* involves perceived susceptibility to an ill-health condition and the

Table 6.1   Major Elements of the Health Belief Model

I.   Perceived Threat
     A. Perceived susceptibility
     B. Perceived severity
II. Outcome Expectations
     A. Perceived benefits
     B. Perceived costs
III. Expectations of Self-Efficacy

perceived seriousness of that condition. In the case of risk for acquiring AIDS, for example, threat would entail believing that one is susceptible to acquiring AIDS and that it is as serious as the medical community portrays it to be.

Outcome expectations are the perceived benefits of a specified action, such as using condoms to prevent the transmission of HIV, and the perceived barriers to taking that action. The benefit of taking action to reduce the risk of acquiring AIDS might be staying alive, whereas barriers might be the cost of buying condoms or fear that one will be rejected after asking a partner to use them.

The Health Belief Model has been used with a variety of health behaviors and conditions. These include medication adherence among psychiatric outpatients (Kelly, Mamon, & Scott, 1987), obtaining influenza vaccination by individuals at high risk for acquiring life-threatening complications of influenza (Larson, Bergman, Heidrich, Alvin, & Schneeweiss, 1982), screening behaviors for breast and cervical cancer (Ingledue, Cottrell, & Bernard, 2004; Ko, Sadler, Ryujin, & Dong, 2003; Tanner-Smith & Brown, 2010), and adherence by lower-socioeconomic-status mothers to weight-loss regimens for their obese children (Becker, Maiman, Kirscht, Haefner, & Drachman, 1977).

Empirical evidence supports the ability of the Health Belief Model to predict health outcomes. Becker and colleagues (1977) were able to explain 39% of the variance in dietary adherence using the Health Belief Model's components in multiple regression analysis. This means that when components of the model, such as perceived susceptibility, were measured in a group of people whose dietary adherence was also measured, the model's components were relatively important to understanding dietary adherence. Although other factors must be considered to fully explain what determines dietary adherence, the Health Belief Model adds significantly to our ability to understand the phenomenon.

Janz and Becker (1984) published a meta-analysis of 18 prospective and 28 retrospective applications of the Health Belief Model completed during the first 30 years of its use. The ability of each component of the model to predict health outcomes, such as adopting health preventive behaviors, was calculated by dividing the number of positive, statistically significant findings for a component by the number of studies for which significant results were obtained. Perceived threat was the most and perceived costs the least significant predictor of outcomes, with perceived susceptibility and perceived benefits intermediate between the two. This finding suggests that the perceived impediments to engaging in a behavior to improve health (whether they are

real or not), such as fear of losing one's hair from radiation therapy for cancer, are more significant than other factors (e.g., perceptions of severity, susceptibility, and benefit) in determining whether a person will engage in the behavior. Perceived severity is the least significant factor in determining behavior.

Theory of Reasoned Action

The Theory of Reasoned Action (Fishbein, 1967; Fishbein & Ajzen, 1975) extends the Health Belief Model to include the influences of significant others in the environment on individual health behavior. The theory assumes that behavior is determined immediately by behavioral intention (see Figure 6.1). Behavioral intention is, in turn, determined by a person's attitude toward the behavior and the influence of significant others in the environment, or social norm. Attitude toward the behavior consists of two things: (1) an individual's belief that if a behavior is performed, a given outcome

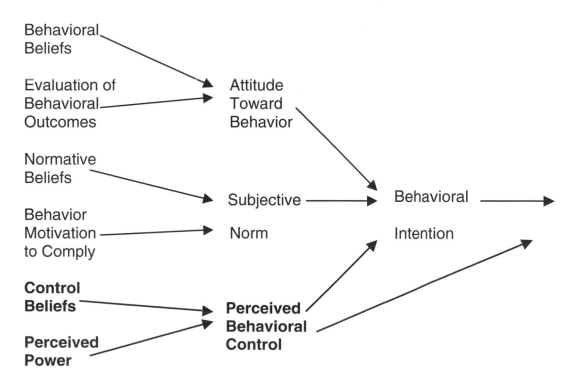

Figure 6.1   Combined Theory of Reasoned Action (TRA) and Theory of Planned Behavior (TPB)

Components shared by the TRA and TBP are shown in regular type. Those unique to the TPB are shown in bold type.

will accrue, and (2) how important the individual considers the outcome to be.

Social norm comprises beliefs about what valued others will think about one's performing a behavior coupled with the individual's motivation to comply with their opinions. For example, a practitioner might consider a young woman's perceptions of what her boyfriend, closest friend, mother, and physician would think about her having an abortion and her motivation to comply with their opinions in attempting to understand or predict her behavior.

The Theory of Reasoned Action has been applied to many health behaviors and conditions, including substance abuse (Beck, 1981), weight loss (Sejwacz, Ajzen, & Fishbein, 1980), and hypertension (Norman, Marconi, Schezel, Schechter, & Stolley, 1985). Because it includes others who hold influence over the individual, the Theory of Reasoned Action has been widely used in studies of the health behavior of adolescents, often in the area of contraception decision making (Albarracín, Johnson, Fishbein, & Muellerleile, 2001; Baker, 1988), abortion (Smetana & Adler, 1986), and AIDS risk behavior (Jemmott, Jemmott, & Fong, 1992). Baker was able to predict 36% of the variance in intention to use condoms with steady partners and 8% with new or infrequent partners by taking into account attitudes toward condom use and subjective norm among patients in a sexually transmitted disease clinic. Jemmott and colleagues designed an intervention for African American adolescent males that emphasized knowledge, attitudes, and skill building based on the Theory of Reasoned Action to decrease intentions to engage in AIDS risk behavior and the behavior itself. Adolescents who received the intervention reported significantly fewer occasions of coitus, fewer partners, more frequent condom use, and a lower incidence of heterosexual anal intercourse than did adolescents in the control condition. A recent meta-analysis conducted by Cooke and French (2008) also found that the Theory of Reasoned Action was able to successfully predict participation in a variety of screening behaviors, such as for breast and colorectal cancer and prenatal screening.

Theory of Planned Behavior

Ajzen and Madden (1986; Ajzen, 1991) extended the Theory of Reasoned Action to include perceived control over behavior. Their idea was that intention alone could not predict behavior if the behavior was one over which the individual did not have complete control (see Figure 6.1). Perceived behavioral control is assumed to reflect past problems encountered in behavioral performance. That is, if a person has been unsuccessful in engaging in a behavior in the past, such as losing weight, and thus has demonstrated poor control over the behavior, it is less likely that he will be able to maintain the behavior no matter how strong his intentions.

The Theory of Planned Behavior has been widely used to predict behaviors as diverse as the administration of opioids for pain relief by nurses (Edwards et al., 2001), cervical cancer screening (Sheeran & Orbell, 2000), and fighting by adolescents (Jemmott, Jemmott, Hines, & Fong, 2001). In a review of studies in which behavior was predicted via intentions alone, as in the Theory of Reasoned Action, and in combination with perceived behavioral control, as in the Theory of Planned Behavior, behaviors that required more volitional control and with which the individual had negative experiences in the past, such as losing weight and getting high grades, were better predicted by the combination of intentions and perceived behavioral control than by intentions alone (Ajzen, 1991). A meta-analysis of 96 studies found that the Theory of Planned Behavior predicted condom use less accurately than did the Theory of Reasoned Action (Albarracín et al., 2001). A meta-analysis of 185 studies using the Theory of Planned Behavior prior to the end of 1997 found the theory to account on average for 27% of the variance in health behavior (Armitage & Conner, 2001). In addition, findings of the previously mentioned meta-analysis by Cooke and French (2008), which considered the Theory of Planned Behavior in addition to the Theory of Reasoned Action, were consistent with analyses of the Theory of Planned Behavior, except that perceived behavioral control did not contribute significantly to behavior.

THEORETICAL APPROACHES BASED ON SOCIAL NETWORKS

The impetus for approaches based on social networks came from critiques that rational choice approaches did not adequately take into account environmental influences on behavior. The Health Belief Model is entirely intrapersonal, and even the Theory of Reasoned Action and Theory of Planned Behavior fail to acknowledge influences on health behavior outside the individual's immediate environment. Missing is an appreciation for the influences of social networks and structures on health behavior. In a second category of theoretical approaches—approaches based on social networks—the emphasis shifts from individual mental events to social relationships, recognizing the social nature of individuals (Tilly, 1984). This shift in emphasis helps to avoid another criticism of approaches based on rational choice—namely, that they ignore the influence of culture on health behavior.

If we conceptualize health decisions made by individuals as the centermost of three concentric circles, approaches based on social networks add two adjacent bands or layers (see Figure 6.2). The middle layer comprises social networks and the outer layer the larger social system, which includes governmental and economic entities and forces. Two approaches that consider the middle and outer layers of influences on health behavior are Social Action Theory (Ewalt, 1991) and the Behavioral Model of Health Services Use (Andersen, 1968, 1995).

Social Action Theory

Social Action Theory (Ewalt, 1991) represents a marriage of psychological and public health models and principles. The prevailing model in public health is a three-way interaction among host, agent, and environment. Whereas approaches based on rational choice are concerned exclusively with the host, Social Action Theory encourages a social-contextual analysis of personal change by suggesting pathways by which social and other environmental factors influence cognitive processes. The model contains three dimensions: (1) self-regulation as a desired action state, (2) a system of interrelated change mechanisms, and (3) larger environmental systems that contextually determine how personal change mechanisms operate (see Box 6.1; Ewalt, 1991, p. 932). Individuals' desired states are influenced by what is necessary to achieve goals, such as social influence, personal safety, material resources, and intimacy (Ewalt, 1991, p. 936).

The health routines and habits that ensue are entwined with those of others, and how these relationships develop has the potential to either promote or inhibit the goals of individuals or the prescriptions of health providers. Recommended change in diet for a child with diabetes, for example, would require a parent to shop for and prepare different foods or serve two separate meals to the family. Health decisions, therefore, are viewed as being embedded in the social network. Although the Theory of Reasoned Action views social networks as influences on health behavior, Social Action Theory considers them to be mechanisms of action. Other people are viewed as active players rather than as outside influences on behavior and are thus inside the lens of inquiry.

Social Action Theory holds that social ties strongly influence the success of attempts to alter behavioral routines, such as lowering dietary fat, increasing physical activity, or engaging in less risky sexual practices. Failure to adhere to health-enhancing regimens has been linked to conflicts that arise when family members' routines are disrupted (Oldridge, 1982). This finding provides guidance for the choice, development, and targeting of interventions, often by specifying when and how significant others should be included in the treatment process.

Because Social Action Theory is a fairly new approach, its applications have been fewer. McCree (1997) found high relationship

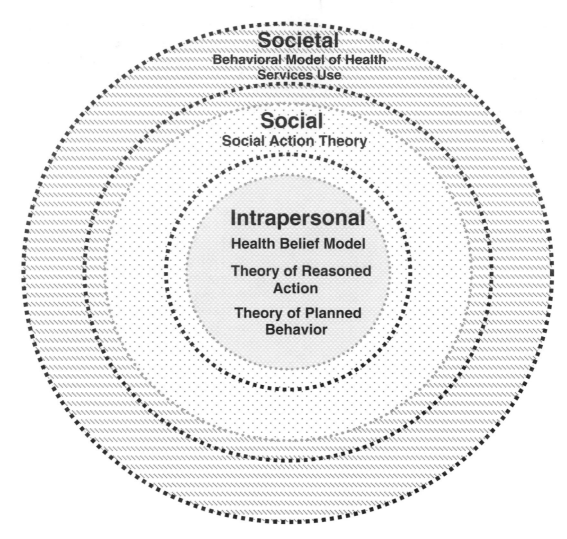

Figure 6.2   Concentric Circles Representing the Three Layers of Influence on Health Behavior, With Theories and Models Superimposed

The Behavioral Model of Health Services Use is on a stippled background. Social Action Theory is on a dotted background. The Health Belief Model, Theory of Reasoned Action, and Theory of Planned Behavior are on a clear background.

Box 6.1 Social Action Theory

Influences on Health Behavior

- Personal level (health habits, personal projects, action states, motivation)
- Social level (social and biological contexts, social interdependence, social interaction processes, action linkages)
- Societal level (organizational structures at the level of government; economic, educational, and health-care systems; laws; policies)

closeness, favorable attitudes toward condom use, high self-esteem, and a secure attachment style to best predict condom use among a sample of African American women. This finding suggests interventions focused on increasing self-efficacy, improving sexual responsibility, and creating more favorable attitudes toward condom use among women and their sexual partners. Social Action Theory also has been applied successfully to the promotion of more healthful behavior and well-being after heart attacks (Ewalt & Fitzgerald, 1995).

BEHAVIORAL MODEL OF HEALTH SERVICES USE

The Behavioral Model of Health Services Use has gone through three phases since its development in the 1960s (Andersen, 1968, 1995) and fairly recently underwent another major revision—the Behavioral Model for Vulnerable Populations (Gelberg, Andersen, & Leake, 2000). The model differs somewhat from the approaches outlined previously in its emphasis on health services use and the outcomes of health behavior. Originating in medical sociology, it considers a bigger picture of the influences on health behavior, such as aspects of the health-care system.

The original model (Andersen, 1968) divided determinants of health service use into three groups of variables: predisposing, enabling, and need. *Predisposing* variables were ones such as demographic factors and health beliefs and attitudes that influenced an individual's use of health services. *Enabling* factors included insurance coverage, social support, and family income. *Need* variables usually included perceived and objectively determined health problems. The model's second phase in the 1970s (see, e.g., Aday & Andersen, 1974) saw predisposing, enabling, and need variables subsumed under the category of population characteristics and the addition of a category of variables, the health-care system, which included policy and resources and organization of the health-care system. Consumer satisfaction was included as an outcome of the use of health services. Phase 3 of the model, in the 1980s and 1990s, brought the addition of the external environment to an expanded category of determinants of health behavior (see Figure 6.3). Use of health services was no longer the end point of the model but was subsumed, with personal health practice, under a new category titled *health behavior.* The outcomes of health behavior became the model's new end point, which was made up of perceived and evaluated health status and consumer satisfaction (Andersen, Davidson, & Ganz, 1994).

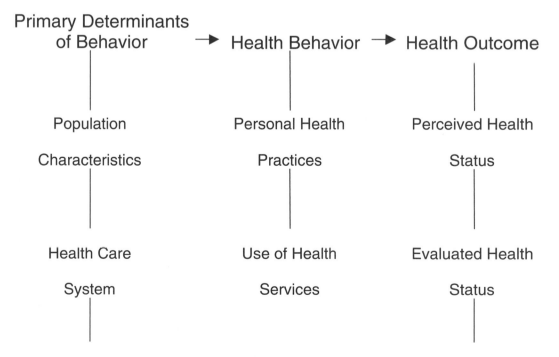

Figure 6.3   Components of Phase 3 of the Behavioral Model of Health Services Use.
Source: From "Revisiting the Behavioral Model and Access to Medical Care: Does It Matter?" by R. Andersen, 1995, *Journal of Health and Social Behavior, 36,* 7. Copyright © 1995 by SAGE. Reprinted with permission.

Empirical support for the Behavioral Model of Health Services Use has been strong. Andersen and Aday (1978) used the model to understand levels of health services use of a probability sample of 7,787 noninstitutionalized people in the United States. These authors were able to explain 22% of the variance in physician visits using (a) age, race, and education of the head of household as predisposing variables; (b) family income, physician visit insurance, number of physicians per 1,000 in population, and if a particular physician was seen as enabling variables; and (c) perceived health and number of illness symptoms in the prior year as need variables. Level of illness and age were related most strongly to the number of physician visits. The most significant policy-related variable was having a regular source of care.

The Behavioral Model for Vulnerable Populations (Gelberg et al., 2000) is an especially valuable tool for the field of social work because of its focus on the health services use of disadvantaged people. Adding residential history, mental health, substance abuse, victimization history, and competing needs to the original model increased the model's efficacy with vulnerable people in a longitudinal study of homeless individuals (Gelberg et al., 2000).

TRANSTHEORETICAL MODEL: STAGES OF CHANGE

Although not itself a theory of health behavior, the Transtheoretical Model (TTM) (DiClemente & Prochaska, 1982; Prochaska, 1984) adds a dimension to existing theories, namely the readiness of individuals to make proposed changes in health behavior. Six stages of change are considered: precontemplation, contemplation, preparation, action, maintenance, and termination (Prochaska, Redding, & Evers, 2008).

The Transtheoretical Model incorporates both intrapersonal and social components of health behaviors and includes various processes of change in its approach to understanding and changing health behavior. These processes include consciousness raising, the use of dramatic relief, and utilization of helping relationships. Change is seen as ongoing and incremental rather than static or occurring at one fixed point in time. This concept adds to the social worker's ability to intervene to change behavior by virtue of respecting "where the client is" and understanding the client within the context of a larger social environment and an ongoing process of change. The Transtheoretical Model has been used with a vast array of health behaviors, including smoking cessation (Dijkstra, Conijm, & DeVries, 2006), stress management (Evers et al., 2006), and condom use (Redding, Morokoff, Rossi, & Meier, 2007).

DISCUSSION

In the early years of the 20th century, Richard Cabot, the Massachusetts physician who helped found the first hospital social work department, urged social workers to build a solid theoretical basis for their profession (Evison, 1995). The profession of social work may have overlooked this advice, focusing on maintaining a respected profile in medicine instead. Building its own theoretical base is an enormous undertaking that arguably is too much to ask of health social work. Employing well-founded theoretical approaches from other disciplines, then, represents a reasonable and prudent compromise with which Cabot likely would have been satisfied.

The theoretical approaches reviewed in this chapter are all relatively sound empirically. They differ more in scope than in content. Approaches based on rational choice focus on the center of a model consisting of three concentric circles, with social networks and relationships forming the middle, and societal level influences forming the outer layers (see Figure 6.2). Although they take into consideration only a part of what we know to influence health behavior, they have utility for understanding that layer well. Whereas some have criticized these approaches for focusing on the intrapersonal, it can be argued that, in certain situations, focusing on smaller constellations of behavior can be useful clinically. To gain an understanding of what goes on within an individual in decision making, a smaller framework, such as that provided by the Health Belief Model, could, for example, be very useful.

Since approaches based on rational choice focus largely on the individual, it is important that the social worker does not engage in the fundamental attribution error (i.e., overlooking environmental causes of the behavior of others) or victim blaming but instead embeds this microcosm of behavior within the larger arena of environmental influences on behavior.

A major strength of Social Action Theory is that it considers in detail influences on behavior from an individual's social network (the middle of our three concentric circles of influence). This focus provides a useful tool for pinpointing how others in the environment are facilitating or impeding the efforts of patients and providers to implement health behavior change. The Behavioral Model of Health Services Use extends our analytic lens to include several systems levels (e.g., the health-care system). The principal disadvantage of approaches based on social networks is that their inclusiveness renders them more cumbersome to implement in practice and research.

Behavioral theory is a powerful tool that allows us to apply existing knowledge of internal and external determinants of health behavior to the clinical situations with which we are faced. The Health Belief Model offers insight into individual's health decision making. The Theory of Reasoned Action extends that insight to include anticipated opinions of valued others. The Theory of Planned Behavior increases the power of the Theory of Reasoned Action when the behavior in question requires a great deal of volition, such as in weight loss or smoking cessation. Social Action Theory is particularly useful when the behavior (rather than opinions) of others is a factor in an individual's behavior change. The Behavioral Model of Health Services Use, by virtue of its

taking into consideration influences at various systems levels, provides assistance in health planning. Taken together, this set of theories and models is a resource that can heighten the ability of health social workers to succeed in an increasingly demanding health-care environment.

SUGGESTED LEARNING EXERCISE

The purpose of this assignment is to apply one of the theories of health behavior discussed in this chapter to a specific health issue or problem. Students should choose one of the three listed vignettes and use it as a tool for analyzing one theory discussed in the chapter. Students should explain the health behavior from the vignette in detail as it relates to the chosen theory and justify why the theory was chosen over others. What features or elements of the theory add to its ability to explain the health behavior described in the specific vignette and would help a health social worker intervene optimally?

In this assignment, students should first include a brief outline of the theory and of the issue or problem as it affects the chosen case. Students should write succinctly, with enough detail to assess their understanding of the theory and the issue or problem. Next, students should explain in detail how well the theory fits the case chosen. Are all of the salient elements of the case covered by the theory? Does the theory allow for a better understanding of the client's behavior? If not, why not? This should be the crux of the assignment. Last, students should address the implications for social work practice of using the theory to understand behavior surrounding the health issue or problem.

Learning Exercise 6.1

A 42-year-old White male who moved to Seattle from Texas one year ago is a patient in the cardiac care unit of your hospital. He was admitted after a second myocardial infarction

(MI), which occurred within a month of a previous MI. Notes from his prior admission indicate that the patient works as an investigator for the state liquor board. He is married for the second time and lives with his unemployed wife and 15-year-old stepson. They reside with a distant relative and were in the process of moving into a rented house when the second MI occurred. He has one biological child, who lives with his first wife in Texas. His father died suddenly of an MI at 55 years of age, without making it to the hospital. You note that the patient is a stocky man, moderately overweight, and a heavy smoker.

During his first admission to the hospital, nurses' notes indicate that the patient presented in an angry manner to the health-care team, threatening to sign out of the hospital and mumbling and interrupting the nurse during cardiac class. He was fairly impulsive, defensive, and, according to the chart notes, very physically active before the MI. When threatening to sign out of the hospital during the hospitalization, he said he was "too young to have a heart attack . . . . I can't work, I can't smoke, I can't eat what I want. . . . I don't care if I die. . . . This hospitalization has placed my family in financial danger. We're supposed to move. . . . I need to help them." At the time of his second admission to the hospital, you note that the patient seems to have tested the limits at home. He now says that he needs to return to Texas, and he has not followed up with the interdisciplinary team's recommendation from his first hospitalization.

Learning Exercise 6.2

A middle-age, African American woman with a history of breast cancer in her family finds a suspicious lump in her breast. Upon interview, she relates to you that her mother died from breast cancer at a young age and that she is familiar with breast cancer, although she says that her family never talked much about the illness when she was growing up. You gather from the interview that she works two jobs, which require her to work many long, late hours. As a single mother with a

busy and changing schedule, she has difficulty finding time to see a doctor and says that she is "just so frustrated by it all." You ask her about the reasons for her frustration, and she says that she recently had a lapse in health insurance because she has been unable to afford the monthly premium. The bills and rent payment have been backing up, and she is having difficulty providing for her family's basic needs. This additional stressor is more than she can deal with at this time.

Understanding her lapse in health insurance and restricted financial situation, you recommend the free health clinic that offers cancer screening to women with low incomes. She says that although she is familiar with this clinic, it is difficult to reach from her apartment. The woman says that she must take two buses and wait for her bus transfer in an extremely unsafe neighborhood in order to get there. In addition, she tells you that she has gone to this particular clinic a couple of times in the past when she lacked health insurance and was disheartened by the lack of consistency in her care. Even when she was able to make the trip across the city to see a doctor, she was never able to see the same physician twice, and explaining her situation multiple times was wearisome. You sense her frustration at the societal barriers that are restricting her ability to follow up with her health concerns. She decides to ignore the lump and hope that it will just go away so that she can continue working to pay the bills and care for her young daughter.

Learning Exercise 6.3

An elderly widow struggles with hypertension, diabetes, and arthritis, and lives alone in a second-floor apartment. She frequently finds herself in need of assistance around the house as her chronic illnesses become progressively worse, and she is having difficulty knowing how to manage these tasks alone. It is now difficult to climb the stairs up to the apartment, and she often feels nervous about falling while getting into the bathtub; however, she tells you that she is unsure of what to do about this situation. She is very indecisive about spending money on home health care, and she does not know where to turn to access these resources. The events coordinator at the local senior center informs you that the woman's husband died about a year ago, and she seems to be having trouble making decisions on her own. The woman did everything with her spouse and says that she relied heavily on him to help her know what to do. The woman's husband paid all of the bills, maintained the finances, and drove her to her routine doctor appointments, but now that he is gone, she rarely keeps these appointments and has trouble filling her prescriptions.

The woman tells you that her two adult children live out of town, and although she speaks to them on the phone almost every week, they seem to be very busy. The woman expresses her desire to talk with them more frequently, but they are full-time professionals with young families of their own and rarely return her multiple calls. From her description, it seems that she calls her children multiple times a day and that they have begun to avoid most of these calls assuming that she is being overly needy. The woman tells you during a home visit that since the death of her husband, she has found a lot of solace in attending church. She speaks to the pastor regularly and appears to look to him for guidance on many issues. She states that he has a lot of wisdom and that she hopes to talk to him more about some of her concerns.

REFERENCES

Abramson, L. Y., Seligman, M. E. P., & Teasdale, J. D. (1978). Learned helplessness in humans: Critique and reformulation. *Journal of Abnormal Psychology, 87,* 49–74.

Aday, L. A., & Andersen, R. M. (1974). A framework for the study of access to medical care. *Health Services Research, 9,* 208–220.

Ajzen, I. (1991). The theory of planned behavior. *Organizational Behavior and Human Decision Processes, 50,* 179–211.

Ajzen, I., & Madden, T. J. (1986). Prediction of goal-oriented behavior: Attitudes, intentions, and perceived behavioral control. *Journal of Experimental Social Psychology, 22,* 453–474.

Albarracín, D., Johnson, B. T., Fishbein, M., & Muellerleile, P. A. (2001). Theories of reasoned action and planned behavior as models of condom use: A meta-analysis. *Psychological Bulletin, 127,* 142–161.

Andersen, R. (1968). *Behavioral model of families' use of health services* (Research Series No. 25). Chicago, IL: Center for Health Administration Studies, University of Chicago.

Andersen, R. (1995). Revisiting the behavioral model and access to medical care: Does it matter? *Journal of Health and Social Behavior, 36,* 1–10.

Andersen, R., & Aday, L. A. (1978). Access to medical care in the United States: Realized and potential. *Medical Care, 16,* 533–546.

Andersen, R. M., Davidson, P., & Ganz, P. (1994). Symbiotic relationships of quality of life, health services research, and other health research. *Quality of Life Research, 3,* 365–371.

Armitage, C. J., & Conner, M. (2001). Efficacy of the theory of planned behavior: A meta-analytic review. *British Journal of Social Psychology, 40,* 471–499.

Baker, S. A. (1988). *An application of the Fishbein model for predicting behavioral intentions to use condoms in a sexually transmitted disease clinic population* (Unpublished doctoral dissertation). University of Washington.

Beck, K. (1981). Driving under the influence of alcohol: Relationships of attitudes and beliefs in a college population. *American Journal of Drug and Alcohol Abuse, 8,* 377–388.

Becker, M. H., Maiman, L. A., Kirscht, J. P., Haefner, D. P., & Drachman, R. H. (1977). The health belief model and prediction of dietary compliance: A field experiment. *Journal of Health and Social Behavior, 18,* 348–366.

Blythe, B. J., & Erdahl, J. C. (1986). Using stress inoculation to prepare a patient for open-heart surgery. *Health & Social Work, 11,* 265–274.

Cooke, R., & French, D. P. (2008). How well do the theory of reasoned action and theory of planned behavior predict intentions and attendance at screening programmes? A meta-analysis. *Psychology and Health, 23*(7), 745–765.

Copeland, V. C., Jackson, V., Jarman-Rohde, L., Rosen, A. J., & Stone, G. (Eds.). (1999). *Approaches to health care in social work: A compendium of model syllabi.* Alexandria, VA: Council on Social Work Education.

DiClemente, C. C., & Prochaska, J. O. (1982). Self change and therapy change of smoking behavior. A comparison of processes of change in cessation and maintenance. *Addictive Behavior, 7,* 133–142.

Dijkstra, A., Conijm, B., & DeVries, H. (2006). A match-mismatch test of a stage model of behavioral change in tobacco smoking. *Addiction, 101,* 1035–1043.

Edwards, H. E., Nash, R. E., Najman, J. M., Yates, P. M., Fentiman, B. J., Dewar, A.,…Skerman, H. M. (2001).

Determinants of nurses' intention to administer opioids for pain relief. *Nursing Health Science, 3,* 149–159.

Evers K. E., Prochaska, J. O., Johnson, J. L., Mauriello, L. M., Padula, J. A., & Prochaska, J. M. (2006). A randomized clinical trial of a population- and transtheoretical model-based stress-management intervention. *Health Psychology, 25*(4), 521–529.

Evison, I. S. (1995). *Pragmatism and idealism in the professions: The case of Richard Clarke Cabot* (Unpublished doctoral dissertation). University of Chicago, IL.

Ewalt, C. K. (1991). Social action theory for a public health psychology. *American Psychologist, 46,* 931–946.

Ewalt, C. K., & Fitzgerald, S. T. (1995). Changing behaviour and promoting well-being after heart attack: A social action theory approach. *Irish Journal of Psychology, 15,* 219–241.

Fishbein, M. (1967). Attitude and the prediction of behavior. In M. Fishbein (Ed.), *Readings in attitude theory and measurement* (pp. 477–492). New York, NY: Wiley.

Fishbein, M., & Ajzen, I. (1975). *Belief, attitude, intention, and behavior: An introduction to theory and research.* Reading, MA: Addison-Wesley.

Gehlert, S. (1994). Perceptions of control in adults with epilepsy. *Epilepsia, 35,* 81–88.

Gehlert, S. (1995). Cognitive restructuring for psychosocial problems in epilepsy. *Epilepsia, 36*(Suppl. 3), S190.

Gehlert, S. (1996). Attributional style and locus of control in adults with epilepsy. *Journal of Health Psychology, 1,* 469–477.

Gelberg, L., Andersen, R. M., & Leake, B. D. (2000). The behavioral model for vulnerable populations: Application to medical care use and outcomes for homeless people. *Health Services Research, 34,* 1273–1302.

Glanz, K., Rimer, B. K., & Viswanath, K. (2008). Theory, research, and practice in health education. In K. Glanz, B. K. Rimer, & K. Viswanath (Eds.), *Health behavior and health education: Theory research and practice* (pp. 21-40). San Francisco, CA: Jossey-Bass.

Hauser, W. A., & Hesdorffer, D. C. (1990). *Epilepsy: Frequency, causes and consequences.* New York, NY: Demos.

Heider, F. (1958). *The psychology of interpersonal relations.* New York, NY: Wiley.

Hepworth, D. H., Rooney, R. H., Rooney, G. D., Strom-Gottfried, K., & Larsen, J. A. (2010). *Direct social work practice: Theory and skills* (2nd ed.). Pacific Grove, CA: Brooks/Cole.

Hochbaum, G. M. (1958). *Public participation in medical screening programs: A sociopsychological study* (Public Health Service Publication No. 572). Washington, DC: U.S. Department of Health and Human Services, United States Public Health Service.

Ingledue, K., Cottrell, R., & Bernard, A. (2004). College women's knowledge, perceptions, and preventive behaviors regarding human papillomavirus infection and cervical cancer. *American Journal of Health Studies, 19,* 28–34.

Janz, N., & Becker, M. (1984). The health belief model: A decade later. *Health Education Quarterly, 11,* 1–47.

Jemmott, J. B., III, Jemmott, L. S., & Fong, G. T. (1992). Reductions in HIV risk-associated sexual behaviors among Black male adolescents: Effects of an AIDS prevention intervention. *American Journal of Public Health, 82,* 372–377.

Jemmott, J. B., III, Jemmott, L. S., Hines, P. M., & Fong, G. T. (2001). The theory of planned behavior as a model of intentions for fighting among African American and Latino adolescents. *Journal of Maternal and Child Health, 5,* 253–263.

Kelley, H. H. (1967). Attribution in social psychology. *Nebraska Symposium of Motivation* (Vol. 15, pp. 192–238). Lincoln: University of Nebraska Press.

Kelly, G. R., Mamon, J. A., & Scott, J. E. (1987). Utility of the health belief model in examining medication compliance among psychiatric outpatients. *Social Science and Medicine, 11,* 1205–1211.

Kerlinger, F. N. (1986). *Foundations of behavioral research.* New York, NY: Holt, Rinehart and Winston.

Kneebone, I. I., & Dunmore, E. (2004). Attributional style and symptoms of depression in persons with multiple sclerosis. *International Journal of Behavior Medicine, 11*(2), 110–115.

Ko, C. M., Sadler, G. R., Ryujin, L., & Dong, A. (2003). Fillipina American women's breast cancer knowledge, attitudes, and screening behaviors. *BMC Public Health, 3*(27), 1–6.

Larson, E. B., Bergman, J., Heidrich, F., Alvin, B. L., & Schneeweiss, R. (1982). Do postcard reminders improve influenza vaccination compliance? *Medical Care, 20,* 639–648.

McCree, D. H. (1997). *The effect of social interdependence on condom use self-efficacy in a college population of African-American females.* Dissertation Abstract International, 58(4-B), 2106 (UMI No. AAM9730752).

Morrison, T., Waller, G., & Lawson, R. (2006). Attributional style in the eating disorders. *Journal of Nervous and Mental Disease, 194*(4), 303–305.

Norman, S. A., Marconi, K. M., Schezel, G. W., Schechter, C. F., & Stolley, P. D. (1985). Beliefs, social normative influences and compliance with antihypertensive medication. *American Journal of Preventive Health, 1,* 10–17.

Oldridge, N. B. (1982). Compliance and exercise in primary prevention of coronary heart disease: A review. *Preventive Medicine, 11,* 56–70.

Peterson, C., Bettes, B. A., & Seligman, M. E. P. (1985). Depressive symptoms and unprompted causal attributions: Content analysis. *Behaviour Research and Therapy, 23,* 379–382.

Peterson, C., Seligman, M. E. P., & Vaillant, G. E. (1988). Pessimistic explanatory style is a risk factor for physical illness: A thirty-five-year longitudinal study. *Journal of Personality and Social Psychology, 55,* 23–27.

Peterson, C., Semmel, A., von Baeyer, C., Abramson, L. Y., Metalsky, G. I., & Selgiman, M. E. P. (1982). The attributional style questionnaire. *Cognitive Therapy and Research, 6,* 287–300.

Prochaska, J. O. (1984). *Systems of psychotherapy: A transtheoretical analysis* (2nd ed.). Pacific Grove, CA: Brooks-Cole.

Prochaska, J. O., Redding, C. A., & Evers, K. E. (2008). The transtheoretical model and stages of change. In K. Glanz, B. K. Rimer, & K. Viswanath (Eds.), *Health behavior and health education: Theory research and practice* (pp. 21–40). San Francisco, CA: Jossey-Bass.

Redding, C. A., Morokoff, P. J., Rossi, J. S., & Meier, K. S. (2007). A TTM-tailored condom use intervention for at-risk women and men. In T. Edgar, S. M. Noar, & V. Freimuth (Eds.), *Communication Perspectives on HIV/AIDS for the 21st Century* (pp. 423–428). Hillsdale, NJ: Erlbaum.

Robertson, M. M. (1997). Suicide, parasuicide, and epilepsy. In J. Engel & T. A. Pedley (Eds.), *Epilepsy: A comprehensive textbook* (pp. 2141–2151). Philadelphia, PA: Lippincott-Raven.

Rosenstock, I. M. (1960). What research in motivation suggests for public health. *American Journal of Public Health, 50,* 295–301.

Rosenstock, I. M. (1966). How people use health services. *Milbank Memorial Fund Quarterly, 44,* 94–124.

Rosenstock, I. M. (1974). Historical origins of the health belief model. *Health Education Monographs, 2,* 328–335.

Sejwacz, D., Ajzen, I., & Fishbein, M. (1980). Predicting and understanding weight loss. In I. Ajzen & M. Fishbein (Eds.), *Understanding attitudes and predicting behavior* (pp. 102–112). Englewood Cliffs, NJ: Prentice-Hall.

Sheafor, B. W., & Horejsi, C. (2006). *Techniques and Guidelines for Social Work Practice.* Boston, MA: Allyn & Bacon.

Sheeran, P., & Orbell, S. (2000). Using implementation intentions to increase attendance for cervical cancer screening. *Health Psychology, 19,* 283–289.

Smetana, J., & Adler, M. (1986). Understanding the abortion decision: A test of Fishbein's value expectancy model. *Journal of Population, 2,* 338–357.

Tanner-Smith, E. E., & Brown, T. N. (2010). Evaluating the health belief model: A critical review of studies predicting mammographic and pap screening. *Social Theory & Health, 8*(1), 95–125.

Tilly, C. (1984). *Big structures, large processes, huge comparisons.* New York, NY: Russell Sage.

Weiner, B. (1985). "Spontaneous" causal thinking. *Psychological Bulletin, 97,* 74–84.

PART II

Health Social Work Practice: A Spectrum of Critical Considerations

7

Community and Health

CHRISTOPHER MASI

Beginning at gestation and continuing through adulthood, day-to-day social and environmental experiences have important positive and negative health effects. The pathways of influence are several and include the effects of air, water, and food quality as well as exposure to physical, social, and psychological stressors. Access to and quality of medical care also affect the onset and course of disease. It has been estimated that, in first-world countries, shortfalls in medical care account for 10% of early mortality, adverse social circumstances account for 15%, and environmental exposure accounts for 5%. Behavioral patterns and genetic predisposition may account for as much as 40% and 30% of early mortality, respectively (McGinnis, Williams-Russo, & Knickman, 2002). Not surprisingly, each of these factors, including genetic predisposition, can be strongly influenced by the resources and characteristics of a community. As counselors, coordinators, and advocates, social workers have unique opportunities to maximize the positive and minimize the negative effects of communities on health.

This chapter reviews the ways in which communities affect health and addresses several questions, including the extent to which neighborhoods differ with respect to ethnic composition and resources that are important to health. The chapter discusses the distinction between contextual and compositional neighborhood features and addresses the relationship between community characteristics and each of the major domains of health determinants. In some cases, the connection between the social/physical environment and health is obvious. In other cases, the pathways of influence

are less straightforward and are explained in greater detail. This chapter uses a life-course model to demonstrate the potential effects of the social and physical environment on each stage of the life cycle. Finally, implications of the neighborhood–health connection for social work practice are discussed.

Chapter Objectives
- Document key differences in community characteristics.
- Illustrate ethnicity and income related health disparities.
- Define *social determinants of health*.
- Review the distinction between contextual and compositional community features.
- Demonstrate pathways through which community characteristics influence health.
- Describe the effects of homelessness on health.
- Identify community effects on health throughout the life course.
- Describe community-based participatory research.
- Outline the implications of the relationship between neighborhood quality and health for social work practice in health-care settings.

COMPOSITION OF U.S. NEIGHBORHOODS

Neighborhood characteristics in the United States, whether urban or rural, vary widely in terms of ethnic makeup and income. This is due to many factors, including resources, personal preferences, and discrimination. With some exceptions, individuals tend to live near those in similar economic circumstances, while individuals of a particular ethnicity or cultural background often prefer to live near others of similar ethnicity or culture. Residency patterns also are influenced by discrimination in realty and lending practices. In the United States, these practices have limited the housing opportunities of many groups and resulted in neighborhood differences that do not reflect the wishes or best interests of all populations.

Although it is not always apparent, racial segregation still is practiced in the United States. In 2000, the typical White American person lived in a neighborhood that was 80.2% White, 6.7% African American, 7.0% Hispanic, and 3.9% Asian. In contrast, the typical African American person lived in a neighborhood that was 51.4% African American, 33% White, 11.4% Hispanic, and 3.3% Asian. The average Hispanic person lived in a neighborhood that was 45.5% Hispanic, 36.5% White, 10.8% African American, and 5.9% Asian. The typical Asian person lived in a neighborhood that was 17.9% Asian, 54% White, 9.2% African American, and 17.4% Hispanic (Mumford Center, 2001).

The five U.S. cities with the highest degree of Black–White segregation are Detroit, Milwaukee, New York, Chicago, and Newark (Mumford Center, 2001). Each city has an Index of Dissimilarity of 80 or greater, meaning that 80% of either group would have to move to different census tracts for the two groups to become equally distributed throughout each city. Although segregation has declined over the past 20 years, the slow rate of change suggests it will take another 40 years before the level of Black–White segregation in the United States declines to the level of Hispanic–White segregation (Mumford Center, 2001).

Economic and school segregation are also prevalent in the United States. According to the 2000 U.S. census, 3.5 million people live in neighborhoods with poverty concentrations of 40% or greater (Orr et al., 2003). In public schools attended by the average African American student, 38.3% of the students are poor, whereas in schools attended by the average Hispanic student, 44% of the students are poor. In contrast, in public schools attended by the average White American student, only 19.6% of the students are poor (Orfield, 2001).

Unfortunately, there is evidence that public school segregation is increasing in the United States. In 1980, 62.9% of African American students attended schools with minority enrollment over 50%. In 1998, this figure had risen to 70.2%, while more than one-third of African American students attended schools with minority enrollment of 90% to 100%. School segregation also has increased for Hispanic students. Between 1968 and 1998, the proportion of Hispanic students who attended schools with minority enrollments of 90% to 100% increased from 23.1% to 36.6% (Orfield, 2001).

Employment discrimination is another source of neighborhood disparity. In the United States, communities with high proportions of minority residents often have higher unemployment rates and lower average incomes. Among Chicago's 77 community areas, unemployment rates in the most economically depressed areas varied from 25.8% to 33.5% in 2000. In these communities, the proportion of African American residents varied from 85.5% to 97.8%, and median household income was $17,209. The five Chicago community areas with the lowest unemployment rates (2.8%–3.4%) had populations that were 79.4% to 93.3% White, and the median household income was $56,455 (Kouvelis, Harper, & Thomas, 2003).

Although diversity is part of the fabric of the United States, diversity between neighborhoods is often greater than diversity within them. Segregation and unequal distribution of resources, in the form of housing quality, green space for exercise, health-care access, and food quality all have important health ramifications.

Does Health Differ by Income and Race or Ethnicity?

Income-related health disparities have been noted for several centuries. Reference to the relationship between health and wealth can be found in ancient Chinese and Greek texts (Krieger, 2001; Porter, 1997). In the early 20th century, Chapin (1924) found that the annual death rate among nontaxpayers was over twice that of taxpayers in Providence, RI. More recently, health outcome differences by income have been documented in the United States, the United Kingdom, and throughout the world.

According to a 2007 U.S. survey of 23,393 adults, poor health continues to affect lower-income individuals to a greater extent than those with higher incomes (Pleis & Lucas, 2009). Among those with household incomes below the federal poverty line, 29.5% reported having hypertension and 4.2% reported having had a stroke. In contrast, only 21.9% and 1.9% of those with incomes greater than or equal to 200% of the poverty threshold reported having hypertension or stroke, respectively. The rates of diabetes and kidney disease were 12.2% and 2.6% among the poor and 6.6% and 1.1% among the not poor, respectively. Obesity among those with incomes of less than $35,000 was also more prevalent (28.9%) compared with those who had incomes of $100,000 or more (19.8%) (Pleis & Lucas, 2009).

Differences in health behaviors and access to care may contribute to differences in income-related disease prevalence. In 2007, 26.8% of those with annual incomes less than $35,000 smoked while 12.4% of those with annual incomes of $100,000 or more did so (Pleis & Lucas, 2009). Of those with incomes of $100,000 or more, 92.2% had a usual place of care while 77.4% of those with incomes less than $35,000 reported a usual place of care (Pleis & Lucas, 2009).

Both disease prevalence and access to care vary by ethnicity. According to the National Health Interview Survey (Pleis & Lucas, 2009), the prevalence of obesity (defined as a body mass index greater than or equal to 30) was 35.1% among African Americans, 27.5% among Hispanics, and 25.4% among White Americans. The prevalences of hypertension and stroke were 22.2% and 2.2% among White Americans, 31.7% and 3.7% among African Americans, and 20.6% and 2.5% among Hispanic Americans, respectively, while the rates

of diabetes and kidney disease were 6.8% and 1.4% among White Americans, 12.3% and 2.5% among African Americans, and 11.1% and 1.8% among Hispanic Americans, respectively. Among White respondents, 84.5% reported a usual place of care. This percentage was slightly higher for African Americans (85.5%) and lower for Hispanic Americans (74.4%) (Pleis & Lucas, 2009).

Given the strong relationship between ethnicity and illness, it is not surprising that ethnicity is related to both life expectancy and mortality. In 2006, the life expectancy at birth was 73.2 years for African American infants and 78.2 years for white infants. Contributing to this difference in life expectancy are differences in infant death and death due to chronic disease. For deaths of infants younger than 1 year, the rate per 100,000 was lower among White infants (576.0) compared to African American (1,303.1) and Hispanic infants (590.6) in 2006. For cause-specific mortality, the age-adjusted Black:White ratio was 1.3 for diseases of the heart, 1.2 for malignant neoplasms, 1.5 for cerebrovascular disease, 2.1 for diabetes mellitus, and 2.7 for hypertensive disease. The overall age-adjusted death rate (per 100,000) was higher among African Americans (982.0) compared to White Americans (764.4) and Hispanic Americans (564.0) in 2006 (Heron et al., 2009).

When considering the ways in which income and race are related to illness and mortality, some links are more obvious than others. Health behaviors, including diet and access to care, mediate this relationship to some extent. Less well understood is the mechanism by which psychological distress also may mediate income- and ethnicity-related differences in health outcomes. In the 2007 National Health Interview Survey (Pleis & Lucas, 2009), those with household incomes less than $35,000 reported higher rates of psychological distress compared with those with incomes of $100,000 or greater in these areas: feeling sad all or most of the time (5.7% versus 0.7%), feeling hopeless all or most of the time (4.3% versus 0.5%), feeling worthless all or most of the time (3.8% versus 0.4%), or reporting everything is an effort all or most of the time (9.0% versus 1.7%). Ethnic differences also existed in some of these domains. Feeling sad all or most of the time was higher among African American people (3.7%) compared to White people (2.6%). Reporting everything is an effort all or most of the time was also more common among African American respondents (6.8%) compared to White respondents (4.4%) (Pleis & Lucas, 2009).

There is some evidence that education may modify the relationship between income/ethnicity and health. Specifically, those with higher education, regardless of income or ethnicity, tend to have lower mortality rates compared with those who have less education. In 2006, the age-adjusted mortality rate (per 100,000) among those with fewer than 12 years of education was 528.8. Among those with 13 or more years of education, the rate was 200.0 (Heron et al., 2009). The effect of education on health is not completely understood, but it appears to operate through such important mediators as health behaviors, access to care, place of residence, and ability to cope with stressful situations.

Low income and low educational attainment are also risk factors for homelessness, which is associated with poor health, including higher rates of human immunodeficiency virus (HIV), tuberculosis, hypertension, diabetes, substance abuse, and trauma. Homeless individuals also are more likely to experience complications from chronic diseases (Sadowski, Kee, VanderWeele, & Buchanan, 2009). These phenomena are due to several factors, including increased exposure to adverse environmental conditions, reduced access to regular medical care, prioritizing food and shelter above medical concerns, and exposure to violence (Sadowski et al., 2009). Not surprisingly, minority populations have higher rates of homelessness compared to White Americans, thereby contributing to racial disparities in health. A recent survey of homeless shelters in 16 cities found that 47% of residents were African American, a proportion higher than in the general population (United States Conference of Mayors, 2007).

Research clearly demonstrates that health differs by income, race, and ethnicity.

How Are Neighborhood Effects Identified?

Given the myriad factors that affect health, it is not surprising that particular neighborhood features, including health-care resources, the presence of green space for exercise, availability of healthy foods, quality of housing, norms and values, and crime all have been associated with health outcomes. But how important are these factors when compared to individual characteristics, such as genetic predisposition and health behaviors? That is, what are the relative health effects of contextual (i.e., neighborhood-level) characteristics compared with compositional (i.e., individual-level) characteristics? Contextual features include neighborhood norms and values, number of parks, quality of schools, and amount of crime in a given neighborhood. Compositional features include individual ethnicity, income, education, and health behaviors. One way to distinguish contextual from compositional effects is by performing multilevel analysis, a statistical approach that categorizes data by level (e.g., individual, classroom, school) and assesses the relative effect of each level on the outcome. If two communities differ in terms of an important health outcome, such as infant mortality, a key question addressed by multilevel analysis would be: Is the difference in infant mortality due to contextual factors (such as community health care resources or quality of community drinking water), or does the difference exist because mothers in these two communities are different in important ways (i.e., income, smoking behavior)? When contextual effects are found, it suggests that there is something about a community or neighborhood (e.g., contaminated drinking water) that exerts an effect on the outcome (e.g., cancer incidence) over and above the effects related to individual characteristics.

In the absence of obvious culprits, such as contaminated drinking water, multilevel analysis cannot always separate individual from community-level effects. For example, multilevel studies have demonstrated significant contextual effects on a variety of health outcomes, but the strength of these effects often is diminished when multiple individual characteristics are considered (Pickett & Pearl, 2001). This fact suggests that either the contextual effect is weak or the relationship between the contextual feature and the health outcome is mediated by one or more individual characteristics, such as diet or tobacco use. Although not negating neighborhood effects, their mediation by health behaviors makes contextual effects more difficult to identify.

Another way to distinguish contextual from compositional effects is to perform an experiment in which individuals living in a community are randomly assigned to either remain in the community or move to a new community with different characteristics. If both groups are similar with respect to individual characteristics at the beginning of the study, then postintervention interviews and analyses permit an assessment of the contextual effects on health. Such studies are difficult to perform because of financial and ethical constraints, but experiments of this type are occasionally undertaken. One example is the Moving to Opportunity (MTO) for Fair Housing Demonstration Program. Conducted by the U.S. Department of Housing and Urban Development, MTO is a randomized social experiment designed to assess the effects of moving out of poor neighborhoods. Families with very low incomes with children younger than 18 years living in public housing or private assisted housing in poor neighborhoods of five cities—Baltimore, Boston, Chicago, Los Angeles, and New York City—were eligible. Between 1994 and 1998, eligible families were randomly assigned to one of three groups: the experimental group, the Section 8 group, or the control group. Individuals in the experimental group were offered housing vouchers that could be used only in low-poverty areas. This group also received assistance finding and leasing units. In addition, to retain their vouchers, families were required to stay in their new neighborhoods for at least one year. Those in the Section 8 group

were offered housing vouchers with no restrictions on where the vouchers could be used and no assistance finding or leasing units. Control group members were not offered housing vouchers; they continued to live in public housing or receive project-based housing assistance (Orr et al., 2003).

In 2002, nearly 8,900 participating adults and children were contacted to assess follow-up status in several domains, including physical and mental health, child educational achievement, youth delinquency and risky behavior, and adult and youth employment and earnings. On average, individuals in the experimental and Section 8 groups reported significant increases in their perceptions of safety and substantial decreases in their risk of observing or being a victim of a crime. Compared with the control group, the intervention group also reported less difficulty getting police to respond to their calls and large reductions in the presence of abandoned buildings, public alcohol consumption, litter, trash, and graffiti.

Adult health differences noted on follow-up included significant reductions in the prevalence of obesity, psychological distress, and depression among the experimental but not the Section 8 group compared with the control group. Calmness and peacefulness were reportedly significantly increased in the experimental group. Among girls age 12 to 19 years, researchers noted reductions in psychological distress and generalized anxiety disorder in the experimental group compared with the control group. Among girls age 15 to 19 years, those in the experimental group were significantly less likely to use marijuana or smoke cigarettes compared with the control group (Orr et al., 2003).

MTO is important in that it assessed the relationship among neighborhood characteristics, health, and health behaviors. Because of randomization, those in the intervention group were not different from those in the control group. Therefore, differences noted in health and health behaviors were due to contextual factors, not individual differences. These results provide evidence that neighborhood features, including neighborhood wealth, can affect health independent of individual characteristics. In this case, greater availability of police and decreased exposure to crime and delinquency appear to have had a positive impact on psychological well-being.

MECHANISMS BY WHICH COMMUNITIES INFLUENCE HEALTH

An individual's social circumstances and physical environment represent two ways communities can influence health. *Social circumstances* include neighborhood educational level, employment, income disparities, poverty, crime, and social cohesion. A community in which social relationships are easy to make and maintain is likely to be a healthier environment than a community in which residents are afraid to venture from their homes because of concerns about crime. A study from the United Kingdom found that individuals who recently had a heart attack and who had a confidant or intimate partner were about half as likely to die or have a further cardiac event compared with similar patients without a confidant or partner (Dickens et al., 2004).

Number and type of social relationships also depend on neighborhood norms and expectations. Laumann, Ellingson, Mahay, Paik, and Youm (2004) recently documented this in four Chicago communities: one predominantly African American community on the South Side, one Mexican American community on the West Side, one mixed but predominantly Puerto Rican community on the Northwest Side, and one primarily White community on the North Side with large heterosexual and homosexual populations. Each neighborhood had distinct opportunities, or "markets," for social relationships, some more supportive of relational or committed encounters and others more amenable to transactional (i.e., relatively uncommitted and often short term) relationships. In this study, market type was influenced by the neighborhood's economy as well as the ethnicity and sexual orientation of its residents. For example, family, friends, and

church played an important role in forming committed relationships in Hispanic communities. In contrast, the transactional market in the North Side community was important for gay men but not for lesbians, who preferred the relational market.

Physical environment refers to sanitation; quality of housing, food, and water; and exposure to environmental toxins and pathogens. Public health and safety programs often monitor these environmental characteristics. Statistics regarding life expectancy and causes of death indicate that environmental problems pose less of a risk in developed countries compared with third-world countries. For example, the life expectancy of an infant born in 2006 in the United States is 80.2 years for females and 75.1 years for males, and the leading causes of death are heart disease (26%), cancer (23.1%), and stroke (5.7%) (Heron et al., 2009). The remaining causes, including chronic lung disease, accidents, diabetes, and infections, each account for fewer than 10% of deaths, and only a very small percentage of deaths are directly attributable to environmental conditions.

In contrast, the most common causes of childhood mortality in developing countries are related to communicable diseases. These include pneumonia, diarrheal diseases, malaria, measles, and HIV/AIDS (acquired immune deficiency disease) (World Health Organization [WHO], 2008). In 2009, the estimated life expectancy at birth was 62 years for females and 59 years for males. That year it was estimated that 80% of Haitians lived in poverty and the per capita gross domestic product (GDP) was $1,300. By comparison, the estimated poverty rate in the United States that year was 12% and the per capita GDP was $46,400. In 2000, the freshwater withdrawal rate per capita was 116 cubic meters per year in Haiti compared with 1,600 cubic meters per year in the United States (Central Intelligence Agency, 2010). Lack of potable water and inadequate sewage disposal are risk factors for infections such as hepatitis A, typhoid, and cholera; poor housing conditions and overcrowding are risk factors for airborne diseases, including influenza and tuberculosis. In Haiti, there were 299 cases of tuberculosis per 100,000 in 2006 compared with 4 cases per 100,000 in the United States that year (WHO, 2008).

It is important to remember that the relationship between national wealth and public health infrastructure is not always positive or linear. Living conditions and environmental quality also reflect national priorities and the relative amount of resources dedicated to public health programs. A comparison of the United States and Cuba is illustrative. Despite having a per capita GDP that is less than one-quarter that of the United States ($9,700 versus $46,400 in 2009), Cuban health statistics compare favorably. In Cuba, female life expectancy at birth is 79.85 years, and male life expectancy at birth is 75.19 years. At nine cases of tuberculosis per 100,000 per year, the Cuban tuberculosis rate is much closer to that of the United States than of Haiti. In fact, low-income communities in the United States with high numbers of immigrants have tuberculosis rates that exceed the Cuban rate. The tuberculosis rate among foreign-born U.S. residents was 18.6 per 100,000 in 2009 (Centers for Disease Control and Prevention, 2010). Despite fewer resources per capita, Cuba has developed a public health system that controls many of the environmentally associated diseases that plague third-world countries and continue to afflict low-income communities in the United States.

Although immunization against disease and separating drinking water from waste water continue to be important strategies in first-world countries, these countries have increasingly embraced the medical model of health care, which focuses on treatment of disease after it is established. Although this model has led to tremendous advances in surgery and medicine, the recent epidemics of obesity, hypertension, cardiovascular disease, and osteoarthritis in wealthy nations suggest that the pendulum may have swung too far away from disease prevention and toward disease intervention (Masi & Gehlert, 2009). Not only does the medical model deemphasize disease prevention, but treatment of disease after it is established is extremely expensive. Cuba often

is cited as an example of the health success that can be attained through public health practices. In 2006, the United States spent over $2 trillion on health care, or roughly $6,714 per person. In comparison, Cuba spent approximately $363 per person on health care and had health outcomes that were similar, if not better, than those in the United States (WHO, 2010).

The public health approach is effective not only because it controls infectious diseases but also because it addresses many of the social determinants of health. Shortfalls in medical care account for approximately 10% of early mortality, and adverse social circumstances and environmental exposures account for 15% and 5% of premature mortality, respectively, in first-world countries (McGinnis et al., 2002). In third-world countries, access to and quality of medical care as well as social circumstances and environmental exposures likely play much greater roles in early mortality. WHO refers to these factors as *social determinants of health* and defines them as access to high-quality health care, education, and housing as well as opportunities for social and economic flourishing (Commission on the Social Determinants of Health [CSDH], 2008). According to the CSDH, reduced access to these factors is due to a "toxic combination of poor social policies and programmes, unfair economic arrangements, and bad politics" (p. 1). Social determinants of health thus explain a major part of health inequities between and within countries. In its 2008 report, the CSDH delineates the political steps that are needed to address the social determinants of health and improve health in developing nations. Although this report does not mention neighborhood factors specifically, it is easy to imagine that new policies regarding health-care access and quality, education, and housing ultimately would be implemented and have effects at the community level.

Despite the nation's first-world status and emphasis on the medical model, some experts in the United States are beginning to advocate for changes in education, housing, and employment policies as ways to improve national health (Schoeni, House, Kaplan, & Pollack,

2008). To an increasing number of policy makers, it is apparent that whether a person exercises, eats a balanced diet, smokes, or engages in high-risk sexual practices is often a function of a neighborhood's social, economic, and physical environment. For example, studies have shown that adults are more likely to exercise in their neighborhood if they perceive it to be safe (Wilbur, Chandler, Dancy, & Lee, 2003) or if they have access to parks, trails, and other areas conducive to physical activity (Huston, Evenson, Bors, & Gizlice, 2003). Other studies have found that healthy foods, such as fruits and vegetables, are less available (Mooney, 1990; Morland, Wing, & Diez Roux, 2002) and more expensive (Sooman, MacIntyre, & Anderson, 1993) in poor neighborhoods compared with wealthy neighborhoods. Obesity has been linked to increased portion sizes and consumption of high-fat foods, such as those served at fast-food restaurants. One study of restaurant density found that people living in the poorest socioeconomic status category had 2.5 times the exposure to fast-food restaurants compared with those living in the wealthiest category (Reidpath, Burns, Garrard, Mahoney, & Townsend, 2001). In the United States, low-income individuals are exposed to more outdoor tobacco advertising than individuals with higher income (Hackbarth, Silvestri, & Cosper, 1995; Stoddard, Johnson, Sussman, Dent, & Boley-Cruz, 1998).

In addition, patterns of social relationships and sexual practices are tied to the economy and culture of the community. Laumann and colleagues (2004) found that residents of higher-income communities tend to meet their partners at school or work and form longer-term relationships more frequently than residents of lower-income communities. In contrast, residents of low-income communities are more likely to be in polygamous or short-term, transactional relationships. The links among poverty, prostitution, and sexually transmitted disease are well established and add to the disease burden of low-income communities (Edlund & Korn, 2002; Girard, 2000; Satz, 2003).

Access to medical care often reflects the resources and provider practices within particular communities. Newer tests and procedures may be available in urban areas long before they become standard practice in rural communities. For example, a recent study of U.S. patients with cardiac arrest found that survival differed markedly by location of arrest. The survival rate was 9% in rural areas, 14% in suburban areas, and 23% in urban sites. These differences were attributed to several factors related to the communities, including medical response time, transport time, resuscitative skill, and type of medical intervention (Vukmir, 2004). In a comparison of diabetes care in urban versus rural clinics in Alabama, Andrus, Kelley, Murphey, and Herndon (2004) found that rural patients were less likely to be at their goals for glycosylated hemoglobin (a measure of blood glucose control), cholesterol level, and blood pressure. Compared with their counterparts at urban clinics, these patients also were less likely to receive screening and preventive services, such as eye examinations, urinary protein screening, aspirin therapy, and vaccinations. In Mexico, the mortality rate from cervical cancer is 3 times higher in rural areas than it is in urban areas. In the rural state of Chiapas, the cervical cancer mortality relative risk was 10.99 times that of the risk in Mexico City. This difference has been attributed to lack of formal education and insufficient access to medical care (Palacio-Mejia, Rangel-Gomez, Hernandez-Avila, & Lazcano-Ponce, 2003).

Type and quality of care also differ markedly across urban settings in the United States. Studies of so-called small-area variations in care were pioneered by Dr. Jack Wennberg at Dartmouth in the 1980s. Since that time, the Dartmouth group has documented regional variations in Medicare spending, use of cancer screening tests, physician adherence to national health-care guidelines, and frequency of surgical procedures (McAndrew-Cooper, Wennberg, & Center for the Evaluative Clinical Sciences Staff,1999). For example, regional rates of mammography screening in the United States vary from 12.5% to over 50%, with women in the northeastern United States, Florida, and Michigan being more likely to receive mammography than women elsewhere. Annual screening for colorectal cancer also varies by geography, from 2.4% among Medicare enrollees in Terre Haute, IN, to 22.2% in Takoma Park, MD. In general, compliance with national colorectal cancer screening is higher in the East and South compared with the Midwest and West in the United States. Medicare enrollees in some areas of the country are also more likely to undergo coronary angiography and carotid endarterectomy than in others. A significant proportion of these procedures are performed unnecessarily. The Dartmouth group has shown that use of medical care resources often reflects capacity (i.e., number of physicians, number of hospital beds) more than need for care. The causes of these small-area variations are numerous and likely reflect the effects of prominent physicians who influence local practice through lectures and consultation (Wennberg et al., 1997).

There is growing evidence that societal factors also can influence the onset and course of several diseases, including type 2 diabetes mellitus, cancer, and cardiovascular disease. For example, obesity leads to insulin resistance, which is a significant trigger for type 2 diabetes mellitus. As the prevalence of obesity has increased in the United States, so too has the prevalence of diabetes. During the period from 1988 to 1994, 24.5% of U.S. adults were obese. By the period from 1999 to 2004, this proportion had increased to 32.1% (Lopez-Jimenez et al., 2009). Between 1988 to 2004, the percentage of adults in a national survey who reported being diagnosed with diabetes increased from 8.2% to 9.6% (Lopez-Jimenez et al., 2009). This study also revealed that diabetes rates vary by state in the United States. In the period from 2003 to 2006, the rate was 11.4% and 27.7% among those age 30 to 59 years and 60 years and older, respectively, in Mississippi and 6.5% and 19.3% among the same age groups, respectively, in Montana

(Danaei, Friedman, Oza, Murray, & Ezzati, 2009). The increasing prevalence of obesity appears to have several causes, including the decrease in cost of food as a percentage of income, a shift toward higher-calorie diets, and a decrease in physical activity (Philipson & Posner, 2003). State-to-state variation in cost of food, dietary patterns, and physical activity likely contribute to state differences in obesity and diabetes prevalence.

Not only can community resources affect diet and disease onset among adults, these same factors can affect disease onset in subsequent generations. For example, fetuses of diabetic mothers appear to be at higher risk of developing diabetes as adults. In a study of Pima Indians, the children of women with type 2 diabetes were more obese and had a higher rate of diabetes (50%) compared with the children of women who developed diabetes after the pregnancy (8.6%) (Pettitt, Nelson, Saad, Bennett, & Knowler, 1993). These findings suggest that predisposition to disease can be modified in utero by maternal diet and blood glucose control. This modification has been labeled fuel-mediated teratogenesis (Freinkel, 1980).

The "thrifty gene" hypothesis contends that higher rates of obesity and diabetes among ethnic minorities, including Pima Indians and African American populations in the United States and Aborigines in Australia, arise from a genetic predisposition to energy storage in abdominal fat in these populations. In times of famine or when diets consist of low-fat foods that are not nutrient dense, such a trait confers survival advantage. However, when food is plentiful (as in modern United States and Australia) and diets are high in carbohydrates and fats, efficient energy storage becomes a liability and leads to obesity. Although there is evidence for this theory, it is unclear whether a thrifty gene influences health outcomes among ethnic minorities to the same extent as other important factors, such as the dietary and psychological changes that can occur with discrimination and economic marginalization (McDermott, 1998).

COMMUNITY EFFECTS AND THE LIFE COURSE

The community effects described can impact individual health at any or all stages of the life course, including gestation, childhood, adolescence, adulthood, and end of life. Interest in community effects on health has spurred interest in health geography and area analysis of epidemiological data. Examples of studies that analyze the relationship between neighborhood or community characteristics and health outcomes at each stage of life are presented next.

Gestation

Because maternal health is a strong predictor of fetal and infant health, many investigators have examined the relationship between the social experience of pregnant women and the health of their newborns. In a study of 176 U.S. cities with a population of 50,000 or more, LaVeist (1989) found that mortality among African American infants was positively associated with the city's index of segregation. The mean morality rate in this study was 19.31 per 1,000 live births among African American infants and 11.09 per 1,000 live births among White infants. In cities with the lowest level of segregation, mortality among African American infants was almost 5% below the mean for all African American infants; in cities with the highest index of segregation, the rate was almost 3% above the overall mean. LaVeist suggested that higher African American infant mortality rates in highly segregated cities reflect older housing stock, higher levels of stress and environmental toxins, and reduced levels of city and medical care services in minority communities. According to LaVeist, these effects are ameliorated as the level of ethnic integration increases.

The notion that ambient stressors can adversely affect pregnancy outcomes is supported by several studies. In Santiago, Chile, women living in high-violence neighborhoods in 1985 and 1986 were 5 times more likely to experience pregnancy complications (including gestational hypertension, fetal growth retardation, and miscarriage) compared with women living in less violent neighborhoods (Zapata, Rebolledo, Atalah, Newman, & King, 1992). Collins and colleagues (1998) found the odds ratio of very low birth weight (less than 3.3 pounds) was 1.7 to 3.2 for African American mothers in Chicago who rated their neighborhoods unfavorably in terms of police protection, protection of property, personal safety, friendliness, delivery of municipal services, cleanliness, quietness, and schools compared with controls. Using multilevel statistical techniques, which account for maternal as well as neighborhood characteristics, another study found mean birth weight decreased among African American infants as the neighborhood level of economic disadvantage increased (Buka, Brennan, Rich-Edwards, Raudenbush, & Earls, 2003). Maternal factors considered in this study were number of times a woman has given birth, prenatal care, education, age, marital status, and smoking history. Neighborhood disadvantage reflected an aggregate measure of the proportion of residents in a neighborhood who lived below the poverty line, were on public assistance, or were unemployed. A similar multilevel analysis found a significant inverse association between birth weight and census-tract violent crime among African American, White, and Hispanic populations (Masi, Hawkley, Piotrowski, & Pickett, 2007).

The links between maternal psychological stress, preterm delivery (less than 37 weeks' gestation), and low birth weight (less than 5.5 pounds) are not well understood. We do know, however, that maternal stress can lead to increased fetal cortisol, a stress hormone that stimulates placental corticotropin-releasing hormone (Chrousos, Torpy, & Gold, 1998; Norwitz, Robinson, & Callis, 1999). Corticotropin-releasing hormone has been labeled a "placental clock" because elevations of this hormone appear to be crucial to the initiation of labor (McLean et al., 1995). Preterm delivery is the primary determinant of low birth weight, and both are risk factors for health problems later in life. Approximately three quarters of neonatal mortality and almost one half of long-term neurological impairment in children have been linked to preterm birth (Alexander, 1998). In a series of studies, Barker (1998) found evidence that low birth weight is a risk factor for coronary artery disease, stroke, diabetes, and hypertension later in life. These studies and others point to the importance of maternal health, including psychological well-being, to the health of offspring during infancy and later in life.

Childhood

Positive and negative childhood experiences can have both immediate and long-term health effects. These experiences usually reflect the child's care environment as well as neighborhood characteristics. Effects on health can be direct, involving physiologic pathways, or indirect, involving long-term health behaviors. Using a retrospective cohort design, Rauh, Parker, and Garfinkel (2003) found that third-grade reading scores in the New York City public schools were significantly related to both individual- and community-level predictors. At the individual level, male gender, low birth weight, unmarried mother, and low maternal education predicted lower reading scores. Controlling for individual-level risk, lower reading scores were significantly associated with concentrated community poverty, defined as more than 40% of families in the community living below the federally defined poverty level. Research suggests that preschool educational interventions lead to improved subsequent educational attainment and avoidance of high-risk health behaviors later in life (Heckman & Masterov, 2007).

Childhood exposure to lead dust is strongly associated with housing materials, which itself is related to the date of housing construction and neighborhood resources. Using National Health and Nutrition Examination Survey data from 1988 to 1994, Bernard and McGeehin (2003) found blood lead levels (BLL) were greater than or equal to 5 micrograms per deciliter (mcg/dL) in 42.5% of children living in housing built before 1946 but in only 14.1% of children living in housing built after

1973. In this study, non-Hispanic Black children were 3 times more likely to have BLL greater than or equal to 5 mcg/dL compared with non-Hispanic White children. Cognitive changes associated with lead toxicity include a decrease in IQ, distractibility, poor organizational skills, and hyperactivity. The effects of lead toxicity among children appear to be irreversible and may contribute to adverse behaviors, including delinquency and teen pregnancy (Bellinger, 2004).

Childhood maltreatment, including neglect, physical abuse, and sexual abuse, also appear to be related to community social organization. Coulton, Korbin, Su, and Chow (1995) found that the highest risk of maltreatment occurred among children who lived in neighborhoods characterized by poverty, high numbers of children per adult resident, population turnover, and concentration of female-headed households. The psychological and physiological effects of childhood maltreatment can be long lasting. In a study of 49 women age 18 to 45 years, Heim, Newport, and colleagues (2000) found that women with a history of childhood abuse demonstrated increased pituitary-adrenal and autonomic responses to stress compared with controls. Stress-related peak levels of adrenocorticotropic hormone (ACTH) were 6 times higher among women with a history of childhood abuse and current major depression compared with age-matched controls. Dysregulation of the hypothalamic-pituitary-adrenal (HPA) axis has been associated with several diseases in adults, including chronic fatigue syndrome, fibromyalgia, rheumatoid arthritis, and asthma (Heim, Ehlert, & Hellhammer, 2000). Developmental neurobiologists currently are examining pathways through which childhood stress and trauma influence brain development and function later in life (Teicher, Anderson, Polcari, Anderson, & Navalta, 2002).

Adolescence

Several studies have found positive associations among neighborhood socioeconomic status and adolescent educational attainment (including years of schooling completed), probability of completing high school, and likelihood of attending college (Leventhal & Brooks-Gunn, 2000). Depending on the study, neighborhood socioeconomic status comprises one or more of these community characteristics: percentage of college-educated residents, percentage of residents living below poverty, percentage of managerial/professional residents, high school dropout rate, levels of female family headship, and female employment. Coulton and Pandey (1992) found that teen birth and juvenile delinquency rates were higher among adolescents living in Cleveland census tracts in which more than 40% of the population lived below the poverty threshold.

An evaluation of a scattered-site public housing program in Yonkers, NY, revealed that youths who remained in low-income neighborhoods were more likely to have used marijuana in the prior year and show signs of problem drinking in the previous month compared with adolescents who moved to middle-income neighborhoods (Briggs, 1997). In the National Survey of Adolescent Males, a high rate of neighborhood unemployment was associated with impregnating someone and fathering a child (Ku, Sonenstein, & Pleck, 1993).

Mediation of the relationship between neighborhood characteristics and adolescent behaviors likely involves several pathways. In a review of this literature, Jencks and Mayer (1990) described five conceptual models or pathways of influence, each emphasizing a different neighborhood construct: institutional resources, collective socialization, contagion or epidemic effects, competition, and relative deprivation. In their study of 877 Los Angeles adolescents, Aneshensel and Sucoff (1996) found evidence for some of these effects. In this study, youth in low-socioeconomic-status (SES) neighborhoods perceived greater ambient crime, violence, drug use, and graffiti compared with youth living in neighborhoods with high SES. This effect was independent of individual SES, and the perception of neighborhood hazard was associated with symptoms of depression, anxiety, oppositional defiant

disorder, and conduct disorder. These results suggest that neighborhood characteristics can have important effects on adolescent physical health and social behavior.

Adulthood

Several dimensions of the neighborhood environment have been linked to illness and mortality among adults. These dimensions include crime rates, ratio of homeowners to renters, percentage of residents receiving public assistance, index of segregation, percentage of unemployment, percentage of households headed by women, income, education, collective efficacy, and housing value. As with studies of children and adolescents, the central question is whether neighborhoods truly influence health outcomes or if differences in health simply are due to differences in the residents' age, race/ethnicity, and health behaviors. In other words, do contextual effects exist above and beyond the compositional associations with health? As mentioned, one way to address this question is to perform multilevel analysis, which simultaneously accounts for individual- and neighborhood-level variables.

One of the earliest studies demonstrating a contextual, or area, effect examined mortality over a 9-year period in Alameda County, CA (Haan, Kaplan, & Camacho, 1987). From the 1,811 study participants, data were obtained regarding baseline health conditions, socioeconomic factors, health practices, social networks, and psychological factors. The researchers also noted if the participants lived in a designated poverty area. Analysis revealed the age-, sex-, and race-adjusted relative risk of mortality was 1.71 times higher among those living in poverty areas compared with those living in nonpoverty areas. The addition of baseline health conditions and other individual characteristics to the analysis lowered the relative risk of mortality slightly, but it remained significantly higher among poverty-area residents. The authors speculated that adverse health outcomes in poverty areas were mediated by higher crime rates, poorer housing, lack of transportation, higher levels of environmental contaminants, or a combination of these factors.

In another study, individual- and family-level information from the 1986 national Americans' Changing Lives study was linked to 1980 census information to assess the relative effects of personal and neighborhood characteristics on three health outcomes: number of chronic conditions experienced in the previous year, level of functional limitation, and self-rated health (Robert, 1998). The individual-level indicators were age, race, gender, and education, and the family-level indicators were income and level of assets. At the community level, four indicators were included: percentage of households receiving public assistance, percentage of families with an income of $30,000 or more, percentage of adult unemployment, and a composite index of the three.

Initial bivariate analysis indicated that education and family income were more highly correlated with all three measures of health compared with the community-level variables. Controlling for individual-level and family-level SES, the percentage of households receiving public assistance had an independent association with self-rated health. In addition, percentage of families earning $30,000 or more, percentage of adult unemployment, and a composite economic disadvantage index each had associations with several chronic conditions when individual- and family-level SES were controlled. Robert (1998) concluded that while individual-level variables are stronger predictors of health, community-level indicators appear to have significant associations with health.

LeClere, Rogers, and Peters (1998) used multilevel analysis to assess neighborhood effects on female heart disease mortality. Data from the National Health Interview Survey (1986–1990) were linked to death certificate information from the National Death Index and the 1990 U.S. census at the census tract level. Individual-level information from the National Health Interview Survey included age, race, body mass index, preexisting conditions, income, education, marital status,

and employment status. Census information included percentage of families in the census tract headed by women, percentage of persons in the census tract who were Black, median family income, percentage of households who received public assistance, and unemployment rate.

For both White Americans and African Americans, heart disease rates were higher in the poorest census tracts. Adjusting for individual-level characteristics in the multilevel model, this study found that women living in communities where more than one quarter of the families were headed by women were more likely to die of heart disease compared with women who lived in neighborhoods with fewer female-headed households. The authors hypothesized that neighborhoods with high proportions of female-headed households may be associated with increased financial, physical, and emotional stress. Stress and other psychosocial risk factors may contribute to heart disease either directly, through acceleration of the atherosclerotic process, or indirectly, through adverse coping behaviors, such as smoking, increased caloric intake, or increased alcohol intake (Williams, Barefoot, & Schneiderman, 2003).

These studies provide evidence that the neighborhood environment exerts an effect on health independent of individual characteristics. However, as more individual characteristics are included in multilevel models, the neighborhood effects on health seem to diminish. In addition, some neighborhood effects may be more deleterious than others. Among the studies reviewed, the most commonly cited culprits are poor housing quality, exposure to toxins, and psychological stress.

End of Life

Among older individuals, the intensity of medical care received at the end of life varies by community. McAndrew-Cooper and colleagues (1999) used 1995–1996 Medicare billing information to compare frequency and types of care delivered to older adults in the last six months of life. They found that end-of-life issues "are resolved in ways that depend on where the patient happens to live, not on the patient's preferences or the power of care to extend life" (p. 42). For example, in some communities, the chance of being hospitalized at the time of death was 20%; in other communities, this proportion was 50%. During the last 6 months of life, the chance of spending a week or more in an intensive care unit also varied by community, ranging from less than 4% to over 20% of patients. The number of physicians who care for patients in the last 6 months of life, also called "intensity of care," varies by community. In some areas, 30% of patients were seen by 10 or more physicians, whereas in other areas, fewer than 3% received care from this number. Interestingly, variations in intensity of care reflected amount of health-care resources more than underlying levels of illness in the community. Also, variations in intensity of care did not predict improved outcomes. That is, mortality rates among older sick individuals were not lower in communities providing more intensive medical care.

McAndrew-Cooper and colleagues (1999) acknowledged that while mortality was not associated with intensity of care, increased spending and services at the end of life may be associated with improved comfort measures and quality of death. Comfort measures are obviously desirable, but do most people want to be in an intensive care unit at the end of life? A study of patients with life-threatening illnesses indicated that 82% would prefer to die at home rather than in the hospital if they were told by their physician they had "very little time to live" (SUPPORT Principal Investigators, 1995). Given the results of these studies, it appears that some communities are better at allocating resources and addressing the needs and wishes of gravely ill Medicare recipients than others.

IMPLICATIONS FOR SOCIAL WORK PRACTICE

The studies reviewed in this chapter suggest that neighborhoods can influence health positively by providing access to high-quality medical care, healthy foods, and green space for exercise as well as by minimizing exposure to crime, toxins, and infectious disease. Neighborhoods also can negatively influence health through poor housing stock, exposure to chemical and biological pathogens, decreased access to medical care, promotion of adverse health behaviors, and ambient psychological stressors. These effects raise important questions for social work practice. For example, from a social work perspective, is it more efficient to help individuals improve their living situation on a case-by-case basis or through community-wide interventions? If a neighborhood is physically or psychologically unhealthy, does it make more sense to help individuals move out of the neighborhood or to advocate community change? The answers to these questions are reflected in the diversity of strategies currently used by social workers. That is, some social workers address problems at the individual level, others work for change at the community level, and still others do both. Neighborhood improvement is a slow process and often requires political, administrative, and community organizing abilities. Providing services to individuals also requires administrative ability as well as knowledge of resources and persistence. Both community- and individual-level development strategies are essential, and both should be supported to a greater extent by public policy.

MacIntyre, MacIver, and Sooman (1993) believe neighborhood improvement has received short shrift in the policy arena. They argue that unhealthy behaviors and many diseases arise from adverse environments and that improvements in the physical and social environment can lead to improved health behaviors and health. Instead of encouraging working-class populations to act more like middle-class populations, MacIntyre and colleagues believe that public policy should foster the transformation of working-class neighborhoods into middle-class neighborhoods.

However, garnering support for investment in low-income communities is time consuming and often is viewed as a low priority by private and public institutions. Even when support is obtained and a plan is in place for community improvement, several pitfalls must be avoided. One of them is the population displacement that can occur with gentrification. For example, a $150 million project to build 550 new single-family homes in Chicago's economically depressed Englewood neighborhood was opposed by some working-class and senior residents who were concerned that rent and property tax increases would force them out. Although about 20% of the proposed homes were set aside for low-income families, local residents were concerned that overall housing costs would be too high (Olivo, 2004). These concerns turned out to be valid, as the low-income units were designed for families earning up to 100% of the Chicago Area Median Family Income, which was $72,400 in 2008. At that time, the median family income in Englewood was $34,902, effectively making the low-income units inaccessible to the average Englewood community resident (Developing Government Accountability to the People Network, 2008). This example demonstrates that although neighborhood improvement can be beneficial for many, the unintended consequences for low- and fixed-income residents must be considered.

Helping individuals or families find housing in healthy environments is an important service provided by many social workers. In some cases, such assistance can mean the difference between health and illness or even life and death. But relocation also has pitfalls. Moving to a new neighborhood can lead to disruption of social networks and loss of support systems. Minorities or individuals with lower incomes also may feel stressed in high-income neighborhoods, especially if there is little ethnic or economic diversity. Analyzing 11 years of data from Alameda County, CA, Yen and Kaplan (1999) found that low-income individuals living in a neighborhood with high SES had significantly higher mortality rates compared with low-income individuals living in neighborhoods with low SES. The authors hypothesize that differential access to resources and psychological stress contributed to this disparity. The implication for social workers

and other service providers is that relocation is not without cost, and every effort should be made to help individuals access services and develop support networks in their new communities.

An additional cost of relocation can be incurred by those who remain in impoverished communities. Typically, individuals who leave economically depressed neighborhoods are either employed or have higher levels of education and job skills. Out-migration of human capital means that those who remain have fewer community resources and fewer successful role models (Wilson, 1996). This can result in further community deterioration, including loss of educational and health-care services and exacerbation of health problems among those left behind.

This problem is mitigated partially if all members of a community leave or are relocated. For example, the Chicago Housing Authority recently relocated all residents of the Robert Taylor Homes (a series of 28 high-rise public housing buildings on Chicago's South Side) to subsidized housing throughout the city. The subsidized housing includes mixed-income units being constructed on the site of the former Robert Taylor Homes. In contrast to neighborhoods that have suffered from out-migration of social capital, this program will result in the evolution of an impoverished area into a middle-class community. However, it will occur at the expense of near complete turnover of neighborhood residents and the disruption of many family and social network ties.

Neighborhood change in the other direction (from middle class to working class) also can occur when economic and ethnic integration occurs too rapidly. The early history of Chicago's Englewood neighborhood is an example. In the first half of the 20th century, Englewood was a popular destination for German, Swedish, and Irish immigrants pursuing the American dream of home ownership. When African American residents moved to Englewood to pursue the same dream in the 1960s and 1970s, "White flight" ensued, and the population decreased from 90,000 in 1960 to 40,000 in 2000 (Kouvelis et al., 2003). Majority exodus when a tipping point is reached is a common problem and presents a recurring challenge for politicians and community planners. How can neighborhoods be integrated without inducing rapid turnover and without incurring property tax and rent increases that overburden low-income residents? In her study of the history of integration, Cashin (2004) notes that rapid neighborhood turnover is less likely to occur when the minority percentage does not exceed a certain proportion or when three or more ethnic groups coexist, none more dominant than the other. Although integration control is not always necessary, many communities closely monitor the status and effects of integration. Some have done so to enhance integration while others have done so to discourage it. Working at planning and administrative levels, social workers can monitor and help influence patterns of integration in their own communities. They also can help families and individuals negotiate the often arcane rules of subsidized housing and ensure that new residents have access to community resources.

Another strategy to improve neighborhoods is through Empowerment Zones—economic development programs begun during the Clinton administration. Through this initiative, urban Empowerment Zones (EZs) and Enterprise Communities receive federal tax credits and Block Grants to design and fund economic development, housing, job training, and social programs (Dixon, 2000). Since 1993, this program has had several successes, including the creation of new businesses, job-training programs, and new or rehabilitated housing for homeless persons. However, a perception exists that ineffective oversight and improper handling of funds have limited the success of this program (McDavid, 1998). Many community residents report that EZ funds have not reached the street level, where they are needed most (Dixon, 2000). In collaboration with administrators and community leaders, social workers can help ensure that EZ jobs and resources reach the street level and provide resources to small business owners, entrepreneurs, and job seekers. All citizens should take an interest in taxpayer-funded programs

such as the EZ initiative. Social workers have the training and skills to monitor and deploy them as originally designed.

A recent report indicates that approximately 3.5 million Americans are likely to experience homelessness in a given year (National Coalition for Homelessness, 2009). As a result, 860 cities and counties have enacted 10-year plans to end homelessness, and 49 states have created Interagency Councils on Homelessness (Interagency Council on Homelessness, 2009). Social workers can play important roles in reducing the adverse health effects of homelessness, as demonstrated by two recent studies. In the first, homeless individuals treated in emergency rooms were randomized to long-term housing and social worker–directed case management versus usual care, which consisted of standard discharge planning (Sadowski et al., 2009). After 18 months, individuals in long-term housing had fewer emergency department visits, fewer hospitalizations, and fewer days spent in the hospital. In a similar study of homeless emergency room patients with HIV, a higher proportion of individuals who entered long-term housing and received social worker–directed case management were alive at one year compared with the usual care group, who received standard discharge planning (Buchanan, Kee, Sadowski, Garcia, 2009).

Using progressive taxation policies, many nations in Europe have had success in pursuing economic parity. These policies have enhanced social security and reduced income-related health differences. Published in 1998, Britain's Acheson report on health disparities recommends specific steps to reduce these disparities further, including increased cash and services to poor women, expectant mothers, children, and elderly people. Additional resources for schools and job training programs as well as improved housing for the poor are also recommended (Acheson, 1998). In the United States, many politicians decry the "offshoring" of jobs to low-wage locales and have called for tax incentives to retain American jobs. Some of these efforts reflect increasing recognition of the growing disparities in employment, income, and community resources in the United States. Whether this rhetoric reflects an appreciation of the link between neighborhood characteristics and health remains to be seen, but efforts in this direction have gained momentum in other countries and some argue that they also should be supported in the United States.

Social workers can play a key role in advocating economic reform and directing community improvement. As professionals who work on the front lines, social workers observe firsthand the effects of unemployment, low wages, and lack of health insurance. Inability to afford housing, strained family relationships, and deferred treatment for illnesses are just a few of the outcomes social workers encounter on a daily basis. Recognizing the need for systemic change, social workers often lead the way in bringing attention to resource-poor communities. This attention can occur in many ways, including through community-based participatory research (CBPR). CBPR is a powerful tool for initiating change because it identifies community resources, needs, and solutions, with community stakeholders who are experiencing problems. Developed over the past two decades, the key features of CBPR are that it:

- Recognizes a community as a unit of identity
- Builds on strengths and resources within the community
- Facilitates collaborative, equitable involvement of all partners in all phases of the research
- Integrates knowledge and action for mutual benefit of all partners
- Promotes a collaborative and empowering process that attends to social inequalities
- Involves a cyclical and iterative process
- Addresses health from both positive and ecological perspectives
- Disseminates findings and knowledge gained to all partners
- Involves a long-term commitment by all partners (Israel, Schulz, Parker, & Becker, 2001)

Recent studies have used CBPR to raise awareness of the importance of community characteristics to health outcomes, including the built environment and health (Redwood et al., 2010), health-care resources and breast cancer treatment (Masi & Gehlert, 2009), and the role of tribal customs in promoting health and preventing substance abuse (Thomas, Donovan, Sigo, Austin, & Marlatt, 2009). Other ways in which social workers can advocate reform and enhance community capacity include testifying before city and state legislatures, writing editorials in local newspapers, highlighting deficient city services, and forming community-based service organizations.

A large volume of evidence indicates that individual health is influenced by community characteristics and resources. Because so many communities face economic and resource challenges, the opportunities for social workers to have a significant impact are enormous. This impact can occur at the individual level as well as at the community and national levels. Whatever strategy is chosen, those who strive to improve the social and physical environment of others can be assured that such efforts will have long-lasting and significant health benefits.

SUGGESTED LEARNING EXERCISES

Learning Exercise 7.1

Identify the characteristics of a local neighborhood that appear to have the most important effects on the health of its residents.

Learning Exercise 7.2

List the physical, social, and health-care needs of individuals who live in an economically depressed community.

Learning Exercise 7.3

Compare and contrast the advantages and disadvantages of the public health and medical models of health care.

Learning Exercise 7.4

List the advantages of community-based participatory research in identifying community resources, needs, and solutions.

Learning Exercise 7.5

Describe the potential impact of education, employment, housing, and food policy on health outcomes in the United States.

SUGGESTED RESOURCES

Berkman, L. F., & Kawachi, I. (Eds.). (2000). *Social epidemiology.* New York, NY: Oxford University Press.

Commission on the Social Determinants of Health. (2008). *Closing the gap in a generation: Health equity through action on the social determinants of health.* Geneva, Switzerland: World Health Organization.

Diez Roux, A. V. (2001). Investigating neighborhood and area effects on health. *American Journal of Public Health, 91,* 1783–1789.

Ellen, I. G., Mijanovich, T., & Dillman, K. (2001). Neighborhood effects on health: Exploring the links and assessing the evidence. *Journal of Urban Affairs, 23*(3/4), 391–408.

Schoeni, R. F., House, J. S., Kaplan, G. A., & Pollack, H. (Eds.). (2008). *Making Americans healthier: Social and economic policy as health policy.* New York, NY: Russell Sage.

World Health Organization: http://www .who.int/en/

REFERENCES

Acheson, D. (1998). *Independent inquiry into inequalities in health report.* London, UK: Her Majesty's Stationery Office.

Alexander, G. R. (1998). Preterm birth: Etiology, mechanisms, and prevention. *Prenatal and Neonatal Medicine, 3,* 3–9.

Andrus, M. R., Kelley, K. W., Murphey, L. M., & Herndon, K. C. (2004). A comparison of diabetes care in rural and urban medical clinics in Alabama. *Journal of Community Health, 29*(1), 29–44.

Aneshensel, C. S., & Sucoff, C. A. (1996). The neighborhood context of adolescent mental health. *Journal of Health and Social Behavior, 37*(4), 293–310.

Barker, D. (1998). *Mothers, babies and health in later life.* London, UK: Churchill Livingstone.

Bellinger, D. C. (2004). Lead. *Pediatrics, 113*(4), 1016–1022.

Bernard, S. M., & McGeehin, M. A. (2003). Prevalence of blood lead levels >5 mu g/dL among U.S. children 1 to 5 years of age and socioeconomic and demographic factors associated with blood lead levels of 5 to 10 mu g/dL. Third National Health and Nutrition Examination Survey, 1988–1994. *Pediatrics, 112*(6), 1308–1313.

Briggs, X. S. (Ed.). (1997). *Yonkers revisited: The early impacts of scattered-site public housing on families and neighborhoods.* New York, NY: Teachers College.

Buchanan, D., Kee, R., Sadowski, L. S., & Garcia, D. (2009). The health impact of supportive housing for HIV-positive homeless patients: A randomized controlled trial. *American Journal of Public Health, 99,* S675–S680.

Buka, S. L., Brennan, R. T., Rich-Edwards, J. W., Raudenbush, S. W., & Earls, F. (2003). Neighborhood support and the birth weight of urban infants. *American Journal of Epidemiology, 157*(1), 1–8.

Cashin, S. (2004). *The failures of integration: How race and class are undermining the American dream.* New York, NY: Public Affairs.

Centers for Disease Control and Prevention. (2010). Decrease in reported tuberculosis cases—United States, 2009. *Morbidity and Mortality Weekly Report, 59*(10), 289–294.

Central Intelligence Agency. (2010). *The world factbook.* Washington, DC: Office of Public Affairs.

Chapin, C. (1924). Deaths among taxpayers and non-taxpayers in Providence, RI, 1865. *American Journal of Public Health, 9,* 647–651.

Chrousos, G. P., Torpy, D. J., & Gold, P. W. (1998). Interactions between the hypothalamic-pituitary-adrenal axis and the female reproductive system: Clinical implications. *Annals of Internal Medicine, 129,* 229–240.

Collins, J. W., David, R. J., Symons, R., Hadler, A., Wall, S., & Andes, S. (1998). African-American mothers' perception of their residential environment, stressful life events, and very low birthweight. *Epidemiology, 9*(3), 286–289.

Commission on the Social Determinants of Health. (2008). *Closing the gap in a generation: Health equity through action on the social determinants of health.* Geneva, Switzerland: World Health Organization.

Coulton, C. J., Korbin, J. E., Su, M., & Chow, J. (1995). Community level factors and child maltreatment rates. *Child Development, 66,* 1262–1276.

Coulton, C. K., & Pandey, S. (1992). Geographic concentration of poverty and risk to children in urban neighborhoods. *American Behavioral Scientist, 35*(3), 238–257.

Danaei, G., Friedman, A. B., Oza, S., Murray, C. J. L., & Ezzati, M. (2009). Diabetes prevalence and diagnosis in US states: Analysis of health surveys. *Population Health Metrics, 7*(16), 1–13.

Developing Government Accountability to the People Network. (2008). *Local implementation: Chicago, Illinois: Response to the periodic report of the United States to the United Nations Committee on the Elimination of Racial Discrimination.* Chicago, IL: Author.

Dickens, C. M., McGowan, L., Percival, C., Douglas, J., Tomenson, B., Cotter, L., . . . Creed, F. H. (2004). Lack of a close confidant, but not depression, predicts further cardiac events after myocardial infarction. *Heart, 90,* 518–522.

Dixon, J. (2000, January 17). Residents in Detroit's empowerment zone see no progress in 5 years. *Detroit Free Press.* Retrieved from www.freep.com/news /locway/dzone17_20000117.htm

Edlund, L., & Korn, E. (2002). A theory of prostitution. *Journal of the Political Economy, 110*(1), 181–214.

Freinkel, N. (1980). Of pregnancy and progeny. *Diabetes, 29,* 1023–1035.

Girard, M. (2000). Emerging infectious diseases. *Medicine Sciences, 16*(8/9), 883–891.

Haan, M., Kaplan, G. A., & Camacho, T. (1987). Poverty and health: Prospective evidence from the Alameda County Study. *American Journal of Epidemiology, 125*(6), 989–998.

Hackbarth, D. P., Silvestri, B., & Cosper, W. (1995). Tobacco and alcohol billboards in 50 Chicago neighborhoods: Market segmentation to sell dangerous products to the poor. *Journal of Public Health Policy, 16,* 213–230.

Heckman, J. J., & Masterov, D. V. (2007). The productivity argument for investing in young children. *Review of Agricultural Economics, 29*(3), 446–493.

Heim, C., Ehlert, U., & Hellhammer, D. H. (2000). The potential role of hypocortisolism in the pathophysiology of stress-related bodily disorders. *Psychoneuroendocrinology, 25,* 1–25.

Heim, C., Newport, D. J., Heit, S., Graham, Y. P., Wilcox, M., Bonsall, R., . . . Nemeroff, C. B. (2000). Pituitary-adrenal and autonomic responses to stress in women after sexual and physical abuse in childhood. *JAMA, 284*(5), 592–597.

Heron, M., Hoyert, D. L., Murphy, S. L., Xu, J., Kochanek, K. D., & Tejada-Vera, B. (2009). Deaths: Final data for 2006. *National Vital Statistics Reports, 57*(14), 1–135.

Huston, S. L., Evenson, K. R., Bors, P., & Gizlice, Z. (2003). Neighborhood environment, access to places for activity, and leisure-time physical activity in a diverse North Carolina population. *American Journal of Health Promotion, 18*(1), 58–69.

Interagency Council on Homelessness. (2009). Home page. Retrieved from www.ich.gov

Israel, B.A., Schulz, A.J., Parker, E.A., & Becker, A.B. (2001). Community-based participatory research: Policy recommendations for promoting a partnership approach in health research. *Education for Health, 14,* 182–197.

Jencks, C., & Mayer, S. (1990). The social consequences of growing up in a poor neighborhood. In L. E. Lynn & M. F. H. McGeary (Eds.), *Inner-city poverty in the United States* (pp. 111–186). Washington, DC: National Academy Press.

Kouvelis, A., Harper, D. M., & Thomas, S. (2003). *Community area health inventory, 1989–1999.* Chicago, IL: Chicago Department of Public Health.

Krieger, N. (2001). Theories for social epidemiology in the twenty-first century: An ecosocial perspective. *International Journal of Epidemiology, 30*(4), 668–677.

Ku, L., Sonenstein, F. L., & Pleck, J. H. (1993). Neighborhood, family, and work: Influences on the premarital behaviors of adolescent males. *Social Forces, 72,* 479–503.

Laumann, E. O., Ellingson, S., Mahay, J., Paik, A., & Youm, Y. (Eds.). (2004). *The sexual organization of the city.* Chicago, IL: University of Chicago Press.

LaVeist, T. A. (1989). Linking residential segregation to the infant mortality race disparity in U.S. cities. *Social Science Review, 73*(2), 90–94.

LeClere, F. B., Rogers, R. G., & Peters, K. (1998). Neighborhood social context and racial differences in women's heart disease mortality. *Journal of Health and Social Behavior, 39,* 91–107.

Leventhal, T., & Brooks-Gunn, J. (2000). The neighborhoods they live in: The effects of neighborhood residence on child and adolescent outcomes. *Psychological Bulletin, 126*(2), 309–337.

Lopez-Jimenez, F., Batsis, J. A., Roger, V. L., Brekke, L., Ting, H. H., & Somers, V. K. (2009). Trends in 10-year predicted risk of cardiovascular disease in the United States, 1976–2004. *Circulation: Cardiovascular Quality and Outcomes, 2,* 443–450.

MacIntyre, S., MacIver, S., & Sooman, A. (1993). Area, class and health: Should we be focusing on places or people? *Journal of Social Policy, 22*(2), 213–234.

Masi, C. M., & Gehlert, S. (2009). Perceptions of breast cancer treatment among African American women and men: Implications for interventions. *Journal of General Internal Medicine, 24*(3), 408–414.

Masi, C. M., Hawkley, L. C., Piotrowski, Z. H., & Pickett, K. E. (2007). Neighborhood economic disadvantage, violent crime, group density, and pregnancy outcomes in a diverse, urban population. *Social Science & Medicine, 65,* 2440–2457.

McAndrew-Cooper, M., Wennberg, J. E., & Center for the Evaluative Clinical Sciences Staff. (1999). *The Dartmouth Atlas of Health Care 1999.* Chicago, IL: American Hospital Association.

McDavid, N. L. (1998, October). HUD auditing empowerment zone. *Chicago Reporter.* Retrieved from http:// www.chicagoreporter.com/index.php/c/Inside_Stories /d/HUD_Auditing_Empowerment_Zone

McDermott, R. (1998). Ethics, epidemiology and the thrifty gene: Biological determinism as a health hazard. *Social Science and Medicine, 47*(9), 1189–1195.

McGinnis, J. M., Williams-Russo, P., & Knickman, J. R. (2002). The case for more active policy attention to health promotion. *Health Affairs, 21*(2), 78–93.

McLean, M., Bisits, A., Davies, J., Woods, R., Lowry, P., & Smith, R. (1995). A placental clock controlling the length of human pregnancy. *Nature Medicine, 1*(5), 460–463.

Mooney, C. (1990). Cost and availability of healthy food choices in a London health district. *Journal of Human Nutrition and Dietetics, 3,* 111–120.

Morland, K., Wing, S., & Diez Roux, A. (2002). The contextual effect of the local food environment on residents' diets: The Atherosclerosis Risk in Communities Study. *American Journal of Public Health, 92,* 1761–1768.

Mumford Center. (2001). Ethnic diversity grows, neighborhood integration lags behind. Retrieved from www.albany.edu/mumford/census

National Coalition for Homelessness. (2009). How many people experience homelessness? Retrieved from www.nationalhomeless.org/factsheets/How_Many .html

Norwitz, E. R., Robinson, J. N., & Callis, J. R. G. (1999). The control of labor. *New England Journal of Medicine, 341*(1), 660–666.

Olivo, A. (2004, May 6). Englewood rebirth plan brings hope and anxiety. *Chicago Tribune,* p. 1, 32.

Orfield, G. (2001). Schools more separate: Consequences of a decade of resegregation. The Civil Rights Project, Harvard University. Retrieved from www .civilrightsproject.ucla.edu/research/k-12-education /integration-and-diversity/schools-more-separate -consequences-of-a-decade-of-resegregation/?search term=resegregation

Orr, L., Feins, J. D., Jacob, R., Beecroft, E., Sanbonmatsu, L., Katz, L. F.,…Kling, J. R. (2003). Moving to opportunity for fair housing demonstration: Interim impacts evaluation. Retrieved from www.huduser.org /Publications/pdf/MTOFullReport.pdf

Palacio-Mejia, L. S., Rangel-Gomez, G., Hernandez-Avila, M., & Lazcano-Ponce, E. (2003). Cervical cancer, a disease of poverty: Mortality differences between urban and rural areas in Mexico. *Salud Publica De Mexico, 45*(Suppl. 3), S315–S325.

Pettitt, D. J., Nelson, R. G., Saad, M. F., Bennett, P. H., & Knowler, W. C. (1993). Diabetes and obesity in the offspring of Pima Indian women with diabetes during pregnancy. *Diabetes Care, 16,* 482–486.

Philipson, T. J., & Posner, R. A. (2003). The long-run growth in obesity as a function of technological change. *Perspectives in Biology and Medicine, 46*(Suppl. 3), S87–S107.

Pickett, K., & Pearl, M. (2001). Multilevel analyses of neighborhood socioeconomic context and health outcomes: A critical review. *Journal of Epidemiology and Community Health, 55,* 111–122.

Pleis, J. R., & Lucas, J. W. (2009). *Summary health statistics for U.S. adults: National Health Interview Survey, 2007.* Washington, DC: National Center for Health Statistics.

Porter, N. (1997). *The greatest benefit to mankind: A medical history of humanity.* New York, NY: Norton.

Rauh, V. A., Parker, F. L., & Garfinkel, R. S. (2003). Biological, social, and community influences on third-grade reading levels of minority head start children: A multilevel approach. *Journal of Community Psychology, 31*(3), 255–278.

Redwood, Y., Schulz, A. J., Israel, B. A., Yoshihama, M., Wang, C., & Kreuter, M. (2010). Social, economic, and political processes that create built environment inequities: Perspectives from urban African Americans in Atlanta. *Family & Community Health, 33*(1), 53–67.

Reidpath, D. D., Burns, C., Garrard, J., Mahoney, M., & Townsend, M. (2001). An ecological study of the relationship between social and environmental determinants of obesity. *Health and Place, 8,* 141–145.

Robert, S. A. (1998). Community-level socioeconomic status effects on adult health. *Journal of Health and Social Behavior, 139,* 18–37.

Sadowski, L. S., Kee, R. A., VanderWeele, T. J., & Buchanan, D. (2009). Effect of housing and case management on emergency department visits and hospitalizations among chronically ill homeless adults: A randomized trial. *JAMA, 301*(17), 1771–1778.

Satz, D. (2003). Child labor: A normative perspective. *World Bank Economic Review, 17*(2), 297–309.

Schoeni, R. F., House, J. S., Kaplan, G. A., & Pollack, H. (Eds.). (2008). *Making Americans healthier: Social and economic policy as health policy.* New York, NY: Russell Sage.

Sooman, A., MacIntyre, S., & Anderson, A. (1993). Scotland's health: A more difficult challenge for some? The price and availability of healthy foods in socially contrasting localities in the West of Scotland. *Health Bulletin, 51,* 276–284.

Stoddard, J. L., Johnson, C. A., Sussman, S., Dent, C., & Boley-Cruz, T. (1998). Tailoring outdoor tobacco advertising to minorities in Los Angeles County. *Journal of Health Communication, 3,* 137–146.

SUPPORT Principal Investigators. (1995). A controlled trial to improve care for seriously ill hospitalized patients. *JAMA, 274,* 1591–1598.

Teicher, M. H., Anderson, S. L., Polcari, A., Anderson, C. M., & Navalta, C. P. (2002). Developmental neurobiology of childhood stress and trauma. *Psychiatric Clinics of North America, 25*(2), 397–426.

Thomas, L. R., Donovan, D. M., Sigo, R. L. W., Austin, L., & Marlatt, G. A. (2009). The community pulling together: A tribal-university partnership project to reduce substance abuse and promote good health in a reservation tribal community. *Journal of Ethnicity in Substance Abuse, 8*(3), 1–13.

United States Conference of Mayors. (2007). *A status report on hunger and homelessness in America's cities: A 23-city survey.* Washington, DC: Author.

Vukmir, R. B. (2004). The influence of urban, suburban, or rural locale on survival from refractory prehospital cardiac arrest. *American Journal of Emergency Medicine, 22*(2), 90–93.

Wennberg, D. E., Dickens, J. D., Biener, L., Fowler, F. J., Soule, D. N., & Keller, R. B. (1997). Do physicians do what they say? The inclination to test and its association with coronary angiography rates. *Journal of General Internal Medicine, 12,* 172–176.

Wilbur, J., Chandler, P. J., Dancy, B., & Lee, H. (2003). Correlates of physical activity in urban Midwestern African-American women. *American Journal of Preventive Medicine, 25*(2), 45–52.

Williams, R. B., Barefoot, J. C., & Schneiderman, N. (2003). Psychosocial risk factors for cardiovascular disease: More than one culprit at work. *JAMA, 290*(16), 2190–2192.

Wilson, W. J. (1996). *When work disappears: The world of the new urban poor.* New York, NY: Random House.

World Health Organization. (2008). *World health statistics 2008.* Geneva, Switzerland: Author.

World Health Organization (2010). Countries. Retrieved from http://who.int/countries

Yen, I. H., & Kaplan, G. A. (1999). Neighborhood social environmental and risk of death: Multilevel evidence from the Alameda County Study. *American Journal of Epidemiology, 149,* 898–907.

Zapata, B. C., Rebolledo, A., Atalah, E., Newman, B., & King, M. (1992). The influence of social and political violence on the risk of pregnancy complications. *American Journal of Public Health, 82,* 685–690.

8

Physical and Mental Health: Interactions, Assessment, and Interventions

MALITTA ENGSTROM

Interactions between physical and mental health are among the most complex issues that are brought to social workers in health-care settings. The complexity stems from the dynamic mind–body relationship; the numerous possible combinations of physical and mental health conditions; differentiation of psychological reactions to physical illness; psychological effects of physical conditions and treatments and psychiatric disorders; intervention during mental health crises; and provision of ongoing intervention to support physical and mental well-being. While considering these issues, the social worker formulates assessments and offers interventions that reflect the unique family and ecological contexts of people in their environments. With particular focus on differential assessment, this chapter provides guidance for social workers navigating these complexities.

It is important to recognize the limitations inherent in using the terms *physical health* and *mental health* (U.S. Department of Health and Human Services [DHHS], 1999, p. 5). This language implies a false division of these related elements of overall health (Angell, 2002; DHHS, 1999; Kerson, 2002). In fact, these two elements are not only interrelated but also exert mutual influences on each other (Rolland, 1994). Recognizing this mutual influence and the ongoing emergence of knowledge about the mind–body connection, this chapter uses these terms for both illustrative purposes and toward the goal of developing knowledge with adequate specificity so that practitioners can engage effectively

in evidence-based assessment and intervention (Angell, 2002; Williams, 1998).

Chapter Objectives
- Provide a framework for considering the intersections of health, psychosocial well-being, and ecological factors (e.g., race, ethnicity, cultural background, gender, socioeconomic status, age, sexual orientation, family relationships, social support).
- Offer guidance for differential assessment of psychological reactions to physical illness, psychological symptoms associated with physical illness or treatment, and clinical mood and anxiety disorders.
- Provide a conceptual overview and clinical tools for the assessment of suicide risk and for intervention in this area.
- Highlight general intervention strategies to support overall health, coping, and well-being and targeted intervention strategies to assist people experiencing psychological distress associated with depression and anxiety disorders in health-care settings.

PSYCHOSOCIAL CONDITIONS AND INCREASED RISK FOR ILLNESS

Stress

Psychological distress, including stress, anger, hostility, depression, and anxiety, is associated with numerous negative health outcomes across a wide range of illnesses (Institute of Medicine [IOM], 2001). The role of stress in particular has been well documented in its relationship to risk for numerous health problems, including cardiovascular disease, cancer, autoimmune and inflammatory disorders, and wound healing. Although stress and its effects on physiology can be beneficial and enable a person to respond to a threat—to "fight or flee" (IOM, 2001)—an individual will experience allostatic load when faced with chronic exposure to undefined stress that is unresolved and thus perpetuates the stress response. *Allostatic load* refers to the cumulative physiological toll of repeated responses to stress (McEwen & Stellar, 1993). Allostatic load also can occur when the stress response fails to activate (McEwen, 1998; McEwen & Gianaros, 2010). *Allostasis* involves the body's physiological responses to stressors to foster adaptation to challenge and to maintain homeostasis (Sterling & Eyer, 1988). However, as the body continues to engage in allostasis, allostatic load results and can contribute disease (McEwen, 1998; McEwen & Stellar, 1993). Allostatic load is influenced not only by chronic stress but also by behavioral factors, including substance use, physical activity, sleep, and diet; individual temperament; and genetics and developmental variations (IOM, 2001; McEwen, 1998).

There are two primary ways to consider the relationship between stress and health: through a biological pathway and through behavior. Through a biological pathway, stress directly influences the body's physiology. Responding to stress releases hormones that influence the central nervous, cardiovascular, and immune systems (IOM, 2001). Exposure to chronic stress in particular negatively influences the immune system (Segerstrom & Miller, 2004). The concept of allostatic load—the cumulative physiological cost of responding to stress— provides a compelling framework for understanding ways in which responding to stress affects well-being, in general, and perpetuates health disparities, in particular (McEwen & Gianaros, 2010). Coping with stress may lead to behaviors, such as eating a higher-fat diet,

smoking cigarettes, and reducing exercise, all of which increase the risk for illness (Ng & Jeffrey, 2003). Through both physiology and behavior, stress intersects with health. In addition, the psychosocial and physical demands of illness may increase stress and warrant intervention to address biological and behavioral effects on overall health.

Popular notions of stress may discount its impact on well-being, as reflected in such statements as "He's just stressed out." However, a growing body of science suggests that being stressed out, particularly if one repeatedly experiences stress, has far-reaching implications for physical health (McEwen & Gianaros, 2010). Social workers in health-care settings are well positioned to help people who are experiencing psychological stress. Such intervention may be critical to supporting physical and mental health. One powerful framework for guiding intervention in this area is Lazarus and Folkman's (1984) model of stress, appraisal, and coping. This model and its implications for physical and mental health are further discussed in the "Psychosocial Intervention Strategies in Health-Care Settings" section of this chapter.

Social Relationships

Social networks, support, integration, and capital also have strong implications for physical and mental health (IOM, 2001; McGinnis, Williams-Russo, & Knickman, 2002). The term *social networks* generally refers to the composition of a person's social relationships (e.g., number of people, types of relationships, relationships among the people in a social network); *social support* generally refers to a person's sense of feeling warmly regarded and respected or to the type of support available (e.g., emotional support, material assistance, instrumental or practical support) (Cobb, 1976; House & Kahn, 1985; IOM, 2001). Social integration can be conceptualized as the number of intimate relationships a person has with both individuals (including family and friends) and groups (including voluntary and religious organizations) as well as a person's sense of having multiple social roles and communal connections with others (IOM, 2001; McEwen & Gianaros, 2010). *Social capital* reflects a societal conceptualization of its members' integration. Measures of social capital can include reported trust among people and degree of civic participation. Greater social integration is associated with a host of health outcomes, including improved quality of life, reduced mortality, fewer suicides, and less crime (IOM, 2001). Furthermore, enhancing social integration may be particularly helpful in reducing the long-term physiological costs of repeatedly responding to stress (McEwen & Gianaros, 2010).

Social ties and support are far reaching in their power to strengthen health. They support survival in infancy, buffer stress in life transitions, increase one's ability to fight off a cold, reduce advancement of carotid atherosclerosis, slow the decline of immune functioning in persons with human immunodeficiency virus (HIV), and contribute to lower levels of allostatic load. Alternatively, isolation, loss, conflict within relationships, and the potential for disease transmission are aspects of social ties that can negatively affect physical and mental health (IOM, 2001). For social workers in health-care settings, these findings highlight the importance of exploring available social support, augmenting it when needed, enhancing interactions among social network members as indicated, and facilitating social integration. In addition, social workers can play an important role in preventing disease transmission between social network members through education and counseling efforts.

PHYSICAL ILLNESS AND THE ROLE OF MENTAL HEALTH

Among people who are experiencing physical illness, mental health can play an important role in physical outcomes across the life span. For example, among adolescents, depression, low-self-esteem, and parent–child conflict can influence nonadherence to oncology regimens (Kennard et al., 2004). Among adults who have experienced myocardial infarction, depression, state anxiety, and psychological distress can increased the risk of 5-year cardiac-related mortality (Frasure-Smith & Lesperance, 2003). Among older women with cancer, depression can lower the likelihood of receiving appropriate treatment and increase the risk of death (Goodwin, Zhang, & Ostir, 2004). In addition, treating depression can reduce intensity of pain and disability associated with osteoarthritis among older adults (Lin et al., 2003).

The next example of research among women living with HIV is provided to illustrate the relationship between mental and physical health, to consider possible pathways through which mental and physical health interact, and to consider implications for social work practice. In this study, Ickovics and colleagues (2001) found that women with chronic depression were twice as likely to die as women with limited or no depressive symptoms. In addition, when controlling for sociodemographic background, clinical status, and substance use, chronic depression predicted decline in CD4 cell counts among women in the study. Although the causal mechanisms in this relationship remain unclear, the authors propose four possible explanations:

1. The previously established impact of depression on morbidity and mortality via changes in neuroendocrine and immunological functioning may have an interaction effect with the medical illness (see also Cohen & Herbert, 1996; Kemeny et al., 1994; Miller, Cohen, & Herbert, 1999).

2. Depression may contribute to engagement in risk behaviors, such as alcohol and tobacco use, and to disengagement in health care, which may negatively influence health status.

3. The negative impact of depression on medication adherence among people living with HIV may contribute to declines in health.

4. Although protease inhibitors have been shown to be associated with reductions in

symptoms of depression, fewer than half the women in the study received highly active antiretroviral therapy for HIV (Ickovics et al., 2001; Low-Beer et al., 2000). With suboptimal treatment experiences, women may have reduced access to both the physical and the mental health gains associated with protease inhibitor treatment.

This example of the relationship between depression and mortality among women living with HIV underscores both the relevance of mental health in physical health outcomes and the complexity of possible pathways between mental and physical health. Although medical intervention to address physical illness may be the priority among the health-care team, mental health assessment and intervention is likely to be closely linked with physical health outcomes. In terms of social work practice, this linkage highlights the critical role of assessing psychosocial conditions, including mental health and risk behaviors, and formulating interventions that can support individuals' overall health.

ASSESSING PSYCHOSOCIAL CONDITIONS IN HEALTH-CARE SETTINGS

Accurate assessment is at the heart of effective social work intervention. As described by Meyer (1993), assessment involves "the thinking process that seeks out the meaning of case situations, puts the particulars of the case in some order, and leads to appropriate interventions" (p. 2). In addition, the assessment is a relationship-building process with clients. The effort to identify the client's presenting concern, factors that contribute to it, resources that can alleviate it, and how to address it is ideally a collaborative endeavor (Berlin & Marsh, 1993). As the social worker seeks to understand the client in his situation, her expression of interest and empathy and her engagement with the client as a respected collaborator can facilitate a positive helping relationship. Such

an alliance is an important component of effective services (Horvath, 1995).

In health-care settings, social workers are likely to encounter people with a range of mental health experiences. Some people may be experiencing mild psychological distress and may benefit from psychoeducation regarding their physical conditions and supportive counseling to enhance coping and stress management. Others may be experiencing severe psychological distress and may benefit from intensive psychosocial interventions, including psychotherapy and psychopharmacology (DHHS, 1999; IOM, 2001). The process through which a social worker or other professional considers the nature of a client's mental health issues and their influencing factors is called *differential assessment*. When the process is intended to identify a psychiatric diagnostic category, it is called *differential diagnosis* (American Psychiatric Association, 2000). This chapter uses the term *differential assessment* to reflect a comprehensive focus that extends beyond diagnostic considerations. To guide differential assessment and thus appropriate intervention, this discussion covers several intersecting domains, including ecological factors, mental health symptoms, physical conditions, medications, and substance use. Figure 8.1 illustrates various domains related to mental health symptoms; Figure 8.2 provides a more real-world depiction of the complex intersections among each of these domains.

Ecological Factors: Macrosystems, Exosystems, and Mesosystems

Although conceptualizations of the connections between the person and the environment have varied, social workers have a long-standing history of recognizing the importance of a person-in-environment perspective (Berlin & Marsh, 1993; Germain & Gitterman, 1980; Hollis, 1939; Jordan & Franklin, 1995; Kondrat, 2002; Perlman, 1957; Richmond, 1917). *Ecological systems theory* (Bronfenbrenner, 1977, 1979, 1989) provides a lens through which

Figure 8.1   Domains Related to Mental Health Symptoms

*For example, race, ethnicity, cultural background, SES, employment status, sexual orientation, spiritual background, family, social support, gender, and age.

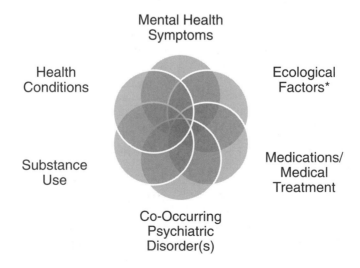

Figure 8.2   Mental Health Symptoms

*For example, race, ethnicity, cultural background, SES, employment status, sexual orientation, spiritual background, family, social support, gender, and age.

to employ this perspective in considering the transactional intersections of ecological factors and physical and mental health. According to ecological systems theory, each individual experiences life within a unique intersecting web of systems. These intersecting systems can include the microsystem (i.e., individual activity, roles, physical and mental health status) and then broaden to the mesosystem (i.e., relationships with family, significant others, peers), then to the exosystem (i.e., work, neighborhood, community), and finally to the macrosystem (i.e., culture and dominant patterned processes that inform numerous configurations, including politics, government, education, and law). Through this perspective, one can consider the relationships between physical and mental health within the context of relationships with significant others and peers; interactions with community, school, work, or unemployment; and connections to broader cultural frameworks and governmental institutions.

The importance of this perspective is not only its consistency with social work practice, which recognizes that individuals and their environments exist in dynamic, mutually influencing interaction (Kondrat, 2002), but also in the conclusion reached by the seminal report from the IOM (2001) that focuses on the interactions among biology, behavior, and social influences. After reviewing evidence gathered across numerous disciplines, the report concludes:

> [H]ealth and behavior are influenced by factors at multiple levels, including biological, psychological, and social. Interventions that involve only the person—for example, using self-control or willpower—are unlikely to change long-term behavior unless other factors, such as family relationships, work situation, or social norms, happen to be aligned to support a change. (p. 27)

To formulate an accurate assessment that will lead the social worker in the direction of effective intervention, multisystemic influences need to be considered. Lack of attention to the various components of an ecologically informed assessment may lead the social worker to focus excessively on either individual characteristics or environmental factors and result in faulty explanations regarding how to be most helpful (Berlin & Marsh, 1993).

A dispositional bias that focuses excessively on individual-level explanations of presenting problems is a common assessment error (Berlin & Marsh, 1993; Gambrill, 2006); however, complex social, political, and economic systems influence health behaviors and access to health-supporting resources (IOM, 2001). Effective assessment requires deliberate attention to multisystemic considerations. The ecological framework provides an efficient way to consider the numerous systems with which individuals interact and their mutual influence with physical and mental health.

This overview of an ecological approach to assessment begins with the macrosystem and concludes with in-depth attention to aspects of the microsystems of physical and mental health. This sequence of assessments acknowledges that complex, multisystemic factors influence physical and mental health. Beginning with the macrosystem places social and environmental considerations in the foreground of the assessment and intervention processes. The critical importance of culturally competent services and the growing body of evidence regarding health disparities based on race and socioeconomic background further support starting at the macrosystem and proceeding to exo-, meso-, and microlevel components of the assessment.

Macrosystems

Beginning with the broadest level, the macrosystem, McGoldrick (1982) states that neither physical nor mental health problems can be assessed appropriately without understanding "the frame of reference of the person seeking help" (p. 6). A person's cultural context informs this frame of reference and influences how she will identify and label problems (McGoldrick, 1982). In addition, cultural influences may shape the experience and communication of pain, expected or desired treatment, understanding of illness causes, coping styles, and perspectives regarding whom to turn to for help (e.g., primary care physician, mental health provider, traditional healer, clergy) (DHHS, 2001a; McGoldrick, 1982). In the context of assessing and intervening to address mental health in health-care settings, these considerations become particularly salient in several ways.

The ways in which symptoms are experienced and described will intersect with the social worker's understanding of what is the matter and how to help (Berlin & Marsh, 1993; McGoldrick, 1982). Generalized statements regarding culture and cultural norms, values, and expectations run the risk of conveying stereotyped information that may obscure individual differences and experiences and may overlook diversity within a culture (Yellow Bird, Fong, Galindo, Nowicki, & Freeman, 1996); however, such information, when provided and used appropriately, can broaden the social worker's cultural knowledge base and inform efforts to reach a shared understanding of the client's experiences (Kerson, 2002). With this caveat in mind, somatization—the expression of feelings of distress through physical symptoms—reflects an important intersection between culture and physical and mental health (DHHS, 2001a). Powerful influences are likely to contribute to somatization across cultural groups, including the culture's understanding of the connection between mind and body, culturally accepted ways of expressing distress, and culturally informed stigma regarding mental illness (DHHS, 2001a). For example, a limited body of research suggests that, among people who are American Indian and Alaska Native, there is not a clear distinction between mind and body, and it is likely that such people express distress in both somatic and psychological terms (DHHS, 2001a). Among several Asian cultures, mental illness carries significant stigma; the weight of this stigma may influence the likelihood of people from Asian backgrounds expressing psychological distress in physical symptoms (DHHS, 2001a). Cultural perspectives regarding the connection between mind and body also may influence this likelihood (Lin & Cheung, 1999); however, when asked explicitly about mental health, research suggests that Asian clients will report symptoms in psychological terms (DHHS, 2001a; Lin & Cheung, 1999).

Common examples of somatization among people who are Puerto Rican, Mexican, and White include stomach-related problems, chest pain, and palpitations. Among people in Africa and South Asia, somatization may involve sensations of "burning hands and feet," "worms in the head," or "ants crawling under the skin." Among some Asian groups, somatization may involve blurred vision, dizziness, and vertigo (DHHS, 2001a, p. 11). In terms of social work practice in health-care settings, the possible somatization of psychological distress underscores the importance of routine screening for mental health concerns.

To provide culturally competent assessment and intervention, it is critical that social workers become informed about their own and their clients' cultural beliefs about experiences of physical and mental health (DHHS, 2001a; Pinderhughes, 1989; Rolland, 1994). Such competence is vital to recognize and support normative coping in the midst of physical or mental illness and to avoid misassessment of physical and mental health symptoms (Lin & Cheung, 1999). The next paragraphs discuss some strategies to assist social workers with increasing their cultural competence in addressing mental health in health-care settings.

Becoming more mindful of one's own cultural beliefs about physical and mental health may enhance self-awareness and capacity to engage in culturally competent assessment and intervention (Pinderhughes, 1989; Rolland, 1994). Social workers should consider specific ways in which their cultural background influences their values regarding expressions of distress and mental and physical illness. One particularly significant domain in the assessment of mental health pertains to cultural expectations regarding expression of emotion. To what degree does a person's cultural background encourage open expression of emotion or limit its direct expression? Social workers' own beliefs about expected displays of emotion are likely to influence the lens through which they assess client experiences. For example, a social worker whose cultural background encourages direct expression of emotion may view a person who is reserved in emotional expression as having a problematic restricted range of affect, when, in fact, the behavior is consistent with the person's cultural context and does not reflect a problem in emotional expression. Awareness of this lens can foster reflection regarding culturally informed assessment and the recognition that "cultural differences are not deviances" (Pinderhughes, 1989, p. 17). Additional salient domains for social workers to consider include their own culturally informed expectations regarding how people respond to physical pain and values regarding mental illness and psychological distress.

Exploring clients' cultural identity with them can explain implications of culture in their presenting concerns and service preferences, including culturally informed ways of expressing distress and preferred types of help. Furthermore, explorations of culture, immigration, and acculturation contribute salient information to ecologically informed assessments (American Psychiatric Association, 2000).

Becoming better informed about the cultures of the people social workers serve and about evidence-based interventions that are culturally relevant to them can be important avenues to enhancing intervention effectiveness (Carlton-LaNey, 1999; DHHS, 2001a; Pinderhughes, 1989).

As outlined in Chapter 10 of this book, exploring clients' beliefs about their illnesses, their desired outcomes, and their service preferences may be facilitated by using these questions (Kleinman, Eisenberg, & Good, 1978, p. 256):

What do you think has caused your
   problem?
Why do you think it started when it did?
What do you think your sickness does to
   you? How does it work?
How severe is your sickness? Will it have
   a short or long course?

What kind of treatment do you think you
   should receive?
What are the most important results you
   hope to receive from this treatment?
What are the chief problems your sickness
   has caused for you?
What do you fear most about your
   sickness?

Becoming better attuned to issues of commonality and difference, including race, ethnicity, culture, socioeconomic status (SES), gender, sexual orientation, age, physical ability, and power, between the social worker and the clients served may facilitate addressing these elements within the helping relationship (American Psychiatric Association, 1994; Pinderhughes, 1989).

Actively considering clients' spiritual beliefs can contribute to the provision of culturally competent services. As described by Kerson (2002), spiritual beliefs and health beliefs often are intertwined and warrant attention that is comparable to other cultural beliefs. Walsh (2004) further describes the role of prayer, meditation, and faith in numerous positive health outcomes, including reduced stress, decreased blood pressure and cortisol levels, improved management of chronic pain, reduced problems with alcohol or other drugs, and reduced depression. Walsh also asserts, "Over 350 studies point to religion as the forgotten factor in physical and mental health" (p. 198). Beliefs may provide a powerful source of cognitive assistance to people who are experiencing physical and mental health difficulties. They may facilitate a sense of coherence, meaning, and control (Walsh, 2004).

In addition to supporting a worldview that facilitates meaning, Musick, Traphagan, Koenig, and Larson (2000) provide three further pathways through which religion may positively influence health: (1) supporting positive health behaviors (e.g., healthier diets, reduced drinking and smoking, increased physical activity); (2) fostering social integration and support (e.g., shared beliefs, larger social network, opportunities for conversation, learning, support); and (3) providing comfort (e.g., emotional and instrumental support, religious rituals for assistance in difficult times, source of hope and coping). Spirituality and religion may be important resources, but assessment should be sensitive to these topics as potential sources of conflicted or negative feelings (Gotterer, 2001). Open-ended inquiry that is sensitive to a diversity of experiences and that elicits the client's unique experiences can be a useful starting point for active consideration of spiritual beliefs. Chapter 11 of this book may help in addressing these issues further; the chapter provides additional detail regarding ways in which culture intersects with health, including ways in which bodily sensations are recognized as symptoms of illness.

Although cultural competence facilitates the recognition of strengths of cultural influences and coping in the midst of health challenges (McGoldrick, 1982), the influences of race-related health disparities are particularly salient in the context of physical and mental health. An ecologically informed assessment requires contextual knowledge of these disparities and their implications for effective services. The extent of race-related disparities in physical and mental health is staggering. For example, in comparison to their White counterparts, people who are African American are more than twice as likely to experience infant mortality and to give birth to a low-weight infant; they also have considerably higher prevalence of tuberculosis, greater exposure to unhealthy air, and considerably higher death rates associated with heart disease, stroke, all cancers, and homicide (Keppel, Pearcy, & Wagener, 2002; Weir et al., 2003). Although African American people have lower rates of major depression and alcohol dependence than their White counterparts, they are likely to experience more severe, persistent symptoms and to receive less treatment (Grant, 1997; D. R. Williams et al., 2007; D. R. Williams, Mohammed, Leavell, & Collins, 2010). Furthermore, in addition to increased risk of dying from cardiovascular disease, people who are African American experience increased risk of burden associated with the condition than do people who are

White (Hahn, Heath, & Chang, 1998; Office of Minority Health, Centers for Disease Control and Prevention [CDC], n.d.; Parmley, 2001). Although epidemiological studies indicate increased prevalence of cardiovascular-disease risk factors among people who are African American (e.g., physical inactivity, being overweight, hypertension, diabetes mellitus) (Hahn et al., 1998), it is also important to consider the ways in which such disparities are shaped by structural inequities that influence access to health care and to resources that support health, including safe living, working, and exercising environments and healthy dietary options (Keppel et al., 2002; Winkleby, Kraemer, Ahn, & Varady, 1998; Wyatt et al., 2003; also see Chapter 7 in this book). In addition, although race and socioeconomic inequalities intersect and additional research is needed to identify the ways in which they (along with gender) influence health, several studies indicate that race-related health disparities persist even when controlling for socioeconomic factors (for discussion, see Williams et al., 2010).

Racial discrimination is another salient macrolevel consideration related to physical and mental health disparities (Krieger, 2003; D. R. Williams, Neighbors, & Jackson, 2003). A large body of research conducted across diverse cultural groups indicates that discrimination is associated with health problems and, in particular, with mental health problems (D. R. Williams et al., 2003; D. R. Williams & Mohammed, 2009; Yoo, Gee, & Takeuchi, 2009); however, the mechanisms through which discrimination influences health are still being explored (Krieger, 2003; D. R. Williams et al., 2003; D. R. Williams & Mohammed, 2009). One conceptualization of this relationship suggests that experiencing discrimination is a source of stress that can negatively influence health through physiological pathways and through behaviors that increase illness risk (D. R. Williams et al., 2003; D. R. Williams & Mohammed, 2009).

Building on this conceptualization are examinations of the mediating role of coping in the relationship between discrimination and health (Noh & Kaspar, 2003). As described by Noh and Kaspar, this body of research considers differences in health based on whether people exposed to discrimination employ emotion-focused coping or problem-focused coping. Emotion-focused coping generally includes cognitions that aim to reduce distress, including minimization, avoidance, distancing, and finding positive elements of negative circumstances (Lazarus & Folkman, 1984). Problem-focused coping generally involves steps to solve a problem, including specifying the problem, considering potential solutions, evaluating strengths and limitations of potential solutions, choosing a solution, and taking action (Lazarus & Folkman, 1984). There have been divergent findings regarding the health effects of emotion- and problem-focused coping among members of diverse culture and gender groups. Noh and Kaspar (2003) assert that the effectiveness of coping is likely shaped by the nature of the stressor and the individual's resources, social context, cultural background, and degree of acculturation.

Another conceptualization of the possible mechanisms through which discrimination negatively affects health comes from the work of Krieger (2003). She argues that the influence of racism on health should be examined through research on these issues: "(1) economic and social deprivation; (2) toxic substances and hazardous conditions; (3) socially inflicted trauma...; (4) targeted marketing of commodities that can harm health, such as junk food and psychoactive substances...; and (5) inadequate or degrading medical care" (p. 196). Although Krieger recognizes the role of individual- and community-level coping and action to counter discrimination, these five potential pathways underscore systemic and multilevel influences of racism on health. This body of knowledge is evolving, but implications for social work practice include attention to individual coping strategies to manage stress and support health and systemic factors that negatively influence physical and mental health. Additional considerations on how to support psychological well-being and coping when experiencing serious illness are addressed in the "Psychosocial Intervention

Strategies in Health-Care Settings" section of this chapter.

Exosystems

Exosystem issues regarding SES, including income, education, and employment, are also likely to intersect with microlevel physical and mental health issues. In fact, as described by McGinnis and colleagues (2002), "for the population as a whole, the most consistent predictor of the likelihood of death in any given year is level of education; persons ages 45 to 64 in the highest levels of education have death rates 2.5 times lower than those in the lowest level" (p. 81). Individual poverty and societal inequality of income distribution also negatively affect mortality among people with lower incomes (McGinnis et al., 2002). In addition to mortality risks associated with lower SES is an increased risk of mental health problems (DHHS, 1999; Siefert, Bowman, Heflin, Danziger, & Williams, 2000). Comparisons between people in the extremes of SES suggest that annual prevalence of mental disorders among people at the lower end are approximately twice that of those at the higher end (World Health Organization [WHO], 2001).

The increased prevalence of mental health problems among people with lower SES has been explained in two primary ways. The first explanation is that the increased risk of acute and chronic stressors among people living in poverty may contribute to their increased risk of mental health problems (Siefert et al., 2000). This explanation is referred to as *social causation*, in which social circumstances have a causal link with mental health problems. The second explanation, referred to as *social selection*, argues that mental health problems cause people to move downward in SES (Dohrenwend et al., 1992; Saraceno & Barbui, 1997). Social causation appears most relevant for women experiencing depression and for men experiencing antisocial personality and substance use disorders while social selection appears most relevant among those experiencing schizophrenia (Dohrenwend et al., 1992; Siefert et al., 2000). Among children, recent research suggests that social causation may be most relevant for young people experiencing oppositional or conduct disorders and that parental monitoring mediates this relationship, such that changing poverty level is associated with increased parental monitoring, which in turn is associated with decreased mental health symptoms (Costello, Compton, Keller, & Angold, 2003). This study did not find that social causation was as relevant for symptoms of anxiety and depression among the participants.

SES also is associated with the course of mental health problems. Numerous factors may influence this relationship, including obstacles related to accessing care, lack of health insurance, and lack of culturally and linguistically appropriate services (WHO, 2001). For social workers addressing mental health issues in health-care settings, the increased risk of physical and mental health problems among people with lower SES underscores the importance of designing and delivering services to reach this population.

Research on stress and coronary artery disease provides an example of the specific ways in which SES intersects with mental and physical health. Krantz and colleagues (2000) discuss factors that may contribute to the inverse relationship between SES and cardiac morbidity and mortality, including limited access to health care, increased prevalence of risks (e.g., smoking, high blood pressure), inadequate nutrition, and social and environmental stress. The hypothetical case example below illustrates this point in regard to implications for social work practice.

As this case depicts, supporting Joseph's physical and mental well-being involves consideration not only of individual coping and stress management strategies but also of broader systems, including employment and socioeconomic resources. Furthermore, as the case depicts, the relationship between socioeconomic resources and health can be a bidirectional one (Adler & Stewart, 2010; Kawachi, Adler, & Dow, 2010).

Mesosystems

Attention to clients' family and social contexts reflects the mesosystem from an ecological

---

CASE EXAMPLE

Joseph is a 52-year-old, heterosexual, single man of Italian American ancestry who has worked in various construction positions for the past 20 years. Although Joseph earns enough money to pay most of his monthly bills, his employer does not provide health insurance, and his income exceeds the eligibility criteria for Medicaid. Joseph recently presented in the emergency room reporting chest pains and shortness of breath, which ultimately were diagnosed as symptoms of myocardial infarction. Upon consultation with the health-care team, Joseph was encouraged to begin a medication regimen and urged to reduce his work hours, to reduce the stress in his life, and to improve his eating habits because he generally relied on low-cost, high-fat takeout for lunch and dinner. Upon discharge from the hospital, Joseph agreed to follow the health-care

team's recommendations and enrolled in the hospital's stress management program.

Within two weeks of beginning the stress management program, Joseph reports that his bills are accumulating due to his efforts to work fewer hours and that he has just received a hefty bill for his hospital services in addition to expensive prescribed medications. Joseph reports that he feels better since reducing his work hours and attending the stress management program but fears he will be unable to pay his bills and might lose his house if he does not return to his prior work schedule. He also says that he thinks returning to work might reduce his general level of stress, because much of it originates with financial pressures and pressure from his boss to work longer days. Joseph fears his boss might replace him with another worker who can maintain the demanding hours.

perspective. Numerous empirical studies support the vital role of family and social support in physical and mental health outcomes (for examples, see Allgšwer, Wardle, & Steptoe, 2001; Bagner, Fernandez, & Eyberg, 2004; DiMatteo, 2004a; McFarlane et al., 1995; for reviews, see Campbell, 2003; Weihs, Fisher, & Baird, 2002). When considering issues of physical and mental health in the context of family and social relationships, it is important to pay attention to the meaning, diversity, and strengths of these relationships. In her discussion of the course of psychotherapeutic intervention with a lesbian woman struggling with infertility, Brown (1991) writes, "[D]uring the process of infertility treatments and fertility testing, Carla [the client] always had to anticipate having to explain to yet another person where her husband wasn't and who Susan [her partner] was" (p. 25). Such anticipation of a heterosexist bias is likely to fuel a client's emotional disengagement from the health-care team and unlikely to facilitate effective intervention to support the mesolevel intimate relationships in the client's life. To support clients in their intimate relationships and to support their physical and mental health, information gathering should proceed with open-ended, inclusive questions that do not presume particular responses.

In addition and as previously described, it is likely that macrosystemic issues such as homophobia may interact with microsystem physical and mental health conditions. Brown (1991) describes this complexity in relation to dominant cultural expectations of women to be wives and mothers. Women who are lesbian and struggling with infertility may confront complex issues regarding their identity in this dominant cultural context. These intersecting cultural and personal experiences may create "difficulties both in valuing herself and being valued by others, difficulties that may be distressing enough to merit psychotherapeutic intervention" (Brown, 1991, p. 15). In Chapter 13 of this book, Rolland discusses relationships among individuals, families, and health and ways in which social workers can intervene to foster coping and positive health outcomes among families in health-care settings.

Informed by relational theory, the research of Kayser and Sormanti (2002a) suggests that women's psychosocial response to cancer is likely to be influenced by close connections with others and that these connections are interwoven with women's sense of identity. In addition, their research suggests that experiencing cancer may influence identity by affecting the ways in which women who are mothers alter their priorities (Kayser & Sormanti, 2002b). For example, women in this study described: enjoying their families and their lives with greater intensity; learning about their identities apart from their functions as workers, partners, and mothers; finding deep personal strength and self-efficacy; experiencing greater empathy and authenticity in their relationships; and examining the balance between caring for self and others.

Interventions to help people experiencing changes in their sense of identity and to support their social relationships as they face illness are important aspects of the social worker's role in health-care settings. Such interventions are likely to have important implications for positive health outcomes. In fact, social isolation is said to increase the risk of mortality by 2 to 5 times compared with the presence of relationships with family, friends, and community (McGinnis et al., 2002). Given that a number of mental health conditions may contribute to social withdrawal and social isolation (American Psychiatric Association, 2000), individuals experiencing concurrent physical and mental health conditions may be a particularly vulnerable group. As part of a comprehensive assessment, social workers should explore clients' social support, including attention to composition and size of the person's social network, types of social support available, positive and negative components of available support, and strengths and obstacles to engaging with others and sharing support.

Microsystems

Bearing in mind the complex intersections between the multiple systems in the ecological framework, this discussion now turns to microsystems of physical and mental health. Given the high prevalence of depression and anxiety disorders across all age groups and their increased prevalence among people experiencing chronic illnesses, they will be the primary focus of this discussion of assessment and intervention. It should be noted that although this discussion focuses on depression and anxiety disorders as discrete conditions, they frequently co-occur with each other and with other psychiatric and substance use disorders. There is growing recognition of these concurrent conditions, the challenges associated with them, and the importance of integrated treatment to assist people experiencing them (American Academy of Child and Adolescent Psychiatry [AACAP], 2010; Campbell et al., 2007; Center for Substance Abuse Treatment [CSAT], 2005, 2009; Engstrom, El-Bassel, Go, & Gilbert, 2008; Engstrom, Shibusawa, El-Bassel, & Gilbert, 2011; National Institute of Mental Health [NIMH], 2008). Implications for assessment and intervention with children experiencing co-occurring conduct disorder and health conditions are discussed in Box 8.1. Further information that focuses entirely on children and older adults can be found in Chapters 15 and 16 of this book.

Box 8.1 Intersections Between Disruptive Disorders and Health Conditions: Assisting Parents and Children

Each year approximately 1 out of 10 children is likely to experience a disruptive disorder, such as attention-deficit/hyperactivity disorder, conduct disorder, or oppositional defiant disorder (DHHS, 1999; Shaffer et al., 1996). The symptoms associated with disruptive disorders, including significant difficulties following directions, limited tolerance for frustration, impulsive behavior, and opposition to authority figures, pose particular challenges for children who are experiencing co-occurring health conditions. In addition, children's ability to benefit from health-care services may be limited by their difficulties following through with adult requests to adhere to medical recommendations (e.g., diet, medicine, other treatment) and to avoid behaviors that worsen illness or interfere with treatment (e.g., engaging in restricted activities, removing bandages, moving around during exams or treatment) (Bagner et al., 2004; Matthews, Spieth, & Christophersen, 1995). Although the study presented here focuses on a child experiencing a disruptive disorder and bladder cancer, it likely has relevance for those experiencing other conditions commonly seen among children in health-care settings, including asthma, diabetes, and epilepsy.

Based on a case study of a 4-year-old boy, "Robert Smith," experiencing oppositional defiant disorder and bladder cancer, Bagner and colleagues (2004) suggest that parent–child interaction therapy (PCIT) holds promise as an effective intervention to address co-occurring disruptive behavior and persistent physical illness. On referral for psychological services, Robert was screaming, yelling, and hitting during medical visits. His behavioral difficulties were exacerbated when he began chemotherapy. In one instance, he swung the bag filled with his chemotherapy over his head, resulting in its spilling on his mother and one of the nurses.

The two phases of PCIT include an initial focus on child-directed interaction (CDI) that aims to enhance the relationship between the parent and child, the degree of positive parental communication with the child, and the child's social skills through play therapy. In the CDI phase, parents are guided to use nondirective skills outlined by the acronym PRIDE: *p*raise for the child, *r*eflection of the child's statements, *i*mitation of the child's play, *d*escription of the child's behavior, and *e*nthusiasm in the play (Bagner et al., 2004, p. 3). Parents are coached during this phase to employ PRIDE skills while ignoring negative behaviors and avoiding criticism, questions, and commands directed toward the child. The second phase focuses on parent-directed interaction. Similar to behavioral intervention, this phase aims to enhance parenting skills in these domains: expectations of their children, limit-setting ability, and consistent discipline.

After 12 sessions of PCIT, Robert displayed numerous clinically significant improvements in his behavior as measured by the Child Behavior Checklist and the Eyberg Child Behavior Inventory, and his behavior was no longer consistent with a diagnosis of oppositional defiant disorder. Robert's behavioral gains transferred to medical visits, as noted by his physician and social worker, who described increased adherence and an absence of aggression in his behavior. In addition, Ms. Smith experienced clinically significant reduction in her parenting stress.

Although this case example presents but one illustration of the effectiveness of PCIT with a child experiencing co-occurring oppositional defiant disorder and a serious health condition, its efficacy with several other populations of children experiencing disruptive behaviors and disorders (Brestan & Eyberg, 1998; Eisenstadt, Eyberg, McNeil, Newcomb, & Funderburk, 1993; Hood & Eyberg, 2003; McNeil, Eyberg, Eisenstadt, Newcomb, & Funderburk, 1991; Nixon, Sweeney, Erickson, & Touyz, 2003; Schuhmann, Foote, Eyberg, Boggs, & Algina, 1998) further suggests that PCIT may be useful for clinicians, parents, and children to address such co-occurring health issues.

Prevalence

According to the Surgeon General's Report on Mental Health, each year approximately 1 in 5 people of all ages is likely to experience psychiatric symptoms that meet criteria for a diagnosable mental health condition (DHHS, 1999). Anxiety disorders, which can include posttraumatic stress disorder, simple phobia, social phobia, agoraphobia, generalized anxiety disorder, panic disorder, and obsessive-compulsive disorder, have the highest annual prevalence among children (ages 9–17 years, 13%), adults (ages 18–54 years, 16.4%), and older adults (over age 55 years, 11.4%) (DHHS, 1999). Among children, disruptive disorders follow in annual prevalence, with an estimated 10.3% of children meeting diagnostic criteria and experiencing mild global impairment (DHHS, 1999). Annual prevalence of mood disorders, which can include major depressive episode, unipolar major depression, dysthymia, and bipolar disorder, is estimated to be 6.2% among children, 7.1% among adults, and 4.4% among older adults (DHHS, 1999). Psychiatric and substance use disorders often are described and classified based on the diagnostic criteria of the *Diagnostic and Statistical Manual of Mental Disorders, Fourth Edition, Text Revision (DSM-IV-TR)* (American Psychiatric Association, 2000), as described in Box 8.2.

Among people with serious and persistent illnesses, prevalence rates of mental health conditions that meet *DSM-IV-TR* diagnostic criteria are likely to be elevated (Aben et al., 2003; American Psychiatric Association, 2000; Bing et al., 2001). For example, among a large, representative sample of adults engaged in HIV-related medical care, prevalence of psychiatric disorders was 47.9%, which is higher than twice the prevalence among community participants (Bing et al., 2001; DHHS, 1999). Among people living with HIV, major depression and dysthymia were the most common conditions, and 21% experienced both conditions; generalized anxiety disorders and panic attacks followed in prevalence (Bing et al., 2001). Prevalence estimates of depressive symptoms and major depression among people experiencing cancer vary considerably— between 1% and 42% (Patrick et al., 2003). Prevalence estimates of anxiety disorders also encompass a broad range, 10% to 30%, based on large-scale research that employed

Box 8.2 *DSM* and Multiaxial Assessment

A commonly used method for describing and classifying the types of mental health symptoms a person is experiencing, along with additional information regarding other health conditions, environmental stressors, and their overall functioning, is the multiaxial assessment contained in the *Diagnostic and Statistical Manual of Mental Disorders, Fourth Edition, Text Revision* (*DSM-IV-TR*) (American Psychiatric Association, 2000). Although there are numerous critiques of the *DSM-IV-TR* (Kirk & Kutchins, 1992; Mechanic, 1999; Saleebey, 2002; Wakefield, 1999), its wide usage as a classification and communication system in physical and mental health settings supports developing familiarity with it (Kerson, 2002; Williams, 1998). Components of the *DSM-IV* multiaxial assessment tool are introduced here. More detailed information and the most recent text revisions of the *DSM-IV* can be found in the *DSM-IV-TR*. A comprehensive revision of the *DSM* currently is under way. The *Diagnostic and Statistical Manual of Mental Disorders: Fifth Edition* (DSM-5) is expected to be published in May 2013.

The *DSM-IV* multiaxial assessment (American Psychiatric Association, 1994, 2000) generally focuses on describing and communicating the problems people are experiencing; however, social workers have a commitment to recognize and to build on people's strengths (Saleebey, 2002). In multiaxial assessment, it is important to be attuned to, to recognize, and to formulate interventions that build on clients' strengths. No matter how dire a situation may be, people have strengths that have fueled their perseverance and survival to the point at which they come into contact with the social worker. Actively reflecting on and engaging people's strengths, which may include their knowledge, capacities, and resources, are arguably central components of clients "achieving their goals and visions and...[having] a better quality of life on

their terms" (Saleebey, 2002, pp. 1–2). Developing a specific notation regarding client strengths may provide a useful tool for active consideration of and engagement with clients' strengths as part of the multiaxial assessment.

According to the *DSM-IV-TR*, multiaxial assessment includes these domains:

- Axis I—Clinical Disorders Other Disorders That May Be a Focus of Clinical Attention
- Axis II—Personality Disorders, Mental Retardation
- Axis III—General Medical Conditions
- Axis IV—Psychosocial and Environmental Problems
- Axis V—Global Assessment of Functioning (American Psychiatric Association, 1994, p. 25; American Psychiatric Association, 2000, p. 27)

This discussion of the differential assessment of physical and mental health focuses primarily on Axis I, Clinical Disorders, such as major depressive episode or generalized anxiety disorder; Axis III, General Medical Conditions, such as cardiovascular disease or HIV; and Axis IV, Psychosocial and Environmental Problems, such as homelessness, long-standing poverty, or recent loss. Because social workers have specialized training in addressing the interactions between people and their environments, they are likely to have particular ability to address issues related to Axis IV; however, it is worth noting that in addition to this expertise, estimates suggest that there are more social workers in the psychotherapy workforce (192,814) than psychologists (73,018), psychiatrists (33,486), and psychiatric nurses (15,330) combined (Center for Mental Health Services, 2001; Insel, 2004). As described throughout this chapter, social workers' attention to the interface between the person and environment is an important aspect of both differential assessment and intervention in mental and physical health; however, the ability to understand and to intervene to address these complex co-occurring issues also requires substantive background and training in additional psychotherapeutic interventions, some of which are discussed in the "Psychosocial Intervention Strategies in Health-Care Settings" section of this chapter.

Axis II identifies personality disorders and mental retardation. There are 10 specific personality disorders: paranoid personality disorder, schizoid personality disorder, schizotypal personality disorder, antisocial personality disorder, borderline personality disorder, histrionic personality disorder, narcissistic personality disorder, avoidant personality disorder, dependent personality disorder, and obsessive-compulsive personality disorder. Personality disorders that do not meet diagnostic criteria for any of the 10 types identified are categorized as personality disorder not otherwise specified (NOS). People with a personality disorder generally experience "an enduring pattern of inner experience and behavior that deviates markedly from the expectations of the individual's culture, is pervasive and inflexible, has an onset in adolescence or early adulthood, is stable over time, and leads to distress or impairment" (American

Psychiatric Association, 2000, p. 685). As with the clinical disorders recorded on Axis I, the *DSM-IV-TR* includes specific diagnostic criteria for each of the personality disorders.

Axis V includes the Global Assessment of Functioning (GAF) scale, which reflects the clinician's assessment of the client's overall functioning in psychological, social, and occupational domains. The GAF does not consider the influence of physical and environmental conditions. The GAF is a constructed continuum in which functioning associated with mental health is ranked on a scale of 1 to 100 (a ranking of 0 indicates inadequate information). A GAF rating of 10 is associated with "persistent danger of severely hurting self or others"; a GAF rating of 50 is associated with "serious symptoms (e.g., suicidal ideation, severe obsessional rituals, frequent shoplifting) or any serious impairment in social, occupational, or school functioning (e.g., no friends, unable to keep a job)"; and a GAF rating of 91 is associated with "superior functioning in a wide range of activities" (American Psychiatric Association, 2000, p. 34). Detailed information and guidance regarding how to formulate a GAF rating can be found in the *DSM-IV-TR* (American Psychiatric Association, 2000).

standardized interviews and diagnostic criteria (Stark et al., 2002). Methodological limitations likely contribute to these wide ranges; however, the National Institutes of Health's State-of-the-Science Panel (Patrick et al., 2003) states that "the most common symptoms of cancer and treatments for cancer are pain, depression, and fatigue" (p. 110). Among people experiencing stroke or myocardial infarction, new cases of depression were identified in 38.7% and 28.4% of a group of people receiving care in the Netherlands; when adjusted for age, sex, and degree of disability, the rates of depression were comparable (Aben et al., 2003).

It is also important to consider trauma in the context of health and comprehensive assessment. Lifetime exposure to trauma—including exposure to seeing someone being seriously injured or killed; a fire, flood, or natural disaster; a life-threatening accident; combat; physical attacks; and sexual assaults—is estimated to occur among 61% of men and 51% of women in the United States (Kessler, Sonnega, Bromet, Hughes, & Nelson, 1995); however, in the current context of post-9/11 experiences, a global war on terror, and homeland security alerts within the United States, perceived risk or threat to one's safety and related psychological sequelae may be more prevalent than earlier estimates (Susser, Herman, & Aaron, 2002). Estimates from 1995 suggest that approximately 5.0% of men and 10.4% of women ages 18 to 54 years experience psychological effects of trauma that meet the diagnostic criteria for posttraumatic stress disorder (PTSD), a type of anxiety disorder, in their lifetime (American Psychiatric Association, 2000; Kessler et al., 1995).

In the context of U.S. involvement in current military conflicts, the risk of PTSD and other mental health concerns among military members and veterans is particularly salient. Recent estimates indicate that among veterans who served in Operation Iraqi Freedom or Operation Enduring Freedom and sought services at the Veterans Administration (VA), 25% met diagnostic criteria for a mental health condition. In addition, 13% of men and 11% of women in the study met diagnostic criteria for PTSD. Veterans younger than 40 years, especially those ages 18 to 25 years, are more likely to experience PTSD and other mental health conditions when compared with those older than 40 years (Seal, Bertenthal, Miner, Sen, & Marmar, 2007).

In addition to risks associated with their military service, female veterans' experiences may be complicated by exposure to sexual harassment and assault within the military. Among a nationally representative sample of 3,632 female veterans seeking care at the VA, an estimated 55% experienced sexual harassment and 23% experienced sexual assault in the military (Skinner et al., 2000). These experiences are associated with increased risk for PTSD, problematic substance use, other mental health concerns, health problems, and employment difficulties (Skinner et al., 2000; Surís, Lind, Kashner, Borman, & Petty, 2004).

Despite the significant mental health needs of many veterans, active military members, and their families, stigma, concerns regarding professional ramifications, and inadequate funding limit the availability and use of mental health services (Department of Defense Task Force on Mental Health, 2007; Hoge et al., 2004; DHHS, 2001a). A recent report by the

Department of Defense Task Force on Mental Health calls for strategies to strengthen resilience, to reach military members and their families across a continuum of care, and to reduce stigma by ensuring that mental health care is an integrated component of military service. Give an Hour, an organization committed to linking current military personnel and their families with free mental health services, is a resource that addresses some of these calls to action (www.giveanhour.org). Additional information regarding assessing and responding to veterans' and family members' mental health needs can be found online through the National Center for PTSD (www.ptsd.va.gov/index.asp).

The connections between trauma and health are numerous.

1. Preexisting trauma exposure and its psychological sequelae are likely to interact with experiences of physical illness.

2. People may be seeking medical care as a direct result of a traumatic experience, such as a motor vehicle accident, sexual assault, or other physical attack.

3. Consistent with the traumatic events identified in the *DSM-IV-TR* as potential precipitants of PTSD (American Psychiatric Association, 2000), Mundy and Baum (2004) underscore the utility of broadening the definition of trauma to include some medical conditions such as myocardial infarctions, which may be considered traumatic events because they represent a serious threat to a person's life.

4. Research regarding PTSD and health-care usage suggests significantly elevated rates of medically related hospitalization, visits to the emergency department, and visits to a medical provider among people experiencing PTSD (Stein, McQuaid, Pedrelli, Lenox, & McCahill, 2000).

Given the high prevalence of exposure to traumatic events, their powerful intersection with individual health and medical care, and the potential for people to experience clinically significant symptoms of posttraumatic stress, even if they do not meet *DSM-IV-TR* diagnostic criteria for PTSD (American Psychiatric Association, 2000), this chapter includes discussion of posttraumatic stress in health-care settings.

Detection

Several factors contribute the importance of routine mental health screening in health-care settings:

- The high prevalence of depression and anxiety in the general population and among people with serious and persistent physical illnesses
- The significant number of people, particularly people from racial and ethnic minority backgrounds, who seek mental health-care solely through primary care services
- The high prevalence (30%–50%) of people experiencing psychiatric disorders who go undetected in usual primary care
- The potential negative impact of psychiatric disorders on health outcomes (DHHS, 2001a; Lecrubier, 2004; Pignone et al., 2002; Regier et al., 1993)

Depression and anxiety can be expressed in health-care settings in a variety of ways. For example, a father may comment to a social worker or other health-care provider that his teenage son "does not seem to be himself." The father might say that his son has been short-tempered lately, is sleeping more than usual, has experienced a decline in his grades, and has lost interest in social activities that formerly interested him. The father has attempted to offer him incentives to improve his academic performance and to encourage him to spend time with friends to no avail. Another individual may describe feeling fatigued, having sore muscles, and experiencing difficulty falling asleep but attribute these symptoms to recent stress at work. As part of conducting a comprehensive assessment, the social worker would recognize that depression among children and adolescents may present

as irritability (American Psychiatric Association, 2000), and that symptoms of anxiety that are attributed to normalized conditions, such as stress at work, may not be detected accurately (Culpeper, 2003; Kessler, Lloyd, & Lewis, 1999). Equipped with the knowledge that detection of mood and anxiety disorders requires the consideration of atypical presentation of symptoms or behaviors, the social worker would understand that further assessment would be warranted for both individuals.

In health-care settings, depression and anxiety also may be expressed through frequent medical visits (more than five per year) and through physical changes, such as weight gain or loss or sleeping problems (Institute for Clinical Systems Improvement, 2002). Anxiety in particular may be expressed through medically unexplained physical symptoms, such as chest pain, gastrointestinal problems, headache, or dizziness (Culpeper, 2003; Institute for Clinical Systems Improvement, 2002). Physical concerns, rather than explicit concerns about anxiety, are expressed frequently by people experiencing panic disorders (Institute for Clinical Systems Improvement, 2002). Although it is important not to invalidate an individual's physical symptoms, recognizing that such symptoms may have a relationship with mental health concerns and, as discussed, may reflect culturally informed somatization of distress can provide avenues to appropriate intervention and relief. However, some medical conditions, including coronary insufficiency, chronic obstructive pulmonary disease, pancreatic tumor, hypoparathyroidism, pheochromocytoma, pulmonary emboli, certain cases of coronary artery disease, and certain epilepsies, may be eclipsed by symptoms of anxiety and would warrant assessment by a physician. Culpeper suggests that if a person older than 35 years previously in good health does not have a history of prior anxiety symptoms, and describes new onset of anxiety, evaluation for possible medical conditions should be pursued. Such medical evaluation also would be indicated (a) when a client presents with symptoms of anxiety without a personal or family history of anxiety; (b) in the absence of a stressful life event; and potentially (c) when a client describes a high level of concern about the feelings of anxiety, which may suggest the presence of a physical condition rather than a mental health condition. Social workers are well situated to refer clients for appropriate physical care and to further explore mental health issues that may manifest as physical symptoms. In addition to asking open-ended questions about the client's mood, coping strategies, and daily functioning, screening instruments and a formal mental status exam are two structured ways in which social workers can explore mental health in health-care settings.

Screening Instruments

Screening instruments, which identify mental health symptoms warranting additional assessment, may facilitate the detection of mood, anxiety, and trauma-related disorders in health-care settings. Such instruments can include standardized scales with numerous items or just a few questions. They often are used in health-care settings in which certain psychosocial responses are seen frequently and in which their early detection is thought important for the achievement of optimal outcomes of care.

According to the U.S. Preventive Services Task Force (USPSTF; 2009), these screening questions may identify the majority of adults experiencing depression with effectiveness that is comparable to detailed instruments (p. 760):

- Over the last two weeks, have you felt down, depressed, or hopeless?
- Have you felt little interest or pleasure in doing things?

Positive responses to these questions suggest that additional assessment of depression and concurrent concerns (e.g., substance use problems, other psychological distress) should be conducted to inform appropriate intervention (USPSTF, 2009).

Screening for specific anxiety disorders may be facilitated by the next questions proposed

by Levinson and Engel (1997). Each question aims to screen for a particular anxiety disorder. A positive response to any of these questions warrants further assessment of anxiety and of its impact on the individual's daily life (Institute for Clinical Systems Improvement, 2002, pp. 2–3).

- Would you describe yourself as a nervous person? Do you feel nervous or tense? (Generalized Anxiety Disorder)
- Have you ever had a sudden attack of rapid heartbeat or rush of intense fear, anxiety, or nervousness? (Panic Disorder)
- Have you ever avoided important activities because you were afraid you would have a sudden attack like the one I just asked you about? (Agoraphobia)
- Some people have strong fears of being watched or evaluated by others. For example, some people do not want to eat, speak, or write in front of people because they fear embarrassing themselves. Is anything like this a problem for you? (Social Phobia)
- Some people have strong fears, or phobias, about heights, flying, bugs, or snakes. Do you have any phobias? (specific phobia)
- Some people are bothered by intrusive, silly, unpleasant, or horrible thoughts that keep repeating over and over. For example, some people have repeated thoughts of hurting someone they love even though they don't want to; that a loved one has been seriously hurt; that they will yell obscenities in public; or that they are contaminated by germs. Has anything like this troubled you? (Obsession)
- Some people are bothered by doing something over and over. They can't resist the urge, even when they try. They might wash their hands every few minutes or repeatedly check to see that the stove is off or the door is locked or count things excessively. Has anything like this been a problem for you? (Compulsion)
- Have you ever seen or experienced a traumatic event when you thought your life

was in danger? Have you ever seen someone else in grave danger? What happened? (Acute Stress and Posttraumatic Stress Disorders).

PTSD is associated with several health conditions, including hypertension, atherosclerotic heart disease, chronic pain, and vulnerability to infections; frequently involves increased health-care utilization; and often goes undetected. The National Center for PTSD (2010) suggests taking steps to identify and assist people experiencing PTSD. Detection of this "hidden diagnosis," as described by Lecrubier (2004), can be facilitated with a four-item screening instrument, the Primary Care PSTD Screen (Prins et al., 2004). The yes-no, self-reported screening questions can be completed via paper and pencil by the client and are (www.ptsd.va.gov/professional/pages/assessments/pc-ptsd.asp):

In your life, have you ever had any experience that was so frightening, horrible, or upsetting that, in the past month, you

1. Have had nightmares about it or thought about it when you did not want to?
2. Tried hard not to think about it or went out of your way to avoid situations that reminded you of it?
3. Were you constantly on guard, watchful, or easily startled?
4. Felt numb or detached from others, activities, or your surroundings?

In primary care settings, positive responses to two of these screening questions would warrant further assessment for PTSD (Prins et al., 2004). The National Center for PTSD provides detailed information regarding proceeding with further assessment and intervention (www.ptsd.va.gov/index.asp).

Substance misuse is a serious health concern that often co-occurs with mental health problems (CSAT, 2005) and complicates other health issues. Chapter 17 provides detailed discussion of screening, assessment, and interventions with which to assist people experiencing substance use problems.

Formal Mental Status Exam

The mental status exam is a systematic, semistructured method for gathering information about and describing a person's mental health status at the current time. It includes observation and inquiry to assess a person's mental status and frequently involves a written summary of the examination. Unlike a biopsychosocial assessment, the mental status exam does not explore comprehensive elements of the person in her environment and her history but focuses primarily on her mental status at the present time. In addition, the mental status exam involves not only eliciting the client's perspective but also actively drawing on and incorporating the social worker's observations (Lukas, 1993). Finally, although it is not a diagnostic tool, the mental status exam may alert the social worker to mental health problems that warrant further assessment (Trzepacz & Baker, 1993).

The mental status exam addresses these domains: appearance, attitude, and activity (sometimes simply referred to as appearance and behavior); mood and affect; speech and language; thought processes, thought content, and perception; cognition; and insight and judgment (Trzepacz & Baker, 1993). A mental status exam may be conducted as a discrete assessment or as part of a clinical interview. For example, when a social worker begins talking with an older adult client, the client may describe recent difficulties with remembering to take his medication and a recent event in which he forgot where he parked his car at the grocery store and wandered around the parking lot for an hour. His description would be a cue to pursue exploration of his cognitive capacities and of his memory, in particular. Especially when a client introduces an area that is worthy of further exploration through a mental status exam, it can be useful to follow up empathetically with the client, explain the nature of the questions you will ask, and proceed with the exam. This sort of follow-up conveys both attentiveness to the client and your professional capacity to further assess and intervene appropriately (Shea, 1988).

Appearance, Attitude, and Activity. The mental status exam typically begins with the social worker's observations of the client's appearance, attitude, and activity (Lukas, 1993; Trzepacz & Baker, 1993). This part of the mental status exam includes attention to these considerations:

- Client's degree of consciousness (Is the person alert? Does she respond to stimuli?)
- Congruence between the client's age and appearance (Does she appear to be her "stated age"? Does she seem older or younger?)
- Client's posture and position (Does the client's posture appear rigid or relaxed? Is the client in a hospital bed? Is the client able to sit down during the interview?)
- Client's attire and personal hygiene (Is the client dressed appropriately for the season? Are there any significant observations regarding the client's personal hygiene?)
- Notable physical characteristics, in addition to race, ethnicity, and gender
- Client's attitude toward the social worker and toward the interview (How does the client respond to you? Are there changes in this response during your meeting?)
- Significant movement or paralysis (Does the client have difficulty sitting still? Does the client seem to move quickly or slowly? Does the client appear to have any tremors or involuntary movements?)

Mood and Affect. Consideration of the client's mood and affect generally follows these observations in the mental status exam. *Mood* commonly refers to the client's subjective report of his emotional state in general or in the present moment, and *affect* commonly refers to the social worker's observations of the ways in which the client demonstrates his emotional state during the clinical interview (Lukas, 1993). Exploration of the client's mood can begin with open-ended questions, such as "How have you been feeling lately?"

or "How do you feel right now?" (Trzepacz & Baker, 1993, p. 40). Asking the client to describe his mood over the previous 30 days can follow these beginning questions and can add additional specific information. It is important to listen closely to the client's descriptions; follow up with questions that elicit greater detail and specificity regarding his mood, especially its intensity and the degree to which it reflects his usual mood; and, whenever possible, include direct phrases from the client in a mental status exam summary. The next hypothetical interaction illustrates such follow-up.

> **Social worker:** Can you tell me about how you've been feeling lately?
>
> **Client:** I've been very nervous.
>
> **Social worker:** In what ways have you been feeling nervous?
>
> **Client:** I feel sick to my stomach. I can't eat. I feel very restless and uneasy. I'm tired, but I can't sleep. I sleep a short time and then I'm up again. I can barely focus at work.
>
> **Social worker:** Is feeling this way new for you, or have you been feeling this way for a while?
>
> **Client:** Sometimes I worry, but it wasn't like this until I got sick. Waiting for all of the test results is very stressful, and it's got me very worried.
>
> **Social worker:** How intense are the feelings that you're having?
>
> **Client:** Like I said, I worry now and then, but I've never felt anything like this.
>
> **Social worker:** It seems like this worry is pretty intense for you. If you were to rank how you're feeling right now on a scale of 1 to 10, where 1 is the best you've ever felt and 10 is the most nervous you've ever felt, what would be your ranking?
>
> **Client:** I feel pretty far from the best I've ever felt (laughs). I would probably say that my nervousness feels like it's about an 8. It could go higher depending on what the test results say.

Social worker: It sounds like this nervousness feels very intense and out of the ordinary for you. It also sounds like you feel it quite physically, in your stomach, with your sleep, and in the restlessness you describe; and it sounds like it's affecting your concentration at work.

In this situation, in addition to the information the client provided regarding his mood, the social worker likely would observe that his affect appeared congruent with his mood—he appeared tense and nervous as he talked about feeling worried. Through the injection of humor, the client also may have displayed a range of affect even while predominantly expressing anxiety. Finally, the psychological distress the client is experiencing would warrant additional assessment to inform appropriate intervention.

Speech and Language. When observing speech and language, social workers focus on how information is being expressed and what is being said. Of particular interest is the speed with which a person speaks, any notable aphasia (difficulty expressing and understanding language, which may be evidenced by word-finding problems and more severe inability to express oneself), comprehension of language, volume of speech, prolonged silences, effort in speaking, poverty of speech, and any significant speech-related impairment (Lukas, 1993; Trzepacz & Baker, 1993). One way to assess comprehension is to ask the client to complete tasks that begin simply and increase in complexity. For example, a person could be asked to point to her eyes and then touch her left hand to her right ear, as described by Trzepacz and Baker (1993). These authors also offer a more complex, three-stage request that could involve asking a person to pick up a paper clip, put it on the table, and cross her arms. Asking clients to name objects in the room or in a complex picture is a way to assess aphasia. The assessment of mental status, and of speech and language in particular, should be informed by an awareness of the client's primary language and should be conducted with linguistic competence (Trzepacz & Baker, 1993). A person whose primary language is Spanish may display limited comprehension and difficulty naming objects; however, this may be due to limited fluency in English rather than a mental health issue. Linguistic competence is a central component of accurate assessment. When a social worker's language ability hinders provision of linguistically competent services, professional interpreters who are able to facilitate communication and cultural understanding should be employed (Hepworth, Rooney, & Larsen, 2002).

The information gathered regarding speech and language can inform inferences regarding mental health problems a person may be experiencing. For example, a person experiencing symptoms of depression may speak slowly and quietly with long pauses in the rhythm of speech. A person who recently has experienced a stroke, severe head trauma, brain surgery, or an infection may demonstrate difficulty finding words but still may exhibit comprehension. Alternatively, the person may demonstrate loss of the ability to understand or express language. In addition, with the range of difficulties associated with aphasia, individuals may have variable awareness of their language difficulties. When individuals evidence aphasia, collaboration with the transdisciplinary health-care team is a key element of ongoing assessment and intervention. Finally, when individuals are experiencing aphasia related to Alzheimer's and other progressive dementias, they likely will demonstrate gradual deterioration in language ability (Trzepacz & Baker, 1993). Routine assessment of mental status among older adults provides a way to monitor changes in mental status over time and to engage in early intervention (Rabins, 1991); however, it should be noted that based on currently available evidence, the United States Preventive Services Task Force (2009) neither endorses nor discourages routine screening for dementia among older adults. The Task Force does support assessment of cognitive functioning among older adults who display cognitive impairment or deterioration.

Thought Processes, Thought Content, and Perception. When assessing thought processes, content, and perception, social workers are focusing primarily on "how a person thinks and...what a person thinks about" (Lukas, 1993, p. 20) as well as any perceptual difficulties (e.g., hearing ability, eyesight, hallucinations, illusions) the person is experiencing (Lukas, 1993; Trzepacz & Baker, 1993). Thought processes are assessed by attending to the "organization, flow, and production of thought" (Trzepacz & Baker, 1993, p. 84). Specifically, the social worker attends to the degree of tangentiality, circumstantiality, flight of ideas, and looseness of associations in the person's verbal expressions. The primary areas of interest regarding thought content include obsessions, compulsions, paranoia, delusions, violent ideation, and poverty of content (Lukas, 1993; Trzepacz & Baker, 1993). Given the increased suicide risk among people with chronic or terminal illnesses (Trzepacz & Baker, 1993), an entire section of this chapter is dedicated to suicide assessment and intervention. In terms of risk of injury to another person through homicide, abuse, or neglect, social workers should familiarize themselves with their organization's protocols for assisting such an individual and preventing harm to another person. In addition, social workers should familiarize themselves with state laws regarding their mandates to warn third parties in the event of risk of imminent harm to an identified person and to report suspected abuse or neglect of children or elders (Lukas, 1993; Trzepacz & Baker, 1993). If a social worker has reason to believe that a person may be at risk of harming another person, it is important to consult a supervisor and to formulate a plan to help the identified potential victim remain safe.

Cognition. Assessment of cognition focuses on orientation, perceived level of intelligence, concentration, memory, and abstract thinking (Lukas, 1993; Trzepacz & Baker, 1993). A phrase frequently used in mental status exams is "the person is oriented x 3." This statement indicates that a person is oriented to person (i.e., who he is; immediate family members), place (i.e., where he is, both specific setting and city and state), and time (i.e., time, day, date, and season) (Trzepacz & Baker, 1993). An additional dimension can include orientation to

activity (i.e., what he is currently doing). For the mental status exam, perceived level of intelligence is based on the social worker's assessment of the client's apparent intelligence, described as above average, average, or below average (Lukas, 1993). Concentration typically is assessed by asking the person to engage in a task, such as counting backward from 20, counting down from 100 by 7s (this request is called serial 7 subtractions), or spelling "WORLD" backward. With these tasks, the person should be encouraged to complete the task without the use of paper, pencil, or other tools. Short-term memory can be assessed by asking a person to remember three words. This process begins with telling the person the words, asking him to repeat the words (which indicates that information has been registered), and then asking him to recall the words after five minutes have passed (Trzepacz & Baker, 1993). Long-term memory can be assessed by inquiring about significant aspects in the person's past, for example, the city where he grew up or details of major life events (Lukas, 1993; Trzepacz & Baker, 1993).

In addition to observing the degree of concrete and abstract thinking reflected in the client's communication, asking him to interpret a proverb can be another way to assess abstract thinking. For example, an interpretation of the phrase "The grass is greener on the other side" that demonstrates abstraction would be "Things that seem better elsewhere are not necessarily so," while a more concrete interpretation would be "His lawn is greener than mine" (Trzepacz & Baker, 1993, p. 144). Numerous factors may influence the degree to which a person interprets a proverb, including age, cultural relevance, level of education, IQ, psychosis, delirium, injury to the head, damage to the frontal lobe, and dementia (Trzepacz & Baker, 1993).

Insight and Judgment. The final component of the mental status exam, which attends to insight and judgment, assesses a person's awareness of a problem and her ability to pursue action with awareness of consequences (Lukas, 1993; Trzepacz & Baker, 1993). The mental status exam enables a social worker to assess a number of elements of a person's mental status and can facilitate detection of mental health problems that warrant further assessment. After mental health issues are identified, the social worker proceeds with differential assessment to guide appropriate interventions.

Differential Assessment: Depression and Anxiety

Feelings of sadness and worry are part of the human experience (American Psychiatric Association, 2000) and are likely to accompany a number of physical illnesses, including cancer, HIV, stroke, diabetes, heart disease, and Parkinson's disease (NIMH, 2002a–f). Psychological distress associated with physical illness is likely to range from transient worry and sadness to clinical mood and anxiety disorders. This discussion focuses on differentiating feelings of sadness and worry from more persistent mental health problems, including those that meet *DSM-IV-TR* diagnostic criteria (American Psychiatric Association, 2000) for anxiety and mood disorders, to formulate appropriate interventions to assist individuals and their families. As described previously, interventions may range from psychoeducation and supportive counseling (to support positive coping) to psychotherapy and psychopharmacology (to assist people who are experiencing more persistent and severe mental health issues) (DHHS, 1999; IOM, 2001).

People experiencing concurrent physical and psychiatric conditions may be particularly vulnerable to social isolation, medication nonadherence, and negative health outcomes (DiMatteo, 2004a; Frasure-Smith & Lesperance, 2003; Ickovics et al., 2001; IOM, 2001). In addition, people with psychiatric conditions have higher rates of illness and mortality. For example, in addition to high rates of suicide, people with mood disorders experience high rates of death due to cardiovascular and cerebrovascular conditions, accidents, and intoxication. Furthermore, treatment can reduce some of these risks, including suicide, vascular conditions, and cancer (Angst, Stassen, Clayton, & Angst, 2002). It is important for social workers to reach not only these vulnerable

groups but also people whose mental health concerns do not meet *DSM-IV-TR* diagnostic criteria (American Psychiatric Association, 2000). Subsyndromal psychological concerns can involve significant distress that warrants assistance. Psychosocial interventions can have powerful effects even when targeting a population based on physical, rather than mental, health conditions. For example, a meta-analysis of 37 studies published between 1974 and 1997 suggests that psychoeducational interventions focusing on stress management and health education among people with coronary disease are associated with reduced risk of cardiac mortality and subsequent myocardial infarction as well as improvements in dietary habits, smoking, exercise, cholesterol, and blood pressure (Dusseldorp, van Elderen, Maes, Meulman, & Kraaij, 1999). In addition, research suggests that quality of life, social support, and group therapeutic interventions that focus on education, coping, support, and stress management are associated with increased cancer survival (Butow, Coates, & Dunn, 1999; Fawzy et al., 1993; Fawzy, Fawzy, Arndt, & Pasnau, 1995; Spiegel, Sephton, Terr, & Stites, 1998). Attending to psychosocial elements of overall health can extend and improve life. Social workers often play a vital role in this process.

Although understanding the unique situation of the individual in his ecological context is at the core of assessment, appropriate action also depends on accurate differentiation of emotional reactions associated with adjustment to various health conditions and psychiatric disorders. Understanding the severity, daily functioning impact, and duration of psychiatric symptoms is critical to this process (American Psychiatric Association, 2000; J. W. Williams, Hitchcock, Cordes, Ramirez, & Pignone, 2002). The following section provides an overview of steps involved in differentiating the etiology and scope of mental health symptoms so that appropriate interventions can be formulated. The steps are based on the decision trees included in the *DSM-IV-TR*. These decisions guide differential diagnosis and take into consideration the possible contribution of medical conditions or substances in the mental health difficulties a person is experiencing. This discussion builds on the decision trees of the *DSM-IV-TR* by also addressing the potential contribution of ecological factors to a person's mental health difficulties. It should be noted that although etiological factors are presented separately, it is possible for a person to experience psychological distress due to multiple causes (American Psychiatric Association, 2000). Such a situation would require attention to each contributing factor.

Medical Conditions

When mental health symptoms have been detected, the decision trees of the *DSM-IV-TR* can provide helpful guidance regarding initial steps in the differential assessment process. The first step is to determine whether or not the symptoms may be due to a general medical condition. Many medical conditions have an underlying association with depression or anxiety. For example, Cushing disease or hypothyroidism can cause symptoms of depression (American Psychiatric Association, 2000; J. W. Williams et al., 2002). Several physical illnesses may be obscured by symptoms of anxiety (Culpeper, 2003). Because of the vast number of potential health conditions people may experience, collaborating with the transdisciplinary health-care team (e.g., nurses, physicians, and others with specialized training) and obtaining condition-specific information are necessary for making this determination. If it is determined that the mental health symptoms are due to an underlying medical condition, intervention should first address that condition, and mental health symptoms should be reassessed following such intervention. When physical conditions are associated with, rather than cause, psychological distress (e.g., diabetes mellitus, coronary heart disease, autoimmune disorders), intervention should concurrently target both the physical and psychological difficulties the person is experiencing (J. W. Williams et al., 2002).

Medications

If mental health symptoms do not appear to be due to a medical condition, the next step is to assess whether or not the symptoms are due to ingesting or withdrawing from a substance, either a prescribed medication, a toxin, alcohol, or other drugs (American Psychiatric Association, 2000). Side effects of numerous medications, including interferon alfa, anabolic steroids, glucocorticoids, and reserpine in high dosage, may involve psychological distress (Strader, Wright, Thomas, Seeff, & American Association for the Study of Liver Diseases, 2004; J. W. Williams et al., 2002). Comprehensive and differential assessment requires that social workers ask about and familiarize themselves with the medications or other substances clients are taking. Gathering substance-specific information and collaborating with the transdisciplinary health-care team are key elements in understanding the potential contribution of substances to psychological distress and in considering options for intervention.

Substance Use

The use of alcohol and other drugs also may influence mental health symptoms. Alcohol use is widely prevalent, with an estimated 51.6% of people 12 years and older in the United States reporting current use; 23.3% report binge drinking at least once in the past 30 days (Office of Applied Studies, 2009). The highest rates of both heavy and binge drinking are found among young adults aged 18–25 years, at 14.5% and 41.0%, respectively (Office of Applied Studies, 2009). Although the effect of alcohol in small amounts can produce feelings of confidence and a positive mood, alcohol is a central nervous system depressant that leads to slowed reaction, reflexes, and muscular response. In addition, higher dosages of alcohol lead to greater slowing of the central nervous system, which typically results in sleep followed by feelings of shakiness, headaches, depression, and difficulty concentrating upon waking (Weil & Rosen, 1993).

Cigarette smoking is also widely practiced. More than 1 in 4 people 12 years and older in the United States uses tobacco (Office of Applied Studies, 2009). Tobacco is a plant whose active ingredient, nicotine, is highly addictive and has significant pharmacological effects on the brain (Henningfield, 1998; Weil & Rosen, 1993). As a stimulant, nicotine may lead some people to feel more energized and alert while others may feel jittery and nervous. Stimulants also may affect sleep and eating. Following the use of stimulants, a person is likely to feel sleepy, fatigued, and depressed (Weil & Rosen, 1993). The National Institute on Drug Abuse (NIDA, 2009) describes numerous psychological effects associated with withdrawal of nicotine (e.g. intense tobacco cravings, attention difficulties, irritability).

This discussion of the physiological effects of alcohol and tobacco in relation to mental health symptoms provides just two examples of the numerous ways in which substance use and mental health symptoms may intersect. As part of a comprehensive assessment of a person's mental health symptoms, a social worker should consider the potential influence of substances on these symptoms. For example, a person recently diagnosed with lung cancer who has been a long-term smoker may describe difficulty concentrating. With further exploration, you learn that he recently stopped smoking. Although this recent discontinuation of smoking is not likely to be the only factor contributing to his psychological distress, it would be an important consideration in a comprehensive assessment. Similarly, a person seeking assistance with feelings of depression may describe heavy alcohol consumption. As alcohol is a central nervous system depressant, its consumption may be contributing to her feelings of depression.

This conceptualization of the relationship between mental health and substance use suggests a unidirectional, causal relationship in which substance use predates and causes the mental health symptoms a person is experiencing; however, this type of relationship is but one of several ways in which substance use and mental health symptoms may intersect. For example, it is possible for a person to experience mental health difficulties that predate her substance use, and the substance use may not meet criteria for a diagnosis of abuse or dependence (American Psychiatric

Association, 2000; Hien, Zimberg, Weisman, First, & Ackerman, 1997). Alternatively, a person may experience concurrent mental health and substance use disorders that are independent of each other and do not necessarily share etiology; however, increased symptoms of either disorder may intensify symptoms of the other (Hien et al., 1997). For social workers engaged in differential assessment, teasing apart the relationship between mental health and substance use issues involves obtaining a comprehensive history of the person's mental health symptoms, substance use, and the relationship between them. This comprehensive history and assessment can facilitate provision of or referral to appropriate services, depending on the social worker's setting.

Conceptualizing co-occurring psychiatric and substance use disorders in terms of severity of each condition (e.g., more severe psychiatric disorder, less severe substance use disorder) can assist with identifying the appropriate treatment setting (CSAT, 2005). Detailed general guidance for addressing substance use in health-care settings can be found in Chapter 17. Additional information for assisting people experiencing concurrent substance use and psychiatric disorders can be found online in the CSAT's 2005 publication *Substance Abuse Treatment for Persons with Co-Occurring Disorders.*

Ecological Context

Although the *DSM-IV-TR* does not identify ecological factors in its decision trees to inform differential diagnosis of psychiatric disorders (American Psychiatric Association, 2000), the centrality of the person-in-environment perspective in social work suggests that a comprehensive assessment of factors contributing to a person's mental health symptoms should include explicit consideration of ecological context. Inadequate housing, nutrition, financial resources, health insurance, access to medical care, and social support are likely to contribute to feelings of stress, sadness, and worry as well as to negative health outcomes. For example, research suggests that adults who are homeless have greater risk for mental illness, substance use disorders, physical illness, lack of health insurance, and death than the U.S. general population (Barrow, Herman, Cordova, & Streuning, 1999; Fischer & Breakey, 1991; Hibbs et al., 1994; Hwang et al., 1998; Kessler et al., 1994; Kushel, Vittinghoff, & Hass, 2001; Regier et al., 1993). Research involving children experiencing food insecurity indicates that this experience is associated with numerous social, emotional, behavioral, and physical health problems. (For a summary, see Wight, Thampi, & Briggs, 2010.) Furthermore, research involving mothers receiving welfare suggests that increased environmental and social risks (such as living in an unsafe neighborhood, not having enough food, experiencing domestic violence, and stressful life experiences associated with meeting basic needs) are associated with increased risk of depression, and social support and a sense of control over one's life are associated with reductions in this risk (Siefert et al., 2000). Some service providers and scholars also have described unmet basic needs and homelessness as sources of psychological trauma (Engstrom, Gunn, Petersen, 2011; Goodman, Saxe, & Harvey, 1991). The health concerns associated with unmet basic needs and ecological risks underscore the importance of strategies that help clients in these areas. Attention to concrete needs and ecological risks often is undervalued, but it is part of social work's "uncelebrated strength" (Johnson, 1999). Such attention can provide critical pathways to improved quality of life, reduced psychological distress, and improved physical health. If a comprehensive assessment indicates that ecological factors are contributing to a person's mental health difficulties, intervention should target them. Identifying potential resources and services, discussing them with the client, and facilitating referrals are important aspects of addressing ecological factors that may be fueling mental health symptoms; these are important functions of meeting the ethical responsibilities of social work (Johnson, 1991) and fulfill one of social workers' key roles: linking people to resources (Hepworth et al., 2002).

After medical conditions, substance use, and ecological factors are addressed as potential contributors to the client's mental health symptoms, the process of differentiating feelings of sadness and worry from psychiatric disorders moves to further consideration of the severity, duration, and functional impact of these experiences (American Psychiatric Association, 2000; Williams et al., 2002). These considerations inform the differential assessment process and can guide strategies to help people experiencing psychological distress. Furthermore, these considerations reflect elements of the diagnostic criteria for psychiatric disorders according to the *DSM-IV-TR* (American Psychiatric Association, 2000).

Diagnostic Criteria: Depression

When inquiring about a person's mental health experiences, it is useful to explore the nature of the difficulty a person is having, its intensity, history, precipitating events or stressors, and any prior mental health difficulties or treatment. The *DSM-IV-TR* identifies clusters of mental health symptoms for each disorder and thresholds for the number of symptoms that must be met, their duration, and their impact on functioning. For example, a diagnosis of major depressive disorder would be made if a person's symptoms meet these criteria (American Psychiatric Association, 2000, p. 356):

1. The patient experiences more than two weeks of daily or near daily experiences of symptoms that cause significant distress or impaired functioning.
2. The symptoms are not due to a medical condition, substance, or bereavement.
3. The symptoms include depressed mood (in children and adolescents, it may be irritable mood) or loss of pleasure or interest in activities and at least four of these symptoms:

   • Significant change in weight or appetite
   • Insomnia or hypersomnia
   • Psychomotor agitation or retardation

- Fatigue or loss of energy
- Feelings of worthlessness or excessive or inappropriate guilt
- Impaired concentration or indecision
- Recurrent thoughts of death, suicidal ideation, or suicide attempt.

A person experiencing fewer symptoms with less impact on functioning may meet the criteria for depressive disorder not otherwise specified. Other diagnostic categories that may be considered when a person presents with symptoms of depression that are not due to a general medical condition or substance include dysthymia, which involves depressed mood and two additional symptoms of depression for more than two years that cause significant distress or impairment, and adjustment disorder with depressed mood, which involves symptoms of depression following a stressful life event and significant distress or impaired functioning (American Psychiatric Association, 2000; J. W. Williams et al., 2002).

Diagnostic Criteria: Anxiety

Anxiety disorders not due to a general medical condition or to a substance include generalized anxiety disorder, panic attack and disorder, phobias, obsessive-compulsive disorder, acute stress disorder, posttraumatic stress disorder, and anxiety disorder not otherwise specified (American Psychiatric Association, 2000). For illustrative purposes, the diagnostic criteria for generalized anxiety disorder and posttraumatic stress disorder are outlined here. Additional information can be found in the *DSM-IV-TR*. With both of these conditions, the attention to severity, duration, and functional impact is again part of differentiating worry that might be part of the human experience from generalized anxiety disorder or differentiating responses that might be expected based on exposure to a traumatic event from posttraumatic stress disorder (American Psychiatric Association, 2000; J. W. Williams et al., 2002). In the case of generalized anxiety disorder, in addition to experiencing excessive worry or

anxiety that is difficult to control for six or more months, the person also experiences at least three (only one required with children) of these symptoms (American Psychiatric Association, 2000, p. 476):

1. Restlessness or feeling keyed up or on edge
2. Experiences of becoming easily fatigued
3. Difficulty concentrating or mind going blank
4. Irritability
5. Muscle tension
6. Sleep disturbance (difficulty falling or staying asleep or restless unsatisfying sleep)

In addition, the anxiety is generalized and not focused on a single domain. The symptoms fuel significant distress or impairment in functioning and are not due to a general medical condition or substance.

Diagnostic Criteria: Posttraumatic Stress Disorder

Diagnostic criteria for posttraumatic stress disorder include exposure to a traumatic event in which the person experienced "intense fear, helplessness, or horror." Among children this experience may be expressed as agitation or disorganization of behavior (American Psychiatric Association, 2000, p. 467). In addition, the person reexperiences the traumatic event, avoids stimuli associated with it or experiences numbed responsiveness evidenced in at least three symptoms, and experiences heightened arousal evidenced in at least two symptoms. Finally, the symptoms are present for more than one month and involve significant distress or impairment in functioning (American Psychiatric Association, 2000, pp. 467–468).

Diagnostic Hierarchy

It should be noted that when a person's symptoms overlap across conditions, the diagnosis that holds a higher place in the diagnostic hierarchy of the *DSM-IV-TR* (e.g., explanations of mental health symptoms due to a general medical condition or to substances are addressed first) or that has greater pervasiveness (e.g., secondary symptoms related to the primary diagnosis are not diagnosed as separate conditions) is applied (J. B. W. Williams, 1998). Exclusion criteria found in each diagnostic category will facilitate the application of these principles (American Psychiatric Association, 2000; J. B. W. Williams, 1998). As described by Williams, "A small forest of decision trees is provided [in the *DSM-IV-TR*] to make the differential diagnostic process easier by helping clinicians understand the organization and hierarchic structure of the classification" (pp. 37–38).

Suicide

Suicide is a serious, preventable public health issue and is ranked as the 11th overall cause of death in the United States (DHHS, 1999, 2001b; NIMH, 2009; Xu, Kochanek, Murphy, & Tejada-Vera, 2010). Numerous risk factors are associated with suicidal behavior and completed suicide, including differences by gender, age, race, and marital status (Heron, 2010; Moscicki, 1997, 2001; NIMH, 2009). In general terms, women are more likely to attempt suicide, and men are more likely to complete suicide. Firearms represent the most common method of suicide among men and second most common method among women. Poisoning is the most prevalent method of suicide among women (NIMH, 2009).

People older than 65 years are at high risk of suicide, and the highest rate of suicide is among White men older than 85 years (NIMH, 2007, 2009). Young adults age 15 to 24 years are also at risk. For this group, suicide is the third leading cause of death and in 2006 accounted for more deaths among this group than the next seven causes, including heart diseases, cancers, HIV, congenital problems, and diabetes, combined (Heron, 2010; U.S. Public Health Service, 1999). Although suicide rates among those 10 to 24 years old declined between 1990 and 2003, recent increases have been documented among those younger than 20

years (Bridge, Greenhouse, Weldon, Campo, & Kelleher, 2008; CDC, 2007). Historically, research suggested that White youth have higher suicide rates than African American youth, but recent increases in suicide among African American youth, particularly among African American young men, have reduced the differences in rates between these groups (Cash & Bridge, 2009; Joe, Baser, Neighbors, Caldwell, & Jackson, 2009). Although African American male youth have higher rates of suicide completion than their female counterparts (Heron, 2010), recent research documents higher rates of attempted suicide among females in this group (Joe et al., 2009).

Among males and females of all ages, suicide ranked among the top 10 causes of death in 2006 among people from American Indian (8th) and Asian or Pacific Islander (9th) backgrounds and among White Americans (10th) (Heron, 2010). Two important considerations should be noted in reviewing these data. First, Heron advises caution in interpreting reports for groups other than African Americans or White Americans because of race-related misreports on death certificates. Second, although suicide did not appear in the top 10 causes of death among all sexes and ages for people who were African American or Hispanic, this ranking differed by age and by gender in both groups. Finally, in her review of epidemiologic studies to identify risk factors for suicide, Moscicki (2001) identified research suggesting that rates of suicide among people who are divorced or widowed are higher than among people who are married across age groups and that being widowed earlier in life poses particular risk.

In addition to differences in prevalence of suicidal behavior and completed suicide by age, gender, race, and marital status, there is a growing body of literature regarding increased risk of suicidal behavior among gay, lesbian, bisexual, and transgender (LGBT) youth and adults. Although there appears to be general agreement that gay, lesbian, and bisexual youth and adults experience increased risk of suicidal ideation and attempts (Fergusson, Horwood, & Beautrais, 1999; Frankowski & Committee on

Adolescence, 2004; Jesdale & Zierler, 2002; King et al., 2008; Remafedi, 1999; Russell & Joyner, 2001), the literature is less conclusive regarding increased risk of completed suicide among gay, lesbian, and bisexual youth and adults compared with their heterosexual counterparts because of methodological limitations (Jesdale & Zierler, 2002; Remafedi, 1999). An emerging body of literature also indicates that transgender individuals are at higher risk for suicidality (Clements-Nolle, Marx, & Katz, 2006; Mathy, 2002; Wells, Freedenthal, & Wisneski, 2008). Although the empirical literature on completed suicide among people who are LGBT is limited, a prior suicide attempt is considered a significant risk factor for suicide (Gliatto & Rai, 1999; Moscicki, 1997; Nock et al., 2008; Zametkin, Alter, & Yemini, 2001). Accordingly, health-care professionals should be aware of the potential for heightened suicide risk among LGBT youth and adults.

Research suggests an increased risk of suicide is associated with several physical illnesses, including "HIV/AIDS, Huntington's disease, malignant neoplasms, multiple sclerosis, peptic ulcer, renal disease, spinal cord injuries, and systemic lupus erythematosus"; however, "there is no evidence that medical disorders are independent risk factors for suicide outside the context of depression and substance abuse" (Moscicki, 1997, p. 511). In terms of social work practice in health-care settings, these findings suggest that strategies to address mental health conditions among people with physical illness, including routine screening, assessment, and intervention, are central components of suicide prevention.

Experiencing a psychiatric or substance use disorder is associated with attempted and completed suicide. The risk is increased for those who have more than one disorder, particularly co-occurring mood and substance use disorders (Kessler, Borges, & Walters, 1999; Moscicki, 1997, 2001; Nock et al., 2008). Other widely recognized risk factors for suicidality include:

- Hopelessness
- Previous suicide attempts
- Firearms in one's home

- Incarceration
- Recent loss
- Significant stressful events (e.g., diagnosis of terminal illness, loss of employment, financial or legal difficulties)
- Family history of mood or substance use disorders or suicidal behavior
- Family stress
- Limited social support
- Physical or sexual abuse
- Models of suicidal behavior among one's family or peer group or among celebrities
- History of impulsive behavior
- Stigma or other obstacles to seeking help (DHHS, 2001b; Hirschfeld & Russell, 1997; Ivanoff & Smyth, 1992; Moscicki, 1997, 2001; NIMH, 2009; New York State Department of Health, 2007; Nock et al., 2008; Sanchez, 2001; Shaffer et al., 2001; U.S. Public Health Service, 1999; Zametkin et al., 2001)

In addition to these considerations, suicide risk factors among youth include domestic violence, rejection, and disciplinary stress (Moscicki, 1997; Zametkin et al., 2001). The National Cancer Institute (NCI, 2010) asserts that people with cancer may be at increased risk for suicide and that additional suicide risk factors to consider include:

- Oral, pharyngeal, and lung cancers (often associated with heavy alcohol and tobacco use)
- Advanced stage of disease and poor prognosis
- Confusion/delirium
- Inadequately controlled pain
- Presence of deficit symptoms (e.g., loss of mobility, loss of bowel and bladder control, amputation, sensory loss, paraplegia, inability to eat and to swallow, exhaustion, fatigue) (NCI, 2010)

The presence of a suicide risk factor does not mean that a person will engage in suicidal behavior (Ivanoff & Smyth, 1992); however, if a person is experiencing numerous factors, the risk may increase (Moscicki, 1997, 2001). Evaluating a person's risk for suicide begins with an awareness of risk factors but relies on an individualized assessment. Suicide assessment involves employing relevant knowledge and finely tuned skills to assess a person's ability to stay safe and to refrain from self-harm. In this process, generalized information should be considered in the context of the unique experiences of each particular individual.

Assessment of Suicide

The first step in suicide assessment is the identification of suicidal ideation. Many people who complete suicide, particularly older adults, have seen a primary care provider in the month prior to their deaths (Andersen, Andersen, Rosholm, & Gram, 2000; Luoma, Martin, & Pearson, 2002), and physicians often are unaware of clients' history or risk of suicidality (Gliatto & Rai, 1999; Murphy, 1975a,b). Research also suggests that patients support routine mental health inquiries by their physicians and that people with a history of suicidality may be particularly supportive of such inquiry at each visit (Zimmerman et al., 1995). Although some individuals may readily identify their thoughts about suicide, others may keep them to themselves or may convey them in indirect language. Indirect communication may include expressions of hopelessness, an inability to see a solution to a problem, a feeling that others might be better off without them, a desire to give up, or a feeling that current problems are insurmountable (Ivanoff & Smyth, 1992).

Direct inquiry about suicidal ideation has not been shown to cause suicidal behavior (J. W. Williams et al., 2002; Zimmerman et al., 1995). Although the U.S. Preventive Services Task Force (2009) recommends depression screenings in settings with appropriate follow-up services, it neither recommends nor discourages routine screening for suicide based on available evidence. However, particularly in settings where people may be at high risk of suicide, routine inquiry about suicidal ideation as part of a mental health assessment may

facilitate early detection and assistance for people at risk (Ivanoff & Smyth, 1992). Furthermore, results from a recent systematic review also indicate that training primary care physicians to identify and address suicidality and depression is associated with significant (22%–73%) reductions in suicides. Finally, psychiatric evaluation guidelines from the American Psychiatric Association (2006) include assessment of risk to self or others as a standard domain in an overall clinical assessment.

Although a number of standardized suicide assessment instruments are available and widely used in research, the American Psychiatric Association (2006) notes their limited predictive abilities. As such, this discussion focuses on direct inquiry about potential self-harm and individualized follow-up questions to assess suicidality. Direct inquiry that is coupled with empathy can provide an inroad into assessing suicidal ideation and intention. For example, interwoven with a discussion in which a client expresses hopelessness and difficulty identifying solutions to a pressing problem, a follow-up question might be: "It sounds like you've been feeling pretty discouraged, and maybe a bit desperate. Have you thought about hurting yourself?" Or another follow-up question might be: "It sounds like you're having a hard time finding a way out of this situation and that you're feeling like you have no options. You mentioned wanting to give up. Have you thought about wanting to die?" If the client reports wanting to die, then the social worker could follow up by asking "You've described feeling so down you've wanted to die. Have you thought about hurting yourself?" (For additional examples, see American Psychiatric Association, 2006; Gliatto & Rai, 1999; Hirschfeld & Russell, 1997; Ivanoff & Smyth, 1992; Lukas, 1993; Shaffer et al., 2001).

If a client reports suicidal ideation, the social worker's next questions aim to (a) gather additional information about components of the ideation (e.g., content, timing, onset, frequency, intensity) and (b) identify the level of imminent risk associated with it (American Psychiatric Association, 2006; Hirschfeld

& Russell, 1997; Ivanoff & Smyth, 1992). Bearing in mind the risk factors previously discussed, the imminence of suicide risk increases with the intensity of the suicidal ideation and the presence of these factors:

- A developed plan for hurting one's self, with particular attention to plans that involve violence or irreversibility
- Access to the means to carry out the plan
- Intention to harm one's self or to carry out the plan
- Consideration of efforts to avoid being discovered or interrupted
- Completion of or in process of writing a suicide note
- Alcohol or other substance use
- Presence of psychotic symptoms, with particular attention to command hallucinations that may be instructing the person to engage in self-harm
- Hopelessness (American Psychiatric Association, 2006; Hirschfeld & Russell, 1997; Ivanoff & Smyth, 1992; USPSTF, 2009)

Making a determination regarding a client's level of suicide risk can be facilitated by five additional factors.

1. Gathering specific information in the course of the suicide assessment will enable the social worker to further consider the person's level of risk, to describe it to others from whom consultation may be sought, and to coordinate services as indicated (Lukas, 1993).
2. Consultation with a supervisor or with colleagues often is a vital element in making this assessment and in formulating appropriate intervention.
3. Before conducting a suicide assessment, social workers should familiarize themselves with their organization's policies and procedures regarding assessment and intervention with clients at risk of suicide. They also should familiarize themselves

with the state laws and regulations in this area.

4. Although social workers should be mindful of the potential negative aspects of inpatient hospitalization (e.g., stigma, loss of control) and the centrality of supporting clients' self-control (Ivanoff & Smyth, 1992; Lukas, 1993), Lukas asserts that "you should make a practice—both for the client's well-being and your own—of never letting a client leave your office until you have used all necessary resources to satisfy yourself that she is not at imminent risk of trying to kill herself" (p.119).
5. Clear, thorough documentation can be useful in recording events, decisions made, and actions taken and in serving as a risk management practice (Ivanoff & Smyth, 1992).

Interventions to Address Suicide Risk

If a client is at immediate risk of suicide, intervention should focus on physical safety (Hirschfeld & Russell, 1997; Ivanoff & Smyth, 1992); however, throughout the process, Ivanoff and Smyth (1992) recommend "a bias toward maintaining the client's sense of self-control and personal management whenever possible" (p. 123). This stance suggests that social workers should pursue collaboration and empowerment rather than unilateral action when working with clients at risk for suicide. In social work practice, this perspective would involve seeking clients' input regarding available intervention options and empowering them to take action—for example, voluntarily pursuing inpatient hospitalization rather than involuntary commitment. However, if a person is unable to pursue action that will uphold his safety and there is imminent risk of suicide, it is the social worker's responsibility, or the responsibility of another direct service provider, to intervene to support his physical safety.

When a client is at imminent risk of suicide, someone should remain with him, and, in most cases, an evaluation for inpatient hospitalization should be made (Hirschfeld & Russell, 1997). If the contact with the client is over the phone, the social worker should remain on the phone with the client and not place the client on hold (Millman, Strike, Van Soest, Rosen, & Schmidt, 1998). It may be helpful to involve a reassuring person to stay with the client so that he is not left alone and so that emotional support can begin to be mobilized (Ivanoff & Smyth, 1992; New York State Department of Health, 2007). If the client says that he has a gun or pills during the phone contact, Millman and colleagues (1998) recommend that he should be asked to place the gun (unloaded) in another part of the room or, likewise, to move pills, to dispose of them in the toilet, or to ask another person to keep them temporarily. Contacting emergency medical services or the police would be warranted if a suicide attempt has occurred or is in the process of occurring or if needed to transport the client for inpatient hospitalization evaluation (Hirschfeld & Russell, 1997; Ivanoff & Smyth, 1992). A client who needs to be evaluated for inpatient hospitalization should not drive himself there (Holkup, 2002).

Shaffer and colleagues (2001) further specify that with children and adolescents experiencing suicidality, the social worker should be in contact with the client's family and should address the importance of treatment as well as its feasibility and family preferences. In addition, they recommend gathering information from multiple sources (e.g., interviews with the client and people who know the client, observation of behavior, completion of standardized scales) and consulting with the client's caregiver. Consultation with the client and caregiver should focus on these topics: (a) restricting access to alcohol or drugs because of their disinhibiting effects, (b) securing or removing any firearms or lethal medications, (c) identifying that someone supportive will be at home, (d) discussing stressful situations that may precipitate suicidality and coping strategies to address them, and (e) confirming that an appointment for follow-up care has been made.

Verbal and written safety contracts often are made with clients and their families when their risk of suicide is found to not be imminent (American Psychiatric Association, 2006; Shaffer et al., 2001). These contracts typically include an agreement that the client will not harm himself and that the client will take action to stay safe, including contact numbers and whom to call if he is not able to stay safe (Holkup, 2002; Ivanoff & Smyth, 1992). Written contracts typically are signed by both the client and the social worker, and each retains a copy (Holkup, 2002). Although such contracts may be widely used, there are important caveats to consider in their use, perhaps most important of which are that they lack empirical research support (Garvey, Penn, Campbell, Esposito-Smythers, & Spirito, 2009; Rudd, Mandrusiak, & Joiner, 2006; Shaffer et al., 2001) and that the American Psychiatric Association (2006) cautions against their use as evidence of a client's ability to stay safe or of his eligibility for discharge from outpatient services or inpatient hospitalization. In addition, the American Psychiatric Association does not recommend the use of safety contracts with clients who display impulsivity, agitation, psychosis, or substance intoxication or with clients who are not well known to the provider or who are seen in emergency contexts. Garvey and colleagues (2009) also caution clinicians regarding the use of such contracts. In particular, they emphasize their limited evidence base, the client's ability to give informed consent, the importance of a comprehensive suicide risk assessment, and the legal liabilities that may be involved with such contracts. In recognition of the limitations of safety contracts, Rudd and colleagues (2006) propose a commitment-to-treatment statement (CTS) that includes attention to roles and expectations of the client and clinician, clear communication about treatment and suicide, and a plan to access crisis services as needed. The authors note that the CTS requires empirical investigation; however, it may address some of the limitations of safety contracts. McMyler and Pryjmachuk (2008) also suggest alternate strategies to the safety contract, including safety and crisis planning, nonintrusive observation and reducing environmental risks on inpatient units, addressing precipitants to suicidality, and attending to the centrality of communication between the client and clinician. The available evidence base of these alternatives varies.

When a client is at risk for suicide but not imminently, recommended interventions include mobilizing her support system by asking her permission to contact and involve a person with whom she has a close relationship; acting to restrict her access to any firearms, ammunition, lethal medication, or other potentially lethal methods of self-harm; thoroughly following up with her through additional contacts (including phone contact, visits, letters, or scheduled meetings); and providing appropriate intervention or referral to address any co-occurring psychiatric or substance use disorders she may be experiencing (Hirschfeld & Russell, 1997; Ivanoff & Smyth, 1992; New York State Department of Health, 2007; Shaffer et al., 2001). The Substance Abuse and Mental Health Services Administration (Office of Applied Studies, 2009) has developed a five-step pocket guide to suicide assessment and immediate intervention that may be useful for quick reference (see http://download.ncadi .samhsa.gov/ken/pdf/SMA09-4432/SMA09 -4432.pdf for this resource).

A growing body of evidence-based information guides intervention with people at risk of suicide. Effective strategies generally include intensive follow-up and a combination of psychotherapy and pharmacotherapy (American Psychiatric Association, 2006; Hirschfeld & Russell, 1997; Ivanoff & Smyth, 1992; Shaffer et al., 2001). Because repeat suicide attempts often occur within the first weeks following intake or hospital discharge (Hunt et al., 2009; Meehan et al., 2006), active and immediate follow-up is warranted. It is important to note that while some studies of chain-of-care networks, follow-up mailings, and easy access to psychiatric care (Morgan, Jones, & Owen, 1993) indicate that such follow-up is helpful in reducing suicidality, other types of follow-up have not consistently been more effective than usual care (Mann et al., 2005). In particular, there have been mixed findings regarding the added value of phone-based interventions. For example, a Swedish study found no added benefit

of two phone interventions (contact at 4- and 8-month follow-up) among 216 people who had attempted suicide and received psychiatric care (Cedereke, Monti, & Öjehagen, 2002). Another study conducted in the United States found that three phone contacts over one year, together with two visits with a depression specialist and personalized mailings, improved medication adherence and depressive symptoms among 386 people with major depression or dysthymia who received primary care. (Katon et al., 2001). Although the second study did not examine effects on suicidality, the combined intervention shows promise to improve medication adherence and depression, which may reduce suicidality. These findings suggest that phone-based interventions may be more effective when part of a multifaceted follow-up plan. Furthermore, the effectiveness of more intensive follow-up by phone cannot be assessed by this research that focuses on highly specified interspersed phone contacts. Of critical importance is timely therapeutic follow-up for people at risk of suicide (Hunt et al., 2009).

Cognitive-behavioral therapy (CBT) and interpersonal psychotherapy may be useful with persons experiencing depression and suicidality; dialectical behavior therapy and psychodynamic therapy may be useful for persons experiencing borderline personality disorder, which often is associated with suicidal and self-harming behavior (American Psychiatric Association, 2000, 2006; Mann et al., 2005). For example, in a study with 120 adults who recently attempted suicide, cognitive therapy (10 sessions) was associated with 50% lower likelihood of reattempting suicide than the usual care condition (Brown et al., 2005). An eight-year follow-up of psychodynamic partial hospitalization (18 months) and outpatient group treatment (18 months) with 41 people experiencing borderline personality disorder found approximately 60% lower likelihood of suicidality among those in the experimental group compared with those in usual treatment (Bateman & Fonagy, 2008). Medication, including lithium, neuroleptics, and antidepressants, also has been shown to reduce the risk of suicide (Angst, Angst, Gerber-Werder,

& Gamma, 2005; Angst, Stassen, Clayton, & Angst, 2002; Baldessarini et al., 2006; Isacsson, Holmgren, Ösby, & Ahlner, 2009). In some cases, when a person is experiencing severe unremitting depression, electroconvulsive therapy (ECT) may be indicated (American Psychiatric Association, 2006; Hirschfeld & Russell, 1997; NIMH, 2008).

Research with older adults experiencing depression suggests that interpersonal psychotherapy or medication (primarily citalopram, a selective serotonin reuptake inhibitor [SSRI]) provide more timely relief from suicidal ideation than does usual care while also facilitating improvements in depression (Bruce et al., 2004). In their practice parameters for intervention with children and adolescents experiencing suicidality, Shaffer and colleagues (2001) draw on research with adolescents experiencing depression to cite evidence for the use of these approaches to assist youth at risk of suicide: CBT, interpersonal psychotherapy, dialectical behavior therapy, and family psychoeducation (Brent et al., 1997; Brent, Poling, McKain, & Baugher, 1993; A. L. Miller, Rathus, Linehan, Wetzler, & Leigh, 1997; Mufson, Weissman, Moreau, & Garfinkel, 1999). The American Academy of Child and Adolescent Psychiatry's (2007) recent practice parameters to assist children and adolescents experiencing depression also recognize the usefulness of CBT, interpersonal psychotherapy, family therapy, and psychodynamic psychotherapy to address depression among youth, however, its review suggests the need for additional research regarding family therapy and psychodynamic psychotherapy.

Shaffer and colleagues (2001) discuss several psychopharmacological interventions to assist children and adolescents experiencing suicidality, including lithium, valproate, carbamazepine, SSRIs, and, in particular, fluoxetine. Concerns regarding increased risk of suicidality with the use of antidepressants among youth have received considerable attention in recent years (March, Silva, Vitiello, & TADS Team, 2006; Olfson, Marcus, & Shaffer, 2006; Schneeweiss et al., 2010; Simon, Savarino, Operskalski, & Wang, 2006; Tiihonen et al.,

2006) and influenced the Food and Drug Administration's (FDA) 2005 decision to request that drug manufacturers include a black-box warning on antidepressants regarding increased risk of suicidal ideation and behavior among children and adolescents (FDA, 2007). In 2007, the FDA proposed revised warnings, including language to indicate that elevated risk continues until age 24 years and that psychiatric disorders play the primary role in suicide risk. Upon review of available science, the AACAP (2007) provided this summary:

> [I]t appears that spontaneously reported events are more common in SSRI treatment. Nevertheless, given the greater number of patients who benefit from SSRIs than who experience these serious adverse effects, the lack of any completed suicides, and the decline in overall suicidality in rating scales, the risk/benefit ratio for SSRI use in pediatric depression appears to be favorable with careful monitoring. (p. 1516)

Close monitoring should include routine inquiry regarding suicidality and attention to worsening depressive symptoms, behavioral changes, and akathisia, a side effect that may increase risk of suicidality (NIMH, 2010b; Shaffer et al., 2001).

For social workers in health-care settings, these findings suggest that, depending on one's role and setting, training in the provision of CBT, interpersonal, psychodynamic, dialectical behavior, and family therapies or referring clients to such therapies may be indicated. In addition, collaboration with physicians who can evaluate the use of psychotropic medications, in particular medications that are not lethal in overdose, would be warranted (Hirschfeld & Russell, 1997; Murphy, 1975a).

PSYCHOSOCIAL INTERVENTION STRATEGIES IN HEALTH-CARE SETTINGS

Social work practitioners strive to match intervention strategies to individuals in their ecological contexts and to the identified problems (Berlin & Marsh, 1993). They do this with the best available evidence and the client's preferences for intervention (Culpeper, 2003; Gambrill, 2000; J. W. Williams et al., 2002). Comprehensive assessment enables social workers to fully consider the range of factors that may be contributing to the problem and the range of interventions that may resolve it effectively. Furthermore, it enables social workers to discuss intervention options with the client (Gambrill, 2000). As described above, differential assessment involves identifying the type of mental health issue a person is experiencing, its possible influences, and possible ways to address it. The psychosocial interventions described next begin with strategies to support coping and overall well-being and then address strategies to assist people who are experiencing depression and anxiety disorders.

Routine Screening of Psychosocial Conditions

Because of the significant implications of mental health in health-care settings, including the relationship between psychological distress and physical health conditions, the role of behavior in health, the importance of suicide prevention, and the power of social ties in supporting health, routine screening of psychosocial conditions is highly relevant in health-care settings. Program planning and policy-level initiatives are warranted to ensure the availability of this core element of overall health care.

Transdisciplinary Collaboration and Coordination of Services

Another central component of supporting mental health in health-care settings involves transdisciplinary collaboration with the team of providers working with the client. Transdisciplinary collaboration is particularly relevant in underscoring the importance of mental health in physical health conditions and outcomes, examining intersections between the client's mental health and physical condition, and coordinating comprehensive care with numerous providers. When a client is experiencing psychological distress that warrants consultation for psychopharmacological intervention, transdisciplinary collaboration can be helpful in accessing this service and in considering the possible interactions between psychotropic medications and any medications the client currently is taking for another condition.

Social workers often serve as brokers of services (Hepworth et al., 2002). In this role social workers can facilitate referrals and access to needed resources, including physical and mental health care, health insurance coverage, housing, food, and community-based case management when indicated. Gambrill (2000) highlights the importance of being aware of the effectiveness of services to which clients are referred. Beyond simply linking a client to a given service, the social worker should consider the overall quality of that resource. In some communities, available resources may be limited and may require macro-level advocacy to adequately meet the needs of people within the community. In addition to simply providing a phone number or a contact name, the social worker may help facilitate the referral by obtaining written consent from the client to contact the referral agency, by following up with the agency directly, and then by following up with the client to ensure that the contact was made.

Information and Psychoeducation

Information and psychoeducation are central components of helping individuals and families understand the physical or mental health condition, including its course, expected outcome, treatment, and psychosocial components (A. Johnson, Sandford, & Tyndall, 2003; Rolland, 1994). Educational and psychoeducational approaches typically differ by scope, focus, and qualifications of the service provider. Education generally focuses on providing information about an illness, including expected course, treatment, and components of self-care by a person who may not necessarily have professional training. Psychoeducation generally builds on these components by also including psychotherapeutic strategies, such as behavioral and cognitive interventions, led by a person with professional training in mental health services (Lukens & Thorning, 1998). Psychoeducational approaches support the emotional and cognitive processing of information and may assist people with developing a psychosocial understanding of the condition and its meaning in their lives (Rolland, 1994).

Based on a review of studies that compared the usefulness of written and verbal information for parents of children discharged from acute hospitals, A. Johnson and colleagues (2003) concluded that greater satisfaction and knowledge were associated with the provision of both written and verbal information. In addition, they underscore the potential for client involvement in creating the written information, the importance of its culturally relevant presentation, and attention to the literacy level of written material. Written and verbal information and psychoeducational interventions are important components of facilitating knowledge and strengthening coping with physical and mental health conditions. Furthermore, as described in the sections titled "Stress Management" and "Strengthening Health-Supporting Behaviors," such interventions also may play an important role in reducing health risks and promoting longevity.

Adherence Counseling

Adherence to medication and treatment are key contributors to health outcomes. However, nonadherence is highly prevalent, impacting approximately 1 in 4 people (DiMatteo, 2004b). Social workers often assist people with adherence to medications and treatment. For comprehensive guidance to support adherence in health-care settings, see Chapter 20 in this book.

Stress Management

Several strategies have shown promise in helping people to manage stress and in supporting overall health, including mindfulness-based stress reduction (MSBR; Kabat-Zinn, 2003; Weissbecker et al., 2002), exercise (McEwen & Gianaros, 2010), and relaxation training. Research on these approaches includes compelling findings regarding their ability to affect not only mood and quality of life but also physical functioning and outcomes. For example, a recent randomized controlled trial of MBSR with 84 women who survived breast cancer found that MBSR was associated with greater reductions in depression and fears of recurrence and greater improvements in energy and physical functioning compared with usual care (Lengacher et al., 2009). In a nonrandomized controlled study involving 75 women with early-stage breast cancer, MBSR was associated with greater improvements in quality of life, coping, and immune functioning and reduced cortisol levels compared with the control group (Witek-Janusek et al., 2008). Similarly, research involving 133 adults experiencing chronic pain found MBSR to be associated not only with improved mental health but also with improved pain and physical functioning (Rosenzweig et al., 2010). A recent meta-analysis indicated small physical effects of MBSR among people with cancer, but it found greater mental health effects (Ledesma & Kumano, 2009). Another meta-analysis found small but significant mental health effects of MBSR among people with chronic physical illness. The authors suggest that mindfulness-based cognitive therapy may be associated with greater gains, particularly in depression, among people with serious and persistent physical illness (Bohlmeijer, Prenger, Taal, & Cujipers, 2010).

There have been mixed findings about the effectiveness of some relaxation training and stress management interventions among people with cardiac problems (IOM, 2001). A comprehensive review of 36 studies by Rees, Bennett, West, Davey, and Ebrahim (2004), 18 of which examined the effectiveness of stress management strategies, suggested that psychological and stress management interventions among people with coronary heart disease were associated with some decreased depression and anxiety; however, findings did not demonstrate reductions in cardiac mortality, which may be due to methodological limitations of the published research and the range of interventions included in the review. In contrast to these findings, as previously discussed, a meta-analysis of 37 studies found that stress management and health education interventions were, in fact, associated with reduced risk of cardiac mortality as well as reductions in associated risk factors such as smoking, dietary habits, cholesterol, and blood pressure (Dusseldorp et al., 1999). These findings, in conjunction with additional research conducted with people experiencing cancer and other serious illnesses, seem to suggest that stress management interventions are best partnered with psychoeducation to reduce risk factors and to enhance coping and survival (Butow et al., 1999; Conn, Hafdahl, Brown, & Brown, 2008; Dusseldorp et al., 1999; Fawzy et al., 1993, 1995; Spiegel et al., 1998).

Strengthening Health-Supporting Behaviors

Smoking cessation, healthful eating, and weight management are key behaviors that can help improve health (IOM, 2001). Engaging people in the change process and facilitating motivation to change behavior are central elements of supporting such health behaviors. Two paradigms—the transtheoretical/stages of change model (Prochaska & DiClemente, 1983) and motivational interviewing (Miller & Rollnick, 1991, 2002; Rollnick, Miller, & Butler, 2008)—have received considerable attention as models to inform assisting people with behavior change efforts. Although empirical research has prompted questions regarding the theoretical validity of Prochaska and DiClemente's transtheoretical model (IOM, 2001; Littell & Girvin, 2002), and further research suggests that perceptions of self-efficacy, expectations about outcomes, and self-control of behavior may predict behavioral changes more effectively, the stages of change model may be useful as a framework for conceptualizing readiness for change (IOM, 2001).

The stages of change model proposes that a person's readiness for behavior change can be understood in the context of five stages: precontemplation, contemplation, preparation, action, and maintenance (Prochaska, DiClemente, & Norcross, 1992). The stages reflect (a) the degree of awareness a person has about making a behavioral change (e.g., a move from precontemplation to contemplation reflects increasing awareness of a behavior to be changed and increasing consideration of the possibility of change), (b) the time frame in which behavioral change will happen (e.g., a move from contemplation to preparation reflects increased intention to take action in the near future), and (c) the action a person is taking to achieve behavioral change (e.g., preparation involves planning for change, action involves active modification of behavior or environment to support behavioral change, and maintenance involves steps to uphold change) (Prochaska et al., 1992). Together, Miller and Rollnick's (1991, 2002) model of motivational interviewing and the stages of change model may provide useful tools for conceptualizing and enhancing motivation and for helping people change behaviors (IOM, 2001). Both of these models are discussed further in Chapter 17 of this book. In addition, more detailed information regarding motivational interviewing in the context of health care can be found in a recent book by Rollnick, Miller, and Butler (2008). As noted earlier, connecting individually focused behavior change interventions with attention to familial, social, and environmental factors, including access to safe places to exercise and availability of healthful food, is likely to strengthen their effectiveness (IOM, 2001).

Coping Enhancement

A large body of research suggests that interventions to enhance coping can assist people experiencing psychological stress (Noh & Kaspar, 2003). Rather than focusing on specific mental health symptoms among people experiencing physical illness, Folkman and Greer (2000) focus on "psychological well-being and the coping processes that support it"

(p. 11). Informed by Lazarus and Folkman's (1984) cognitive model of stress and coping and relevant research that focuses on elements of effective coping while experiencing illness, Folkman and Greer propose an approach that relies heavily on pursuing meaningful goals to support coping when faced with illness. In essence, this model focuses on continuing to seek goals that matter; facing the inspiring yet potentially frightening possibility that the goal may or may not be realized; and taking action to achieve the goal. Implicit in this model is the notion that pursuing goals that matter and that are not necessarily illness specific can be an important mechanism for fostering coping and continued engagement with positive aspects of life in the midst of illness.

In this model, the social worker first focuses on creating "conditions for challenge" which reflect a positive appraisal that something valuable can be gained through the experience (Folkman & Greer, 2000, p.16). The importance of challenge in this model is based on the premise that such appraisal holds the possibility of achieving a meaningful goal through the client's own efforts and of enhancing the client's sense of control and ability. This challenge combines the exciting possibility of achieving the goal and the potentially worrisome risk of striving without success. Normalizing this combination of emotions may be helpful. To create the conditions for challenge, Folkman and Greer (2000) suggest exploring what matters to the client, whether it relates to his illness or to other parts of his life. The social worker "needs to help the patient define what is important now, what matters most" (p. 16). Probing recent events and specific aspects of those events that have meaning and that matter to the client will help create conditions for challenge. Identification of what matters to the client also may be fostered even as clients discuss negative events. Negative events can be explored and followed with inquiry regarding positive events or personal strengths. Folkman and Greer (2000) offer these specific questions: "Tell me about a time when something happened that made you feel good" or "Tell me about a time when things

were really going well. What was going on?'" (p. 16). Other sample questions might include "What are some of your strengths? When was a time that you used that strength?" Exploration of what was involved in those times, of how the client was feeling, and of "what mattered" to the client can help identify what is important to him (p. 16).

Identifying what matters to the client then informs the creation of a realistic goal that has meaning to him. The goal may be created independently by the client or with input from the social worker or significant others. Most relevant is that the goal matters to the client and that it emphasizes personal control. Folkman and Greer (2000) describe the goal of a person experiencing metastatic bowel cancer to make tea for his companion although he was feeling weak physically and somewhat powerless emotionally. They go on to describe that in setting this goal and considering steps to achieve it, "the patient realized that there were still things he could control, and this helped lift his spirits" (p. 16). Goals may involve reading a book to a loved one, having a conversation with a friend, pursuing a cherished hobby, formulating a system to manage medical treatments or side effects, or writing a letter to a partner; what is important is that the goal has value to the client and strengthens a sense of control.

The next step focuses on encouraging the client's achievement of the goal, including continued support or revision of the goal if the task seems overwhelming. Key elements of this step include active engagement of the client in pursuing a goal that has meaning to him, focusing on steps to achieve the goal, and continuing to create the conditions of positive challenge. The final component of the model involves maintaining "background positive mood" (Folkman & Greer, 2000, p. 17), which may include asking clients to talk about positive happenings in their lives and encouraging them to plan activities that yield feelings of enjoyment and accomplishment.

This theoretically informed and research-guided model provides a framework for enhancing coping and psychological well-being when a person is experiencing serious illness. Key elements of this model include its attention to normative coping and supporting a sense of control and mastery in the context of illness. This model has the potential to support meaning, growth, and well-being in the midst of challenges associated with significant illness (Cordova, Cunningham, Carlson, & Andrykowski, 2001; Folkman & Greer, 2000; Towsley, Beck, & Watkins, 2007).

Family and Social Support and Spiritual Resources

Psychosocial responses to physical and mental illness among individuals and their families are likely to vary according to the timing, onset, course, degree of incapacitation, and anticipated outcome of the illness (Rolland, 1994). Family and social support influence health outcomes via these pathways: direct biology (e.g., airborne, bloodborne, and genetic conditions), health behavior (e.g., lifestyle, caregiving, and medical adherence support), and psychophysiology (e.g., physiological effects of emotions and cognitions). Generally evidence-based family interventions include illness-specific education and psychoeducation to support knowledge and coping and therapy to address relational problems, as indicated (Campbell, 2003). Multiple family groups, ongoing assessment of family members' psychosocial experiences, support for normative coping, early intervention in the event of psychological distress, self-help or professionally facilitated support groups, and the structuring of services to actively involve family members also are recommended (IOM, 2001; Fobair, 1998; Rolland, 1994; Weihs et al., 2002). Enhancing social support and coping skills through support groups and peer support also is likely to improve quality of life and health status. Finally, involvement in religious organizations is linked with positive health outcomes (IOM, 2001). Additional information regarding families and health can be found in Chapter 13, and information regarding spiritual resources among families can be found in a recent book by Walsh (2009).

Targeted Interventions for People With Depression and Anxiety Disorders

There is a growing body of evidence to guide intervention with people experiencing depression and anxiety disorders (DHHS, 1999). Unfortunately, most people in the United States who likely need care do not receive appropriate treatment, even when "appropriate treatment" is defined based on minimal recommended levels of antidepressant medication or at least four meetings focusing on mental health with a mental health specialist or primary care provider (Young, Klap, Sherbourne, & Wells, 2001). With a nationally representative sample of those likely experiencing a depressive or anxiety disorder, only 30% received appropriate treatment, although 83% had seen a health-care provider. Likelihood of not receiving appropriate care was associated with being male, African American, less well educated, younger than 30 years, or older than 59 years. Income and insurance status were not associated with appropriate treatment, although insurance was associated with seeking care. No difference in accessing care was found between people who were White American or African American, but African Americans were less likely to receive appropriate treatment; this discrepancy underscores the importance of addressing cultural competence in mental health care. In addition, the research also underscores the importance of addressing mental health-care disparities associated with race and SES (DHHS, 2001a; Young et al., 2001).

These treatment recommendations to assist people experiencing depression and anxiety disorders are informed by empirical studies and consensus statements (Ballenger et al., 2000, 2004; DHHS, 1999; Hollon, Thase, & Markowitz, 2002; NIMH, 2008, 2009; Young et al., 2001). For depression, CBT and interpersonal therapy (IPT) are evidence-based psychotherapeutic interventions that have demonstrated effectiveness with adolescents, adults, and older adults (DHHS, 1999; Hollon et al., 2002; NIMH, 2008). A recent review of effective approaches to depression among older adults also recognizes the value of problem-solving therapy and supportive psychotherapy. A new approach, ecosystem-focused therapy, recently has been developed and aims to assist older adults whose cognitive or physical challenges limit gains in therapies that rely heavily on problem-solving strategies (Alexopoulos & Kelly, 2009). NIMH (2010a) notes that light therapy, melatonin, and expressive or creative arts therapy have shown promise in the treatment of depression.

Antidepressant medications including SSRIs, serotonin and norepinephrine reuptake inhibitors (SNRIs), tricyclics, and monoamine oxidase inhibitors (MAOIs) may be helpful for people experiencing depression. It is important to note that antidepressants can take several weeks to achieve therapeutic effects and that if one medication is ineffective, an effective alternative often can be found. Furthermore, some people require additional medications, particularly to address co-occurring physical and mental health conditions (NIMH, 2008). When people are experiencing severe unremitting depression for which other treatments are not effective or that co-occurs with psychotic symptoms, consideration of electroconvulsive therapy (ECT) may be indicated (DHHS, 1999; Hollon et al., 2002; NIMH, 2008).

For people experiencing anxiety disorders, CBT has been demonstrated to be effective as have several antidepressant and antianxiety medications and beta-blockers (DHHS, 1999; NIMH, 2009; Young et al., 2001). A recent clinical trial found that both CBT and short-term psychodynamic psychotherapy improved anxiety among 57 adults with generalized anxiety disorder, but the CBT group experienced greater gains related to worry, depression, and trait anxiety (Leichsenring et al., 2009). A growing body of empirical research suggests that psychodynamic psychotherapy, long used to assist people experiencing a range of mental health concerns, outperforms wait-list or usual-treatment control groups and often is comparable to CBT and other psychotherapies across psychiatric conditions. Further research is needed to examine the efficacy and

effectiveness of psychodynamic psychotherapy to assist people with specific mental health conditions and to assess the optimal match between clients and approaches (Leichsenring & Leibing, 2007; Leichsenring, Rabung, & Leibing, 2004; Leichsenring et al., 2009).

Recommended intervention for people experiencing PTSD differs based on when the traumatic event occurred. Immediately following the traumatic event, recommendations include attending to safety, providing education about trauma, accessing natural support systems, and providing supportive counseling (Ballenger et al., 2000; Foa, Hembree, Riggs, Rauch, & Franklin, 2005; National Center for PTSD, 2010). Psychological first aid is a research- and culturally informed model for addressing these and related considerations with children, adults, older adults, and families in the wake of natural disasters or terrorism (Brymer et al., 2006). A detailed guide to providing psychological first aid is available electronically at the National Center for PTSD Web site (www.ptsd.va.gov/professional/manuals /psych-first-aid.asp).

Psychoeducation regarding trauma, normal responses, coping strategies, and, when indicated, psychotherapeutic and psychopharmacologic interventions may be particularly useful in primary care. Neither single sessions of critical incident stress debriefing nor benzodiazepines are recommended as early intervention strategies (Ballenger et al., 2004). Ballenger and colleagues underscore the importance of encouraging clients who may access Internet information to pursue it from reputable health-care or advocacy organizations rather than commercial, nonspecialist, or chat room Web sites.

People experiencing high levels of distress with psychological or somatic symptoms should be assisted with relief of symptoms; CBT may be useful in reducing the risk of later PTSD (Ballenger et al., 2004). If after three or four weeks and two assessment sessions the client continues to experience significant distress and symptoms of PTSD, treatment that includes either SSRIs, CBT, or a blend of these strategies is recommended. Further research is needed to address possible relapse upon completion of treatment. People experiencing persistent PTSD may benefit from medication regimens lasting one year or more. CBT may help enhance gains during pharmacotherapy and sustain gains after treatment concludes (Ballenger et al., 2004).

As noted by the National Center for PTSD (Hamblen, Schnurr, Rosenberg, & Eftkhari, 2010), available treatment guidelines are unanimous in their support of CBT to assist people experiencing PTSD. Exposure-based therapy has been studied most and has strong empirical support (Hamblen et al., 2010; IOM, 2008). A recent study of brief eclectic psychotherapy (BEP), which draws upon CBT and psychodynamic therapies, found that BEP outperformed a wait-list control group among 24 Dutch adults experiencing PTSD (Lindauer et al., 2005). Although further research is needed, the findings suggest that this approach holds promise for helping people experiencing PTSD. Another approach with wide support is eye movement desensitization and reprocessing (EMDR) (Hamblen et al., 2010).

Recommended interventions with children and adolescents experiencing PTSD include trauma-focused psychotherapies that may draw on CBT, psychodynamic, and attachment theories; active involvement of primary caregivers in the helping process; and attention to resilience, functioning, and positive development in addition to psychological distress. Trauma-focused cognitive behavioral treatment (TF-CBT) has the strongest evidence base and is employed most frequently. Several studies suggest that Cognitive-Behavioral Intervention for Trauma in Schools (CBITS), a group model that is similar to TF-CBT, can be adapted for use with diverse cultural groups and can reduce symptoms of posttraumatic stress and depression (AACAP, 2010; Ngo et al., 2008). Psychoeducation with children and caregivers, a component of TF-CBT, is recommended to provide information about PTSD and treatment, facilitate coping, and aid parental efforts to support the child or adolescent (AACAP, 2010; Cohen et al., 1998). Although EMDR has some research support for use with children, recent practice parameters note significant limitations of much of the currently available research. Finally, SSRIs combined with psychotherapy may assist children and adolescents experiencing PSTD. Other medications including risperidone, clonidine, propranalol, and morphine (used with children experiencing burns in one study) also may be helpful (AACAP, 2010). Further information can be found online through the AACAP (http://www.aacap.org/).

Substance use problems and mental health concerns often co-occur. In general, integrated treatment that addresses these concerns simultaneously is preferred (CSAT, 2005; NIDA, 2009). Promising treatment approaches and the value of trauma-informed and trauma-specific services are discussed in Chapter 17. More detailed information can be found in two electronically available treatment improvement protocols (CSAT, 2005, 2009).

CONCLUSION

This chapter addresses myriad intersections between physical and mental health in health-care settings. In many ways, we end where we started—the recognition of the complexity of the mutual influences between physical and mental health and ecological contexts. Although the general information provided can contribute to one's evidence-based practice knowledge, it is critical that any knowledge base be informed by the unique preferences and ecological contexts of the people served. When crossing the many intersections between physical and mental health in health-care settings, it is important to proceed with engaged, thoughtful attention to assessments and interventions that reflect competence to serve individuals and families across culture, race, ethnicity, SES, sexual orientation, spiritual background, physical ability, gender, and age. This engaged, thoughtful attention, in conjunction with leading-edge, evidence-based practice knowledge, will enable social workers to provide the high-quality services that all people deserve.

SUGGESTED LEARNING EXERCISES

Learning Exercise 8.1

Discuss the following questions: How do physical and mental health conditions intersect? How can attention to psychosocial and ecological concerns influence health? What challenges exist in addressing psychosocial and ecological concerns in your practice setting? What resources are available to assist with these challenges? What is one step you can take to improve your and your organization's ability to address intersections between physical and mental health among the clients you serve?

Learning Exercise 8.2

Discuss the following questions: How does your cultural background influence your understanding of physical and mental health, expressions of emotion and pain, and appropriate paths to help? How might these understandings influence your direct practice with clients and your interactions with the transdisciplinary health-care team? How do you address culture in your direct practice with clients? What are your strengths and areas for growth in this area? How might you and your organization strengthen the cultural competence of provided services?

Learning Exercise 8.3

Discuss the following questions: What are key components of differential assessments in health-care settings? How do assessments inform interventions? Either discuss or role-play how you would engage in differential assessment and subsequent intervention in the next hypothetical cases.

Exercise 8.3.1

Darren is a 25-year-old man of African American background. He and his wife, Paula, have been married for 2 years. Last year he was diagnosed with HIV and hepatitis C. He recently was prescribed a combination of protease inhibitors and interferon-alfa. He was referred to the social worker by his physician because his feelings of depression are causing him distress; he feels easily fatigued and recently has missed several days of work because he "could not get going." He is worried about his job and about being able to pay his bills if he does not go to work. He describes having experienced feelings of sadness and worry as a teenager, but prior to two months ago, those feelings had not surfaced for several years.

Exercise 8.3.2

Sandy is a 40-year-old woman of Native American background. She and her partner of 15 years, Racquel, have two children, ages 11 and 9. Sandy has experienced asthma since her early 20s; she entered the hospital yesterday with exacerbated symptoms. While talking with you, she describes intense fears about the possibility of another asthma attack. She also describes that she has felt increased difficulty breathing over the past couple of weeks. She was so busy with household and child-care responsibilities that she did not have time to see the doctor to adjust her medication regimen. She describes feeling worried and restless when you meet with her. She has no prior history of mental health difficulties or of mental health treatment.

Learning Exercise 8.4

Discuss the following questions: How might you proceed in direct practice with Joseph, who was described in the first case example in this chapter? What additional information might you need to inform the assessment? What goals might be collaboratively set with Joseph? How might you intervene to address these goals?

Learning Exercise 8.5

In small groups, define *mental health* and *mental illness*. Half of your group should develop a principled argument in support of the utility of the *DSM-IV-TR* and the other half should develop a principled argument against the utility of the *DSM-IV-TR*. Return to one large group to discuss the strengths and limitations of the *DSM-IV-TR* in direct social work practice.

Learning Exercise 8.6

Discuss the following questions: What factors are associated with suicide risk? What are key ingredients of suicide assessment and intervention? In pairs, role-play the assessment of Georgina's suicide risk in the next hypothetical case. What might short- and long-term intervention involve?

Exercise 8.6.1

Georgina is a 45-year-old widowed woman of Mexican American background who was diagnosed with breast cancer 5 years ago. At that time she had a mastectomy followed by reconstructive surgery, radiation, and chemotherapy. She recently has been diagnosed with a recurrence of cancer. Georgina describes a deep sense of sadness and hopelessness about this diagnosis. She fears feeling pain, going through chemotherapy, and losing her hair again and believes "it won't do any good anyway." She also describes feeling alone. Although her son and her daughter live nearby, they are both busy with their families and jobs. Georgina and her long-time companion separated 6 months ago. Georgina feels overwhelmed by her hopelessness, does not feel it will get better, and says that she wants to die. She has thought about notes that she would write to her family to say good-bye, and she has stored pain medication at her home that she plans to take.

Learning Exercise 8.7

Discuss the following questions: What practice theories currently guide your clinical work with clients? How do these theories fit with the evidence-based approaches addressed in this chapter? What are the implications of this fit for providing optimal clinical services to clients?

Learning Exercise 8.8

Discuss the following questions: What additional information would be helpful for you to gain in order to enhance the effectiveness of your assessments and interventions with people experiencing physical and mental health difficulties?

Learning Exercise 8.9. Homework

You have been asked to conduct a comprehensive assessment of your organization's capacity to effectively address co-occurring physical and mental health concerns among its clients. This assessment should consider the organization's strengths and challenges in this area. Although the assessment will readily address the availability and accessibility of appropriate screening, assessment, and intervention, it also should address other factors that influence clients' experiences in the organization. Based on your comprehensive assessment, you are asked to provide a thorough action plan that prioritizes steps the organization can take to improve its effectiveness in serving clients with co-occurring physical and mental health concerns.

SUGGESTED RESOURCES

Condition-Specific Organizations

American Cancer Society—www.cancer.org

American Heart Association—www.heart.org/HEARTORG

Join Together—www.jointogether.org

National Alliance for the Mentally Ill—www.nami.org

National Center for PTSD—www.ptsd.va.gov/index.asp

National Child Traumatic Stress Network—www.nctsn.com/nccts/nav.do?pid=hom_main

Cultural Competence

Association of Black Cardiologists, Inc.—www.abcardio.org

Cross Cultural Health Care Program—www.xculture.org

Cultural Competence in Care with Older Adults—www.stanford.edu/group/ethnoger

Office of Minority Health—minorityhealth.hhs.gov

www.stanford.edu/group/ethnoger

Evidence-Based Practice

Evidence-Based Practice in Health Care -Cochrane Collaboration—www.cochrane.org

National Registry of Evidence-Based Programs and Practices—www.nrepp.samhsa.gov

Practice Guidelines—Consumers and Patients—www.ahrq.gov/consumer

Practice Guidelines—National—www.guideline.gov

U.S. Preventive Services Task Force—www.ahrq.gov/clinic/pocketgd.htm

Gay, Lesbian, Bisexual, and Transgender Resources

Gay and Lesbian Health—American Public Health Association—www.apha.org/about/Public+Health+ Links/LinksGay andLesbianHealth.htm

Gay and Lesbian Medical Association—www.glma.org

Parents, Families, and Friends of Lesbians and Gays—www.pflag.org

Government Organizations

Agency for Health Care Quality and Research—www.ahrq.gov

Bureau of Primary Health Care—http://bphc.hrsa.gov

National Institute on Drug Abuse—http://drugabuse.gov/nidahome.html

National Institute of Mental Health—www.nimh.nih.gov

Office of Minority Health—http://minorityhealth.hhs.gov

Substance Abuse and Mental Health Services Administration—www.samhsa.gov

Medication Information

U.S. National Library of Medicine and National Institutes of Health—www.nlm.nih.gov/medlineplus/aboutmedlineplus.html

Search Engines

Google Scholar—http://scholar.google.com

PubMed—www.ncbi.nlm.nih.gov/pubmed

Suicide

Suicide Prevention—National Institute of Mental Health—www.nimh.nih.gov/health/topics/suicide-prevention/index.shtml

Suicide Prevention—Substance Abuse and Mental Health Services Administration (SAMHSA)—National Suicide Prevention Lifeline, 1-800-273-TALK; http://mentalhealth.samhsa.gov/suicideprevention/

REFERENCES

Aben, I., Verhey, F., Strik, J., Lousberg, R., Lodder, J., & Honig, A. (2003). A comparative study into the 1 year cumulative incidence of depression after stroke and myocardial infarction. *Journal of Neurology, Neurosurgery, and Psychiatry, 74*, 581–585.

Adler, N. E., & Stewart, J. (2010). Preface to the biology of disadvantage: Socioeconomic status and health. *Annals of the New York Academy of Sciences, 1186*, 1–4.

Alexopoulos, G. S., & Kelly, R. E. (2009). Research advances in geriatric depression. *World Psychiatry, 8*(3), 140–149.

Allgšwer, A., Wardle, J., & Steptoe, A. (2001). Depressive symptoms, social support, and personal health behaviors in young men and women. *Health Psychology, 20*(3), 223–227.

American Academy of Child and Adolescent Psychiatry. (2007). Practice parameter for the assessment and treatment of children and adolescents with depressive disorders. *Journal of the American Academy of Child and Adolescent Psychiatry, 46*(100), 1503–1526.

American Academy of Child and Adolescent Psychiatry. (2010). Practice parameter for the assessment and treatment of children and adolescents with posttraumatic stress disorder. *Journal of the American Academy of Child and Adolescent Psychiatry, 49*(4), 414–430.

American Psychiatric Association. (1994). *Diagnostic and statistical manual of mental disorders* (4th ed.). Washington, DC: Author.

American Psychiatric Association. (2000). *Diagnostic and statistical manual of mental disorders* (4th ed., text revision). Washington, DC: Author.

American Psychiatric Association. (2006). *Practice guidelines for the assessment and treatment of patients with suicidal behaviors.* Washington, DC: Author.

Andersen, A. U., Andersen, M., Rosholm, J. U., & Gram, L. F. (2000). Contacts to the health care system prior to suicide: A comprehensive analysis using registers for general and psychiatric hospital admissions, contacts to general practitioners and practising specialists and drug prescriptions. *Acta Psychiatrica Scandinavica, 102*(2), 126–134.

Angell, B. (2002). Boundary spanning: An ecological reinterpretation of social work practice in health and mental health systems [Book review]. *Social Service Review, 76*(4), 703–705.

Angst, F., Stassen, H. H., Clayton, P. J., & Angst, J. (2002). Mortality of patients with mood disorders: Follow-up over 34–48 years. *Journal of Affective Disorders, 68,* 167–181.

Angst, J., Angst, F., Gerber-Werder, R., & Gamma, A. (2005). Suicide in 406 mood-disorder patients with and without long-term medication: A 40–44 years' follow-up. *Archives of Suicide Research, 9,* 279–300.

Bagner, D. M., Fernandez, M. A., & Eyberg, S. M. (2004). Parent-child interaction therapy and chronic illness: A case study. *Journal of Clinical Psychology in Medical Settings, 11*(1), 1–6.

Baldessarini, R. J., Tondo, L., Davis, P., Pompili, M., Goodwin, F. K., & Hennen, J. (2006). Decreased suicides and attempts during long-term lithium treatment: A meta-analytic review. *Bipolar Disorders, 8,* 625–639.

Ballenger, J. C., Davidson, R. T., Lecrubier, Y., Nutt, D. J., Foa, E. B., Kessler, R. C.,... Shalev, A. Y. (2000). Consensus statement on posttraumatic stress disorder from the international consensus group on depression and anxiety. *Journal of Clinical Psychiatry, 61*(Suppl. 5), S60–S66.

Ballenger, J. C., Davidson, J. R., Lecrubier, Y., Nutt, D. J., Marshall, R. D., Nemeroff, C. B.,... Yehuda, R. (2004). Consensus statement update on posttraumatic stress disorder from the international consensus group on depression and anxiety. *Journal of Clinical Psychiatry, 65*(Suppl. 1), S55–S62.

Barrow, S. M., Herman, D. B., Cordova, P., & Streuning, E. (1999). Mortality among homeless shelter residents in New York City. *American Journal of Public Health, 89*(4), 529–534.

Bateman, A., & Fonagy, P. (2008). 8-year follow-up of patients treated for borderline personality disorder: Mentalization-based treatment vs. treatment as usual. *American Journal of Psychiatry, 165*(5), 631–638.

Berlin, S., & Marsh, J. (1993). *Informing practice decisions.* New York, NY: Macmillan.

Bing, E., Burnam, A., Longshore, D., Fleishman, J. A., Sherbourne, C. D., London, A. S.,... Shapiro, M. (2001). Psychiatric disorders and drug use among human immunodeficiency virus-infected adults in the United States. *Archives of General Psychiatry, 58,* 721–728.

Bohlmeijer, E., Prenger, R., Taal, E., & Cuijpers, P. (2010). The effects of mindfulness-based stress reduction on mental health of adults with a chronic medical disease: A meta-analysis. *Journal of Psychosomatic Research, 68,* 539–544.

Brent, D. A., Holder, D., Kolko, D., Birmaher, B., Baugher, M., Roth, C.,...Johnson, B. A. (1997). A clinical psychotherapy trial for adolescent depression comparing cognitive, family, and supportive therapy. *Archives of General Psychiatry, 54*(9), 877–885.

Brent, D. A., Poling, K., McKain, B., & Baugher, M. (1993). A psychoeducational program for families of affectively ill children and adolescents. *Journal of the American Academy of Child and Adolescent Psychiatry, 32,* 770–774.

Brestan, E. V., & Eyberg, S. M. (1998). Effective psychosocial treatments of conduct-disordered children and adolescents: 29 years, 82 studies, and 5,272 kids. *Journal of Clinical Child Psychology, 27*(2), 180–189.

Bridge, J. A., Greenhouse, J. B., Weldon, A. H., Campo, J. V., & Kelleher, K. J. (2008). Suicide trends among youths aged 10–19 years in the United States, 1996–2005. *JAMA, 300*(9), 1025–1026.

Bronfenbrenner, U. (1977, July). Toward an experimental ecology of human development. *American Psychologist, 32*(7), 513–531.

Bronfenbrenner, U. (1979). *Ecology of human development.* Cambridge, MA: Harvard University.

Bronfenbrenner, U. (1989). Ecological systems theory. *Annals of Child Development, 6,* 187–249.

Brown, G. K., Ten Have, T., Henriques, G. R., Xie, S. X., Hollander, J. E., & Beck, A. T. (2005). Cognitive therapy for the prevention of suicide attempts: A randomized controlled trial. *JAMA, 294*(5), 563–570.

Brown, L. S. (1991). Therapy with an infertile lesbian client. In C. Silverstein (Ed.), *Gays, lesbians and their therapists* (pp.15–30). New York, NY: Norton.

Bruce, M. L., Ten Have, T. R., Reynolds, C. F., Katz, I. I., Schulberg, H. C., Mulsant, B. H.,...Alexopoulos, G. S. (2004). Reducing suicidal ideation and depressive symptoms in depressed older primary care patients. *JAMA, 291*(9), 1081–1091.

Brymer, M., Jacobs, A., Layne, C., Pynoos, R., Ruzek, J., Steinberg, A.,...Watson, P. (2006). Psychological first aid: Field operations guide (2nd ed.). Retrieved from http://www.ptsd.va.gov/professional/manuals/psych-first-aid.asp

Butow, P. N., Coates, A. S., & Dunn, S. M. (1999). Psychosocial predictors of survival in metastatic melanoma. *Journal of Clinical Oncology, 17*(7), 2256–2263.

Campbell, D. G., Felker, B. L., Liu, C., Yano, E. M., Kirchner, J. E., Chan, D.,...Chaney, E. F. (2007). Prevalence of depression-PTSD comorbidity: Implications for clinical practice guidelines and primary-care based interventions. *Journal of General Internal Medicine, 22,* 711–718.

Campbell, T. L. (2003). The effectiveness of family intervention for physical disorders. *Journal of Marital and Family Therapy, 29*(2), 262–281.

Carlton-LaNey, I. (1999). African-American social work pioneers' response to need. *Social Work, 44*(4), 311–321.

Cash, S. J., & Bridge, J. A. (2009). Epidemiology of youth suicide and suicidal behavior. *Current Opinion in Pediatrics, 21*, 613–619.

Cedereke, M., Monti, K., & Öjehagen, A. (2002). Telephone contact with patients in the year after a suicide attempt: Does it affect treatment attendance and outcome? A randomized controlled study. *European Psychiatry, 17*, 82–91.

Center for Mental Health Services, Substance Abuse and Mental Health Services Administration, U.S. Department of Health and Human Services. (2001). *Mental health, United States, 2000* (DHHS Publication No. SMA 01-3537). Washington, DC: U.S. Government Printing Office. Retrieved from http://www.eric.ed.gov:80/PDFS/ED469203.pdf

Center for Substance Abuse Treatment, Substance Abuse and Mental Health Services Administration, U.S. Department of Health and Human Services. (2005). *Substance abuse treatment for persons with co-occurring disorder* (Treatment Improvement Protocol [TIP] Series, 42; DHHS Publication No. SMA 05-3922). Rockville, MD: Author.

Center for Substance Abuse Treatment, Substance Abuse and Mental Health Services Administration, U.S. Department of Health and Human Services. (2009). *Substance abuse treatment: Addressing the specific needs of women* (Treatment Improvement Protocol [TIP] Series, 51; DHHS Publication No. SMA 09-4426). Rockville, MD: Author.

Centers for Disease Control and Prevention. (2007). Suicide trends among youths and young adults aged 10–24 years: United States, 1990–2004. *Morbidity and Mortality Weekly Report, 56*(35), 905–908.

Clements-Nolle, K., Marx, R., & Katz, M. (2006). Attempted suicide among transgender persons: The influence of gender-based discrimination and victimization. *Journal of Homosexuality, 51*(3), 53–69.

Cobb, S. (1976). Social support as a moderator of life stress. *Psychosomatic Medicine, 38*, 300–314.

Cohen, J. A., Bernet, W., Dunne, J. E., Adair, M., Arnold, V., Benson, S., Sloan, L. E. (1998). Practice parameters for the assessment and treatment of children and adolescents with posttraumatic stress disorder. *Journal of the American Academy of Child and Adolescent Psychiatry, 37*(Suppl. 10), S4–S26.

Cohen, S., & Herbert, T. B. (1996). Health psychology: Psychological factors and physical disease from perspectives of human psychoneuroimmunity. *Annual Review Psychology, 47*, 114–132.

Conn, V. S., Hafdahl, A. R., Brown, S. A., & Brown, L. M. (2008). Meta-analysis of patient education interventions to increase physical activity among chronically ill adults. *Patient Education and Counseling, 70*, 157–172.

Cordova, M. J., Cunningham, L. L. C., Carlson, C. R., & Andrykowski, M. A. (2001). Posttraumatic growth following breast cancer: A controlled comparison study. *Health Psychology, 20*(3), 176–185.

Costello, E. J., Compton, S. N., Keller, G., & Angold, A. (2003). Relationships between poverty and psychopathology: A natural experiment. *JAMA, 290*(15), 2023–2029.

Culpeper, L. (2003). Use of algorithms to treat anxiety in primary care. *Journal of Clinical Psychiatry, 64* (Suppl. 2), S30–S33.

DiMatteo, M. R. (2004a). Social support and patient adherence to medical treatment: A meta-analysis. *Health Psychology, 23*(2), 207–218.

DiMatteo, M. R. (2004b). Variations in patients' adherence to medical recommendations. *Medical Care, 42*, 200–209.

Dohrenwend, B. P., Levav, I., Shrout, P. E., Schwartz, S., Naveh, G., Link, B. G.,…Stueve, A. (1992). Socioeconomic status and psychiatric disorders: The causation-selection issue. *Science, 255*(5047), 946–952.

Dusseldorp, E., van Elderen, T., Maes, S., Meulman, J., & Kraaij, V. (1999). A meta-analysis of psychoeducational programs for coronary heart disease patients. *Health Psychology, 18*(5), 506–519.

Eisenstadt, T. H., Eyberg, S., McNeil, C. B., Newcomb, K., & Funderburk, B. (1993). Parent-child interaction therapy with behavior problem children: Relative effectiveness of two stages and overall treatment outcome. *Journal of Clinical Child Psychology, 22*(1), 42–51.

Engstrom, M., El-Bassel, N., Go, H., & Gilbert, L. (2008). Childhood sexual abuse and intimate partner violence among women in methadone treatment: A direct or mediated relationship? *Journal of Family Violence, 23*(7), 605–617.

Engstrom, M., Gunn, A., & Petersen, S. (2011, January). *Homelessness, unmet basic needs, and social marginalization: Expanding conventional definitions of trauma.* Poster presentation at the 15th Annual Conference of the Society for Social Work and Research, Tampa, FL.

Engstrom, M., Shibusawa, T., El-Bassel, N., & Gilbert, L. (2009). Age and HIV sexual risk among women in methadone treatment. *AIDS and Behavior, 15*(1), 103–113.

Fawzy, F. I., Fawzy, N. W., Arndt, L. A., & Pasnau, R. O. (1995). Critical review of psychosocial interventions in cancer care. *Archives of General Psychiatry, 52*(2), 100–113.

Fawzy, F. I., Fawzy, N. W., Hyun, C. S., Elashoff, R., Guthrie, D., Fahey, J. L.,…Morton, D. L. (1993). Malignant melanoma: Effects of an early structure psychiatric intervention, coping, and affective state on recurrence and survival 6 years later. *Archives of General Psychiatry, 50*(9), 681–689.

Fergusson, D. M., Horwood, L. J., & Beautrais, A. L. (1999). Is sexual orientation related to mental health problems and suicidality in young people? *Archives of General Psychiatry, 56,* 876–880.

Fischer, P. F., & Breakey, W. R. (1991). The epidemiology of alcohol, drug, and mental disorders among homeless persons. *American Psychologist, 46*(11), 1115–1128.

Foa, E. B., Hembree, E. A., Riggs, D., Rauch, S., & Franklin, M. (2005). Guidelines for mental health professionals' response to the recent tragic events in the United States: National Center for PTSD fact sheet. Washington, DC: U.S. Department of Veterans Affairs.

Fobair, P. (1998). Cancer support groups and group therapies. In J. B. Williams & K. Ell (Eds.), *Advances in mental health services research: Implications for practice* (pp. 365–398). Washington, DC: National Association of Social Workers.

Folkman, S., & Greer, S. (2000). Promoting psychological well-being in the face of serious illness: When theory, research and practice inform each other. *Psychooncology, 9,* 11–19.

Food and Drug Administration. (2007). New warnings proposed for antidepressants. Retrieved from www .fda.gov/ForConsumers/ConsumerUpdates/ucm 048950.htm

Frankowski, B. L., & Committee on Adolescence. (2004). Sexual orientation and adolescents. *Pediatrics, 113*(6), 1827–1832.

Frasure-Smith, N., & Lesperance, F. (2003). Depression and other psychological risks following myocardial infarction. *Archives of General Psychiatry, 60,* 627–636.

Gambrill, E. (2000). The role of critical thinking in evidence-based social work. In P. Allen-Meares & C. Garvin (Eds.), *The handbook of social work direct practice* (pp. 43–64). Thousand Oaks, CA: Sage.

Gambrill, E. (2006). Social work practice: A critical thinker's guide. New York, NY: Oxford University Press.

Garvey, K. A., Penn, J. V., Campbell, A. L., Esposito-Smythers, C., & Spirito, A. (2009). Contracting for safety with patients: Clinical practice and forensic implications. *Journal of the American Academy of Psychiatry Law, 37*(3), 363–370.

Germain, C. B., & Gitterman, A. (1980). *Life model of social work practice.* New York, NY: Columbia University Press.

Gliatto, M. F., & Rai, A. K. (1999). Evaluation and treatment of patients with suicidal ideation. *American Family Physician, 67*(6), 1500–1513. Retrieved from www.aafp.org/afp/990315ap/1500.html

Goodman, L., Saxe, L., & Harvey, M. (1991). Homelessness as psychological trauma. *American Psychologist, 46,* 1219–1225.

Goodwin, J. S., Zhang, D. D., & Ostir, G. V. (2004). Effect of depression on diagnosis, treatment and survival of older women with breast cancer. *Journal of the American Geriatric Society, 52*(1), 106–111.

Gotterer, R. (2001). The spiritual dimension in clinical social work practice: A client perspective. *Families in Society: Journal of Contemporary Human Services, 82*(2), 187–193.

Grant, B. F. (1997). Prevalence and correlates of alcohol use and DSM-IV alcohol dependence in the United States: Results of the National Longitudinal Alcohol Epidemiologic Survey. *Journal on Studies of Alcohol, 58,* 464-473.

Hahn, R. A., Heath, G. W., & Chang, M. (1998, December 11). Cardiovascular disease risk factors and preventive practices among adults—United States, 1994: A behavioral risk factor atlas [CDC Surveillance Summaries]. *Morbidity and Mortality Weekly Report, 47*(No. SS-5), 35–69.

Hamblen, J. L., Schnurr, P. P., Rosenberg, A., & Eftkhari, A. (2010). Overview of PTSD treatment research. Retrieved from www.ptsd.va.gov/professional/pages /overview-treatment-research.asp

Henningfield, J. E. (1998). *Addicted to nicotine—A national research forum: Section 1. History and pharmacology.* Retrieved from www.nida.nih.gov /MeetSum/Nicotine/henningfield.html

Hepworth, D. H., Rooney, R. H., & Larsen, J. A. (2002). *Direct social work practice: Theory and skills* (6th ed.). Pacific Grove, CA: Brooks/Cole.

Heron, M. (2010). Deaths. Leading causes for 2006. *National Vital Statistics Reports, 58*(14).

Hibbs, J. R., Benner, L., Klugman, L., Spencer, R., Macchia, I., Mellinger, A., & Fife, D. K. (1994). Mortality in a cohort of homeless adults in Philadelphia. *New England Journal of Medicine, 331*(5), 304–309.

Hien, D., Zimberg, S., Weisman, S., First, M., & Ackerman, S. (1997). Dual diagnosis subtypes in urban substance abuse and mental health clinics. *Psychiatric Services, 48,* 1058–1063.

Hirschfeld, R. M. A., & Russell, J. M. (1997). Current concepts: Assessment and treatment of suicidal patients. *New England Journal of Medicine, 337*(13), 910–915.

Hoge, C. W., Castro, C. A., Messer, S. C., McGurk, D., Cotting, D. I., & Koffman, R. L. (2004). Combat duty in Iraq and Afghanistan, mental health problems, and barriers to care. *New England Journal of Medicine, 351*(1), 13–22.

Holkup, P. (2002). *Evidence-based protocol: Elderly suicide—Secondary prevention.* Iowa City, Iowa: University of Iowa Gerontological Nursing Interventions Research Center, Research Dissemination Core.

Hollis, F. (1939). *Social case work in practice: Six case studies.* New York, NY: Family Welfare Association of America.

Hollon, S. D., Thase, M. E., & Markowitz, J. C. (2002). Treatment and prevention of depression. *Psychological Science in the Public Interest, 3*(2), 39–77.

Hood, K. K., & Eyberg, S. M. (2003). Outcomes of parent-child interaction therapy: Mothers' reports of maintenance 3 to 6 years after treatment. *Journal of Clinical Child and Adolescent Psychology, 32*(3), 419–429.

Horvath, A. (1995). The therapeutic relationship: From transference to alliance. *In Session: Psychotherapy in Practice*, 1, 1–17.

House, J. S., & Kahn, R. (1985). Measures and concepts of social support. In S. Cohen & S. L. Syme (Eds.), *Social support and health* (pp. 83–108). Orlando, FL: Academic Press.

Hunt, I. M., Kapur, N., Webb, R., Robinson, J., Burns, J., Shaw, J., & Appleby, L. (2009). Suicide in recently discharged psychiatric patients: A case-control study. *Psychological Medicine, 39,* 443–449.

Hwang, S. W., Lebow, J. M., Bierer, M. F., O'Connell, J. J., Orav, E. J., & Brennan, T. A. (1998). Risk factors for death in homeless adults in Boston. *Archives of Internal Medicine, 158*(13), 1454–1460.

Ickovics, J. R., Hamburger, M. E., Vlahov, D., Schoenbaum, E. E., Schuman, P., Boland, R. J.,... HIV Epidemiology Research Study Group. (2001). Mortality, CD4 cell count decline, and depressive symptoms among HIV-seropositive women: Longitudinal analysis from the HIV epidemiology research study. *JAMA, 285*(11), 1466–1474.

Insel, T. R. (2004, January). *Science to service: Mental health care after the decade of the brain.* Paper presentation at the eighth annual conference of the Society for Social Work and Research, New Orleans, LA.

Institute for Clinical Systems Improvement. (2002). *Major depression, panic disorder and generalized anxiety disorder in adults in primary care.* Bloomington, MN: Author. Retrieved from www.guideline.gov

Institute of Medicine. (2001). *Health and behavior: The interplay of biological, behavioral, and societal influences.* Washington, DC: National Academy Press.

Institute of Medicine. (2008). *Treatment of posttraumatic stress disorder: An assessment of the evidence.* Washington, DC: National Academies Press.

Isacsson, G., Holmgren, A., Ösby, U., & Ahlner, J. (2009). Decrease in suicide among the individuals treated with antidepressants: A controlled study of antidepressants in suicide, Sweden, 1995–2005. *Acta Psychiatrica Scandinavia, 120,* 37–44.

Ivanoff, A. J., & Smyth, N. J. (1992). Intervention with suicidal individuals. In K. Corcoran (Ed.), *Structuring change: Effective practice for common client problems* (pp. 111–137). Chicago, IL: Lyceum Books.

Jesdale, B. M., & Zierler, S. (2002). Enactment of gay rights laws in the United States and trends in adolescent suicides: An investigation of non-Hispanic White boys. *Journal of the Gay and Lesbian Medical Association, 6*(2), 61–69.

Joe, S., Baser, R. S., Neighbors, H. W., Caldwell, C. H., & Jackson, J. S. (2009). 12-month and lifetime prevalence of suicide attempts among Black adolescents in the National Survey of American Life. *Journal of the American Academy of Child & Adolescent Psychiatry, 48*(3), 271–282.

Johnson, A., Sandford, J., & Tyndall, J. (2003). Written and verbal information versus verbal information only for patients being discharged from acute hospital settings to home. *Cochrane Database of Systematic Reviews, 4.*

Johnson, Y. (1999). Indirect work: Social work's uncelebrated strength. *Social Work, 44*(4), 323–334.

Jordan, C., & Franklin, C. (1995). *Clinical assessment for social workers: Quantitative and qualitative methods.* Chicago, IL: Lyceum Books.

Kabat-Zinn, J. (2003). Mindfulness-based interventions in context: Past, present, and future. *Clinical Psychology: Science and Practice, 10*(2), 144–156.

Katon, W., Rutter, C., Ludman, E. J., Von Korff, M., Lin, E., Simon, G.,... Unutzer, J. (2001). A randomized trial of relapse prevention of depression in primary care. *Archives of General Psychiatry, 58,* 241–247.

Kawachi, I., Adler, N. E., & Dow, W. H. (2010). Money, schooling, and health: Mechanisms and causal evidence. *Annals of the New York Academy of Sciences, 1186,* 56–68.

Kayser, K., & Sormanti, M. (2002a). A follow-up study of women with cancer: Their psychosocial well-being and close relationships. *Social Work in Health Care, 35*(1/2), 391–406.

Kayser, K., & Sormanti, M. (2002b). Identity and the illness experience: Issues faced by mothers with cancer. *Illness, Crisis and Loss, 10*(1), 10–26.

Kemeny, M. E., Weiner, H., Taylor, S. E., Schneider, S., Visscher, B., & Fahey, J. L. (1994). Repeated bereavement, depressed mood, and immune parameters in HIV seropositive and seronegative gay men. *Health Psychology, 13,* 14–24.

Kennard, B. D., Stewart, S. M., Olvera, R., Bawdon, R. E., O'Hailin, A., Lewis, C. P., & Winick, N. (2004). Nonadherence in adolescent oncology patients: Preliminary data on psychological risk factors and relationships to outcome. *Journal of Clinical Psychology in Medical Settings, 11*(1), 31–39.

Keppel, K. G., Pearcy, J. N., & Wagener, D. K. (2002, January). *Trends in racial and ethnic-specific rates for the health status indicators: United States, 1990–1998* (Healthy People Statistical Notes, No. 23). Hyattsville, MD: National Center for Health Statistics.

Kerson, T. S. (2002). *Boundary spanning: An ecological reinterpretation of social work practice in health and mental health systems.* New York, NY: Columbia University Press.

Kessler, D., Lloyd, K., & Lewis, G. (1999). Cross sectional study of symptom attribution and recognition of depression and anxiety in primary care. *British Medical Journal, 318,* 436–439.

Kessler, R. C., Borges, G., & Walters, E. E. (1999). Prevalence of and risk factors for lifetime suicide attempts in the National Cormorbidity Survey. *Archives of General Psychiatry, 56,* 617–626.

Kessler, R. C., McGonagle, K. A., Zhao, S., Nelson, C. B., Hughes, M., Eshlerman, S.,... Kendler, K. S.

(1994). Lifetime and 12-month prevalence of DSM-II-R psychiatric disorders in the United States. *Archives of General Psychiatry, 51,* 8–19.

Kessler, R. C., Sonnega, A., Bromet, E., Hughes, M., & Nelson, C. B. (1995). Posttraumatic stress disorder in the National Comorbidity Survey. *Archives of General Psychiatry, 52*(12), 1048–1060.

King, M., Semlyen, J., Tai, S. S., Killaspy, H., Osborn, D., Popelyuk, D., & Nazareth, I. (2008). A systematic review of mental disorder, suicide, and deliberate self harm in lesbian, gay and bisexual people. *BMC Psychiatry, 8*(70).

Kirk, S. A., & Kutchins, H. (1992). *The selling of the DSM: The rhetoric of science in psychiatry.* New York, NY: Aldine de Gruyter.

Kleinman, A., Eisenberg, L., & Good, B. (1978). Culture, illness, and care: Clinical lessons from anthropologic and cross-cultural research. *Annals of Internal Medicine, 88*(2), 251–258.

Kondrat, M. E. (2002). Actor-centered social work: Re-visioning "person-in-environment" through a critical theory lens. *Social Work, 47*(4), 435–448.

Krantz, D. S., Sheps, D. S., Carney, R. M., & Natelson, B. H. (2000). Effects of mental stress in patients with coronary artery disease: Evidence and clinical implications. *JAMA, 283*(14), 1800–1802.

Krieger, N. (2003). Does racism harm health? Did child abuse exist before 1962? On explicit questions, critical science, and current controversies: An ecosocial perspective. *American Journal of Public Health, 93*(2), 194–199.

Kushel, M. B., Vittinghoff, E., & Haas, J. S. (2001). Factors associated with the health care utilization of homeless persons. *JAMA, 285*(2), 200–206.

Lazarus, R. S., & Folkman, S. (1984). *Stress, appraisal and coping.* New York, NY: Springer.

Lecrubier, Y. (2004). Posttraumatic stress disorder in primary care: A hidden diagnosis. *Journal of Clinical Psychiatry, 65*(Suppl. 1), S49–S54.

Ledesma, D., & Kumano, H. (2009). Mindfulness-based stress reduction and cancer: A meta-analysis. *Psycho-Oncology, 18,* 571–579.

Leichsenring, F., & Leibing, E. (2007). Psychodynamic psychotherapy: A systematic review of techniques, indications and empirical evidence. *Psychology and Psychotherapy: Theory, Research and Practice, 80,* 217–228.

Leichsenring, F., Rabung, S., & Leibing, E. (2004). The efficacy of short-term psychodynamic psychotherapy in specific psychiatric disorders. *Archives of General Psychiatry, 61,* 1208–1216.

Leichsenring, F., Salzer, S., Jaeger, U., Kächele, H., Kreische, R., Leweke, F.,…Leibing, E. (2009). Short-term psychodynamic psychotherapy and cognitive-behavioral therapy in generalized anxiety disorder: A randomized, controlled trial. *American Journal of Psychiatry, 166*(8), 875–881.

Lengacher, C. A., Johnson-Mallard, V., Post-White, J., Moscoso, M. S., Jacobsen, P. B., Klein, T. W.,… Kip, K. E. (2009). Randomized controlled trial of mindfulness-based stress reduction (MBSR) for survivors of breast cancer. *Psycho-Oncology, 18,* 1261–1272.

Levinson, W., & Engel, C. C. (1997). Anxiety. In M. D. Feldman & J. F. Christensen (Eds.), *Behavioral medicine in primary care: A practical guide* (pp. 193–211). Stamford, CT: Appleton & Lange.

Lin, E., Katon, W., Von Korff, M., Tang, L., Williams, J. W., Kroenke, K.,…IMPACT Investigators. (2003). Effect of improving depression care on pain and functional outcomes among older adults with arthritis: A randomized controlled trial. *JAMA, 290*(18), 2428–2434.

Lin, K., & Cheung, F. (1999). Mental health issues for Asian Americans. *Psychiatric Services, 50*(6), 774–780.

Lindauer, R. J. L., Gersons, B. P. R., van Meijel, E. P. M., Blom, K., Carlier, I. V. E., Vrijlandt, I., & Olff, M. (2005). Effects of brief eclectic psychotherapy in patients with posttraumatic stress disorder: Randomized clinical trial. *Journal of Traumatic Stress, 18*(3), 205–212.

Littell, J. H., & Girvin, H. (2002). Stages of change: A critique. *Behavior Modification, 26*(2), 223–273.

Low-Beer, S., Chan, K., Yip, B., Wood, E., Montaner, J. S. G., O'Shaughnessy, M. V., & Hogg, R. S. (2000). Depressive symptoms decline among persons on HIV protease inhibitors. *Journal of Acquired Immune Deficiency Syndromes and Human Retrovirology, 23*(4), 295–301.

Lukas, S. (1993). *Where to start and what to ask: An assessment handbook.* New York, NY: Norton.

Lukens, E. P., & Thorning, H. (1998). Psychoeducation and severe mental illness: Implications for social work practice and research. In J. B. Williams & K. Ell (Eds.), *Advances in mental health services research: Implications for practice* (pp. 343–364). Washington, DC: National Association of Social Workers.

Luoma, J. B., Martin, C. E., & Pearson, J. L. (2002). Contact with mental health and primary care providers before suicide: A review of the evidence. *American Journal of Psychiatry, 159,* 909–916.

Mann, J. J., Apter, A., Bertolote, J., Beautrais, A., Currier, D., Haas, A.,…Hendin, H. (2005). Suicide prevention strategies: A systematic review. *JAMA, 294*(16), 2064–2074.

March, J., Silva, S., Vitiello, B., & TADS Team. (2006). The treatment for adolescents with depression study (TADS): Methods and message at 12 weeks. *Journal of the American Academy of Child and Adolescent Psychiatry, 45*(12), 1393–1403.

Mathy, R. M. (2002). Transgender identity and suicidality in a nonclinical sample: Sexual orientation, psychiatric history, and compulsive behaviors. *Journal of Psychology and Human Sexuality, 14*(4), 47–63.

Matthews, J. R., Spieth, L. E., & Christophersen, E. R. (1995). Behavior compliance in a pediatric context. In M. Roberts (Ed.), *Handbook of pediatric psychology* (2nd ed., pp. 617–632). New York, NY: Guilford Press.

McEwen, B. S. (1998). Stress, adaptation and disease: Allostasis and allostatic load. *Annals of the New York Academy of Sciences, 840,* 33–44.

McEwen, B. S., & Gianaros, P. J. (2010). Central role of the brain in stress and adaptation: Links to socioeconomic status, health, and disease. *Annals of the New York Academy of Sciences, 1186,* 190–222.

McEwen, B. S., & Stellar, E. (1993). Stress and the individual: Mechanisms leading to disease. *Archives of Internal Medicine, 153,* 2093–2101.

McFarlane, W. R., Lukens, E., Link, B., Dushay, R., Deakins, S. A., Newmark, M.,...Toran, J. (1995). Multiple-family groups and psychoeducation in the treatment of schizophrenia. *Archives of General Psychiatry, 52,* 679–687.

McGinnis, J. M., Williams-Russo, P., & Knickman, J. R. (2002). The case for more active policy attention to health promotion. *Health Affairs, 21*(2), 78–93.

McGoldrick, M. (1982). Ethnicity and family therapy: An overview. In M. McGoldrick, J. K. Pearson, & J. Giordano (Eds.), *Ethnicity and family therapy* (pp. 3–30). New York, NY: Guilford Press.

McMyler, C., & Pryjmachuk, S. (2008). Do 'no-suicide' contracts work? *Journal of Psychiatric and Mental Health Nursing, 15,* 512–522.

McNeil, C., Eyberg, S., Eisenstadt, T., Newcomb, K., & Funderburk, B. (1991). Parent-child interaction therapy with behavior problem children: Generalization of treatment effects to the school setting. *Journal of Clinical Child Psychology, 20*(2), 140–151.

Mechanic, D. (1999). Mental health and mental illness: Definitions and perspectives. In A. V. Horwitz & T. L. Scheid (Eds.), *A handbook for the study of mental health: Social contexts, theories, and systems* (pp. 12–28). Cambridge, UK: Cambridge University Press.

Meehan, J., Kapur, N., Hunt, I. M., Turnbull, P., Robinson, J., Bickley, H.,...Appleby, L. (2006). Suicide in mental health in-patients and within 3 months of discharge. *British Journal of Psychiatry, 188,* 129–134.

Meyer, C. H. (1993). *Assessment in social work practice.* New York, NY: Columbia University Press.

Miller, A. L., Rathus, J. H., Linehan, M. M., Wetzler, S., & Leigh, E. (1997). Dialectical behavior therapy adapted for suicidal adolescents. *Journal of Practical Psychiatry and Behavioral Health, 3,* 78–86.

Miller, G. E., Cohen, S., & Herbert, T. (1999). Pathways linking major depression and immunity in ambulatory female patients. *Psychosomatic Medicine, 61,* 850–860.

Miller, W. R., & Rollnick, S. (1991). *Motivational interviewing: Preparing people to change addictive behavior.* New York, NY: Guilford Press.

Miller, W. R., & Rollnick, S. (2002). *Motivational interviewing: Preparing people for change* (2nd ed.). New York, NY: Guilford Press.

Millman, J., Strike, D. M., Van Soest, M., Rosen, N., & Schmidt, E. (1998). *Talking with the caller: Guidelines for crisis line and other volunteer counselors.* Thousand Oaks, CA: SAGE.

Morgan, H. G., Jones, E. M., Owen, J. H. (1993). Secondary prevention of non-fatal deliberate self-harm. *British Journal of Psychiatry, 163,* 111–112.

Moscicki, E. K. (1997). Identification of suicide risk factors using epidemiologic studies. *Psychiatric Clinics of North America, 20*(3), 499–517.

Moscicki, E. K. (2001). Epidemiology of completed and attempted suicide: Toward a framework for prevention. *Clinical Neuroscience Research, 1,* 310–323.

Mufson, L., Weissman, M. M., Moreau, D., & Garfinkel, R. (1999). Efficacy of interpersonal psychotherapy for depressed adolescents. *Archives of General Psychiatry, 56,* 573–579.

Mundy, E., & Baum, A. (2004). Medical disorders as a cause of psychological trauma and posttraumatic stress disorder. *Current opinion in psychiatry, 17*(2), 123–127.

Murphy, G. E. (1975a). The physician's responsibility for suicide: Pt. 1. An error of commission. *Annals of Internal Medicine, 82*(3), 301–304.

Murphy, G. E. (1975b). The physician's responsibility for suicide: Pt. 2. Errors of omission. *Annals of Internal Medicine, 82*(3), 305–309.

Musick, M. A., Traphagan, J. W., Koenig, H. G., & Larson, D. B. (2000). Spirituality in physical health and aging. *Journal of Adult Development, 7*(2), 73–86.

National Cancer Institute. (2010). Suicide risk in cancer patients. Retrieved from www.cancer.gov/cancertopics/pdq/supportivecare/depression/HealthProfessional/page4

National Center for PTSD. (2010). Trauma, PTSD, and the primary care provider. Retrieved from http://www.publichealth.va.gov/docs/vhi/posttraumatic.pdf

National Institute of Mental Health. (2002a). *Depression and cancer.* Bethesda, MD: National Institute of Mental Health, National Institutes of Health, U.S. Department of Health and Human Services (NIH Publication No. 02-5002).

National Institute of Mental Health. (2002b). *Depression and diabetes.* Bethesda, MD: National Institute of Mental Health, National Institutes of Health, U.S. Department of Health and Human Services (NIH Publication No. 02-5003).

National Institute of Mental Health. (2002c). *Depression and heart disease.* Bethesda, MD: National Institute of Mental Health, National Institutes of Health, U.S. Department of Health and Human Services (NIH Publication No. 02-5004).

National Institute of Mental Health. (2002d). *Depression and HIV/AIDS.* Bethesda, MD: National Institute of

Mental Health, National Institutes of Health, U.S. Department of Health and Human Services (NIH Publication No. 02-5005).

National Institute of Mental Health. (2002e). *Depression and Parkinson's disease.* Bethesda, MD: National Institute of Mental Health, National Institutes of Health, U.S. Department of Health and Human Services (NIH Publication No. 02-5007).

National Institute of Mental Health. (2002f). *Depression and stroke.* Bethesda, MD: National Institute of Mental Health, National Institutes of Health, U.S. Department of Health and Human Services (NIH Publication No. 02-5006).

National Institute of Mental Health. (2007). *Older adults: Depression and suicide facts.* Retrieved from www.nimh.nih.gov/health/publications/older-adults-depression-and-suicide-facts-fact-sheet/index.shtml

National Institute of Mental Health. (2008). *Depression* [NIH Publication No. 08-3561]. Bethesda, MD: U.S. Department of Health and Human Services.

National Institute of Mental Health. (2009). *Anxiety disorders* [NIH Publication No. 09-3879]. Bethesda, MD: U.S. Department of Health and Human Services.

National Institute of Mental Health. (2010a). Psychotherapies. Retrieved from www.nimh.nih.gov/health/topics/psychotherapies/index.shtml

National Institute of Mental Health. (2010b). What medications are used to treat depression? Retrieved from www.nimh.nih.gov/health/publications/mental-health-medications/what-medications-are-used-to-treat-depression.shtml

National Institute on Drug Abuse. (2009). Cigarettes and other tobacco products. Retrieved from www.drugabuse.gov/infofacts/tobacco.html

New York State Department of Health. (2007). Suicidality and violence in patients with HIV/AIDS. New York, NY: Author. Retrieved from www.guideline.gov/content.aspx?id=10413&search=suicidality+and+violence+in+patients+with+hiv%2faids

Ng, D. M., & Jeffrey, R. W. (2003). Relationships between perceived stress and health behaviors in a sample of working adults. *Health Psychology, 22*(6), 638–642.

Ngo, V. M., Langley, A., Kataoka, S. H., Nadeem, E., Escudero, P., & Stein, B. D. (2008). Providing evidence-based practice to ethnically diverse youths: Examples from the cognitive behavioral intervention for trauma in schools (CBITS) program. *Journal of the American Academy of Child and Adolescent Psychiatry, 47*(8), 858–862.

Nixon, R. D. V., Sweeney, L., Erickson, D. B., & Touyz, S. W. (2003). Parent-child interaction therapy: A comparison of standard and abbreviated treatment for oppositional defiant preschoolers. *Journal of Consulting and Clinical Psychology, 71*(2), 251–260.

Nock, M. K., Borges, G., Bromet, E. J., Cha, C. B., Kessler, R. C., & Lee, S. (2008). Suicide and suicidal behavior. *Epidemiologic Reviews, 30,* 133–154.

Noh, S., & Kaspar, V. (2003). Perceived discrimination and depression: Moderating effects of coping, acculturation, and ethnic support. *American Journal of Public Health, 93*(2), 232–238.

Office of Applied Studies, Substance Abuse and Mental Health Services Administration, U.S. Department of Health and Human Services. (2009). *Results from the 2008 National Survey on Drug Use and Health: National Findings* [DHHS Publication No. SMA 09-4434]. Rockville, MD: Author.

Office of Minority Health, Centers for Disease Control and Prevention. (n.d.). Eliminate disparities in cardiovascular disease (CVD). Retrieved from www.cdc.gov/omhd/amh/factsheets/cardio.htm

Olfson, M., Marcus, S. C., & Shaffer, D. (2006). Antidepressant drug therapy and suicide in severely depressed children and adults. *Archives of General Psychiatry, 63,* 865–872.

Parmley, W. W. (2001). African American patients and heart disease [Editor's page]. *Journal of the American College of Cardiology, 38*(5), 1577.

Patrick, D. L., Ferketich, S. L., Frame, P. S., Harris, J. J., Hendricks, C. B., Levin, B.,…Vernon, S. W. (2003). National Institutes of Health state-of-the-science conference statement: Symptom management in cancer—Pain, depression, and fatigue, July 15–17, 2002. *Journal of the National Cancer Institute, 95*(15), 1110–1117.

Perlman, H. H. (1957). *Social casework: A problem-solving process.* Chicago, IL: University of Chicago Press.

Pignone, M. P., Gaynes, B. N., Rushton, J. L., Burchell, C. M., Orleans, C. T., Mulrow, C. D., Lohr, K. N. (2002). Screening for depression in adults: A summary of the evidence for the U.S. Preventives Services Task Force. *Annals of Internal Medicine, 136*(10), 760–764.

Pinderhughes, E. (1989). *Understanding race, ethnicity, and power: The key to efficacy in clinical practice.* New York, NY: Free Press.

Prins, A., Ouimette, P., Kimerling, R., Cameron, R. P., Hugelshofer, D. S., Shaw-Hegwer, J.,…Sheikh, J. I. (2004). The primary care PTSD screen (PC–PTSD): Development and operating characteristics. *Primary Care Psychiatry, 9*(1), 9–14.

Prochaska, J. O., & DiClemente, C. C. (1983). Stages and processes of self-change of smoking: Toward an integrative model of change. *Journal of Consulting and Clinical Psychology, 51,* 390–395.

Prochaska, J. O., DiClemente, C. C., & Norcross, J. C. (1992). In search of how people change: Applications to addictive behaviors. *American Psychologist, 47*(9), 1102–1114.

Rabins, P. (1991). *Assessing the mental status of the older person* [Videorecording]. Baltimore, MD: University of Maryland at Baltimore.

Rees, K., Bennett, P., West, R., Davey, S. G., & Ebrahim, S. (2004). Psychological interventions for coronary heart disease. *Cochrane Database of Systematic Reviews, 2,* 1.

Regier, D. A., Narrow, W. E., Rae, D. S., Manderscheid, R. W., Locke, B. Z., & Goodwin, F. K. (1993). The de facto U.S. mental and addictive disorders service system: Epidemiologic catchment area prospective 1-year prevalence rates of disorders and services. *Archives of General Psychiatry, 50*(2), 85–94.

Remafedi, G. (1999). Sexual orientation and youth suicide. *JAMA, 282*(13), 1291–1292.

Richmond, M. (1917). *Social diagnosis.* New York, NY: Russell Sage.

Rolland, J. S. (1994). *Families, illness, and disability: An integrative treatment model.* New York, NY: Basic Books.

Rollnick, S., Miller, W., & Butler, C. C. (2008). *Motivational interviewing in health care: Helping patients change behavior.* New York, NY: Guilford Press.

Rosenzweig, S., Greeson, J. M., Reibel, D. K., Green, J. S., Jasser, S. A., & Beasley, D. (2010). Mindfulness-based stress reduction for chronic pain conditions: Variation in treatment outcomes and role of home meditation practice. *Journal of Psychosomatic Research, 68,* 29–36.

Rudd, M. D., Mandrusiak, M., & Joiner, T. E. (2006). The case against no-suicide contracts: The commitment to treatment statement as a practice alternative. *Journal of Clinical Psychology: In Session, 62*(2), 243–251.

Russell, S. T., & Joyner, K. (2001). Adolescent sexual orientation and suicide risk: Evidence from a national study. *American Journal of Public Health, 91*(8), 1276–1281.

Saleebey, D. (2002). Introduction: Power to the people. In D. Saleebey (Ed.), *The strengths perspective in social work practice* (3rd ed., pp. 1–22). Boston, MA: Allyn & Bacon.

Sanchez, H. G. (2001). Risk factor model for suicide assessment and intervention. *Professional Psychology: Research and Practice, 32*(4), 351–358.

Saraceno, B., & Barbui, C. (1997). Poverty and mental illness. *Canadian Journal of Psychiatry, 42,* 285–290.

Schneeweiss, S., Patrick, A. R., Solomon, D. H., Mehta, J., Dormuth, C., Miller, M.,…Wang, P. S. (2010). Variation in the risk of suicide attempts and completed suicides by antidepressant agent in adults: A propensity score-adjusted analysis of 9 years' data. *Archives of General Psychiatry, 67*(5), 497–506.

Schuhmann, E. M., Foote, R. C., Eyberg, S. M., Boggs, S. R., & Algina, J. (1998). Efficacy of parent-child interaction therapy: Interim report of a randomized trial with short-term maintenance. *Journal of Clinical Child Psychology, 27*(1), 34–45.

Seal, K. H., Bertenthal, D., Miner, C., Sen, S., & Marmar, C. (2007). Mental health disorders among 103,788 US veterans returning from Iraq and Afghanistan seen at Department of Veterans Affairs facilities. *Archives of General Psychiatry, 167,* 476–482.

Segerstrom, S. C., & Miller, G. E. (2004). Psychological stress and the human immune system: A meta-analytic study of 30 years of inquiry. *Psychological Bulletin, 130*(4), 601–630.

Shaffer, D., Fisher, P., Dulcan, M. K., Davies, M., Piacentini, J., Schwab-Stone, M. E.,…Regier, D. (1996). The NIMH diagnostic interview schedule for children (Version 2.3, DISC-2.2): Description, acceptability, prevalence rates, and performance in the MECA study. *Journal of the American Academy of Child and Adolescent Psychiatry, 35*(7), 865–877.

Shaffer, D., Pfeffer, C. R., Bernet, W., Arnold, V., Beitchman, J., Benson, R. S.,…Shaw, J. (2001). Practice parameter for the assessment and treatment of children and adolescents with suicidal behavior. *Journal of the American Academy of Child and Adolescent Psychiatry, 40*(Suppl.), S24–S51.

Shea, S. C. (1988). *Psychiatric interviewing: The art of understanding.* Philadelphia, PA: Saunders.

Siefert, K., Bowman, P. J., Heflin, C. M., Danziger, S., & Williams, D. R. (2000). Social and environmental predictors of maternal depression in current and recent welfare recipients. *American Journal of Orthopsychiatry, 70*(4), 510–522.

Simon, G. E., Savarino, J., Operskalki, B., & Wang, P. S. (2006). Suicide risk during antidepressant treatment. *American Journal of Psychiatry, 163*(1), 41–47.

Skinner, K. M., Kressin, N., Frayne, S., Tripp, T. J., Hankin, C. S., Miller, D. R., & Sullivan, L. M. (2000). The prevalence of military sexual assault among female Veterans' Administration outpatients. *Journal of Interpersonal Violence, 15*(3), 291–310.

Spiegel, D., Sephton, S. E., Terr, A. I., & Stites, D. P. (1998). Effects of psychosocial treatment in prolonging cancer survival may be mediated by neuroimmune pathways. *Annals of New York Academy of Science, 840,* 674–683.

Stark, D., Kiely, M., Smith, A., Velikova, G., House, A., & Selby, P. (2002). Anxiety disorders in cancer patients: Their nature, association, and relation to quality of life. *Journal of Clinical Oncology, 20*(14), 3137–3148.

Sterling, P. & Eyer, J. (1988) Allostasis: a new paradigm to explain arousal pathology. In S. Fisher & J. Reason (Eds.), *Handbook of Life Stress, Cognition and Health* (pp. 629–649). New York, NY: Wiley.

Stein, M. B., McQuaid, J. R., Pedrelli, P., Lenox, R., & McCahill, M. E. (2000). Posttraumatic stress disorder in the primary care medical setting. *General Hospital Psychiatry, 22,* 261–269.

Strader, D. B., Wright, T., Thomas, D. L., Seeff, L. B., & American Association for the Study of Liver Diseases (2004). Diagnosis, management, and treatment of Hepatitis C. *Hepatology, 39*(4), 1147–1171.

Surís, A., Lind, L., Kashner, T. M., Borman, P. D., & Petty, F. (2004). Sexual assault in women veterans: An examination of PTSD risk, health care utilization, and cost of care. *Psychosomatic Medicine, 66*(5), 749–756.

Susser, E. S., Herman, D. B., & Aaron, B. (2002). Combating the terror of terrorism. *Scientific American, 287*(2), 70–78.

Tiihonen, J., Lönnqvist, J., Wahlbeck, K., Klaukka, T., Tanskanen, A., & Haukka, J. (2006). Antidepressants and the risk of suicide, attempted suicide, and overall mortality in a nationwide cohort. *Archives of General Psychiatry, 63,* 1358–1367.

Towsley, G. L., Beck, S. L., & Watkins, J. F. (2007). "Learning to live with it": Coping with the transition to cancer survivorship in older adults. *Journal of Aging Studies, 21,* 93–106.

Trzepacz, P. T., & Baker, R. W. (1993). *The psychiatric mental status examination.* New York, NY: Oxford University Press.

U.S. Department of Defense Task Force on Mental Health. (2007). *An achievable vision: Report of the Department of Defense Task Force on Mental Health.* Falls Church, VA: Defense Health Board.

U.S. Department of Health and Human Services. (1999). *Mental health: A report of the surgeon general.* Rockville, MD: Author.

U.S. Department of Health and Human Services. (2001a). *Mental health: Culture, race, and ethnicity—A supplement to mental health: A report of the surgeon general.* Rockville, MD: Author.

U.S. Department of Health and Human Services. (2001b). *National strategy for suicide prevention: Goals and objectives for action.* Rockville, MD: Author. Retrieved from http://www.sprc.org/library/nssp.pdf

U.S. Preventive Services Task Force, Agency for Health care Research and Quality, U.S. Department of Health and Human Services. (2009). *Guide to clinical preventive services, 2009.* Retrieved from www.ahrq.gov/clinic/pocketgd.htm

U.S. Public Health Service. (1999). *The Surgeon General's call to action to prevent suicide.* Washington, DC: Author. Retrieved from www.surgeongeneral.gov/library/calltoaction/default.htm

Wakefield, J. (1999). The measurement of mental disorder. In A. V. Horwitz & T. L. Scheid (Eds.), *A handbook for the study of mental health: Social contexts, theories, and systems* (pp. 29–57). Cambridge, UK: Cambridge University Press.

Walsh, F. (2004). Spirituality, death, and loss. In F. Walsh & M. McGoldrick (Eds.), *Living beyond loss: Death in the family* (2nd ed., pp. 182–210). New York, NY: Norton.

Walsh, F. (Ed.). (2009). *Spiritual resources in family therapy* (2nd ed.). New York, NY: Guilford Press.

Weihs, K., Fisher, L., & Baird, M. (2002). Families, health and behavior: A section of the commissioned report by the Committee on Health and Behavior (Research, Practice, and Policy Division of Neuroscience and Behavioral Health and Division of Health Promotion and Disease Prevention Institute of Medicine, National Academy of Sciences). *Families, Systems, and Health, 20*(1), 7–46.

Weil, A., & Rosen, W. (1993). *From chocolate to morphine: Everything you need to know about mind-altering drugs* (2nd ed.). Boston, MA: Houghton Mifflin.

Weir, H. K., Thun, M. J., Hankey, B. F., Ries, L. A. G., Howe, H. L., Wingo, P. A.,…Edwards, B. K. (2003). Annual report to the nation on the status of cancer, 1975–2000, featuring the uses of surveillance data for cancer prevention and control. *Journal of the National Cancer Institute, 95*(17), 1276–1299.

Weissbecker, I., Salmon, P., Studts, J. L., Floyd, A. R., Dedert, E. A., & Sephton, S. E. (2002). Mindfulness-based stress reduction and sense of coherence among women with fibromyalgia. *Journal of Clinical Psychology in Medical Settings, 9*(4), 297–307.

Wells, N. E., Freedenthal, S., & Wisneski, H. (2008). Suicidal ideation and attempts among sexual minority youths receiving social services. *Social Work, 53*(1), 21–29.

Wight, V. R., Thampi, K., & Briggs, J. (2010). *Who are America's poor children? Examining food insecurity among children in the United States.* New York, NY: National Center for Children in Poverty.

Williams, D. R., González, H., Neighbors, H. W., Nesse, R., Abelson, J. M., Sweetman, J., & Jackson, J. S. (2007). Prevalence and distribution of major depressive disorder in African Americans, Caribbean Blacks, and Non-Hispanic Whites: Results from the national survey of American Life. *Archives of General Psychiatry, 64,* 305–315.

Williams, D. R., & Mohammed, S. A. (2009). Discrimination and racial disparities in health: Evidence and needed research. *Journal of Behavioral Medicine, 32,* 20–47.

Williams, D. R., Mohammed, S. A., Leavell, J., & Collins, C. (2010). Race, socioeconomic status, and health: Complexities, ongoing challenges, and research opportunities. *Annals of the New York Academy of Sciences, 1168,* 69–101.

Williams, D. R., Neighbors, H. W., & Jackson, J. S. (2003). Racial/ethnic discrimination and health: Findings from community studies. *American Journal of Public Health, 93*(2), 200–208.

Williams, J. B. W. (1998). Classification and diagnostic assessment. In J. B. Williams & K. Ell (Eds.), *Advances in mental health services research: Implications for practice* (pp. 25–48). Washington, DC: National Association of Social Workers.

Williams, J. W., Hitchcock, P., Cordes, J. A., Ramirez, G., & Pignone, M. (2002). Is this patient clinically depressed? *JAMA, 287*(9), 1160–1170.

Winkleby, M. A., Kraemer, H., Ahn, D. K., & Varady, A. N. (1998). Ethnic and socioeconomic differences in cardiovascular disease risk factors: Findings from the third national health and nutrition examination survey, 1988–1994. *JAMA, 280*(4), 356–362.

Witek-Janusek, L., Albuquerque, K., Rambo Chroniak, K., Chroniak, C., Durazo-Arvizu, R., & Matthews, H. L.

(2008). Effect of mindfulness-base stress reduction on immune function, quality of life and coping in women newly diagnosed with early stage breast cancer. *Brain, Behavior and Immunity, 22,* 969–981.

World Health Organization. (2001). *World Health Report 2001: Mental health—New understanding, new hope.* Geneva, Switzerland: Author.

Wyatt, S. B., Williams, D. R., Calvin, R., Henderson, F. C., Walker, E. R., & Winters, K. (2003). Racism and cardiovascular disease in African Americans. *American Journal of the Medical Sciences, 325*(6), 315–331.

Xu, J. Q., Kochanek, K. D., Murphy, S. L., & Tejada-Vera, B. (2010). Deaths: Final data for 2007. *National Vital Statistics, 58*(19). Hyattsville, MD: National Center for Health Statistics.

Yellow Bird, M., Fong, R., Galindo, P., Nowicki, J., & Freeman, E. M. (1996). The multicultural mosaic. In P. L. Ewalt, E. M. Freeman, S. A. Kirk, & D. L. Poole (Eds.), *Multicultural issues in social work* (pp. 3–13). Washington, DC: National Association of Social Workers.

Yoo, H. C., Gee, G. C., & Takeuchi, D. (2009). Discrimination and health among Asian American immigrants: Disentangling racial from language discrimination. *Social Science and Medicine, 68,* 726–732.

Young, A. S., Klap, R., Sherbourne, C. D., & Wells, K. B. (2001). The quality of care for depressive and anxiety disorders in the United States. *Archives of General Psychiatry, 58*(1), 55–61.

Zametkin, A. J., Alter, M. R., & Yemini, T. (2001). Suicide in teenagers: Assessment, management, and prevention. *JAMA 286*(24), 3120–3125.

Zimmerman, M., Lish, J. D., Lush, D. T., Farber, N. J., Plescia, G., & Kuzma, M. A. (1995). Suicidal ideation among urban medical outpatients. *Journal of General Internal Medicine, 10*(10), 573–576.

9

Social Work Practice and Disability Issues

REBECCA BRASHLER

Disability bridges the study of health care and the study of diversity within the social work curriculum. People with disabilities generally have a greater number of health-care encounters than do people without disabilities; therefore, they have a considerable stake in issues such as access to medical care, insurance, quality of care, and the delivery of health services (De-Jong & Basnett, 2001). *Disability studies*, however, is a distinct, emerging field in academia that embraces the examination of humanities, social science, and the history of people with disabilities and is analogous to identity studies or group studies, such as women's studies, African American studies, or Jewish studies. For social workers, the study of disability often focuses on the psychology and the politics of difference—the stigma associated with those who fall outside the mainstream as well as the benefits found when differences are embraced and societal barriers eliminated. This chapter presents a review of these issues for social workers who provide counseling to individuals with disabilities in a variety of settings.

Chapter Objectives

- Discuss the challenges faced when attempting to define disability.
- Review disability models and discuss their assumptions as well as their power to influence our perspectives as social workers.
- Provide an overview of common challenges social workers encounter when working with clients who have disabilities.
- Explore societal values regarding difference and disability that influence both personal perspectives and clinical approaches.

DEFINING *DISABILITY*

Depending on one's perspective, disability may be viewed as a personal characteristic, much like blue eyes, brown skin, or curly hair—an identifying but not necessarily defining feature. Others may view disability as a disease or an abnormality—something to be avoided at all costs; something that will bring with it hardship, suffering, and stigma. Still others may view disability as a source of pride, an entrée into the rich world of disability culture and a disability community that celebrates differences while empowering people with disabilities to demand their rights. When discussing disability, examining one's perspective becomes critical. Doing this can be challenging because our perspective is ever changing, influenced by life experiences, age, and health as well as societal norms, historical context, and our own self-image as people with or without disabilities.

To make matters more complex, there is no universally accepted definition of the word *disability*. Oxford's *Concise Medical Dictionary* defines *disability* as "a loss or restriction of functional ability or activity as a result of impairment of the body or mind" (Martin, 2010). The Americans with Disabilities Act defines a person with a disability as a person who "meets at least one of the three criteria: (1) having a physical or mental impairment that substantially limits one's ability to perform one or more major life activities, (2) having a record of such an impairment, or (3) being regarded as having such an impairment" (National Council of Disability, 1997, Appendix F).

The Social Security Administration (SSA) will consider a person disabled if "you cannot do work you did before and we decide that you cannot adjust to other work because of your medical conditions(s). Your disability also must last or be expected to last for at least a year or to result in death" (www.benefits.gov /benefits/benefit-details/4343).

The widely quoted definition of disability by the World Health Organization (WHO) in the *International Classification of Impairments, Disabilities, and Handicaps* (*ICIDH*) distinguishes among the three related concepts of *impairment*, *disability*, and *handicap*:

> Impairments are defined as "disturbances of body structures or processes." A disability "is any restriction or lack (resulting from an impairment) of ability to perform an activity in the manner or within the range considered normal for a human being." And a handicap is "the social disadvantage individuals experience as a result of impairment or disability." (WHO, 1980)

This definition was revised subsequently by WHO's *ICIDH-2* classification, which places further emphasis on the role of environmental or social factors in "personal activity limitations" and "social participation restrictions."

Because disability identification is so elusive, attempts to count the number of people with disabilities in our communities are "subject to methodological bias and the distortion of the cultural lens" (Fujiura & Rutkowski-Kmitta, 2001, p. 72). The U.S. Census Bureau (2010) indicates that 19% of the population 5 years and older have some type of disability. Global estimates abound in popular literature, and often people with disabilities are referred to as the nation's "largest minority" or as "a minority that we all, if we live long enough, join" (Shapiro, 1994, p. 13). Some of us may never have a disability ourselves yet will spend a large portion of our lives caring for and loving a family member with a disability. Furthermore, disability happens to people at different times; some will be born with a disability while others will acquire one through illness or accident. Many people will spend most of the time as individuals without a disability only to experience alterations in functioning as they enter the final years of their lives.

Disabilities can be sorted by impairment type (e.g., mobility impairments, cognitive impairments, sensory impairments), or they can be viewed on a continuum from mild to moderate to severe, depending on the limitations they cause. Some disabilities are unnoticable by others while others are immediately obvious. Complex typologies have been developed, such as John Rolland's, which classify disabilities according to onset, course, outcome, and incapacity (Rolland, 1994). Although they are of interest to clinicians, most people with disabilities seem largely indifferent to these statistics, definitions, and classification schemes. What may matter most to people with disabilities is that they are fully included in schools, communities, and workplaces and that they are viewed by others as people with value. The perspective that others embrace dramatically shapes the lives of people with disabilities.

HISTORICAL CONTEXT

In the early 19th century, many in the Western world viewed disease and disability in the same way that they viewed poverty and disaster—as "a visitation of a just God upon a frail and erring person ... a direct consequence of undesirable personal or social behavior" (Trattner, 1974, p. 73). It is not surprising, given this view, that people with disabilities were historically shunned, institutionalized, and feared. What may be surprising are how these same views, left unchallenged and fueled by social Darwinism, led to the eugenics movement in the United States during the early 20th century (Braddock, 2002; Pfeiffer, 1999). American physicians during this period routinely facilitated the deaths of babies with birth defects and sterilized institutionalized residents with intellectual disabilities so that their "inferior genes" would not weaken our society. The true horror of the eugenics movement became evident in Nazi Germany during the 1930s and 1940s, when hundreds of thousands of German citizens with disabilities were murdered after being "unworthy of life" (Lifton, 1986, p. 128). This program of euthanasia carried out by physicians under the guise of medical treatment often is seen as the prelude to the mass killings of Jews in concentration camps during World War II.

Throughout the 20th century in the United States, people with disabilities, when not locked away in large, poorly funded institutions, often were exploited as curiosities, paraded before the public for amusement and profit in circuses and freak shows that remained popular well into the 1950s and 1960s (Thomson, 1996). Given this backdrop, the advent of religious and secular organizations that presented people with disabilities as objects of pity and deserving of charity seemed comparatively humane. However, the era of telethons and poster children offered a view of people with disabilities only as victims of tragic circumstances. Telethons and other charity fundraisers created sympathy by manipulating the fears of their viewers in order to get them to "open their wallets" (Shapiro, 1994, p. 13). The viewers' sense of vulnerability could be relieved by sending money that would fund a cure for the unfortunate children—the only acceptable solution, for rarely were images of adults with disabilities shared with the public.

Today we find ourselves in innovative times as the disability rights movement replaces the charity movement and people with disabilities claim their right to equal opportunities and full participation in all aspects of society (Bickenbach, 2001). Through hard-fought legislative battles, the grassroots independent living movement, and individual efforts to change attitudes, the prevailing view of people with disabilities has changed dramatically in recent years. People with disabilities, previously seen as "the embodiment of misery and lost opportunity," now claim pride in their identities, willingly embrace a disability subculture, and force us to question our preconceived ideas of capacity and value (Trent, 2000, p. 214). These changing views of disability challenge social workers and other mental health professionals to reevaluate their roles and reassess traditional thoughts about treatment.

DISABILITY MODELS

Medical Model

The medical model of treatment can be illustrated clearly by following a person who wakes up with acute abdominal pain. The person may go to the emergency room, where she becomes a "patient"—someone in need of care from an expert medical professional. The transformation from "person" to "patient" during hospital admissions was described by Goffman (1961) in his study of institutions as a "leaving off and a taking on, with the midpoint marked by physical nakedness" (p. 18). The physician completes an assessment, usually consisting of a physical examination and history, sometimes augmented by further tests to determine the problem or pathology. The physician then arrives at a diagnosis, which in turn leads to a course of treatment or intervention. Often during the intervention phase the patient is asked to give up a fair amount of autonomy and control to health-care professionals. This is easily seen in a patient hospitalized for an appendectomy who is instructed on what to eat, what to wear, when to get out of bed, and when to interact with visitors. In the best scenario, the treatment leads to a cure or a resolution of the problem, returning the patient to an existence without pain or dysfunction. In the case of abdominal pain diagnosed as appendicitis and leading to an appendectomy, the medical model seems to provide a satisfactory process for delivering care.

For individuals with chronic illnesses and disabilities, however, the medical model holds some troubling challenges. The diagnosis of a chronic or permanent condition, one not amenable to cure, seems to trap the individual in the "patient" or "sick" role forever. As a perpetual patient, people with disabilities may never be well and are forever stuck in a position of reduced status and power. Furthermore, because the intervention phase is prolonged for months or years, the person with a chronic illness or disability is asked to give up autonomy to the "expert" health-care professional for an undetermined period, a position that may foster feelings of dependency and helplessness. In addition, the failure of the person with a chronic illness or disability to be cured—a failure to be "a good patient"—often elicits unexpected and negative reactions from physicians and caregivers. Health-care professionals treating patients who cannot be cured may become disheartened and retreat behind an impersonal technical approach (Halpern, 2001). Professionals also may abandon incurable patients in order to protect themselves from feelings of failure and vulnerability and may move on to treat others who are more likely to have successful outcomes (Gans, 1983; Gunther, 1994).

The diagnostic phase of the medical model also holds some troubling risks for people with disabilities. Diagnostic labels and words used to describe people with disabilities often have served to stigmatize them. As Zola writes, people with disabilities are "de-formed, diseased, dis-ordered, ab-normal, and most telling of all…in-valid" (Zola, 1982, p. 206). Diagnoses such as "imbecile," "moron," and "Mongoloid idiot" were used historically to describe people with cognitive impairments. The self-fulfilling prophecy and low expectations associated with some diagnoses encouraged institutionalization for many people who later would prove capable of living successfully in the community. It is critical to note that the desire for differential diagnosis schemes and classification systems for physical and mental diseases has never been driven by patient needs. The goal of these diagnostic manuals is to "enable clinicians and investigators to diagnose, communicate about, study, and treat people with various [mental] disorders" (APA, 1994, p. 4). For example, the introduction to the *Diagnostic and Statistical Manual of Mental Disorders (DSM-IV)* cautions readers that it is not a "classification of people" but a "classification of disorders that people have" (p. 7).

Although this distinction is an important one, it offers no assurance that clinicians and others will not view the individual differently once the label or diagnosis has been determined. The labeling process appears to be inevitably stigmatizing, and in the case of chronic illness and disability, the stigma it creates may last a lifetime.

In the medical model, disability resides within the individual—the model assumes that there is something wrong with the person. People with disabilities are deviant or abnormal. They may be missing body parts, lacking in function, unable to perform typical tasks, and incapable of going through life like their able-bodied peers. This model focuses exclusively on the pathology and, some would argue, reduces people to laundry lists of ailments while ignoring their value and humanity.

Rehabilitation and Biopsychosocial Models

The field of rehabilitation medicine evolved in the mid-1900s and adopted a multidisciplinary team approach with physical therapists, occupational therapists, speech pathologists, social workers, vocational counselors, and psychologists joining physicians and nurses to treat people with disabilities (Albrecht, 1992). Rehabilitation professionals realized that the medical model did not necessarily fit the needs of their patients and began to ask if "in chronic illness and disability, is it the professional who treats the illness, or is it the patient (or the patient and his family) who actually carries out the routine treatment day after day" (Anderson, 1975, p. 19). The rehabilitation model of treatment acknowledges that the patient is not a passive recipient of care but an active member of the treatment team and that the goal of rehabilitation is not a cure but restoration of the best possible physical and psychological functioning. Furthermore, in rehabilitation medicine, there was a distinct shift from focusing solely on the individual with a disability to focusing on the individual, the family, and the community in which that individual resided. Rehabilitation in this sense embraced the biopsychosocial model of health care (Engel, 1977).

The biopsychosocial model expanded thinking beyond the narrow confines of bodily pathology and greatly shifted the focus to psychological and family issues. However, this shift in focus sometimes led to a tendency to pathologize patients' psychological makeup along with their bodies. It is not difficult to find literature that promotes the belief that physical disability invariably inflicts horribly disruptive and negative psychological consequences and leads to a whole host of personality disorders. For example, a review of the literature reveals that patients with arthritis

> have been said to have weak egos; to repress hostility; to be compliant and subservient; to be potentially psychotic; to be depressed, dependent, conscientious, masochistic, emotionally labile, compulsive, introverted, conservative, perfectionistic, moody, nervous, worried, tense, overconcerned about personal appearance, and prone to express psychopathology in physical symptoms. (Shontz, 1970, p. 112)

For years, the mind-set among many mental health professionals seemed to be that pathological bodies led to pathological personalities, and they set out to analyze the "disabled personality" in spite of having limited research data to back up their assumptions. Far from freeing patients from the stigma of labels, early applications of the biopsychosocial model may have added to the stigma of disability by labeling patients first physically and then psychologically.

Relatives, particularly mothers, of individuals with disabilities also found themselves being labeled and diagnosed as the focus of treatment widened to encompass the entire family system. The classic example of this phenomenon may be Bruno Bettleheim's theory, later disputed, that autism was actually a psychological disturbance arising from cold and detached mothering (Bettleheim, 1967). Others wrote about "narcissistic mothers" of children with asthma who were unable to be "consistently giving" or of the "overprotective mothers" of hemophiliacs whose denial and guilt feelings were "manifested in severe, undisguised anxiety" (Travis, 1976, p. 178).

The biopsychosocial model leads one to think about the interactions between the person with a disability and the person's family, community, and social system. It highlights the connection between biological and psychological functioning. It also challenges some underlying principles of traditional medical thinking, allowing people with disabilities to be seen as active participants in their care and to have legitimate goals and needs even in the absence of a cure. It suggests that people with disabilities are much more than their functional limitations, but it remains at heart a medical paradigm, one that is prone to misinterpretation and not completely free from the dangers of labeling.

Social Model and Minority Group Paradigm

The social model of disability shifts the focus from the impairment within an individual or family system to the environment in which the individual interacts. Advocates for the social model challenge traditional beliefs that physical and cognitive differences are inherently bad and generally lead to a lifetime of suffering. According to this model, "the culprit is not the biological, psychic, or cognitive equipment but the social, institutional, and physical world in which people with impairments must function—a world designed with the characteristics and needs of the nondisabled majority in mind" (Asch, 2001, p. 300).

Using the medical model approach, a child who uses a wheelchair and cannot enter a school with a flight of stairs at its entrance is seen as suffering from a "mobility impairment." Furthermore, the medical model would classify her mobility impairment as having a neurological basis (spinal cord injury) with a predictive course (static), a traumatic onset (motor vehicle accident at the age of 5 years), and a distinct prognosis (permanent but not terminal). The child's inability to walk creates her problem and limits her ability to go to class with "normal" children, leading to a host of social and psychological difficulties. Using the social model, however, the same child in that situation is seen as healthy and whole but socially excluded and unable to exercise her rights to a free public education by a system unwilling to accommodate her needs. The focus moves from the person to the environment and in the process forces us to examine social norms, issues of discrimination, and political concerns.

It can be difficult to switch frameworks and think about disability as a purely socially constructed concept. We are taught to think about health and wellness as ideal states and to view all variation from the norm as undesirable. Often anthropological studies can help dissect medical model assumptions. In her book *Everyone Here Spoke Sign Language*, Groce (1985) writes about hereditary deafness on Martha's Vineyard in the 18th and 19th centuries. Because the island was populated by large numbers of individuals with hearing impairments, the general population was fluent in Island Sign Language, which eliminated the typical communication barriers. Individuals with deafness often were sent off the island to school and therefore received more extended formal education, making them more literate than their neighbors and generally financially secure. They were completely integrated into society to the point that oral historians had difficulty remembering who had deafness and who did not. In essence, the disability disappeared because it was no longer seen as a limitation or a significant characteristic. The study led Groce to conclude that if disability "is a question of definition, rather than a universal given, perhaps it can be redefined, and many of the cultural preconceptions summarized in the term 'handicapped,' as it is now used, eliminated" (Groce, 1985, p. 108).

The social model helps us recognize parallels between people with disabilities and people of other recognized minority groups defined by race, gender, sexual orientation, or nationality. Like other minority groups, people with disabilities often are judged solely by a single characteristic. They are segregated in nursing homes and institutions, they receive separate and unequal education, and they have limited access to jobs, which, in turn, leaves them with less power and money than those with majority status. People with disabilities have to fight to protect their most basic civil rights and in this regard truly share the experiences of other oppressed groups.

Critics of the social model, however, argue that it ignores the real and often distressing aspects of living life with limitations and illness. It is difficult for some to view their disability as a neutral characteristic or based solely in society when they are struggling to live with chronic pain, caring for a loved one who is minimally conscious, or attempting to adjust to the progressive loss of physical and cognitive abilities that accompany, for example, amyotophic lateral sclerosis (ALS, Lou Gehrig's disease) or Alzheimer's disease. In general, we recognize that "all of the problems associated with disability cannot be entirely eliminated by any imaginable form of social arrangements" (Shakespeare, 2006, p. 56).

INTEGRATING MODELS FOR SOCIAL WORK PRACTICE

Undeniable tensions exist among these different models, and whether one truly can find a synthesis between medical and social frameworks is not clear (Shakespeare, 2006; Turner, 2001). For example, it is difficult to advocate for medical advances or searches for a cure, as the actor Christopher Reeve did after his spinal cord injury, without sometimes offending those working in the arena of disability rights. Some fear that "Reeve, perhaps inadvertently, bolstered the case against disability rights by offering a story of the disability experience that concurred with those who insisted that what people with severe disabilities faced were personal, medical problems, that what they needed was compassion—and a cure" (Johnson, 2003, p. 129).

However, it may be equally closed-minded to think that everyone with a disability will or should approach their situation from the same perspective or that we should make no attempt to mitigate the medical conditions that lead to disability as we advocate for social changes (Kirschner, 2000). Some well-adjusted individuals will choose to celebrate their disabilities and view their disability as a "central element of their identity" while others who seem equally well adjusted may choose to minimize their differences and shy away from the disability rights movement (Glastris, 1997). The challenge for many social workers, particularly those who practice in medical facilities, is to balance the skill set needed to negotiate their practice setting while remaining ever cognizant of the lessons learned from years of social oppression, institutional discrimination, and attitudinal barriers.

CLINICAL PRACTICE ISSUES AND THE ROLE OF THE SOCIAL WORKER

Initial Counseling and Framing the Disability

Social workers in many settings will be called on to provide support and counseling for individuals who are encountering disability for the first time. Whether counseling parents who have learned that their unborn child will have a congenital disability, meeting a child who recently was diagnosed with juvenile diabetes at school, seeing a patient in the intensive care unit who has sustained a spinal cord injury and will not walk again, or helping a family in a private medical practice whose grandmother is disabled from a stroke, the primary challenge is to frame the event in a way that will promote a positive adjustment.

It is important to recognize that social workers are rarely, if ever, capable of simply relaying facts and communicating a diagnosis without revealing their own bias. The professionals involved in presenting disability news to individuals must appreciate that the words

they choose, the tone they adopt, their affect, their body language, and their message intertwine to create a subtle but sometimes lasting influence. The parents of a child with Down syndrome might be told:

I'm afraid we have some very bad news about your child. He has Down syndrome. This is an incurable genetic disorder due to a mutation in one of his chromosomes. He has many of the characteristic physical features associated with this syndrome, including epicanthal folds, a sloping forehead, a flat nose, and short limbs. Children with this disorder are also moderately to severely mentally retarded and sometimes have other associated medical complications. We will need to consult with several specialists before you leave the hospital to make sure that appropriate care can be provided for him.

Alternatively, the parents could be told:

We just saw baby Elizabeth and have to say that she is quite beautiful and wonderfully alert! She looks perfectly healthy, but we recommend that she see another physician because she has Down syndrome and may have some associated medical problems. Children with Down syndrome typically lead very normal lives, go to regular school, and are capable of developing very close relationships. However, she also may have some special learning needs and physical delays, so it will be important that you have an opportunity to talk with other parents who have children with Down syndrome in order to fully understand some of the programs and services that can help Elizabeth.

Although neither introduction to Down syndrome is ideal, complete, or without bias, the first clearly frames the disability as a tragedy due to a host of abnormalities and requiring a future of specialized medical care. The emphasis is on the child's differences, and the explanation focuses solely on medical concerns. The second presentation frames the disability as a manageable set of challenges that will be faced by a beautiful child and her loving parents. The emphasis is on the child's relationship to others, and the identified experts needed for consultation are other families who have experienced life with a child who has Down syndrome.

During the framing process, which can encompass multiple conversations, social workers and other professionals must realize that they carry preconceived ideas about what life with a disability is like. The literature on attitudes toward disability clearly indicates that health-care providers often harbor extremely negative views about disability, including beliefs that death is preferable to life with extensive disability and that incurable disability causes irremediable suffering. In fact, research studies have found quality of life to be only weakly correlated with level of impairment and that people with disabilities repeatedly rate their quality of life higher than others would predict they might (Bach & Tilton, 1994; Craig, Hancock, & Dickson, 1994; Fuhrer, Rintala, Kare, Clearman, & Young, 1992; Gerhart, Koziol-McLain, Lowenstien, & Whiteneck, 1994; Longmore, 1995; Sprangers & Aaronson, 1992). In light of this knowledge, it is imperative that social workers who engage in initial counseling closely examine their own perceptions.

One of the most valuable commodities during the framing process is access to a nonjudgmental counselor who is willing to provide information based on "the views of a wide range of health professionals involved in caring for people affected by the condition, together with the views of individuals and families affected by the condition" (Marteau & Anionwu, 2000, p. 126). It seems critical that at some point during the framing process people with newly defined disabilities have an opportunity to interact with others who actually live with similar conditions. Support groups, peer counselors, or access to first-person narratives about life with disabilities can be invaluable when constructing a value-neutral frame. The overriding message always must be that, although the individual now belongs to a specific diagnostic class, he or she remains a "distinct and idiosyncratic human," one who will not by virtue of a single diagnosis share all the characteristics of others with the same genetic mutation, physical limitation, or chronic illness (Berube, 1996).

Providing adequate time and a safe environment during these sensitive counseling sessions is also vital. Too often, initial conversations are hurried and take place in hospital hallways or school classrooms. There is often a rush to send the family on to the next expert or to refer them immediately for additional examinations and further treatment. The clinician's own discomfort in the face of disability may be what leads to this kind of truncated interaction when, in fact, what individuals need most is the "opportunity to ask their own questions in their own way; to go over difficult, often insoluble, problems in an unhurried manner; and to feel supported" (Harper, 2000, p. 59). One mother's advice to professionals in similar situations should be heeded carefully: "Do not disappear. Do not leave the room. Make eye contact. Look me in the eye and ask me what you can do to help me deal with this" (Berube, 1996, p. 38).

Responses to Disability

Therapists over the years have searched for concrete models that predict and explain the experience of people as they encounter disability and adapt to changes in appearance or altered functioning. Various models of adjustment to disability can be found in the literature, but it is important to recognize that there is limited empirical data in this area and no universally accepted theory regarding disability adjustment.

Stage models of adjustment to disability are derived from Elisabeth Kübler-Ross's work with terminally ill patients with cancer (Kübler-Ross, 1969). These models suggest that individuals confronted with a new diagnosis of disability experience predictable stages or reactions, such as shock, denial, anger, bargaining, or depression, and that the desired end point is a final stage of adaptation or acceptance. The value of stage theories is that they can depathologize the process of adjustment by emphasizing that even healthy and ultimately well-adjusted individuals may experience periods of disruption in functioning when first confronting a disability. However, in order to have any utility, stage theories cannot be taken literally and must account for individual differences. The adjustment process is rarely linear, and individuals with disabilities have both good and bad days along their journey. Not everyone will pass through the stages in the same order; some individuals may skip a stage completely while others will linger longer than expected in a particular stage without experiencing a negative outcome (Gunther, 1969; Livneh, 1992; Olkin, 1999).

Grief models compare reactions to disability with the process of bereavement following a death. *Mourning* often is defined as the adaptation to loss (Worden, 1991) and can have relevance to the loss of a limb, the loss of function, or the loss of the dream for a healthy child. The primary difference between bereavement and adaptation to disability is that death by its very nature is finite while disability is ongoing or chronic. The concept of *chronic sorrow,* or periods of grief that resurface from time to time (often associated with key developmental milestones), acknowledges this distinction. Although on the surface the idea of chronic sorrow may seem depressing and pessimistic, it does serve to caution professionals not to become impatient during the adjustment process and not to think of prolonged adjustment periods as evidence of neurosis. It also challenges professionals "to abandon the simplistic and static concept of…acceptance," at least acceptance that will be reached through a handful of therapy sessions (Olshansky, 1970, p. 22). Others have remarked that the losses associated with disability, particularly those that accompany disabilities like severe brain injury and late-stage Alzheimer's disease, are more ambiguous and complex than those that surround death (Boss, 2000). In these situations, the individual survives but often has lost the essence of the person he had previously been. There is a death of sorts, but one that often is devoid of any comforting rituals and that is largely unrecognized by society.

Crisis intervention models emphasize the temporary disruption in functioning and emotional stability that is created whenever one experiences an event that is perceived to be a threat to one's life or the life of a loved one or that has the potential to become overwhelming (Aguilera & Messick, 1978). This framework has some utility when thinking about disability because it values the perception of the person involved in the crisis. A young couple learning that their toddler has been diagnosed with cerebral palsy may indeed feel that they are in the midst of a crisis, while a single parent who chooses to bring home a child with a similar disability from an adoption agency may view the event as joyful. A professional violinist who loses a finger in an accident may feel that she is facing a crisis of great magnitude while a machinist may view the same injury as minor and unimportant. A crisis can be defined only by the person, not by others who may have a different perspective of the same experience. Because crises are viewed as turning points or opportunities for growth, this framework also reminds the client and the therapist that people frequently emerge from crisis with improved coping skills and greater feelings of competence. The notion that people actually benefit from adversity is one that can be very reassuring to people experiencing disability challenges (Elliot, Kurylo, & Rivera, 2002; McMillen, 1999).

Regardless of which adjustment model frames their work, it remains critical that social workers not become so distracted by the disability adjustment process that they fall into the trap of blaming the disability for any and all difficulties an individual experiences. Individuals with disabilities experience marital problems, life-adjustment issues, child-rearing challenges, and emotional problems that may bring them to a therapist's office. Assuming that disability is the root cause of any of these difficulties is dangerous. This assumption may be particularly lethal for situations in which individuals with disabilities present with suicidal ideation and are treated less aggressively because of beliefs that anyone in their physical condition rationally would prefer to be dead.

People with disabilities turn to suicide in response to the same triggers as people without disabilities, and "there is no evidence of a unique death-seeking dynamic associated with disability that...is somehow more rational than 'ordinary' suicide" (Gill, 2004, p. 185).

In 1986, Elizabeth Bouvia, a woman in her 20s with cerebral palsy and arthritis, requested that a California hospital admit her and allow her to die by keeping her sedated while she stopped her gastric feedings. Although individuals without disabilities with suicidal intentions are routinely hospitalized and treated for their emotional distress, the courts in this case ruled that Ms. Bouvia should be allowed to facilitate her death because her life with disabilities was regarded as intolerable (Asch, 2001). They were completely willing to overlook the fact that this young woman had lived successfully with her disability since birth but recently had experienced multiple losses, including the death of her brother, a miscarriage, a divorce, and withdrawal from her master's-level graduate school program in social work. The presence of a disability is often only one of many factors that will prompt an individual to question the value of life and exhibit signs of depression, hopelessness, and anxiety.

The most useful of adjustment perspectives are those that can account for the paradoxical feelings and ideas that most individuals have toward disability (Larson, 1998). They acknowledge that an individual can hold simultaneously seemingly contradictory thoughts about life with differences. Individuals do not really move through stages; they live in two or more stages at the same time. They do not experience distinct, easily defined periods of grieving; distress about losses may come and go in unpredictable patterns for years. Often people with disabilities experience a series of crises rather than a single event followed by adjustment. One can be absolutely devastated about not being able to walk yet simultaneously hopeful about the future. One can truly love a child unconditionally yet simultaneously pray that she will be cured miraculously. One can bitterly grieve for the lost capacity to talk yet simultaneously be grateful to be alive. One can

be angry about the barriers created by society yet simultaneously be joyful about newfound resourcefulness in the face of those barriers. One can completely dismiss a physician's prognosis as overly pessimistic yet simultaneously engage in prescribed therapies. Adaptation to disability is never simple, it is rarely black and white, and, in this sense, it does not lend itself well to any single theory or model.

There are several critical points for clinicians to remember when assessing adjustment and thinking about structuring interventions:

- When confronted by disability, individuals are likely to encounter a period of disrupted functioning that, in and of itself, is not pathological or abnormal. Repeatedly normalizing the process may be the single most important service a social worker can provide.

- There is no right or wrong way for patients to approach disability adjustment.

- Each individual will perceive his or her disability differently, and it is the individual's perceptions, not ours, that are most relevant. Social workers must listen carefully to their clients' perceptions, inform them that their perceptions may be fluid, and expose them to other perspectives when appropriate.

- People's perceptions of their disability change over time, and people often hold paradoxical views regarding disability.

- The adaptation process cannot be defined in terms of weeks or years. It may ebb and flow throughout one's lifetime. Just as individuals adjust to different stages of life, individuals adjust to different stages of life with a disability. Social workers should remain available well beyond the initial adjustment phase yet not associate this availability with the notion that our clients will never be psychologically well.

- Individuals may experience periods of depression or anxiety that require treatment at any point during their experience with disability, but therapists cannot assume that these symptoms are caused solely by the disability; rather, they may be related to and interwoven with other life issues or be the result of frustration over societal barriers.

- People with disabilities often have a history of unsatisfactory health-care encounters and may be distrustful or disillusioned about the benefits of seeking treatment. Be prepared to review this history with them to learn about their experiences, build rapport, and create a solid therapeutic alliance.

- There is no idealized state of final adaptation or acceptance with a disability, just as there is no idealized state of adjustment to life without a disability.

DISABILITY AND ETHICS

Some of the most pressing ethical issues of our times involve disability on some level. Physician-assisted suicide, stem cell research, genetic engineering, health-care resource allocation, and end-of-life care are just a few examples. Examining a landmark case in detail can help tease apart how the disability perspective alters one's thinking about ethical dilemmas and may lead to asking different questions and possibly drawing different conclusions.

On February 25, 1990, Terri Schiavo had a cardiac arrest resulting in severe hypoxic-ischemic encephalopathy. Fifteen years later, her name and face became widely known as physicians, lawyers, journalists, and the general public discussed the many complex and controversial issues that surrounded her situation and the choice of removing her from life support. Her private family conflict became painfully public, and political lines were drawn based on "right to life" and "right to die" slogans. Legal and legislative history was made when the case was debated in Congress, and journalists struggled to summarize some of the most complex ethical issues into sound bites suitable for the nightly news. In the midst of this activity, many were surprised to find that disability advocates were among those deeply invested in the outcome of the proceedings that were taking place to determine if Schiavo's feeding tube could be withdrawn.

Furthermore, the disability perspective brought a unique way of viewing the feeding tube that was keeping Schiavo alive—one that others may not have considered previously (Brashler, Savage, Mukherjee, & Kirschner, 2007).

The prevailing medicolegal view is that the "right of competent patients to refuse unwanted medical treatment, including artificial hydration and nutrition, is a settled ethical and legal issue" (Quill, 2005, p. 1631). Furthermore, the courts have ruled that this right is not lost when a patient becomes incompetent as long as there is clear and convincing evidence that withdrawal of the artificial feeding is consistent with the patient's prior wishes. The Catholic church and many others, however, viewed the removal of Schiavo's feeding tube as inhumane. Pope John Paul II stated that there was a "moral obligation" to provide tube feedings to patients in vegetative states (Vatican, 2004). Those who adhered to this viewpoint felt that removal of the feeding tube could be considered euthanasia by omission and worried that Schiavo would "starve to death."

A third view, articulated by individuals with disabilities, was that Schiavo's feeding tube was simply a disability accommodation, not much different from a wheelchair for an individual who cannot walk. People with chronic conditions who use feeding tubes on a daily basis because of swallowing problems often begin to think of the tube as a tool or an implement similar to a fork. The tube gradually becomes devoid of medical meaning and simply allows them to ingest food efficiently and safely. For example, wheelchairs may seem frightening to individuals who walk, and feeding tubes may seem equally foreign to those who ingest food orally. But the insider perspective of those who use these items routinely is dramatically different. Some individuals with disabilities felt a kinship to Schiavo, not only because they shared her dependence on adaptive equipment but also because of the judgments being made about her quality of life. Some worried that if it was acceptable to remove Schiavo's feeding tube, it also would be permissible to remove feeding tubes from people who were still conscious or who used them for other reasons. They feared that "we would be starting down a slippery slope where we might eventually wind up removing tubes from people who are profoundly disabled but not in a permanent vegetative state" (Shepherd, 2009, p. 12).

The Schiavo case had many observers thinking carefully about that slippery slope and trying to determine for themselves what makes life worth living and when they would want life-sustaining treatments to be withdrawn. The disability concerns embedded in this case became intertwined with profound questions about the value of life and our obligation to protect vulnerable individuals in society.

ADVOCACY

Most social workers provide not only counseling but concrete case management services to clients with disabilities. Counseling and advocacy efforts ideally are provided in an integrated fashion rather than being packaged as discrete functions. Counseling an individual experiencing the recent onset of a disability that prevents a return to work without providing information and advocacy around income maintenance would be fruitless, just as assisting an older person with a nursing home placement without addressing the issues of losses associated with aging and illness would be irresponsible. Throughout the United States, there are confusing arrays of fragmented financial, legal, educational, medical, and family services available to people with disabilities, many of which have complex application and eligibility requirements. Social workers in private practice, in schools, and in medical settings must educate themselves about the community resources available to their clients to assist them to navigate the overwhelming maze of disability services that are available.

Disability can bring devastating financial burdens in three areas: (1) hospital/medical expenses, (2) loss of income or earning potential for the individual and her family caregiver, and (3) additional community/living expenses. Medicare, Medicaid, managed care,

indemnity, worker's compensation, veterans' benefits, and other forms of health insurance may cover medical expenses related to disability, but people often are unfamiliar with their coverage, uncertain how to apply for coverage, and unaware of what types of medical care may not be paid for under their policies. In cases of catastrophic injuries, fears about financial ruin may be very real. People who are uninsured and underinsured are certain to have concerns about access to quality health care. For many people, managing the overwhelming amount paperwork required to file a claim or navigate the bureaucracy of a large managed care company is more than they can handle while in the midst of a medical crisis. Social work assistance in this area is invaluable.

Income maintenance may be available from Social Security disability insurance, supplemental security income, the Veteran's Administration, crime victims' compensation, private disability insurance, and worker's compensation. These programs are complex, and services sometimes are difficult to secure. When returning to work, individuals with a disability also may encounter challenges related to employer biases, disincentives built into the system, and inflexible benefits. Knowing both entitlement eligibility and legal protections is important for social workers in this area.

Community living expenses include the cost of transportation, affordable/accessible housing, and attendant care services. Advocating for better transportation, housing, and attendant care consumes many local disability rights groups, which understand that access to these basic services frequently mean the difference between being able to live freely in the community and having to live in an institution or nursing home. The politics that surround community living programs are complex, and a bias toward the institutionalization of people with disabilities in our current government programs remains. Even when it may cost less to care for people with a disability in the community, they may end up in a nursing home because they cannot piece together the support systems needed to allow for independent living. Attendants are difficult to find and keep because the job often pays less than other non-skilled jobs in the community and often does not include health-care coverage or other benefits. Family members willing to provide care in their homes often do so at the expense of their own careers and at the risk of their own health. They remain an invisible source of free labor that goes unrecognized and unaccounted for by traditional economic measures (Gould, 2004).

The right to free and appropriate public education for children regardless of the type or extent of their disability has been secured in the United States through passage of Public Law 94-142 (1975), later amended and renamed the Individuals with Disabilities Act in 1990. Before this law was enacted, it was estimated that "at least 1 million children in the United States were being excluded from public schools because of their disabilities" (Switzer, 2003, p. 61). With this law, parents became participants in planning for their children's education through the use of Individual Education Programs, and schools were mandated to place children in the "least restrictive environment." However, these government regulations also led to a complex system of registration, case study evaluations, multidisciplinary conferences, placement protocols, and procedural safeguards. Parents often feel the need for an advocate to help them through the process, particularly if there are disagreements about their child's needs. Controversies still surround the move from no education to separate schools to mainstreaming in regular schools with separate classrooms and finally to full inclusion. Social workers can help parents and children in their quest to secure the most appropriate and inclusive educational program available in their community.

Advocating for clients who have disabilities—whether they face discrimination in the workplace, difficulties accessing health care, or problems researching available community services—is a critical role for most social workers. During this process, however, social workers must remain sensitive to the very real power differential that invariably exists between the professional and the client seeking services, particularly when the client is a member of a vulnerable and oppressed group. Social service professionals who work with vulnerable groups often are seen as extensions of the bureaucracies that employ them or gatekeepers who must be manipulated in order to receive needed services. This has been particularly true for many people with disabilities. Patients with disabilities are not "cases," and they do not need to be "managed." They need information and support at times, but "help is useful only when it leads to empowerment" (Charlton, 1998, p. 5). True empowerment for people with disabilities, as with other minority groups, will be realized only when they reach positions of status in hospitals, universities, legislative bodies, and governmental agencies in meaningful numbers. Making sure that people with disabilities represent themselves and assume a primary role in shaping the services they require must be the ultimate goal of social workers whenever we act as advocates.

FINDING MEANING

The search for meaning is a journey than can take many years. It is a universal process in which every person engages, but for people with disabilities, it may have some added poignancy and importance. Many mental health professionals have noted the need to shift our focus from examining the parameters of patients' physical conditions or analyzing clients' psychological makeup to helping them clarify their values in an effort to create positive meaning. Trieschmann (1999) writes:

> I have become increasingly dissatisfied with the conceptual models of traditional western medicine and psychology because they do not offer me comfortable viewpoints or strategies that are really helpful in teaching people to find happiness. When people do find happiness, it derives from a reevaluation of what is important in their lives, usually accompanied by a deepening of their spirituality and usually accomplished by themselves without help from professionals. (p. 32)

The work of Victor Frankl, a psychiatrist who developed a therapy model he called logotherapy, is particularly helpful when thinking about the process of finding meaning. Frankl wrote extensively about his experiences in a concentration camp during World War II and how survival became dependent on finding acceptable meaning for an unacceptable atrocity. He wrote that if "one cannot change a situation that causes his suffering, he can still choose his attitude" (Frankl, 1984, p. 148). Frankl and others emphasize that the meaning people create must be uniquely theirs based on their own life experiences, religion, culture, family structure, worldviews, and belief systems. Health-care professionals can facilitate this search for meaning, but it will be different for each individual.

First-person narratives from people living with a disability illustrate how varied their individual meanings can be, yet they all seem to reflect changing perspectives, a reassessment of values, or a process of "sifting out the trivial from the important" (Wright, 1983, p. 191). One father takes comfort in the randomness of the universe by saying:

> I've come to believe that there's no design for tragedy nor a design whereby the sins of the past return to punish the sinner....This means that there's no method to the madness and sadness found here on Earth. Life is as random and unpredictable as the shape of the next snowflake, and we all must take our chances if we are to stick. (Seerman, 1995, p. 89)

Others find meaning in religious terms:

> I have a higher power, my God, who is with me always, even though I may not feel that presence all the time. I know that I can make it; I know that I can keep up hope; I know that even if things do not turn out as they should, I am not alone....What more could a person want? (Kahlback, 2001)

Another father writes about the essence of humanity:

> Peering into the crib of a child with disability in the predawn moonlight can bring tears of truly unconditional love, love that will not be based on the report card performance, scores as a star quarterback or excellent performance as a trial lawyer. This love is for who the person *is*, for their qualities, their trials and for the inner strength they must develop to take their place. (Kappes, 1995, p. 25)

A writer with a facial difference due to cancer surgery struggles to tease out the difference between internal and external images. She once thought:

> I was my face, I was ugliness...the one immediately recognizable place to point to when asked what was wrong with my life. (Grealy, 1994, p. 7)

She later writes:

> I experienced a moment of the freedom I'd been practicing for behind my Halloween mask all those years ago. As a child I had expected my liberation to come from getting a new face to put on, but now I saw it came from shedding something, shedding my image. (Grealy, 1994, p. 222)

A mother of a son with autism who lives and works on a university campus writes:

> To have an autistic child is to learn to love difference, the humanity that runs far deeper than the success and achievement we are all taught to value....I was forced to confront my deepest prejudices....Living all my adult life in an academic environment, I had never been forced to consider that intellect is not the same as merit, it is not the same as virtue. It is a gift of nature as surely as any other. (McDonnell, 1993, p. 324)

A man with a spinal cord injury finds meaning by shifting his focus from the negative to the positive and says:

> Before I was paralyzed, there were ten thousand things I could do, ten thousand things I was capable of doing. Now there are nine thousand. I can dwell on the one thousand or

concentrate on the nine thousand I have left. And of course the joke is that none of us in our lifetime is going to do more than two or three thousand of these things in any event. (Corbet, 1980, p. 32)

An important social work role is to help people formulate a meaning that works for them, a meaning that brings them to a place where the disability becomes understood and therefore less frightening. American society places a premium on youth, athleticism, independence, power, wealth, beauty, and achievement. Helping people look beyond these ubiquitous values and treasure the spirit that they and their loved ones bring to our world, a spirit uniquely theirs that transcends the mundane issues of how one walks or talks or eats or looks or thinks, can be tremendously rewarding work.

SUGGESTED LEARNING EXERCISE

This learning exercise helps students explore their personal values related to people with disabilities and facilitate an open discussion of societal ideals.

Learning Exercise 9.1

Students are told that they comprise the board of directors of a small community hospital. Their community has been hit with a new illness that is 100% fatal—usually within a few hours. The only successful treatment is an injection of a new drug that has just been developed and cures the patient almost immediately. Unfortunately, the drug is in short supply, and difficult decisions have to be made regarding which patients will be treated and which patients will be left to die from the infection. The hospital currently houses 10 patients who have the infection and are in dire need of treatment. The hospital has just received a shipment of five doses of the medication. The board members must decide which of the patients, based only on the next profiles, will get the injection.

1. A 65-year-old nun who has spent her entire life in a secluded convent and has devoted herself to a life of prayer and poverty.

2. A 44-year-old African American, single, foster mother who has adopted five hard-to-place children with disabilities and is raising them on her own.

3. A 24-year-old male model who recently was voted one of the 10 most beautiful people in the United States. He is single and has just been cast in his first film.

4. A 5-year-old Hispanic American boy who is blind, deaf, and mentally retarded. He is well adjusted and lives with his mother, grandmother, and six siblings in a loving and secure home.

5. A 23-year-old woman who is working on her MSW and is engaged to be married. She sustained a spinal cord injury in a car accident 10 years ago. She uses a wheelchair for mobility and is independent in self-care.

6. A 77-year-old Nobel Prize–winning researcher who is working on a cure for arthritis and has made several important breakthroughs in recent months.

7. A 10-year-old Caucasian boy who likes to play soccer and video games. He lives in the suburbs with his parents and his sister in an upper-middle-class home. He has learning disabilities and sometimes struggles with impulse control/anger management.

8. A 50-year-old accomplished concert pianist. He is moody, temperamental, and a self-described loner. Never married, he has few friends and lives for his music.

9. A 40-year-old beloved coach of the U.S. Women's Olympic Softball team, which is preparing to compete in the next Olympics in 18 months.

10. A 21-year-old African American teen currently incarcerated on drug charges. He is due to be paroled in 6 months. While in jail, he completed his general equivalency diploma and started an innovative program to help teens stay out of gangs.

After the exercise, the group should list the deciding factors that drove their choices. Is age more important than lifestyle? Is intellectual capacity more important than artistic ability? Did patients without obvious disabilities fare better than others? Is past behavior more critical than future potential? What value do we place on the patient's capacity to relate to others? Assuming that the board of directors will have its choices scrutinized by the community at large, will any of its decisions meet with community disagreement or outrage? Why or why not?

REFERENCES

Aguilera, D., & Messick, J. (1978). *Crisis intervention: Theory and methodology* (3rd ed.). Saint Louis, MO: Mosby.

Albrecht, G. (1992). *The disability business: Rehabilitation in America*. Newbury Park, CA: Sage.

American Psychiatric Association. (1994). *Diagnostic and statistical manual of mental disorders, fourth edition*. Washington, DC: Author.

Anderson, T. (1975). An alternative frame of reference for rehabilitation: The helping process versus the medical model. *Archives of Physical Medicine and Rehabilitation, 56*, 101–104.

Asch, A. (2001). Disability, bioethics and human rights. In G. Albrecht, K. Seelman, & M. Bury (Eds.), *Handbook of disability studies* (pp. 297–326). Thousand Oaks, CA: Sage.

Bach, J. R., & Tilton, M. C. (1994). Life satisfaction and well-being measures in ventilator assisted individuals with traumatic tetraplegia. *Archives of Physical Medicine and Rehabilitation, 75*, 626–632.

Berube, M. (1996). *Life as we know it: A father, a family, and an exceptional child*. New York, NY: Pantheon.

Bettleheim, B. (1967). *The empty fortress: Infantile autism and the birth of the self*. New York, NY: Free Press.

Bickenbach, J. (2001). Disability human rights, law, and policy. In G. Albrecht, K. Seelman, & M. Bury (Eds.), *Handbook of disability studies* (pp. 565–584). Thousand Oaks, CA: Sage.

Boss, P. (2000). *Ambiguous loss: Learning to live with unresolved grief*. Cambridge, MA: Harvard University Press.

Braddock, D. (Ed). (2002). *Disability at the dawn of the 21st century*. Washington, DC: American Association on Mental Retardation.

Brashler, R., Savage, T. A., Mukherjee, D., & Kirschner, K. L. (2007). Feeding tubes: Three perspectives. *Topics in Stroke Rehabilitation, 14*(6), 74–77.

Charlton, J. (1998). *Nothing about us without us: Disability oppression and empowerment*. Berkeley, CA: University of California Press.

Corbet, B. (1980). *Options: Spinal cord injury and the future*. Denver, CO: A. B. Hirschfeld.

Craig, A. R., Hancock, K. M., & Dickson, H. G. (1994). Spinal cord injury: A search for determinants of depression two years after the event. *British Journal of Clinical Psychology, 33*(Pt. 2), 221–230.

DeJong, G., & Basnett, I. (2001). Disability and health policy: The role of markets in the delivery of health services. In G. Albrecht, K. Seelman, & M. Bury (Eds.), *Handbook of disability studies* (pp. 610–632). Thousand Oaks, CA: Sage.

Elliot, T. R., Kurylo, M. & Rivera, P. (2002). Positive growth following acquired physical disability. In C. R. Snyder & S. J. Lopez (Eds.), *Handbook of positive psychology* (pp. 687–699). Oxford, UK: Oxford University Press.

Engel, G. (1977). The need for a new medical model. *Science, 196,* 129–136.

Frankl, V. (1984). *Man's search for meaning: An introduction to logotherapy* (3rd ed.). New York, NY: Simon & Schuster.

Fuhrer, M. J., Rintala, D. H., Hart, K. A., Clearman, R., & Young, M. E. (1992). Relation of life satisfaction to impairment, disability, and handicap among persons with spinal cord injury living in the community. *Archives of Physical Medicine and Rehabilitation, 73,* 552–557.

Fujiura, G., & Rutkowski-Kmitta, V. (2001) Counting disability. In G. Albrecht, K. Seelman, & M. Bury (Eds.), *Handbook of disability studies* (pp. 69–96). Thousand Oaks, CA: Sage.

Gans, J. (1983). Hate in the rehabilitation setting. *Archives in Physical Medicine and Rehabilitation, 64,* 176–179.

Gerhart, K., Koziol-McLain, J., Lowenstien, S., & Whiteneck, G. (1994). Quality of life following spinal cord injury: Knowledge and attitudes of emergency care providers. *Annals of Emergency Medicine, 23*(4), 807–812.

Gill, C. J. (2004). Depression in the context of disability and the "right to die." *Theoretical Medicine, 25,* 171–198.

Glastris, P. (1997, May 5). Spoiling a proper memorial. *U.S. News & World Report,* 9.

Goffman, E. (1961). *Ayslums*. New York, NY: Anchor Books.

Gould, D. (2004). Measuring what matters: Levers for change. In C. Levine (Ed.), *Family caregivers on the job: Moving beyond ADLs and IADLs*. New York, NY: United Hospital Fund of New York.

Grealy, L. (1994). *Autobiography of a face*. New York, NY: HarperCollins.

Groce, N. (1985). *Everyone here spoke sign language: Hereditary deafness on Martha's Vineyard*. Cambridge, MA: Harvard University Press.

Gunther, M. (1969). Emotional aspects. In D. Ruge (Ed.), *Spinal cord injuries* (pp. 93–108). Springfield, IL: Charles C Thomas.

Gunther, M. (1994). Countertransference issues in staff caregivers who work to rehabilitate catastrophic-injury survivors. *American Journal of Psychotherapy, 48*(2), 208–220.

Halpern, J. (2001). *From detached concern to empathy: Humanizing medical practice.* Oxford, UK: Oxford University Press.

Harper, P. (2000). Personal experiences of genetic diseases: A clinical geneticist's reaction. In T. Marteau & M. Richards (Eds.), *The troubled helix: Social and psychological implications of the new genetics* (pp. 54–59). Cambridge, UK: Cambridge University Press.

Johnson, M. (2003). *Make them go away: Clint Eastwood, Christopher Reeve & the case against disability rights.* Louisville, KY: Avocado Press.

Kahlback, D. (2001). *Religion and Ethics in America* [Television broadcast out takes]. Chicago, IL: WTTW.

Kappes, N. (1995). Matrix. In D. J. Meyer (Ed.), *Uncommon fathers: Reflections on raising a child with a disability* (pp. 13–28). Bethesda, MD: Woodbine House.

Kirschner, K. (2000, May 7). My view: Literature fumbles a tough lesson. *Chicago Tribune,* 13.

Kübler-Ross, E. (1969). *On death and dying.* New York, NY: Macmillan.

Larson, E. (1998). Reframing the meaning of disability to families: The embrace of paradox. *Social Science Medicine, 47*(7), 865–875.

Lifton, R. (1986). *The Nazi doctors: Medical killing and the psychology of genocide.* New York, NY: Basic Books.

Livneh, H. (1992). A unified approach to existing models of adaptation to disability: A model of adaptation. In R. Marinelli & A. Dell Orto (Eds.), *The psychological and social impact of disability* (3rd ed., pp. 241–248). New York, NY: Springer.

Longmore, P. (1995). Medical decision making and people with disabilities: A clash of cultures. *Journal of Law, Medicine & Ethics, 23,* 82–87.

Marteau, T., & Anionwu, E. (2000). Evaluating carrier testing: Objectives and outcomes. In T. Marteau & M. Richards (Eds.), *The troubled helix: Social and psychological implications of the new genetics* (pp. 123–139). Cambridge, UK: Cambridge University Press.

Martin, E. A. (Ed.). (2010). *Concise medical dictionary* (8th ed.). Oxford, UK: Oxford University Press.

McDonnell, J. (1993). *News from the border: A memoir.* Northfield, MN: Black Willow.

McMillen, J. C. (1999). Better for it: How people benefit from adversity. *Social Work, 44*(5), 455–468.

National Council of Disability. (1997). *Equality of opportunity: The making of the Americans with Disabilities Act.* Washington, DC: Author.

Olkin, R. (1999). *What psychotherapists should know about disability.* New York, NY: Guilford Press.

Olshansky, S. (1970). Chronic sorrow: A response to having a mentally defective child. In R. Nolland (Ed.), *Counseling parents of the mentally retarded: A sourcebook* (pp. 328–331). Springfield, IL: Charles C Thomas.

Pfeiffer, D. (1999). Eugenics and disability discrimination. In R. Marinelli & A. Dell Orto (Eds.), *The psychological and social impact of disability* (4th ed., pp. 12–31). New York, NY: Springer.

Quill, T. (2005). Terri Schiavo—A tragedy compounded. *New England Journal of Medicine, 352,* 1630–1633.

Rolland, J. (1994). *Families, illness and disability: An integrative treatment model.* New York, NY: Basic Books.

Seerman, D. (1995). The loneliness of the long-distance daddy. In D. J. Meyer (Ed.), *Uncommon father: Reflections on raising a child with a disability* (pp. 79–90). Bethesda, MD: Woodbine House.

Shakespeare, T. (2006). *Disability rights and wrongs.* New York, NY: Routledge.

Shapiro, J. (1994). *No pity.* New York, NY: Three Rivers.

Shapiro, M., Spece, R., Dresser, R., & Clayton, E. (Eds). (2003). *Bioethics and law: Cases, materials and problems* (2nd ed.). St. Paul, MN: West.

Shepherd, L. (2009). *If that ever happens to me: Making life and death decisions after Terri Schiavo.* Chapel Hill, NC: University of North Carolina Press.

Shontz, F. (1970). Physical disability and personality: Theory and recent research. *Rehabilitation Psychology, 17,* 51–69.

Social Security Administration. (2007). *Supplemental security income (SSI)* [Publication no .05-11000]. Retrieved from www.ssa.gov/pubs/11000.pdf

Sprangers, M. A. G., & Aaronson, N. K. (1992). The role of health care providers and significant others in evaluating the quality of life of patients with chronic disease: A review. *Journal of Clinical Epidemiology, 45*(7), 743–760.

Switzer, J. V. (2003). *Disabled rights: American disability policy and the fight for equality.* Washington DC: Georgetown University Press.

Thomson, R. (Ed.). (1996). *Freakery: Cultural spectacles of the extraordinary body.* New York: New York University Press.

Trattner, W. (1974). *From poor law to welfare state: A history of social welfare in America.* New York, NY: Free Press.

Travis, G. (1976). *Chronic illness in children: Its impact on child and family.* Stanford, CA: Stanford University Press.

Trent. J. (2000). Disability, subculture (culture) of. In *The encyclopedia of criminology and deviant behavior: Self destructive behavior and devalued identity* (Vol. 4, pp. 213–216). London, UK: Taylor & Francis.

Trieschmann, R. (1999). The energy model: A new approach to rehabilitation. In R. Marinelli & A. Dell Orto (Eds.),

The psychological and social impact of disability (4th ed., pp. 32–42). New York, NY: Springer.

Turner, B. (2001), Disability and the sociology of the body. In G. Albrecht, K. Seelman, & M. Bury (Eds.), *Handbook of disability studies* (pp. 252–266). Thousand Oaks, CA: Sage.

U.S. Census Bureau. (2010). *U.S. Census Bureau Facts for Features: 20th Anniversary of Americans With Disabilities Act: July 26.* Retrieved from www .prnewswire.com/news-releases/us-census-bureau -facts-for-features--20th-anniversary-of-americans -with-disabilities-act-july-26-94914034.html

Vatican. (2004, March 20). Address to the participants in the international congress: Life-sustaining treatments and vegetative state: Scientific advances and ethical dilemmas. Retrieved from www.vatican.va/holy _father/john_paul_ii/speeches/2004/march/documents /hf_jp-ii_spe_20040320_congress-fiamc_en.html

Worden, J. (1991). *Grief counseling and grief therapy: A handbook for the mental health practitioner* (2nd ed.). New York, NY: Springer.

World Health Organization. (1980). *International classification of impairments, disabilities and handicaps.* Geneva, Switzerland: Author.

Wright, B. A. (1983). *Physical disability—A psychosocial approach* (2nd ed.). New York, NY: Harper & Row.

Zola, I. (1982). *Missing pieces: A chronicle of living with a disability.* Philadelphia, PA: Temple University Press.

10

Communication in Health Care

SARAH GEHLERT

Good communication is central to the provision of effective health care. If patient and provider are able to communicate in a way that leads to the accurate exchange of information, health outcomes will be enhanced in several ways. Diagnosis is more accurate, for example, when social workers and other health-care providers are able to establish rapport with patients, take cues from them, and pose questions in a way that is understandable. Likewise, when patients are able to express their symptoms and concerns in a way that can be understood by providers, it is more likely that their conditions will be diagnosed and any problems assessed with accuracy. Treatment plans based on those assessments will be more effective because they will better reflect patients' unique health-care and social needs. It therefore is easy to agree with Fisher's (1992) assessment that the best scientific knowledge in the world is insufficient if communication between patient and provider is flawed.

In this chapter, the goal of health communication is defined as obtaining and disseminating the maximum amount of information with the minimum amount of distortion and discomfort for the communicators. The chapter's purpose is to describe (a) the negotiations inherent in health-care encounters, (b) common sources of communication error, and (c) ways in which communication can be enhanced in a variety of clinical settings.

Chapter Objectives
- Convey the structure and dynamics of the clinical encounter between patient (or patient system) and provider in health-care settings.
- Convey how health beliefs impact health communication.
- Determine how group differences by race, ethnicity, gender, socioeconomic status, religion, and geography can affect health beliefs.
- Discuss the dynamics of health-care teams.
- Outline evidence-based methods for improving how health messages and information are communicated to patients and their families and how information is solicited by health-care providers.
- Outline evidence-based methods for improving how patients and families present information to and question health-care providers.
- Distinguish *interpretation* from *translation*.
- Provide guidelines for accurate translation of health-care information between patients and providers in health-care settings.

This chapter is designed to be used in concert with other chapters in this book, especially those on physical and mental health (Chapter 8), chronic illness (Chapter 20), and alternative health (Chapter 12). Active cross-referencing of these chapters by readers will optimize their learning of how communication can be enhanced to maximize health-care outcomes.

STRUCTURE AND DYNAMICS OF THE CLINICAL ENCOUNTER IN HEALTH CARE

In a seminal article on communication in health care, Kleinman, Eisenberg, and Good (1978) described the clinical encounter between patient and provider as a negotiation between two cultural constructions of reality that yields clinical reality. The authors defined *clinical reality* as the interactions between patients and providers that occur during the health-care encounter and the outcomes that accrue from those interactions. Outcomes may include: (a) the development of treatment plans; (b) adherence to those plans; (c) health consequences, such as reduction in asthma attacks or seizures; and (d) social consequences, such as a child's ability to return to school.

Kleinman et al. (1978, 2006) noted that patients bring to their encounters with providers sets of beliefs, expectations, values, and goals that are culturally constructed in the sense that they are determined by each individual's life experiences. The authors note that illness is shaped by cultural factors governing the perception, labeling, explanation, and evaluation of discomforting experiences, the latter of which are analogous to symptoms. These processes are embedded in complex family, social, and cultural nexuses. Prior experience with the illnesses of family members and how these illnesses were managed, for instance, has a significant effect on the ways in which individuals approach or deal with their own illnesses and those of their families. These prior experiences can be as subtle as a child overhearing her parents talk about the serious illness of a family member.

As described by Rolland in Chapter 13 on families and chronic illness, families vary greatly in their approaches to illness. They vary in the extent to which and how they work together to deal with the management of an illness, how they work with providers, and how they communicate with one another and others about the illness. The parents of a child with epilepsy in one family, for instance, may not talk about the condition within the family, may attempt to hide seizures from others, and may take a passive role with the child's physician. Another set of parents might organize the family around the child's seizures, talking freely about the condition, with all members responsible for monitoring symptoms, becoming active in advocacy groups, and joining the child at clinic visits. A third family may have integrated the child's seizures into family life so that the condition is neither hidden nor dominates activities. Each of these three approaches to dealing with a child's epilepsy likely would have a unique effect on the lifetime responses to illness of the child with epilepsy and his siblings. Determining an individual's family illness history thus can be a powerful tool for health social workers because it provides valuable insights into how prior experiences might have shaped the individual's cultural construction of reality.

Pachter (1994) says that patients' cultural constructions of reality almost never differ entirely from the biomedical constructions held by health-care providers but instead vary on a continuum between lay or ethnocultural constructions on one end and biomedical constructions on the other. In fact, most patients' cultural constructions of reality represent combinations of "ethnocultural beliefs, personal and idiosyncratic beliefs, and biomedical concepts" (p. 690). The farther that patients' constructions diverge from those of providers, the greater the likelihood that communication problems will occur.

Providers, too, bring to clinical encounters sets of beliefs, expectations, values, and goals that are shaped by their own unique life experiences as well as the professional cultures into which they have been socialized (Hall, 2005). Professional cultures, such as those of physicians, nurses, health social workers, and physical therapists, entail shared language, rules of behavior, dress, and ways of acknowledging status. Rosenthal (1993, p. B1) described the socialization of medical students, for instance, in this way: "[F]rom the beginning, medical students are told that they are in school to learn to think like a doctor. And when they emerge 4 years later, many will have adopted a professional demeanor such that they not only think like one, but talk like one, and dress like one, too." Some have gone so far as to suggest that providers' socialization and culture may contribute to health disparities in the United States (Institute of Medicine [IOM], 2002; van Ryn & Fu, 2003).

Health Beliefs and Communication

Health beliefs are components of cultural constructions of reality that guide health behavior and communication. They are guided by culture and dictate (a) how symptoms are identified and which are considered appropriate to take to providers, (b) how patients understand the causes and treatment of their illnesses, (c) what patients expect of providers, and (d) what personal and moral meanings patients ascribe to their illnesses and how they address questions such as "Why me? What did I do to deserve this?" (Weston & Brown, 1989, p. 77).

Leventhal (1985) adds that the natural history of illnesses can shape patients' health beliefs and constructions of reality in much the same way that culture shapes health beliefs. This is particularly true with chronic illnesses. Patients' awareness and understanding of illness increase through time as they are exposed to health information and become more familiar with how their bodies respond to chronic illness. This heightened awareness can influence how symptoms are evaluated and in which situations patients deem it appropriate to seek formal treatment. A patient who initially was frightened by symptoms and sought treatment frequently may in time feel capable of illness self-management as she becomes more familiar with the pattern of her symptoms.

From a global perspective, illness is seen as due either to natural causes, such as infection or accident, or to supernatural causes, such as spirit aggression, sorcery, witchcraft, or mystical retribution (Erasmus, 1952; Foster, 1976; see Table 10.1). Although supernatural causes may seem exotic to many, they are part of the health belief systems of many residents of the United States, especially those who were born outside the country. In 2000, 1 in 10 U.S. residents (28.4 million) was born outside the country (Lollock, 2001). According to data from the 2000 U.S. census (Spector, 2004), 51% were from Latin America, 25.5% from Asia, 15.3% from Europe, and 8.2% from other areas; these figures do not include undocumented immigrants. Although their numbers are difficult to estimate, around 10.9 million undocumented immigrants were thought to be living in the United States in the first quarter of 2009 (Camarota & Jensenius, 2009).

Health beliefs, like cultural constructions of reality in general, are learned through socialization. They are often long-held cultural beliefs that remain with a group, especially one that is cut off from mainstream society for socioeconomic, religious, geographic, or political reasons. Religious and political groups might, for example, have reason to hold on to certain beliefs and to eschew mainstream constructions. Jehovah's Witnesses, for example, hold strong beliefs against the sharing of blood products and come into conflict with healthcare providers who prescribe transfusions during surgery or after accidents. A number of high-profile court cases have resulted from situations in which parents who are Jehovah's

Table 10.1   Four Theories of Supernatural Causation by Region of the World

Theory	Definition	Region
Mystical retribution	Acts in violation of some taboo or moral injunction causing disease indirectly	Africa
Sorcery	Ascription of impairment of health to the aggressive use of magical techniques by a human being, either independently or with the assistance of a specialized magician or shaman	North America
Spirit aggression	Aspiration to the direct, hostile, arbitrary, or punitive action of some malevolent or affronted supernatural being, such as nature spirits, disease, demons, departed ancestors, or ghosts	East Asia, insular Pacific, South America
Witchcraft	Ascription of impairment of health to the suspected voluntary or involuntary aggressive action of a member of a special class of human beings believed to be endowed with a special power and propensity for evil	Circum-Mediterranean

Witnesses refused to allow their children to receive transfusions prescribed by physicians. Orthodox Jews who observe strict dietary laws may come into conflict with staff members when admitted to hospitals that are not equipped to provide kosher meals.

Geography can act to maintain traditional health beliefs by limiting access to mainstream sources. Rural areas of the United States are characterized by lower population density, fewer specialized health-care providers, and greater distance between health-care facilities (Coward & Kout, 1998). Because exposure to mainstream culture is likely to be limited to media sources, fewer mainstream health messages are received, and traditional health beliefs are less likely to be challenged. Christakis and Fowler (2007) examined a densely interconnected social network of 12,067 people assessed repeatedly from 1971 to 2003 through the Framingham (Massachusetts) Health Study and found evidence that obesity spreads through person-to-person social ties. A network member's chances of becoming obese during a certain period of time increased 57% if that person had a friend who became obese during the same period of time. Similar results were found for the spread of alcohol-consumption behavior (Rosenquist, Murabito, Fowler, & Christakis, 2010).

Residents born outside the United States are more likely than their native-born counterparts to live in the center of cities and to live in poverty (Lollock, 2001). They, like many native-born residents of inner cities, often live in homogeneous groups with strong within-group social network ties. These strong ties are beneficial to health in that they provide opportunities for support from other group members. If others in the group are similarly impoverished, however, they might not be able to provide financial support in times of need or assist with travel to health-care facilities. Also, strong within-group ties are often at the expense of weak ties to mainstream culture, which represent important sources of health information (Pescosolido & Levy, 2002). Women with weak ties to mainstream culture, for example, are much less likely to receive information on breast self-examination and where to obtain free mammograms. Parents with weak ties to mainstream culture are less likely to know about health-care funding opportunities for their children (see Chapter 5 in this book).

In her book *Walkin' over Medicine* (1993), Loudell Snow describes the impact of patients' health beliefs on their health behavior, observed during her work at a community health clinic serving predominantly African American patients in Lansing, MI. Clinic providers were concerned about nonadherence to prescribed medications, such as medications to lower blood pressure (called antihypertensive medications). Through interviews with clinic patients, Snow found that a number of patients included anemia under the rubric of "low blood." Many patients in this group had discontinued their medications after providers made statements such as "Congratulations, you've brought your blood pressure down. It's low now!" What seemed to providers to be a healthy state (i.e., low blood pressure among those prone to hypertension) seemed unhealthy to patients, causing them to discontinue taking their medications.

In another example, Snow (1993) was consulted on high rates of unplanned pregnancy among young African American women. As part of clinical practice, women were being prescribed oral contraceptives and trained in the rhythm method of contraception. Through interviews, Snow determined that the two means of birth control conflicted with the beliefs of a number of women that menstruation was important to health because it allowed toxins and pollutants to be eliminated that might otherwise cause ill health. Oral contraceptives were viewed as deleterious to health because they diminished menstrual flow. The rhythm method similarly was seen as dangerous to health because of its prescription that sex should occur near menstruation, a time when women felt that their bodies were particularly open and thus more vulnerable to toxins and pollutants. According to the group's health beliefs, the days most distant from menstruation were safest for sex because the body was least open. This was problematic because days distant in time from menstruation are when women ovulate and are most likely to become pregnant.

In both of these examples, a clinical reality could be negotiated that addressed the incongruities between the health beliefs of patients and providers. In the case of antihypertensive medications, the task was as simple as identifying the two meanings of "low blood" and advising providers to use instead "normal blood pressure" or "good blood pressure." In the case of conflicting views of birth control, methods that neither restricted menstrual flow, as was the case with oral contraception, nor involved having sex during menstruation, when women considered the body to be particularly vulnerable (e.g., the rhythm method), were emphasized.

Numerous empirical studies have supported the link between health beliefs and success of behavior-change efforts. Patterson, Kristal, and White (1996) measured the baseline beliefs about the association between diet and cancer of a population-based sample of 607 people in Washington state. They found those with stronger beliefs significantly decreased their percentage of fat consumed and significantly increased their fiber intake. In a second study, low-income, rural, African American women who did not believe themselves to be at risk for breast cancer, whether they had positive family histories or not, were less likely to get mammograms than women who believed themselves to be at risk (West et al., 2003).

ILLNESS VERSUS DISEASE

The clinical encounter can be seen as a set of transactions or negotiations between patients and providers. Success is determined at least partly by the extent to which the two can reach a measure of congruence. In general, the more dissimilar the cultural constructions of reality of the two, the more difficult will be the negotiation. A gross example of dissimilarity between the patient's and the provider's cultural constructions of reality is that patients experience illness while physicians treat disease. *Disease* is defined by Kleinman and colleagues (2006) as malfunctioning or maladaptation of biologic and psychophysiologic processes in the individual. Helman (1985) says that a disease construction reduces ill health to physicochemical terms and overemphasizes biological (as opposed to social or psychological) information in reaching a diagnosis. *Illness,* however, represents personal, interpersonal, and cultural reactions to disease or discomfort (Kleinman et al., 2006). According to Helman (1985), illness is a wider and more diffuse concept that is patterned by social, psychological, and cultural factors.

Disease is determined objectively while illness is determined subjectively. Thus, disease can exist in the absence of illness, for example, when a patient has a biological abnormality of which she is not aware. A woman could, for instance, have a malignant ovarian tumor in the absence of symptoms. Likewise, illness can occur in the absence of disease. Common complaints such as headache and gastrointestinal distress may be very problematic for patients and cause disruption in social functioning, such as the ability to work or go to school, yet occur in the absence of any abnormality in the structure or function of body organs or systems.

Illness conditions that are specific to certain cultures, such as susto in Mexico (Rubel, 1977), koro in Malaysia, and pibloktoq among Eskimos (Foulks, 1972; see Table 10.2), fall

Table 10.2   Culture-Specific Syndromes

Syndrome	Description	Cultural Origins
Koro	An episode of sudden, intense anxiety in which the penis recedes into the body and that may cause death	Malaysia
Pibloktoq (Arctic hysteria)	Sudden-onset bizarre behavior that is short lived and thought to be induced by fright	Circumpolar regions
Susto	Illness arising from fright in which the soul is thought to leave the body	Mexico

under the rubric of illness rather than disease. Although these culture-specific syndromes are considered real by the culture groups that recognize them, providers do not universally recognize them. They are not included in the *International Statistical Classification of Diseases and Related Health Problems* (*ICD*), a compendium of internationally recognized diseases published by the World Health Organization. The *ICD*, now in its tenth revision (*ICD-10*; World Health Organization, 2003), is the international standard diagnostic classification used for monitoring the incidence and prevalence of diseases worldwide and allowing the compilation of mortality and morbidity statistics by member nations.

That illness and disease are not directly correlated with one another can be a source of miscommunication and lead to nonadherence to medical treatment recommendations. Conditions such as brain cancers are considered serious diseases by physicians, yet in their early stages, they may cause less distress and social disruption for patients than muscle spasms of the lower back. In addition, patients with the same degree of organ or system pathology (i.e., disease) report different levels of well-being and social dysfunction (i.e., illness). In other words, some patients with rheumatoid arthritis might report adequate well-being and are able to perform their own activities of daily living (ADLs) while others at the same stage of the disease might report that their well-being is diminished markedly and that they require assistance to perform ADLs.

Optimal patient and provider communication can influence health outcomes in a number of direct and indirect ways (Street, Makoul, Arora, & Epstein, 2009). Clinical encounters in which providers focus on disease and patients focus on illness are likely to result in frustration, mistrust, and less favorable health outcomes because providers may feel that their recommendations are not being given due consideration by patients and patients may perceive that their complaints are not being taken seriously. A poignant real-life example comes from a book entitled *The Spirit Catches You*

and You Fall Down (Fadiman, 1997). This book describes non-English-speaking Hmong immigrant parents of a young girl with epilepsy who viewed her illness through the eyes of their culture, namely as the flight of her soul from her body. They treated the condition according to their beliefs, with animal sacrifices and traditional remedies. The Merced County, CA, physicians who were treating the child focused on her condition as a disease (epilepsy) requiring fine-tuned dosages of prescribed anticonvulsant medications. Both sides were operating with the best intentions and compassion, yet their inability to communicate with one another and subsequent mutual mistrust and blaming resulted in a situation in which the two sides could only watch impotently as the child's situation deteriorated to the point of serious disability.

Social workers who are aware of incongruent understandings between patients and providers can help to remedy the situation by pointing out the discrepancy, interpreting each side's frustration to the other, and helping to establish a clinical accord. Setha Low (1984, p. 13) wrote: "[O]ften the social worker is the only person who can see both sides of the cultural picture—the bureaucratic, mainstream, and the ethnic or subcultural perspective—and from this vantage point may be the single most critical actor in the provision of care and information." This is congruent with Richard Cabot's notion of social workers as translators in healthcare environments (see Chapter 1 in this book).

A list of questions developed by Kleinman (1980) can serve as a valuable tool for social workers and other providers in their efforts to elicit patients' health beliefs. These questions include:

- What do you think caused your problem?
- How severe do you think the problem is?
- Do you think that its course will be short or long?
- What difficulties is the problem causing for you?
- About what are you most concerned?

- What treatment do you think is warranted for your problem?
- What benefits do you expect to receive from the treatment?

A vivid example of what might occur if a provider is not aware of a patient's health beliefs comes from the work of Young and Flower (2001, p. 91). A young man named Pete who worked in a fast-food restaurant went to the emergency room after injuring his ankle. He assumed that his ankle was fractured because he was in a great deal of pain and heard the same cracking sound that he had heard when he had fractured his ankle in the past. His greatest concern was that he would lose his job if he missed work. Pete lost trust in the physician when he was told that his ankle was sprained rather than fractured and that the only possible treatment was to stay off it for 5 days. He had framed the problem very differently from the physician and had given the situation different meaning. Because his cultural construction of reality weighted serious sprains and fractures differently, he assumed that he would not be granted sick leave from his employer if his ankle were sprained rather than broken. The clinical situation deteriorated rapidly with the physician, who had given Pete no opportunity to tell his story, perceiving Pete as being uncooperative and wanting to get off work for no reason. Pete left the encounter assuming that the physician had made a mistake. He promptly threw away the Ace bandage that he had been given for his sprain and returned to work. This left his ankle prone to reinjury and his view of physicians compromised. The physician's view of patients as malingerers was reinforced.

Social Workers on Health-Care Teams

Although written over 20 years ago, Cleora Roberts's (1989) observations on the strain inherent in the professional relationship between social workers and physicians still rings true today. Roberts suggested that an appreciation of this strain and the necessary tension that it produces could catalyze successful collaboration between social workers and physicians. The five areas of major difference in perspectives are that:

1. A physician's goal is to save lives while the social worker's focus is more on quality than quantity of life.
2. Physicians are more likely to base decisions on objective data, such as laboratory tests, while social workers consider patients' subjective interpretations of events.
3. Physicians are likely to develop treatment plans based on the assumption that the goal of treatment is improved health and the longest possible life, while social workers are trained to encourage self-determined treatment goals.
4. Social workers are more likely than physicians to feel comfortable in dealing with patients' emotional problems.
5. Physicians are more likely to take charge on health-care teams while social workers are accustomed to collaboration.

A few studies have examined social worker and physician collaborations. Mizrahi and Abramson (1985) examined self-reports of collaborations between 50 social worker–physician pairs and found the two professions to have similar perspectives in many cases. Social workers were more likely to identify family problems with adjustment to illness and problems with availability of and access to resources than were their physician collaborators. This finding is congruent with Roberts's observation that social workers are more likely than physicians to consider quality rather than quantity of life and less likely to focus on objective data.

Turner (1990) describes social work in health care as a transcultural resource. He implicates three phenomena in Western medicine as particularly culture specific and value laden and thus potential obstacles to health communication. Each of the three conflicts with the values of social work. The "scientification" of medicine is a trend toward addressing the somatic aspects of health at the expense of behavioral and social aspects. Turner describes the "recurrent, unofficial, and popular 'antiscientific' theme" (p. 14) of social work as counter to the trend toward scientification. A second trend is toward increased specialization, which Turner says leads to decreased sensitivity to the whole person. Social work's holistic perspective broadens the health-care team's view to consider the individual as a whole. The third trend noted by Turner is medicine's increasingly patient-only focus, to the exclusion of salient others, events, and issues in the environment. Again, the emphasis of social work on person in environment broadens the scope of the health-care team.

An appreciation of the complex interplay of biological, social, and behavioral factors in health (see, e.g., McGinnis, Williams-Russo, & Knickman, 2002) has led to new conceptualizations of team science and disciplinary collaboration (Abrams, 2006; Hiatt & Breen, 2008). In 2003, Elias Zerhouni, the director of the National Institutes of Health (NIH), initiated the Roadmap for 21st Century Medical Research, which for the first time encouraged professionals from different disciplines to work together in new ways and to include community members as active participants in scientific investigations. NIH personnel, scientists, and community members are all considered stakeholders in research.

New professional collaborations fostered by the NIH Roadmap take research from the multidisciplinary and interdisciplinary approach to the new concept of transdisciplinary (see Table 10.3). In the latter, investigators from the biological, social, and behavioral sciences work so closely together in addressing major health issues that they must develop new shared languages that incorporate key words from their separate disciplines, pool the best of their disciplinary theories, and forge new methodologies and analytical approaches that allow inclusion of factors at multiple levels in the same analyses (Gehlert et al., 2010). Kahn and Prager (1994) point out that, for

Table 10.3   Types and Descriptions of Health-Care Teams

Type	Description
Multidisciplinary	Team members represent a variety of professional backgrounds. Although part of the same team, they have separate bodies of professional knowledge and maintain different disciplinary languages.
Interdisciplinary	Team members from a variety of professional backgrounds share their bodies of knowledge and disciplinary languages.
Transdisciplinary	Team members from a variety of professional backgrounds develop a shared language based on their separate disciplinary languages, pool bodies of knowledge and theories, and jointly develop new methods and analytical techniques.

true transdisciplinary teams to be successful, university structures, such as rewards for publishing frequently and on narrow topics, must be modified, a sentiment echoed in a report by the National Academies (National Academy of Sciences, National Academy of Engineering, & IOM, 2005).

Social work education faces similar challenges, especially in providing sufficient biological and genetic training to students interested in working in health care so that they can operate effectively on transdisciplinary teams. Toward that purpose, a guide to understanding medical terminology is located in an appendix to this chapter.

Additional challenges presented by the transdisciplinary approach to health include preparing students to work with professionals from other disciplinary cultures (Hall, 2005) and teaching them new ways to include community members in health-care decision making. The tradition of family support in social work education can provide guidance for the latter.

Although the NIH Roadmap addresses research directly, it has major implications for how health care is viewed and delivered in the United States. NIH is the largest funder of medical research in the world, and hospitals and other health-care facilities depend on research funding for their operations. This has been the case with teaching hospitals for some time but is increasingly becoming the case for community clinics, other outpatient facilities, illness-specific consumer organizations (e.g., the American Heart Foundation), and advocacy groups. The broad view of health as a complex interplay of biological, social, and behavioral factors and of community residents as important contributors presented by the NIH Roadmap is significant for how social work is viewed in health care for two major reasons: It forces a broader view of health that includes social and behavioral factors, and it places a premium on being able to establish and access community ties. Because social work is recognized by other health-care professionals as particularly expert in these two areas, the profile of the profession is likely to rise.

Group theory traditionally has been used by social workers in health care to understand patients as members of groups. It also serves them well in helping to understand the dynamics of the teams on which they serve. The often-used classification of group roles that include opinion giver, coordinator, gatekeeper, and special-interest pleader (Benne & Sheets, 1948) works as well for health-care teams as for patient groups. Likewise, the phases of small groups (see e.g., Northouse & Northouse, 1997)—namely orientation, conflict, cohesion, working, and termination—work equally well for patient and provider groups in health care, although health-care teams often are ongoing and not time limited.

Yalom (1998) provides a list of factors through which groups work to achieve therapeutic aims. Understanding factors such as (a) catharsis, which occurs when team members are able to express openly or ventilate their frustrations; (b) the corrective recapitulation of the primary family group, in which group members experience interactions that mimic those they experienced with their parents and siblings but in a more positive way; and (c) interpersonal learning, in which members

learn from one another through observation, can be useful in understanding why members of a health-care team are behaving as they are. Many social workers report anecdotally that they have become team diagnosticians and that other professionals turn to them for advice on personal matters.

Beginning in the 1980s, a number of authors have examined the role of social workers on health-care teams. Sands, Stafford, and McClelland (1990), for example, echoed the sources of conflict between social workers and physicians noted by Roberts (1989) and Turner (1990; also see Mizrahi & Abramson, 1985) and added others germane to social workers' relationships with other health-care team professionals. These include status differences between disciplines that interfere with democratic functioning and the competition that arises when professional roles and functions overlap.

At the same time, there is evidence that interprofessional collaborations involving social workers are effective. In an experimental study, Sommers, Marton, Barbaccia, and Randolph (2000) compared teams of primary care physicians, nurses, and social workers to primary care physicians working alone in terms of number of hospital admissions; readmissions; office visits; emergency department visits; and changes in self-rated physical, mental, and social functioning of patients. The collaborative team approach resulted in significantly fewer hospitalizations, readmissions, and office visits for patients as well as an increase in their levels of social activity. As noted in Chapter 1, social workers in health care have been less likely than other professionals to have roles identified as uniquely their own. This phenomenon was noted originally in a 1980 study by Lister in which health professionals from 13 disciplines were surveyed on role expectations. No role was assigned uniquely to social work. This leads to confusion when psychologists, nurses, and therapists perform some of the same functions, such as taking social histories or helping patients prepare psychologically for medical procedures. Overlap of roles is more likely in some settings than others. Settings that rely more on technology, such as emergency departments or intensive care units, generally exhibit more role distinction and more hierarchical decision making. In settings less tied to technology, such as long-term care facilities or nursing homes, professionals' roles are less distinct and more likely to overlap. Decision making is more likely to be democratic.

Sands et al. (1990) note that conflict has a function in health-care teams: to ensure that situations and issues facing the team are viewed from a variety of perspectives. Conflict can be a catalyst for growth and contribute to good decision making if team members are able to speak freely, negotiate effectively, and achieve resolution. Group think (Janus, 1972), which occurs when group members feel pressured to conform, has been implicated in some of the worst disasters in history, including the Bay of Pigs invasion and the escalation of the war in Vietnam.

A number of authors have offered suggestions for improving interprofessional functioning while minimizing pressure to conform (Freeth, 2001; Satin, 1987; Vanclay, 1996). Vanclay suggests that the keys to sustaining effective collaboration between social workers and physicians are interprofessional education, a clear understanding of the roles and responsibilities of other disciplines, regular face-to-face contact, shared information on structures and procedures, and support from senior management.

Communication Patterns in Health-Care Settings

A landmark study of communication in outpatient settings noted a pattern in which patients were cut off by physicians before they were able to express all of their health concerns. Beckman and Frankel (1984) recorded 74 outpatient return visits and measured physicians' questioning style and whether they interrupted patients during their opening statements of concern. In 8% of visits, physicians failed to solicit patients' concerns entirely and asked only closed-ended questions. In 69% of visits,

physicians interrupted patient within 18 seconds of their beginning to talk and redirected interviews. In only 1 of 74 instances (less than 1%) did a physician allow a patient to return to his initial statement of concerns. In the remaining 23% of visits, patients were allowed to complete their opening statement of concerns without interruption. The authors cautioned that the physician-directed style observed in their study would almost certainly result in the exclusion of information pertinent to diagnosis and treatment planning. In a subsequent interview, Frankel (Goleman, 1991) stated that physician interruptions are particularly troubling in light of the fact that patients rarely list their most troubling complaint first but instead submerge it in a list of less troubling concerns. The third complaint listed by patients is generally the most troubling for them.

Clinical encounters are even more problematic when providers and patients are from different racial or ethnic groups or different socioeconomic status (SES), especially when providers are White American and patients are low income or members of a minority group. A 2002 report issued by the IOM implicated physician behavior in the growth of health disparities in the United States, which often are based on racial, ethnic, or SES differences. McGinnis and colleagues (2002), based on a review of the best available empirical studies, attributed 10% of early deaths in the United States to shortfalls in medical care; a portion of that percentage was thought to be due to provider behavior.

Johnson, Roter, Powe, and Cooper (2004) conducted a study to determine the extent to which patient race and ethnicity affect communication between providers and patients. The outpatient clinic visits of 458 White American and African American patients and 61 physicians in the Washington, DC/Baltimore area were rated by experts in terms of physician verbal dominance (measured by dividing the total number of physician statements by the total number of patient statements), patient-centeredness (measured by dividing the total amount of socioemotional talk by the total amount of biomedical talk), and emotional tone (affect) of the interviews. Physicians were 23% more verbally dominant and communication was 33% less patient-centered during physician visits with African American patients than with White American patients. African American patients and their physicians also were rated as exhibiting lower levels of positive affect than were White American patients and their physicians.

Beach and colleagues (2010) analyzed 354 encounters between patients infected with human immunodeficiency virus (HIV) and their providers across four HIV care sites (Portland, OR; Detroit, MI; Baltimore, MD; and New York, NY) using the Roter Interaction Analysis System to explore racial differences in communication. As was the case in the 2004 study by Johnson and colleagues, physicians were more verbally dominant with African American than with White American patients. The total number of socioemotional statements made did not differ between the two groups, however, in the study by Beach and colleagues.

In attempting to tease out the sources of unintentional provider bias that might be impacting health disparities, Burgess, Fu, and von Ryn (2004) outlined a number of possible explanations. They suggest that White American providers unknowingly may convey negative affect toward African American patients, which triggers the patients' own negative affect, resulting in a situation that is suboptimal for communication. They suggest that the majority of providers hold conscious beliefs on equality that are inconsistent with their automatic, unconscious reactions to low-income and minority patients. The authors go on to say that in clinical situations in which the time allotted for information gathering is almost never sufficient, providers tend to fill in the gaps with information based on group stereotypes and behave in ways that confirm those stereotypes.

An example of this phenomenon comes from a study by Lewis, Croft-Jeffreys, and David (1990). In this study, 139 psychiatrists completed a questionnaire after reading one of two versions of a case that varied only by whether the patient was Afro-Caribbean or White American. Another two versions of the vignette varied only in terms of the patient's gender. All vignettes described the behavior of a patient with psychosis. Respondents rated the Afro-Caribbean case as more violent and criminal and less likely to need narcoleptics than the White American case. Female cases were rated as less violent, less criminal, and less likely to need narcoleptic medications than male cases.

Two additional studies linked patient race to physicians' treatment recommendations. In the first, van Ryn and Burke (2000) gathered survey data from 618 patients visiting 193 physicians after an angiogram. Physicians tended to rate African American patients as lower in intelligence and less likely to adhere to treatment recommendations and more likely to exhibit risk behaviors than White American patients. They attributed patients of lower and middle SES less favorably than upper-SES patients on measures of personality, ability, role demands, and behavioral tendencies. In a second study (Schulman et al., 1999), 720 primary care physicians attending two national meetings viewed a taped interview with a patient and reviewed hypothetical data on the same patient. They were then surveyed about how they would manage the patient's chest pain. Women and African American patients were less likely than men and White American patients to be referred for cardiac catheterization. African American women were significantly less likely to be referred for the procedure than White American men.

Little work has focused on how SES differences between providers and patients might impact communication, and thus health outcomes, above and beyond the effect of racial and ethnic differences. Jensen, King, Guntzviller, and Davis (2010) surveyed 131 low-income adults living in Indiana about their satisfaction with their communication with health-care providers. Interestingly, satisfaction was lower among younger White American patients with higher levels of literacy than among older patients with lower rates of literacy who were African American or Hispanic

Americans. The authors suggest that the former group may be more assertive while the latter group may withdraw during health-care encounters.

Biases in communication by gender have been observed in the few studies that have addressed the topic. Although little is known about variation in communication by gender of patient, a number of studies have demonstrated differences in communication between male and female physicians. Roter, Hall, and Aoki (2002) reviewed available studies from 1967 to 2001 and found 26 that used a communication database that could be analyzed by raters. They found no gender differences in the quantity or quality of biomedical communication or social conversation between male and female physicians. Female physicians, however, exhibited significantly more patient-centered talk than their male colleagues, specifically emotionally focused talk, psychosocial counseling, psychosocial question asking, active partnership behaviors, and positive talk. Clinic visits to female physicians were on average two minutes longer (10%) than visits to male physicians.

The 2001 IOM report and empirical studies by Roter and colleagues (2002) and Burgess, Fu, and von Ryn (2004) are aimed at physicians, despite the fact that the latter authors use the generic term *provider*. Yet issues of cross-cultural communication are equally important to social workers in health care. Although the perspectives and values of social workers differ from those of physicians, as aptly pointed out by Roberts (1989) and Turner (1990), social workers are as vulnerable to stereotyping and heuristics as other professions and therefore have to grapple with the same issues and biases when attempting to communicate with people with other cultural constructions of reality.

There is evidence that being ill equipped to communicate with patients from different cultural backgrounds has consequences for providers as well as patients. Ulrey and Amason (2001) measured the cultural sensitivity, intercultural communication skills, and levels of state anxiety of 391 employees of two hospitals and four clinics in the U.S. South and found low levels of sensitivity and communication skills to be significantly correlated with high levels of anxiety. In other words, providers who were high in cultural sensitivity and better intercultural communicators experienced less anxiety than providers who were less sensitive and less adept at intercultural communication.

The idea that communication problems can be as problematic for providers as patients is supported by a Dutch study (Zandbelt, Smets, Oort, Godfried, & de Haes, 2004) in which the authors measured the same five visit-specific relationship phenomena in 30 physicians and 330 patients following outpatient clinic visits. They found physicians to be less satisfied in general with health encounters than patients. Patients were most satisfied with physicians whom they thought attended better to their health concerns and from whom they were able to obtain information. Physicians reported greater satisfaction after medical encounters with patients who were better educated, had better mental health, and preferred to receive fewer details about their care.

Patient–Provider Communication and Health Outcomes

A number of empirical studies have linked improved provider and patient communication to positive changes in physiological and behavioral measures of health status. In addition to helping to ensure an accurate exchange of information, enhanced provider communication skills are thought to improve health outcomes by motivating patients to engage actively in their treatment and increasing their confidence in their ability to influence their health. Maguire and Pitceathly (2002, p. 697) add that patients' propensity for anxiety and depression is lessened when communication is effective; effective communication also enhances providers' well-being.

Several studies have linked better communication between patients and providers with improved adherence to treatment regimens and other favorable health-care outcomes.

Schneider, Kaplan, Greenfield, Li, and Wilson (2004), for instance, linked better communication to improved adherence (measured on a 4-point scale) to antiretroviral therapy in a sample of 554 patients treated at 22 outpatient HIV clinics. The study's seven independent variables were (1–6) quality of physician-patient communication, measured using six available scales—general communication, HIV-specific information, egalitarian decision-making style, overall physician satisfaction, willingness to recommend physician, and physician trust—and (7) the extent to which patients thought their physicians understood and were able to solve problems with their antiretroviral regimens. Six of the seven physician-patient communication variables (all but egalitarian decision-making style) were significantly associated with adherence to antiretroviral therapy. Conteh, Stevens, and Wiseman (2007) found better communication to be associated with increased adherence to malaria treatment in rural Gambia.

In another study (Stewart et al., 2000), the outpatient visits of 315 patients and their 39 family physicians were audiotaped and rated on patient-centered communication (measured as the extent to which the physicians explored patients' disease and illness experiences, understood patients as whole persons, and discussed and sought agreement with patients on treatment plans). Patients were asked to rate their encounters for patient-centered communication independently. Outcomes measured were patients' health and health care, specifically diagnostic tests taken, referrals made, and visits to the family physician in the two months following the audiotaped visit, all of which were extracted from patients' charts. Higher rates of patient-centered communication were associated significantly with better recovery from the complaint that brought the patient to the physician in the first place, fewer diagnostic tests, and fewer referrals. Additional empirical studies link better communication to reduced pain after surgery (Egbert, Battit, Welch, & Bartlett, 1964) and other physiological outcomes (Orth, Stiles, Scherwitz, Hennrikus, & Vallbona, 1987; Skipper & Leonard, 1968).

METHODS FOR IMPROVING HEALTH COMMUNICATION

The body of literature on interventions that improve providers' and patients' communication skills has grown in recent years.

Changing Providers' Behavior

Interventions range from prompting physicians to check patients' understanding of information to complex, comprehensive training programs that address a number of factors thought to improve communication.

Based on data obtained from observations of the clinical performance of 25 physicians, Sideris, Tsouna-Hadjis, Toumanidis, Vardas, and Moulopoulos (1986) developed a four-hour training seminar for physicians on health communication. Physicians were taught how to: (a) explain diagnoses, treatment objectives, and prognoses; (b) provide oral and written instructions; (c) check patients' comprehension; and (d) convey positive affect. Communication scores were obtained prior to and after the training seminar by asking dyads of participating and nonparticipating physicians and their patients a series of complementary questions about the medical encounter. Adherence was measured by comparing patients' behavior with instructions given. Both communication and adherence scores of the dyads of physicians who participated in training and their patients were statistically significantly higher than those of dyads in which the physicians did not participate in training.

Maiman, Becker, Liptak, Nazarian, and Rounds (1988) tested an intervention in which pediatricians were trained to use simple informational and motivational techniques for enhancing mothers' adherence to prescribed treatment recommendations. The intervention focused on how to: (a) express sincere concern and empathy; (b) provide information in a way that can be understood and remembered; (c) simplify treatment regimens; (d) elicit, assess, and modify health beliefs; (e) elicit and meet mothers' expectations for treatment; and (f) monitor adherence to prescribed treatment recommendations. Mothers whose physicians were in the intervention group were significantly more likely to adhere to medication recommendations and to keep follow-up appointments than mothers whose physicians were in the control condition.

Kinmonth, Woodcock, Griffin, Spiegal, and Campbell (1998) tested a 1.5-day training program for nurses and physicians aimed at increasing levels of patient-centered communication. Teams of physicians and nurses from 41 practices were randomly assigned to an experimental or a control condition. Nurses in the experimental condition were offered a half day of training to review evidence for patient-centered interviewing and a full day of facilitated practice in implementing patient-centered interviewing skills. Physicians in the experimental group received a half day of training in active listening and negotiating behavioral change. Nurses received two additional support sessions with the facilitator. Nurse/physician dyads in the control condition received no training. The quality of life, well-being, hemoglobin A1c and lipid concentrations, blood pressure, and body mass index (BMI) of 250 patients with type 2 diabetes from the same practices as the nurse-physician dyads were measured one year after training. Patients also were asked to rate the quality of communication of their nurses and physicians and their satisfaction with care. Patients of dyads in the experimental condition reported better communication, greater satisfaction with care, and greater well-being than did patients of dyads in the control condition. Patients whose nurses and physicians were in the experimental group did not, however, exhibit more favorable hemoglobin A1c or lipid concentrations, blood pressure readings, or BMI than the control group.

A second study (Brown, Boles, Mullooly, & Levinson, 1999) failed to find gains in patient satisfaction after a communication skills training program titled "Thriving in a Busy Practice: Physician-Patient Communications." Sixty-nine primary care physicians, surgeons, medical subspecialists, physician-assistants, and nurse practitioners participated in a 4-hour interactive workshop focused on skills for building effective relationships with patients (active listening, expressing concern, understanding, respect, and responding to feelings) followed by 2 hours of homework in which they were asked to audiotape at least two patient interviews and listen to the recordings. A 4-hour follow-up session focused on teaching skills for effective negotiation with patients was conducted one month after the first 4-hour session. Patients of the providers who received training were asked to complete the Art of Medicine survey, which measures both satisfaction with providers' communication abilities and global visit satisfaction. No difference was seen in the Art of Medicine survey scores of patients whose providers had or had not participated in the communication skills training program.

A systematic review by Rao, Anderson, Inui, and Frankel (2007) assessed 21 randomized clinical trials published between 1996 and 2005 (none of the studies mentioned earlier were included in this group of 21) that tested an intervention to change physicians' communication behaviors. Most interventions included multiple modalities, such as information, feedback, modeling, and practice, and were delivered in one or more sessions. In 17 of these trials, physicians practiced and received feedback on their communication. Most studies reported improvement in physicians' behavior. Those that did not, however, involved interventions in which physicians had little or no opportunity to practice and receive feedback on their communication skills.

Changing Patient Behavior

A number of studies have focused on modifying patient behavior during interviews with physicians to improve health-care communication and outcomes. Most focus on increasing patients' participation in treatment.

Roter (1977) developed a 10-minute intervention in which a health educator assisted patients in formulating questions for their physicians and asking the questions early in clinic visits. Patients in a control condition were provided only with information on services. Interestingly, patients in the experimental condition reported more anxiety than did control patients but were significantly more likely to keep appointments during the 4-month follow-up period of the study. Although patients in the experimental group asked significantly more direct questions of their physicians than did control patients, their visits were no longer than those of patients in the control condition. In other words, the intervention changed the nature of the clinic visit without increasing its length.

In another early study of patient and physician communication, Greenfield, Kaplan, and Ware (1985) developed and tested an intervention in which patients were helped to read the medical records from their last clinic visit. In a 20-minute session, patients were taught to identify relevant medical issues and decisions from their records, devise ways to negotiate these decisions with their physicians, and ask questions. The audiotaped interviews of patients who participated in the intervention were compared with those who did not. No significant difference in length of visits was found between the two groups. Patients who received training, however, were found to be significantly more assertive in their interactions with physicians. They exhibited a 48% higher ratio of patient-to-physician utterances than the control group and elicited about twice the number of factual statements from their physicians.

Kaplan, Greenfield, and Ware (1989) reported the results of an intervention study in which patients with ulcer disease, hypertension, breast cancer, and diabetes were given copies of their medical records and an algorithm for interpreting the information and coached in behavioral strategies for increasing their participation in clinical interviews with their physicians. The interviews prior to and after the intervention were audiotaped and coded by experts. More patient control and more affect, especially negative affect on the part of both the patient and physician, and more information provided by physicians in response to patients' seeking of information were associated with better health status, including better control of diabetes and hypertension. The authors interpreted negative physician affect, such as tension, nervous laughter, frustration, and anxiety, as beneficial because it conveyed caring on the part of the physician.

Thompson, Nanni, and Schwankovsky (1990) tested a simple intervention to improve patients' participation in communication during outpatient clinic visits. Sixty-six women were randomly assigned to a control group or a group that was asked to prepare three written questions for their physician. The group that prepared questions asked significantly more questions during their clinic visits and reported less anxiety after the visits than did women in the control group.

McCann and Weinman (1996) prepared a pamphlet explaining how patients could increase their participation in interviews with their primary care physicians. The pamphlet encouraged patients to take a more active part in their interactions with their physicians. The pamphlet first asked patients to describe the nature of their problems and to consider the problems' possible causes and treatments and likely impacts. The pamphlet then outlined how to voice concerns during visits as well as how to ask questions about diagnosis and treatment and check understanding. The 59 patients who received the intervention materials prior to their visits asked significantly more questions of their physicians than did the 61 individuals in the control condition who received an educational pamphlet.

In another study (Davison & Degner, 1997), 60 men newly diagnosed with prostate cancer in a community urology clinic were randomly assigned to either an experimental group that received written information about prostate cancer, a list of questions to ask their physicians, and an audiotape of the medical consultation or to a control group that received only information on prostate cancer. Although the two groups did not differ significantly in levels of depression, the men in the intervention group took a more active role in treatment decision making and reported significantly lower levels of anxiety 6 weeks after the intervention than did men in the control condition.

Another study included 205 patients with chronic health conditions who were randomly assigned to experimental and control conditions. Those in the experimental condition were given copies of their medical record progress notes and asked to prepare two questions about their conditions that would be attached to the front of their charts. Patients in the control conditions received educational materials and completed suggestion lists for improving clinic care. Those in the experimental group reported significantly better overall physical functioning and satisfaction with their physicians' care and were significantly more interested in seeing their medical records than those in the control group. In addition, patients in the experimental group reported a significantly better overall health status than they had prior to the intervention (Maly, Bourque, & Engelhardt, 1999).

Additional Techniques for Improving Health Communication

Several techniques have been suggested for improving health-care communication. They can be divided roughly into individual-level techniques that address building empathy and elicit patients' thoughts and feelings and group- or community-level techniques.

Coulehan and colleagues (2001) devised a method for improving empathy, which they defined as "the ability to understand the patient's situation, perspective, and feelings and to communicate that understanding to the patient" (p. 221). Their method involved active listening, framing or signposting, reflecting the content, identifying and calibrating the emotion, and accepting and requesting correction. Active listening involves verbal and nonverbal techniques, such as the mirroring of facial expression, making direct eye contact, assuming a posture indicating attention, and exhibiting facilitative responses such as nods of understanding. Framing or signposting is analogous to the empathic responding advocated by social work clinicians (see, e.g.,

Hepworth, Rooney, & Larsen, 2002) and may take forms such as "Sounds like you are saying...." *Reflecting the content* is another term for paraphrasing. Identifying and calibrating the emotion is a means of eliciting the nature of emotion through the use of statements such as "I have the sense that you feel strongly, but I'm not sure I understand exactly what the feeling is. Can you tell me?" (p. 222). Requesting and accepting correction comes after statements of providers' understanding of what patients have said through phases such as "Did I get that right?" The sequence—patient's narrative, provider's statement of understanding and request for correction—is repeated until the provider's understanding is validated by the patient.

DuPre (2001) outlines four additional techniques to elicit patients' feelings and thoughts, which she gleaned from a review of interviews conducted by a physician well known for her communication skills. These are: (1) involving patients in decision making, (2) talking openly about patients' fears, (3) asking open-ended questions, and (4) self-disclosing. The latter is appreciated more by some patients than others based on their personal preferences and cultural expectations. The decision to self-disclose always should be based on cues and responses from patients.

A category of techniques in which providers partner with groups or communities to achieve health-care goals have gained popularity. These techniques fall under the rubric of community-engaged research (CEnR), a major category of which is community-based participatory research. The hallmark of CEnR approaches is the active involvement of community members at every stage of the research process. They share an aim to "enhance understanding of a given phenomenon and the social and cultural dynamics of the community and integrate the knowledge gained with action to improve the health and well-being of community members" (Israel et al., 2003, p. 54). CEnR approaches have been used with a variety of culture groups and illness conditions.

A novel approach was developed in the Wai'anae Cancer Research Project (Matsunaga et al., 1996) to test the effectiveness of a culturally appropriate intervention for increasing the participation of native Hawaiian women in cervical and breast cancer screening. The impetus for the intervention was that native Hawaiians had the second highest cancer rates in Hawaii. An advisory committee made up of community residents was selected to work collaboratively with project scientific investigators to devise and test an intervention over a period of years. The intervention was a series of health-focused support groups using existing social networks based on the traditional Hawaiian value of a mutual willingness to help others without expectation of reciprocity and without having to be asked. Native Hawaiian paraprofessionals recruited women to host groups, presented information to the groups, and facilitated discussion about breast and cervical cancer screening. Peer group leaders, who volunteered to host groups, helped investigators access community groups. Group discussion took traditional "talk story" form, which was familiar to the women and thus more acceptable. Vouchers for free mammograms, breast examinations, and Pap smears were provided to each participant and one of each woman's friends who was unable to participate. An evaluation of the program indicated that it had a positive impact on community knowledge, attitudes, and behaviors about breast and cervical cancer screening. In addition, investigators learned a great deal about traditional Hawaiian health beliefs and forged positive relationship with community members and groups.

Recent efforts have aimed at improving the patient–physician partnership by working with the two groups independently and in patient–physician dyads. An example is the Patient-Physician Partnership Study (Cooper et al., 2009), a culturally tailored, multicomponent intervention aimed at improving health outcomes for members of racial and ethnic minority groups and people of lower SES. The intervention, which will be tested using a randomized clinical trial, includes a computerized self-study communication skills training program for physicians.

Working With Patients With Limited or No English-Language Proficiency

Perhaps the greatest challenge to health communication comes when patients and families have very limited or no English-language skills. This is an issue in health care today because, according to data from the 2000 census, 19 million people in the United States have limited proficiency in English (Marcus, 2003).

The optimal approach to working with a patient and family who have limited or no English-language skills is to work with a professional medical interpreter. In fact, federal law mandates that health-care facilities that receive Department of Health and Human Services funding provide interpreter services to all people seeking or receiving medical care. The mandate is enforced by the federal Office for Human Rights. Some states also require the use of interpreters. Illinois, for example, passed the Language Assistance Services Act, which requires that nursing homes and hospitals make interpreter services available in person or by telephone 24 hours a day.

Professional medical interpreters are specially trained individuals who can take a spoken message in one language and render it into another language (Luckman, 2000, p. 152). Their task is not merely to change a word in one language to one in another but they are supposed to accurately reflect differences in culture that influence communication. For this reason, Luckman refers to professional medical interpreters as culture brokers. Interpretation differs from translation in that it deals with spoken language while translation deals with written language.

Several points are known to enhance the accuracy of interpretation. It is important for the provider to face and speak directly to the patient instead of to the interpreter. Doing this helps to ensure that some measure of relationship and rapport is established between patient and provider. Providers should make eye contact with patients when they are speaking or listening unless it is inappropriate for the patients' culture group. Appropriateness of eye contact can be determined from the professional interpreter or from family members. Questions and comments should be interpreted exactly as they are stated by the provider and in the same voice (i.e., in first person). If the provider said, for example, "I would like to know why you came in today," the interpreter should interpret the statement in the first person rather than saying "The doctor would like to know why you came in today." The provider should avoid asking more than one question at a time (e.g., "How are you feeling and why did you come in today?") and avoid using acronyms or colloquialisms (e.g., "Did you hurt your noggin?"), which might be difficult to interpret.

The interpreter should be positioned behind and to the side of the patient and between the patient and the provider, so that the three form a triangle. If the interpreter has questions for the provider, they should be spoken directly to the provider in English after informing the patient that this will occur. Similarly, questions or requests for clarification from patients should be made directly to the patients, after informing the provider that this is to occur.

Because interpreting from one language to another entails more than merely rendering a word from one language into a second language, some interpretation may entail additional explanation. This might occur when a phenomenon does not take the same form in one culture as it does in another. If a patient refers to a culture-specific condition, such as evil eye, for instance, a direct word-for-word interpretation would not be sufficient to convey the patient's meaning to the provider. In these situations, after interpreting word for word, the interpreter should tell the provider that the words do not have the same meaning in English as in the patient's language and provide an explanation (e.g., "mal ojo or evil eye is a condition in Mr. Garcia's culture in which illness is thought to occur suddenly when one person casts his gaze on another"). The patient also should be informed that the interpreter is explaining a condition that does not occur in the same way in the two cultures. Otherwise, the patient may wonder why the length of the interpreter's statement to the provider in English took twice or three times as long his response in his own language.

Some facilities contract with telephone interpretation services, especially for unusual languages. An example is the AT&T Language Line, a 24-hour service available in all parts of the country that employs interpreters in 140 languages. In some states, Medicaid covers the cost of this service. The interview usually is done using the telephone's speaker feature. The disadvantage of using telephone interpretation services is that they do not provide the interpreter with valuable nonverbal cues. Also, people who work for telephone interpretation services often are not familiar with medical terminology.

A key advantage to using in-person professional medical interpreters is that they have no stake in patients' answers to physicians because they presumably are strangers. When no interpreter is available, such as in community health centers, it may be necessary to use a family member of the patient or someone working in the facility who is bilingual. Using family members as interpreters poses problems with objectivity, and patients may be reluctant to discuss sensitive information in front of their relatives. Families also might want to make a patient look good to providers and thus minimize problems they think are socially less acceptable, such as hallucinations (Slomski, 1993). Finally, a family member's English skills may be only slightly better than those of the patient.

Using nonfamily members who speak the patient's language, such as workers in other units of the hospital, may be expeditious but yield poor results, because they may be unfamiliar with medical terminology and may not understand how to interpret precisely and objectively (Luckman, 2000). Using nonfamily members also can cause serious privacy issues in the health setting. Regional differences in word use between different countries or cultures that speak the same language also may present problems. In a review of audiotaped transcripts of interviews with six Spanish-speaking patients in which a nonprofessional interpreter was used (either a bilingual employee or family member), 165 errors were noted, 77% of which had the potential to cause serious clinical problems (Flores et al., 2003). These included telling a mother to put antibiotics in a child's ears instead of his mouth and failing to translate questions about drug allergies.

Although it may be necessary to use bilingual relatives or employees to interpret in situations in which a patient has no or very limited English skills, it is preferable to use a professional medical interpreter who is familiar with medical terminology. Telephone interpreting services, with the interpreter participating via telephone, are viable options, especially if they employ interpreters with expertise in medical terminology. In situations involving bilingual family members or employees or telephone interpreters who have not been trained in medical terminology, the provider should (a) take time to explain the importance of interpreting objectively and without editing what the provider says and (b) use less technical terms that are more likely to be understood by the person interpreting and the patient (e.g., "Have you been running a temperature?" rather than "Have you been febrile?" or "Have you gone to the bathroom today?" instead of "Have you voided today?"). The more technical the language, the less likely it is that it will be understood in the same way by provider, interpreter, and patient.

CONCLUSION

Clinical encounters in health care are problematic and require negotiation when patient and provider come with markedly different cultural constructions of reality and hold different health beliefs. Good communication between patient and provider can help to overcome divergent beliefs and smooth the path toward a negotiated clinical reality that optimizes the flow of information, motivates patients to engage actively in their treatment, increases patients' confidence in their ability

to influence their own health, and enhances the well-being of both patient and provider. This type of communication has the potential to decrease group differences in health in the United States.

A number of techniques for promoting effective communication were outlined and discussed. A number of techniques for increasing patients' participation in treatment have demonstrated empirical support and show promise for use in clinical settings. Techniques for improving providers' communication skills by attending more to the nonsomatic aspects of patients' health and making interviews more patient-centered have stood up less well in empirical testing.

Social work input is needed in the development and testing of interventions to improve communication in health care. Although the majority of studies reviewed in this chapter had strong research designs, they were almost exclusively atheoretical. Interventions based on strong social science theory constructed by social workers with experience in health care likely would fare better. Similarly, techniques for maximizing the accuracy of communication with people with no or limited English-language skills need empirical testing.

More challenging for social work and other disciplines is how to acknowledge and minimize often subtle provider bias toward patients from sociodemographic groups that are very different from the provider's own. This is as much a challenge for social workers as for any other professional group. Empirical evidence of the outcomes of health encounters between majority providers and patients from minority and lower- and middle-SES groups is sobering, especially in terms of its potential negative impact on health outcomes. A great deal more work is needed to develop interventions for providers to sensitize them to the dangers of unacknowledged bias and provide guidance for overcoming that bias. Social workers clearly have a role in developing and testing these interventions and in serving as models of good practice through their positions on transdisciplinary health-care teams. The success of these efforts could profoundly diminish the contribution of the shortfalls in health care noted by McGinnis and colleagues (2002) to health disparities in the United States and other parts of the world.

SUGGESTED LEARNING EXERCISES

Learning Exercise 10.1

Determine what groups of recent immigrants or refugees are in your area or in the metropolitan area closest to your college, university, or place of work. Choose the group that is greatest in number. Investigate the group's culture by consulting library and Internet services. Interview a health provider who serves the group. This might be someone from the local health department, a community clinic, or a federally qualified health center. Ask if it would be possible to interview a member of the group. Obtain answers to the next questions and include them in a five-page paper:

1. What are the major health problems faced by the group (both in its country of origin and in the United States)?
2. What are the barriers to treating these health problems?
3. How has communication between providers and members of the group progressed?
4. What are the major barriers to communication between providers and members of the group?
5. What medical interpretation services are available?
6. How easy or difficult are these services to access?

Conclude your paper by outlining your reactions to the situation and what recommendations you would suggest to improve it. For extra credit, suggest for how group members might be included in decision making using a CEnR approach. You can supplement practitioner interviews with written materials, academically published or otherwise, but be careful to distinguish and attribute sources of information throughout your paper.

Learning Exercise 10.2

Using the procedure for understanding medical terminology that is outlined in the appendix that follows, determine the meanings of the next 20 terms:

1. Retroperitoneal
2. Neoplasia
3. Hypertrophy
4. Paranasal sinuses
5. Microcephaly
6. Cardiac arrhythmia
7. Myalgia
8. Bronchitis
9. Visceroptosis
10. Splenomegaly
11. Prostatic hypoplasia
12. Arteriosclerosis
13. Hemolysis
14. Prenatal
15. Mammography
16. Metastasis
17. Epigastric
18. Nephritis
19. Cardiomyopathy
20. Bradycardia

APPENDIX 10.1 MEDICAL TERMINOLOGY

This appendix describes how medical terms can be understood by breaking them into their component parts and following a few decision rules. Breaking down medical words into their components and learning the meaning of those components allows a person to understand the meaning of a wide range of terms. This is especially important in preparing social workers to work in transdisciplinary environments in which they must communicate with team members from a variety of disciplines.

In analyzing medical terms, begin with the end of the word (the suffix). For example, the word *neurology* ends in -LOGY, which means "the study of." Next, go to the beginning of the word. NEUR- is the word root, or the component of the word that provides its essential meaning. The root NEUR- means "nerve." The third part of the word, the letter O, has no meaning of its own but connects the suffix and the root. It is called a combining vowel. Putting it all together, we get "the study of nerves."

Another word is *gastroenteritis*. The suffix -ITIS means "inflammation." The root is GASTR-, which means "stomach." The word has a second root, ENTR-, which means "intestines." The connector is O. The word is read from the suffix, back to the beginning, and then across, from left to right. *Gastroenteritis* thus means "inflammation of the stomach and intestines."

It helps to look for the connector in dividing the word into its component parts. The combining vowel and root together are referred to as the combining form. Some words have two combining forms. In this case, the rule is to drop the combining vowel before a suffix that starts with a vowel. In *gastroenteritis*, for example, the root ENTER- does not have a combining vowel before it joins with -ITIS, because -ITIS begins with a vowel. The combining vowel between root components is kept (as in GASTR-O-ENTER), even if the root begins with a vowel. Another example of a word with two combining forms is *electroencephalogram*. The suffix -GRAM means "record of." The combining form ELECTRO- means "electricity." The combining form ENCEPHALO- means "brain." So the word *electroencephalogram* means "record of the electricity in the brain."

In addition to suffixes, roots, combining vowels, and combining forms, some words have components attached to their beginnings, which are called *prefixes*. Prefixes can change the meanings of words to which they are attached. An example is the word *pericardial*. The suffix -AL means "pertaining to." CARDI- is a root that means "heart." PERI- is a prefix that means "surrounding." So *pericardial* means "pertaining to the area that surrounds the heart." RETRO- is a prefix means "behind." Thus, *retrocardial* means "pertaining to the area behind the heart." Because the prefix EPI- means "above," the word *epicardial* means "pertaining to the area above the heart."

Tables 10.4 to 10.6 provide a number of common medical suffixes, prefixes, and roots. The information provided is general because of space considerations and should be seen as a resource for learning rather than a complete list of medical terms. A number of excellent manuals are available that can supplement the information in this text and provide medical terms germane to specialty areas. A number of these manuals are listed in the "Suggested Resources" at the end of this appendix.

The information in these three tables should allow social workers in health care to deconstruct and understand medical terms that they encounter. Remember these five steps in identifying medical terms:

1. Identify the suffix and determine its meaning.

2. Identify any prefix that may occur and determine its meaning.

3. Identify the first root and combining vowel, which make up the combining form, that occur after a prefix or in the absence of a prefix. Determine its meaning.

4. Identify additional combining forms that may occur after the first combining form that was identified. Determine their meanings. Recall that the last root before a suffix that begins with a vowel will not have a combining vowel.

5. Read the word from its suffix to its prefix to its combining forms or roots.

Table 10.4   Common Medical Prefixes, Their Meanings, and Examples of Their Use

Prefix	Definition	Example
a-, an-	not, without	apnea
ante-	before, forward	antepartum
anti-	against	antibiotic, antiseptic
auto-	self, own	autoimmune
bi-	two	bilateral, bifurcation
brady-	slow	bradycardia
cata-	down	catabolism
con-	with, together	congenital
contra-	against, opposite	contralateral
de-	down, lack of	dehydration
dia-	through, apart, complete	dialysis, diarrhea
dys-	bad, painful, difficult	dyspnea
ec-, ecto-	out, outside	ectopic
en-, endo-	in, within	endoscope
epi-	upon, on, above	epithelium
eu-	good, well	euphoria
ex-	out, away from	exopthalmia
hemi-	half	hemiplegia
hyper-	excessive, above	hyperplasia
hypo-	below	hypothermia
in-	not, in	insomnia, incision
infra-	beneath	infracostal
macro-	large	macrocephalia
mal-	bad	malignant
meta-	change, beyond	metastasis
micro-	small	microscope
neo-	new	neoplasm
pan-	all	pancytopenia
para-	alongside of, near, beside, beyond	parathyroid, paralysis
peri-	surrounding	pericardial
poly-	many, much	polyneuritis
post-	after, behind	postmortem, postnatal
pre-	before, in front of	prenatal, precancerous
pro-	before, beyond	prodrome, prolapse
pseudo-	false	pseudocyesis
re-	back, again	relapse
retro-	behind, backward	retroperitoneal
sub-	below, under	subcutaneous
supra-	above, upper	supracutaneous
syn-, sym-	together, with	synthesis, symphysis
tachy-	fast	tachycardia
trans-	across, through	transfusion
uni-	one	unilateral

Table 10.5   Common Medical Roots and Connecting Vowels and Their Definitions

Root	Definition
abdomin/o	abdomen
aden/o	gland
angi/o	vessel
arthr/o	joint
carcin/o	cancer
cardi/o	heart
cerebr/o	cerebrum (largest part of the brain)
chondr/o	cartilage
cutane/o	skin
encephal/o	brain
enter/o	intestines
gastr/o	stomach
gynec/o	women, female
hepat/o	liver
hemat/o	blood
lapar/o	abdominal wall
mamm/o	breast
mast/o	breast
nephr/o	liver
neur/o	nerve
onc/o	tumor
opthalm/o	eye
orch/o	testes
oste/o	bone
ovari/o	ovary
ped/o	child
psych/o	mind
pulmon/o	lung
rhin/o	nose
sarc/o	flesh
thel/o	nipple
thorac/o	thorax
thyr/o	thyroid
trache/o	trachea
urethr/o	urethra

Table 10.6   Common Medical Suffixes, Their Meanings, and Examples of Their Use

Suffix	Meaning	Example of use
-algia	pain	neuralgia
-centesis	surgical puncture to remove fluid for analysis	amniocentesis
-coccus	berry-shaped bacterium	streptococcus
-cyte	cell	lymphocyte
-dynia	pain	mastodynia
-ectomy	removal of, excision	tonsillectomy
-genesis	producing, forming	carcinogenesis
-genic	producing, produced	carcinogenic
-gram	record	mammogram
-itis	inflammation	tonsillitis
-logy	study of	morphology
-lysis	breakdown, separation	paralysis
-malacia	softening	osteomalacia
-megaly	enlargement	splenomegaly
-oma	tumor, collection	myoma
-osis	condition, usually abnormal	necrosis
-pathy	disease condition	cardiopathy
-penia	deficiency	leucopenia
-plasia	development, growth	achondroplasia
-plasty	surgical repair	angioplasty
-ptosis	sagging, drooping	visceroptosis
-sclerosis	hardening	arteriosclerosis
-stasis	stopping, control	metastasis

Stedman, J. M.. (2008). *Stedman's medical dictionary for the health professions and nursing.* Philadelphia, PA: Lippincott, Williams & Wilkins.

Steiner, S. S. (2002). *Quick medical terminology: A self-teaching guide.* Hoboken, NJ: Wiley.

SUGGESTED RESOURCES

Chabner, D. (2008). *Medical terminology: A short course.* Philadelphia, PA: Elsevier.

Chabner, D. (2010). *The language of medicine.* Philadelphia, PA: Elsevier.

REFERENCES

Abrams, D. B. (2006). Applying transdisciplinary research strategies to understanding and eliminating health disparities. *Health Education & Behavior, 33*(4), 515–531.

Beach, M. C., Saha, S., Korthuis, P. T., Sharp, V., Cohn, J., Wilson, I. B.,...Moore, R. (2010). Patient-provider communication differs for Black compared to White HIV-infected patients. *AIDS and Behavior*, January 10 [E-pub ahead of print], doi:10.1007/s10461-009-9664-5.

Beckman, H. B., & Frankel, R. M. (1984). The effect of physician behavior on the collection of data. *Annals of Internal Medicine, 101,* 692–696.

Benne, K. D., & Sheets, P. (1948). Functional roles of group members. *Journal of Social Issues, 4,* 41–49.

Brown, J. B., Boles, M., Mullooly, J. P., & Levinson, W. (1999). Effect of clinician communication skills training on patient satisfaction. *Annals of Internal Medicine, 131,* 822–829.

Burgess, D. J., Fu, S. S., & von Ryn, M. (2004). Why do providers contribute to disparities and what can be done about it? *Journal of General Internal Medicine, 19,* 1154–1159.

Camarota, S. A, & Jensenius, K. (2009, July). A shifting tide: Recent trends in the illegal immigrant population. Retrieved from www.cis.org/IllegalImmigration-ShiftingTide

Christakis, N. A., & Fowler, J. H. (2007). The spread of obesity in a large social network over 32 years. *New England Journal of Medicine, 357*(4), 370–379.

Conteh, L., Stevens, W., & Wiseman, V. (2007). The role of communication between clients and health care providers: Implications for adherence to malaria treatment in rural Gambia. *Tropical Medicine and International Health, 12*(3), 382–391.

Cooper, L. A., Roter, D. L., Bone, L. R., Larson, S. M., Miller, E. R., III, Barr, M. S.,…Levine, D. M. (2009). A randomized controlled trial of interventions to enhance patient-physician partnership, patient adherence and high blood pressure control among ethnic minorities and poor persons: Study protocol NCT00123045 [Electronic version]. *Implementation Science, 4,* doi: 10.1186/1748-5908-4-7

Coulehan, J. L., Platt, F. W., Egener, B., Frankel, R., Lin, C.-T., Lown, B., & Salazar, W. H. (2001). "Let me see if I have this right …" Words that help build empathy. *Annals of Internal Medicine, 135,* 221–227.

Coward, R. T., & Kout, J. A. (Eds.). (1998). *Aging in rural settings: Life circumstances and distinctive features.* New York, NY: Springer.

Davison, B. J., & Degner, L. F. (1997). Empowerment of men newly diagnosed with prostate cancer. *Cancer Nursing, 20,* 187–196.

DuPre, A. (2001). Accomplishing the impossible: Talking about body and soul and mind in a medical visit. *Health Communication, 14,* 1–21.

Egbert, L. D., Battit, G. E., Welch, C. E., & Bartlett, M. K. (1964). Reduction of postoperative pain by encouragement and instruction of patients. *New England Journal of Medicine, 270,* 825–827.

Erasmus, C. J. (1952). Changing folk beliefs and the relativity of empirical knowledge. *Southwestern Journal of Anthropology, 8,* 411–428.

Fadiman, A. (1997). *The spirit catches you and you fall down: A Hmong child, her American doctors, and the collision of two cultures.* New York, NY: Noonday.

Fisher, N. L. (1992). Ethnocultural approaches to genetics. *Pediatric Clinics of North America, 39,* 55–64.

Flores, G., Laws, M. B., Mayo, S. J., Zuckerman, B., Abreu, M., Medina, L., & Hardt, E. J. (2003). Errors in medical interpretation and their potential clinical consequences in pediatric encounters. *Pediatrics, 111,* 6–14.

Foster, G. M. (1976). Disease etiologies in non-western medical systems. *American Anthropologist, 78,* 773–782.

Foulks, E. F. (1972). *The Arctic hysterias of the North Alaska Eskimo.* Washington, DC: American Anthropological Association.

Freeth, D. (2001). Sustaining interprofessional collaboration. *Journal of Interprofessional Care, 15*(1), 37–46.

Gehlert, S., Murray, A., Sohmer, D., McClintock, M., Conzen, S., & Olopade, O. (2010). The importance of transdisciplinary collaborations for understanding and resolving health disparities. *Social Work in Public Health, 25*(3), 408–422.

Goleman, D. (1991, November 13). All too often, the doctor isn't listening, studies show. *New York Times.* Retrieved from www.nytimes.com/1991/11/13/health/all-too-often-the-doctor-isn-t-listening-studies-show.html?scp=72&sq=&st=nyt

Greenfield, S., Kaplan, S., & Ware, J. E. (1985). Expanding patient involvement in care: Effects on patient outcomes. *Annals of Internal Medicine, 102,* 520–528.

Hall, P. (2005). Interprofessional teamwork: Professional cultures as barriers. *Journal of Interprofessional Care, 19*(Suppl. 1), 188–196.

Helman, C. G. (1985). Communication in primary care: The role of patient and practitioner explanatory models. *Social Science and Medicine, 20,* 923–931.

Hepworth, D. H., Rooney, R. H., & Larsen, J. (2002). *Direct social work practice: Theory and skills.* Pacific Grove, CA: Brooks/Cole.

Hiatt, R. A., & Breen, N. (2008). The social determinants of cancer: A challenge for transdisciplinary science. *American Journal of Preventive Medicine, 35*(Suppl. 2), S141–S150.

Institute of Medicine. (2002). *Unequal treatment: What healthcare providers need to know about racial and ethnic disparities in health care.* Washington, DC: National Academy Press.

Israel, B. A., Schulz, A. J., Parker, E. A., Becker, A. B., Allen, A. J., III, & Guzman, J. R. (2003). Critical issues in developing and following community based participatory research principles. In M. Winkler & N. Wallerstein (Eds.), *Community-based participatory research for health* (pp. 53–76). San Francisco, CA: Jossey-Bass.

Janus, I. L. (1972). *Victims of groupthink.* Boston, MA: Houghton Mifflin.

Jensen, J. D., King, A. J., Guntzviller, L. M., & Davis, L. A. (2010). Patient–provider communication and low-income adults: Age, race, literacy, and optimism predict communication satisfaction. *Patient Education and Counseling, 79,* 30–35.

Johnson, R. L., Roter, D., Powe, N. R., & Cooper, L. A. (2004). Patient race/ethnicity and quality of patient-physician communication during medical visits. *American Journal of Public Health, 94,* 2084–2090.

Kahn, R. L., & Prager, D. J. (1994, July 11). Interdisciplinary collaborations are a scientific and social imperative. *Scientist,* p. 12.

Kaplan, S. H., Greenfield, S., & Ware, J. E. (1989). Assessing the effects of physician–patient interactions on the outcomes of chronic disease. *Medical Care, 27,* S110–S127.

Kinmonth, A. L., Woodcock, A., Griffin, S., Spiegal, N., & Campbell, M. J. (1998). Randomised controlled trial of patient centered care of diabetes in general practice: Impact on current wellbeing and future disease risk. *British Medical Journal, 31,* 1202–1208.

Kleinman, A. (1980). *Patients and healers in the context of culture: An exploration of the borderland between anthropology, medicine, and psychiatry.* Berkeley, CA: University of California Press.

Kleinman, A., Eisenberg, L., & Good, B. (1978). Clinical lessons from anthropologic and cross-cultural research. *Annals of Internal Medicine, 88,* 251–258.

Kleinman, A., Eisenberg, L., & Good, B. (2006). Culture, illness, and care: Clinical lessons from anthropologic and cross-cultural research. *Focus, 4*(1), 140–149.

Leventhal, H. (1985). The role of theory in the study of adherence to treatment and doctor-patient interactions. *Medical Care, 23,* 556–563.

Lewis, G., Croft-Jeffreys, C., & David, A. (1990). Are British psychiatrists racist? *British Journal of Psychiatry, 157,* 410–415.

Lister, L. (1980). Role expectations of social workers and other health professionals. *Health & Social Work, 5,* 41–49.

Lollock, L. (2001). *The foreign born population of the United States: March 2000. Current population reports* (pp. 20–534). Washington, DC: U.S. Census Bureau.

Low, S. M. (1984). The cultural basis of health, illness and disease. *Social Work in Health Care, 9,* 13–23.

Luckman, J. (2000). *Transcultural communication in health care.* Scarborough, Ontario, Canada: Delmar Thomson Learning.

Maguire, P., & Pitceathly, C. (2002). Key communication skills and how to acquire them. *British Medical Journal, 325,* 697–700.

Maiman, L. A., Becker, M. H., Liptak, G. S., Nazarian, L. F., & Rounds, K. A. (1988). Improving pediatricians' compliance-enhancing practices: A randomized trial.

American Journal of Disease of Children, 142, 773–779.

Maly, R. C., Bourque, L. B., & Engelhardt, R. F. (1999). A randomized controlled trial of facilitating information giving to patients with chronic medical conditions: Effects on outcomes of care. *Journal of Family Practice, 48,* 273–276.

Marcus, E. N. (2003, April 8). When a patient is lost in the translation. *New York Times,* p. D7. Retrieved from www.nytimes.com/2003/04/08/health/cases-when-a-patient-is-lost-in-the-translation.html

Matsunaga, D. S., Enos, R., Gotay, C. C., Banner, R. O., DeCambra, H., Hammond, O. W.,...Tsark, J. (1996). Participatory research in a native Hawaiian community: The Wai'anae cancer research project. *Cancer, 78,* 1582–1586.

McCann, S., & Weinman, J. (1996). Empowering the patient in the consultation: A pilot study. *Patient Educational Counseling, 27,* 227–234.

McGinnis, J. M., Williams-Russo, P., & Knickman, J. R. (2002). The case for more active policy attention to health promotion. *Health Affairs, 21,* 78–93.

Mizrahi, T., & Abramson, J. (1985). Sources of strain between physicians and social workers: Implications for social workers in health care settings. *Social Work in Health Care, 10,* 33–51.

National Academy of Sciences, National Academy of Engineering, and Institute of Medicine. (2005). *Facilitating interdisciplinary research.* Washington, DC: National Academies Press.

Northouse, P. G., & Northouse, L. L. (1997). *Health communication: A handbook for health professionals.* Englewood Cliffs, NJ: Prentice-Hall.

Orth, J. E., Stiles, W. B., Scherwitz, L., Hennrikus, D., & Vallbona, C. (1987). Patient exposition and provider explanation on routine interviews and hypertensive patients' blood pressure control. *Health Psychology, 6,* 29–42.

Pachter, L. M. (1994). Culture and clinical care: Folk illness beliefs and behaviors and their implications for health care delivery. *JAMA, 271,* 690–694.

Patterson, R. E., Kristal, A. R., & White, E. (1996). Do beliefs, knowledge, and perceived norms about diet and cancer predict dietary change? *American Journal of Public Health, 86,* 1394–1400.

Pescosolido, B. A., & Levy, J. A. (2002). The role of social networks in health, illness, disease and healing: The accepting present, the forgotten past, and the dangerous potential for a complacent future. *Social Networks and Health, 8,* 3–25.

Rao, J. K., Anderson, L. A., Inui, T. S., & Frankel, R. M. (2007). Communication interventions make a difference in conversations between physicians and patients: A systematic review of the evidence. *Medical Care, 45*(4), 340–349.

Roberts, C. S. (1989). Conflicting professional values in social work and medicine. *Health & Social Work, 14,* 211–218.

Rosenquist, J. N., Murabito, J., Fowler, J. H., & Christakis, N. A. (2010). The spread of alcohol consumption behavior in a large social network. *Annual Review of Internal Medicine, 152,* 426–433.

Rosenthal, E. (1993, November 28). How doctors learn to think they're doctors. *New York Times,* pp. B1, B4. Retrieved from www.nytimes.com/1993/11/28/weekinreview/how-doctors-learn-to-think-they-re-doctors.html?scp=1&sq=How%20doctors%20learn%20to%20think%20they%E2%80%99re%20doctors&st=cse

Roter, D. L. (1977). Patient participation in patient–provider interaction: The effects of patient question-asking on the quality of interaction, satisfaction, and compliance. *Health Education Monographs, 5,* 281–315.

Roter, D. L., Hall, J. A., & Aoki, Y. (2002). Physician gender effects in medical communication. *JAMA, 288,* 756–764.

Rubel, A. J. (1977). The epidemiology of a folk illness: Susto in Hispanic America. In D. Landy (Ed.), *Culture, disease, and healing: Studies in medical anthropology* (pp. 119–128). New York, NY: Macmillan.

Sands, R. G., Stafford, J., & McClelland, M. (1990). "I beg to differ": Conflict in the interdisciplinary team. *Social Work in Health Care, 14,* 55–72.

Satin, D. G. (1987). The difficulties of interdisciplinary education: Lessons from three failures and a success. *Educational Gerontology, 13,* 53–69.

Schneider, J., Kaplan, S. H., Greenfield, S., Li, W., & Wilson, I. B. (2004). Better physician-patient relationships are associated with higher reported adherence to antiretroviral therapy in patients with HIV infection. *Journal of General Internal Medicine, 19,* 1096–1103.

Schulman, K. A., Berlin, J. A., Harless, W., Kerner, J. F., Sistrunk, S., Gersh, B. J., . . . Escarce, J. J. (1999). The effect of race and sex on physicians' recommendations for cardiac catheterization. *New England Journal of Medicine, 25,* 618–626.

Sideris, D. A., Tsouna-Hadjis, P., Toumanidis, S. T., Vardas, P. E., & Moulopoulos, S. D. (1986). Attitudinal educational objectives at therapeutic consultation: Measures of performance, educational approach and evaluation. *Medical Education, 20,* 307–313.

Skipper, J. J., & Leonard, R. C. (1968). Children, stress, and hospitalization: A field experiment. *Journal of Health and Social Behavior, 9,* 275–287.

Slomski, A. J. (1993, May 24). Making sure that your care doesn't get lost in translation. *Medical Economics,* pp. 122–139.

Snow, L. (1993). *Walkin' over medicine.* Boulder, CO: Westview Press.

Sommers, L. S., Marton, K. I., Barbaccia, J. C., & Randolph, J. (2000). Physician, nurse, and social worker collaborations in primary care for chronically ill seniors. *Archives of Internal Medicine, 160,* 1825–1833.

Spector, R. (2004). *Cultural diversity in health and illness.* Upper Saddle River, NJ: Pearson Education.

Stewart, M., Brown, J. B., Donner, A., McWhinney, I. R., Oates, J., Weston, W. W., & Jordan, J. (2000). The impact of patient-centered care on outcomes. *Journal of Family Practice, 49,* 796–804.

Street, R. L., Makoul, G., Arora, N. K., & Epstein, R. M. (2009). How does communication heal? Pathways linking clinician-patient communication to health outcomes. *Patient Education and Counseling, 74*(3), 295–301.

Thompson, S. C., Nanni, C., & Schwankovsky, L. (1990). Patient-oriented interventions to improve communication in a medical office visit. *Health Psychology, 9,* 390–404.

Turner, F. J. (1990). Social work practice theory: A transcultural resource for health care. *Social Science and Medicine, 31,* 13–17.

Ulrey, K. L., & Amason, P. (2001). Intercultural communication between patients and health care providers: An exploration of intercultural communication effectiveness, cultural sensitivity, and anxiety. *Health Communication, 13,* 449–463.

van Ryn, M., & Burke, J. (2000). The effect of patient race ad socio-economic status on physician perceptions of patients. *Social Science and Medicine, 50,* 813–828.

van Ryn, M., & Fu, S. S. (2003). Paved with good intentions: Do public health and human service providers contribute to racial/ethnic disparities in health? *American Journal of Public Health, 93*(2), 248–255.

Vanclay, L. (1996). *Sustaining collaboration between general practitioners and social workers.* London, UK: CAIPE.

West, D. S., Greene, P. G., Kratt, P. P., Pulley, L., Weiss, H. L., Siegfried, N., & Gore, S. A. (2003). The impact of a family history of breast cancer on screening practices and attitudes in low-income, rural, African American women. *Journal of Women's Health, 12,* 779–787.

Weston, W. W., & Brown, J. B. (1989). The importance of patients' beliefs. In M. Stewart & D. Roter (Eds.), *Communicating with medical patients* (pp. 77–85). Newbury Park, CA: Sage.

World Health Organization. (2003). *International classification of diseases and related health problems,* Revision 10 (ICD-10). Geneva, Switzerland: Author. Retrieved from www.who.int/classifications/icd/en

Yalom, I. D. (1998). *The Yalom reader.* New York, NY: Basic Books.

Young, A., & Flower, L. (2001). Patients as partners, patients as problem-solvers. *Health Communication, 14,* 69–97.

Zandbelt, L. C., Smets, E. M., Oort, F. J., Godfried, M. H., & de Haes, H. C. (2004). Satisfaction with the outpatient encounter: A comparison of patients' and physicians' views. *Journal of General Internal Medicine, 19,* 1088–1095.

Zerhouni, E. (2003). Medicine: The NIH roadmap. *Science, 3,* 63–72.

11

Religion, Spirituality, Health, and Social Work

TERRY A. WOLFER

This chapter provides information to assist social workers in developing religious and spiritual competence. It begins by briefly summarizing data regarding the importance of religion for Americans. Then it defines *religion* and *spirituality* and summarizes a variety of terms associated with a multidimensional conceptualization of these overlapping terms. Next it summarizes some empirical research on the relationships among religion, spirituality, and aspects of physical and mental health. Finally, it introduces a variety of assessment strategies for use in clinical practice ranging from brief tools to in-depth interviews.

Chapter Objectives

- Describe levels of religiosity in the American population and why this matters to health social workers and other health professionals.
- Define the concepts of religion and spirituality, their multiple dimensions, and how they interrelate.
- Discuss the major pathways that link religion and spirituality to physical and mental health and the empirical evidence to support these pathways.
- Outline a rationale for assessing client spirituality and major methods of spiritual assessment (including brief screening instruments, pictorial tools, and in-depth interview formats).
- Discuss the importance for health social workers of understanding a client's religion and spirituality.

Several recent and ongoing controversies demonstrate the complex relationship between religion and health in American society. For example, Oregon was the first state in the United States to legalize euthanasia—allowing people to choose and hasten their own deaths—usually in the context of a terminal illness. Euthanasia remains illegal in most other states partly because of religiously based concern for the value of human life.

A recent court case in Oregon involved similar issues but in a different context. The case involved members of the Followers of Christ Church (Mayes, 2010). A couple was charged with criminal negligence in the death of their 16-year-old son for failing to obtain medical care for his urinary tract infection. In this case, the parents rejected medical care in favor of prayer, anointing with oil, and the ceremonial laying on of hands. The Followers of Christ Church is one of several groups, including the better-known Church of Christ, Scientist, that refuse medical care on religious grounds. For most Americans, including most religious people, the group's refusal of medical care seems extreme and unwarranted. But it also represents the significant diversity of religious belief and practice in America related to health care and social services. (A child welfare worker had visited the family only months before the teen died.) Health social workers in situations like this need to balance respect for the religious rights of patients and their families with protecting the individual lives, especially those of minors.

Obviously, euthanasia, or physician-assisted suicide, differs from refusing medical treatment on religious grounds. Nevertheless, the two situations have some important things in common: profound religious or ethical disagreements about issues regarding the value of preserving human life, quality of life, patient self-determination, religious freedom, and paternalism.

Another example of religiously based controversy in health care involves organ donation. Because almost all organ donations come from patients who are brain dead rather than cadavers, organ procurement teams often must obtain consent from family members for organ removal. Intense debate has arisen regarding religious and ethical issues surrounding brain death and organ donation. Two facts make this debate more intense: (1) The number of donations remains steady; and (2) the number of people awaiting organ transplants each year continues to grow. As a result, the pressure to donate organs is on the rise.

Bresnahan and Mahler (2010) identify the perspectives of the five major religious traditions regarding organ donation in the context of brain death and then compare the perspectives to information readily available online. These authors found that health-care workers and most Internet sources typically report that major religious traditions support organ donation. However, some Internet Web sites may contradict this information. This matters because consumers increasingly turn to the Internet for information. A health social worker might be flummoxed by the refusal of family members to consider donation for religious reasons if the social worker knows that major religious groups generally approve of organ donation but does not know of this contradictory information online. As a result, the social worker might be less able to assist the family in respectfully exploring their concerns and reaching a satisfactory decision. Health practitioners who wish to establish and maintain trust with deeply religious families must treat their religious arguments and points of view with respect (Röcklinsberg, 2009).

Currently there is heated debate about another ethical issue involving religious perspectives: whether health-care practitioners may refuse to provide medical treatments that

they personally oppose on ethical or religious grounds. This issue was heightened during the recent debates about national health-care reform. Many Americans agree that health-care professionals should have a right to refuse to provide services to which they have moral or religious objections. At the same time, many Americans also believe that patients have a right to information about all legal options for medical treatment. Occasionally these expectations are in conflict. Curlin, Lawrence, Chin, and Lantos (2007) surveyed a national sample of physicians regarding controversial procedures, such as "administering terminal sedation in dying patients, providing abortion for failed contraception, and prescribing birth control to adolescents without parental approval" (p. 593). They found that most physicians believe it acceptable to express reservations regarding treatments they find personally objectionable but also that most feel obligated to provide information to their patients about all legal options and willingly refer their patients to other practitioners for treatments they oppose. Nevertheless, Curlin and colleagues (2007) report that a substantial number of physicians "do not believe they are obligated to disclose information about or provide referrals for legal yet controversial treatments" (p. 597).

Health social workers may encounter this ethical issue in two ways. Like physicians, some social workers may struggle with deciding whether to help patients obtain interventions they find morally objectionable, or whether to inform patients of such interventions. Or they may work with physicians or other health-care professionals who oppose certain interventions that they do not. This puts them in a position to discuss these controversial interventions with their mutual patients. Health social workers must be aware of these controversies, draw their own conclusions, and be prepared to work with professional colleagues whose beliefs may differ from their own.

It should not be surprising that health and health care are fraught with religious, spiritual, and moral issues. In one form or another, physical and mental health often involve pain and suffering and questions regarding meaning and the beginning and ending of life. Health and health care involve profound aspects of human existence, aspects historically addressed by religion and religious institutions, and increasingly addressed by scientific research. At the same time, medical innovations have pressed boundaries and opened doors previously unimagined, often raising profound religious and spiritual concerns. For all these reasons, social workers who work in health care need to be aware of and sensitive to religion and spirituality in the lives of their clients, the families of these clients, their colleagues, and themselves.

This chapter provides information to assist social workers in developing religious and spiritual competence. Before going further, it may be helpful to reflect on what is known and not known about religion and spirituality. What individuals know and believe, to a large extent, is influenced, if not determined, by personal experience. Individuals, including health social workers and patients, have positive or negative experiences within their families, with friends, and with colleagues. They also have learned things from formal education and cultural media of many types. They use their own experiences and education to understand others. Although that is true with any topic, it seems uniquely difficult with religion and spirituality, because it often happens with less awareness and self-reflectiveness. Because people have such different experiences, it is important to avoid assumptions and work hard at understanding others. A Brazilian physician and researcher put it this way:

> Studying spirituality scientifically is a very exciting although somewhat precarious enterprise. This is a field filled with prejudices, biases for and against spirituality. Many people have opinions to give, but usually these judgments are not based on an in-depth analysis of the evidence available. It is easy to slip into an intolerant and Pyrrhonean skepticism or to give a naive acceptance of doubtful claims. Regardless of whether we hold spiritual or materialistic beliefs, religious or anti-religious postures or not, we have a responsibility to explore the

relationship between spirituality and health in order to improve our knowledge and our care for human beings. (Moreira-Almeida, 2007, pp. 3–4)

RELIGIOSITY AND SPIRITUALITY IN THE AMERICAN POPULATION

There are a variety of ways to gauge the importance of religion for Americans. Perhaps the simplest and most direct is simply to ask. For example, according to the Pew Forum on Religion and Public Life (2009), more than half (56%) of Americans state that religion is "very important" in their lives. The percentage of people stating that religion is "very important" ranges from a low of 36% in New Hampshire and Vermont to a high of 82% in Mississippi. As another example, according to Pew, nearly two fifths (39%) of Americans report that they "attend worship services at least once a week," while many others attend worship services less frequently. By comparison, according to the 2008 General Social Survey (www.norc.uchicago.edu/GSS), more than one quarter (27.5%) of the population attends worship services at least weekly while nearly half (48.3%) attend at least monthly. Again, weekly attendance varies by state, from a low of 22% in Alaska to a high of 60% in Mississippi (Pew Forum, 2009). Nearly half (48%) of Americans report that they "pray at least once a day," with a low of 40% in Maine and a high of 77% in Mississippi (Pew Forum, 2009). By comparison, according to the 2008 General Social Survey, a majority (57.6%) of Americans pray at least daily, and others (17.7%) pray at least once a week (Association of Religion Data Archives [ARDA], n.d.). More than 90% of Americans state that they "believe in God or a universal spirit," and more than two thirds (71%) state that they are "absolutely certain" in this belief (Pew Forum, 2009).

There is considerable disparity in these variables across the United States. In general, these surveys suggest that southern states have higher rates on each of these measures, while northeastern and western states have lower rates. But the rates suggest that social workers in any geographical area are likely to encounter some patients who consider religion important, who attend worship services on a weekly basis, and who pray daily. Culturally competent health social work practice requires that social workers be prepared to understand and take account of these realities.

The region in which a social worker practices will influence the likelihood of encountering people from certain religious traditions. "The Midwest most closely resembles the religious makeup of the overall population. The South, by a wide margin, has the heaviest concentration of members of evangelical Protestant churches. The Northeast has the greatest concentration of Catholics, and the West has the largest proportion of unaffiliated people, including the largest proportion of atheists and agnostics" (Pew Forum, 2009, p. 8). Nevertheless, given the nation's significant religious diversity, social workers may encounter people with little or no religious faith in any region of the United States. That is clearly true in metropolitan areas but often is also true in rural areas. For example, one may encounter atheists or agnostics in rural areas and small towns in Nebraska or conservative evangelicals in Southern California.

This religious diversity is evident in another way. Although more than 3 out of 4 Americans (78.4%) identify themselves as "Christian," this diverse grouping includes Protestants (including evangelical, mainline, and historically African American denominations), Catholics, Mormons, Jehovah's Witnesses, Orthodox, and others (Pew Forum, 2009). About 1 in 6 (16.1%) Americans report no religious affiliation, including atheists and agnostics (1.6% and 2.4%, respectively). Slightly fewer than 1 out of 20 Americans (4.7%) identify with all other religions, including Jewish, Muslim, Buddhist, Hindu, and others. More than 4 out of 5 (80.8%) Americans identify with one of the three Abrahamic traditions (i.e., Christian, Jewish, Muslim). Looked at another way, 97.2% of Americans who identify themselves as religious identify with one of the Abrahamic traditions, including 93.4% who identify as Christian (Pew Forum, 2009).

Research on religion and spirituality over the life span is confounded by age, cohort, and period effects (Smith, 2009, p. 10). In other words, some changes in religiosity apparently result from the aging process itself (i.e., life cycle experience and concern with mortality) while others result from conditions and experiences shared by people born at about the same time or by events that occur at the time of survey or interview (Smith, 2009). For example, research on Millennials—people born after 1980—shows they are generally less religious in terms of belief, attendance, and practice than previous generations of adults (Pond, Smith, & Clement, 2010). However, it also finds them similar to previous generations, when they were a similar age. Pond et al. (2010) conclude: "This suggests that some of the religious differences between younger and older Americans today are not entirely generational, but result in part from people's tendency to place greater emphasis on religion as they age" (p. 2). If previous trends continue, we may expect young people to become somewhat more religious as they age.

In summary, while sizable groups within the American population do not self-identify as religious, attend worship services, or pray, large groups of Americans do. Furthermore, this is true in every region of the country. It is also true for people across the life span and appears to increase with age. Finally, people experiencing severe stress, disability, illness, or dying (and their family members) often have heightened interest in spirituality, and these are the very people encountered by health social workers.

These data suggest that health social workers must be prepared to work with people of faith. In the United States, that usually will mean people who identify themselves as Christian, although that designation itself includes great diversity. But social workers also must be prepared to work with people of other faiths or no religious faith.

The United States often is referred to as a religiously diverse nation (Eck, 2001). Indeed, the United States has been religiously diverse since colonial times. In the early 1600s, for example, there were "Huguenots in Charleston, Anglicans in Tidewater Virginia, Catholics in St. Mary's City, Swedish Lutherans along the Delaware River, Quakers and Presbyterians further up the river, Dutch Reformed in Manhattan, Puritans in New England, Baptists, and Heaven-knows-what-else in Rhode Island" (Gaustad, 1968, p. 835). Notably, this diversity occurred primarily within the Christian tradition. But from the beginning, American religious diversity also included and was influenced by Native American and African religious traditions. "Since then," as Smith (2002) writes, "America has continued to both import foreign and spawn indigenous religions" (p. 1).

Historically, changes in U.S. immigration laws significantly increased the flow of immigrants, many of who come from non-Christian traditions. In particular, the Immigration and Nationality Act of 1965 substantially increased the flow of followers of other religious traditions. According to the 2000 census, 11.1% of the U.S. population was foreign born. After Mexico, the leading countries are China, the Philippines, India, and Vietnam. "While Americans still overwhelmingly adhere to their traditional faiths, the United States is home to all of the world's religions and non-Judeo-Christian religions make up a small, but growing, share of America's religious mosaic" (Smith, 2002, p. 4).

WHY CONSIDER RELIGION AND SPIRITUALITY IN HEALTH CARE?

Demographics alone suggest that social workers must consider religion and spirituality when conducting psychosocial assessments with patients. Because so many Americans report that religion and spirituality are important parts of their lives and regularly participate in individual and corporate religious activities, it seems important that social workers routinely inquire about those activities. In health-care settings, however, it is even more important. For many people, religion and spirituality have numerous profound connections with their health

and well-being as well as their illnesses, suffering, disability, recovery, coping, and dying. According to the 2004 General Social Survey, more than half of Americans (51.2%) agree that at least daily, "I find comfort in my religion or spirituality" (ARDA, n.d.). Another quarter (26.9%) agree with this statement "some days" or "most days." Likewise, the same survey found that nearly half (48%) agree that at least daily, "I find strength in my religion or spirituality," and another quarter (28.5%) agree with this statement "some days" or "most days" (ARDA, n.d.). Indeed, religion and spirituality often represent important resources for preventing or coping with illness and dying. "By keeping patients' beliefs, spiritual/religious needs and supports separate from their care, we are potentially ignoring an important element that may be at the core of patients' coping and support systems and may be integral to their well-being and recovery" (D'Souza, 2007, p. S57). More than that, "religion provides things that are good for health and well-being, including social support, existential meaning, a sense of purpose, a coherent belief system and a clear moral code" (Eckersley, 2007, p. S54). Of course, these benefits also can come from other sources, but they often are associated with religion. "The process of 'humanizing' health care involves the consideration of individuals' unique psychosocial resources, including their spirituality, during illness and recovery. Spirituality encompasses feelings of connection to others and finding meaning in life" (Dalmida, Holstad, Dilorio, & Laderman, 2009, p. 120).

DEFINING *RELIGION* AND *SPIRITUALITY*

It may be helpful to consider formal definitions for the terms *religion* and *spirituality* and how they are related. In fact, there are many conflicting definitions for these terms. More than a decade ago, Scott (1997) scanned 20th-century social science for definitions of religion and spirituality. She found 31 definitions of religiousness and 40 definitions of spirituality.

Interestingly, she found that these definitions were quite evenly distributed across nine content categories, suggesting both considerable diversity within definitions for either religiousness or spirituality and considerable overlap between the two. Scott's findings should alert health social workers to the difficulty and complexity of defining the terms.

Adding to this complexity, in recent decades, popular and scholarly understandings of *religion* and *spirituality* have changed. "The word 'religion' comes from the Latin root *religio* which signifies a bond between humanity and some greater-than-human power" (Hill et al., 1998, p. 15). Historically, it was understood to mean: "(1) a supernatural power to which individuals must respond; (2) a feeling present in the individual who conceives such a power; and (3) the ritual acts carried out in respect of that power" (p. 15). These meanings depict religion as a profound and pervasive part of human experience. However, growing secularism and disillusionment with religious institutions have disrupted the historically close relationship between religion and spirituality. Many people now differentiate spirituality and religion, associating *spirituality* with personal experience of the transcendent and *religion* with possible restrictions and barriers to such experience. As a result, they tend to view spirituality more positively and religion more negatively (p. 16) and also to emphasize spirituality as subjective (i.e., individualized) and religion as institutional.

Distinguishing between religion and spirituality makes it possible for people to identify themselves as either religious or spiritual, both religious and spiritual, or neither. In fact, the General Social Survey found that while most Americans identify themselves as equally religious and spiritual, a growing minority in 2008 identify themselves as more spiritual than religious, compared with the number who did so in 1998 (Smith, 2009).

Despite the trend, dichotomizing religion and spirituality in this way may be problematic. Hill and colleagues (1998) argued that dichotomizing religion and spirituality poses several dangers. "The first subtle danger can be expressed in two forms of polarization: individual vs. institutional and good vs. bad" (p. 18). They go on to explain that speaking of individual spirituality and institutional religion ignores two basic facts: "(1) virtually all religions are interested in matters spiritual, and (2) every form of religious and spiritual expression occurs in some social context." In other words, religions consistently address matters of transcendent or ultimate concern, and all beliefs and practices, whether religious or spiritual, occur in a social and cultural environment. Furthermore, Hill et al. (1998) write, "to argue that spirituality is good and religion is bad (or vice-versa) is to deny a substantial body of research demonstrating that both religion and spirituality can be manifested in both healthy and unhealthy ways" (p. 18). A simple dichotomy obscures this complexity.

Hill and colleagues (1998) identify yet another danger, one they argue is perhaps most serious: losing the distinctive sacred core of religion and spirituality. In religion, the sacred "has to do with a higher power, God, or ultimate truth. This sacred content is often defined through institutional mechanisms, such as ecclesiastical authority, sacred writings, and traditions" (p. 19). In spirituality, the sacred also has to do with matters of transcendent or ultimate concern (i.e., beyond ordinary experience or material existence). Yet spirituality often emphasizes a highly individualized, experiential path for each person. This potentially trivializes, and may even obscure, the search for the sacred by individuals. In light of these issues, the authors agree that the sacred core is central to the experience of both religion and spirituality. Furthermore, they agree that both religion and spirituality involve a search for the sacred. Thus, they define spirituality and religion in ways that highlight their similarities (see Table 11.1).

These definitions highlight the significant overlap these constructs have in the lives of people. Spirituality involves a search for the sacred. Likewise, religion involves a search for the sacred, a search for other, nonsacred goals in a context primarily concerned with the sacred, or both. Religion also involves the means

Table 11.1 Defining Religion and Spirituality

Criterion for Spirituality

The feelings, thoughts, and behaviors that arise from a search for the sacred. The term "search" refers to attempts to identify, articulate, maintain, or transform. The term "sacred" refers to a divine being, ultimate reality, or ultimate truth as perceived by the individual.

Criterion for Religion/Religiousness

The feelings, thoughts, and behaviors that arise from a search for the sacred (a divine being, ultimate reality, or ultimate truth as perceived by the individual); and/or a search or quest for non-sacred goals (such as identity, belongingness, meaning, health, or wellness).

Source: From "Definitions of Religion and Spirituality," by P. C. Hill, K. I. Pargament, J. P. Swyers, R. L. Gorsuch, M. E. McCullough, R. W. Hood, and R. F. Baumeister, 1998. In D. B. Larson, J. P. Swyers, and M. E. McCullough (Eds.), *Scientific Research on Spirituality and Health: A Consensus Report* (p. 21). Rockville, MD: National Institute of Healthcare Research.

and methods of this search, supported by a group. In short, while spirituality and religion both involve a search for the sacred, religion also incorporates the sociocultural context (and other goals in that context). Defined in this way, spirituality for an individual always involves a search for the sacred. But religion for an individual may involve a search for the sacred or a search for nonsacred goals (e.g., social identity, health) in the context of a group organized to search for the sacred. The group may legitimate nonsacred goals, the search for either sacred or nonsacred goals, and the methods or means of the search. By these criteria, spirituality may be considered as the more fundamental category, with religion being the more concrete one. Consistent with these definitions, Hufford (2005) defines *spirituality* most simply as "personal relationship to the transcendent" and *religion* as "the community, institutional aspects of spirituality" (p. 2).

The importance of this emphasis on the sacred in both religion and spirituality becomes more apparent when one considers it in terms of research. Without this emphasis on the sacred, spirituality cannot be readily distinguished from humanism or positive psychology (Koenig, 2008). If that is the case, researchers cannot distinguish between and draw clear conclusions about the relationships

among spirituality, humanism, positive psychology, and health. These distinctions become especially difficult in relation to mental health. As Koenig notes, spirituality researchers sometimes confuse causes and consequences. "Simply defining spirituality as good mental health and including mental health indicators as part of the measures of spirituality precludes any ability to actually study the relationship between spirituality and mental health" (p. 18). The result would be tautological, essentially correlating a concept with itself.

Koenig (2008) argues that the meaning of spirituality has changed and currently is too vague for research purposes. But this ambiguity actually may be useful in clinical care settings. In clinical practice, social workers must attend to the idiosyncratic perspectives and needs of individual clients. Thus, Koenig advocates the use of primarily religious categories for research purposes—because they lend themselves to more reliable operationalization—with the addition of spiritual categories for clinical care—because these encourage and enable understanding of client uniqueness.

Before reviewing research on the relationships among religion, spirituality and health, it is helpful to explore further how these concepts can be operationalized, whether for research or for clinical assessment. The next section clarifies the numerous ways people can be involved with religion and spirituality.

Dimensions of Religiosity and Spirituality

Early research on religion and health typically focused on the patient's religious affiliation or denomination. In approximately 250 studies conducted between 1937 and 1984, the "investigation of religion [was] confined to comparisons of morbidity and mortality rates across religious denominations" (Levin & Markides, 1986, p. 589). Often these distinctions went no further than Catholics, Protestants, and Jews. Beginning in the 1960s, some health researchers began asking respondents how often they attended religious services, generally referred to as "church attendance" in the research literature. It usually was measured by a single survey item, such as "How often do you attend Sunday worship services?" (Hall, Meador, & Koenig, 2008, p. 140). Subsequently, researchers began to use self-reported, global assessments of religion. These often take the form of a question asking "To what extent do you consider yourself to be a religious person?" (p. 142) or "How important is religion for you?" (Veenhoven, 2003, p. 145). In the past decade, however, researchers have attempted to conceptualize and measure numerous additional dimensions of religion and spirituality. This section briefly reviews these dimensions as a basis for understanding current empirical research and, more generally, expanding our recognition and understanding of religion and spirituality in the lives of patients.

Table 11.2 compares domains of religiousness identified by several groups of scholars. King and Hunt (1972) led an early attempt to identify domains empirically by factor-analyzing numerous religiously oriented items. Larson, Swyers, and McCullough (1998) present a "consensus report," based on a series of conferences sponsored by the John Templeton Foundation and the National Institute for Healthcare Research. Their report reflects the thinking of more than 70 prominent researchers in the area of religion and spirituality. One chapter of the report provides a definition of *religion* and *spirituality* (Hill et al., 1998). Funded by the Fetzer Institute and the National Institute on Aging (NIA), a smaller national working group of scholars created a new tool, the Multidimensional Measurement of Religiousness/Spirituality for Use in Health Research (Fetzer Institute/National Institute of Aging, 1999). This measure includes 11 domains of religion and spirituality. The instrument has been embedded in the General Social Survey, and domain-specific components have been widely used in health research. Hill and Hood (1999) compiled what remains the largest collection of standardized measures of religiosity and developed a list of domains. Likewise, Koenig, McCullough, and Larson (2001) identified a variety of domains based on their comprehensive review of the empirical

literature through 2000. Their review included more than 1,200 studies and 400 research reviews. Table 11.2 lists the various domains identified by these groups to highlight unique and overlapping categories.

Going well beyond demographic variables reported earlier, the concepts listed in Table 11.2 allow a fine-grained understanding of religiosity and spirituality in people's lives. Of these dimensions, religious affiliation is the most widely used by researchers. As recently as four decades ago, scholars and health professionals were content to inquire whether people were Catholic, Protestant, or Jewish. But changes in religious demographics resulting from social dynamics and immigration have made these categories inadequate. Likewise, another common measure of religious participation—weekly worship attendance—has been recognized as an overly crude measure of religiosity.

Table 11.2 makes clear that numerous other dimensions of religion and spirituality may be significant for particular populations of patients seen in health or other settings. A religious or spiritual history may be the best means of assessing these intertwined and overlapping dimensions. A history identifies crucial, often idiosyncratic, formative factors in the client's experience. Religious and spiritual histories are especially well suited to clinical practice, but because they are highly qualitative, they are less amenable to research on religion and health outcomes. These dimensions are interrelated. For example, besides participating in weekly worship services, many people participate in private religious activities, such as prayer, watching religious television, listening to religious radio, meditation, or reading scripture or other religious literature. Such activity may be encouraged by organizational participation but also may occur in its absence. Religious activities—both organizational and private—probably contribute to people's religious knowledge, beliefs, and values (three separate yet overlapping dimensions). Religious knowledge, beliefs, and values may foster religious meaning making and appraisals regarding one's own life. Furthermore, they

Table 11.2   Dimensions of Religion and Spirituality

King and Hunt (1972)	Larson, Swyers, and McCullough (1998)	Fetzer Institute/ National Institute of Aging (1999)	Hill and Hood (1999)	Koenig, McCullough, and Larson (2001)
Creedal assent	Beliefs and values	Beliefs	Belief and practice	Belief
				Belief versus nonbelief
				Certainty of belief
				Orthodoxy of belief
Religious knowledge		Values	Moral values	
	Preference or affiliation	Religious preference		Affiliation or denomination
Organizational activity	Social participation	Organizational religiousness	Institutional religion	Organizational religiosity
Congregational involvement				Membership
Church attendance				Attendance at religious services
				Social activity
				Study/Prayer groups
				Church leadership (elder, deacon)
				Sacramental/Ritual participation
Financial support				Financial support
Devotionalism	Private practices	Private religious practices	Spirituality and mysticism	Nonorganizational religiosity
				Private prayer
				Private reading (scripture/theology)
				Religious television/ radio
Salience				Subjective religiosity
Behavior				Importance of religion
Cognition				Self-rating religiosity
Orientation to religion	Commitment	Commitment	Commitment orientation	Commitment and motivation
Growth and striving				Intrinsic
Extrinsic				Extrinsic
		Meaning		"Quest" (search for truth)
	Experiences	Daily spiritual experiences	Experience	Experience
				Religious well-being
	Coping	Coping	Coping and problem solving	Coping
	History	History		History (spiritual history)
			Development	Maturity

(continued)

Table 11.2   Dimensions of Religion and Spirituality (*Continued*)

King and Hunt (1972)	Larson, Swyers, and McCullough (1998)	Fetzer Institute/ National Institute of Aging (1999)	Hill and Hood (1999)	Koenig, McCullough, and Larson (2001)
			Attitudes	Attitudes and Practices
	Motivation for regulating and reconciling relationships	Forgiveness	Forgiveness	
	Support	Support		
			Concept of God	
			Fundamentalism	
			View of afterlife	
			Divine intervention	

Source: Adapted from "Measuring Religiousness in Health Research: Review and Critique," by D. E. Hall, K. G. Meador, and H. G. Koenig, 2008, *Journal of Religion and Health, 47*(2), 134–163.

may contribute to religious and spiritual coping (i.e., the use of religious ideas and practices to deal with stressors). Furthermore, participation in organized religiosity may specifically contribute to exchange of religious and spiritual support (i.e., support within religious groups or for religious reasons, a form of social support). Religious and spiritual thinking and behavior also may lead to religiously influenced motivation. For example, religiosity may provide substantive content for ideals and goals (e.g., honesty, fidelity, apology, forgiveness). Over time, it may encourage behavior consistent with these ideals and, subsequently, build commitment to their achievement. Some people report experiences of the sacred, ranging from a sense of peace or awe to more explicit and direct involvement, such as conversion or healing. Just as people vary in their experience of the sacred, they also differ in their sense of subjective or personal religiosity. Some people experience a sense of quest and adventure in relation to religious and spiritual experience, and many people can identify the presence or absence of spiritual well-being in their lives.

Do religion and spirituality do all of these things? Perhaps not on the individual level, but for groups of people in various combinations, they probably do. Although religious and spiritual involvement may vary dramatically

between individuals and groups, these differences provide some of the key dimensions for understanding and assessing them. As Krause (2008) argues, it is time to move beyond simple conceptualizations of religion and spirituality. "If researchers hope to better understand the relationship between religion and health, then more attention must be given to the complex ways in which religion is measured" (pp. 5–6).

A complete list of religiosity domains may serve four purposes.

1. It reveals the multifaceted nature of the underlying concepts of religion and spirituality.

2. It provides a starting point for researchers wishing to operationalize these concepts, and for practitioners considering how to include them in client assessment.

3. It provides a basis for understanding and interpreting empirical research on the relationships between religion and spirituality and health.

4. More generally, it may help to untangle vague and overlapping conceptualizations of religion and spirituality and to develop more precise understanding of these important concepts. This will provide a foundation for exploring how religion and spirituality relate to health.

EMPIRICAL RESEARCH ON RELIGION AND HEALTH

In 2001, Koenig et al. published the *Handbook of Religion and Health*, a 700-page review of empirical research on the relationship between religion and a variety of physical and mental health conditions. The authors examined more than 1,200 research studies and 400 research reviews, with the goal of including all English-language published studies available at that time. Koenig and his colleagues published the second edition of the *Handbook* in 2011, and the current edition reviews research from the past decade. Reflecting the dramatic growth of scholarly interest in the topic, more research has been conducted in the decade since the first edition was published than in the entire previous century (H. Koenig, personal communication, February 8, 2008). Rather than provide a comprehensive review, this section discusses the major pathways through which religion and spirituality are theorized to influence health.

In the burgeoning empirical literature, several potential pathways have been theorized for the influence of religion and spirituality on health. Some of these are less inclusive while others involve biological and physiological mechanisms. The latter are not reviewed in this chapter.

First, some religious groups prescribe and encourage what Oman and Thoreson (2005) refer to generally as lifestyle health behaviors. For example, George, Ellison, and Larson (2002) note that Mormons prohibit use of alcohol and illegal drugs, cigarette smoking, and nonmarital sex. Mormons also provide guidelines for diet and sleep. Likewise, Seventh Day Adventists prohibit consumption of alcohol, illegal drugs, tobacco, and caffeine and encourage a vegetarian diet and Sabbath keeping. Less directly, many religious groups promote gratitude for the gift of life and encourage respect and care for the human body as the temple of God (Park, 2007, p. 322) or as an instrument of God's service (Oman & Thoreson, 2005). These positive messages are assumed to contribute to healthy choices (George et al., 2002).

Indeed, empirical data supports this psychosocial mechanism. Based on their review of evidence-based literature, for example, Powell, Shahabi, and Thoreson (2003) conclude that "the relationship between religion or spirituality and cardiovascular death is, to a large extent, explained by the encouragement that religion or spirituality provides for living a healthier lifestyle" (p. 42). As another example, religious prohibitions regarding smoking represent a major factor for some religious groups in lowered tobacco-related cancers. Despite substantial recent declines in smoking, tobacco-related cancers remain the leading cause of cancer deaths in the United States (Centers for Disease Control [CDC], 2010). Building on recent psychological research, Geyer and Baumeister (2005) proposed spiritual self-regulation as a means of understanding how people use religion to increase their self-control in an attempt to align their lives with important values.

Related to healthy behaviors, religion is associated with increased use of preventive health care and adherence to medical regimens (Oman & Thoreson, 2005, p. 446). For example, in a nationally representative sample of older adults, Benjamins and Brown (2004) found that people who reported high levels of religiosity were more likely to use preventive services (flu shots, cholesterol screening, breast self-exams, mammograms, pap smears, and prostate screening). They speculate that religious beliefs may motivate healthier living and use of preventive care, or that religious settings may directly provide information, instrumental support (e.g., transportation), or on-site preventive services. Either by encouraging use of preventive health care or facilitating access to such care, religious involvement appears to increase older adults' use of preventive health care and to improve their health outcomes.

More broadly, most religious groups provide significant social support for their members, especially when members need it most (Koenig, 2008, p. 57f). "This is not surprising because virtually all religions in the world extol the virtues of loving one another and caring for those who are in need. In fact, this is one reason why some researchers maintain that social ties in the church are specially close-knit and may be more beneficial than social relationships that arise in secular setting" (Krause, 2008, p. 1216). Like religion and spirituality, social support is a complex, multidimensional construct. This creates the possibility of numerous relationships. For example, religious and spiritual involvement correlates with larger and more stable social networks, more interaction within social networks, greater perception of social and emotional support, and greater satisfaction with support (George, Larson, Koenig, & McCullough, 2000; Oman & Thoreson, 2005).

Social support provides a context for individuals to be open and disclose their health conditions and concerns. In turn,

> disclosure evokes cognitive and affective responses, which can ameliorate stress and moderate its deleterious effects on human physiology. In addition, confiding in others, human or divine, and reinforcing reciprocal bonds of assistance among individuals, or with divine others, has both health-promotive and disease-preventive consequences for populations, as shown through decades of social and epidemiologic research on social support. (Levin, 2009, p. 90)

Religious groups often promote what Krause (2008) terms "close companion friends," an intense type of relationship uncommon outside of families.

In research on religion and health, a commonplace finding is that people's religious involvement is related to both the amount and the quality of social support they experience (Koenig, 2008). This is especially true for older adults and for people with health problems. For example, older adults are more likely to be involved with religious groups than other social groups, and controlling for other factors, this involvement has greater effects on their happiness and health (Koenig, 2008; Krause, 2008).

Religious traditions provide significant resources to help members find meaning and purpose in their struggles, to make sense of their experience, and to establish a sense of coherence (George et al., 2002). Through religion, "people understand their role in the universe, the purpose in life, and develop the courage to endure suffering" (George et al., 2000, p. 111). Interestingly, there is no assumption that the meanings are positive. It appears that simply being able to make sense of experience is most critical.

Likewise, religious traditions provide a variety of coping resources to assist people in dealing with illness, suffering, and death (Koenig, 2008). Somewhat ironically, for many people, trust in God appears to enhance their sense of control and to promote active coping (Hood, Hill & Spilka, 2009; Pargament, 1997). "For example, persons adopting a 'collaborative' coping orientation with the divine, viewing God as a partner, experienced better outcomes than persons using either a primarily 'deferring' coping style (involving passive attitude toward problems) or a primarily 'self-directive' coping style" (Oman & Thoreson, 2005, p. 445).

Although religious coping may be beneficial in general, it appears especially beneficial for people dealing with chronic illness or with the loss of a loved one (Hood et al., 2009). There is limited evidence for beneficial effects of religious coping on physical health; it appears that the effects may be obscured by the failure to distinguish negative and positive coping (Park, 2007). Nevertheless,

> an impressive number of studies done in a wide range of social settings indicate that people who rely on positive religious coping responses are more likely to avoid the pernicious effects of stress than individuals who do not turn to religion in an effort to deal with the adversity that confronts them. (Krause, 2004, p. 1217)

Psychosocial resources, such as self-esteem, self-efficacy, and mastery, also may partly explain the health benefits of religious participation. Religious participation is associated with higher levels of these psychosocial resources, although the evidence to support this connection is based on cross-sectional data (Krause, 2008). There also is evidence that these psychosocial resources are associated with better health, although, again, this conclusion rests largely on the results of cross-sectional studies

Most religious traditions endorse forgiving attitudes and behaviors (McCullough, Bono & Root, 2005; Oman & Thoreson, 2005). Krause (2004) suggests that forgiveness may help people in several ways. First, those unwilling to forgive "often relive the hurtful act over and over" (p. 1218). This rumination may produce stress and lead to poor health outcomes. Conversely, "forgiving others helps restore and renew social ties that were previously a source of significant support." These ties may produce better health. Finally, "forgiving others promotes positive emotions." At noted previously, these actions exert a beneficial effect on health. Furthermore, interventions to promote forgiveness improve psychological well-being, reduce chronic stress and anger, reduce anxiety and depressive symptoms, and increase self-esteem and hope (Enright & Coyle, 1998; as cited in McCullough et al., 2005). For these reasons, it seems plausible that forgiveness may contribute to improved health.

Likewise, religious traditions promote altruism and service to others by offering both reasons and opportunities for involvement. For example, volunteering, philanthropy, altruism, and other kinds of helping behavior are generally higher among religious people, and these activities are associated with both mental and physical health (Koenig, 2008). "Regular church attendance may encourage meaningful social roles that provide a sense of self-worth and purpose through the act of helping. This is in contrast to the more common conceptualizations of social support where the emphasis is on being helped" (Powell et al., 2003, p. 48). Beyond this, religious involvement promotes formal volunteer work and informal helping, both of which may be associated with improved health outcomes.

Religious and spiritual people often exhibit qualities such as gratitude, hope, optimism, and compassion (referring to, respectively, an appreciation for life, expectancies of favorable outcomes, a sense that one can achieve these outcomes, and a deep and abiding sense of love for all of humankind) may provide individuals with a deeper sense of meaning in life and a source of direction and comfort in difficult times. (Park, 2007, p. 322)

Furthermore, they may experience positive psychological states as a result of better coping, meaning derived from religious goals, the experience of forgiveness, helping others, and faith-related expectancy (Oman & Thoreson, 2005). If so, these positive psychological states may contribute to positive health outcomes.

These positive emotional states, in turn, may affect health by reducing allostatic load (AL). AL represents the cumulative wear and tear on one's body from adapting to the demands of everyday living. These demands require ongoing adjustments to maintain physiological systems within normal operating ranges. The adjustment process itself may become damaged, especially when the demands are chronic, the adjustment is inadequate, or for other reasons it does not shut off. Thus, AL is conceptualized as a failure of bodily systems to regulate normally and posited to mediate the relationship between stress and health, thus increasing the risk of illness (Maselko, Kubzansky, Kawachi, Seeman, & Berkman, 2007).

Oman and Thoreson (2005) speculate that attachment styles also provide a plausible pathway between religion and health. Secure attachment to God is linked with greater life satisfaction and lower levels of anxiety, depression, and loneliness, and these, in turn, are related to better physical health (Oman & Thoreson, 2005).

Considering macro-level relationships between religion and health, faith-based efforts to improve community health are becoming more popular. Griffith and colleagues (2010) describe a community health promotion effort that was successful in partnering with African American churches in the Flint, MI, area to reduce HIV/AIDS. Working with these churches, the community groups were able to reach over 4,000 congregants across 11 churches to increase awareness, knowledge, and understanding of human immunodeficiency virus (HIV)/acquired immunodeficiency syndrome (AIDS). Duru, Sarkisian, Leng, and Mangione (2010) conducted the first randomized controlled trial of a faith-based physical activity program to increase physical activity in older African American women at three Los Angeles churches. As part of that trial, congregants followed a curriculum that included Bible reading and prayer in addition to walking. Their research suggests that a church-based physical activity program may be successful in promoting physical activity among members. A majority of the participants in rural North Carolina focus groups about community kidney disease screenings by Jennette, Vupputuri, Hogan, Falk, and Harward (2010) suggested that such screenings would be most successful if held in community churches. One focus group member stated: "I think the church is a good place if you want to start in the community because that's a common place, no matter how poor or rich we are" (p. 7). Campbell et al. (2007) suggest that collaborative partnerships with churches can improve community health and that program leaders of such partnerships should incorporate key components of community-based participatory research (such as involving churches in program design and delivery) to be most effective.

This brief summary of potential pathways linking religion and health reflects a growing body of empirical evidence. "To summarize, we conclude that a relationship between religion or spirituality and physical health does exist but that it may be more limited and more complex than has been suggested by others" (Powell et al., 2003, p. 50). As Park (2007) notes, "[W]hile it is useful to keep [the pathways] conceptually distinct, they likely interact and overlap in many ways" (p. 321).

Suicide

Social workers in many settings, including health care, encounter clients who contemplate or attempt suicide. It is well known that in the United States suicide attempts and suicide rates

vary significantly by gender, age, and ethnicity (CDC, 2010). Suicide is a leading cause of death among young people but actually occurs more frequently among older adults. Non-Hispanic Whites, American Indians, and Native Alaskans are twice as likely to commit suicide as other ethnic groups (CDC, 2010). It may be less known that suicide risk and suicide rates are also associated with religion.

Research consistently has demonstrated that suicide rates vary by religious tradition and by level of participation: Both religious affiliation and religious participation serve as protective factors for suicide (Gearing & Lizardi, 2009; Lizardi & Gearing, 2010). In a review of 68 studies, Koenig and Larson (2001) report that 84% found lower rates of suicide or more negative attitudes toward suicide among more religious persons. Most religious traditions condemn taking one's own life, provide reasons for living, and discourage aggressive behavior and hostility. More broadly, religious participation also may contribute to social support and increase emotional well-being. Because of this protective potential, psychosocial assessment for suicide risk should consider religion. Indeed, Gearing and Lizardi (2009) recommend that social workers ask a variety of questions to assess: the importance of religion to the client, the role of religiosity in previous times of stress and difficulty, how suicide is conceptualized in the client's religion, and the potential benefit of encouraging the client's religiosity (pp. 237–238).

SPIRITUAL ASSESSMENT

The previous discussion about components of religion and spirituality alerts us to the multiple ways that religion and spirituality may relate to health. Furthermore, it suggests ways that religion and spirituality may influence the development and course of particular diseases and psychosocial problems across the life course. It suggests the importance of considering religion and spirituality as an integral part of a thorough psychosocial assessment process. Indeed, several authors have offered a variety of reasons for including religion and spirituality in the assessment process.

If the spiritual and religious diversity present in the United States is taken seriously, data may be overwhelming. But it may be less important that social workers know details about specific religions and spiritual approaches and more important that they know how to ask about a patient's religious and spiritual beliefs and involvement. As a subset of cultural competence, religious and spiritual competence requires the ability to explore the unfamiliar. Given time and attention, patients often are willing to teach health-care providers about their health concerns and how these relate to religion or spirituality. Barnes and Harris (2001) recommend "respectful curiosity" as an important way to approach clients. "The broader skill—as in all effective medical care—involves developing the capacity to listen differently, in a way that is personally respectful, clinically insightful, and aimed at understanding rather than agreement or disagreement" (pp. 7–8).

In a brief chapter such as this, it is impossible to provide an adequate introduction to the variety of religious and spiritual beliefs and practices that health social workers may encounter in their professional practices. Furthermore, there is great diversity within as well as between religious groups. Thus, religiously competent practice requires continual efforts to individualize assessments and to avoid stereotyping and making assumptions.

Rationale for Spiritual Assessment

There are a number of reasons for social workers to address religion and spirituality with patients and their families. As previously discussed, many Americans identify themselves as religious or spiritual and indicate that this is important for them. Things that are important for people, such as religion and spirituality, likely will have implications for their health care. If so, it appears that social workers will want to determine whether this is true for particular patients and incorporate this information into their work with those patients. For example, religion and spirituality may shape people's beliefs about pain and suffering, quality of life, meaning and purpose, and mortality. Those beliefs also may influence patients' access to social support and other resources. The purpose of conducting religious or spiritual assessment is to clarify their roles in the lives of patients, which allow the development of more complete and better-informed treatment plans.

Why should we assess and attempt to address religious and spiritual issues with our patients? Koenig (2008) and others give several reasons (for additional information, see Canda & Furman, 2010). As discussed previously, many patients are religious, and most would like to have their faith considered in their health care (Cloninger, 2006; Koenig, 2008). Also, a large proportion of Americans identify themselves as religious or spiritual, and of these, a large percentage report religion or spirituality is an important part of their lives. For these patients, inquiring about religion and spirituality signals an interest in the whole person and may further enhance the treatment relationship and the therapeutic effects of treatment (D'Souza, 2007).

Religion and spirituality influence people's efforts and ability to cope with illness, whether physical or mental. More specifically, religion may influence "motivation toward self-care, willingness to cooperate with plan treatments, and ability to comply with medical therapies" (Koenig, 2008, p. 157). Because these are important contributors to treatment success, it is important for social workers and other health-care providers to take religion into account. In particular, religion may be critical for discharge planning and aftercare—a frequent focus for social workers in health settings—because religious groups often represent a significant source of concrete assistance (e.g., transportation, meals) and social support for their newly discharged members. Many churches, for example, have health ministries or outreach efforts.

In addition, religious beliefs and practices may influence medical outcomes (Koenig, 2008). As Koenig suggests, unmet spiritual and emotional needs may create physiological stress, thus impacting body systems. These, in turn, influence the way patients respond to surgical and medical treatments. Thus, identifying and trying to address spiritual needs may reduce stress and enhance medical treatment.

Hospitalized patients often are isolated from their usual spiritual care and support. Patients may be hospitalized far from home and their spiritual communities. Even when they are not distant, their clergy may have limited time and ability to visit. In such situations, social workers may play a critical role in helping patients acquire spiritual care and support, by initiating contact with the patient's clergy, clergy within the community, or the hospital chaplain. In addition, most clergy will have limited understanding of medical conditions and medical procedures and thus have limited ability to connect these with spiritual concerns. In these situations, social workers may serve as intermediaries among patients, clergy, and other health professionals. This may be of considerable importance when patients wish for spiritual counsel regarding certain procedures (e.g., starting or stopping life support).

As outlined by Koenig (2008), religious beliefs and rituals may conflict with or otherwise influence medical decisions that patients make, particularly when they are seriously ill. Religious beliefs and rituals may influence medical decisions by family members as well, in ways that may or may not be consistent with the patient's wishes. Although uncommon, such conflicts often are high profile and attract disproportionate attention. These include avoidance of medical care by Christian Scientists, suspicion of psychiatric care by fundamentalist Christians, refusal of blood transfusions by Jehovah's Witnesses, and so on. Health social workers must be prepared to work with people holding these views and intercede with healthcare administrators, attorneys, and members of the judicial system.

Whether and to what extent a patient participates in a religious congregation may have significant implications for follow-up care. For example, religious communities may provide a variety of significant material and emotional supports. Potential supports include meals, transportation, social visits, prayers, telephone calls, supervision, caregiving, and respite for caregivers. Such supports may hasten and facilitate discharge to the community, prolong community stay, and improve the quality of life. These congregational supports may be especially important for patients who do not have many family members nearby or whose family members cannot provide much support.

Major professional organizations now recommend or even require practitioners to conduct routine spiritual assessment as part of competent practice. In recognition of the foregoing benefits, the Joint Commission for the Accreditation of Hospital Organizations requires a spiritual assessment of all patients in hospitals, nursing homes, and home-health agencies (Hodge, 2006). Related to this, the Joint Commission also requires that medical, nursing, and psychiatric training programs prepare their students to provide culturally sensitive health care, including sensitivity to deeply held religious beliefs (Koenig, 2008). Likewise, the World Health Organization (WHO) has emphasized the importance of addressing religion and spirituality in clinical practice (WHO, 1998; WHOQOL SRPB Group, 2006). Other groups of health professionals also have recommended spiritual assessment as part of competent practice in palliative care (e.g., American College of Physicians; Qaseem et al., 2008), cancer care (National Cancer Institute, 2009), and mental health (Substance Abuse and Mental Health Services Administration, 2006; Royal College of Psychiatrists, 2010).

The National Association of Social Workers (NASW) has promulgated standards in several areas of professional practice that recommend assessment of spirituality. These include NASW Standards for Services in Long-Term Care Facilities (NASW, 2003), Social Work Practice in Health Care Settings (NASW, 2005b), and Social Work Practice with Clients with Substance Use Disorders (NASW, 2005a). The standards for health-care settings include this assertion: "Social workers recognize that ethnic, cultural, spiritual, and religious factors can have an impact on healthcare choices and adherence to regimens of care" (NASW, 2005b, p. 18). More generally, NASW recommends spiritual assessment as an essential aspect of cultural competence (NASW, 2001, 2007). Thus, professional competence will require assessment of spiritual and religious factors.

Approaches to Assessment

This chapter has identified numerous dimensions of religion and spirituality. Scholars have developed a variety of standardized measures for assessing religion and spirituality in empirical research, even though they tend to focus on only a few of the specified dimensions. The Multidimensional Measurement of Religiousness/Spirituality for Use in Health Research is one of the best measures for studying the relationships between religion, spirituality, and health. It can be used in its entirety or particular sections can be selected for more focused investigations. Hill and Hood (1999) compiled a large collection of religious measures developed for research purposes, many of which are appropriate for health research. More recently, Hill and Maltby (2009) identified measures of religion and spirituality related to well-being. The National Cancer Institute (NCI, 2010) also identified several measures for research on religion and health. To add religion and spirituality to a larger health study, the Duke University Religion Index (DUREL) is a simple five-item measure that taps several key dimensions (Koenig & Büssing, 2010). Developed for use in epidemiological studies, it can be easily incorporated into health research.

At the same time, scholars have developed a variety of tools for assessing religion and spirituality in clinical practice. This chapter provides a set of categories for such tools and discusses exemplars in each category. Tools for assessing spirituality in clinical practice can be categorized as brief screening tools, pictorial interview tools, and in-depth interviews. By including several tools in each category, this chapter enables practitioners to select an approach that fits client needs and priorities, and the practitioner's own preferences. These tools

may be included with a conventional intake procedure or used as part of a more thorough psychosocial assessment process.

Health social workers have several ways to address religious and spiritual concerns with patients. They can wait for patients to bring up spiritual concerns. They can routinely use brief paper-and-pencil assessment or oral screening tools with patients. Or they can use a spiritual inquiry or assessment to explicitly address these issues and indicate their openness to further discussion (NCI, 2010). These approaches have different strengths and weaknesses. Uncertain of how their social worker will respond, some patients may be reluctant or fearful to raise spiritual concerns on their own. Some may think it inappropriate to discuss their spiritual concerns with a social worker while others wish to do so. Some patients may be relieved to have their social worker indicate openness to address these issues. For these reasons, a brief routine inquiry may adequately signal practitioner interest and openness without putting undue pressure on the patient. As the NCI suggests,

> simply inquiring about an area such as religious or spiritual coping may be experienced by the patient as an opening for further exploration and validation of the importance of this experience. Evidence suggests that such an inquiry will be experienced as intrusive and distressing by only a very small proportion of patients. (NCI, 2010)

Brief Screening Tools

Several brief screening tools are available for use by health-care practitioners, including physicians, nurses, and social workers. Most provide an acronym to remind practitioners of the recommended questions or topics. For example, the HOPE questions (Anandarajah & Hight, 2001, p. 86) address:

H Sources of *h*ope, meaning, comfort, strength, peace, love, and connection

O *O*rganized religion

P *P*ersonal spirituality and *p*ractices

E *E*ffects on medical care and *e*nd-of-life issues

These few questions highlight the existential, social, and personal aspects of religion and spirituality and invite patients to comment on how these might be related to their medical care.

Similarly, another set of four questions for physicians focus on "the meaning and effect of spirituality in the patient's life and coping system" (Frick, Riedner, Fegg, Hauf, & Borasio, 2006, p. 238). The SPIR questions (p. 240) address:

S Would you describe yourself—in the broadest sense of the term—as a believing/spiritual/religious person?
P What is the place of spirituality in your life? How important is it in the context of your illness?
I Are you integrated in a spiritual community?
R What role would you like to assign to your doctor, nurse, or therapist in the domain of spirituality?

These questions emphasize patients' preferences regarding spiritual identity and its significance, their involvement with a spiritual community, and the role of health-care professionals in spirituality.

Yet another set of four questions may be the most widely used as a brief screening tool in health care (Puchalski, 2004; Puchalski & Romer, 2000). Puchalski's model uses the acronym FICA and provides specific questions to guide spiritual assessment (Pulchalski & Romer, 2000, p. 131):

F Faith and Belief: "Do you consider yourself spiritual or religious?" or "Do you have spiritual beliefs that help you cope with stress?" If the patient responds "No," the health-care provider might ask, "What gives your life meaning?" Sometimes patients respond with answers such as family, career, or nature.
I Importance: "What importance does your faith or belief have in our life? Have your beliefs influenced how you take care of yourself in this illness? What role do your beliefs play in regaining your health?"

C Community: "Are you part of a spiritual or religious community? Is this of support to you and how? Is there a group of people you really love or who are important to you?" Communities such as churches, temples, and mosques, or a group of like-minded friends can serve as strong support systems for some patients.
A Address in Care: "How would you like me, your health-care provider, to address these issues in your health care?"

Like previous models, FICA invites patients to: self-identify whether they are religious or spiritual and let health-care professionals know what terminology they prefer, indicate how important religion and spirituality is and how it may relate to their illness, identify their religious or spiritual communities as potential support networks for patients, and indicate their comfort with and preferences for health-care professionals to engage openly these matters. In short, the FICA helps health-care professionals determine what may be not only permissible but also desirable in their collaboration with patients.

Any of these brief screening tools elicit basic information about a patient's spirituality and provide a foundation for initiating the professional/patient relationship. Of course, professionals still must decide whether and how to use this information. If a health-care professional has reason to believe that religion and spirituality play a significant role in a patient's history, medical condition, or potential response to treatment, then she may decide to pursue additional information using one of the methods discussed next.

Pictorial Interview Tools

Although brief screening tools provide a good place to begin, they generally provide only limited information about religion and spirituality in patients' lives. To go further, social workers need additional, interview-based tools. Starting with assessment tools widely used in social work direct practice, Hodge (2005a) has adapted assessment tools for use in social work practice. Specifically, he has proposed several pictorial tools for supplementing verbal interviews regarding religion and spirituality, something that many patients will appreciate for disclosing sensitive religious and spiritual experiences.

Spiritual Life Maps

Hodge (2005a,c) proposed spiritual life maps as an alternative to exclusively verbal spiritual histories. Hodge (2005a) notes that life maps have several advantages for clinical practice: (a) They encourage an active role for clients in the assessment process; (b) they provide a respectful context for discussing potentially sensitive matters; (c) they may facilitate communication by less verbal clients and those for whom English is not the first language and provide a concrete focus for subsequent exploration; and (d) they help to make concrete what otherwise may seem amorphous and subjective, thus making it more readily available for intervention. Furthermore, construction of a life map may itself represent a form of intervention. The process of selecting and reflecting on past experience may promote insight and help patients to articulate things they have not understood previously, reinterpret or reframe themselves and their experience more positively, and generally encourage greater narrative coherence. Many of these advantages apply to other pictorial interview tools as well.

Constructing a spiritual life map simply requires a large sheet of paper and writing instruments. Along a line representing the client's life, the client can draw or paste pictures and write words representing key events and experiences that have spiritual significance. These events may be positive or negative, great or small, public or private. The process of constructing the life map serves as a trigger for memory and a focus for conversation in the clinical encounter. To encourage greater creativity, practitioners may provide color pencils or crayons, construction paper, magazines for cutting photos, scissors, and glue. They can continue clinical conversation while the patient works on the life map, inviting patients to talk about the events chosen for inclusion.

Although clients and practitioners may learn most from constructing life maps in a clinical session, they also can be assigned as homework and discussed in the next session. In either case, the life map provides a concrete point of reference to which practitioners may return in treatment (i.e., to discuss particular incidents, strengths, responses). Of several pictorial tools, spiritual life maps probably are least structured and, thus, most flexible and client directed.

Canda and Furman (2010) suggest spiritual development timelines, a similar tool that has slightly more structure than the life map. Their timelines also are designed to help clients tell the story of their lives; however, they assume a developmental process that brings some narrative coherence to the story. Their timelines include a horizontal axis that marks the passage of time and a vertical axis that represents developmental stages of spiritual consciousness.

Spiritual Genograms

Much as spiritual life maps focus on the life course of an individual patient, spiritual genograms frame the patient's life in its historical family context. Building on the traditional portrayal of family trees, family genograms capture additional qualitative information about family relationships and highlight family patterns over time (McGoldrick, Gerson, & Shellenberger, 1999). Going further, spiritual genograms emphasize the spiritual and religious aspects of family experience within and across generations (Frame, 2000; Hodge, 2001b, 2005a). Because genograms usually include information about three or more generations of a family system, they can illuminate the ways that religion and spirituality have both strengthened and disrupted family functioning. For example, genograms can help patients to recognize those members who have been key contributors to their spiritual socialization and support and how religion may relate to alliances and conflict in the family system, and can highlight patterns of continuity and change over time. They also may trigger memories of how family members used religion and spirituality to deal with illness positively.

As described by Hodge (2001b, 2005a), spiritual genograms resemble traditional genograms, except that they use additional symbols to represent religion and spirituality and specifically include information about religion and spirituality. For example, in addition to the traditional squares for males and circles for females, practitioners can use triangles to represent key religious figures from outside the family system. By using different colors for different religious traditions, they can highlight interfaith marriages and the multiplicity of religious backgrounds in an extended family. Likewise, they can use lines to reflect spiritual and religious bonds between individuals. They also include words and symbols to convey other important information about people, relationships, and events. See Hodge (2001b) and Frame (2000) for vignettes demonstrating use of a spiritual genogram and for possible interview questions to explore completed genograms more deeply.

Spiritual Ecomaps

In contrast to spiritual life maps and genograms, spiritual ecomaps emphasize patients' current ecological contexts rather than personal or relational histories. In short, they focus attention on religious and spiritual resources as well as relationships in which patients currently are involved. By doing so, ecomaps highlight and affirm what is already present and may clarify what is absent. Both types of information can be useful for intervention planning. As Hodge (2000) notes, patients who may be skeptical of exploring past relationships nevertheless may appreciate how current relationships influence their situations. Indeed, spiritual ecomaps fit well with the emphasis on relationships and social support prevalent in most religion traditions.

The ecomap was first developed by Hartman (1995) to depict a client's ecological context, for example, including connections with the extended family, work, school, and social services. Spiritual ecomaps essentially bring a focus on religious and spiritual aspects of this context. The ecomap consists of a central circle depicting the patient and patient's family with a series of additional circles arranged around the perimeter of the page. The surrounding circles are labeled to represent key elements in the patient's environment and then connected to the central circle with different types of lines to represent the nature of each relationship. For a spiritual ecomap, Hodge (2000) suggests these categories for the surrounding circles: God/transcendence, religious community, spiritual leader, transpersonal beings, ritual/practice, and religious traditions of patient's parents. He also discusses how the categories may be applied and provides a vignette to demonstrate use of the ecomap.

Spiritual Ecogram

Hodge (2005b) also describes the spiritual ecogram, a combination of the spiritual genogram and ecomap. The spiritual ecogram provides a dual focus on history and current context and thus helps patients and practitioners to recognize complex interactions. But this tool is also the most complex and time-consuming of the pictorial ones described here. For that reason, practitioners must decide whether its completion warrants the effort and time required. The spiritual ecogram can be constructed following guidelines already provided for both ecomaps and genograms.

In-Depth Interviews

In situations where religion and spirituality loom significant, it may be appropriate to conduct an in-depth interview focused on relevant aspects. Nelson-Becker, Nakashima, and Canda (2007) recommend beginning an interview on religion and spirituality with two prefatory questions:

1. Is spirituality, religion, or faith important in your life?
2. What terms do you prefer to talk about spirituality, religion, or faith? Please explain.

Such questions ensure that the social worker can use the patient's preferred language for discussing these issues.

Canda and Furman (2010) provide guidance for exploring the role of religion or spirituality in the lives of patients in depth. Although their interview suggestions are not specifically targeted to health-care settings, most are relevant to such practice environments. They distinguish among three types of spiritual assessment: implicit, brief explicit, and detailed explicit. For example, questions for implicit spiritual assessment include:

- What currently brings a sense of meaning and purpose to your life?
- Where do you go to find a sense of deep inspiration or peace?
- What are the important sources of strength and help for you in getting through times of difficulty or crisis?
- What are the deepest questions your situation raises for you? (p. 102)

For remembering their brief explicit spiritual assessment, Canda and Furman offer the acronym MIMBRA. This stands for: *m*eaning, *i*mportance, *m*embership, *b*eliefs, *r*elevance, and *a*ction. The corresponding questions are:

- What helps you to experience a deep sense of *meaning*, purpose, morality, hope, connection, joy, or peace in your life?
- Are spirituality, religion, or faith *important* to you? Please explain why or why not.
- Are you a *member* of any groups or communities (such as a religious group, support group, or cultural group) that give you a sense of belonging and help you find meaning and support in life? Please explain.
- Please describe any important *beliefs*, practices (such as prayer, meditation, rituals, or holistic therapies), or values that shape your understanding and response to your current situation.
- From what we discussed so far, what if anything is *relevant* to your current situation and your goals for our work together?
- Is there anything we discussed that you would like us to *act* on in our work together? For example, is there anything that has been helpful that we could apply or unhelpful that we should avoid or deal with? Are there close friends, relatives,

mentors, clergy, or spiritual teachers who I should be aware of or contact? Please explain. Thank you. (Canda & Furman, 2010, p. 267)

In an appendix, Canda and Furman (2010) provide a more complete set of interview questions organized in 10 categories:

1. Spiritual group membership and participation
2. Spiritual beliefs
3. Spiritual activities
4. Spiritual experiences and feelings
5. Moral and value issues
6. Spiritual development
7. Spiritual sources of support
8. Spiritual sources of transformation
9. Spiritual well-being
10. Extrinsic/intrinsic styles of spiritual propensity

Within these categories, they provide more than 50 questions. Depending on what seems important for a particular patient, a health social worker could select one or more of these categories for further exploration.

Nelson-Becker et al. (2007) identify a similar set of interview categories and provide a smaller set of questions for each category. But they also provide helpful vignettes to demonstrate how client responses to questions in each category may yield increased understanding of clients and their unique situations. For that reason, their article may be especially helpful for understanding the potential payoff of questions in particular categories. Although the vignettes portray older adults, social workers can use the interview questions with other populations as well.

Specifically formulated for oncology settings, the NCI (2009) recommends that spiritual assessment interviews with patients address these categories:

- Religious denomination, if any
- Beliefs or philosophy of life
- Important spiritual practices or rituals

- Using spirituality or religion as a source of strength
- Being part of a community of support
- Using prayer or meditation
- Loss of faith
- Conflicts between spiritual or religious beliefs and cancer treatments
- Ways that health-care providers and caregivers may help with the patient's spiritual needs
- Concerns about death and afterlife
- Planning for the end of life

No assessment approach will work with all patients (Hodge, 2005b). For this reason, it seems important that practitioners be familiar with several different assessment approaches, so they can choose the appropriate approach for individual patients. Beyond the choice of a brief screening tool or initial interview questions, the preferred assessment approach will require practitioner judgment regarding client preferences, areas of substantive importance, and time constraints.

APPROACHES TO INTERVENTION

Koenig and colleagues (2001) identify several ways in which health professionals can address or incorporate religion and spirituality in health care. As suggested, clinicians should assess the role of religion and spirituality in a patient's life. Besides gathering basic information that may guide treatment, doing so will communicate that the health professional is open to discussing religious and spiritual concerns. If a patient's religious beliefs and practices appear helpful, the professional may encourage or "support those that the *patient finds helpful*" (p. 441). It may be helpful to ensure that the patient has access to desired religious resources, ranging from religious reading or listening material to hospital chaplains. It may be even more helpful to ensure that patients have visits with clergy and other members of their religious communities. As a related

matter, health professionals should recognize chaplains or community religious leaders as part of the health-care teams, especially in hospitals, residential institutions, and hospice agencies. Health professionals also should be prepared to address spiritual concerns directly and substantively when chaplains or other clergy are unavailable. Finally, health professionals may wish to use spiritual interventions in particular situations with specific patients. But they must do so with caution. "Patients and situations should be carefully selected and the interventions highly individualized to fit the patient's religious background and spiritual need" (Koenig et al., 2001, p. 443).

Potential Spiritual Interventions

Besides these efforts to incorporate spiritual concerns of clients in health care, there is an emerging category of explicitly religious or spiritual therapies. In a recent article, Hook et al. (2010) conducted a systematic review of studies reporting on empirically supported and explicitly religious and spiritual therapies. The criteria for inclusion in the study specified mental health interventions for direct practice with individuals or groups and excluded medical interventions or religious interventions outside a therapy context. Further, the review included only those interventions that explicitly integrate religion or spirituality, thus excluding many interventions that have a basis in spirituality (i.e., mindfulness). Finally, the review included only randomized clinical trials. A total of 24 studies met these selection criteria. The studies included treatments for depression (8 studies), anxiety (6), unwillingness to forgive (3), eating disorders (2), schizophrenia (1), alcoholism (1), anger (1), and marital issues (1). The religions represented were Christianity (10 studies), Islam (7), Taoism (1), Buddhism (1), and a generic spirituality (5). Most of the interventions consisted of a religious or spiritual add-on to standard secular interventions.

Several of the treatments were found to be beneficial for clients, with gains maintained at follow-up. One study found that religious therapy was effective for highly religious clients but no more effective than secular alternatives for other clients. Given the generally positive findings but small number of studies, the authors suggest that selecting religious or spiritual therapies may be primarily a matter of client preference or therapist comfort. The authors conclude with a call for more research on these therapies.

CONCLUSIONS

In an article on religion, aging, and health, Krause (2004) makes three general observations that seem relevant here as well.

1. The associations between religion and health are imperfect. Religion appears to have some benefits, but not for everyone or for all conditions. Given the multidimensional nature of religion and spirituality, we need to know much more about the specific relationships between health and religion.

2. It is important to remember that everyone dies, including those who are religious or spiritual, and most people become ill before they die. That means there are obvious limits to any benefits of religion.

3. "[S]ome (but not all) deeply religious people strongly believe that religion should not be pursued for the purpose of improving one's health" (Krause, 2004, p. 1220). In other words, an instrumental focus on the health benefits of religion and spirituality may lead to extrinsic rather than intrinsic religion, undermining the essential and primary purposes of religion and spirituality.

SUGGESTED LEARNING EXERCISES

Learning Exercise 11.1

The Association for Religion Data Archives (n.d.) provides a fascinating, easy-to-use tool for understanding religious diversity in

the United States. Using a Graphic Information System (GIS), it maps population statistics by zip code for the years 1980, 1990, and 2000. For example, it reports percentages of the population by major religious groups (Catholic, mainline Protestant, evangelical Protestant, Jewish, Muslim, Orthodox) as well as by more than 130 specific denominations (e.g., Baha'i, Roman Catholic, Presbyterian Church, Southern Baptist, Unitarian Universalist Association). In small groups or pairs, spend some time with its online GIS resource to learn about religious affiliation in the area where you live or work. Discuss how this resource may be helpful to health social workers in settings in which social workers collaborate with a team to help individuals *and* those in which social workers work with a community, neighborhood, and other organizations.

Learning Exercise 11.2

The Pluralism Project at Harvard (Eck, 2010) provides an introduction to numerous religious traditions present in the United States. Among other things, this Web site includes extensive information organized by either state or religious tradition. Individually, read about one spiritual tradition with which you are unfamiliar. In small or large groups, share the information you learned from this project, and discuss how this information can help health social workers intervene on both an individual patient level and a community/organization level.

Learning Exercise 11.3

To learn more about spiritual assessment and how to use one brief screening tool, go to the George Washington Institute on Spirituality and Health Web site (www.gwish.org/). It offers a free, multimedia training module, *Spiritual Assessment in Clinical Practice*, for "assessing the spiritual beliefs, values, and practices important in your patients' responses to illness or stress." The course provides detailed information about how to use the FICA, one of the tools mentioned in this chapter. Using this module and tool, role-play a spiritual assessment with a partner.

Learning Exercise 11.4

For additional resources on spiritual assessment in health care, browse the Spirituality and Health Online Education and Resource Center (SOERCE). Funded by the John Templeton Foundation, "SOERCE aims to be the premiere online location for educational and clinical resources in the fields of spirituality, religion, and health." It is available at www.gwumc.edu /gwish/soerce/. The Web site includes articles; assessment tools; case studies; teaching modules, methods, or exercises; guides, handbooks, and manuals; video or audio presentations; and patient or caregiver educational materials.

Learning Exercise 11.5

For in-depth group discussion, facilitators may select cases from *Spirituality and Religion in Social Work Practice: Decision Cases for Social Work Practice*, a casebook published by the Council on Social Work Education. All of the open-ended decision cases in this collection were based on interviews with actual social workers, and most come from health-care settings.

SUGGESTED RESOURCES

Print

Canda, E. R., & Furman, L. D. (2010). *Spiritual diversity in social work practice: The heart of helping*. New York, NY: Oxford University Press.

Fetzer Institute/National Institute of Aging. (1999). *Multidimensional measurement of religiousness/spirituality for use in health research*. Kalamazoo, MI: Fetzer Institute.

Hill, P. C., & Hood, R. W., Jr. (1999). *Measures of religiosity*. Birmingham, AL: Religious Education Press.

Koenig, H. G. (2007). *Spirituality in patient care: Why, how, when, and what* (2nd ed.). West Conshohocken, PA: Templeton Foundation Press.

Koenig, H. G. (2008). *Medicine, religion, and health: Where science and spirituality meet*. West Conshohocken, PA: Templeton Foundation Press.

Koenig, H. G., King, D. E., & Carson, V. B. (2011). *Handbook of religion and health* (2nd ed.). New York, NY: Oxford University Press.

Koenig, H. G., McCullough, M. E., & Larson, D. B. (2001). *Handbook of religion and health*. New York, NY: Oxford University Press.

Krause, N. M. (2008). *Aging in the church: How social relationships affect health*. West Conshohocken, PA: Templeton Foundation Press.

Pargament, K. I. (1997). *The psychology of religion and coping: Theory, research, practice*. New York, NY: Guilford Press.

Pargament, K. I., Exline, J. J., & Jones, J. (Eds.). (Forthcoming). *APA handbook of psychology, religion and spirituality* (Vol. 1). Washington, DC: American Psychological Association.

Puchalski, C. M., & Ferrell, B. (2010). *Making health care whole: Integrating spirituality into patient care*. West Conshohocken, PA: Templeton Press.

Richards, P. S., & Bergin, A. E. (Eds.). (1999). *Handbook of psychotherapy and religious diversity*. Washington, DC: American Psychological Association.

Online

Barnes, L. L. (2010). Boston Healing Landscape Project: A program for the study of cultural, therapeutic and religious pluralism. Available at www.bu.edu/bhlp/

Center for Spiritual Development in Childhood and Adolescence, Search Institute. (2010). Spirituality measures. Available at www.spiritualdevelopmentcenter.org /Display.asp?Page=measure2#intrinsic

Center for Spirituality and Healing, University of Minnesota. (2003). Spirituality in health care. Available at www.csh.umn .edu/modules/spirituality/index.html

Center for Spirituality, Theology and Health, Duke University. (2007). Center for Spirituality, Theology and Health. Available at www.spiritualityandhealth.duke.edu/index.html

Eck, D. (2010). The Pluralism Project at Harvard University. Available at http://pluralism.org

Ehman, J. (2009). Spiritual assessment and health care: A select bibliography of Medline-indexed articles published 2001–2009. Available at www.uphs.upenn.edu/pastoral/cpe/Res_Bib_Spiritual_Asessment_MEDLINE_2009.pdf

George Washington Institute for Spirituality & Health. (n.d.). Spirituality and Health Online Education and Resource Center (SOERCE). Available at www.gwumc.edu/gwish/soerce/

George Washington Institute on Spirituality and Health. (n.d.). Spiritual assessment in clinical practice. Available at: www.gwish.org

Harrington, A. (2009). Health and spirituality. Available at http://nccam.nih.gov/training/videolectures/spirituality.htm

National Cancer Institute: PDQ®. (2010). Spirituality in cancer care [Professional version]. Bethesda, MD: National Cancer Institute. Available at www.cancer.gov/cancertopics/pdq/supportivecare/spirituality/HealthProfessional

Free online course from National Center for Complementary and Alternative Medicine, National Institutes of Health.

Maloof, P. S. (n.d.). Body/mind/spirit: Toward a biopsychosocial-spiritual model of health. Available at http://nccc.georgetown.edu/body_mind_spirit/

Pew Forum on Religion and Public Life. (2008). U.S. religious landscape survey. Religious affiliation: Diverse and dynamic. Washington, DC: Author. Available at http://religions.pewforum.org/pdf/report-religious-landscape-study-full.pdf

Pew Forum on Religion and Public Life. (2009). How religious is your state? Available at http://pewforum.org/How-Religious-Is-Your-State-.aspx

REFERENCES

Anandarajah, G., & Hight, E. (2001). Spirituality and medical practice: Using the HOPE questions as a practical tool for spiritual assessment. *American Family Physician, 63*(1), 81–88.

Association of Religion Data Archives [ARDA]. (n.d.). Quickstats. Available at www.thearda.com/quickstats/

Barnes, L., & Harris, G. (2001, November/December). A changing medical landscape: Religious pluralism and competent care. *The Park Ridge Center Bulletin,* 7–8.

Benjamins, M. R., & Brown, C. (2004). Religion and preventative health care utilization among the elderly. *Social Science & Medicine, 58,* 109–118.

Bresnahan, M. J., & Mahler, K. (2010). Ethical debate over organ donation in the context of brain death. *Bioethics, 24*(2), 54–60.

Campbell, M. K., Hudson, M. A., Resnicow, K., Blakeney, N., Paxton, A., & Baskin, M. (2007). Church-based health promotion interventions: Evidence and lessons learned. *Annual Review of Public Health, 28,* 213–234.

Canda, E. R., & Furman, L. D. (2010). *Spiritual diversity in social work practice: The heart of helping.* New York, NY: Oxford University Press.

Centers for Disease Control and Prevention [CDC]. (2010). Diseases & conditions. Available at http://www.cdc.gov/DiseasesConditions/.

Cloninger, C. R. (2006). The science of well-being: An integrated approach to mental health and its disorders. *World Psychiatry, 5*(2), 71–76.

Curlin, F. A., Lawrence, R. E., Chin, M. H., & Lantos, J. D. (2007). Religion, conscience, and controversial clinical practices. *New England Journal of Medicine, 356*(6), 593–600.

Dalmida, S. G., Holstad, M. M., Dilorio, C., & Laderman, G. (2009). Spiritual well-being, depressive symptoms, and immune status among women living with HIV/AIDS. *Women Health, 49*(2–3), 119–143.

D'Souza, R. (2007). The importance of spirituality in medicine and its application to clinical practice. *Medical Journal of Australia, 186*(10), S57–S59.

Duru, O. K., Sarkisian, C. A., Leng, M., & Mangione, C. M. (2010). Sisters in motion: A randomized controlled trial of a faith-based physical activity intervention. *Journal of the American Geriatrics Society, 58*(10), 1863–1869.

Eck, D. (2001). *A new religious America: How a "Christian country" has become the world's most religiously diverse nation.* New York, NY: HarperCollins.

Eck, D. (2010). The Pluralism Project at Harvard University. Retrieved from http://pluralism.org/index.php

Eckersley, R. M. (2007). Culture, spirituality, religion and health: Looking at the big picture. *Medical Journal of Australia, 186*(10), S54–S56.

Enright, R. D., & Coyle, C. T. (1998). Researching the process model of forgiveness within psychological interventions. In *Dimensions of Forgiveness: Psychological Research & Theological Forgiveness.* E. L. Worthington, (Ed.), pp. 139–161. Philadelphia, PA: Templeton Foundation Press.

Fetzer Institute/National Institute of Aging. (1999). *Multidimensional measurement of religiousness/ spirituality for use in health research.* Kalamazoo, MI: Fetzer Institute.

Frame, M. W. (2000). The spiritual genogram in family therapy. *Journal of Marriage and Family Therapy, 26*(2), 211–216.

Frick, E., Riedner, C., Fegg, M., Hauf, S., & Borasio, G. D. (2006). A clinical interview assessing cancer patients' spiritual needs and preferences. *European Journal of Cancer Care, 15,* 238–243.

Gaustad, E. S. (1968). America's institutions of faith. In D. R. Cutler (Ed.), *The religious situation: 1968* (pp. 835–870). Boston, MA: Beacon Press.

Gearing, R. E., & Lizardi, D. (2009). Religion and suicide. *Journal of Religion and Health, 48*(3), 332–341.

George, L. K., Ellison, C. G., & Larson, D. B. (2002). Explaining the relationships between religious involvement and health. *Psychological Inquiry, 13*(3), 190–200.

George, L. K., Larson, D. B., Koenig, H. G., & McCullough, M. E. (2000). Spirituality and health: What we know, what we need to know. *Journal of Social and Clinical Psychology, 19*(1), 102–116.

Geyer, A. L., & Baumeister, R. F. (2005). Religion, morality, and self-control: Values, virtues, and vices. In R. F. Paloutzian & C. L. Park (Eds.), *Handbook of the Psychology of Religion and Spirituality* (pp. 412–432). New York, NY: Guilford Press.

Griffith, D. M., Allen, J. O., DeLoney, E. H., Robinson, K., Lewis. E. Y., Campbell, B.,…Reischl, T. (2010). Community-based organizational capacity building as a strategy to reduce racial health disparities. *Journal of Primary Prevention, 31,* 31–39.

Hartman, A. (1995). Diagrammatic assessment of family relationships. *Families in Society, 76,* 111–122.

Hall, D. E., Meador, K. G., & Koenig, H. G. (2008). Measuring religiousness in health research: Review and critique. *Journal of Religion and Health, 47*(2), 134–163.

Hill, P. C., Pargament, K. I., Swyers, J. P., Gorsuch, R. L., McCullough, M. E., Hood, R. W.,…Baumeister, R. F. (1998). Definitions of religion and spirituality. In D. B. Larson, J. P. Swyers, & M. E. McCullough (Eds.), *Scientific research on spirituality and health: A consensus report* (pp. 14–30). Rockville, MD: National Institute of Healthcare Research.

Hill, P. C., & Hood, R. W., Jr. (1999). *Measures of religiosity.* Birmingham, AL: Religious Education Press.

Hill, P. C., & Maltby, L. E. (2009). Measuring religiousness and spirituality: Issues, existing measures, and the implications for education and wellbeing. In M. de Souza, L. J. Francis, J. O'Higgins-Norman, & D. Scott (Eds.), *International handbook of education for spirituality, care and wellbeing* (Vol. 3, pp. 33–50). New York, NY: Springer.

Hodge, D. R. (2000). Spiritual ecomaps: A new diagrammatic tool for assessing marital and family spirituality. *Journal of Marital and Family Therapy, 26*(2), 217–228.

Hodge, D. R. (2001a). Spiritual assessment: A review of major qualitative methods and a new framework for assessing spirituality. *Social Work, 46*(3), 203–214.

Hodge, D. R. (2001b). Spiritual genograms: A generational approach to assessing spirituality. *Families in Society: Journal of Contemporary Social Services, 82*(1), 35–48.

Hodge, D. R. (2005a). Developing a spiritual assessment toolbox: A discussion of the strengths and limitations of five different assessment methods. *Health & Social Work, 30*(4), 314–323.

Hodge, D. R. (2005b). Spiritual ecograms: A new assessment instrument for identifying clients' spiritual strengths in space and across time. *Families in Society, 86*(2), 287–296.

Hodge, D. R. (2005c). Spiritual lifemaps: A client-centered pictorial instrument for spiritual assessment, planning, and intervention. *Social Work, 50*(1), 77–87.

Hodge, D. R. (2006). A template for spiritual assessment: A review of the JCAHO requirements and guidelines for implementation. *Social Work, 51*(4), 317–326.

Hood, R. W., Jr., Hill, P. C., & Spilka, B. (2009). Religion, health, psychopathology, and coping. In K. I. Pargament (Ed.), *The psychology of religion: An empirical approach* (4th ed., pp. 435–476). New York, NY: Guilford Press.

Hook, J. N., Worthington, E. L., Jr., Davis, D. E., Jennings, D. J., II, Gartner, A. L., & Hook, J. P. (2010). Empirically supported religious and spiritual therapies. *Journal of Clinical Psychology, 66*(1), 46–72.

Hufford, D. J. (2005). *An analysis of the field of spirituality, religion and health (S/RH).* Retrieved from www .templetonadvancedresearchprogram.com/pdf/TARP -Hufford.pdf

Jennette, C., Vupputuri, S., Hogan, S. L., Falk, R. J., & Harward, D. H. (2010). Community perspectives on kidney disease and health promotion from at-risk populations in rural North Carolina, USA. *Rural and Remote Health, 10,* 1388.

King, M. B., & Hunt, R. A. (1972). Measuring the religious variable: National replication. *Journal for the Scientific Study of Religion, 14*(1), 13–22.

Koenig, H. G. (2008). *Medicine, religion, and health: Where science and spirituality meet.* West Conshohocken, PA: Templeton Foundation Press.

Koenig, H. G., & Büssing, A. (2010). The Duke University Religion Index (DUREL): A five-item measure for use in epidemological studies. *Religions, 1*(1), 78–85.

Koenig, H. G., & Larson, D. B. (2001). Religion and mental health: Evidence for an association. *International Review of Psychiatry, 13*, 67–78.

Koenig, H. G., McCullough, M. E., & Larson, D. B. (2001). *Handbook of religion and health*. New York, NY: Oxford University Press.

Koenig, H. G., McCullough, M. E., & Larson, D. B. (2011). *Handbook of religion and health, 2nd Edition*. New York, NY: Oxford University Press.

Krause, N. (2004). Religion, aging and health: Exploring new frontiers in medical care. *Southern Medical Journal, 97*(12), 1215–1222.

Krause, N. M. (2008). *Aging in the church: How social relationships affect health*. West Conshohocken, PA: Templeton Foundation Press.

Larson, D. B., Swyers, J. P., & McCullough, M. E. (Eds.). (1998). *Scientific research on spirituality and health: A consensus report*. Rockville, MD: National Institute of Health care Research.

Levin, J. S. (2009). How faith heals: A theoretical model. *Explore, 5*(2), 77–95.

Levin, J. S., & Markides, K. S. (1986). Religious attendance and subjective health. *Journal for the Scientific Study of Religion, 25*(1), 31–40.

Lizardi, D., & Gearing, R. E. (2010). Religion and suicide: Buddhism, Native American and African religions, atheism, and agnostism. *Journal of Religion and Health, 49*(3), 377–384.

Maselko, J., Kubzansky, L., Kawachi, I., Seeman, T., & Berkman, L. (2007). Religious service attendance and allostatic load among high-functioning elderly. *Psychosomatic Medicine, 69*, 464–472.

Mayes, S. (2010, January 9). Oregon City trial raises new questions in faith-healing debate. *The Oregonian*.

McCullough, M. E., Bono, G., & Root, L. M. (2005). Religion and forgiveness. In R. F. Paloutzian & C. L. Park (Eds.), *Handbook of the psychology of religion and spirituality* (pp. 394–411). New York, NY: Guilford Press.

McGoldrick, M., Gerson, R., & Shellenberger, S. (1999). *Genograms: Assessment and intervention* (2nd ed.). New York, NY: Norton.

Moreira-Almeida, A. (2007). Spirituality and health: Past and future of a controversial and challenging relationship. *Revista de Psiquiatria Clinica, 34*(S1), 3–4.

National Association of Social Workers. (2001). *NASW Standards for cultural competence in social work practice*. Washington, DC: Author. Available at www.socialworkers.org/practice/standards/NASW CulturalStandards.pdf

National Association of Social Workers. (2003). *NASW Standards for social work in long-term care facilities*. Washington, DC: Author. Available at www.socialworkers.org/practice/standards/NASW LongTermStandards.pdf

National Association of Social Workers. (2005a). *NASW Standards for social work practice with clients with substance use disorders*. Washington, DC: Author. Available at www.socialworkers.org/practice/standards /NASWATODStatndards.pdf

National Association of Social Workers. (2005b). *NASW Standards for social work practice in health care settings*. Washington, DC: Author. Available at www.socialworkers.org/practice/standards/NASW HealthCareStandards.pdf

National Association of Social Workers. (2007). *Indicators for the achievement of the NASW Standards for cultural competence in social work practice*. Washington, DC: Author. Available at www.socialworkers.org/practice /standards/NASWCulturalStandardsIndicators2006 .pdf

National Cancer Institute. (2009). *Spirituality in cancer care (PDQ®): Health professional version*. Bethesda, MD: National Cancer Institute. Retrieved from http://cancer.gov/cancertopics/pdq/supportivecare /spirituality/HealthProfessional

National Cancer Institute. (2010). *Spirituality in cancer care (PDQ®): Health professional version*. Retrieved from www.cancer.gov/cancertopics/pdq /supportivecare/spirituality/HealthProfessional /allpages

Nelson Becker, H., Nakashima, M., & Canda, E. R. (2007). Spiritual assessment in aging: A framework for clinicians. *Journal of Gerontological Social Work, 2*(3/4), 331–347.

Oman, D., & Thoreson, C. E. (2005). Do religion and spirituality influence health? In R. F. Paloutzian & C. L. Park (Eds.), *Handbook of the psychology of religion and spirituality* (pp. 435–459). New York, NY: Guilford Press.

Pargament, K. I. (1997). *The psychology of religion and coping: Theory, research, practice*. New York, NY: Guilford Press.

Park, C. L. (2007). Religiousness/spirituality and health: A meaning systems perspective. *Journal of Behavioral Health, 30*, 319–328.

Pew Forum on Religion and Public Life. (2009). How religious is your state? Retrieved from http:// pewforum.org/How-Religious-Is-Your-State-.aspx

Pond, A., Smith, G., & Clement, S. (2010). *Religion among the Millennials: Less religiously active than older Americans, but fairly traditional in other ways*. Washington, DC: Pew Forum on Religion & Public Life. Available at: http://pewforum.org /docs/?DocID=510

Powell, L. H., Shahabi, L., & Thoreson, C. E. (2003). Religion and spirituality: Linkages to physical health. *American Psychologist, 58*(1), 36–52.

Puchalski, C. M. (2001). The role of spirituality in health care. *Baylor University Medical Center Proceedings, 14*(4), 352–357.

Puchalski, C. M. (2004). A conversation with Dr. Christina Puchalski. *Spirituality and Health International, 5*(2), 82–87.

Puchalski, C., & Romer, A. L. (2000). Taking a spiritual history allows clinicians to understand patients more fully. *Journal of Palliative Medicine, 3*(1), 129–137.

Qaseem, A., Snow, V., Shekelle, P., Casey, D. E., Jr., Cross, J. T., Jr., & Owens, D. (2008). Evidence-based interventions to improve the palliative care of pain, dyspnea, and depression at the end of life: A clinical practice guideline from the American College of Physicians. *Annals of Internal Medicine, 148,* 141–146.

Röcklinsberg, H. (2009). The complex use of religion in decisions on organ transplantation. *Journal of Religion and Health, 48*(1), 62–78.

Royal College of Psychiatrists. (2010). Spirituality and mental health. Retrieved from http://www.rcpsych .ac.uk/mentalhealthinfo/treatments/spirituality.aspx

Scott, A. B. (1997). Categorizing definitions of religion and spirituality in the psychological literature: A content analytic approach. Unpublished Manuscript.

Smith, T. W. (2002). Religious diversity in America: The emergence of Muslims, Buddhists, Hindus, and others [GSS Social Change Report No. 4]. Chicago, IL: National Opinion Research Center. Retrieved from http://publicdata.norc.org:41000/gss/DOCUMENTS /REPORTS/Social_Change_Reports/SC47.pdf

Smith, T. W. (2009). *Religious change around the world* [Report for the Templeton Foundation]. Chicago, IL: National Opinion Research Center/University of Chicago. Available at: http://news.uchicago.edu/files /religionsurvey_20091023.pdf

Substance Abuse and Mental Health Services Administration. (2006). National consensus statement on mental health recovery. Retrieved from http://store .samhsa.gov/shin/content//SMA05–4129/SMA05 –4129.pdf

Veenhoven, R. (2003). *Findings on happiness & religion* [World Database on Happiness]. Retrieved from http:// publishing.eur.nl/ir/repub/asset/655/Religion.pdf

World Health Organization. (1998). *WHOQOL and spirituality, religiousness and personal beliefs: Report on WHO consultation*. Geneva, Switzerland: Author.

WHOQOL SRPB Group. (2006). A cross-cultural study of spirituality, religion, and personal beliefs as components of quality of life. *Social Science & Medicine, 62*(6), 1486–1497.

12

Developing a Shared Understanding: When Medical Patients Use Complementary and Alternative Approaches

PENNY B. BLOCK

The use of alternative medicine in this country represents neither a passing trend nor a marginal sociological phenomenon. National surveys conducted in the 1990s trumpeted the substantial and escalating use of alternative treatments among Americans but profiled the typical user of such care by drawing from a limited population sampling, thus misidentifying the adults who seek such therapies as primarily White, middle-age females with higher education and income (Astin, 1998b; Eisenberg et al., 1993, 1998). A later corrective report that relied on data representative of wider demographics came up with a different conclusion: Use of at least one alternative therapy was prevalent across all ethnic groups, income levels, and age ranges (MacKenzie, Taylor, Bloom, Hufford, & Johnson, 2003). Only the patterns of preferred healing modalities varied among different ethnic groups; these findings were echoed by comparable conclusions from a later analysis (Hsiao et al., 2006). To be truly effective in our professional role with ethnically and socially diverse clients and to respond with genuine respect and helpful sensitivity to individuals from many cultural backgrounds presenting in a medical setting, it is essential to reach beyond our own predominantly biomedical backgrounds and augment our understanding of divergent health philosophies and practices. Knowing about and demonstrating regard for nonconventional modalities that are important to clients is a precondition to developing confidence, trust, and mutual respect. Doing so should help engage clients and patients in the cooperative planning of their treatment strategy by bridging conventional thinking with individual health beliefs and strengthen therapeutic alliances that enhance adherence to comprehensive and individually meaningful medical treatments. Moreover, when informed about beneficial synergies or problematic interactions among therapies, social workers can coordinate services for optimal health care more completely.

Chapter Objectives
- Learn about the patterns and prevalence of alternative and complementary use among different populations.
- Distinguish alternative, complementary, and integrative categories.
- Discuss divergent health models and therapies grouped under the alternative umbrella.
- Understand the rationale for use of alternative therapies, examples of supporting research, and effective applications.
- Learn about potentials for engaging clients in an open discussion about their personal health practices.
- Identify appropriate applications of mind–body strategies as stress-mitigating tools.
- Provide resources for more detailed information and evaluation of nonallopathic therapies.

ALTERNATIVE AND COMPLEMENTARY PRACTICES IN THE UNITED STATES

Although some experts have predicted that the popularity of unconventional practices might fade, increasing numbers of Americans are seeking health treatments outside modern Western medicine. Adults across the United States schedule more sessions with nonconventional providers (600 million annually) than medical visits with physicians. In the 1998 follow-up to their eye-opening 1993 report, Eisenberg and colleagues documented a 25% increase in the use of alternatives among Americans, expanding from 33% in 1990 to 42.1% in 1997. During this same time period, the number of estimated annual visits to unconventional practitioners swelled from 427 million to 629 million, an upsurge of 47.3%, or a projected 243 million more visits than to all U.S. primary care physicians that same year. This escalating trend continued so that by 2002, national surveys indicated that 74.6% of U.S. adults had used at least one form of complementary and alternative medicine (CAM) (Barnes, Powell-Griner, McFann, & Nahin, 2004). The concomitant financial outlay had become substantial. Reflecting only data from 1997, those Americans using alternative care were spending approximately $27 billion, which was not reimbursed, on unconventional therapies—up 45.2% from 1990, a total that slightly exceeded out-of-pocket expenditures on total physician services (Eisenberg et al., 1998). Later surveys revealed that 33.9 billion out-of-pocket dollars had been spent by U.S. adults for CAM treatments during the preceding 12 months alone (Nahin, Barnes, Stussman, & Bloom, 2009). In a sample of 453 patients with different cancer diagnoses, 69% reported using at least one type of nonstandard practice or product within the preceding year (Sparber et al., 2000). Variant rates appear in the records for pediatric use, with some surveys showing approximately 21% of parents treating their children with alternative or complementary practices but seeking unconventional

modalities for 73% of children diagnosed with cancer (Noonan, 2002).

Represented in these surveys were a range of relaxation techniques, herbal treatments, massage therapies, chiropractic practices, spiritual healing, megavitamins, self-help groups, imagery, dietary plans and other lifestyle programs, folk remedies, energy healing, homeopathy, hypnosis, biofeedback, and acupuncture (Eisenberg et al., 1998). Although biofeedback, hypnosis, guided imagery, relaxation techniques, lifestyle, diet, and vitamin supplementation fall closer to conventional medicine on a continuum (i.e., seem more readily accepted by mainstream medicine for specific chronic conditions), these therapies accounted for less than 10% of alternative practitioner visits (Eisenberg et al., 1998). What usually propels people toward modalities outside the conventional armamentarium are chronic disorders unrelieved by allopathic methods (e.g., back problems, allergies, fatigue, arthritis, headaches, neck problems, high blood pressure, insomnia, skin problems, digestive difficulties, depression, anxiety), but unremitting back pain or annoying allergies top the list as the disorders most commonly treated with unconventional techniques (Eskinazi, 1998).

These combined data reflect a consumer-driven revolution in the health-care system that seems to be gaining momentum—not a simple fascination with exotic practices or passing fad but a manifestation of the growing public demand for a broader medical armamentarium than the more limited inventory in the conventional medicine cabinet. In response to rather startling survey data and certain political pressures, a 1998 congressional mandate led the National Institutes of Health (NIH) to redesign its Office of Alternative Medicine to the National Center for Complementary and Alternative Medicine (NCCAM) with a budget that grew from an initial $2 million (1992 total) to more than $100 million allocated to research the efficacy and safety of alternative treatments and to develop a public clearinghouse of information (Goldberg, Anderson, & Trivieri, 2002). Federal appropriations for NCCAM grants continued to expand gradually so that by 2010, they had reached $125,471,000, representing an increase of 2.7% over what had been allocated in 2009.

Even with a surge in patient use of nonconventional therapies in conjunction with a continuation of conventional treatments, only a small proportion of patients actually divulged or discussed their use of these alternatives with their medical doctor. The 1998 report revealed that 1 in 3 adults consulting a conventional doctor for a serious condition simultaneously utilized an alternative therapy, but less than 40% of those patients ever mentioned such therapies to their physicians; specifically, 39.8% of alternative therapies were disclosed to physician in 1990, with a slight downward trend to 38.5% in 1997 (see Table 12.1). A follow-up 2008 paper emphasized that as many as 72% of Americans never revealed their use of CAM therapies. The authors of this study emphasized that the percentage of disclosure was estimated to be substantially lower among racial/ethnic minorities (Chao, Wade, & Kronenberg, 2008). What is perhaps even more problematic is a 1994 assessment that indicated that 83% of those diagnosed with a serious medical condition combined unconventional along with conventional treatment but often did so surreptitiously—that is, 72% of these patients withheld this information from their doctor (Brown, Cassileth, Lewis, & Renner, 1994). Believing that their primary care physician would not be interested or approve and thus would dismiss CAM practices summarily, or feeling too embarrassed and deeming their traditional or alternative practices irrelevant to medical dialogue, many patients will not broach the subject in medical consultations (Brown et al., 1994; Richardson, Sanders, Palmer, Greisinger, & Singletary, 2000). Chao and colleagues (2008) found that most patients would discuss their nonconventional practices more readily and openly if they perceived this discussion would be acceptable to their physicians. Disclosure of CAM utilization might well affect treatment outcomes by virtue of physicians being biased against complementary and alternative practices.

Accompanying this picture of nondisclosure and contributing to legitimate medical

Table 12.1   Reasons for Nondisclosure of Complementary Therapies Utilization

Not important for doctor to know	61%
Doctor never asked	60%
None of doctor's business	31%
Doctor wouldn't understand	20%
Doctor would disapprove or discourage use of alternatives	14%

Source: From "Perceptions about Complementary Therapies Relative to Conventional Therapies Among Adults Who Use Both: Results from a National Survey," by D. M. Eisenberg et al., 2001, *Annals of Internal Medicine, 135*(5), 344–351.

worry are statistics showing soaring herbal use. The percentage of Americans taking herbal remedies almost quadrupled in 1998–2008, and growth in high-dose vitamin supplementation has surged 130%, which Sullivan (2000) speculates places an estimated 15 million adults taking prescription medicines concurrently with supplemental agents at risk for possible adverse interactions. Specific supplements possibly could produce drug-action inhibition, substantial interference with efficacy, or magnification of the bioavailability of certain pharmaceuticals, resulting in serious complications that demand attention. Too often, contraindicated practices remain unknown and unaccounted for in the medical setting. It is here, at the nexus of alternative use and medical implications, that the social worker, intervening on behalf of the patient as liaison/coordinating presence with the medical provider, is so critical to the larger health needs of individual clients.

ALTERNATIVE USE AMONG ETHNIC MINORITIES

One finding echoed in several surveys but inconsistent with expectations is that alternative use is uncommon among ethnic minorities. Although Eisenberg and colleagues' data (1993, 1998) described the typical CAM user as White, female, and of higher educational and socioeconomic status (SES), this description belies what we know from ethnomedicine and is contradicted by data in medical anthropology research (Barnes et al., 2004; Becerra & Iglehart, 1995; Hsiao et al., 2006; MacKenzie et al., 2003; Ni, Simile, & Hardy, 2002) and experience with populations using traditional healing techniques (Culliton & Kiresuk, 1996). The Eisenberg teams acknowledged that their database was neither sufficiently large nor adequately inclusive of different ethnicities to reflect minority use (MacKenzie et al., 2003). Even though the Eisenberg team (1998) reported that the typical users of CAM—48% of those surveyed—were in a higher income bracket (with an annual income of $50,000 or more), their data revealed that 43% of those utilizing CAM interventions were in the lowest income bracket (earning less than $20,000 annually). In addition, the three earlier national surveys of CAM trends (Astin, 1998a; Eisenberg et al., 1993, 1998) were conducted only in English, whereas MacKenzie and colleagues' 2003 data relied on surveys conducted in multiple languages (e.g., Spanish, Mandarin, Cantonese, Vietnamese, Korean). Analyzing the 1995 National Comparative Survey of Minority Health Care, the MacKenzie team found that use of nonstandard approaches did not differ by ethnicity; 43.1% of adults surveyed used at least one such therapy with no statistically significant difference in percentage of use among African Americans, Hispanic Americans, Asian Americans, Native Americans, and non-Hispanic Whites. With their analysis, they concluded that earlier prevalence studies that reported that CAM practices were not medically significant among ethnic minorities, and especially among lower-SES populations, were as a result inaccurate. Only preferences for specific alternatives—categorized as herbal medicines, acupuncture, chiropractic, traditional healer, and home remedies—were found to vary among ethnic populations (e.g., using herbal formulations was more common or popular among Asian and Native Americans, whereas White Americans were found to use chiropractic services more frequently). Even with MacKenzie and colleagues' recharacterization of CAM demographics, surveys may be prone to underestimation because some

cultural traditions consider home remedies such as special foods, botanicals, herbals, and spices as the norm and thus do not report them as "alternative" (Committee on the Use of Complementary and Alternative Medicine by the American Public, 2005).

The MacKenzie investigation clearly asserts that aggregate statistics of alternative and complementary use, ignoring divergent modalities, obscure actual usage among different minorities. For data to mirror the true profile of users, surveys must distinguish divergent practices lumped summarily under the CAM umbrella (see Table 12.2).

CAM use, they conclude, does not belong to any single demographic—not ethnicity, income, age, or being foreign-born predicted

Table 12.2   Patterns of Alternative Use Among Racial Groups

Categories of Practice	Prevalence of Use
Herbal medicines	Asian Americans 3 times more likely than White Americans to use Latino Americans 2 times more likely than White Americans to use African Americans 1.5 times more likely than White Americans to use
Acupuncture	Asian Americans 12.84 times more likely than White American counterparts Uninsured respondents 2 times higher rate than insured
Traditional healer[a]	Beyond high school education—about 3 times more likely
Home remedy	African Americans 1.24 times more likely to use than White Americans Women 1.24 times more likely to use than men Uninsured 1.5 times more likely to use than insured

[a]This label is more academic than commonly used and understood terms such as *curandero* (medicine man or root-worker).

Source: From "Ethnic Minority Use of Complementary and Alternative Medicine (CAM): A National Probability Survey of Cam Utilizers," by E. R. MacKenzie, L. Taylor, B. S. Bloom, D. J. Hufford, and J. C. Johnson, 2003, *Alternative Therapies, 9*(4), 50–56.

use—so understanding these various practices and their true prevalence is essential to the delivery of culturally competent medical care. Even with their more complete detailing, the MacKenzie team (2003) noted certain deficits that skewed their accounting. For example, they did not survey religious or spiritual healing practices, keystones of most traditional medicines, or home remedies and special diets. In addition, the label *traditional healer*—more of an academic reference than the common terms used in different ethnic circles, such as *curandero*, "medicine man" or "root-worker"—might not have elicited true numbers of followers because of the unfamiliar terminology. Beyond its particulars, MacKenzie and colleagues' (2003) message is a compelling reminder that medicine is always a cultural construct, that the biomedical model is but one paradigm that originated in European science, and that many Americans continue to follow health-care approaches that emerged from nonallopathic medical philosophies. As a final caution, having data on ethnic patterns of medical preferences is essential but should not blind the social worker to individual divergences from cultural norms, which can be identified only with appropriate questions through supportive inquiry (Becerra & Iglehart, 1995; Krajewski-Jaime, 1991; Pachter, 1994).

DEFINITION OF TERMS: DISTINCTIONS AMONG *ALTERNATIVE, COMPLEMENTARY,* AND *INTEGRATIVE*

Alternative, complementary, and *integrative* are labels often used loosely and interchangeably to refer to nonstandard medical practices. But this changing, elusive, and overlapping terminology perpetuates confusion and imprecision in efforts to distinguish the merits of different practices. Surprisingly, despite the swelling proportion of Americans seeking nonconventional therapies in the past decade,

a governmental agency dedicated to studying such treatments with vast expansion in federal funding for this purpose, and significant growth of insurance coverage, no clear or consistent definition of alternative medicine has emerged. Experts still fumble with negative conceptualizations, the most prominent example of which is what is not taught in U.S. medical schools and what is not insurance reimbursed (Eisenberg et al., 1993). Yet even by 1997, several insurance carriers had initiated cost coverage for certain alternative practices (Wetzel, Eisenberg, & Kaptchuk, 1998), and in 2002, complementary and alternative coursework appeared in the curriculum of 98 out of 125 medical schools (Barzansky & Etzel, 2003).

Using terminology such as *alternative, unconventional*, and *unproven* to indicate practices outside the armamentarium of Western medicine implicitly censures such therapies (Scholten & Van Rompay, 2000). What words connote can subtly but effectively sabotage or substantially influence acceptance and credibility. For example, using the label *orthodox* to identify the currently dominant medical system in the United States confers automatic authority because the words *accepted, approved, established*, and *standard* are understood as synonyms for *orthodox*. Even the word *biomedical* presumes that all practices under this umbrella are based on scientific confirmation, obscuring other evidence that the human organism is more than a biochemical entity and obviating the value of mind–body approaches (MacIntosh, 1999). The next discussion is offered to help unravel the tangled meanings of the terms *alternative, complementary*, and *integrative* so that professional dialogue with colleagues and conversations with clients will be less susceptible to misinterpretation.

Alternative Medicine

Alternative medicine is not a singular practice or tradition but divergent systems and practices of health care that emerge from widely disparate medical philosophies. Alternative medical systems are complete diagnostic and treatment approaches with distinctive theoretical foundations, such as those traditional to non-Western cultures (e.g., traditional Chinese medicine [TCM] and Ayurveda) and those developed in Western cultures (e.g., homeopathy and naturopathic medicine). In distinction, alternative practices are specific discrete treatments or modalities independent of comprehensive or coherent medical schema (MacIntosh, 1999). The chief commonality connecting disparate alternative practices and systems is that they differ in some obvious respect from modern biomedicine and therefore are seen as challenges to the prevailing medical paradigm. Indeed, the term *alternative* often is employed to indicate medical practices used in place of modern medical treatments (e.g., iridology used as diagnostic technique instead of conventional blood assays).

Beyond the defining characteristic of alternatives just mentioned, there are several more positive, shared premises. For one thing, these alternative modalities see the human organism as an indivisible system, an ecological whole. This is the fundamental assumption that body, mind, and spirit are not separable but dynamically interconnected, stimulating the healing process as a unified system. In distinction, the Western medical model presumes that the psyche and soma are separate entities to be treated independently; it is believed that a disorder of one organ is not interrelated with the dysfunction of another. Also, in biomedicine, the body as a machine with interworking but semi-independent anatomic parts is assumed and reflected in specialties of medicine that commonly do not interact. Also, alternative practices share a core belief in the body's inherent potential for self-healing with medical regimens designed to encourage and support that process.

Next, the primary objectives of alternative methods are optimal health and total healing, not elimination of symptoms and signs of the presenting complaint. Western medicine maintains a fixation on physical sickness; the concepts of *disease* and *restoring health*, however, are not the same thing. Jonas (1998) refers to this nonallopathic emphasis on health as "salutogenesis" compared to the biomedical fixation on "pathogenesis." Furthermore,

traditional systems presuppose that ill health results from a disturbance or imbalance in life force or energy (e.g., *qi*, pronounced "chee," in China, *ki* in Korea and Japan, *prana* in India, and "vital force" in homeopathy or other traditional Western systems) for which there is no Western anatomical equivalent. Restoring that balance will reestablish health in all dimensions of being. Alternative practices also share the principle of the patient's active engagement or partnership in the healing process. In addition, they share an assumption that spirituality is inseparable from physical and psychological health and is critical to a full resolution of what Western physicians diagnose and treat solely as a biological disorder (see full discussion in Chapter 11). This spiritual underpinning of alternative practices is reflective of each culture's dominant religious and cosmological beliefs; for example, TCM is connected to Taoism, Ayurveda rests on the Hindu belief system, and Tibetan medicine is congruent with specific Buddhist precepts (Eskinazi, 1998).

In some cases, what is casually labeled as alternative actually may mesh effectively with the dominant model of medicine (e.g., hydrazine sulfate treatments for cancer) and therefore may be considered more accurately a complementary adjunct. The same allopathic paradigm still determines the architecture of care, with an herbal or botanical medicament substituted or added alongside a conventionally prescribed drug, but the diagnostic categories and essential treatment planning is consistent with orthodox Western medicine (Pietroni, 1994).

Complementary Approaches

As certain alternatives (e.g., acupuncture, mind/body techniques including meditation, relaxation and biofeedback, chiropractic, massage therapies) gained access to modern medical centers/medical mainstream, new status brought new nomenclature (Brown et al., 1994). Complementary medicine—actually a misnomer—is not a comprehensive system of health care but a heterogeneous assortment of hundreds of treatment modalities lumped under one categorical label. These therapies are used in conjunction with, rather than in lieu of, conventional treatments and often are implemented to relieve discomfort or secondary consequences of modern medical interventions (i.e., specific herbals used with prescription drug therapies to help mitigate untoward effects, relaxation strategies to accompany and alleviate symptomatic distress of surgery or chemotherapy). When applied, the model that prevails over the implementation of complementary treatments is still the Western medical paradigm (Pietroni, 1994). Although many times used interchangeably with the word *alternative, complementary* by definition means something that completes or provides what is lacking (Merriam-Webster, 2003), whereas *alternative* indicates something that is mutually exclusive of, "offering a choice between two incompatible courses." If what was judged alternative is brought in-house—joined to mainstream medicine protocols—and institutionalized, it is assigned a peripheral or ancillary role and therefore is no longer perceived as competitive or challenging to the dominant medical model. *Complementary* is more a designation that identifies the relationship of diverse treatments to the prevailing health system than a term that actually describes different healing techniques.

In records of CAM usage, the most common health complaints have been disorders that seem unremitting, such as chronic back pain, insomnia, arthritic problems, headaches, musculoskeletal difficulties, and psychological distress (Campion, 1993; Institute of Medicine, 2005). Among those who do seek CAM therapies for more severe health concerns, a large majority (83%) continue treatment with their standard provider, but 85% of those using nonstandard therapies choose not to inform their physicians they have done so (Eisenberg et al., 2001). At the time of the Cassileth, Luck, Strouse, and Bodenheimer paper (1984), 60% of CAM practitioners were physicians—that is, those providing unorthodox therapies were not stereotypical untrained charlatans; this proportion has increased steadily, but few CAM practitioners are oncologists (Cassileth

& Chapman, 1996). It is when conventional and nonstandard treatment are uncoordinated that CAM can prove most harmful.

CAM practices are a frequent choice for patients diagnosed with cancer (Campion, 1993; Eisenberg et al., 2001; Ernst & Cassileth, 1998). According to Campion's (1993) report, a full 58% were convinced that such treatments likely would provide a cure. Even data from 1984 revealed that 54% of patients surveyed in a major U.S. cancer center were CAM adherents, but at least 40% of patients at that center at one point had abandoned their standard medical treatments to pursue CAM exclusively (Cassileth & Chapman, 1996). A systematic review found that the proportion of cancer patients using an amalgam of CAM and conventional treatments—either simultaneously or sequentially—was 64% (Ernst & Cassileth, 1998). In another survey of cancer patients queried soon after completing chemotherapy, 91% reported routinely utilizing at least one CAM modality during their treatment cycles (Yates et al., 2005). Certainly a major concern arises if patients desert potentially effective conventional care, opting to use only alternatives, even ones that as complements could prove truly helpful, because these patients could lose their way on an unnecessarily perilous treatment path. Most analyses seem to concur that CAM applications—including diet therapies; healing relaxation programs; metabolic therapies; acupuncture; homeopathy; manual and body therapies; vitamin, herbal, and botanicals or other supplemented compounds (e.g., Iscador, a proprietary cancer treatment formulation derived from mistletoe)—represent a global phenomenon. Eisenberg acknowledges CAM as an "invisible mainstream" within current health care (Cassileth, 1998; Eisenberg, 1997).

Integrative Medicine

Integrative medicine, a term in current parlance, designates an approach to health care that combines, in careful treatment programming, mainstream medical treatments and certain complementary therapies that have demonstrated safety and potential efficacy. Not a specific traditional system of health care based on a distinguishing philosophical or theoretical foundation, integrative medicine is used by providers who are formally trained in allopathic therapies and equally proficient in or knowledgeable about relevant alternative modalities. To produce a truly melded protocol of integrative care, practitioners must be fully versed in and able to anticipate positive synergies as well as problematic interactions that can occur when previously unfused therapies are combined. Even though it is not a single system of medicine, there are certain consistent, identifiable standards of care in this medical field. A true integrative approach requires a systematic fusion of conventional and alternative treatments intended to marshal the body's own recovery processes; it maintains an openness to paradigms other than Western allopathy, focuses on the larger goal of optimal health beyond ameliorating specific disease issues, and begins by creating a partnership of provider and patient. This last principle echoes and is consistent with one of the key practice tenets of social work, reaffirming the true professional fit for the healthcare social worker in the integrative sphere.

Proponents postulate therapeutic advantages if regimens are integrated properly and tailored to each individual's particular health needs. What is required are treatment plans for individual patients that rely on a sound coupling of therapies from both conventional protocols (e.g., prescription medications) and alternative practices (e.g., herbal/botanical agents), a melding guided by evidence-based information, and a watchful eye to potentially problematic interactions (certain combinations contraindicated because of specifics about medical status of a patient or intervention). The totality of an integrative program can yield a better-than-sum-of-its-parts outcome; that is, a comprehensive and coherent treatment plan can produce full synergistic benefits beyond mere adjunctive add-ons of disconnected, exotic practices. Nevertheless, an unanswered conundrum hovers over the enthusiasm of integrative intentions: Can systems shaped by dissimilar, nonparallel paradigms of health and healing ever be fully blended?

REASONS FOR SEEKING ALTERNATIVE TREATMENTS

More than a decade after the Eisenberg and colleagues' initial report (1993), the disagreement surrounding actual determinants of CAM still smolders. Discussing this dispute does not simply serve in the interest of debate or polemics but familiarizes us with proposed reasons to encourage an open but knowledgeable discussion with patients, to act as an informed liaison between patients and the medical team, and to impact an administrative response to cultural and medical pluralism in effective programs.

Some argue, based on results from surveys, that dissatisfaction with orthodox treatments is not a significant predictor of alternative usage. Astin (1998a) cites data showing that 54% of those using alternatives reported feeling very satisfied with their conventional experience. Astin's conclusion supports a "philosophical congruence theory." That is, patients felt aligned with comprehensive treatments designed to promote health rather than oriented wholly on pathology and disease and with approaches that value dietary, mind–spirit, and lifestyle factors in self-care programs. From this perspective, modern medicine represents a necessary but insufficient response to health concerns.

Others contend that even philosophical congruence can be construed as an indicator of disappointment with orthodox care. Although most users of CAM are not distrustful of or totally displeased with mainstream medical treatments, many would concur that electing to use an alternative implicitly signifies some dissatisfaction with results of the conventional armamentarium—that conventional therapies have not been fully effective, prompting the patient to seek other and more (Baldwin, 1998). From this perspective, electing CAM therapies suggests that even if patients do not eschew conventional interventions, they are not fully pleased with their experience in mainstream medical facilities. It has been argued that because Astin (1998b) did not include a direct question about perceived efficacy (i.e., "Has conventional treatment worked for you?") and because satisfaction with treatment is a primary determinant of each individual's medical choice, Astin's conclusions are based on inadequate data. In Baldwin's words, "patients in general would not part with good money unless they felt they were getting better results outside conventional health care" (1998, p. 1660).

Although standard Western medicine is unparalleled at crisis intervention—trauma and emergency care—and battling microbial disease, it has been less successful at identifying how to achieve and maintain optimal health or how to respond to unalleviated chronic ailments: problems that fail to disappear. No doubt the drive toward CAM can be very idiosyncratic, but certain recurring themes lead people to unorthodox practices:

1. Discomfort with an impersonal quality pervasive in institutional settings
2. Discontent with technological procedures that presume a mechanistic and reductionistic model of human health (Borins, 2002)
3. Unresolved chronic medical problems (e.g., arthritis and allergies that often do not respond to conventional interventions) and reduced faith in the ability of medical breakthroughs to eliminate vexing health concerns (Jonas, 1998; Testerman, Morton, Mason, & Ronan, 2004)
4. Growing fascination in spiritual dimensions of health
5. Mounting unease about the toxic potential and adverse consequences of invasive medical practices (Jonas, 1998) combined with confidence in lower toxicity and greater safety of most alternative treatments
6. The repeated experience of dispiriting or perfunctory communications from medical providers
7. The desire to regain a modicum of personal control over the direction and process of care

This last reason—the intent to reclaim responsibility for treatment decisions and

medical care rather than remain passive recipients of medical interventions and invasive technology—frequently propels cancer patients toward nonstandard practices (Lerner & Kennedy, 1992). Beyond avoidance of dreaded side effects and iatrogenic consequences, many people diagnosed with a malignancy suspect that pollution, dietary patterns, and stressors are implicated in the etiology of their disease; the logical recovery strategy requires altering food intake and a personal regimen of lifestyle adjustments (Borins, 2002). Further motivating cancer patients to adopt CAM practices is a desire to augment biological factors deemed vital in battling malignancy to mitigate symptoms, such as fatigue, pain, and nausea; diminish side effects; and enhance emotional well-being (Molassiotis et al., 2005). Although 43% of patients believed that their supplement programs were a truly effective tactic in their cancer battle (Cassileth et al., 1984), when cancer patients elect alternative or complementary modalities, they usually do not limit CAM options to a singular practice. The likelihood of CAM use is heightened the longer a patient has been dealing with their cancer (Lerner & Kennedy, 1992). In addition, oncology patients choose these combination therapies because conventional treatments hold out poor cure and remission statistics—very bleak showings on desired outcomes—and seem unable to deliver desired outcome. All of these reasons indicate dissatisfaction, if not total disillusionment (Borins, 2002; Lerner & Kennedy, 1992). Added to these issues is an increasing frustration among patients—and substantial numbers of doctors—with their experience in standard medicine, perpetuated by a managed care economics that permits too little physician time and encourages a system that often feels impersonal (Weil, 2001). Therefore, although most users of alternatives may not be truly distrustful of mainstream medical treatment—and in fact stay with conventional regimens simultaneous to alternative and complementary modalities—neither are they fully satisfied with the results of their conventional modalities.

SYSTEMS AND PRACTICES

Learning the divergent cultural models of health and medicine that are the philosophical underpinnings of specific alternative interventions is as critical for social workers as is becoming familiar with names and types of single practices, agents, or therapies. Traditional or indigenous health-care systems emerge from centuries-old philosophical principles and fundamentals of health care that differ appreciably from those underlying the model of biomedicine. They developed from ancient texts and medical ideologies embedded in and reflective of the specific traditions and societal and spiritual beliefs of each culture.

Traditional Chinese Medicine

In the traditional Chinese medical system, health is understood as the unimpeded flow of vital energy (qi) traveling through a network of bioelectrical pathways that have no exact correlate in the Western model of anatomy. In addition, health implies a balance of opposed universal forces of yin and yang within all systems—body, mind, and spirit—and with the larger external environment. To reestablish balance and optimize health, traditional Chinese doctors prescribe a complex regimen of dietary adjustments, meditative physical exercises (e.g., tai chi, qi gong), specific massage treatments, herbal formulations, and acupuncture. These recommendations are tailored to match the individual's diagnosis (e.g., hot liver excess; TCM diagnoses bear no exact correspondence to Western disease categories) and are determined by pulse evaluations (again, unlike Western pulse taking or blood pressure readings) and other signature indicators (e.g., tongue signs, vocal tone, skin quality). In diagnosis, the practitioner identifies the underlying cause of body's pattern of disharmony that is unique to that individual and at that time. For example, an individual diagnosed as suffering from cold-deficiency disease will be placed on a regimen of specific foods known as body heating (not synonymous with temperature, but a quality believed to strengthen the blood).

Acupuncture

Because disrupted energy flow is understood as the basis of disease, acupuncture treatment involves the insertion of very thin needles at blockage junctures or specific meridian points to release or restore flow of energy through channels or meridians. It is theorized that there are more than 2,000 points connected to particular organ systems. Although deemed alternative in the United States, acupuncture is a traditional, standard healing practice in China, with origins in the classic text of Chinese medicine, the *Nei Ching* (ca. 2500 B.C.). Currently it is the most commonly used medical practice worldwide, applied as a full diagnostic and healing treatment in Asian cultures (Gerber, 1988; NCCAM, 2000).

A report published in 1998 calculated that more than 5 million visits are made to acupuncture practitioners annually in the United States (Eisenberg et al., 1998). With research primarily on its effectiveness at alleviating different degrees and types of discomfort, acupuncture has earned gradual medical acceptance for certain pain syndromes (NIH, 1992). Even though its specific mechanisms continue to elude scientific explanations, compelling evidence has found acupuncture efficacious beyond placebo in relieving chronic and acute pain (Jackson, 1997; Takeda & Wessel, 1994), easing the severity of drug withdrawal (Gandhi, 1996), and diminishing chemotherapy-induced nausea and vomiting (Beinfield & Korngold, 2003; Ezzo et al., 2005). Beyond analgesic and anesthetic applications, when administered as an adjunct for cerebral vascular episodes, acupuncture reduced recovery time by 50% and per-patient cost by $26,000 (Johansson, Lindgren, Widner, Wiklund, & Johansson, 1993). In broader medical settings, acupuncture has been gaining favor as a therapy for asthma, gastrointestinal problems, and chronic fatigue (Sullivan, 2000) and as an effective treatment for night sweats, diarrhea, vomiting, digestive difficulty, insomnia, and other debilitating symptoms of acquired immunodeficiency syndrome (AIDS) symptoms, particularly when combined with moxibustion (specially heated herbs applied to parts of the body) and herbal formulas (Hudson, 1996). For those who are truly needle phobic, resistance to acupuncture might interfere with and obstruct anticipated benefits (D. P. Lu, Lu, & Kleinman, 2001).

Ayurvedic Medicine (or Ayurveda)

The traditional medical system known as Ayurvedic medicine has roots in 5,000-year-old Indian texts that, similar to TCM, explain illness as disruption of harmony and balance in the vital life force, or prana. Restoration of health—reestablishing balance—depends on individualized dietary, herbal, massage, and meditative therapies that correspond to the individual's predominant constitutional or metabolic body type, known as a *dosha* (e.g., *kapha*, *pitta*, and *vatta*) (Chopra, 1989). Rather than focusing exclusively on disease particulars and their specific treatment, Aurvedic plans of care are equally directed at systematic preventive care and optimization of health.

Alternative Health-Care Systems

Homeopathy

Homeopathy, a complete system of medicine, originated during the latter 1790s and early 1800s in Germany and is founded on the theory that "like cures like," also spoken of as *similia similibus curantur* or "law of similars" (Moore & Schmais, 2000). In this country, homeopathy was not only popular but was highly regarded professionally as a full medical approach during the 1800s and early 20th century. By 1900, homeopathic institutions included 22 medical schools and approximately 200 hospitals; 15% of physicians were homeopathic doctors. The advent of allopathic standards, the pervasive impact of our cultural ideal of empiricism, and the increasing influence of the American Medical Association and its determination of acceptable practices (Wharton, 1999) diminished homeopathy's stature, another manifestation of cultural and social configuration of medical models. However, homeopathy is more widely used globally than any other system of medical care, is commonly applied in Western Europe (Sullivan, 2000), and has been attracting research interest and gaining advocacy once again in the United States.

The principles of homeopathy seem paradoxical and defy conventional pharmacological explanations. That is, homeopathy treats health disorders by administering tiny, dilute doses of natural substances—mineral, plant extracts, metals, even disease-producing germs, diluted in pure water or alcohol (Goldberg et al., 2002)—that, if given in a larger quantity, could produce the undesired symptoms or medical complaint. This doctrine of practice is referred to as the law of infinitesimal doses: The more highly dilute dosages (30 successive dilutions) are considered more potent than less dilute (6×) formulations (Moore & Schmais, 2000). The basic assumption is that these precisely formulated microdosages target the root causes of disease by initiating the body's inherent healing mechanisms. In this system of care, symptoms are viewed as a functional attempt of the organism to right or heal itself (Taylor, 1995) and therefore are not the primary focus of treatment. For instance, two patients presenting with the very same Western medical disease diagnosis might exhibit very different symptoms. After careful analysis of other subtly related indicators, pointing to noncomparable origins of their malady, the practitioner would recommend entirely different homeopathic remedies (choosing among hundreds) in contradistinction to the precise algorithms of Western medicine that would identify a singular protocol for a single diagnosis.

Although homeopathic assumptions contradict Western medical precepts, more than 80 randomized trials show homeopathic efficacy for disorders such as severe diarrhea among young children (Jacobs, Jimenez, Gloyd, Gale, & Crothers, 1994), asthma, dermatitis, and otitis media (Sullivan, 2000). A meta-analysis found measurable benefits for disorders as various as hay fever, asthma, and influenza (Kleijnen, Knipschild, & Riet, 1991).

Naturopathic Medicine

With an ebb-and-flow history, naturopathy is now regaining popular interest and recognition and is formally licensed in 15 states and the District of Columbia. Originating in the United States in the early 1900s (first with Benjamin Lust and later systemized in Henry Lindlahr's texts on natural therapeutics), this is a medical discipline of nontoxic regimens derived from worldwide healing systems. Treatment plans are designed to enhance the body's inherent healing capacity (*vis medicatrix naturae*) and are based on a meticulous composite of therapeutic diet, herbal medicine, homeopathic remedies, acupuncture, detoxification therapies (colonic irrigation, saltwater baths, and fasting), hydrotherapy, physical therapies, spinal/soft tissue manipulation, and hyperthermia—the compendium derived from various traditional healing modalities. The most common application of naturopathy is treatment of chronic and degenerative problems rather than acute or trauma conditions.

A basic principle of naturopathy (*primum no nocere*) and of Western medicine holds that disease symptoms are the body's innate mechanism for correcting unhealthy imbalances. It is believed, for example, that reducing a fever or medicating inflammation—simple manifestations of imbalance—rather than eliminating the root cause (*tolle causam*) of an elevated temperature or the inflammatory condition will perpetuate the disorder and result in chronic disease. Often during the therapeutic regimen to remove causative factors, a patient will experience an acute episode, or a healing crisis, which, according to naturopathic thinking, indicates an expected reaction to treatment and a signal that the therapy is on track. It is assumed that subsequent to this amplification of symptoms, the adverse condition will subside naturally (Goldberg et al., 2002).

Folk Medicines

In dictionary terms, *folk medicine* (or lay medicine) refers to a tradition of health beliefs and illness treatments transmitted orally and by imitation among a group of people with a common cultural or ethnic identity (Hurdle, 2002; Merriam-Webster, 2003). What this term inaccurately seems to conjure is a set of quaint practices predominant among rural or nonacculturated populations. In a 1995 paper, Becerra and Iglehart reported the common practice of folk medicine, particularly for minor disorders or as preventive, among diverse urban populations who do have access to modern scientific interventions. For example, Chinese Americans may selectively apply traditional Chinese practices while continuing to follow modern medical recommendations, deeming each differentially effective with particular health problems. Surprisingly, from surveying parents from different ethnic groups (Chinese American, African American, Mexican American, and non-Hispanic Whites), Becerra and Iglehart (1995) observed that level of assimilation was not predictive of reliance on folk medicine, but personal injury or illness of children during the prior 6 months was. Why these medicines still attract loyal adherents and are resilient even in modern urban societies can be attributed first and foremost to their effectiveness for specific problems plus an unwillingness to abandon heritage and tradition, a desire to preserve self-determination in personal health, affordability, and congruence with spiritual belief systems (Neff, 2004).

Although specific remedies or "cures" embraced by folk medicines often are used in combination with conventional medicine, these practices are not easily tagged as complementary. That is, folk practices will not neatly fit the allopathic model. Their theoretical underpinnings and diagnostic and healing categories can be incompatible with biomedical thinking. This may pose a substantial challenge to professional providers trained in the conventional medical paradigm. Folk medicines represent consistent and coherent patterns of practice, not disconnected assortments of remedies and preventives. Each folk system reflects its cultural source with a distinct explanatory model of sickness appreciably different from that of Western biomedicine that divorces spiritual and religious meaning from disease etiology and treatment.

These folk diagnostics and curatives seem to share the belief that a patient's disorder and subsequent health are embedded in an environment that is simultaneously social, ecological, and spiritual—a tenet that echoes and coheres with the person-in-environment fundamental of professional social work. Another important distinction is that, unlike allopathic medicine, which prescribes treatments even when disease causation is unknown or uncertain, folk systems do not proceed with curative therapies before identifying clear etiology (Krippner, 1995).

Because it is not feasible in one chapter to present a full discussion of the complex topic of folk medicine, examples will be used to highlight certain distinctions among systems and identify possible points of incongruity between modern medical thinking and folk models—ones that reflect vastly different ways of construing health and sickness issues. For the health-care social worker, familiarity with folk practices helps bridge separate cultures of medicine and engender mutual respect for a more effective delivery of services.

As an example, among Mexican Americans, *curanderismo*, or folk healing, is a continuing and stable presence in family health care (Becerra & Iglehart, 1995). Not an assortment of piecemeal remedies, this is a comprehensive tradition that holds religion as a core element with practices that derive from an elaborate classification of maladies. These maladies have no exact corollary in orthodox medicine, thus may not be resolvable by Western medical techniques and, as a result, necessitate folk healer (*curandera* or *curandero*) interventions. Although disease causation is not understood as God's punishment, the divine is viewed as the ultimate source of relief and recovery from illness (Becerra & Iglehart, 1995). Most often, the curandera determines a diagnosis by reading the patient's aura or energy body, by questioning both patient and family about signs or symptoms and peculiar patterns of patient behavior, and ultimately by information from the spirit guide in dreams (Krippner, 1995). In curanderismo diagnostics, there are five principal folk sicknesses, four of which are

deemed natural disorders (*males naturales*)—*caida de la mullera* (fallen fontanel in infants due to mother's neglect), *empacho* (a digestive disorder understood as obstruction in the bowel or stomach by saliva or soft foods), *mal ojo* (the evil eye, which occurs when stared at with envy or desire), and *susto* (shock or fright)—and one with its source in witchcraft or sorcery—*mal puesto*, due to a hex (Becerra & Iglehart, 1995; Krippner, 1995). Symptom patterns can be complex and include fever, headaches, vomiting, and drooping eyes for mal ojo but do not in and of themselves define the problem. Depending on diagnosis, curatives can involve herbals, incantations, manipulations, and spiritual practices with the curandera present to enlist divine assistance or the intercession of helpful spirits (Krippner).

A patient case example of the ethnomedical condition known in Latin American traditions as empacho exemplifies a successful folk-biomedical interface. A 20-month-old Puerto Rican toddler was admitted to a hospital for dietary and behavioral observation because of "failure to thrive"—the diagnosis in biomedical terminology for his continuing weight loss—but assumed by his parents to signify empacho, a disorder with no correspondence in modern medicine. Respecting the conviction and insistence of both parents, the doctors invited a local santiguadora along with the owner of a *botanica* (a local Puerto Rican shop selling herbs, remedies, and specific religious artifacts) into the hospital unit to perform ritual healing with massage and other folk medicaments, concurrent with conventional care. Within days, the boy was able to return home after evidencing appropriate weight gain. Importantly, achieving this successful outcome did not require the parents to relinquish their culturally determined beliefs about illness, nor was the physician compelled to concur with those beliefs. This result suggests how discrepant explanatory models can be negotiated effectively—can peacefully coexist and deliver effective care—in a conventional medical environment that demonstrates openness and the ability to suspend judgmental thinking (Pachter, 1994).

Other folk practices persist in an urban setting. For example, without abandoning their modern medical care, African Americans may specifically seek herbal remedies ("root" work) or spiritual practices to cure sickness ("the misery") when illness is attributed to divine punishment or natural or magical forces. In contradistinction, White non-Hispanics seem to rely more on specific food preparations and mechanical applications (e.g., poultices rather than herbals) as remedies, but, parallel to modern medicine, Anglo popular medicines (as they are labeled by Becerra & Iglehart, 1995) separate spiritual rituals from physical health practices. These authors imply that although not as elaborate and codified as other folk medicines, continuity of Anglo healing measures is ensured because it enables and echoes values of independence and self-reliance.

Among many Native American practices, a rigorous logic informs practice, and, in fact, the Pima Indian model with its specialties and subspecialties is seen by medical anthropologists as perhaps as highly developed as that of Western medical systems (Krippner, 1995). Comparisons, however, are not simple because many diagnostic categories are not comprehensible outside of a particular cultural perspective. The Pima model holds that one category of disease responds to external treatment while other types may heal only with the body's innate mechanisms or might not be remediable, such as infant deformities (Krippner, 1995). According to Pima theory, the body of each patient reflects the accumulative repository of resources and weaknesses to be evaluated and analyzed by the shaman with the assistance of benevolent spirit guides before the individual is assigned to the appropriate intervention of other practitioners. Specific behaviors inform the shaman's diagnostic conclusions. In this system, "wandering sickness" (impurities such as germs, pus, or heat that traverse the body), identified with signs such as fever, hives, piles, and sores, is treated with herbals and spirit entreaties. Another category of maladies, "staying sickness" (manifestation of proscribed behavior toward power object from nature), persists in the body because the

individual has violated sacred laws. This group includes "wind sickness," "deer sickness," and "rabbit sickness" and requires shamanic chanting and ritual removal of toxic substance from the ill person's body, often in conjunction with sand painting and/or special feasting (Krippner, 1995). In some instances, a disease is deemed untreatable (an intrinsic condition that is characterologically induced), obviating interventions, which would interfere with a specific and necessary life lesson (Cohen, 1999).

CAM Practices

As mentioned earlier, what usually is classified as complementary medicine is not a true medical system but an umbrella term for nonstandard practices that can be applied within the allopathic model (i.e., when nonstandard treatments dovetail with, instead of supplanting, conventional plans of care). It is still the conventional biomedical model and theory that determine usage (MacIntosh, 1999). Although a listing of CAM modalities is far too extensive for full coverage in this chapter, some of the more common CAM categories of treatment are mentioned to increase familiarity (Loveland-Cook, Becvar, & Pontious, 2000).

Body and Massage Therapies (Manual Therapies)

The manual therapy modality encompasses multiple distinctive therapies that primarily use physical touch for diagnostic and treatment plans (Loveland-Cook et al., 2000).

Chiropractic is foremost a system of spinal adjustments and is the most immediately identifiable form of CAM (Lawrence & Meeker, 2007). It is estimated that 23 to 38 million Americans visit chiropractors annually (Goldberg et al., 2002). Although the primary chiropractic function remains treatment of back pain, one of the most common health complaints in the United States second only to the common cold, in some states (e.g., Illinois), chiropractors may be licensed to perform certain interventions, such as throat cultures, and to treat minor health issues (Rattenbury, 1995). According to the guiding premise in chiropractic, health ultimately is determined by the central nervous system. Misalignment of the spine, referred to as "subluxation," engenders pain and other health problems, requiring spinal adjustments, achieved with varying methods and equipment, to restore healthier nerve functioning. Numerous studies have found chiropractic to effect better and longer-maintained relief of back pain than that achieved by medical doctors (Meade, Dyer, Browne, Townsend, & Frank, 1990) and at significantly reduced cost (Jarvis, Phillips, & Morris, 1991).

Naprapathy is a back/body modality related to chiropractic, but this practice treats musculoskeletal pain by manipulating connective tissue and muscles rather than bones. Naprapaths most commonly treat muscle spasms, joint pain, inflammation, and scar tissue (Rattenbury, 1995).

Reflexology, another manual therapy, is based on the premise that each body organ or system has one or several corresponding points on the feet and hands. By applying precise pressure to these points, it is believed that the practitioner can unlock disrupted pathways of energy that have produced pain or an unrelieved structural disorder (Stephenson & Dalton, 2003). Research has shown reflexology to be an effective treatment for chronic migraines and tension headaches (Launso, Brendstrup, & Amberg, 1999).

Therapeutic touch (TT) has as its underlying rationale the theory that bioelectrical energy fields make up soma and psyche of each individual, and these fields interact with environmental factors to produce health problems. This practice involves realigning or rebalancing disturbances in this energy field. Studies regarding efficacy have found that gentle TT bolstered weight gain among premature infants (Harrison, Olivet, Cunningham, Bodin, & Hicks, 1996) and helped calm children distressed during hospitalization (Kramer, 1990); other data suggest that TT aids factors that enhance immune response, particularly an increase in helper T4 cells and reduction of suppressor T8 cells (Quinn & Strelkauskas, 1993). Moreover, TT has been associated with reduced pain of tension headaches (Keller & Bzdek,

1986) and has found applications in more than 200 hospitals (Goldberg et al., 2002).

Aromatherapy uses essential oils, distilled from plant oils, to relieve and relax symptoms associated with disease and side effects of treatment and more generally to enhance overall well-being through the olfactory system. The usual routes of aromatherapy are through inhalation of oils dispensed by diffusers or massaged directly on skin. The latter method requires knowledgeable professional guidance as certain oils, such as cinnamon and clove, can burn or irritate the skin. In addition, even the most purified oils should not be ingested because they can be quite toxic. But beneficial effects abound. Lavender induces calming, almost sedative benefits on brain wave activity (Birchall, 1990) and can be very helpful with sleep disorders, particularly sleep-onset problems. During childbirth, lavender and lemon relieved tension in early stages of labor, whereas in later phases peppermint was found to alleviate nausea and vomiting (Burns & Blarney, 1994). In an intensive care unit, aromatherapy combined with massage provided patients with greater observed ease and relaxation than massage alone (Dunn, Sleep, & Collett, 1995).

Therapeutic massage and bodywork includes multiple practices, such as Swedish, deep tissue, sports, and lymphatic massage. Estimates suggest they are used by 20 million Americans annually (Goldberg et al., 2002). Research on various forms of manual therapy has produced substantial documentation that massage therapy can relieve psychological stress and lift mood (Corley, Ferriter, Zeh, & Gifford, 1995; Dunn et al., 1995; Sims, 1986). Physiologically, massage enhances blood and lymph circulation and parasympathetic response (e.g., decreased heart and respiratory rate, relieved muscle tension, lowered blood pressure). It has been associated with better gastrointestinal functioning, diminished reliance on analgesics, and improved active functional levels (DeGood, 1996). In research with another focus, preterm infants have benefited, showing significantly improved weight gain and shortened hospitalization with daily massage (Field et al., 1986). Other physical manipulation therapies—too numerous for this chapter—include deep-tissue work to restructure the body such as Rolfing or the gentler craniosacral therapy, pressure point techniques like acupressure, or health awareness through movement redesign of the Feldenkrais approach.

The term *mind–body* refers to a broad category of techniques—meditation, hypnosis, biofeedback, autogenic training, relaxed abdominal breathing, guided imagery, progressive muscle relaxation—based on the understanding that psyche and soma are interconnected in a dynamic, unified system. The bidirectional communication among autonomic, musculoskeletal, and psychoneuroendocrine systems via neurotransmitters means that stressors can exert a harmful impact on physiology and biochemistry, but inversely, relieving stressor impact can afford salutary effects on the body and total health.

Blumenthal and colleagues at Duke University (1997) assessed patients with angina in a 16-week mind–body program and found fewer subsequent episodes than among controls. Although stressors that initiate damaging physiological reactions may not be perceived or processed consciously, both acute and chronic psychological distress produce symptoms, such as elevated pulse and blood pressure as well as respiratory rates, platelet aggregation, insulin levels, sodium retention, and decrements in immune response (Seaward, 1997; Wells-Federman et al., 1995). Techniques with empirical support of benefits offsetting damaging levels of stress include the techniques discussed next.

- Guided imagery techniques have demonstrated effectiveness, but guided imagery also affords personal customization. For example, a detailed mental image, using all senses—visual, auditory, olfactory, tactile—can be evoked that represents for that individual a safe, comfortable, and healing setting. Strong associations were reported between such practices and mitigation of chronic pain as well as improvements in

immune-influenced diseases (Benson & Stuart, 1993; Hillhouse & Adler, 1991). In cancer settings, guided imagery combined with progressive muscle relaxation was more effective at reducing the experience of pain severity among women with stage II, III, and IV disease than simple supportive communications (Sloman, 1995); cancer patients trained in guided imagery were able to diminish the severe oral mucositis pain that followed chemotherapy (Pan, Morrison, Ness, Fugh-Berman, & Leipzig, 2000). In another study among women with breast cancer, a link was observed with improved killer-cell activity along with mood enhancement (Fawzy et al., 1993; Newton, 1996). Also, with breast cancer patients, enhanced interferon levels accompanied by improved stamina and well-being that was substantially greater than controls resulted with this mind–body technique (Justice, 1996). In addition, guided imagery relieved chemotherapy-induced nausea and vomiting in the oncology setting (Troesch, Rodehaver, Delaney, & Yanes, 1993).

- Meditation is a traditional practice in many cultures with technical variations, but when it is stripped of religious or cultural overlay, it reveals substantial commonalities. Basic guidelines involve keeping the mind calmly focused on the present moment and diminishing painful ruminations about the past and anxious preoccupations with the future. In the concentrative approach of meditation, one is instructed to maintain attention on the breath or the repetition of a special word, phrase, sound (*mantra*), or image; alternatively, the mindfulness approach encourages nonjudgmentally observing sensations and thoughts as they enter the mindscape. The psychophysiological benefits evidenced with mindfulness-based stress reduction, a meditative discipline developed by John Kabat-Zinn and his team at University of Massachusetts and utilized in more than 200 U.S. hospitals, include alleviation of chronic and heretofore unremitting pain (Cassileth, 1998; Hafner, 1982; Kabat-Zinn, Lipworth, & Burney, 1985); 4 times more rapid healing of psoriasis (Kabat-Zinn et al., 1998); and anxiety and stress relief with accompanying physiological benefits (e.g., reduced hypertension).

- Hypnosis is a practice that uses selective attention to induce a specific altered state (trance), which enhances communication between conscious and unconscious processes (e.g., functioning of autonomic nervous system) for therapeutic benefit. All hypnosis is in effect self-hypnosis— that is, to produce a hypnotic state, the client must be engaged actively as a willing participant with the therapist as facilitator. Although it is thought that the brain's limbic system, which influences emotions and controls what is believed to be involuntary body functions, responds to hypnotic suggestions, a precise understanding of how this intervention works still eludes scientific explanation. By 1991, at least 15,000 health professionals practiced hypnotherapy in combination with their conventional medicine to ameliorate many conditions (Goldberg et al., 2002). Hypnotherapy helps to accelerate healing (Ginandes, Brooks, Sando, Jones, & Aker, 2003), triggering the release of endogenous anti-inflammatory properties; curb secretion of excess stomach acids among ulcer patients; soothe chronic and acute pain (Montgomery, DuHamel, & Redd, 2000); relieve side effects of chemotherapy, such as nausea and vomiting (Levitan, 1992; Lynch, 1998; Marchioro et al., 2000; Syrjala, Cummings, & Donaldson, 1992); reduce blood loss and pain medication needs associated with surgery (Disbrow, Bennett, & Owings, 1993; Enqvist, 1991); assist in asthma relief (Hackman, Stern, & Gershwin, 2000); and provide measurable relief with other difficult treatments (Goldberg et al., 2002). Generating important implications, a randomized clinical trial comparing a 15-minute hypnosis session just prior to a breast biopsy or lumpectomy to a control group of patients who did not receive hypnosis resulted in significantly reduced need for anesthetics, reported pain intensity, and postsurgical nausea and fatigue among the experimental group. Another striking benefit of this brief intervention was an institutional cost savings of $773 per patient, which is particularly germane when considering national concerns about runaway health-care expenses (Montgomery et al., 2007). With a different focus, one study demonstrated that burn patients healed more rapidly and with less pain when a light trance was induced soon after the trauma (Findlay, Podolsky, & Silberner, 1991). With pediatric patients, hypnosis was helpful with problems from recurrent migraines to sickle cell anemia (Goldberg et al., 2002). Contrary to earlier estimations, approximately 94% of patients experience some relief, and those more easily hypnotized benefit even more substantially (Podolsky, 1991).

- Biofeedback is a painless procedure in which sensors, attached to electrodes, are slipped on fingers or placed as upper arm cuffs while a client observes signals on a computer monitor indicating that he or she is able to achieve a desired state, for example, reduced heart rate, relief of tension headaches, or warmer peripheral temperature (Long, Machiran, & Bertell, 1986). This technique involves patients learning to control seemingly involuntary body functioning (e.g., skin temperature, brain wave patterns) when they practice relaxation tactics. It has been found useful with Reynaud's disease (in which fingers become painfully cold in cooler but not necessarily frigid conditions). Numerous insurers reimburse the cost of this therapy (Goldberg et al., 2002).

Mind–body techniques are congruent with social work objectives of empowering patients to implement positive changes through self-management and with social work values of respecting and tailoring to individual needs, because each of these techniques is amenable to individual adjustment. Moreover, through professional training programs and workshops, mind–body approaches can be added to clinical skills and incorporated into professional social work practice. By engaging patients and clients in these complementary techniques—training and treating individuals whose health can benefit from mind–body modalities—social workers enlarge their clinical role beyond that of patient advocate and medical liaison and in treatment ideals that echo social work fundamentals.

Nutrition and Lifestyle Regimens

Traditional medical systems rely heavily on dietary adjustments to restore or maintain balance, seen as the essence of health. Depending on environmental factors and the individual's energetic status, specific foods are to be eaten and others are to be deliberately avoided or eliminated.

Macrobiotic regimen is a lifestyle and dietary discipline emerging from Japanese Zen practices that prescribe individualized regimens to restore yin-yang energy balance. Dietary guidelines are based on fresh, whole foods, such as whole cereal grains, fresh vegetables, legumes, seeds, nuts, fruits, and some fish, with adjustments to match the individual's particular imbalanced energy, which is determined by evaluating condition and constitution, and to correspond to changing climate exigencies.

Lifestyle Heart Trial showed patients with substantial coronary artery disease had significant regression of atherosclerosis when following a specific low-fat diet combined with nonimpact exercise and relaxation strategies (Ornish et al., 1983, 1998). Other dietary information from epidemiological and observational research suggests that vegetarian eating may relieve rheumatoid arthritis symptoms and may reduce arthritic incidence and allergy problems by cutting protein triggers (Adam, 1995). Furthermore, high fiber as well as other aspects of whole grain, vegetable, legume, and fresh fruit consumption is linked with healthier gastrointestinal functioning and diminished risk of specific cancers and cardiovascular

problems (Block, 1999; Burkitt, Walker, & Painter, 1974).

Nutritional supplementation has shown a continual and dramatic rise in use among Americans in recent decades, despite medical controversy (Murray & Pizzorno, 1996). This fact reconfirms the public conviction that botanicals, herbals, and nutrients do make a significant difference and are generally less toxic than pharmaceutical drugs. Even in the midst of a media furor, there is little contest that specific agents can improve resistance to and duration of certain infectious sicknesses (Hemila, 1994), even among elderly people (Chandra, 1992). Supplements can augment preventive measures to counter severe disorders (e.g., protective against heart diseases as well as certain cancers), particularly vitamins E and C as well as carotenoids (Loveland-Cook et al., 2000). Preliminary evidence also supports the value of coenzyme Q10 for supportive benefits with cardiovascular problems, such as congestive heart failure (Gaby, 1999), and protection from cardiotoxic chemotherapies like doxorubicin (Mortensen, Aabo, Jonsson, & Baandrup, 1986). Chromium is helpful with type 2 diabetes (Sullivan, 2000).

Bioelectronic therapies depend on the theoretical premise that all living organisms are affected by and exist within electromagnetic (EM) fields. Therapeutic improvement of EM fields—altering the individual's energy for physiological relief—is postulated by creating bodily contact of an individual's EM field with a weak, nonthermal EM field to enhance blood and lymph circulation, cellular oxygenation, and detoxification, thus relieving pain, hastening the healing process, and boosting energy. Enhanced healing of bone fractures was evidenced in studies reported in 1984 (Barker, Dixon, Sharrard, & Sutcliffe), and accelerated wound healing was conferred by this energy modality (Bassett, 1993; Lee, Canaday, & Doong, 1993). Research to verify benefits of magnets applied on the body has not produced statistically significant results.

Biological treatments are chemical formulations for injection or ingestion theorized to achieve very particularized physiological responses, such as enhancing specific immune factors, but are not pharmaceutical drugs that target the elimination of disease-producing organisms or disease processes. Chelation therapy, for example, involves an injectable substance (ethylene diamine tetracetic acid [EDTA]) said to attach to toxic materials in the body (e.g., aluminum and lead) that are then eliminated from the body through excretion rather than reabsorbed. Chelation has been shown useful with cases of lead poisoning and is being assessed for other health problems (Chappell, 1995). EDTA has been added as an effective adjunct for atherosclerotic problems, including strokes and peripheral vascular disease (Goldberg et al., 2002).

Herbal Medicines (Botanical Medicine)

Medicinal herbal applications have a 60,000-year-old history, the most ancient form of medical treatment, with evidence dating as far back as the Neanderthal era (Solecki, 1975). In Europe, herbal therapies hold a long-honored tradition and are more commonly incorporated into standard treatment plans than in American medicine. Even across the United States, herbal regimens are inching into mainstream medical plans with science verifying what medical folklore has long posited. Herbals are plant substances, which can include the root, flower, stem, seeds, or leaves, used to enhance or correct improper functioning of organs and represent a core treatment component in TCM, Ayurvedic medicine, and naturopathy. Garlic (and its compounds), the herb most universally recognized for medicinal value (Blumenthal, Goldberg, & Brinckmann, 2000; Goldberg et al., 2002), takes a lead in varied applications. It is ingested to help reduce problematic cholesterol and elevated blood pressure (Vorberg & Schneider, 1990; Warshafsky, Kramer, & Sivak, 1993), is taken commonly for its antibiotic and antimicrobial properties (Sullivan, 2000), is a popular antidote for gout and rheumatism (Foster, 1991), and has been shown to reverse arterial plaqueing (Koscielny et al., 1999). In addition, in large epidemiological studies, modest intake was linked statistically with reduced intestinal cancer (Lawson,

1997). By 1998, 1,990 research papers had been published on the beneficial activities of garlic (Goldberg et al., 2002). In just one study among heart patients, 6 milligrams garlic daily resulted in a 35% reduction of heart attacks and a 45% reduction in mortality compared with placebo (Lawson, 1997).

RESEARCH DILEMMA

The best potential for increased respect and comprehension of CAM and integrative benefits is continuing controlled research. What impedes full investigation are issues of economics and real methodological conundrums. The bias against full studies can be significant, because unlike testing of single pharmaceutical drugs, the likelihood of financial gain from CAM is minuscule and the cost is great. In addition, most alternative systems, CAM protocols, and integrative regimens are difficult to study because they usually involve complex, multifaceted programs that are difficult to evaluate against single therapies and seem to defy unifocal investigative efforts, the most common scientific investigational approach. One additional puzzle is how to design a true double-blind study on certain practices such as meditation; that is, what can serve as a genuine placebo control? And finding groups to maintain as controls is a thorny task because surveys tell us the vast numbers of patients on their own initiative and in secret are receiving alternative treatments. Finally, even diagnostic categories among alternative systems do not always correspond to those of biomedicine, so comparisons can be inexact.

PROBLEMS AND CONCERNS

What confuses a definitive evidence base is that specifics of treatment vary considerably (e.g., Chinese versus Korean acupuncture). This variance among practices can be very problematic if counseling a client, for example, on the value of acupuncture for musculoskeletal pain based on documented randomized controlled trials due to uncertainty about real correspondence between the methodology used by the local acupuncturist and the precise approach tested in the research. For another example, it is not clear for migraines which precise acupuncture points are most effective, the appropriate duration for needle insertion, or the necessary number of treatments (Vickers, 2003).

An unresolved quandary haunts a full melding of practices: Can different medical models be integrated effectively and truly? That is, when diagnostic and therapeutic systems are based on very different biological and philosophical premises, can treatment plans be merged successfully? For example, a single disease presentation, in Western medicine labeled as stomach cancer, can point to several very different maladies in the Chinese system, such as stomach yin deficiency due to stomach heat, blood stagnation due to chi stagnation, or stomach yang deficiency (Beinfield & Korngold, 2003), each demanding a distinct, even incongruent, treatment. Although an American physician would reasonably and almost automatically prescribe one chemotherapy protocol intended specifically for stomach cancer, the Chinese doctor might advise very dissimilar regimens for this same stomach cancer, determined by the different Chinese diagnostic categories.

Another continuing concern is that formal training, credentialing, and licensure of CAM practitioners remains inconsistently monitored or required across the 50 states. (An exception is chiropractic, licensed in all states with specific training standards.) Even though the risk of toxicity of most herbal preparations is usually very small because many formulations incorporate multiple chemical substances believed to synergistically enhance their therapeutic potential, toxic consequences and adverse herb–drug interactions are possible. However, compared to prescriptive pharmaceuticals, supplements carry fractional hazards. Furthermore, experts acknowledge that at least 51% of prescriptive drugs can produce severe side effects that went undetected even in controlled testing prior to approved use

(Moore, Psaty, & Furberg, 1998). For these reasons, expert guidance is essential when a patient is being treated simultaneously for serious disease.

Because dietary supplements are sold as food compounds, they are unregulated by Food and Drug Administration standards. Quality issues, such as contamination and variation in content and processing, are a continuing worry for an untutored public (De Smet, 1999; Marrone, 1999). Some formulations hit the market with meaningless amounts of identified key ingredients; many do not even dissolve or disintegrate after ingested; and most are not standardized. Even if positive research findings are available on one product (e.g., black cohosh) indicating safety and benefits, there is no assurance that a different cohosh product will produce the same effect because actual dosing might be inconsistent.

Certainly some more aggressive alternative practices do carry the possibility of untoward consequences, but the potential for truly severe side effects from most CAM therapies seems dwarfed by that of pharmaceuticals or more invasive procedures. When CAM therapies are practiced skillfully and applied appropriately, the likelihood of problematic effects is minimized (Jonas, 1998). This consideration does not deny limited but real concerns about problematic interactions between alternative practices and conventional drugs. One such example is the use of special grapefruit preparations (as reported informally by a woman from Jamaica, October 2003) to reduce symptoms of hypertension. Regular grapefruit juice consumption is known to increase blood volume of specific antihypertensives, antihistamines, and antidepressants by down-regulating cytochrome P450, an enzyme that functions in the body to metabolize drugs (Beinfeld & Korngold, 2003). An example of possible herbal contraindication is the use of *Hypericum perforatum* (St. John's wort), available for purchase in health food stores and backed by scientific and popular literature as normally safe and effective with mild to moderate depressive symptoms. This usually benign herb is known to (a) augment the metabolism of protease inhibitors, thus reducing blood levels of such medications; (b) elevate the body's serotonin to potentiate the impact of monoamine oxidase inhibitor and selective serotonin reuptake inhibitor antidepression drugs; and (c) interfere with the full effectiveness of drugs such as cyclosporine and theophylline (Croom, 2000). Another undesired herb-drug complication, Ginkgo biloba, which is commonly used for memory and cognitive enhancement, can inhibit platelet aggregation (as does garlic), elevating anticoagulant effects of some prescription drugs. However, warnings such as these stem from scientific evaluations of each herb as a single agent. The impact observed is moderated when an herb or nutrient is one component in a multiple compound formulation, whereby, for instance, any anticoagulant concern is mitigated by the presence of other herbs. One recommendation for modifying posited drug-supplement problems is taking drugs separately from food consumption to avoid undesired digestive tract interactions (Blumenthal et al., 2000).

INSURANCE COVERAGE ISSUES

Several third-party insurance carriers were reported, even in the prior decade, to have covered 25% of the cost for CAM treatments used by cancer patients (Campion, 1993). One of the appeals of alternative practices to American consumers is financial. Many alternative treatments are less costly than conventional therapies; exceptions may be interventions such as antineoplastons (Ernst, 1994, 1995). In fact, in reporting use of alternatives among ethnic minorities, MacKenzie and her team (2003) noted that being uninsured—paying out of pocket—predicted greater likelihood of unconventional practices. Yet managed care companies, confronted by fierce competition, are now chasing the very lucrative CAM market to attract new enrollees from a public enamored with these once-obscure or seemingly exotic practices. One marketing strategy of managed care corporations to counter a growing

disenchantment with health maintenance organization restrictions is to attach a rider to a general policy to include some alternative care options. Other groups provide discounted access to nonconventional services—25% off practices such as chiropractic, acupuncture, and so on (Rauber, 1998). By 2000, 43 insurers covered alternative care, up from just 2 or 3 a few years earlier, and some are marketing packages with a blend of benefits (Pelletier & Astin, 2002).

CONCLUSION

Today's health-care terrain is a mélange of medical preferences and practices mirroring the nation's cultural plurality. Encouraging evidence implies that deep-rooted prejudices may be fading gradually and a new consensus emerging, one that holds that distinctions between alternative and conventional medicine are detrimental (Fontanarosa & Lundberg, 1998). Advocates of a broader medical philosophy believe that there is only good or bad medicine and that all health professionals are mandated to maintain an open mind to what might be most beneficial for each patient. On this principle, MacKenzie and her coauthors (2003) pointedly ask, "How well do the health systems we have created fit the persons we wish to serve?" (p. 56). One attempt to address this issue has been a corrective response to linguistic problems to untangle and rephrase complex medical terminology and to improve how professionals communicate disease and treatment information to patients from diverse backgrounds. But this effort has been motivated largely by the medical need to persuade patient compliance to seemingly foreign and misunderstood protocols (MacKenzie et al., 2003). Although medical professionals have initiated efforts at greater language congruence, the need to acknowledge and better integrate components of divergent medical practices and thinking into our biomedical paradigm is still unmet. To effectively serve and support individual clients, who embrace culturally diverse or idiosyncratic health beliefs but who might get lost in a labyrinth of technical and personally incongruent medical thinking, social workers are called on in their specialized professional role to build an expanding familiarity with divergent approaches as a bridge to better care.

SUGGESTED LEARNING EXERCISES

Learning Exercise 12.1

Consider this question: Can medical models shaped by dissimilar, nonparallel paradigms of health and healing be integrated effectively? If you believe it is possible, discuss limitations to combining modern conventional modalities with a treatment plan from an alternative system of medicine using detailed examples. Also, how would you propose that a medical team go about helping a client or patient have access to a treatment plan based on this integration of disparate medical models? If this is not possible in your opinion, explain why, with detailed and specific examples from the different alternative systems and how you would communicate this impossibility to a client/patient.

Learning Exercise 12.2

Using material from this chapter in conjunction with issues addressed in Chapter 11 on spirituality in health care and Chapter 6 on health theories, discuss how you would engage one of the next people in an open and supportive conversation of personal health practices to enable better care.

- A 40-year-old Mexican American (or Chinese American) woman diagnosed with stage II breast cancer, which can be treated effectively with chemotherapy, has not shown up for two of her scheduled appointments. Assume for this assignment that you have helped her find appropriate practical support and have communicated effectively the value of treatment and availability of pharmaceuticals to coun-

teract side effects, but you wish to understand what other factors prevent her from continuing with the oncologist's recommendations. Taking into account cultural health values while respecting individual preferences and examining your own medical predispositions, describe your preparatory thinking and your interaction with this woman. What do you need to consider before you actually meet with her? What questions and what suggestions might you offer? Then describe how you might present to her physician the rationale for why she has been using practices he or she might regard as problematic alternatives and how the physician can best create culturally and individually congruent recommendations.

- Consider your advance thinking and subsequent conversations with a 50-year-old African American man with uncontrolled hypertension. Either his disease is unresponsive to medications or, as his doctor implies, he is not adhering to his medical regimen. Alternatively, consider a Native American man in a similar scenario but with diabetes rather than hypertension. What alternative recommendations are worth consideration and investigation? What are some possible barriers to medical effects?

SUGGESTED RESOURCES

Beinfield, H., & Korngold, E. (1992). *Between heaven and earth: A guide to Chinese medicine.* New York, NY: Ballantine Books.

Blumenthal, M. (2003). *The ABC clinical guide to herbs.* Austin, TX: American Botanical Council.

Goldberg, B., Anderson, J.W., & Trivieri, L. (Ed.). (2002). *Alternative medicine: The definitive guide* (2nd ed.). Berkeley, CA: Celestial Arts.

Jonas, W. B., & Levin, J. S. (1999). *Essentials of complementary and alternative medicine.* Philadelphia, PA: Lippincott Williams & Wilkins.

Moss, D. (Ed.). (2003). *Handbook of mind-body medicine for primary care.* Thousand Oaks, CA: Sage.

Pizzorno, J., & Murray, M. T. (1998). *Encyclopedia of natural medicine* (revised 2nd ed.). Roseville, CA: Prima.

INFORMATIONAL WEB SITES

National Center for Complementary and Alternative Medicine (NCCAM)—Toll-free (888) 644-6226; TTY (for deaf or hard-of-hearing callers): (866) 464-3615; e-mail info@nccam.nih.gov

Insurance—www.consumeraction.gov/insurance.shtml

For a client/patient with medical insurance, information on CAM treatment coverage may be provided by state insurance departments.

Ornish, Dean—http://www.pmri.org/index.html

Medicare has proposed coverage for Dr. Dean Ornish's Program (a full diet/fitness/stress care regimen, a possible alternative to surgery) for Reversing Heart Disease, scheduled to begin September 2010.

REFERENCES

Adam, O. (1995). Anti-inflammatory diet in rheumatic diseases. *European Journal of Nutrition, 49*(10), 703–717.

Astin, J. A. (1998a). Why patients use alternative medicine: Results of a national study. *JAMA, 279*(19), 1548–1553.

Astin, J. A. (1998b). In reply. *JAMA, 280*(19), 1660–1661.

Baldwin, L. (1998). Letter to the editor. *JAMA, 280*(19), 1659–1660.

Barker, A. T., Dixon, R. A., Sharrard, W. J., & Sutcliffe, M. L. (1984). Pulsed magnetic field therapy for tibial non-union: Interim results of a double-blind trial. *Lancet, 1*(8384), 994–996.

Barnes, P. M., Powell-Griner, E., McFann, K., & Nahin, R. L. (2004). Complementary and alternative medicine use among adults: United States, 2002. *Vital Health and Statistics, 343,* 130–136.

Barzansky, B., & Etzel, S. I. (2003). Educational programs in U.S. medical schools, 2002–2003. *JAMA, 290,* 1190–1196.

Bassett, C. A. (1993). Beneficial effects of electromagnetic fields. *Journal of Cellular Biochemistry, 51*(4), 387–393.

Becerra, R. M., & Iglehart, A. P. (1995). Folk medicine use: Diverse populations in a metropolitan area. *Social Work in Health Care, 21*(4), 37–58.

Beinfield, H., & Korngold, E. (2003). Chinese medicine and cancer care. *Alternative Therapies, 9*(5), 38–52.

Benson, H., & Stuart, E. (1993). *The wellness book: The comprehensive guide to maintaining health and treating stress-related illness.* New York, NY: Simon & Schuster.

Birchall, A. (1990). A whiff of happiness. *New Scientist, 127,* 45–57.

Block, K. I. (1999). Nutritional biotherapy. In W. B. Jonas & J. S. Levin (Eds.), *Essentials of complementary and alternative medicine* (pp. 490–521). Philadelphia, PA: Lippincott Williams & Wilkins.

Blumenthal, J. A., Jiang, W., Babyak, M. A., Krantz, D. S., Frid, D. J., Coleman, R. E.,…Morris, J. J. (1997). Stress management and exercise training in cardiac patients with myocardial ischemia: Effects on prognosis and evaluation of mechanisms. *Archives Internal Medicine, 157*(19), 2213–2223.

Blumenthal, M., Goldberg, A., & Brinckmann, J. (2000). *Herbal medicine: Expanded Commission E Monographs.* Newton, MA: Integrative Medicine Communications.

Borins, M. (2002, June). *Taking care: Perspectives on complementary and alternative medicine.* Symposium presented at the meeting of the College of Physicians and Surgeons of Nova Scotia, Canada.

Brown, H., Cassileth, B. R., Lewis, J. P., & Renner, J. H. (1994, June 15). Alternative medicine, or quackery? *Patient Care, 28*(11), 80.

Burkitt, D. P., Walker, A. R., & Painter, N. S. (1974). Dietary fiber and disease. *JAMA, 229*(8), 1068–1074.

Burns, E., & Blarney, C. (1994). Using aromatherapy in childbirth. *Nursing Times, 90,* 54–60.

Campion, E. W. (1993). Why unconventional medicine? *New England Journal of Medicine, 328,* 282.

Cassileth, B. R. (1998). Overview of alternative/complementary medicine. *Cancer Practice, 6*(4), 243–245.

Cassileth, B. R., & Chapman, C. C. (1996). Alternative cancer medicine: A 10-year update. *Cancer Investigation, 14*(4), 396–404.

Cassileth, B. R., Luck, E., Strouse, T., & Bodenheimer, B. (1984). Contemporary unorthodox treatments in cancer medicine: A study of patients, treatments, and practitioners. *Annals of Internal Medicine, 101,* 105–113.

Chandra, R. K. (1992). Nutrition and immunity in the elderly. *Nutritional Review, 50*(12), 367–371.

Chao, M. T., Wade, C., & Kronenberg, F. (2008). Disclosure of complementary and alternative medicine to conventional medical providers: Variation by race/ethnicity and type of CAM. *Journal of the National Medical Association, 100*(11), 1341–1349.

Chappell, L. T. (1995). EDTA chelation therapy should be more commonly used in the treatment of vascular disease. *Alternative Therapies Health Medicine, 1*(2), 53–57.

Chopra, D. (1989). *Quantum healing: Exploring the frontiers of mind/body medicine.* New York, NY: Bantam.

Cohen, K. (1999). Native American medicine. In W. B. Jonas & J. S. Levin (Eds.), *Essentials of complementary and alternative medicine* (pp. 233–251). Philadelphia, PA: Lippincott Williams & Wilkins.

Committee on the Use of Complementary and Alternative Medicine by the American Public. (2005). *Complementary and Alternative Medicine in the United States.* Washington, DC: National Academies Press.

Corley, M. C., Ferriter, J., Zeh, J., & Gifford, C. (1995). Physiological and psychological effects of back rubs. *Applied Nursing Research, 8*(1), 39–42.

Croom, E. M. (2000, April 14). Major herbal medicines for which clinical studies appear promising. In D. M. Eisenberg & D. Foster (Eds.), *Recent advances in complementary and alternative medicine.* (Symposium, Harvard Clinical and Translational Science Center, course code PN 12).

Culliton, P. D., & Kiresuk, T. J. (1996). Overview of substance abuse acupuncture treatment research. *Journal of Alternative and Complementary Medicine, 2*(1), 149–165.

DeGood, D. (1996). *Effect of massage therapy and post-surgical outcomes. Research grant abstracts and results.* Rockville, MD: NIH Office of Alternative Medicine.

De Smet, P. A. (1999). The safety of herbal products. In W. B. Jonas & J. S. Levin (Eds.), *Essentials of complementary and alternative medicine* (pp. 108–147). Philadelphia, PA: Lippincott Williams & Wilkins.

Disbrow, E. A., Bennett, H. L., & Owings, J. T. (1993). Effect of preoperative suggestion on postoperative gastrointestinal motility. *West Journal Medicine, 158,* 488–492.

Dunn, C., Sleep, J., & Collett, D. (1995). Sensing an improvement: An experimental study to evaluate the use of aromatherapy, massage and periods of rest in an intensive care unit. *Journal Advances Nursing, 21*(1), 34–40.

Eisenberg, D. M. (1997). Advising patients who seek alternative medical therapies. *Annals of Internal Medicine, 127*(1), 61–69.

Eisenberg, D. M., Davis, R. B., Ettner, S. L., Appel, S., Wilkey, S., Van Rompay, M., & Kessler, R. C. (1998). Trends in alternative medicine use in the United States, 1990–1997: Results of a follow-up national survey. *JAMA, 280*(18), 1569–1575.

Eisenberg, D. M., Kessler, R. C., Foster, C., Norlock, F. E., Calkins, D. R., & Delbanco, T. L. (1993). Unconventional medicine in the United States: Prevalence, costs, and patterns of use. *New England Journal of Medicine, 326*(4), 246–252.

Eisenberg, D. M., Kessler, R. C., Van Rompay, M. I., Kaptchuk, T. J., Wilkey, S. A., Appel, S., & Davis, R. B. (2001). Perceptions about complementary therapies relative to conventional therapies among adults who use both: Results from a national survey. *Annals of Internal Medicine, 135*(5), 344–351.

Enqvist, B. (1991). Preoperative hypnotherapy and preoperative suggestions in general anesthesia: Somatic responses. *Hypnosis, 28,* 72–77.

Ernst, E. (1994). Complementary medicine: Common misconceptions [Editorial]. *Journal Research Sociology of Medicine, 88*(5), 244.

Ernst, E. (1995). Complementary cancer treatments: Hope or hazard? *Clinical Oncology, 7*(4), 259–272.

Ernst, E., & Cassileth, B. R. (1998). The prevalence of complementary/alternative medicine in cancer: A systematic review. *Cancer, 83*(4), 777–782.

Eskinazi, D. P. (1998). Factors that shape alternative medicine. *JAMA, 280*(18), 1621–1623.

Ezzo, J., Vickers, A., Richardson, M. A., Allen, C., Dibble, S. L., Issell, B.,…Zhang, G. (2005). Acupuncture-point stimulation for chemotherapy-induced nausea and vomiting. *Journal of Clinical Oncology, 23*(28), 7188–7198.

Fawzy, F. I., Fawzy, N. W., Hyun, C. S., Elashoff, R., Guthrie, D., Fahey, J. L., & Morton, D. L. (1993). Malignant melanoma: Effects of an early structured psychiatric intervention, coping, and affective state on recurrence and survival 6 years later. *Archives of General Psychiatry, 50*(9), 681–689.

Field, T. M., Schanberg, S. M., Scafidi, F., Bauer, C. R., Vega-Lahr, N., Garcia, R.,…Kuhn, C. M. (1986). Tactile/kinesthetic stimulation effects on preterm neonates. *Pediatrics, 77*(5), 654–658.

Findlay, S., Podolsky, D., & Silberner, J. (1991, September 23). Wonder cures from the fringe. *U.S. News & World Report,* 68–71, 73–74.

Fontanarosa, P. B., & Lundberg, G. D. (1998). Alternative medicine meets science. *JAMA, 280*(18), 1618–1619.

Foster, S. (1991). *Garlic botanical series 311.* Austin, TX: American Botanical Council.

Gaby, A. R. (1999). Orthomolecular medicine and megavitamin therapy. In W. B. Jonas & J. S. Levin (Eds.), *Essentials of complementary and alternative medicine* (pp. 459–471). Philadelphia, PA: Lippincott Williams & Wilkins.

Gandhi, R. (1996). The uses of auricular acupuncture in the field of substance misuse. *Psychiatric Care, 3,* 40–41.

Gerber, R. (1988). *Vibrational medicine: New choices for healing ourselves.* Sante Fe, NM: Bear & Co.

Ginandes, C., Brooks, P., Sando, W., Jones, C., & Aker, J. (2003). Can medical hypnosis accelerate post-surgical wound healing? *American Journal of Clinical Hypnosis, 45*(4), 333–351.

Goldberg, B., Anderson, J. W., & Trivieri, L. (Eds.). (2002). *Alternative medicine: The definitive guide* (2nd ed.). Berkeley, CA: Celestial Arts.

Hackman, R. M., Stern, J. S., & Gershwin, M. E. (2000). Hypnosis and asthma: A critical review. *Journal of Asthma, 37*(1), 1–15.

Hafner, R. J. (1982). Psychological treatment of essential hypertension: A controlled comparison of meditation and meditation plus biofeedback. *Biofeedback & Self-Regulation, 7*(3), 305-316.

Harrison, L., Olivet, L., Cunningham, K., Bodin, M. B., & Hicks, C. (1996). Effects of gentle human touch on pre-term infants: Pilot study results. *Neonatal Network, 15*(2), 35–42.

Hemila, H. (1994). Does vitamin C alleviate the symptoms of the common cold? A review of current evidence. *Scandinavian Journal of Infectious Disease, 26*(1), 1–6.

Hillhouse, J., & Adler, C. (1991). Stress, health, and immunity: A review of the literature and implications for the nursing profession. *Holistic Nurse Practitioner, 5*(4), 22–23.

Hsiao, A. F., Wong, M. D., Goldstein, M. S., Yu, H. J., Andersen, R. M., Brown, E. R.,...Wenger, N. S. (2006). Variation in complementary and alternative medicine (CAM) use across racial/ethnic groups and the development of ethnic-specific measures of CAM use. *Journal of Alternative and Complementary Medicine, 12*(3), 281–290.

Hudson, C. (1996, Spring). Acupuncture and traditional Oriental medicine in the treatment of HIV and AIDS. *STEP Perspective, 8*(1), 2–3.

Hurdle, D. E. (2002). Native Hawaiian traditional healing: Culturally based interventions for social work practice. *Social Work, 47*(2), 183–193.

Institute of Medicine. (2005). *Complementary and alternative medicine in the United States.* Washington, DC. National Academy of Science.

Jacobs, J., Jimenez, L. M., Gloyd, S. S., Gale, J. L., & Crothers, D. (1994). Treatment of acute childhood diarrhea with homeopathic medicine: A randomized clinical trial in Nicaragua. *Pediatrics, 93*(5), 718–725.

Jackson, D. A. (1997). Acupuncture for the relief of pain: An overview. *Physical Therapy Reviews, 2,* 13–18.

Jarvis, K. B., Phillips, R. B., & Morris, E. K. (1991). Cost per case of back injury claims: Chiropractic versus medical management for conditions with identical diagnosis codes. *Journal of Occupational Medicine, 33*(8), 847–852.

Johansson, K., Lindgren, I., Widner, H., Wiklund, I., & Johansson, B. B. (1993). Can sensory stimulation improve the functional outcome in stroke patients? *Neurology, 43*(11), 2189–2192.

Jonas, W. B. (1998). Alternative medicine: Learning from the past, examining the present, advancing to the future. *JAMA, 280*(18), 1616–1617.

Justice, B. (1996). Alternative medicine's relevance to public health practice and research. *Alternative Therapies and Health Medicine, 2*(3), 24–25.

Kabat-Zinn, J., Lipworth, L., & Burney, R. (1985). The clinical use of mindfulness meditation for the self-regulation of chronic pain. *Journal of Behavioral Medicine, 8*(2), 163–190.

Kabat-Zinn, J., Wheeler, E., Light, T., Skillings, A., Scharf, M. J., Cropley, T. G.,...Bernhard, J. D. (1998). Influence of a mindfulness meditation-based stress reduction intervention on rates of skin clearing in patients with moderate to severe psoriasis undergoing phototherapy (UVB) and photochemotherapy (PUVA). *Psychosomatic Medicine, 60*(5), 625–632.

Keller, E., & Bzdek, V. M. (1986). Effects of therapeutic touch on tension headache pain. *Nurse Researcher, 35*(2), 101–106.

Kleijnen, J., Knipschild, P., & Riet, G. (1991). Trials of homeopathy. *British Medical Journal, 302*(6782), 960.

Koscielney, J., Klussendorf, D., Latza, R., Schmitt, R., Siegel, G., & Kiesewetter, H. (1999). The antiatherosclerotic effect of Allium sativum. *Atherosclerosis, 144*(1), 237–249.

Krajewski-Jaime, E. R. (1991). Folk-healing among Mexican-American families as a consideration in the delivery of child welfare and child health care services. *Child Welfare, 70*(2), 157–167.

Kramer, N. A. (1990). Comparison of therapeutic touch and casual touch in stress reduction of hospitalized children. *Pediatric Nursing, 16*(5), 483–485.

Krippner, S. (1995). A cross-cultural comparison of four healing models. *Alternative Therapies, 1*(1), 21–29.

Launso, L., Brendstrup, E., & Amberg, S. (1999). An exploratory study of reflexological treatment for headache. *Alternative Therapies in Health and Medicine, 5*(3), 57–65.

Lawrence, D. J., & Meeker, W. C. (2007). Chiropractic and CAM utilization: A descriptive review. *Chiropractic and Osteopathy, 15*(2), 1–27.

Lawson, L. D. (1997, May). The science and therapeutic effects of garlic and other allium species. Program book entry from the Functional Foods for Health, Sixth Annual Retreat, University of Illinois at Chicago and the University of Illinois at Urbana-Champaign.

Lee, R. C., Canaday, D. J., & Doong, H. (1993). A review of the biophysical basis for the clinical application of electric fields in soft tissue repair. *Journal of Burn Care and Rehabilitation, 14,* 319–335.

Lerner, I. J., & Kennedy, B. J. (1992). The prevalence of questionable methods of cancer treatment in the United States. *CA: A Cancer Journal for Clinicians, 42*(3), 181–191.

Levitan, A. A. (1992). The use of hypnosis with cancer patients. *Psychiatric Medicine, 10*(1), 119–131.

Long, J. M., Machiran, N. M., & Bertell, B. L. (1986). Biofeedback: An adjunct to social work practice. *Social Work, 31,* 476–478.

Loveland-Cook, C. S., Becvar, D. S., & Pontious, S. L. (2000). Complementary alternative medicine in health and mental health: Implications for social work practice. *Social Work in Health Care, 31*(3), 39–47.

Lu, D. P., Lu, G. P., & Kleinman, L. (2001). Acupuncture and clinical hypnosis for facial and head and neck pain: A single crossover comparison. *American Journal of Clinical Hypnosis, 44*(2), 141–148.

Lynch, D. (1998). Applications of clinical hypnosis in cancer therapy. In W. Mathews & J. H. Edgette (Eds.), *The evolution of brief therapy: An annual publication of the Milton H. Erickson Foundation* (pp. 161–203). New York, NY: Brunner/Mazel.

MacIntosh, A. (1999, July). Understanding the differences between conventional, alternative, complementary, integrative and natural medicine. *Townsend Letter for Doctors and Patients,* 60–62.

MacKenzie, E. R., Taylor, L., Bloom, B. S., Hufford, D. J., & Johnson, J. C. (2003). Ethnic minority use of complementary and alternative medicine (CAM): A national probability survey of CAM utilizers. *Alternative Therapies, 9*(4), 50–56.

Marchioro, G., Azzarello, G., Viviani, F., Barbato, F., Pavanetto, M., Rosetti, F.,...Vinante, O. (2000). Hypnosis in the treatment of anticipatory nausea and vomiting in patients receiving cancer chemotherapy. *Oncology, 59*(2), 100–104.

Marrone, C. M. (1999). Safety issues with herbal products. *Annals of Pharmacotherapy, 33*(12), 1359–1362.

Meade, T. W., Dyer, S., Browne, W., Townsend, J., & Frank, A. O. (1990). Low back pain of mechanical origin: Randomized comparison of chiropractic and hospital outpatient treatment. *British Medical Journal, 300*(6737), 1431–1437.

Merriam-Webster. (2003). *Merriam-Webster's Collegiate Dictionary* (11th edition). Springfield, MA: Author.

Molassiotis, A., Fernadez-Ortega, P., Pud, D., Ozden, G., Scott, J. A., Panteli, V.,...Patiraki, E. (2005). Use of complementary and alternative medicine in cancer patients. *Annals of Oncology, 16*(4), 655–663.

Montgomery, G. H., DuHamel, K. N., & Redd, W. H. (2000). A meta-analysis of hypnotically induced analgesia. *International Journal of Clinical and Experimental Hypnosis, 48*(2), 138–153.

Montgomery, G. H., Bovbjerg, D. H., Schnur, J. B., David, D., Goldfarb, A., Weltz, C. R.,...Silverstein, J. (2007). A randomized clinical trial of a brief hypnosis intervention to control side effects in breast surgery patients. *Journal of the National Cancer Institute, 99*(17), 1304–1312.

Moore, K., & Schmais, L. (2000, November/December). The ABCs of complementary and alternative therapies and cancer treatment. *Oncology Issues,* 20–22.

Moore, T. J., Psaty, B. M., & Furberg, C. D. (1998). Time to act on drug safety. *JAMA, 279*(19), 1571–1573.

Mortensen, S. A., Aabo, K., Jonsson, T., & Baandrup, U. (1986). Clinical and non-invasive assessment of anthracycline cardiotoxicity: Perspectives on myocardial protection. *International Journal of Clinical Pharmacological Research, 6*(3), 137–150.

Murray, M. T., & Pizzorno, J. (1996). *Encyclopedia of nutritional supplements: The essential guide for improving your health naturally.* New York, NY: Random House.

Nahin, R. L., Barnes, P. M., Stussman, B. J., & Bloom, B. (2009). Costs of complementary and alternative medicine (CAM) and frequency of visits to CAM practitioners: United States, 2007. *National Health Statistics Reports, 18.*

National Center for Complementary and Alternative Medicine. (2000, June). *General information about complementary and alternative medicine and the National Center for Complementary and Alternative Medicine* (Pub. M-42). Silver Spring, MD: NCCAM Clearinghouse.

National Institutes of Health. (1992). *Alternative medicine: Expanding medical horizons.* Washington, DC: U.S. Government Printing Office.

Neff, N. (2004). Folk medicine in Hispanics in the southwestern United States (Module VII). Retrieved from www.rice.edu/projects/HispanicHealth/Courses /mod7/mod7.

Newton, P. (1996). *Hypnotic imagery and immunity. Research grant abstracts and results.* Rockville, MD: NIH Office of Alternative Medicine.

Ni, H., Simile, C., & Hardy, A. M. (2002). Utilization of complementary and alternative medicine by United States adults: Results from the 1999 National Health Interview Survey. *Medical Care, 40*(4), 353–358.

Noonan, D. (2002, December 2). For the littlest patients. *Newsweek,* 58–62.

Ornish, D., Scherwitz, L. W., Billings, J. H., Brown, S. E., Gould, K. L., Merritt, T. A., Brand, R. J. (1998). Intensive lifestyle changes for reversal of coronary heart disease. *JAMA, 280*(23), 2001–2007.

Ornish, D., Scherwitz, L. W., Doody, R. S., Kesten, D., McLanahan, S. M., Brown, S. E.,...Gotto, A. M., Jr. (1983). Effects of stress management training and dietary changes in treating ischemic heart disease. *JAMA, 249*(1), 54–59.

Pachter, L. (1994). Culture and clinical care: Folk illness beliefs and their implications for health care delivery. *JAMA, 271,* 690–694.

Pan, C. X., Morrison, R. S., Ness, J., Fugh-Berman, A., & Leipzig, M. (2000). Complementary and alternative medicine in the management of pain, dyspnea, and nausea and vomiting near the end of life: A systematic review. *Journal of Pain and Symptom Management, 20*(5), 374–387.

Pelletier, K. R., & Astin, J. A. (2002). Integration and reimbursement of complementary and alternative medicine by managed care and insurance providers: 2000 update and cohort analysis. *Alternative Therapies in Health Medicine, 8*(1), 38–39.

Pietroni, P. C. (1994). The interface between complementary medicine and general practice. *Journal of the Royal Society of Medicine* (Suppl. 22), S28–S30.

Podolsky, D. (1991, September 23). Big claims, no proof. *U.S. News & World Report,* 77.

Quinn, J. F., & Strelkauskas, A. J. (1993). Psychoimmunological effects of therapeutic touch on practitioners and recently bereaved recipients: A pilot study. *Advances in Nursing Science, 15*(4), 13–26.

Rattenbury, J. (1995, January). The other health care reform: From acupuncture to massage therapy and beyond—A guide to alternative treatments that are winning patients and even, in some cases, the grudging acceptance of the medical establishment. *Chicago,* 62–65.

Rauber, C. (1998). HMO: Open to alternatives. *Modern Healthcare, 28*(36), S7.

Richardson, M. A., Sanders, T., Palmer, J. L., Greisinger, A., & Singletary, S. E. (2000). Complementary/alternative medicine use in a comprehensive cancer center and the implications for oncology. *Journal of Clinical Oncology, 18,* 2505–2521.

Scholten, R., & Van Rompay, M. (2000, January). *Complementary and alternative medical (CAM) therapies: Information resources for health professionals.* Boston, MA. Beth Israel Deaconess Medical Center, Center for Alternative Medicine Research and Education.

Seaward, B. L. (1997). *Managing stress: Principles and strategies for health and well-being* (2nd ed.). Boston, MA: Jones and Bartlett.

Sims, S. (1986). Slow stroke back massage for cancer patients. *Nursing Times, 82*(13), 47–50.

Sloman, R. (1995). Relaxation and the relief of cancer pain. *Nursing Clinics of North America, 30*(4), 697–709.

Solecki, R. S. (1975). Shanidar IV, a Neanderthal flower burial of northern Iraq. *Science, 190*(28), 880–881.

Sparber, A., Bauer, L., Curt, G., Eisenberg, D., Levin, T., Parks, S., . . . Wootton, J. (2000). Use of complementary medicine by adult patients participating in cancer clinical trials. *Oncology Nurses Forum, 27*(4), 623–630.

Stephenson, L. N., & Dalton, J. (2003). Using reflexology for pain management: A review. *Journal of Holistic Nursing, 21*(2), 179–191.

Sullivan, M. J. (2000, October). Integrative medicine: Making it work for you. *Emergency Medicine, 10,* 76–83.

Syrjala, K. L., Cummings, C., & Donaldson, G. W. (1992). Hypnosis or cognitive behavioral training for the reduction of pain and nausea during treatment: A controlled clinical trial. *Pain, 63*(2), 189–198.

Takeda, W., & Wessel, J. (1994). Acupuncture for the treatment of pain of osteoarthritic knees. *Arthritis Care and Research, 7*(3), 118–122.

Taylor, E. (1995). Homeopathic medicine. *Alternative Therapies in Health and Medicine, 1*(1), 72–73.

Testerman, J. K., Morton, K. R., Mason, R. A., & Ronan, A. M. (2004). Patient motivations for using complementary and alternative medicine. *Complementary Health Practice Review, 9*(2), 81–92.

Troesch, L. M., Rodehaver, C. B., Delaney, E. A., & Yanes, B. (1993). The influence of guided imagery on chemotherapy-related nausea and vomiting. *Oncology Nursing Forum, 20,* 1179–1185.

Vickers, A. (2003). *Introduction to evidence-based complementary medicine.* Retrieved from http://ktclearinghouse.ca/cebm/syllabi/complementary/intro

Vorberg, G., & Schneider, B. (1990). Therapy with garlic: Results of a placebo-controlled, double-blind study. *British Journal of Clinical Practice Supplement, 69,* 7–11.

Warshafsky, S., Kramer, R., & Sivak, S. (1993). Effect of garlic on total serum cholesterol: A meta-analysis. *Annals of Internal Medicine, 119*(7), 599–605.

Weil, A. (2001). CAM and continuing education: the future is now. *Alternative Therapies in Health and Medicine, 7*(3), 32–34.

Wells-Federman, C. L., Stuart, E. M., Deckro, J. P., Mandle, C. L., Baim, M., & Medich, C. (1995). The mind-body connection: The psychophysiology of many traditional nursing interventions. *Clinical Nursing Specialist, 9*(1), 59–66.

Wetzel, S., Eisenberg, D. M., & Kaptchuk, T. J. (1998). Courses involving complementary and alternative medicine at U.S. medical schools. *JAMA, 280*(9), 784–787.

Wharton, J. C. (1999). The history of complementary and alternative medicine. In W. B. Jonas & J. S. Levin (Eds.), *Essentials of complementary and alternative medicine* (pp. 16–45). Philadelphia, PA: Lippincott Williams & Wilkins.

Yates, J. S., Mustian, K. M., Morrow, G. R., Gillies, L. J., Padmanaban, D., Atkins, J. N., . . . Colman, L. K. (2005). Prevalence of complementary and alternative medicine use in cancer patients during treatment. *Supportive Care in Cancer, 13*(10), 806–811.

13

Families, Health, and Illness

JOHN S. ROLLAND

Illness, disability, and death are universal experiences in families. The real question is not *if* we will face these issues but when in our lives they will occur, under what kinds of conditions, how long they will last, and how serious they will be. With major advances in medical technology, people are living much longer with conditions that in the past have been fatal. This means that ever-growing numbers of families are living with chronic disorders over an increasingly long time span and coping with a greater number of conditions, often simultaneously. This chapter provides a normative, preventive model for assessment, psychoeducation, and intervention with families facing chronic and life-threatening conditions. This model offers a systemic view of healthy family adaptation to serious illness as a developmental process over time in relation to the complexities and diversity of contemporary family life, modern medicine, and existing flawed models of health-care delivery and access to care.

Chapter Objectives
- Outline a comprehensive family systems model for assessment and clinical intervention with families facing chronic illness and disability.
- Describe the psychosocial demands of illness based on their pattern of onset, course, outcome, incapacitation, and level of uncertainty.
- Delineate the crisis, chronic, and terminal phases of illness; the transitions between phases; and the psychosocial developmental tasks associated with each phase.
- Discuss the interface of illness, individual, and family development; multigenerational

legacies of illness and loss; and how these legacies relate to coping and adaptation to chronic illness.
- Describe how health belief systems affect a patient's or family's response to illness.

OVERVIEW OF THE FAMILY SYSTEMS-ILLNESS MODEL

Over the past 30 years, family-centered, collaborative, biopsychosocial models of health care have grown and evolved (Blount, 1998; Doherty & Baird, 1983; Engel, 1977; McDaniel, Campbell, Hepworth, & Lorenz, 2005; McDaniel, Hepworth, & Doherty, in press; Miller, McDaniel, Rolland, & Feetham, 2006; Rolland, 1994a; Seaburn, Gunn, Mauksch, Gawinski, & Lorenz, 1996; Wood et al., 2008). There is substantial evidence for the mutual influence of family functioning, health, and physical illness (Carr & Springer, 2010; D'Onofrio & Lahey, 2010; Weihs, Fisher, & Baird, 2002) and the usefulness of family-centered interventions with chronic health conditions (Campbell, 2003). Weihs and colleagues (2002) summarized the increasing body of research regarding the impact of serious illness on families across the life span and the relationship of family dynamics to illness behavior, adherence, and disease course. In this report, a broad definition of *family* was used. *Family* was defined as a "group of intimates with strong emotional bonds...and with a history and a future as a group" (p. 8). Most illness management takes place within the context of the family environment. Social work interventions in health settings aim to help families adjust to and live with the demands of an illness or disability, assist families in navigating the health-care system, and enhance quality of life for the entire family.

There is a clear need for a conceptual model that provides a guide useful to both clinical practice and research, one that allows a dynamic, open communication between these disciplines. What is most needed is a comprehensive way to organize our thinking about all the complex interactions among biological illness, family, individual family members, and professionals involved in providing care. We need a model that can accommodate the changing landscape of interactions between these "parts of the system" over the course of the illness and the changing seasons over the life course.

Families enter the world of illness and disability without a psychosocial map. To master the challenges presented by an illness or disability, families must understand the impact of the condition on the entire family network. The Family Systems-Illness Model that was developed by Rolland (1984, 1987a, b, 1990, 1994a, 1998) is based on a strength-oriented perspective, viewing family relationships as a resource and emphasizing possibilities for resilience and growth, not just liabilities and risks (Walsh, 2006). This model provides social workers with a framework for assessing the impact of an illness or disability on family life and for structuring interventions to meet the needs of family members.

Defined in system terms, an effective psychosocial model for assessing the impact of illness on family life needs to encompass all people affected by the condition. The first step to constructing such a model is to redefine the unit of care to include the family or caregiving system rather than just the ill individual (McDaniel et al., in press). This is a departure from the medical model's narrow focus on the patient alone. By using a broad definition of family as the cornerstone of the caregiving system, we can describe a model of successful coping and adaptation based on family system strengths. By viewing the family as the unit of care, in which a broad range of family forms and dynamics is normative, social workers can apply a model that addresses the fit between family resources and strengths and the demands of the condition over time.

In situations of chronic disorders, a basic task for families is to create a meaning for the illness situation that preserves their sense of competency and mastery. At the extremes, competing ideologies can leave families with a choice between a biological explanation or one of personal responsibility (e.g., illness as retribution for wrongdoing). Families desperately need reassurance that they are handling illnesses appropriately. (Bad things do happen to good people.) These needs often occur in the context of a vague or nonexistent psychosocial map. Many families, particularly those with untimely disorders, find themselves in unfamiliar territory and without guides. This fact highlights the need for a preventive, psychoeducational approach that helps families anticipate normative illness-related developmental tasks over time in a fashion that maximizes their sense of control and mastery.

To create a normative context for their illness experience, families need a four-part foundation:

1. *They need a psychosocial understanding of the condition in systems terms.* This means learning the expected pattern of practical and affective demands of a disorder over the life course of the condition, including a time frame for disease-related developmental tasks associated with different phases of the unfolding disorder.

2. *Families need to understand themselves as a systemic functional unit.*

3. *They need an appreciation of individual and family life-cycle patterns and changes to facilitate their incorporation of changing developmental demands for the family unit and individual members in relation to the demands of a chronic disorder.*

4. *Families need to understand the cultural, ethnic, spiritual, and gender-based beliefs that guide the type of caregiving system they construct.* This includes guiding principles

that define roles, rules of communication, definitions of success or mastery, and fit with beliefs of the health-care providers. Family understanding in these areas facilitates a more holistic integration of the disorder and the family as a functional family-health/illness system evolving over time.

The Family Systems-Illness Model addresses three dimensions: (1) psychosocial types of health conditions, (2) major developmental phases in their natural history, and (3) key family system variables (see Figure 13.1). It attends to the expected psychosocial demands of a disorder through its various phases, family systems dynamics that emphasize family and individual development, multigenerational patterns, and belief systems (including influences of culture, ethnicity, spirituality, and gender; see Figure 13.2). The model emphasizes the match between the psychosocial demands of the disorder over time and the strengths and vulnerabilities of a family.

Psychosocial Types of Illness

The standard disease classification used in medical settings is based on purely biological

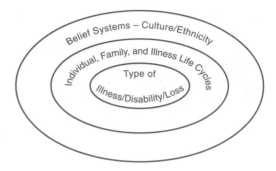

Figure 13.2   Family Systems-Illness Model
Source: From *Families, Illness, and Disability: An Integrative Treatment Model,* by J. S. Rolland, 1994a, New York, NY: Basic Books. Reprinted with permission.

criteria that are clustered in ways to establish a medical diagnosis and treatment plan rather than on the psychosocial demands on patients and their families. The alternative classification scheme presented here provides a better link between the biological and psychosocial worlds and thereby clarifies the relationship between chronic illness and the family (Rolland, 1984, 1994a). The goal of this typology is to define meaningful and useful categories with similar psychosocial demands for a wide array of chronic illnesses affecting individuals across the life span.

Onset

Illnesses can be divided into those that have either an acute onset, such as strokes, or a gradual onset, such as Alzheimer's disease. For acute-onset illnesses, emotional and practical changes are compressed into a short period of time, requiring families to mobilize their crisis-management skills more rapidly. Families that are able to tolerate highly charged emotional situations, exchange roles flexibly, problem-solve efficiently, and utilize outside resources will have an advantage in managing acute-onset conditions. Gradual-onset conditions, such as Parkinson's disease, allow a more gradual period of adjustment.

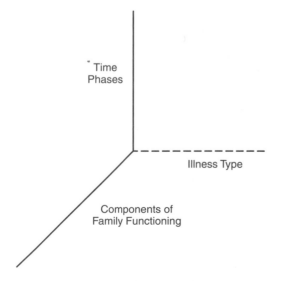

Figure 13.1   Three-Dimensional Model
Source: From "Chronic Illness and the Life Cycle: A Conceptual Framework," by J. S. Rolland, 1987a, *Family Process, 26*(2), 203–221. Reprinted with permission.

Course

The course of chronic diseases generally takes three forms: progressive, constant, or relapsing/episodic. With a progressive disease, such as Alzheimer's or Parkinson's, the family is faced with a perpetually symptomatic family member whose disability worsens in a stepwise or gradual way. The family must live with the prospect of continual role change and adaptation to continued losses as the disease progresses. Increasing strain on family caregiving is caused by exhaustion, with few periods of relief from the demands of the illness, and by new caregiving tasks over time.

With a constant-course illness, the occurrence of an initial event is followed by a stable biological course, such as a single heart attack or spinal cord injury. Typically, after an initial period of recovery, the illness is characterized by some clear-cut deficit or limitation. The family is faced with a semipermanent change that is stable and predictable over a considerable time span. Therefore, the potential for family exhaustion exists without the strain of new role demands over time.

Relapsing, or episodic-course illnesses, such as back problems and asthma, are distinguished by the alternation of stable low-symptom periods with periods of flare-up or exacerbation. Families are strained by both the frequency of transitions between periods of crisis and noncrisis and ongoing uncertainty about when the disorder might recur. Families must develop two modes of operation, one to cope with flare-ups and another to address periods of relative stability. Families must remain flexible as they alternate between these two forms of organization. The wide psychological discrepancy between low-symptom periods versus flare-up is a particularly taxing feature unique to relapsing diseases.

Outcome

The extent to which a chronic illness leads to death or shortens a person's life span has a profound psychosocial impact. The most crucial factor is the initial expectation of whether a disease will cause death. On one end of the continuum are illnesses that do not typically affect the life span, such as allergies

or arthritis. At the other extreme are illnesses that are clearly progressive and fatal, such as metastatic cancer. An intermediate, more unpredictable category includes both illnesses that shorten the life span, such as heart disease, and those that may bring sudden death, such as hemophilia. A major difference between these kinds of outcome is the degree to which the family experiences anticipatory loss and its pervasive effects on family life (Rolland, 1990, 2004).

Incapacitation

Disability can involve impairment of cognition (e.g., Alzheimer's disease), sensation (e.g., blindness), movement (e.g., stroke with paralysis), stamina (e.g., heart disease), disfigurement (e.g., mastectomy), and conditions associated with social stigma (e.g., acquired immunodeficiency syndrome [AIDS]; Olkin, 1999). The extent, kind, and timing of disability imply sharp differences in the degree of family stress. For instance, the combined cognitive and motor deficits caused by a stroke necessitate greater family reorganization than those caused by a spinal cord injury, in which cognitive abilities are unaffected. For some illnesses, such as stroke, disability often is worst at the beginning. For progressive diseases, such as Alzheimer's, disability looms as an increasing problem in later phases of the illness, allowing a family more time to prepare for anticipated changes and an opportunity for the ill member to participate in disease-related family planning while still cognitively able (Boss, 1999).

The predictability of an illness, or the degree of uncertainty about the specific way in which it will unfold, overlays all other variables. For illnesses with highly unpredictable courses, such as multiple sclerosis, family coping and adaptation, especially future planning, are hindered by anticipatory anxiety and ambiguity about what the family will encounter. Families able to put long-term uncertainty into perspective are best prepared to avoid the risks of exhaustion and dysfunction.

By combining the types of onset, course, outcome, and incapacitation into a grid, we generate a typology that clusters illnesses according to similarities and differences in patterns that pose differing psychosocial demands.

Time Phases of Illness

Too often, discussions of "coping with cancer," "managing disability," or "dealing with life-threatening disease" approach illness as a static state and fail to appreciate the dynamic unfolding of illness processes over time. The concept of time phases allows social workers and families to think longitudinally and to understand chronic illness as an ongoing process with normative landmarks, transitions, and changing demands. Each phase of an illness poses its own psychosocial demands and developmental tasks that require significantly different strengths, attitudes, or changes from a family. The core psychosocial themes in the natural history of chronic disease can be described in three major phases: crisis, chronic, and terminal (see Figure 13.3, Table 13.1).

Crisis Phase

The crisis phase includes any symptomatic period before diagnosis through the initial readjustment period after a diagnosis and initial treatment planning. This phase presents a number of key tasks for the ill member and family. Moos (1989) describes certain universal, practical illness-related tasks, including (a) learning to cope with any symptoms or disability, (b) adapting to health-care settings and treatment procedures, and (c) establishing and maintaining workable relationships with

Table 13.1   Phases of Illness Developmental Tasks

Crisis Phase

1. Family understands itself in systems terms.
2. Family has a psychosocial understanding of illness.
   a. In practical and emotional terms.
   b. In longitudinal and developmental terms.
3. Family appreciates developmental perspective (individual, family, illness life cycles).
4. Family experiences crisis reorganization.
5. Family creates meaning that promotes family mastery and competence.
6. Family defines *challenge* as shared one in "we" terms.
7. Family accepts permanence of illness/disability.
8. Family grieves loss of family identity before chronic disorder.
9. Family acknowledges possibilities of further loss while sustaining hope.
10. Family develops flexibility to ongoing psychosocial demands of illness.
11. Family learns to live with symptoms.
12. Family adapts to treatments and health-care settings.
13. Family establishes functional collaborative relationship with health-care providers.

Chronic Phase

1. Maximize autonomy for all family members given constraints of illness.
2. Balance connectedness and separateness of family members.
3. Minimize relationship skews in the family.
4. Maximize mindfulness to possible impact on current and future phases of family and individual life cycles.

Terminal Phase

1. Complete the process of anticipatory grief and unresolved family issues.
2. Support the terminally ill member.
3. Help survivors and dying member live as fully as possible in the time remaining.
4. Begin the family reorganization process.

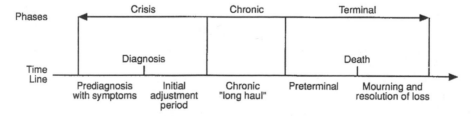

Figure 13.3   Timeline and Phases of Illness

Source: From *Families, Illness, and Disability: An Integrative Treatment Model,* by J. S. Rolland, 1994a, New York, NY: Basic Books. Reprinted with permission.

the health-care team. There also are critical tasks of a more general, existential nature. The family needs to (a) create a meaning for the illness that maximizes a sense of mastery and competency, (b) grieve for the loss of health, (c) gradually accept the illness as permanent while maintaining a sense of continuity between its past and future, (d) pull together to cope with the immediate crisis, and (e) in the face of uncertainty, develop goals for the future.

During this initial adjustment period, health professionals have enormous influence over a family's approach to and sense of competence in accomplishing these developmental tasks. Initial meetings and advice given at the time of diagnosis can be thought of as a "framing event." Because families are so vulnerable at this point, clinicians need to be extremely sensitive in their interactions with family members. They should be aware of messages conveyed by their behavior in interactions with the family. This framing event has a powerful influence on what the family decides is normal. For instance, if a clinician meets with parents separately from adolescents to give them information about a cancer diagnosis and prognosis, the parents may assume they were being instructed implicitly to protect their adolescent from any discussion of the illness. Social workers can encourage physicians to ask patients whom they would like to include in important discussions or can help reframe these experiences for families by asking them about their preferences.

With life-threatening conditions that can cause sudden death (e.g., heart attack), there is a higher premium on early frank conversation. Knowing an ill member's wishes concerning heroic medical efforts and life support can benefit everyone. For example, in one family, the father had serious heart disease. Everyone, including the father, became emotionally paralyzed by fear because end-of-life decision making had been avoided. Family consultations facilitated the father making his wishes known regarding the limits on life-saving efforts. This relieved his family members because they knew his feelings if they had to make life-and-death decisions. For the father, making his wishes known not only gave him a sense of personal control over the end of his life but also freed him to focus on living well and maximizing his physical well-being. Despite the short-run challenge of having end-of-life discussions, it is important to keep in mind that many of the most wrenching end-of-life experiences for families occur when the wishes of a dying member are unknown or have been disregarded. With conditions, such as Alzheimer's disease, involving progressive dementia, there is added incentive for conversations before the affected person's cognitive impairment makes meaningful discussion impossible (Boss, 1999).

Chronic Phase

The chronic phase, whether long or short, is the time span between the initial diagnosis/readjustment and the third phase, when issues of death and terminal illness predominate. This phase can be marked by constancy, progression, or episodic change. It has been referred to as "the long haul" or "day-to-day living with chronic illness" phase. Often the patient and family have come to grips psychologically and organizationally with permanent changes and have devised an ongoing coping stratcgy. The ability of the family to maintain the semblance of a normal life, attending as equitably as possible to both the illness and to normative developmental tasks, is key during this period. If the illness is fatal, this is a time of living in limbo. For certain highly debilitating but not clearly fatal illnesses, such as a massive stroke or dementia, the family can feel saddled by an exhausting problem "without end." Paradoxically, the family may feel its hope to resume a "normal" life can be realized only after the death of the ill member. The maintenance of maximum autonomy for all family members in the face of prolonged adversity helps to offset trapped, helpless feelings.

For long-term disorders, customary patterns of intimacy for couples become skewed by discrepancies between the ill member and the well spouse/caregiver (Rolland, 1994b). As one young husband lamented in a clinical meeting regarding his wife's cancer, "It was hard enough 2 years ago to absorb that, even if Ann was cured, her radiation treatment would make pregnancy impossible. Now I find it unbearable that her continued slow, losing battle with cancer makes it impossible to go for our dreams like other couples our age." Normative ambivalence and escape fantasies often remain underground and contribute to survivor guilt. Psychoeducational family interventions that normalize such emotions related to threatened loss can help prevent destructive cycles of blame, shame, and guilt.

Terminal Phase

In the terminal phase of an illness, the inevitability of death becomes apparent and dominates family life. At this point, the family must cope with issues of separation, death, mourning, and beginning the reorganization process needed for the resumption of "normal" family life beyond the loss (Walsh & McGoldrick, 2004). Families that adapt best to this phase are able to shift their views of hope and mastery from controlling the illness to a successful process of letting go. Optimal coping involves emotional openness as well as dealing with the myriad practical tasks at hand. This includes seeing this phase as an opportunity to share precious time together to acknowledge the impending loss, to deal with unfinished business, and to say good-byes. If they have not decided beforehand, the patient and key family members need to decide about such things as a living will; the extent of medical heroics desired; preferences about dying at home, in the hospital, or at hospice; and wishes about a funeral or memorial service and burial.

Transitions Between Phases

Critical transition periods link the three time phases. These transitions present opportunities for families to reevaluate the appropriateness of their previous life structures in the face of new illness-related developmental demands. Unfinished business from the previous phase can complicate or block movement through the transitions. Families can become

permanently frozen in an adaptive structure that has outlived its utility (Penn, 1983). For example, the usefulness of pulling together in the crisis phase can become maladaptive and stifling for all family members in the chronic phase. An illness timeline delineates psychosocial developmental phases of an illness, each with its own unique developmental tasks. It is important for families to address normative phase-related tasks in sequence to optimize successful adaptation over the long haul of a chronic disorder.

New Genetics and an Extended Illness Timeline

With the mapping of the human genome, burgeoning scientific knowledge is rapidly increasing our understanding of the mechanisms, treatment, and prevention of disease. New genetic technologies are enabling physicians to test for increased risk of developing a serious and life-threatening illness before it actually occurs. This means that individuals and families now can be living with illness risk information long before loved ones have developed symptoms of those illnesses (Miller et al., 2006), which significantly increases the amount of time and energy that families spend considering an illness and lengthens the illness timeline to include nonsymptomatic phases (Rolland & Williams, 2005). The nonsymptomatic phases are awareness, pretesting, test/posttesting, and long-term adaptation. These nonsymptomatic phases are distinguished by questions of uncertainty. Fundamental issues include the potential amount of genetic knowledge medically available, decisions about how much of that information various family members choose to access, and living with the psychosocial impact of those choices.

For some, the nonsymptomatic crisis phase begins when predictive testing becomes available, continuing through the decision to pursue testing and initial posttesting adaptation. For others, this phase begins as individuals reach significant developmental milestones and begin to consider testing. Sometimes, plans for having children raise fears of passing on a mutation and thus spark an interest in testing. Some women decide to be tested for hereditary breast and ovarian cancer genes when they reach an age that coincides with the age at which another blood relative—a mother, aunt, or older sister—was diagnosed. During the posttesting phases, families need to accept the permanence of the genetic information. They must develop meanings that preserve their sense of competency and flexibility in the face of future uncertainty or loss (Rolland, 2006a; Werner-Lin, 2008).

After receiving genetic information, families may live in limbo for years in the long-term adaptation phase. Social workers can help families maintain mastery during this period by leading them to acknowledge the possibility, probability, or inevitability of illness and loss, find meaning that transcends biological outcomes, and build family flexibility into planning that balances illness concerns with normative family developmental milestones.

The involvement of the health-care system is very different with predictive testing than with a diagnosed illness, a fact that presents a major psychosocial challenge. Despite the enormous psychosocial impact of positive testing results, families usually have limited contact with health professionals after initial testing. There is a need for ongoing, family-centered, collaborative approaches to prevent isolation and fear.

We can orient families to the value of prevention-oriented consultations at key future life-cycle transitions, when the experience of genetic risk likely will be heightened. Concerns about loss may surface that family members had postponed or thought they had worked through. It is vital to prepare family members for the fact that concerns about genetic risk and decisions about whether to pursue genetic testing will be more activated during transitional periods, such as launching young adults and marriage or partner commitments. Such feelings also can be reactivated by critical events, such as genetic testing of another family member, diagnosis of a serious illness in immediate or extended families or friends, or death of a loved one. Social workers can help family members decide about circumstances when further family discussion would be helpful, who would be appropriate to include, and how to discuss genetic risk with children or adolescents.

CLINICAL AND RESEARCH IMPLICATIONS

The Family System-Illness Model provides a framework for assessment and clinical intervention by facilitating an understanding of chronic illness and disability in psychosocial terms. The interaction of the time phases and typology of illness provides a framework for a normative psychosocial developmental model for chronic disease that resembles models for human development. The time phases—crisis, chronic, and terminal—can be considered broad developmental periods in the natural history of a chronic disease. Attention to features of onset, course, outcome, and incapacitation provides markers that focus clinical assessment and intervention with a family. For instance, acute-onset illnesses demand high levels of adaptability, problem solving, family reorganization, and balanced cohesion. In such circumstances, helping families to maximize flexibility enables them to adapt more successfully.

This framework can help in research design. The typology and time-phase framework can facilitate research aimed to sort out the relative importance of different psychosocial variables across a spectrum of chronic disorders. Particular "psychosocial types" of disorders can be considered crudely matched as to onset, course, outcome, incapacitation, and level of uncertainty. Specific typology variables can be utilized to analyze and compare individual and family dynamics related to different conditions over time. Time phases can facilitate a methodology for longitudinal studies. Multiple observations can be spaced at intervals that correspond to different time phases.

The model is guided by awareness of the components of family functioning most relevant to particular types or phases of an illness and therefore can inform goal setting and treatment planning. Using a psychoeducational approach, social workers can work with families to create a psychosocial map, deciding on specific goals together to maximize a sense of control and realistic hope. This process empowers families in their journey of living with a chronic disorder. This knowledge also educates family members about warning signs that should alert them to request brief, goal-oriented treatment at appropriate times. The framework is useful for timing family psychosocial checkups to coincide with key transition points over the course of both the illness and individual family members' and the family's development. For families with limited resources or access to psychosocial care, social workers can educate families in their limited time together about what to expect at nodal points in the illness journey to minimize future distress.

The model also informs evaluation of general functioning and illness-specific family dynamics, such as the interface of the illness with individual and family development; the family's multigenerational history of coping with illness, loss, and other adversity; the family's health and illness belief system; the meaning of the illness to the family; social support; use of community resources; and the family's capacity to manage illness-related crises or perform home-based medical care. At a larger systems level, the model provides a lens for clinicians to analyze shifts in relationships among health-care institutions, professionals, the patient, and family members.

Psychoeducational Family Groups

Preventively oriented family psychoeducational or support groups for patients and their families (Gonzalez & Steinglass, 2002; Steinglass, 1998) are an increasingly utilized, cost-effective way to address illness concerns of families and can be designed to deal with different types of conditions (e.g., progressive, life-threatening, relapsing). They can be provided in either as 1-day or as time-limited, weekly or biweekly meetings for three to six sessions. Brief psychoeducational modules, timed for critical phases of particular types of diseases, enable families to digest manageable portions of a long-term coping process. Modules can be tailored to particular phases of the illness and to family coping skills necessary to confront disease-related demands. This method provides a cost-effective preventive service that networks families, counteracts their isolation, and helps identify families at high risk for maladaptation.

Grounded in a family systems-based psychoeducational framework, these groups bring together families facing conditions with similar psychosocial demands. The goals of psychoeducational family groups are to help families cope as a team with the continued demands of chronic illness, to mobilize the ill individuals' natural support networks, and to reduce the negative effects of both normative and illness-related family stressors. In other words, the aim is to find "a place for the illness in the family while at the same time keeping the illness in its place" (Gonzalez, Steinglass, & Reiss, 1989, p. 80). This is achieved by providing informational support through collaboration with health-care providers, social networking, and skill building.

These groups emphasize a resilience perspective, focusing on family strengths and the development of positive coping techniques and problem-solving skills. This allows families to minimize negative and pathologizing views about their adaptation to illness management. Finally, the intervention addresses the needs of all family members, giving each participant the opportunity to voice concerns and to form cross-family alliances with others in similar family roles (Gonzalez & Steinglass, 2002; Steinglass, 1998). Social workers facilitating such groups may use tools such as social skills and problem-solving training, practicing these skills during group sessions, and encouraging families to bring their experiences with these skills back to the group for consideration.

FAMILY ASSESSMENT

As chronic illnesses become incorporated into the family system and all its processes, coping is influenced by illness-oriented family dynamics that concern the dimension of time and belief systems.

Multigenerational Legacies of Illness, Loss, and Crisis: Constructing a Genogram

A family's current behavior, and therefore its response to illness, cannot be understood adequately apart from its history (Boszormenyi-Nagy, 1987; Bowen, 1993; Byng-Hall, 1995; Framo, 1992; McGoldrick, Garcia-Preto, & Carter, 2010; Walsh & McGoldrick, 2004). Social workers can use historical questioning and construct a basic genogram, and timeline to track nodal events and transitions (McGoldrick, Gerson, & Petry, 2008; see Appendix 13.1). This process helps clinicians gain an understanding of a family's organizational shifts and coping strategies as a system in response to past stressors and, more specifically, to past illnesses. Such inquiry helps explain and predict the family's current style of coping, adaptation, and creation of meaning. A multigenerational assessment helps to clarify areas of strength and vulnerability. It also identifies high-risk families burdened by past unresolved issues and dysfunctional patterns that prevent them from adequately addressing the challenges presented by a serious condition.

A genogram oriented toward illness focuses on how a family organizes itself and adapts as an evolving system around major stressors, especially previous illnesses and unexpected crises, in the current and previous generations. A central goal is to bring to light areas of consensus and "learned differences" that are sources of cohesion and conflict. Patterns of coping, replications, discontinuities, shifts in relationships (e.g., triangles, cutoffs), and sense of competence are noted. These patterns can be transmitted across generations as family pride, myths, taboos, catastrophic expectations, and belief systems (Seaburn, Lorenz, & Kaplan, 1992; Walsh & McGoldrick, 2004). In one case involving a couple where the husband was diagnosed with basal cell carcinoma, the oncologist discussed a favorable prognosis. In spite of this reassurance, the wife believed her husband would die from this skin cancer. This resulted in increased marital discord and ultimately a couple's consultation with the oncologist. In the initial interview, when asked about prior experiences with illness and loss, the wife revealed that her own father had died tragically of a misdiagnosed malignant melanoma. This woman had a catastrophic fear based on both sensitization to cancer (particularly any related to the skin) and the possibility of human error by health professionals. Had the oncologist inquired about prior experiences at the time of diagnosis, earlier intervention would have been facilitated.

It also is useful to inquire about other forms of loss (e.g., divorce, migration), crisis (e.g., lengthy unemployment, rape, natural disaster such as Hurricane Katrina), and protracted adversity (e.g., poverty, racism, war, political oppression). These experiences can provide transferable sources of resilience and effective coping skills in the face of a serious health problem (Walsh, 2006).

Illness Type and Time Phase Issues

Whereas a family may have certain standard ways of coping with any illness, there may be critical differences in its styles and success in adaptation to different "types" of diseases. In a social work assessment, it is important to track prior family illnesses for areas of perceived competence, failures, or inexperience. Inquiry about experiences with different types of illness (e.g., life-threatening versus nonlife-threatening) may find, for instance, that a family dealt successfully with nonlife-threatening illnesses but reeled under the weight of metastatic cancer. Such a family might be well equipped to deal with less severe conditions but be particularly vulnerable to the occurrence of another life-threatening illness. Some families may lack familiarity with chronic illness. The next case consultation highlights the importance of family history in uncovering areas of inexperience.

Tracking a family's coping capabilities in the crisis, chronic, and terminal phases of previous chronic illnesses highlights legacies of strength as well as complications in adaptation related

CASE EXAMPLE

Joe, his wife, Ann, and their three teenage children presented for a family evaluation 10 months after Joe's diagnosis with severe asthma. Joe, age 44, had been employed for many years as a spray painter. Apparently, exposure to a new chemical triggered the onset of asthmatic attacks that necessitated hospitalization and occupational disability. Although somewhat improved, he continued to have persistent, moderately severe respiratory symptoms. Initially, his physicians had predicted that improvement would occur but remained noncommittal as to the level of chronicity to be expected. Continued breathing difficulties contributed to increased symptoms of depression, uncharacteristic temperamental outbursts, alcohol abuse, family discord, and finally admission to an alcohol detoxification unit. In the initial assessment, after

Joe's discharge to outpatient psychiatric treatment, the social worker inquired as to the family's prior illness experience. This was the nuclear family's first encounter with chronic illness, and their families of origin had limited experience. Ann's father had died 7 years earlier of a sudden and unexpected heart attack. Joe's brother had died in an accidental drowning. Neither had experience with disease as an ongoing process. Joe had assumed that improvement meant "cure." In addition, Joe had a history of alcoholism that had been in remission for 20 years. Illness for both Joe and his wife had meant either death or recovery. The physician/family system was not attuned to the hidden risks for this family coping with the transition from the crisis to the chronic phase of his asthma, the juncture where the permanency of the disease needed to be addressed.

to different points over the course of the illness. One man grew up with a father who was partially disabled with heart disease and witnessed his parents successfully renegotiate traditional gender-defined roles when his mother went to work while his father assumed household responsibilities. This man, who now has heart disease himself, has a positive legacy about gender roles from his family of origin that facilitated a flexible response to his own illness.

Another family with a member suffering from chronic kidney failure functioned very well in handling the practicalities of home dialysis. However, in the terminal phase, their limitations with emotional expression left a legacy of unresolved grief. Tracking prior illness experiences in terms of time phases helps clinicians see both the strengths and vulnerabilities of a family, which counterbalances the assignment of dysfunctional labels. Social workers need to ask specifically about positive family-of-origin experiences with illness and loss that can be highlighted as family successes and used as models to adapt to the current situation.

Although many families facing chronic disease have healthy multigenerational family patterns of adaptation, any family may falter in the face of multiple superimposed disease and nondisease stressors that occur in a relatively short period of time. With progressive, incapacitating diseases or the concurrence of illnesses in several family members, a pragmatic approach that focuses on expanded or creative use of supports and resources outside the family is most productive.

Interface of the Illness, Individual, and Family Development

Addressing the impact of the illness over the life span provides a powerful way to construct a normative framework for serious illness. Individual and family life cycle perspectives address development over time in discrete phases, each with expectable challenges to be mastered sequentially before continuing on to the next phase. Illness frequently disrupts these normative challenges as family resources are directed toward illness management and treatment. To place the unfolding of chronic disease into a developmental context, it is crucial to understand the intertwining of three evolutionary threads: illness, individual, and family development (see Rolland, 1987a, 1994a, 2010).

Individual and Family Development

It is essential to consider the interaction of individual and family development. A chronic disorder influences the development of the affected person and various family members in distinct ways depending on a number of factors, including age of onset of the illness, the core commitments in the affected person and each family member's life at that time, and the phase of the family life cycle. Life cycle models can facilitate thinking proactively about the timing and nature of strains on the family unit and each member over the course of a major health problem.

Life cycle and life structure are central concepts for both family and individual development. The term *life cycle* refers to a basic sequence and unfolding of the life course within which individual, family, or illness uniquely occurs. *Life structure* refers to the core elements (e.g., work, child rearing, caregiving) of an individual's or family's life at any phase of the life cycle.

Illness, individual, and family development have in common the notion of phases, each with its own developmental challenges. Mc-Goldrick and colleagues (2010) have divided the family life cycle into six phases, where marker events (e.g., marriage, birth of first child, adolescence, children leaving home) herald the transition from one phase to the next. The family life cycle also can be viewed as oscillating between phases where family developmental tasks require intense bonding or relatively higher cohesion (e.g., early child rearing) versus phases during which time the external family boundary is loosened, such as families with adolescents, which often emphasize personal identity and autonomy (Combrinck-Graham, 1985). Levinson (1986), in his description of individual adult development, describes how individuals' and families' life structures can move between periods of

life structure transition and building/stability. Transition periods are sometimes the most vulnerable because previous individual, family, and illness life structures are reappraised in light of new developmental tasks that may require major discontinuous change rather than minor alterations. The primary goal of a life structure building/maintaining period is to form a life structure and enrich life within it based on the key choices an individual/family made during the preceding transition period.

These unifying concepts provide a base to think about the fit among illness, individual, and family development. Each phase in these three kinds of development pose tasks and challenges that move through periods of being more or less in sync with each other. The model distinguishes: (a) the phases of the family life cycle, particularly the kind and degree of cohesion required; (b) the alternation of transition and life structure building/maintaining periods in family and individual development; and (c) periods of higher and lower psychosocial demands, requiring relatively greater and lesser degrees of family cohesion over the course of a chronic condition.

Generally, illness and disability tend to push individual and family developmental processes toward transition and increased cohesion. Analogous to the addition of a new family member, illness onset sets in motion an inside-the-family-focused process of socialization to illness. Symptoms, loss of function, the demands of shifting or acquiring new illness-related roles, and the fears of further disability or death all require a family to focus inward.

The need for family cohesion varies enormously with different illness types and phases. The tendency for a disease to pull a family inward increases with the level of disability or risk of progression and death. Progressive diseases over time inherently require a greater cohesion than constant course illnesses. The ongoing addition of new demands as an illness progresses keeps a family's energy focused inward, often impeding or halting the natural life cycle evolution of other members. After an initial period of adaptation, a constant-course disease (without severe disability) permits a family to get back on track developmentally. Relapsing illnesses alternate between periods of drawing a family inward and periods of release from immediate demands of disease. But the on-call nature of many such illnesses keeps part of the family focus inward despite asymptomatic periods, hindering the natural flow between phases of development.

With major health conditions, previous norms concerning family organization may need greater flexibility. Enmeshment with blurred generational boundaries is touted as the hallmark of family dysfunction. Yet the very real demands on older children and adolescents to assume adult functions in the interest of family survival must be distinguished from rigid pathological descriptions of "parentified" children. For instance, when a parent develops a serious disorder during a child-rearing phase of development, a family's ability to stay on course is most severely taxed. The impact is twofold. A new family burden is added as a parent is "lost." To meet simultaneous child-rearing and caregiving needs, an older child or grandparent may need to assume parental responsibilities. These forms of family adaptation are appropriate, if structural realignments are flexible, shared, and sensitive to competing age-related developmental needs. Frequently, however, family or cultural dictates put children, especially girls, in highly responsible roles before it is developmentally appropriate to do so. Social workers can help families set up culturally appropriate structures that do not overburden any one family member by naming expectations and helping families to delegate tasks across a number of participating family members. Social workers also can aid families in enlisting neighbors, community members, and religious congregations in aiding them during particularly challenging times.

In clinical assessment, two basic questions arise: "What is the fit between the psychosocial demands of a condition and family and individual life structures and developmental tasks at a particular point in the life cycle?" and "How will this fit change as the course of the illness unfolds in relation to the family's and each member's development?"

From a systems viewpoint, at the time of diagnosis, it is important to know the phase of the family life cycle and the stage of individual development of all family members, not just the ill member. Chronic disease in one family member can profoundly affect developmental goals of another member. For instance, an infant disability can be a serious roadblock to parents' preconceived ideas about competent child rearing, or a life-threatening illness in a young married adult can interfere with the well spouse's readiness to become a parent. Family members also frequently do not adapt equally to chronic illness. Each member's ability to adapt, and the rate at which he or she does so, is related to his or her own developmental phase and role in the family. When family members are in tune with each other's developmental processes, and promote flexibility and alternative means to satisfy developmental needs, successful long-term adaptation is maximized.

By adopting a longitudinal developmental perspective, a clinician will stay attuned to future developmental transitions. Imagine a family in which the father (a carpenter) and primary financial provider has a heart attack. Dad's rehabilitation is uneventful and includes appropriate lifestyle modifications and a return to work. The oldest son, age 15, seems relatively unaffected. Two years later, his father experiences a second heart attack, leaving him with a disability. His son, now 17, has dreams of going away to college. The specter of financial hardship and the perceived need for a "man in the family" creates a serious dilemma of choice for the son and the family, which surfaces with the boy's precipitously declining academic performance and alcohol abuse. In this case, there is a fundamental clash between developmental issues of individuation and the ongoing demands of a progressive, life-threatening type of heart disease on the family. Further, there is a resurgence of fears of loss fueled not only by the recurrence but also its timing with a major developmental transition for the oldest son. The son may fear that if he were to move away, he might never see his father alive again. This case demonstrates the potential clash between simultaneous transition periods—the illness transition to a more disabling, progressive, and life-threatening course; the adolescent son's transition to early adulthood; and the family's transition from the "living with teenagers" to "launching young adults" phase. At the time of initial diagnosis, inquiry about anticipated major transitions over the next three to five years and discussing them in relation to the specific kind of heart disease and its related uncertainties would help avert a future crisis.

The timing of chronic illness in the life cycle can be normative (e.g., expectable in relation to chronological and social time) or nonnormative (e.g., "off-time"). Coping with chronic illness and death are considered normally anticipated challenges in late adulthood, whereas their occurrence earlier is out of phase and developmentally more disruptive (Neugarten, 1976). For instance, chronic diseases that occur during the child-rearing period can be most challenging because of their potential impact on family financial and child-rearing responsibilities. The actual impact will depend on the type of illness and pre-illness family roles. Families governed by flexible gender-influenced rules about who is the financial provider and caregiver of children will tend to have an easier adjustment.

When a parent develops a major health condition during the child-rearing phases of the life cycle, a family's ability to stay on course is severely taxed. For more serious and debilitating diseases, such as stroke, the impact of the illness is like the addition of a new infant member, one with "special needs" who will compete with those of the other children for potentially scarce family resources that are diminished by parental loss. Moreover, in two-parent families, the well parent must juggle child-rearing demands with caregiving of a spouse (Rolland, 1994b).

With chronic disorders, an overarching family goal is to deal with the developmental demands of the illness without family members sacrificing their own or the family's development as a system over time. It is important to determine whose life plans were or might be canceled, postponed, or altered and when plans put on hold and future developmental issues will be addressed. In this way, clinicians can anticipate developmental nodal points related to "autonomy within" versus "subjugation to" the condition. Family members can be helped to strike a healthier balance with life plans that resolve feelings of guilt and hopelessness and find family and external resources to enhance freedom, both to pursue personal goals and to provide needed care for the ill member.

HEALTH/ILLNESS BELIEF SYSTEM

When illness strikes, a primary developmental challenge for families is to create meaning for the illness experience that promotes a sense of mastery and competency (Kleinman, 1988; Rolland, 1987b, 1994a, 1997; Wright & Bell, 2009). Because serious illness often is experienced as a betrayal of fundamental trust in our bodies and belief in our invulnerability (Kleinman, 1988), creating an empowering narrative can be a formidable task. Family health beliefs help us grapple with the existential dilemmas of our fear of death, tendency to want to sustain our denial of death, and attempts to reassert control when suffering and loss occur. They serve as a cognitive map guiding decisions and action and provide a way to approach new and ambiguous situations for coherence in family life, facilitating continuity between past, present, and future (Antonovsky & Sourani, 1988; Reiss, 1981). Inquiry into and curiosity about family beliefs is perhaps the most powerful foundation stone of collaboration between families and health professionals (Rolland, 1998; Wright & Bell, 2009). There is growing research evidence that family members' distress about a disease, such as cancer, can be associated more closely to perceived risk or appraisals of seriousness than objective characteristics of the disease (Franks & Roesch, 2006; Hurley, Miller, Rubin, & Weinberg, 2006; Thompson & Kyle, 2000).

In the initial crisis phase, it is essential for clinicians to inquire about key family beliefs that shape the family's illness narrative and coping strategies. This inquiry includes tracking: (a) beliefs about normality and mind-body relationship, control, and mastery; (b) assumptions about what caused an illness and what will influence it's course and outcome; (c) meanings attached by a family, ethnic group, religion, or the wider culture to symptoms (e.g., chronic pain) (J. Griffith & Griffith, 1994; McGoldrick, Pearce, & Garcia-Preto, 2005), types of illnesses (e.g., life threatening), or specific diseases (e.g., AIDS) (Sontag, 2001) that have shaped a family's health beliefs; and (e) anticipated nodal points in illness, individual, and family development when health beliefs are strained or need to shift. A clinician also should assess the congruence of health beliefs within the family and its various subsystems (e.g., spouse, parental, extended family) as well as between the family and the health-care system and wider culture.

Beliefs About Normality

Family beliefs about what is normal or abnormal, and the importance members place on conformity and excellence in relation to the average family, have far-reaching implications for adaptation to chronic disorders. Family values that allow having a "problem" without self-denigration have a distinct advantage, enabling one to seek outside help and yet maintain a positive identity in the face of chronic conditions. Families that define help seeking as weak and shameful undercut this kind of resilience. Essentially, with chronic disorders in which problems are to be expected and the use of professionals and outside resources is necessary, a belief that pathologizes this normative process can be seen as adding insult to injury.

Two excellent questions that can be used to elicit these beliefs are: "How do you think other average families would deal with a similar situation to yours?" and "How would a healthy family ideally cope with your situation?" Families with strong beliefs in high achievement and perfectionism are prone to apply standards in a situation of illness in which the kind of control they are accustomed to is impossible. Particularly with untimely conditions that occur early in the life cycle, there are additional pressures to keep up with normative socially expectable developmental milestones of age peers or other young couples. The fact that developmental goals may take longer to achieve than anticipated or need revision requires a flexible belief about what is normal and healthy. To sustain hope effectively, particularly in situations of long-term adversity, families need to embrace a flexible definition of normality.

Mind–Body Relationships

Varied conceptualizations of the mind–body relationship have been the subject of discourse and debate for millennia. Traditional mental health theories and research endeavors have been pathology based, tending to emphasize character traits or emotional states that affect body chemistry adversely. From this perspective, emotions can be seen to affect the body negatively, but possible positive influences of healthy attitudes are overlooked. More recently, the public has been drawn increasingly to popular literature citing the importance of positive attitudes in healing, emphasizing the unity of mind and body. This literature describes healing as a state of being, involving mind and body, rather than in strictly biomedical terms where something is done to the body. Social workers must be particularly mindful that families may be more familiar with and open to positive attitudes as a powerful source of healing.

As social workers assess family beliefs about illness, it is useful to distinguish beliefs about the mind as a logical, thinking process that can determine actions that may help in healing the body (e.g., seeking medical care, changing diet or activity patterns) from those of the mind as a source of thought or energy that can directly impact body physiology. These beliefs about mind and spirit often extend beyond the individual to include family, community, or a higher spiritual power. Anthropologists have found tremendous diversity in the role of family, community, God, or nature as a source of healing. Such beliefs typically are expressed in the form of rituals (Imber-Black, Roberts, & Whiting, 2003). In our society, for example, a family's religious community often will organize a prayer service to promote healing for an ill member. Social workers can inquire about the role of spirituality in family life (Walsh, 2009), family beliefs regarding healing, and rituals that are important expressions of those beliefs. Sometimes important family healing rituals conflict with hospital rules, leading to power struggles that alienate families and erode a functional collaborative relationship with the health-care team.

Family's Sense of Mastery Facing Illness

It is important to determine how a family defines *mastery* or *control* in general and in situations of illness (Taylor, Helgeson, Reed, & Skokan, 1991; Thompson & Kyle, 2000). Mastery is similar to the concept of health locus of control, which indicates beliefs about influence over the course/outcome of an illness (Lefcourt, 1982). It is useful to distinguish whether a family's beliefs are based on the premise of internal control, external control by chance, or external control by powerful others. Families with an internal locus of control believe they can affect the outcome of a situation. In illness, such families believe they have direct control of their health and have the power to recover from illness (Wallston, 2004). An external orientation entails a belief that outcomes are not contingent on the individual's or family's behavior. Families that view illness in terms of chance believe that illness occurs as a matter of luck and that fate determines recovery. Those who see health control as in the hands of powerful others view health professionals, God, or sometimes powerful family members as exerting control over their bodies and illness course.

Family beliefs about mastery strongly affect each member's relationship with the illness and the health-care system, impacting adherence and preferences about family participation in treatment and healing processes.

Families that view a disease's course/outcome as a matter of chance tend to establish marginal relationships with health professionals largely because their belief system minimizes the importance of their own or the professional's impact on a disease process. Families of lower socioeconomic statuses, especially minorities, also may receive inadequate care or lack insurance or access, leading to a fatalistic attitude and lack of engagement with health-care providers, whom they may not trust to help. Just as any psychotherapeutic relationship depends on a shared belief system about what is therapeutic, a workable accommodation among the patient, family, and health-care team in terms of these fundamental values is essential. Families that feel misunderstood by health professionals often are reacting to a lack of joining at this basic value level. Too often their healthy need to participate has been ignored or preempted by a professional needing unilateral control (Rolland, 1998).

A family may adhere to a different set of beliefs about control when dealing with physical illness as opposed to typical day-to-day issues. Therefore, it is important to assess both a family's basic beliefs and those about control for illnesses in general, for chronic and life-threatening illness, and finally for the specific disease facing the family. For instance, regardless of the actual severity or prognosis in a particular case, cancer may be equated with death or a lack of control because of medical statistics, cultural myth, or prior family history. Alternatively, families may have enabling stories about a member or friend who, in spite of cancer and a shortened life span, lived a "full" life centered on effectively prioritizing the quality of relationships and goals. Clinicians can highlight these positive narratives to help families counteract cultural beliefs that focus exclusively on control of biology as defining success.

The goodness of fit between family beliefs about mastery can vary depending on the time phase of the condition. For some conditions, the crisis phase involves protracted medical interventions outside the family's direct control. This may be stressful for a family that prefers to tackle its own problems without outside control and "interference." The patient's return home may increase the workload but allow members to reassert more fully their competence and leadership. In contrast, a family guided more by a preference for external control by experts can expect greater difficulty when their family member returns home. Recognition of such normative differences in belief about control can guide an effective psychosocial treatment plan tailored to each family's needs and affirming rather than disrespecting their core values.

Social workers must be cautious about judging the relative denial or acceptance of painful realities. Often people need to do both. The healthy use of minimization, or selective focus on the positive, and timely uses of humor should be distinguished from denial. The skilled social worker must support both the usefulness of exaggerated hope and the need for treatment to control the illness or a new complication. There is greater incentive for a family to confront denial when there is hope that preventive action or medical treatment can affect the outcome or when an illness is entering its terminal phase. Yet to cope with an arduous, uncertain course, families often need simultaneously to acknowledge the condition while minimizing treatment risks or the likelihood of a poor outcome.

Family Beliefs About the Cause of an Illness

When a significant health problem arises, it is natural to wonder "Why me (or us)?" and "Why now?" (Roesch & Weiner, 2001; Taylor, 1983). We almost invariably construct an explanation or story that helps organize our experience. With limits of current medical knowledge, tremendous uncertainties persist about the relative importance of myriad factors, leaving individuals and families to make idiosyncratic attributions about what caused an illness. A family's beliefs about the cause of an illness should be assessed separately from its beliefs about what can affect the outcome. It is important to elicit each family member's explanation. Responses generally will reflect a combination of medical information and family mythology. Beliefs might include punishment for prior misdeeds (e.g., an affair), blame of a particular family member ("Your drinking made me sick!"), a sense of injustice ("Why am I being punished? I have been a good person."), genetics (e.g., cancer runs on one side of the family), negligence by the patient (e.g., careless driving) or by parents (e.g., sudden infant death syndrome), or simply bad luck.

Highly adaptive family narratives respect the limits of scientific knowledge, affirm basic competency, and promote the flexible use of multiple biological and psychosocial healing strategies. In contrast, causal attributions that invoke blame, shame, or guilt make it extremely difficult for a family to cope and adapt in a functional way. With a life-threatening illness, a blamed family member is implicitly, if not explicitly, held accountable if the patient dies. Decisions about treatment then become confounded and filled with tension. A husband who believes his drinking caused his wife's coronary and subsequent death may increase self-destructive drinking because of his profound guilt. A mother who secretly blames herself for their daughter's leukemia may be less able to stop a low-probability experimental treatment than the husband who sees further treatment as causing additional suffering to their terminally ill child (see Box 13.1).

Belief System Adaptability

Because illnesses vary enormously in their responsiveness to psychosocial factors, both families and providers need to make distinctions among beliefs about their overall participation in a long-term disease process, beliefs about their ability to control the biological unfolding of an illness, and the flexibility with which they can apply these beliefs. Families' experience of competence or mastery depends on their grasp of these distinctions. Optimal family and provider narratives respect the limits of scientific knowledge, affirm basic competency, and promote the flexible use of multiple biological and psychosocial healing strategies.

Box 13.1 Family Beliefs About Cause of Illness

Lucy and Tom G., a young couple, have a daughter, Susan, age 5, who is terminally ill with leukemia. The pediatric oncologist offered the parents the choice between an experimental treatment with a low probability of success or halting treatment. Tom's position was "Let's stop; enough is enough." Lucy, however, felt, "We must continue; we can't let her die." The couple could not reach an agreement, and the physician was immobilized. He requested a social work consultation for the couple.

When the consultant asked, "What is your explanation of how your daughter got leukemia?" the critical story emerged. Tom basically saw it as bad luck. Lucy, however, had a very different belief. During her pregnancy with Susan, Lucy's father had a heart attack and died several months later from a second episode. Lucy experienced this

as a time of great stress and grief, which she felt adversely affected Susan's intrauterine life. After Susan's birth by normal delivery, Lucy was still mourning the loss of her father and felt that this affected the quality of her bonding with Susan and led to a hidden depression in her infant. Further, Lucy had read research linking depression with a lowering of the effectiveness of the immune system, which could, in turn, decrease normal surveillance and clearing of cancer cells from the body. She believed this combination of factors caused her child's cancer and that if she had been a more competent mother, this never would have happened. Lucy said she had never told this story to anyone (including her husband), because no one had ever asked, and she was very ashamed. She had hoped for a cure, so that the whole issue could be resolved. She could not accept stopping treatment because, to her, it meant that Susan's death then would be her fault.

A family's belief in their participation in the total illness process can be thought of as independent from whether a disease is stable, improving, or in a terminal phase. Sometimes mastery and the attempt to control biological process coincide, as when a family tailors its behavior to help maintain the health of a member with cancer in remission. This might include changes in family roles, communication, diet, exercise, and balance between work and recreation. Optimally, when an ill family member comes out of remission and as the family enters the terminal phase of the illness, participation as an expression of mastery is transformed to a successful process of letting go that eases suffering and allows palliative care to be provided (Lynn, Schuster, Wilkinson, & Simon, 2007).

Families with flexible belief systems are more likely to experience death with a sense of equanimity rather than profound failure. The death of a patient whose long, debilitating illness has heavily burdened others can bring relief as well as sadness to family members.

Because relief over death goes against societal conventions, it can trigger massive guilt reactions that may be expressed through such symptoms as depression and family conflict. Clinicians need to help family members accept ambivalent feelings they may have about the death as natural.

Flexibility within both the family and the health professional system is a key variable in optimal family functioning. Rather than linking mastery in a rigid way with biological outcome (survival or recovery) as the sole determinant of success, families can define control in a more "holistic" sense with involvement and participation in the overall process as the main criteria defining success. This is analogous to the distinction between curing "the disease" and "healing the system." Healing the system may influence the course and outcome, but a positive disease outcome is not necessary for a family to feel successful. This flexible view of mastery permits the quality of relations within the family or between the family and health professionals to become more central to criteria of success. The health provider's competence becomes valued from both a technical and a caregiving perspective not solely linked to the biological course.

Ethnic, Spiritual, and Cultural Beliefs

Ethnicity, race, and spiritual beliefs strongly influence family beliefs concerning health and illness (McGoldrick et al., 2005; Rolland, 2006b; Walsh, 2009). Significant ethnic differences regarding health beliefs typically emerge at the time of a major health crisis. Health professionals need to be mindful of the belief systems of various other ethnic, racial, and religious groups in their community, particularly as these translate into behavioral patterns that differ from their own. Cultural norms vary in such areas as the definition of the appropriate "sick role" for the patient, the kind and degree of open communication about the disease, who should be included in the illness caregiving system (e.g., extended family, friends, professionals), who is the primary caretaker (almost always the wife, mother, daughter, or daughter-in-law), and the kind of rituals viewed as normative at different stages of an illness (e.g., hospital bedside vigils, healing, and funeral rituals). This is especially true for a number of minority groups (e.g., African American, Asian American, and Hispanic American) who experience discrimination or marginalization from the prevailing White American culture. Illness provides an opportunity to encourage role flexibility and shift from defining one female member as the caregiver to a collaborative caregiving team that includes male and female siblings/adult children.

Clinicians need to be mindful of cultural differences between themselves and the patient and family as a necessary step to forging a workable alliance that can endure a long-term illness (Seaburn et al., 1996). Disregarding these issues can lead families to distance themselves from health providers and available community resources, which is a major cause of adherence problems and treatment failure. Accepting that the patient retains final

responsibility for decisions about his body requires a strong commitment to the core social work value of self-determination.

Fit Among Health-Care Provider, Health System, and Family Beliefs

It is a common but unfortunate error to regard "the family" as a monolithic unit that feels, thinks, believes, and behaves as an undifferentiated whole. Social workers should inquire both about the level of agreement and tolerance for differences among family members' beliefs and between the family and the health-care system. Is the family rule "We must agree on all/some values," or are diversity and different viewpoints acceptable? To what degree does the family feel the need to stay in sync with prevailing cultural or societal beliefs or with family tradition?

Family beliefs that balance the need for consensus with diversity and innovation are optimal and maximize permissible options. If consensus is the rule, then individual differentiation implies disloyalty and deviance. If the guiding principle is "We can hold different viewpoints," diversity is allowed. This is adaptive because it facilitates the use of novel and creative forms of problem solving that may be needed in a situation of protracted adversity, such as serious illness. Social workers can facilitate open communication and effective conflict resolution when members differ on major health-care/treatment decisions.

The same questions are relevant to the fit between the family, social worker, and health-care team. What are their attitudes about their own and the family's ability to influence the course/outcome of the disease? How does the health-care team see the balance between its own participation in the treatment process and the family's involvement? If basic differences in beliefs about control exist, how can these differences be reconciled? These questions will inform the types of interventions social workers employ to help families facing chronic and terminal illness.

It is common for differences in beliefs or attitudes to erupt during any major life cycle or illness transition. For instance, in situations of severe disability or terminal illness, one member may want the patient to return home, whereas another prefers long-term hospitalization or transfer to an extended care facility. Because the chief task of patient caregiving usually is assigned to the wife/mother, she is the one most apt to bear the chief burdens in this regard. A family able to anticipate the collision of gender-based beliefs about caregiving with the potential overwhelming demands of home-based care for a dying family member and flexibly modify its rules would avert the risk of family caregiver overload, resentment, and deteriorating family relationships.

The murky boundary between the chronic and the terminal phases highlights the potential for professionals' beliefs to collide with those of the family. Physicians can feel bound to a technological imperative that requires them to exhaust all possibilities at their disposal, regardless of the odds of success. Families may not know how to interpret continued life-saving efforts, assuming real hope where virtually none exists. Health-care professionals and institutions can collude in a pervasive societal wish to deny death as a natural process truly beyond technological control (Becker, 1973). Endless treatment can represent the medical team's inability to separate a general value placed on controlling diseases from their beliefs about participation (separate from cure) in a patient's total care.

CHALLENGES IN IMPLEMENTATION OF FAMILY-BASED RESEARCH

Interventions for families facing medical illness currently are being implemented in a number of settings, including hospitals, community health and mental health clinics, hospices, and wellness organizations (Campbell, 2003). It is important that social workers base the development of interventions on the best available research knowledge. A major challenge for family intervention research is the need to further develop research methods and protocols that demonstrate the relationship of family system dynamics to health status, health-care outcomes, and cost containment (Carr & Springer, 2010; Law & Crane, 2007; Weihs et al., 2002).

Despite advances in evidence-based knowledge, significant challenges persist for conducting such systematic and rigorous intervention research (Kazak, 2002). Often implementation of family-centered biopsychosocial research is more difficult in health-care settings (e.g., hospitals) focused primarily on the treatment and management of the individual with the disease. Although psychosocial care may improve family functioning, this outcome might not be the established goal of medical settings or health insurance corporations, both of which are concerned with biomedical cure and controlling costs. Family-based interventions, such as multifamily discussion groups (McFarlane, 2002) and collaborative family-oriented primary and tertiary care (McDaniel et al., 2005; Weihs et al., 2002), have proven effective in health-care settings to (a) promote patient and family coping and adaptation, (b) reduce medical and psychiatric morbidity for all family members, (c) contain overall health-care costs, and (d) facilitate collaboration between families and health-care teams to increase treatment adherence. Despite these data, these interventions are rarely offered as part of routine care.

In the era of managed health care, evidence-based practice highlighting positive outcomes is essential in social work's effort to maintain a clear and integrated presence in hospitals and medical settings. By illustrating how family-based interventions facilitate illness management, ease the burden on health-care teams, and are cost effective, social workers can join with other health-care professionals to advocate for collaborative models of health care that include such interventions as part of standard practice. Social workers can carve a unique niche for themselves in medical settings by working collaboratively to fill these methodological and clinical gaps and by conducting sound intervention research.

CONCLUSION

The most resilient families are able to harness the experience of facing the risks and burdens of chronic illness or disability to improve the quality of life. Families can achieve a healthy balance between accepting limits and promoting autonomy. For conditions with long-range risks, families can maintain mastery in the face of uncertainty by enhancing their capacities to acknowledge the possibility of loss, sustain hope, and build flexibility into both the family's and each member's life cycle planning that conserves and adjusts major goals and helps circumvent the forces of uncertainty.

A serious illness, such as cancer, or a brush with death, provides an opportunity to confront catastrophic fears about loss. This confrontation can lead family members to develop a better appreciation and perspective on life that results in clearer priorities and closer relationships. Seizing opportunities can replace procrastination for the "right moment" or passive waiting for the dreaded moment. By emphasizing life's fragility and preciousness, major health conditions provide families with an opportunity to heal unresolved issues and develop more immediate, caring relationships. For diseases in a more advanced stage, clinicians should help families emphasize quality of life by defining goals that are attainable more immediately and that enrich their everyday lives.

As the new era of genetics unfolds, families and clinicians are facing unprecedented complex clinical and ethical challenges (Miller et al., 2006). Families increasingly will be able to choose genetically informed knowledge of their future health risks or fate. Some key questions include:

- Which individuals and families will benefit by genetic risk screening and knowledge of their health risks or fate?
- How can we best help family members reach decisions about whether to pursue predictive testing?
- Who are the relevant family members to include in these decisions—spouses or partners? Extended family?

- Our societal fixation on "the perfect healthy body" could meld seamlessly with technology and eugenics, forcing families living with disability, illness, or genetic risk to further hide their suffering in order to demonstrate the value of their lives and avoid increased stigmatization (Rolland, 1997, 1999).

Clinicians also need to consider their own experiences and feelings about illness and loss (McDaniel, Hepworth, & Doherty, 1997). Awareness and ease with our own multigenerational and family history with illness and loss, our health beliefs, and our current developmental phase will enhance our ability to work effectively with families facing serious illness.

Living well with the strains and uncertainties of illness can be a monumental challenge. The Family Systems–Illness model offers a way to address this challenge and make the inevitable strains more manageable. Attending to the psychosocial demands of different kinds of conditions over time within a multigenerational, developmental, and belief system context can provide a strength-based framework—a common language that facilitates collaborative, creative problem solving and quality of life for families facing illness, disability, and loss.

SUGGESTED LEARNING EXERCISES

Learning Exercise 13.1

You are called by the head nurse for the oncology inpatient unit to intervene with a patient and his family who are disrupting the unit. The patient is a 34-year-old African American male who has been diagnosed with stage IV prostate cancer. The patient's mother has been very emotional about his condition and insists on staying in her son's room. This is in conflict with the rules of the oncology unit. The patient, Keith, has been married for 6 months to a White woman named Lisa who is quite distressed by Keith's condition but estranged from her own family. An unpleasant triangular conflict has existed for the couple because of Keith's strong relationship to his family of origin, particularly his mother, which is problematic for his spouse. On admission, his mother began a 24-hour vigil by her son's hospital bed. Lisa greatly resents her mother-in-law's seemingly intrusive and smothering behavior. Keith's mother is critical of what she perceives as Lisa's emotional coldness. Keith feels caught between his mother and wife and complains of anxiety and fatigue.

1. Thinking in terms of different cultural traditions of the family members, including your own, how would you react to this case? Thinking systemically, how would you approach a consultation with the patient and family?

2. Thinking in terms of the intersection of three distinct belief systems—your work setting (hospital), yourself as a social worker, and your personal cultural/ethnic/family values—how might these affect your strategy in this case? What biases might interfere with your effectiveness? How could you avoid taking sides?

Learning Exercise 13.2

Mrs. L. tells you that she is concerned that her daughter Janice, age 5, has been compulsively masturbating for the past 3 months and that it is an indication of sexual abuse. When the child assessment reveals no evidence of abuse, you inquire about other recent stressful events in the family. Only at that point does the mother reveal that her husband had a subtotal gastrectomy 9 months ago because of stomach cancer and that 3 months ago he had been rehospitalized for further tests that proved inconclusive. When Mrs. L. is asked what the children have been told, she reports that, after her husband's surgery, they had told the children only that "Daddy had a tummyache, so the doctors removed Daddy's stomach so he'd feel better." Mrs. L. reveals that she herself worries constantly about her husband's condition but that he will not come in to see the doctor and will not discuss his

problems. She states that, after the surgery, "He was adamant that he did not want ever to talk about it. He went back to work almost immediately and insisted that everything is fine." Asked if this medical crisis had any impact on the children, especially Janice, she replies, "Well, she doesn't tell me about any worries, but now that you ask, at dinner every night, when we say grace, Janice prays out loud for Daddy's stomach. But no one in the family comments on this."

1. Thinking in terms of healthy family communication in the face of threatened loss, how would you intervene in this case? Who would you try to convene, and why?

2. In what ways would you handle communication with the children differently than with the couple?

3. How would you view the husband's personal decision to minimize his problem and keep it private in the context of other symptomatic family members?

Learning Exercise 13.3

Mr. and Mrs. Ellis, both in their early 80s, live alone on a farm in rural Illinois. Mr. Ellis has been experiencing a progressive dementia, which was diagnosed by a consulting neurologist as Alzheimer's disease. At a recent visit to her primary care physician, Mrs. Ellis revealed that Mr. Ellis's confusion has been worsening and that he has hit her on occasion, causing serious bruising. The family physician feels the couple have reached their limits and has suggested a nursing home placement for Mr. Ellis. The family includes three adult children, Amy, John, and Jerry. Amy lives 100 miles away and visits weekly. The two sons live far away and are married and raising children. Amy agrees with the family physician and is very worried about her mother. The sons, however, think that Amy and her mother are exaggerating and have accused their mother of "never understanding our dad." The family is in a stalemate about the current dilemma, and tensions between the two camps are rising.

1. What might explain the differences in perception about Mr. Ellis's condition by his wife and daughter and sons? How might it affect each family member's feelings about placing Mr. Ellis in a nursing home?

2. Would you schedule a family meeting? How would you decide whether to include Mr. Ellis? What about John and Jerry, who are not in town?

3. How might gender norms be a factor in this case? How might you address them with this family?

4. How are life cycle issues (e.g., couple in later life, adult children in child-rearing phase with aging parents) pertinent, and how would you make them part of the consultative process?

5. What do you see as the choices for this family? How would you explore them in a collaborative manner?

APPENDIX 13.1
CONSTRUCTING A FAMILY GENOGRAM

Genograms provide graphic representations of family structure and patterns over several generations that offer social workers a quick sense of a family's strengths and vulnerabilities in relation to the current health situation and places present issues in the context of multigenerational family patterns. Clarification of complex family patterns can be used to generate hypotheses about the evolution of current issues and to develop intervention strategies. Genograms provide a useful clinical tool to frame certain family challenges as developing over generations and, in complex family contexts, minimizing blame, and helping families regain a sense of control as they move forward. Social workers can use a genogram in their practice setting to elicit key family narratives, highlighting important family and community members, patterns of illness and coping, and relational ties. McGoldrick et al. (2008) provide a standardized format for constructing a family genogram that includes (a) mapping the family

structure, (b) recording information about the family, and (c) describing family relationships. The basic family structural map is a pictorial representation of nuclear and extended family members and significant nonfamily people or organizations usually encompassing three generations. This structural map is fleshed out by adding demographic information, functioning, and critical events. Key demographic data include ages, dates of birth and death, occupation, education, ethnic background, religion, and geographic location of key family members who may be involved in caregiving.

Usually a family finds the process of sharing its history a useful way to communicate important family values, and sometimes it is an easier first step than discussing emotionally charged problems. Families typically enjoy constructing a genogram (some may even ask for a copy to take home) and approach it eagerly, giving the social worker clues as to the family's capacity for and interest in collaboration.

Social workers can use genograms creatively, depending on their practice setting and the family's presenting problem. For example, in health-care settings, the genogram can be targeted toward tracking prior family illness experiences and patterns of response to highlight the particular strengths and challenges for the family in confronting a current diagnosis. The genogram promotes continuity and comprehensiveness of care by supplying a versatile, succinct clinical summary that can be used to quickly familiarize other consultants and health-care providers with a case.

REFERENCES

Antonovsky, A., & Sourani, T. (1988). Family sense of coherence and family adaptation. *Journal of Marriage and the Family, 50,* 79–92.

Becker, E. (1973). *The denial of death.* New York, NY: Free Press.

Blount, A. (1998). *Integrated primary care: The future of medical and mental health collaboration.* New York, NY: Norton.

Boss, P. (1999). *Ambiguous loss: Learning to live with unresolved grief.* Boston, MA: Harvard University Press.

Boszormenyi-Nagy, I. (1987). *Foundations of contextual therapy: Collected papers of Borzomenyi-Nagy, MD.* New York, NY: Brunner/Mazel.

Bowen, M. (1993). *Family therapy in clinical practice.* New York, NY: Jason Aronson.

Byng-Hall, J. (1995). *Rewriting family scripts.* New York, NY: Guilford Press.

Campbell, T. (2003). The effectiveness of family interventions for physical disorders. *Journal of Marital and Family Therapy, 29*(2), 263–281.

Carr, D., & Springer, K. W. (2010). Advances in families and health research in the 21st century. *Journal of Marriage and the Family, 72*(3), 743–761.

Combrinck-Graham, L. (1985). A developmental model for family systems. *Family Process, 24,* 139–150.

Doherty, W., & Baird, M. (1983). *Family therapy and family medicine: Towards the primary care of families.* New York, NY: Guilford.

D'Onofrio, B. M., & Lahey, B. B. (2010). Biosocial influences on the family: A decade review. *Journal of Marriage and the Family, 72*(3), 762–782.

Engel, G. L. (1977). The need for a new medical model: A challenge for biomedicine. *Science, 196,* 129–136.

Framo, J. (1992). *Family-of origin therapy: An intergenerational approach.* New York, NY: Brunner/Mazel

Franks, H. M., & Roesch, S. C. (2006). Appraisals and coping in people living with cancer: A meta-analysis. *Psychooncology, 15*(12), 1027–1037.

Gonzalez, S., & Steinglass, P. (2002). Application of multifamily discussion groups in chronic medical disorders. In W. R. McFarlane (Ed.), *Multifamily groups in the treatment of severe psychiatric disorders* (pp. 315–340). New York, NY: Guilford Press.

Gonzalez, S., Steinglass, P., & Reiss, D. (1989). Putting the illness in its place: Discussion groups for families with chronic medical illnesses. *Family Process, 28,* 69–87.

Griffith, J., & Griffith, M. (1994). *The body speaks.* New York, NY: Basic Books.

Hurley, K., Miller, S. M., Rubin, L., & Weinberg, D. S. (2006). The individual facing genetic issues: Information processing, decision making, perception, and health-protective behaviors. In S. M. Miller, S. H. McDaniel, J. S. Rolland, & S. L. Feetham (Eds.), *Individuals, families, and the new era of genetics: Biopsychosocial perspectives.* New York, NY: Norton.

Imber-Black, E., Roberts, J., & Whiting, R. (Eds.). (2003). *Rituals in families and family therapy* (2nd ed.). New York, NY: Norton.

Kazak, A. E. (2002). Challenges in family health intervention research. *Families, Systems, and Health, 20*(1), 51–59.

Kleinman, A. (1988). *The illness narratives: Suffering, healing, and the human condition.* New York, NY: Basic Books.

Law, D., & Crane, R. (2007). The influence of individual, marital, and family treatment on high utilizers of health care. *Journal of Marital and Family Therapy, 29*(3), 353–363.

Lefcourt, H. M. (1982). *Locus of control* (2nd ed.). Hillsdale, NJ: Erlbaum.

Levinson, D. J. (1986). A conception of adult development. *American Psychologist, 41,* 3–13.

Lynn, J., Schuster, J. L., Wilkinson, A., & Simon, L. N. (2007). *Improving care for the end of life: A sourcebook for health care managers and clinicians* (2nd ed.). New York, NY: Oxford University Press.

McDaniel, S., Campbell, T., Hepworth, J., & Lorenz, A. (2005). *Family-oriented primary care* (2nd ed.). New York, NY: Springer.

McDaniel, S., Hepworth, J., & Doherty, W. (Eds.). (in press). *Medical family therapy: A biopsychosocial approach to families with health problems* (2nd ed). New York, NY: Basic Books.

McDaniel, S., Hepworth, J., & Doherty, W. (Eds.). (1997). *The shared experience of illness: Stories of patients, families, and their therapists.* New York, NY: Basic Books.

McFarlane, W. F. (Ed.). (2002), *Multifamily groups in the treatment of severe psychiatric disorders.* New York, NY: Guilford Press.

McGoldrick, M., Garcia-Preto, N., & Carter, B. (2010). *The expanded family life cycle: Individual, family and social perspectives* (4th ed.). New York, NY: Allyn & Bacon.

McGoldrick, M., Gerson, R., & Petry, S. (2008). *Genograms in family assessment* (3rd ed.). New York, NY: Norton.

McGoldrick, M., Pearce, J. K., & Garcia-Preto, N. (2005). *Ethnicity and family therapy* (3rd ed.). New York, NY: Guilford Press.

Miller, S., McDaniel, S., Rolland, J., & Feetham, S. (Eds.). (2006). *Individuals, families, and the new era of genetics: Biopsychosocial perspectives.* New York, NY: Norton.

Moos, R. (Ed.). (1989). *Coping with physical illness. Volume 2: New perspectives.* New York, NY: Plenum Press.

Neugarten, B. (1976). Adaptation and the life cycle. *Counseling Psychologist, 6*(1), 16–20.

Olkin, R. (1999). *What psychotherapists should know about disability.* New York, NY: Guilford Press.

Penn, P. (1983). Coalitions and binding interactions in families with chronic illness. *Family Systems Medicine, 1*(2), 16–25.

Reiss, D. (1981). *The family's construction of reality.* Cambridge, MA: Harvard University Press.

Roesch, S., & Weiner, B. (2001). A meta-analytic review of coping with illness: Do causal attributions matter. *Journal of Psychosomatic Research, 50*(4), 205–219.

Rolland, J. (2006b). Genetics, family systems, and multicultural influences. *Families, Systems, & Health, 24*(4), 425–442.

Rolland, J. (2010). Mastering family challenges in illness, disability, and genetic conditions. In F. Walsh (Ed.), *Normal family processes* (4th ed., pp. 411–439). New York, NY: Guilford.

Rolland, J. S. (1984). Toward a psychosocial typology of chronic and life-threatening illness. *Family Systems Medicine, 2,* 245–263.

Rolland, J. S. (1987a). Chronic illness and the life cycle: A conceptual framework. *Family Process, 26*(2), 203–221.

Rolland, J. S. (1987b). Family illness paradigms: Evolution and significance. *Family Systems Medicine, 5*(4), 467–486.

Rolland, J. S. (1990). Anticipatory loss: A family systems developmental framework. *Family Process, 29*(3), 229–244.

Rolland, J. S. (1994a). *Families, illness, and disability: An integrative treatment model.* New York, NY: Basic Books.

Rolland, J. S. (1994b). In sickness and in health: The impact of illness on couples' relationships. *Journal of Marital and Family Therapy, 20*(4), 327–349.

Rolland, J. S. (1997). The meaning of disability and suffering: Socio-political and ethical concerns. *Family Process, 36*(4), 437–440.

Rolland, J. S. (1998). Beliefs and collaboration in illness: Evolution over time. *Families, Systems and Health, 16*(1/2), 7–27.

Rolland, J. S. (1999). Families and genetic fate: A millennial challenge. *Families, Systems and Health, 16*(1), 123–133.

Rolland, J. S. (2004). Helping families with anticipatory loss and terminal illness. In F. Walsh & M. McGoldrick (Eds.), *Living beyond loss: Death in the family* (2nd ed., pp. 213–236). New York, NY: Norton.

Rolland, J. S. (2006a). Living with anticipatory loss in the new era of genetics: A life cycle perspective. In S. Miller, S. McDaniel, J. Rolland, & S. Feetham. (Eds.), *Individuals, families, and the new era of genetics: Biopsychosocial perspectives* (pp. 139–172). New York, NY: Norton.

Rolland, J. S., & Williams, J. K. (2005). Toward a biopsychosocial model for 21st century genetics. *Family Process, 44*(1), 3–24.

Seaburn, D., Gunn, W., Mauksch, L., Gawinski, A., & Lorenz, A. (Eds.). (1996). *Models of collaboration: A guide for mental health professionals working with physicians and health care providers.* New York, NY: Basic Books.

Seaburn, D., Lorenz, A., & Kaplan, D. (1992). The transgenerational development of chronic illness meanings. *Family Systems Medicine, 10,* 385–395.

Sontag, S. (2001). *Illness as metaphor and AIDS and its metaphors.* New York, NY: Picador.

Steinglass, P. (1998). Multiple family discussion groups for patients with chronic medical illness. *Families, Systems, and Health, 16*(1/2), 55–71.

Taylor, S. (1983). Adjustment to threatening events: A theory of cognitive adaptation. *American Psychologist, 38*(11), 1161–1173.

Taylor, S., Helgeson, V., Reed, G., & Skokan, L. (1991). Self-generated feelings of control and adjustment to physical illness. *Journal of Social Issues, 47*(4), 91–109.

Thompson, S., & Kyle, D. (2000). The role of perceived control in coping with the losses associated with chronic illness. In J. Harvey & E. Miller (Eds.), *Loss and trauma: General and close relationship perspectives.* Philadelphia, PA: Brunner-Routledge.

Wallston, K. A. (2004). Control and Health. In N. Anderson (Ed.), *Encyclopedia of Health & Behavior, Volume 1* (pp. 217–220). Thousand Oaks, CA: Sage.

Walsh, F. (2006). *Strengthening family resilience* (2nd ed). New York, NY: Guilford Press.

Walsh, F. (Ed.). (2009). *Spiritual resources in family therapy* (2nd ed.). New York, NY: Guilford Press.

Walsh, F., & McGoldrick, M. (Eds.). (2004). *Living beyond loss: Death in the family* (2nd ed.). New York, NY: Norton.

Weihs, K., Fisher, L., & Baird, M. (2002). Families, health, and behavior: A section of the commissioned report by the committee on Health and Behavior: Research, Practice and Policy, Division of Neuroscience and Behavioral Health and Division of Health Promotion and Disease Prevention, Institute of Medicine, National Academy of Sciences. *Families, Systems, and Health, 20*(1), 7–47.

Werner-Lin, A. (2008). Beating the biological clock: The compressed family life cycle of young women with BRCA gene alterations. *Social Work in Health Care, 47*(4): 416–437.

Wood, B. L., Lim, J., Miller, B., Cheah, P., Zwetsch, T., Ramesh, S., & Simmens, S. (2008). Testing the biobehavioral model in pediatric asthma: Pathways of effect. *Family Process, 47*(1), 21–40.

Wright, L. M., & Bell, J. (2009). *Beliefs and illness: A model for healing.* Calgary, Alberta, Canada: 4th Floor Press.

14

Human Sexual Health

LES GALLO-SILVER AND DAVID S. BIMBI

Sexuality and physical intimacy contribute to every individual's quality of life. However, many people find these aspects of life difficult to discuss with health-care professionals, particularly those who may feel stigmatized by their sexual identity (e.g., lesbian, gay, bisexual, and transgender [LGBT] people; people who engage in atypical sexual behaviors). Understanding the development of humans as sexual beings, details of the human sexual response, and changes and challenges presented by medical illnesses and traumatic injuries can help social workers in health-care settings feel more comfortable and confident when addressing sexuality with patients and their partners. Often the social worker is the only member of the health-care team who is willing and able to address issues of sexuality and physical intimacy in the context of communication, connection, and healing (Hazan & Shaver, 1987; McCabe, 1994; Schover, 2000). It is crucial for health social workers to help patients preserve this important part of life in the face of injury or illness. This chapter provides a foundation of basic information about human sexuality and the impact of illness or injury.

Many words describe various aspects of sexuality and physical intimacy. For the purposes of this chapter, *sexuality* refers to the desire to have sexual contact and intercourse and the body's responses to sexual stimulation; *physical intimacy* refers to physical acts of affection, comfort, and support. *Sensuality* refers to types of stimulation that are pleasurable but are not necessarily sexual.

Chapter Objectives
- Introduce social workers to a perspective that focuses on psychosexual developments

in the context of verbal and nonverbal communication and interpersonal relationships.
- Guide social workers in strategies to become comfortable addressing sexual issues and exploring sexual content with patients.
- Guide social workers through an assessment that includes the questions needed to understand life, behavior, sexual relationships, and activities appropriate to health social work settings.
- Provide an understanding of the human sexual response, and identify areas of preserved sexual functioning in people with medical illness or injury in order to address issues of disenfranchisement (see Box 14.1).
- Introduce social workers to sexual rehabilitation counseling techniques that focus on

> **Box 14.1 Institutional Obstacles to Physical Intimacy**
>
> Health facilities and related environments that assist the medically ill or injured often have policies and procedures that present obstacles to physical intimacy. These policies and procedures reflect a lack of basic knowledge about human sexuality and an avoidance of sexual issues. An example is rules that discourage the partners of adult patients from sleeping or resting in bed with them. The same institution may consider it routine for parents to share the beds of their pediatric patients. This incongruity is most apparent in cancer treatment centers where both the adult and pediatric patients receive chemotherapy and may have a weakened immune system yet face disparate policies for overnight visitation and bed sharing.

difficulties in sexual functioning and recovering functioning or creatively accommodating for the impairment.

- Introduce social workers to concerns unique to LGBT people.
- Introduce social workers to cultural and faith-based issues that may impact sexual rehabilitation.
- Introduce social workers to macrolevel issues of creating sex-positive care environments, and encourage social workers to learn how to provide sex-positive education, advocacy, and leadership in both inpatient and outpatient settings.

DEMYSTIFYING HUMAN SEXUAL DEVELOPMENT

Social workers are obligated by the National Association of Social Workers Code of Ethics to explore issues of suicidal thinking, domestic violence, and substance abuse. This exploration might be difficult for some, but few social workers would argue that they are not important to social work practice. Sexuality and physical intimacy, as healthy and potentially healing aspects of the quality of life, require the same professional attention from social workers.

The natural biological sexual capabilities of humans are evident throughout the life cycle, even at an early age, before the concept of sexual desire develops or intercourse occurs. For instance, infant boys may experience erections and infant girls may become lubricated (Horner, 2004; Kelly & Hockenberg-Eaton, 1999; Ryan, 2000; Walker & Casale, 1997). From a very young age, children may explore their bodies, including their genitals, because of the pleasurable sensation it provides (Kaplan, 1974; Zoldbrod, 2003).

Early Theories of Sexual Development

Freud's pleasure principle, introducing the concept of libido, has influenced many social workers' professional thoughts about sexual development (Freud, 1922). *Libido* is a concept that includes sexual desire, fantasy, and the initial sensations of being sexually stimulated. Freud believed that libido was concerned with pleasure seeking to relieve sexual tension. He presented a theory that seems devoid of many interpersonal processes, such as love seeking, comfort, and receiving pleasure from another person. It is thus incongruent with social work's philosophy of preserving and enhancing the quality of life. An unfortunate consequence of viewing sexual feelings primarily as a way to release tension is that issues of sexuality and physical intimacy are considered to be outside of a person's day-to-day functioning and thus, by definition, less important than activities such as going to work or school or caring for children.

Erickson's (1968) work on the formation of a person's identity from childhood to adulthood better represents sexuality and physical intimacy as aspects of the human experience by which people connect and communicate their thoughts and feelings. At each developmental stage, people express their wish to be close to others through displays of physical affection, comforting, and, at times, sexual desire (Erickson, 1968).

The gap between Freud's and Erickson's perspectives arguably may be bridged by the work of W. Ronald D. Fairbairn (1946), who suggested that libido was not concerned simply with seeking release but rather with an object or person with whom to connect intimately. The need to connect physically is rooted in the infant–parent relationship, which is based partly on touch and is each human's first experience of physical connection. Considering sexuality as relationship-based may lend it deeper meaning than if it is considered a purely pleasure-seeking activity. This idea demystifies human sexuality by placing it in an interpersonal context rather than one that is purely biological. This conceptualization is the basis of Zoldbrod's Milestones in Sexual Development (1998, 2003).

Zoldbrod's Milestones in Sexual Development

Zoldbrod's Milestones in Sexual Development begins with birth and progresses to the parent's initial bonding experience with the infant. Parental love is communicated through touch—the foundation of empathy as the parent searches for the right response to an infant's cry. As the baby's cry is interpreted correctly, the baby develops a sense of trust in the world and a belief that his needs will be met, which allows the infant to be soothed by the parent. Because parents must help their infants with all basic needs, such as bathing and feeding, a parent's attitude toward her baby's body becomes reflected in the baby's own attitude about his body and is therefore the foundation of body image. Body image is ultimately refined to include the establishment of gender identity.

As the growing child becomes more certain of his gender identity, he develops self-esteem and feels accepted. Regardless of later sexual and gender identity, children with atypical gender expression may encounter overt hostility, condemnation, and withdrawal of affection by their parents and same-age peers. As children continue to develop, they become more aware of their effect on other people and realize that their words and actions impact others. Thus begins the process of learning how to manage power within relationships with others. As children enter puberty, they develop a sense of "owning" themselves; that is, they begin to discover the parameters of autonomy and the concept of interdependence with others as an aspect of each being his own person.

Adolescence is a time of sexual exploration. A parent's permission to explore sexual issues is primarily a function of open communication, sharing, and recognition that the adolescent is experiencing intense sexual feelings. The exploration of both sexual and emotional feelings remains within a social and interpersonal context and provides an opportunity to develop more sophisticated social skills. A key part of this journey of sexual development is the creation of sexual fantasies and masturbation. The final milestone in the Zoldbrod model is the development of loving sexual interpersonal relationships.

Zoldbrod's milestones ground sexual development in an interpersonal perspective—the parent–child relationship. The parent's care of the child's bodily needs and functioning and the physical and emotional affection that travels

with the child, as he develops into an adolescent and then a young adult, position sexuality and physical intimacy more as an aspect of human communication and connection than one of sensation or pleasure seeking. Thus these milestones naturally progress from the love and touch of caring parents to loving and sexual relationships with others as adults (Zoldbrod, 1998, 2003). Parental touch responds to the needs of preverbal infants, both emotionally and physically, and becomes the foundation for empathy and trust. We learn that touch will soothe us and help us relax. Parents who talk to their children while diapering and bathing them convey the message that the child and the child's body are beautiful. This experience helps form our first notions of positive body image (Clawson & Reese-Weber, 2003; Connolly, Slaghter, & Mealey, 2004; Ehrenberg & Ehrenberg, 1988). The pleasure of being touched is the basic foundation of human sexuality and physical intimacy (Frohlick & Meston, 2005).

Communication and the Health-Care Team

People with medical conditions often are sexually disenfranchised by the medical establishment. In the 1940s, Alfred Kinsey studied human sexual practices in the United States, providing data on the age of first sexual experience, prevalence and fluidity of same sex practices, frequency of sexual intercourse within marriage, and masturbatory behavior in adolescents and adults (Kinsey, Pomeroy, & Martin, 1948, 1953). Kinsey's research was revisited by Laumann, Gagnon, Michael, and Michaels (1994) at the University of Chicago, who collected data to compare to Kinsey's. Included among the changes indicated by the comparison of the two collections of data are that Americans had their first sexual experience at a younger age, more women were willing to report that they masturbated, heterosexual oral intercourse had become more prevalent, and more unmarried people were living together in sexual relationships. The sexual practices of people with medical illness or injuries, however, were not addressed by either study.

People with medical problems become sexually disenfranchised when their sexual concerns are neither explored nor addressed (Gallo-Silver & Parsonnet, 2001; Kroll & Klein, 2001; McCabe, 1999). Health-care professionals tend to wait for patients and their partners to raise issues of sexuality and do not themselves initiate them (Esmail, Yashima, & Munro, 2002). This silence further isolates patients and their partners, sending the message that questions and concerns about sex are less than appropriate (Katzin, 1990; McInnes, 2003).

Discomfort with issues and discussion of sex and sexual expression may be based on cultural or religious beliefs. Prohibitions about premarital sex, masturbation, and nonprocreative sex may be part of the cultural or faith-based milieu that have been integrated into patients' belief systems. The health social worker needs to be educated about these issues, with the patient being one of the sources of information. At times, the health social worker collaborates with faith-based leaders to help negotiate these restrictions in a respectful and productive manner. Helen Singer Kaplan (1974) described a constrictive upbringing by parents who were uncomfortable with sexual issues as a source of sexual alienation and adult difficulties in sexual functioning.

LGBT people may be uncomfortable discussing their sexual behaviors and expression with social workers outside their communities, and some may avoid the topic altogether. Social workers may have to establish that they are LGBT friendly and demonstrate cultural credibility to facilitate disclosure and discussion from these patients (see Box 14.2).

Box 14.2 Glossary of Terms Used Within the LGBT Community

Members of the LGBT community self-identify using specific terms.

Lesbian: A woman who identifies as someone erotically, romantically, and affectionately attracted to other women.

Gay: An individual who identifies as someone erotically, romantically, and affectionately attracted to the same gender. Typically used by men and frequently interpreted as referring to men but also commonly used by women.

Bisexual: An individual who is erotically, romantically, and affectionately attracted to both genders. Used both as an identity label and as an adjective to describe behavior.

Transgender: Often used to describe all gender-variant people; clinically used to describe a person who lives or identifies as a gender other than that expected based on their anatomical sex.

In addition to these terms, additional self-identifiers are important to understand. *Homosexual* refers to a behavior and not to a person. *Gender identity* is a person's sense of being male, female, or other gendered.

Gender variant: A person who, either by nature or choice, does not conform to gender-based expectations of society.

Intersexed: A person born with ambiguous genitals may self-identify as being a member of both genders. At times this is used to self-identify a woman with an elongated clitoris or a man born with a micropenis and undescended testicles.

Transsexual: Often used interchangeably with the word *transgender*. It clinically describes those who may have surgically modified their secondary and/or primary sexual characteristics to match their gender identity.

Many of these terms have become stigmatized within specific cultures and often are associated with urban communities. People may use other labels to describe their identity and behavior, such as *queer, men who have sex with men, same-gender loving, two-spirited, pansexual,* and *polyamorous,* among others. When in doubt, always ask clients to define the term they use to describe themselves or their behaviors in a respectful and open manner.

CASE EXAMPLE

Ms. King, who is 75 years old, is recovering from a hysterectomy after ovarian cancer and is struggling with feeling less feminine. Her physician indicated that she was recovering nicely and told her that, because she was postmenopausal and therefore beyond childbearing age, the surgery would have a negligible effect on her life. Ms. King decided not to ask her doctor how her surgery might affect her sexual activity with her female partner. With empathy and respect, the social worker seeks a better understanding of Ms. King's relationship with her partner. A joint session with the couple prior to discharge from the hospital helps them explore the issue of physical intimacy in a direct and frank manner. Ms. King's doctor then is asked to explain the medical issues that would impact their sexual functioning and how those issues can be accommodated. The social worker provides the couple with reading material about sexual activity and arranges for them to meet with the physician in order for them to get specific information.

Social Worker's Role

Successful professional intervention is influenced in part by the attitudes of patients and their partners. The functioning of the health-care team also is affected by its members' cultural and religious backgrounds, which may result in a reluctance to focus on the sexual relationships between patients and their partners. In addition, some health-care professionals may be concerned that raising the issue of sex will alarm a patient or partner and be seen as inappropriate or unprofessional. Social workers are trained to address difficult issues, such as family violence, chemical dependence, and suicidal thoughts. Although these issues are difficult to discuss, they are seen as necessary issues for social workers' interventions. Health social workers need to be equally comfortable discussing sexuality and intimacy issues with patients and their partners in order to assess and address patients' psychosocial issues fully as well as to plan effective programs and services for individuals, groups, and communities. In addition, health social workers need to develop a sex-positive approach to people, for example, one that does not assume that everyone is heterosexual or that a person is "too old" for sexual activity. Although currently people who are LGBT are labeled according to their sexual orientation and lifestyle, many are no more or less inhibited and embarrassed about discussing sexual activity than are other Americans. In some instances, LGBT people may be more inhibited than other people because of fear of rejection or stigmatization.

INTIMACY OF HEALTH SOCIAL WORK

Health social work often requires a level of intimacy that social workers in other settings rarely experience. In acute care medical facilities, patients are often in bed and wearing hospital gowns or sleepwear when the social worker is present. In both outpatient and inpatient settings, as well as in nursing homes, the health social worker often must discuss a patient's body and its functions. Health social workers who are part of visiting nurse or hospice programs face situations in which their patients' bodies and functioning become part of the clinical focus, and most contact takes place in or near where patients sleep.

The intimacy of health social workers' practice settings requires an acute sensitivity to the patient's need for privacy and feelings of vulnerability. In most instances, the social worker is well advised to ask the patient's permission to join her at the bedside and to empower her to communicate when would be a comfortable time to be interviewed. Knocking on the door to the hospital or nursing home room, even if the door is open, sets a tone of respect and indicates that one is entering the patient's intimate environment. Some cultures prefer a more formal way of addressing and being addressed by health-care professionals. The social worker should begin the relationship with patients with formal greetings (i.e., using an honorific and the patient's last name) until she is able to assess what is the norm for the person's cultural group. Eye contact is best maintained on an equal plane; that is, if a patient is in bed or seated in a wheelchair, the health social worker also should be seated and at the patient's eye level instead of forcing the patient to look up by standing above her. Even for patients who come from cultures in which eye contact is considered impolite, being at the same level as the patient is almost always considered a sign of respect.

It is within these environments that patients may exchange information on body functioning and sexuality that is rarely, if ever, exchanged with social workers in other practice settings. Within these intimate contexts, it is important that all discussions about sexuality, sexual functioning, and physical intimacy address patients as people with complete adult lives that happen to have been disrupted by illness or injury (Schover, 2000; Schover & Jensen, 1988). In addition, the health social worker must establish some level of privacy, which may be difficult in some medical environments.

Obtaining a Sexual History

Early in the acquired immunodeficiency syndrome (AIDS) epidemic and prior to the development of the current family of antiviral drugs, people with AIDS experienced long hospital stays. The health social worker's role in discharge planning and the profession's commitment to underserved and isolated communities provided an opportunity to educate other health-care professionals (Eagan, 1993; Fahs & Wade, 1996; Mantell, Shulman, Belmont, & Spivak, 1989; Napoleone, 1988). Health social workers on the forefront of AIDS intervention claimed as part of their professional roles counseling to heterosexuals, bisexuals, and gay women and men about safer sex practices and harm reduction (Berkman & Zinberg, 1997; Christ, Moynihan,

& Gallo-Silver, 1995; Gallo-Silver, Raveis, & Moynihan, 1993; Weiner & Siegel, 1990). The counseling uses a sex-positive approach (Furstenberg & Olson, 1984; Samuel & Boyle, 1989). Health social workers accomplish this task by assessing a person's sexual practices with acceptance and respect and view the process as an integral part of their work.

Similarly, a psychosocial assessment of a person challenged by any illness or injury that fails to address sexual issues is incomplete. The health social worker is the one member of the health-care team who is not specifically and exclusively focused on the patient's illness or injury in terms of treatment or procedures. Rather, the health social worker's focus is on emotional coping skills and practical problem solving. The social work relationship provides the most comfortable and safe environment and opportunity for patients and partners to discuss issues of sexuality and physical intimacy. The natural time during a social work assessment to ask patients if they are sexually active and if they have partners is when discussing relationships and social supports (Fuentes, Rosenberg, & Marks, 1983; Gallo-Silver & Parsonnet, 2001; Weerakoon, Jones, Pynor, & Kilburn-Watt, 2004).

These assessments provide health social workers with opportunities to convey the message that sexuality and physical intimacy are natural and normal parts of life (Andrews, 2000). As a rule, people who have enjoyed their sexuality and the physical intimacy of their relationships want to recover and resume that aspect of their lives. People who have had long-standing difficulties with their sexuality fear that their medical conditions will render these difficulties intractable. In either case, the support and empathy of a social worker can help individuals feel less alone and overwhelmed by issues of sexuality and physical intimacy. Gaining an understanding of a patient's most recent and current sexual relationships helps the social worker learn what has been lost, or perceived to have been lost, due to adverse health conditions. All assessments should elicit information about significant relationships (see Box 14.3).

Box 14.3 Five Suggested Social Work Assessment Questions and Strategies for Patients

1. A patient's demographics enable the health social worker to integrate questions about sexuality and physical intimacy into a psychosocial assessment. If a patient is married, a social worker can ask, "Your admissions sheet indicates that you are married. How long have you been married? Do you have children? What are their ages? Are you currently sexually active?" or "Your admission sheet lists an emergency contact person; what is this person's relationship to you? Is this person a relative, friend, or partner? Are you currently sexually active with your partner?" Some patients are gay or lesbian. Therefore, discussions of wives and husbands that presume the patient is heterosexual are an obstacle to open and helpful discussions about sexual issues. The term *partner* is more gender neutral.

2. Assessing a couple's emotional intimacy is the first step in assessing their sexual relationship. Emotional intimacy is a good barometer of the couple's abilities to communicate and share intimate details of their lives together with each other. Areas to consider are an understanding of the history of their meeting and how the relationship progressed, the pre-illness/pre-injury sleeping arrangements, special enjoyable milestones, and the recreation/leisure time they spent together.

3. Patients define sexual activity and physical intimacy in an individual way. Asking patients how they define the terms *sexually active* or *physical intimacy* can be accomplished in a respectful and professional manner: "Thank you for sharing with me that you have a partner and that prior to your illness or injury you have been sexually active. Do you feel comfortable enough to share with me what, in particular, you mean by *sexual activity*?"

4. Patients will want to share sexual material with health-care professionals because they have concerns, worries, and distress about the impact of their illnesses or injury on their sexual functioning. Health social workers can share their discomfort with the issue, even their embarrassment, as such a disclosure can help put patients at ease. The reason to explore sexual issues is to diminish a sense of isolation and to help patients gain access to medical information and interventions that might improve their functioning. Health social workers demonstrate this by making clear the purpose of the discussion: "I appreciate you sharing such personal issues with me. It is a little awkward for me to ask you these questions about sexual activity. My goal in exploring the issue with you is to help you identify areas where you may want help and facilitate getting specialized help for your concerns."

5. Sometimes a patient's concerns are not specifically about how her body functions but how she looks to others and her perceived loss of attractiveness and desirability. These feelings can be very discouraging to people as they diminish self-esteem. At times, these feelings can impede a person's commitment to treatment or rehabilitation and can be an aspect of depression (McCabe & Taleporos, 2003; Sundquist & Yee, 2003; Tanyi, 2002) The health social worker's interventions are listening empathically, tolerating silence, and not presenting an obstacle to exploration by quickly reassuring the patient, "Your feelings about the way you look are very important. You have shared with me how much distress this causes for you. I don't think there are any quick or easy solutions, but I do think that discussing these issues can bring us closer to finding some solutions."

Social workers must be particularly attentive to the additional stressors and barriers faced by patients who are LGBT because of the lack of national legal recognition of their relationships. Because of this lack of recognition, members of the LGBT community may use terms such as *boyfriend* or *girlfriend* to describe their partners, even if they are in committed long-term relationships, while some patients may use *husband* or *wife*, even if the relationship is not legally recognized where they live.

The patient's partner is an important participant in understanding the sexual and affectionate aspects of their relationship. Interviewing the partner can elicit more information about a person's life functioning before illness or disability (see Box 14.4; Cagle & Bolte, 2009; Lemieux, Kaiser, Periera, & Meadows, 2004). Partners may be reluctant to approach issues of sex or physical intimacy due to the belief that by doing so, they are selfishly placing their own needs before those of their partner who is ill or has a disability (Soloway, Soloway, Kim, & Kava, 2005; Wimberly, Carver, Laurenceau, Karris, & Antoni, 2005; Zunkel, 2002). The health social worker who is willing to address the issues of sexuality and physical intimacy with a partner can help normalize and validate concerns about how life has changed due to the illness or injury (Esmail et al., 2002).

Box 14.4 Four Suggested Social Work Assessment Questions and Strategies for Partners

1. Social workers should understand the couple's experience of sexuality and physical intimacy during the beginning of their relationship. The health social worker needs to engage the partner in sharing how he met the patient to learn how the relationship unfolded emotionally. Questions such as "What were the reasons the two of you became a couple? At what point did you decide to become a couple? and What was it like in the beginning of the relationship?" focus the partner on the emotional underpinning of the relationship and ultimately its sexual underpinnings as well.

2. Relating emotional commitment to the expression of physical love through sexuality and physical intimacy helps a partner understand the health social worker's interest in this area of their lives. The health social worker's questions need to reflect this interpersonal approach: "My next question is a logical one but also a very personal one, and I want to avoid any embarrassment for you or for me. How has your relationship grown over the years in the areas of sexuality and physical intimacy? What has this been like for the two of you before your partner became ill/was injured? What types of touching and affection can/do the two of you share now?"

3. The health social worker needs to ascertain the importance of sexuality and physical intimacy for the partner at this time in his or her and the patient's life. "How important was making love/sex to you and your partner before the illness/injury? What do you miss now? Are you interested in finding out how you and your partner might be able to return to what the two of you enjoyed before the illness/injury?"

4. The health social worker's interventions are empathic: listening, tolerating silence, and not presenting an obstacle to exploration by quickly reassuring the partner or changing the subject. "Thank you for giving me a very clear understanding of how much the two of you share and how close the two of you are. Sexuality and physical intimacy are an important part of a couple's life. Perhaps as I talk further with you and your partner we can find some solutions and/or specialized services to help you both retain/reclaim the physically intimate aspects of your relationship."

The health social worker's approach to obtaining a sexual history and ultimately helping the patient and her partner problem-solve around sexual issues is based in supportive counseling techniques. The health social worker uses questioning to increase the couple's understanding of their thoughts, feelings, concerns, and needs; identifies patients and partners who want further intervention; and collaborates with other health-care professionals to access specialized services.

In addition to this process-oriented outline for assessment, other interventions are used more commonly in health-care settings that employ a medical model. The health social worker needs to be aware of how other health professionals may approach issues of sexuality and physical intimacy.

The EX-PLISSIT model of assessment has been developed and enhanced by nursing professionals and often is used by health social workers (Cagle & Bolte, 2009). EX-PLISSIT is based on the original PLISSIT model developed by Anon in 1976 (Taylor & Davies, 2006). The acronym stands for

EXtended. Social workers need to take a well-paced, ongoing approach to helping people with sexual issues.

Permission. Social workers need to give patients permission to talk about and consider sexual issues using generalization and normalization interventions.

Limited Information. Social workers need to gather limited information to capture the patient/family education aspects of a sexual assessment.

Specific Suggestions. Social workers need to provide specific suggestions and recommendations to the patient and the couple based on their sexual activity before their illness or injury.

Intensive Therapy. Social workers may suggest and intensive therapy to address an identified need through an appropriate referral.

Many health social workers use the EX-PLISSIT model, but a social work–developed model also can be used. The CARESS model was designed originally to assess sexual issues for patients receiving palliative care or at the end of life (Gallo-Silver, 2011) The acronym stands for:

Counseling. Health social workers often provide a variety of services and psychosocial interventions concurrently, and sexual issues often are presented within the context of ongoing meetings with patients and families focused on adjustment to illness.

Assessment. After the health social worker has developed a therapeutic alliance with the patient and partner, sexual issues should be introduced in a way that enables them to provide a description of their emotional and physical intimacy (see Box 14.4).

Research. The social worker must conduct research to become familiar with the specific needs and sexual issues confronting each patient due to specific illnesses or conditions.

Education. The social worker must provide education to the patient and her partner based on the social worker's research and in collaboration with the health-care team to help the couple understand their current medically related sexual obstacles.

Strategies. The social worker, in collaboration with the patient and her partner, must strategize for solving specific problems, because often the couple are too embarrassed or inhibited to share ideas with each other.

Sustainment. Social workers must make an ongoing commitment to help the couple when medical issues change.

Health social workers help other health professionals understand how certain terminology and phrasing might confuse patients who may be too uncomfortable to ask for clarification. Given the number of euphemisms used for sexual activities, definitions can vary from individual to individual.

CHILDHOOD SEXUAL ABUSE

People's sexual histories can be fraught with joy, contentment, resignation, or disappointment. After a health social worker uses his skill set to normalize issues of sexuality and physical intimacy and validate them as a natural part of life, other issues can be uncovered. Sadly, not all children are touched with parental tenderness and affection. Researchers estimate that 1 in 3 women and 1 in 7 men were sexually abused as children (Finkelhor, 1984; Maltz, 2001, 2003; Russell, 1999). *Childhood sexual abuse* is an umbrella designation for a series of behaviors that include vaginal and anal penetration by a penis, finger, hand, or other object; receptive or active oral sex; fondling and masturbation; invasion of privacy when bathing and toileting; sexually provocative behavior and nudity; and exposure to and involvement in pornography (Johnson, 2004). Survivors of childhood sexual abuse often feel violated by the health-care system (Jehu, 1992). The requirement that patients remove their clothes and appear inadequately dressed in a hospital gown, undergo X-rays and other radiographic tests that require them to stay still or be posed in certain ways, and receive invasive examinations, such as a gynecological or digital rectal exams, all can evoke feelings and thoughts about childhood sexual abuse that previously have been avoided or not acknowledged (Draucker, & Spadlin, 2001; Gallo-Silver & Weiner, 2006; Hobbins, 2004; Sansone, Gaither, & Sansone, 2001; Sansone, Skaife, & Rhodes, 2003).

A health social worker may become aware of a history of childhood sexual abuse when working with a patient who is in distress or having difficulty coping with the health-care environment. Helping a patient feel safe in these circumstances is achieved by increasing her sense of control over a given situation. All medical procedures require some form of consent, that can be rescinded or altered according to the patient's wishes. The next case example depicts how health social workers can use their clinical skills to help this emotionally fragile population.

CASE EXAMPLE

Mr. Allen is slowly recovering from a stem cell transplant to treat cancer. He underwent intensive chemotherapy and needed the transplant to help his bone marrow recover from the treatment. He becomes reluctant to change his pajamas, refuses to bathe, and struggles whenever he is being examined. His social worker, who had provided counseling to him in anticipation of the transplant, indicates that Mr. Allen's behavior is not consistent with how he had coped with his cancer prior to the transplant. After a medical reason for his change in behavior is ruled out, the social worker continues to help Mr. Allen become more aware of his feelings and thoughts. The simple questions "What is troubling you about the staff touching you? Do you think you could put it into words for me?" helps Mr. Allen share that his father fondled him when he was young, telling him that his skin was smooth and soft. Mr. Allen shares with the social worker that the loss of all his body hair frightens him because it makes him feel that his body has reverted back to the body his father molested. Continued counseling and psychiatric intervention with medication helps Mr. Allen manage the remaining course of his treatment.

The exploration of childhood sexual abuse in the health-care setting is appropriate when the history represents an obstacle to care, as illustrated in the last case. The ability to respond empathetically to a patient's disclosure of abuse is the social worker's most important skill when working with this population. The nature of the experiences described is often difficult to hear and can evoke considerable anxiety for the health social worker and other health-care professionals. It is both respectful and supportive for survivors of childhood sexual abuse to know that their histories are hard to hear. The pacing of the questioning is essential; survivors can overwhelm themselves and be retraumatized by sharing too much information at one time. By setting a limit on how much material will be discussed in any one session, the health social worker will help the survivor feel cared for rather than rejected (Gallo-Silver & Weiner, 2006; Schacter, Radomsky, Stalker, & Teram, 2004).

HUMAN SEXUAL RESPONSE

The hormonal surge during adolescence increases the skin's sensitivity to touch (Neufield, Klingbell, Borgen, Silverman, & Thomas, 2002). Sensitivity to touch remains intact as people age and become ill (Gelfand, 2000; Kingsberg, 2000). Even seriously ill people can respond to the sensual experience of bed baths, the application of moisturizers to their feet, and assistance with repositioning their body in bed. For people with spinal cord injury, the part of their body above the point of spinal injury remains highly sensitive. Some people with spinal cord injury report that their skin's sensitivity seems heightened because of the lack of sensation they experience below the point of injury (Sipski, 1998).

Human sexual response also can be seen as a neurological process. The centers of the brain interpret stimulation and send messages to the body to respond. The brain interprets both touch and nontouch types of stimulation. The brain is the repository of learning, experience, and recollection, all of which have a memory component. The brain stores a variety of sexual memories (Karma, Lecours, & Leroux, 2002), including memories of the physical sensations related to excitement, arousal, and orgasm; the memory of sexual and masturbatory fantasies; and the memory of actual sexual experiences (Cranston-Cuebas & Barlow, 1990; Holstege, Georgiadis, & Paans, 2003; McKenna, 1999). Masturbatory fantasies are thought to change only superficially as people mature; their basic concepts remain constant throughout the life span (Green & Mosher, 1985; Hurlbert & Whittaker, 1991; Lukianowicz, 1960; Mosher, 1980; Nutter & Condron, 1985; Rowan, 2000). As part of the long-term memory bank, sexual memories are resilient and retrievable (Jones & Barlow, 1990). Retrieving these memories can help medically ill and injured people enhance their sexual responsiveness through the use of masturbatory fantasies.

Masters and Johnson (1966, 1970) divided the human sexual response into interdependent phases. The four identified phases expanded existing knowledge of human sexuality beyond the previous notions of impotence and frigidity, two terms that have not added to our understanding of sexual dysfunction and have pejorative connotations that may add to patients' feelings of hopelessness and rejection. The phases determined by Masters and Johnson include: (1) the desire phase, which encompasses the feelings and thoughts about sex and sexual feelings; (2) the excitement phase, which involves increased blood supply to the genitals, erection of the penis, and lubrication of the vagina during sexual stimulation; (3) the orgasm phase, with rapid muscle spasms, increased heart and respiratory rates, changes in body temperature, and ejaculation; and (4) the resolution phase, which is marked by the body's return to a resting heart rate and a decrease in the supply of blood to the genitals.

Medical illnesses and injuries can disrupt some of these phases, but it is rare for all to be markedly disrupted (Black, 2004; Boone & Kelly, 1990; Ide, 2004; Katz, 2007; McCabe & Taleporos, 2003; McInnes, 2003). Because not all phases are disrupted, sexual rehabilitation for people with medical illnesses or injuries is possible. Sexual rehabilitation is the process of helping a medically ill or injured person restore and resume sexual functioning. A rehabilitative approach identifies the phase or phases that remain intact and helps patients maximize their responsiveness and enjoyment by building on the strengths of the remaining phases (Gallo-Silver, 2000; Kaplan, 1974, 1983; Schover & Jensen, 1988). Sex therapists using this model focus on cognitive and behavioral techniques that help obviate sexual concerns and worries (Gallo-Silver, 2000).

The phases of sexual response developed by Masters and Johnson are considered to be linear in nature. For this reason, some sex therapists consider them to be more relevant for men than for women. Basson (2001), for example, considers women's sexual responses to be more cyclical than those of men. Basson's sexual response cycle for women begins and ends with emotional intimacy that creates receptivity to sexual stimulation. The cycle continues to subjective arousal that is both emotional and physical, which leads in turn to objective arousal and responsive desire (similar to the Masters and Johnson's phase of excitement), followed by orgasm, resolution, and emotional and physical satisfaction. Emotional and physical satisfaction can engender further emotional intimacy. In Basson's formulation, emotional intimacy is both the beginning and end of the cycle of sexual functioning. Sex therapists whose interventions are based on Basson's conceptualization use a strengths-based approach that identifies those aspects of the response cycle that are intact as building blocks to sexual and emotional satisfaction.

It is easy for a patient challenged by a changed body and functioning to be discouraged about and fearful of sexual issues. A strengths-based approach presents this same patient with a measure of hope and possibilities for a different approach to sexuality. A rehabilitation approach based on Basson's (2001) model would focus on the interpersonal and intrapsychic issues that likely represent obstacles to comfort and enjoyment of physical intimacy. It should be noted that the gender patterns outlined here are not invariable.

DEVELOPMENTAL PERSPECTIVE

Older Adults

Often sexuality is considered the domain of the young, able, slim, and well. Although some baby boomers (individuals born in the post-World War II period from 1945 to 1968) consider sexually active older adults to be a new phenomenon, Kinsey in the 1940s, as well as Laumann in the 1990s, found individuals of both genders to be sexually active and satisfied with the quality of physical intimacy in their lives into their 80s and 90s (Kinsey, Pomeroy, & Martin, 1948, 1953; Laumann et al., 1994). Kinsey's findings are more illuminating, because the median age of survival during the period of his research was lower than it is at present, and medicine was less capable of addressing serious medical problems. Social workers should consider all patients as sexual beings, because sexuality is basic to the human condition. This approach will ensure that no group (e.g., those older than 80 years, those with physical disabilities) is desexualized and assumed to be sexually inactive.

After a certain age, women begin to produce less estrogen. The decreased estrogen levels can diminish vaginal lubrication, and the walls of the vagina may become thicker and less elastic. Desire, which is to some extent hormonally determined, might diminish, and some women report less intense orgasms as they age (Dennerstein & Lehert, 2004; Dennerstein, Lehert, Dudley, & Burger, 1999). However, hormone replacement therapy remains controversial due to empirical evidence that it can increase risk for breast and ovarian cancers (Aubuchon & Santoro, 2004; Chen et al., 2004; Ching & Lip, 2002; Durna et al., 2004).

Postmenopausal women may benefit from vaginal lubricants or moisturizers to facilitate comfortable sexual intercourse. As men age, they may require more tactile stimulation to achieve erections, and erections may be less rigid. The intensity of their orgasm also may diminish, as might the quantity of their ejaculates. Men also may require longer periods of time to achieve erections following orgasm. Erectile dysfunction medications are said to be effective for men who have difficulties due to natural aging, medical problems, or emotional obstacles to becoming aroused.

Laumann and colleagues (1994) suggest that partner availability might be a more important obstacle to sexual activity for older adults than the physical sequelae of aging. Older adults who do not have partners may use masturbation as their primary sexual activity. Masturbation is often a part of their sleep ritual. There is evidence to suggest that masturbation among older adult women without partners is almost as high as among adolescent males (Laumann et al., 1994). Health-care staff who work in congregate living settings often report discomfort when encountering a patient who is masturbating. Social workers can educate staff about masturbation in older adults and, in the process, help normalize the experience.

People in congregate living situations, such as assisted living residences, supportive senior apartments, nursing homes, and chronic care institutions, at times form sexual relationships with other residents. Nursing homes and chronic care facilities often do not permit unmarried patients to share rooms, but couples in love find ways to have private time nonetheless. Although it is important for institutions to protect vulnerable patients from being sexually exploited, some rules about privacy and sexual activity are more reflective of society's discomfort with sex rather than a need to protect. Social workers should advocate for patients who are competent to consent to sexual activity to have the privacy they desire in ways that are still consistent with the institutional policy and procedures.

Gay and lesbian older adults, whether in assisted living facilities, nursing homes, or chronic care environments, may feel particularly isolated (D'Augelli, Grossman, Hershberger, & O'Connell, 2001; Grossman, D'Augelli, & Hershberger, 2000; McMahon, 2003). The AIDS epidemic has left some gay men without the support of groups of male friends. Gay and lesbian adults in congregate or assisted living situations often feel they cannot be themselves or talk openly about their sexual identity or orientation, even though they may have led open lives before entering a facility or group living situation (Spitzer, Neuman, & Holden, 2004). Social workers can enable LGBT people to adjust to new living situations, including feeling safe and able to be themselves without the threat of being ostracized or scapegoated. It is crucial for the social worker to model acceptance for the other residents as well as staff members.

Health social workers can inform other members of the health-care team about

---

CASE EXAMPLE

Mr. Jones, who is 80 years old, is in the hospital's recovery area after a cardiac catheterization to clear several blockages in his arteries. At his bedside is his "friend," Ms. Thomas, who is 75 years old. His doctor visits and tells him that he will recover well and can return to his regular activities a few weeks but that he should not overly exert himself during that time. The doctor does not mention sexual intercourse, and neither Mr. Jones nor Ms. Thomas feels comfortable bringing it up, although they previously had made love a few times a month.

Once home, they are fearful of even cuddling, because they have heard stories of people dying of heart attacks during sexual activity. The social worker reassures them during her session with Mr. Jones by asking about his relationship with Ms. Thomas, and she makes it clear that talking about their sexual relationship is important.

---

patients' need for information about sexuality. At times, the health social worker seems to be the "safest" member of the health-care team to approach about sexual issues. This may be because of the therapeutic bond that health social workers establish around other issues important to their patients.

Young Adults

Adolescence is a time of rapid emotional and physical change. A major feature of adolescence, and the engine for the emotional upheaval during this stage of development, is the increased production of testosterone and estrogen. Adolescents are challenged by intense changes in body image and functioning due to the development of pubic hair, breasts, and muscle mass. Medical illness and injury further complicate young adults' relationships with their own bodies and their developing sexuality (Berman et al., 1999; Greydanus, Rimsza, & Newhouse, 2002).

Health-care professionals are obligated to inform patients that recommended treatment may interrupt or impair fertility. Often these discussions fail to address the sexual challenges that treatment presents, leaving young adults with many unanswered questions about the impact of their illness or treatment on their ability to function sexually. Some illnesses, such as testicular cancer, gynecological cancers, and cancer of the penis, affect both the functioning of the genitals and their appearance (Anderson, Woods, & Copeland, 1997; Katz, 2007; Nazareth, Lewin, & King, 2001; Opjordsmoen, Waehre, Aass, & Fossa, 1994). The health social worker can advocate for complete and comprehensive information to be given to patients, which is a crucial first step in helping them cope.

Advocacy is an important leadership function of social workers on health-care teams. It is essential that health social workers are informed about the impact of the illness, injury, and/or treatment to patients' genitals before the patient is given this information by physicians or nurses (Fuentes et al., 1983; Weerakoon et al., 2004). Being present when this discussion occurs maximizes the health social worker's ability to shape discussions that may be distressing and difficult for patients.

The use of clear and accurate terms is essential in discussing sexual issues to a population that may be sexually naive. It is part of the health social worker's advocacy role to inform other health-care professionals when a patient does not understand the information given to him or when he might misconstrue information.

In addition to issues related to fertility, another psychosocial barrier that young adults may struggle with are issues of attractiveness and desirability. Body image issues can create crises of self-esteem for people who do not currently have a partner or who have had limited sexual experiences (Horgan & MacLachlan, 2004; Ide, Watanabe, & Toyonaga, 2002; Lawrence, Fauerbach, Heinberg, & Doctor, 2004; McCabe & Taleporos, 2003). Changes in appearance are painful for any young adult, regardless of their sex. Many people view young adulthood as a time for entering long-term relationships, getting married, and having children; therefore, people experiencing physical changes during this period may be particularly vulnerable to issues with self-esteem. This may be especially true for young adults coping

---

CASE EXAMPLE

Mr. Crane, a 19-year-old with lymphoma, proudly walks into the clinic and announces to his social worker that the doctors were "wrong" and that his chemotherapy would not prevent him from having children. He reports that he and his girlfriend had made love the night before and that everything was about the same as it always had been. Mr. Crane had been confused by the euphemistic and medical language used to discuss his illness. He thought that infertility meant he could not have an erection.

CASE EXAMPLE

Ms. Dean, a 22-year-old woman, underwent an amputation of her left leg above her knee after a car accident. About the same time, her boyfriend decided to end their relationship. During the period in which she is awaiting a prosthesis, she repeatedly cancels appointments and misses her outpatient physical therapy appointments. She tells her social worker that there is little point in keeping her appointments, because she would rather just stay in a wheelchair.

Counseling with her social worker helps her mourn the loss of both her boyfriend and her leg. Support and education help Ms. Dean feel more in control and willing to accept her prosthesis. Counseling continues as an integral part of her physical therapy. Ms. Dean gradually begins to pay more attention to her appearance. She tells her social worker that she feels more confident when socializing with her friends and that she hopes to meet the "right person" with whom to begin a new relationship.

with an amputation. Amputation of a limb and facial disfigurement can be profoundly disorganizing to a person's self-esteem because it often has an immediate impact on how others interact with the affected person (Horgan & MacLachlan, 1004; Lawrence et al., 2004; McCabe & Taleporos, 2003; Monga, Tan, Ostermann, & Monga, 1997).

Given the many changes that are characteristic of adolescent physical development, the additional changes due to illness and injury serve to separate affected adolescents from their peers. The validation and normalization of adolescents sharing thoughts and concerns about bodily changes with their peers are often unavailable to those challenged by illness or injury. In some ways, the relationship with the health social worker becomes the environment for validation of and normalization to the special circumstances caused by illness or injury.

Although prosthetic devices can help a young adult amputee look "whole" in clothing that covers the affected limb, the loss of a limb becomes apparent in intimate situations. This reality can affect how the young adult approaches and adheres to the required physical therapy and prosthetic fittings. The health social worker's role is often to permit the young adult to mourn the lost body part, bear witness to the loss, and confront fears about how the loss will affect sexual relationships. Education about the normal or typical process of adjusting to an amputation and the provision of supportive counseling either before or directly after a physical therapy session can help young adults with amputations begin to integrate their experiences (Bodenheimer, Kerrigan, Garber, & Monga, 2000; Shell & Miller, 1999). The goal of the health social worker's interventions is for the patient to accept the loss of the limb as part of an ongoing process of adjustment.

The young adult's adjustment to facial disfigurement is accompanied by a tendency to become socially isolated and anxious about meeting new people, including new healthcare professionals (Bianchi, 1997; Monga et al., 1997; Whitehead, 1993). The health social worker can build a relationship of trust by maintaining eye contact with the patient and acknowledging the discomfort caused by facial disfigurement. Assisting young adults with facial disfigurement to gain social confidence can be accomplished by helping them develop strategies to put people at ease and address hurtful reactions to their disfigurement in an open and direct manner. The health social

---

CASE EXAMPLE

Mr. North, age 15, had been challenged by a variety of physical problems due to cerebral palsy. He shares a friendship with Ms. White, also 15 years old and challenged by cerebral palsy. They met at the medical clinic where they both receive care. The parents are aware that their children have formed a close friendship.

They are observed by a medical assistant kissing and touching each other in what the teens had assumed was a private place. The medical assistant tells Ms. White's mother, believing Ms. White needs to be "protected."

The social worker intervenes after Ms. White's mother complains about Mr. North to clinic staff. Gently but empathically, the social worker helps Ms. White's mother place her daughter's behavior and the behavior of her male friend in the perspective of adolescence. The mother had not focused much on her daughter's body changes, beyond helping her understand her menstrual cycles, purchase a bra, and learn to address her personal hygiene activities. The mother admits to the social worker that she never considered that her daughter might have "those" thoughts. Similarly, Mr. North's parents were aware that he was masturbating but had not discussed sexual development or feelings with him.

The health social worker can help these two families communicate with one another about many difficult issues using empathy as well as even-handed neutrality. In this instance, normalizing adolescent behavior helps the parents realize that all parents of adolescents struggle with the same issues.

worker can help young adults who are challenged by amputation or facial disfigurement consider issues of sexuality and physical intimacy and manage social situations in general.

Social workers should not assume heterosexuality, because many lesbian, gay, and bisexual people are "coming out" or becoming self-aware of their sexual orientation in middle and high school (Grov, Bimbi, Nanin, & Parsons, 2006). In addition, many transgender people begin to struggle with their gender identity during adolescence (Koken, Bimbi, & Parsons, 2009).

Finally, adolescents with complex medical needs often struggle with intensified issues of independence from parents, who necessarily are involved in their ongoing care. Parents' increased involvement in adolescents' lives and physical needs may delay their acknowledgment of their child's maturation and sexual development. Health social workers often educate parents about the additional struggles experienced by their adolescent and the adolescent's experiences with sexuality and physical intimacy. Heterosexual and LGBT youth may use sexual contact to affirm their sense of self and identity.

SPECIFIC ISSUES RELATED TO WORKING WITH COUPLES

"Parentification" of the Well Partner

Hospital stays have become progressively shorter because of improvements in medicine's ability to treat illnesses, the expansion of outpatient services, and the demands of medical insurers. Families have become more involved in the practical care of people with both acute and chronic illness. The shift in care from health-related facilities to patients' homes may have unintended, negative consequences for couples.

Medical illnesses and traumatic injuries place patients in a vulnerable position and increase their dependence on others, both practically and emotionally. The well partner often must monitor the patient's condition, supervise medications, provide transportation to physician

visits and treatments, assist with bathing and toileting, and participate in physical and occupational therapies. As the level of practical and personal care increases, partners may report that they feel like parents rather than romantic partners. Other health-care professionals are often unaware of this shifting dynamic in couple relationships as the well partner begins to focus on the details of the care, treatment, and progress. A health social worker's awareness of this potential "parentification" of the well partner can help diminish the isolation and loneliness that develops among couples. The health social worker's use of problem-solving skills

---

CASE EXAMPLE

Ms. Richards is recovering from a gunshot wound that left her paralyzed from the waist down. Her partner, Mr. Barry, visits her daily and participates in her therapy at the acute care rehabilitation center. Ms. Richards complains to her social worker that, while Mr. Barry is attentive and helpful, the affection and physicality of their relationship has suffered.

The social worker meets with Mr. Barry and asks him how well he thinks he and his partner are adjusting to her spinal cord injury. He reports that he has learned a lot, wants to help Ms. Richards in every way, but misses aspects of their previous life together. When the social worker questions further, Mr. Barry begins to cry, relating how he feels more like his partner's father than her lover. He recalls to the social worker how he loved to hold her and caress her breasts. Mr. Barry seems quite embarrassed when sharing this with the social worker. The social worker reassures him and suggests that because the spinal cord injury did not change Ms. Richards's breasts in any way, and because touching them would not hurt her in any way, perhaps that is something they can still share. She suggests that he pull the curtain around her bed, giving them enough privacy to show how much they love each other.

CASE EXAMPLE

Mr. Wong is a 28-year-old man recovering from the surgical treatment of testicular cancer. He was referred to the health social worker when a nurse walked in on him while he was trying to masturbate. He explains to the health social worker that he wanted to make "sure it [his penis]" still worked. He was reassured by his surgeon prior to his surgery that his erectile capacity would be unchanged. Mr. Wong reports fearing that his boyfriend of two years, Mr. Perez, would leave him if he could not sexually "perform." Although he is fearful of talking at all to Mr. Perez, he is more fearful of returning home without some discussion of the issue. The health social worker facilitates a couple's session that helps them rediscover the vast number of ways they enjoy each other's bodies. Specifically, Mr. Perez's hugs and kisses reassure Mr. Wong of his emotional commitment to him and their relationship.

engages the partner in an exploration of what aspects of physical intimacy could be integrated into daily care routines. The activity is identified by the partner, and the health social worker works on helping the couple consider ways to incorporate physical intimacy into these activities. This might include adding massage to bathing activities or kissing when helping the patient with meals.

Straightforward suggestions can give couples permission to demonstrate their love physically. The health social worker can work collaboratively with occupational therapists to help couples feel more "normal" in the face of traumatic injuries that affect day-to-day self-care functioning as well as issues of sexuality.

Physical Intimacy as an Aspect of Couples' Communication

Medical illness and traumatic injury can have an enormous impact on a couple's ability to communicate, share, and understand each other.

If communication problems existed before the health crisis, they likely will not improve under the challenge of poor health or disability. Physical intimacy for people with medical conditions requires verbal communication. Often couples need to relearn how to listen to each other so they can rekindle the physical intimacy they enjoyed before the crisis. Adjusting to a changed body and body image requires sensitivity and clarity, both of which are best achieved through good communication.

The Speaker/Listener Technique (Markham, Stanley, & Blumberg, 1994) was developed to help couples improve their ability to communicate and share their thoughts, concerns, and worries. The technique entails teaching couples how to concentrate on the words that the other person is saying instead of focusing on how they should respond. Couples are instructed to try to paraphrase what their partner has said and then inquire whether their interpretation accurately reflected their partner's statement. The couple takes turns completing the exercise. For couples who need more structure, the speaker may hold a card, which is called the "floor." The term *holding the floor* means that only the person with the card is allowed to speak at that time. The Speaker/Listener Technique can be taught at the bedside or in a clinic exam room.

EFFECTS OF MEDICAL ILLNESSES AND TRAUMATIC INJURIES

Impact on Sexuality and Physical Intimacy

Illness and injury often disrupt aspects of the human sexual response, but rarely do they disrupt them entirely. Many people retain functioning in at least one of the major phases (i.e., desire, excitement, and orgasm) of the response.

Many anecdotal stories exist about people who suffer heart attacks during sexual activity. Although instances of cardiac arrest during sexual intercourse are uncommon, people with heart disease often approach the issue of physical intimacy with fear and dread (Debusk, 2000). Cardiovascular disease, hypertension, and diabetes often diminish the body's sensitivity to touch and stimulation, secondary to diminished blood flow. This has its greatest impact on the genitals, which require increased blood supply to achieve erection of the penis or lubrication of the vagina. At the same time, however, diminished blood flow would not likely affect the desire for sexual stimulation or the overall quality of orgasm.

Although desire is highly governed by hormones, it also may be affected by systemic problems. This is because emotional vibrancy and vigor also play a part in the desire phase. People in renal failure lose energy and stamina due to the buildup of impurities in the blood that would ordinarily be cleaned by the kidneys. Dialysis can assume the functioning of the kidneys, but the process leaves the body fatigued and diminishes its overall response to stimulation. Therefore, erectile and lubrication capabilities are impaired, although orgasm is largely unaffected (Schover, 2000; Schover & Jensen, 1988).

Pulmonary disease robs the body of energy, which in turn diminishes feelings of desire. Although they are able to be stimulated to the excitement or arousal phase of response, people with pulmonary disease sometimes do not have the lung capacity to tolerate orgasm, and the quality and intensity of their orgasms are diminished (F. Haas & Haas, 2000; Walbroehl, 1992).

Cancer is a generic term for a number of illnesses, all of which involve cells multiplying and growing out of control (see Chapter 19). Women with breast or gynecological cancers may experience diminished desire, problems with excitement or arousal, and diminished quality of orgasm. Men with prostate cancer are challenged by diminished desire and erectile difficulties, yet they retain orgasmic functioning. Men with testicular cancer retain desire and erectile capabilities but report some diminished quality of orgasm. People with colorectal cancers and bladder cancer experience problems with erection and lubrication but retain desire and orgasm. Women treated for bladder, cervical, and other gynecological cancers may experience changes in the shape or size of the vaginal vault. This may necessitate the use of dilators to maintain and stretch the contours of the vagina. Dilators are used until the penis can be inserted comfortably into the vagina. Health-care professionals may recommend vaginal intercourse as a way of preserving the vagina's contours. This is a sex-negative recommendation because it places women in the position of having uncomfortable and painful intercourse in the short run for longer-term sexual comfort. People with leukemia or lymphomas experience a loss of desire and some fatigue-related erectile or lubrication dysfunctions yet retain orgasm. People with brain tumors can experience a loss of desire but often retain some ability to achieve erection or lubrication as well as orgasm (American Cancer Society, 1998; Schover, 1999).

Spinal cord injury disrupts the individual's ability to feel below the injury. Desire remains intact, and erections and lubrication occur, but the individual is not able to feel these changes. Because orgasm is a total body response not confined to the genitals, people can experience orgasmic feelings in parts of the body that are above the injury. Kroll and Klein (2001) report that skin over areas that retain feeling express some of the orgasmic reactions.

The social work profession encourages a strengths-based perspective. Supportive and educational social work interventions focus on the aspects of sexual functioning that remain intact while at the same time respecting the loss or impairment of certain sexual abilities. The health social worker who is able to help people feel comfortable with sharing their sexual feelings can help them locate reactions that can serve as building blocks to more satisfying physical intimacy.

Impact on Stamina

The loss of overall physical stamina caused by cancer, AIDS, pulmonary disease, multiple sclerosis, and other chronic medical problems can impair the body's ability to respond to sexual stimulation (Ferrando et al., 1998; Harden, 2005; Parish, 2002; Schmidt, Hofmann, Niederwieser, Kapfhammer, & Bonelli, 2005; Walbroehl, 1992). As the body moves from an aroused state to orgasm, heartbeat and respiration increase. Cardiologists have compared the energy needed for sexual activity to that of climbing two flights of stairs or walking three miles on level ground (Brody & Pruet, 2003; Debusk, 2000; Thorson, 2003). Energy conservation is a crucial element in enabling people with a medical illness or injury to resume or return to sexual activity. Accommodations in lovemaking positions transfer more of the "work" of sexual intercourse to the well partner (Haas & Haas, 2000).

Fatigue is a major obstacle to sexual activity for people with challenging medical conditions. Fatigue is a physiological phenomenon that does not respond to sleep or rest and often is intensified by increased inactivity. Tiredness is usually muscular in nature and can be resolved by sleep and rest. Although it is counterintuitive to be active when fatigued, exercise can work to offset fatigue. It is important that people can identify the times at which they experience higher energy levels so they can plan for physical intimacy.

For people with pulmonary disease, the morning is a time to clear secretions that have built up in the lungs during sleep. After secretions have been cleared, many people feel more energetic. For people who are challenged by paralysis due to either stroke or spinal cord injury and are wheelchair-bound, energy levels may seem higher when they move from bed to their wheelchairs. Physical intimacy for people who require the use of wheelchairs is often more easily undertaken while they are in their chairs rather than in bed because the chair provides both physical and emotional support (a person may feel more confident in the wheelchair), and offers more mobility than the bed.

People on kidney dialysis usually undergo the procedure three days a week. Usually people will experience a bit more energy on the morning of the second day after dialysis (Camsari et al., 1999; Reynolds & Postlethwaite, 1996; Uttley, 1996). Those

undergoing chemotherapy for cancer also have breaks between treatments during which their body recovers from the side effects of the chemotherapy. The days just before the next administration of chemotherapy are often days of higher energy (Burt, 1995; Hughes, 2000; Wood & Tombrink, 1983). Health social workers aware of the relationship between treatment and energy level are better able to help couples preserve the sense of normalcy achieved when they are able to resume being physically intimate.

People with human immunodeficiency virus (HIV) often have few symptoms in the early stages of their infections. Medications that inhibit the growth of the virus may present side effects, such as fatigue and some gastric complaints that may diminish sexual vibrancy (Roak, Webster, Darrow, & Stempel, 2005). The challenge for people with HIV is integrating harm-reduction practices into their sexual routines to limit the chance that they will infect others. The use of barriers, including condoms for men, dental dams for women, and spermicidal preparations, requires a thoughtful and planned approach to sexual activity.

Impact of Complications From Medications

Medicines that affect sexual functioning are said to have sexual side effects. Medications can disrupt any of the phases of sexual response (Dickman, 2003; Kaplan, 1983).

Because medical illness and traumatic injury can cause mood disorders, patients may be prescribed antidepressant or anxiolytic medications. Antidepressant medications may diminish sexual desire. Men who experience erectile dysfunction due to prostate cancer, diabetes, or cardiovascular disease may experience depression in response to their inability to achieve an erection. The treatment of prostate cancer, diabetes, and cardiovascular disease may include the prescription of additional medications, such as hormonal treatment and antihypertensive medications, which can diminish desire, cause erectile dysfunction, and diminish the intensity of orgasm. The inclusion of antidepressant medication to the list that may inhibit sexual desire may cause men to feel sexually "shut down." Although erectile dysfunction medications can help a man achieve higher-quality erections, and thus rekindle his desire, such medications cannot improve the quality of orgasms that has been impaired by other medications or nerve damage.

Like men, women can experience depression in reaction to cancer, diabetes, and cardiovascular disease. This depression compounds the impact of illness on the body's ability to function sexually. Chemotherapy induces permanent menopause in women ages 35 to 40 years in about half of cases. Chemotherapy-induced menopause occurs about 70% of the time in women ages 40 to 45 years and 80% of the time in women between the ages of 45 and 50 (Poniatowski, Grimm, & Cohen, 2001). Transient menopause is much more common.

Some gynecological cancers require removing a woman's ovaries, a procedure called an oopherectomy (Schover, 1997). The treatment for breast cancer that is estrogen-receptor positive can lead to early menopause in women (Chen et al., 2004; Schover, 1997, 1999). By virtue of their effects on estrogen production and metabolism, these treatments may affect vaginal lubrication and the elasticity of the vaginal walls.

Most antidepressants, beta blockers, and antihypertensive medications cause problems in women similar to those in men (Dickman, 2003; Schover, 2000). Diminished desire, loss of ability to lubricate naturally, and diminished quality of orgasm have been reported by women who are taking these medications. Currently no widely accepted treatment for female sexual dysfunction has been developed that appreciably improves women's response to stimulation. Some herbal combinations depend on plant estrogens to improve a woman's sexual functioning (Rowland & Tai, 2003). These preparations come as a salve to be applied directly to the vaginal wall and clitoris. Some of these preparations have a mild irritant that draws blood to the genitals, and others contain progesterone. The latter come either in a salve form applied to the abdomen or in a ring-shaped vaginal insert that slowly releases hormones. It should be cautioned, however, that none of these methods has approval from the Food and Drug Administration, and health social workers should refer patients who are contemplating using these approaches to their physicians.

Health social workers should ensure that patients are aware of the sexual side effects of their medications and medical regimes and feel empowered to talk to their physicians about their concerns. This is important even if no viable alternatives to the prescribed medications are available. When patients are able to mourn the losses that illness, injury, and treatment cause, they feel more in control of their conditions. Requesting erectile dysfunction medications or asking a physician to revisit the issue of hormonal replacement or enhancement requires self-advocacy. An important role of health social workers is to help people learn how to communicate with their physicians about sexual issues. At times, role-playing can be an effective method to help people practice new ways of communicating in stressful situations.

Sexual Rehabilitation of People With Medical Illness or Traumatic Injuries

Sex therapy addresses pervasive problems and obstacles to physical intimacy that may be psychogenic or emotional in nature. The goal of sex therapy is to help patients establish a new, improved baseline of functioning. Sexual rehabilitation counseling also focuses on the impact of medical illness or injury on sexual functioning and intimacy. Its goal is to help individuals restore or return to their baseline functioning or to accommodate a changed baseline of functioning (Gallo-Silver, 2000).

Sexual rehabilitation counseling includes a number of cognitive and behavioral interventions, including safe-touch exercises, the prolonged kiss, "dressing" for bed in new pajamas, self-exploration and self-pleasuring exercises, sensate focus or sensual massage exercises, and altering coital positions to accommodate a changed body (Gallo-Silver & Parsonnet,

2001; Schover, 2000). Safe-touch exercises and body mapping are consistent with the concept that physical intimacy and sexuality have their foundations in touch. Sexual rehabilitation counseling may employ a series of safe-touch exercises, which were devised to help people who were sexually traumatized by rape, incest, and childhood sexual abuse regain comfort with being touched (Maltz, 2003). Several of these exercises can be useful in helping couples challenged by illness or injury. *Back-writing* involves having the person with the medical challenge trace a word on the back of his partner using the tip of his finger. The person traces the word over and over again until the partner is able to identify the word correctly. The exercise is then reversed with the partner tracing a word on the back of the person with the medical challenge.

Another exercise is a variation of the child's game Red-Light-Green-Light, in which the person with the medical challenge gives cues to her partner about where on her body it feels good to be touched (green light), which touches are not comfortable (red light), and which touches are okay at times (yellow light). Body mapping is based on a similar concept. An outline of the body is drawn in green, red, and yellow, and the partner then has a map of the parts of the body where the person with the medical challenge enjoys being touched.

The prolonged kiss and the second kiss exercises recognize that couples under duress due to medical problems may kiss each other in a quick, almost perfunctory and, at times, parental manner. The second kiss exercise is based on the premise that the couple will be more aware and connected to each other if they kiss a second time. Typically, the second kiss is held for a longer period of time, and the couple tends to feel greater emotional resonance from the second kiss.

Self-exploration and self-pleasuring, or masturbation, are basic behaviors to discover enjoyable sensations (Lukianowicz, 1960; Rowan, 2000). Although many cultures and religions prohibit masturbation, it remains a primary way in which men and women discover their sexuality and orgasmic capabilities.

Sexual rehabilitation counseling gives people with medical challenges permission to explore and regain comfort with their changed bodies. Self-pleasuring exercises are included as part of bathing (Gallo-Silver & Parsonnet, 2001). The exercises are then duplicated in a bed or chair. Ultimately the person with the medical challenge instructs the partner on what feels good and how to best stimulate her body.

From this foundation, couples frequently turn to sensate focus exercises. Sensate focus exercises are a series of sensual massage techniques that help couples whose sexual activity has been interrupted by illness or injury. Developed by Masters and Johnson (1970), the exercises avoid direct genital massage until the couple has become more comfortable caressing other parts of the body (Kaplan, 1974, 1987; Masters & Johnson, 1970). Altering coital positions to avoid injured or "red-light" areas of the body helps people with medical challenges conserve energy and helps couples feel safe and secure so they can enjoy physical intimacy with each another.

Sexual rehabilitation exercises have a self-help aspect to them as well. Instructional texts provide easy-to-follow, systematic instructions with drawings that help couples understand exercises. Many of these materials focus on opposite-sex couples but can be easily adapted for same-sex couples.

Creating Sex-Positive Environments of Care

The health social worker is a problem solver. Privacy is a major obstacle to physical intimacy in institutional settings. Policies and procedures that insist that hospital room doors remain open at all times are changed when patients have a communicable infection or need protection, such as when they are recovering from a bone marrow or organ transplant. Policies and procedures that frown on adult visitors climbing into bed with adult patients are not used on pediatric floors, where it is routine for parents and their children to be in bed together. Discomfort about physical displays of affection also changes on obstetric units, on which the staff helps to provide a romantic setting for new parents. The contradiction between how intimacy is fostered in these settings for everyone but adults with medical illnesses or injuries is not always apparent to other health professionals. Health social workers advocate for "bending the rules" on an individual, case-by-case basis. Often, educating the staff about the patient's and partner's needs for privacy emphasizes the couple's love and devotion for one another. Social workers can define a couple's privacy as part of a supportive-care plan that addresses the symptoms of loneliness and sadness about separation. At times, the health social worker is able to change policy with a creative idea that helps coprofessionals understand patients' needs for privacy and physical contact.

Hospital libraries for patients and professionals generally contain few, if any, books on physical intimacy and sexuality. Health social workers can advocate for enriching the libraries by including these materials. Social workers who perform home visits can provide a list of books or pamphlets that can help patients and their partners remain physically close. People with chronic and acute illness

---

CASE EXAMPLE

The health social worker reports in oncology multidisciplinary rounds that patients frequently want more "alone" time with their partners. Even when patients' doors are closed, staff members sometimes enter without knocking or while they are knocking. The social worker points out that health-care staff are used to looking at closed doors for special instructions related to protecting the patient and others from infection. The social worker proposes that when a partner is visiting, the patient or partner could place a cardboard cutout of a cupid on the door so that the staff would be aware that the partner was with the patient and wanted privacy. The staff institutes the change, and the social worker's suggestion becomes part of the facility's marketing campaign.

---

or injuries do not have routine access to urologists and gynecologists with a knowledge base in sexual difficulties. Social workers can address these gaps by developing educational programs to which they invite local experts to meet with patients and their partners in a group setting.

CONCLUSION

Issues of sexuality and physical intimacy are greatly affected by cultural norms. It is beyond the scope of this chapter to explore these issues in detail, but it is important to consider how cultural norms change depending on a mixture of scientific discovery and political influences. Homosexuality was once considered a psychiatric illness by many in the mental health professions. Physicians once believed that masturbation caused a host of physical and psychological conditions and that the only "healthy" reason for sexual intercourse was procreation. Specialists in child abuse and health-care professionals once believed that childhood sexual abuse rarely, if ever, occurred. Transgenderism still is not widely understood, and debates are ongoing about etiology and whether it is a condition requiring a *DSM* diagnosis. Nonetheless, the changes in attitudes about these and other sexual issues are by no means universal. The ideas of health-care professionals and the community often are based on religious beliefs, cultural conventions at the time, beliefs of the person's specific ethnic or cultural group, and the basic scientific understanding of people as sexual beings. All of these factors may change, become more widely influential, or lose influence depending on the political and cultural climate at the time. Nonetheless, sexual issues are quintessentially human issues. When, by reason of culture, politics, or ignorance, the human aspects of sexuality are overlooked or replaced by viewing it as a completely biological function, an important aspect of quality of life is diminished. People challenged by medical illnesses and injuries suffer many losses, among them a sense of being entitled to be sexual beings. One of the health social worker's roles is to humanize the health-care experience. Helping medically ill and injured patients reclaim their ability to connect with their loved ones, communicate their love physically, receive the loving touch of others, and feel pleasurable physical sensations is a part of humanizing the health-care environment.

SUGGESTED LEARNING EXERCISES

Learning Exercise 14.1

Your sibling or cousin tells you that he is transgendered. Write down how you would feel about learning this. What would be the impact on your relationship with him? What would be the impact on your family? Would your sibling's/cousin's partner of choice be welcomed by you and by the family?

Learning Exercise 14.2

Identify one policy or procedure at your current internship or practice setting that is an obstacle to physical intimacy. Develop a strategy to change the policy. With whom must you meet with to begin this process? What would be the best environment for this discussion: a private meeting, team meeting, or rounds? How many alternatives can you devise that preserve some of the policy but enhance a person's opportunities for physical intimacy?

Learning Exercise 14.3

Write down your own sexual history. Read it silently to yourself. How difficult would it be to share this information with a stranger? What would a stranger need to do, say, or demonstrate to help you feel more comfortable with a discussion of your history? Share your thoughts with the class either in a small or a large group.

Learning Exercise 14.4

With what type of client or patient would you feel most comfortable discussing sexual issues,

and why? With what type of client or patient would you feel most uncomfortable discussing sexual issues, and why?

SUGGESTED RESOURCES

Professional Education

American Association of Sex Educators, Counselors and Therapists (ASSECT)—www.assect.org

ASSECT sponsors and provides continuing education credits through a number of training seminars and workshops throughout the United States for professionals at various levels of skill development.

LGBT Communities Education

Advocates for Youth (LGBT Adolescents)—www.advocatesforyouth.org

Family Caregiver Alliance (LGBT frequently asked questions)—www.caregiver.org

LAMBDA (LGBT Adults)—www.lambda.org

Illness- or Condition-Specific Sex Education

American Association of Kidney Patients—www.aakp.org

American Cancer Society—www.cancer.org

American Heart Association—www.americanheart.org

American Lung Association—www.lungusa.org

American Social Health Association (Sexually Transmitted Diseases, Hepatitis, HIV/AIDS)—www.ashastd.org

American Spinal Injury Association—www.asia-spinalinjury.org/

Instructional Books for Professionals and Patients/Partners

Altman, C. (1997). *You can be your own sex therapist.* San Francisco, CA: Caper.

Britton, P. (2005). *The art of sex coaching.* New York, NY: Norton.

DeVillers, L. (2002). *Love skills.* Marina Del Rey, CA: Aphrodite Media.

Westheimer, R. K. (2005). *Sex after 50: Revving up the romance, passion & excitement.* Sanger, CA: Quill Driver Books/Works Dancer Press.

REFERENCES

American Cancer Society. (1998). *For the man/woman with cancer and their partners: Companion booklets.* Atlanta, GA: Author.

Anderson, B. L., Woods, X. A., & Copeland, L. J. (1997). Sexual self esteem and sexual morbidity among gynecologic cancer survivors. *Consulting Clinical Psychology, 65*(2), 221–229.

Andrews, W. C. (2000). Approaches to Taking a Sexual history. *Journal of Women's Health & Gender-Based Medicine, 9*(Suppl.), S21–S24.

Aubuchon, M., & Santoro, N. (2004). Lessons learned from WHI; HRT requires a cautious individualized approach. *Geriatrics, 59*(1), 22–26.

Basson, R. (2001). Human sex response cycles. *Journal of Sex and Marital Therapy, 27,* 33–43.

Berkman, C. S., & Zinberg, G., (1997). Homophobia and heterosexism in social workers. *Social Work, 42*(4), 319–332.

Berman, H., Harris, D., Enright, R., Gilpin, M., Cathers, T., & Bukovy, G. (1999). Sexuality and the adolescent with a physical disability: Understandings and misunderstandings. *Issues in Comprehensive Pediatric Nursing, 22*(4), 189–196.

Bianchi. T. L. (1997). Aspects of sexuality after burn injury: Outcomes in men. *Journal of Burn Care Rehabilitation, 18*(2), 183–186.

Black, P. K. (2004). Psychological, sexual and cultural issues for patients with a stoma. *British Journal of Nursing, 3*(2), 692–697.

Bodenheimer, C., Kerrigan, A. J., Garber, S. L., & Monga, T. N. (2000). Sexuality in persons with lower extremity amputations. *Disability and Rehabilitation, 22*(9), 409–415.

Boone T., & Kelly, R. (1990). Sexual issues and research in counseling the post myocardial infarction patient. *Journal of Cardiovascular Nursing, 4*(4), 65–75

Brody, S., & Pruet, R. (2003). Vaginal intercourse and heart rate variability. *Journal of Sex and Marital Therapy, 29*(5), 371–380.

Burt K. (1995). The effects of cancer on body image and sexuality. *Nursing Times, 91*(7), 36–37.

Cagle, J. G., & Bolte, S. (2009). Sexuality and life-threatening illness: Implications for social work and palliative care. *Health & Social Work, 34*(3), 223–232.

Camsari, T., Cavdar, C., Yemez, B., Ozkahya, M., Atabay, G., Alkin, T., & Akçiçek, F. (1999). Psychosexual function in CAPD and hemodialysis patients. *Peritoneal Dialysis International, 19*(6), 585–588.

Chen, W. Y., Hankinson, S. E., Schnitt, S. J., Rosner, B. A., Holmes, M. D., & Colditz, G. A. (2004). Association of hormone replacement therapy to estrogen and progesterone receptor status in invasive breast carcinoma. *Cancer, 101,* 1490–1500.

Ching, A. Y., & Lip, G. Y. (2002). Hormone replacement therapy and cardiovascular risk. *Treatment Endocrinology, 1*(2), 95–103.

Christ, G. H., Moynihan, R. T., & Gallo-Silver, L. (1995). Crisis intervention with AIDS patients and their families (pp. 231–247). In A. R. Roberts (Ed.), *Crisis intervention and time-limited cognitive treatment.* London, UK: Sage.

Clawson, C. L., & Reese-Weber, M. (2003). The amount and timing of parent-adolescent sexual communication as predictors of late adolescent sexual risk-taking behaviors. *Journal of Sex Research, 40*(3), 256–265.

Connolly, J. N., Slaghter, V., & Mealey, L. (2004). The development of preferences for specific body shapes, *Journal of Sex Research, 41*(1), 5–15.

Cranston-Cuebas, M. A., & Barlow, D. H. (1990). Cognitive and affective controls to sexual functioning. *Annual Review of Sex Research, 1,* 119–161.

D'Augelli, A. R., Grossman, A. H., Hershberger, S. L., & O'Connell, T. S. (2001). Aspects of mental health among older lesbian, gay and bisexual adults. *Aging Mental Health, 5*(2), 149–158.

Debusk, R. F. (2000). Evaluating the cardiovascular tolerance for sex. *American Journal of Cardiology, 86*(Suppl. 2A), 51F–56F.

Dennerstein, L., & Lehert, P. (2004). Modeling mid-aged women's sexual functioning: A prospective population based study. *Journal of Sex and Marital Therapy, 30*(3), 175–184.

Dennerstein, L., Lehert, P., Dudley, E., & Burger, H. (1999). Factors affecting sexual functioning of women in the mid-life years. *Climacteric, 2,* 254–262.

Dickman, G. (2003). A role for sexologists: Helping manage the medication induced sexual dysfunctions associated with treatment of depression. *Contemporary Sexuality, 37*(5), i–viii.

Draucker, C. B., & Spadlin, D. (2001). Women sexually abused as children: Implications for orthopaedic nursing care. *Orthopaedic Nursing, 20*(6), 41–48.

Durna, E. M., Heller, G. Z., Leader, L. R., Sjoblom, P., Eden, J. A., & Wren, B. G. (2004). Breast cancer in premenopausal women: Recurrence and survival rates and relationship to hormone replacement therapy. *Climacteric, 7*(3), 284–291.

Eagan, M. (1993). Resilience at the front lines: Hospital social work with AIDS patients and burnout. *Social Work in Health Care, 18*(2), 109–125.

Ehrenberg, M., & Ehrenberg, O. (1988). *The intimate circle of sexual dynamics of family life*. New York, NY: Simon & Schuster.

Erickson, E. H. (1968). *Identity, youth and crisis*. New York, NY: Norton.

Esmail, S., Yashima, E., & Munro, B. (2002). Sexuality and disability: The role of health care professionals in providing options and alternatives for couple. *Sexuality and Disability, 9*(4), 267–282.

Fahs, M. C., & Wade, K. (1996). An economic analysis of two models of hospital care for AIDS patients: Implications for hospital discharge planning. *Social Work in Health Care, 22*(4), 21–34.

Fairbairn, W. R. D. (1946). Object-relationships and dynamic structure. *International Journal of Psycho-Analysis, 27*(1–2), 30–37.

Ferrando, S., Evans, S., Goggin, K., Sewell, M., Fishman, B., & Rabkin, J. (1998). Fatigue in HIV illness: Relationship to depression, physical limitations and disability. *Psychosomatic Medicine, 60*(6), 759–764.

Finkelhor, D. (1984). *Child sexual abuse: New theory and research*. New York, NY: Free Press.

Freud, S. (1922). *Beyond the pleasure principle*. London, UK: International Psycho-Analytic Press.

Frohlick, P. F., & Meston, C. M. (2005). Tactile sensitivity in women with sexual arousal disorder. *Archives of Sexual Behavior, 34*(2), 207–217.

Fuentes, P., Rosenberg, J., & Marks, R. (1983). Sexual side effects: What to tell your patients, what not to say. *Registered Nurse, 46*(2), 35–41.

Furstenberg, A. L., & Olson, M. M. (1984). Social work and AIDS. *Social Work in Health Care, 9*(4), 45–62.

Gallo-Silver, L. (2000). The sexual rehabilitation of people with cancer. *Cancer Practice: A Multidisciplinary Journal of Cancer Care, 8*(1), 10–15.

Gallo-Silver, L. (2011). Sexuality and physical intimacy for people receiving palliative care. In S. Otis-Green & T. Altilio (Eds.), *Handbook of palliative social work* (pp. 261–270). New York, NY: Oxford University Press.

Gallo-Silver, L., & Parsonnet, L. (2001). Sexuality and fertility. In M. M. Lauria, E. J. Clark, J. F. Hermann, & N. M. Stearns (Eds.), *Social work in oncology: Supporting survivors, families and caregivers* (pp. 279–298). Atlanta, GA: American Cancer Society.

Gallo-Silver, L., Raveis, V. H., & Moynihan, R. T. (1993). Psychosocial issues in adults with transfusion-related HIVB infection and their families. *Social Work in Health Care, 18*(2), 63–74.

Gallo-Silver, L., & Weiner, M. (2006). Survivors of childhood sexual abuse with cancer: Managing the impact of early trauma on cancer treatment. *Journal of Psychosocial Oncology, 24*(1), 107–134.

Gelfand, M. M. (2000). Sexuality among older women. *Journal of Women's Health and Gender Based Medicine, 9*(Suppl.), S15–S20.

Green, S. E., & Mosher, D. L. (1985). A causal model of sexual arousal to erotic fantasies. *Journal of Sex Research, 21*(1), 1–23.

Greydanus, D. E., Rimsza, M. E., & Newhouse, P. A. (2002). Adolescent sexuality and disability. *Adolescent Medicine, 13*(2), 223–247.

Grossman, A. H., D'Augelli, A. R., & Hershberger, S. L. (2000). Social support networks of lesbian, gay and bisexual adults 60 years of age and older. *Journal of Gerontology Behavioral Psychology and Social Science, 55*(3), 171–179.

Grov, C., Bimbi, D. S., Nanin, J. E., & Parsons, J. T. (2006). Race, ethnicity, gender, and generational factors associated with the coming out process among gay, lesbian, and bisexual individuals. *Journal of Sex Research, 4*, 115–121.

Haas, F., & Haas, S. S. (2000). *The chronic bronchitis and emphysema handbook*. New York, NY: Wiley.

Harden, J. (2005). Developmental life stage and couples' experiences with prostate cancer: A review of the literature. *Cancer Nursing, 28*(2), 85–98.

Hazan, C., & Shaver, P. (1987). Romantic love conceptualized as an attachment process. *Journal of Personality and Social Psychology, 52*, 511–524.

Hobbins, D. (2004). Survivors of childhood sexual abuse: Implications for perinatal nursing care. *Journal of Obstetrics, Gynecology and Neonatal Nursing, 33*(4), 485–497.

Holstege, G., Georgiadis, J. R., & Paans, A. M. J. (2003). Brain activation during human male ejaculation. *Journal of Neuroscience, 23*(27), 9185–9193.

Horgan, O., & MacLachlan, M. (2004). Psychosocial adjustment to lower-limb amputation: A review. *Disability and Rehabilitation, 26*(14–15), 837–850.

Horner, G. (2004). Sexual behavior in children: Normal or not? *Journal of Pediatric Health Care, 18*(2), 56–64.

Hughes, M. K. (2000). Sexuality and the cancer survivor: A silent coexistence. *Cancer Nursing, 23*(6), 477–482.

Hurlbert, D. F., & Whittaker, K. E. (1991). The role of masturbation in marital satisfaction: A comparative study of female masturbators and non-masturbators. *Journal of Sex Education and Therapy, 17*, 272–282.

Ide, M. (2004). Sexuality in persons with limb amputation: A meaningful discussion of re-integration. *Disability and Rehabilitation, 14–15*, 939–949.

Ide, M., Watanabe, T., & Toyonaga, T. (2002). Sexuality in persons with limb amputation. *Prosthetics and Orthotics International, 26*(3), 189–194.

Jehu, D. (1992). Long-term consequences of childhood sexual abuse: Presentation and management in gynaecological practice. In K. Wijma & B. von Schoultz (Eds.), *Reproductive life: Advances in research in psychosomatic obstetrics and gynaecology* (pp. 513–520). Stockholm, Sweden: Parthenon.

Johnson, C. F. (2004). Child sexual abuse. *Lancet, 364,* 462–470.

Jones, J. C., & Barlow, D. H. (1990). Self reported frequency of sexual urges, fantasies and masturbatory fantasies in heterosexual males and females. *Archives of Sexual Behavior, 19,* 269–279.

Kaplan, H. S. (1974). *The new sex therapy: Active treatment of sexual dysfunction.* New York, NY: Brunner/Mazel.

Kaplan, H. S. (1983). *The evaluation of sexual disorders: Psychological and medical aspects.* New York, NY: Brunner/Mazel.

Kaplan, H. S. (1987). *The illustrated manual of sex therapy.* New York, NY: Brunner/Mazel.

Karma, S., Lecours, A. R., & Leroux, J. M. (2002). Areas of brain activation in males and females during viewing of erotic film excerpts. *Human Brain Mapping, 16,* 1–16.

Katz, A. (2007). *Breaking the silence on cancer and sexuality: A handbook for healthcare providers.* Pittsburgh, PA: Oncology Nursing Society.

Katzin, L. (1990). Chronic illness and sexuality. *American Journal of Nursing, 90*(1), 54–59.

Kelly, D. C., & Hockenberg-Eaton, M. (1999). Communication about sexual issues: Mothers, fathers and friends. *Journal of Adolescent Health, 24*(3), 181–189.

Kingsberg, S. A. (2000). The psychological impact of aging on sexuality and relationships. *Journal of Women's Health and Gender Based Medicine, 9*(Supp), S33–S38.

Kinsey, A. C., Pomeroy, W. B., & Martin, C. E. (1948). *The sexual behavior in the adult male.* Philadelphia, PA: Saunders.

Kinsey, A. C., Pomeroy, W. B., & Martin, C. E. (1953). *The sexual behavior of the adult female.* Philadelphia, PA: Saunders.

Koken, J. A., Bimbi, D. S., & Parsons, J. T. (2009). Experiences of familial rejection-acceptance among transgender women. *Journal of Family Psychology, 23,* 853–860.

Kroll, K., & Klein, E. L. (2001). *Enabling romance: A guide to love, sex, and relationships for people with disabilities.* Horsham, PA: No Limits Communications.

Laumann, E. O., Gagnon, J. H., Michael, R. T., & Michaels, S. (1994). *The social organization of sexuality: Sexual practices in the United States.* Chicago, IL: University of Chicago Press.

Lawrence, J. W., Fauerbach, J. A., Heinberg, L., & Doctor, M. (2004). Visible vs. hidden scars and their relationship to body esteem. *Journal of Burn Care and Rehabilitation, 25*(1), 25–32.

Lemieux, L., Kaiser, S., Periera, J., & Meadows, L. M. (2004). Sexuality in palliative care: Patient perspectives. *Palliative Medicine, 18,* 630–637.

Lukianowicz, N. (1960). Imaginary sexual partners and visual masturbatory fantasies. *Archives of General Psychiatry, 3,* 429–449.

Maltz, W. (2001). *The sexual healing journey: A guide for survivors of sexual abuse.* New York, NY: Quill.

Maltz, W. (2003). Treating the sexual intimacy concerns of sexual abuse survivors. *Contemporary Sexuality, 37*(7), i–viii.

Mantell, J. E., Shulman, L. C., Belmont, M. F., & Spivak, H. B. (1989). Social workers respond to the AIDS epidemic in an acute care hospital. *Health Social Work, 14*(1), 41–51.

Markham, H., Stanley, S., & Blumberg, S. L. (1994). *Fighting for your marriage.* San Francisco, CA: Jossey-Bass.

Masters, W. H., & Johnson, V. E. (1966). *Human sexual response.* Boston, MA: Little Brown.

Masters, W. H., & Johnson, V. E. (1970). *Human sexual inadequacy.* Boston, MA: Little Brown.

McCabe, M. P. (1994). The interrelationship between intimacy, sexual functioning and sexuality among men and women in committed relationships. *Canadian Journal of Human Sexuality, 8,* 31–38.

McCabe, M. P. (1999). Sexual knowledge, experience and feelings among people with disability. *Sexuality & Disability, 17*(2), 157–170.

McCabe, M. P., & Taleporos, G. (2003). Sexual esteem, sexual satisfaction and sexual behavior among people with physical disabilities. *Archives of Sexual Behavior, 32*(4), 359–369.

McInnes, R. A. (2003). Chronic illness and sexuality. *Medical Journal of Australia, 179*(5), 263–266.

McKenna, K. (1999). The brain is the master organ in sexual functioning: Central nervous system control of male and female sexual functioning. *International Journal of Impotence Research, 11,* 48–55.

McMahon, E. (2003). The older homosexual: Current concepts of lesbian, gay, bisexual, and transgender older Americans. *Clinical Geriatric Medicine, 19*(3), 587–593.

Monga, U., Tan, G., Ostermann, H. J., & Monga, T. N. (1997). Sexuality in head and neck cancer patients. *Archives of Physical and Medical Rehabilitation, 78*(3), 298–304.

Mosher, D. (1980). The dimensions of depth involvement in human sexual response. *Journal of Sex Research, 16,* 1–42.

Napoleone, S. (1988). Inpatient care of persons with AIDS. *Social Casework, 69*(6), 376–379.

Nazareth, I., Lewin, J., & King, M. (2001). Sexual dysfunction after treatment for testicular cancer: A systemic review. *Journal of Psychosomatic Research, 51*(6), 735–743.

Neufield, J. A., Klingbell, F., Borgen, D. N., Silverman, B., & Thomas, A. (2002). Adolescent sexuality and disability. *Physical Medicine and Rehabilitation Clinics of North America, 13*(4), 857–873.

Nutter, D. E., & Condron, M. C. (1985). Sexual fantasy and activity patterns of males with inhibited sexual desire and males with erectile dysfunction versus normal controls. *Journal of Sex and Marital Therapy, 11*, 91–98.

Opjordsmoen, S., Waehre, H., Aass, N., & Fossa, S. D. (1994). Sexuality in patients treated for penile cancer: Patients' experience and doctors' judgment. *British Journal of Urology, 73*(5), 554–560.

Parish, K. L. (2002). Sexuality and haemophilia: Connections across the lifespan. *Haemophilia, 8*(3), 353–359.

Poniatowski, B. C., Grimm, P., & Cohen, G. (2001). Chemotherapy-induced menopause: A literature review. *Cancer Investigations, 19*, 641–648.

Reynolds, J. M., & Postlethwaite, R. J. (1996). Psychosocial burdens of dialysis treatment modalities: Do they differ and does it matter. *Peritoneal Dialysis International, 16*(Suppl. 1), S548–S550.

Roak, R. A., Webster, R. D., Darrow, W. W., & Stempel, R. R. (2005). HIV testing among men who have sex with men: How often should one test? *Journal of Public Health Management Practice, 11*, 18–24.

Rowan, E. L. (2000). *The joy of self pleasuring.* Amherst, NY: Prometheus Books.

Rowland, D. L., & Tai, W. (2003). A review of plant-derived and herbal approaches to the treatment of sexual dysfunctions. *Journal of Sex and Marital Therapy, 29*, 185–206.

Russell, D. (1999). *The secret trauma: Incest in the lives of girls and women.* New York, NY: Basic Books.

Ryan, G. (2000). Childhood sexuality: A decade of study, Part II, dissemination and future direction. *Child Abuse and Neglect, 24*, 49–69.

Samuel, J. C., & Boyle, M. (1989). AIDS training and social services. *AIDS Care, 1*, 287–296.

Sansone, R. A., Gaither, G. A., & Sansone, L. A. (2001). Childhood trauma and adult somatic preoccupation by body area among women in an internal medicine setting: A pilot study. *International Journal of Psychiatry in Medicine, 31*, 147–154.

Sansone, P., Skaife, K., & Rhodes, J. (2003). Abuse, dissociation and somatization in irritable bowel syndrome: Toward an explanatory model. *Journal of Behavioral Medicine, 1*, 1–18.

Schacter, C. L., Radomsky, N. A., Stalker, C. A., & Teram, E. (2004). Women survivors of child sexual abuse: How can health care professionals promote healing? *Canadian Family Physician, 50*, 341–346.

Schmidt, E. Z., Hofmann, P., Niederwieser, G., Kapfhammer, H. P., & Bonelli, R. M. (2005). Sexuality and multiple sclerosis. *Journal of Neural Transmission, 112*(9), 1201–1211.

Schover, L. R. (1997). *Sexuality and fertility after cancer.* New York, NY: Wiley.

Schover, L. R. (1999). Counseling cancer patients about changes in sexual function. *Oncology, 13*, 1585–1596.

Schover, L. R. (2000). Sexual problems in chronic illness. In S. R. Leiblum & R. C. Rosen (Eds.), *Principles and practice of sex therapy* (pp. 57–81). New York, NY: Guilford Press.

Schover, L. R., & Jensen, J. B. (1988). *Sexuality and chronic illness: A comprehensive approach.* New York, NY: Guilford Press.

Shell, J. A., & Miller, M. E. (1999). The cancer amputee and sexuality. *Orthopeadic Nursing, 18*, 62–65.

Sipski, M. (1998). Sexual functioning in the spinal cord injured. *International Journal of Impotence Research, 10*(Suppl. 2), 128–130.

Soloway, C. T., Soloway, M. S., Kim, S. S., & Kava, B. R. (2005). Sexual, psychological, and dyadic qualities of the prostate cancer "couple." *British Journal of Urology International, 95*, 780–785.

Spitzer, W. J., Neuman, K., & Holden, G. (2004). The coming of age for assisted living: New options for senior housing and social work practice. *Social Work in Health Care, 38*, 21–45.

Sundquist, K., & Yee, L. (2003). Sexuality and body image after cancer. *Australian Family Physician, 32*, 19–23.

Tanyi, R. A. (2002). Sexual unattractiveness: A patient's story. *Medsurg Nursing, 11*, 95–99.

Taylor, B., & Davies, S. (2006). Using the extended PLISSIT model to address sexual healthcare needs. *Nursing Standards, 21*(11), 35–40.

Thorson, A. I. (2003). Sexual activity and the cardiac patient. *American Journal of Geriatric Cardiology, 12*, 38–40.

Uttley, L. (1996). Treatment of sexual dysfunction. *Peritoneal Dialysis International, 16*(Suppl. 1), S402–S405.

Walbroehl, G. S. (1992). Sexual concerns of the patient with pulmonary disease. *Postgraduate Medicine, 91*, 455–460.

Walker, J. R., & Casale, A. J. (1997). Prolonged penile erection in the newborn. *Urology, 50*, 796–799.

Weerakoon, P., Jones, M. K., Pynor, R., & Kilburn-Watt, E. (2004). Allied health professional students' perceived level of comfort in clinical situations that have sexual connotations. *Journal of Allied Health, 33*, 189–193.

Weiner, L. S., & Siegel, K. (1990). Social worker's comfort in providing services to AIDS patients. *Social Work, 35*, 18–25.

Whitehead, T. L. (1993). Sexual health promotion of the patient with burns. *Journal of Burn Care and Rehabilitation, 14*, 221–226.

Wimberly, S. R., Carver, C. S., Laurenceau, J. P., Karris, S. D., & Antoni, M. H. (2005). Perceived partner reactions to diagnosis and treatment of breast cancer: Impact on psychosocial and psychosexual development. *Journal of Consulting and Clinical Psychology, 73*, 300–311.

Wood, J. D., & Tombrink, J. (1983). Impact of cancer on sexuality and self-image: A group program for patients and partners. *Social Work in Health Care, 8,* 45–54.

Zoldbrod, A. (2003). Assessing intrapsychic blocks to pleasure using the Milestones of Sexual Development Model. *Contemporary Sexuality, 37,* 7–14.

Zoldbrod, A. P. (1998). *SexSmart: How your childhood shaped your sexual life and what to do about it.* Oakland, CA: New Harbinger.

Zunkel, G. (2002). Relational coping process: Couples response to a diagnosis of early stage breast cancer. *Journal of Psychosocial Oncology, 20,* 39–55.

PART III

Health Social Work: Selected Areas of Practice

15

Social Work With Children and Adolescents With Medical Conditions

NANCY BOYD WEBB AND ROSE A. BARTONE

Utilizing a strengths perspective that acknowledges the stress and trauma factors associated with medical conditions and their treatment, this chapter illustrates various methods social workers can use to help children and adolescents who have serious and chronic medical conditions. The chapter reviews the knowledge base needed by social workers to collaborate effectively with medical and school personnel as well as methods for helping the child and family members (with *family* defined broadly) understand and cope with the numerous stressors associated with the youth's medical reality. Detailed examples of both hospital-based social work interventions and those occurring while the child is living at home illustrate helping methods at different stages of illness. Work with the family is an essential part of helping medically compromised children, as is transdisciplinary collaboration. This chapter illustrates the necessity and value of collaborative teamwork, often initiated by the social worker who interfaces with schools and other community organizations in addition to hospital-based medical practitioners for the purpose of providing competent, comprehensive, and compassionate care for youth with medical conditions.

Chapter Objectives
- Understand the prevalence and scope of children's health conditions.
- Understand the influence of a child's age and level of development on the attribution of meaning in medical diagnosis and prognosis.

- Recognize the necessary collaboration among the family, school, and medical setting in providing care to youth with medical conditions.
- Learn of interventions that social workers can employ to help children with medical conditions in the hospital, home, and community.
- Explore palliative care and end-of-life issues for the child, family, and interdisciplinary team.
- Understand issues and challenges for the social worker dealing with youth who have medical conditions, including vicarious traumatization.
- Discover resources in the community and on the Internet to help children and families challenged by medical conditions.

PREVALENCE AND SCOPE OF CHILDREN'S HEALTH PROBLEMS

Children's health problems range from those that cause pain and discomfort for a few days (such as the chicken pox or the flu) to others that require ongoing monitoring and periodic hospitalizations over the course of the child's life (such as cancer or diabetes; see Table 15.1). This section focuses on the most prevalent serious childhood conditions, indicating the frequency of each, the course of each illness, and the typical range of treatments.

Table 15.1   Most Frequent Pediatric Illnesses in the United States

Medical Condition	Prevalence	Usual Course of Illness	Range of Treatment
Asthma	6.7 million U.S. children under 18 years; highest among children 11 to 17 (Akinbami, Moorman, Garbe, & Sondik, 2009)	Lifelong	Short-acting relievers Long-acting inhalers Environmental control Clinical trials
Cancer	Approximately 12,400 American children under the age of 20 (Mariotto et al., 2009)	Sudden onset	Chemotherapy Steroids Antinausea medications Radiation therapy Surgery Clinical trials
Diabetes	Type 1 is more prevalent in ages 0 to 19, affecting 182 per 100,000 U.S. children Type 2 is more prevalent in ages 10 to 19, affecting 174 per 100,000 U.S. children (SEARCH for Diabetes in Youth Study, 2006)	Type 1 (juvenile onset) autoimmune; develops under 21 years Type 2 nonautoimmune; develops in overweight children under 21	All types: diet and exercise Type 1: insulin Type 2: may require insulin
Juvenile rheumatoid arthritis	1.6–86.1 per 100,000 U.S. children (Helmick et al., 2008)	Lifelong; degenerative	Steroids
Obesity	16.9% of U.S. children ages 2 to 19 (Ogden, Carroll, Curtin, Lamb, & Flegal, 2010)	Genetic; lifestyle; cultural; medical conditions	Diet Exercise Medications

Children with special health-care needs comprise 12.8% of all children younger than 18 years in the United States, and half a million young adults with special health-care needs reach their 18th birthdays each year (Oftedahl, Benedict, & Katcher 2004). Special health-care needs may result from premature birth, illness, injury, or congenital causes.

DEVELOPMENTAL CONSIDERATIONS AND CHILD AND FAMILY ATTRIBUTION OF MEANING TO MEDICAL DIAGNOSES

The formal diagnosis of a medical condition may occur unexpectedly or following a series of symptoms or problems that have disturbed the child and family for a period of weeks, months, or years. Parents may have suspected that something was seriously wrong and may have awaited a formal diagnosis with great trepidation. Other times, families may downplay a child's symptoms and remain unaware of the possible significance of the child's complaints.

A diagnosis gives parents and youth a reason about the reason for the complaints but also may confer a reality requiring substantial changes in the lifestyle of the family and the child for many years or even a lifetime. Often the diagnosis brings a cruel awareness that things will never again be the same as they have been. The knowledge that a child has a serious medical condition results in a shocking and major loss for all concerned, who realize that they will need to find a way to adapt and cope with this new reality, which will impact the lives of all the family members (see Chapter 13 for a full discussion of families and health).

Researchers who have studied the family impact of medical diagnoses propose a four-stage model to describe the typical adjustment to a youth's medical condition. According to Clarke-Steffen (1993; Dell Clark, 2010), the stages are:

Stage 1: First clue. The family and child begin to have some awareness that "something is definitely wrong."

Stage 2: Limbo. The family and child react to the diagnosis with varying degrees of uncertainty and feelings of vulnerability.

Stage 3: Reconstructing meaning. The family reorganizes its lifestyle and routines to manage the requirements of the therapeutic program.

Stage 4: New normal. The family and child operate with a shared tolerance of the new routines and uncertainties, even though this state differs from their prior, "normal" experiences.

Although this model seems to progress logically toward an end point of acceptance, all families do not move consistently through the stages. Some families persist in denial of the diagnosis and may insist on additional tests and procedures. Likewise, the unpredictability of the child's illness may cause relapses and impair coping even when all are doing their best to comply with medical regimens.

The case of Carl, age 13, provides an example of a family's and child's positive and ideal adjustment to the diagnosis of asthma. It is presented as an ideal situation. Asthma is the most common chronic childhood illness, affecting over 6 million children younger than 18 years in the United States (Brown, Daly, & Rickel, 2007; Clay, 2004). It causes more school absences per year than any other chronic illness and is the third most common reason for hospitalization among children younger than 15 years (Taylor & Newacheck, 1992). Social workers and others who deal with children with medical conditions such as asthma must be aware that the youth's friends will notice and sometimes worry about their friend's need to use an inhaler or other treatments. The case illustrates a successful adaptation of a child and family who were motivated to make their personal experiences public in the hope

---

CASE EXAMPLE: Child with Asthma, Carl, Age 13

This summary is based on a preadolescent boy's account of his reaction to receiving a diagnosis of asthma when he was 3 years old and his experiences growing up with the disease (Huegel, 1998). He documents his daily need for medications and frequent need to confer with his physician. Despite his condition, Carl manages to engage in sports and other school activities, including gym class. His mother has been a very positive presence in Carl's life and started a support group for parents and children with asthma in their community.

Carl reports that he has been responsible for taking his own daily medications (with parental monitoring) since the fourth grade. He makes it very clear that he lives within the ongoing constraints of his asthma and prepares himself for a possible attack by wearing a Medic Alert bracelet and carrying his medications and an EpiPen in a pouch. When he participates in sports, his physical education teachers and coaches are informed that he will use an inhaler before playing vigorous games and that he may have to sit out part of the game. He attends sleep-away camp for 3 weeks every summer, well supplied with instructions for counselors and with extra medications and inhalers to permit him to carry out the daily activities of camp life.

Carl has helped other young people with asthma, both by talking with and encouraging them and by writing his personal story. He makes it very clear that although he does not like living with asthma, he is determined not to let it interfere with his success in life. This positive attitude represents an ideal to which others may aspire.

that it might inspire others to maintain hope despite the considerable necessary adaptations required by the disease (Huegel, 1998).

TYPICAL RESPONSES OF CHILDREN AND THEIR PARENTS WHEN DEALING WITH A CHILD'S MEDICAL CONDITION

Children and families react very differently to a serious medical diagnosis. Although Carl reported that when he was diagnosed with asthma at age 3, he was too young to comprehend the meaning of his condition, an older child in the same situation might assume that the diagnosis will lead to certain death. This was the case for a 10-year-old girl whose mother told her at age 7 that she had diabetes. She burst into tears, and even after her parents convinced her that she was not going to die, she remained convinced that her life was going to change completely (Krementz, 1992; Webb, 2009).

Because children take their cues from the adults around them, it is important for social workers to be informed about various illnesses so that they in turn can help to inform parents. Often parents may not accurately recall the doctor's recommendations and prognostic statements about the management of illness and its likely course. This is why written explanations and guidelines are helpful, together with an offer by the social worker to be available to answer future questions about the illness and its management or to act as a go-between with other providers. It is also critical for the social worker to maintain a relationship with the patient and family to ensure that they understand instructions for medications, diet, and follow-up visits. The resource list at the end of this chapter provides some Web sites with helpful information about the most typical chronic medical conditions.

It is understandable that diagnosis of a medical condition inevitably arouses questions and anxiety for parents, which may not be verbalized to the provider. Parents may wonder why their child became ill and in some cases may feel responsible, especially if there is a genetic component to the disease. They may try to present a positive front to the child despite their mixed feelings of anger, worry, and loss. However, the child usually senses the parents' feelings. When parents feel overwhelmed and anxious, it is helpful for them to become involved in individual or group counseling to help mourn their losses and feel more able to support their children. Groups for the children also can be very helpful, as are Internet contacts with other parents and children confronting similar medical challenges. Internet support and information groups moderated by social workers trained in the area of a specific disorder can be helpful resources for those who live in rural areas or at great distance from the treatment centers; for example, see: http://healthfinder.gov/scripts/SearchContext .asp?topic=833&section=3

Young people may be more focused on their current lives than on the future ramifications of their illnesses. Nonetheless, they will need to understand the details of their daily medical routines that may involve taking medications and making periodic office or hospital visits for checkups that sometimes will require regular blood work and other tests. It is common for young people to resist all or some of these procedures, and parents will need help in dealing firmly with this resistance in a manner that emphasizes its necessity. Goodman (2007) presents an account of a boy's transition from extreme distress when anticipating upcoming treatments for his cancer to a subsequent attitude of acceptance and wanting to help other kids facing procedures such as spinal taps. This change was due at least partly to his therapy with a sympathetic art therapist, who encouraged him to express his feelings symbolically through drawing. Support groups specific to certain medical conditions may be very helpful for children who, without such contacts, would feel very isolated and discouraged about their conditions (see the chapter resource list for a listing of organizations that sponsor specialized support groups).

Although living with a medical condition brings with it stressors and constraints on activities, it is important that young people do not identify themselves primarily in terms of their diagnoses. Some adolescent survivors of cancer and their parents report positive attitudes a year after supportive treatment (Barakat, Alderfer, & Kazak, 2006). This phenomenon, called *posttraumatic growth*, refers to positive changes in views about oneself, others, and plans for the future following a medical diagnosis. Although this may not occur in all cases, it does provide convincing evidence that a medical crisis need not bring with it a legacy of negative consequences.

COLLABORATION AMONG FAMILY, SCHOOL, AND MEDICAL SETTING IN CARING FOR YOUTH WITH MEDICAL CONDITIONS

Because children live in worlds that include networks of school, community, and family members, the social worker needs to facilitate connections with these networks after a medical diagnosis. Confidentiality always must be observed, and written permission from the parent should be obtained before sharing any medical information with the school or others. The Health Insurance Portability and Accountability Act of 1996 (U.S. Department of Health and Human Services, n.d.) provides legal protection for the confidentiality of medical information. Although parents may want school personnel to be informed of a child's diagnosis, it is advisable for parents to refrain from disclosing details of the medical condition because what they tell the school becomes part of the permanent school record. The school nurse is pivotal in coordinating the child's medical care at school. The social worker, parents, student, and nurse can collaborate on care while protecting the privacy of the child's medical information.

Educating any child with a chronic or acute medical condition is a difficult task for all involved, especially the child. However, educating a child with cancer or other diagnosis that is life threatening presents special challenges. At diagnosis, the parents' initial focus likely is directed toward the child's survival and perhaps the cost of care. After the shock of diagnosis abates, attention shifts to the realization that treatment and its side effects may interfere with the educational process and likelihood of success later in life (Keene, 2003). Chemotherapeutic agents, radiation therapy, and surgical interventions can affect memory and cognitive functioning (CureSearch, 2008). The effects of treatment may, in fact, cause a host of impairments in cognitive and physical functioning well into adulthood (Leukemia & Lymphoma Society, 2007).

Treatment for brain tumors, tumors of the eye and ear, acute lymphoblastic leukemia, and non-Hodgkin's lymphoma are more likely to cause learning and memory problems because of the nature of treatment. Methotrexate; cytosine arabinoside; brain surgery; and radiation therapy to the brain, ear, or total body put children at higher risk of learning difficulties. Cisplatin or carboplatin can affect hearing. Neuropsychological testing is important to identify learning losses so that they may be diagnosed in a timely manner and an appropriate education plan can be developed. Even if initial testing is normal, it is imperative to repeat testing at regular intervals over the school year so that adjustments can be made to educational plans (CureSearch, 2008).

It is crucial for social workers to understand the legal rights of students under federal law so that they and parents can advocate for minor patients; see Table 15.2 for some laws that assist and protect student rights. Social workers can act both as educators and advocates in this area. They have the opportunity to teach the parents and school personnel about the laws that affect a student's rights. They also have the chance to communicate effectively and collaborate with those who will directly impact the current life and future endeavors of the student. The outcome of this intervention

Table 15.2   Laws That Assist and Protect Student Rights

Rehabilitation Act of 1973, Section 504[a]	Federal assistance is provided through the Department of Education to protect against discrimination and provides services for individuals with a physical or mental impairment in at least one major life activity.
American with Disabilities Act (ADA) of 1990	The ADA guarantees the civil rights of a person with a disability; see http://www.usdoj.gov/crt/ada/adahom1.htm
Individuals with Disabilities Education Act (IDEA)[a]	The IDEA guarantees a free and appropriate education, including preschool, elementary, and secondary (ages 3 to 21). An Individualized Education Plan (IEP) is developed to assist students to achieve their maximum potential.
Family Education and Privacy Act (FERPA)	This 1974 act ensures the confidentiality of the student's written record, making it available only to those with legitimate concerns and only with the student's express permission.

[a]Under Section 504 and IDEA, colleges and universities that receive federal money are required to provide accommodations for their students.

Source: Beyond the Cure: The Mountain You Have Climbed, National Children's Cancer Society, Saint Louis, MO: Author, 2008.

has the potential to positively affect the child's quality of life for years.

FERTILITY

Young adulthood brings many changes and challenges. Although young people take for granted the possibility of having children when they wish to do so, a cancer diagnosis may challenge that assumption. Certain chemotherapies and high-dose radiation therapies can cause infertility. The social worker's role is to provide the patient and his family with information and resources so that they are ready for the transition to adulthood and the obstacles that it may bring. This is best done early in the diagnostic period and addressed periodically as needed through and beyond the period of treatment.

Sperm cryopreservation and embryo freezing offers the highest likelihood of success for cancer survivors who have reached puberty. Sperm collection is a relatively simple process. The patient donates sperm cells by masturbating, and the sperm is then frozen and stored for future use. Embryo freezing, while offering the best chance at reproduction, is less likely to happen for a female patient because an embryo must be fertilized before it is frozen and stored. Egg freezing, where mature eggs are surgically removed, frozen, and stored, may be a more viable option for females.

Other methods of preserving reproductive ability are available for those who are prepubescent, such as testicular tissue freezing for males and ovarian tissue freezing for females. The process involves removal of testicular tissue surgically, which is then frozen. Females may have part or all of the ovary surgically removed for later use. These procedures remain experimental, and their costs are high (Leukemia & Lymphoma Society, 2007). Chapter 21 presents the special dilemmas of young women who find that they are positive for breast cancer mutations that greatly heighten their risks for the disease.

SELECTED INTERVENTIONS FOR HOSPITAL-BASED AND COMMUNITY-BASED SOCIAL WORKERS WHO HELP YOUTH WITH MEDICAL CONDITIONS

A young person who is hospitalized for medical treatment faces many stressors. First and foremost is a fear of the unknown. These young people are in unfamiliar environments and surrounded by strangers, many of whom subject them to painful or uncomfortable procedures. Even when a parent is present, the child comes to realize that in this particular setting the parent is no longer "in charge," and this reality may further confuse and upset the youngster. Recognizing that their parent is relatively helpless with very little control or choice over what will happen to them magnifies the young person's fears. Furthermore, the treatment that is supposed to help often causes pain, which can be very confusing to very young children. Often children will fear damage to their bodies and wonder if they will ever be able to return home and to function normally. A hospital can be a very scary place for a child, and even an adolescent who understands the necessity of treatment may strongly resent having to submit to it.

Joan Lovett, a behavioral pediatrician, lists these factors that can make a medical experience traumatic for a child (Lovett, 2010):

- Helplessness and vulnerability
- Discomfort and pain
- Confusion
- Parental distress
- Uncertainty about outcome

Social workers can help young patients and their families cope with these psychosocial stressors that accompany illness. Social work interventions should include collaboration with the family, including the patient's siblings, who often are overlooked because of the focus on the designated patient. In addition to the family, the social worker also gives attention to hospitalized patients and tries to address their major concerns, including anxiety and fear about the future.

The role of the social worker may encompass using play therapy approaches and rehearsal to help alleviate the child's anxieties during various phases of the hospitalization. Some hospitals employ child-life specialists whose function includes preparing children for medical procedures and interacting with him after the procedures have been performed

to provide opportunities for mastery. Vilas (2010) describes in detail the role of the child-life professional in using play and expressive therapies to assist hospitalized children. Many of these functions are very similar to those carried out by social workers, who typically interact with the patient, the family, and the medical staff to provide needed services. Social work interventions may include play and expressive therapies and anxiety management techniques, or these interventions may be used by other specialists with whom social workers collaborate.

Play and Expressive Therapies

Because all children have difficulty expressing their emotions in words, play therapists work with them using dolls, puppets, and a variety of toys. The assumption of play therapy is that when the child knows that the purpose of the play therapist's visit is to help with "troubles and worries" and that it is acceptable to either talk or play, children will use the toys to express their anxieties symbolically.

Any therapist working with children with medical conditions (in a hospital setting, in a school, or elsewhere in the community) will need to have a supply of medical equipment, such as that found in toy medical kits. This equipment usually includes tongue depressors, toy syringes, thermometers, blood pressure gauges, and surgical masks. Often young children repeatedly use a doll or puppet to act out the procedures that they have experienced. In the process of doing this, the play therapist encourages the child to verbalize the feelings and questions of the doll patient under the assumption that through this process, the children actually are expressing their own emotions and concerns. During this play, the therapist can provide some educational information to clarify any of the child's confusion about the medical condition and to help the child anticipate the future. The next interaction is typical.

Therapist: Alice, this doll has had some pains in his tummy like yours, and he had to go to the hospital. Would you like to show him what might happen so he will be ready to go?

Child: Give me the doctor's bag. [Takes out a toy syringe, and speaks to the doll] Hold out your arm; you have to get a shot.

Therapist: [Speaking for the doll] Is it going to hurt?

Child: Yes, but only for a minute. Then you go to sleep, and then the doctor takes out part of your stomach.

Therapist: [Talking as the doll] How can I eat if I don't have a stomach?

Child: This is your punishment for eating too much Halloween candy!

Therapist: [As doll] My mommy said I had a big lump in my tummy. I don't think it came from the candy, because I know that candy and everything we eat gets changed into poop and comes out when we go to the bathroom.

Child: So where did the big lump come from?

Therapist: The doctors aren't sure, but it's not from your food, and they are sure that they can take it out, then you won't feel that pain anymore.

Child: [To doll] Okay. You can wake up now, and you can go home soon.

Therapist: You will have to come back for checkups later, so we can be sure you are okay, but you will be able to go back to school soon and do your regular activities.

This brief excerpt demonstrates how play therapy can help clarify points of confusion and misinformation while also permitting the child to express some fears.

Social workers and other professionals can use drawings and board games with older children for a similar purpose in play therapy. Goodman (2007) and Webb (2009) discuss a drawing by a boy taking prednisone who drew a cactus family in which the needles of the cactus represented the frequent injections he received. Play therapy also can be effective using the Milton Bradley board game *Operation*. For example, with a 10-year-old girl whose mother was terminally ill, the game provided a wonderful stimulus for a play therapist to engage the girl in a discussion (through playing the game) about the doctors' inability to help (Webb, 2002). See Hart and Rollins (2011) for a complete overview of play activities appropriate for children with medical conditions.

Most play and expressive therapy methods can be used on an inpatient or an outpatient basis. Some hospitals have play therapy rooms that are equipped with a variety of toys. When a child is ambulatory, the therapist will escort the child to the play therapy room for a session. Other times, if the child is confined to bed, the play therapist may wheel a cart with a variety of toys into the child's room and invite the child to pick a toy. Some hospitals also employ music therapists, who ask children to choose from a variety of instruments and then to make up their own words to a familiar song, such as "The Wheels on the Bus." An example of music therapy with a 7-year-old boy involved playing scary music to chase away the monsters that were interfering with his sleep. After the boy thought the monsters had left, the therapist played and sung a gentle lullaby, soothing the child and enabling him to fall asleep peacefully (Loewy & Stewart, 2004).

The power of play therapy rests in its ability to engage children symbolically with a situation that is similar to their own and to reveal and discuss related feelings without requiring children to identify these feelings as their own. It is possible to work out solutions with dolls or with drawings or music, and children then can generalize these solutions to their own situations.

Anxiety Management Techniques

Although play therapy methods may be intrinsically relaxing to children, at times it may be appropriate and more effective to employ specific methods that are intended to reduce anxiety. Some of these techniques include:

- Breathing exercises
- Self-control methods, such as "Stop Sign" and "Change the Channel"
- Safe-place imagery

Breathing Exercises

Although breathing slowly and counting one's breaths does help to calm the body, most children find it boring merely to focus on their breathing. Therefore, creative play therapists and others have created methods to help children engage in deliberate breathing exercises while still having fun. For example, the therapist asks children to pretend that they are blowing bubbles, using a wand and a jar of bubble mixture. While also pretending to blow bubbles, the therapist engages the child in blowing a series of pretend bubbles and talks about their color and size. After a few minutes of this exercise, the child may feel calmer.

Self-Control Methods

Two easy self-control exercises entail cognitive therapy methods that begin with an explanation to the child that everyone's head is like a television set. The social worker can say to patients, "Lots of pictures go through your head, and some are nice pictures and some are not nice and may be even scary or terrible." The children are told that they can be the boss of what goes on in their own head. To do this, they can learn to "change the channel" if they do not like the pictures in their head. The therapist can then say, "Think of and put up a picture of a stop sign in the front of your head. This means that the bad pictures have to stop."

Next, the social worker instructs children to close their eyes and think of a place, either real or imaginary, where they can go to feel totally safe and where nothing bad or scary can happen to them. The therapist asks them to think about how it looks, smells, feels, and sounds. After a few moments, the social worker asks the children to open her eyes and draw the safe place. It is important for the youngsters to take time to draw all the details. When the drawing is complete, the social worker refers to it as "your own safe place where no one can harm or hurt you." The social worker can then tell the children to use this safe place when they are worried or upset after first thinking about the stop sign to push away worries and scary pictures. It is helpful for the social worker to emphasize that this is within the children's control. The social worker may say: "Some kids like to repeat to themselves this statement when they put up the stop sign and change the channel: 'I'm the boss of me!'" These cognitive therapy–related activities encourage children's own natural resiliency. They do not take away the pain of the medical condition or the need for ongoing procedures, but they do provide an alternative to feeling helpless and vulnerable.

PALLIATIVE CARE AND END-OF-LIFE ISSUES

Approximately 53,000 children die each year in the United States, and at least 400,000 more live every day with chronic, life-threatening conditions (Friebert & Huff, 2009, p. 9). Currently only about 10% to 20% of dying children receive hospice services, and a similar number of children with life-threatening conditions receive palliative care support and interventions (Friebert & Huff, 2009). See Table 15.3 for more information about the primary causes of death for 1- to 19-year-olds.

For adults, hospice care is offered once the medical team has determined that the patient has six or fewer months to live. However, this time frame is less relevant for children, whose course of illness is more difficult to predict. In fact, only 20% of American hospice programs offer services to children and their parents (Corr, 2009), which may represent a desire to continue treatments for children and to attempt to cure their conditions until the time of death. Hospice and palliative care programs for children slowly are gaining favor among the medical community, and families are becoming more open to receiving the services. A growing number of pediatric palliative care programs in children's hospitals have developed in recent years to "fill the gap between traditional hospital care and

Table 15.3   Causes of Death in 1- to 19-Year-Olds

All Children 1–19 Years Old	Children 1–19 Years Old with Chronic Health Conditions
1. Accidents	1. Malignancy
2. Assault	2. Neuromuscular
3. Malignancy	3. Cardiovascular

Source: "A Key Step in Advancing Care for America's Children," by S. Freibert and S. Huff, 2009, *Newsline,* pp. 9–13. Retrieved from www.dcppcc.org/dp/sites/default/files/A%20Key%20Step%20in%20Advancing%20Care%20for%20 Americas%20Children.pdf

community-based hospice care" (Himelstein, Hilden, Boldt, & Weissman, 2004, p. 17). Working collaboratively to change the perception of palliative care with children may expedite referrals and help children to get services sooner (Thompson, Knapp, Madden, & Shenkman, 2009).

Hospice and pediatric palliative care share the same goal of alleviating pain and suffering. Pain management, nursing and social work support, pastoral care, and the ongoing support and bereavement services provided after the death of the patient all argue for offering these services sooner rather than later. Hospice also offers an aide in the home and volunteer visitors to provide respite for caregivers and greater comfort for patients. These programs serve patients well because they give them nonfamily outlets for talking about their impending death, something that patients often have trouble doing with loved ones (see Chapters 22 and 23 for more details).

When no further treatment options are available for a child, it may be devastating to all concerned, including caregivers, doctors, nurses, social workers, child-life staff, and even auxiliary staff who take vital signs and clean hospital rooms. Social workers can intervene by establishing a link among the patient, family, and care team early on and create a smooth transition for patients and their families facing palliative and end-of-life care needs.

It is difficult to acknowledge or witness both the sudden death of a young person in the emergency room or the steady deterioration of a child or young person after the medical team has come to the conclusion that there is nothing further it can do to help. At

that point, the goal becomes one of managing pain and helping the family plan for the future. Doing this may involve a referral to a hospice program or a spiritual counselor who can meet with family members separately and as a group. Social workers can engage terminally ill children in a life-review process that may include journal writing and a plan for the distribution of the youth's special possessions. This needs to happen after the prognosis has been discussed and before the child is intubated or heavily sedated, as may occur in the later stages of illness.

A hospital-based social worker may play a critical role in all these processes, which also entail collaboration with other professionals involved with the child and the family. Often the professionals who work together to help children and families at the end of life refer to themselves as the "palliative care team." They may include the physician, the nurses, the chaplain, and the medical social worker and child-life specialist. A physician whose specialty comprises both ethics and palliative care has stated that "the transition to palliative care involves the exchange of curative goals for comfort measures" (Finn, 2006, p. 86). This can feel like a massive shift to the family, who may or may not have been anticipating the ultimate decline of their child into death.

The most complete definition of palliative care comes from the National Hospice and Palliative Care Standards (http://www.nhpco .org/i4a/pages/index.cfm?pageid=4900). These standards state that pediatric palliative care is both a philosophy and an organized method for delivering care to children with life-threatening conditions. It involves effective management of pain and other distressing symptoms together with the provision of psychosocial and spiritual care. Pediatric palliative care is planned and delivered through the collaborative efforts of a transdisciplinary team, including the child, family, and caregivers, which attempts to guide and assist the child and family in making decisions that enable them to work toward their goals in whatever time they have.

End-of-Life Care in the Emergency Room

Some young people have serious accidents that are life threatening and result in their admission to the emergency room or the pediatric intensive care unit. Examples of such injuries include falls that cause massive traumatic head injury or car or bicycle accidents that cause significant injury that may result in death either during or following surgery. Families typically are shocked and may not believe the news that their child will not recover. Fortunately, emergency rooms have established protocols for sudden bereavement (see Heggar, 1993; Meyer, 2009). These protocols involve using clear and direct communication with the parents about the fact that the youth died despite all medical efforts (Wind, 2009). Often the facts of the death will have to be repeated compassionately until families understand what happened. Many families also benefit from the assistance of the hospital chaplain or other clergy at this very difficult time.

The role of the social worker in situations of sudden death may include the completion of required paperwork and notification of the family physician, providing transportation and other details, helping family members deal with their feelings, and finding follow-up bereavement care. These circumstances are very stressful for everyone, including the medical team. The social worker and others must pay attention to their own feelings and find appropriate ways to avoid or mitigate vicarious traumatization, which is discussed later in this chapter.

End-of-Life Care in the Pediatric Intensive Care Unit

Play therapy has been used to ease the pain of dying children, as depicted in a moving case example of 7-year-old Nathan, who was hospitalized with a life-threatening illness (Shelby, 2010). The child enjoyed playing on his bed with miniature castles, figurines, and horses and would create play scenes involving battles with powerful knights and invading armies. The play therapist observed the play and made some comments about its main themes. In Nathan's play, the brave men always won, and this represented his own battle and hope for survival.

In time, as Nathan grew weaker, he wanted to play only with the horses and developed a special relationship with one white stallion that he said was going to escape. Soon before his death, Nathan told the horse that he would have to go on without him. This poignant story illustrates how a child used play to prepare for his own death and how the play therapist in her role as witness gave the child the support and understanding he needed.

Methods to Help Families and Youth at the End of Life

The death of a young person is very hard to accept, but the reality is that children and adolescents die, and social workers and others can play an important role in making the dying process dignified and meaningful for all concerned. Some of the methods that should be considered in facilitating a death with dignity include:

- Acknowledging the spiritual needs of the dying person
- Facilitating a life review and identify a legacy
- Creating meaningful rituals
- Connecting with family, friends, and community

Spiritual Needs of the Dying Person

The word *spirituality* refers to the universal need to understand what lays beyond human experience, including the meaning of life, the quest for vision, and some kind of inspiration (Thayer, 2009). Although the spiritual needs of children may be overlooked or minimized, professionals who work with children with chronic illnesses have found that young people often create personal narratives about their unique struggles with illness and their efforts to find meaning in their experiences.

Facilitating a Life Review and Identifying a Legacy

Children, like adults, often have the need to feel that they have made some difference through their actions and that others will remember them because of some of their special qualities or talents. It can be very self-affirming for the social worker to offer to help children create a book of memories, which contains the activities and messages that they want other people to think about when they remember them. For some children, this may involve their accomplishments in sports, music, cooking, or taking care of animals. Whatever is of special importance should be included in the children's own words, if possible. The social worker can introduce this subject by saying that sometimes she helps kids make a very special and personal book about their lives, and, if the child wants to do that, they can begin by talking about one thing about which the child is especially proud. The social worker can record the child's statements, make a video, or write down what the child says. The social worker can encourage the child to give this document to parents or family.

Creating Meaningful Rituals

A ritual can be created to serve the needs of terminally ill children. For those who are religious, it may involve saying a prayer and singing a special comforting song. Often the parents may be involved and will be able to suggest and participate in meaningful activities with the child. For example, a child-life music therapist helped a young patient cope with his pain by helping him to write a song that he used to ameliorate his discomfort. To the tune of "Rain, Rain, Go Away," young Billy rewrote the words as "Pain, pain, go away. Don't come back another day. Little Billy wants to play, so pain go away." As his pain increased, he added different stanzas to his song. This ritual soothed the boy, and as he lay dying the music therapist visited his bedside and sang him his song. It brought comfort both to the caregivers and to his parents.

Pastoral care also can provide the family of a dying child with the opportunity to express their unique rituals of grief. Understanding and being open to divergent cultural and religious ritual helps the patient and family cope during the last stages of life.

Connecting With Family, Friends, and Community

It is very important for parents and siblings to have quiet, intimate times with a child who has a life-threatening illness. These times help parents with the anticipatory grieving process, and they help the child feel a sense of safety and connection. The child should be reassured that the parents will try to see to it that the child does not experience pain, and they may wish to let the child know that some medications that reduce the pain also may make them drowsy. Both the child and the family should be encouraged to express their love for one another with verbal assurance that they will always remember these special moments.

ISSUES AND CHALLENGES FOR THE MEDICAL SOCIAL WORKER

Working on a daily basis with youth who have medical challenges and their families is not easy. Some young clients will have physical limitations or conditions that will affect their lives forever, and the social worker must find a way to emphasize what the child can achieve rather than focusing on all the limitations. Many children respond favorably to this positive approach because children usually do not want to view themselves as having physical limitations. Autobiographies written by chronically ill or terminally ill young people give numerous examples of a positive frame of mind that others may label as "transformational." For example, Matthew Stepanek (2001) wrote poems conveying his sense of hope for the future despite his serious and terminal diagnosis of muscular dystrophy.

Not all social workers will be able to function well knowing that a certain percentage of their young clients will die over the course of weeks or months. Although most social work positions include a certain amount of stress, the reality of trauma, pain, and loss pervade the medical field. This field of practice clearly makes special demands on its professionals and requires that they learn to function in highly stressful environments.

Social workers have different methods for dealing with this stress. Some take pride in the fact that they have helped a young person and family achieve a peaceful, dignified death. Sometimes a child or family member who expresses faith in religion and belief in an afterlife makes the separation process inspirational despite the pain.

Some pediatric care facilities encourage members of the medical staff to attend a child's funeral. Typically hospitals have a protocol for reaching out to families of deceased children. The end-of-life helping process often involves sharing the experience of loss with others who also participated in providing comfort to the child and the family. Therefore, some hospitals have memorial services for staff, other patients, and family members. The ritual of a remembrance service is critical to helping the staff of caregivers cope with the loss of the patient. Children who have been in care for a long period of time develop relationships with their caregivers, and giving those caregivers the opportunity to express their thoughts and feelings helps them to grieve the loss.

Avoiding Vicarious Traumatization

The high degree of stress involved in trying to help children and families deal with the special circumstances of a medical condition can be very taxing to all involved, including the professional helpers. Research suggests that all medical procedures are traumatizing to children (Lovett, 2010), yet they also may be traumatizing for practitioners.

The term *vicarious traumatization* refers to the experience of the helper who identifies and empathizes with the physical or psychological pain of the client to the extent that the practitioner becomes traumatized. The expression was developed in 1990 by McCain and Pearlman to describe the impact on therapists of working with traumatized individuals because of the empathetic engagement of therapists with their clients. Often the helpers are not aware of their own traumatization, but their behavior and views about the world and their work may change in a negative direction. For example, a social worker who previously had felt proud and enthusiastic about working in a children's cancer facility began to fear for the well-being of the patients because the doctors did not seem to be able to restore all of them to their previous levels of functioning. The social worker began to dread returning to work on Mondays, and her family was increasingly aware that she seemed irritable and angry with them for no discernible reason. She was exercising less, watching television more, and drinking excessive amounts of alcohol. Fortunately, a staff training session on the topic of vicarious traumatization helped this social worker realize that she had become a victim of the condition. She made a promise to herself that she would follow some of the guidelines for avoiding vicarious traumatization that were discussed in the training (Gamble, 2002; Ryan & Cunningham, 2007; Webb, 2009). These guidelines are:

- Create boundaries between home and work and maintain a personal (as opposed to only a professional) identity.
- Seek supervision from professionals who understand the stresses of health social work with children and families.
- Locate professional colleagues who work in medical settings and who will agree to meet together twice a month to discuss the stresses and trauma of hospital work and who will support each other through a mutual debriefing process.

- Spend time with children who do not have medical challenges to help maintain perspective on the wide range of typical child and youth behavior.
- Engage in rejuvenating experiences and relationships.
- Find a way to relieve stress, such as prayer, meditation, listening to music, gardening, talking a walk, or engaging in physical exercise.
- Accept one's own limitations and the reality that medicine cannot save everyone from pain and untimely death.
- Take comfort in knowing that the children and families whom the social worker helps received the best efforts of the medical team.

Practitioners who follow these guidelines will be more likely to separate their work and personal lives and, as a consequence, return to their work with a sense of optimism and hope.

CONCLUSION

The role of the social worker in dealing with children and youth with serious medical conditions is very complex and challenging. On a daily basis, health social workers must deal with systems (both the child's family and organizations such as the school) on behalf of clients who are in pain and whose young age makes it difficult for them to advocate for themselves. The social worker attempts to facilitate the best possible interventions to enhance the youth's quality of life within the constraints and reality of the medical situation.

The social worker often serves a very important role as someone with whom the family can discuss the implications and prognosis of the child's condition. A strong bond often develops between the family and the social worker, and this helping relationship may serve to assist the family through many difficult phases of their child's illness. Because of the intensity of the situation, a degree of intimacy may develop that comforts the family and permits them to focus on their child because they feel emotionally stronger by virtue of the social worker's assistance. By contrast, the social worker's empathy with the child and the family may create an unforeseen negative effect on the practitioner and, at times, result in the social worker feeling a degree of traumatization. This work is difficult, and self-care is essential for the social worker to preserve his or her mental health.

Collaboration with other professionals is critical in carrying out the multifaceted responsibilities associated with serving youth with medical challenges and their families. Working with a transdisciplinary team on the child's behalf means that the burden and responsibility is shared. However, the high level of stress associated with daily exposure to end-of-life issues may exhaust and deplete the emotional resources of social workers, whose very job makes them vulnerable to the debilitating effects of vicarious traumatization. Thus, social workers are at risk for empathizing with the family's pain without addressing their personal grief and loss related to the frequent exposure to end-of-life realities and stressors. Hospitals and other facilities that deal with dying patients must acknowledge the risk for their staff and provide training on methods for coping with this inevitable component of medical work. Fortunately, there are well-documented methods of self-care to prevent the phenomenon of burnout that sometimes accompanies work in this field. The goal for health social workers is to feel a sense of pride and achievement in carrying out a difficult job in a compassionate manner that conveys meaning and dignity to children and families who are coping with a serious medical condition.

SUGGESTED LEARNING EXERCISES

Learning Exercise 15.1

Find a partner and discuss the challenges faced by a health social worker working with a pediatric population. After these conversations, the pairs should report back to the larger group about their discussion. Sample questions to include in this discussion are:

- What unique issues arise when working with children in health-care settings?
- How is working with children in health-care settings different from working with adults?
- When working with children in health-care settings, what would you do if a parent does not want to disclose a diagnosis or prognosis to a child?
- How is working with an adolescent or young adult different from working with a young child?
- How can a social worker learn all the specialized medical language to communicate with one's colleagues in other professions?
- How can a social worker respond to someone who thinks that health social workers spend most of their time on discharge planning?

Learning Exercise 15.2

Do you think that vicarious traumatization is an appropriate term for describing the burnout that some health social workers report experiencing? If you noticed one of your colleagues who seemed uncharacteristically abrasive and unable to connect effectively with patients and their families, how could you broach the topic and suggest that the colleague seek help? Describe your personal plan to avoid vicarious traumatization.

SUGGESTED RESOURCES

Child-Youth/Family-Related and Health-Related Professional Organizations

American Academy of Pediatrics—www .aap.org

American Art Therapy Association—www .arttherapy.org

American Cancer Society—www.cancer.org/

American Medical Association—www .ama-assn.org

American Music Therapy Association—www.musictherapy.org

American Professional Society on the Abuse of Children—www.apsac.org

American Psychological Association—www.apa.org

Association for Play Therapy, Inc.— www .a4pt.org

Association of Pediatric Oncology Social Workers—www.aposw.org

Asthma and Allergy Foundation of America—www.aafa.org

Brain Injury Association www.biausa.org

Children's Neuroblastoma Cancer Foundation—info@cncf-childcancer.org

Child Welfare League of America—www .cwla.org

Eye Movement Desensitization and Reprocessing International Association—www.emdria.org

International Society for Traumatic Stress Studies—www.istss.org

Leukemia and Lymphoma Society—www .lls.org

Make-A-Wish Foundation—www.wish .org/

National Association of Perinatal Social Workers—www.napsw.org

National Association of Social Workers—www.naswdc.org

National Childhood Cancer Foundation—www.nccf.org

National Parent Network on Disabilities—www.npnd.org

Starlight Starbright Children's Foundation—www.starbrightworld.org

Resources for Youth and Families

American Cancer Society (ACS)—www .cancer.org

This site can provide the telephone number of local ACS offices. It provides general information related to disease and may provide reimbursement for transportation, medicine, and medical supplies. This organization also organizes summer camps for children age 6 to 19.

Believe in Tomorrow—www.believeintomorrow.org

This national, nonprofit organization has unique programs that provide support to children and their families facing cancer. This program offers respite vacations to families with an ill child.

Cancer Care, Inc.—www.cancercare.org

This national nonprofit agency offers a range of support services including counseling to cancer patients and their families, financial assistance, and transportation.

Children's Hopes and Dreams Foundation—www.childrenswishes.org

The foundation provides educational booklets for terminally and chronically ill children who suffer any kind of illness, such as cancer, cystic fibrosis, acquired immunodeficiency syndrome, Hodgkin's lymphoma, leukemia, muscular dystrophy, and sickle cell disease.

National Children's Cancer Society (NCCS)—www.nationalchildrenscancersociety.com

NCCS assists by providing some financial assistance for medical treatment, lodging, and travel.

Support Groups for Children, Teens, and Families

List of support groups compiled by the U.S. Department of Health and Human Services—healthfinder.gov/scripts/SearchContext.asp?topic=833&section=3

Gilda's Club—www.gildasclub.org

This free cancer support community offers a wide range of therapeutic activities and educational programs. It offers teen support groups and Noogieland, a magical space with fun activities and support for children.

Starlight Starbright Children's Foundation—www.starlight.org, www.myspace.com/starlightfriends

Starlight has launched My Life, an extension of the Starbright World online social network for seriously ill teens

and teen siblings. My Life was developed specifically to help teens with life-threatening illnesses acknowledge and cope with the possibility of death.

Internet Teen Support Groups

Group Loop—www.grouploop.org

I'm Too Young for This—i2y.com/

Planet Cancer—www.planetcancer.org

Teens Living with Cancer—www.teenlivingwithcancer.org

For Siblings

Supersibs!—www.supersibs.org

Camps

Camp Make A Dream—www.campdream.org

This camp offers a free weeklong camp for patients and their families.

Camp Sunshine—www.campsunshine.org

This camp offers free weeklong camping experience for patients and families.

For Parents and Teachers

Learning Disabilities OnLine—www.ldonline.com

Parenting Tips, Activities for Children, and Current Research about Learning Disabilities

Cancervive—www.cancervive.org/

This group is dedicated to providing support, public education, and advocacy to those who have experienced cancer.

Starlight Children's Foundation—www.starlight.org/sicklecell

This foundation offers a comprehensive menu of outpatient, hospital-based, and Internet resources that provide ongoing support for children with sickle cell anemia and families.

Miscellaneous

Adapting Motor Vehicles for People with Disabilities—www.nhtsa.dot.gov/cars/rules/adaptive/brochure/index.html

Books and Workbooks

Alexander-Azlin, M. L. (2000). *Beyond the rainbow*. Enumclaw, WA: Wine Press.

Best, C. (2002). *Goose's story*. New York, NY: Farrar, Straus & Giroux.

Brown, B. S. (1997). *Oliver's high five*. Albuquerque, NM: Health Press.

Brown, L. K., & Brown, M. (1996). *When dinosaurs die: A guide to understanding death*. New York, NY: Little, Brown.

Carion, H. S. (2008). *Sixty-five roses: A sister's memoir*. Toronto, Canada: McArthur & Co.

Foss, K. S. (1996). *The problem with hair*. Omaha, NB: Centering Corporation.

Heegaard, M. E. (2003). *Living well with my serious illness*. Lanham, MD: Fairview Press.

Gerner, M. (1990). *For bereaved grandparents*. Omaha, NE: Centering Corporation.

Gordan, M. A. (1999). *Let's talk about sickle cell anemia*. New York, NY: Rosen.

Gouss, D. J., & Leeds, E. M. *Tool box of hope*. Atlanta, GA: Healing Hearts Communications.

Keane, N., Hobbie, W., & Ruccione, K. (2006) *Childhood cancer survivors: A practical guide to your future* (2nd ed.). Sebastopol, CA: O'Reilly.

Keene, N. (2003). *Chemo, craziness, and comfort*. Kensington, MD: Candlelighters.

Keene, N. (Ed.) (2003). *Educating the child with cancer*. Kensington, MD: Candlelighters.

Klein, S. D., & Schive, K. (2001). *You will dream new dreams: Inspiring personal stories by parents of children with disabilities*. New York, NY: Kensington Books.

Krishner, T., Levine, A. & Westcott. B. (1992). *Kathy's hats: A story of hope*. Atlanta, GA: Whitman & Co.

McCue, K. (1996). *How to help children through a parent's serious illness*. New York, NY: St Martin's Press.

Miles, B. S., & Wong, N. (2006). *Imagine a rainbow: A child's guide to soothing pain*. Washington, DC: Magination Press.

Mills, J. C. (2003). *Little tree: A story for children with serious medical problems*. Washington, DC: Magination Press.

North, S. (2003). *My brand new leg*. Thousand Oaks, CA: Northstar Entertainment.

O'Toole, D. (1995). *Facing change: Falling apart and coming together again in the teen years*. Burnsville, NC: Compassion Press.

O'Toole, D., & Corr, J. (2004). *Helping children grieve and grow: A guide for those who care*. Omaha, NB: Centering Corporation.

Platt, A. (2003). *Hope and destiny: A patient's and parent's guide to sickle cell disease*. Munster, IN: Hilton.

Sacerdote, A., Platt, A, and Sacerdote, A. (2002). *Hope and destiny: The patient and parent's guide to sickle cell disease and sickle cell trait*. Munster, IL: Hilton.

Salloum, A. (1998). *Reactions: A workbook to help young people who are experiencing trauma and grief*. Omaha, NE: Centering Corporation.

Samuel-Trailsman, E. (1992). *Fire in my heart, ice in my veins: A journal for teens experiencing loss*. Omaha, NE: Centering Corporation.

Scherago, M. G. (1987). *Sibling grief*. Redmond, WA: Medic.

Schmidt, R. C. (2003). *My book about cancer: A workbook to help children deal with the diagnosis and treatment of a father with cancer*. Pittsburgh, PA: Oncology Nursing Society.

Schultz, C. M. (2002).*Why, Charlie Brown, why? A story about what happens when a friend is very ill*. New York, NY: Ballantine Books.

Schwiebert, P., & DeKlyen, C. (1999). *Tear soup*. Portland, OR: ACTA Publications.

Shavatt, D., & E. (2002). *My grieving journey book*. Mahwah, NJ: Paulist Press.

Silverman, J. (1999). *Help me say goodbye*. Lanham, MD: Fairview Press.

Sonnenblick, J. (2006). *Drums, girls, and dangerous pie*. New York, NY: Scholastic.

Temes, R. (1992). *The empty place: A child's guide through grief.* Far Hills, NJ: New Horizon Press.

REFERENCES

Akinbami, L. J., Moorman, J. E., Garbe, P. L., & Sondik, E. J. (2009). Status of childhood asthma in the United States, 1980–2007. *Pediatrics, 123,* S131–S145.

Barakat, L., Alderfer, M., & Kazak, A. (2006). Posttraumatic growth in adolescent survivors of cancer and their families. *Journal of Pediatric Psychology, 31,* 413–419.

Brown, R. T., Daly, B. P., & Rickel, A. U. (2007). *Chronic illness in children and adolescents.* Cambridge, MA: Hogrefe & Huber.

Clarke-Steffen, L. (1993). A model of family transition to living with childhood cancer. *Cancer Practice, 1*(4), 285–292.

Clay, D. L. (2004). *Helping schoolchildren with chronic health conditions: A practical guide.* New York, NY: Guilford Press.

Corr, C. A. (2009). Children's hospice care. In K. J. Doka & A. S. Tucci, *Living with grief: Children and adolescents* (pp. 59–74). Washington, DC: Hospice Foundation of America.

CureSearch. (2008). *Healthy living after treatment for childhood Cancer, Educational issues, Version 3.0.* Retrieved from www.childrensoncologygroup.org

Dell Clark, C. (2010). The emotional impact of a young person's illness on the family. In N. B. Webb (Ed.), *Helping children and adolescents with chronic and serious medical conditions: A strengths-based approach* (pp. 21–34). Hoboken, NJ: Wiley.

Finn, J. J. (2006). *A palliative ethic of care: Clinical wisdom at life's end.* Boston, MA: Jones & Bartlett.

Friebert, S., & Huff, S. (2009). A key step in advancing care for America's children. *Newsline* (pp. 9–13). Retrieved from http://www.dcppcc.org/dp/sites/default/files/A%20Key%20Step%20in%20Advancing%20Care%20for%20Americas%20Children.pdf

Gamble, S. J. (2002). Self-care for bereavement counselors. In N. B. Webb (Ed.) *Helping bereaved children: A handbook for practitioners* (2nd ed., pp. 346–362). New York, NY: Guilford Press.

Goodman, R. (2007). Living beyond the crisis of childhood cancer. In N. B. Webb (Ed.), *Play therapy with children in crisis. Individual, group, and family treatment* (pp. 197–227). New York, NY: Guilford Press.

Hart, R., & Rollins, J. (2011). *Therapeutic activities for children and teens coping with health issues.* Hoboken, NJ: Wiley.

Heggar, A. (1993). Emergency room: Individuals, families and groups in trauma. *Social Work in Health Care, 18*(3/4), 161–168.

Helmick, C. G., Felson, D. T., Lawrence, R. C., Gabriel, S., Hirsch, R., Kwoh, C. K.,…Stone, J. H. (2008). Estimates of the prevalence of arthritis and other rheumatic conditions in the United States. *Arthritis & Rheumatism, 58*(1), 15–25.

Himelstein, B. P., Hilden, J. M., Boldt, A. M., & Weissman, D. (2004). Medical progress—pediatric palliative care. *New England Journal of Medicine, 350*(17), 1752–1762.

Huegel, K. (1998). *Young people and chronic illness: True stories, help, and hope.* Minneapolis, MN: Free Spirit.

Keene, N. (Ed.). (2003). *Educating the child with cancer: A guide for parents and teachers.* Kensington, MD: Candlelighters Childhood Cancer Foundation.

Krementz, J. (1992). *How it feels to fight for your life.* New York, NY: Simon & Schuster.

Leukemia & Lymphoma Society. (2007). *Fertility: Fact Sheet No. 23.* Retrieved from www.leukemia-lymphoma.org/attachments/National/br_1192020700.pdf

Loewy, J. V., & Stewart, K. (2004). Music therapy to help traumatized youth and caregivers. In N. B. Webb (Ed.), *Mass trauma and violence: Helping families and children cope* (pp. 191–213). New York, NY: Guilford Press.

Lovett, J. (2010). A behavioral pediatrician's perspective on helping children recover from traumatic medical experiences. In N. B. Webb (Ed.), *Helping children and adolescents with chronic and serious medical conditions: A strengths-based approach* (pp. 59–72). Hoboken, NJ: Wiley.

Mariotto, A. B., Rowland, J. H., Yabroff, K. R., Scoppa, S., Hachey, M., Ries, L., & Feuer, E. J. (2009). Long-term survivors of childhood cancers in the United States. *Cancer Epidemiology, Biomarkers & Prevention, 18*(4), 1033–1040.

McCain, L. A., & Pearlman, L. (1990). Vicarious traumatization. A framework for understanding the psychological effects of working with victims. *Journal of Traumatic Stress, 3*(1), 131–149.

Meyer, E. C. (2009). Hospital treatment of children and youth with life-threatening conditions. In N. B. Webb (Ed.), *Helping children and adolescents with chronic and serious medical conditions: A strengths-based approach* (pp. 269–284). Hoboken, NJ: Wiley.

National Children's Cancer Society. (2008). *Beyond the cure: The mountain you have climbed.* Saint Louis, MO: National Children's Cancer Society.

Oftedahl, E., Benedict, R., & Katcher, M. L. (2004). National survey of children with special health care needs: Wisconsin-specific data. *Wisconsin Medical Journal, 103*(5), 88–90.

Ogden, C. L., Carroll, M. D., Curtin, L. R., Lamb, M. M., & Flegal, K. M. (2010). Prevalence of high body mass index in US children and adolescents, 2007–2008. *JAMA, 303*(3), 242–249.

Ryan, K., & Cunningham, M. (2007). Helping the helpers. Vicarious traumatization of play therapists working with traumatized children. In N. B. Webb (Ed.), *Play therapy with children in crisis. Individual, group, and family treatment 3d ed.* (pp. 443–460). New York, NY: Guilford Press.

SEARCH for Diabetes in Youth Study. (2006). The burden of diabetes mellitus among us youth: Prevalence estimates from the search for diabetes in youth study. *Pediatrics, 118*(4), 1510–1518.

Shelby, J. (2010). Cognitive-behavioral therapy and play therapy for childhood trauma and loss. In N. B. Webb (Ed.), *Helping bereaved children: A handbook for practitioners* (3rd ed., pp. 263–277). New York, NY: Guilford Press.

Stepanek, M. J. T. (2001). *Journey through heartsongs.* New York, NY: Hyperion.

Taylor, L., & Newacheck, P. W. (1992). Impact of childhood asthma on health. *Pediatrics, 90,* 657–662.

Thayer, P. (2009). Meeting the spiritual needs of children with chronic and life-threatening illness. In N. B. Webb (Ed.), *Helping children and adolescents with chronic and serious medical conditions: A strengths-based approach* (pp. 171–185). Hoboken, NJ: John Wiley & Sons.

Thompson, L. A., Knapp, C., Madden, V., & Shenkman, E. (2009). Pediatricians' perceptions of and preferred timing for pediatric palliative care. *Pediatrics, 123,* e777–e782.

U.S. Department of Health and Human Services. (n.d.) The Health Insurance Portability and Accountability Act of 1996 (HIPAA) Privacy and Security Rules. Retrieved from http://www.hhs.gov/ocr/privacy

Vilas, D. (2009). Child life practice in hospitals. In N. B. Webb (Ed.), *Helping children and adolescents with chronic and serious medical conditions: A strengths-based approach* (pp. 73–88). Hoboken, NJ: Wiley.

Webb, N. B. (2002). (Ed.). *Helping bereaved children: A handbook for practitioners* (2nd ed.). New York, NY: Guilford Press.

Webb, N. B. (2009). (Ed.). *Helping children and adolescents with chronic and serious medical conditions: A strengths-based approach.* Hoboken, NJ: Wiley.

Wind, L. H. (2009). Helping in the emergency room after accidents and traumatic injury. In N. B. Webb (Ed.), *Helping children and adolescents with chronic and serious medical conditions: A strengths-based approach* (pp. 285–301). Hoboken, NJ: Wiley.

16

Social Work With Older Adults in Health-Care Settings

SADHNA DIWAN, SHANTHA BALASWAMY, AND SANG E. LEE

Using a biopsychosocial approach to understanding health and well-being, this chapter presents an introduction to issues relevant to social work with older adults in health-care settings. It focuses on knowledge needed by social workers to comprehensively assess the needs and resources of diverse groups of older people, provides a review of the available empirical literature on various domains of assessment, and describes the nature of social work practice with older adults in a variety of health-care settings. The subject matter of this chapter overlaps to some degree with that of other chapters in this book, such as those addressing policy, disability, nephrology, oncology, chronic illness, end-of-life care, and pain management, as they relate to work with older adults. The reader is urged to treat the chapters as overlapping bodies of information rather than discrete and separate entities.

Chapter Objectives
- Provide an overview of the demographic changes related to aging and their implications for social workers in health care.
- Describe the concept of comprehensive geriatric assessments and discuss the available empirical literature on their efficacy.
- Describe the core components of culturally relevant ethnogeriatric assessment.
- Using a biopsychosocial approach, provide an overview of the domains of knowledge necessary to assess the needs and resources of older adults.
- Describe the nature of social work practice with older adults in selected health-care

settings, such as primary care, inpatient acute care, hospital-to-home transitional care, home health care, and nursing homes.
- Discuss the issues and challenges related to working with older individuals that are encountered by social workers in the current health-care environment.

CHARACTERISTICS OF THE AGING POPULATION

The Administration on Aging (AoA, 2010) provides these facts in *A Profile of Older Americans: 2009.*

Demographics
- Older adults (people 65 years or older) numbered 38.9 million in 2008, representing 12.8% of the U.S. population—about 1 in every 8 Americans.
- The older population itself is getting older, and in 2009, people reaching age 65 years had an average life expectancy of an additional 18.6 years (19.8 years for females and 17.1 years for males).
- The population of adults 65 years of age and older increased from 35 million in 2000 to 40 million in 2010 (a 15% increase), and is expected to increase to 55 million in 2020 (a 36% increase for that decade). The number of individuals 85 years and over is expected to more than double by 2030.

- In 2008, 19.6% of people age 65 years and older were racial and ethnic minorities—8.3% were African Americans, Hispanics represented 6.8%; about 3.4% were Asian or Pacific Islander; and fewer than 1% were American Indian or Native Alaskan. About 0.6% of people age 65 years and older identified themselves as being of two or more races.

Health and Health Care

- Most older people have at least one chronic health condition, and many have multiple conditions. Among the most frequently occurring conditions for the time period 2005 to 2007 were hypertension (41%), diagnosed arthritis (49%), all types of heart disease (31%), any cancer (22%), diabetes (18%), and sinusitis (15%).

- In 2008, 39% of noninstitutionalized older people rated their health as excellent or very good. Among the older population, African Americans (25%), American Indians/Alaska Natives (23.2%), and Hispanics (28%) were less likely to rate their health as excellent or very good than were White (41.8%) or Asian Americans (35.2%).

- In 2008, 38% of older people reported having some type of disability (i.e., difficulty in hearing, vision, cognition, ambulation, self-care, or independent living). Some of these disabilities may be relatively minor, but others result in the need for assistance in meeting important personal needs.

- Limitations on ability to perform specific activities of daily living (ADLs) because of chronic conditions increase with age. Fifty-six percent of people older than 80 years reported a severe disability, and 29% of this population reported that they needed assistance. Disability status and reported health status are strongly correlated. Among those people 65 years and older with a severe disability, 64% report their health as fair or poor.

- In 2006, over 13.1 million people 65 years and older were discharged after short stays in hospitals. The rate of hospital discharge for people 65 years and older is more than three times the comparable rate for people of all ages.

- The average length of stay for people 65 years and older was 5.5 days; the comparable rate for people of all ages was 4.8 days. The average length of stay for older people has decreased by 5 days since 1980.

- Older people averaged more annual physician office visits than did younger people in 2005: 6.5 office visits for those ages 65 to 74 and 7.7 office visits for people older than 75 years; people age 45 to 65 years averaged only 3.9 office visits during that year.

- In 2008, over 96% of older people reported that they did have a usual source of medical care and only 2.4% said they failed to obtain needed medical care during the previous 12 months because of financial barriers.

- Older Americans spent 12.5% of their total expenditures on health, more than twice the proportion spent by all consumers (5.9%).

Implications of Demographic Changes for Social Work in Health Care

Within the next decade, a larger proportion of individuals seen in all parts of the health-care system (e.g., primary care, specialty care, inpatient hospital, nursing home) will be older adults. Given the shortened length of stay in hospitals and the changing nature of nursing home stays (short stay, postacute care), there will be a heavy emphasis on appropriate post–hospital discharge planning and development of community-based care models to help maintain older adults in community settings. These community-based care models will need to address physical, functional, psychological, and social needs of older adults and their families, and social workers will need to pay increasing attention to the development of culturally competent models of care to address the needs of the growing number of minority elders.

As noted by the Bureau of Labor Statistics (2010):

> [G]rowth of medical and public health social workers is expected to be about 22 percent, which is much faster than the average for all occupations. One of the major contributing factors is the rise in the elderly population. These social workers will be needed to assist in finding the best care and assistance for the aging, as well as to support their families. Employment opportunities for social workers with backgrounds in gerontology should be excellent, particularly in the growing numbers of assisted-living and senior-living communities. The expanding senior population also will spur demand for social workers in nursing homes, long-term care facilities, home care agencies, and hospices. (p. 3)

Although Medicare has enabled access to health care for those 65 years and older, older adults have significantly higher out-of-pocket expenditures related to health care, especially for prescription drugs, compared with other groups, and older adults spend a greater proportion of their expenditures on health care (AoA, 2010). Policy advocacy and resource development for health-care products and services also will remain important tasks for social workers in health-care settings.

COMPREHENSIVE GERIATRIC ASSESSMENT

Comprehensive assessment of needs and resources has become a fundamental aspect of providing care to older people. The principles of comprehensive geriatric assessments (CGAs) in health care originated in England in the 1930s in the work of Marjory Warren, who created a specialized geriatric assessment unit in a workhouse infirmary that housed a large number of older patients who were neglected and bedridden (Wieland & Hirth, 2003). Through systematic assessments, Warren determined who might benefit from medical and rehabilitation efforts. She remobilized

a majority of these patients and in many cases discharged them to their homes. These experiences led her to become a leading proponent of comprehensive assessment of older adults before they were placed in chronic hospital or nursing home facilities (Wieland & Hirth, 2003).

Over time, the National Health Service in the United Kingdom established geriatric assessment units as a point of entry into the health-care system, and these assessments were offered to all older patients through universal health coverage. Many other developed countries (e.g., Canada, Australia, Italy, the Netherlands, Norway) have followed the British model (Urdangarin, 2000). In the United States, however, the use of comprehensive geriatric assessment has been restricted to academic centers and Veterans Administration (VA) hospitals (Urdangarin, 2000).

The concept of a CGA in health-care settings such as primary care, inpatient care, and nursing homes is based on the assumption that older adults simultaneously experience problems in multiple domains—physical, social, and psychological—which results in many unmet health-care needs. These problems and needs require a more thorough assessment than what is possible in a routine diagnostic examination provided by the physician. The hallmark of a CGA is that it is performed by a multidisciplinary or transdisciplinary team consisting primarily of physicians, nurses, and social workers and can include specialists from fields such as occupational and physical therapy, nutrition, pharmacy, audiology, and psychology (Agostini, Baker, & Bogardus, 2001; American Geriatrics Society, n.d.; Wieland & Hirth, 2003).

According to the American Geriatrics Society (n.d.):

> [A] geriatric assessment is more involved and comprehensive than the standard medical exam and includes a health "history" and a physical exam, often also including a review or assessment of the person's activities of daily living (ADLs), medications, immunizations, mobility, cognition and signs of

anxiety or depression.... While the geriatrician often serves as the "point person," each member of the geriatrics team is a skilled health professional. All play an important role in the proper assessment and care of an older patient. (p. 1)

Although a CGA is very helpful in making a diagnosis and understanding a patient's needs, the value of a comprehensive assessment in improving patient outcomes often is limited because the assessment team does not have control over the implementation of the recommendations and treatment plan, which usually are initiated by a primary care physician. Researchers in the United States have noted that many of the recommendations made during the assessment were not followed either by the primary care physician or the patient (Shah, Maly, Frank, Hirsch, & Reuben, 1997; Urdangarin, 2000), resulting in unmet needs and compromised health situations.

Because of the disconnect between the assessment and the actual treatment or care provided to the patient, in the United States, there has been increasing recognition that needs assessment should be combined with care management. For this reason, the VA has adopted the geriatric evaluation and management (GEM) approach as a basic component of clinical geriatric care (Urdangarin, 2000). The VA system first established GEM units in inpatient hospital care and later in ambulatory care to identify, assess, and treat frail and older veterans with disabilities in the system who were at risk for institutionalization and failing to benefit from usual care (Wieland & Hirth, 2003). Early studies of the GEM approach within the VA system suggested that it was highly cost effective, leading to its adoption throughout the system. By the mid-1990s, over three fourths of the 172 VA medical centers reported having a GEM program (Wieland & Hirth, 2003).

In GEM programs, patients receive most of their care from the GEM team. The team consists of (a) the physician, who provides medical care and generally supervises the team; (b) the nurse, who provides some medical care and education about the condition or disease, treatments and medications, and the use of home health and emergency services; and (c) the social worker, who provides psychosocial counseling for the patient and caregiver; referral to appropriate financial, social, psychological, and community services; and appropriate discharge planning if the patient is hospitalized (Urdangarin, 2000).

The principles of GEM have been incorporated and tested in other care coordination models, such as Geriatric Resources for Assessment and Care of Elders (GRACE) and the Program of All Inclusive Care for the Elderly. Although the implementation of comprehensive geriatric assessment and evaluation has increased in other inpatient units and outpatient departments, 80% of Medicare beneficiaries do not have access to such programs (see American Geriatrics Society, n.d.). Some of the barriers to providing this service have been the difficulty in obtaining adequate reimbursement for it, the lack of trained geriatric physicians to run these units, and the difficulty in maintaining interdisciplinary teams (Wieland & Hirth, 2003). Another issue has been the mixed evidence on the effectiveness of these approaches in influencing a variety of outcomes, such as functional status, cognitive ability, affect, use of services, cost of care, satisfaction with care, and mortality.

The most commonly reported positive outcomes of CGA and GEM are a reduction in mortality, favorable effects on cognitive and physical functioning, increased likelihood of living at home, and decreased likelihood of hospitalization during follow-up (Urdangarin, 2000). The attempt to move this field forward through research on CGA and GEM has been limited by the diversity of patients in the interventions, the differing nature of both interventions as well as "usual care" practices, the inherent complexity of geriatric evaluation and management, inconsistent measurement of outcomes and use of assessment tools, and the difficulty in replicating successful single-site studies (Van Craen et al., 2010; Wieland & Hirth, 2003). A multisite controlled trial is needed to address some of these difficulties. Despite these issues, comprehensive geriatric assessment has become an accepted component of geriatric primary care and inpatient consultation services, especially with the spread of managed health-care programs. Box 16.1 describes the GRACE model of assessment and care coordination (Counsell et al., 2007) in which social worker and nurse practitioner teams collaborate with a larger interdisciplinary team and primary care physicians to assess, develop, and implement individualized care plans for low-income seniors. The model has been recognized and described in the Healthcare Innovations Exchange of the Agency for Health Care Research and Quality (AHRQ, 2010) and is being disseminated to other health-care systems.

According to R. L. Kane (2000a, p. 3), "the key to good assessment is using a strong conceptual model" that should identify not only specific client attributes of interest but also related factors, such as the physical environment and informal support. Using the biopsychosocial lens, various domains of assessment, their influence on the lives of older individuals, and the implications of their inclusion for social work practice are discussed. Table 16.1 at the end of the section on assessment domains provides a list of tools that are commonly used to assess patients and families in each of the domains. Readers are referred to R. L. Kane and R. A. Kane (2000) for details on the items and psychometric properties of the scales.

Physiological Well-Being and Health

Assessment of an individual's health status is the most basic feature of a comprehensive evaluation in health-care settings. As individuals age, the prevalence of chronic disease conditions increases significantly, with the most common health problems being arthritis, cardiovascular disease, cancer, and diabetes (AoA, 2010). Beyond the genetic or familial predispositions that contribute to developing these chronic conditions, all of these diseases or conditions influence and are influenced by what individuals do or don't do in their daily lives (Centers for Disease Control and Prevention [CDC], 2004). Other common health

measures that are important to assess are an older individual's overall health status; presence of pain; nutritional status; risk for falling; incontinence; sleep; alcohol and drug use; dental or oral health; and sensory perception, especially vision and hearing (McInnis-Dittrich, 2009). These health conditions may significantly influence other domains, such as lowering psychological well-being, limiting functional ability, and diminishing quality of life. For example, arthritis can be painful, limit mobility, and lead to depression. Similarly, complications from diabetes can result in a loss of limbs that requires modification of the home, access to assistive devices, and personal care assistance. Social workers generally are called on to help older individuals and their families address these issues.

One important problem associated with having multiple health conditions is polypharmacy; that is, an individual may visit different doctors and receive prescriptions for different medications that may have significant interactions and side effects. Physicians may not be aware that the patient has seen other providers. A review of all medications should be a standard component of every geriatric evaluation (R. L. Kane, 2000a). Social workers need to be aware of the common medications prescribed for older adults and have some knowledge of side effects. Problems experienced with medications or with compliance often can be spotted in the context of home visits and conversations with family caregivers. Another significant issue related to medication use is the cost of medications. Mojtabal and Olfson (2003) report that low-income Medicare beneficiaries with higher out-of-pocket spending for drugs were more likely to not adhere to prescribed medications because of their cost.

Cost-related nonadherence with medication use was associated with poorer health outcomes in terms of worsening chronic conditions such as arthritis, heart disease, hypertension, and depressive symptoms (Mojtabal & Olfson, 2003). For social workers, advocating for individuals to obtain prescribed medications has become an important feature of their practice in health-care settings. Social

Box 16.1 Geriatric Resources for Assessment and Care of Elders (GRACE)

Key Components

- *Initial, at-home comprehensive geriatric assessment by support team of a certified nurse practitioner and licensed clinical social worker.* The assessment includes medical and psychosocial history, medication review, functional assessment, review of social support and advance directives, and home safety evaluation.
- *Meetings with interdisciplinary team (geriatrician, pharmacist, physical therapist, mental health social worker, and community-based services liaison) to develop an individualized, integrated care plan based on protocols for evaluating and managing 12 common geriatric conditions.* The conditions include: advance care planning, health maintenance, medication management, difficulty walking/falls, malnutrition/weight loss, visual impairment, hearing loss, dementia, chronic pain, urinary incontinence, depression, and caregiver burden.
- *Team-led implementation, ongoing care coordination supported by a common electronic medical record (EMR) and longitudinal tracking system.* The coordination includes in-home follow-up visit by support team to review the care plan and goals.
- *Ongoing care coordination and case management.* The team encourages goal setting and self-care, teaches problem-solving skills, provides education using low-health-literacy materials that correspond to each GRACE protocol, prepares

patients and physicians to address problems and team suggestions during office visits, and assists with transportation arrangements. Each patient receives a minimum of a monthly phone contact to check for and address any new problems, such as changes in medications, social supports, and/or living arrangements. The social worker plays a critical role throughout this process, helping patients to access community-based resources (e.g., discounted fitness classes) and navigate the health and social services system.
- *Periodic interdisciplinary care team reviews and annual reassessments.*

Results

The GRACE program: improved the provision of evidence-based care; led to significant improvements in measures of general health, vitality, social functioning, and mental health; reduced emergency visits; and generated high levels of physician and patient satisfaction. Overall hospital admission rates were not affected, but admission rates for high-risk participants were lower than for comparable patients in the usual-care group. A recent analysis found that the program was cost neutral over a 2-year period and yielded cost savings in the third year for high-risk enrollees.

Source: From "Team-Developed Care Plan and Ongoing Care Management by Social Workers and Nurse Practitioners Result in Better Outcomes and Fewer Emergency Department Visits for Low-Income Seniors." Washington, DC: Agency for Health Care Research and Quality, Innovations and Tools to Improve Quality and Reduce Disparities, 2010. Retrieved from www.innovations.ahrq.gov/content.aspx?id=2066

workers need to remain informed about local and national resources (e.g., Medicare drug discount cards, pharmaceutical company programs) as well as medication assistance programs, which vary from state to state (see Chapter 5 for more information).

Psychological Well-Being and Mental Health

Although older adults experience many of the same mental disorders as other adults, the prevalence, nature, and course of each disorder may vary significantly (U.S. Department of Health and Human Services, 1999). Depression, anxiety, and dementia are some of the pathological disorders that can develop in older age (McInnis-Dittrich, 2009). These problems often are underdiagnosed in large part because of several challenges that clinicians encounter when assessing the mental health of older people. These challenges include comorbidity (the presence of other health conditions), wherein many symptoms of mood disorders (e.g., sleeplessness, fatigue) could be misattributed to health problems. Other challenges include stereotypes about aging; for example, the belief that normal aging is associated with increased negative affect is likely to lead to a lack of attention to the symptoms of mood disorders (Grann, 2000). Family members may believe "senility" is a normal part of aging and delay seeking care for the older individual. Older adults themselves may be less willing to talk about their feelings, as different cohorts and cultures may view psychological symptoms very negatively, and instead focus on somatic complaints (see Chapter 10). For example, older individuals, especially those from Asian cultures, may be more willing to admit to sleep and memory problems than feeling sad or anxious (Kleinman, 2004). Finally, the overlap between the symptoms of dementia and depression makes it difficult to assess them separately.

Substance abuse, particularly the abuse of alcohol, prescription drugs, and over-the-counter medications, is another disorder that is underdiagnosed in the older adult population. Because often decreased activity by an older adult is attributed to other age-related factors, substance abuse is not seen as the cause of a disruption from work or social activities (Widlitz & Marin, 2002). Furthermore, clinicians are often unaware of an older person's drinking problems because the topic is rarely discussed by the physician (Kane, 2000c). Specialized assessment tools, such as the CAGE or the Michigan Alcoholism Screening Test, that specifically target symptoms relating to older people are essential to screen for substance abuse. These symptoms include mood swings, loss of physical mobility, progressive isolation, unexplained accidents, and a decline in cognitive functioning. Left undiagnosed and untreated, substance abuse can decrease overall health because it is associated with immunodeficiency; arrhythmia; and increased risk for cancer, gastritis, and new seizure activity (Widlitz & Marin, 2002). See Chapter 17 for further information.

In the assessment of an older individual's mental health, positive aspects of psychological well-being often are overlooked. That is, assessments of depression, stress, anxiety, and other disorders generally do not address an individual's subjective well-being, such as the presence of positive affect, hope, optimism, and life satisfaction. Folkman and Moskowitz (2000) suggest that positive affect in the context of chronic stress may help prevent worse outcomes, such as clinical depression or adverse physiological consequences of stress. Hope is conceptualized as a future-oriented positive expectation that motivates an individual and provides a means of coping with uncertainty (Raleigh & Boehm, 1994). The lack of hope is predictive of suicidal thoughts among older adults with depression (Uncapher, Gallagher-Thompson, Osgood, & Bonger, 1998).

Although the rate of suicide among those 65 years and older has declined since 1991, suicide rates among seniors are among the highest of all age groups (CDC, 2009). See Box 16.2 for more facts about older adult suicide, as well as Chapter 8 for further information.

Cognitive Capacity

Changes in cognitive capacity occur as people age. Two types of cognitive changes should be noted. The first has to do with small declines in memory, selective attention, information processing, and problem-solving ability that occur with normal aging, although the amount of change varies greatly (Siegler, Poon, Madden & Welsh, 1996). The consequences of these cognitive changes may be a slower pace

Box 16.2 Facts About Suicide Among Older Adults

- Suicide rates increase with age and are highest among individuals age 65 years and over.
- Eighty-five percent of the suicides in this age group were by males. Caucasian males have the highest rates of completed suicide.
- As compared to younger suicide victims, older adults who complete suicide are more likely to have lived alone, be widowed, and have had a physical illness.
- About 70% of older suicide victims had visited their primary care provider in the month prior to their suicide attempt, representing a missed opportunity for intervention.
- Firearms were used in 73% of suicides committed by adults over the age of 65 in 2001 (CDC, 2004).
- In one study, only 58% of physicians asked their depressed and suicidal older patients about their access to firearms (Kaplan, Adamek, & Rhoades, 1998).

Prevention of Suicide in Primary Care Elderly: Collaborative Trial (PROSPECT) Study

Most older suicide victims are seen by their primary care provider within a few weeks of their suicide and are experiencing a first episode of mild to moderate depression. One promising intervention (see Alexopoulos et al., 2009) for reducing suicidal ideation among seniors is a care management intervention involving trained depression care managers (social workers, nurses, and psychologists) who collaborate with primary care physicians by helping the physicians in:

- Recognizing depression
- Offering guideline-based treatment recommendations for patients
- Monitoring patients' depressive symptoms, medication adverse effects, and treatment adherence
- Providing interpersonal psychotherapy when a patient declines medication therapy

A randomized trial evaluation of the intervention found it to be effective in significantly reducing suicidal ideation among those with major depression and noted that treatment response occurred earlier among those receiving the intervention. Despite the promise of this intervention, Conwell (2009) notes that two thirds of the patients in the trial were women; the efficacy of this intervention in reducing suicidal ideation and behavior among older depressed men (who are at highest risk) remains to be examined.

---

of learning and an increased need for repetition of new information (U.S. Department of Health & Human Services, 1999). The second type of cognitive change is a progressive, irreversible, global deterioration in capacity that occurs as a result of dementing illnesses such as Alzheimer's disease, vascular dementia, and subcortical dementia. It is estimated that about 3% of men and women ages 65 to 74 years old have Alzheimer's, and nearly 50% of those 85 years and older may have the disease (National Institute on Aging, 2004).

Another important issue is the determination of the competence of people with impaired cognitive capacity to make their own decisions regarding care. Usually this is accomplished by having either a family member or a social worker (if no family member is available) petition the court for guardianship of the patient's finances and/or person. The decision to grant guardianship is a legal determination made by the court but usually also involves a physician's and social worker's assessment of the client's capacity for making decisions that do not cause harm to self or others (Cummings & Jackson, 2000).

As the dementia progresses, profound changes occur in memory, language, object recognition, and executive functioning (i.e., the ability to plan, organize, sequence, and abstract). Behavioral symptoms such as agitation, hallucinations, and wandering are also common. These cognitive changes necessitate increasing supervision of the older individual, leading to considerable strain and burden for both formal and informal caregivers (Alzheimer's Association, 2004). Much of social workers' effort is directed toward finding resources, such as caregiver support groups, behavior management training, counseling, personal care services, respite, and alternative living arrangements (e.g., foster care, assisted living facilities, nursing homes) to support the informal caregivers. Medications also can be helpful in managing some behavioral symptoms, such as agitation and hallucinations. Social workers should encourage family members to discuss all symptoms and changes in behavior with the physician, social worker, and caregiver support group because many behavior management techniques can be learned from listening to the experiences of other caregivers.

Functional Ability

Functional ability is usually defined as an individual's ability to perform certain basic ADLs. The activities classified as basic ADLs refer to personal care (e.g., dressing, bathing, eating, grooming, toileting, getting in and out of bed or a chair, urinary and bowel continence); the term *instrumental activities of daily living* (IADLs) refer to activities that need to be performed in order to live in a community setting (e.g., cooking, cleaning, shopping, money management, use of transportation, telephone, medication administration). Mobility, which addresses walking, climbing stairs, balance, and transferring in and out of a chair or bed, often is included in the ADLs. The performance of these activities usually is assessed in terms of being independent, needing assistance (human help or mechanical devices), and being unable or completely dependent on human help to perform the various activities. The progression of disability in performing these activities predicts an individual's movement along the continuum of care, ranging from independent living, to assisted living (assistance could be informal, formal, or both), to nursing home care.

A variety of factors contribute to an individual's ability to perform ADLs and IADLs. Pearson (2000) notes: "[F]unctional ability can be conceptualized as the dynamic interaction of an older adult's physiological status, the emotional or psychological environment, and the external or physical and social environment" (p. 19). For example, many of the health conditions discussed earlier could contribute to limitations in functional ability. Psychological issues such as depression, anxiety (including a fear of falling), and hopelessness may lead to a decreased motivation to perform these activities. Cognitive changes such as dementia also limit an individual's functional ability. Finally, the external physical environment (type of dwelling or neighborhood) as well as the social support available to an individual may promote or hinder the ability to perform ADLs and necessitate a change in living conditions. For social workers, the implications are clear: An assessment of functional status requires an evaluation of all of these factors that may contribute to an individual's disability. Limitations in ADLs and IADLs are a prerequisite for eligibility for services in all publicly funded home and community-based services programs.

Another significant issue in the area of functional limitation is the ability to drive a motor vehicle. According to Stutts, Martell, and Staplin (2009), drivers age 60 to 69 years (i.e., the "young-old") do not show any increase in automobile crashes. The rate begins to rise for those 70 years and older and increases rapidly at 80 years. Thus, it is the oldest drivers who pose more risk to themselves and to public safety. The conditions that substantially increase the risk for crashes among older drivers include those that require navigating complex situations, such as intersections and left turns and reacting to an imminent crash.

A variety of age-related and other changes in vision, hearing, reaction time, and cognitive function can interfere with an individual's ability to drive. As Stutts and colleagues (2009) note:

> Situations that have proven risky for older drivers often include complex visual searches,

and information from multiple sources that must be processed rapidly under divided attention conditions. These are conditions where context-appropriate driver behavior often depends less upon conformity to formal or informal rules than to judgment or "executive function." (p. 42)

These findings about particular risk factors can help target educational materials to the appropriate age cohorts and suggest that older adults may be able to extend the safe driving years through engagement in health/wellness programs (Stutts et al., 2009).

In the United States in particular, the ability to drive is one of the most significant components of the ability to remain independent. Some communities have undertaken environmental modifications, such as lengthening the time of traffic signals and increasing the size of lettering and visibility of street signs. Organizations such as the Automobile Association of America and the American Association of Retired Persons (AARP) offer a Mature Driver Safety program to retrain older drivers. Based on a study of older drivers, the Hartford Financial Services Group, in partnership with the Massachusetts Institute of Technology AgeLab, developed a brochure that prepares family members for how to have a conversation with an older person about driving decisions (Hartford, 2005). Older people generally preferred to be approached by individual family members as opposed to those outside the family (such as a close friend or the police) when having conversations about their driving. Most married older adults preferred to hear first from a spouse, although over 18% of those who were married with a spouse in the household reported that they absolutely did not want to hear from their spouse about driving concerns. Doctors and adult children also were preferred choices for conversations. In cases where older adults lived alone, doctors, followed by adult children, were most often selected (Coughlin, Mohyde, D'Ambrosio, & Gilbert, 2004). Social workers can be helpful in educating and engaging family members and physicians about addressing this issue with an older patient.

Social Functioning

When assessing social function, it is important to remember the subjective and objective components to social functioning. Objective measures would include social support (support or help received), social networks (number of people in the individual's social circle), social activities (attendance at social events, frequency of contact with others), and social roles (the number and type of roles performed). Subjective measures of social function ask individuals to report on their satisfaction with their social situation and their perception that support is available when needed. Individuals may vary considerably in objective measures of social function yet express similar amounts of satisfaction. In fact, there is a large body of evidence to suggest that subjective evaluations of support are more strongly related to psychological well-being than objective indicators of social functioning, such as the frequency of contact with others (Krause, 1995). Different aspects of social functioning can be addressed depending on the goal of treatment or care planning. For example, social workers may focus on an increase in the frequency of contact with existing social networks (e.g., finding transportation to attend social or church activities) or an increase in social roles (e.g., finding employment or volunteer opportunities), depending on which aspects of social function are most salient to the older person.

Among older individuals, social integration (i.e., having social ties, roles, and activities) is associated with better health outcomes, such as a lower risk of mortality, cardiovascular disease, cancer mortality, and functional decline (Unger et al., 1999). However, health also affects social functioning in that individuals who are confined to a bed or have severe mobility impairments are likely to disengage from social activities that involve leaving the home. Thus, as Levin (1994) points out, social functioning is both an outcome as well as a predictor of physical and psychological well-being.

Negative interaction or support is also an important area for assessment. Negative interaction typically occurs with individuals who have a close relationship with the older person (Antonucci, Sherman, & Vandewater, 1997) and can take the form of disagreements, emotional and financial abuse, and even physical abuse and neglect (discussed in the section "Assessment of Family and Informal Support").

One issue that overlaps social, physical, and psychological domains is the expression of sexuality and the experience of intimacy among older people (see Chapter 14 for more details). In a review of the literature, Hooyman and Kiyak (2002) note that contrary to the misperceptions about the cessation of sexual activity as individuals grow older, researchers have found that sexual activity continued into older ages and that sexual inactivity appeared to depend more on life circumstances rather than decreases in interest or desire. For example, the influence of marital status and interpersonal relationships on sexual behavior is greater for women than for men (Matthias, Lubben, Atchison, & Schweitzer, 1997), whereas physical conditions resulting in sexual dysfunction appear to be the major difficulty influencing sexual activity for men (Wiley & Bortz, 1996). A psychosocial assessment of factors that influence sexual activity in older adults should include an individual's past history of sexual activity, attitudes toward sexual activities and intimacy, availability of a partner, anxiety about sexual performance, opportunities for privacy, and attitudes of staff toward sexual activity in institutional settings (Hooyman & Kiyak, 2002). Given the rates of human immunodeficiency virus (HIV) and acquired immunodeficiency syndrome (AIDS) among older people—10% of those with HIV are over age 50 and about 3% are older than 60 years (Linsk, 2000)—knowledge about HIV and the practice of risky behaviors also should be part of the assessment.

Physical Environment

As individuals age, social workers often see a widening in the gap between the demands of the environment and the individual's competence to address those demands. The aging process brings with it many physiological changes in sensory perception, gait, reaction time, and strength, all of which may compromise an individual's ability to negotiate the existing environment. For example, changes in vision and depth perception make it difficult to negotiate stairs, which may lead individuals to restrict their trips out of the house, leading to further dependence on assistance and increased social isolation. Inadequacies in the physical environment also may necessitate relocation from a house or residence, which could negatively influence an individual's psychological well-being, especially if the older person opposes the move. This is particularly true in the case of many nursing home admissions.

Although independent homes are the most obvious targets of an assessment of the adequacy of the physical environment, Cutler (2000) suggests that "all residential environments can be measured against the principles of universal design, wherein a residential setting should be adaptable, supportive, accessible, and safe" (p. 360). In 2000, about 78% of older adults (65 years and older) owned their home (U.S. Census Bureau, 2004), and about 89% of respondents age 55 years and older strongly or somewhat agreed that they would like to remain in their current residence for as long as possible (AARP, 2000). Among older adults, falls are the leading cause of injury deaths and the most common cause of injuries and hospital admissions for trauma. Each year, about 35% to 40% of adults 65 years and older fall at least once, and about two thirds to one half of falls occur in or around the home (CDC, 2001). Among community-dwelling older adults, the risk of falling is greater for those who live alone and have some type of functional impairment (Elliott, Painter, & Hudson, 2009).

Assessing the fit of the home environment with the capabilities of the individual is an important assessment domain, and the prevention of falls is a critical area of intervention. Typical home assessments will examine the condition, adequacy, and accessibility of lighting; flooring and carpeting, including obstacles or potential hazards for falling; bath and toilet, including need for assistive devices; kitchen; heating and cooling; access to home from outside; access to rooms within the home; and personal safety issues, such as neighborhood conditions. Similar issues are also important when evaluating assisted living or foster care facilities.

Assessment of Family and Informal Support

Family members play an important role in organizing or providing for the care of an older adult. About two thirds (64%) of people who live in the community and need long-term care rely solely on family and friends (i.e., informal support) for help; 28% receive a combination of informal and formal care; and only 8% use formal care or paid help only (Liu, Manton, & Aragon, 2000). Family members of older adults most likely to be caregivers are adult daughters (27%), other female relatives (18%), sons (15%), wives (13%), husbands (10%), and others. About 30% of people caring for older long-term care users were themselves age 65 years or older, and another 15% were between ages 45 and 54 years (Spector, Fleishman, Pezzin, & Spillman, 2000).

The assessment of informal support generally focuses on the number and relationship of family helpers, amount and type of help provided, the expected permanence of family help, the strain or burden experienced by caregivers, and more recently on the positive aspects of caregiving (Gaugler, Kane, & Langlois, 2000; Pearson, 2000). Many caregivers have competing demands, such as employment and caring for young children. With the declining functional ability that occurs with chronic illnesses and dementia, along with the need for increased vigilance, caregivers experience considerable strain, which puts the older person at greater risk for entering a nursing home and also increases the likelihood of abuse or neglect. It is thus important to assess both objective and subjective components of caregiver strain to gain a better understanding of the needs of the caregiver. The term *objective components of burden* refers to the disruption

in finances, family life, and social relations; the term *subjective components* refers to the caregiver's appraisal of the situation as stressful (Gaugler et al., 2000).

There is some evidence of race/ethnic differences in the appraisal of strain due to caregiving, such as evidence that African American caregivers have a lower likelihood of viewing caregiving as stressful compared with Caucasian caregivers (Pinquart & Sörenson, 2005). However, much of the research on race/ethnicity is confounded with socioeconomic status, and little data are available on caregiver perspectives from different socioeconomic strata within racial and ethnic groups. In many long-term care programs, formal services are provided only when family members are not in a position to do so. Thus it is important that social workers attend to both objective and subjective components of caregiver strain when developing a long-term care plan.

In the health-care system, the assessment of family support often is constrained by legal definitions of who is a family member. This creates significant structural and legal barriers for older gay and lesbian couples in various health-care settings. For example, partners may be denied access to medical records or visits to intensive care; in matters of medical decision making, health-care professionals may restrict themselves to dealing with family members rather than partners despite the fact that family members may know less about the preferences of the older patient than the partner; and staff may hold negative attitudes toward gay and lesbian couples (Hooyman & Kiyak, 2002). Social workers should be aware of their own values and practices related to this issue and act in accordance with the professional code of ethics to not discriminate against individuals on the basis of a variety of factors, including sexual orientation (National Association of Social Workers, 2003).

Elder abuse often occurs when family members are overwhelmed with caregiving responsibilities, particularly if the care recipient and the care provider are living in the same household and there is a past history of family abuse. Additional risk factors for elder abuse include being older than 75 years; being female; having physical or cognitive limitations; living in a lower socioeconomic household; and caregiver vulnerability to problems such as substance use, mental illness, or financial dependency on the care recipient (McInnis-Dittrich, 2009; National Center on Elder Abuse [NCEA], 2004). A survey of states by the NCEA in 2000 notes that social workers are mandated reporters of elder abuse in 30 states or territories in this country. This fact is important in part because signs of elder abuse may be overlooked in health-care settings when bruises, bone fractures, or painful body symptoms might be attributed to changes due to normal aging, unexpected falls, or pain related to illness.

Economic Resources

Typically the assessment of economic resources (i.e., income, pension, health insurance, other assets) is necessary to determine eligibility for publicly funded home- and community-based services. Almost every state operates a Medicaid waiver–funded home- and community-based services program that provides for home care services to older adults who are at risk of entering a nursing home. The actual assessment and eligibility criteria vary from state to state, but in general they include limitations in functional ability and an income at or near poverty (Centers for Medicare and Medicaid [CMS], 2010a). Individuals whose incomes exceed the criteria are required to "spend down" their assets until they reach the eligibility level (CMS, 2010b). See Chapter 5 for additional information. Assessing income and assets can be a frustrating and time-consuming activity because of the reluctance of older people and their family members to divulge such information, often leading to an increased use of social work time and delays in the Medicaid application process (Diwan, 1999).

Values and Preferences

There is little systematic evaluation of the values and preferences of older adults in most health and long-term care settings (R. L. Kane, 2000c).

Kane outlines several areas in which some systematic ways of eliciting individual preferences are desirable. These areas include preferences:

- For end-of-life care that address whether individuals would want various procedures performed, such as resuscitation, ventilator care, intubation, and hydration, and also whether they would like to designate a proxy decision maker in the event they cannot make these decisions

- About outcomes associated with alternative hospital discharge plans; for example, preferences related to particular types of home care services needed or the location of post-hospital care

- About housing arrangements, such as those related to independent as well as various types of congregate living arrangements, such as assisted living facilities, small group homes, continuing care retirement communities, or nursing homes

- For how routines of everyday life are conducted, especially with ADLs and IADLs

- Related to religious practices

- Related to privacy, especially in congregate settings where individuals may share rooms and be observed by others when being helped with ADLs

- Related to safety versus freedom; for example, older adults may choose to live in situations that professionals consider less than adequate

In keeping with social work values that promote the principles of client self-determination and autonomy, assessment of values and preferences of older adults can help social work practitioners be more attentive to these issues when working with older adults in institutional settings that tend to minimize the opportunity for self-determination.

Spiritual Assessment

A growing body of literature documents the positive link among religiosity, spirituality, participation in religious activities, and health

Table 16.1 Assessment Domains and Some Commonly Used Assessment Tools

Major Domains of Assessment	Some Commonly Used Assessment Tools
Physiological well-being and health	*Get Up and Go Test* (Mathias et al., 1986) and *Expanded Timed Get Up and Go* (Wall, Bell, Campbell, & Davis, 2000). Widely used as screens for risk for falls.
	Medical Outcomes Study—Short Form-36 Health Survey (SF-36) (Ware & Sherbourne, 1992). Covers eight areas: physical function, role limitations due to physical problems, social function, pain, general mental health, role limitations due to emotional problems, vitality, and general health perceptions.
Psychological well-being and mental health	*CAGE Questionnaire* (Ewing, 1984). Assesses alcohol problems.
	Center for Epidemiological Studies Depression Scale (CES-D) (http://chipts.cch.ucla .edu/assessment/Assessment_Instruments/Assessment_pdf_new/assess_cesd_pdf.pdf). Assesses depressed affect, positive affect, somatic/vegetative signs, and interpersonal distress. Available in shorter versions.
Cognitive capacity	*Global Deterioration Scale (GDS)*. (Reisberg, Ferris, de Leon, & Crook, 1982). Assesses the severity of dementia related to cognition, functional ability, and problem behaviors.
	Mini Mental State Exam (MMSE) (Folstein, Folstein, & McHugh, 1975). Assesses immediate and delayed memory recall; orientation; calculation/working memory; visuospatial abilities; language.
Ability to perform various ADLs	*Katz Index of Independence in Activities of Daily Living* (Katz et al., 1963). Measures performance in ADLs: dressing, bathing, eating, grooming, toileting, transferring from bed or chair, mobility, and continence.
	Older Americans Resources and Services, Instrumental Activities of Daily Living (OARS-IADL) (Fillenbaum & Smyer, 1981). Measures performance in IADLs: cooking, cleaning, shopping, money management, use of transportation, telephone, medication administration.
Social functioning	*Lubben's Social Network Scale* (Lubben, 1988). Can be used as a screening tool for an older person's risk for isolation.
	Social Support Questionnaire (Sarason et al., 1983). Measures objective and subjective aspects of support received: global, informational, perceived, structural, and provisional.
Physical environment	*Elderly Resident Housing Assessment Program (ERHAP)* (Brent & Brent, 1987). Assesses safety, functioning, comfort in various domains through interviews with homeowner, direct observation, and photographs by rater.
Assessment of family caregivers	*Caregiver Strain Index* (Robinson, 1983). Assesses physical, personal, family, and financial strain related to caregiving.
	Revised Memory and Problem Behavior Checklist (RMBPC) (Teri et al., 1992). Assesses frequency of memory, mood, and problem behaviors in care the older patient and how much these bother the caregiver.
Economic resources	*Older Americans Resources and Services (OARS-Economic Resources)* (Fillenbaum & Smyer, 1981). Assesses income, pension, Social Security, health insurance, and other assets, such as a house, cars, and savings.
Values and preferences	*Desire for Choice and Control in Nursing Homes* (Kane et al., 1997). Assesses preferences for choice and control in everyday life in nursing homes.
	Values Assessment Protocol (Degenholtz, Kane, & Kivnick, 1997). Assesses values and preferences of older people in case-managed home care programs. Could be useful in developing care plans.
Spiritual assessment	*The Daily Spiritual Experience Scale* (Underwood & Teresi, 2002). Attempts to measure experience rather than particular beliefs or behaviors.

and psychological well-being among older adults (Koenig, 1990; Levin, 1994). Assessment of preferences for religious and spiritual activity is important because these factors are known to influence an individual's psychological and social functioning, ability to cope with stress, and overall quality of life. Spiritual beliefs and religious worldviews also may influence health- and illness-related beliefs. For many African Americans, spiritual beliefs are a foundation for understanding disease conditions and making treatment decisions (e.g., they believe that God is ultimately responsible for physical health, the physician is God's instrument, and only God has the power to decide life and death) (Johnson, Elbert-Avila, & Tulsky, 2005). Many Muslims are taught that illness is a test of faith and a way to strengthen character and that God is responsible for health care. Therefore, Muslims may choose to not cooperate at all with practitioners who discuss the probable course of a disease or death (Gorder & Ellor, 2008). The actual domains of assessment may include religious affiliation, beliefs, commitment, participation in religious activities, and private daily experience (Olson & Kane, 2000). The salience of these domains to an individual (e.g., religious strictures for food [kosher for observant Jews, halal for observant Muslims], the availability of religious services) could significantly influence care plans for community-based care as well as for institutional long-term care arrangements.

ETHNOGERIATRIC ASSESSMENT

Increasing ethnic and cultural diversity in the older population and the growing demand for culturally competent care have contributed to the development of *ethnogeriatics*, which is a synthesis of aging, health, and cultural concerns about health-care and social services for ethnic older adults (McBride & Lewis, 2004; Yeo, David, & Llorens, 1996). Ethnogeriatric assessment involves adding cultural exploration (Andrulis & Brach, 2007) or cultural

investigation (Gorder & Ellor, 2008) to the CGA. Ethnogeriatric assessment is the first step to providing culturally competent care and requires knowledge and skills in several areas, including culturally defined health beliefs, historical and cohort experience, the role of the family in the cultural context, culturally appropriate ways of nonverbal communication (showing respect), ability to address clients with language barriers, and use of linguistic and culturally appropriate assessment instruments.

Cultural Context of Health and Illness

Older clients and families from various ethnic and cultural backgrounds may have culturally defined health belief systems that do not exactly match with or exist in the Western health-care system, which is based on the biomedical model (Yeo, 2009). The biomedical model uses definitions and explanations of health and illness that are based on scientific assumptions and processes whereas ethnic older clients and families may consider factors such as balance, nature, or spirits in explaining their conditions. As a result, social workers may encounter clients who describe culturally defined somatic disorders or culture-bound syndromes during assessment (Stanford Geriatric Education Center [SGEC], 2001). For example, in Chinese and other traditional medicine, health is maintained by balancing forces in the body (e.g., yin and yang balance, cold or hot concepts) and free flow of *qi* (Lin, 1980; McBride, Morioka-Douglas, & Yeo, 1996). Vietnamese and other Southeast Asian refugee populations identify "wind illness" as a common cause of various illnesses and also believe that karma from past lives and supernatural or ancestral spirits contribute to health or illness (Yeo, 1996). Older Hmong refugees from Cambodia believe spirit and soul loss affect health (Gerdner, Xiong, & Yang, 2006).

Historical Context and Cohort Experience

Historical context and cohort experience, such as immigration patterns, experience of certain events (e.g., war, torture, refugee status), and discrimination, may be reflected in health beliefs and illness behaviors. Not knowing such experience can result in inaccurate assessment of clients' conditions (Rosich, 2007; Xakellies et al., 2004; Yeo et al., 1998). For example, the most commonly reported symptom by older Cambodians, severe headaches frequently combined with dizziness, may be related to their unique cohort experience of the genocide under the Khmer Rouge. Their frequent thinking about loss of and separation from family members during wartime results in headaches (Handelman & Yeo, 1996). Alaska Natives who experience separation from others through death or school in their childhood and are now seniors may exhibit trauma-like symptoms (Rosich, 2007). Knowing about these unique experiences can help in interpreting symptoms expressed as well in establishing trust with older ethnic clients and their families (SGEC, 2001).

Acculturation, which is the degree to which individuals are influenced by and actively engage in the traditions, norms, and practices of one or more cultures, can vary by the amount of exposure to those cultures. Cohort experience, length of residence in the United States, and language proficiency influence degree of acculturation (Diwan, 2008). Acculturation thus should be regarded as a continuum rather than a category, and social workers should assess the degree of acculturation in thoughts, behaviors, and attitudes to better understand the older person's frame of reference (Organista, 2009; Yeo, 2009).

Role of Family in Cultural Context

In assessment of ethnic older clients, cultural expectations of their families that guide the family members' responses, such as levels of involvement and decision making, must be recognized (Yeo, 1996). Values and ethical principles emphasized in U.S. health care, such as independence, autonomy, privacy, and confidentiality, may not apply in some cultures. For example, in traditional Mexican and Filipino families, physical dependence in old age may be expected, and taking care of dependent older members is considered to be a family's responsibility. In many cultures, the family (and not the older client) is responsible for deciding the older person's health care, and sometimes family members ask providers not to reveal a serious diagnosis or bad news as a way of protecting elders (Yeo, 1996, 2009). Gender roles may be traditional (e.g., in Muslim families, men often are regarded as protectors by women, and men are responsible for all health-care decisions) (Gorder & Ellor, 2008).

When working with older clients from family-centered cultures, it is useful to invite family members to participate in the assessment process in addition to the older adult (Andrulis & Brach, 2007). Likewise, it is useful to identify information related to family composition and structure, kinship patterns, expectations of and for family members, decision-making practices and roles (e.g., individualistic versus collectivistic, family centered, matriarchal or patriarchal), gender role allocation, and the like (SGEC, 2001; Xakellies et al., 2004). Family members can help provide insightful information about clients' problems and contribute to collaborative problem solving (Organista, 2009).

Culturally Appropriate Nonverbal Communication

Cultural preferences about showing respect through nonverbal communication vary greatly across groups, and social workers should be familiar with culturally appropriate behaviors, gestures, and styles (Xakellies et al., 2004). Appropriate physical proximity between a practitioner and a client varies across cultures. Physical contact in greeting and examination by the opposite gender are limited or prohibited in many cultures, and direct eye contact is appropriate in some cultures but can be considered impolite or disrespectful in others (Gorder & Ellor, 2008; SGEC, 2001). Practitioners should keep these variations in mind and carefully determine what to do or not do during assessment. If in doubt about the appropriateness of an action, ask clients' for guidance and about their preferences (Yeo, 1996).

Language Barriers

Clear communication is critical for accurate assessment, but it can be a challenge when working with older clients and families with limited English proficiency and when practitioners do not speak the same language as clients (Yeo, 1996). Language barriers can contribute to misunderstanding and errors in communication during assessment and undermine the practitioner-client relationship (Min, 2005). Likewise, accurate assessment about preferred language and degree of English proficiency is essential in deciding on whether to use interpreter services and translated materials (Andrulis & Brach, 2007; Hasnain-Wynia & Baker, 2006). Please see Chapter 10 on communication for information and resources about using interpreters.

Using Standardized Assessment Instruments

When using standardized assessment instruments (e.g., depression and other mental status, health literacy), practitioners need to ensure that instruments have been tested psychometrically to determine their appropriateness with the individual or group in question (Tran, Ngo, & Conway, 2003). Relying on translated instruments may be problematic because items on the instruments may not have the same meaning to all groups, and level of education and literacy also may impact scores (Andrulis & Brach, 2007; Douglas & Lenahan, 1994; Yeo, 1996).

Choice of format of the instrument can vary based on the ethnic group of clients. For example, expectation about expressing emotion varies across cultures. Face-to-face interview will be appropriate for clients from cultures encouraging expressing feelings. Self-reporting will be more appropriate for those who are influenced by cultural norms of suppressing emotion because ways of keeping harmony and face-saving may cause individuals to be reluctant to be interviewed or respond using socially desirable response biases (SGEC, 2001).

Implications of Ethnogeriatric Assessment for Social Work in Health Care

Factors shaping individuals' cultural attitudes are not limited to the areas just mentioned, and social workers should try to solicit extensive information in a sensitive and unobtrusive way that is culturally appropriate (Gorder & Ellor, 2008). Use of cultural liaisons (e.g., health workers, personal care workers) or cultural brokers can help social workers resolve difficult interactions and communications (Xakellies et al., 2004; Yeo, 2009). As stated earlier, medical interpretation should be undertaken by people who are specially trained and licensed (see Chapter 10).

ASSESSMENT VERSUS SCREENING

Although comprehensive assessment of older people and their families is desirable, it is not feasible to assess individuals in depth in all possible areas. Typically the content of an assessment is determined by its purpose and the setting in which it occurs. An abbreviated form of assessment often is used for the purposes of screening or case finding. Screening usually is done to identify individuals who may have difficulties or problems in certain areas of functioning. These individuals then are assessed in greater depth and often referred to specific disciplines for continuing care (Finch-Guthrie, 2000). For example, many health maintenance organizations screen all of their older patients by sending surveys at the time of enrollment. Individuals who meet certain "risk" criteria (e.g., those at risk for falling, breakdown of informal support, those likely to be frequent users of emergency room services) then are referred to case managers who develop, implement, and monitor a care plan to address their particular risk factors. Screening, or case finding, is also important in primary care settings, where the needs of many older patients may be overlooked because of the lack of time or training to assess psychosocial needs of older patients with chronic illness (Berkman et al., 1999). Another example of screening occurs in inpatient units where social workers screen "high-risk" individuals, or those who may require earlier intervention and intensive attention, for the purpose of developing a viable discharge plan (Cummings & Jackson, 2000).

SOCIAL WORK WITH OLDER ADULTS IN HEALTH-CARE SETTINGS

Social work practice with older adults occurs in a range of health-care settings: outpatient clinics, hospitals, emergency rooms, public health departments, home health-care agencies, agencies providing home- and community-based services, and residential and rehabilitation facilities such as nursing homes and assisted living facilities. Some essential social work practice skills that are needed to work with older adults in these settings are described in Table 16.2.

Primary Health-Care Settings

The term *primary care* refers to the initial entry of the patient into the health-care system and implies a holistic approach to care focusing on health promotion, disease prevention, and integration of mental and physical

health services (Cowles, 2003; Oktay, 1995). Primary health-care centers are considered important one-stop services because they can assist patients and families in navigating other health-care services and promote continuity of care and linkages among patient, family, and community (Donaldson, Yordy, Lohr, & Vaneselow, 1996). Most older patients in primary health-care settings have two or more comorbid chronic illnesses, such as those described earlier in this chapter.

Generally, social workers come in contact with older people through referral from physicians or nurse case managers or via high-risk screening methods. The social worker completes a psychosocial assessment to determine the strengths and service needs of the patient, develops a care plan in partnership with the patient and family, and seeks input from all of the health-care professionals involved in the delivery of care. The social worker's level of collaboration with health-care professionals varies depending on the type of primary care setting and availability of a geriatric consultation team. The GRACE model described in Box 16.1 is an example of interdisciplinary collaboration for assessment and care planning in a primary care setting. Social workers may advocate for access to identified gaps in services and resources within or outside the primary care setting on behalf of the older person to ensure successful implementation of

Table 16.2   Essential Social Work Practice Skills in Health Service Settings

Screening	High-risk, service eligibility, special problems
Assessment	Problem identification, needs, strengths, resources—individual and community
Communication skills	Verbal and nonverbal; interviewing—patient and family; special groups, other professionals and service providers
Interpersonal engagement skills	Conveying values—autonomy, empathy, trust; clarifying roles; empowerment
Clinical skills	Crisis intervention, counseling and therapy—individual, family, and group
Group facilitation	Support groups, psychoeducational groups
Mediation/Negotiation	Advocacy, dispute resolution
Documentation	Health insurance, medical records, mandated assessments

the care plan. They also provide information on available resources in the community and refer older patients to community agencies that offer services such as housing, transportation, home health care, counseling/psychotherapy, durable medical equipment, and health insurance. The goal is to facilitate comprehensive care that meets the needs of the patient. As direct service practitioners, social workers may provide emotional support and counseling to older people to foster coping and adaptation to their illness, treatment, and prognosis. They also help identify and mobilize the social support system (family, friends, and significant others) in the community.

A new approach to increasing access to primary health-care providers that has been used involves house calls made to homebound, high-risk, frail seniors by interdisciplinary teams of geriatricians, nurse practitioners, and social workers. This approach has produced favorable outcomes, such as reduced inpatient hospital services, nursing home placements, and cost of care (Maynard & Stein, 2008). Furthermore, to improve access and adherence to recommended preventive care services among older adults, experts suggest the need for education of the older adults about the diagnosis and treatment of emotional health problems, which can be achieved through the use of mental health specialists in primary care settings (De Jonge, Taler, & Boling, 2009; Thrope, Patterson, & Sleath, 2006).

As provision of health care is shifting rapidly to ambulatory settings, social work experts envision a need for expanding the role of social workers in primary care settings to include more multidisciplinary and transdisciplinary team approaches, organizational networking, case management services, participation in medical ethics consultations, therapeutic and crisis interventions, and other supportive counseling and group work interventions (Berkman & Harootyan, 2003; Cowles, 2003; Netting, 1992).

Inpatient Hospital Settings

In hospitals, social workers typically see older patients through referrals from physicians and nurses or through case finding using high-risk screening methods. Characteristics of high-risk patients may include living alone, terminal or chronic illness, suicidal tendencies, mental health problems (Becker & Becker, 1986; Thrope et al., 2006), and lack of supports (Berkman et al., 1999). Hospitalized older patients are referred to social workers for a wide range of issues and problems, such as anxiety over being hospitalized; pre- or postsurgical concerns about procedures, treatment, recovery, and discharge; lack of support and resources after discharge; family and patient consent on use of life-sustaining equipment; suspected abuse; and cognitive or functional impairments that require intervention. Acute health problems for which older people may be admitted to the hospital include falls and fractures, physical impairment, iatrogenic illness, nutritional problems, and surgery.

Hospital social workers in inpatient settings are responsible for screening and case finding, psychosocial assessment, discharge planning, postdischarge follow-up, outreach, counseling (individual, group work), documentation and record keeping, and collaboration. Depending on the hospital, they may provide emergency services through on-call programs.

The psychosocial assessment evaluates the patient's level of functioning, service needs, social history, and availability of support, if needed, from family and friends. The process of discharge planning and developing a posthospitalization care plan involves coordinating input from the various members of a multidisciplinary team. Social workers coordinate this effort in their important role on the team as liaison for the patient and family (Cotti & Watt, 1989; Cowles, 2003; see Cummings & Jackson, 2000).

Social workers can help inform or educate older individuals about the seriousness of their illness, consequences if the illness is left untreated, resources available to assist in continuity of care, options for alternative care, legal rights, and other matters. Such information can help patients become effective consumers of services and gain a sense of self-efficacy, which is often lost when a person experiences losses in functioning and when dealing with large and complex health-care systems. Through referrals to community services and family conferences, social workers may engage in informing other formal and informal support networks to help the client after discharge or advocating for specialized services within or outside the hospital. Doing this requires knowledge of the availability and eligibility requirements of various community resources. Social workers also are expected to have knowledge and skill in determining the method of reimbursement, such as private or public insurance or out-of-pocket costs.

Social workers often are involved in counseling older patients regarding adjustment-to-illness issues and may provide crisis counseling to help the family and older person reestablish an emotional equilibrium, begin to understand the medical condition, prioritize tasks, and develop a short-term action plan (McInnis-Dittrich, 2009). Social workers also may develop support groups (e.g., bereavement, cancer, dementia, high-risk health behaviors) to assist patients and their families with their losses and illness and undertake family counseling when needed. Facilitation of support groups for older patients in this setting requires skills such as relationship building, counseling, and communication (Ross, 1995).

The level of social work involvement in discharge planning may vary depending on hospital size, location, number of social workers employed, policies, protocols, and organizational culture. In general, physicians refer patients to hospital social workers for concrete services, such as assistance with IADLs, or social-environmental problems, such as those involving financial needs, posthospital care, and transportation, rather than for primarily expressive problems involving attitudes, feelings, or behaviors related to health (Cowles & Lefcowitz, 1995). However, in a study by Holliman, Dziegielewski, and Datta (2001), social workers in the field perceived their role in discharge planning as requiring specific skills related to communication and assessment of social and financial issues, and not just provision of concrete services.

Care Transitions Settings

"Care transitions refer to the movement of patients from one health-care practitioner or setting to another as their conditions and care needs change. These may include transitions from hospitals to nursing homes or home care after an acute illness, or transitions from nursing homes to home care" (California Health Care Foundation, 2008, p. 1). During care transitions, older patients with multiple comorbid conditions are particularly at risk for medical errors, service duplication, patient and caregiver distress, and having critical elements of the care plan fall through the cracks. Ineffectively managing care transitions leads to poor clinical outcomes; dissatisfaction among patients; and inappropriate use of hospital, emergency, postacute, and ambulatory services (Coleman & Boult, 2003).

A number of efforts have been undertaken to intervene with transitions of care between providers to prevent relapse, reduce rehospitalizations, and ensure safe and continuous care (Kanaan, 2009; Naylor & Keating, 2008; Parry, Kramer, & Coleman, 2006). The primary goal of transition care is to improve communication among hospital or nursing facility providers, primary care physicians, and other community providers. The secondary goal is to establish a follow-up care plan at the time of discharge to ensure quality of care and safety through education and support.

The Coleman Transition Care Intervention (CTI) model, developed and implemented by Dr. Eric Coleman and colleagues, is a brief intervention designed specifically to address the immediate needs of the patient following discharge from health-care settings through patient empowerment, support, and education (Coleman, 2006). Specifically, the intervention utilizes a transition coach, who is responsible for empowering patients by helping them develop skills in managing their care and well-being as well as developing skills in navigating and communicating with health-care providers. In particular, a transition coach facilitates development of skills in patients and caregivers in four areas: (1) medication management (being knowledgeable about medications and having a medication management system), (2) use of a personal health record (PHR) (understanding and using the PHR to facilitate communication and continuity of care across settings), (3) knowledge of "red flags" (knowing and recognizing health indicators that suggest their condition is worsening and how to respond), and (4) primary care and specialist follow-up (scheduling follow-ups and communicating their conditions). Transition care is accomplished through at least one visit in the hospital or nursing facility before discharge, a home visit, and a series of follow-up phone calls to help the patient make the successful transition. Several tools are available to help transition care coaches perform their tasks (e.g., the patient activation assessment tool, which assesses the progress of the patient during follow-up visits; the PHR documentation maintained by the patient on medical conditions and medications; a list of questions that patients can ask of their primary care physicians) (Coleman, 2006).

The CTI model is flexible in its implementation as it promotes engagement of professionals from various disciplines including nurses, pharmacists, community workers, or social workers as the designated transition coach (California Health Care Foundation, 2008). This model has been field-tested by several organizations as a strategy for improving postdischarge patient care across settings (Adler, Lipkin, Cooper, Agolino, & Jones, 2009; California Health Care Foundation, 2008; Graham, Ivey, & Neuhauser, 2009; Naylor & Keating, 2008; Parry et al., 2006), and is supported as a strategy to improve care transition by major health-care organizations, including the Medicare Payment Advisory Commission, Centers for Medicare and Medicaid Services, Joint Commission for Hospitals and Quality Improvement, and the American Board of Internal Medicine (California Health Care Foundation, 2008).

Evidence suggests that while most older patients face difficulties in making a successful transition from one setting to another, the barriers are even more pronounced for older adults from minority ethnic groups, recent immigrants, older people without spouses, and those who have limited English-language skills (Graham et al., 2009). The CTI model can benefit these patients, especially if a culturally competent transition coach is available. Box 16.3 describes the CTI model in greater detail.

Although the transition coach role for social workers is innovative, there are challenges to its full implementation in health-care settings. These include lack of adequate staffing, high turnover among staff, lack of resources in the community, collaborating effectively with community providers, convincing patients and families to take part in the process, and making follow-up home visits within two days of discharge (California Health Care Foundation, 2008).

Home Health-Care Settings

In 2007, 7.6 million individuals in the United States received home health services from more than 17,000 providers (National Association of Home Care, 2001). The major sources of funding for home health-care are through Medicare and Medicaid, followed by private out-of-pocket payments. Certified Medicare home health-care providers have to meet the minimum federal standards of patient care and are expected to maintain an electronic Outcome and Assessment Information Set (OASIS) database. This database consists of core elements of a clinical assessment for all the adult home care patients served. The major components of the OASIS are living arrangements, supportive assistance, sensory status, skin condition, respiratory status, elimination, neuro/behavioral/emotional status, ADLs and IADLs, medications, medical equipment management, and emergent care (Kane, 2000b).

The federal government utilizes this information for cost reimbursement and ongoing monitoring to measure patient outcomes for purposes of outcome-based quality improvement. A physician has to refer an older patient for home health-care services in order

Box 16.3 Coleman Care Transitions Intervention

The next elements are the essence of the CTI using a transitional coach.

- *Identification of patients.* Generally, patients who are at high risk for relapse postdischarge are identified through referral or direct recruitment through high-risk screening based on routine screening and assessment by social workers, nurses, or other community health-care workers. High-risk patients can be identified in settings such as hospitals or nursing care facilities.
- *Discharge planning.* Conduct an initial visit to prepare patient for discharge. Prior to discharge introduce personal health record and the discharge preparation checklist to patient. The PHR includes the patient's demographic information, medical history, primary care physician, caregiver contact information, advance directives, medications and allergies, and a list of warning signs (red flags). The discharge preparation checklist is completed prior to discharge to ensure that patients understand the discharge process and recommendations.
- *Follow-up postdischarge.* Conduct home visit(s) and/or phone calls within 24 to 48 hours postdischarge depending on patient needs and risk of relapse. Remind the patient to share PHR with the primary care physician/specialist and discuss outcome of this visit with patient to ensure care compliance and reduce potential relapse risk. During home visits, the transition coach

can undertake patient assessment, education, and activation in self-management skills and gather important information on the patient's functional abilities, mental abilities, social support, and environmental challenges that inform decisions related to self-management capabilities and needs.

- *Termination.* Length of intervention is approximately four weeks following discharge. Prior to termination, assess patient's stability and refer the patient to complementary resources in the community to ensure continuity of care and support as needed.

In contrast to traditional case management approaches, the CTI is a self-management model where a transition coach utilizes modeling techniques rather than "doing" it for the patient. To help the patient and caregiver assume greater involvement and control over postdischarge care, the focus is on patient education and training by providing information on health care, symptom management, medication management, follow-up with doctors, and maintenance of the PHR based on self-assessment. Patients who participated in the CTI were significantly less likely to be readmitted to the hospital, and the benefits were sustained for at least five months after the end of the one-month intervention.

Source: Adapted from "The Care Transitions Intervention: A Patient-Centered Approach to Ensuring Effective Transfers between Sites of Geriatric Care," by C. Parry, E. Coleman, J. Smith, J. Frank, and A. Kramer, 2003, *Home Health Services Quarterly, 22*(3), pp. 1–17; and the Care Transitions Program at www.caretransitions.org/

to receive Medicare and Medicaid reimbursement. Similarly, Medicare mandates that social workers' services are covered only if they are ordered by physician. The goal of home health-care services for an older person is to reduce the length of inpatient hospital stays and delay of discharge or prevent nursing home placement or hospital readmission through the

provision of a range of health and social services within the home setting (Dyeson, 2004). Recent reports on home health care show an overall increase in the number of home care agencies since 2001. Estimates are that about 12,564 social workers currently are employed, with an average of 3.31 visits per client (National Association for Home Health Care and Hospice, 2008). More than three fourths of beneficiaries reported having no problems accessing home health-care services, which confirms the existence of a well-coordinated linkage of services to meet client needs. Minority older adults, however, are less likely to use home care services because of lack of awareness of their availability (Choi, Crist, McCarthy, & Woo, 2010).

Home health-care users are more likely to be White, female, poor, widowed, and divorced or single; live alone; have functional limitations in ADLs; and reside in urban areas (Kadushin, 2004). About 69% of all Medicare beneficiaries are 65 years older, with most receiving home health care because of an acute episode of a chronic illness, such as diabetes, hypertension, heart failure, chronic skin ulcer, or osteoarthritis (National Association for Home Health Care and Hospice, 2008). In addition, many have psychosocial issues that compound their illnesses and require care from multiple professionals, including social workers (Lee & Gutheil, 2003).

Following hospital discharge, a homebound patient may require multiple services by a variety of health-care providers. Nurses and physical therapists may assist with medication and rehabilitation; home health aides may assist the patient with personal care activities, such as bathing and transferring (i.e., getting in and out of bed or a chair); and homemakers may assist with light housekeeping, such as meal preparation, shopping, and laundry. In addition to coordinating these supportive services, home health social workers can arrange for community services, such as transportation and friendly visitor volunteers. They help the family and older person adjust to having providers enter the home and often provide supportive or therapeutic counseling services or arrange for similar services from other agencies in the community (Dziegielewski, 2004; Lee & Gutheil, 2003; McInnis-Dittrich, 2009).

A critical function of the social worker is to assess and facilitate the caregiver's involvement in the patient's recovery and rehabilitation. Social workers may help caregivers identify, secure, and utilize other community

services, such as adult day health care, to meet the changing needs of the patient (Rossi, 1999). Social workers frequently are engaged in negotiating with health-care providers for specific services, service units, time slots, requesting for specific staff, and the like, to match the patient's needs with services. The frequency of denial of requested services is greater in home health settings due to changes in cost reimbursement policies (conversion from a cost-based reimbursement system to a prospective payment system), and social workers feel ethically obligated to advocate for their patients (Kadushin & Egan, 2001).

Nursing Home Settings

According to the National Nursing Home Survey, 16,000 nursing homes were operating in the United States in 2004 with about 1.5 million residents, 88.3% of whom were age 65 years and over (National Center for Health Statistics, 2004). Historically, nursing homes were viewed only as long-term care facilities. However, the past decade has seen greater use of nursing homes for short stays for rehabilitation and care after discharge from the hospital with a concomitant increase in the role of Medicare in financing nursing home care (Rhoades & Sommers, 2003). Residents who are married or living with a partner tend to stay in nursing homes for the least amount of time, compared with widowed, divorced, single, or never-married residents (Talley & Crew, 2007). Seventy-one percent of nursing home residents are female, 57% are widowed, and more than half require assistance in all five areas of ADLs—bathing, dressing, eating, transferring, and toileting—indicating a high level of dependence of care. Evidence suggests that nearly a third of residents are bowel incontinent and over three fourths of them have stage 2 pressure ulcers, which are painful and may lead to other health complications and infections. A quarter of the residents have the circulatory problems as their primary diagnosis, followed by mental disorder (22%) and disease of the nervous system and sense organs (National Center for Health Statistics,

2004). In addition, residents older than 75 years frequently are diagnosed with dementia and psychiatric conditions, such as schizophrenia and mood disorders. According to the report, the most common mental health disorders residents suffer are delirium, dementia, and depression.

Depression is common among nursing home residents (Jakubiak & Callhan, 1995–1996; Masand, 1995), especially in patients diagnosed with Alzheimer's disease. Often it is attributed to coexisting conditions or simply to aging, and thus fails to receive appropriate intervention (Adamek, 2003). The most frequently received services by residents include nursing, medicines, medical, personal care, nutritional, social services, and equipment or assistive devices. Other services commonly received from other outside sources include hospice, therapy, podiatry services, dental and oral services, and diagnostic services (National Nursing Home Survey, 2004, www.cdc.gov/nchs/nnhs/nnhs.htm). Residents who are older and more functionally and cognitively impaired are more likely to receive end-of-life care; three quarters of residents have at least one advance directive on their records (National Center for Health Statistics, 2008).

Private for-profit nursing facilities employ more full-time social workers (19%) than not-for-profit homes (7%) and government-run nursing homes (6%) (Center for Health Workforce Studies, 2006) with social workers employed as administrators, specialized unit directors (e.g., dementia care) or direct practitioners. Within the nursing home setting, social workers perform a variety of functions, such as doing psychosocial assessments (Nathanson & Tirrito, 1998), working to resolve family conflicts with facility staff and administration (Iecovich, 2000; Vinton, Mazza, & Kim, 1998), and addressing problem behaviors of nursing home residents (Tirrito, 1996). In most nursing homes, social workers are responsible for conducting the preadmission screenings to determine if patients have any major mental disorders (mental retardation, developmental disability, or related disorders) in order to provide appropriate referrals and treatment (Cowles, 2003; Dziegielewski, 2004).

All Medicare- and Medicaid-certified nursing home facilities require a comprehensive assessment of residents within 14 days of admission. In response to public and professional concern about the quality of care in nursing homes across the country in the 1980s, Congress directed the Health Care Financing Administration to study how to improve nursing home regulation. That administration contracted with the Institute of Medicine, which issued a report in 1986 titled "Improving the Quality of Care in Nursing Homes." Congress included many of the institute's recommendations from this report as part of the 1987 Omnibus Budget Reconciliation Act. Based on the institute's report, the act's regulations require the assessment of nursing home residents in 18 functional areas. The Minimum Data Set was developed as a recommended format for that comprehensive assessment (American Geriatrics Society, 2000). In most facilities, social workers complete the psychosocial assessment of the minimum data set to develop the care plan for the resident (Cowles, 2003; Dziegielewski, 2004).

Among the most frequently cited sources of distress that older patients face in transitioning into nursing home settings are feelings of loss and abandonment; adjustment to new environments; fear and anxiety related to life changes, illness, and prognosis; and loss of privacy, independence, and family connection. Social workers can help residents adjust to their environments by providing emotional support and initiating appropriate interventions (individual, family, and group) to enhance psychosocial functioning. They also can facilitate social integration within nursing homes through planned recreational activities in that setting. In conjunction with the provision of direct services to residents, involvement of family is especially critical during admission and discharge (Kruzich & Powell, 1995; Vourlekis, Gelfand, & Greene, 1992). Informal support networks can provide valuable assistance to older people during their stays in nursing homes by providing support and monitoring the quality of care provided by the staff.

Because family members are considered an integral part of care plans, social workers may want to provide meaningful services to them— for example, therapeutic caregiver support groups or educational groups on illness or end-of-life issues. In settings like nursing homes, where the patients and family members may be unable to negotiate the client's care due to frailty, inability to make personal decisions, or bureaucracy, social workers can advocate on behalf the patient and empower families to voice their concerns and to negotiate the patient's treatment needs and care. They also may work with resident councils to improve the quality of care in facilities. In other situations, where there may be conflict between family members and nursing home staff, social workers can mediate to help resolve the conflict and facilitate improved communication.

ISSUES AND CHALLENGES TO SOCIAL WORK WITH OLDER INDIVIDUALS IN THE CURRENT HEALTH-CARE ENVIRONMENT

Demographic trends make clear that within the next decade, older adults will represent a larger proportion of individuals seen in all parts of the health-care system (primary care, specialty care, inpatient hospital stays, nursing care). As the costs of health care continue to skyrocket, attempts to manage these costs have altered the context in which health care is delivered and significantly influenced the practice of social work in a variety of health-care settings. The principal idea underlying managed care has been to control the costs by decreasing "unnecessary utilization" of health-care services, which is accomplished through budget restrictions, case management and utilization review, incentives to providers for limiting services, and using the primary care provider as the gatekeeper for access to care (Berkman, 1996). Managed care, however, presents social workers with a dilemma of being a patient advocate while, to a certain

extent, a gatekeeper of resources. For example, can social workers adequately assess the needs of patients and their families given prevailing time restraints? Can they attend to the preferences of the patient and the family given the institutional mandate to develop and implement a discharge plan that minimizes length of stay (Moody, 2004)?

Although Medicare has enabled access to health care for the population that is 65 and older, older adults have experienced significantly higher out-of-pocket expenditures related to health care through time, especially for prescription drugs, compared to other age groups, and spend a greater proportion of their income on health care (Administration on Aging, 2010). Thus, advocacy and resource development for health-care products and services will remain important tasks for social workers in health-care settings.

Given the shortening of inpatient stays in hospitals and the changing nature of nursing home stays (short stay, postacute care), community-based care models will need to be developed to help maintain older adults in community settings. However, the ability to maintain older individuals in the community depends on the availability and pulling together of several community resources. In communities where resources are underdeveloped or where services are financially beyond the reach of clients, case management may simply become a referral service that fails to adequately address the needs of older adults and their families (Netting, 1992). Policy advocacy for supporting family caregivers will remain an important area of social work practice to support community-based care for older adults. In addition, with increasing frailty among the population as it ages, the need for advocacy to integrate physical care with in-home psychiatric care will be critical, to increase access to psychiatric service, reduce hospital readmissions, and save cost. Finally, health promotion and disease prevention activities at the individual and community levels that help older people maintain functional autonomy and physical and psychological well-being will be important areas of social work intervention.

SUGGESTED RESOURCES

Administration on Aging—www.aoa.gov

This site provides information about programs, services, and opportunities for older adults and their caregivers. Also links to: Eldercare Locator, www.eldercare.gov, which furnishes information on state and local area agencies on aging as well as community-based service organizations that provide services to older adults and their care providers.

American Association of Retired Persons (AARP)—www.aarp.org

AARP is a national, nonprofit advocacy organization for adults age 50 and over. Main topic areas include: care and family, health and wellness, legislation and elections, money and work, policy and research, and travel and leisure. The information on the AARP Web site is also available in Spanish.

American Geriatrics Society (AGS)—www.americangeriatrics.org/

AGS is a not-for-profit organization of health professionals (primarily physicians) devoted to improving the health, independence, and quality of life of all older people. The Web site has useful information especially on policy advocacy and publications on ethnogeriatrics, such as *Doorway thoughts: Cross-cultural health care for older adults,* vols. 1–3 (AGS 2004, 2006, 2008).

Benefits Checkup—www.benefitscheckup.org

This online service allows individuals (age 55 and over) to check whether they may qualify for a variety of program benefits. The service screens over 1,100 programs for federal, state, and local public and private benefits.

Care Transitions Program—www.caretransitions.org/

This program provides descriptions, tools, references, and evidence for the effectiveness of the Care Transitions Intervention designed to improve quality of care and patient safety during care handoffs.

Centers for Disease Control and Prevention—www.cdc.gov/

This is the official Web site for the federal agency that monitors American's health and safety. Health and safety topics applicable to older adults include: disabilities, diseases and conditions, environmental health, health promotion, and vaccines and immunizations. State and national health and safety data and statistics are also available on this Web site.

Centers for Medicare & Medicaid—www.cms.hhs.gov/

This is the agency's official Web site. It describes programs, benefits, and eligibility rules for Medicare and Medicaid.

Council on Social Work Education Gero-Ed Center—www.cswe.org/CentersInitiatives/GeroEdCenter.aspx

This site contains evidence-supported resource reviews, teaching modules, and practice demonstration videos on aging-related topics in the advanced social work practice areas of health, mental health, and substance use. The *Health Resource Review* is an excellent resource review on social work with older adults.

Family Caregiver Alliance (FCA)—www.caregiver.org

FCA is a national advocacy organization. The Web site's topic areas include: public policy and research, caregiving information, fact sheets and publications, newsletters, online discussion and support groups (including specialized groups, such as LGBT support groups), and news releases. The Web site information is also available in Chinese and Spanish.

Hartford Geriatric Nursing Institute—consultgerirn.org/resources

This site is an excellent resource offering articles, case studies, and videos demonstrating the use of assessment tools for a variety of topics relevant to the care of older adults.

Massachusetts Institute of Technology Age Lab—agelab.mit.edu/

The Age Lab was created to invent new ideas and creatively translate technologies into practical solutions that improve people's health and enable them to "do things" throughout the life span. The site describes numerous projects that are in process.

Medicare Rights Center—www.medicarerights.org/

Subtitled "Your Guide through the Medicare Maze," this national, nonprofit organization provides information on Medicare plan options and current policy changes.

Psychosocial Measures for Asian-American Populations: Tools for Direct Practice and Research—www.columbia.edu/cu/ssw/projects/pmap/about.htm

This site, maintained by the School of Social Work at Columbia University, contains information on the validity and reliability of a number of assessment instruments with Asian American populations.

Social Security Administration—www.socialsecurity.gov

This is the official SSA Web site. It offers information on Social Security programs and policies. In addition, individuals can process online claims, estimate their future benefits, and apply for replacement Social Security cards.

Stanford Geriatric Education Center—sgec.stanford.edu/

This Web site provides a comprehensive curriculum in ethnogeriatrics (a five-module core curriculum with 11 ethnic-specific modules. The primary focus of the SGEC is to provide training on culturally sensitive geriatric care. It is an excellent source of ethnogeriatric information.

Veterans Administration (VA)—www.va.gov

This is the VA's official Web site. It supplies information on veterans' health benefits and services, vocational rehabilitation and employment services, pension benefits, and burial and memorial benefits.

Volunteers in Health Care (VIH)—www.volunteersinhealth care.org/home.htm

This is the national resource center funded by the Robert Wood Johnson Foundation for organizations and clinicians caring for the uninsured. The Web site contains useful information on prescription drug assistance programs at: www.rxassist.org

SUGGESTED READINGS

Beaulieu, E. M. (2002). *A guide for nursing home social workers*. New York, NY: Springer.

Provides a comprehensive overview of issues that social workers need to know and address in nursing homes.

Hooyman, N., & Kiyak, A. (2010). *Social gerontology: A multidisciplinary perspective* (9th ed.). Boston, MA: Allyn & Bacon.

Reviews the literature on various aspects of aging and discusses implications for a multidisciplinary audience in the allied health and mental health professions.

Kane, R. L., & Kane, R. A. (Eds.). (2000). *Assessing older persons: Measures, meanings, and practical applications.* New York, NY: Oxford University Press.

An edited book providing an excellent review of available assessment tools for each of the domains of assessment discussed in this chapter.

Knight, B. G. (2004). *Psychotherapy with older adults* (3rd ed.). Thousand Oaks, CA: Sage.

Provides a practical account of the knowledge, technique, and skills necessary to work with older adults in a therapeutic relationship. Case examples illustrate the dynamics of the therapeutic task and issues covered in therapy and stress the human element in working with older adults.

LEARNING EXERCISE 16.1

Mr. and Mrs. C are an older Caucasian couple who came to the attention of a hospital social worker after Mrs. C had been hospitalized for dehydration. She was brought to the hospital based on the recommendation of her primary care physician, who had found her to be quite confused and delirious during her visit to the doctor's office. Mrs. C had been stable over the past few days, but her age (73) and her confusion had flagged her as an at-risk patient who would need additional attention to develop an adequate discharge plan. The social worker learned that the Cs lived in their own home and their only son lived about 200 miles away from them. The Cs lived modestly on their pension and Social Security. Mr. C indicated that he wanted his wife discharged to their home as he was quite capable of looking after her. Mr. C himself did not appear to have any observable limitations in his ability to carry out activities of daily living, although he did look tired. The social worker was not entirely convinced of Mr. C's ability to care adequately for his wife—she did, after all, have to be hospitalized due to dehydration. According to the patient's chart, Mrs. C's confusion still seemed to persist, although she seemed quite lucid when talking to the social worker. The physician and the nursing staff wanted the social worker to develop a discharge plan fairly quickly. The hospital social worker decided that Mrs. C should be discharged to her home in the care of her husband. However, she recommended that the physician order home health care for Mrs. C as a nurse could monitor her condition and a social worker could do a more comprehensive assessment in the client's home. This way, at least someone could monitor this situation for several weeks.

Did the hospital social worker do everything she could have done with planning for the couple? What were some of the constraints or dilemmas the social worker experienced?

ABC Home Health is the agency selected to provide in-home care to Mrs. C. The home health social worker visits the home once to make an assessment. The house seems a little cluttered. Mr. C notes that he does all of the housework but because of the pain caused by his arthritis, he cannot get things done quickly. The social worker suggests that they try to get some homemaker assistance. She gives Mr. C the contact information for the local Area Agency on Aging and also suggests that Mr. C call his son to discuss long-term care plans since they would likely need more assistance as time went by. Mr. C. calls the Area Agency on Aging for homemaker assistance but is put on a waiting list. One month later, Mr. C trips on an area rug, which results in a leg fracture, and he ends up in the hospital.

How could this fall have been prevented? What are some of the resources in the community that could have been helpful to the couple? What are the options for Mrs. C now? Research your community's resources to learn more about how you could help the couple.

Additional Discussion Questions

To use the case for an ethnogeriatric assessment exercise: Change the ethnic background/context of the client (e.g., monolingual Mexican American, Vietnamese American who immigrated to the United States for family unification), and integrate the ethnogeriatric principles described in the chapter for assessment of the case.

To use the case for a care transition coach exercise: Incorporate the use of a transitional coach and discuss issues to be addressed in assisting the client to maintain stability and reduce relapse of the primary condition.

REFERENCES

AARP. (2000). *Fixing to stay: A national survey of housing and home modification issues*, Washington, D.C., AARP. Retrieved from http://research.aarp.org /il/home_mod.pdf

Adamek, M. E. (2003). Late-life depression in nursing home residents: Opportunities to prevent, educate, and alleviate. In B. Berkman & L. Harootyan (Eds.), *Social work and health care in an aging society: Education, policy, practice and research* (pp. 15–48). New York, NY: Springer.

Adler, A., Lipkin, C., Cooper, L., Agolino, M., & Jones, V. (2009). Effect of social work intervention on hospital discharge transition planning in a special needs population. *Managed Care, 18*(11), 50–43.

Administration on Aging. (2010) *A profile of older Americans: 2009.* Washington, DC: U.S. Department of Health and Human Services. Retrieved from http://www .aoa.gov/aoaroot/(S(42nfwo55qzegvw45pkhesp45)) /aging_statistics/Profile/2009/2.aspx

Agency for Health Care Research and Quality. (2010). *Team-developed care plan and ongoing care management by social workers and nurse practitioners result in better outcomes and fewer emergency department visits for low-income seniors.* AHRQ Innovations Exchange. Retrieved from http://www .innovations.ahrq.gov/

Agostini, J. V., Baker, D. I., & Bogardus, S. T. (2001). Geriatric evaluation and management units for hospitalized patients. In K. G. Shojania, B. W. Duncan, K. M. McDonald, & R. M. Wachter (Eds.), *Making health care safer: A Critical analysis of patient safety practices.* Evidence Report/Technology Assessment No. 43. AHRQ Publication No. 01-E058. Rockville, MD: Agency for Healthcare Research and Quality.

Alexopoulos, G. S., Reynolds, C. F., Bruce, M. L., Katz, I. R., Raue, P. J., Mulsant, B. H., … Ten Have, T. (2009). Reducing suicidal ideation and depression in older primary care patients: 24-Month outcomes of the PROSPECT Study. *American Journal of Psychiatry, 166,* 882–890.

Alzheimer's Association. (2004). *About Alzheimer's.* Retrieved from www.alz.org/

American Geriatrics Society. (n.d.). *The principles of geriatric care.* Retrieved from www.americangeriatrics .org/files/documents/Adv_Resources/PayReform _fact3.pdf

American Geriatrics Society. (2000). *Regulation of nursing facilities position statement.* Retrieved from www.americangeriatrics.org/products/positionpapers /regulnl.shtl

Andrulis, D. P., & Brach, C. (2007). Integrating literacy, culture, and language to improve health care quality for diverse populations. *American Journal of Health Behavior, 31*(suppl. 1), S122–S133.

Antonucci, T. C., Sherman, A. M., & Vandewater, E. A. (1997). Measures of social support and caregiver burden. *Generations, 21*(1), 48–51.

Becker, N., & Becker, F. (1986). Early identification of high social risk. *Health & Social Work, 11*(1), 26–35.

Berkman, B. (1996). The emerging health care world: Implications for social work practice and education. *Social Work, 41*(5), 541–551.

Berkman, B., Chauncey, S., Holmes, W., Daniels, A., Bonander, E., Sampson, S., & Robinson, M. (1999). Standardized screening of elder patients' needs for social work assessment in primary care: Use of the SF 36. *Health & Social Work, 24*(1), 9–16.

Berkman, B., & Harootyan, L. (2003). *Social work and health care in an aging society: Education, policy, practice and research* (pp. 1–15). New York, NY: Springer.

Brent, E. E., & Brent, R. S. (1987). ERHAP: An artificial intelligence expert system for assessing the housing of elderly residents. *Housing and Society, 14*(3), 215–230.

Bureau of Labor Statistics. (2010). *Occupational outlook handbook*, 2010–11 ed. Social Workers. Retrieved from www.bls.gov/oco/pdf/ocos060.pdf

California Health Care Foundation. (2008). *Navigating care transitions in California: Two models for change.* Retrieved from www.caretransitions.org/documents/CA _Two_Models.pdf

Center for Health Workforce Studies and NASW Center for Workforce Studies. (2006). *Licensed social workers in the United States, 2004.* Rensselaer, NY: University at Albany School of Public Health, and Washington, DC: National Association of Social Workers. Retrieved from http://workforce.socialworkers.org /studies/fullStudy0806.pdf

Centers for Disease Control and Prevention. (2001). *Falls among older adults: Summary of research findings.* Retrieved from www.cdc.gov/ncipc/pub-res/toolkit /SummaryOfFalls.htm

Centers for Disease Control and Prevention. (2004). *Health Information for older adults: Chronic diseases.* Retrieved from www.cdc.gov/aging /health_issues.htm

Centers for Disease Control and Prevention. (2009). *National suicide statistics at a glance.* National Center for Injury Prevention and Control, Division of Violence Prevention. Retrieved from www.cdc.gov /violenceprevention/suicide/statistics/aag.html#5

Centers for Medicare and Medicaid. (2010a). *Home and community-based services waiver program.* Retrieved from www.cms.gov/home/medicaid.asp

Centers for Medicare and Medicaid. (2010b). *Medicaid eligibility.* Retrieved from www.cms.gov/Medicaid Eligibility/

Choi, M., Crist, J. D., McCarthy, M., & Woo, S. H. (2010). Predictors of home health care service use by Anglo American, Mexican American and South Korean elders. *International Journal of Research in Nursing, 6*(1), 8–16.

Coleman, E. A. (2006). *Geriatric interdisciplinary teams in practice care transitions model*. Retrieved from www.jhartfound.org/ar2007html/pdf/Hart07_care _transitions_model.pdf

Coleman, E. A., & Boult, C. (2003). Improving the quality of transitional care for persons with complex care needs. Position statement of the American Geriatrics Society Health Care Systems Committee. *Journal of the American Geriatrics Society, 51*(4), 556–557.

Conwell, Y. (2009). Suicide prevention in later life: A glass half full, or half empty? *American Journal of Psychiatry, 166,* 845–848.

Cotti, M., & Watt, S. (1989). Discharge planning. In M. J. Holosko & P. A. Taylor (Eds.), *Social work practice in health care settings* (pp. 469–487). Toronto, Ontario, Canada: Canadian Scholars' Press.

Coughlin, J. F., Mohyde, M., D'Ambrosio, L.A. & Gilbert, J. (2004). *Who drives older driver decisions?* Retrieved from http://web.mit.edu/agelab/news_ events/pdfs/AgeLab_driver_decision.pdf

Counsell, S. R., Callahan, C. M., Clark, D. O., Tu, W., Buttar, A. B., Stump, T. E., & Ricketts, G. D. (2007). Geriatric care management for low-income seniors: A randomized controlled trial. *JAMA, 298*(22), 2623–2633.

Cowles, L. A. (2003). *Social work in the health field: A care perspective.* New York, NY. Haworth Press.

Cowles, L. A., & Lefcowitz, M. J. (1995). Interdisciplinary expectations of the medical social worker in the hospital setting. Part 2. *Health & Social Work, 20*(4), 279–286.

Cummings, S. R., & Jackson, D. L. (2000). Hospital discharge planning. In R. L. Schneider, N. P. Kropf, & A. J. Kisor (Eds.), *Gerontological social work: Knowledge, service settings, and special populations* (2nd ed., pp. 191–224). Belmont, CA: Brooks-Cole.

Cutler, L. J. (2000). Assessment of physical environments of older adults. In R. L. Kane & R. A. Kane (Eds.), *Assessing older persons: Measures, meanings, and practical applications* (pp. 360–382). New York, NY: Oxford University Press.

Degenholtz, H. D., Kane, R. A., & Kivnick, H. Q. (1997). Care-related preferences and values of elderly community-based LTC consumers: Can case managers learn what is important to clients? *Gerontologist, 37*(6), 767–776.

De Jonge, K. E., Taler, G., & Boling, P.A. (2009). Independence at home: community-based care for older adults with severe chronic illness. *Clinical Geriatric Medicine, 25*(1), 155–169.

Department of Health and Human Services. (1999). *The Surgeon General's call to action to prevent suicide*. Washington, DC: Author. Retrieved from www .surgeongeneral.gov/library/calltoaction/default.htm

Diwan, S. (1999). Allocation of case management resources in long-term care: Predicting high use of case management time. *Gerontologist, 39*(5), 580–590.

Diwan, S. (2008). Limited English proficiency, patterns of social integration, and depressive symptoms among older Asian Indian immigrants in the U.S. *Journal of Gerontology: Social Sciences, 63B*(3), S184–S191.

Donaldson, M. S., Yordy, K. D., Lohr, K. N., & Vaneselow, N. A. (Eds.). (1996). *Primary care: America's health in new era*. Washington, DC: National Academy Press.

Douglas, K. C., & Lenahan, P. (1994). Ethnogeriatric assessment clinic in family medicine. *Family Medicine, 26,* 372–375.

Dyeson, T. B. (2004). The home health care social worker: A conduit in the care continuum for older adults. *Home Health Care Management & Practice, 16*(4), 290–292.

Dziegielewski, S. (2004). *The changing face of health social work: Professional practice in managed behavioral health care* (2nd ed.). New York, NY: Springer.

Elliott, S., Painter, J., & Hudson, S. (2009). Living alone and fall risk factors in community-dwelling middle age and older adults. *Journal of Community Health, 34,* 301–310.

Ewing, J. A. (1984). Detecting alcoholism: The CAGE questionnaire. *JAMA, 252,* 1905–1907.

Fillenbaum, G. G., & Smyer, M. A. (1981). The development, validity, and reliability of the OARS Multidimensional Functional Assessment Questionnaire. *Journal of Gerontology, 36,* 428–434.

Finch-Guthrie, P. (2000) Care planning for older adults in health care settings. In R. L. Kane & R. A. Kane (Eds.), *Assessing older persons: Measures, meanings, and practical applications* (pp. 406–437). New York, NY: Oxford University Press.

Folkman, S., & Moskowitz, J. T. (2000). Positive affect and the other side of coping. *American Psychologist, 55*(6), 647–654.

Folstein, M. F., Folstein, S. E., & McHugh, P. R. (1975). Mini-mental State: A practical method for grading the cognitive state of patients for the clinician. *Journal of Psychiatric Research, 12,* 189–198.

Gaugler, J. E., Kane, R. A., & Langlois, J. (2000). Assessment of family caregivers of older adults. In R. L. Kane & R. A. Kane (Eds.), *Assessing older persons: Measures, meanings, and practical applications* (pp. 320–359). New York, NY: Oxford University Press.

Gerdner, L. A., Xiong, X., & Yang, D. (2006). Working with Hmong American families. In G. Yeo & D. Gallagher-Thompson (Eds.), *Ethnicity and the dementias* (pp. 209–230). New York, NY: Routledge.

Gorder, A. C., & Ellor, J. W. (2008). Ethnogeriatrics and comparative religions methods for gerontological research into topics of religion and spirituality. *Journal of Religion, Spirituality & Aging, 20*(3), 206–219.

Graham, C. L., Ivey, S. L., & Neuhauser, L. (2009). From hospital to home: assessing the transitional care needs of vulnerable seniors. *Gerontologist, 49*(1), 23–33.

Grann, J. D. (2000). Assessment of emotions in older adults: Mood disorders, anxiety, psychological well-being, and hope. In R. L. Kane & R. A. Kane (Eds.), *Assessing older persons: Measures, meanings, and practical applications* (pp. 129–169). New York, NY: Oxford University Press.

Handelman, L., & Yeo, G. (1996). Using explanatory models to understand chronic symptoms of Cambodian refugees. *Family Medicine, 28*(4), 271–276.

The Hartford. (2005). *We need to talk…Family conversations with older drivers.* Retrieved from www.thehartford.com/talkwitholderdrivers/brochure/brochure.htm

Hasnain-Wynia, R., & Baker, D. W. (2006). Obtaining Data on patient race, ethnicity, and primary language in health care organizations: Current challenges and proposed solutions. *Health Services Research, 41*(4), 1501–1518.

Holliman, D. C., Dziegielewsk, S. F., & Datta, P. (2001). Discharge planning and social work practice. *Social Work in Health Care, 32*(3), 1–19.

Hooyman, N., & Kiyak, A. (2002). *Social gerontology: A multidisciplinary perspective* (6th ed.). Boston, MA: Allyn & Bacon.

Iecovich, E. (2000). Sources of stress and conflicts between elderly patients, their family members and personnel in care settings. *Journal of Gerontological Social Work, 34,* 73–88.

Jakubiak, C., & Callhan, J. (1995–1996). Treatment of mental disorder among nursing home residents: Will the market provide? *Generations, 19*(4), 39–42.

Johnson, K., Elbert-Avila, K. I., & Tulsky, J. (2005). The influence of spiritual beliefs and practices on the treatment preferences of African Americans: A review of the literature. *Journal of American Geriatrics Society, 53*(4), 711–719.

Kadushin, G. (2004). Home health care utilization: A review of the research for social work. *Health & Social Work, 29,* 219–244.

Kadushin, G., & Egan, M. (2001). Ethical dilemmas in home health care: A social work perspective. *Health & Social Work, 26*(3), 136–161.

Kanaan, B. K. (2009). *The CHCF care transition projects: Final progress report and meeting summary.* Retrieved from http://www.chcf.org/projects/2009/coleman-care-transitions-intervention

Kane, R. A. (2000). Values and preferences. In R. L. Kane & R. A. Kane (Eds.), *Assessing older persons: Measures, meanings, and practical applications* (pp. 237– 260). New York, NY: Oxford University Press.

Kane, R. A., Caplan, A., Urv-Wong, E., Freeman, I., Aroskar, M. A. & Finch, M. (1997). Everyday matters in the lives of nursing home residents: Wish for and perception of choice and control. *Journal of the American Geriatrics Society, 45*(9), 1086–1093.

Kane, R. L. (2000a). Choosing and using an assessment tool. In R. L. Kane & R. A. Kane (Eds.), *Assessing older persons: Measures, meanings, and practical applications* (pp. 237–260). New York, NY: Oxford University Press.

Kane, R. L. (2000b). Mandated assessments. In R. L. Kane & R. A. Kane (Eds.), *Assessing older persons: Measures, meanings, and practical applications* (pp. 458–482). New York, NY: Oxford University Press.

Kane, R. L. (2000c). Physiological well-being and health. In R. L. Kane, & R. A. Kane (Eds.), *Assessing older persons: Measures, meanings, and practical applications* (pp. 237–260). New York, NY: Oxford University Press.

Kane, R. L., & Kane, R. A. (Eds.). (2000). *Assessing older persons: Measures, meanings, and practical applications.* New York, NY: Oxford University Press.

Kaplan, M. S., Adamek, M. E., & Rhoades, J. A. (1998). Prevention of elderly suicide: Physicians' Assessment of firearm availability. *American Journal of Preventive Medicine, 15,* 60–64.

Katz, S., Ford, A. B., Moskowitz, R. W., Jackson, B. A., Jaffe, M. W., & Cleveland, M. A. (1963). Studies of illness in the aged: The index of ADL—a standardized measure of biological and psychosocial function. *JAMA, 185,* 914–919.

Kleinman, A. (2004). Culture and depression. *New England Journal of Medicine, 351*(10), 951–953.

Koenig, H. G. (1990). Research on religion and mental health in later life: A review and commentary. *Journal of Geriatric Psychiatry, 23*(1), 23–53.

Krause, N. (1995). Negative interaction and satisfaction with social support among older adults. *Journal of Gerontology,* Series B: *Psychological Sciences & Social Sciences, 50,* 59–74.

Kruzich, J. M., & Powell, W. E. (1995). Decision-making influence: An empirical study of social workers in nursing homes. *Health & Social Work, 20*(3), 215–223.

Lee, J. S., & Gutheil, I. A. (2003). The older patient at home: Social work services and home health care. In B. Berkman & L. Harootyan, *Social work and health care in an aging society: Education, policy, practice and research* (pp. 73–95). New York, NY: Springer.

Levin, J. S. (1994). Religion and health: Is there an association, is it valid, and is it causal? *Social Science and Medicine, 38,* 1475–1482.

Lin, K.-M. (1980). Traditional Chinese medical beliefs and their relevance for mental illness and psychiatry. In A. Kleinman & T.-Y. Lin (Eds.), *Normal and abnormal behavior in Chinese culture* (pp. 95–111). Dordrecht, Holland: D. Reidel.

Linsk, N. L. (2000). HIV Among older adults: Age-specific issues in prevention and treatment. *AIDS Reader, 10*(7), 430–440.

Liu, K., Manton, K. G., & Aragon, C. (2000). Changes in home care use by disabled elderly persons 1982–1994. *Journal of Gerontology–Series B Psychological Sciences and Social Sciences, 55*(4), S245–S253. doi: 10./1093/geronb/55.4

Lubben, J. E. (1988). Assessing social networks among elderly populations. *Family Community Health, 11*(3), 42–52.

Masand, P. S. (1995). Depression in long-term care facilities. *Geriatrics, 50*(Suppl. 1), S16–S24.

Mathias, S., Nayak, U. S. & Isaacs, B. (1986). Balance in elderly patients: The "get up and go" test. *Archives of Physical Medicine and Rehabilitation, 67*(6), 387–389.

Matthias, R. E., Lubben, J. E., Atchison, K. A., & Schweitzer, S. O. (1997). Sexual activity and satisfaction among very old adults: Results from a community-dwelling Medicare population survey. *Gerontologist, 37,* 6–14.

Maynard, G., & Stein, J. (2008). *Preventing hospital-acquired venous thromboembolism: A guide for effective quality improvement.* Rockville, MD: Agency for Healthcare Research and Quality.

McBride, M. R., & Lewis, I. D. (2004). African American and Asian American elders: An ethnogeriatric perspective. In J. J. Fitzpatrick (Ed.), *Annual review of nursing research* (Vol. 22) (pp. 161–214). New York, NY: Springer.

McBride, M. R., Morioka-Douglas, N., & Yeo, G. (1996). *Aging and health: Asian and Pacific Island American elders* (SGEC Working Paper Series No. 3, 2nd ed.). Stanford, CA: Stanford Geriatric Education Center.

McInnis-Dittrich, K. (2009). *Social work with older adults* (3rd ed.) Boston, MA: Allyn and Bacon.

Min, J. W. (2005). Cultural competency: A key to effective future social work with racially and ethnically diverse elders. *Families in Society: Journal of Contemporary Social Services, 86*(3), 347–358.

Mojtabal, R., & Olfson, M. (2003). Medication costs, adherence, and health outcomes among Medicare beneficiaries. *Health Affairs, 22*(4), 220–229.

Moody, H. R. (2004). Hospital discharge planning: Carrying out orders? *Journal of Gerontological Social Work, 43*(1), 107–118.

Nathanson, I., & Tirrito, T. (1998). *Gerontological social work: Theory into practice.* New York, NY: Springer.

National Association for Home Health Care and Hospice. (2008). *Basic statistics about home care.* Washington, DC: Author.

National Association of Social Workers. (2003). Lesbian, gay, and bisexual issues. *Social work speaks: National Association of Social Workers policy statements, 2003–2006* (6th ed., pp. 224–235). Washington, DC: NASW Press.

National Center for Health Statistics. (2004). Health status of older adult. Findings from National Health and Nutrition Examination Survey 1999–2004. Retrieved from http://media.pfizer.com/files/products/The_Health _Status_of_Older_Adults_2007.pdf

National Center for Health Statistics. (2008). *End of life care.* Report by National Nursing Home Survey, No. 9 (pp. 1–24). Washington, DC: Centers for Disease Control and Prevention.

National Center on Elder Abuse. (2004). NCEA: The source of information and assistance on elder abuse. Retrieved from www.elderabusecenter.org

National Institute on Aging. (2004). *General information: How many Americans have AD?* Alzheimer's Disease Education & Referral Center. Retrieved from www .alzheimers.org/generalinfo.htm

National Nursing Home Survey (2004). Retrieved from www.cdc.gov/nchs/nnhs.htm

Naylor, M. D., & Keating, S. A. (2008). Transitional care: Moving patients from one care setting to another. *American Journal of Nursing, 8*(9), 58–63.

Netting, E. F. (1992). Case management: Service or symptom? *Social Work, 37*(2), 160–164.

Oktay, J. S. (1995). Primary health care. In R. L. Edwards (Ed.), *The encyclopedia of social work* (19th ed., pp. 1887–1894). Washington, DC: NASW Press.

Olson, D. M., & Kane, R. A. (2000). Spiritual assessment. In R. L. Kane & R. A. Kane (Eds.), *Assessing older persons: Measures, meanings, and practical applications* (pp. 300–319). New York, NY: Oxford University Press.

Organista, K. C. (2009). New practice model for Latinos in need of social work services. *Social Work, 54*(4), 297–305.

Parry, C., Coleman, E., Smith, J., Frank, J., & Kramer, A. (2003). The care transitions intervention: A patient-centered approach to ensuring effective transfers between sites of geriatric care. *Home Health Services Quarterly, 22*(3), 1–17.

Parry, C., Kramer, H., & Coleman, E. A. (2006). A qualitative exploration of a patient-centered coaching intervention to improve care transitions in chronically ill older adults. *Home Health Care Services Quarterly, 25*(3–4), 39–53.

Pearson, V. I. (2000). Assessment of function in older adults. In R. L. Kane & R. A. Kane (Eds.), *Assessing older persons: Measures, meanings, and practical applications* (pp. 17–48). New York, NY: Oxford University Press.

Pinquart, M., & Sörensen, S. (2005). Ethnic differences in stressors, resources, and psychological outcomes of family caregiving: A meta-analysis. *Gerontologist, 45*(1), 90–106.

Raleigh, E. H., & Boehm, S. (1994). Development of a Multidimensional Hope Scale. *Journal of Nursing, 2*(2), 155–167.

Reisberg, B., Ferris, S. H., de Leon, M. J., & Crook, T. (1982). The Global Deterioration Scale for assessment of primary degenerative dementia. *American Journal of Psychiatry, 139,* 1136–1139.

Rhoades, J., & Sommers, J. P. (2003). Trends in nursing home expenses, 1987–1996. *Health Care Financing Review, 25*(1), 99–114.

Robinson, B. (1983). Validation of a Caregiver Strain Index. *Journal of Gerontology. 38,* 344–348.

Rosich, R. M. (2007). The human mosaic. Cultural beliefs and health professions training. *Annals of the New York Academy of Sciences, 1114,* 310–316.

Ross, J. W. (1995). Hospital work. In R. L. Edwards (Ed.), *The encyclopedia of social work,* (19th ed., pp. 1365–1377). Washington, DC: NASW Press.

Rossi, P. (1999). *Case management in health care.* Philadelphia, PA: WB. Saunders.

Sarason, I. G., Levine, H. M., Basham, R. B., & Sarason, B. R. (1983). Assessing social support: The Social Support Questionnaire. *Journal of Personality and Social Psychology, 44*(1), 127–139. doi: 10.1037/0022–3514.44.1.127

Shah, P. N., Maly, R. C., Frank, J. C., Hirsch, S. H., & Reuben, D. B. (1997). Managing geriatric syndromes: What geriatric assessment teams recommend, what primary care physicians implement, what patients adhere to. *Journal of the American Geriatrics Society, 45,* 413–419.

Siegler, I. C., Poon, L. W., Madden, D. J., & Welsh, K. A. (1996). Psychological aspects of normal aging. In E. W. Busse & D. G. Blazer (Eds.), *The American Psychiatric Press textbook of geriatric psychiatry* (2nd ed., pp. 105–128). Washington, DC: American Psychiatric Press.

Spector, W. D., Fleishman, J. A., Pezzin, L. E., & Spillman, B. C. (2000, September). *The characteristics of long-term care users* (AHRQ Publication No. 00–0049). Agency for Healthcare Research and Policy, Rockville, MD. Retrieved from http://www.ahrq.gov/research/ltcusers/

Stanford Geriatric Education Center. (2001). *Curriculum in ethnogeriatrics. Core curriculum and ethnic-specific modules.* Retrieved from http://www.stanford.edu/group/ethnoger/index.html

Stutts, J., Martell, C., & Staplin, L. (2009). Identifying behaviors and situations associated with increased crash risk for older drivers. Washington, DC: Office of Behavioral Safety Research, National Highway Traffic Safety Administration. Report No. DOT HS 811 093.

Talley, R. C., & Crew, J. E. (2007). Framing the public health of caregiving. *American Journal of Public Health, 97*(2), 224–228.

Teri, L., Truax, P., Logsdon, R., Uomoto, J., Zarit, S., & Vitaliano, P. P. (1992). Assessment of behavioral problems in dementia: The Revised Memory and Behavior Problems Checklist. *Psychology of Aging, 7,* 622–631.

Thrope, M., Patterson, M. E., & Sleath, B. L. (2006). Psychological distress as a barrier to preventive care in community-dwelling elderly in the United States. *Medical Care, 44*(2), 187–191.

Tirrito, T. (1996). Mental health problems and behavioral disruptions in nursing homes: Are social workers prepared to provide needed services? *Journal of Gerontological Social Work, 27*(1–2), 73–87.

Tran, T. V., Ngo, D., & Conway, K. (2003). A cross-cultural measure of depressive symptoms among Vietnamese Americans. *Social Work Research, 27,* 56–65.

U.S. Department of Health and Human Services. (1999). *Mental health: A report of the Surgeon General.* Rockville, MD: Author. Retrieved from www.surgeongeneral.gov/library/mentalhealth/home.html

U.S. Census Bureau, (2004). *The Older population in the United States: March 2002.* Retrieved from www.census.gov/hhes/www/housing/homeown/tab4.html

Unger, J. B., McAvay, G., Bruce, M. L., Berkman, L., & Seeman, T. (1999) Variation in the impact of social network characteristics on physical functioning in elderly persons: MacArthur Studies of Successful Aging. *The Journals of Gerontology: Series B, 54*(5): S245-51.

Uncapher, H., Gallagher-Thompson, D., Osgood, N., & Bonger, B. (1998). Hopelessness and suicidal ideation in older adults. *Gerontologist, 38*(1), 62–70.

Underwood, L., & Teresi, J. (2002). The Daily Spiritual Experience Scale: Development, theoretical description, reliability, exploratory factor analysis, and preliminary construct validity using health-related data. *Annals of Behavioral Medicine, 24*(1), 22–33.

Urdangarin, C. F. (2000). Comprehensive geriatric assessment and management. In R. L. Kane & R. A. Kane (Eds.), *Assessing older persons: Measures, meanings, and practical applications* (pp. 383–405). New York, NY: Oxford University Press.

Van Craen, K., Braes, T., Wellens, N., Denhaerynck, K., Flamaing, J., Moons, P.,...Milisen, K. (2010). The effectiveness of inpatient geriatric evaluation and management units: A systematic review and meta-analysis. *Journal of the American Geriatrics Society, 58,* 83–92. doi: 10.1111/j.1532–5415.2009.02621.x

Vinton, L., Mazza, N., & Kim Y. (1998). Aggression perpetrated by family members in nursing homes: An investigation of dynamics and interventions. *Clinical Gerontologist, 19,* 45–68.

Vourlekis, B. S., Gelfand, D., & Greene, R. R. (1992). Psychosocial needs and care in nursing homes: Comparison of views of social workers and home administrators. *Gerontologist, 32*(1), 113–119.

Wall, J. C., Bell, C., Campbell, S., & Davis, J. (2000). The timed Get-up-and-go Test revisited: Measurement of the component tasks. *Journal of Rehabilitation Research and Development, 37* (1), 109–114.

Ware, J. E., & Sherbourne, C. D. (1992). The MOS 36-item short form health survey (SF-36). Conceptual framework and item selection. *Medical Care, 30,* 473–483.

Widlitz, M., & Marin, D. B. (2002). Substance abuse in older adults: An overview. *Geriatrics, 57*(12), 29–34.

Wieland, D., & Hirth, V. (2003). Comprehensive geriatric assessment. *Cancer Control, 10*(6), 454–462.

Wiley, D., & Bortz, W. M. (1996). Sexuality and aging—Usual and successful. *Journals of Gerontology, 51,* M142–M146.

Xakellies, G., Brangman, S. A., Hinton, W. L., Jones, V. Y., Masterman, D., Pan, C. X.,...Yeo, G. (2004). Curricular framework: Core competencies in multicultural geriatric care. *Journal of American Geriatric Society, 52*(1), 137–142.

Yeo, G. (1996). Ethnogeriatrics: Cross-cultural care of older adults. *Generations, 20*(1), 72–77.

Yeo, G. (2009). How will the U.S. health care system meet the challenge of the ethnographic imperative? *Journal of American Geriatric Society, 57*(7), 1278–1285.

Yeo, G., David, D., & Llorens, L. (1996). Faculty development in ethnogeriatrics. *Educational Gerontology, 22*(1), 79–91.

Yeo, G., Hikoyeda, N., McBride, M., Chin, S.-Y., Edmonds, M., & Hendrix, L. (1998). *Cohort analysis as a tool in ethnogeriatrics: Historical profiles of elders from eight ethnic populations in the United States* (SGEC Working Paper Series No.12). Stanford, CA: Stanford Geriatric Education Center.

17

Substance Use Problems in Health Social Work Practice

MALITTA ENGSTROM, COLLEEN A. MAHONEY, AND JEANNE C. MARSH

Substance use problems are widespread in our society and are present across diverse age, gender, sexual orientation, racial, cultural, and socioeconomic backgrounds. Social workers, regardless of the setting in which they work, are likely to encounter clients with substance use problems. Given the health effects of substance use, social workers in health-care settings are particularly likely to encounter this population. Whether patients present with physical illnesses directly related to substance use (e.g., cirrhosis of the liver) or with health problems with no obvious link to substance use, it is crucial that health social workers be aware of the potential role of substance use in clients' health, treatment, and social needs (Abbott, 2002). This chapter provides social workers with basic knowledge and core skills necessary to address substance use problems across a variety of clients and health-care settings.

Chapter Objectives

- Define terms and diagnostic categories used to describe substance use problems.
- Identify the prevalence of substance use and problems across sociodemographic groups.
- Present information about the psychoactive and health effects of substances that are commonly used.

- Provide an overview of practice and research regarding prominent approaches to assist people experiencing substance use problems.
- Provide general information to guide screening for substance use problems and brief intervention to address these problems in health-care settings.

DEFINITION OF TERMS

A variety of expressions are used to describe substance use problems in lay and professional writing and conversation. *Addiction, drug abuse*, and *alcoholism* are but a few common terms. It is widely agreed, however, that these and other terms are not always used in a consistent fashion (National Institute on Alcohol Abuse and Alcoholism [NIAAA], Center for Substance Abuse Prevention [CSAP], & Public Health Service, 1995; White, 1998). Yet the use of a stable vocabulary is essential. In addition, because of the particular role of health social workers as translators between health-care systems and patients (see Chapter 10 in this book for a discussion of communication), it is especially important to use language in a clear, concise, and consistent manner. This chapter begins with a clarification of terms and expressions.

This entire domain often is referred to as the substance abuse field or the addictions field (van Wormer & Davis, 2003). Although both labels provide a shortcut to describing

ACKNOWLEDGMENT: The authors thank Scott Petersen for his helpful comments on an earlier version of this chapter.

the field, it is important to note that they also can take on other meanings depending on the context. *Substance abuse*, although commonly used to denote a range of substance use problems, distinguishes a specific disorder in the *Diagnostic and Statistical Manual of Mental Disorders, Fourth Edition, Text Revision* (*DSM-IV-TR*; American Psychiatric Association, 2000). *Addiction* most commonly implies a severe level of problematic substance use that involves dependence and continued pursuit and use of substances in the midst of negative consequences. Furthermore, *addiction* often is applied to problematic behaviors other than substance use (e.g., gambling). In this chapter, the discussion is limited to the behavior of problematic psychoactive substance use; however, it is not restricted to substance use that meets the criteria for specific disorders but includes all levels of problematic use. Accordingly, the expression *substance use problems* is used to designate the entire range of problematic substance use. At times, when brevity and grammar require it, the term *substance abuse* is used in a general way to denote all levels of substance use problems.

The term *substance* refers to both legal and illegal psychoactive substances that affect the central nervous system (CNS) when consumed. Users experience pleasure or diminished pain through the alteration of mood, cognition, perception, memory, or consciousness. Alcohol, nicotine, and caffeine are legal psychoactive substances. The term *drug* is used most often to refer to illegal "street" psychoactive substances (e.g., marijuana, cocaine, heroin) and prescribed medications used illegally. The acronyms *AOD* (alcohol and other drugs) and *ATOD* (alcohol, tobacco, and other drugs), however, emphasize that alcohol and tobacco are themselves drugs. These acronyms assist in countering the popularly held myth that street drugs are different from, and more dangerous than, alcohol and tobacco. In this chapter, the term *substance* denotes both legal and illegal psychoactive substances. Although caffeine, a stimulant, is widely used, it "does not ordinarily pose a threat to health or an impairment to functioning" (McNeece & Barbanell, 2005,

p. 16) and therefore is not included in the discussion of legal drugs.

Certain levels of problematic substance use do not meet the criteria for a diagnosable disorder but nonetheless may require attention. Standard terminology exists for designating amount of use and potential risk. For example, research on and clinical screening for problematic alcohol use generally defines current use as at least one drink in the past 30 days, binge use as five or more drinks on the same occasion at least once in the past 30 days, and heavy use as five or more drinks on the same occasion at least five different days in the past 30 days, according to the Substance Abuse and Mental Health Services Administration [SAMHSA] (2009). However, NIAAA (2004a) recently has revised the definition of *binge drinking* to consumption that elevates blood alcohol concentration (BAC) to .08 gram percent and higher. This BAC is typically achieved among men by consuming five drinks or more in a 2-hour period and among women by consuming four drinks or more in a 2-hour period.

Intoxication, withdrawal, craving, tolerance, dependence, and *addiction* are important terms that describe various aspects of the experience of using psychoactive substances. *Intoxication* describes a reversible state caused by the recent use of a substance that typically is characterized by a substance-specific constellation of physiological, behavioral, and cognitive-emotional changes. *Withdrawal,* however, describes substance-specific behavioral, physiological, and cognitive-emotional changes that result from stopping or reducing substance use, particularly when use has been significant and long term. *Withdrawal* typically involves the opposite experiences that are associated with intoxication of the substance consumed (e.g., the euphoria of cocaine intoxication is countered by feelings of depression in cocaine withdrawal) and occurs with these psychoactive substances: alcohol; nicotine; cocaine; opioids; amphetamines and related substances; and sedatives, hypnotics, or anxiolytics. *Craving,* or the intense desire to use the substance, often occurs while in the state of withdrawal to alleviate symptoms (American Psychiatric Association, 2000). After using a substance over time, individuals develop tolerance when they must use more of the substance to achieve the same effect previously achieved with a smaller amount (Wilcox & Erickson, 2005). The terms *addiction* and *dependence* are not defined consistently. As noted by O'Brien and Volkow (2006), it is important to distinguish between the normal physical dependence that is associated with numerous psychoactive medications (e.g., opioids, beta-blockers, and antidepressants) and addiction. Tolerance and withdrawal, which are anticipated physiological responses to numerous psychoactive substances, do not necessarily indicate that a person is experiencing addiction, which involves problematic pursuit of drugs despite negative consequences. Such confusion, according to O'Brien and Volkow, can keep clinicians from providing appropriate pain medication when clients display tolerance and withdrawal even though addiction is not present. In addition, they argue, some clients may needlessly avoid appropriate pain medication because they equate physical dependence with addiction. Finally it is important to note that the *DSM* diagnosis of substance dependence does not necessarily require the experience of tolerance or withdrawal (American Psychiatric Association, 2000).

DIAGNOSTIC CATEGORIES

The *DSM-IV-TR* (American Psychiatric Association, 2000) classifies substance-related disorders into two groups. *Substance use disorders* are defined by a pattern of problematic substance use and include the diagnostic categories of substance abuse and substance dependence. *Substance-induced disorders* refer to the patterns of physiological, behavioral, cognitive, and emotional responses to substance ingestion and substance use cessation. These include substance intoxication and substance withdrawal as well as substance-induced mental disorders (e.g., delirium, persisting dementia, persisting amnestic disorder,

psychotic disorder, mood disorder, anxiety disorder, sexual dysfunction, sleep disorder).

The *DSM-IV-TR* (American Psychiatric Association, 2000) provides general criteria that apply across substances for substance abuse, dependence, intoxication, and withdrawal. In addition, it provides specific information for each of these diagnoses across 11 different classes of substances. This section describes general criteria for substance use disorders.

Substance Abuse

This disorder is characterized by repeated use of a substance that leads to negative consequences but is not severe enough to meet the criteria for substance dependence diagnosis. Nicotine and caffeine are not included among the substances that can meet criteria for abuse. Specific *DSM-IV-TR* criteria for substance abuse can be found in the *Diagnostic and Statistical Manual of Mental Disorders, Fourth Edition, Text Revision* (American Psychiatric Association, 2000).

Substance Dependence

This disorder is characterized by a constellation of symptoms indicating that the individual continues to use the substance although significant negative consequences result. The individual repeatedly seeks and consumes the substance and may experience tolerance for and withdrawal from the substance. Individuals who meet the criteria for substance dependence disorder are not diagnosed with substance abuse disorder. Specific criteria can be found in the *Diagnostic and Statistical Manual of Mental Disorders, Fourth Edition, Text Revision* (American Psychiatric Association, 2000).

The terms *alcoholism* and *drug addiction* are generally interchangeable with *substance dependence*. *Alcoholic* and *addict* are terms used to describe the person with alcohol dependence disorder or another substance (generally illegal) dependence disorder, respectively. These terms are part of a common vocabulary within many self-help groups, such as Alcoholics Anonymous (AA), and can be important identifying labels for those active in these groups. Nonetheless, these labels also can be stigmatizing. It is preferable to replace the terms *alcoholic* and *addict* with person-first language, such as "a person experiencing alcohol (or other substance) dependence." Person-first language, which often is used with other physical, psychological, and developmental conditions, assists in conveying the fact that the health condition does not define the person's entire identity. In addition, such language assists with emphasizing that one is a person rather than a health condition. There are efforts under way to replace the term *substance dependence* with *addiction* in the development of the *DSM-5* (O'Brien & Volkow, 2006). If such change occurs, person-first language that describes a person experiencing addiction still can be employed.

COMMONLY USED SUBSTANCES

Media representations of substance abuse tend to convey stereotypes that focus on people with limited incomes in inner cities selling and using illegal drugs (Cornelius, 2002). Although there is no question that drug use is a problem for the inner city, its reach and magnitude go far beyond the confines of urban areas with high rates of poverty and include diverse racial, cultural, gender, and income groups. Furthermore, the use of legal drugs—tobacco and alcohol—across socioeconomic groups and regions represents the most prevalent and costly component of drug-related problems (SAMHSA, 2009). This section provides information about the epidemiology and the psychoactive and health effects of legal and illegal substances that are commonly used in problematic ways.

Alcohol

The 2008 NSDUH indicates that just over half of all Americans 12 years and older report current use of alcohol (SAMHSA, 2009). More than 50% of American adults have a close family member who has met the diagnostic criteria for alcohol dependence (Dawson & Grant, 1998). Among children younger than 18 years in the United States, approximately 1 in 4 is exposed to alcohol abuse or alcohol dependence in the family (Grant, 2000). In the United States and worldwide, alcohol is one of the most widely used and dangerous drugs. Problematic use of alcohol leads to deleterious effects on biological, psychological, and social well-being. Furthermore, its effects may extend beyond the individuals engaged in problematic alcohol use to their families and communities.

Alcohol is a CNS depressant that, unlike many other psychoactive substances, is thought to affect multiple CNS neurotransmitter systems (Moak & Anton, 1999). Kranzler and Anton (1994) suggest that the relationships between alcohol and neurotransmitter systems are likely to vary across subtypes of persons with alcohol use problems. Relatedly, individuals vary in their levels of vulnerability toward alcohol use disorders. Research suggests that genetics account for approximately 60% of total vulnerability (Prescott & Kendler, 1999). Thus, close relatives of persons with alcohol use disorders should be educated about their increased risk.

Epidemiology

The 2008 NSDUH indicates that young adults age 18 to 25 years experience the highest rates of problem drinking (SAMHSA, 2009). Approximately 41% of this group reported binge drinking in the past month, and 14.5% reported heavy alcohol use in the same time period. Within this group, men were more likely than women to report binge (48.4% versus 33.6%) and heavy (19.9% versus 9.0%) alcohol use. Asian American young adults were least likely to report binge (24.9%) and heavy (6.4%) use. White American young adults age 18 to 25 years reported the highest rates of problematic alcohol use (47.1% and 18.1% for binge and heavy use, respectively).

In the same survey, adolescents age 12 to 17 years reported alcohol use at rates that are cause for concern. Approximately 30.8% used alcohol in the past year, and 8.8% of the same group had engaged in binge drinking in the past month. Gender differences in drinking rates were less significant among adolescents than among young adults. Interestingly, girls age 12 to 17 years reported greater lifetime alcohol use than boys (39.1% versus 37.6%). Rates of past-month binge use were comparable for boys and girls (8.9% and 8.7%, respectively). Among diverse racial/ethnic groups, Asian adolescents reported the lowest rates of lifetime use (25.2%) and past-month binge use (2.0%). African American youth also reported relatively low binge use rates (4.0%). American Indian, Hispanic, and White American adolescents reported the highest levels of lifetime use (46.6%, 39.3%, and 39.8%, respectively).

After a peak in young adulthood, rates of alcohol use, binge use, and heavy use slowly decline as people age (SAMHSA, 2009). Between the ages of 26 and 64 years, current alcohol use decreases from 67.4% to 50.3%. Likewise, rates of binge and heavy alcohol use slowly decrease as adults become older (from 42.6% to 14.6% for binge drinking and from 13.2% to 3.6% for heavy drinking). Men and women age 26 years and older differed in their reported rates of binge drinking (31.7% versus 13.2%). Among racial groups within the same age range, Hispanic adults report the highest rate of binge drinking (26.4%), Asian adults report the lowest rate of binge drinking (10.7%), and all other racial groups report rates between 21.4% and 24.0%.

Over 8% (8.2%) of adults 65 years and older reported binge drinking, and 2.2% reported heavy drinking (SAMHSA, 2009). Although these rates are relatively low when compared with younger and middle-age adults, alcohol use in older populations constitutes a serious problem that should not be overlooked. Older adults have unique vulnerabilities that put them at greater risk of negative outcomes when using even relatively small amounts of alcohol. For example, individuals in this group may reach higher BAC with less alcohol consumption than individuals in other groups (NIAAA, 2004a). In addition, alcohol use may increase the risk of falls among older adults, and recovery from such incidents can be difficult (Center for Substance Abuse Treatment [CSAT], 1998).

Health Effects

The health effects of alcohol use are wide ranging and staggering. Alcohol has an effect on multiple organs and systems and is associated with several types of cancer. Illnesses that are a direct result of or are severely exacerbated by alcohol use account for 20% to 40% of patients in urban hospitals (NIAAA, 2000). Alcohol often is involved in episodes of violence, injury, and trauma, which leads to significant and repeated contacts with the health-care system. Research suggests that alcohol is associated with 67% of partner assaults, 50% of homicides, 40% of traffic fatalities, and 37% of rapes (NIAAA, 2000). Perhaps the most telling evidence of alcohol's negative impact on health is the fact that average life span is decreased by 10 to 15 years for persons with alcohol dependence (Schuckit & Tapert, 2004).

Considerable research demonstrates that chronic heavy drinking is a leading cause of cardiovascular illnesses (NIAAA, 2000). In fact, heart disease is the leading cause of early mortality among those with alcohol dependence (Schuckit & Tapert, 2004). Men with alcohol dependence are two times more likely than men without alcohol dependence to die from atherosclerotic and degenerative heart disease; women with alcohol dependence are four times more likely to die from these diseases than those who do not have alcohol dependence (McNeece & DiNitto, 2005). Based on a review of available evidence, the Dietary Guidelines Advisory Committee (DGAC, 2010), appointed by the U.S. Drug Administration (USDA) and the U.S. Department of Health and Human Services (DHHS), cites the association between low to moderate amounts of drinking (i.e., average alcohol consumption of not more than two drinks per day for men and one drink per day for women) and reduced risk of coronary heart disease, diabetes, and all causes of mortality among middle-age and older adults; however, as discussed by Williams, Mohammed, Leavell, and Collins (2010), African Americans, particularly African American men, do not experience the same gains. In addition, the effects of even low or moderate levels of alcohol on risk of breast cancer, colon cancer, liver cancer, and unintentional injuries complicate the risk-benefit considerations of alcohol use. It should be noted that gender, diet, lifestyle, and other health factors may differentially influence the relationship between alcohol and these cancers (DGAC, 2010).

Liver disease commonly is associated with alcohol use. According to the 10th Special Report to the U.S. Congress on Alcohol and Health (NIAAA, 2000), "long-term heavy alcohol use is the leading cause of illness and death from liver disease in the United States" (p. 198). The liver is central to human survival and health because it both processes key nutrients and assists the body's defense system to filter toxins from the blood. Long-term moderate to heavy alcohol use is associated with changes in the liver that are described in three phases, together known as alcoholic liver disease. Fatty liver, the first phase of the disease, is generally reversible with abstinence. The second phase of alcoholic liver disease, alcoholic hepatitis, is characterized by inflammation of the liver. Cirrhosis, or scarring of the liver, is the final phase of this disease. The prognosis for persons who have both alcoholic hepatitis and cirrhosis is poor, with a death rate over a four-year period greater than 60% (Chedid et al., 1991). Alcohol also plays a significant role in other types of liver diseases. For example, alcohol consumption may enhance acetaminophen liver toxicity, and although the specific mechanism is unknown, alcohol consumption is associated with greater severity of hepatitis C (NIAAA, 2000).

People who have alcohol dependence are at increased risk for cancer, especially of the head, neck, esophagus, and stomach; lung cancer occurs at higher rates in this group even after controlling for smoking status. Although not yet well understood at a physiological level, it is clear that heavy alcohol use has a significant effect on the immune system. Infections that are a result of immune deficiency, such as pneumonia, occur at higher rates among persons who are heavy alcohol users than among the general population. Human immunodeficiency virus (HIV) rates are higher among persons who abuse alcohol. Several factors may contribute to this finding, including high-risk sexual activity and injection drug use associated with alcohol use and alcohol's immune-suppressing effect, which may increase susceptibility to HIV.

Chronic alcohol use can lead to multiple neurological disorders. Neuropathy, a disorder of the nerves in which an individual experiences pain and numbness in the legs and feet, is associated with heavy alcohol use. Wernicke's syndrome and Korsakoff's psychosis also are related to heavy use. They often occur in combination and are characterized by confusion, inability to learn new material, and other cognitive deficits (McNeece & DiNitto, 2005).

Risk of fetal alcohol syndrome and other alcohol exposure–related disorders are of particular concern for women of childbearing age. Drinking alcohol during pregnancy increases the risk of spontaneous abortion, low birth weight, small brain volume, heart defects, varying levels of mental retardation, and facial abnormalities. Although binge drinking is associated with increased risk to the fetus, no amount of alcohol consumption during pregnancy has been established as safe (Stratton, Howe, & Battaglia, 1995).

Tobacco

Although it is common knowledge that tobacco is toxic and that its nicotine component is extremely addictive, tobacco use is not always included in the substance abuse literature. Nevertheless, no other psychoactive substance is associated with the morbidity and mortality of tobacco (Slade, 1999). The National Institute on Drug Abuse (NIDA, 2001a) reports that "tobacco kills more than 430,000 U.S. citizens each year—more than alcohol, cocaine, heroin, homicide, suicide, car accidents, fire, and AIDS [acquired immunodeficiency syndrome] combined" (p. 3). In spite of high rates of use, known negative health consequences, and the fact that treatment works (NIDA, 2001a), health providers rarely offer smokers assistance with quitting (U.S. Public Health Service [USPHS], 2000). Furthermore, individuals who have other substance use problems or serious mental illness are offered assistance with smoking cessation even less frequently, even though they may have a greater need for services than the general population (Grant, Hasin, Chou, Stinson, & Dawson, 2004).

The reasons for this treatment failure are complex. Until recently, few effective treatments for smoking cessation had been identified. Furthermore, health-care systems did not support their consistent delivery (USPHS, 2000). However, research conducted by Lemon, Friedman, and Stein (2003) with 2,316 participants from the Drug Abuse Treatment Outcome Study (DATOS) who reported consumption of cigarettes at the beginning of the study and who participated in follow-up interviews suggests that smoking cessation is positively associated with increased abstinence from illegal drug use 12 months after completing substance use treatment. Although it should be noted that those who smoke less were more likely to stop and that those who completed treatment were more likely to be in this sample, the research can "raise questions about the clinical myth that nicotine dependence should be treated only after stabilization of the primary drug dependence" (p. 1330). Similarly, smoking cessation efforts may be particularly relevant among people living with HIV, for whom smoking may negatively affect immune functioning over time and increase risk of infections of the respiratory tract (Chiasson, 1994).

Initial ingestion of nicotine can result in unpleasant experiences, such as headaches and nausea. Tolerance for these symptoms develops quickly, however, and regular users report that tobacco helps with relaxation and concentration (Slade, 1999). Addiction occurs with regular use, and withdrawal symptoms, such as irritability, sleep disturbances, craving, and cognitive deficits, can occur for a month or more following cessation of use (NIDA, 2001a).

Epidemiology

The 2008 NSDUH estimated that 28.4% of the U.S. population 12 years and older were current users of tobacco products. Adolescents age 12 to 17 years reported current use rates of 11.4%. Boys were more likely than girls to report use (12.6% versus 10.2%). American Indian adolescents reported the highest rates of tobacco use (22.0%) and Asian youth the lowest rates (4.4%) of all racial groups.

Similar to patterns of alcohol use, current tobacco use rates peaked during young adulthood. Among persons age 18 to 25 years, 41.4% reported using tobacco in the past month. Rates of use among gender and racial groups in this age group varied similarly to those seen among adolescents. Men used at rates greater than women (48.8% versus 33.8%). Asian and African American young adults reported the lowest rates of current use (20.0% and 30.7%, respectively); American Indian and White American young adults reported the highest rates of current use (52.8% and 47.5%).

Among people 26 years and older, 28.3% reported current tobacco use. Men continued to use at rates greater than women (35.0% versus 22.2%).

Health Effects

The negative effects of tobacco on health and the health-care system are legion. In fact, NIDA (2010b) reports that "tobacco use is the leading preventable cause of disease, disability, and death in the United States." Approximately 8.6 million Americans suffer from at least one serious illness caused by smoking, and annual estimates indicate that smoking is responsible for economic losses of $75 billion in excess medical expenditures (Centers for Disease Control and Prevention [CDC], 2004). Cigarette use is strongly associated with lung cancer, heart disease, and chronic obstructive pulmonary disease (emphysema and chronic bronchitis). Smokers are at increased risk for stroke and peripheral vascular disease, and many cancers of the mouth, throat, larynx, and esophagus are related to cigarette use (NIDA, 2001a; Slade, 1999). In 2001, NIDA (2001a) reported that "cigarette smoking is the most important preventable cause of cancer in the United States" (p. 5).

It is estimated that approximately 20% of pregnant women in the United States smoke throughout their pregnancies (NIDA, 2001a), an alarming statistic given that maternal smoking is associated with a variety of adverse pregnancy outcomes, including abruption of the placenta (separation from the uterine wall), low birth weight, premature delivery, and increased risk of sudden infant death syndrome (SIDS; NIDA, 2001a; Slade, 1999). In a large study examining the prenatal effects of multiple substances, Shiono and colleagues (1995) concluded, "[I]n the United States, cigarette smoking remains the single largest preventable cause of adverse pregnancy outcomes" (p. 26).

Cannabis

Among the U.S. population 12 years and older, approximately 10.3% and 6.1% reported marijuana use in the past year and month, respectively (SAMHSA, 2009). These prevalence rates make marijuana the most commonly used illegal drug. Literature examining the effects of marijuana is conflicting, and most purported findings are in need of replication. For example, some longitudinal studies have found that heavier marijuana use in adolescence is associated with less stability in adult roles (Kandel, Davies, Karus, & Yamaguchi, 1986); however, it is unclear whether these outcomes are due to marijuana use or if they are better explained by other substance use or preexisting differences between heavy marijuana users and others (Stephens, 1999).

Cannabis is most often smoked but sometimes is mixed into food. Users may experience mild euphoria, relaxation, and enhancement or distortion of perceptual experiences. Intoxication often involves impairment in attention and short-term memory. Typically lethargy and sleepiness occur as the effects wear off (Stephens, 1999). Addiction can occur as a result of long-term use in some people (NIDA, 2004a), and some authors report that clinicians are encountering "more marijuana-dependent patients than ever before" (Gold, Frost-Pineda, & Jacobs, 2004, p. 177).

Epidemiology

As previously noted, the 2008 NSDUH reported that 6.1% of persons 12 years and older were current users of marijuana. Among illicit-substance users specifically, 75.7% reported that they had used marijuana, making it the most commonly used illegal substance. This finding was true across broad age groups; however, it is interesting to note that 12- and 13-year-olds reported current use of psychotherapeutics (prescription-type medications used nonmedically; 1.5%) and inhalants (1.3%) at rates greater than marijuana (1.0%). Rates of cannabis use peaked for 18- to 25-year-olds, with 16.5% reporting current use. Male young adults reported higher current use rates (20.1%) than female young adults (12.8%). This gender difference continued among people 26 years and older, with 5.8% of men and 2.8% of women reporting current use. Among adolescents, the gender differences were in the same direction but were less substantial, with 7.3% of boys and 6.0% of girls reporting current use.

Asian and African American youth age 12 to 17 years reported the lowest rates of current use (1.0% and 5.9%, respectively), whereas youths who identified as two or more races or as White American reported the highest rates (10.6% and 7.2%, respectively). Among 18- to 25-year-olds, persons identifying as two or more races or as American Indian reported the highest rates of current use (22.8% and 20.4%, respectively), whereas White and African American young adults reported lower, but still substantial, rates of use (17.8% and 18.2%, respectively).

Health Effects

Few conclusive negative health effects directly related to marijuana use exist. One primary concern is related not to the psychoactive ingredients of marijuana but to the preferred mode of its administration (Stephens, 1999). Like tobacco, marijuana frequently is smoked and appears to pose similar health risks, such as increased rates of respiratory problems and cancer (NIDA, 2002a; Slade, 1999). Research examining marijuana use during pregnancy has produced mixed findings (Keegan, Parva, Finnegan, Gerson, & Belden, 2010). Some studies have shown that smoking marijuana during pregnancy is associated with low birth weight (Hatch & Bracken, 1986; Zuckerman et al., 1989); however, a large multicenter study found that when tobacco use was controlled for, marijuana use was not related to low birth weight or preterm delivery (Shiono et al., 1995).

Increasing attention is being given to the positive or medicinal effects of marijuana use; however, it is not without controversy. Proponents state that marijuana is effective in treating a range of symptoms associated with cancer, HIV/AIDS, multiple sclerosis, and glaucoma. Detractors emphasize the potential harm and suggest that medicalizing marijuana is simply a strategy to allow easier access for recreational use. By 2010, 15 states had active medical marijuana programs, but their laws stand in contrast to federal law, which prohibits all use of cannabis. A review of the evidence by the Institute of Medicine (IOM) culminated in a report issued in 1999. The report summarized research examining the effectiveness of marijuana to treat pain, wasting syndrome, nausea, muscle spasticity, movement disorders, epilepsy, and glaucoma. Evidence is strongest for alleviating pain, nausea, and appetite loss such that "for patients such as those with AIDS or who are undergoing chemotherapy, and who suffer simultaneously from severe pain, nausea, and appetite loss, cannabinoid drugs might offer broad-spectrum relief not found in any other single medication" (Joy, Watson, & Benson, 1999, p. 177). However, the report also is cautious to recommend smoking marijuana as "good medicine" (p. 177). Although tetrahydrocannabinol (THC), the active ingredient in marijuana, is shown to have therapeutic effects, marijuana also delivers other toxic substances, including

many found in tobacco smoke. Thus, the report recommends that future research include clinical trials with the aim of developing safer delivery systems of cannabinoid drugs.

Cocaine

Cocaine is a powerful stimulant currently used by approximately 0.7% of persons 12 years and older in the United States (SAMSHA, 2009). It is sold as a white powder or in crack form and can be snorted, injected, or smoked. Immediate effects include mental alertness; increased energy; euphoria; and increased heart rate, blood pressure, and body temperature. With high duration and doses of stimulants, individuals may experience stimulant delirium, which can include symptoms of disorientation, confusion, anxiety, and fear; in episodes of high doses, individuals also may experience symptoms of psychosis and paranoia and behavioral compulsions (Kosten & Sofuoglu, 2004).

The onset, duration, and intensity of these effects depend on the route of administration. For example, crack cocaine, easily made by cooking powder cocaine with water and ammonia or sodium bicarbonate (baking soda), is smoked, resulting in an intense high within a matter of seconds (Kosten & Sofuoglu, 2004; NIDA, 1999a). Snorting powder cocaine generally elicits effects within 20 minutes; intravenous injection generally elicits effects in 30 seconds (Kosten & Sofuoglu, 2004).

Epidemiology

In 2008, 14.7% of U.S. persons 12 years and older reported that they had used cocaine during their lifetimes. Men were more likely than women to report both lifetime use (17.7% versus 11.9%) and current use (1.0% versus 0.5%). Among adolescents 12 to 17 years old, however, girls reported greater lifetime use than boys (2.1% versus 1.7%), but boys reported greater current use (0.5% versus 0.3%). Youth who identified as being of two or more races or as White American reported a current cocaine use rate of 0.5%, the highest in this age group. The lowest rates of current use were reported by Asian (0.0%) and African American (0.1%) adolescents.

Current cocaine use peaked among 21-year-olds (2.3%). Young adult men (18–25 years old) reported current use rates of 1.8% whereas 1.3% of women age 18 to 25 years reported current use. As with adolescent racial groups, Asian and African American young adults reported the lowest rates of current cocaine use at 0.2% and 0.3%, respectively. This trend changed, however, among adults 26 years and older, with African Americans reporting the highest current use rate (1.2%).

Health Effects

Some of cocaine's health effects differ with the route of administration (NIDA, 2010a). For example, intranasal use (snorting) may result in nosebleeds, lost sense of smell, and a persistently runny nose, and injecting cocaine may result in allergic reactions and risk of contracting HIV and other blood-borne infections, including viral hepatitis. Sharing drug-related equipment for intranasal and inhalation use of cocaine also may increase the risk of contracting viral hepatitis (Aaron et al., 2008; Macias et al., 2008; NIDA, 2010a).

Heavy use of cocaine and other stimulants often results in health problems involving multiple systems. Cardiovascular and gastrointestinal illnesses are common, as are problems with the CNS and reproductive system (Weaver & Schnoll, 1999). Research suggests that cocaine is particularly dangerous when used in combination with alcohol. The body transforms cocaine and alcohol into a substance (cocaethylene) that is more toxic than either drug alone. This mixture results in more deaths than any other two-drug combination (NIDA, 1999a).

Some have argued that the primary negative effects of problematic cocaine use are psychological and social rather than physiological (Weil & Rosen, 1993), but it is important to note that cocaine abuse is associated with acute cardiovascular and cerebrovascular events, including heart attack and stroke, that may result in death (NIDA, 2010a). Two recent studies—one in New Mexico and one in British Columbia—found elevated rates of cocaine overdose since the 1990s (Buxton et al., 2009; Shah, Lathrop, Reichard, & Landen, 2007). Recent research from New York City suggests that elevated ambient temperature (above 24°C—approximately 75°F) is associated with accidental, fatal overdose of cocaine and that public health efforts to reach at-risk populations during warm weather are particularly important (Bohnert, Prescott, Vlahov, Tardiff, & Galea, 2010).

Many studies have documented that babies born to women who use cocaine during pregnancy are prematurely delivered, have low birth weight, and have smaller head circumferences than babies not exposed to cocaine in utero (NIDA, 1999a). Because of methodological limitations, however, it has been difficult for research to tease out the effects of cocaine from those of other co-occurring conditions, such as maternal use of other substances, lack of prenatal care, and low socioeconomic status (Singer, 1999). Furthermore, NIDA (1999a) asserts that predictions about "crack babies" suffering profound irreversible damage has proven to be a "gross exaggeration" because most of these children have been able to recover from earlier deficits (p. 6). They do caution, however, that more sophisticated research techniques now are demonstrating an association between fetal cocaine exposure and later subtle deficits in behaviors such as concentration and blocking out distractions.

Heroin

In 2008, approximately 213,000 Americans (0.1% of the population) older than 12 years reported current heroin use (SAMHSA, 2009). In spite of the relatively small number of users, it represents a serious and significant public health problem. Heroin can be smoked, snorted, injected under the skin ("skin-popping"), or injected into a vein ("mainlining"). Users generally experience a pleasurable sensation, or "rush," followed by a period of drowsiness and mental cloudiness. Although heroin long has been associated with marginalized groups of people, the 1990s saw its use spread to people from middle and upper-middle socioeconomic classes (Stine & Kosten, 1999).

Heroin, derived from morphine, belongs to a class of substances known as opioids, which are used for relieving pain. Prescription medications belonging to this class include morphine, codeine, oxycodone (OxyContin), hydrocodone (Vicodin), propoxyphene (Darvon), meperidine (Demerol), and hydromorphone (Dilaudid) (NIDA, 2009b, 2010b). For epidemiological purposes, these prescription medications are covered in the "Psychotherapeutics" section; they tend to produce effects similar to those of heroin.

Epidemiology

In 2008, 1.5% of persons in the United States 12 years and older reported that they had used heroin in their lifetime. Predictably, lifetime use rates were highest for those 26 years and older (1.7%) and lowest for those 12 to 17 years old (0.3%). Young adults age 18 to 25 reported a lifetime heroin use rate of 1.4%.

Health Effects

NIDA (2000) states: "[O]ne of the most detrimental long-term effects of heroin is addiction itself" (p. 3). Regular users experience tolerance, need to administer higher doses to get the desired effects, and develop physical dependence. If heroin is not readministered, painful physiological withdrawal symptoms may occur for up to a week. Some people continue to experience withdrawal symptoms for months (NIDA, 2010b). These symptoms include restlessness, muscle and bone pain, insomnia, gastrointestinal disturbance, involuntary leg movements, and cold flashes (NIDA, 2005a). Overdose leading to death is possible and is a significant risk for street users who do not know the purity level of the heroin they have obtained. Heroin injectors run the risk of acquiring blood-borne viruses, such as HIV and hepatitis C, particularly when needles are shared. Intranasal use also may increase the risk of viral hepatitis (Aaron et al., 2008). Collapsed veins, liver disease, abscesses, infection of the heart lining and valves, and pulmonary complications are possible outcomes of long-term heroin use (NIDA, 2000).

Studies indicate that infants born to women with heroin dependence are more frequently premature, tend to have low birth weight, and often experience a range of perinatal complications and abnormalities (McNeece & DiNitto, 2005). Maternal heroin use also is associated with miscarriage and a greater risk of SIDS. Maternal and infant outcomes can be improved with a combination of comprehensive methadone treatment and prenatal care (NIDA, 2010b). Infants born to women who are engaged in methadone treatment can be treated safely if they show signs of physical dependence (NIDA, 2000). Buprenorphine is emerging as a promising treatment during pregnancy. Detoxification from opioids during pregnancy should be considered carefully in light of risk to the fetus (NIDA, 2010c).

Hallucinogens

Hallucinogens comprise a broad group of over 100 different substances that share the capacity to effect a variety of sensory distortions and hallucinations. Historically, select hallucinogens have been used among some groups as part of religious and spiritual rituals. For example, mescaline, derived from the peyote cactus, is used by certain Native Indian peoples of Mexico and is also a central component of rituals in the Native American Church (Durrant & Thakker, 2003).

Hallucinogens commonly known in the United States include LSD, PCP, mushrooms, and ecstasy (MDMA). Ecstasy is a designer drug that is tailor-made to produce specific effects. It is known as a party drug and a yuppie psychedelic and can produce both stimulant and hallucinogenic effects (McNeece & DiNitto, 2005). Users may experience mild euphoria and expanded mental perspective and insight. Negative effects include confusion, sleep disruption, anxiety, and paranoia, sometimes weeks after taking the substance. Physiological symptoms such as dehydration, blurred vision, teeth clenching, chills, sweating, and nausea have been observed (McNeece & DiNitto, 2005).

Epidemiology

In 2008, an estimated 1.06 million Americans 12 years and older reported current hallucinogen use, and about 3.7 million people reported using hallucinogens in the past year. Among past-year users, approximately 640,000 people reported using ecstasy, 154,000 reported using LSD, and 24,000 people reported using PCP (SAMHSA, 2009).

Among racial groups, younger Asian and African American people reported the lowest rates of lifetime hallucinogen use. Specifically, they reported rates of 0.8% and 1.4% as adolescents and 7.5% and 9.5% as young adults. Among people 26 years and older, their reported lifetime use rates remained low (5.2% and 9.9%, respectively), along with those of Latinos (9.4%). Estimates of reported lifetime hallucinogen use were not available for American Indians 26 years and older; however, among adolescents and young adults, their reported rates were highest (13.8% and 31.9%).

Health Effects

With the exception of ecstasy, hallucinogens pose few known health risks. The use of LSD has been associated with enduring psychoses, but it is unclear the extent to which LSD is causal (Abraham, Aldridge, & Gogia, 1996). During the acute hallucinogenic state, there is the risk of accidental injury or death. This is particularly true with PCP use because paranoia and confusion are associated with its acute effects (Stephens, 1999).

Taken in high dosages, ecstasy is associated with hyperthermia and can lead to cardiovascular, kidney, and liver failure. Neurotoxicity has been demonstrated in animals, and although studies have not definitively shown the same results in humans (NIDA, 2005c), clinical reports have documented toxic effects and fatality associated with ecstasy use (Dar & McBrien, 1996).

Inhalants

Inhalants are breathable chemical vapors found in many common items and household substances. Examples include gasoline, paint, cleaning fluids, glue, marking pens, lighter fluid, and lacquer thinner. These substances are sniffed, or "huffed," for their psychoactive effects. Although the effects of each of the particular substances can vary, intoxication generally resembles that of alcohol and may include stimulation and euphoria, followed by disinhibition, agitation, and light-headedness. With increased volume of vapor inhalation, anesthesia and unconsciousness can result (NIDA, 2005b).

Epidemiology

Because of their accessibility and affordability, inhalants are often a substance of choice for young people. In 2008, an estimated 1.1% of American youth age 12 to 17 years reported current inhalant use (SAMHSA, 2009). Among the same group, 9.3% reported lifetime use. Lifetime rates were higher for girls (10.1%) than for boys (8.4%), and American Indians reported the highest rate (16.8%) in this age group among ethnic/racial groups. Among all adolescents, 14-year-olds were the most likely to report inhalant use in the past month (1.5%) and past year (5.1%) (SAMHSA, 2009).

Health Effects

Inhalants are extremely toxic and potentially lethal. Over 700 deaths, mostly of teens and preteens, were reported to the National Inhalant Prevention Coalition between 1996 and 2001 (CSAP, 2003). Negative health effects include damage to the brain, lungs, kidneys, and liver. Inhalant use has been associated with sudden death, known as sudden sniffing death syndrome (NIDA, 2005b).

Psychotherapeutics

Psychotherapeutic medication is the second most commonly used illegal substance today. In 2008, 2.5% of Americans 12 years and older reported current use of these substances. Psychotherapeutics include the nonmedical use of prescription-type pain relievers, tranquilizers, stimulants, and sedatives. They comprise numerous kinds of substances that are obtained either with a prescription or illegally, "on the street." Classes of these substances most commonly abused include opioids (e.g., morphine, codeine, oxycodone), CNS depressants (barbiturates and benzodiazepines), and stimulants (e.g., dextroamphetamine [Dexedrine], methylphenidate [Ritalin], methamphetamine) (NIDA, 2001b). Depending on the dose administered, opioid users often experience euphoria followed by a significant decrease in tension and anxiety (Stine & Kosten, 1999). CNS depressants provide a calming and sedating function (Brady, Myrick, & Malcolm, 1999), whereas stimulants cause an increase in alertness, attention, and energy along with a feeling of euphoria (Weaver & Schnoll, 1999).

Epidemiology

Among those 12 years and older in the United States, 20.8% reported that they had used psychotherapeutics in their lifetime (SAMHSA, 2009). Men reported slightly higher lifetime rates than women (22.4% versus 19.3%), and young adults age 18 to 25, when compared with other age groups, reported the highest lifetime use rate (29.2%). Young adults also reported the highest current use rate (5.9%) among age groups. People 26 years and older reported the lowest current use rate at 1.9%. Almost 3% of adolescents (12- to 17-year olds) reported current use of psychotherapeutics.

Overall, men reported slightly greater current and lifetime use rates of psychotherapeutics than women (2.6% versus 2.4% and 22.4% versus 19.3%). This gender pattern varied, however, when examined by age groups. Girls 12 to 17 years old were more likely than boys of the same age to report current use and lifetime use (3.3% versus 2.5% and 12.4% versus 9.9%, respectively). This gender pattern switched, however, among 18- to 25-year-olds, with men reporting current and lifetime use rates (6.3% and 30.8%) higher than those of women (5.5% and 27.6%). Among adults 26 years and older, women and men were similar in their current use (1.8% and 1.9%), but men were more likely than women to report lifetime use (22.6% versus 18.8%).

Among youth age 12 to 17 years, Asian adolescents reported the lowest current rate of psychotherapeutic use (0.7%). Youth identifying as two or more races or as American Indian reported the highest rates of use (4.2% and 4.0%, respectively). During young adulthood, White Americans joined American Indians and people identifying as two or more races to report the highest rates of current psychotherapeutic use (7.2%, 5.9%, and 7.7%, respectively) while Asian American persons continued to report the lowest rates (3.0%). Among people older than 26 years, Asian Americans again reported the lowest rates of current psychotherapeutic use (0.7%) while American Indians and White Americans retained their position as reporting the highest rates of current use (2.2% and 2.1%, respectively).

Health Effects

The health consequences of psychotherapeutics vary widely because the substances themselves have such wide variation in chemical and psychoactive properties. Opioids, prescribed to treat pain, include morphine, codeine, oxycodone, meperidine, and propoxyphene. Long-term use of these and other opioids can result in tolerance, physical dependence, and addiction. If use is reduced or stopped abruptly, withdrawal symptoms such as restlessness, insomnia, irritability, diarrhea, nausea, and cold flashes may occur (NIDA, 2001b). Severe intoxication or overdose is potentially lethal and requires immediate medical attention (Stine & Kosten, 1999). Recent research suggests increasing rates of overdose from prescription opioids (Compton & Volkow, 2006; Hu & Baker, 2009; Paulozzi, Ballesteros, & Stevens, 2006).

A particular challenge in health-care settings involves balancing attention to opioid medication risks with appropriate pain management (Savage, Kirsh, & Passik, 2008; Zacny et al., 2003). The physical dependence associated with opioid medications does not in and of itself demonstrate problematic use of the medication (O'Brien & Volkow, 2006); however, as noted by Zacny and colleagues, opiophobia, driven by inadequate medication information and intense fears of medication misuse, persists and contributes to poor treatment of pain. Although social workers do not prescribe medication, they may play an important role in assessing clients' current and past substance use, intervening to support clients' pain management strategies, assisting clients experiencing problematic substance use, referring clients for additional services and self-help programs, and collaborating with the entire treatment team (Savage et al., 2008). A recent publication by Savage and colleagues (2008) provides more detailed guidance for social workers engaged in balancing pain management and substance use concerns with clients in their settings.

CNS depressants, prescribed to treat sleep and anxiety disorders, include barbiturates and benzodiazepines such as diazepam (Valium), chlordiazepoxide (Librium), alprazolam (Xanax), and clonazepam (Klonopin). Tolerance for these substances develops when they are taken over time, and physical dependence, withdrawal, and addiction are also risks. Sleep disorder medications such as zolpidem (Ambien), eszopiclone (Lunesta), and zaleplon (Sonata) are also CNS depressants, although they seem to be associated with reduced risk of problematic use. If used in combination with alcohol, pain medications, some cold and allergy medications, or other substances that make one drowsy, CNS depressants can slow one's breathing and heart rate, possibly leading to death (NIDA, 2009a). Benzodiazepines must be used cautiously with older adults because their use is a risk factor for falls causing fractures and for cognitive impairment (NIDA, 2001b).

Prescription-type stimulants include amphetamines such as dextroamphetamine and Adderall and methylphenidate as found in Ritalin and Concerta. Users may experience euphoria, decreased appetite, and heightened energy and attention. Irregular heartbeat, high body temperature, and cardiovascular failures or seizures are associated with high dosages of stimulants. Combining stimulants with decongestants may result in dangerous elevations in blood pressure or heart arrhythmias; combining them with antidepressants may heighten the stimulant's effects (NIDA, 2009a).

Methamphetamine is closely related to the substance amphetamine; however, its effects on the CNS are greater (NIDA, 2004b). Highly addictive, it produces a high of longer duration than that of cocaine. It can cause a variety of serious health effects including rapid heart rate, increased blood pressure, hyperthermia, and, over time, changes in brain functioning, significant weight loss, dental problems, psychosis, and various problems related to mood and behavior. Methamphetamine overdose can lead to hyperthermia and convulsion and, without proper medical attention, can be fatal. Research suggests that use during pregnancy may lead to prenatal complications, premature delivery, and heart and brain problems for the baby; further research is needed in this area to address methodological limitations of the available research as well as altered patterns of neonatal behavior (NIDA, 2002b).

PROMINENT APPROACHES TO CONCEPTUALIZE AND ADDRESS SUBSTANCE USE PROBLEMS

Interventions to address substance use problems are informed and shaped by a variety of factors. Conceptual models that explain the development of substance use problems tend to articulate and advocate for specific interventions and desired outcomes. For example, a conceptualization of substance use problems as the result of a complex illness that requires God's power for healing (AA, 2001) is prominent in spiritually based, 12-step approaches, such as AA (Miller & Hester, 1995; Schilling & El-Bassel, 1998) while conceptualizations of substance use problems as the result of learning processes are prominent in cognitive-behavioral approaches (Longabaugh & Morgenstern, 1999; Marlatt & Gordon, 1985). With attention to evidence-based practices (Miller, Zweben, & Johnson, 2005), this section briefly describes prominent approaches and modalities to assist people experiencing substance use problems. It then provides more detailed discussion of screening and brief interventions that are likely to be employed by social workers in health-care settings.

Reconciling Diverse Perspectives

Proponents of particular approaches are divided as to their efficacy (Miller & Hester, 1995). Commitment to particular approaches and conceptual frameworks is shaped in complex ways. For example, such commitments may be shaped by evaluation of available evidence, personal preferences, one's own treatment and recovery experiences, and affiliations based on training and association (Borden, 2000). The overview of prominent approaches presented here focuses specifically on their conceptual tenets, implications for intervention, and available evidence that supports them. Furthermore, although intense divisions exist among proponents of particular approaches, no one approach has been shown to be effective in serving all persons (Miller & Hester, 1995; NIDA, 2009b).

The term *systematic* or *informed eclecticism* has been used to describe the process through which social workers and other service providers should approach making decisions about which models to employ to help people effectively (Hepworth, Rooney, & Larsen, 2002; Miller & Hester, 1995). This process involves systematically considering available evidence to guide intervention, with preference for approaches that are evidence based, comprised of clearly described strategies and techniques, consistent with social work ethics, within the social worker's competencies, and culturally competent (Hepworth et al., 2002). To facilitate this process of systematic or informed eclecticism, this discussion addresses available evidence regarding each of the approaches.

Moral and Temperance Perspectives

Throughout the course of history, many perspectives have informed approaches to understanding and addressing substance use problems. Numerous authors describe the evolution of understanding regarding problematic substance use (McNeece & DiNitto, 2005; Miller & Hester, 1995; Schilling & El-Bassel, 1998). Early models conceptualized problematic substance use as a moral issue, reflecting moral weakness, sin, and volitional disregard for social norms of behavior (McNeece & DiNitto, 2005; Miller & Hester, 1995). The temperance movement emerged in the United States in the late 1800s and advocated for the judicious, moderate use of alcohol, based on its potential for harmful consequences (Miller & Hester, 1995). Differing perspectives exist on the role of the temperance movement in contributing to a moralistic view of problematic substance use. Some authors assert that "the core of the temperance model is that the cause of alcohol problems is alcohol itself" (Miller & Hester, 1995, p. 3). This conceptualization would suggest that limiting access to alcohol by making it more costly or less available and encouraging moderation and abstinence would be useful interventions (Miller & Hester, 1995). Others assert, "[P]rior to the activities of the Temperance Movement, a force that eventually led to the adoption of Prohibition in the United States, the consumption of alcohol was not necessarily considered to be a sinful act" (Marlatt, 1985b, p. 182). This view of the role of the temperance movement puts particular emphasis on the moral perspective of problematic substance abuse, with attention to the individual's lack of self-control (Marlatt, 1985b). The moral perspective informs interventions that focus on punishment through social and legal consequences for substance use (Miller & Hester, 1995).

Disease Models

Early in the 19th century, Benjamin Rush, a physician in the United States, proposed a disease framework for understanding alcohol use problems (Marlatt, 1985a). This framework further evolved through the 20th century. In 1935, AA began and contributed to disseminating the concept of alcoholism as a disease rather than a moral failing (Kinney &

Leaton, 1991; Schilling & El-Bassel, 1998). In the 1940s, E. M. Jellinek and his colleagues at Yale University also contributed to the formulation of the current disease model of alcoholism (Kinney & Leaton, 1991; Marlatt, 1985a). One way of considering elements of the disease model is reflected in the perspective of William Silkworth, known as a friend of AA: "an obsession of the mind and an allergy of the body" (Kinney & Leaton, 1991, p. 54). This conceptualization reflects recognition of the psychological and biological components of the disease perspective; however, as argued by Miller and Hester (1995), the 12-step approach also incorporates considerable emphasis on spirituality as a primary component of recovery. In fact, the 12-step approach of AA views alcoholism as "an illness which only a spiritual experience will conquer" (AA, 2001, p. 21).

The conceptualization of problematic substance use as a persistent medical condition has continued to evolve with recognition that it is influenced by biological, environmental, behavioral, and genetic components (Alterman, McLellan, O'Brien, & McKay, 1998; O'Brien & McLellan, 1996). A similar view is presented by the Center for Substance Abuse Treatment (CSAT; 1999b), which describes "an emerging biopsychosocial-spiritual model" (p. 8). These viewpoints recognize that complex, intersecting factors influence the onset and course of substance use problems and, as with other chronic health conditions, require multifaceted intervention strategies (CSAT, 1999b; Leshner, 1997; NIDA, 2009b). Furthermore, as with other chronic health conditions, long-term treatment is required to address addiction as "a chronic, relapsing illness" (Leshner, 1997, p. 45; O'Brien & McLellan, 1996). Although risk for relapse often dominates common understanding of addiction, rates of relapse with addiction (40%–60%) are comparable to relapse rates associated with type 1 diabetes (30%–50%), hypertension (50%–70%), and asthma (50%–70%; NIDA, 2009b). Although a complex combination of factors can influence the effectiveness of treatment (e.g., type and severity of client's presenting problems,

capacity of available services to address the client's presenting problems, nature of the client's interactions with service providers), NIDA (2009c) notes that "according to research that tracks individuals in treatment over extended periods of time, most people who get into and remain in treatment stop using drugs, decrease their criminal activity, and improve their occupational, social, and psychological functioning" (p. 11).

Several intervention strategies emerge from the conceptualization of substance use disorders as a disease. Although there are distinctions between a dispositional disease model and the more comprehensive perspective of AA (Miller & Kurtz, 1994), AA and other 12-step approaches are among the most promising to emerge from disease conceptualizations of substance use disorders. Research regarding 12-step approaches is limited, but a 2004 research review suggests that participation in AA and Narcotics Anonymous is associated with increased abstinence and self-efficacy and enhanced socialization. Augmenting 12-step meeting attendance with participation in additional group-related activities seems to add to effects (Humphreys et al., 2004). In addition, findings from this review also suggest that self-help group participation is best considered as continuing care rather than as a replacement for acute professional treatment. Findings from a more recent research review indicate that several aspects of AA participation are associated with better outcomes, including connecting with a sponsor, attending meetings frequently and over a longer period of time, affiliating with AA more rapidly, and receiving support from other AA members (Krentzman, 2007). In addition, recent research with adolescents indicates that 12-step involvement is associated with drug and alcohol abstinence at three years after treatment (Chi, Kaskutas, Sterling, Campbell, & Weisner, 2009). Finally, while focused on facilitating attendance at AA meetings and incorporating elements of the 12-step approach, findings of Project MATCH, a large clinical trial of alcohol treatment conducted with 1,726 clients over 10 years, suggest that 12-step facilitation conducted by a therapist is as effective as cognitive-behavioral and motivational enhancement therapy (Donovan, Carroll, Kadden, DiClemente, & Rounsaville, 2003).

Numerous pharmacotherapies have emerged to assist people experiencing substance use problems. Among the best known are:

- Nicotine lozenges, patches, or gum or oral medications such as bupropion (Zyban) or varenicline (Chantix), which can be helpful to people with nicotine addiction. (Note, however, that the transdermal patch is the only addiction medication approved by the Food and Drug Administration [FDA] for use with adolescents.)
- Disulfiram (Antabuse), which may help people with alcohol use disorders who have high motivation, are entering a treatment contract with a significant other, or are attending events where alcohol is served.
- Acamprosate (Campral) and topiramate (Topamax), which can help people abstain from or reduce drinking. (Topiramate is not yet approved by the FDA.)
- Naltrexone (Revia), which has shown promise in treating alcohol and opiate use problems.
- Methadone and Subutex, which have been effective in treating opioid dependence.
- Selective serotonin reuptake inhibitors, which have been effective in enhancing alcohol treatment retention, reducing alcohol consumption among clients experiencing co-occurring anxiety, and reducing cocaine consumption among clients engaged in methadone treatment (Alterman et al., 1998; NIDA, 2009b).

Combining medication with psychosocial interventions, which are discussed further next, reflects a multifaceted approach to address "addiction as a prototypical psychobiological illness, with critical biological, behavioral, and social-context components" (Leshner, 1997, p. 46).

Psychological Models

Prominent psychological models for understanding substance abuse include behavioral and cognitive perspectives (Miller & Hester, 1995). One such model is Relapse Prevention, in which "addictive behaviors are viewed as overlearned habits that can be analyzed and modified in the same manner as other habits" (Marlatt, 1985a, p. 9). As described by Marlatt, analysis of these habits involves the examination of factors that contribute to maintaining the behavior, such as antecedents in the situation or environment (e.g., relational conflicts, social influences, emotions), expectations about the outcome of substance use (e.g., anticipation of positive consequence of consumption), and previous experiential learning about the substance (e.g., observations of peers and family members using substances, positive reinforcement of behavior through enjoyable effects of consumption, negative reinforcement of behavior through relief of distress with consumption). The analysis also includes examination of consequences of the behavior (e.g., ways in which substance use is reinforced to encourage the behavior and ways in which negative outcomes may discourage behavior), with particular attention to the social context and interpersonal components associated with substance using behavior.

Another central element of this model is its perspective on relapse, or reengaging in substance use behavior. In fact, Marlatt (1985a) distinguishes a lapse, or a single experience of returning to prior behavior, from a relapse, a more complete experience of returning to prior behavior. In this model "a single slip (mistake)" is not seen "as an indication of total failure" (p. 32). Thus, the notion of being in or out of control of substance use is not viewed dichotomously, and efforts are made to use lapses and relapses as learning experiences that can inform future relapse-prevention strategies (Larimer, Palmer, & Marlatt, 1999; Marlatt, 1985a).

The phrase *abstinence violation effect* is used by Marlatt (1985a) to describe the cognitive and affective responses people may experience when they are committed to absolute abstinence but then engage in substance use. After committing to total abstinence, people who engage in substance use may be more likely to experience negative affective states (e.g., guilt) and cognitions that involve self-blame or that reinforce lack of self-control. Such experiences may increase their risk for relapse (Larimer et al., 1999; Marlatt, 1985a; Miller, Westerberg, Harris, & Tonigan, 1996; for review, see Dimeff & Marlatt, 1998). Interventions based on the model's conceptualization of substance use problems focus on assisting clients to identify situations that may increase their risk of relapse, strengthen their ability to cope with or modify such situations, address expectations regarding anticipated outcomes of substance use, strengthen self-efficacy, reduce the intensity of the abstinence violation effect through cognitive interventions, and foster learning from lapses and relapses (Larimer et al., 1999).

NIDA (2009b) notes the effectiveness of cognitive-behavioral treatment with people experiencing problematic use of alcohol, nicotine, marijuana, cocaine, and methamphetamine and highlights that people often experience sustained retention of skills in the year following treatment. Findings from Project MATCH suggest that cognitive-behavioral therapy was as effective as 12-step facilitation and motivational enhancement therapy (Miller & Longabaugh, 2003). In addition, a review of research on cognitive-behavioral relapse prevention presents positive findings of several studies that suggest that this approach can help increase the period of abstinence, reduce the severity of relapse, and have comparable effectiveness with a 12-step approach with both alcohol and other drug use (Dimeff & Marlatt, 1998). Although there is research support for relapse prevention, Dimeff and Marlatt note that there have been some mixed findings. For example, in a review by Miller and Hester (1995), three of seven studies that specifically examined "relapse prevention" yielded positive findings, but four yielded mixed findings, including findings that indicated improvements in both experimental groups. Miller and Hester (1995) also note findings indicating that supportive therapy may be more effective in alcohol-related outcomes than relapse prevention for clients who have lower levels of verbal learning ability (Dimeff & Marlatt, 1998; Jaffe et al., 1996).

Motivation and Change Theory Perspectives

Motivation and change theory perspectives emphasize understanding the motivation for and the nature and processes of change.

Motivational Interviewing

First published in 1991, Miller and Rollnick's (1991, 2002) motivational interviewing model focuses on why people change behavior rather than why they do not. Although specific principles and methods are associated with motivational interviewing, Miller and Rollnick's revised edition places greater weight on the spirit of the approach. The authors focus on three primary components that contribute to the spirit of the approach: collaboration, evocation, and autonomy (p. 34). These components are contrasted with their opposing counterparts: confrontation, education, and authority (p. 35). A spirit of collaboration aims to create an egalitarian partnership rather than a context of confrontation and argument between the social worker and the client. The aim is "to create a positive interpersonal atmosphere that is conducive but not coercive to change" (p. 34). Rather than presuming that clients lack awareness, information, or competence and then attempting to impart them to clients, the worker engaged in motivational interviewing aims to evoke from clients their perspectives, interests, and sources of motivation. The presumption of evocation is that change is facilitated by eliciting intrinsic motivation regarding what is most meaningful to clients and their aims. Finally, rather than focusing on an authoritarian relationship in which the social worker tells clients what to do, motivational interviewing recognizes that clients have a choice regarding accepting assistance and that ultimately they will be responsible for making a behavior change.

As further described by Miller and Rollnick (2002), "when motivational interviewing is done properly, it is the client rather than the counselor who presents the arguments for change" (p. 34). Building on the spirit of the approach, Miller and Rollnick (p. 36) suggest four principles that can inform motivational interviewing: (1) express empathy, (2) develop discrepancy, (3) roll with resistance, and (4) support self-efficacy.

As described by Miller and Rollnick (2002), the expression of empathy draws on the work of Carl Rogers with an emphasis on reflective listening and the recognition that ambivalence about change is normal. In developing discrepancy, the social worker aims to assist clients with exploration of the difference between the current situation and their future goals. In this process, it once again is the clients rather than the social worker who provide the reasons for change. This process is facilitated by eliciting client perspectives regarding the discrepancies and then amplifying their perspectives to facilitate change and to resolve ambivalence. Central to the idea of rolling with resistance is that "argumentation is counterproductive" (Miller & Rollnick, 2002, p. 39). In fact, according to Miller and Rollnick, when clients display "resistance," it should be taken as a cue to the social worker that the current approach should be modified. Finally, self-efficacy is supported by two main elements: The social worker's belief that change is possible and the recognition that ultimately clients will be responsible for the change. These two ideas are interwoven: "To assert that a person is responsible for deciding and directing his or her own change is to assume that the person is capable of doing so" (Miller & Rollnick, 2002, p. 41).

Motivational interviewing has been evaluated in more than 200 clinical trials, showing promise with a wide range of substance use problems and other health concerns, including physical inactivity, HIV risk, HIV medication adherence, co-occurring substance use and mental health problems, hypertension, cardiovascular rehabilitation, and diabetes management (Britt, Hudson, & Blampied, 2004; Miller & Rose, 2009; Miller, Yahne,

& Tonigan, 2003; Parsons, Golub, Rosof, & Holder, 2007; Weir et al., 2009). Findings from recent meta-analyses indicate that motivational interviewing facilitates positive outcomes related to substance use, although there appear to be differential effects by substance. In these studies, the comparative effects were greater with weak comparison groups; however, it should be noted that motivational interviewing involved fewer sessions than usual treatment, which suggests that motivational interviewing may require less cost and time to achieve gains (Hettema, Steele, & Miller, 2005; Lundahl & Burke, 2009; Lundahl, Kunz, Brownell, Tollefson, & Burke, 2010; Vasilaki, Hosier, & Cox, 2006). The effects of motivational interviewing were not shown to differ by gender or problem severity in the meta-analyses that examined these variables; some analyses do indicate that people from racial/ethnic minority groups and those who are older may experience greater effects of motivational interviewing (Hettema et al., 2005; Lundahl et al., 2010).

Motivational enhancement therapy (MET), a four-session adaptation of motivational interviewing, was conducted over 12 weeks of treatment in Project MATCH (Donovan et al., 2003; Miller & Longabaugh, 2003). Findings of Project MATCH indicate that MET is as effective as cognitive-behavioral therapy and 12-step facilitation; however, given the brevity of the MET intervention, it is deemed a more cost-effective intervention (Miller & Longabaugh, 2003). In its recent review of effective treatments, NIDA (2009b) indicates that MET's success appears to differ by drug used, with greater effectiveness for alcohol and marijuana, and it is particularly useful in enhancing treatment engagement rather than altering drug use.

Understanding the mechanisms through which motivational interviewing facilitates and sustains change and its intersections with environmental factors (e.g., familial and social support of change efforts) are central questions to be addressed in ongoing research (Dunn, Deroo, & Rivara, 2001; Heather, 2005; Vasilaki et al., 2006). Emerging efforts to identify mechanisms of change in motivational interviewing suggest that several factors may be particularly important, including: relational elements (e.g., empathy and motivational interviewing spirit); technical elements (e.g., consistency with motivational interviewing, capacity for evoking and supporting change talk, use of decisional balance exercise, providing feedback); and client experiences (e.g., demonstration of change talk and intention to change, sense of discrepancy between the present situation and valued goals). The scholarship in this area draws conflicting conclusions regarding the role of relational elements, including empathy and the spirit of motivational interviewing, in facilitating change (Apodaca & Longabaugh, 2009; Miller & Rose, 2009). Continued knowledge development in this area is likely to strengthen theoretical understandings of motivational interviewing, direct practice that draws on this approach, and positive outcomes for people facing substance use and other health concerns.

Transtheoretical/Stages of Change Model

The transtheoretical model provides a framework for understanding the incremental processes that facilitate intentional changes in behavior (DiClemente & Velasquez, 2002). Central to this model is the idea that people experience five stages in the process of making changes in their behaviors, hence the name stages of change (DiClemente & Velasquez, 2002; Prochaska, DiClemente, & Norcross, 1992). The five stages of change include precontemplation, contemplation, preparation, action, and maintenance (see Box 17.1).

Key tenets of the stages of change model involve three concepts.

1. The change process can begin before people have identified that they have a problem (precontemplation) and proceeds with increased recognition of a problematic behavior (contemplation), to considerations about how change might be approached (preparation), to engaging in behavior change (action), and finally to making a sustained behavioral change (maintenance).

Box 17.1 Five Stages of Change

1. *Precontemplation.* No intention of changing behavior in the foreseeable future. Many people are unaware or underaware of their problems during this stage.
2. *Contemplation.* Awareness that a problem exists and serious consideration about overcoming it but no commitment to take action at this time. Contemplators typically experience ambivalence and often weigh the pros and cons of the problem and its solution.
3. *Preparation.* Intention to take action in the next month; unsuccessful in taking action during the past year.
4. *Action.* Modification of behavior, experiences, or environment to overcome problems. This stage involves successful alteration of the addictive behavior for a period of one day to six months.
5. *Maintenance.* Prevention of relapse and consolidation of gains attained during action.

Source: Adapted from "In Search of How People Change: Applications to Addictive Behaviors," by J. O. Prochaska, C. C. DiClemente, and J. C. Norcross, 1992, *American Psychologist, 47*(9), pp. 1103–1114.

---

2. Relapse, as "the rule rather than the exception with addictions," leads to a spiral model of progression through the stages of change (Prochaska et al., 1992, p. 1104). In this spiral model, a person who has taken action and experienced a relapse may return to the contemplation or preparation phase and then continue to proceed through the stages of change (Prochaska et al., 1992). As in the Relapse Prevention model, relapse is viewed as an opportunity for learning rather than as a failure (Prochaska & Prochaska, 1999). As further described by Prochaska and Prochaska (1999), people who attempt to stop smoking typically engage in three or four action efforts over a period of 7 to 10 years before achieving sustained maintenance.

Although the social worker does not set people up for failure by expecting relapse, it is important to frame relapse in terms of lessons that can be learned, to provide feedback for clients regarding the time required to achieve sustained behavioral change, and to assist clients with maintaining self-efficacy and reengaging in change efforts (DiClemente, 1991; DiClemente & Velasquez, 2002; Prochaska & Prochaska, 1999; Prochaska et al., 1992).

3. DiClemente and Velasquez (2002) describe the importance of matching the intervention strategy to the client's stage of change. For example, clients who do not view their drinking habits as problematic and are not considering changing them would be considered to be in the precontemplation stage. In this stage, action-oriented steps are likely to be premature and to yield limited success (Prochaska et al., 1992). Rather than proceeding with action-oriented steps, motivational interviewing strategies (e.g., empathic, reflective listening; recognizing client autonomy to make decisions about accepting assistance; weighing out the benefits and drawbacks of current alcohol use; providing a menu of options) that facilitate movement from precontemplation to contemplation would be indicated (DiClemente & Velasquez, 2002).

Although the stages of change model can be useful in conceptualizing a person's readiness to change along a continuum, with implications for numerous populations and settings (e.g., to address substance use, partner violence exposure, health behaviors, and mental health), recent scholarship demonstrates mixed findings regarding its effectiveness in practice (Bridle et al., 2005) and critiques the validity of some of its theoretical underpinnings (IOM, 2001; Littell & Girvin, 2002). Bridle et al. (2005) reviewed behavioral outcomes of 35 trials based on the transtheoretical model. Of the 35 studies, which focused on a range of health issues including smoking, dietary change, and treatment adherence,

the model was favored in approximately one-quarter of the comparisons. In approximately half of the comparisons, the intervention and control group outcomes were similar, and in another quarter, the findings were inconclusive. Based on a review of 87 studies that examined the stages of change with diverse target problems, Littell and Girvin (2002) concluded that this model is limited in two main ways. First, their review suggests that there is a lack of distinction between each of the discrete stages and that there is limited clarity regarding the relationship between readiness for change and the stages. Second, their review suggests that there is a lack of evidence to suggest that people move through the stages in a stepwise fashion. Little and Girvin propose that conceptualizing change along a continuum that may not reflect linear progression may be useful and that the model may have heuristic utility; however, they caution against intervention matched to stages, and they argue that future research should further explore change processes across diverse problems and sociocultural contexts.

Public Health: Harm Reduction Approach

Emerging out of the Netherlands in the 1980s, the harm reduction approach is relatively new in the substance abuse field. Although a growing body of literature addresses the potential of harm reduction and traditional approaches to work in complementary and integrated ways (Denning, 2001; Futterman, Lorente, & Silverman, 2004; Housenbold Seiger, 2004; Kellogg, 2003; Lee, Engstrom, & Petersen, in press; Marlatt, Blume, & Parks, 2001), harm reduction sometimes is seen as at odds with abstinence-oriented traditional approaches. Harm reduction philosophy, however, does not dismiss the fact that abstinence is often an ideal goal for many substance-using individuals (Marlatt, 1998). In addition, prominent scholars in the addictions field argue that because addiction is a chronic health condition, "improvement rather than cure" is "the only realistic expectation for the treatment of addiction" (O'Brien & McLellan, 1996, p. 237). The approach recognizes that many clients are not ready to pursue abstinence at the time they come into contact with treatment systems. Rather than arguing with this group of clients about appropriate goals or, worse, turning them away from treatment, harm reduction is a method of engaging clients as they are. It recognizes that people who currently are using substances have strengths, and it draws on these strengths to empower clients to reduce harms in their lives and to achieve goals that are important to them. As noted by Miller and Miller (2009), "[C]lients themselves have priorities, and the extent to which we address them is likely to influence our success with engagement, retention, and outcomes" (p. 685). Their perspective that treatment should focus on improving people's lives, not just the suppression of substance use, is consistent with a harm perspective. Harm reduction values positive changes in clients' lives, including those who may not focus on their substance use. The Harm Reduction Coalition (n.d.) describes that this approach "establishes quality of individual and community life and well-being—not necessarily cessation of all drug use—as the criteria for successful interventions and policies." Finally, in many ways, a harm reduction approach is consistent with social work values (Brocato & Wagner, 2003; MacMaster, 2004). By meeting clients where they are, the worker acknowledges the inherent worth and dignity of each person regardless of the substances they may use. Furthermore, this approach embodies the value of social justice by recognizing that all substance users, regardless of their motivation to abstain from using, deserve treatment services (Brocato & Wagner, 2003).

The public health approach of harm reduction has numerous key components. As described by the Harm Reduction Coalition (n.d.), harm reduction "does not attempt to minimize or ignore the real and tragic harm and danger associated with licit and illicit drug use"; however, it also "accepts, for better and for worse, that licit and illicit drug use is part of our world and chooses to work to minimize its harmful effects rather than simply ignore

or condemn them." Harm reduction strategies that aim to reduce harmful effects of drug use include direct practice or treatment interventions, environmental modifications or public health approaches, and public policy and advocacy initiatives (Marlatt, 1998; Rotgers, Little, & Denning, 2005). Direct practice and treatment interventions can involve these strategies: low-threshold service access; motivational interviewing; education conducted with a collaborative, participatory spirit; relapse prevention strategies informed by cognitive-behavioral approaches; pharmacotherapy, such as methadone treatment and nicotine replacement; and integration of substance use screening, brief intervention, and referral in emergency departments and trauma centers (Hunt, 2003; Logan & Marlatt, 2010; Marlatt, 1998; Marlatt & Witkiewitz, 2010; Rotgers et al., 2005).

Environmental modifications and public health approaches can involve making clean needles and condoms available; facilitating designated driver programs; facilitating access to health care and to safe, affordable housing without treatment and abstinence contingencies; and preventing overdose with administration training and distribution of naloxone (Narcan) (Harm Reduction Coalition, n.d.; Marlatt, 1998; Marlatt & Witkiewitz, 2010; Rotgers et al., 2005). Public policy and advocacy initiatives can involve reducing barriers and facilitating access to services, working to eliminate discrimination against people with substance use problems, reforming legal consequences for substance consumption, and addressing sentencing disparities (Marlatt, 1998; Rotgers et al., 2005).

One such sentencing disparity is the 100 to 1 disparity for the federal mandatory minimum sentence for possession of crack and powder cocaine that disproportionately affects people who are African American (Hatsukami & Fischman, 1996). Under this policy, a person with a first-time offense of possession of 5 g of crack cocaine would be mandated to a minimum sentence of five years; this sentence would require possession of 500 g of cocaine hydrochloride (Hatsukami &

Fischman, 1996). The U.S. Senate and House of Representatives passed a bill to reduce this disparity, and President Obama signed the Fair Sentencing Act in 2010. In this bill, the 5-year sentence would be enacted with 28 g of crack cocaine (Fields, 2010). Addressing such disparities reflects public policy initiatives to reduce harm and to pursue social justice. Last, harm reduction values a range of positive outcomes that reflect reduced harm associated with drug use at multiple levels (e.g., individual, community, society), and it favors individualized approaches to reflect the unique experiences and interests of individuals and communities (Harm Reduction Coalition, n.d.; Hunt, 2003).

Research regarding harm reduction has focused heavily on needle exchange and methadone treatment interventions (Hunt, 2003). In a review of 42 studies of syringe exchange programs, Gibson, Flynn, and Perales (2001) identified positive outcomes with 28 of them. The authors discuss methodological issues, such as the design of the research and selection and dilution biases, which may have influenced the negative (2 studies) and null or mixed (14 studies) findings; however, based on their review, the authors conclude that "there is substantial evidence that syringe exchange programs are effective in preventing HIV risk behavior and HIV seroconversion among IDUs [injection drug users]" (p. 1338). Methadone treatment has been researched for nearly 40 years; findings indicate positive effects on reductions in the use of heroin and HIV risk behaviors (Hunt, 2003). In their more recent review, Marlatt and Witkiewitz (2010) conclude that opioid substitution therapy not only reduces illicit opiate use and HIV risk behaviors but also illegal activity and death related to opioid use. Furthermore, they note that for every dollar spent on treatment for opioid use, there is a $12 cost savings. Finally, as described by NIDA (2009b), "patients stabilized on adequate, sustained dosages of methadone or buprenorphine can function normally" (p. 39).

There are numerous additional harm reduction strategies with empirical support. These strategies include motivational interviewing (Britt et al., 2004; Hettema et al., 2005; Lundahl & Burke, 2009; Lundahl et al., 2010; Miller & Rose, 2009; Miller et al., 2003; Parsons et al., 2007; Vasilaki et al., 2006; Weir et al., 2009); cognitive-behavioral relapse prevention (Dimeff & Marlatt, 1998; Larimer et al., 1999; Miller & Hester, 1995); behavioral self-control training, overdose prevention (Seal et al., 2005); housing programs without treatment or abstinence requirements (Larimer et al., 2009; Tsemberis, Gulcur, & Nakae, 2004); and substance use screening, brief intervention, and treatment referral in medical settings (Madras et al., 2009).

Additional Evidence-Based Approaches

The prominent approaches discussed in this section are not exhaustive. They provide an introduction to various ways of thinking about and intervening to address substance use problems. Additional approaches that are described by NIDA (2009b) as evidence based include: (a) behavioral strategies that incorporate vouchers or incentives to support abstinence from cocaine, alcohol, stimulants, opioids, marijuana, and nicotine and (b) the Matrix model, which incorporates relapse prevention, group therapy, self-help, education about drugs, and family therapy to assist people with reduction of stimulant and other drug use. Much of the research regarding family-oriented intervention in the substance abuse field has focused on adolescents, and the next models have a developing evidence base: multisystemic treatment, multidimensional family therapy, and brief strategic family therapy (Henggeler, Schoenwald, Borduin, Rowland, & Cunningham, 1998; Liddle & Hogue, 2001; Liddle, Rowe, Dakof, Henderson, & Greenbaum, 2009; NIDA, 2009b; Szapocznik & Williams, 2000). A growing body of evidence also supports the use of family-oriented interventions with adults experiencing substance use problems. Gains associated with such interventions include reductions in substance use, greater treatment engagement and attendance, improved family member well-being, and enhanced family relationships (NIDA,

2009b; O'Farrell & Fals-Stewart, 2008; O'Farrell, Murphy, Alter, & Fals-Stewart, 2010; Smith, Meyers & Austin, 2008). In addition, as noted by O'Farrell & Fals-Stewart (2008), behavioral couples therapy, a NIDA-recognized evidenced-based treatment, results in a 5-to-1 reduction in social costs, meaning that for every dollar invested in this treatment, $5 are saved in social costs, including healthcare, criminal justice, and public assistance expenditures.

Mental illness frequently co-occurs with substance use problems, affecting an estimated 50% to 75% of people with substance use disorders (CSAT, 2005; NIDA, 2009b). Among people experiencing co-occurring substance use and psychiatric disorders, integrated treatment that focuses on both conditions simultaneously is recommended (NIDA, 2009b; CSAT, 2005). Promising approaches to assist people with co-occurring substance use and mental health concerns include motivational interviewing, contingency management, cognitive-behavioral treatment, relapse prevention, assertive community treatment, intensive case management, and the modified therapeutic community model (CSAT, 2005). In addition, trauma-informed programming may be critical to support engagement and treatment success of clients, particularly women, affected by co-occurring trauma and substance use concerns (CSAT, 2005; Elliott, Bjelajac, Fallot, Markoff, & Reed, 2005; Finkelstein et al., 2004; Harris & Fallot, 2001). A growing body of evidence supports the use of trauma-specific treatments to address co-occurring trauma and substance use (Cook, Walser, Kane, Ruzek, & Woody, 2006; Cusack, Morrissey & Ellis, 2008; Gilbert et al., 2006; Hien, Cohen, Miele, Litt, & Capstick, 2004; Hien et al., 2010; Morrissey et al., 2005; Najavits, 2002; Najavits, Schmitz, Gotthardt, & Weiss, 2005; Zlotnick, Johnson, & Najavits, 2009). The Center for Substance Abuse Treatment has published two Treatment Improvement Protocols, one focused on co-occurring substance use and mental health conditions (2005) and one focused on treatment needs of women (2009), which provide detailed practice guidance.

Intervention Modalities

Interventions vary not only according to the etiological models that inform them but also in their functions, modalities, and organizational structures. For example, interventions may vary according to focus (e.g., detoxification, long-term rehabilitation, aftercare), location (e.g., hospital, community), intensity (e.g., inpatient, residential, outpatient, self-help groups), identity of the helping system (e.g., substance abuse services, mental health center, child welfare, family and social support), client system (e.g., individual, group, family), and public or private funding sources (McNeece & DiNitto, 2005). Knowledge of various treatment modalities and locally available resources is particularly relevant for social workers in health-care settings, who often facilitate referrals for additional specialized and comprehensive services that people with substance use problems frequently need and that can affect treatment outcomes (El-Bassel, Gilbert, Wu, Chang, & Fontdevila, 2007; Engstrom, El-Bassel, Go, & Gilbert, 2008; Engstrom, Shibusawa, El-Bassel, & Gilbert, 2009; Grella & Stein, 2006; Marsh, Cao, & D'Aunno, 2004; McLellan et al., 1998). Detailed guidance for referring adolescent and adult clients to an appropriate level of care given their substance use characteristics, biopsychosocial conditions, and environmental context is provided by the American Society of Addiction Medicine's 2001 *Patient Placement Criteria for the Treatment of Substance-Related Disorders.*

SCREENING AND BRIEF INTERVENTION COORDINATION IN HEALTH-CARE SETTINGS

For health social workers to incorporate consideration of potential substance use problems into their clients' care, they must skillfully gather information about their clients' substance-using behaviors. For a variety of reasons, many health and social service providers simply do not inquire and thus inadvertently overlook possible substance use problems. The IOM (1990) recommends that questions about substance use be included with routine lifestyle and behavioral questions, such as those about diet and exercise, with all people who come into contact with health-care systems. Especially in light of the large numbers of people with substance use problems who do not identify that they have a problem or seek treatment (approximately 95.5%; IOM, 1990; Madras et al., 2009), substance use screening, brief intervention, and referral to treatment (SBIRT) provides an excellent opportunity to reach this population. In addition, research regarding SBIRT demonstrates powerful findings (Babor et al., 2007; Madras et al., 2009). A recent study involving 459,599 people employed the SBIRT model across diverse health-care settings (e.g., emergency rooms, trauma centers, primary care, school health clinics) and diverse populations (e.g., diversity by race/ethnicity, gender, age, substances used). In this study, alcohol and drug use screening identified people who needed brief intervention, brief treatment, or referral to specialized treatment. Of those who screened positively for drug use at baseline, rates of drug use and heavy alcohol use were 67.7% and 38.6% lower at six-month follow-up. Furthermore, brief treatment or referral to specialized treatment generally was associated with gains in other domains as well, including health status, emotional problems, employment, arrests, and homelessness (Madras et al., 2009).

The next section provides information and tools necessary for detecting potential substance use problems. First it discusses issues related to professional use of self when talking with clients about substance use behaviors. Then it offers some basic considerations about gathering information. Finally it presents information about established screening tools and protocols and how to consolidate information gathered to conduct brief interventions or to make referrals for other services as needed.

Screening

Although screening and assessment are presented separately from interventions in this chapter, it is important to note that, just as in other types of social work practice, they are actually overlapping activities. More often than not, assessment continues during the intervention process. In fact, NIAAA (2004b) includes both screening and assessment activities as part of a brief intervention framework. Furthermore, the interpersonal experience of asking clients about their behaviors and providing feedback based on their answers can be a potent intervention in and of itself (Miller, 2000).

This chapter focuses more on screening than on assessment. In general, screening is a relatively brief process and is aimed at identifying individuals with potential substance use problems (Abbott & Wood, 2000; Donovan, 1999). When an individual is identified as being at risk, further assessment is required. The assessment process is more comprehensive in scope and aims to diagnose substance use disorders, assess related health and psychosocial effects, and inform specialized and comprehensive services (Cooney, Zweben, & Fleming, 1995). This section presents information to incorporate substance use screening into a more general psychosocial assessment and to make appropriate referrals for further assessment and intervention when necessary.

Empathic, Invitational, and Supportive Stance

Because of the stigma and shame often associated with substance use problems, the manner in which social workers ask about potential problems is critical. McCrady (1993) identified several provider characteristics that appear to be conducive to successful treatment with persons with alcohol problems. These characteristics are relevant for accurate screening as well.

(1) The clinician must be empathic and recognize that it is often embarrassing and difficult for clients to talk about their

substance use. If they have struggled with substance use over time, it is likely that they have encountered criticism and disapproval from family, friends, and previous treatment providers. In addition, it is important that clinicians have an appreciation for how difficult it can be to change substance-using behavior. Often clients have made multiple attempts at stopping their use of alcohol, tobacco, or other drugs only to relapse and feel as if they have failed, thus leading to greater demoralization. The ability to empathize with both the stigma of substance use and the difficulty in changing substance-using behavior is critical.

(2) The clinician needs to be able to discriminate between the person and his or her substance-using behavior. McCrady (1993) notes that this process can involve a "delicate" balance. First and foremost, clinicians need to convey a sense of respect for the person, acknowledging her inherent dignity, value, and worth. At the same time, however, McCrady cautions that clinicians should be careful not to dismiss or overlook the problematic substance-using behavior. Furthermore, given that substance use problems are so common, it is not unusual for professional service providers to have had personal experiences of problematic substance use in their own families and social networks. Some treatment programs prefer providers who have gone through their own recovery. Although personal experience often can facilitate empathy, it also carries the potential to narrow the provider's beliefs about what works (Imhof, 1995). Ongoing clinical supervision is critical to facilitate providers' capacity to honestly acknowledge their own beliefs and biases and to encourage the use of emerging knowledge to support informed engagement, screening, assessment, and intervention.

(3) It is important to be mindful that recent research has not supported numerous myths that have influenced strategies to assist people experiencing substance use problems. For example, evidence does not support that there is such a thing as an "addictive personality," that people with substance use problems have more enhanced defense mechanisms that are displayed as resistance or denial, or that aggressive confrontation facilitates change (CSAT, 1999b).

Sources of Information

Health social workers gather important information about clients' substance use–related behaviors from a variety of sources. First and especially, they gather information from the clients themselves. In addition, they may gather information from involved family and friends and other treatment providers. Finally, they also may gather information from existing medical/treatment records, from biological tests such as toxicology screenings, and from other service providers. The next sections answer two important questions about the process of gathering information: (1) What is the purpose of gathering this information? and (2) What kinds of information should be gathered?

Purpose of Gathering Information About Substance Use Behavior

It is important to understand the purpose of gathering information about clients' substance use history and patterns. Clearly, strong associations exist between substance use and a variety of health and social problems that may bring people into contact with health-care systems. Often the identified health problem cannot be treated fully unless the associated substance use problem is addressed simultaneously. Thus, screening for potential substance use problems is central to recommending and providing comprehensive treatment for clients' identified health problems. For example, active use of alcohol and other substances may contraindicate certain pharmacotherapies and medical procedures. Specific information about the frequency and amount of use, as well as consequences of use, allows the health social worker to make appropriate recommendations and referrals.

What Information to Gather

When screening for substance use problems, social workers may gather information that falls into several different categories: substances being used, frequency of use, amount of use, consequences of use, and circumstances in which one uses. In addition, because of the genetic influence for substance dependence, social workers may want to ask about substance use by close family members (NIAAA, 2004b). Established tools, which are discussed next, may include questions from one or more of these categories. In general, questions that ask about consequences of alcohol and other drug use tend to be effective for detecting people who have substance use disorders; however, such questions may miss identifying people who are at risk for developing a substance use disorder. Questions about frequency and amount are typically important for detecting persons at risk (CSAT, 1997).

Because it may be particularly difficult for clients to respond honestly about using illicit substances, it is generally helpful to begin with inquiring about alcohol use (IOM, 1990) and then to discuss other drug use. Questions regarding other drug use may be less stigmatizing when paired with questions regarding alcohol use. Risk factors for other drug use include psychiatric illness, genetic predisposition, peers who use alcohol and other drugs, familial conflict, and HIV-positive status (CSAT, 1997).

NIAAA (2007) recommends simply beginning by asking "Do you sometimes drink beer, wine, or other alcoholic beverages?" Negative answers should be followed up with the question "What made you decide not to drink?" (CSAT, 1997, p. 15). If the client has been a lifelong abstainer or reports abstinence for five years or longer, the screening, with a few exceptions discussed next, can be concluded. Regardless of what they report about drinking alcohol, adolescents should be asked about use of other drugs, particularly marijuana. Women who are pregnant or who have experienced a major life transition should be asked about

prescription drug use and over-the-counter sleep aids (CSAT, 1997). Finally, all older adults (those 60 years and older) also should be asked about over-the-counter and prescription drug use (CSAT, 1998).

NIAAA (2007) recommends that positive answers to "Do you sometimes drink beer, wine, or other alcoholic beverages?" should be followed with a question about frequency and amount. Such questions can begin with "How many times in the year have you had five or more drinks in a day [for men] or four or more drinks in a day [for women]?" If the person reports one or more days of heavy drinking, the next questions should include "On average, how many days a week do you drink?" and "On a typical drinking day, how many drinks do you have?" (p. 4). It can be useful to ask the client "What is the maximum number of drinks you consumed on any given occasion during the past month?" With this question in particular, standard drink measures should be clearly identified. One drink is equivalent to 12 oz of beer or wine cooler; 8–9 oz of malt liquor; 5 oz of table wine; 3–4 oz of fortified wine (such as sherry or port); 2–3 oz of cordial, liqueur, or aperitif; and 1.5 oz of spirits (NIAAA, 2004b).

With information about the frequency and amount of alcohol use, the social worker is able to determine if the client's alcohol consumption is within a safe range or is potentially problematic. In defining "at risk" alcohol use, NIAAA (2004b, 2007) states that criteria differ by age, gender, pregnancy/health/medication status, and family history of substance dependence. Consumption of alcohol according to these conditions is considered "at risk":

- More than 14 drinks per week or more than 4 drinks on a given occasion by men
- More than 7 drinks per week or more than 3 drinks on a given occasion by women
- Any amount of alcohol consumption by pregnant women
- More than 7 drinks per week or more than 3 drinks on any given occasion by older adults
- Any alcohol consumption by children or adolescents

In addition, problematic substance use may intersect with a variety of health and psychosocial problems. The presence of the following factors may suggest increased risk of substance use problems:

- Mental health problems
- Presence of infectious diseases such as HIV, hepatitis B and C, and tuberculosis
- Trauma exposure
- Involvement with peers who use drugs and alcohol
- Homelessness/housing instability
- Significant familial conflict or instability
- Familial history of substance use problems
- Vocational instability
- Legal problems (CSAT, 1997)

Although the presence or absence of any of these risk factors cannot predict whether a person will experience substance use problems, their presence can cue the social worker to further consider possible risk (CSAT, 1997). In addition, these health and psychosocial risk factors likely would be points of intervention for social workers in health-care settings as part of comprehensive biopsychosocial assessment and intervention.

Established Tools

Multiple measures have been developed to screen and assess for problems with substance use. These clinical tools include structured interviews and self-administered questionnaires. It is essential that these tools demonstrate accuracy in their screening ability as reflected by the measure's sensitivity and specificity. *Sensitivity* refers to the measure's ability to identify all persons with the designated problem (i.e., to avoid false negatives). *Specificity* refers to the instrument's ability not to include people who do not have the designated problem (i.e., to avoid false positives) (NIAAA, 2004b). For example, if a measure included the single question "Do you drink alcohol?" and identified any person who answered positively as having an alcohol use

disorder, it would have very high sensitivity and low specificity. A measure that identifies a person as having a problem with alcohol use by a positive response to the single question "Have you ever blacked out or lost time when you were drinking alcohol?" would have low sensitivity and high specificity. The sensitivity and specificity of instruments can be altered by shifting their cut-off scores, changing their designated problem, and deleting or adding items. The next discussion illustrates some of these principles.

CAGE

The CAGE is one of the most widely used short screening tools in the substance abuse field. Originally designed to detect alcohol dependence, it consists of four questions about aspects of alcohol use (http://pubs.niaaa.nih.gov/publications/arh28-2/78-79.htm):

1. Have you ever felt that you should cut down on your drinking?
2. Have people annoyed you by criticizing your drinking?
3. Have you ever felt bad or guilty about your drinking?
4. Have you ever had a drink first thing in the morning to steady your nerves or get rid of a hangover ("eye opener")?

A positive answer to two or more questions is considered clinically significant (Ewing, 1984). Research suggests that this measure has high levels of sensitivity and specificity for identifying persons with alcohol use disorders (Buchsbaum, Buchanan, Centor, Schnoll, & Lawton, 1991). Because it does not include questions about frequency or amount of alcohol use, however, it is likely to miss some persons who do not meet diagnostic criteria yet are at-risk drinkers (Adams, Barry, & Fleming, 1996). In an attempt to increase the CAGE's sensitivity for a wider range of substance use problems, both NIAAA (2004b) and CSAT (1997) recommend using the CAGE in conjunction with questions about frequency and amount of alcohol use. Furthermore, both agencies recommend that a positive answer to one question prompt further assessment.

The CAGE has been modified to screen for other drugs in addition to alcohol. The CAGE-AID (CAGE Adapted to Include Drugs) consists of the original CAGE questions, but rather than focusing solely on drinking, the CAGE-AID inquires about drinking or drug use with each of the questions previously identified. With the CAGE-AID, the questions should be preceded by the instruction "When thinking about drug use, include illegal drug use, and the use of prescription drugs other than as prescribed" (Brown, Leonard, Saunders, & Papasouliotis, 1998, p. 102). Because the CAGE-AID, like the CAGE, inquires about negative consequences only, CSAT (1997) recommends asking the additional question "Have you used street drugs more than five times in your life?" (p. 17). A positive answer to this question or to any of the CAGE-AID questions suggests the need for further assessment.

The CAGE and CAGE-AID have been tested with older adults and shown to be effective in screening for both alcohol and other drug use problems among this population. Buchsbaum and colleagues (1991) used a score of 2 or greater on the CAGE to define problem drinking in a sample of medical outpatients over the age of 60 years and found it to have reasonable sensitivity (.70) and very good specificity (.91). Another study examining the utility of the CAGE-AID for use with older adults demonstrated high sensitivity for detecting persons with alcohol or other drug use disorders (.91 and .92, respectively) but low specificity (.48) (Hinkin et al., 2001). The authors noted that many older adults, regardless of whether they had a substance use disorder, answered positively to the question "Have you ever felt you ought to cut down on your drinking or drug use?" By omitting this question, specificity was significantly increased to .69 although sensitivity decreased to .83. Taken together, these findings suggest that providers may want to make adjustments in how they use the CAGE depending on the population, setting, and goals.

AUDIT

The Alcohol Use Disorders Identification Test (AUDIT) includes 10 items that can be completed in an interview or written format. It was designed through a six-country, multicultural, collaborative project of the World Health Organization to detect alcohol use–related problems (Saunders, Aasland, Amundsen, & Grant, 1993). The work group's initial intent was to create a screening tool that detected problems before the development of dependence or serious harm to provide early intervention. The measure covers three conceptual domains: level of consumption (items 1–3), dependence symptoms (items 4–6), and alcohol-related consequences (items 7–10). It is scored by summing the numbers of the answers to each question.

1. How often do you have a drink containing alcohol?
   (0) Never
   (1) Monthly or less
   (2) Two to four times a month
   (3) Two to three times a week
   (4) Four or more times a week
2. How many drinks containing alcohol do you have on a typical day when you are drinking?
   (0) 1 or 2
   (1) 3 or 4
   (2) 5 or 6
   (3) 7 to 9
   (4) 10 or more
3. How often do you have six or more drinks on one occasion?
   (0) Never
   (1) Less than monthly
   (2) Monthly
   (3) Weekly
   (4) Daily or almost daily
4. How often during the last year have you found that you were not able to stop drinking once you had started?
   (0) Never
   (1) Less than monthly

(2) Monthly

(3) Weekly

(4) Daily or almost daily

5. How often during the last year have you failed to do what was normally expected from you because of drinking?

(0) Never

(1) Less than monthly

(2) Monthly

(3) Weekly

(4) Daily or almost daily

6. How often during the last year have you needed a first drink in the morning to get yourself going after a heavy drinking session?

(0) Never

(1) Less than monthly

(2) Monthly

(3) Weekly

(4) Daily or almost daily

7. How often during the last year have you had a feeling of guilt or remorse after drinking?

(0) Never

(1) Less than monthly

(2) Monthly

(3) Weekly

(4) Daily or almost daily

8. How often during the last year have you been unable to remember what happened the night before because you had been drinking?

(0) Never

(1) Less than monthly

(2) Monthly

(3) Weekly

(4) Daily or almost daily

9. Have you or someone else been injured as a result of your drinking?

(0) No

(2) Yes, but not in the last year

(4) Yes, during the last year

10. Has a relative or friend or a doctor or other health worker been concerned about your drinking or suggested you cut down?

(0) No

(2) Yes, but not in the last year

(4) Yes, during the last year

Scores range from 0 to 40. In general, a score of 8 or greater points to the strong likelihood of problematic alcohol use (Saunders, Aasland, Babor, De La Fuente, & Grant, 1993).

Recent research suggests that, in general, the AUDIT has utility across gender and racial groups, although some differences in performance between groups have been found (Reinert & Allen, 2002). For example, Cherpitel (1998) found that when used with a standard cut-off score of 8, the AUDIT was less sensitive for women than for men. NIAAA (2007) recommends that a cut-off score of 8 or higher reflects a positive screening for men and a cut-off score of 4 or higher reflects a positive screening for women.

TICS

The Two-Item Conjoint Screening (TICS) for alcohol and other drug use has shown strong sensitivity and specificity (approximately 81%) in an evaluation with 434 adults in primary care (Brown, Leonard, Saunders, & Papasouliotis, 1997). The TICS involves two questions:

1. In the last year, have you ever drank or used drugs more than you meant to?

2. Have you felt you wanted or needed to cut down on your drinking or drug use in the last year?

As noted by Brown and colleagues (1997), a positive response to either question is likely to accurately identify the presence of a current substance use disorder among 80% of adults (age 18–59 years) who are screened.

Additional Tools

Many other tools have been developed for screening and comprehensive assessment of substance use–related problems. Although there are too many to describe here, a few are mentioned. The Michigan Alcoholism Screening Test (MAST) is a 25-item instrument designed to detect alcohol problems (Selzer, 1971). Two shorter versions are available, the 13-item Short MAST (SMAST; Selzer, Vinokur, & van Rooijen, 1975) and the 10-item Brief MAST (B-MAST; Pokorny, Miller, & Kaplan, 1972). The MAST-Geriatric Version (MAST-G; Blow et al., 1992) has been validated for use with older adults. Finally, the Drug Abuse Screening Test (DAST; Skinner, 1982) was designed to identify problems related to the use of drugs other than alcohol.

From Screening to Brief Intervention

If the screening process indicates that a person may have a possible substance use problem, the social worker will then want to follow up with further assessment for substance use disorders, conduct a brief intervention, and, depending on the severity of the problem, make a referral for more comprehensive assessment and services (Babor et al., 2007; Madras et al., 2009; NIAAA, 2007; SAMHSA, 1999). Brief interventions, which are discussed next, provide a means by which social workers talk with clients about risks related to their use and enhance their motivation to take positive steps toward addressing their substance use problems. Feedback about the screening results is the first step of an initial brief intervention. CSAT (1997, 1999a,b) recommends that feedback be given promptly, in a direct and nonjudgmental manner, and framed in a way that conveys respect, relates to the client's medical health, and is delivered with cultural competence.

Brief Interventions

Opportunities for addressing substance use problems frequently occur in nonsubstance abuse treatment settings. Health social workers and other professionals can be equipped to act on these opportunities through the use of brief interventions. Brief interventions are defined as "those practices that aim to investigate a potential problem and motivate an individual to begin to do something about his substance abuse, either by natural, client-directed means or by seeking additional treatment" (SAMSHA, 1999, p. 5). Brief interventions are informed by general guidelines and include a variety of strategies and techniques.

General Goals and Guidelines

The general goal of all brief interventions is based on a philosophy of harm reduction: "to lower the likelihood of damage that could result from continued use of substances" (SAMHSA, 1999, p. 5). Goals specific to individuals depend on their aims, the characteristics of their use (e.g., substance of choice, severity of use, history of use), their readiness for change, and the setting in which the intervention is offered (CSAT, 1999a). Although eliciting goals that are of interest to the client should guide the goal-setting process, specific goals might include these examples: participating in a more comprehensive assessment, identifying costs and benefits of substance use, recording amount of use over a given time period, decreasing amount of use over a given time period, declining an offer for a drink or other substance, attending an AA or NA meeting, expanding a supportive social network, and identifying positive activities that can be substituted for substance use (CSAT, 1999a). These possibilities are only a few examples. The social worker and client can creatively brainstorm to identify other goals appropriate for the particular circumstances of the client. Social workers should emphasize the positive quality of any goal that decreases the risk of harm resulting from substance use.

In an extensive review of 32 studies in 14 countries, the findings of Bien, Miller, and Tonigan (1993) provide substantial support for the effectiveness of brief interventions to assist people experiencing problematic alcohol use. In 11 out of 12 trials, brief intervention enhanced referrals and engagement in specialized services. In seven out of eight trials, brief interventions were effective in reducing alcohol use or problems associated with use in comparison to no intervention. Miller and Sanchez (1993) examined the brief intervention strategies employed in these outcome studies to determine common ingredients among the interventions. Six components of effective brief interventions were identified and are summarized by the now widely known and recommended FRAMES acronym: "Feedback, Responsibility, Advice, Menu, Empathy, and Self-efficacy" (Bien et al., 1993, p. 326; Britt et al., 2004; CSAT, 1999a; Miller & Sanchez, 1993). Such brief interventions, including the FRAMES approach, are important ingredients in the SBIRT model addressed earlier (Madras et al., 2009).

(1) Providers offer feedback to clients to inform them about the risks associated with their substance use; however, this feedback process should be interactive, with incremental provision of information and elicitation of the client's responses to it (CSAT, 1999a,b). Effective brief interventions typically include structured screening, such as those discussed earlier. Following this screening, clients receive information about the status of their substance use. In addition to educating clients about their general status, health social workers also should provide clients with information regarding the health interactions and consequences of their substance use. For example, active substance use contraindicates many medical interventions (e.g., organ transplants, particular medications).

(2) Responsibility for change is placed with the clients (CSAT, 1999a). It is important for clients to know that while the professional is concerned and interested in their welfare, ultimately it is the decision and responsibility of clients to make changes in substance use behavior. Care must be taken so that clients do not feel alone in trying to change or blamed for their problems. Rather, social workers should recognize that this step is about self-determination and empowerment (CSAT, 1999b), which reflects the spirit of autonomy, a central component of motivational interviewing (Miller & Rollnick, 2002).

(3) The provider gives advice to clients to change their behavior (Bien et al., 1993; CSAT, 1999b). This advice will vary depending on the client and can range from suggesting a change in substance use behavior to providing relevant information about substance use (CSAT, 1999b). Key elements of giving advice in a way that is consistent with motivational interviewing include asking permission from clients to provide the advice (e.g., "Can I tell you what I've seen in the past in these situations?" (CSAT, 1999b, p. 27), providing information in culturally relevant ways, and attending to the way in which the suggestions are made (Britt et al., 2004; CSAT, 1999b).

(4) The social worker provides a menu of various options to facilitate change (Bien et al., 1993; CSAT, 1999b). Such options may include treatment services, self-help, and other change strategies. Providing clients with information about the options and discussing their perspectives about them are central elements of assisting clients with making an informed decision about how they would like to proceed (CSAT, 1999b).

(5) The social worker should use an empathetic stance that conveys respect, caring, warmth, and reflective listening (Bien et al., 1993; CSAT, 1999b).

(6) Social workers should seek to enhance clients' sense of self-efficacy, that is, the belief that they can and will accomplish goals they set for themselves (CSAT, 1999b). Conveying hope, optimism, and recognition of clients' strengths are meaningful ways in which to achieve this goal (Bien et al., 1993; CSAT, 1999b).

CONCLUSION

Health social workers face many challenges in providing effective assistance to persons struggling with substance use problems. The knowledge base is expansive, the field sometimes is perceived as in flux, and substance use problems can seem impermeable to change. In addition, such problems have a far-reaching presence across persons of diverse age, gender, sexual orientations, and racial, cultural, and socioeconomic backgrounds. This chapter orients the provider to foundational information that is useful for offering hopeful and effective interventions with clients experiencing substance use problems. Information about short-term psychoactive and long-term health effects of commonly used substances, along with current prevalence data, is aimed to equip health social workers with the ability to identify individuals who may be at risk for difficulties with use of particular substances. In addition, such information can assist with strengthening the developmental and cultural competence of services to reach affected groups. The overview of prominent approaches to conceptualizing and addressing substance use problems familiarizes the health social worker with intervention options and their research support. It is essential that social workers be aware of the existing evidence base for particular approaches and, when possible, provide or refer clients to services that utilize evidence-based practice strategies. Finally, the chapter provides screening knowledge and tools as well as a framework for brief intervention strategies. This information offers guidance so that the social worker can assist people experiencing substance use problems in ways that offer hope, enhance motivation, reduce harm, and strengthen efforts to pursue and sustain change.

SUGGESTED LEARNING EXERCISES

Learning Exercise 17.1

How would you define *tolerance, withdrawal, physical dependence*, and *addiction*? How can clarity regarding these concepts be helpful in health social work practice?

Learning Exercise 17.2

How can knowledge regarding the epidemiology and effects of various substances be used in health social work practice with clients?

Learning Exercise 17.3

What are some of the prominent approaches to conceptualizing and addressing substance use problems? Do you prefer particular approaches? What informs your preference for particular approaches? What does research suggest about the effectiveness of the approaches discussed in this chapter, and how does that information fit with your perspective of "what works"? How might the research findings and your preferences inform your direct practice with people experiencing substance use problems? What additional evidence can inform your direct practice in this area?

Learning Exercise 17.4

What does the acronym *SBIRT* represent? What is known about its effectiveness? To what degree do you and the agency you work or intern at engage in SBIRT activities with the clients you serve? How might SBIRT efforts be strengthened in your own practice and in your agency?

Learning Exercise 17.5

In pairs, role-play how might you draw on the FRAMES model in brief intervention with Alex in the next hypothetical situation.

Alex is a 25-year-old, heterosexual, Caucasian man of Italian American descent who resides with his mother, who is 60 years old. His brother, Carl, brought him to the community health clinic because he is concerned about his drinking, his use of cocaine, his overall health, and the worry their mother is experiencing about Alex. After seeing a primary care physician, Alex was referred to you. Your brief screening with Alex indicates that he has made numerous attempts to stop using cocaine and to reduce his drinking. He explains that these efforts "have not quite worked out," but he feels he can address this issue on his own. He also feels angry with his brother for "making such a big deal about all of this," but at the same time he describes feeling guilty about his behavior when he drinks and uses cocaine. Alex states that he usually drinks a six-pack of beer four or five times a week, but he recently has increased this amount and has not "really kept track of it." Alex describes that he uses cocaine less often since he lost his job a month ago and cannot afford it. Currently Alex does not have health insurance or regular income.

Learning Exercise 17.6

What do you consider your strengths and challenges in working with people experiencing substance use problems? What additional information would help strengthen your ability to effectively assist people experiencing substance use problems?

Learning Exercise 17.7

If you were asked to develop one of the groups listed next, how might you proceed? What approach(es) would guide the group, and how would you structure it? How might you recruit participants? Who would be included in the group? How would you measure the success of the group? What would be the rationale for these decisions? What challenges might you face with implementing this group, and how might you address them proactively?

Group Topics

- Substance use and health for a general population
- Pain management for people at risk of developing substance use
- Problems while managing persistent pain
- Overdose prevention for people at risk and their loved ones

SUGGESTED RESOURCES

Al-Anon and Alateen—www.al-anon.alateen.org

Alcoholics Anonymous—www.aa.org

Alcoholism and Drug Addiction Counselor Information and Certification—www.naadac.org/index.php?option=com_content&view=article&id=478&Itemid=129 Current Clinical Trials—www.clinicaltrials.gov

Double Trouble in Recovery—www.doubletroubleinrecovery.org

Based on a 12-step approach, this program assists people experiencing co-occurring substance use and mental health problems.

Harm Reduction Coalition—www.harmreduction.org

Health Effects of Substance Use—www.drugabuse.gov/consequences

International Harm Reduction Association—www.ihra.net

Join Together—www.jointogether.org

Motivational Interviewing—www.motivationalinterview.org

Narcotics Anonymous—www.na.org

National Clearinghouse for Alcohol and Drug Information (NCADI)—www.health.org

This clearinghouse contains information and resources about alcohol and other drugs available from NIAAA, NIDA, and SAMHSA. Resources include videos, posters, pamphlets, educational tools and kits, and reports. Information geared toward a range of audiences (e.g., families, youth, health providers, educators, researchers) are available. Many of the resources are free.

National Institute on Alcoholism and Alcohol Abuse—www.niaaa.nih.gov

This branch of the National Institutes of Health (NIH) researches the effects and treatment of problematic alcohol use.

National Institute on Drug Abuse—www.nida.nih.gov

This branch of the NIH researches the effects and treatment of drug abuse.

National Registry of Evidence-Based Programs and Practices—www.nrepp .samhsa.gov

Substance Abuse and Mental Health Services Administration—www.samhsa.gov

This branch of the Department of Health and Human Services is charged with developing and disseminating effective prevention and treatment programs. SAMHSA includes both the Center for Substance Abuse Prevention (CSAP) and the Center for Substance Abuse Treatment (CSAT).

Substance Abuse Treatment for Gay, Lesbian, Bisexual, and Transgender Individuals—http://kap.samhsa.gov/products /manuals/pdfs/lgbt.pdf

Treatment Locator (NCADI)—http:// dasis3.samhsa.gov

This resource locates substance abuse treatment providers sorted by geographic location, population, and type of treatment.

World Health Organization—http:// whqlibdoc.who.int/hq/1992/WHO_PSA _92.4. pdf

This site provides guidelines for using the AUDIT in primary health care.

University of Washington Alcohol and Drug Abuse Institute—https://depts .washington.edu/adai

REFERENCES

Aaron, S., McMahon, J. M., Milano, D., Torres, L., Clatts, M., Tortu, S.,...Simm, M. (2008). Intranasal transmission of hepatitis C virus: Virological and clinical evidence. *Clinical Infectious Diseases, 47,* 931–934.

Abbott, A. A. (2002). Health care challenges created by substance abuse: The whole is definitely bigger than the sum of its parts. *Health & Social Work, 27,* 162–165.

Abbott, A. A., & Wood, K. M. (2000). Assessment: Techniques and instruments for data collection. In A. A. Abbott (Ed.), *Alcohol, tobacco, and other drugs: Challenging myths, assessing theories, individualizing interventions* (pp. 159–186). Washington, DC: National Association of Social Workers Press.

Abraham, H. D., Aldridge, A. M., & Gogia, P. (1996). The psychopharmacology of hallucinogens. *Neuropsychopharmacology, 14,* 285–298.

Adams, W. L., Barry, K. L., & Fleming, M. F. (1996). Screening for problem drinking in older primary care patients. *JAMA, 276,* 1964–1967.

Alcoholics Anonymous. (1972). *A brief guide to Alcoholics Anonymous.* New York, NY: Alcoholics Anonymous World Services. Retrieved from www .alcoholics-anonymous.org

Alcoholics Anonymous. (2001). *Alcoholics Anonymous: The story of how many thousands of men and women have recovered from alcoholism* (4th ed.). New York, NY: Author.

Alterman, A. I., McLellan, A. T., O'Brien, C. P., & McKay, J. R. (1998). Differential therapies and options. In R. J. Frances & S. I. Miller (Eds.), *Clinical textbook of addictive disorders* (2nd ed., pp. 447–478). New York, NY: Guilford Press.

American Psychiatric Association. (2000). *Diagnostic and statistical manual of mental disorders* (4th ed., text revision). Washington, DC: Author.

American Society of Addiction Medicine. (2001). *ASAM patient placement criteria for the treatment of substance-related disorders* (2nd ed.). Chevy Chase, MD: Author.

Apodaca, T. R., & Longabaugh, R. (2009). Mechanisms of change in motivational interviewing: A review and preliminary evaluation of the evidence. *Addiction, 104,* 705–715.

Babor, T. F., McRee, B. G., Kassebaum, P. A., Grimaldi, P. L., Ahmed, K., & Bray, J. (2007). Screening, brief intervention, and referral to treatment (SBIRT): Toward a public health approach to the management of substance abuse. *Substance Abuse, 28*(3), 7–30.

Bien, T. H., Miller, W. R., & Tonigan, J. S. (1993). Brief interventions for alcohol problems: A review. *Addiction, 88,* 315–336.

Blow, F. C., Brower, K. J., Schulenberg, J. E., Demo-Dananberg, L. M., Young, J. P., & Beresford, T. P. (1992). The Michigan Alcoholism Screening Test—Geriatric Version (MAST-G): A new elderly-specific screening instrument. *Alcoholism: Clinical and Experimental Research, 16,* 372.

Bohnert, A. S. B., Prescott, M. R., Vlahov, D., Tardiff, K. J., & Galea, S. (2010). Ambient temperature and risk of death from accidental drug overdose in New York City, 1990–2006. *Addiction, 105,* 1049–1054.

Borden, W. (2000, September). The relational paradigm in contemporary psychoanalysis: Toward a psychodynamically informed social work perspective. *Social Service Review,* 352–379.

Brady, K. T., Myrick, H., & Malcolm, R. (1999). Sedative-hypnotic and anxiolytic agents. In B. S. McCrady & E. E. Epstein (Eds.), *Addiction: A comprehensive guidebook* (pp. 95–104). New York, NY: Oxford University Press.

Bridle, C., Riemsma, R. P., Pattenden, J., Sowden, A. J., Mather, L., Watt, I. S., & Walker, A. (2005). Systematic review of the effectiveness of health behavior interventions based on the Transtheoretical Model. *Psychology and Health, 20*(3).

Britt, E., Hudson, S. M., & Blampied, N. M. (2004). Motivational interviewing in health settings: A review. *Patient Education and Counseling, 53,* 147–155.

Brocato, J., & Wagner, E. F. (2003). Harm reduction: A social work practice model and social justice agenda. *Health & Social Work, 28*(2), 117–125.

Brown, R. L., Leonard, T., Saunders, L. A., & Papasouliotis, O. (1997). A two-item screening test for alcohol and other drug problems. *Journal of Family Practice, 44*(2), 151–160.

Brown, R. L., Leonard, T., Saunders, L. A., & Papasouliotis, O. (1998). The prevalence and detection of substance use disorders among inpatients ages 18 to 59: An opportunity for prevention. *Preventive Medicine, 27,* 101–110.

Buchsbaum, D. G., Buchanan, R. G., Centor, R. M., Schnoll, S. H., & Lawton, M. J. (1991). Screening for alcohol abuse using CAGE scores and likelihood ratios. *Annals of Internal Medicine, 115,* 774–777.

Buxton, J. A., Skutezky, T., Tu, A. W., Waheed, B., Wallace, A., & Mak, S. (2009). The context of illicit drug overdose deaths in British Columbia, 2006. *Harm Reduction Journal, 6*(9). Retrieved from http://harmreductionjournal.com/content/6/1/9

Center for Substance Abuse Prevention. (2003). Here's the latest on inhalants. *CSAP Prevention Alert, 6*(11), 1–3.

Center for Substance Abuse Treatment. (1997). *A guide to substance abuse services for primary care clinicians* (Treatment Improvement Protocol [TIP] Series, No. 24, DHHS Pub. No. SMA 03–3807). Washington, DC: U.S. Government Printing Office.

Center for Substance Abuse Treatment. (1998). *Substance abuse among older adults* (Treatment Improvement Protocol [TIP] Series, No. 26, DHHS Pub. No. SMA 98–3179). Rockville, MD: Substance Abuse and Mental Health Services Administration.

Center for Substance Abuse Treatment. (1999a). *Brief interventions and brief therapies for substance abuse* (Treatment Improvement Protocol [TIP] Series, No. 34, DHHS Pub. No. SMA 04–3952). Rockville, MD: Substance Abuse and Mental Health Services Administration.

Center for Substance Abuse Treatment. (1999b). *Enhancing motivation for change in substance abuse treatment* (Treatment Improvement Protocol [TIP] Series, No. 35, DHHS Pub. No. SMA 04–3922). Rockville, MD: Substance Abuse and Mental Health Services Administration.

Center for Substance Abuse Treatment. (2005). *Substance abuse treatment for persons with co-occurring disorder* (Treatment Improvement Protocol [TIP] Series, 42. DHHS Pub. No. SMA 05–3922). Rockville, MD: Substance Abuse and Mental Health Services Administration.

Center for Substance Abuse Treatment. (2009). *Substance abuse treatment: Addressing the specific needs of women* (Treatment Improvement Protocol [TIP] Series, 51 DHHS Pub. No. SMA 09–4426). Rockville, MD: Substance Abuse and Mental Health Services Administration.

Centers for Disease Control and Prevention. (2004). January 11, 2004 marks the 40th anniversary of the inaugural surgeon general's report on smoking and health. Retrieved from www.cdc.gov/tobacco/overview/anniversary.htm

Chedid, A., Mendenhall, C. L., Gartside, P., French, S. W., Chen, T., & Rabin, L. (1991). Prognostic factors in alcoholic liver disease. *American Journal of Gastroenterology, 86,* 210–216.

Cherpitel, C. J. (1998). Differences in performance of screening instruments for problem drinking among Blacks, Whites and Hispanics in emergency room population. *Journal of Studies on Alcohol, 59,* 420–426.

Chi, F. W., Kaskutas, L. A., Sterling, S., Campbell, C. I., & Weisner, C. (2009). Twelve-step affiliation and 3-year substance use outcomes among adolescents: Social support and religious service attendance as potential mediators. *Addiction, 104*(6), 927–939.

Chiasson, R. E. (1994). Smoking cessation in patients with HIV. *JAMA, 272*(7), 564.

Compton, W. M., & Volkow, N. D. (2006). Major increases in opioid analgesic abuse in the United States: Concerns and strategies. *Drug and Alcohol Dependence, 81,* 103–107.

Cook, J. M., Walser, R. D., Kane, V., Ruzek, J. I., & Woody, G. (2006). Dissemination and feasibility of a cognitive-behavioral treatment for substance use disorders and posttraumatic stress disorder in the Veterans Administration. *Journal of Psychoactive Drugs, 38,* 89–92.

Cooney, N. L., Zweben, A., & Fleming, M. F. (1995). Screening for alcohol problems and at-risk drinking in health-care settings. In R. K. Hester & W. R. Miller (Eds.), *Handbook of alcoholism treatment approaches: Effective alternatives* (2nd ed., pp. 45–60). Boston, MA: Allyn & Bacon.

Cornelius, L. J. (2002). Defining substance abusers using a prism: What you see is what you get. *Health & Social Work, 27,* 234–237.

Cusack, K. J., Morrissey, J. P., & Ellis, A. R. (2008). Targeting trauma-related interventions and improving outcomes for women with co-occurring disorders. *Administration and Policy in Mental Health and Mental Health Services Research, 35*(3), 147–158.

Dar, K. J., & McBrien, M. E. (1996). MDMA induced hyperthermia: Report of a fatality and review of current therapy. [Review]. *Intensive Care Medicine, 22,* 995–996.

Dawson, D. A., & Grant, B. F. (1998). Family history of alcoholism and gender: Their combined effects on DSM-IV alcohol dependence and major depression. *Journal of Studies of Alcohol, 59,* 97–106.

Denning, P. (2001). Strategies for implementation of harm reduction in treatment settings. *Journal of Psychoactive Drugs, 33*(1), 23–26.

DiClemente, C. C. (1991). Motivational interviewing and the stages of change. In W. R. Miller & S. Rollnick, *Motivational interviewing: Preparing people to change addictive behavior* (pp. 191–202). New York, NY: Guilford Press.

DiClemente, C. C., & Velasquez, M. M. (2002). Motivational interviewing and the stages of change. In W. R. Miller & S. Rollnick (Eds.), *Motivational interviewing: Preparing people for change* (2nd ed., pp. 201–216). New York, NY: Guilford Press.

Dietary Guidelines Advisory Committee. (2010). Report of the DGAC on the dietary guidelines for Americans, 2010. Retrieved from www.cnpp.usda .gov/DGAs2010-DGACReport.htm

Dimeff, L. A., & Marlatt, G. A. (1998). Preventing relapse and maintaining change in addictive behaviors. *Clinical Psychology: Science and Practice, 5,* 513–525.

Donovan, D. M. (1999). Assessment strategies and measures in addictive behaviors. In B. S. McCrady & E. E. Epstein (Eds.), *Addictions: A comprehensive guidebook* (pp. 187–215). New York, NY: Oxford University Press.

Donovan, D. M., Carroll, K. M., Kadden, R. M., DiClemente, C. C., & Rounsaville, B. J. (2003). Therapies for matching: Selection, development, implementation and costs. In G. Edwards (Series Ed.), T. F. Babor & F. K. Del Boca (Vol. Eds.), *International Research Monographs in the Addictions (IRMA): Treatment matching in alcoholism* (pp. 42–61). Cambridge, UK: Cambridge University Press.

Dunn, C., Deroo, L., & Rivara, F. (2001). The use of brief interventions adapted from motivational interviewing across behavioral domains: A systematic review. *Addiction, 96,* 1725–1742.

Durrant, R., & Thakker, J. (2003). *Substance use and abuse: Cultural and historical perspectives.* Thousand Oaks, CA: Sage.

El-Bassel, N., Gilbert, L., Wu, E., Chang, M., & Fontdevila, J. (2007). Perpetration of intimate partner violence among men in methadone treatment programs in New York City. *American Journal of Public Health, 97*(7), 1230–1232.

Elliott, D. E., Bjelajac, P., Fallot, R. D., Markoff, L. S., & Reed, B. G. (2005). Trauma-informed or trauma-denied: Principles and implementation of trauma-informed services for women. *Journal of Community Psychology, 33*(4), 461–477.

Engstrom, M., El-Bassel, N., Go, H., & Gilbert, L. (2008). Childhood sexual abuse and intimate partner violence among women in methadone treatment: A direct or mediated relationship? *Journal of Family Violence, 23*(7), 605–617.

Engstrom, M., Shibusawa, T., El-Bassel, N., & Gilbert, L. (2009). Age and HIV sexual risk among women in methadone treatment. *AIDS and Behavior, 15*(1), 103–113.

Ewing, J. A. (1984). Detecting alcoholism: The CAGE Questionnaire. *JAMA, 252,* 1905–1907.

Fields, G. (2010, July 29). House passes bill easing crack-cocaine sentences. *Wall Street Journal.*

Finkelstein, N., VandeMark, N., Fallot, R., Brown, V., Cadiz, S., & Heckman, J. (2004). Enhancing substance abuse recovery through integrated trauma treatment. Sarasota, FL: National Trauma Consortium. Available at www.nationaltraumaconsortium.org/documents /IntegratedTrauma.pdf

Futterman, R., Lorente, M., & Silverman, S. (2004). Integrating harm reduction in abstinence-based substance abuse treatment in the public sector. *Substance Abuse, 25*(1), 3–7.

Gibson, D. R., Flynn, N. M., & Perales, D. (2001). Effectiveness of syringe exchange programs in reducing HIV risk behavior and HIV seroconversion among injecting drug users. *AIDS, 15,* 1329–1341.

Gilbert, L., El-Bassel, N., Manuel, J., Wu, E., Go, H., Golder, S., … Sanders, G. (2006). An integrated relapse prevention and relationship safety intervention for women on methadone: Testing short-term effects on intimate partner violence and substance use. *Violence and Victims, 21*(5), 657–672.

Grant, B. F. (2000). Estimates of U.S. children exposed to alcohol abuse and dependence in the family. *American Journal of Public Health, 90,* 112–115.

Grant, B. F., Hasin, D. S., Chou, S. P., Stinson, F. S., & Dawson, D. A. (2004). Nicotine dependence and psychiatric disorders in the United States. *Archives of General Psychiatry, 61,* 1107–1115.

Grella, C. E., & Stein, J. A. (2006). Impact of program services on treatment outcomes of patients with comorbid mental and substance use disorders. *Psychiatric Services, 57*(7), 1007–1015.

Harm Reduction Coalition. (n.d.). Principles of harm reduction. Retrieved from www.harmreduction.org

Harris, M., & Fallot, R. D. (Eds.) (2001). *Using trauma theory to design service systems.* San Francisco, CA: Jossey-Bass.

Hatch, E. E., & Bracken, M. B. (1986). Effect of marijuana use in pregnancy on fetal growth. *American Journal of Epidemiology, 124,* 986–993.

Hatsukami, D. K., & Fischman, M. W. (1996). Crack cocaine and cocaine hydrochloride: Are the differences myth or reality? *JAMA, 276,* 1580–1588.

Heather, N. (2005). Motivational interviewing: Is it all our clients need? *Addiction Research and Theory, 13,* 1–18.

Henggeler, S. W., Schoenwald, S. K., Borduin, C. M., Rowland, M. D., & Cunningham, P. B. (1998). *Multisystemic treatment of antisocial behavior in children and adolescents.* New York, NY: Guilford Press.

Hepworth, D. H., Rooney, R. H., & Larsen, J. A. (2002). *Direct social work practice: Theory and skills* (6th ed.). Pacific Grove, CA: Brooks/Cole.

Hettema, J., Steele, J., & Miller, W. R. (2005). Motivational interviewing. *Annual Review of Clinical Psychology, 1,* 91–111.

Hien, D. A., Cohen, L. R., Miele, G. M., Litt, L. C., & Capstick, C. (2004). Promising treatments for women with comorbid PTSD and substance use disorders. *American Journal of Psychiatry, 161*(8), 1426–1432.

Hien, D. A., Jiang, H., Campbell, A. N. C., Hu, M.-C., Miele, G. M., Cohen, L. R., ... Nunes, E. V. (2010). Do treatment improvements in PTSD severity affect substance use outcomes? A secondary analysis from a randomized clinical trial in NIDA's Clinical Trials Network. *American Journal of Psychiatry, 167*(1), 95–101.

Hinkin, C. H., Castellon, S. A., Dickson-Fuhrman, E., Daum, G., Jaffe, J., & Jarvik, L. (2001). Screening for drug and alcohol abuse among older adults using the modified version of the CAGE. *American Journal on Addiction, 10*(4), 319–326.

Housenbold Seiger, B. (2004). The clinical practice of harm reduction. In S. L. A. Straussner (Ed.), *Clinical work with substance abusing clients* (2nd ed., pp. 65–81). New York, NY: Guilford Press.

Hu, G., & Baker, S. P. (2009). Trends in unintentional injury deaths, U.S., 1999–2005: Age, gender and racial/ethnic differences. *American Journal of Preventive Medicine, 37*(3), 188–194.

Humphreys, K., Wing, S., McCarty, D., Chappel, J., Gallant, L., Haberle, B., ... Weiss, R. (2004). Self-help organizations for alcohol and drug problems: Toward evidence-based practice and policy. *Journal of Substance Abuse Treatment, 26,* 151–158.

Hunt, N. (2003). A review of the evidence-base for harm reduction approaches to drug use. Retrieved from www.ihra.net/files/2010/05/31/HIVTop50Documents11.pdf

Imhof, J. E. (1995). Overcoming countertransference and other attitudinal barriers in the treatment of substance abuse. In A. M. Washton (Ed.), *Psychotherapy and substance abuse: A practitioner's handbook* (pp. 3–22). New York, NY: Guilford Press.

Institute of Medicine. (1990). *Broadening the base of treatment for alcohol problems.* Washington, DC: National Academy Press.

Institute of Medicine. (2001). *Health and behavior: The interplay of biological, behavioral, and societal influences.* Washington, DC: National Academy Press.

Jaffe, A. J., Rounsaville, B., Chang, G., Schottenfeld, R. S., Meyer, R. E., & O'Malley, S. S. (1996). Naltrexone, relapse prevention, and supportive therapy with alcoholics: An analysis of patient treatment matching. *Journal of Consulting and Clinical Psychology, 64,* 1044–1053.

Joy, J. E., Watson, S. J., Jr., & Benson, J. A., Jr. (Eds.). (1999). *Marijuana and medicine: Assessing the scientific base.* Washington, DC: National Academy Press.

Kandel, D. B., Davies, M., Karus, D., & Yamaguchi, K. (1986). The consequences in young adulthood of adolescent drug involvement. *Archives of General Psychiatry, 43,* 746–754.

Keegan, J., Parva, M., Finnegan, M., Gerson, A., & Belden, M. (2010). Addiction in pregnancy. *Journal of Addictive Diseases, 29,* 175–191.

Kellogg, S. H. (2003). On "gradualism" and the building of the harm reduction-abstinence continuum. *Journal of Substance Abuse Treatment, 25,* 241–247.

Kinney, J., & Leaton, G. (1991). *Loosening the grip: A handbook of alcohol information.* St. Louis, MO: Mosby-Year Book.

Kosten, T. R., & Sofuoglu, M. (2004). Stimulants. In M. Galanter & H. D. Kleber (Eds.), *Textbook of substance abuse treatment* (3rd ed., pp. 189–197). Washington, DC: American Psychiatric Press.

Kranzler, H. R., & Anton, R. F. (1994). Implications of recent neuropsychopharmacologic research for understanding the etiology and development of alcoholism. *Journal of Consulting and Clinical Psychology, 62,* 1116–1126.

Krentzman, A. (2007). The evidence base for the effectiveness of Alcoholics Anonymous: Implications for social work practice. *Journal of Social Work Practice in the Addictions, 7*(4), 27–48.

Larimer, M. E., Malone, D. K., Garner, M. D., Atkins, D. C., Burlingham, B., Lonczak, H. S., ... Marlatt, G. A. (2009). Health care and public service use and costs before and after provision of housing for chronically homeless persons with severe alcohol problems. *JAMA, 301*(13), 1349–1357.

Larimer, M. E., Palmer, R. S., & Marlatt, G. A. (1999). Relapse prevention: An overview of Marlatt's cognitive-behavioral model. *Alcohol Research and Health, 23,* 151–160.

Lee, H., Engstrom, M., & Petersen, S. (in press). Harm reduction and twelve steps: Complementary, oppositional, or something in-between? *Substance Use & Misuse.*

Lemon, S. C., Friedman, P. D., & Stein, M. D. (2003). The impact of smoking cessation on drug abuse treatment outcome. *Addictive Behaviors, 28,* 1323–1331.

Leshner, A. I. (1997). Addiction is a brain disease, and it matters. *Science, 278,* 45–47.

Liddle, H. A., & Hogue, A. (2001). Multidimensional family therapy for adolescent substance abuse. In E. F. Wagner & H. B. Waldron (Eds.), *Innovations in adolescent substance abuse interventions* (pp. 227–261). London, UK: Pergamon/Elsevier Science.

Liddle, H. A., Rowe, C. L., Dakof, G. A., Henderson, C. E., & Greenbaum, P. E. (2009). Multidimensional family therapy for young adolescent substance abuse: Twelve-month outcomes of a randomized controlled trial. *Journal of Consulting and Clinical Psychology, 77*(1), 12–25.

Littell, J. H., & Girvin, H. (2002). Stages of change: A critique. *Behavior Modification, 26*(2), 223–273.

Logan, D. E., & Marlatt, G. A. (2010). Harm reduction therapy: A practice-friendly review of research. *Journal of Clinical Psychology: In Session, 66*(2), 201–214.

Longabaugh, R., & Morgenstern, J. (1999). Cognitive-behavioral coping-skills therapy for alcohol dependence. *Alcohol Research and Health, 23,* 78–85.

Lundahl, B., & Burke, B. L. (2009). The effectiveness and applicability of motivational interviewing: A practice-friendly review of four meta-analyses. *Journal of Clinical Psychology: In Session, 65*(11), 1232–1245.

Lundahl, B. W., Kunz, C., Brownell, C., Tollefson, D., & Burke, B. L. (2010). A meta-analysis of motivational interviewing: Twenty-five years of empirical studies. *Research on Social Work Practice, 20*(2), 137–160.

Macias, J., Palacios, R. B., Claro, E., Vargas, J., Vergara, S., Mira, J. A., . . . Pineda, J. A. (2008). High prevalence of hepatitis C virus infection among noninjecting users: Association with sharing the inhalation implements of crack. *Liver International, 28*(6), 781–786.

MacMaster, S. A. (2004). Harm reduction: A new perspective on substance abuse services. *Social Work, 49*(3), 356–363.

Madras, B. K., Compton, W. M., Avula, D., Stegbauer, T., Stein, J. B., & Clark, H. W. (2009). Screening, brief interventions, referral to treatment (SBIRT) for illicit drug and alcohol use at multiple health care sites: Comparison at intake and 6 months later. *Drug and Alcohol Dependence, 99,* 280–295.

Marlatt, G. A. (1985a). Theoretical rationale and model. In G. A. Marlatt & J. R. Gordon (Eds.), *Relapse prevention* (pp. 3–70). New York, NY: Guilford Press.

Marlatt, G. A. (1985b). Cognitive factors in the relapse process. In G. A. Marlatt & J. R. Gordon (Eds.), *Relapse prevention* (pp. 128–200). New York, NY: Guilford Press.

Marlatt, G. A. (1998). Basic principles and strategies of harm reduction. In G. A. Marlatt (Ed.), *Harm reduction: Pragmatic strategies for managing high-risk behaviors* (pp. 49–66). New York, NY: Guilford Press.

Marlatt, G. A., Blume, A. W., & Parks, G. A. (2001). Integrating harm reduction therapy and traditional substance abuse treatment. *Journal of Psychoactive Drugs, 33*(1), 13–21.

Marlatt, G. A., & Gordon, J. R. (Eds.). (1985). *Relapse prevention.* New York, NY: Guilford Press.

Marlatt, G. A., & Witkiewitz, K. (2010). Update on harm-reduction policy and intervention research. *Annual Review of Clinical Psychology, 6,* 591–606.

Marsh, J. C., Cao, D., & D'Aunno, T. (2004). Gender differences in the impact of comprehensive services in substance abuse treatment. *Journal of Substance Abuse Treatment, 27,* 289–300.

McCrady, B. S. (1993). Alcoholism. In D. S. Barlow (Ed.), *Clinical handbook of psychological disorders* (2nd ed., pp. 362–395). New York, NY: Guilford Press.

McLellan, A. T., Hagan, T. A., Levine, M., Gould, F., Meyers, K., Bencivengo, M., & Durell, J. (1998). Supplemental social services improve outcomes in public addiction treatment. *Addiction, 93*(10), 1489–1499.

McNeece, C. A., & Barbanell, L. D. (2005). Definitions and epidemiology of substance use, abuse, and disorders. In C. A. McNeece & D. M. DiNitto (Eds.), *Chemical dependency: A systems approach* (3rd ed., pp. 3–24). Boston, MA: Pearson Education.

McNeece, C. A., & DiNitto, D. M. (2005). *Chemical dependency: A systems approach* (3rd ed.). Boston, MA: Pearson Education.

Miller, P. G., & Miller, W. R. (2009). What should we be aiming for in the treatment of addiction? *Addiction, 104,* 685–686.

Miller, W. R. (2000). Rediscovering fire: Small interventions, large effects. *Psychology of Addictive Behaviors, 14,* 6–18.

Miller, W. R., & Hester, R. K. (1995). Treatment for alcohol problems: Toward an informed eclecticism. In R. K. Hester & W. R. Miller (Eds.), *Handbook of alcoholism treatment approaches: Effective alternatives* (2nd ed., pp. 1–11). Boston, MA: Allyn & Bacon.

Miller, W. R., & Kurtz, E. (1994). Models of alcoholism used in treatment: Contrasting AA and other perspectives with which it is often confused. *Journal of Studies on Alcohol, 55,* 159–166.

Miller, W. R., & Longabaugh, R. (2003). Summary and conclusions. In G. Edwards (Series Ed.), T. F. Babor, & F. K. Del Boca (Vol. Eds.), *International research monographs in the addictions (IRMA): Treatment matching in alcoholism* (pp. 207–237). Cambridge, UK: Cambridge University Press.

Miller, W. R., & Rollnick, S. (1991). *Motivational interviewing: Preparing people to change addictive behavior.* New York, NY: Guilford Press.

Miller, W. R., & Rollnick, S. (2002). *Motivational interviewing: Preparing people for change* (2nd ed.). New York, NY: Guilford Press.

Miller, W. R., & Rose, G. S. (2009). Toward a theory of motivational interviewing. *American Psychologist, 64*(6), 527–537.

Miller, W. R., & Sanchez, V. C. (1993). Motivating young adults for treatment and lifestyle change. In G. Howard & P. E. Nathan (Eds.), *Issues in alcohol use and misuse by young adults* (pp. 55–82). Notre Dame, IN: University of Notre Dame Press.

Miller, W. R., Westerberg, V. S., Harris, R. J., & Tonigan, J. S. (1996). What predicts relapse? Prospective testing of antecedent models. *Addiction, 91*(Suppl.), S155–S171.

Miller, W. R., Yahne, C. E., & Tonigan, J. S. (2003). Motivational interviewing in drug abuse services: A randomized trial. *Journal of Consulting and Clinical Psychology, 71,* 754–763.

Miller, W. R., Zweben, J., & Johnson, W. R. (2005). Evidence-based treatment: Why, what, where, when and how? *Journal of Substance Abuse Treatment, 29,* 267–276.

Moak, D. H., & Anton, R. F. (1999). Alcohol. In B. S. McCrady & E. E. Epstein (Eds.), *Addictions: A comprehensive guidebook* (pp. 75–94). New York, NY: Oxford University Press.

Morrissey, J. P., Ellis, A. R., Gatz, M., Amaro, H., Reed, B. G., Savage, A.,…Banks, S. (2005). Outcomes for women with co-occurring disorders and trauma: Program and person-level effects. *Journal of Substance Abuse Treatment, 28*(2), 121–133.

Najavits, L. M. (2002). *Seeking safety: A treatment manual for PTSD and substance abuse.* New York, NY: Guilford Press.

Najavits, L. M., Schmitz, M., Gotthardt, S., & Weiss, R. D. (2005). Seeking safety plus exposure therapy: An outcome study on dual diagnosis men. *Journal of Psychoactive Drugs, 37*(4), 425–435.

National Institute on Alcohol Abuse and Alcoholism, Center for Substance Abuse Prevention, & Public Health Service. (1995). *The alcohol and other drug thesaurus: A guide to concepts and terminology in substance abuse and addiction* (2nd ed., Vol. 1). Washington, DC: U.S. Department of Health and Human Services.

National Institute on Alcohol Abuse and Alcoholism (NIAAA). (2000). *The economic costs of alcohol and drug abuse in the United States 1992.* Rockville, MD: National Institutes of Health.

National Institute on Alcohol Abuse and Alcoholism. (2004a). NIAAA council approves definition of binge drinking. Retrieved from http://pubs.niaaa.nih .gov/publications/newsletter/winter2004/newsletter _number3.pdf

National Institute on Alcohol Abuse and Alcoholism. (2004b). Social work curriculum on alcohol use disorders. Retrieved from http://pubs.niaaa.nih.gov /publications/social/main.html

National Institute on Alcohol Abuse and Alcoholism. (2007). Helping patients who drink too much (NIH Publication No. 07–3769). Retrieved from http://pubs.niaaa.nih.gov/publications/practitioner /cliniciansguide2005/clinicians_guide.htm.

National Institute on Drug Abuse. (1999a). *Cocaine abuse and addiction* (NIDA Research Report Series, NIH Publication No. 99–4342). Retrieved from www .drugabuse.gov/PDF/RRCocaine.pdf

National Institute on Drug Abuse. (1999b). *Principles of drug addiction treatment: A research-based guide* (NIH Publication No. 99–4180). Retrieved from www .drugabuse.gov/PODAT/PODATindex.html

National Institute on Drug Abuse. (2000). *Heroin abuse and addiction* (NIDA Research Report Series, NIH Publication No. 00–4165). Retrieved from www .drugabuse.gov/PDF/RRHeroin.pdf

National Institute on Drug Abuse. (2001a). *NIDA Research Report Series: Nicotine Addiction* (NIH Publication No. 01–4342). Washington, DC: Author.

National Institute on Drug Abuse. (2001b). *Prescription drugs: Abuse and addictions* (NIDA Research Report Series, NIH Publication No. 01–4881). Retrieved from www.drugabuse.gov/PDF/RRPrescription.pdf

National Institute on Drug Abuse. (2002a). *Marijuana abuse* (NIDA Research Report Series, NIH Publication No. 99-4342). Retrieved from www.drugabuse.gov /PDF/RRMarijuana.pdf

National Institute on Drug Abuse. (2002b). *Methamphetamine abuse and addiction* (NIDA Research Report Series, NIH Publication No. 02–4210). Retrieved from www. drugabuse.gov/PDF/RRMetham.pdf

National Institute of Drug Abuse. (2004a). *Marijuana.* Retrieved from www.nida.nih.gov/tib/marijuana.html

National Institute of Drug Abuse. (2005a). *NIDA InfoFacts: Heroin.* Retrieved from http://nida.nih.gov/infofacts/ heroin.html

National Institute on Drug Abuse. (2005b). *Inhalant abuse* (NIDA Research Report Series, NIH Publication No. 05–3818). Retrieved from www.drugabuse.gov/PDF /RRInhalants.pdf

National Institute of Drug Abuse. (2005c). *Research report series-MDMA (ecstasy) abuse.* Retrieved from http:// nida.nih.gov/researchreports/mdma/MDMA6.html

National Institute on Drug Abuse. (2009a). Prescription and over-the-counter medications (NIDA InfoFacts). Retrieved from www.drugabuse.gov/PDF/Infofacts /PainMed09.pdf

National Institute on Drug Abuse. (2009b). *Principles of drug addiction treatment: A research-based guide* (2nd edition). Retrieved from www.drugabuse.gov /podat/podatindex.html

National Institute on Drug Abuse. (2009c). Principles of drug addiction treatment. Retrieved from http:// drugabuse.gov/PDF/PODAT/PODAT.pdf

National Institute on Drug Abuse. (2010a). Cocaine (NIDA InfoFacts). Retrieved from www.drugabuse .gov/pdf/infofacts/Cocaine10.pdf

National Insitute on Drug Abuse. (2010b). *NIDA InfoFacts: Cigarettes and other tobacco products.* Retrieved from www.nida.nih.gov/inforfacts/tobacco.html

O'Brien, C. P., & McLellan, A. T. (1996). Myths about the treatment of addiction. *Lancet, 347*(8996), 237–240.

O'Brien, C. P., & Volkow, N. (2006). What's in a word? Addiction versus dependence in DSM-V. *American Journal of Psychiatry, 163*(5), 764–765.

O'Farrell, T. J., & Fals-Stewart, W. (2008). Behavioral couples therapy for alcoholism and other drug abuse. *Alcoholism Treatment Quarterly, 26*(1), 195–219.

O'Farrell, T. J., Murphy, M., Alter, J., & Fals-Stewart, W. (2010). Behavioral family counseling for substance abuse: A treatment development pilot study. *Addictive Behaviors, 35,* 1–6.

Parsons, J. T., Golub, S. A., Rosof, E., & Holder, C. (2007). Motivational interviewing and cognitive-behavioral intervention to improve HIV medication adherence among hazardous drinkers: A randomized controlled trial. *Journal of Acquired Immune Deficiency Syndrome, 46*(4), 443–450.

Paulozzi, L. J., Ballesteros, M. F., & Stevens, J. A. (2006). Recent trends in mortality from unintentional injury in the United States. *Journal of Safety Research, 37,* 277–283.

Pokorny, A. D., Miller, B. A., & Kaplan, H. B. (1972). The brief MAST: A shortened version of the Michigan Alcoholism Screening Test. *American Journal of Psychiatry, 129,* 342–345.

Prescott, C., & Kendler, K. (1999). Genetic and environmental contributions to alcohol abuse and dependence in a population-based sample of male twins. *American Journal of Psychiatry, 156,* 34–40.

Prochaska, J. O., & Prochaska, J. M. (1999). Why don't continents move? Why don't people change? *Journal of Psychotherapy Integration, 9,* 83–101.

Prochaska, J. O., DiClemente, C. C., & Norcross, J. C. (1992). In search of how people change: Applications to addictive behaviors. *American Psychologist, 47*(9), 1102–1114.

Reinert, D. F., & Allen, J. P. (2002). The Alcohol Use Disorders Identification Test (AUDIT): A review of recent research. *Alcoholism: Clinical and Experimental Research, 26*(2), 272–279.

Rotgers, F., Little, J., & Denning, P. (2005). Harm reduction and traditional treatment: Shared goals and values. *Addiction Professional,* July, 20–26.

Saunders, J. B., Aasland, O. G., Amundsen, A., & Grant, M. (1993). WHO Collaborative Project on Early Detection of Persons with Harmful Alcohol Consumption: Pt. I. Alcohol consumption and related problems among primary health care patients. *Addiction, 88,* 349–362.

Saunders, J. B., Aasland, O. G., Babor, T. F., De La Fuente, J. R., & Grant, M. (1993). Development of the Alcohol Use Disorders Identification Test (AUDIT): WHO Collaborative Project on Early Detection of Persons with Harmful Alcohol Consumption-II. *Addiction, 88,* 791–804.

Savage, S. R., Kirsh, K. L., & Passik, S. D. (2008). Challenges in using opioids to treat pain in persons with substance use disorders. *Addiction Science and Clinical Practice, 4*(2), 4–25.

Schilling, R. F., & El-Bassel, N. (1998). Substance abuse interventions. In J. B. Williams & K. Ell (Eds.), *Advances in mental health services research: Implications for practice* (pp. 437–481). Washington, DC: National Association of Social Workers Press.

Schuckit, M. A., & Tapert, S. (2004). Alcohol. In M. Galanter & H. D. Kleber (Eds.), *Textbook of substance abuse treatment* (3rd ed., pp. 151–166). Washington, DC: American Psychiatric Press.

Seal, K. H., Thawley, R., Gee, L., Bamberger, J, Kral, A. H. Ciccarone, D.,...Edlin, B. R. (2005). Naloxone distribution and cardiopulmonary resuscitation training for injection drug users to prevent heroin overdose death: A pilot intervention study. *Journal of Urban Health, 82*(2), 303–311.

Selzer, M. L. (1971). The Michigan Alcoholism Screening Test: The quest for a new diagnostic instrument. *American Journal of Psychiatry, 127,* 1653–1658.

Selzer, M. L., Vinokur, A., & Van Rooijen, L. (1975). A self-administered Short Michigan Alcoholism Screening Test (SMAST). *Journal of Studies on Alcohol, 36,* 117–126.

Shah, N. G., Lathrop, S. L., Reichard, R. R., & Landen, M. G. (2007). Unintentional drug overdose death trends in New Mexico, USA, 1990–2005: Combinations of heroin, cocaine, prescription opioids and alcohol. *Addiction, 103,* 126–136.

Shiono, P. H., Klebanoff, M. A., Nugent, R. P., Cotch, M. F., Wilkins, D. G., Rollins, D. E.,...Behrman, R. E. (1995). The impact of cocaine and marijuana use on low birth weight and preterm birth: A multicenter study. *American Journal of Obstetrics and Gynecology, 172,* 19–27.

Singer, L. T. (1999). Advances in redirections in understanding effects of fetal drug exposure. *Journal of Drug Issues, 29*(2), 253–262.

Skinner, H. A. (1982). The Drug Abuse Screening Test. *Addictive Behaviors, 7,* 363–371.

Slade, J. (1999). Nicotine. In B. S. McCrady & E. E. Epstein (Eds.), *Addictions: A comprehensive guide* (pp. 162–170). New York, NY: Oxford University Press.

Smith, J. E., Meyers, R. J., & Austin, J. L. (2008). Working with family members to engage treatment-refusing drinkers: The CRAFT program. *Alcoholism Treatment Quarterly, 26*(1), 169–193.

Stephens, R. S. (1999). Cannabis and hallucinogens. In B. S. McCrady & E. E. Epstein (Eds.), *Addictions: A comprehensive guidebook* (pp. 121–140). New York, NY: Oxford University Press.

Stine, S. M., & Kosten, T. R. (1999). Opioids. In B. S. McCrady & E. E. Epstein (Eds.), *Addictions: A comprehensive guidebook* (pp. 141–161). New York, NY: Oxford University Press.

Stratton, K., Howe, C., & Battaglia, F. (1995). *Fetal alcohol syndrome: Diagnosis, epidemiology, prevention, and treatment.* Washington, DC: Institute of Medicine, National Academy Press.

Substance Abuse and Mental Health Services Administration [SAMSHA]. (2009). *Results from the 2008 National Survey on Drug Use and Health: National findings* (Office of Applied Studies, NSDUH Series H-36, DHHS Publication No. SMA 09-4434). Rockville, MD: Author.

Szapocznik, J., & Williams, R. A. (2000). Brief strategic family therapy: Twenty-five years of interplay among theory, research and practice in adolescent behavior problems and drug abuse. *Clinical Child and Family Psychology Review, 3,* 117–134.

Tsemberis, S., Gulcur, L., & Nakae, M. (2004). Housing first, consumer choice, and harm reduction for homeless individuals with a dual diagnosis. *American Journal of Public Health, 94*(4), 651–656.

U.S. Public Health Service. (2000, June). Treating tobacco use and dependence. Retrieved from www .surgeongeneral.gov/tobacco/smokesum.htm

van Wormer, K., & Davis, D. R. (2003). *Addiction treatment: A strengths perspective.* Pacific Grove, CA: Brooks/Cole.

Vasilaki, E., Hosier, S. G., & Cox, W. M. (2006). The efficacy of motivational interviewing as a brief intervention for excessive drinking: A meta-analytic review. *Alcohol and Alcoholism, 41*(3), 328–335.

Weaver, M. F., & Schnoll, S. H. (1999). Stimulants: Amphetamines and cocaine. In B. S. McCrady & E. E. Eptstein (Eds.), *Addictions: A comprehensive guidebook* (pp. 105–120). New York, NY: Oxford University Press.

Weil, A., & Rosen, W. (1993). *From chocolate to morphine: Everything you need to know about mind-altering drugs* (Rev. ed.). Boston, MA: Houghton Mifflin.

Weir, B. W., O'Brien, K., Bard, R. S., Casciato, C. J., Maher, J. E., Dent, C. W., ... Stark, M. J. (2009). Reducing HIV and partner violence risk among women with criminal justice system involvement: A randomized controlled trial of two motivational interviewing-based interventions. *AIDS and Behavior, 13,* 509–522.

White, W. L. (1998). *Slaying the dragon: A history of addiction treatment and recovery in America.* Bloomington, IL: Chestnut Health Systems/ Lighthouse Institute.

Wilcox, R. E., & Erickson, C. K. (2005). The brain biology of drug abuse and addiction. In C. A. McNeece & D. M. DiNitto (Eds.), *Chemical dependency: A systems approach* (pp. 42–60). Boston, MA: Pearson Education.

Williams, D. R., Mohammed, S. A., Leavell, J., & Collins, C. (2010). Race, socioeconomic status, and health: Complexities, ongoing challenges, and research opportunities. *Annals of the New York Academy of Sciences, 1186,* 69–101.

Zacny, J., Bigelow, G., Compton, P., Foley, K., Iguchi, M., & Sannerud, C. (2003). College on Problems of Drug Dependence taskforce on prescription opioid non-medical use and abuse: Position statement. *Drug and alcohol dependence, 69,* 215–232.

Zlotnick, C., Johnson, J., & Najavits, L. M. (2009). Randomized controlled pilot study of cognitive-behavioral therapy in a sample of incarcerated women with substance use disorder and PTSD. *Behavior Therapy, 40*(4), 325–336.

Zuckerman, B., Frank, D., Hingson, R., Amaro, H., Levenson, S., Kayne, H., ... Bauchner, H. (1989). Effects of maternal marijuana and cocaine use on fetal growth. *New England Journal of Medicine, 320,* 762–768

18

Nephrology Social Work

TERI BROWNE

End-stage renal disease (ESRD) is a chronic condition that requires lifelong treatment via hemodialysis, peritoneal dialysis, or a kidney transplant. ESRD is a significant American public health issue. It is also an important practice focus for health social work because it provides the only Medicare mandate for MSW service provision for a disease or treatment category. This chapter presents an overview of psychosocial issues related to ESRD and a discussion of the role of the nephrology social worker in various arenas.

Chapter Objectives

- Explore psychosocial aspects of renal failure and its treatment regimes.
- Identify roles and responsibilities of nephrology social workers.
- Explore nephrology social work assessment and intervention recommendations.
- Examine the history of nephrology social work in dialysis and transplantation.
- Define professional issues of nephrology social workers.

END-STAGE RENAL DISEASE AS A PUBLIC HEALTH ISSUE

ESRD is a significant and growing American public health issue, as evidenced by these findings from the U.S. Renal Data System Annual Data Report (2010):

- In 2008, 547,982 U.S. residents had ESRD (354,600 on hemodialysis; 26,517 on peritoneal dialysis; 165,639 with a kidney transplant). It is projected that by 2030, the number of ESRD patients will increase to 2.24 million.
- The total spending for ESRD care in 2008 was $39.46 billion.
- ESRD care represents a significant proportion of federal health-care costs, comprising 5.9% of the Medicare budget in 2008.
- Medicare contributions to the ESRD program rose from $5.8 billion in 1991 to $26.8 billion in 2008. Non-Medicare expenditures for ESRD care from Medicaid, private insurers and state kidney programs rose from $2.2 billion in 1991 to $12.66 billion in 2008.

ESRD is a chronic illness that results in kidney failure and necessitates renal replacement therapy via dialysis or kidney transplantation. ESRD also is referred to as "chronic kidney disease stage 5." When an individual's kidneys fail, waste products and fluids accumulate in the body, urine output decreases (and may cease entirely), and red blood cell production diminishes. ESRD may develop suddenly or over many years; without treatment, a patient with ESRD will die. ESRD has many causes, with diabetes and hypertension being the two greatest. Other causes of ESRD include lupus, gout, chemotherapy, cancer, substance use, and kidney diseases such as

Note: The author would like to thank her USC College of Social Work research assistants, Sonya Davis-Kennedy, Lesley Jacobs, Olivia Jones, Derrick Jordan, Cassidy Shaver, Valerie Stiling, Felix Weston, and Jennifer Worthington, for reviewing this chapter and making suggestions for added content.

glomerulonephritis, nephritis, and polycystic kidney disease.

Dialysis is mostly provided by large for-profit national dialysis chains, usually on an outpatient basis at free-standing dialysis clinics. Transplants are provided in hospitals that have transplant centers. The average 2010 Medicare cost per patient for hemodialysis was $77,506 per year; the cost for peritoneal dialysis was $57,639; the cost for kidney transplantation was approximately $116,100 for the year in which the transplant was received and $26,668 per year after the transplant (U.S. Renal Data System, 2010). Two types of dialysis currently are available: hemodialysis and peritoneal dialysis.

Hemodialysis is a medical treatment in which a patient is connected to a dialysis machine via tubing joined to an external catheter in the patient's chest or needles that are inserted into a permanent vascular access (called a fistula or graft, which is usually in the patient's arm), which is attached to tubing that leads to the machine. The hemodialysis machine consists of tubing, solutions, monitors, and a filtering device called a dialyzer that removes excess fluid from the patient and cleanses the blood prior to its return to the body through tubing connected to the catheter or access. Hemodialysis usually is performed three times a week (referred to as in-center dialysis), for at least 3 hours per treatment in an outpatient dialysis clinic by nurses and patient care technicians. Hemodialysis patients see their healthcare team while receiving treatments.

The hemodialysis regime can vary, and daily, overnight, and home hemodialysis are available patient treatment options. Research suggests that hemodialysis received more frequently than three times a week provides patients with better outcomes, including improved mortality, morbidity, and quality of life. In the Frequent Hemodialysis Network (FHN) Trial Group's 2010 investigation reported in the *New England Journal of Medicine*, 125 patients were randomly assigned to a clinical trial and received hemodialysis six times per week while 120 patients were randomly assigned to a group receiving the standard three-times-per-week hemodialysis. After a year of this randomized clinical trial, patients who received more frequent dialysis were found to have lower mortality rates and better cardiac status.

In his meta-analysis of the research related to the benefits of home hemodialysis, Rosner (2010) concludes that patients who receive hemodialysis at home rather than in a dialysis center have significantly better outcomes, including improved mortality, morbidity, nutritional status, and quality of life. This and other research that evaluates the benefits of home hemodialysis suggests that the improved outcomes related to this treatment modality can be attributed to the longer dialysis treatment times that home hemodialysis patients usually receive compared to patients who dialyze in outpatient centers only three times per week.

Home hemodialysis is a treatment option that allows patients to perform their own dialysis at home. Patients and social support network members receive comprehensive training to master their own hemodialysis. Dialysis centers arrange for equipment and supplies needed for home hemodialysis to be delivered and set up, using the small hemodialysis machines that the technology related to this modality now supports. Patients are trained to insert their own hemodialysis needles, set up and run hemodialysis machines, and troubleshoot any concerns. Patients can dialyze in the comfort of their homes or perform hemodialysis when traveling. Patients who receive home hemodialysis see the members of their dialysis teams when they return to the dialysis clinic for laboratory testing and follow-up visits.

Peritoneal dialysis is also a renal replacement treatment modality conducted by patients themselves. A catheter is surgically implanted in patients that protrudes from the abdomen and is used to attach tubing to containers of dialysate fluid, which is drained into patients' abdomens. Using the peritoneal membrane surrounding the abdominal cavity, the fluid filters patients' blood and attracts excess fluids and is drained and refilled periodically. Peritoneal dialysis is done daily, either several times throughout the day or overnight via a machine.

Peritoneal dialysis patients see their health-care team during monthly visits to the clinic.

Research suggests that patients who receive peritoneal dialysis instead of in-center hemodialysis have better outcomes, including improved mortality and morbidity rates. A study of 9,277 dialysis patients from across the United States demonstrated that peritoneal patients have a 40% decrease in risk of mortality, compared to patients who received hemodialysis three times a week (Charnow, 2010). Interestingly, a recent anonymous survey of nephrologists suggests that the overwhelming majority of nephrologists would choose peritoneal or home hemodialysis if they themselves needed renal replacement treatment (Schatell, Bragg-Gresham, Mehrotra, Merighi, & Witten, 2010). When asked what treatment modality they would choose for themselves if they had kidney failure and a 5-year wait for a kidney transplant, only 6.4% of the 660 nephrologists indicated that they would choose standard three-times-per-week in-center hemodialysis. Forty-five percent responded that they would choose peritoneal dialysis for themselves, and 45% that they would choose home hemodialysis.

Kidney transplantation is a surgical procedure in which a donor kidney is placed in the ESRD patient's body. The donor kidney can come from a deceased (also known as cadaveric) or a living donor. To get a transplant, a patient must undergo extensive evaluation and testing. If a living donor cannot be located, the patient is placed on a waiting list for a deceased donor kidney. Patients with living donors may be scheduled for surgery at a future date. A person whose kidneys are healthy can function with only one kidney, making a living donation an increasingly popular form of transplantation. Although it usually occurs between patients and donors who have a relationship with one another, altruistic donations from donors who do not know transplant recipients are becoming more common.

These altruistic kidney donations include "paired donors," which is a growing phenomenon in kidney transplantation. In its simplest form, paired donation matches strangers who need kidney transplants and have kidney donors in their social support networks who are not good matches for transplantation. These donors are paired with other patients, who receive their kidneys for transplantation. For example, Joe is an ESRD patient who needs a kidney transplant. His wife, Doris, wants to donate a kidney to Joe and is suitable in most ways to donate, yet her kidney would not be compatible with Joe's blood type. Ann is another ESRD patient in the same situation—her sister Nancy wants to donate a kidney to Ann, but she is not compatible with Ann's blood type. Transplant centers facilitate a pairing between these two patients, so that Joe receives Nancy's kidney (because they are a good match) and Ann receives Doris's kidney (because they have the same blood type). Paired donations are becoming increasingly complicated. Rees and colleagues (2009) report on a paired donor chain that resulted in 10 different kidney transplants at six different transplant centers in five different states. In November 2010, Georgetown University Hospital set the record for the size of a paired donation kidney swap, transplanting 16 different ESRD patients with organs from donors who included spouses, aunts, parents, children, cousins, and strangers to these 16 patients. The donors were not biologically compatible with their family members with ESRD (or were strangers with benevolent motives for donating a kidney) and were matched in this "kidney swap" with one of the 16 patients by Georgetown University's kidney transplant center. Because of the scarcity of deceased organ donors in the United States, transplant centers and the United Network of Organ Sharing want to increase future rates of paired kidney donation (Georgetown University Hospital, 2010).

Transplantation is considered a form of ESRD treatment, not a cure, because patients must take immunosuppressant medications for the life of the kidney to ensure that their bodies do not reject the donor kidney. Transplants may fail, requiring a patient to return to dialysis. In an ESRD patient's lifetime, he may experience all three forms of ESRD treatment.

Kidney transplantation is the most cost-effective treatment for ESRD and provides patients with enhanced physical and mental health, especially when compared to dialysis (Becker et al., 2000). An objective of Healthy People 2010 and a proposed objective of Healthy People 2020 is to increase the number of dialysis patients who get kidney transplants (U.S. Department of Health and Human Services, 2000). Transplants may not be possible, however, in situations where patients are not medically suited for transplant surgery or in which they prefer another form of treatment.

Acute dialysis was first done in the 1940s, the first kidney transplant was performed in 1951, and chronic outpatient dialysis was first available in the early 1960s. In 1965, there were only 200 dialysis patients in the world; prior to 1972, hemodialysis machines were scarce, and dialysis was largely paid for by patients or with donated funds (Fox & Swazey, 1979). Selection committees chose individuals for dialysis, and lack of funding and scarcity of treatment venues prevented many ESRD patients from having dialysis. Selection committees were comprised of lay individuals who chose dialysis patients based on their perceived "social worth," with preference given to family breadwinners and community leaders (Jonsen, 2000). On October 30, 1972, the national ESRD program, Public Law 92–601, was passed after significant lobbying by patients, their families, and the community in response to the rationing of dialysis care (Fox & Swazey, 1979). This law provides Medicare coverage of dialysis or kidney transplantation for all ESRD patients regardless of age. Medicare also pays for the expenses for kidney donors, including paired donors. This coverage is unique, because ESRD is the only disease category that guarantees Medicare eligibility (with sufficient work history of the patient or spouse/parent).

DEMOGRAPHICS OF RENAL PATIENTS

The demographics of the renal patient population have changed dramatically since the start of widespread ESRD care in the United States. The majority of dialysis patients used to be younger heads of families. Today, individuals 65 years and older comprise the fastest-increasing population among ESRD patients (Kutner, 1994). Older adults with ESRD have more comorbidities, greater psychosocial issues and needs, and more physical problems than do younger adults with the condition (Chen, Wu, Wang, & Jaw, 2003).

ESRD affects certain groups in the United States disproportionately; African Americans, Hispanics, American Indians, and Alaskan Natives are dramatically more likely to develop renal failure than are White Americans. Compared to White Americans with an ESRD incidence of 273 per million, African Americans have an incidence rate of ESRD of 998 per million, Hispanics have an incidence of 508 per million for ESRD, Native Americans have an incidence of 495 per million, and Asians have an incidence of 296 per million (U.S. Renal Data System, 2009). Higher incidence of ESRD in minority populations generally is attributed to the greater prevalence of diabetes and hypertension in these populations, leading to ESRD.

Disparity in kidney transplantation also exists, with White American males more likely to receive a kidney transplant than any other demographic group in the United States. African American ESRD patients are much less likely than White Americans to be referred for renal transplant, placed on a waiting list for a kidney, or to receive a kidney transplant (U.S. Renal Data System, 2010). Reasons for this disparity include a lack of preventive care, patient preference, socioeconomic disadvantage, distrust of the medical community, a lack of knowledge about kidney transplantation, and medical reasons. Further research on ESRD disparity is needed.

PSYCHOSOCIAL ASPECTS

Eighty-nine percent of ESRD patients report experiencing significant lifestyle changes from the disease (Kaitelidou et al., 2005). The chronicity of ESRD and the intrusiveness of its required treatment provide renal patients with multiple disease-related and treatment-related psychosocial stressors that affect their everyday lives (Devins et al., 1990). Illness intrusiveness related to ESRD is defined as "the extent to which the illness and/or its treatment interfere with important facets of a patient's life" (Landsman, 1975, p. 328). Researchers have found that psychosocial issues negatively impact health outcomes of patients and diminish patient quality of life (Auslander, Dobrof, & Epstein, 2001; Burrows-Hudson, 1995; Kimmel et al., 1998). Social workers can help patients ameliorate psychosocial barriers to ESRD care such as:

- Adjustment and coping to the illness and treatment regime(s)
- Medical complications and problems
- Issues related to pain, palliative care, and end-of-life care
- Social role adjustment: familial, social, and vocational
- Concrete needs: financial loss, insurance problems, and prescription coverage
- Diminished quality of life
- Body image issues
- Numerous losses, such as financial security, health, libido, strength, independence, mobility, schedule flexibility, sleep, appetite, freedom with diet and fluid

Disease-Related Psychosocial Aspects

ESRD may impair sense of taste, diminish appetite, and cause bone disease that can require surgery and impair a person's ability to walk. A buildup of toxins in the blood may cause patients to be anemic and uremic. Uremia and anemia lead to symptomatology such as confusion, lethargy, and sleep problems that have psychosocial sequelae. Anemia is common among ESRD patients and impairs activities of daily living, diminishes energy, and consequently can affect quality of life (Gerson et al., 2004). ESRD patients have a comprised nutritional status, and a subsequent low blood albumin level also decreases patient quality of life (Frank, Auslander, & Weissgarten, 2003).

Moreover, ESRD usually occurs along with chronic illnesses, such as hypertension and diabetes. These illnesses bring their own psychosocial issues that require ESRD patients to access health services from a number of community sources frequently (Merighi & Ehlbrcht, 2004c).

ESRD patients often require complex medication regimes due to kidney failure and other health conditions. Medications and blood transfusions may be needed during dialysis to address anemia and iron deficiency. Dialysis patients often must take several phosphorous-binding tablets with every meal as well as numerous other medications related to ESRD and its side effects, such as cramping and restless legs syndrome. Transplant patients may, in fact, have to take dozens of pills a day to manage their transplant and prevent rejection of the organ. Self-management of oral medications is a significant problem among the ESRD population (Browne & Merighi, 2010). Chiu and colleagues (2009) conclude that dialysis patients take the highest number of pills per day of all patients with chronic illness—25% of hemodialysis patients must take at least 25 pills per day (median 19 pills).

The toll of these disease-related stressors is great. Some researchers have found ESRD patients to be significantly more likely than persons in the general population to commit suicide (Kurella, Kimmel, Young, & Chertow, 2005). Others have noted that ESRD results in anxiety and depression. Auslander and colleagues (2001) found that 52% of ESRD patients had significant anxiety; Wuerth and colleagues (2001) found that 49% of patients were depressed. Depression in ESRD patients is a significant issue because:

- Kimmel, Peterson, Weihs, and their fellow researchers (2000) determined that ESRD patients who are depressed are more likely to have poor nutritional outcomes and have a higher mortality rate. Koo and colleagues (2003) also have found that depression leads to malnutrition. Patients who are depressed are not likely to eat properly. Depression is linked to higher mortality rates

(Hedayati et al., 2004). In addition, DeOreo (1997) found that depressed patients were less likely to adhere to their recommended treatment regimes than nondepressed patients and were more likely to have a higher level of morbidity and mortality.

- Paniagua, Amato, Vonesh, Guo, and Mujais (2005) found that ESRD patients who are depressed are more likely to be hospitalized.

Depression can also diminish patients' quality of life (Frank et al., 2003; Mollaoglu, 2004). This is relevant to public policy and is a public health concern because DeOreo (1997) and Mapes and colleagues (2004) have shown that a low quality of life in ESRD patients is significantly related to a higher hospitalization rate, greater morbidity, and higher mortality.

ESRD patients have a lower functional status than the population as a whole and are likely to need assistance with activities of daily living (Kimmel, 2000). ESRD patients often have insomnia and sleeping problems (Valdez, 1997). They also may have body image issues related to their dialysis access and medication side effects (Beer, 1995). Vascular accesses for hemodialysis can become quite large and visible on patients' arms. Peritoneal accesses and catheters used for hemodialysis are surgically implanted and protrude from the body. Medications, especially transplant immunosuppressant drugs, can cause weight gain or other changes in patients' physical appearance.

Sexual functioning may be diminished due to ESRD, another major source of concern for patients (Wu et al., 2001). ESRD female patients have decreased rates of fertility because the disease impairs reproductive endocrine functioning. This impaired endocrine functioning results in numerous complications of pregnancy, and ESRD patients are unlikely to have a successful pregnancy (Holley & Reddy, 2003).

Poor adjustment to ESRD may be exacerbated by what Landsman (1975) refers to as "the marginal man syndrome." Most ESRD patients may appear "healthy" despite being chronically ill. Others may therefore have

unrealistic expectations of their abilities and expect more of them than is appropriate. Friends, neighbors, and coworkers may not understand why patients cannot participate in a pizza party due to the renal diet or other social functions due to the dialysis schedule. Landsman (1975) describes the necessity of coping with the "concept of perpetual treatment without cure, suspended in a state of limbo between the world of the sick and the world of the well, belonging to neither, yet a part of both, [questioning], am I sick or am I well?" (p. 268).

Restless legs syndrome, in which patients have persistent tremors in their extremities, is common in ESRD patients (Takaki et al., 2003). Acute and chronic pain is very common among ESRD patients and can impair quality of life (Devins et al., 1990). Pain can result from surgeries, cramping, needle sticks, neuropathy, and bone disease. Iacono (2003, 2004) found that 60% of dialysis patients have chronic pain and that 66% of these patients were using prescription medication for pain. Lori Hartwell (2002), an ESRD patient and advocate, describes her own experiences with pain:

> During my many medical procedures, I've had to endure hundreds of needle pricks. When I was younger, I would never complain about the number of sticks the nurses made. Consequently, they repeatedly told me what a good patient I was. In reality, those needles hurt! I wanted to cry and scream at the person who kept poking me. Most often I was silent and tried to be as accommodating as possible. (p. 8)

Palliative care and end-of-life issues are prevalent in ESRD. The life expectancy of patients is 75% lower than similar individuals without ESRD (Moss, 2005). Discontinuing dialysis is a recognized treatment choice, and patients may opt to stop their treatment, which will lead to death. Without dialysis, the median number of days that patients will survive is eight, although there is much variability in survival time after stopping dialysis

(Germain & Cohen, 2007). A study of 115,239 deceased dialysis patients found that 96% of patients who stopped dialysis died within a month (Murray, Arko, Chen, Gilbertson, & Moss, 2006). In the United States, fewer than 5% of patients opt not to start dialysis (Germain & Cohen, 2007). Kidney disease teams are encouraged to discuss realistic expectations of prognosis and quality of life related to starting this life-extending treatment. Russ, Shim, and Kaufman (2007) recommend that nephrologists have frank discussions with their patients about their prognoses, how long they can expect to live on dialysis, and how dialysis will impact their quality of life and that of their families. Many ESRD patients have psychosocial problems and concerns prior to death, including significant pain in the last week of life (Cohen, Germain, Woods, Mirot, & Burleson, 2005). See Browne (2011) for a full discussion about palliative and end-of-life care for kidney disease patients.

Finally, there are particular disease-related challenges for children suffering from ESRD. Pediatric ESRD patients and their families face unique psychosocial stressors. Infants born with ESRD require frequent hospitalization and medical visits. Their development is impaired, and they may need supplemental nourishment or a feeding tube. Parents of pediatric ESRD patients are more likely to have anxiety, depression, and coping problems than parents of well children (Fukunishi & Honda, 1995). This is in part because ESRD alters normal infant care. Infants with ESRD may not produce urine, for instance, which can be anxiety provoking for parents (Brady & Lawry, 2000).

Children and adolescents with ESRD may be concerned especially about body image related to dialysis accesses (Fielding et al., 1985). Along with body image issues, they may have a difficult time adjusting to the ESRD regime of treatment and a special diet. Kurtin, Landgraf, and Abetz (1994) found that 59% of ESRD adolescents have poor adherence to medical regimes.

ESRD has significant psychosocial ramifications for patients' families as well (see Box 18.1). Dialysis patients' partners have problems coping with the illness and its treatment regimes (White & Greyner, 1999). MacDonald (1995) found that families of ESRD patients have problems adjusting to the impact of the illness on their lifestyle. Other authors have noted spouses' and partners' increased levels of stress and problems with managing role reversal and the need to assume more responsibilities than usual due to ESRD (Gudes, 1995; Pelletier-Hibbert & Sohi, 2001). The family also must cope with the possible financial burden of ESRD. Because of the time needed to care for patients and transport them to treatments, a spouse or child may need to limit work hours. Kaitelidou and colleagues (2005) found that 51% of ESRD family members reported absences from work related to the patient's illness.

ESRD may present patients and families with a loss of income, which is another very important concern of patients and their families (Wu et al., 2001). One study found that only 13% of ESRD patients were able to resume employment after starting dialysis (Dobrof, Dolinko, Lichtiger, Uribarri, & Epstein, 2000). Sixty percent of a sample of hemodialysis patients in Greece had to change professions or retire due to ESRD (Kaitelidou et al., 2005). Thus, it may be particularly important for renal social workers to consider the employment options of their patients. Maintaining employment and being active after a diagnosis of ESRD can be beneficial. Working patients are less depressed than their unemployed counterparts (Chen et al., 2003). Patients with a good rehabilitation status who stay active through employment or other activities also may have a better quality of life (Mollaoglu, 2004).

Treatment-Related Psychosocial Aspects

The treatment regimes related to ESRD can have serious psychosocial ramifications. Dialysis patients are required to assume strict diets due to their inability to process food products with high levels of potassium and phosphorous and a need for sodium restrictions. Poor self-management of the standard

Box 18.1 ESRD Case Example

Dan is a 17-year-old peritoneal dialysis patient. The nephrology social worker had been working with Dan and his father, Chris, for over a year to improve his adherence to the renal diet and medication regime in order to have him physically prepared for kidney transplantation surgery and recovery. Dan has not been taking his phosphorus-binding medication with his meals, which indicates a lack of potential commitment to take his immunosuppressive medications posttransplant. If Dan fails to take these medications as prescribed, his kidney transplant would be at serious risk of failure. Dan's father and the social worker met several times about this matter with little success. Chris was emotionally debilitated due to two jobs and sole custody of his three children, and had little energy to follow through with the constant monitoring that Dan required.

Because Dan was the oldest child and Chris was often working or asleep, Dan had been the primary caregiver of his siblings since he was 7 years old. The combination of an overwhelming age-inappropriate sense of responsibility and the normal growth and development of adolescence was not mixing well. Chris had come to rely on Dan a great deal and found Dan's illness to be a major interference in their routine. He brought Dan to the appointments but remained disengaged and angry; Dan and his father were in open conflict much of the time. The social worker intervened on a number of clinic visits to reduce the conflict between the two.

The social worker was able to gain Dan's and his father's agreement to attend one of the groups she held to educate and support youth and their parents as they prepared for transplant. Fortunately, one of her other challenging patients, Jeff, also attended that group with his mother. Jeff, a 15-year-old, had struggled with his own adherence issues. With social work counseling and education, Jeff had been able to manage his medications and a year ago had received a successful transplant. As the group progressed, it was clear that Dan found the group "lame" and wanted to leave. Jeff confronted Dan directly, one teen to another. Jeff's mother, Denise, offered to bring Dan lunch every day at school to make sure he took his phosphorus binders with his meals. Chris cried as Denise told them that she truly understood what he was dealing with and how overwhelmed she often felt trying to care for Jeff. The social worker was able to direct the discussion to facing challenges with the benefit of a support system.

Dan's school grades improved and both Dan and his father began to come out of their self-imposed isolation. They kept appointments on time and eagerly reported on things they were doing to have fun. A couple of group sessions later, Dan, Chris, Jeff, and Denise arrived together. They had had an early supper in the cafeteria, where Denise asked Dan about his medications. Rather than the surly responses he was famous for, he laughed and produced his pills. It was clear that the four had connected and felt they could help each other within the support group as well as outside the hospital milieu. Within the year, Dan's phosphorous level was within range, and he was emotionally ready for his transplant. His level of responsibility, as demonstrated by his adherence with the treatment plan, was an accomplishment that he reveled in and has shared with the group on a routine basis.

Source: Prepared by Sandra Coorough, Phoenix Children's Hospital Kids Kidney Center, Phoenix, AZ.

renal diet can have significant consequences because potassium levels outside the range considered appropriate can lead to heart failure. High phosphorous levels can lead to permanent bone disease and calcification of the heart. Dialysis patients therefore are placed on diets that severely limit foods such as bananas, melons, dried fruit, tomatoes, oranges, potatoes, nuts, dairy, cola products, and sodium. Patients also may require a high protein diet due to their low albumin levels. Efforts toward optimal diet often are hampered by patients' impaired appetite and a diminished sense of taste.

Because of their inability to produce urine effectively, patients have very strict fluid restrictions, as little as 48 ounces per day. Otherwise, excess liquid will build up and cause patients' extremities to swell and their lungs to fill with fluid. Extreme weight gain between dialysis treatments can lead to discomfort during hemodialysis, and removal of excessive fluid results in severe cramping and low blood pressure. Dry mouth and thirst are common among dialysis patients. Peritoneal dialysis patients have much less restrictive dietary and fluid intake restrictions, and transplant patients normally are not required to follow renal diets or limit their fluids.

Poor self-management of ESRD treatment regimes can have serious ramifications for patients. Missed treatments and high fluid weight gains between treatments are associated with increased mortality in dialysis patients (Saran et al., 2003). Failing to take transplant immunosuppressant medications leads to transplant rejection (Russell & Ashbaugh, 2004). Many dialysis patients may not adhere to medical recommendations about diet, prescriptions, or fluid restrictions (Friend, Hatchett, Schneider, & Wadhwa, 1997). A study of hemodialysis patients found that:

- 27% to 31% of patients missed one dialysis treatment per month.
- 35% to 41% of patients signed off of dialysis early and did not receive their full treatment.
- 76% to 85% patients had problems following their recommended diet.
- 75% of patients who were coping poorly were likely to miss treatments.
- 50% of patients who were coping poorly did not follow recommended fluid restrictions (Dobrof et al., 2000).

The ESRD treatment regime is both very intrusive and unrelenting (see Box 18.2). Patients may find it difficult to travel, because dialysis must be done while they are away

---

Box 18.2 A Day in the Life of a Hemodialysis Patient

Florence is a 65-year-old patient who attends dialysis every Monday, Wednesday, and Friday. Her treatment begins at 5:00 in the morning, so she must awaken at 3:30 in the morning to begin the 25-mile journey to her dialysis unit. Because she is diabetic, Florence must eat breakfast before leaving her home. She must get to the dialysis unit by 4:45 in the morning so that she can weigh herself (so that the treatment team will know how much fluid to remove during hemodialysis), have her blood pressure taken, set up the pillow and blanket she will use during her treatment, tune the television that is above her dialysis chair to her favorite morning news channel, and greet her fellow patients before the technician puts the needles in her forearm that connect her to the machine. During her four-hour treatment, her vital signs will be taken, her medications will be given, and she likely will be visited by her physician, nurses, dietitian, and social worker. After dialysis, Florence sometimes has problems with excessive bleeding or low blood pressure, so she may have to wait for her problems to stabilize to go home. Florence takes the local senior citizen van to her home (because the van does not operate before 9:00 in the morning, Florence must pay her neighbor to take her there) and often must wait over 30 minutes for the van to arrive at the dialysis center. Many times the van does not take Florence home directly, because other people are traveling to doctor appointments or shopping. Because of this, Florence usually does not get home from dialysis until noon. This means that it has been almost eight hours since she initially left her house.

from home. It can be difficult to access dialysis treatment services while traveling in rural areas, areas in which the number of patients exceeds treatment possibilities, or in areas experiencing staff shortages. Payment can be challenging for dialysis patients who are traveling. Some private insurers refuse to pay for out-of-network procedures, Medicaid coverage is specific to the state in which the patient resides, and dialysis in territories outside the United States is not covered by Medicare and most insurers. Hemodialysis usually takes between 4 and 6 hours, including transportation, pre- and posttreatment procedures, and attention to complications, three times per week.

Common side effects of hemodialysis include cramping, nausea, and vomiting. A serious complication of peritoneal dialysis is an infection called peritonitis, which is painful and occasionally fatal. Transplantation requires significant workup, frequent post-surgical visits, and numerous daily immunosuppressant medications. Transplantation is a serious surgery and may lead to complications. Long-term immunosuppressant usage may cause serious negative physical outcomes.

RAMIFICATIONS OF PSYCHOSOCIAL ISSUES

Many psychosocial factors can negatively impact renal patients' nutritional status and albumin management (Vourlekis & Rivera-Mizzoni, 1997). Barriers to a quality diet may include patients' education and literacy level because they may not comprehend the diet instructions. Insurance may not allow patients to obtain recommended nutritional supplements. Social support availability is another psychosocial attribute related to poor diet in ESRD patients because they may need assistance to purchase groceries and prepare meals. Patients also may have decreased appetite due to depression or anxiety. These factors are very important for social workers to address because a poor nutritional status has been clearly linked to death in ESRD patients (Lowrie & Lew, 1990).

ESRD patients with psychosocial problems who are less cognizant of the illness and its treatment are more likely to have high fluid gains and missed treatments, which lead to poor health outcomes. Patients with poor psychological status are less likely to be adherent to treatment regimes and to have more hospitalizations and higher rates of mortality (DeOreo, 1997). ESRD patients who feel they are less in control of their illness tend to cope less effectively and have a lower quality of life (Mapes et al., 2004).

Patients are likely to experience several different treatment regimes during the course of the disease, including unsuccessful kidney transplants. As they cope with numerous losses, repeated lifestyle adjustments, and difficult transitions between transplant and dialysis, these changes can lead to the compounding effect of the burden of ESRD (Levine, 1999). One patient describes her experience in this way:

> I lived through dialysis treatments, three transplants, and two rejections. Each transplant brought renewed hope; each rejection would send me reeling. It took me years to learn how to manage the feelings that came along with the constant diagnoses, the seemingly endless stream of bad news. (Hartwell, 2002, p. 7)

SOCIAL WORK INTERVENTION

The significant psychosocial issues faced by ESRD patients and their families require social work intervention, referred to as nephrology social work or renal social work. ESRD is the only disease category or treatment regime with a public policy inclusion for master's-level social workers on health teams. Medicare regulations mandate that a master's-level social worker be on staff in every dialysis center and kidney transplant program (*Federal Register*, 1976, 2008). These social workers focus on "improving the patient's ability to adjust to and cope with chronic illness and the health-care system's ability to meet the needs of the patient" (McKinley & Callahan, 1998, p. 123).

Megan Prescott, MSW, LCSW is an example of a nephrology social worker who works at both an inpatient hospital setting and an outpatient dialysis clinic setting. She works for the University of Colorado Hospital at both its outpatient dialysis unit and inpatient acute dialysis unit. She splits her time between the two units each week. In the chronic outpatient setting, her population is primarily Medicaid eligible and disadvantaged. She finds that her patients have low health literacy. Most did not have access to health care before kidney failure and many were unaware of kidney problems prior to starting dialysis. She helps patients to adjust to the dialysis treatment regimen; this includes helping them to identify and utilize available support sources, develop effective coping strategies, and understand and engage in educational support from the team, to maximize self-management and outcomes. Prescott conducts psychosocial assessments to determine barriers to optimal psychosocial functioning and health-care outcomes. One important aspect of this assessment is a quality-of-life survey, which helps the team, with the patient at the center, to set goals for the coming year.

Prescott assists patients in accessing available resources, including Medicare, Medicaid, vocational rehabilitation services, housing, and other community resources. In the acute care setting, she works as a social worker and discharge planner for hospitalized dialysis patients. With her knowledge of the chronic care setting, she can help develop safe strategies for discharge, keeping in mind the patients' dialysis schedule and associated needs. She coordinates with staff at the patient's established dialysis center to follow up on any new medical needs for continuity of care. Some patients will leave the hospital without any changes in routine while others may need home health assistance or nursing home care following their hospitalizations. In addition to this role, Prescott also works with patients newly diagnosed with kidney failure who need to begin treatment. She is often their first social work contact after discovering that they will need renal replacement therapy. She

introduces patients to the variety of modalities and with other members of the care team provides education to choose the best modality to begin treatment and help coordinate the start of that treatment. Prescott initiates conversations about immediate patient concerns, such as eligibility for Medicare, transportation, and other resources in the community. These conversations will continue when patients establish care with their dialysis team.

Social workers are included on renal medical teams, which also include patients, their family members, nephrologists (kidney doctors), nurses, dietitians, and patient-care technicians. Teams also may include transplant surgeons and pharmacists. The inclusion of a number of specialists reflects the complexity of the needs and issues renal patients face and has been linked empirically with optimal service delivery (Goldstein, Yassa, Dacouris, & McFarlane, 2004). For example, Lindberg and colleagues (2005) found that a team approach to patient education about vascular accesses that included a social worker was more successful than a single-disciplinary approach. A report on morbidity and mortality of dialysis by the National Institutes of Health (1993) states: "[T]he social and psychological welfare and the quality of life of the dialysis patient are favorably influenced by the involvement of a multidisciplinary team" (p. 1). Although many teams provide patient care in a collaborative transdisciplinary environment (see Chapter 2 in this volume), the Medicare policies for this unique practice setting use the term *interdisciplinary* to describe these teams. It is important to note that the 2008 Medicare Conditions for Coverage for dialysis and kidney transplant settings mandate that patients and their family members should be considered important members of the team, and patients have the right to participate in assessments and care planning and to refuse any aspect of their treatment (*Federal Register*, 2008).

Nephrology social work interventions tend to be valued by patients. Siegal, Witten, and Lundin's 1994 survey of ESRD patients found that 90% of respondents "believed that access to a nephrology social worker was important"

(p. 33) and that patients relied on nephrology social workers to assist them with coping, adjustment, and rehabilitation. According to Rubin and colleagues (1997), dialysis patients have ranked a "helpful social worker" as being more important to them than nephrologists or nurses. One study reported that 70% of patients said that social workers gave the most useful information about treatment modalities compared to nurses and physicians (Holley, Barrington, Kohn, & Hayes, 1991). These researchers also found that patients thought that social workers were twice as helpful as nephrologists in helping them to choose between hemodialysis and peritoneal dialysis for treatment.

Nephrology Social Work Tasks

Social workers can help renal patients with their psychosocial needs in a variety of ways in collaboration with the renal health team. The activities conducted by nephrology social workers may include assessment, counseling, education, crisis intervention, end-of-life care, case management, rehabilitation assistance, and patient advocacy. Social workers also intervene at the community level.

Assessment

Comprehensive individual psychosocial assessment of ESRD patients is central to the achievement of optimal patient outcomes (Fox & Swazey, 1979). Nephrology social workers conduct an assessment of patients' psychosocial status to identify their strengths, needs, and the areas for social work intervention. Social work assessments are completed for every dialysis and transplant patient and take into account each patient's social, psychological, financial, cultural, and environmental needs.

A unique attribute of ESRD social work care is that it is provided on a chronic, rather than episodic, basis. Nephrology social workers are fortunate to work in settings that allow them to develop long-term relationships with patients. Long-term relationships provide them the opportunity to evaluate the effectiveness of services and reassessment of clients'

needs through time. In her article for the *New Social Worker*, Devon Rocha (2010) explains her view of being a dialysis social worker:

> There are many advantages to social work in this setting. One of these is getting to work with a consistent client base for potentially several years. Since I work full time at one dialysis unit, I get to see everyone a couple of times each week. This is especially helpful if or when a patient is experiencing a particularly difficult time. It gives a nice opportunity to at least "check in" on how the patient is doing, instead of having to wait a full week in a typical counseling/therapeutic relationship. There can also be a real opportunity for collaboration with the patient's outside support system. A teamwork approach involving the patient's loved ones can be very effective for difficulties such as medication management, nutrition, or adherence to the treatment regimen. It is also rewarding to be there with a person who is undergoing such a significant life change, as when a person is newly diagnosed with end-stage renal disease and needs to start dialysis. Some patients have never even known they were at risk for kidney failure. Then all of a sudden they must deal with this new self-image as someone who is "sick." This can be very anxiety provoking, with so many new terms, routines, and new people involved. There is often a great sense of loss and always there is a huge lifestyle change.

Social workers also assess transplant donors. Living donor kidney transplants, including donations from strangers, have become increasingly popular in the United States. Social workers assess donors and recipients to gauge any normative pressures on donors that may influence their decisions to donate as well as their motivations for donating and their ability to make informed consent. This is important because kidney donation requires significant surgery and recovery. If individuals feel pressured to donate a kidney, a social worker may recommend that they not donate, pending further assessment. Social workers investigate the nature of relationships between donors and recipients as well as their psychosocial and mental health statuses and developmental and substance use histories in order to make a recommendation to the transplant team regarding surgery (Leo, Smith, & Mori, 2003). The 2007 Medicare guidelines for transplant centers mandate that every transplant center have an independent living donor advocate (*Federal Register*, 2007). This advocate is in place to ensure that living donors are evaluated independently and to maximize their informed consent. In some transplant centers, social workers serve as the living donor advocates.

Nephrology social workers use various standardized assessment tools with demonstrated validity and reliability, including those to measure depression and quality of life. The 2008 Medicare Conditions for Coverage for dialysis units mandate that every dialysis unit that bills Medicare for services must have the social worker assess patients' quality of life (*Federal Register*, 2008). This mandate was in response to research findings that suggest that quality of life can independently predict dialysis patients' morbidity and mortality (DeOreo, 1997; Knight, Ofsthun, Teng, Lazarus, & Curhan, 2003). Because future Medicare clinical performance measures for dialysis units suggest using the Kidney Disease Quality of Life, most dialysis social workers use this measurement to assess patient quality of life.

Counseling and Education

Nephrology social workers provide emotional support, encouragement, and counseling to patients and members of their support networks. ESRD patients and their families may have difficulty adjusting to the illness and treatment regimes. Social workers can help them cope through individual, family, and group counseling as well as through support groups.

Social workers can provide counseling and education to decrease patient depression. Depression is a serious issue that often is experienced by ESRD patients. Chen and colleagues (2003) recommend that "a good psychosocial support program should be incorporated into the treatment of patients with chronic renal failure to reduce the possibility and severity of depression" (p. 124). In an empirical study,

Beder (1999) found that nephrology social work counseling and cognitive-behavioral education interventions significantly lower patient depression. In her experimental study, Cabness (2005) found that a cognitive-behavioral education group led by social workers is significantly linked to lower depression. Johnstone and LeSage (1998) found that 76% of depressed dialysis patients indicate that they prefer to seek counseling from the nephrology social worker on their treatment team rather than pursue care from an outside mental health practitioner.

Nephrology social workers help patients deal with emotional concerns that stem from the numerous losses associated with ESRD. These include failed vascular accesses and transplants, schedule and dietary restrictions, the death of fellow patients, decreased activity levels, and employment and professional losses. Kidney transplant patients also require social work assistance when coping with anxiety and frustration over being on a transplant waiting list because it can take several years to get a kidney transplant. Transplant patients may need help with feeling guilty about accepting a deceased donor organ. They also may have concerns about receiving a kidney from a living donor because the donor is placed at risk from the surgery.

Through patient education and other interventions, nephrology social workers are successful in improving patient's adherence to the ESRD treatment regime (see Box 18.3). For example, Rita-An Kiely and her social work colleagues counseled patients on the importance of attending all hemodialysis treatments, tracked attendance, and provided ongoing encouragement for adhering to the treatment regime. As a result of this social work education and counseling, there was a 50% decrease in missed hemodialysis treatments (Medical Education Institute, 2004). Auslander and Buchs (2002) and Root (2005) have shown that social work counseling and education led to reduced fluid weight gains in patients. Johnstone and Halshaw (2003) found that social work education and encouragement were associated with a 47% improvement in fluid restriction adherence.

Box 18.3 Outcomes-Oriented Nephrology Social Practice

Nephrology social workers at Fresenius Medical Care in San Diego, CA, have created an exemplar of outcomes-oriented dialysis social work intervention. They also provide "wellness programs" for patients with ESRD. Because of the barriers that arise for people to attend these programs, they have started a telephonic group for depression management. Patients will meet once to establish supportive relationships and then complete five telephonic sessions with a social worker. Similar to programs offered to cancer patients, wellness programming for the patient with ESRD focuses on three areas:

1. These programs highlight the key role of patients as part of the renal team and invite them to participate actively in their care.
2. The programs focus on imparting life skills that help patients learn to manage the complex medical regime in order to improve survival and quality of life.
3. The programs, often featured as wellness classes, launch patients out with a sense of empowerment over their own medical destiny. The perception of control and self-efficacy that improve with these programs, combined with the additional social support that the classes offer, are seen as the key change agents to their improved outcomes. This group of social workers also conducts a number of research projects related to various psychosocial interventions and are frequent contributors to renal publications and presentations.

Source: Prepared by Stephanie Johnstone, Fresenius Medical Care, San Diego, CA.

Beder, Mason, Johnstone, Callahan, and LeSage (2003) conducted an experimental research study to determine the effect of cognitive-behavioral social work services. They found that patient education and counseling by nephrology social workers was significantly associated with increased medication compliance. This study also determined that such interventions improved patients' blood pressure. Sikon (2000) discovered that social work counseling can reduce patients' anxiety level. Several researchers have determined that nephrology social work counseling significantly improves ESRD patient quality of life (Chang, Winsett, Gaber, & Hathaway, 2004; Frank et al., 2003; Johnstone, 2003).

Nephrology social workers play an important role in educating patients about the different treatment modalities for ESRD and in helping patients pursue different treatment options. This is particularly important in assisting dialysis patients with getting a kidney transplant. Despite evidence that a kidney transplant is the ESRD treatment with the best outcome, research has demonstrated that vulnerable patients, particularly African Americans, are less likely to be successful in receiving a kidney transplant (Browne, 2008). The 2008 Medicare Conditions for Coverage recognize that patients need extra help from their dialysis team in navigating the pathway to getting a kidney transplant and now mandate that all dialysis teams specifically and methodically help all patients who are interested in a kidney transplant to get one (*Federal Register*, 2008). Nephrology social workers are well suited to oversee this task and help patients get kidney transplants.

Crisis Intervention

Nephrology social workers provide crisis intervention services in dialysis and transplant units. Patients may act inappropriately during hemodialysis, yelling at staff or patients, threatening violence, or trying to pull the needles out of their arms. Social workers also resolve crises with peritoneal dialysis and transplant patients. Social workers often effectively mediate conflicts in dialysis settings (Johnstone, Seamon, Halshaw, Molinair, & Longknife, 1997). Merighi and Ehlebracht (2004a) found that more than 75% of nephrology social workers mediate conflicts.

End-of-Life Care

Social work has an important role in the palliative and end-of-life care of ESRD patients. Social workers provide end-of-life information to patients and their families (Promoting Excellence in End-of-Life Care, 2002). Yusack (1999) found that patient education provided by social workers about advance directives led to a 51% increase in the use of such documents. Terminally ill ESRD patients and their families said that they would like more emotional support and other interventions from social workers and requested that social workers make contact with their families after they died (Woods et al., 1999).

The National Program Office of the Robert Wood Johnson Foundation created an ESRD workgroup entitled "Promoting Excellence in End-of-Life Care" in 2002. It recommends that nephrology social workers:

- Provide education to ESRD patients and their families on palliative and end-of-life care.
- Create palliative care programs that include attention to pain and symptom management, advance care planning, and psychosocial and spiritual support.
- Advocate for the adoption of patient self-determination policies.
- Create peer-mentoring initiatives and bereavement programs.

Case Management

Renal social workers provide information to patients and their families about resources and information that are unknown to the family (McKinley & Callahan, 1998). They routinely provide case management services, including information, referrals, and linkages to local, state, and federal agencies and programs.

Rehabilitation Assistance

Social workers help patients maximize their rehabilitation status. Doing this includes assessing barriers to patient goals of rehabilitation, providing patients with education and

encouragement, and providing case management with local or state vocational rehabilitation agencies. Helping patients maximize the achievement of their rehabilitation goals is very important for this patient population and is included in the Medicare Conditions for Coverage as a required focus for all dialysis units (*Federal Register*, 2008). Research suggests that many patients do not return to work after starting dialysis. A survey of 296 randomly selected dialysis clinics in the United States determined that only 33% of all patients who were working prior to starting dialysis maintained employment after the start of treatment (Kutner, Zhang, Huang, & Johansen, 2010).

In a literature review about nephrology social work and rehabilitation, Romano (1981) outlines different roles for social workers related to rehabilitation:

- *Enabler/facilitator.* Social workers can encourage patients to be as active as possible with work, social activities, and exercise. In addition to helping patients maintain employment after starting ESRD treatment, social workers also can encourage patients who are unable to or are not interested in working to be involved in other activities, such as volunteering and exercise.
- *Educator/advocate.* Social workers can educate patients and their families about vocational rehabilitation resources available for ESRD patients. They also can educate schools, workplace settings, and vocational rehabilitation agencies about the needs of ESRD patients and advocate for patients within these settings (Raiz, 1999). At times, patients may think they cannot work because of the intrusive dialysis schedule. Social workers can provide patient education about home dialysis treatment options that may be more conducive to employment and allow a more flexible daily schedule. Social workers also can advocate with facility administrators at dialysis units to offer patients dialysis schedules that allow them to work, such as late-night or overnight dialysis shifts.

• *Administrator*. Social workers can develop and oversee programs that offer rehabilitation opportunities for ESRD patients as well as conduct relevant research. Many social workers are involved as board members and advisors for the national organization Life Options, which provides the ESRD community with information about rehabilitation.

Team Collaboration

Nephrology social workers collaborate with the renal team in providing patient care. They participate in quality assurance programs and team care planning, and train other health-care professionals on the topic of psychosocial issues. The 2008 Medicare Conditions for Coverage for dialysis units mandate that every unit implement a Quality Assessment and Performance Improvement (QAPI) program to assess patient and clinic outcomes (*Federal Register*, 2008). The QAPI initiatives, often called QA (Quality Assessment) or CQI (Continuous Quality Improvement) programs, must be interdisciplinary and include the dialysis social worker's participation.

Advocacy

Social workers advocate for their patients within their clinics as well as with community agencies (see Box 18.4). For example, a social worker can explain to the nurse manager that a patient's hemodialysis schedule cannot be changed because the patient would like to attend a computer class in the afternoons. A transplant team may hesitate to transplant a patient with a history of substance use; a social worker can advocate for this patient and explain that her four years of sobriety and her three years of demonstrated adherence to a dialysis regime merits her consideration for transplant. Social workers also advocate for patients on a systems level, with various organizations and governmental agencies. Arthur, Zalemski, Giermek, and Lamb (2000) found that nonrenal medical professionals, such as home care or nursing home care providers,

are unfamiliar with the psychosocial issues associated with ESRD. Renal social workers can help patients navigate complex systems of service provision, educate nonrenal community care providers on the unique issues related to ESRD care, and advocate for patients with community providers not familiar with their special needs.

Community-Level ESRD Social Work Intervention

Nephrology social workers are committed to social reform and influencing policy and programs affecting renal patients. Arizona dialysis social worker Kay Smith organized weekly garage sales to raise money for patients and persistently lobbied for dialysis services for undocumented workers. She was suspended temporarily from her job at a for-profit dialysis center because of these activities. Smith was named the 2003 "Social Worker of the Year" by the National Association of Social Workers (NASW). Her award noted that "she made an outstanding difference in areas of advocacy for clients, social policy, social work practice, program development, administration, and research, while demonstrating outstanding leadership and contributing to a positive image for the profession" (NASW, 2003). Social worker Steve Bogatz (2000) successfully advocated with a managed care organization to secure payment of a kidney transplant for a patient.

Social workers also are employed in macrolevel services to the ESRD community (see Box 18.5). They may be clinical managers of treatment facilities, social work directors of dialysis corporations, regional social work coordinators, academic researchers, members of boards of directors of community agencies, or independent consultants to ESRD organizations. Nephrology social workers are employed by nondirect patient care organizations, including the Centers for Medicare and Medicaid, the National Kidney Foundation (national and regional offices), the American Kidney Fund, the American Association of Kidney Patients, the ESRD Networks, and state kidney programs.

Box 18.4 Social Workers as Advocates: Changing Health Policy

In 1982, Arizona Medicaid coverage for organ transplantation was limited to kidney transplants only. Many poor and working poor individuals were enrolled in Medicaid who needed heart, liver, and bone marrow transplants, but Medicaid would not provide coverage for those life-saving treatments. By the late 1980s and early 1990s, Medicaid patients eligible for Medicaid based on federal entitlement, such as Supplemental Security Income (SSI) or Aid to Families with Dependent Children (AFDC), were covered for life-saving organ transplants. But those working poor individuals not federally entitled but eligible based on low income and high medical costs or "spend down" still were not covered for life-saving transplants, even though they were enrolled in Medicaid. It was not uncommon for patients to become disabled and receive SSI for the first six months of disability and be eligible for Medicaid coverage of their transplant only to lose SSI and that coverage once they began receiving Social Security Disability Income (SSDI). Patients receiving SSDI then had to wait two years before becoming eligible for Medicare that would cover their life-saving transplant. Many did not live that long. In 1985, the social workers from the Arizona transplant hospitals were able to document that in the previous several years, over 50 people enrolled in Medicaid had died as a result of this policy.

In November 1994, transplant social workers joined with support group leaders to form a coalition to lobby the Arizona State Legislature and the governor to change the Medicaid policy that denied heart, liver, and bone marrow transplants to the working poor enrolled in Medicaid (Thomas, 1999). The coalition met regularly and invitations were sent to every transplant support group in Arizona, administrators from the transplant programs, the State Organ Procurement Organization, the Coalition

on Donation, the Health Departments from the major metropolitan counties, the State Health and Medicaid Departments, the National Kidney Foundation (NKF), the American Liver Foundation, the American Association of Kidney Patients, the lobbyists from the transplant hospitals, the American Hospital Association, the Legislative Liaisons (lobbyists) from the counties, and individuals denied transplants by Medicaid and their families. The social workers from the transplant centers functioned as community organizers.

Rothman's (1968) principles of social work practice were utilized: locality development, social planning, and social action. Locality development occurred in developing the coalition of concerned stakeholders. The social planning principle was important because the coalition was able to document that Medicaid was paying more to provide medical services to individuals dying than it would have to provide a heart, liver, or bone marrow transplant. For example, one woman who received extensive media coverage died needing a bone marrow transplant that would have cost $130,000; Medicaid paid over $800,000 to provide services as she was dying. The coalition identified three alternative funding sources: additional federal funds, unused Medicaid funds in the annual budget, and revenue from a new tobacco tax. The social action phase included the development of a policy brief or white paper that documented how Medicaid "discriminated" against the working poor in its transplant policy, contacting the media, and training coalition members and others on the legislative process and how to engage the legislature.

The legislature and Medicaid were slow to respond to the coalition, and many of the coalition members were in urgent need of a transplant. Utilizing a tactic from Alinsky (1971)—"The threat is usually more terrifying than the thing itself"—the coalition threatened media coverage every time a Medicaid patient who had been denied a transplant died. As noted, the media previously had reported on several individuals who had died after Medicaid denied coverage for the transplant. This proved to be very effective in getting the legislature's attention. The coalition increased its direct lobbying of the legislature, the governor, and the media.

In March 1995, five months after organizing the coalition, the Arizona State Legislature passed emergency legislation authorizing the immediate appropriation of $8.2 million from the tobacco tax to pay for 63 heart, liver, and bone marrow transplants for the working poor. The governor personally came to the floor of the state senate to sign the bill into law. In October 1995, the coalition persuaded the governor to call the legislature into special session when an additional $2.7 million from the tobacco tax was appropriated to fund 17 heart-lung and lung transplants. In 1996, the legislature expanded the state renal medication program from $100,000 per year to $250,000 per year. In 1997, an additional $100,000 was added to the renal medication program for a total of $350,000 per year. In 1998, legislation was passed that created a new $200,000 per-year nonrenal medication program for heart, liver, and lung transplant patients. One unexpected outcome of this process was the development of a policy that allowed transplant candidates on waiting lists to remain on the lists if they lost their Medicaid eligibility and Medicaid was the payer when the transplant eventually occurred. By 2004, over 120 working poor individuals were transplanted. The average

cost to the state was approximately $5 million annually, and over $4 million of state appropriations have helped needy transplant recipients with the costs of their medications.

In 2010, due to the economic recession, the Arizona State Legislature eliminated Medicaid coverage of liver transplants for hepatitis C, all lung transplants, all single pancreas transplants, and reduced coverage for certain heart transplants and certain bone marrow transplants. There were also budget cuts to other areas of Medicaid as well as to public education and the universities. Social workers and the transplant community mobilized but were not able to stop this reduction in transplants. Unlike the earlier success of expanding Medicaid coverage for transplants, the state was in a fiscal crisis, and no funds were available. The campaign expanded beyond the Arizona transplant community to the national organizations such as the American Society for Transplantation, the American Society for Transplant Surgeons, and the United Network for Organ Sharing. Serious concerns arose that other states would follow Arizona's example and that Medicaid coverage of life-saving transplants in other states would be threatened. This issue has not been resolved to date. Social workers, transplant hospitals, patients and families, and now national organizations continue the advocacy.

Source: Prepared by Charles M. Thomas, Banner Good Samaritan Medical Center Transplant Services, Phoenix, AZ.

PROFESSIONALIZATION OF NEPHROLOGY SOCIAL WORKERS

Social workers are very involved in providing effective intervention with ESRD patients. However, nephrology social workers may face professional challenges, and they may be assigned tasks inappropriately by their employers. Tasks that are clerical in nature or involve

admissions, billing, and determining insurance coverage prevent nephrology social workers from performing the clinical tasks central to their mission (Callahan, Witten, & Johnstone, 1997). Russo (2002) found that all of the nephrology social workers he surveyed felt that transportation was not an appropriate task for them, yet 53% of respondents were responsible for making transportation arrangements for patients. He found that 46% of the nephrology social

Box 18.5 Social Work and the End-Stage Renal Disease Networks

The ESRD Network system was established by law on June 3, 1976, after Medicare coverage was extended on October 30, 1972, to individuals younger than 65 years of age with permanent kidney failure to promote the efficient and equitable distribution of quality medical care to persons with end-stage renal disease. On June 13, 1978, the Social Security Act was amended establishing the ESRD Networks.

The current 18 ESRD Networks, operating as contractors to the Centers for Medicare and Medicaid Services (CMS), manage a computerized patient registry system, ensure quality of care through continuous quality improvement methodology and data analysis, provide community education, process patient beneficiary complaints, and provide regulatory guidance for providers. The mission of ESRD Network Patient Services professionals is to provide a patient-centered perspective in the design and implementation of ESRD Network programs and to meet the needs of ESRD patients by assuring quality of care through communication, education, and conflict resolution.

Full-time Patient Services Coordinator (PSC) positions were mandated by CMS at each network in 2003. PSCs must be master's-prepared social workers or equally qualified individuals (experienced nephrology nurses or counselors). Most of the networks utilize social workers for the position, who are responsible for addressing challenging patient situations. This practice creates a strong social work perspective in the network system and allows facility social workers to serve as contacts for assistance. Network organizations are viewed by many as resources far beyond regulatory concerns.

A *challenging patient* is defined as an individual who is nonadherent to the treatment regimen and can be verbally abusive, physically threatening, or physically violent. In some instances, staff response is not appropriate and exacerbates the situation. All PSCs, regardless of discipline, assume a proactive role in the prevention, facilitation, and resolution of difficult patient and facility situations. This role may include implementing educational programs that will assist facility staff in handling difficult situations and advocating for individual patient rights and rights of all patients at a facility, depending on the situation presented.

Although regional differences due to geography, cultural concerns, and density of population create network-specific PSC tasks, the overall purpose is the same. Some of these tasks include visits to facilities to meet with patients, staff, and administrators for the purposes of patient education, staff training, and responding to grievances; attending regional conferences as a participant or presenter; and creating network-wide patient newsletters. Some networks have a patient advisory committee (PAC) consisting of patients who volunteer their time to help improve the quality of care in their facilities. The network PSC usually coordinates the PAC.

Most PSCs process grievances at the network level and seek resolution through interactions with the facility or follow through with appropriate agency referrals while maintaining a database that is used to track trends. Network vocational rehabilitation efforts to assist facilities to encourage patients to return to work are under the purview of most PSCs, as are efforts to encourage patient exercise programs. Some PSCs communicate network policies, concerns, and goals to other professional organizations, such as the NKF, Kidney and Urology Foundation of America, American Kidney Fund, American Association of Kidney Patients, Society for Social Work Leadership in Health Care, and the national and local Councils of Nephrology Social Workers.

In this environment, PSCs respond to patient needs with an expanded view of quality of care, embracing psychosocial as well as medical concerns. The social work perspective has enhanced the awareness of patient needs in national discussions on quality-of-care issues for renal patients. These discussions have had impact in meetings with CMS officials and in developing network policies that support patient health and address quality of life concerns.

ESRD Network resources and newsletters can be accessed through its Web sites. Links to all networks can be found at the Forum of ESRD Networks Web site, http://www.esrd

networks.org. In addition, publications by Network PSCs (E. Anderson, R. Bachelder, B. K. Campbell, R. Bova-Collis, B. Dyson, L. Hall, M. Meir, K. Niccum, M. L. Pederson, D. Perez, R. Russo, K. Thompson, R. Valdez, among others) have added to social work literature, as well as that of other disciplines, via numerous articles in nephrology publications and journals.

Source: Prepared by Rick Russo, MSW, LSW, Media, PA.

workers in his survey were responsible for making dialysis transient arrangements (which involved copying and sending patient records to out-of-town units) yet only 20% were able to do patient education. The 2002 report of Promoting Excellence in End-of-Life Care recommends that dialysis units discontinue using master's-level social workers for clerical tasks to ensure that they will have sufficient time to provide clinical services to their patients and their families. The 2005 Department of Health and Human Services' proposed conditions for coverage of ESRD facilities recognize this issue:

> [W]e recognize that dialysis patients also need other essential services including transportation and information on Medicare benefits, eligibility for Medicaid, housing, and medications, but these tasks should be handled by other facility staff in order for the MSW to participate fully with the patient's interdisciplinary teams so that optimal outcomes of care may be achieved. (*Federal Register*, 2005, p. 6222)

Merighi and Ehlebracht (2004a,b, 2005), in a survey of 809 randomly sampled dialysis social workers in the United States, found that:

- 94% of social workers did clerical tasks and 87% of those respondents considered these tasks to be outside the scope of their social work training.
- 61% of social workers were solely responsible for arranging patient transportation.

- 57% of social workers were responsible for making travel arrangements for patients who were transient, taking 9% of their time.
- 26% of social workers were responsible for initial insurance verification.
- 43% of social workers tracked Medicare coordination periods.
- 44% of social workers were primarily responsible for completing admission packets.
- 18% of social workers were involved in collecting fees from patients. Respondents noted that this could significantly diminish therapeutic relationships and decrease trust.
- Respondents spent 38% of their time on insurance, billing, and clerical tasks versus 25% of their time on counseling and assessing patients.
- Only 34% of the social workers thought that they had enough time to sufficiently address patient psychosocial needs.

The study also noted that as nephrology social workers increased their involvement in insurance and billing, their job satisfaction decreased. This was true particularly for social workers who collected fees from patients. Nephrology social work job satisfaction was correlated positively with the amount of time spent in counseling and patient education and negatively with insurance-related, clerical tasks. Nephrology social workers who spent more time on insurance, billing, and clerical activities reported increased emotional exhaustion. Those who spent more time doing counseling and patient education reported less emotional exhaustion. The authors posited that providing education and direct counseling to patients and family members were more congruent with the professional training and education of master's-level social workers and thus more satisfying for them.

Another professional concern for nephrology social workers is high patient caseloads. The Council of Nephrology Social Workers (CNSW) conducted an anonymous online salary and caseload survey of nephrology social workers from March 31 to June 21, 2010 (Merighi, Browne, & Bruder, in press). This survey ($n = 1,037$) indicates that full-time dialysis social workers have caseloads ranging from 1 and 711 patients (median 125). Transplant social workers can be responsible for hundreds of patients and organ donors. Large nephrology social work caseloads have been linked to decreased patient satisfaction and less successful patient rehabilitation outcomes (Callahan, Moncrief, Wittman, & Maceda, 1998). Social workers report that high caseloads prevent them from providing adequate nephrology clinical services, most notably counseling (Merighi, & Ehlebracht, 2002, 2005).

The CNSW (2002) recommends an acuity-based social worker-to-patient ratio that takes into consideration the psychosocial risks of patients and recommends a maximum of 75 patients per full-time dialysis social worker. The state of Texas mandates a load of 75 to 100 patients per full-time social worker. Nevada likewise has a mandated ratio of 1 full-time social worker per 100 dialysis patients. However, Merighi and Ehlebracht's (2004c) national survey of social workers found that only 13% of full-time dialysis social workers had caseloads of 75 or fewer, 40% had caseloads of 76 to 100 patients, and 47% had caseloads of more than 100 patients.

As of 2010, no nephrology social work ratios had been mandated by federal authorities. However, the 2008 Medicare Conditions for Coverage for dialysis units do indicate that every dialysis unit needs to make sure that all professionals have caseloads that allow them to fulfill their duties (*Federal Register*, 2008). Specifically, condition 494.180 states:

> An adequate number of qualified personnel are present whenever patients are undergoing dialysis so that the patient/staff ratio is appropriate to the level of dialysis care given and meets the needs of patients; and the registered nurse, social worker, and dietitian members of the interdisciplinary team are available to meet patient clinical needs. (p. 20483)

Nephrology social workers have reported that large caseloads hindered their ability to provide clinical interventions (Bogatz, Colasanto, & Sweeney, 2005). Social work respondents in this study reported caseloads as high as 170 patients; 72% had a median caseload of 125 patients. The researchers found that 68% of social workers did not have enough time to do casework or counseling; 62% did not have enough time to do patient education; and 36% said that they spent excessive time doing clerical, insurance, and billing tasks. One participant in their study stated: "The combination of a more complex caseload and greater number of patients to cover make it impossible to adhere to the federal guidelines as written. I believe our patients are being denied access to quality social work services" (p. 59).

COUNCIL OF NEPHROLOGY SOCIAL WORKERS

The CNSW, a professional council affiliated with the NKF, is the largest organization of nephrology social workers in the world. The organization's goals are to: (1) develop and promote patient and public education; (2) support and promote the profession and education of renal social work; (3) impact regulatory and legislative issues; (4) ensure that qualified social workers are employed in ESRD settings; and (5) provide ongoing support and education to renal patients. In 2010, more than

900 members belonged to the organization, the majority of whom were from the United States. More than 55 local CNSW chapters are located around the country, all of which are overseen by the national organization. Nephrology social workers may belong to other professional organizations, including:

- The Society for Transplant Social Workers, which was founded in 1986 and is active in the United States and Canada
- The European Dialysis and Transplant Nurses Association, which has a social work component
- The Kidney Foundation of Canada, which includes a nephrology social work organization

The CNSW became a national entity and an advisory board to the NKF in April 1973. Prior to this time, nephrology social workers had met regionally to discuss common issues and concerns. Early CNSW activities included providing input on the ESRD federal regulations and lobbying for the inclusion of master's-level social workers on renal teams. Since then, CNSW has developed a number of professional resources, including an annual training program for nephrology social workers, as well as publications such as "Standards of Practice for Nephrology Social Work" and "Continuous Quality Improvement for Nephrology Social Workers." When the Medicare Conditions for Coverage of dialysis and transplant facilities were being revised in 2005, a CNSW-directed initiative resulted in social workers being the profession that commented most frequently on the proposed conditions, which set policy and practice in all ESRD facilities. The CNSW partners with the other NKF professional councils, such as the Council of Renal Nutrition, Council of Advanced Practitioners, and Council of Nephrology Nurses and Technicians, on various projects and to publish a quarterly professional newsletter. Since 1981, the CNSW has provided funding for research projects initiated by nephrology social workers.

Addressing the professional challenges discussed here and providing outcomes-oriented nephrology social work care is a major emphasis of CNSW. In 1995, CNSW collaborated with the NASW to create the "NASW/ CNSW Clinical Indicators for Social Work and Psychosocial Services in Nephrology Settings," a set of guidelines for measuring social work outcomes. CNSW also has a series of 18 training sessions entitled "Refocusing Nephrology Social Work: An Outcomes Training Program," which consist of live presentations, regional continuing education trainings via videotape, and Internet-based professional education programs on these topics:

- "Assessment of Cultural Barriers and Design for Effective Care Plans"
- "Assessment and Management of the Patient with Altered Mental Status"
- "Conducting a Comprehensive Clinical Assessment"
- "Conducting Interventions to Improve Adherence"
- "Continuous Quality Improvement"
- "Delivering, Scoring, and Interpreting Biopsychosocial Instruments to Enhance Assessment, Monitor Treatment Outcomes, and Guide Continuing Interventions"
- "Developing Individualized Plans for Rehabilitation"
- "End-of-Life Issues"
- "Providing Case Management Services"
- "Facilitating Support, Psychoeducational, and Brief Therapy Groups"
- "Interdisciplinary Team Collaboration and Teaching"
- "Marital and Family Counseling to Enhance Patient Adaptation to Illness"
- "Patient Education"
- "Providing Protective Services"
- "Treating Depression"
- "Understanding and Assessing for Depression in the ESRD Patient"
- "Understanding Psychosocial Predictors of Treatment Outcome"

A major CNSW emphasis is legislative advocacy. CNSW is an active member of the National Consortium of Health Care Social Work Organizations and works with the NKF to lobby for improvement in health insurance coverage for ESRD patients as well as to extend Medicare coverage for transplant recipients to include immunosuppressive medications. Another focus of CNSW is professional advocacy; the organization has created a number of documents to clarify the role of a nephrology social worker. The council has four very active e-mail listservs, one each for general membership, regional chapter chairpersons, kidney transplant social workers, and pediatric social workers. These Internet resources allow members quick access to their colleagues.

In October 2008, Medicare enacted the first update to the conditions of coverage for transplant and dialysis facilities in 30 years. These regulations specify the care provided in all ESRD facilities in the United States and its territories, and are used by state and federal surveyors to determine if facilities are performing adequately. The CNSW organized its members to provide a response to these conditions, advocating for attention to ESRD psychosocial issues and appropriate utilization of MSWs on renal teams.

CONCLUSION

ESRD is a significant public health concern with serious biopsychosocial ramifications. Nephrology social work interventions have demonstrated effectiveness in addressing the psychosocial barriers to optimal ESRD patient care. Nephrology social workers practice in all types of settings and levels of practice and work with patients of all ages and backgrounds. This chapter presents information that can guide social work practice in nephrology as well as inform all health social workers about ESRD and its psychosocial issues.

SUGGESTED LEARNING EXERCISES

Learning Exercise 18.1

Increasingly, kidney transplant patients are older (over 65 years) or have chronic illnesses such as human immunodeficiency virus (HIV) and hepatitis. In the United States, there is a significant shortage of organs for patients on the kidney transplant waiting list. Because of this, in some areas of the country, patients wait as long as 8 years to receive a deceased donor kidney transplant. Recently there has been a debate about changing the allocation system for kidney transplants. Historically, children have been given preference for organs, followed by perfect antigen matches (i.e. if a donated kidney perfectly matches the antigens of someone on the transplant waiting list, that person usually will get the kidney), and length of time someone has been on the list (i.e., the longer you are on the list, the more likely you are to receive a transplant). The proposed new kidney allocation policy would emphasize "life years from transplant" and prioritize the distribution of deceased donor kidneys to those on the waiting list who would be most likely to live the longest after a kidney transplant. Proponents of this new allocation system argue that because deceased donor kidneys are in short supply, changes to the system are necessary in order to maximize utility from this scarce commodity. Opponents of this system argue that this new procedure would disadvantage older patients or patients with comorbid illnesses and in effect prohibit such patients from timely transplantation. Through small or large group discussion (or a written assignment), have students discuss or debate these questions (refer to Chapter 3 for more information about ethics; also see http://optn.transplant.hrsa.gov /kars.asp for more information about the kidney transplant allocation proposal):

1. What do you think about a 75-year-old patient, or a patient with HIV or hepatitis, receiving a kidney transplant from a deceased

donor? How does the fact that there are thousands of people (many of whom are younger or less ill) waiting for a kidney transplant influence your decision?

2. What do you think about the new proposal for kidney allocation that would emphasize "life years from transplant"? What social work ethical considerations should be taken into account when thinking about this?

3. If you agree with the new proposal and think that life years from transplant should be the primary consideration when allocating kidneys for transplant, how would you explain this new system to a healthy 70-year-old patient or to a 30-year-old patient with hepatitis or HIV who is interested in a kidney transplant?

Learning Exercise 18.2

Healthy People 2020 is a set of health objectives for the United States that relates to many different health areas, including kidney disease (U.S. Department of Health and Human Services, 2000; see Chapter 4 for more information). Have group members investigate Healthy People 2020 and report back to the group on (or write a paper addressing) these questions:

1. What is Healthy People 2020?

2. What recommendations for kidney disease patients are included in Healthy People 2020? (Students can find this information at http://www.healthypeople.gov)

3. What are at least five ways that social workers can help the United States achieve the kidney disease objectives in Healthy People 2020? Be sure to include individual- and family-level roles with policy-level roles for social workers in this discussion.

Learning Exercise 18.3

Divide the students into six groups. Within these groups, half of the group will take

---

Case Example 18.1

Joseph is a 52-year-old White American male with hypertension who just started dialysis. He did not know that his kidneys were failing and was shocked to be admitted to the hospital with ESRD after going to the emergency room because he was short of breath. Before that, he had not been to see a doctor for over 10 years. After spending a week in the hospital, he started dialysis at an outpatient hemodialysis clinic three times per week. He is newly married, and had been working full time as a construction worker. He is concerned about how the dialysis schedule will work around his job duties, and is also very upset that he may not even be able to return to his physically demanding job because he is so weak. He does not know about the different treatment options for kidney failure and tells you that he is afraid he is going to die.

Case Example 18.2

Rita is a 32-year-old Hispanic female who has been on dialysis for 6 months in a busy urban area. She is interested in a kidney transplant and went to the hospital for an evaluation by the transplant social worker. Her family already has been tested as possible living donors for the transplant; as no one is a good blood match, she must go on the transplant waiting list for a deceased donor kidney. She is concerned about the waiting time for a kidney, as some of her friends from the dialysis clinic have been waiting for a kidney for more than six years. Her dialysis unit reported to the transplant clinic that Rita has not adhered completely to her dialysis regime, as she does not always stay for her recommended treatment time or may miss treatments altogether. This concerns the unit staff, who are unsure whether Rita would take all of her immunosuppressant medications if she got a transplant, which would put her at risk for rejecting a transplanted kidney.

Case Example 18.3

John is a 42-year-old African American male who came to the transplant center for a social work assessment from the living donor advocate, in preparation for donating a kidney to his sister Monique, who has been on dialysis for a year. Monique has three small children and has had many hospitalizations since starting dialysis. Of all his siblings, family, and parents, Joe is the only person who matches Monique for a kidney donation. The family reports that this match is a "miracle." John is very ambivalent about transplantation, however, because he is concerned about missing work due to the kidney donation workup, surgery, and recovery period. He has never been very close to Monique and feels pressured by his family to donate his kidney to his sister.

Case Example 18.4

Mary is a 20-year-old single White American female dialysis patient. She receives hemodialysis at an outpatient clinic three times a week. She started dialysis 2 years ago after the failure of a transplant she received at the age of 14. The dialysis-unit team is very fond of Mary. She has been on the deceased donor waiting list for another kidney transplant and has no family members who are able to donate a kidney to her. (Her kidney failure is due to a genetically inherited disease, which precludes family members from donating a kidney.) In Mary's city, the wait for a kidney transplant is about six years. Inspired by a television news story about a grocery store clerk who donated a kidney to one of his customers, Mary has been asking the dialysis team members if they would donate a kidney to her. One of the patient care technicians, Kim, is interested in donating a kidney to Mary. After role-playing an assessment with Mary, discuss the ethical issues that may be related to Kim donating a kidney to Mary.

the role of a nephrology social worker and complete a social work assessment of the other half of the group (who will role-play one of the patient scenarios in case examples 18.1–18.3, improvising details as they wish). Each group will report back to the class about the unique psychosocial issues identified in the role-play. If time allows, the groups can create an intervention plan for the hypothetical patient.

SUGGESTED RESOURCES

Nephrology Social Work

Canadian Association of Nephrology Social Workers—www.cansw.org

National Kidney Foundation—www.kidney.org/professionals/CNSW/index.cfm

Society for Transplant Social Workers—www.transplantsocialworker.org/

Kidney Disease, Psychosocial Issues, and Treatment Options

American Association of Kidney Patients—www.aakp.org

American Kidney Fund—www.akfinc.org

American Society of Nephrology—www.asn-online.org

American Society of Pediatric Nephrology—www.aspneph.com

American Society of Transplant Surgeons—www.asts.org

Centers for Medicare and Medicaid Services www.cms.gov/

Dialysis from the sharp end of the needle (Patient-created Web site about kidney disease—www.billpeckham.com/from_the_sharp_end_of_the)

Healthy People 2020—www.healthypeople.gov

Home Dialysis Central—www.homedialysis.org

Institute on Rehabilitation Issues—www.rcep6.org/IRI_PublicaNational

Kidney and Urology Foundation of America—www.kidneyurology.org

Kidney Directions: For Research in Polycystic Kidney Disease—www.kidneydirections.com

KDQOL Complete—www.kdqol-complete
.org
> Resource to help administer and score
> KDQOL assessments.

Kidney Disease Quality of Life (KDQOL)
Working Group—http://gim.med.ucla
.edu/kdqol/

Kidney School—www.kidneyschool.org

Life Options—www.lifeoptions.org

National Institute of Diabetes and Digestive
and Kidney Diseases—www.niddk.nih
.gov

National Kidney Disease Education
Program —www.nkdep.nih.gov/

National Kidney Foundation—www
.kidney.org

Nephron Information Center—www
.nephron.com

NephrOnline—www.nephronline.com

NephroWorld: The Whole World of Nephrology—www.nephroworld.com

PKD Foundation: For Research in Polycystic Kidney Disease www.pkdcure.org
/home.html

Promoting Excellence in End of Life
Care—www.promotingexcellence.org

RenalWeb: Vortex Web Site of the Dialysis
World—www.renalweb.com

United Network of Organ Sharing—www
.unos.org

United States Renal Data System—www
.usrds.org

International Nephrology

European Dialysis and Transplant Society—
www.era-edta.org/

International Society for Hemodialysis—
www.ishd.net

International Society of Nephrology—
www.isn-online.org

International Society of Peritoneal
Dialysis—www.ispd.org

Kidney Foundation of Canada—www
.kidney.ca

Kidney Health Australia—www.kidney
.org.au

National Kidney Research Fund—www
.nkrf.org.uk

U.K. National Kidney Federation—www
.kidney.org.uk

World Kidney Fund—www.worldkidneyfund
.org

REFERENCES

Alinsky, S. (1971). *Rules for radicals.* New York, NY: Random House.

Arthur, T., Zalemski, S., Giermek, D., & Lamb, C. (2000). Educating community providers changes beliefs towards caring for the ESRD patient. *Advances in Renal Replacement Therapy, 7*(1), 85–91.

Auslander, G. K., & Buchs, A. (2002). Evaluating an activity intervention with hemodialysis patients in Israel. *Social Work in Health Care, 35*(1/2), 407–423.

Auslander, G., Dobrof, J., & Epstein, I. (2001). Comparing social work's role in renal dialysis in Israel and the United States: The practice-based research potential of available clinical information. *Social Work in Health Care, 33*(3/4), 129–151.

Becker, B. N., Becker, Y. T., Pintar, T., Collins, B. H., Pirsch, J. D., Friedman, A.,…Brazy, P. C. (2000). Using renal transplantation to evaluate a simple approach for predicting the impact of end-stage renal disease therapies on patient survival: Observed/ expected life span. *American Journal of Kidney Diseases, 35*(4), 653–659.

Beder, J. (1999). Evaluation research on the effectiveness of social work intervention on dialysis patients: The first 3 months. *Social Work in Health Care, 30*(1), 15–30.

Beder, J., Mason, S., Johnstone, S., Callahan, M. B., & LeSage, L. (2003). Effectiveness of a social work psychoeducational program in improving adherence behavior associated with risk of CVD in ESRD patients. *Journal of Nephrology Social Work, 22,* 12–22.

Beer, J. (1995). Body image of patients with ESRD and following renal transplantation. *British Journal of Nursing, 4*(10), 591–598.

Bogatz, S. (2000). Winning an HMO appeal: A case studying social work advocacy. *Journal of Nephrology Social Work, 20,* 61–67.

Bogatz, S., Colasanto, R., & Sweeney, L. (2005, January). Defining the impact of high patient/staff ratios on dialysis social workers. *Nephrology News and Issues,* 55–60.

Brady, D., & Lawry, K. (2000). Infants, families and end stage renal disease: Strategies for addressing psychosocial needs in the first 2 years of life. *Journal of Nephrology Social Work, 20,* 17–20.

Browne, T. (2008). *Social networks and pathways to kidney transplantation* (Doctoral dissertation). Retrieved from ProQuest.

Browne, T. (2011). Palliative care in chronic kidney disease. In T. Altilio & S. Otis-Green (Eds.), *Oxford textbook of palliative social work* (pp. 339–350). New York, NY: Oxford University Press.

Browne, T., & Merighi, J. R. (2010). Barriers to adult hemodialysis patients' self-management of oral medications. *American Journal of Kidney Diseases, 56*(3), 547–557.

Burrows-Hudson, S. (1995). Mortality, morbidity, adequacy of treatment, and quality of life. *American Nephrology Nurses Association Journal, 22*(2), 113–121.

Cabness, J. (2005). *National Kidney Foundation second quarter research progress report.* New York, NY: National Kidney Foundation.

Callahan, M. B., Moncrief, M., Wittman, J., & Maceda, M. (1998). Nephrology social work interventions and the effect of caseload size on patient satisfaction and rehabilitation interventions. *Journal of Nephrology Social Work, 18,* 66–79.

Callahan, M. B., Witten, B., & Johnstone, S. (1997). Improving quality of care and social work outcomes in dialysis. *Nephrology News and Issues, 2*(4), 42–43.

Chang, C. F., Winsett, R. P., Gaber, A. O., & Hathaway, D. K. (2004). Cost-effectiveness of post-transplantation quality of life intervention among kidney recipients. *Clinical Transplantation, 18*(4), 407–415.

Charnow, J. A. (2010, April 10). Death risk is lower with peritoneal dialysis. *Renal & Urology News.* Retrieved from http://www.renalandurologynews.com/death-risk-is-lower-with-peritoneal-dialysis/article/168306/

Chen, Y. S., Wu, S. C., Wang, S. Y., & Jaw, B. S. (2003). Depression in chronic hemodialysed patients. *Nephrology, 8*(3), 121–126.

Chiu, Y. W., Teitelbaum, I., Misra, M., de Leon, E. M., Adzize, T., & Mehrotra, R. (2009). Pill burden, adherence, hyperphosphatemia, and quality of life in maintenance dialysis patients. *Clinical Journal of the American Society of Nephrology, 4*(6), 1089–1096.

Cohen, L. M., Germain, M. J., Woods, A. L., Mirot, A., & Burleson, J. A. (2005). The family perspective of ESRD deaths. *American Journal of Kidney Diseases, 45*(1), 154–161.

Council of Nephrology Social Workers. (2002). *Standards of practice for nephrology social work* (5th ed.). New York, NY: National Kidney Foundation.

DeOreo, P. B. (1997). Hemodialysis patient-assessed functional health status predicts continued survival, hospitalization, and dialysis-attendance compliance. *American Journal of Kidney Diseases, 30*(2), 204–212.

Devins, G. M., Mandin, H., Hons, R. B., Burgess, E. D., Klassen, J., Taub, K.,...Buckle, S. (1990). Illness intrusiveness and quality of life in end-stage renal disease: Comparison and stability across treatment modalities. *Health Psychology, 9*(2), 117–142.

Dobrof, J., Dolinko, A., Lichtiger, E., Uribarri, J., & Epstein, I. (2000). The complexity of social work

practice with dialysis patients: Risk and resiliency factors, interventions and health-related outcomes. *Journal of Nephrology Social Work, 20,* 21–36.

Federal Register. (1976, June). *Conditions for coverage for ESRD facilities,* 42 CFR Part 405, Subpart U. Washington, DC: U.S. Government Printing Office.

Federal Register. (2005). *Proposed conditions for coverage for ESRD facilities,* 42 CFR Parts 400, 405, 410, 412, 413, 414, 488, and 494. Washington, DC: U.S. Government Printing Office.

Federal Register. (2007, March). *Hospital Conditions of participation: Requirements for approval and re-approval of transplant centers, to perform organ transplants,* 42 CFR Parts 405, 482, 488, & 498. Washington, DC: U.S. Government Printing Office.

Federal Register. (2008, April). *Conditions for coverage for end stage renal disease facilities,* 42 CFR Part 405, Subpart U. Washington, DC: U.S. Government Printing Office.

Fielding, D., Moore, B., Dewey, M., Ashley, P., McKendrick, T., & Pinkerton, P. (1985). Children with end-stage renal disease: Psychological effects on patients, siblings and parents. *Journal of Psychosomatic Research, 29,* 457–465.

Fox, R. C., & Swazey, J. P. (1979). Kidney dialysis and transplantation. In E. Fox (Ed.), *Essays in medical sociology* (pp. 105–145). New York, NY: Wiley.

Frank, A., Auslander, G. K., & Weissgarten, J. (2003). Quality of life of patients with end-stage renal disease at various stages of the illness. *Social Work in Health Care, 38*(2), 1–27.

Friend, R., Hatchett, L., Schneider, M. S., & Wadhwa, N. K. (1997). A comparison of attributions, health beliefs, and negative emotions as predictors of fluid adherence in renal dialysis patients: A prospective analysis. *Annals of Behavioral Medicine, 19,* 344–347.

Fukunishi, I., & Honda, M. (1995). School adjustment of children with end-stage renal disease. *Pediatric Nephrology, 9,* 553–557.

Georgetown University Hospital. (2010). *32 participants in paired kidney exchange get an early start on the season of Thanksgiving.* Georgetown University Hospital Press & Media. Retrieved from www .georgetownuniversityhospital.org/body.cfm?id =15&action=detail&ref=215

Germain, M., & Cohen, L. M. (2007). Renal supportive care: View from across the pond: The United States perspective. *Journal of Palliative Medicine, 10*(6), 1241–1244.

Gerson, A., Hwang, W., Fiorenza, J., Barth, K., Kaskel, F., Weiss, L.,...Furth, S. (2004). Anemia and health-related quality of life in adolescents with chronic kidney disease. *American Journal of Kidney Diseases, 44*(6), 1017–1023.

Goldstein, M., Yassa, T., Dacouris, N., & McFarlane, P. (2004). Multidisciplinary predialysis care and morbidity and mortality of patients on dialysis. *American Journal of Kidney Diseases, 44*(4), 706–714.

Gudes, C. M. (1995). Health-related quality of life in end-stage renal failure. *Quality of Life Research, 4*(4), 359–366.

Hartwell, L. (2002). *Chronically happy: Joyful living in spite of chronic illness.* San Francisco, CA: Poetic Media Press.

Healthy People 2020. (n.d.). *Healthy People 2020.* Retrieved from www.healthypeople.gov

Hedayati, S. S., Jiang, W., O'Connor, C. M., Kuchibhatla, M., Krishnan, K. R., Cuffe, M. S.,…Szczech, L. A. (2004). The association between depression and chronic kidney disease and mortality among patients hospitalized with congestive heart failure. *American Journal of Kidney Diseases, 44*(2), 207–215.

Holley, J. L., Barrington, K., Kohn, J., & Hayes, I. (1991). Patient factors and the influence of nephrologists, social workers, and nurses on patient decisions to choose continuous peritoneal dialysis. *Advances in Peritoneal Dialysis, 7,* 108–110.

Holley, J. L., & Reddy, S. S. (2003). Pregnancy in dialysis patients: A review of outcomes, complications, and management. *Seminars in Dialysis, 16,* 384–388.

Iacono, S. A. (2003). Coping with pain: The dialysis patient's perspective. *Journal of Nephrology Social Work, 22,* 42–44.

Iacono, S. A. (2004). Chronic pain in the hemodialysis patient population. *Dialysis and Transplantation, 33*(2), 92–101.

Johnstone, S. (2003). Evaluating the impact of a physical rehabilitation program for dialysis patients. *Journal of Nephrology Social Work, 22,* 28–30.

Johnstone, S., & Halshaw, D. (2003). Making peace with fluid: Social workers lead cognitive-behavioral intervention to reduce health-risk behavior. *Nephrology News and Issues, 17*(13), 20–27, 31.

Johnstone, S., & LeSage, L. (1998). *The key role of the nephrology social worker in treating the depressed ESRD patient: Patient utilization preferences and implications for on-site staffing practices.* Unpublished manuscript.

Johnstone, S., Seamon, V. J., Halshaw, D., Molinair, J., & Longknife, K. (1997). The use of medication to manage patient-staff conflict in the dialysis clinic. *Advances in Renal Replacement Therapy, 4*(4), 359–371.

Jonsen, A. (2000). *A short history of medical ethics.* New York, NY: Oxford University Press.

Kaitelidou, D., Maniadakis, N., Liaropouls, L., Ziroyanis, P., Theodorou, M., & Siskou, O. (2005). Implications of hemodialysis treatment on employment patterns and everyday life of patients. *Dialysis and Transplantation, 34*(3), 138–147, 185.

Kimmel, P. (2000). Psychosocial factors in adult end-stage renal disease patients treated with hemodialysis:

Correlates and outcomes. *American Journal of Kidney Diseases, 35*(Suppl.), S132–S140.

Kimmel, P. L., Peterson, R. A., Weihs, K. L., Simmens, S. J., Alleyne, S., Cruz, I., & Veis, J. H. (1998). Psychosocial factors, behavioral compliance and survival in urban hemodialysis patients. *Kidney International, 54,* 245–254.

Kimmel, P. L., Peterson, R. A., Weihs, K. L., Simmens, S. J., Alleyne, S., Cruz, I., & Veis, J. H. (2000). Multiple measurements of depression predict mortality in a longitudinal study of chronic hemodialysis outpatients. *Kidney International, 57*(3), 2093–2098.

Knight, E. L., Ofsthun, N., Teng, M., Lazarus, J. M., & Curhan, G. C. (2003). The association between mental health, physical function, and hemodialysis mortality. *Kidney International, 63*(5), 1843–1851.

Koo, J. R., Yoon, J. W., Kim, S. G., Lee, Y. K., Oh, K. H., Kim, G. H.,…Son, B. K. (2003). Association of depression with malnutrition in chronic hemodialysis patients. *American Journal of Kidney Diseases, 41*(5), 1037–1042.

Kurella, M., Kimmel, P. L., Young, B. S., & Chertow, G. M. (2005). Suicide in the United States end-stage renal disease program. *Journal of the American Society of Nephrology, 16,* 774–781.

Kurtin, P. S., Landgraf, J. M., & Abetz, L. (1994). Patient-based health status measurements in pediatric dialysis: Expanding the assessment of outcome. *American Journal of Kidney Diseases, 24*(2), 376–382.

Kutner, N. G. (1994). Psychosocial issues in end-stage renal disease: Aging. *Advances in Renal Replacement Therapy, 1*(3), 210–218.

Kutner, N. G., Zhang, R., Huang, Y., & Johansen, K. L. (2010). Depressed mood, usual activity level, and continued employment after starting dialysis. *Clinical Journal of the American Society of Nephrology, 5*(11), 2040–2045.

Landsman, M. K. (1975). The patient with chronic renal failure: A marginal man. *Annals of Internal Medicine, 82*(2), 268–270.

Leo, R. J., Smith, B. A., & Mori, D. L. (2003). Guidelines for conducting a psychiatric evaluation of the unrelated kidney donor. *Psychosomatics, 44*(6), 452–460.

Levine, B. J. (1999). "The emerald city complex" transitional depression in adjustment to organ transplant: A review of the literature and implications for transplant social work. *Journal of Nephrology Social Work, 18,* 12–17.

Lindberg, J. S., Husserl, F. E., Ross, J. L., Jackson, D., Scarlata, D., Nussbam, J.,…Elzein, H. (2005). Impact of multidisciplinary early renal education on vascular access placement. *Nephrology News and Issues, 19*(3), 35–43.

Lowrie, E. G., & Lew, N. L. (1990). Death risk in hemodialysis patients: The predictive value of commonly measured variables and an evaluation of death rate differences between facilities. *American Journal of Kidney Diseases, 15,* 458–482.

MacDonald, H. (1995). Chronic renal disease: The mother's experience. *Pediatric Nursing, 21,* 503–507, 574.

Mapes, D., Bragg-Gresham, J. L., Bommer, J., Fukuhara, S., McKevitt, P., & Wikstrom, B. (2004). Health-related quality of life in the Dialysis Outcomes and Practice Patterns Study (DOPPS). *American Journal of Kidney Diseases, 44*(Suppl. 5), S54–S60.

McKinley, M., & Callahan, M. B. (1998). Utilizing the case management skills of the nephrology social worker in a managed care environment. In National Kidney Foundation (Ed.), *Standards of practice for nephrology social work* (4th ed., pp. 120–128). New York, NY: Author.

Medical Education Institute. (2004). Social work project reduces missed treatments. *Control, 1*(3), S2, S8.

Merighi, J. R., Browne, T., & Bruder, K. (in press). 2010 nephrology social work salary and caseload survey summary results. *Journal of Nephrology Social Work.*

Merighi, J. R., & Ehlebracht, K. (2002). Advocating for change in nephrology social work practice. *Nephrology News and Issues, 16*(7), 28–32.

Merighi, J. R., & Ehlebracht, K. (2004a). Issues for renal social workers in dialysis clinics in the United States. *Nephrology News and Issues, 18*(5), 67–73.

Merighi, J. R., & Ehlebracht, K. (2004b). Unit-based patient services and supportive counseling. *Nephrology News and Issues, 18*(6), 55–60.

Merighi, J. R., & Ehlebracht, K. (2004c). Workplace resources, patient caseloads, and job satisfaction of renal social workers in the United States. *Nephrology News and Issues, 18*(4), 58–63.

Merighi, J. R., & Ehlebracht, K. (2005). Emotional exhaustion and workload demands in renal social work practice. *Journal of Nephrology Social Work, 24,* 14–20.

Mollaoglu, M. (2004). Depression and health-related quality of life in hemodialysis patients. *Dialysis and Transplantation, 33*(9), 544–555.

Moss, A. H. (2005). Improving end-of-life care for dialysis patients. *American Journal of Kidney Diseases, 45*(1), 209–212.

Murray, A., Arko, C., Chen, S., Gilbertson, D., & Moss, A. (2006). Use of hospice in the United States dialysis population. *Clinical Journal of the American Society of Nephrology, 1,* 1248–1255.

National Association of Social Workers. (2003). Hospital social worker, Kay Smith, recognized as the NASW social worker of the year 2003. Retrieved from www.socialworkers.org/pressroom/2003/070103_swoty.asp

National Institutes of Health. (1993). *Morbidity and mortality of dialysis: NIH Consensus Statement, 11*(2). Bethesda, MD: Author.

Paniagua, R., Amato, D., Vonesh, E., Guo, A., & Mujais, S. (2005). Health-related quality of life predicts outcomes but is not affected by peritoneal clearance: The ADEMEX trial. *Kidney International, 67*(3), 1093–2005.

Pelletier-Hibbert, M., & Sohi, P. (2001). Sources of uncertainty and coping strategies used by family members of individuals living with end stage renal disease. *Nephrology Nursing Journal, 28*(4), 411–419.

Promoting Excellence in End-of-Life Care. (2002). *End-stage renal disease workgroup recommendations to the field.* Missoula, MT: Robert Wood Johnson Foundation.

Raiz, L. R. (1999). Employment following renal transplantation: The employer perspective. *Journal of Nephrology Social Work, 19,* 57–68.

Rees, M. A., Kopke, J. E., Pelletier, R. P., Segey, D. L., Rutter, M. E., Fabrega, A. J.,...Montgomery, R. A. (2009). A nonsimultaneous, extended, altruistic-donor chain. *New England Journal of Medicine 360*(111), 1096–1101.

Rocha, D. (2010). *Rewards & challenges in dialysis social work. New Social Worker, 17*(3). Retrieved from www.socialworker.com/home/Feature_Articles/General/Rewards_%26_Challenges_in_Dialysis_Social_Work/

Romano, M. (1981). Social worker's role in rehabilitation: A review of the literature. In J. Brown, B. Kirlin, & S. Watt (Eds.), *Rehabilitation services and the social work role: Challenge for change* (pp. 13–21). Baltimore, MD: Williams & Wilkins.

Root, L. (2005). Our social work group's process of conducting an outcomes-driven project. *Journal of Nephrology Social Work, 24,* 9–13.

Rosner, M. H. (2010). Home hemodialysis: Present state of the evidence. *Dialysis & Transplantation, 39*(8), 330–334.

Rothman, J. (1968). *Social work practice.* New York, NY: Columbia University Press.

Rubin, H., Jenckes, M., Fink, N., Meyer, K., Wu, A., Bass, E., ... Powe, N. R. (1997). Patient's view of dialysis care: Development of a taxonomy and rating of importance of different aspects of care. *American Journal of Kidney Disease, 30*(6), 793–801.

Russell, C. L., & Ashbaugh, C. (2004). The experience of immunosuppressive medication on compliance: A case study. *Dialysis and Transplantation, 33*(10), 610–621.

Russ, A. J., Shim, J. K., & Kaufman, S. R. (2007). The value of "life at any cost": Talk about stopping kidney dialysis. *Social Science and Medicine, 64*(11), 2236–2247.

Russo, R. (2002). The role of the renal social worker in the 21st century. *Nephrology News and Issues, 16*(3), 38, 40.

Saran, R., Bragg-Gresham, J. L., Rayner, H. C., Goodkin, D. A., Keen, M. L., Van Dijk, P. C.,...Port, F. K. (2003). Nonadherence in hemodialysis: Associations with mortality, hospitalization, and practice patterns in the DOPPS. *Kidney International, 64*(1), 254–263.

Schatell, D. R., Bragg-Gresham, J. L., Mehrotra, R., Merighi, J. R., & Witten, B. (2010, November). *A description of nephrologist training, beliefs, and practices from the national nephrologist dialysis practice survey*. Proceedings from the 2010 American Society of Nephrology Annual Meeting & Scientific Exposition, Denver, CO.

Siegal, B., Witten, B., & Lundin, A. P. (1994, April). Patient access and expectations of nephrology social workers. *Nephrology News and Issues, 40,* 32–33.

Sikon, G. M. (2000). Pre-dialysis education reduces anxiety in the newly diagnosed chronic renal failure patient. *Dialysis and Transplantation, 6*(346), 344–345.

Takaki, J., Nishi, T., Nangaku, M., Shimoyama, H., Inada, T., Matsuyama, N.,...Kuboki, T. (2003). Clinical psychological aspects of restless legs syndrome in uremic patients on hemodialysis. *American Journal of Kidney Diseases, 41*(4), 833–839.

Thomas, C. (1999). The Arizona experience: Empowering patients and families. *Transplantation Proceedings, 31*(Suppl. 4A), 7–12.

U.S. Department of Health and Human Services. (2000). *Healthy People 2020*. Washington, DC: U.S. Government Printing Office.

U.S. Renal Data System. (2009). *Annual data report*. Bethesda, MD: National Institutes of Health, National Institute of Diabetes and Digestive and Kidney Diseases.

U.S. Renal Data System. (2010). *Annual data report*. Bethesda, MD: National Institutes of Health, National Institute of Diabetes and Digestive and Kidney Diseases.

Valdez, R. (1997). A comparison of sleep patterns among compliant and noncompliant chronic hemodialysis patients. *Journal of Nephrology Social Work, 17,* 28–36.

Vourlekis, B., & Rivera-Mizzoni, R. (1997). Psychosocial problem assessment and ESRD patient outcomes. *Advances in Renal Replacement Therapy, 4*(2), 136–144.

White, Y., & Greyner, B. (1999). The biopsychosocial impact of end-stage renal disease: The experience of dialysis patients and their partners. *Journal of Advanced Nursing, 30*(6), 1312–1320.

Woods, A., Berzoff, J., Cohen, L. M., Cait, C. A., Pekow, P., German, M., & Poppel, D. (1999). The family perspective of end-of-life care in end-stage renal disease: The role of the social worker. *Journal of Nephrology Social Work, 19,* 9–21.

Wu, A. W., Fink, N. E., Cagney, K. A., Bass, E. B., Rubin, H. R., Meyer, K. B.,...Powe, N. R. (2001). Developing a health-related quality-of-life measure for end-stage renal disease: The CHOICE health experience questionnaire. *American Journal of Kidney Diseases, 37,* 11–21.

Wuerth, D., Finkelstein, S. H., Ciarcia, J., Peterson, R., Kliger, A. S., & Finkelstein, F. O. (2001). Identification and treatment of depression in a cohort of patients maintained on chronic peritoneal dialysis. *American Journal of Kidney Diseases, 37*(5), 1011–1017.

Yusack, C. M. (1999). The effectiveness of a structured education program on the completion of advance directives among hemodialysis patients. *Journal of Nephrology Social Work, 19,* 51–56.

19

Oncology Social Work

DANIEL S. GARDNER AND ALLISON WERNER-LIN

Oncology social work is a specialization in social work that addresses the psychosocial responses and needs of individuals and families affected by cancer. Emerging from a long tradition of social work in health care, the subspecialty of oncology social work flourished in the 20th century as biomedical advances transformed cancer from a terminal to a chronic disease. The conceptual foundations of oncology social work are found in a number of disciplines, including psychosocial oncology, an area of clinical practice and research that addresses the psychological, social, behavioral, spiritual, and other dynamics of cancer among individuals, families, and communities. Through multisystemic and holistic practice, research, education, and advocacy, social workers are integral to adding to the knowledge base of cancer and the provision of comprehensive care to people with and affected by cancer. This chapter will introduce readers to the foundations of oncology social work and to social work's unique contributions to comprehensive and integrated cancer care.

Chapter Objectives
- Provide an introduction of cancer epidemiology, treatment, and the psychosocial, behavioral, and spiritual impact of the disease on individuals and families.
- Describe the history, conceptual foundations, and functions of oncology social work in general, and the field of psychosocial oncology.
- Describe the contributions of social work to oncology research.
- Define the scope of practice knowledge, skills, and interventions that oncology

social workers use to assess and ameliorate psychosocial and quality of life concerns.
- Address emerging issues in psychosocial oncology including cancer survivorship, family decision making, genetic testing, and end-of-life care.
- Present selected resources available for patient education and support, and professional development.

CANCER EPIDEMIOLOGY

Over an average American life span, 44% of men and 38% of women will develop some form of cancer during their lifetimes, and an estimated 1.5 million new cases will be diagnosed this year alone (Altekruse et al., 2010). *Cancer* is an umbrella term for hundreds of diseases characterized by uncontrollable growth of abnormal cells in the body. Oncologists classify the diseases according to the type of cell or the organ in which the cancer originated. Although incidence rates vary by gender, race, and ethnicity, non-Hodgkin's lymphoma and melanoma, in addition to cancers of the prostate, breast, lung, colon and rectum, uterus, bladder and kidney, and ovary, are the most common cancers in men and women of all races (Altekruse et al., 2010; see Tables 19.1 and 19.2).

Cancer typically begins with damage to genetic material that leads to the growth of abnormal cells, at times because of the failure to repair mutations. These cells act in a disorganized manner, divide more rapidly than healthy cells, and lack the requisite programming to complete their genetically assigned functions. Cancer cells form tumors (also

Table 19.1   Leading Cancer Sites for Females by Site, Race

Cancer Site	U.S. Prevalence 2007 (SEER)	Estimated New Cases, 2010 (ACS)	U.S. Prevalence, White	U.S. Prevalence, Black	U.S. Prevalence, Hispanic	U.S. Prevalence, Asian
ALL SITES	6,360,682	739,940	5,614,748	479,368	268,580	133,712
Breast (female)	2,591,855	207,090	2,296,698	201,276	102,436	58,562
Uterine corpus	575,108	43,470	523,613	26,175	19,390	10,533
Colon & Rectum	571,857	70,480	489,901	58,546	21,186	14,223
Melanoma	408,229	26,260	391,407	1,605	6,063	750
Non-Hodgkin Lymphoma	211,470	30,160	188,249	15,490	10,719	4,382
Lung & Bronchus	197,878	105,770	172,551	17,957	4,795	4,049
Ovary	177,162	21,880	156,821	12,072	8,061	8,061
Kidney	116,651	22,870	102,098	13,778	7,288	1,816
Thyroid	100,521	338,026	298,625	19,155	21,041	10,761
Pancreas	16,939	21,770	13,718	2,330	1,082	589

Source: Adapted from *SEER Cancer Statistics Review, 1975–2007*, edited by S. Altekruse et al., 2008. Bethesda, MD: National Cancer Institute.

known as malignancies) that spread via the blood or lymphatic system in a process called metastasis, invading and destroying healthy tissue. If the growth of invasive cells continues unabated, the affected areas cease to function (Eyre, Lange, & Morris, 2001). In fast-growing or aggressive cancers, this process often leads to death. In many cancers, however, tumor growth is slow, and the disease can be stopped or controlled with medical treatment.

Table 19.2   Leading Cancer Sites for Males by Site, Race

Cancer Site	U.S. Prevalence 2007 (SEER)	Estimated New Cases, 2010 (ACS)	U.S. Prevalence, White	U.S. Prevalence, Black	U.S. Prevalence, Hispanic	U.S. Prevalence, Asian
ALL SITES	5,353,054	789,620	4,688,195	462,999	233,031	94,285
Prostate	2,276,112	217,730	1,923,891	273,813	99,902	35,457
Colon & Rectum	540,636	72,090	472,191	43,302	23,519	15,315
Urinary Bladder	395,480	52,760	370,034	12,835	9,507	4,559
Melanoma	385,054	38,870	371,219	1,083	3,723	595
Non-Hodgkin Lymphoma	226,855	35,380	203,436	15,559	11,662	4,732
Lung & bronchus	172,739	116,750	145,246	17,728	4,879	4,504
Kidney	164,839	35,370	144,338	15,097	9,831	2,881
Oral cavity & Pharnyx	161,112	25,420	141,976	10,436	5,218	4,324
Leukemia	137,398	24,690	122,770	7,877	10,181	2,685
Pancreas	16,057	21,370	14,093	1,291	451	840

Source: Adapted from *SEER Cancer Statistics Review, 1975–2007*, edited by S. Altekruse et al., 2008. Bethesda, MD: National Cancer Institute.

Malignant cell types present, behave, and are treated differently, so accurate diagnosis of type is critical. Diagnosis can involve careful examination, blood tests, scans, or surgical biopsy, after which the cancer generally is classified as one of five types. *Carcinoma*, a term sometimes used to describe all cancers, specifically refers to malignancies that originate in the epithelial linings of organs such as the skin, lung, breast, liver, colon, or prostate. *Sarcomas* affect bones, cartilage, muscle, or connective tissues. *Adenomas* begin in the adrenal, pituitary, and hormonal glands. *Lymphomas* are cancers of the lymphatic system and affect the organs affiliated with the immune system. *Leukemias* are blood cancers that arise in the bone marrow where stem cells mature and travel through the bloodstream. Some cancers, such as melanomas and small-cell lung carcinomas, do not fit into any of these broad categories (Beers, Porter, Jones, Kaplan, & Berkwits, 2006).

Etiology and Mortality

Cancers are caused by multiple mechanisms and operate along a variety of pathways, including interactions among genetic, environmental, or behavioral processes. Some malignancies are caused by genetic damage or mutations that occur randomly or sporadically, and others are due to hereditary mutations that are passed from generation to generation. Other cancers are strongly associated with age, gender, ethnicity, race, or ancestry. Environmental influences (e.g., exposure to toxic chemicals, air pollutants, viruses, or sunlight and ultraviolet rays), behavioral patterns (such as the use of alcohol or tobacco, obesity and dietary habits, sexual and reproductive behaviors), and social circumstances (e.g., poverty, racial disparities in treatment, or the lack of access to adequate housing and nutrition, clean air, education, and health-care and preventive screening) also can contribute to cancer expression, treatment response, and mortality (Ghafoor et al., 2003; McGinnis, Williams-Russo, & Knickerman, 2002; Shavers & Brown, 2002).

Approximately 570,000 Americans die each year from cancer, representing nearly 25% of all deaths (American Cancer Society [ACS], 2010a). Because of prevention efforts, improved early screening, and treatment advances, mortality rates from cancer overall have decreased since the 1990s (Altekruse et al., 2010; Edwards et al., 2009). Although survival rates vary by cell type and stage at diagnosis, fewer than half of all people diagnosed with cancer will die from the disease (Eyre et al., 2001). Despite these trends, incidence and mortality rates demonstrate significant health disparities based on gender, age, race/ethnicity, ancestry, geography, and socioeconomic status (SES). According to the Centers for Disease Control and Prevention (CDC, 2010), while different cancers affect men and women at different rates, men are at an overall greater risk than women for developing the disease. Incidence for all cancers combined is significantly higher for African American men than for men of other races/ethnicities, and cancer mortality is higher for African American men and women than for other men and women. In general, lower SES puts people at increased risk for developing cancer (Ghafoor et al., 2003), and older adults are 10 times more likely to develop cancer than those younger than 65 years (Altekruse et al., 2010).

Although well documented, the causes of health disparities in cancer and other chronic diseases are not fully understood and likely reflect complex interactions among biological, social, and behavioral factors, including genetic differences, exposure to environmental toxins, and lack of access to good nutrition, preventive screening, and health insurance (Link & Phelan, 1995; Williams, 1997). Factors such as bias among health-care providers and skepticism about mainstream medicine among some individuals and lack of access to primary and preventive care services have increased cancer risks for vulnerable communities and marginalized populations (Shavers & Brown, 2002). African American women, for example, are less likely to have breast cancer than White women but are significantly more likely to die from the disease (Chu et al., 1997;

Box 19.1 Cancer Staging

Staging is the process of determining the severity and invasiveness of disease to inform treatment decisions, determine prognosis, identify clinical trials that might be appropriate, and facilitate communication between providers. Commonly, staging integrates information about the location and size of primary tumor(s), whether the cancer has spread into the surrounding lymph nodes, and whether cancer cells have invaded other organs.

Because criteria for stages vary by cancer type, the American Joint Committee on Cancer developed the TNM classification system to provide common language. *T* describes the size (in millimeters or centimeters) or extent of the original tumor; *N* indicates whether cells have traveled to the surrounding lymph nodes, and *M* indicates the presence of metastases. Each criterion has grades to indicate the degree of severity.

Generally, however, cancer staging is discussed differently with patients and families. This staging system is shown next.

Staging	Type	Description
Stage 0	in situ	Abnormal cells are contained to the primary organ. Generally, Stage 0 cancers are curable.
Stage 1	localized	Cancer is limited to the organ in which it began, without evidence of spread.
Stages 2–3	regional	Cancer is locally advanced, may have spread to local lymph nodes.
Stage 4	distant	Cancer has spread from the primary site to distant organs or distant lymph nodes. Generally, Stage 4 cancers are referred to as metastatic and may be inoperable.
	recurrent	Disease that recurs either in the area of the primary tumor (locally recurrent) or as metastasis (distant recurrence).

Source: From www.cancer.gov/cancertopics/factsheet/Detection/staging and www.cancerstaging.org/mission/whatis.html

Dignam, 2000). Gehlert and colleagues (2008) propose a "downstream" model of disease that links structural and environmental variables (e.g., poverty, poor nutrition, exposure to crime, and substandard housing) with social isolation, depression, and stress-hormone reactions, creating pathways to illness and higher mortality among lower socioeconomic and racial/ethnic communities.

Cancer Treatment

A variety of conventional and experimental treatments are designed to eliminate or shrink tumors and to prevent the spread or recurrence of cancer. Oncologists base treatment decisions primarily on the type and the invasiveness of the disease, or its stage of de-velopment (see Box 19.1). Other important considerations include the effectiveness of a particular treatment option; the overall health of the individual; the short- and long-term side effects of treatments, which may vary across groups; and financial considerations, such as insurance coverage (Eyre et al., 2001). Physicians generally discuss treatment alternatives with the patient, who then makes decisions in consultation with health-care professionals and family members. Treatment may include some combination of surgery, chemotherapy, and radiation.

Surgery is used for prevention, diagnosis, and treatment of cancer. Surgical biopsies provide visual confirmation of tumor size and extent of spread and obtain tissue for analysis of cell type and disease stage. When the cancer is contained or easily removed, surgery remains the most effective treatment. Surgery frequently is used in combination with other treatment modalities, including radiation, chemotherapy, and/or hormonal therapy. Radiation therapy uses ionizing radiation to destroy or minimize malignancies and is used to target precisely and reach cancer cells and tumors that often are difficult to reach. Used successfully in curative and palliative treatment, radiation treatment can be prescribed alone or as an adjuvant treatment to surgery or chemotherapy. Radiation often requires daily treatments that last for many weeks. It is time consuming and fatiguing and can result in localized skin reactions, hair loss, or internal scarring in the areas of the body that are treated (Eyre et al., 2001; Weinberg, 2006).

In contrast to more localized treatment, chemotherapy, a broad term describing hundreds of medications that attack cancer cells throughout the body, often affects healthy organs and functions during treatment. Like radiation therapy, chemotherapy can be used for curative or palliative purposes, and is used alone or as an adjuvant to other treatments, depending on cancer type and staging. Chemotherapy uses specific combinations of cancer-fighting agents, provided via a range of methods (e.g., transfusions, injections, oral medications), schedules, and dosages, to maximize the effects of treatment while minimizing the impact on healthy organs (Beers et al., 2006). Although chemotherapy plays a large role in reducing mortality among cancer patients, its physical side effects can be severe and cause great anxiety. A nonexhaustive list includes nausea and vomiting, suppression of immune systems, hair loss, mouth sores, fatigue, and decreased libido (Weinberg, 2006).

Experimental approaches to treating cancer may be offered to people with cancers that do not respond well to conventional treatments and to those experiencing metastatic growth or recurrences (Eyre et al., 2001). Patients can try new treatments by participating in clinical trials that test the effectiveness of newly developed protocols. Access to clinical trials often is limited because of strict exclusion and inclusion criteria for protocols, meaning that not everyone who might be helped by an experimental treatment will qualify. Rural residents who live a distance from comprehensive cancer centers are less likely to have the opportunity to use experimental approaches. Clinical trials generally are performed at a handful of research and teaching hospitals, and travel requirements may be prohibitive for people with financial or instrumental constraints. Psychosocial and structural barriers such as these frequently prevent ethnic and racial minorities from participating in clinical trials (Wells & Zebrack, 2008). Experimental treatments often are tested against placebo or Food and Drug Administration–approved protocols in double-blind tests.

Many people with cancer supplement their conventional treatments with complementary or alternative therapies. An estimated 53% to 68% of all adults in the United States have reported using prayer or spiritual practices, naturopathic supplements, breathing and relaxation exercises, yoga, and chiropractic to enhance their health (Richardson et al., 2000; Tilden, Drach & Tolle, 2004). The use of less conventional remedies to complement treatment has risen steadily in recent years, and the National Center for Complementary and Alternative Medicine at the National Institutes for Health anticipates that the trend will continue as the baby boom generation ages (Kessler et al., 2001). See Chapter 12 in this volume for more discussion of complementary and alternative treatments.

BRIEF HISTORY OF PSYCHOSOCIAL ONCOLOGY

Fight Against a Devastating Disease

Although cancer has affected individuals for much of recorded history, prior to the 20th century, a definitive diagnosis was difficult to make, and the disease was nearly always fatal (Mukherjee, 2010). People diagnosed with cancer often experienced uncontrolled pain, incapacitation, disfigurement, foul-smelling tumors, social isolation, and loss of self-esteem (Holland, 1998). Because little was known about the disease or its etiology, cancer engendered fears of contagion and stigmatization (Sontag, 2001; Waskul & van der Riet, 2002). Cancer was a shameful secret; until the late 20th century, social mores dictated that a cancer diagnosis was rarely discussed publicly and often not even disclosed to the patient by physicians and family members. The introduction of anesthesia in the late 19th century allowed surgical intervention, the first potentially curative treatment for cancer. Early surgeries often were devastating, however, and carried long-term physical and functional side effects. In the 1920s, radiation therapy was found to be effective in shrinking some tumors and was used in conjunction with surgery. Following World War II, compounds initially developed by the military for use in chemical warfare were found to be successful in treating acute leukemia in children (Mukherjee, 2010). This discovery presaged the development of widespread chemotherapy treatments beginning in the early 1950s (ACS, 2010c).

Public and private funding for cancer research and training began to increase once effective treatments became more common. The federal government established the National Cancer Institute (NCI) in 1937 to centralize efforts to understand and reduce cancer morbidity and mortality. After World War II, not-for-profit organizations dedicated to improving cancer care and prevention, such as the American Society of Clinical Oncology (ASCO) and ACS, increased public education about cancer prevention and testing and helped fund a generation of research that produced significant breakthroughs in early detection and treatment of a variety of cancers (ACS, 2010c; Fobair et al., 2009). In 1970, President Nixon declared a "War on Cancer," and Congress enacted legislation to focus efforts to find a cure for the disease (NCI, 2010). The National Cancer Act of 1971 broadened the scope and responsibilities of the NCI, created a National Cancer Program, and organized the development of 12 (currently expanded to over 40) comprehensive cancer centers around the country to integrate research and clinical practice. The National Cancer Act created the infrastructure for the generation and collection of data on cancer etiology, treatment, and biological and psychological impact that have fueled remarkable advances in cancer screening, treatment, and survivorship over the past 40 years.

Progress and Hope in the Late 20th Century

Because of continuing advances in cancer screening and detection, diagnosis, and treatment technologies, the 1960s and 1970s saw increased long-term survivorship of cancer. According to the ACS (2010a), the 5-year survival rate for the 15 most common cancers increased from 50% to 66% across race and gender over the past two decades. This translates to an estimated 540,000 deaths that have been avoided because of advances in cancer treatment and early detection (Jemal et al., 2010). Approximately 10.5 million people nationwide have survived cancer, and mortality rates from the four leading cancers—lung, breast, prostate, and colorectal—have fallen for over a decade (Altekruse et al., 2010). As greater numbers of people are living with cancer and experiencing the long-term side effects of treatment, it has come to be considered a chronic, episodic illness rather than a terminal condition (Witter & LeBas, 2008). Although curing cancer remains the goal, long-term survival has broadened the aims of treatment to include controlling symptoms and optimizing patient quality of life (Gunnars, Nygren, & Glimelius, 2001; Holland & Lewis, 2000).

Growing public awareness about behavioral and environmental aspects of cancer (e.g., smoking, exposure to ultraviolet rays and other carcinogens) and increasing survivorship helped stimulate the development of psycho-oncology, a medical subspecialty that deals with psychological responses to the disease and treatment and the biopsychosocial determinants of cancer morbidity and mortality (Holland, 1998; Montgomery, 1999). The transdisciplinary field of psycho-oncology aims to develop and evaluate interventions that alleviate distress, increase supports, and maximize quality of life among individuals with cancer and their families. Efforts to integrate psychosocial care for cancer patients and their families have increased significantly over the past 30 years. The ACS, ASCO, Institute of Medicine (IOM), and NCI all have promoted research, conferences, and scholarly publications that have advanced the field of psychosocial oncology, addressing topics such as cancer prevention, coping and adaptation, survivorship, quality-of-life assessment, family caregiving, cultural differences and health disparities, psychoneuroimmunology, and cancer genetics (Montgomery, 1999).

The hospice and end-of-life care movement in the 1970s developed in response to concerns about the need to improve the quality of care in chronic and terminal illness (Connor, 2007). Advocating for enhanced patient autonomy, pain and symptom control, communication with patients about their medical status and treatment options, and the importance of social support networks at the end of life, hospice advocates and early programs had a pronounced effect on the field of oncology, leading to increased public awareness and funding of pain management teams and psychosocial care services. In the ensuing 20 years, the hospice movement spurred the development of palliative medicine, which has brought a more patient- and family-centered, holistic approach to cancer treatment, beginning at the time of diagnosis (Connor, 2007; National Hospice and Palliative Care Organization, 2010). See Chapters 22 and 23 for more details about palliative and hospice care.

Social Work's Contribution to Practice

Health social workers have helped individuals and their families cope with the biopsychosocial aspects of illness in hospitals and outpatient clinics since the early 20th century (Beder, 2006; Fobair et al., 2009; see Chapter 1 for more information). Pioneering social workers like Ida Cannon and Harriet Bartlett applied a holistic, "person-in-environment" perspective to their clinical practices, which

led the way for the subspecialty of oncology social work (Fobair et al., 2009). In the 1940s, social workers developed the first hospital departments dedicated to addressing the psychosocial concerns of cancer patients and their families, and oncology social workers have become integral members of interdisciplinary health-care teams at major hospitals around the nation since that time (Holland, 2002). Today, oncology social workers provide comprehensive psychosocial assessment; case management; and supportive individual, family, and group interventions that help patients and their families navigate medical systems, make use of community resources, and attain optimal adjustment to the disease and treatment (Hermann & Carter, 1994)

Oncology social work leaders are deeply committed to enhancing patient care. Many of them helped to refine and disseminate clinical knowledge and skills in the 1980s by building accomplished and highly respected departments, developing standards of care, and promoting professional training and research programs (Fobair et al., 2009). These include Grace Christ, who was the director of social work at Memorial Sloan-Kettering Cancer Center in New York; Joan Hermann, formerly at the Fox Chase Cancer Center in Philadelphia; and Naomi Stearns, currently the director of social work at Dana-Farber Cancer Institute in Boston. With the support of the ACS, these and other pioneers formed the National Association of Oncology Social Work in 1983 (renamed the Association of Oncology Social Work [AOSW] in 1993), which has grown into a major professional organization representing social workers in the subspecialty. Psychosocial support services are increasingly being integrated into standard medical guidelines for oncology (Blum, Clark & Marcusen, 2001; Holland, 2002). National and international oncology social work organizations have helped lead efforts to improve psychosocial care of cancer patients and their families through the creation of professional standards of practice specific to social work in oncology; position papers on areas such as euthanasia and pain management; national conferences and research awards; and formal continuing education in areas such as end-of-life care and family-centered practice (Fobair et al., 2009).

PSYCHOSOCIAL IMPACT OF CANCER

Despite the advances in early detection and treatment, a diagnosis of cancer can be an emotionally devastating and life altering experience (IOM, 2007). Newly diagnosed patients experience a range of emotions, including fear, shock, uncertainty, and grief, and many struggle to mobilize the coping skills needed to manage these emotions (Hermann & Carter, 1994). Patients and family members must absorb and comprehend a great deal of information and medical terminology about the disease, undergo blood tests and diagnostic procedures, manage the disease and treatment regimens, navigate complex health-care systems, ask informed questions and make critical treatment decisions, and adapt to often-extensive dietary and behavioral restrictions. Cancer patients and their families struggle to become experts in managing the illness, keeping track of medical appointments and procedures, interacting with a variety of health-care providers, and monitoring insurance benefits, including short- and long-term disability policies (Smith, Walsh-Burke, & Crusan, 1998). Psychosocial stressors associated with cancer and its sequelae can undermine an individual's sense of self and self-worth, provoke fears and anxieties, and test coping mechanisms, values, and social support systems like never before. Coping with the emotional impact of the disease over time involves adapting to changes in self and identity, living with uncertainty and a heightened sense of mortality, and radical disruptions in all arenas of one's life, including work, leisure, and social relationships (Holland & Lewis, 2000; Waskul & van der Riet, 2002).

Treatment often is associated with greater discomfort and disruption of the patient's life than the disease itself. Cancer surgery can result in short-term complications, such as pain and discomfort, lack of mobility, bleeding, or infection, and long-term side effects, such as scarring, nerve and tissue damage, and significant functional limitations (e.g., disruption of gastrointestinal, respiratory, or sexual functioning, and limited mobility or range of motion) (Eyre et al., 2001). Despite the development of interventions and protocols that moderate symptomatic responses to treatment, treatment effects of chemotherapy and radiation therapy, such as fatigue, pain, nausea, and vomiting, are still quite common (IOM, 2007). Treatment effects can affect quality of life significantly because they diminish energy and limit mobility, autonomy, and the ability to carry out day-to-day activities. Side effects, such as hair loss and appetite and weight fluctuations, and radical surgical procedures carry additional stigma by displaying visible clues of a serious illness (Rosman, 2004).

Individuals with cancer have higher rates of mental illness than their peers, especially adjustment disorders, anxiety, and depression (Carlson et al., 2004; Spiegel, 1996). Psychological distress may be preexisting or a response to the diagnosis and can be exacerbated by ongoing disease and treatment. Anxiety and depression are not related specifically to different types of cancer, but cancers with poorer prognoses (e.g., pancreatic) tend to be associated with greater levels of distress (Carlson et al., 2004; Zabora, Brintzenhofeszoc, Curbow, Hooker, & Piantadosi, 2001). Depression in cancer patients often is underdiagnosed or viewed by health-care professionals as a "natural" response to life-threatening disease (Spiegel, 1996). The failure to accurately detect and treat psychosocial difficulties or mental illness can exacerbate patient and family distress, get in the way of disease management and adherence to treatment protocols, and decrease quality of life (IOM, 2007).

Research on psychosocial response to cancer suggests that several factors may enhance the patient's adaptation to the disease. Cancer patients who approach their illness with an internal sense of control over the disease process and an optimistic or hopeful attitude generally experience less emotional distress and higher psychological adjustment than do other cancer patients (Ell, Nishimoto, Mediansky, Mantell, & Hamovitch, 1992; Livneh, 2000). Using active engagement-oriented coping styles that emphasize problem solving, seeking information and social support, processing and expressing emotions, and adopting a fighting spirit also may enhance psychological adaptation to the cancer experience (Stanton et al., 2000). In addition, patients who report higher levels of social support, and those who turn to religion or faith in coping with the disease, may experience less distress and improved well-being (Wright, 1999). This literature has many inconsistencies, however, and the role of neuroimmunological changes, illness factors, and sociodemographic variables such as gender, age, and race/ethnicity in coping and psychological adjustment have yet to be fully explored (Livneh, 2000).

Cancer and the Family

Cancer is considered a disease that affects families because of the many ways in which an individual's illness affects and is affected by the functioning of families and extended kin. Cancer and its treatment can disrupt family and social roles, causing emotional upheaval and requiring changes in all family members to manage the disease and maintain normal family functioning (Weihs & Politi, 2006). Families adapt to chronic and advanced illness through complex and often unconscious changes in structure, rules, and communication with one other and with those outside the family (Gardner, 2008; Patterson & Garwick, 1994). Having a parent, for example, who is too ill or exhausted to care for her children, a family breadwinner who is temporarily unable to work, or a partner who has significant changes in appearance or sexual desire can bring about devastating changes in family interactions, resources, and health.

Family caregivers provide the bulk of care for cancer patients (Rabow, Hauser, & Adams, 2004; Wolff, Dy, Frick, & Kasper, 2007) and play a significant role in providing hands-on, day-to-day care; ensuring adherence with

medications and care plans; and maintaining communication with health-care team members, friends, and family about the patient's daily status, needs, and concerns. This is particularly salient when the cancer patient is a child, elderly, or has advanced cancer (Glajchen, 2004; Hauser & Kramer, 2004; Waldrop, Kramer, Skretny, Milch, & Finn, 2005). A rich empirical literature suggesting that family caregivers share much of the emotional, physical, and financial strains of living with a chronic and progressive illness, often at the risk of their own physical and mental health (Hudson, Aranda, & Kristjanson, 2004; Waldrop, 2007). Despite the potential benefits of providing care for family members with chronic illness (Kramer, 1997), doing so significantly increases the caregiver's vulnerability to a range of mental and physical health problems (Braun, Mikulincer, Rydall, Walsh, & Rodin, 2007).

Family adaptation to cancer is influenced by family dynamics, such as communication, flexibility, mutuality, cohesion, and family life stage, as well as illness variables, including disease course (i.e., acute or chronic, and progressive, constant, or relapsing), anticipated outcome, and patient's level of functioning (Rolland, 2005; see Chapter 13 for further discussion). Flexibility of family roles and boundaries, which allows families to use outside supports while maintaining some consistency in family functioning, is associated with coping and resilience (F. Walsh, 2006). Living with cancer changes family communication patterns and requires families to talk about things they often have little or no experience in talking about. Although open and intimate communication is thought to be helpful in families living with chronic illness, barriers to effective communication include preexisting family conflicts, differing health beliefs or care preferences, family secrets, or conflicting family narratives (Kramer, Boelk, & Auer, 2006; Werner-Lin & Gardner, 2009). Dyadic and relational stressors can compound the tasks of the cancer experience and negatively affect marital or partner relationships (Kayser, Watson, & Andrade, 2007; Manne, 1998).

Genetic Testing and Reproductive Decision Making

Recent advances in mapping the human genome have uncovered alterations in the genetic code that predispose carriers to increased risk for a variety of adult-onset cancers (see Chapter 21). According to the National Human Genome Research Institute (n.d), genetic cancers account for approximately 5% to 15% of all cancer diagnoses. A blood test can identify the presence of one of these mutations, and receiving results is complex and frequently distressing (Meiser, 2005). Because of the nature of genetic inheritance, test results provide information about an entire family bloodline. Because every generation is at risk for inheriting mutations, a major motivation for young adults to pursue genetic testing is to inform family planning (Decruyenaere et al., 1996; Denayer, Evers-Kiebooms, Tejpar, Legius, & Van Cutsem, 1999; Werner-Lin, 2010). Genetic counseling and testing can reduce anxiety for patients by clarifying risk perceptions (Meiser & Halliday, 2002), increasing control over inherited risk, and opening avenues to pursue advanced and targeted preventive medical care (Gooding, Organista, Burack, & Beisecker, 2006). Yet patients frequently have trouble understanding, interpreting, and using complex genetic health information. Furthermore, although preventive measures do exist, they provide no guarantees and may significantly impact quality of life, identity, self-esteem, sexuality (Lostumbo, Carbine, Wallace, Ezzo, & Dickersin, 2004; Lux, Fasching, & Beckmann, 2006; Metcalfe, Lynch, Ghadirian, & Nadine, 2004), and long-term health outcomes (Kauff et al., 2008; Rebbeck, 2002).

A mutation of the *BRCA* gene, just one of the gene mutations that has been implicated in inherited breast cancer risk, confers an estimated 14% to 87% lifetime risk for breast cancer to women as well as a 10% to 68% lifetime risk of ovarian cancer (Antoniou et al., 2003; Szabo & King, 1997). High rates of cancer expression suggest that extended family systems may have experienced many cancer-related diagnoses and losses with few periods of respite between one diagnosis and the next. Experiences with cancer treatment and loss may become a familiar backdrop for family life and may shape perceptions of cancer risk and decisions about prevention and early detection for asymptomatic family members (Werner-Lin, 2010).

Cancer Over the Life Course

Childhood and Adolescence

The psychosocial impact of cancer on individuals, families, and communities depends to a great extent on the biological, developmental, historical, and culturally defined age of the patient. Children of different ages, for example, interpret and experience illness and treatment differently, according to their cognitive and developmental capacities and in the context of their family and peer relationships. Children with cancer often experience increased anxiety, depression, social isolation, and regression (Zebrack & Chesler, 2001). As a result, a cancer diagnosis in childhood or adolescence may impede the resolution of normal developmental tasks, such as individuation from caregivers, identity development, and building intimate friendships. Children may experience anticipatory symptoms, including nausea and vomiting, prior to treatment as a result of classical conditioning or anxiety. Nonadherence to cancer treatment is reported in 33% of children younger than 13 years and 59% of adolescents (Keene, Hobbie, & Ruccione, 2000; Richardson & Sanchez, 1998). Although parents are responsible for their children's adherence to treatment, a child may still refuse treatment. Social workers can intervene by refocusing the child's need for control toward other, less harmful behaviors and by assessing how parenting styles may be problematic for the child. Referral for individual and family counseling is crucial if ongoing difficulties persist.

School experiences have a significant impact on development and support during childhood and adolescence (Patenaude & Kupst, 2005). Children often miss significant amounts of school, which impacts their classroom learning, peer relationships, and sense of mastery and autonomy. For adolescents, cancer can interfere with sexual development. Psychosexual losses surround issues of physical development, menses, fertility, and libido (Zebrack, Casillas, Nohr, Adams, & Zeltzer, 2004). Cancer also can interfere with adolescents' exploration of their sexual identities; an estimated half of adolescent survivors of cancer feel uncomfortable with the opposite sex and avoid dating (Zebrack & Chesler, 2001).

Parents of School-Age Children

When parents of school-age children are diagnosed with cancer, balancing parenting and self-care may be problematic. Parents with cancer worry about what and how to tell their children about their illness, how to continue meeting the demands of parenting throughout treatment, and how to plan for their children's care if they die from the disease (Biank & Sori, 2003). At times, cancer patients rely on their children and teens for treatment or emotional support; this "parentification" can add to the child's burden and is associated with negative mental health outcomes (Hermann, 2001). Children, adolescents, and parents can benefit from education and support, including support groups in which their needs and concerns can be addressed (Werner-Lin, Biank, & Rubenstein, 2010).

Cancer in Later Life

Older adults account for approximately 77% of new cases of cancer each year (ACS, 2010a). Older cancer patients are more likely than those younger than 65 years to live with concurrent, chronic illnesses, such as diabetes, cardiovascular disease, respiratory disease, kidney disease, and Alzheimer's disease or other dementing illnesses. The pervasiveness of comorbid chronic conditions in later life poses distinct health and psychosocial challenges to older cancer patients, their families, and health-care providers. Chronic illness in later life is associated with increased pain, depression, and mortality and with diminished quality of life (Kane & Kane, 2005; Lawton, 2001). Co-occurring chronic and degenerative diseases often cause or exacerbate functional limitations that threaten older adults' ability to care for themselves or live independently. Age-related functional concerns, such as vision and hearing loss, difficulties with balance and walking, falls, eating and nutritional problems, cognitive losses, and incontinence, can significantly limit an older adult's ability to carry out daily activities and manage medical treatments (Inouye, Studenski, Tinetti, & Kuchel, 2007). Frailty—a condition defined by muscle weakness, limited mobility, and fatigue—is increasingly common with age and is associated with higher risks of falls, disability, hospitalization, and premature death (Feldt, 2004; Woods et al., 2005; see Chapter 16).

Older patients share many physical, psychological, social, and spiritual concerns that shape their aging and illness experiences, quality of life, and palliative care needs. Older adulthood is often a time of significant life transitions, including retirement, changing family roles, the death of a partner and other loved ones, and declining health, functioning, autonomy, and independence. Although there is wide variability in how older patients experience chronic and progressive illness, some view a life-threatening diagnosis as an "expected" and developmentally consistent phenomenon. Many older adults report that they fear the process of dying more than death itself; frequent concerns include the possibility of experiencing uncontrollable pain, growing incapacity, loss of autonomy and control, and becoming a burden on family members (Cicirelli, 1999; Gardner & Kramer, 2009/10). Elders who have or expect to experience more physical pain, who fear abandonment, or who lack social and spiritual support report having more difficulty coping with progressive illness and dying (Fortner & Neimeyer, 1999).

Fixed incomes and inadequate insurance benefits can limit an older cancer patient's access to the resources needed for coping with the demands of cancer treatment, particularly when older individuals themselves are caring for adult children, grandchildren, or ill spouses. Common challenges include paying for treatments not covered by Medicare and other insurances, finding transportation to medical appointments, and needing assistance in performing daily self-care activities. Medicare and third-party insurers rarely cover new or experimental medications and procedures, making it difficult for older patients to take full advantage of emerging treatment options. In addition, a growing literature identifies ageism as a factor in the undertreatment of older patients with a range of cancer diagnoses (Dale, 2003; Peake, Thompson, Lowe, & Pearson, 2003). Older cancer patients frequently are excluded from clinical trials solely on the basis of age, and physicians may refrain from offering aggressive treatments to them under the assumption that older patients cannot physically handle adverse side effects (Marcusen & Clark, 2001; Rohan, Berkman, Walker, & Holmes, 1994).

Feeling that one has reliable, reciprocal social supports and a community or social network (e.g., church congregations, friends, and extended family) is a significant predictor of health and well-being in later life (L. Berkman, 2000; Krause, 2006), and it may mediate the impact of serious illness and stressful life events (Cohen, 2001). Conversely, older adults who are socially isolated, live alone, and report few social resources are more vulnerable to illness, disability, and mortality (Lyyra & Heikkinen, 2006; Moren-Cross & Lin, 2006). Yet older adults generally cope with advanced illness and the threat of dying by turning inward (Atchley, 2009; Werth, Gordon, & Johnson, 2002), engaging in inquiry about life's meaning, their legacy, and the afterlife (Bolmsjo, 2000; Nelson-Becker, 2005). Some elders experience renewed faith that can strengthen their connections to family and community and help them adapt to loss, chronic illness, functional decline, dying, and death (Atchley, 2009).

Cancer Survivorship

Outliving a life-threatening condition like cancer often requires managing long-term effects that can cause emotional distress, functional limitations, and further chronic health problems. Some survivors live with "minor" annoyances, such as a dry skin, lymphedema (i.e., fluid retention, often in the arms or legs), or mild neuropathy in their hands and feet. For others, surviving cancer comes at the cost of developing other serious health concerns, such as cardiac disorders, cognitive deficits, chronic renal disease, secondary cancers, and infertility (Kornbluth, 1998; Oeffinger et al., 2006; Pizzo, 2001). These chronic conditions and side effects act as ongoing reminders of the negative emotional experiences associated with cancer.

Survivors of childhood cancer face unique medical and psychosocial issues. They frequently worry about recurrence (Zebrack & Chesler, 2001) and may need support with separation from parents and reintegration into peer groups. Learning disabilities can develop as a result of chemotherapy and radiation treatment and may impede academic progress and cause loss of mastery and self-esteem, social isolation, depression, anxiety, and family problems (Shilds et al., 1995; Zebrack, Jaehee, Petersen, & Ganz, 2007). School reintegration is a major area of concern for children and families. Realistic standards should be set for such children, combining appropriate school rules to maintain normalcy while making specific illness-related allowances.

As survivors grow into adulthood, they become more vulnerable to long-term treatment side effects and early mortality (Mertens et al., 2001). Families and providers may not fully discuss the long-term side effects of cancer treatment with children and adolescent cancer patients, due either to a focus on the immediate goals of helping the child to survive or to difficulty in broaching emotionally charged and potentially painful future losses. Common treatment side effects experienced by childhood cancer survivors in adulthood include the development of secondary cancers, ongoing fatigue and pain, uncertainty about fertility, and challenges to sexual functioning (Zebrack et al., 2007). Sexuality and reproductive functioning present ongoing reminders of childhood cancer experiences. Concerns about fertility and sexual function require young adult survivors to wonder whether they can or should have children and how to discuss these issues with romantic partners (Zebrack, Casillas, Nohr, Adams, & Zeltzer, 2004).

ONCOLOGY SOCIAL WORK

Oncology social workers provide psychosocial support that maximizes the health and functioning of individuals, families, groups, and communities affected by cancer. In a variety of oncology settings and across the cancer continuum, they access psychosocial and instrumental resources, support adaptive coping capacities, and alleviate emotional and environmental stressors (AOSW, 2010). Social workers draw on the profession's person-in-environment perspective to treat "the whole person" in the context of social and environmental factors that can enhance or exacerbate the illness experience. This approach addresses biopsychosocial and spiritual concerns that pose barriers to managing the illness, adhering to treatment protocols, and persevering through treatment, and makes the oncology social worker an essential member of the health-care team (IOM, 2007).

Scope and Functions

Social workers intervene at multiple levels and across systems (see Box 19.2) to enhance patient care and quality of life (Raveis, Gardner, Berkman, & Harootyan, 2010). Psychosocial support at the micro level includes:

- Conducting comprehensive assessments of individual and family emotional, behavioral, and social functioning
- Assessing patient and family coping, emotional and social resources, and response to the illness; educating and answering questions about medical, practical, and psychosocial aspects of cancer and treatment
- Fostering adaptive coping
- Helping patients and families navigate complex health-care and community systems

- Mobilizing supportive resources and services to improve the quality of care
- Teaching strategies to manage and reduce symptoms and side effects
- Providing supportive and therapeutic interventions to individuals, groups, and families to address uncertainty, reduce anxiety and emotional distress, and enhance quality of life throughout the illness course (AOSW, 2010)

Oncology social workers use a variety of interventions and provide a range of services, from clinical case management, to intensive psychotherapy, to meet the unique needs of cancer patients and their families at different points on the cancer continuum.

Traditionally, oncology social workers have practiced primarily in inpatient and ambulatory hospital settings, but the subspecialty has grown to a range of inpatient and outpatient programs (e.g., oncology, pain medicine and palliative care, and other specialty services), home health and hospice services, community-based cancer support programs, private practice, and community-based mental health settings (AOSW, 2010). The profession's emphasis on social context and working across multiple systems positions social workers well to provide care coordination and enhance continuity of care for patients who commonly experience multiple transitions over the course of the illness (Raveis et al., 2010).

Support groups can be an effective resource for cancer patients, caregivers, and other family members to find answers to illness-related questions and ameliorate psychosocial concerns. Social group work often is used in cancer care to reduce social isolation and build social supports, facilitate the sharing of emotional concerns, and provide safe places to exchange strategies for managing symptoms, interacting with family members and health-care providers, and coping with multiple illness-related changes (Fobair, 1998; Spiegel & Classen, 2000). Patients and caregivers participating in support groups feel less distress about cancer and cope with illness-related concerns more social relationships that patients turn to most for support when facing life-threatening, chronic illness. Family-centered care engages family members as allies in providing quality treatment, treats families with dignity and respect, and helps patients and families make more informed and consensual care decisions (Johnson, 2000). Oncology social workers help families adapt to illness-related changes in family roles and responsibilities, provide emotional support and resources to reduce the burdens of family caregiving, assist with financial and other logistical concerns, and empower families to stay informed about a patient's status. They also advocate for patients through the course of the illnesses. Family caregivers benefit from clinical case management, resource referral, respite, and support around transitions. Families also benefit from psychotherapeutic support and psychoeducation around problem solving and decision making, working through family conflicts, and communicating more effectively with one another and with team members (Hudson et al., 2004; Johnson, 2000).

Family conferences are used extensively by oncology social workers to increase communication and enhance management of the illness among patients, family members, and members of the health-care team (Hudson, Thomas, Quinn, & Aranda, 2009). Social workers often coordinate and facilitate family meetings and help families and health-care team members create an environment in which they can connect with one another and address the concerns of all participants. Effective family meetings provide opportunities for communicating about changing medical information and discussing treatment options, provide emotional support to patients and families, and facilitate communication and decision making about goals and care preferences (Glajchen, 2004). Family meetings also allow social workers to bring together patients, families, friends, neighbors, and representatives of community institutions (e.g., workplaces, schools, and houses of worship) to lend instrumental and emotional assistance to families as they adapt to living with cancer.

efficiently (Goodwin et al., 2001; Spiegel & Classen, 2000). Support groups can help to keep children and adolescents on track developmentally, support overburdened and exhausted parents, and provide continuity during chaotic or uncertain transitions (Werner-Lin et al., 2010).

Oncology social workers emphasize the family as the unit of care, a perspective that expands the traditional focus on the physician–patient relationship to include the primary

The scope of oncology social work practice extends beyond the patient and family to include service to other professionals on the oncology team, health-care systems, communities, the social work profession, and society at large. Oncology social workers act as a bridge between patients and the health-care system, advocate for patients and families, and help keep the oncology team informed about the unique concerns, strengths, cultural beliefs, and care preferences that affect the patient's experience with cancer. Social work contributes to the advancement of cancer prevention and quality care by working to develop and strengthen community resources; developing and implementing social services and programs that are responsive to the needs of cancer patients and survivors; promoting public education about early cancer screening and treatment options; and conducting research on the impact of the disease on individuals and families, the effectiveness of psychosocial oncology interventions, and the long-term experiences of cancer survivors and family members (AOSW, 2010; Hermann & Carter, 1994). In addition, social workers in oncology are active in professional development, creating and disseminating guidelines for ethical and competent practice, providing clinical supervision, and working to educate the next generation of oncology health-care professionals.

Conceptual Foundations

Oncology social work practice is grounded in a variety of theoretical frameworks and empirical literatures, including psychosocial oncology, attachment and loss, stress and coping models (Livneh, 2000), family systems and relational coping (Boss, 2001; Kayser et al., 2007), child and adult development, and narrative and meaning making (Fife, 1994; Werner-Lin & Gardner, 2009). In addition, an ecosystems perspective (Germain & Gitterman, 2008; Meyer, 1995) and commitment to treating the person in environment are integral to social work in oncology, sensitizing social workers to team and organizational issues, community processes, and macro-level policy

while they simultaneously attend to the intrapsychic and interpersonal needs of individuals and families. For the oncology social worker, "the ecosystems perspective is a way of seeing case phenomena (the person and the environment) that are interconnected and multilayered to order and comprehend complexity and avoid oversimplification" (Meyer, 1995, p. 18).

Oncology social work practice reflects the ethics and values that guide the social work profession, such as promoting service to clients, individual dignity and self-determination, social justice, the importance of social relationships, and integrity in professional conduct (NASW, 2008). The profession's commitment to meeting the needs of the most vulnerable and oppressed members of society is particularly important in the cancer context, where social workers work to mobilize resources for individuals, families, and groups and work toward the elimination of health disparities and inequities in treatment. The aims of oncology social work are consistent with those of palliative care, gerontology, and health social work, in that they focus on enhancing individual and family functioning, autonomy and choice in decision making, communication and access to resources, and quality of life in chronic and end-of-life care.

Essential Knowledge and Skills

Although cancer diagnoses, treatment protocols, and symptoms vary greatly, and each patient's experience is unique, the knowledge and competencies presented in Box 19.3 are fundamental to providing quality psychosocial care for cancer patients and their families.

Medical and Psychosocial Knowledge About Cancer and Oncology

Social workers in oncology must be well informed about common types of cancer, symptoms, treatment protocols, medical procedures, short- and long-term side effects, illness trajectories, and survivorship. Knowing the fundamentals of cancer and oncology is important in tracking a patient's changing medical situation, assessing the extent to which patients and

Box 19.3 Essential Knowledge and Skills for Oncology Social Workers

Knowledge about cancer, symptoms, treatment, and side effects

Biopsychosocial impact of chronic and life-threatening illness on individuals, families, and communities

Health-care and social service systems and resources

Mental health diagnoses and treatment

Ethical and legal concerns

Conducting comprehensive biopsychosocial assessment

Clinical case management

Direct clinical practice across the cancer continuum

Family-centered practice

Educating patients and family members about cancer prevention, health promotion, and disease self-management

End-of-life and palliative care

Interdisciplinary and ethical practice

Cultural competence and advocacy

Research- and evidence-based practice

families understand disease and treatment, and helping them to prepare and ask appropriate questions of their health-care and psychosocial service providers. Having a basic understanding of cancer prevention and control, including early screening, genetic testing, and physical and behavioral predictors of different cancers, is also important for oncology social workers. Research suggests that social workers can help with cancer prevention by tailoring individual, behaviorally oriented interventions to target harmful behaviors among groups (Gotay, 2005).

Understanding the physical, emotional, psychological, social, spiritual, and practical effects of living with cancer across the course of the illness represents the fundamental knowledge base of oncology social work. It is essential that social workers continually build on their command of developmental dynamics, ego functions, coping skills, family

dynamics and adaptation to illness, the exceptional needs of family caregivers, financial and other concrete needs, the role of social support, and community responses to cancer and its sequelae to effectively assess and develop plans that respond to the needs of patients and families (Hermann & Carter, 1994). Oncology social workers should be familiar with scientific publications, professional listservs, and opportunities for continuing education that expose them to evidence-based research and practice.

Oncology social workers also must keep abreast of current knowledge about mental health and illness, particularly regarding manifestations of psychopathology and psychiatric symptoms associated with chronic and life-threatening illness. Such knowledge, along with a familiarity with the *Diagnostic and Statistical Manual of Mental Disorders* and psychopharmacology, is essential for comprehensive assessment, case planning, and provision of appropriate services or referrals. Individuals with cancer may be vulnerable to anxiety and depression, and these and other serious mental health concerns may be underdiagnosed and undertreated among people with cancer. As the member of the transdisciplinary care team who may have the most expertise in mental and behavioral health, oncology social workers should be familiar with risk factors and treatment options for mental health conditions that are common among cancer patients and caregivers.

Health-Care and Social Service Systems and Resources

To help patients and families navigate complex systems and access resources necessary to ensure quality care, oncology social workers must be familiar with health-care organizations and services, service delivery systems, and financial structures and processes (i.e., health insurance, managed care, Medicare, and Medicaid). Oncology social workers are trained to understand the aspects of the continuum of care from health promotion and disease prevention to critical and end-of-life care, including programs and services ranging from community-based clinics to inpatient hospitals, rehabilitation, and long-term care facilities. Linking patients with essential programs and resources (e.g., information, financial or transportation assistance, home-care and home health aides, Medicaid and third-party insurance, etc.) requires up-to-date knowledge of ever-changing policies and services, including eligibility requirements, application procedures, and strategies for communicating information to cancer patients and their caregivers. Oncology social workers often also work closely with patient navigators to provide information and services to patients and families. Navigators are individuals hired by hospitals and clinics to help patients operate within treatment systems efficiently and effectively.

Ongoing Assessment of Individuals and Families

The skills needed to conduct comprehensive biopsychosocial assessments are fundamental to understanding and addressing the psychosocial resources, challenges, and unmet needs facing cancer patients and their families. Early assessments help identify and resolve problematic coping and health behaviors (Brintzenhofszoc, Smith, & Zabora, 1999; Zabora et al., 2001). Comprehensive assessments can predict morbidity and mortality in older patients with cancer (Extermann & Hurria, 2007). Assessment should be ongoing as cancer progresses, remits, or recurs. For example, assessment of survivorship experiences may mitigate ongoing distress (Zebrack et al., 2007) or help to address complicated bereavement after a patient dies (Brintzenhofszoc et al., 1999). Although many standardized assessment instruments are designed to measure adjustment to cancer and patient quality of life (e.g., FACT, COPES; see Goodwin et al., 2001, for a review), a comprehensive assessment should include (IOM, 2007; Walsh, 2005; Zebrack, Walsh, Burg, Maramaldi, & Lim, 2008):

- Current medical situation and symptoms, including illness course and trajectory,

multidimensional assessment of pain and other symptoms, and patient and family perceptions of illness and care

- Cognitive and functional status
- Individual and family illness history (including physical and mental illness and use of medical and psychosocial support services)
- Family and relational processes (family structure, communication, problem solving, adaptability, cohesion, and conflict, etc.)
- Developmental capacities and concerns
- Coping skills and ego functioning
- Social supports (informational, emotional, and practical) and resources
- Cultural, spiritual, and religious beliefs, values, and practices
- Financial status and resources
- Access to community programs and services
- Family meaning making
- Mental health and coping concerns

Cultural Competence and Advocacy

In an increasingly diverse and aging society, the ability to practice with people from a variety of cultural, ethnic, racial, socioeconomic, and religious backgrounds is a requisite skill for oncology social workers. Social workers are trained to provide culturally sensitive assessment, care planning, and psychosocial support services (Bonder, Martin, & Miracle, 2001). Oncology social workers must remain attentive to differences in the way patients and families perceive of and cope with illness, medical treatment, grief, and loss based on ethnicity, culture, religion, life history, and SES. Effective pain and symptom management, for example, is impossible without understanding individual, familial, and cultural perceptions, values, and beliefs about pain and developing interventions that respect the unique, individualized experiences of patients with chronic illness and their families (Altilio, 2004; Davidhizar & Gige, 2004). Competent social workers should be aware of their own cultural assumptions and biases, engage in exploring and appreciating the worldviews of their diverse clients, and strive, develop, and practice appropriate, relevant, and sensitive intervention strategies in helping all clients (Pérez Foster, 1998).

Social work's core value of respect for the dignity and worth of those they serve draws attention to the dynamics of difference and social inequities that affect individuals, families, and communities (NASW, 2008). Understanding health disparities and the pervasive effects of racism, xenophobia, sexism, ageism, economic oppression, and cumulative disadvantage thus are essential to oncology social work practice. Promoting awareness of the unique perspectives and concerns of diverse cancer patients and their families, advocating for their needs and concerns, and educating members of the palliative care team about distinct beliefs and values regarding aging, illness, pain, and treatment can expand the reach and enhance the quality of care (Del Rio, 2004). Social workers have a professional mandate to intervene on multiple levels (i.e., individual, familial, institutional, community, and societal), ensure the provision of just and equitable care to all patients, and advocate within health-care systems to balance the desire for cost efficiency and measurable outcomes with services that are accessible and affordable to all cancer patients and their families (Christ & Diwan, 2008; Harootyan & O'Neill, 2006).

Clinical Practice With Multiple Modalities Through the Cancer Continuum

Oncology social workers provide psychosocial support to individuals, families, and communities from the point of screening through the period of long-term survivorship. Many cancer patients experience turning points along the disease continuum at which they feel vulnerable, frightened, and uncertain about their futures. These points may occur at the time of cancer diagnosis, the inception of treatment, remission, recurrence or metastasis, the conclusion of treatment, and, for many, when facing death from the disease or its complications.

Social workers are familiar with the challenges specific to various cancer diagnoses and are skilled at crisis intervention and supportive counseling to help patients and families cope with the emotional, practical, and existential crises that often arise at this time.

Education and psychosocial support are critical to helping patients understand medical information and procedures, clarify the roles of different health-care providers, and manage the demands of undergoing diagnostic workups, navigating health-care systems, and making informed decisions about treatment, providers, and care settings. At the beginning of treatment, oncology social workers continue to support patients and family caregivers around the fears and uncertainties inherent in adhering to medical protocols, dealing with side effects, and adjusting to new routines at home and in the hospital or clinic. During treatment, social workers help patients marshal their strengths and adhere to often complex and demanding treatment regimens and their accompanying anxiety, uncertainty, and emotional exhaustion (Eyre et al., 2001).

The termination of treatment presents an existential crisis for some patients, who feel they are no longer actively fighting the cancer and become anxious about its recurrence (Holland & Lewis, 2000). The extraordinarily taxing nature of cancer treatment makes the prospect of a recurrence devastating for the cancer survivor, and each diagnostic test or exam in the ensuing months and years can raise fears of having to resume treatment. Oncology social workers help survivors understand and adapt to a new "normal" (Rolland, 2005) by providing individual, group, and family therapy to enhance adaptation to long-term physical, functional, and emotional effects of the disease and its treatment. This helps survivors to anticipate concerns and mobilize the resources needed to resume their previous roles and activities.

Oncology social workers must be skilled in a variety of direct practice methods. Social workers are trained in using multiple modalities, such as cognitive-behavioral, psychodynamic, family and group therapy, to address illness related concerns. Being familiar with treatment guidelines and evidence-based practices for patients with mental health concerns, such as anxiety, depression, or chronic mental illness, is essential to providing effective psychosocial care. These skills enable social workers to move fluidly between modalities and methods to support patients and their families at different points along the cancer continuum.

Clinical practice with families and family caregivers is a central component of oncology social work. Given dramatic changes in health care, families have increasingly assumed the burden of providing care for loved ones with cancer and other chronic illnesses. Conducting comprehensive family assessments, developing family-centered care plans, providing family counseling around illness-related changes and concerns, and arranging and facilitating family conferences to apprise everyone of the patient's medical condition and treatment options are essential to supporting the psychosocial needs of patients and family members (Given, Charles, Given, & Kozachik, 2001). Oncology social workers support family caregivers through a range of evidence-based caregiver interventions and respite services, and link families to such resources as home care, medication and financial assistance, transportation, and social supports.

Case Management and Coordination of Care

Case management has long been a critical role for oncology social workers. Given their professional skills in working with multiple community and institutions, social workers are well suited to assist cancer patients in making transitions between care settings as they recover, receive rehabilitation, or need additional medical and psychosocial assistance. Social workers, who have long practiced in the context of community and institution-based health-care teams, bring well-established skills of collaboration, advocacy, and leadership to their work with physicians, nurses, and allied health professionals (Raveis et al., 2010). Care coordination and case management require

collaboration across multiple settings (e.g., hospital, home, long-term care) to support patients and families through the course of their illness. In an increasingly fragmented health-care environment, case managers ensure integration across health-care settings and promote continuity of care that benefits patients, families, and health-care teams. Oncology social workers support timely and effective discharge planning by coordinating services among various providers and settings; managing insurance and helping to access eligible benefits; providing transportation services and family and community support and services; and procuring equipment and services to support home-based care.

Patient Education

Throughout the course of disease, oncology social workers are involved in educating patients and their families about cancer and its anticipated disease trajectory, treatment, common psychosocial responses, community resources, and symptom management. Oncology social workers help families to access reliable resources online and in the community (AOSW, 2010). Through ongoing guidance, clarification, and psychoeducation, oncology social workers provide cancer patients and their caregivers with tools to navigate health-care and social service systems and teach them strategies for communication, problem solving, and decision making around patients' changing needs, concerns, and preferences (Glajchen, 2004; Hermann & Carter, 1994).

Oncology social workers empower patients and families to be more engaged in their care by helping them ask to questions and make informed decisions about all aspects of medical treatment. Changing medical technology has opened new areas of decision making, such as reproductive choices prior to treatment. An example is whether to harvest eggs or collect sperm prior to radiation therapy for later use. Although such procedures are costly (Keene et al., 2000; Richardson & Sanchez, 1998), they have the potential to provide the cancer patient with some control over future family planning. Furthermore, social workers encourage adult survivors to seek accurate information about their own fertility as well as cancer-related pregnancy risks for themselves and their off-spring. For survivors, obtaining accurate information can significantly reduce ongoing distress and damage to self-esteem (Zebrack & Chesler, 2001).

Palliative and End-of-Life Care

Oncology social workers are aware of transitions at the end of life and with services to control pain and discomfort for chronically and terminally ill cancer patients. Hospice is an innovative model of care that assumes primary management of dying patients care to provide state-of-the-art medical care and pain management to reduce physical, psychological, and spiritual suffering in the last months of life. Palliative care teams and programs provide integrated and holistic care at any point during a serious chronic illness, with the aim of enhancing patient autonomy and functioning, managing pain and other symptoms, and working to improve the quality of care and quality of life for seriously ill and dying individuals and their families. Unlike hospice, palliative medicine often is provided simultaneously with curative treatment, until the patient's condition improves or hospice services are recommended (National Hospice and Palliative Care Organization, 2010).

Although cancer mortality has decreased (Altekruse et al., 2010), oncology social workers should be skilled and comfortable in working with patients who are chronically ill and dying. In palliative and end-of-life care, oncology social workers may serve as consultants, mediators, and advocates on transdisciplinary teams addressing complex ethical dimensions of medical decision making, family communication, and care preferences. Requisite skills include psychoeducation for families and patients about symptom management and end of life, advanced care planning and family therapy to help synchronize the patient's end-of-life care preferences and wishes with those of the family, and supportive counseling around grief and bereavement (Blacker et al., 2004).

Social workers are uniquely trained to address complex ethical dilemmas involving individual autonomy and quality of life and to mediate among the individual needs, perspectives, values, and responsibilities of patients, their family members, and health-care providers (Csikai, 2004). In the case of terminal cancer, social workers may provide end-of-life care to patients and family members by facilitating discussion of the patient's end-of-life wishes and supporting the selection of a health-care proxy, if indicated. Finally, when patients are dying, oncology social workers can support families in funeral preparation and providing bereavement counseling or bereavement resources. See Chapters 22 and 23 for more information about palliative and end-of-life care.

Research on Evidence-Based Practice

An important way in which oncology social workers can improve psychosocial care is by engaging in research that addresses the cancer experience for individuals and families across the cancer care continuum (Brintzenhofszoc et al., 1999; Clark, 2001; Institute for the Advancement of Social Work Research, 2003). Social workers can conduct primary research on the biopsychosocial aspects of cancer, with the goal of enhancing our understanding of patient and family needs, and developing and evaluating psychosocial interventions. This breadth of focus and the profession's holistic perspective of individual and family functioning makes social work research particularly important in cancer care.

Social work research provides an opportunity for producing evidence of the effectiveness of social work and other interventions. Important areas of inquiry include health status and quality of life in cancer survivorship, the interface of cancer and aging, the impact of disparities and strategies to reduce these disparities, improving the quality of care, enhancing communications among families and between patients and health-care providers, the needs of family caregivers, improving palliative care, behavioral interventions to enhance cancer prevention and screening, and identifying genetic contributions cancer and treatment outcomes. Social workers have been active in developing these interventions and testing them for their efficacy and effectiveness. Social workers contribute to knowledge building, too, by conducting primary research on how the social environment contributes to worse cancer outcomes (Gehlert et al., 2008).

CHALLENGES TO ONCOLOGY SOCIAL WORK

Despite how much is known about the psychological and emotional toll of living with cancer, the health-care system has not addressed adequately the psychosocial concerns of cancer patients, cancer survivors, and their families. A report by the IOM (2007) suggests that many health-care providers do not address these concerns or consider psychosocial support to be an integral part of quality oncology care. It is not surprising, therefore, that cancer patients and families often are dissatisfied with the amount of supportive information and psychosocial care that they receive from their health-care teams and that they report that their emotional, psychological, behavioral and spiritual needs are largely unmet by the health-care system (Christ, 2010; IOM, 2007).

Although transdisciplinary teams in oncology settings are increasingly common, social workers are not always part of oncology teams. The medical model traditionally has focused primarily on biological and clinical aspects of cancer to the exclusion of social and psychological factors (IOM, 2007). Significant changes in the treatment of cancer and the structure and delivery of health care also have complicated the work of social workers in oncology. Traditional functions, such as crisis and long-term counseling, case management, and discharge planning become problematic as inpatient stays are shortened. Technological advances in genetic screening, complex and specialized treatment options, and life-sustaining technology, coupled with a shift toward greater patient choice in treatment decision making, simultaneously have

provided opportunities and placed additional strains on individuals and families and present important new roles for oncology social workers. These developments in cancer care serve as an impetus and opportunity for social workers to develop innovative interventions to meet the needs of their clients.

CONCLUSION

Social workers in oncology contribute significantly to the provision of high-quality, family-centered, biopsychosocial care for cancer patients and their families in a wide variety of settings. This subspecialty within health social work includes many roles, such as helping patients and families to communicate with one another and with providers about their needs and care preferences and how to participate in advance care planning. Oncology social workers also help with decision making and serve as advocates for patients and families within the health-care system. Their distinct knowledge, skills, and values make social workers a resource for cancer patients, families, and health-care teams.

Self-advocacy, a cornerstone of social work practice, is essential for social workers in oncology to survive in the field, both personally and professionally (Stearns, 2001). Oncology social workers who are hospital-based face the effects of downsizing, and accessible psychosocial resources continue to be scarce for cancer patients and their families in all domains. Institutional and social advocacy on behalf of the profession and clients is essential to maintaining adequate and high-quality services (Institute for the Advancement of Social Work Research, 2003). Political activity and policy development, particularly through or in partnership with national organizations, continues to be a powerful tool for change to improve the lives of our clients and to advance the profession.

Given the high incidence of cancer and the growing number of adult survivors, all social workers should expect to work with at least one person affected by cancer at some point in their careers. Discoveries in science and technology, early detection, cancer genetics, health disparities, and translational research will continue to transform cancer into a chronic disease that is managed primarily in the community (NCI, 2010). Oncology social workers will be at the forefront of addressing psychosocial and spiritual concerns and enhancing quality-of-life among cancer patients and their families, all done through research, policy making, and practice.

SUGGESTED LEARNING EXERCISES

Learning Exercise 19.1

Using common genogram notation,* construct a multigenerational genogram (for your family or a client's family) focused on experiences of illness, family caregiving, and loss. Include at least three generations.

1. Begin by adding basic demographic information: dates of birth and death, marriage, separation, and divorce; geographic location; dates of immigration; and religious or spiritual orientation.
2. Identify major illnesses or health-related incidents. Include dates of onset, significant medical intervention (such as hospitalization or surgery), and cause of death.
3. Add select family dynamics related to illness and caregiving roles, alliances, or losses related to illness treatment or loss.

Reflect on this genogram. Possible questions to explore include:

- How do the etiology, treatment, and required care from physicians and family caregivers impact coping and family life?

---

* For guidance constructing a family genogram, refer to information from your social work practice courses or see R. Gerson, M. McGoldrick, and S. Petry (2008), *Genograms: Assessment and intervention*, 3rd ed. (New York, NY: Norton Professional Books).

- How did the family adjust to the demands of the illness? What was helpful in coping? What might have facilitated greater coping?
- How did health or spiritual beliefs play into the story of the disease?

Learning Exercise 19.2

One common psychosocial intervention to help people coping with cancer is a support group. These groups frequently are composed of participants coping with different types of cancer at various stages. Members bring unique family and work concerns to the group for consideration. The role of the oncology social worker is to provide a safe place for participants to discuss these concerns, find common elements in their stories, and facilitate connections.

For this exercise, ask six students from the class to role-play a session of such a support group. Write descriptions of six roles, including group facilitator and five group participants, on slips of paper and place them, folded, in a hat. The slips should include basic cancer and demographic information. The volunteer facilitator should not take on a role but should come to the role-play with her own personal history and lead the group as she would in a real clinical setting.

Each student pulls one slip of paper from the hat and then acts out that role for 15 minutes in a group role-play. Once the role-play is complete, the students and facilitator should take 10 minutes to process the experience of leading, participating in, or observing the interaction. Students should be encouraged to provide constructive feedback to each other.

This activity can be modified to address different populations (e.g., family caregivers, children with cancer, siblings of cancer patients, or bereaved adolescents).

SUGGESTED RESOURCES

Oncology Social Work Support Organizations

American Psychosocial Oncology Society— www.apos-society.org

Association of Oncology Social Work—www.aosw.org

Association of Pediatric Oncology Social Worker—www.aposw.org

International Psycho-Oncology Society—www.ipos-society.org/

Society of Behavioral Medicine—www.sbm.org

National Cancer Organizations

American Cancer Society—www.acs.org (800) ACS-2345

Cancer Care, Inc.—www.cancercare.org (800) 813-HOPE

Cancer Support Community—www.thewellnesscommunity.org (202) 659–9709

National Cancer Institute—www.cancer.gov (800) 4-CANCER

Professional Organizations and Support Networks

American Society of Clinical Oncology—www.asco.org

Association of Cancer Online Resources—www.acor.org

Cancer News—www.cancernews.com

National Association of Social Workers—www.naswwebed.org

Online continuing education.

National Center for Complementary and Alternative Medicine—nccam.nih.gov

National Chronic Care Consortium—www.nccconline.org

National Coalition for Cancer Survivorship—www.canceradvocacy.org/

National Registry of Evidence-Based Programs and Practices—www.nrepp.samhsa.gov

Oncolink at the University of Pennsylvania Cancer Center—www.oncolink.org

Resources for Family Caregivers

Caregiver Resource Directory—www.stoppain.org/caregivers/resource_form.html

National Alliance for Caregiving—www.caregiving.org

National Family Caregiver Association—www.nfcacares.org

U.S. Administration on Aging, National Family Caregiver Support Program—www.aoa.gov/aoaroot/aoa_programs/oaa/resources/faqs.aspx#Caregiver

REFERENCES

Altekruse, S., Kosary, C., Krapcho, M., Neyman, N., Aminou, R., Waldron, W.,...Edwards, B. (2010). *SEER cancer statistics review, 1975–2007*. Bethesda, MD: National Cancer Institute.

Altilio, T. (2004). Pain and symptom management: An essential role for social work. In J. Berzoff & P. R. Silverman (Eds.), *A handbook for end-of-life healthcare practitioners* (pp. 380–408). New York, NY: Columbia University Press.

American Cancer Society. (2010a). *Cancer facts & figures 2010*. Atlanta, GA: Author.

American Cancer Society. (2010b). *Glossary*. Retrieved from www.cancer.org

American Cancer Society. (2010c) *The history of cancer*. Retrieved from www.cancer.org/acs/groups/cid/documents/webcontent/002048-pdf.pdf

Antoniou, A., Pharoah, P., Narod, S., Risch, H., Eyfjord, J., Hopper, J.,...Easton, D. F. (2003). Average risks of breast and ovarian cancer associated with BRCA1 or BRCA2 mutations detected in case series unselected for family history: A combined analysis of 22 studies. *American Journal of Human Genetics, 72*, 1117–1130.

Association of Oncology Social Workers. (2010). *Standards of practice*. Retrieved from www.aosw.org

Atchley, R. (2009). *Spirituality and aging*. Baltimore, MD: Johns Hopkins University Press.

Beder, J. (2006). *Hospital social work: the interface of medicine & caring*. New York, NY: Routledge, Taylor & Francis.

Beers, M. H., Porter, R. S., Jones, T. V., Kaplan, J. L., & Berkwits, M. (2006). *The Merck manual of diagnosis and therapy,* 18th ed. Whitehouse Station, NJ: Merck Research Laboratories.

Berkman, L. (2000). Social support, social networks, social cohesion, and health. *Social Work & Health Care, 31,* 3–14.

Biank, N., & Sori, C. (2003). A child's impossible and scariest task. In C. F. Sori & L. Hecker, (Eds.), *The therapist's notebook for children and adolescents: Homework, handouts, and activities for use in psychotherapy* (pp. 18–24). Binghamton, NY: Haworth.

Blacker, S., et al. (2004). *NASW standards for palliative and end of life care*. Washington, DC: NASW Press. Retrieved from www.naswdc.org/practice/bereavement/standards/standards0504New.pdf

Blum, D., Clark, E. J., & Marcusen, C. P. (2001). Oncology social work in the 21st century. In M. M. Lauria, E. J. Clark, J. F. Hermann, & N. M. Stearns (Eds.), *Social work in oncology: Supporting survivors, families, and caregivers* (pp. 45–72). Washington, DC: American Cancer Society.

Bolmsjo, I. (2000). Existential issues in palliative care; Interviews with cancer patients. *Journal of Palliative Care, 16,* 20–24.

Bonder, B., Martin, L., & Miracle, A. (2001). Achieving cultural competence: The challenge for clients and healthcare workers in a multicultural society. *Generations, 25*(1), 35–42.

Boss, P. (2001). *Family stress management: A contextual approach*. New York, NY: Sage.

Braun, M., Mikulincer, M., Rydall, A., Walsh, A., & Rodin, G. (2007). Hidden morbidity in cancer: Spouse caregivers. *Journal of Clinical Oncology, 25*(30), 4829–4834.

Brintzenhofszoc, K., Smith, E., & Zabora, J. (1999). Screening to predict complicated grief in spouses of cancer patients. *Cancer Practice, 7*(5), 233–239.

Carlson, L., Angen, M., Cullum, J., Goodey, E., Koopmans, J., Lamont, L.,...Bultz, B. D. (2004). High levels of untreated distress and fatigue in cancer patients. *British Journal of Cancer, 90*(12), 2297–2304.

Centers for Disease Control, Office of Cancer Prevention and Control. (2010). *Health disparities in cancer— basic information*. Retrieved from www.cdc.gov/cancer/healthdisparities/basic_info/index.htm

Christ, G. (2010). Cancer as a chronic life-threatening condition. In S. Diwan (Ed.), *Health care and older adults resource review*. CSWE Gero-Ed Center, Master's Advanced Curriculum Project. Retrieved from www.cswe.org/CentersInitiatives/GeroEdCenter/Programs/MAC/Reviews/Health/22419/22536.aspx

Christ, G., & Diwan, S. (2008). Role of social work in managing chronic illness care. In S. Diwan (Ed.), *Health care and older adults resource review*. CSWE Gero-Ed Center, Master's Advanced Curriculum Project. Retrieved from http://depts.washington.edu/geroctr/mac/1_6health.html

Chu, K., Tarone, R., Kessler, L., et al. (1997). Recent trends in U.S. breast cancer incidence, survival, and mortality rates. *Journal of the National Cancer Institute, 88,* 1571–1579.

Cicirelli, V. (1999). Personality and demographic factors in older adults' fear of death. *Gerontologist, 39*(5), 569–579.

Cohen, E. (2001). The complex nature of ageism: What is it? Who does it? Who perceives it? *Gerontologist, 41,* 576–577.

Clark, E. (2001). The importance of research in oncology social work. In M. Lauria, E. J. Clark, J. Hermann, & N. Stearns (Eds.), *Social work in oncology* (pp. 193–210). Atlanta, GA: American Cancer Society.

Connor, D. (2007). Development of hospice and palliative care in the United States. *Omega: Journal of Death & Dying, 56*(1), 89–99.

Csikai, E. (2004). Social workers' participation in the resolution of ethical dilemmas in hospice care. *Health & Social Work, 29*(1), 67–76.

Dale, D. (2003). Poor prognosis in elderly patients with cancer: The role of bias and undertreatment. *Journal of Supportive Oncology, 1*(Suppl. 2), S11–S17.

Davidhizar, R., & Gige, J. (2004). A review of the literature on care of clients in pain who are culturally diverse. *International Nursing Review, 51*(1), 47–55.

Del Rio, N. (2004). A framework for multicultural end-of-life care: Enhancing social work practice. In J. Berzoff & P. Silverman (Eds.), *Living with dying: A handbook for end-of-life practitioners* (pp. 439–461). New York, NY: Columbia University Press.

Decruyenaere, M., Evers-Kiebooms, G., Boogaerts, A., Cassiman, J. J., Cloostermans, T., Demyttenaere, K.,...Van den Berghe, H. (1996). Prediction of psychological functioning one year after the predictive test for Huntington's disease and impact of the test result on reproductive decision making. *Journal of Medical Genetics, 33,* 737–743.

Denayer, L., Evers-Kiebooms, G., Tejpar, S., Legius, E., & Van Cutsem, E. (1999). Illness perception, transfer of information and risk perception in familial adenomatous polyposis families. *Gedrag & Gezondheid: Tijdschrift voor Psychologie en Gezondheid, 27,* 244–254.

Dignam, J. (2000). Differences in breast cancer prognosis among African-American and Caucasian women. *CA: Cancer Journal for Clinicians, 50*(10), 50–64.

Edwards, B., Ward, E., Kohler, B., Eheman, C., Zauber, A. G., Anderson, R. N.,...Ries, L. A. G. (2009). Annual report to the nation on the status of cancer, 1975–2006, featuring colorectal cancer trends and impact of interventions (risk factors, screening, and treatment) to reduce future rates. *Cancer, 116*(3), 544–573.

Ell, K., Nishimoto, R., Mediansky, L., Mantell, J., & Hamovitch, M. (1992). Social relations, social support and survival among patients with cancer. *Journal of Psychosomatic Research, 32,* 531–541.

Extermann, M., & Hurria, A. (2007). Comprehensive geriatric assessment for older patients with cancer. *Journal of Clinicians in Oncology, 25*(14), 1824–1831.

Eyre, H., Lange, D. P., & Morris, L. B. (2001). *Informed decisions: The complete book of cancer diagnosis, treatment, and recovery*. Washington, DC: American Cancer Society.

Feldt, K. (2004). The complexity of managing pain for frail elders. *Journal of the American Geriatrics Society, 52,* 840–841.

Fife, B. (1994). The conceptualization of meaning in illness, *Social Science & Medicine, 38,* 309–316.

Fobair, P. (1998). Cancer support groups and group therapies. In K. Ell & J. Williams (Eds.), *Advances in mental health research* (pp. 365–398). Washington, DC: NASW Press.

Fobair, P., Stearns, N. N., Christ, G., Dozier-Hall, D., Newman, N. W., Zabora, J.,…Desonier, M. (2009). Historical threads in the development of oncology social work. *Journal of Psychosocial Oncology, 27,* 155–215.

Fortner, B., & Neimeyer, R. (1999). Death anxiety in older adults: A quantitative review. *Death Studies, 23*(5), 387–411.

Gardner, D. (2008). Cancer in a dyadic context: Older couples' negotiation of ambiguity and meaning in end-of-life. *Journal of Social Work in End-of-Life and Palliative Care, 4*(2), 1–25.

Gardner, D., & Kramer, B. J. (2009/10). End-of-life challenges, fears and care preferences: Congruence in reports of low-income elders and their family members. *OMEGA: Journal of Death and Dying, 60*(3), 273–297.

Gehlert, S., Somer, D., Sacks, T., Miniger, C., McClintock, M., & Olopade, O. (2008). Targeting health disparities: A model linking upstream determinants to downstream interventions. *Health Affairs, 27*(2), 339–349.

Germain, C. B., & Gitterman, A. (2008). *The life model of social work practice: Advances in theory & practice* (3rd ed.). New York, NY: Columbia Press.

Gerson, R., McGoldrick, M., & Petry, S. (2008). *Genograms: Assessment and intervention,* 3rd ed. New York, NY: Norton Professional Books.

Ghafoor, A., Jemal, A., Ward, E., Cokkinides, V., Smith, R., & Thun, M. (2003). Trends in breast cancer by race and ethnicity. *CA: Cancer Journal for Clinicians, 53*(6), 342–355.

Given, B., Charles, W., Given, C., & Kozachik, S. (2001). Family support in advanced cancer. *CA: Cancer Journal for Clinicians, 51,* 213–231.

Glajchen, M. (2004). The emerging role and needs of family caregivers in cancer care. *Journal of Supportive Oncology, 2*(2), 145–155.

Gooding, H. C., Organista, K., Burack, J., & Biesecker, B. B. (2006). Genetic susceptibility testing from a stress and coping perspective. *Social Science & Medicine, 62,* 1880–1890.

Goodwin, P., Leszcz, M., Ennis, M., Koopmans, J., Vincent L., Guther, H.,…Hunter, J. (2001). The effect of group psychosocial support on survival in metastatic breast cancer. *New England Journal of Medicine, 345*(24), 1719–1726.

Gotay, C. C. (2005). Behavior and cancer prevention. *Journal of Clinical Oncology, 23,* 301–310.

Gunnars, B., Nygren, P., & Glimelius, B. (2001). Assessment of quality of life during chemotherapy. *Acta Oncologica, 40*(2:3), 175–184.

Hauser, J., & Kramer, B. J. (2004). Family caregivers in palliative care. *Clinics in Geriatric Medicine, 20,* 671–688.

Harootyan, L., & O'Neill, G. (2006). National advocacy groups for older adults. In B. Berkman (Ed.), *Handbook of social work in health and aging* (pp. 817–822). New York, NY: Oxford University Press.

Hermann, J., & Carter, J. (1994). The dimensions of oncology social work: Intrapsychic, interpersonal, and environmental interventions. *Seminars in Oncology, 21*(6), 713–717.

Hermann, J. F. (2001). Children of cancer patients: Issues and interventions. In M. M. Lauria, E. J. Clark, J. F. Hermann, & N. M. Stearns (Eds.), *Social work in oncology: Supporting survivors, families, and caregivers* (pp. 73–92). Washington, DC: American Cancer Society.

Holland, J. C. (1998). Societal views of cancer and the emergence of psycho-oncology. In J. C. Holland (Ed.), *Psycho-oncology* (pp. 3–15). New York, NY: Oxford University Press.

Holland, J. C. (2002). History of psycho-oncology: Overcoming attitudinal and conceptual barriers. *Psychosomatic Medicine, 64*(2), 206–221.

Holland, J. C., & Lewis, S. (2000). *The human side of cancer.* New York, NY: HarperCollins.

Hudson, P., Aranda, S., & Kristjanson, L. (2004). Meeting the supportive needs of family caregivers in palliative care: Challenges for health professionals. *Journal of Palliative Medicine, 7*(1), 19–25.

Hudson, P., Thomas, T., Quinn, K., & Aranda, S. (2009). Family meetings in palliative care: Are they effective? *Palliative Medicine, 23,* 150–157.

Inouye, S., Studenski, S., Tinetti, M., & Kuchel, A. (2007). Geriatric syndromes: Clinical, research, and policy implications of a core geriatric concept. *Journal of the American Geriatrics Society, 55*(5), 780–791.

Institute for the Advancement of Social Work Research. (2003). *Social Work's Contribution To Research On Cancer Prevention, Detection, Diagnosis, Treatment And Survivorship.* Retrieved from www.charityadvantage.com/iaswr/images/nci_final_report_9_15_03.pdf

Institute of Medicine. (2007). *Cancer care for the whole patient: Meeting psychosocial health needs.* Washington, DC: National Academies Press.

Jemal, A., Siegel, R., Ward, E., Hao, Y., Xu, J., Murray, T., & Thun, M. (2010). Cancer statistics: 2008. *CA—Cancer Journal for Clinicians, 58,* 71–96.

Johnson, B. H. (2000). Family-centered care: Four decades of progress. *Family Systems & Health, 18*(2), 133–156.

Kane, R., & Kane, R. (2005). Ageism in healthcare and long-term care. *Generations, 29*(3), 49–54.

Kauff, N. D., Domchek, S. M., Friebel, T. M., Robson, M. E., Lee, J., Garber, J. E.,…Rebbeck, T. R. (2008). Risk-reducing salpingo-oophorectomy for the prevention of BRCA1- and BRCA2-associated breast and gynecologic cancer: A multicenter, prospective study. *Journal of Clinical Oncology, 26,* 1331–1337.

Kayser, K., Watson, L., & Andrade, J. (2007). Cancer as a "we" disease: Examining the process of coping from a relational perspective. *Families, Systems, & Health, 25*(4), 404–418.

Keene, N., Hobbie, W., & Ruccione, K. (2000). *Childhood cancer survivors: A practical guide to your future.* Cambridge, MA: O'Reilley.

Kessler, R., Davis, R., Foster, D., Van Rompay, M. I., Walters, E. E., Wilkey, S. A.,…Eisenberg, D. M. (2001). Long-term trends in the use of complementary and alternative medical therapies in the United States. *Annals of Internal Medicine, 135*(4), 262–268.

Kornbluth, A. B. (1998). Psychosocial adaptation of cancer survivors. In J. C. Holland (Ed.), *Psycho-oncology* (pp. 223–241). New York, NY: Oxford University Press.

Kramer, B. J. (1997). Gain in the caregiving experience: Where are we? What next? *Gerontologist, 37*(2), 218–232.

Kramer, B. J., Boelk, A., & Auer, C. (2006). Family conflict at the end of life: Lessons learned in a model program for vulnerable older adults. *Journal of Palliative Care, 9*(3), 791–801.

Krause, N. (2006). Social relationships in late life. In R. Binstock & L. George (Eds.), *Handbook of aging and the social sciences,* 6th ed. (pp. 182–201). New York, NY: Academic Press.

Lawton, M. (2001). Quality of life and the end of life. In J. Birren & K. W. Schaie (Eds.), *Handbook of the psychology of aging* (5th ed., pp. 593–616). New York, NY: Academic Press.

Link, B., & Phelan J. (1995). Social conditions as fundamental causes of disease. *Journal of Health & Social Behavior, 35,* 80–94.

Livneh, H. (2000). Psychosocial adaptation to cancer: The role of coping strategies. *Journal of Rehabilitation, 66*(2), 40–50.

Lostumbo, L. N., Carbine, N. E., Wallace, J., Ezzo, J., & Dickersin, K. (2004). Prophylactic mastectomy for the prevention of breast cancer. *Cochrane Database of Systematic Reviews, 4,* CD002748.

Lux, M. P., Fasching, P. A., & Beckmann, M. W. (2006). Hereditary breast and ovarian cancer: Review and future perspectives. *Journal of Molecular Medicine, 84,* 16–28.

Lyyra, T., & Heikkinen, R. (2006). Perceived social support and mortality in older people. *Journals of Gerontology, 61B,* S147–S153.

Manne, S. (1998). Cancer in the marital context: A review of the literature. *Cancer Investigation, 16*(3), 188–202.

Marcusen, C., & Clark, E. (2001). Cancer and the elderly population. In M. Lauria, E. Clark, J. Hermann, & N. Stearns (Eds.), *Social work in oncology: Supporting survivors, families, and caregivers* (pp. 269–278). Washington, DC: American Cancer Society.

McGinnis, J. M., Williams-Russo, P., & Knickerman, J. R. (2002). The case for more active policy attention to health promotion. *Health Affairs, 21*(2), 78–93.

Meiser, B. (2005). Psychological impact of genetic testing for cancer susceptibility: An update of the literature. *Psycho-Oncology, 14,* 1060–1074.

Meiser, B., & Halliday, J. L. (2002). What is the impact of genetic counselling in women at increased risk of developing hereditary breast cancer? A meta-analytic review. *Social Science & Medicine, 54*(10), 1463–1470.

Mertens, A. C., Yasui, Y., Neglia, J. P., Potter, J. D., Nesbit, M. E., Jr., Ruccione, K.,…Robison, L. L. (2001). Late mortality experience in five-year survivors of childhood and adolescent cancer: The Childhood Cancer Survivor Study. *Journal of Clinical Oncologists, 19,* 3163–3172.

Metcalfe, K., Lynch, H. T., Ghadirian, P., & Nadine, T. (2004). Contralateral breast cancer in BRCA1 and BRCA2 mutation carriers. *Journal of Clinical Oncology, 22,* 2328–2335.

Meyer, C. (1995). The ecosystems perspective: Implications for practice. In C. Meyer & M. Mattaini (Eds.), *The foundations of social work practice* (pp. 72–89). Washington, DC: National Association of Social Workers.

Montgomery, C. (1999) Psycho-oncology: A coming of age. *Psychiatric Bulletin, 23*(7), 431–435.

Moren-Cross, J., & Lin, N. (2006). Social networks and health. In R. Binstock & L. George (Eds.), *Handbook of aging and the social sciences,* 6th ed., (pp. 111–127). New York, NY: Academic Press.

Mukherjee, S. (2010). *The emperor of all maladies: A biography of cancer.* New York, NY: Scribner.

National Association of Social Workers. (2008). *Code of ethics of the National Association of Social Workers.* Retrieved from www.socialworkers.org/pubs/code/code.asp

National Cancer Institute. (2010). *The nation's investment in cancer research: 2011 plan.* Retrieved from plan.cancer.gov/pdf/nci_2011_plan.pdf

National Hospice and Palliative Care Organization. (2010). *The history of hospice care.* Retrieved from www.nhpco.org/i4a/pages/index.cfm?pageid=3285

National Human Genome Research Institute. (n.d). Retrieved from www.genome.gov/

Nelson-Becker, H. (2005). Spiritual, religious, nonspiritual, and nonreligious narratives in marginalized older adults: A typology of coping styles. *Journal of Religion, Spirituality and Aging, 17*(1 & 2), 21–38.

Oeffinger, K., Mertens, A., Sklar, C., Kawashima, T., Hudson, M. M., Meadows, A. T.,…Robison, L. L. (2006). Chronic health conditions in adult survivors of childhood cancer. *New England Journal of Medicine, 355*(15), 1572–1582.

Patenaude, A., & Kupst, M. (2005). Psychosocial functioning in pediatric cancer. *Journal of Pediatric Psychology, 30*(1), 9–27.

Patterson, J., & Garwick, A. (1994). The impact of chronic illness on families: A family systems perspective. *Annals of Behavioral Medicine, 16*(2), 131–142.

Peake, M., Thompson, S., Lowe, D., & Pearson, M. (2003). Ageism in the management of lung cancer. *Age and Ageing, 32*(2), 171–177.

Pérez Foster, R. M. (1998). The clinician's cultural countertransference: The psychodynamics of culturally competent practice. *Clinical Social Work Journal, 26*(3), 253–270.

Pizzo, P. A. (2001). The medical diagnosis and treatment of childhood cancer. In M. M. Lauria, E. J. Clark, J. F. Hermann, & N. M. Stearns (Eds.), *Social work in oncology: Supporting survivors, families, and caregivers* (pp. 93–116). Washington, DC: American Cancer Society.

Rabow, M., Hauser, J., & Adams, J. (2004). The role of nurse practitioners in end-of-life care. *JAMA, 291*(4), 483–491.

Raveis, V., Gardner, D., Berkman, B., & Harootyan, L. (2010). Linking the NIH strategic plan to the research agenda for social workers in health and aging. *Journal of Gerontological Social Work, 53*(1), 77–93.

Rebbeck, T. R. (2002). Prophylactic oophorectomy in BRCA1 and BRCA2 mutation carriers. *European Journal of Cancer, 38*(6), 15–17.

Richardson, J. L., & Sanchez, K. (1998). Compliance with cancer treatment. In J. Holland (Ed.), *Psycho-oncology* (pp. 67–77). New York, NY: Oxford University Press.

Richardson, M. A., Sanders, T., Palmer, J. L., Greisinger, A., & Singletary, S. E. (2000). Complementary/alternative medicine use in a comprehensive cancer center and the implications for oncology. *Journal of Clinical Oncology, 18,* 2505–2521.

Rohan, E., Berkman, B., Walker, S., & Holmes, W. (1994). The geriatric oncology patient: Ageism in social work practice. *Journal of Gerontological Social Work, 23*(1/2), 201–221.

Rolland, J. S. (2005). Cancer and the family: An integrative model. *Cancer, 704*(Suppl.), S2584–S2595.

Rosman, S. (2004). Cancer and stigma: experience of patients with chemotherapy-induced alopecia. *Patient Education & Counseling, 4*(52), 333–339.

Shavers, V., & Brown, M. (2002). Racial and ethnic disparities in the receipt of cancer treatment. *Journal of the National Cancer Institute, 94*(5), 334–357.

Shilds, G., Schondel, C., Barnhart, L., Fitzpatrick, V., Sidell, N., Adams, P.,…Gomez, S. (1995). Social work in pediatric oncology: A family needs assessment. *Social Work in Health Care, 21*(1), 39–54.

Smith, E. D., Walsh-Burke, K., & Crusan, C. (1998). Principles of training social workers in oncology. In J. C. Holland (Ed.), *Psycho-oncology* (pp. 1061–1068). New York, NY: Oxford University Press.

Sontag, S. (2001). *Illness as metaphor and AIDS and its metaphors.* New York, NY: Picador USA.

Spiegel, D. (1996). Cancer and depression. *British Journal of Psychiatry, 168* (Supp. 30), 109–116.

Spiegel, D., & Classen, C. (2000). *Group therapy for cancer patients: A research-based handbook of psychosocial care.* New York, NY: Basic Books.

Stanton, A., Cameron, C., Danoff-Burg, S., Bishop, M., Collins, C., Kirk, S.,…Twillman, R. (2000). Emotionally expressive coping predicts psychological and physical adjustment to breast cancer. *Journal of Consulting and Clinical Psychology, 68*(5), 875–882.

Stearns, N. (2001). Professional issues in oncology social work. In M. M. Lauria, E. J. Clark, J. F. Hermann, & N. M. Stearns (Eds.), *Social work in oncology: Supporting survivors, families, and caregivers* (pp. 213–232). Washington, DC: American Cancer Society.

Szabo, C. I., & King, M. C. (1997). Population genetics of BRCA1 and BRCA2. *American Journal of Human Genetics, 60,* 1013–1020. Retrieved from www.ncbi.nlm.nih.gov/pmc/articles/PMC1712447/

Tilden, V., Drach, L., & Tolle, S. (2004). Complementary and alternative therapy use at end-of-life in community settings. *Journal of Alternative and Complementary Medicine, 10*(5), 811–817.

Waldrop, D. (2007). Caregiver grief in terminal illness and bereavement: A mixed-methods study. *Health & Social Work, 32*(3), 197–206.

Waldrop, D., Kramer, B. J., Skretny, J., Milch, R., & Finn, W. (2005). Final transitions: Family caregiving at the end of life. *Journal of Palliative Medicine, 8*(3), 623–638.

Walsh, F. (2006). *Strengthening family resilience,* 2nd ed. New York, NY: Guilford Press.

Walsh, K. (2005). *Oncology social work roles and functions across the continuum of care.* Washington, DC: National Patient Advocate Foundation.

Waskul, D., & van der Riet, P. (2002). The abject embodiment of cancer patients: Dignity, selfhood and the grotesque body. *Symbolic Interaction, 25,* 487–513.

Weihs, K., & Politi, M. (2006). Family development in the face of cancer. In D. Crane & E. Marshall (Eds.), *Handbook of Families and Health* (pp. 3–18). Thousand Oaks, CA: Sage.

Weinberg, R. (2006). *The biology of cancer.* Florence, KY: Garland Science.

Wells, A., & Zebrack, B. (2008). Psychosocial barriers contributing to the under-representation of racial/ethnic minorities in cancer clinical trials. *Social Work in Health Care, 46*(2), 1–14.

Werner-Lin, A. (2010). Building the cancer family: Family planning in the context of inherited breast and ovarian cancer risk. *Journal of the Society of Social Work and Research, 1*(1), 14–27.

Werner-Lin, A., Biank, N., & Rubenstein, B. (2010). There's no place like home: Preparing children for geographical and relational attachment disruptions following parental death to cancer. *Clinical Social Work Journal, 38,* 132–143.

Werner-Lin, A., & Gardner, D. (2009). Family illness narratives of inherited cancer risk: Continuity and transformation. *Families, Systems & Health, 27*(3), 201–212.

Werth, J., Gordon, J., & Johnson, R. (2002). Psychosocial issues near the end of life. *Aging and Mental Health, 6,* 402–412.

Williams D. (1997). Race and health: Basic questions, emerging directions. *Annals of Epidemiology, 7,* 322–333.

Witter, D., & LeBas, J. (2008). *Cancer as a chronic disease. OncoLog, 53*(4). Retrieved from www2 .mdanderson.org/depts/oncolog/articles/08/4-apr /4-08-1.html

Wolff, J., Dy, S., Frick, K., & Kasper, J. (2007). End-of-life care: Findings from a national survey of informal caregivers. *Archives of Internal Medicine, 167*(1), 40–46.

Woods, N., LaCroix, A., Gray, S., Aragaki, A., Cochrane, G., Brunner, R.,...Newman, A. (2005). Frailty: Emergence and consequences in women aged 65 and older in the Women's Health Initiative Observational Study. *Journal of the American Geriatrics Society, 53*(8), 1321–1330.

Wright, L. (1999). Spirituality, suffering and beliefs: The soul of healing with families. In F. Walsh (Ed.), *Spiritual resources in family therapy* (pp. 61–75). New York, NY: Guilford Press.

Zabora, J., Brintzenhofeszoc, K., Curbow, B., Hooker, C., & Piantadosi, S. (2001). The prevalence of psychological distress by cancer site. *Psycho-Oncology, 10*(19), 19–28.

Zabora, J., Brintzenhofeszoc, K., Jacobsen, P., Curbow, B., Piantadosi, S., Hooker, C.,...Derogatis, L. (2001). A new psychosocial screening instrument for use with cancer patients. *Psychosomatics, 42*(3), 241–246.

Zebrack, B., Casillas J., Nohr, L., Adams, H., & Zeltzer, L. (2004). Fertility issues for young adult survivors of childhood cancer. *Psycho-Oncology, 13*(10), 689–699.

Zebrack, B., & Chesler, M. (2001). Health-related worries, self-image, and life outlooks of long-term survivors of childhood cancer. *Health & Social Work, 26*(4), 245–256.

Zebrack, B., Jaehee, Y., Petersen, L., & Ganz, P. A. (2007). The impact of cancer and quality of life for long-term survivors. *Psycho-Oncology, 17*(9), 891–900.

Zebrack, B., Walsh, K., Burg, M. A., Maramaldi, P., & Lim, J. (2008). Oncology social worker competencies and implications for education and training. *Social Work in Health Care, 47*(4), 355–375.

20

Adherence and Mental Health Issues in Chronic Disease: Diabetes, Heart Disease, and HIV/AIDS

WENDY AUSLANDER AND STACEY FREEDENTHAL

Direct practice issues increasingly present challenges for social workers who treat people with chronic disease. Rates of chronic disease continue to grow, and psychosocial problems often accompany or arise from chronic disease. People with chronic diseases face many difficulties maintaining sometimes complex and burdensome treatment regimens. As members of the health-care team who have expertise in mental health and behavioral issues, social workers are in a unique position to help people who have a chronic disease.

This chapter provides an overview of the epidemiology of heart disease, diabetes, and human immunodeficiency virus (HIV)/acquired immunodeficiency syndrome (AIDS), three common chronic diseases that social workers encounter within health-care and community settings. Then it describes a systematic practice model with which social workers can promote patient adherence to treatment, provides a review of strategies that enhance patients' recall of information, and provides instructions for social workers to use in their role as educators. Finally, the chapter describes the relationship between mental health problems and chronic disease etiology and management.

Many other direct practice issues are important for social workers who treat persons with chronic disease, such as family and individual coping, social support, developmental issues as they relate to illness and economic and cultural factors that influence disease management; these issues are discussed in detail elsewhere in this book (see Chapters 7, 10, and 13).

Chapter Objectives
- Exhibit knowledge about the epidemiology of heart disease, HIV/AIDS, and diabetes in the United States, including racial and ethnic disparities.
- Identify and assess psychosocial factors that influence adherence to treatment among individuals with chronic disease.
- Incorporate a systematic model of adherence counseling in practice with individuals with chronic disease.
- Understand the importance of communication techniques in patient education and adherence counseling for individuals with chronic disease.
- Understand the relationship between mental health and chronic disease.

CURRENT TRENDS IN THE CARE OF PATIENTS WITH A CHRONIC DISEASE

Significant changes in the health status of Americans have occurred within the past century due to some relatively recent trends.

For one thing, individuals are living longer than ever before. The average life span in the United States increased by 27 years in the past century—from 49.2 years in 1900 to 76.5 years in 2000 (Guyer, Freedman, Strobino, & Sondik, 2000)—largely due to public health measures such as vaccinations, antibiotics, and other methods for controlling infectious diseases (Centers for Disease Control and Prevention [CDC], 1999a). A second trend is an increase in the number of individuals living with chronic diseases because of advances in medical treatment and technology and the increasing average life span. In addition, chronic diseases have replaced infectious diseases as the leading causes of death in the United States (Guyer et al., 2000). For example, in 1900, the top causes of death were pneumonia, tuberculosis, and intestinal problems such as diarrhea (CDC, 1999b). Combined with diphtheria, these acute diseases accounted for one-third of all deaths in the United States (CDC, 1999b). Today, heart disease, diabetes, and AIDS are chronic diseases that are among the top causes of death; heart disease is the number-one cause of death in the United States, diabetes ranks 7th, and HIV/AIDS ranks 20th (CDC, 2010b) Although still incurable, these diseases often respond to medications, surgery, or other types of medical management.

The increasing prevalence of chronic disease in the United States has led to a major shift from viewing individuals as consumers of health care to seeing them for what they really are—*providers* of health care. Most of the responsibility for preventing and managing chronic disease lies with the patient and the patient's family. Individuals with chronic disease and their families are the members of the health-care team who are most responsible for the day-to-day activities necessary to carry out treatment regimens. Because of this shift in perspective, understanding how to promote patient adherence to treatment has become increasingly important in the past two decades. In particular, diabetes, HIV/AIDS, and heart disease are chronic diseases that, once diagnosed, require adherence to complex and challenging treatment regimens. Prevention

of these diseases involves behavioral changes such as weight loss, exercise, dietary changes, and reduction of risky sexual behaviors, all of which patients may have difficulty maintaining in the long term.

In addition to the importance of patient adherence in chronic disease prevention and management, three other issues related to chronic disease are also important for social workers to understand.

1. *There are no known cures for chronic diseases such as diabetes, heart disease, and HIV/AIDS, and they are usually progressive in nature.* Unlike some disabilities or acute illnesses, chronic diseases fluctuate in symptoms and disease-related complications. Disease-specific complications for individuals with chronic disease can be viewed as "predictable crises" (Hamburg & Inoff, 1983) because they can cause a state of anxiety and disequilibrium that is expected, given what we know about how the diseases progress.

2. *Because of the progressive nature of chronic disease, the patient and family must adjust to continual treatment changes.* For example, new medications continually are being developed that often subject the patient to new side effects. The past few decades have seen new medical technologies for the management of diabetes (e. g., insulin infusion pumps and home glucose monitoring), yet they all include some costs (e. g., financial and physical pain) along with the benefits they provide for patients.

3. *Because chronic diseases usually continue throughout the patient's lifetime, developmental and lifestyle changes (such as pregnancy, puberty, divorce, or college) often influence or pose additional challenges to the person with a chronic disease.*

Each of these challenges (i.e., disease, treatment regimens, and developmental changes), unique to chronic diseases, offers opportunities for social work intervention to promote positive adaptation and management behaviors among patients.

EPIDEMIOLOGY OF DIABETES, HEART DISEASE, AND HIV/AIDS

Social workers encounter people with heart disease, diabetes, and HIV/AIDS in virtually all health-care settings, including emergency rooms, hospitals, outpatient clinics, community centers, hospices, nursing homes, and rehabilitation centers. Before describing some practice issues for social workers who work with individuals who have been diagnosed

with diabetes, heart disease, and HIV/AIDS, we first present an overview of disease rates, risk factors, racial and ethnic disparities and other information related to these three major killers in the United States and worldwide (see Table 20.1).

Heart Disease: A Leading Killer

The term *heart disease* can refer to any of several cardiac conditions including coronary artery disease, congestive heart failure, and heart

Table 20.1   Epidemiology of Chronic Diseases in the United States

	Heart Disease	Diabetes	HIV/AIDS
Deaths (in 2007)[a]			
Ranking	1	7	20[b]
Number	616,067	71,382	11,295
Percentage in the United States	25.4%	2.9%	0.5%
People living with disease	18 million[c]	13.4 million (6.6%)[d] 16.7 million (8.3%)[c]	HIV: 800,000[e] AIDS: 362,827[d]
Possible symptoms	Chest pain or tightness Shortness of breath Fluid retention	Excessive thirst Frequent urination Extreme hunger Unusual weight loss Fatigue Blurry vision	Rapid weight loss Recurring fever or night sweats Profound fatigue Swollen lymph glands Chronic diarrhea Pneumonia
Risk factors	Diabetes High cholesterol High blood pressure Smoking Physical inactivity Obesity Older age Family history	*Type 2 only* Obesity Physical inactivity Older age Family history Black, Hispanic, or American Indian/Alaska Native High blood pressure	Unprotected sex Injection drug use
Preventive measures	Exercise Diet rich with fiber, fruits, and vegetables No smoking	*Type 2 only* Weight control Healthy diet	Condom use Clean needles Blood donor screening

[a]From "WISQARS Leading Cause of Death Reports: 1981–1998," by Centers for Disease Control and Prevention (2010b), retrieved from http://webappa.cdc.gov/sasweb/ncipc/leadcaus9.html
[b]HIV ranks as the 8th leading cause of death for the 15- to 54-year-old age group.
[c]From "Prevalence of Diabetes and Impaired Fasting Glucose in Adults: United States, 1999–2000," by C. C. Cowie, K. F. Rust, D. Byrd-Holt, M. S. Eberhardt, S. Saydah, L. S. Geiss, et al., 2003, *Morbidity and Mortality Weekly Report, 52,* pp. 833–837.
[d]From *Summary Health Statistics for U.S. Adults: National Health Interview Survey, 2002* (DHHS Publication No. PHS 2004–1550), by U.S. Department of Health and Human Services, 2004, Hyattsville, MD: Author.
[e]From *HIV/AIDS Surveillance Report*, 13th ed. (pp. 1–44), Centers for Disease Control and Prevention, 2001. Atlanta, GA: Author.

attack. Heart disease itself is a type of cardiovascular disease, along with hypertension and stroke. Stroke also is a major leading cause of death in the United States and results from the brain being deprived of oxygen, usually due to plaque in the arteries (CDC, 2010b). Although stroke and hypertension are themselves important public health problems, this section focuses only on chronic diseases directly related to the heart (see Table 20.2).

Gender

Many people mistakenly believe that heart disease primarily affects men, when in fact men have experienced a decline in heart fatalities in recent years. However, the rate of heart disease in women continues to increase (American Heart Association, 2002), and heart disease has become the leading cause of death for women (CDC, 2010b). Hormones, particularly estrogen, appear to protect many women from heart disease until after menopause, although a causal relationship is not certain (Barrett-Connor, 2003). Research indicates that hormone replacement therapy for postmenopausal women actually may increase the risk of heart disease (Manson et al., 2003). This negative effect may increase with age, with estrogen having a positive effect in the years immediately following menopause (Manson et al., 2007).

Racial and Ethnic Disparities

Like diabetes and HIV/AIDS, heart disease disproportionately affects certain racial and ethnic minority groups. Of the 700,000 people who died of heart disease in the U.S. general population in 2007, 19.5% were younger than 65 years (CDC, 2010b). Yet among American Indians and Alaska Natives, 38.1% of people who died of heart disease were younger than 65 years (CDC, 2010b). The rates were 35.4% and 26.5% for African Americans and Hispanic Americans, respectively (CDC, 2010b). The reasons for these disparities are not fully understood but may include factors such as differences in access to medical and emergency care, diet, exercise, risk behaviors such as smoking, and health behaviors such as checking blood pressure regularly. For example, the proportion of American Indians who smoke is twice that of White Americans; African Americans are more likely than White Americans to have high blood pressure; and African Americans, American Indians, and Hispanic Americans are more likely than White Americans to lack health insurance coverage (Bolen, Rhodes, Powell-Griner, Bland, & Holtzman, 2000). Physician bias also may contribute to racial and ethnic disparities in heart disease fatalities. In an experiment using videotaped, hypothetical case scenarios, physicians were almost twice as likely to recommend a heart

Table 20.2   Major Types of Heart Disease

Name	Description
Coronary artery disease	Arteries become hardened and narrowed by plaque (arteriosclerosis), decreasing blood flow to the heart and oxygen to the heart muscle.
Acute myocardial infarction ("heart attack")	A blood clot cuts off blood to part of the heart, resulting in damage to the heart muscle and sometimes death.
Congestive heart failure	The heart fails to pump blood effectively, resulting in shortness of breath, fluid retention, and fatigue.
Congenital heart defects	The heart or blood vessels around the heart failed to develop properly at birth.
Cardiomyopathy	The heart muscle is weakened.
Angina	Chest pain or discomfort is caused by the heart not getting enough blood, usually as a result of arteriosclerosis (hardening of the arteries).

procedure to White Americans and men than to African Americans and women despite identical symptoms among all the characters (Schulman et al., 1999).

Diabetes: A Global Epidemic

Diabetes mellitus affects the body's ability to metabolize blood glucose (sugar). A healthy person's pancreas produces sufficient insulin for cells to absorb and convert food into blood sugar. With diabetes, the person's body either fails to use insulin properly or produce it at all. Many people with diabetes must therefore limit their sugar intake or take insulin by either giving themselves injections or using an insulin infusion pump. When diabetes is uncontrolled and blood sugar levels get too high (hyperglycemia), the individual may experience shortness of breath; nausea; vomiting; excessive thirst; and a life-threatening, precoma condition called diabetic ketoacidosis. Controlled diabetes always carries the risk of hypoglycemia (low blood sugar) caused by too much insulin or medication. Symptoms and signs of hypoglycemia include shakiness, irritability, heart palpitations, hunger, and sweating. Left untreated, severe hypoglycemia can lead to loss of consciousness, seizures, and coma.

Most people with diabetes live and function for many years with the disease. Many people with diabetes are not even aware they have it because the onset of symptoms is gradual. Yet diabetes can take an enormous toll on a person's health and quality of life. People with diabetes commonly develop an array of complications that can include cardiovascular disease, vision problems (including blindness), amputations, kidney failure, and nerve damage. Ultimately, diabetes can be fatal. It ranked as the seventh leading cause of death in the United States in 2007, resulting in 71,382 deaths (CDC, 2010b). Mortality rates underestimate the true extent of diabetes's lethality because the damage it exacts on lungs, tissues, and organs contributes to other major causes of death—heart disease, stroke, and kidney disease, to name a few (National Center for Health Statistics [NCHS], 2010). Half of people with diabetes eventually die of heart disease or stroke (World Health Organization [WHO], 2009a).

Types of Diabetes

There are four major types of diabetes. *Type 1 diabetes,* formerly called juvenile diabetes, frequently is diagnosed in children and young adults and accounts for 5% to 10% of all diabetes cases (National Institute of Diabetes and Digestive and Kidney Diseases [NIDDK], 2008). Type 1 diabetes is an autoimmune disease, whereby a person's immune system inappropriately attacks necessary tissues. In type 1 diabetes, the immune system destroys the cells that produce the hormone insulin, which metabolizes blood sugar. People with type 1 diabetes must take insulin every day, sometimes before every meal, via injections or an insulin infusion pump.

Type 2 diabetes accounts for 90% to 95% of all diabetes cases (NIDDK, 2008). In type 2 diabetes, formerly called adult-onset diabetes, the body still may produce insulin, but the body's cells cannot absorb it. Eventually the pancreas may lose the ability to produce insulin altogether. This type of diabetes frequently is associated with being overweight and physically inactive. Many people with type 2 diabetes control their blood sugar by managing their diet, losing weight, exercising regularly, and taking oral medications. Roughly 10% to 15% of people with type 2 diabetes require insulin, either alone or in combination with oral medication (NIDDK, 2008).

Gestational diabetes is a form of glucose intolerance that occurs in about 14% of women during pregnancy (Kim, Newton, & Knopp, 2002). The condition typically disappears after childbirth, but various studies have shown that, 2.6% to 7% of women with gestational diabetes develop type 2 diabetes (Kim et al., 2002).

Other types of diabetes include conditions caused by genetic defects, drug use, infection, or less common forms of autoimmune illness (American Diabetes Association, 2004). These types of diabetes are the least common, making up only 1% to 5% of diabetes cases in the United States (NIDDK, 2008).

Epidemiology

Diabetes has been diagnosed in more than 17.9 million people in the United States, and an additional 5.7 million people are believed to have diabetes without being aware of their condition (NIDDK, 2008). Diabetes rates have increased substantially in recent years, including a 50% increase in the United States from 1997 to 2004 (CDC, 2006). Rates are increasing so rapidly nationally and worldwide that the WHO regards it as an epidemic with premature deaths of a similar magnitude, although less recognized, to HIV/AIDS (WHO, 2004). More than 1.1 million people worldwide died from diabetes in 2005 (WHO, 2009a). About 220 million people worldwide have been diagnosed with diabetes (WHO, 2009a), and the number is expected to increase to 366 million by 2030 (Wild, Roglic, Green, Sicree, & King, 2004). The number of Americans with diabetes is expected to grow to 38 million during the same time period (Mainous et al., 2007).

Risk Factors

Type 2 diabetes is considered to be largely preventable. The increasing prevalence of type 2 diabetes parallels increases in obesity, sugar and fat consumption, and physical inactivity in today's society (Mokdad et al., 2000). Diabetes is almost twice as common in developed countries than in developing countries (Black, 2002), reflecting the excess fat consumption and lack of exercise that often accompany higher socioeconomic status.

Racial and Ethnic Disparities

People from certain racial and ethnic minority groups are especially vulnerable to diabetes (Black, 2002). Compared to non-Hispanic White populations, Hispanic people in the United States are 1.5 times more likely to have diabetes, African Americans are 1.6 times more likely, and American Indians and Alaska Natives are 2.3 times more likely (CDC, 2004a). For example, almost 1 in 4 African American women between the ages of 65 and 74 years have diabetes (Tull & Roseman, 1995). In some areas of the country, more than 1 in 3 American Indians have type 2 diabetes (Lee et al., 2000). Pima Indians in southern Arizona have the highest rate of diabetes in the world, with 1 of every 2 tribal members diagnosed with the disease (Black, 2002; Knowler, Saad, Pettitt, Nelson, & Bennett, 1993). The higher rates of diabetes among minorities are attributed to having less access to health care and genetic differences in glucose tolerance in addition to the other primary risk factors of diabetes, including higher rates of obesity and inactivity (Black, 2002).

Racial and ethnic minorities in the United States also tend to suffer greater negative effects from diabetes than White Americans. For example, compared to White Americans in the United States, rates of death attributable to diabetes among African Americans and Hispanic Americans are twice as high and, among American Indians, 3 times as high (CDC, 2000).

HIV/AIDS: FROM TERMINAL ILLNESS TO CHRONIC DISEASE

HIV and AIDS are two different but overlapping disorders. HIV infects the body's immune system, in particular cells called T4 lymphocytes (T cells), which protect the body against infection and other threats. AIDS is the most advanced stage of HIV infection and is defined as a specific group of diseases or conditions that severely suppress the body's immune system (CDC, 2001). An HIV-positive person is diagnosed with AIDS when he or she has fewer than 200 T cells per cubic millimeter of blood, in comparison to levels of more than 1,000 in healthy adults (National Institute of Allergy and Infectious Diseases [NIAID], 2003). It can take 10 or more years for an HIV-positive person to develop AIDS (NIAID, 2003). This lag time makes the virus especially dangerous, because infected individuals may unknowingly pass HIV to others.

HIV is transmitted through contact with infected blood, which can occur from sexual contact, sharing needles, or blood transfusions.

Women also can pass the virus on to their infants during pregnancy, birth, or breast milk. The use of condoms during sexual intercourse may prevent the transmission of HIV. Public health approaches to preventing HIV include screening blood donations, promoting non-sharing of needles, and distributing free condoms on college campuses.

Epidemiology

The first case of AIDS was reported in 1981 in the United States (NIAID, 2003). Within just four years, AIDS was diagnosed in 16,000 people in the United States, 8,000 of whom died (Center for Infectious Diseases, 1985). A diagnosis of HIV or AIDS used to be a virtual death sentence. The median survival time for a person in the United States newly diagnosed with AIDS in the mid-1980s was 11.6 months (Jacobson et al., 1993). No effective treatments existed, and patients' suppressed immune systems made them vulnerable to dying from infections not typically deadly among young individuals, such as pneumonia.

The death rate from HIV/AIDS in the United States slowed in 1996, when patients began taking potent medications called highly active antiretroviral therapy (HAART). This therapy combines different types of medications in what is frequently called a *drug cocktail.* The medications in a drug cocktail are reverse transcriptase inhibitors, which prevent the virus from making copies of itself, and protease inhibitors, which control the enzyme in HIV that spreads infectious viral particles. Antiretroviral therapy does not cure HIV or AIDS, but it does reduce the amount of virus and prolong both the quality and length of life. After the introduction of antiretroviral therapy in the United States, deaths from HIV declined dramatically—from 31,130 deaths in 1996 to 16,516 in 1997 (CDC, 2010b). That same year, HIV/AIDS fell out of the top 10 causes of death. A study of AIDS deaths in 12 high-income countries found that antiretroviral therapy reduced mortality by 85% overall (Bhaskaran et al., 2008).

In recent years, AIDS deaths in the United States have consistently declined, dropping from 14,478 deaths in 2000 to 11,295 in 2007, the most recent year with available statistics (CDC, 2010b). Most deaths from AIDS occur in younger people; among youth and adults age 15 to 54 years, HIV is the eighth leading cause of death in the United States (CDC, 2010b).

AIDS Worldwide: A Leading Cause of Death

At least 20 million people worldwide have died from AIDS since the very first case was reported almost 30 years ago (Joint United Nations Programme on HIV/AIDS [UNAIDS], 2004). HIV/AIDS now ranks as the sixth leading cause of death worldwide (WHO, 2008). The devastation is enormous, particularly in southern Africa, which accounts for 22 million of the world's 33 million AIDS cases (WHO, 2009b). In 2008 alone, 1.4 million people in southern Africa died of AIDS (UNAIDS, 2009). New, potent antiretroviral medications have only recently become available to people in these poorer countries; only 7% of southern Africans with HIV received antiretroviral medications in 2003, compared with 48% in 2008 (UNAIDS, 2009). Furthermore, rates of HIV continue to increase. In 2008, an estimated 2.7 million people in the world acquired HIV (UNAIDS, 2009).

Almost all new HIV infections occur in the world's developing countries, and they spread most commonly through heterosexual contact. In Africa, more than 80% of HIV infections among women result from heterosexual contact, and the remainder are transmitted from mother to child or via blood transfusion (Lamptey, 2002).

Gender and AIDS

For many years, AIDS was identified in the United States, often pejoratively, as a "gay disease" because the majority of AIDS-related cases occurred among men who had sex with men without using a condom to protect against sexually transmitted diseases (CDC, 2001; Herek & Glunt, 1988). Yet even from its earliest days, the disease also claimed the lives of women who had sex with HIV-positive men, infants and children born to mothers who had AIDS, people who received tainted blood transfusions, and people who used injectable drugs and shared contaminated needles.

The disease still disproportionately afflicts men who have sex with men in the United States, but that is changing. In 2008, one-third of people newly infected with AIDS contracted the disease through heterosexual contact (CDC, 2010a). Nationally, HIV is more common among men than women, with 75% of cases occurring in men (CDC, 2010a). Worldwide, almost half of all people with AIDS are female, and heterosexual contact is the primary means of infection (UNAIDS, 2009). For example, 60% of people infected with HIV in southern Africa are women and girls (UNAIDS, 2009). Gender inequalities, especially including violence against women, are blamed for women's disproportionate burden of the disease in Africa (UNAIDS, 2009).

Racial and Ethnic Disparities

In wealthier, industrialized countries such as the United States, deaths from AIDS have dropped for all racial and socioeconomic groups since antiretroviral therapies began, but the progress has been smaller for some vulnerable groups. The decline in deaths was lowest among African American women and highest among White American men and residents of more affluent areas (Karon, Fleming, Steketee, & DeCock, 2001). Furthermore, HIV rates are increasing among African Americans, Asian Americans, and American Indians (CDC, 2010a). Although African Americans make up 13% of the U.S. population, they accounted for 52% of all new HIV infections in 2008 (CDC, 2010a). A study of 38 states that keep track of HIV cases found that the highest rates of HIV infection occur among African Americans (CDC, 2010a). The disparities largely reflect differences in HIV-testing patterns and access to new drugs (Karon et al., 2001). Minorities, women, and people with low income may be less likely to have access to and receive effective therapy for HIV and AIDS (Andersen et al., 2000).

AIDS in the United States: A Continuing Public Health Problem

Although more people with HIV and AIDS in the United States survive and function well with antiretroviral therapy, the conditions still represent major, national public health problems (Arias, Anderson, Kung, Murphy, & Kochanek, 2003). Even though AIDS deaths have declined, the number of HIV cases reported each year continues to grow (CDC, 2010b). HIV primarily affects young people, especially minorities. Medical researchers caution that the new drug therapies have resulted in treatment-resistant types of HIV. Even when the drug cocktails are effective and accessible, many people fail to take them properly because of complicated dosing regimens and side effects (Conway, 2007; Fleming, Wortley, Karon, DeCock, & Janssen, 2000). Immediate side effects can include rash, recurrent or chronic diarrhea, vomiting, and fatigue; long-term effects can include pancreatic, liver, and kidney dysfunction (Sax & Kumar, 2004). Although some writers disagree (e.g., Elford, 2006), others have suggested that the new, effective treatments lead to complacency among high-risk groups who used to protect themselves against HIV infection (Fleming et al., 2000). For these reasons, social workers in health-care settings will continue to encounter people who are HIV-positive or living with AIDS.

ADHERENCE TO TREATMENT REGIMENS

The successful management of diabetes, heart disease, and HIV/AIDS depends largely on the extent to which patients adhere to and take responsibility for their treatment regimens. As such, facilitating patient adherence to medical regimens has emerged as an important function for the social worker on the health-care team. *Adherence* is defined broadly as the extent to which a patient's behavior corresponds with medical advice (Meichenbaum & Turk, 1987). Although the terms *adherence* and *compliance* sometimes are used interchangeably, *adherence* implies an active and collaborative role with health-care professionals whereas *compliance* connotes a more passive, submissive role. Treatment effectiveness for many chronic diseases, such as diabetes, heart disease, and HIV/AIDS, is strongly influenced by the patient's willingness and ability to adhere to a complicated medical regimen.

For example, the diabetes treatment regimen involves multiple daily insulin injections or use of an insulin infusion pump for type 1 diabetes or oral medications for type 2 diabetes, frequent daily blood glucose testing, adherence to a meal plan, and a regular exercise program. Adherence to treatment for heart disease involves diet and exercise as well as oral medications, blood pressure and lipid monitoring, and regular visits to the cardiologist for routine stress tests and electrocardiograms. For HIV/AIDS, adherence to preventive behaviors (e.g., use of condoms and clean needles) is necessary to reduce the risk of transmission or infection; once infected, adherence to treatment is critical for slowing progression and delaying complications of HIV. Current treatment guidelines for HIV recommend HAART, a complex regimen of usually three or four antiretroviral drugs (Deeks, Smith, Holodniy, & Kahn, 1997).

The magnitude of nonadherence to medical regimens has been studied for decades. In a review of 50 years of research across 569 studies, nonadherence ranged from 4.6% to 100%, with an average of 75.2% (DiMatteo, 2004). In this review, adherence was significantly higher in more recent smaller studies, those involving pharmacological treatment rather than modified health behaviors, and populations with greater resources such as higher education and income. The IOM revealed that approximately 90 million adults have low literacy, the literacy proficiency needed to understand and respond to health information (Kindig, Nielsen-Bohlman, & Panzer, 2004). Individuals with low income, ethnic minorities, and those who live in rural areas are more likely to face health literacy barriers (Kirsch, Jungeblut, Jenkins & Kolstad, 1993).

Many studies have examined the correlates or predictors of adherence among individuals with diabetes, heart disease, and HIV/AIDS, such as familial, mental health, health beliefs, literacy, and demographic factors (Anderson, Auslander, Jung, Miller, & Santiago, 1990; Auslander, Thompson, Dreitzer, White, & Santiago, 1997; DiMatteo, Haskard, & Williams, 2007; Frain, Bishop, Tschopp, Ferrin, & Frain, 2009; Glasgow & Toobert, 1988; Jacobson et al., 1990). Results from several studies indicate that the degree of adherence to one aspect of the diabetic regimen is unrelated to adherence to other aspects of the regimen (Glasgow, Wilson, & McCaul, 1985). These data suggest that there are multiple influences on patient adherence and highlight the complexities involved in facilitating behavioral changes among individuals with chronic disease.

More recently, there has been an increase in the number of studies about adherence to HAART in patients infected with HIV. This is due in part to the fact that effective treatment requires at least a 95% adherence rate to HAART to reduce viral loads and prevent drug-resistant HIV variants (Chesney, 2003). Because nonadherence among these patients can increase the risk of death significantly, studies have focused on the barriers to adherence as well as factors that promote adherence behaviors (Chesney, 2003; Garcia & Cote, 2003; Steele & Grauer, 2003). Identified barriers to adherence include complicated dosing schedules and food restrictions, medication side effects, psychosocial issues (i.e., substance abuse, depression, stress), and unsupportive relationships with providers (Altica, Mostashari, & Friedland, 2001; Chesney, 2003; Gonzalez et al., 2004).

Likewise, a review of the literature on the antecedents of adherence of cardiovascular risk reduction (Cohen, 2009) indicated that the collaborative relationship between the practitioner and patient is very important. Adherence is influenced by perception of personal risk, decision support, motivation, self-efficacy, and credible health information.

Systematic Model of Adherence Counseling

Many studies have evaluated the efficacy or effectiveness of interventions designed to improve adherence to treatment regimens, particularly for patients with diabetes and HIV/AIDS (Anderson, Brackett, Ho, & Laffel, 1999; Smith-Rogers, Miller, Murphy, Tanney, & Fortune, 2001; Wysocki et al., 2000), and there are numerous systematic reviews of adherence interventions (van Dulmen et al., 2007). Yet few studies have specified the processes of adherence counseling that are common across these interventions. The adherence counseling process described in this chapter is not an evidence-based intervention, but rather a comprehensive and systematic overview of strategies that have been shown to improve adherence in clinical settings (Auslander, 1993; Auslander, Bubb, Peelle, & Rogge, 1989; Bubb, Auslander, & Manthei, 1989; Lorenz et al., 1996). The approach has a cognitive-behavioral orientation and integrates classic works by Becker (1974; Becker & Maiman, 1980), Meichenbaum and Turk (1987), and Marlatt and Gordon (1985). Typically, evidence-based interventions to improve adherence target a portion of the behavioral change strategies outlined in this model, such as encouraging peer and family support, assessing and modifying health beliefs, or encouraging joint decision making. In practice, social workers often use all of the strategies, either singly or in various combinations, depending on the adherence-related problem. As shown in Table 20.3, adherence counseling includes four distinct phases that the social worker implements: (1) assessment and identification of adherence problems, (2) planning the medical treatment regimen, (3) facilitating behavioral change, and (4) maintaining patient adherence.

Phase 1: Assess and Identify Adherence Problems

The assessment phase focuses on those factors that are most likely to influence adherence. Clinical experience and health behavior research have identified several areas that are associated with a patient's willingness and ability to follow a treatment regimen (Marlatt & Gordon, 1985; Meichenbaum & Turk, 1987). These areas include social support, lifestyle, financial status, psychological well-being, health beliefs, past adherence history, and satisfaction with the treatment regimen (see Table 20.3). Assessment of these factors provides information that is important in developing a realistic treatment plan designed to increase the probability of regimen adherence.

Social Support. The family assessment is designed to identify family strengths and risk factors associated with adherence. The family assessment should include: (a) the family's social and economic status; (b) the family's willingness to be supportive and competence to do so (i.e., family member's disease knowledge, technical skills, ability to learn, problem-solving ability, and organizational skills); (c) family stressors, such as divorce, remarriage, loss of a job, a new baby, or a death in the family; and (d) observation of family interactions to gain information about the family's ability to work together and resolve conflict. This is an important area, given the wealth of research that shows significant associations between family characteristics and adherence (Anderson et al., 1990; Glasgow & Toobert, 1988; Thompson, Auslander, & White, 2001a,b). Patients spend a great deal of their time at work or school, and, as at home, they need cooperation from those around them to create an environment that promotes adherence. Patients also need competent assistance in the case of a medical emergency. Therefore, it is crucial to assess the extent of support available from friends, teachers, coworkers, employers, and others outside of the family.

Lifestyle/Daily Schedule. Assessment of patients' and families' daily routines frequently reveals conflicts between lifestyle and treatment regimens that can undermine or prevent adherence. The lifestyle/daily schedule assessment can be accomplished by asking the patient to recall the events of a typical day, hour by hour, from waking until bedtime, as well as asking her to describe how weekends differ

Table 20.3   Adherence Counseling for Chronic Disease Management

Phase 1: Patient and Family Assessment
Lifestyle and daily schedule.
Psychological factors.
Health beliefs.
Prior adherence history and treatment satisfaction.

Phase 2: Planning the Treatment Regimen
Promote a realistic medical regimen.
Encourage patient participation in regimen planning.
Facilitate communication.
Encourage joint decision making.

Phase 3: Facilitate Behavioral Change
Initiate new behaviors.
    Translate treatment goals into behavioral goals.
    Encourage self-management strategies.
    Teach patients to plan for high-risk situations.
Activate social support.
    Family support. Increase family involvement, promote shared responsibility.
    Strengthen emotional support.
    Social support outside of the family. Enhance patient's ability to activate social and medical support

Phase 4: Strategies for Long-Term Adherence
Develop skills for maintaining adherence.
Teach how to cope with lapses in adherence.
Increase accessibility to health care.
Reinforce positive health-care behaviors.

from weekdays. This methodology, a 24-hour recall, has been widely used in research to assess adherence to diet in patients with diabetes and heart disease (Anding, Kubena, McIntosh, & O'Brien, 1996; Johnson, Perwien, & Silverstein, 2000). Often, knowledge of the small details of a patient's life will lead to the understanding of major adherence problems.

Psychological Factors. As discussed earlier in this chapter, several psychological problems have been associated with adherence to medical regimens: depression (Anderson, Freedland, Clouse, & Lustman, 2001; Lustman et al., 2000; Starace et al., 2002), anxiety disorders (Anderson et al., 2002), eating disorders (Jones, Lawson, Daneman, Olmsted, & Rodin, 2000), and substance use (Arnsten et al., 2002). It is critical to assess for psychological factors, because many of these conditions may adversely affect adherence.

Beliefs. In his Health Belief Model, Becker (1974; Becker & Maiman, 1980) suggested that patients' health-related decisions and behaviors are influenced more by personal medical experiences, beliefs, and attitudes than by recommendations from health-care professionals. It is important for members of the health-care team to understand a patient's health beliefs so they can correct misinformation and misconceptions that could undermine adherence. Becker's model points to several key assessment areas: (a) the patient's beliefs about whether the disease is serious enough to warrant the effort involved in following the treatment regimen, (b) the patient's beliefs about the probability of the treatment regimen improving the medical condition, and (c) the patient's beliefs about the likelihood that the benefits of treatment will outweigh the difficulties and inconveniences of adherence.

Adherence History/Treatment Satisfaction. A review of the patient's past adherence performance is important because practitioners consider past adherence behaviors good predictors of future adherence. Adherence behavior patterns can be assessed by asking the patient specific questions about how often he follows each aspect of his prescribed regimen. For example, the patient can be asked how frequently during the previous day, week, or month he exercised. It also should be determined when and where adherence is most difficult. During the assessment of the patient's adherence history, the social worker also can identify why the patient did not follow a specific area of treatment. The social worker can determine if, for example, nonadherence resulted from the patient's misunderstanding of the prescribed regimen. In the assessment of prior adherence history, it is important to determine the patient's satisfaction with his adherence performance. If the patient is dissatisfied with his performance, he already may have a plan and be motivated to change adherence behaviors. In contrast, if the patient is nonadherent according to the assessment but satisfied with his performance, his readiness to change will be limited. This situation demands renegotiation of treatment goals between the health-care provider and patient, which is discussed in Phase 2.

Phase 2: Plan the Medical Treatment Regimen

Social workers must take an active role in treatment planning because they often can enhance the plan's effectiveness and increase patient adherence by ensuring that psychosocial and behavioral factors are not overlooked or disregarded.

Promote the Development of a Realistic Medical Regimen. By encouraging patients and health-care professionals to utilize the social worker's adherence assessment, a medical regimen can be developed that is feasible for a patient in terms of her life. Patients are more likely to be adherent if their regimens are tailored to their specific lifestyle, behavioral changes are minimized, and convenience is enhanced (Chesney, 2003; DiMatteo, 2004).

Encourage Patient Participation in Regimen Planning. Adherence can be enhanced by developing individualized medical regimens that reflect patient preference. It is important that the social worker urge the health-care team to actively involve the patient in treatment planning and to seriously consider the patient's desires and expectations. The social worker should ensure that the patient has been informed of all treatment options, including the risks and benefits of each option.

Facilitate Communication. Several research studies have found positive correlations between a physician's communication style and the patient's comprehension, satisfaction, and adherence (Roter & Hall, 1997). Physicians and other health-care providers may communicate more effectively with a patient after the social worker consults with the health-care team regarding the patient's individual life demands and adherence difficulties. Patients, too, must be willing to listen to and understand their health-care providers. To ensure accurate understanding, social workers should encourage health professionals routinely to ask patients to restate important medical information and instructions; misunderstandings then can be corrected. At the end of this chapter, we review strategies that social workers can use to enhance patient recall of information.

Encourage Joint Decision Making. After effective communication is established, the social worker can encourage and guide health-care professionals in negotiating a treatment plan with the patient. Research has shown that actively engaging patients in treatment decision making or shared decision making has potential to improve adherence and health outcomes (Fraenkel & McGraw, 2007; Heisler, 2008; Stacey, Samant, & Bennett, 2008). Shared decision making is important because patients' treatment goals often differ from those of their health-care professionals. For example, in the case of diabetes treatment planning, the diabetes team might prescribe a treatment designed to normalize blood sugar levels when the patient's goal is to prevent uncomfortable episodes of low blood glucose, thus intentionally keeping blood sugars higher than normal. The patient may then be adherent in terms of behaviors to reach goals, but nonadherent from the perspective of the health-care professional.

Phase 3: Facilitate Behavioral Change

Patients with recently diagnosed chronic disease often must develop new behaviors and change established behaviors to most effectively implement the recommended treatment regimen. Strategies that can be used by social workers to facilitate behavioral change can be grouped into two categories: initiating new behaviors, and activating social support.

Initiating New Behaviors. Early success in the process of behavioral change reinforces and motivates patients. The techniques described here are designed to ensure that patients feel a sense of accomplishment as soon as possible after they begin to establish new adherence behaviors (Meichenbaum & Turk, 1987). The first technique is to assist patients in translating treatment goals into behavioral goals. Patients must understand exactly what new or changed behaviors are required in order to achieve their treatment goals. They must plan specifically how, when, and where the new behavior(s) will occur. If the treatment goal is to increase exercise, simply advising the patient to exercise more frequently will not be as effective as guiding her in devising a plan specifying, for instance, the type of activity, exercise frequency, and when and where she will engage in the activity. Meichenbaum and Turk warn that the plans should be moderately specific, but not overly rigid, for best results.

A second technique is to encourage patients to use self-management strategies. After behavioral goals are set, patients can be encouraged to establish a daily self-monitoring or self-recording system. Changes seem easier to achieve when taken day by day. Daily monitoring or recording also reinforces patients' efforts by giving them a sense of immediate achievement. In addition, patients and healthcare providers can use information from self-monitoring forms to manage treatment regimens more effectively. Small changes are easier to make than big changes. Patients may be more successful if they graduate the treatment plan; that is, change their behaviors in a step-by-step fashion. For example, a patient who is instructed to exercise five times per week may be overwhelmed by the task. It may seem less daunting to the patient to begin by exercising twice per week, gradually adding more activity. Another self-management strategy is to structure the physical environment by organizing the home and work site. Doing this often entails encouraging patients to make

simple adjustments, such as keeping tempting, high-fat foods out of the house, setting up an exercise mat in a convenient place, or keeping blood-testing equipment in a convenient place. Last, *cueing* is another self-management strategy that has been successful in increasing patient adherence. Patients can be taught to use cues to prompt them to remember new behaviors. Patients can use routine events, such as a favorite television show or the evening news, as a prompt to take medication. Medication containers separated into daily doses are also helpful. Be creative, even humorous, in helping patients identify behavioral cues.

A third technique to foster the initiation of new behaviors is to teach patients to plan ahead for high-risk situations (Marlatt & Gordon, 1985). During the assessment, the patient may have identified or given clues to behaviors, situations, events, or persons that are likely to interfere with adherence to the treatment regimen. Anticipating these obstacles to adherence and planning ways to manage them are key strategies to successful behavioral change. Role-play and rehearsal are useful in preparing patients to cope with the challenges of everyday living.

Activating Social Support. Results of a wide range of studies strongly suggest that social support and social relationships positively affect health, in part through health behaviors (Heaney & Israel, 1997). Strengthening and expanding a patient's support network, within the family and without, is an essential component of the third phase of adherence counseling.

Knowledge of family strengths and risk factors revealed in the initial adherence assessment enables the social worker to focus interventions on areas where the need is greatest. In general, to activate effective family support, the social worker can encourage family involvement and competence, promote shared responsibility among family members, and strengthen the family's emotional support for the patient (Anderson et al., 1990; Glasgow & Toobert, 1988). To encourage family involvement and competence, it is crucial that the social worker encourage the health-care team to include family members in disease-related education and regimen planning, especially those members who play key roles in areas related to adherence. For example, family members who do the shopping and cooking must learn about the recommended diet for individuals with heart disease or diabetes and help the health-care team tailor the patient's diet to the at-home situation. In order to accomplish this type of involvement, classes or meetings must be scheduled at a time convenient not only for the patient and health-care team, but for family members as well. If family members are reluctant to learn about the disease or seem hesitant about helping with the regimen, the social worker can talk with them about the reasons for their reluctance to become involved. Do they fear medical procedures? Do they know how to help? Are they resentful of the demands being placed on them? Once these issues surface, the social worker and family can openly deal with them. Family members are more likely to want to continue helping if they know their efforts have made a difference and are appreciated.

Promoting shared responsibility among family members is another way to improve the effectiveness of family support. Because research has shown that disagreements between family members regarding the division of responsibility for disease-related tasks have been associated with problems with adherence (Anderson et al., 1990), patients and their families should be encouraged to discuss and decide on the tasks and roles each person is willing to assume. Families often are anxious about handling medical emergencies, so often it is useful to devote the first meeting to helping them plan what must be done in an emergency and who will carry out each task.

Emotional support can be strengthened by encouraging family members to openly share their feelings. Often the patient and family try to hide painful emotions, such as sadness, grief, or anxiety, in order to protect each other. In doing so, they miss an opportunity to comfort one another and grow closer as a family. Social workers also can encourage families to share angry feelings so that differences can be negotiated and conflicts resolved. Many studies have found that cohesive families with low levels of conflict have better adherence and improved medical outcomes (Hanson, De Guire, Schinkel, & Kolterman, 1995; Herskowitz et al., 1995).

Adhering to a treatment regimen for heart disease, diabetes, or HIV/AIDS may be difficult, if not impossible, if the patient has uninformed or unsympathetic friends, coworkers, bosses, or teachers. Encouraging the patient to educate at least one or two coworkers or fellow students can strengthen the supportive atmosphere and increase the probability of adherence. Support from others at work or school can be encouraged by educational efforts by the patient. In children with diabetes, personal contacts by a member of the health-care team may be used to reinforce parental education of school personnel.

Linking patients with support groups frequently reduces the sense of isolation and provides opportunities for learning practical ways of dealing with adherence problems. Linking patients with appropriate community resources, a traditional and essential social work function, helps patients access supplies and services that are important for regimen adherence.

Patients will be better served in the long run if they learn how to activate their own support. Social workers can guide patients to identify those persons who might provide social support by having them recall people who have helped them in the past and by asking them to think of those who might be willing to help in the future. Further, social workers can prepare patients to ask for support and cope with refusals by using role-play and rehearsal techniques as described by Marlatt and Gordon (1985). Patients who are uncomfortable about "bothering the doctor" can be taught patient activation or assertiveness skills to obtain medical support. One patient activation strategy is to encourage patients to prepare a list of questions before they make telephone calls to the doctor or go to office visits (Roter, 1977). Other strategies include encouraging patients to learn about their medical condition by reading their medical charts and helping them negotiate medical treatment decisions with their health-care providers. In a study of the cognitive and behavioral determinants of adherence to the diabetes regimen, Amir, Rabin, and Galatzer (1990) found that a patient's ability to assertively request follow-up with a specific doctor was significantly correlated with adherence.

Phase 4: Maintaining Patient Adherence

Marlatt and Gordon (1985) observed that the high rate of failure associated with attempts to change behaviors may stem from a lack of emphasis on the maintenance phase of treatment. Chronic disease patient education and management programs commonly suffer from a lack of attention to maintenance issues. Health-care professionals often are naive in assuming that their job is done once the patient has been educated and launched onto a new treatment regimen. However, for patients, the challenges are just beginning. The next strategies have been helpful in facilitating long-term adherence.

Assist in Maintenance Skills. Many of the strategies described previously as effective in initiating behavioral change are also effective in maintaining behavioral change. In general, the most successful strategies will be those directed toward helping patients develop a sense of personal responsibility for their own adherence and helping them acquire the skills needed to carry out this responsibility (Meichenbaum & Turk, 1987). One of the most crucial of these skills, described earlier in this chapter, is the ability to anticipate and plan ahead for situations that are likely to result in nonadherent behaviors. This skill is particularly important in light of Marlatt and Gordon's (1985) findings that most episodes of nonadherence occur in a limited number of high-risk situations that are unique to each individual.

Other skills that will help patients independently maintain adherence are problem-solving skills, assertiveness skills, interpersonal skills, and stress management skills (Meichenbaum & Turk, 1987). When a patient is deficient in these areas, the social worker's role is to

strengthen these skills as they relate to adherence. The patient also can be referred to skills training programs offered by community agencies. The social worker then can help the patient apply the knowledge and skills learned from the training program to his personal regimen adherence problems.

Teach Techniques for Coping with Lapses. To maintain long-term adherence, patients must learn to cope successfully with lapses in adherence. Marlatt and Gordon (1985) stress the importance of cognitive reframing for patients who view each slip in adherence as a sign of personal inadequacy or as an indication that adherence is not achievable. Patients who think this way become easily discouraged and lose motivation. Cognitive reframing involves helping patients view lapses as errors or mistakes in the process of learning new behaviors, not as indications of personal deficiencies, so they can understand, as with any mistake, the possibility of corrective learning. The social worker can then assist patients in reviewing and debriefing the lapse so that causes can be identified and strategies devised to prevent recurrences. Marlatt and Gordon (1985) also suggest lapse rehearsal as a technique for preparing patients to handle lapses in adherence. Lapse rehearsal gives patients an opportunity to anticipate an adherence lapse, to imagine their response to the lapse, and to receive feedback and coaching from the social worker.

Utilize Follow-up Techniques. There are a number of very direct ways that the health-care team can encourage long-term maintenance, some of which involve ongoing communication between patient and health-care professional. Regular phone calls, text messages, e-mails, and reminders help some patients keep on track.

Social workers can utilize strategies to reduce health-care costs, such as locating low-cost sources of medications and supplies and making referrals to state and federal agencies for financial and medical assistance. Chronic diseases, such as HIV/AIDS, diabetes, and heart disease, can be very expensive to manage because of the high cost of prescription drugs, blood glucose testing supplies, dietary restrictions, frequent doctor visits, medical transportation, child care, and laboratory tests. Patients frequently fail to maintain their regimen because of the hardships these expenses cause for their families over time. In the long term, other financial demands may take priority over disease-related expenses. Social workers should be aware that changes in adherence over time may be due to competing financial needs.

Social workers must consistently recognize and reinforce patients' positive health-care behaviors. Reinforcement will be more effective if done in such a way that patients realize their successes are due to their own efforts rather than those of their health professionals (Meichenbaum & Turk, 1987). Patients need self-confidence and a belief in their own self-efficacy to follow the treatment regimen successfully for a lifetime.

Applicability to Diverse Populations

This approach holds promise for individuals from diverse socioeconomic and ethnic backgrounds because it uses an ecological approach for assessing barriers and facilitators to adherence. This approach also acknowledges and examines the influence of the broader social context, such as societal and cultural factors, that affect adherence behaviors. For example, cultural factors, such as health beliefs and extended family social support networks among minority patients, may differ from those of the majority culture and are crucial to successful adherence counseling. Furthermore, this approach to adherence counseling can be used as a strategy to prevent adherence problems from developing with newly diagnosed patients or patients who are changing their regimens. Clinical wisdom, as well as research about chronically ill children, suggests that it is easier to prevent the occurrence of family-related adherence and disease management problems than it is to reverse already existing negative patterns within the family (Auslander, Anderson, Bubb, Jung, & Santiago, 1990; Auslander, Bubb, Rogge, & Santiago, 1993).

ADHERENCE AND PATIENT–PRACTITIONER COMMUNICATION

Outcomes Associated With Positive Patient–Practitioner Communication

After three decades of research about patient–practitioner communication, several consistent findings that characterize interactions between patients and practitioners have been shown to be associated with adherence to treatment. For example, when practitioners engage in more positive and less negative talk, ask fewer questions, and offer more information, patients are more likely to be adherent. In fact, more information giving is associated with better patient recall and more partnership building (Hall, Roter, & Katz, 1988; Roter & Hall, 1997). Although many of these studies have been conducted with physicians as the practitioner, general principles and techniques used to improve communication skills can be extrapolated to other members of the health-care team, such as social workers, nurses, and dietitians.

Likewise, the strongest predictor of patient satisfaction is how much information is provided to the patient; that is, patients who receive more information are more satisfied with medical care than those who receive less information (Hall et al., 1988). The strong relationship between more information and greater satisfaction may be due to the need patients have for knowledge about their condition. It also may be related to patients' perceptions that practitioners who share more information with them are more concerned and caring people. Studies even link patient–practitioner communication with health outcomes such as improved recovery from surgery and decreased use of pain medication (Roter & Hall, 1997). As patients with chronic diseases take greater responsibility for their own treatment and health, their needs for information will increase. Social workers can lead the medical team in changing the interaction between patients and providers to a more collaborative style of communication. (See Chapter 10 for further discussion of these issues.)

Information Giving and the Educator Role

Patients with chronic diseases are continually coping and adapting to changes, whether they are the co-occurrence of a mental health problem, changes in their medical condition, changes in their treatment regimen, or developmental or lifestyle changes. All of these changes pose demands on the patient to continually seek out new information and learn new ways of coping. In response to this patient need, social workers play a large role in delivering information to patients and educating them about disease-related and psychosocial issues. Although there is an emphasis on conducting psychosocial assessments in most social work programs, little attention is spent on training social workers to deliver information to patients. Research in patient–practitioner communication indicates that patients are dissatisfied and nonadherent when (a) they do not understand what they are told and do not ask questions, (b) they forget what they are told, and (c) too much time is spent on assessing personal histories as opposed to providing patient education (Robbins et al., 1993; Roter, 1977; Roter, Hall, & Katz, 1987).

Communication Techniques to Enhance Information Recall

Patients forget much of what practitioners tell them by the time they leave the building. To increase the amount of information recalled by patients, the next communication strategies have been identified as useful in the medical encounter. The first strategy is to use explicit categorization. When giving a lot of information to patients, social workers should present the information in categories or blocks and describe each category in advance. For example, "I am going to tell you the various types of support groups that are available for you and your family, what the potential benefits are to participating in these groups, who facilitates or sponsors each of these groups, and where and when these groups are held and how you can sign up for them."

A second strategy is to use *repetition.* Combined with explicit categorization, repeating the most important information to patients and their families can increase recall. In one of the pioneer studies on patient–practitioner communication, providers asked patients to repeat the information back to the physician to make sure they understood what they were told. Any information that was misunderstood or forgotten was repeated to the patient. Results of this study showed that individuals in the experimental group were better able to recall information from the physicians and also more satisfied with the medical visit (Bertakis, 1977).

Another strategy to enhance recall of information is to provide specific instructions. Patients can remember and more easily follow concrete or specific, detailed advice or information more easily than general, abstract information, because the former better enhances imagery than the latter. For example, the classic general statement, "You should reduce the sugar in your diet," often is ignored by patients not only because it is difficult to achieve but because it does not provide specific enough advice. A more specific statement would be "Substitute fresh fruit and crackers for dessert after meals in your diet." When using specific instructions, social workers should avoid using medical jargon and long sentences that are difficult to follow.

Ley (1982), another pioneer in studying information giving to patients, examined the ordering of information presented to the patient. Results indicated that patients presented with information in a medical encounter remember best what they are told first and what they consider most important. Because practitioners often end their visits with patients by providing them with information and recommendations, patients may be more likely to forget this information. Instead, Ley's early work suggests that social workers should present the most important information early in their visit with patients so that patients are more likely to remember it. Providing a rationale to help patients understand why a treatment is recommended is another strategy that may increase patient recall. Last, practitioners should elicit patient expectations and involvement. None of these techniques will improve the interaction with patients, unless the practitioner asks what the patients want to know and encourages patient involvement in their interactions. A recent study that assessed how frequently recall-promoting physician behaviors are used in primary care settings indicated that repetition was the most common technique used (53.7%), followed by a rationale for treatment (28.2%) (Silberman, Tentler, Ramgopal, & Epstein, 2007). Because longer visits were associated with increased use of recall-promoting techniques, social workers can play a strong role in enhancing recall by having extended visits with patients after the physician completes her interaction.

Previous research on adherence and communication between practitioners and patients has led to the understanding that health-care professionals are most effective when they adopt a collaborative style with patients. When patients choose to not adhere to a treatment regimen, it should be viewed as a logical, motivated choice. The solution is to renegotiate the agreed-on prescribed treatment so that patients can realistically follow it. Lessons learned from a multisite controlled trial of intensive therapy (the Diabetes Control and Complications Trial) for individuals with type 1 diabetes (Lorenz et al., 1996) demonstrated that for intensive therapy to be successful, health professionals must change as much as patients.

RELATIONSHIP BETWEEN MENTAL HEALTH AND CHRONIC DISEASE

One of the most important issues for social workers who work with chronically ill patients is the co-occurrence of mental health problems. People with chronic illnesses, such as heart disease, diabetes, or HIV/AIDS, have higher rates of emotional problems than the general population. Chronic illness can cause functional disabilities, ongoing pain, burdensome medication regimens, reliance on caregivers, and awareness of one's mortality, any of which can lead to feelings of grief, anxiety, and depression. But the relationship between mental disorder and chronic illness goes beyond the easily explainable premise that chronic illnesses cause patients distress. Research also indicates that the relationship occurs in the other direction as well—distress can be a causal factor in the etiology of chronic illness. Depression can increase the risk of heart disease, diabetes, and HIV/AIDS through direct and indirect pathways.

Social workers bring a holistic, person-in-environment perspective to the care of people with chronic illness. Part of this perspective requires knowledge of how mental illness and other physical illnesses can inextricably converge. To summarize such knowledge, this section examines: the prevalence of mental disorders among individuals with heart disease, diabetes, or HIV/AIDS; the bidirectional relationship of these chronic illnesses and mental disorders; factors associated with mental health in people with chronic illness; and approaches to providing social work services for people with a mental disorder and heart disease, diabetes, or HIV/AIDS.

Prevalence of Mental Disorders Among People With Heart Disease, Diabetes, or HIV/AIDS

Heart Disease

An estimated 15% to 20% of people with heart disease also have depression, compared to 4% to 7% in the general population (Lett et al., 2004). Research shows that depression can exacerbate heart disease, perhaps because of behavioral consequences of depression, such as poor eating and exercise habits, or because of physiological correlates, such as decreased heart rate variability and platelet activity in depressed individuals (Ferketich, Schwartzbaum, Frid, & Moeschberger, 2000). In 20 studies that followed patients with heart disease for up to 15 years, people with heart disease and depression were, on average,

2 times more likely to die of cardiac complications than people with heart disease and no depression (Barth, Schumacher, & Herrmann-Lingen, 2004). Studies generally indicate that people who experience coronary artery disease, acute myocardial infarction, congestive heart failure, or heart surgery and who subsequently experience depression are 1.5 to 2.5 times more likely to die from their cardiac condition than people with heart disease and no depression (Lett et al., 2004). Although depression is a major risk factor for suicide (Rihmer, 2007), a review of studies on suicide and medical illness found no increased suicide risk for cardiac conditions such as hypertension and heart transplant (Hughes & Kleespies, 2001).

Diabetes

Studies consistently show the risk for depression is 2 times higher among people with type 1 or type 2 diabetes compared with those who do not have diabetes (Ali, Stone, Peters, Davies, & Khunti, 2006; Anderson et al., 2001). This effect is consistent for women, men, children, and adults, as well as for different types of diabetes. In general, a review of 39 studies including 20,218 participants indicated that 11% of people with diabetes had major depression and an additional 31% had a high number of depression symptoms (Anderson et al., 2001). In a longitudinal study of children with type 1 diabetes, 28% developed depression over a 10-year period (Kovacs, Goldston, Obrosky, & Bonar, 1997). Psychiatric disorders occurred most commonly in the first year after treatment. Depression among people with diabetes is related to poor nutrition, lack of medication adherence, increased health problems, and lower quality of life (Anderson et al., 2001; Ciechanowski, Katon, & Russo, 2000; Lustman & Clouse, 2005). Various studies have shown that depression is related to a greater likelihood of hyperglycemia, eye damage, heart disease, hospitalization, and other complications among people with diabetes (Clouse et al., 2003; Kovacs, Mukerji, Drash, & Iyengar, 1995; Lustman et al., 2000; Lustman & Clouse, 2005; Rosenthal, Fajardo,

Gilmore, Morley, & Naliboff, 1998). The severity of diabetes and functional impairment appears to increase the risk for depression (de Groot, Anderson, Freedland, Clouse, & Lustman, 2001; Lustman et al., 2000).

Other emotional problems and disorders, particularly anxiety and general psychological distress, also occur with higher-than-average frequency among people with diabetes. Anxiety is twice as likely in people with diabetes (Kruse, Schmitz, & Thefeld, 2004), and it is especially associated with hyperglycemia (Anderson et al., 2002). Overall, 14% of people with diabetes also have generalized anxiety disorder, and an additional 40% have elevated symptoms of anxiety (Grigsby, Anderson, Freedland, Clouse, & Lustman, 2002). In a study of almost 10,000 people in New York City, people who had been diagnosed with diabetes were twice as likely as those without diabetes to be in serious psychological distress, defined as having at least 13 symptoms of anxiety, depression, schizophrenia, and other mental disorders (McVeigh, Mostashari, & Thorpe, 2004). Although little research has examined whether psychological disorders occur at equal rates among people with diabetes of different races and ethnicities, one major study in the United States found that American Indians with diabetes had the highest rates of depression, followed by White, Hispanic, and African American patients; Asian American patients with diabetes had the lowest rates (Li, Ford, Strine, & Mokdad, 2008).

Finally, the need to focus on food and exercise continually may give rise to eating disorders in some people with diabetes. Some adolescent and young adult women with type 1 diabetes engage in what is called "insulin purging" (Rydall, Rodin, Olmsted, Devenyi, & Daneman, 1997), by which they regulate their weight by withholding insulin and thus purging themselves of food that would be stored as fat. Perhaps as a result, women with type 1 diabetes have almost twice the risk for bulimia nervosa compared with women without type 1 diabetes (Mannucci et al., 2005).

HIV/AIDS

Because the human immunodeficiency virus invades the central nervous system, numerous types of psychiatric complications can accompany HIV and AIDS (Forstein & McDaniel, 2001). HIV-associated dementia and minor cognitive-motor disorder can result from the involvement of the virus with the central nervous system. Studies have reported high prevalence rates (4%–19%) of HIV/AIDS among people with serious mental illness, but these studies lacked random samples or control groups (Lyon, 2001). The risk for suicide among people with HIV/AIDS is generally 2 times higher than average (Dannenberg, McNeil, Brundage, & Brookmeyer, 1996; Marzuk et al., 1997), although earlier studies produced dramatically larger estimates (Komiti et al., 2001)

Treatment for HIV/AIDS also can trigger psychiatric problems. For example, antiretroviral therapy can induce psychosis in some patients, which may subside once the therapy is withdrawn and antipsychotic medication is introduced (Foster, Olajide, & Everall, 2003). At the same time, antiretroviral therapy has been associated with a marked decline in cases of AIDS-related dementia (Liner, Hall, & Robertson, 2008) and with improvement of depression in people with HIV/AIDS (Low-Beer et al., 2000).

Depression and Other Mental Illness: Cause or Consequence of Chronic Illness?

Chronic illness can engender sufficient stress and anxiety to affect a person's mental health. But what about the possible influence of mental health on the etiology of chronic disease? Indeed, evidence is building that poor mental health can increase the risk for chronic illness. The research involving depression, in particular, is the strongest; studies of many diseases indicate that depression can both directly and indirectly increase the risk of certain health conditions.

Heart Disease

Studies have found that depression increases the risk of subsequent heart disease by an average 1.5 to 2 times, almost as much as smoking, which increases the risk of heart disease by 2.5 times (Lett et al., 2004; Wulsin & Singal, 2003). One of the first studies of this phenomenon, the Epidemiologic Catchment Area study, found that people with no history of heart disease and a history of major depression in 1981 were 4.5 times more likely to have had a heart attack by 1994 than those with no depression history (Pratt et al., 1996). A more recent study discerned that, among adults with no previous history of heart disease, people with depression were 2.7 times more likely than those without depression to die of heart disease within an average of 8.5 years (Surtees et al., 2008). The relationship between depression and heart disease complications may be more profound for men than for women. One study found that men with depression were 2.75 times more likely than men without depression to develop heart disease, but depression did not increase risk of heart disease for women (Hippisley-Cox, Fielding, & Pringle, 1998).

Why depression increases the risk of heart disease and heart-related complications is not known. One hypothesis asserts that behavioral consequences of depression—specifically smoking, alcohol use, or physical inactivity—and physiologic effects increase the risk of heart disease or complications (Lett et al., 2004). Depression's effects on motivation, energy, and hopefulness are known to impair compliance with treatment regimens, which can in turn lead to graver health outcomes. Physiologic effects of depression that may encourage heart problems include alterations in blood platelet activity, serotonin dysregulation, inflammation, and diseases such as diabetes, obesity, and hypertension (Lett et al., 2004). Antidepressant medications that target serotonin (fluoxetine [Prozac], sertraline [Zoloft], and other selective serotonin reuptake inhibitors) provide evidence supporting a relationship between serotonin and heart disease. At the same time, Lett and colleagues caution that factors related to both depression and heart disease need more longitudinal study before any causal relationships can be established.

Diabetes

Although we know that depression may follow a diagnosis of diabetes, depression also is associated with increased risk of acquiring diabetes (Knol et al., 2006; Mezuk, Eaton, Albrecht, & Golden, 2008). It is not clear why depression may increase the risk of diabetes. As with heart disease, one possible explanation is that depression itself leads to poor diet, lack of exercise, smoking, social isolation, and stress, all risk factors for diabetes (Barth et al., 2004; Rozanski, Blumenthal, & Kaplan, 1999). Another possibility is that depression produces biochemical changes that make an individual more susceptible to other types of illness or that depression directly affects cardiac and metabolic regulation.

Diabetes also is associated with other mental illnesses besides depression. People with schizophrenia have higher rates of impaired glucose tolerance than people in the general population, even when no antipsychotic medications that might affect physiology are taken (Ryan, Collins, & Thakore, 2003). In fact, people with schizophrenia who take antipsychotic medications are at an elevated risk for developing diabetes (Koro et al., 2002; Leslie & Rosenheck, 2004; Sacchetti et al., 2005). This relationship is particularly strong among newer antipsychotic medications, such as olanzapine (Zyprexa), risperidone (Risperdal), and quetiapine (Seroquel). One study found that 1% of people developed diabetes within three months of initiating quetiapine (Koro et al., 2002).

Weight gain, which is another side effect of the medications (Allison et al., 1999), may help explain the increased risk for diabetes. For these reasons, it is especially important that people who start taking antipsychotic medications be monitored regularly by a physician, eat low-fat and high-fiber diets, and act preventively in general. Yet schizophrenia itself may affect the metabolic system (Ryan et al., 2003), and the challenges posed by schizophrenia can make it difficult for people to exercise diligently and eat well.

HIV/AIDS

In the case of HIV/AIDS, in which transmission of the disease is preventable with behavioral measures, mental illness indirectly increases the chances of acquiring the sexually transmitted disease. Many people with serious mental illness engage in disproportionately high rates of risky behaviors that can lead to HIV infection, including unprotected sex, drug use involving needles, and prostitution (Meade & Sikkema, 2005). Feelings of hopelessness and lethargy produced by depression can inspire risky sexual behavior. In a study of 460 gay men, those with dysthymic disorder were 2.4 times more likely than those without any depressive disorder to have engaged in unprotected anal intercourse with a casual partner in the previous 6 months (Rogers et al., 2003). Cognitive problems, particularly those associated with schizophrenia, can hinder a person's understanding of the magnitude of HIV/AIDS and methods for prevention (Lyon, 2001).

Even after an individual contracts HIV, depression is associated with graver outcomes. A 7-year study of 1,716 women with HIV found that the proportion of women with chronic symptoms of depression who died of AIDS was double that of those with few or intermittent depression symptoms (Cook et al., 2004).

Mental Illness and Adherence to Treatment Regimens

Not surprisingly, depression, anxiety, schizophrenia, substance use disorders, and other types of mental disorders can negatively affect a person's compliance with treatment recommendations. Depression itself is perhaps the largest culprit (DiMatteo, Lepper, & Croghan, 2000). The nature of depression lessens motivation, concentration, energy, and hopefulness. These problems make it difficult to exercise, eat healthfully, test blood sugar regularly, and maintain medications (Ciechanowski et al., 2000; Rubin, Ciechanowski, Egede, Lin, & Lustman, 2004).

Depression hinders compliance with treatment for heart disease, diabetes, and HIV/AIDS (Ciechanowski et al., 2000; DiMatteo et al., 2000; Starace et al., 2002). In a study of patients with cardiac problems, those with depression were less likely, than those without depression, to take their medications regularly, to quit smoking, to attend cardiac rehabilitation appointments, and to exercise regularly (Kronish et al., 2006). Among adults with depression and HIV, those who took antidepressants were more likely to comply with antiretroviral therapy (Yun, Maravi, Kobayashi, Barton, & Davidson, 2005). Illicit drug use also influences adherence. In a study of 85 current and former drug users infected with HIV, only 27% of cocaine users adhered to their medication regimen compared to 68% of people who reported no cocaine use during the six-month study (Arnsten et al., 2002). Although depression and other mental illnesses may disturb a person's motivation and ability to follow a medical regimen of diet, exercise, and medication, Rubin and Peyrot (2001) stress that many people with depression do adhere to their treatment plan and, likewise, many people who do not follow their medical regimen are not depressed.

Protective Factors and Mental Health in Chronic Illness

Not everybody with a chronic illness develops a mental disorder. Most people with heart disease, diabetes, or HIV/AIDS do *not* merit a diagnosis of major depression, despite managing constant stress and fears related to their illness.

What helps people cope with their chronic illness without experiencing depression, anxiety, or other mental disorder? Studies generally find that marriage and higher levels of education, income, and social support are associated with fewer psychiatric complications with diabetes (Blazer, Moody-Ayers, Craft-Morgan, & Burchett, 2002; McVeigh et al., 2004; Peyrot & Rubin, 1997). In cases of diabetes, well-controlled blood sugar is associated with a decreased risk for depression

(Rubin & Peyrot, 2001), as are lower weight, insulin treatment, and older age (Katon et al., 2004). White Americans with diabetes are less likely to experience major or minor depression than African Americans (Blazer et al., 2002) and other people of color who have diabetes (Katon et al., 2004).

It is hard to know whether depression or poor health habits (such as control of blood sugar) come first because of the reciprocal effect they have on each other. This is also true of exercise, diet, and sleep, which can help prevent depression but also can be dramatically affected by depression. As Rubin and Peyrot (2001) note, "The helplessness and hopelessness often associated with depression may contribute to a vicious cycle of poor self-management, worse glycemic control, and exacerbation of depression" (p. 461). A synergistic effect seems to exist when a person has comorbid physical and mental illnesses: The worse the physical or psychosocial situation, the worse the consequences for one's mental health. Psychological, economic, social, and physical health problems are likely to interact with each other in what can be either a vicious or a productive cycle, depending on the circumstances.

Interventions to Improve Mental Health in People With Chronic Disease

Social workers have numerous interventions available to help people with mental health problems. Medical crisis counseling, psychotherapy, and relaxation training are briefly described here. Antidepressant medication is omitted because social workers do not prescribe medications but rather work with psychiatrists and other physicians who prescribe them. However, it is helpful for social workers to be aware of the benefits and risks of psychiatric medications so that they can educate and advocate for their patients. For example, antidepressants can reduce depression effectively but also carry risks, including increased risk for suicidal behavior in children, adolescents, and young adults (Barbui, Esposito, & Cipriani, 2009).

Medical Crisis Counseling

Medical crisis counseling is a short-term intervention that centers on fears, anxieties, disabilities, and other problems posed by a person's medical condition (Pollin, 1995). The premise of medical crisis counseling is that eight fears impede a person's ability to cope with illness: loss of control, loss of self-image, dependency, stigma, abandonment, expressing anger, isolation, and death. The counseling typically lasts for only 10 or fewer sessions, and an active, problem-solving approach is stressed. The role of the social worker or other therapist "is that of a facilitator, problem-solver, health educator, and coach to the patient with a solution-focused orientation" (Pollin, 1995, p. 53). The ultimate therapeutic goal is to help people with illness feel some sense of control over their situation and, in turn, cope more effectively. A small, randomized controlled trial indicated that crisis counseling may help increase social support for patients with diabetes, heart disease, and other conditions without increasing costs (Koocher, Curtiss, Pollin, & Patton, 2001).

Psychotherapy

Various studies attest to psychotherapy's effectiveness in general (Nathan & Gorman, 2007), but evidence is mixed regarding psychotherapy and people with specific illnesses. Psychotherapy may vary by orientation (e.g., cognitive-behavioral or psychodynamic), mode (individual or group), or focus (cognitive distortions, grief, or stress).

Cognitive-behavioral therapy has reduced depression effectively (Petrak & Herpertz, 2009; Snoek et al., 2008) and improved glycemic control (Ismail, Winkley, & Rabe-Hesketh, 2004) among people with type 2 diabetes. Rubin and Peyrot (2001) propose that interpersonal psychotherapy also would benefit people with diabetes because so much of the illness's management requires effectively interacting with other people. In one of the first studies to examine stress-reduction training and heart disease outcome, men who had a heart attack and received stress-reduction training had lower fatality rates than those with no psychological intervention (Frasure-Smith & Prince, 1985). In addition, psychotherapy delivered over the telephone has demonstrated positive results; in a randomized controlled trial with cardiac patients, patients who received six sessions of telephone therapy reported less depression and anxiety than those who did not receive the intervention (McLaughlin et al., 2005).

Not all studies of psychotherapy effectiveness yield positive results. An intervention including group and individual psychotherapy failed to reduce rates of depression, recurrence of heart attack, or death rates among 2,328 people who had a recent heart attack (Jones & West, 2004). A large study of individual and group cognitive-behavioral therapy for adults with depression and a recent heart attack showed that the intervention was associated with reduced depression and increased social support. However, within the average follow-up period of 29 months, 1 in 4 people had died regardless of whether they received psychotherapy (Berkman et al., 2003). More research is needed into the effectiveness of different types, modes, and foci of psychotherapy, specifically for people with chronic illness.

Relaxation Training

Relaxation techniques have generated considerable evidence of effectiveness among people with chronic health conditions. In his classic book *The Relaxation Response,* Benson (1976) showed that meditating for 10 to 20 minutes a day can produce physiologic changes, such as lower blood pressure and heart rate. Relaxation techniques are associated with improved blood glucose control among people with diabetes (McGinnis, McGrady, Cox, & Grower-Dowling, 2005). Deep relaxation techniques can help children and adolescents with type 1 diabetes feel less fear and anxiety when receiving injections and other stressful medical procedures (Sewell, 2004).

Numerous types of relaxation training exist. In meditation, a person sits still while concentrating on counting, repeating a phrase, or visualizing an object. In progressive muscle relaxation, a person breathes deeply and relaxes specific muscle groups one at a time, starting either from the head and going down to the feet or vice versa. In hypnotherapy, also called deep relaxation (Sewell, 2004), another person induces relaxation in the patient by directing the patient to focus attention on an object or a visualization. For detailed instructions on how to use relaxation techniques with clients, see Bernstein, Borkovec, and Hazlett-Stevens (2000) or Payne and Donaghy (2010).

CONCLUSION

Social workers in all types of health-care settings frequently work with people who have heart disease, diabetes, HIV/AIDS, or some other chronic disease. Chronic disease brings ongoing challenges to patients, particularly in the form of issues with mental health, treatment adherence, and gathering information to better cope with ongoing changes associated with the disease. Chronic illness may lead to mental health problems, such as depression and anxiety, which in turn can exacerbate physical complications of chronic illness. Mental health problems such as depression also can negatively affect a patient's ability to follow through with medication, diet, and other components of the medical regimen. Adherence to medical treatment is of utmost importance for people with chronic illness. How patients live on a daily basis—whether they eat, exercise, take medication regularly, or act preventively—can profoundly impact the course and outcome of their illness.

Social workers have multiple roles in their work with chronically ill patients: adherence counselor, mental health specialist, and educator. Each of these roles demands that social workers are knowledgeable about the patients' diseases and treatments in addition to their unique psychosocial issues. Perspectives on nonadherence have changed from one of blame to one of choice, whereby the practitioner and patient must take responsibility for renegotiating the agreed-on treatment.

Future trends in health care may influence the roles that social workers assume in health-care settings and in the community. For example, increased rates of obesity and diabetes among individuals of all age groups, even children and adolescents, will strengthen social work's role in promoting lifestyle changes and adherence. The relatively new emphasis on prevention of heart disease, diabetes, and HIV/AIDS will enhance social workers educational role in community-based public health settings, such as schools, primary care clinics, and mental health and social service agencies. Finally, the continued disparities in health found between people of color and White Americans will highlight the need for social workers' expertise in sociocultural and family factors that influence health outcomes. Knowledge of heart disease, diabetes, and HIV/AIDS is critical for social workers who work with growing numbers of individuals who are actively preventing and managing these chronic diseases.

SUGGESTED LEARNING EXERCISES

Read a book about an individual's struggle to cope or adapt to a chronic disease. The book can be a personal account (autobiographical) or written by someone else.

Suggested Learning Exercise 20.1

In a case study presentation or paper, analyze the individual's ability to manage the disease using the adherence counseling model described in this chapter. First, describe the disease by its etiology, symptoms, treatment, and progression. Then analyze how various factors, such as family social support, lifestyle, cultural factors, mental health status, emotional reaction to the diagnosis, health beliefs, and treatment satisfaction, may affect the character's ability to manage the disease and adhere to treatment. Based on this assessment, how might a social worker intervene with the client and family to facilitate behavioral changes, activate social support, and help them cope more effectively?

Suggested Learning Exercise 20.2

In pairs, assume the role of the individual from the book that you read, and role play by taking turns conducting a social work assessment with one other. Once you have completed this assessment, individuals can take turns completing a social work intervention plan based on strengths and challenges identified in the role-plays. After the work done in pairs, individuals can share information and feedback from the role-play experience with the larger group.

Suggested Learning Exercise 20.3

Considering the information in this chapter, along with information from Chapter 15 ("Social Work With Children and Adolescents With Health Conditions") and Chapter 16 ("Social Work With Older Adults in Health-Care Settings") from this book, have small- or large-group discussions about the unique (1) psychosocial barriers and (2) social work intervention issues related to chronic illnesses, such as diabetes, HIV/AIDS, and heart disease among children, adolescents, and older adults. Among each of these populations, what may be unique issues related to adhering to medical recommendations?

REFERENCES

Ali, S., Stone, M. A., Peters, J. L., Davies, M. J., & Khunti, K. (2006). The prevalence of co-morbid depression in adults with type 2 diabetes: A systematic review and meta-analysis. *Diabetic Medicine, 23,* 1165–1173.

Allison, D. B., Mentore, J. L., Heo, M., Chandler, L. P., Cappelleri, J. C., Infante, M. C., & Weiden, P. J. (1999). Antipsychotic-induced weight gain: A comprehensive research synthesis. *American Journal of Psychiatry, 156,* 1686–1696.

Altica, F. L., Mostashari, F., & Friedland, G. H. (2001). Trust and acceptance of and adherence to antiviral therapy. *Journal of Acquired Immune Deficiency Syndromes, 28,* 47–58.

American Diabetes Association. (2004). Diagnosis and classification of diabetes mellitus. *Diabetes Care, 27,* S5–S10.

American Heart Association. (2002). *Heart disease and stroke statistics—2003 update.* Dallas, TX: Author.

Amir, S., Rabin, C., & Galatzer, A. (1990). Cognitive and behavioral determinants of compliance in diabetics. *Health & Social Work, 15,* 144–151.

Andersen, R., Bozzette, S., Shapiro, M., St. Clair, P., Morton, S., Crystal, S.,…Cunningham, W. (2000). Access of vulnerable groups to antiretroviral therapy among persons in care for HIV disease in the United States. *Health Services Research, 2,* 389–416.

Anderson, B. J., Auslander, W. F., Jung, K. G., Miller, J. P., & Santiago, J. V. (1990). Assessing family sharing of diabetes responsibilities. *Journal of Pediatric Psychology, 15,* 477–492.

Anderson, B. J., Brackett, J., Ho, J., & Laffel, L. M. (1999). An office-based intervention to maintain parent-adolescent teamwork in diabetes management: Impact on parental involvement, family conflict, and subsequent glycemic control. *Diabetes Care, 22,* 713–721.

Anderson, R. J., Freedland, K. E., Clouse, R. E., & Lustman, P. J. (2001). The prevalence of comorbid depression in adults with diabetes: A meta-analysis. *Diabetes Care, 24,* 1069–1078.

Anderson, R. J., Grigsby, A. B., Freedland, K. E., de Groot, M., McGill, J. B., & Clouse, R. E. (2002). Anxiety and poor glycemic control: A meta-analytic review of the literature. *International Journal of Psychiatry in Medicine, 32,* 235–247.

Anding, J. D., Kubena, K. S., McIntosh, W. A., & O'Brien, B. (1996). Blood lipids, cardiovascular fitness, obesity, and blood pressure: Presence of potential coronary heart disease risk factors in adolescents. *Journal of the American Dietetic Association, 96*(3), 238–242.

Arias, E., Anderson, R. N., Kung, H., Murphy, S. L., & Kochanek, K. D. (2003). Deaths: Final data for 2001. *National Vital Statistics Reports, 52,* 1–116.

Arnsten, J. H., Demas, P. A., Grant, R. W., Gourevitch, M. N., Farzadegan, H., Howard, A. A., & Schoenbaum, E. E. (2002). Impact of active drug use on antiretroviral therapy adherence and viral suppression in HIV-infected drug users. *Journal of General Internal Medicine, 17,* 377–381.

Auslander, W. F. (1993). Brief family interventions to improve family communication and cooperation regarding diabetes management. *Spectrum, 6*(5), 330–333.

Auslander, W., Anderson, B. J., Bubb, J., Jung, K. G., & Santiago, J. V. (1990). Risk factors to health in diabetic children: A prospective study from diagnosis. *Health & Social Work, 15,* 133–142.

Auslander, W., Bubb, J., Peelle, A., & Rogge, M. (1989, August). *Intervention to improve family role sharing in high risk diabetic adolescents.* Paper presented at the annual meeting of the American Association of Diabetes Educators, Seattle, WA.

Auslander, W. F., Bubb, J., Rogge, M., & Santiago, J. V. (1993). Family stress and resources: Potential areas of intervention in recently diagnosed children with diabetes. *Health & Social Work, 18,* 101–113.

Auslander, W. F., Thompson, S., Dreitzer, D., White, N., & Santiago, J. V. (1997). Disparity in glycemic control and adherence between African American and Caucasian youths with diabetes: Family and community contexts. *Diabetes Care, 20*(10), 1569–1575.

Barbui, C., Esposito, E., & Cipriani, A. (2009). Selective serotonin reuptake inhibitors and risk of suicide: A systematic review of observational studies. *Canadian Medical Association Journal, 180,* 291–297.

Barrett-Connor, E. (2003). An epidemiologist looks at hormones and heart disease in women. *Journal of Clinical Endocrinology and Metabolism, 88,* 4031–4042.

Barth, J., Schumacher, M., & Herrmann-Lingen, C. (2004). Depression as a risk factor for mortality in patients with coronary heart disease: A meta-analysis. *Psychosomatic Medicine, 66,* 802–813.

Becker, M. H. (1974). The health belief model and personal health behavior. *Health Education Monographs, 2.*

Becker, M. H., & Maiman, L. A. (1980). Strategies for enhancing patient compliance. *Journal of Community Health, 6,* 113–135.

Benson, H. (1976). *The relaxation response.* New York, NY: HarperTorch.

Berkman, L. F., Blumenthal, J., Burg, M., Carney, R. M., Catellier, D., Cowan, M. J.,…Enhancing Recovery in Coronary Heart Disease Patients Investigators. (2003). Effects of treating depression and low perceived social support on clinical events after myocardial infarction: The Enhancing Recovery in Coronary Heart Disease Patients (ENRICHD) randomized trial. *JAMA, 289,* 3106–3116.

Bernstein, D. A., Borkovec, T. D., & Hazlett-Stevens, H. (2000). *New directions in progressive relaxation: A guidebook for helping professionals.* Westport, CT: Praeger.

Bertakis, K. D. (1977). The communication of information from physician to patient: A method for increasing patient retention and satisfaction. *Journal of Family Practice, 5*(2), 217–222.

Bhaskaran K., Hamouda, O., Sannes, M., Boufassa, F., Johnson, A. M., Lambert, P. C., & Porter, K. (2008). Changes in the risk of death after HIV seroconversion compared with mortality in the general population. *JAMA, 300,* 51–59.

Black, S. A. (2002). Diabetes, diversity, and disparity: What do we do with the evidence? *American Journal of Public Health, 92,* 543–548.

Blazer, D. G., Moody-Ayers, S., Craft-Morgan, J., & Burchett, B. (2002). Depression in diabetes and obesity: Racial/ethnic/gender issues in older adults. *Journal of Psychosomatic Research, 53,* 913–916.

Bolen, J. C., Rhodes, L., Powell-Griner, E. E., Bland, S. D., & Holtzman, D. (2000). State-specific prevalence of selected health behaviors, by race and ethnicity: Behavioral Risk Factor Surveillance System, 1997. *Morbidity and Mortality Weekly Report, 49,* 1–60.

Bubb, J., Auslander, W. F., & Manthei, D. (1989, November). *A model of adherence counseling for chronically ill patients.* Paper presented at the annual meeting of the National Association of Social Workers, San Francisco, CA.

Center for Infectious Diseases. (1985). Acquired immunodeficiency syndrome (AIDS) weekly surveillance report—United States. Retrieved from www.cdc.gov/hiv/stats/surveillance85.pdf

Centers for Disease Control and Prevention. (1999a). Achievements in public health, 1900–1999: Control of infectious diseases. *Morbidity and Mortality Weekly Report, 48,* 621–629.

Centers for Disease Control and Prevention. (1999b). Ten great public health achievements—United States, 1900–1999. *Morbidity and Mortality Weekly Report, 48,* 241–243.

Centers for Disease Control and Prevention. (2000). *Data on health disparities.* Washington, DC: National Center for Health Statistics.

Centers for Disease Control and Prevention. (2001). *HIV/AIDS Surveillance Report* (13th ed., Vol. 2). Atlanta, GA: Author.

Centers for Disease Control and Prevention. (2004a) *National diabetes fact sheet: General information and national estimates on diabetes in the United States, 2003.* Rev. ed. Atlanta, GA: U.S. Department of Health and Human Services, Centers for Disease Control and Prevention. Retrieved from www.cdc.gov/diabetes/pubs/pdf/ndfs_2003.pdf

Centers for Disease Control and Prevention. (2006). QuickStats: Number of persons with diagnosed diabetes and number of ambulatory care visits related to diabetes: United States, 1997–2004. *Morbidity and Mortality Weekly Report, 55,* 825.

Centers for Disease Control and Prevention. (2010a). HIV surveillance report, 2008, vol. 20. Retrieved from www.cdc.gov/hiv/topics/surveillance/resources/reports

Centers for Disease Control and Prevention. (2010b). WISQARS leading cause of death reports: 1999–2007. Retrieved from http://webappa.cdc.gov/sasweb/ncipc/leadcaus10.html

Chesney, M. (2003). Adherence to HAART regimens. *AIDS Patient Care and STDs, 17,* 169–177.

Ciechanowski, P. S., Katon, W. J., & Russo, J. E. (2000). Depression and diabetes: Impact of depressive symptoms on adherence, function, and costs. *Archives of Internal Medicine, 160,* 3278–3285.

Clouse, R. E., Lustman, P. J., Freedland, K. E., Griffith, L. S., McGill, J. B., & Carney, R. M. (2003). Depression and coronary heart disease in women with diabetes. *Psychosomatic Medicine, 65,* 376–383.

Cohen, S. M. (2009). Concept analysis of adherence in the context of cardiovascular risk reduction. *Nursing Forum, 44*(1), 25–36.

Conway, B. (2007). The role of adherence to antiretroviral therapy in the management of HIV infection. *Journal of Acquired Immune Deficiency Syndromes, 45,* S14–S18.

Cook, J. A., Grey, D., Burke, J., Cohen, M. H., Gurtman, A. C., Richardson, J. L.,…Hessol, N. A. (2004). Depressive symptoms and AIDS-related mortality among a multisite cohort of HIV-positive women. *American Journal of Public Health, 94,* 1133–1140.

Cowie, C. C., Rust, K. F., Byrd-Holt, D., Eberhardt, M. S., Saydah, S., Geiss, L. S.,…Gregg, E. W. (2003). Prevalence of diabetes and impaired fasting glucose in adults: United States, 1999–2000. *Morbidity and Mortality Weekly Report, 52,* 833–837.

Dannenberg, A. L., McNeil, J. G., Brundage, J. F., & Brookmeyer, R. (1996). Suicide and HIV infection: Mortality follow-up of 4147 HIV seropositive military service applicants. *JAMA, 276,* 1743–1746.

Deeks, S. G., Smith, M., Holodniy, M., & Kahn, J. O. (1997). HIV-1 protease inhibitors: A review for clinicians. *JAMA, 277,* 145–153.

de Groot, M., Anderson, R., Freedland, K. E., Clouse, R. E., & Lustman, P. J. (2001). Association of depression and diabetes complications: A meta-analysis. *Psychosomatic Medicine, 63,* 619–630.

DiMatteo, M. R. (2004). Variations in patients' adherence to medical recommendations. *Medical Care, 42,* 200–209.

DiMatteo, M. R., Haskard, K. B., & Williams, S. L. (2007). Health beliefs, disease severity, and patient adherence: A meta-analysis. *Medical Care, 45*(6), 521–528.

DiMatteo, M. R., Lepper, H. S., & Croghan, T. W. (2000). Depression is a risk factor for noncompliance with medical treatment: Meta-analysis of the effects of anxiety and depression on patient adherence. *Archives of Internal Medicine, 160,* 2101–2107.

Elford, J. (2006). Changing patterns of sexual behaviour in the era of highly active antiretroviral therapy. *Current Opinion in Infectious Diseases, 19,* 26–32.

Ferketich, A. K., Schwartzbaum, J. A., Frid, D. J., & Moeschberger, M. L. (2000). Depression as an antecedent to heart disease among women and men in the NHANES I study. *Archives of Internal Medicine, 160,* 1261–1268.

Fleming, P. L., Wortley, P. M., Karon, J. M., DeCock, K. M., & Janssen, R. S. (2000). Tracking the HIV epidemic: Current issues, future challenges. *American Journal of Public Health, 90,* 1037–1041.

Forstein, M., & McDaniel, J. S. (2001). Medical overview of HIV infection and AIDS. *Psychiatric Annals, 31,* 16–20.

Foster, R., Olajide, D., & Everall, I. (2003). Antiretroviral therapy-induced psychosis: Case report and brief review of the literature. *HIV Medicine, 4,* 139–144.

Fraenkel, L., & McGraw, S. (2007). What are the essential elements to enable patient participation in medical decision making? *Society of General Internal Medicine, 22,* 614–619.

Frain, M. P., Bishop, M., Tschopp, M. K., Ferrin, M. J., & Frain, J. (2009). Adherence to medical regimens: Understanding the effects of cognitive appraisal, quality of life, and perceived family resiliency. *Rehabilitation Counseling Bulletin, 52,* 237–250.

Frasure-Smith, N., & Prince, R. (1985). The ischemic heart disease life stress monitoring program: Impact on mortality. *Psychosomatic Medicine, 47,* 431–445.

Garcia, P. R., & Cote, J. K. (2003). Factors affecting adherence to antiretroviral therapy in people living with HIV/AIDS. *Journal of the Association of Nurses in AIDS Care, 14*(4), 37–45.

Glasgow, R. E., & Toobert, D. J. (1988). Social environment and regimen adherence among type II diabetic patients. *Diabetes Care, 11,* 377–386.

Glasgow, R. E., Wilson, W., & McCaul, K. D. (1985). Regimen adherence: A problematic construct in diabetes research. *Diabetes Care, 8,* 300–301.

Gonzalez, J. S., Penedo, F. J., Antoni, M. H., Duran, R. E., Fernandez, M. I., McPherson-Baker, S.,…Schneiderman, N. (2004). Social support, positive states of mind, and HIV treatment adherence in men and women living with HIV/AIDS. *Health Psychology, 23,* 413–418.

Grigsby, A. B., Anderson, R. J., Freedland, K. E., Clouse, R. E., & Lustman, P. J. (2002). Prevalence of anxiety in adults with diabetes: A systematic review. *Journal of Psychosomatic Research, 53,* 1053–1060.

Guyer, B., Freedman, M. A., Strobino, D. M., & Sondik, E. J. (2000). Annual summary of vital statistics: Trends in the health of Americans during the twentieth century. *Pediatrics, 106,* 1307–1317.

Hall, J. A., Roter, D. L., & Katz, N. R. (1988). Meta-analysis of correlates of provider behavior in medical encounters. *Medical Care, 26,* 657–675.

Hamburg, B. A., & Inoff, G. E. (1983). Coping with predictable crises of diabetes. *Diabetes Care, 6,* 409–416.

Hanson, C. L., De Guire, M. J., Schinkel, A. M., & Kolterman, O. G. (1995). Empirical validation for a family-centered model of care. *Diabetes Care, 18,* 1347–1356.

Heaney, C. A., & Israel, B. A. (1997). Social networks and social support. In K. Glanz, F. M. Lewis, & B. K. Rimer (Eds.), *Health behavior and health education* (pp. 179–205). San Francisco, CA: Jossey Bass.

Heisler, M. (2008). Actively engaging patients in treatment decision making and monitoring as a strategy to improve hypertension outcomes in diabetes mellitus. *Circulation, 117,* 1355–1357.

Herek, G. M., & Glunt, E. K. (1988). An epidemic of stigma: Public reactions to AIDS. *American Psychologist, 43,* 886–891.

Herskowitz, D. R., Jacobson, A. M., Cole, C., Hauser, S. T., Wolfsdorf, J. I., Willett, J. B.,…Wertlieb, D.

(1995). Psychosocial predictors of acute complications of diabetes in youth. *Diabetic Medicine, 12,* 612–618.

Hippisley-Cox, J., Fielding, K., & Pringle, M. (1998). Depression as a risk factor for ischaemic heart disease in men: Population based case-control study. *British Medical Journal, 316,* 1714–1719.

Hughes, D., & Kleespies, P. (2001). Suicide in the medically ill. *Suicide and Life-Threatening Behavior, 31*(Suppl.), S48–S59.

Ismail, K., Winkley, K., & Rabe-Hesketh, S. (2004). Systematic review and meta-analysis of randomized controlled trials of psychological interventions to improve glycaemic control in patients with type 2 diabetes. *Lancet, 363,* 1589–1597.

Jacobson, A. M., Hauser, S. T., Lavori, P., Wolfsdorf, J. I., Herskowitz, R. D., Milley, J. E.,...Stein, J. (1990). Adherence among children and adolescents with insulin-dependent diabetes mellitus over a 4-year longitudinal follow-up: Pt. 1. The influence of patient coping and adjustment. *Journal of Pediatric Psychology, 15,* 511–526.

Jacobson, L. P., Kirby, A. J., Polk, S., Phair, J. P., Besley, D. R., Saah, A. J.,...Schrager, L. K. (1993). Changes in survival time after acquired immunodeficiency syndrome (AIDS): 1984–1991. *American Journal of Epidemiology, 138,* 952–964.

Johnson, S. B., Perwien, A. R., & Silverstein, J. H. (2000). Response to hypo- and hyperglycemia in adolescents with type 1 diabetes. *Journal of Pediatric Psychology, 25,* 171–178.

Joint United Nations Programme on HIV/AIDS. (2004). *2004 report on the global AIDS epidemic: 4th global report.* Geneva, Switzerland: Author. Retrieved from www.unaids.org

Joint United Nations Programme on HIV/AIDS. (2009). *AIDS epidemic update: November 2009.* Geneva, Switzerland: Author. Retrieved from http://data.unaids .org/pub/Report/2009/JC1700_Epi_Update_2009 _en.pdf

Jones, D. A., & West, R. R. (2004). Psychological rehabilitation after myocardial infarction: Multicentre randomised controlled trial. *British Medical Journal, 313,* 1517–1521.

Jones, J. M., Lawson, M. L., Daneman, D., Olmsted, M. P., & Rodin, G. (2000). Eating disorders in adolescent females with and without type 1 diabetes: cross-sectional study. *British Medical Journal, 320,* 1563–1566.

Karon, J. M., Fleming, P. L., Steketee, R. W., & DeCock, K. M. (2001). HIV in the United States at the turn of the century: An epidemic in transition. *American Journal of Public Health, 91,* 1060–1068.

Katon, W., Von Korff, M., Ciechanowski, P., Russo, J., Lin, E., Simon, G.,...Young, B. (2004). Behavioral and clinical factors associated with depression among individuals with diabetes. *Diabetes Care, 27,* 914–920.

Kim, C., Newton, K. M., & Knopp, R. H. (2002). Gestational diabetes and the incidence of type 2 diabetes: A systematic review. *Diabetes Care, 25,* 1861–1868.

Kindig, D. A., Nielsen-Bohlman, L., & Panzer, A. (Eds.) (2004). *Health literacy: A prescription to end confusion.* Washington DC: National Academy Press.

Kirsch, I., Jungeblut, A., Jenkins, L., & Kolstad, L. (1993). *Adult literacy in America: A first look at the results of the National Adult Literacy Survey.* Washington, DC: National Center for Education Statistics, U.S. Department of Education.

Knol, M. J., Twisk, J. W., Beekman, A. T., Heine, R. J., Snoek, F. J., & Pouwer, F. (2006). Depression as a risk factor for the onset of type 2 diabetes mellitus: A meta-analysis. *Diabetologia, 49,* 837–845.

Knowler, W. C., Saad, M. F., Pettitt, D. J., Nelson, R. G., & Bennett, P. H. (1993). Determinants of diabetes mellitus in the Pima Indians. *Diabetes Care, 16,* 216–227.

Komiti, A., Judd, F., Grech, P., Mijch, A., Hoy, J., Lloyd, J. H., & Street, A. (2001). Suicidal behavior in people with HIV/AIDS: A review. *Australian and New Zealand Journal of Psychiatry, 35,* 747–757.

Koocher, G. P., Curtiss, E. K., Pollin, I. S., & Patton, K. E. (2001). Medical crisis counseling in a health maintenance organization: Preventive intervention. *Professional Psychology: Research and Practice, 32,* 52–58.

Koro, C. E., Fedder, D. O., L'Italien, G. J., Weiss, S. S., Magder, L. S., Kreyenbuhl, J.,...Buchanan, R. W. (2002). Assessment of independent effect of olanzapine and risperidone on risk of diabetes among patients with schizophrenia: Population based nested case-control study. *British Medical Journal, 325,* 243–251.

Kovacs, M., Goldston, D., Obrosky, D. S., & Bonar, L. K. (1997). Psychiatric disorders in youths with IDDM: Rates and risk factors. *Diabetes Care, 20,* 36–44.

Kovacs, M., Mukerji, P., Drash, A., & Iyengar, S. (1995). Biomedical and psychiatric risk factors for retinopathy among children with IDDM. *Diabetes Care, 18,* 1592–1599.

Kronish, I. M., Rieckmann, N., Halm, E. A., Shimbo, D., Vorchheimer, D., Haas, D. C., & Davidson, K. W. (2006). Persistent depression affects adherence to secondary prevention behaviors after acute coronary syndromes. *Journal of General Internal Medicine, 21,* 1178–1883.

Kruse, J., Schmitz, N., & Thefeld, W. (2004). On the association between diabetes and mental disorders in a community sample: Results from the German National Health Interview and Examination Survey. *Diabetes Care, 26,* 1841–1846.

Lamptey, P. R. (2002). Reducing heterosexual transmission of HIV in poor countries. *British Medical Journal, 324,* 207–211.

Lee, E. T., Howard, B. V., Go, O., Savage, P. J., Fabsitz, R. R., Robbins, D. C., & Welty, T. K. (2000). Prevalence of undiagnosed diabetes in three American Indian populations: The Strong Heart Study. *Diabetes Care, 23,* 181–186.

Leslie, D. L., & Rosenheck, R. A. (2004). Incidence of newly diagnosed diabetes attributable to atypical antipsychotic medications. *American Journal of Psychiatry, 161,* 1709–1711.

Lett, H. S., Blumenthal, J. A., Babyak, M. A., Sherwood, A., Strauman, T., Robins, C., & Newman, M. F. (2004). Depression as a risk factor for coronary artery disease: Evidence, mechanisms, and treatment. *Psychosomatic Medicine, 66,* 305–315.

Ley, P. (1982). Giving information to patients. In J. R. Eiser (Ed.), *Social psychology and behavioral science* (pp. 339–373). Hoboken, NJ: John Wiley & Sons.

Li, C., Ford, E. S., Strine, T. W., & Mokdad, A. H. (2008). Prevalence of depression among U.S. adults with diabetes: Findings from the 2006 behavioral risk factor surveillance system. *Diabetes Care, 31,* 105–107.

Liner, K. J., Hall, C. D., & Robertson, K. R. (2008). Effects of antiretroviral therapy on cognitive impairment. *Current HIV/AIDS Reports, 5,* 64–71.

Lorenz, R. A., Bubb, J., Davis, D., Jacobson, A., Jannasch, K., Kramer, J.,…Schlundt, D. (1996). Changing behavior. *Diabetes Care, 19,* 648–652.

Low-Beer, S., Chan, K., Yip, B., Wood, E., Montaner, J. S., O'Shaughnessy, M. V., & Hogg, R. S. (2000). Depressive symptoms decline among persons on HIV protease inhibitors. *Journal of Acquired Immune Deficiency Syndromes, 23,* 295–301.

Lustman, P. J., Anderson, R. J., Freedland, K. E., de Groot, M. K., Carney, R. M., & Crouse, R. E. (2000). Depression and poor glycemic control: A meta-analytic review of the literature. *Diabetes Care, 23,* 934–942.

Lustman, P. J., & Clouse, R. E. (2005). Depression in diabetic patients: The relationship between mood and glycemic control. *Journal of Diabetes Complications, 19,* 113–122.

Lyon, D. E. (2001). Human immunodeficiency virus (HIV) disease in persons with severe mental illness. *Issues in Mental Health Nursing, 22,* 109–119.

Mainous, A. G., Baker, R., Koopman, R. J., Saxena, S., Diaz, V. A., Everett, C. J., & Majeed, A. (2007). Impact of the population at risk of diabetes on projections of diabetes burden in the United States: An epidemic on the way. *Diabetologia, 50,* 934–940.

Mannucci, E., Rotella, F., Ricca, V., Moretti, S., Placidi, G. F., & Rotella, C. M. (2005). Eating disorders in patients with type 1 diabetes: A meta-analysis. *Journal of Endocrinological Investigation, 28,* 417–419.

Manson, J. E., Allison, M. A., Rossouw, J. E., Carr, J., Langer, R. D., Hsia, J.,…WHI and WHI-CACS Investigators. (2007). Estrogen therapy and coronary-artery calcification. *New England Journal of Medicine, 356,* 2591–2602.

Manson, J. E., Hsia, J., Johnson, K. C., Rossouw, J. E., Assaf, A. R., Lasser, N. L.,…Women's Health Initiative Investigators. (2003). Estrogen plus progestin and the risk of coronary heart disease. *New England Journal of Medicine, 349,* 523–534.

Marlatt, G. A., & Gordon, J. R. (1985). *Relapse prevention: Maintenance strategies for addictive behavior change.* New York, NY: Guilford Press.

Marzuk, P. M., Tardiff, K., Leon, A. C., Hirsch, C. S., Hartwell, N., Portera, L., & Iqbal, M. I. (1997). HIV seroprevalence among suicide victims in New York City, 1991–1993. *American Journal of Psychiatry, 154,* 1720–1725.

McGinnis, R. A., McGrady, A., Cox, S. A., & Grower-Dowling, K. A. (2005). Biofeedback-assisted relaxation in type 2 diabetes. *Diabetes Care, 28,* 2145–2149.

McLaughlin, T. J., Aupont, O., Bambauer, K. Z., Stone, P., Mullan, M. G., Colagiovanni, J.,…Locke, S. E. (2005). Improving psychologic adjustment to chronic illness in cardiac patients: The role of depression and anxiety. *Journal of General Internal Medicine, 20,* 1084–1090.

McVeigh, K. H., Mostashari, F., & Thorpe, L. E. (2004). Serious psychological distress among person with diabetes—New York City, 2003. *Morbidity and Mortality Weekly Report, 53,* 1089–1090.

Meade, C. S., & Sikkema, K. J. (2005). HIV risk behavior among adults with severe mental illness: A systematic review. *Clinical Psychology Review, 25,* 433–457.

Meichenbaum, D., & Turk, D. C. (1987). *Facilitating treatment adherence: A practitioner's guidebook.* New York, NY: Plenum Press.

Mezuk, B., Eaton, W. W., Albrecht, S., & Golden, S. H. (2008). Depression and type 2 diabetes over the lifespan. *Diabetes Care, 31,* 2383–2390.

Mokdad, A. H., Ford, E. S., Bowman, B. A., Nelson, D. E., Engelgau, M. M., Vinicor, F., & Marks, J. S. (2000). Diabetes trends in the United States: 1990 to 1998. *Diabetes Care, 23,* 1278–1283.

Nathan, P. E., & Gorman, J. M. (2007). *A guide to treatments that work* (3rd ed.). Oxford, UK: Oxford University Press.

National Center for Health Statistics. (2010). *Health, United States, 2009: With special feature on medical technology.* Hyattsville, MD: Author. Retrieved from www.cdc.gov/nchs/data/hus/hus09.pdf

National Institute of Allergy and Infectious Diseases. (2003). *HIV infection and AIDS: An overview.* Hyattsville, MD: U.S. Dept. of Health and Human Services. Retrieved from www.niaid.nih.gov/fact sheets/hivinf.htm

National Institute of Diabetes and Digestive and Kidney Diseases. (2008). National diabetes statistics, 2007. Bethesda, MD: National Institutes of Health. Retrieved from http://diabetes.niddk.nih.gov/dm/pubs /statistics/

Payne, R. A., & Donaghy, M. (2010). *Payne's handbook of relaxation techniques: A practical handbook for the health care professional* (4th ed.). Edinburgh, Scotland: Churchill Livingstone.

Petrak, F., & Herpertz, S. (2009). Treatment of depression in diabetes: An update. *Current Opinion in Psychiatry, 22,* 211–217.

Peyrot, M., & Rubin, R. R. (1997). Levels and risks of depression and anxiety symptomatology among diabetic adults. *Diabetes Care, 20,* 585–590.

Pollin, I. (1995). *Medical crisis counseling: Short-term treatment for long-term illness.* Evanston, IL: Norton.

Pratt, L. A., Ford, D. E., Crum, R. M., Armenian, H. K., Gallo, J. J., & Eaton, W. W. (1996). Depression, psychotropic medication, and risk of myocardial infarction: Prospective data from the Baltimore ECA follow-up. *Circulation, 94,* 3123–3129.

Rihmer, Z. (2007). Suicide risk in mood disorders. *Current Opinion in Psychiatry, 20,* 17–22.

Robbins, J. A., Bertakis, K. D., Helms, L. J., Azari, R., Callahan, E. J., & Creten, D. A. (1993). The influence of physician practice behaviors on patient satisfaction. *Family Medicine, 25*(1), 17–20.

Rogers, G., Curry, M., Oddy, J., Pratt, N., Beilby, J., & Wilkinson, D. (2003). Depressive disorders and unprotected casual anal sex among Australian homosexually active men in primary care. *HIV Medicine, 4,* 271–275.

Rosenthal, M. J., Fajardo, M., Gilmore, S., Morley, J. E., & Naliboff, B. D. (1998). Hospitalization and mortality of diabetes in older adults: A 3-year prospective study. *Diabetes Care, 21,* 231–235.

Roter, D. L. (1977). Patient participation in the patient-provider interaction: The effects of patient question asking on the quality of interaction, satisfaction and compliance. *Health Education Monographs, 5*(4), 281–315.

Roter, D. L., & Hall, J. A. (1997). Patient-provider communication. In K. Glanz, F. M. Lewis, & B. K. Rimer (Eds.), *Health behavior and health education* (pp. 206–226). San Francisco, CA: Jossey-Bass.

Roter, D. L., Hall, J. A., & Katz, N. R. (1987). Relations between physicians' behaviors and patients' satisfaction, recall, and impressions: An analogue study. *Medical Care, 25,* 437–451.

Rozanski, A., Blumenthal, J. A., & Kaplan, J. (1999). Impact of psychological factors on the pathogenesis of cardiovascular disease and implications for therapy. *Circulation, 99,* 2192–2217.

Rubin, R. R., Ciechanowski, P., Egede, L., Lin, E. H. B., & Lustman, P. J. (2004). Recognizing and treating depression in patients with diabetes. *Current Diabetes Reports, 4,* 119–125.

Rubin, R. R., & Peyrot, M. (2001). Psychological issues and treatments for people with diabetes. *Journal of Clinical Psychology, 57,* 457–478.

Ryan, M. C. M., Collins, P., & Thakore, J. H. (2003). Impaired fasting glucose tolerance in first episode, drug naive patients with schizophrenia. *American Journal of Psychiatry, 160,* 284–289.

Rydall, A. C., Rodin, G. M., Olmsted, M. P., Devenyi, R. G., & Daneman, D. (1997). Disordered eating behavior and microvascular complications in young women with insulin-dependent diabetes mellitus. *New England Journal of Medicine, 336,* 1849–1854.

Sacchetti, E., Turrina, C., Parrinello, G., Brignoli, O., Stefanini, G., & Mazzaglia, G. (2005). Incidence of diabetes in a general practice population: A database cohort study on the relationship with haloperidol, olanzapine, risperidone or quetiapine exposure. *International Clinical Psychopharmacology, 20,* 33–37.

Sax, P. E., & Kumar, P. (2004). Tolerability and safety of HIV protease inhibitors in adults. *Journal of Acquired Immune Deficiency Syndromes, 37,* 1111–1124.

Schulman, K. A., Berlin, J. A., Harless, W., Kerner, J. F., Sistrunk, S., Gersh, B. J., ... Escarce, J. J. (1999). The effect of race and sex on physicians' recommendations for cardiac catheterization. *New England Journal of Medicine, 340,* 618–626.

Sewell, G. (2004). Using deep relaxation in children and adolescents with diabetes. *Journal of Diabetes Nursing, 8,* 309–313.

Silberman, J., Tentler, A., Ramgopal, R., & Epstein, R. M. (2007). Recall-promoting physician behaviors in primary care. *Journal of General Internal Medicine, 23*(9), 1487–1490.

Smith-Rogers, A., Miller, S., Murphy, D. A., Tanney, M., & Fortune, T. (2001). The TREAT (Therapeutic Regimens Enhancing Adherence in Teens) Program: Theory and preliminary results. *Journal of Adolescent Health, 298,* 30–38.

Snoek, F. J., van der Ven, N. C., Twisk, J. W., Hogenelst, M. H., Tromp-Wever, A. M., & van der Ploeg, H. M. (2008). Cognitive behavioural therapy (CBT) compared with blood glucose awareness training (BGAT) in poorly controlled type 1 diabetic patients: Long-term effects on HbA moderated by depression: A randomized controlled trial. *Diabetic Medicine, 25,* 1337–1342.

Stacey, D., Samant, R., & Bennett, C. (2008). Decision making in oncology: A review of patient decision aids to support patient participation. *CA: A Cancer Journal for Clinicians, 58,* 293–304.

Starace, F., Ammassari, A., Trotta, M. P., Murri, R., De Longis, P., Izzo, C., ... AdICoNA and the NeuroIcoNA Study Groups. (2002). Depression is a risk factor for suboptimal adherence to highly active antiretroviral therapy. *Journal of Acquired Immune Deficiency Syndromes, 31,* S136–S139.

Steele, R. G., & Grauer, D. (2003). Adherence to antiretroviral therapy for pediatric HIV infection: Review of the literature and recommendations for research. *Clinical Child and Family Psychology Review, 6,* 17–30.

Surtees, P. G., Wainwright, N. W. J., Luben, R. N., Wareham, N. J., Bingham, S. A., & Khaw, K. (2008). Depression and ischemic heart disease mortality: Evidence from the EPIC-Norfolk United Kingdom Prospective Cohort Study. *American Journal of Psychiatry, 165,* 515–523.

Thompson, S., Auslander, W. F., & White, N. (2001a). Comparison between single-mother and two-parent families on metabolic control of youths with diabetes. *Diabetes Care, 24,* 234–238.

Thompson, S., Auslander, W. F., & White, N. (2001b). Influence of family structure on health among youths with diabetes. *Health & Social Work, 26,* 7–14.

Tull, E. S., & Roseman, J. M. (1995). Diabetes in African Americans. In National Diabetes Data Group (Ed.), *Diabetes in America* (NIH Publication No. 95–1468, 2nd ed.). Washington, DC: National Institute of Diabetes and Digestive and Kidney Diseases.

U.S. Department of Health and Human Services. (2004). *Summary health statistics for U.S. adults: National Health Interview Survey, 2002* (DHHS Publication No. PHS 2004–1550). Hyattsville, MD: Author.

van Dulmen, S., Sluijs, E., van Dijk, L., de Ridder, D., Heerdink, R., & Bensing, J. (2007). Patient adherence to medical treatment: a review of reviews. *BMC Health Services Research, 7,* 55.

Wild, S., Roglic, G., Green, A., Sicree, R., & King, H. (2004). Global prevalence of diabetes: Estimates for the year 2000 and projections for 2030. *Diabetes Care, 27,* 1047–1053.

World Health Organization. (2004). *Diabetes action now: An initiative of the World Health Organization and International Diabetes Federation.* Geneva, Switzerland: Author. Retrieved from www.who.int /diabetes/actionnow/en/DANbooklet.pdf

World Health Organization. (2008). *Fact sheet: The top ten causes of death.* Geneva, Switzerland: Author. Retrieved from www.who.int/mediacentre/factsheets /fs310_2008.pdf

World Health Organization. (2009a). *Diabetes.* Geneva, Switzerland: Author. Retrieved from www.who.int /mediacentre/factsheets/fs312/en/print.html

World Health Organization. (2009b). *Global health risks: Mortality and the burden of disease attributable to selected major risks.* Geneva, Switzerland: Author. Retrieved from www.who.int/healthinfo/global_burden _disease/GlobalHealthRisks_report_full.pdf

Wulsin, L., & Singal, B. (2003). Do depressive symptoms increase the risk for the onset of coronary disease? A systematic quantitative review. *Psychosomatic Medicine, 65,* 201–210.

Wysocki, T., Harris, M. A., Greco, P., Bubb, J., Danda, C. E., Harvey, L. M.,...White, N. H. (2000). Diabetes mellitus in the transition to adulthood: Adjustment, self-care, and health status. *Journal of Developmental and Behavioral Pediatrics, 25,* 23–33.

Yun, L. W., Maravi, M., Kobayashi, J. S., Barton, P. L., & Davidson, A. J. (2005). Antidepressant treatment improves adherence to antiretroviral therapy among depressed HIV-infected patients. *Journal of Acquired Immune Deficiency Syndrome, 38,* 432–438.

21

Social Work and Genetics

ALLISON WERNER-LIN AND KATE REED

Historically, social workers in health care have helped families cope with the psychosocial implications of genetic conditions (Schild & Black, 1984). The earliest articles that address how to integrate genetic concepts and concerns into social work practice were published over 45 years ago. Two seminal articles, one by Schild (1966) and the other by Schultz (1966), outlined advances in genetics and their potential influence on social work practice. Both emphasized the importance of psychosocial support for individuals and families dealing with genetic disorders and suggested that social workers are particularly well suited to provide counseling about genetics.

Since then, scientific advances have altered the landscape of genetic medicine dramatically. Most notably, the Human Genome Project was launched in 1990 to determine the exact makeup of the human genome with the hope of improving health by identifying genetic variants that contribute to disease. Completed in 2003, the Human Genome Project (www.ornl.gov/sci/techresources/Human _Genome/home.shtml) allows us to read the human genetic blueprint. This opens the door for improved methods of understanding the underlying biology and genetics of disease and the development of effective interventions for both rare and common genetic conditions. Scientists have made great strides in identifying genetic contributions that cause or predispose individuals to specific disorders. Identifying these genetic variants has enabled the development of genetic tests for individuals interested in learning whether they carry specific gene variants (commonly called mutations or alterations) that predispose or cause illness.

Yet the ability to identify genetic contributions to disease continues to outpace the development of targeted therapies. Furthermore, our understanding of the relationship between single gene variants and disease expression has increased in complexity, and the interplay between multiple genes and environmental factors further complicates prediction. Thus an unintended result of the Human Genome Project was the creation of a new class of patients for whom we can detect risk variants but cannot determine whether or when disease will develop.

The identification of genetic variations that predispose individuals to a variety of conditions means that social workers must contend with a new risk concept, one that is microscopic. Our person-in-environment lens must be broadened to include consideration of genetic variation as a core feature of developmental, social, and environmental assessment without essentializing genetic contributions to conditions or traits. As scientists identify genes linked to stigmatized disorders, such as mental illness and addiction, or personality traits, such as aggression and anxiety, the ability to identify genetic predispositions comes with a potent ethical, social, and personal cost. Knowledge of basic genetic concepts and how they are presented and understood in medical care is critical to competent practice, especially with marginalized and vulnerable populations, such as those with limited health literacy and inadequate resources.

The genetic revolution offers a variety of opportunities for social workers to participate in the comprehensive care of patients and families to address an entire range of health concerns, including genetic aspects of well-being. The strengths perspective and person-in-environment lens suggest a potent role for social workers to participate in designing information-sharing models and approaches to genetic services that are tailored to the specific needs of individuals, families, and communities (Kent, 2003). The aim of this chapter is to present an overview of basic genetic concepts and dilemmas most relevant to social work practice.

Chapter Objectives

- Introduce basic concepts and recent developments in genetic medicine.
- Identify variation and gene–environment interaction as a foundation for building strengths-based knowledge and practice in genetics.
- Discuss opportunities and challenges for integrating social work into transdisciplinary clinical and research teams in genetic medicine.
- Introduce common ethical issues faced by providers and patients involved in genetic medicine.
- Examine recent policy developments in the area of genetic medicine.
- Suggest roles for social work in developing and implementing research, advocacy, education, and intervention protocols in genetics.

INTRODUCTION TO GENETIC VARIATION

No two people or environments are identical. Even twins born with identical genetic blueprints develop distinct personalities, interests, and social networks. Researchers have long studied twin pairs in an attempt to identify the impact of varied environmental conditions on the ways genes are expressed (their phenotype) (Rose & Kaprio, 2008; Shih, Belmonte, & Zandi, 2004). Yet great variation exists in how specific genes are expressed and in how those genes interact with similar and diverse environmental factors to shape the ways humans grow and develop. For example, only a subset of people exposed to tobacco become addicted. Genetic variants influence how nicotine is processed in the body; people with one variant experience the effects of nicotine for longer than others because it is metabolized more slowly. These individuals need to smoke fewer cigarettes during the course of a day than people who metabolize nicotine more rapidly. These genetic variants interact with other environmental and behavioral factors, such as access to cigarettes and composition of the social network, to determine whether an individual develops an addiction.

Genetic variation refers to the differences that exist in the genetic code across individuals and groups. Those differences contribute to diversity in physical appearance, health, and behavior and affect the ways individuals respond to their environment. The code that determines the basic instructions for growth and development, DNA (deoxyribonucleic acid), is grossly the same among all individuals because those instructions are necessary to support life. For example, all humans have the same basic body shape and develop organs in the same order and at around the same time. Beyond these fundamental instructions, though, variation is the rule, not the exception.

A rapidly growing body of literature addresses genetic variation and the interplay between genes and environments (Manolio, 2009). This literature tells us that genetic variation contributes to the array of personality and behavioral traits we develop, to illness expression and treatment response, and to the development of psychopathology. Genetic factors play a role in an individual's stress and coping response, thus shaping the way individuals engage with and respond to environmental stressors (Caspi, Hariri, & Holmes, Uher, & Moffitt, 2010). Social workers are trained to assess environments and to hypothesize and test links between environmental strengths and constraints and mental health and health outcomes. Recognizing genetic as well as environmental factors will allow social workers, in partnership with other health and mental health professionals, to develop interventions and resources that are targeted to an individual's specific circumstances across a variety of presenting problems. Thus, with respect to social work practice in the age of genetic discovery, social workers are in the ideal position to identify the environmental, behavioral, and familial factors that provide the context for gene expression.

The Basics

Variation ultimately occurs at the level of DNA, which is the source of all genetic information. DNA carries genetic information encoded in four different chemicals bases— adenine, thymine, cytosine, and guanine, or, more familiarly, A, T, C, and G—which pair (A-T and C-G) together. Each pair is called a *nucleotide*, and the sequence of nucleotides conveys specific instructions about the growth, function, and development of the cells. Genes are segments of DNA with a unique combination of nucleotides that contain instructions for making a specific protein required for cell growth, development, and/or maintenance. Human beings have about 20,000 to 25,000 genes. All human beings have roughly the same genes, but no two people, except identical twins, have the same versions (*alleles*) of each of those genes. Each person generally has two copies of each gene, one inherited from each parent (see Figure 21.1).

Chromosomes provide the organizational structure for DNA. They are composed of complexes of genes and proteins found in the nucleus of the cell. A normal human cell has 46 chromosomes. We inherit 23 chromosomes from each parent, which means we have 23 pairs of chromosomes and two copies of every gene. The chromosomes that we inherit from each parent are grossly the same for 22 pairs. The 23rd pair of chromosomes determines biological sex of the individual. Females have two X chromosomes and males have one X and one Y chromosome.

Sources of Genetic Variation

Genetic variation refers to the changes that exist in the genetic code across individuals and groups that affect the function of the gene. These changes can be small or large, and their effect on an individual depends on their location in the genome and whether the change has functional significance. Variation itself is neutral; not all changes lead to negative health consequences. Some genetic changes have no effect, some make individuals less susceptible to certain diseases, and some increase the risk for disease.

There are two main types of genetic variation, reproductive and structural. Structural variation, in many ways, can be thought of as "mistakes" that occur during the replication of DNA. By contrast, we all have genes that facilitate the process of increasing variation through reproduction. The following explanations are designed to provide an overview of the mechanics of variation that have significance for how individuals, families, and groups present for treatment, the kinds of questions or medical decisions they may be facing, and the scope of psychosocial intervention that may facilitate positive health and mental health outcomes.

Reproductive Variation

The union of genetically distinct egg and sperm produces a unique combination of genetic information, thereby increasing variation. During the process of reproduction, genetic material from each biological parent is sorted randomly

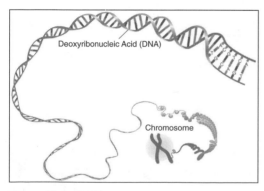

Figure 21.1   DNA

to ensure a full complement of genes from each parent. Therefore, each egg or sperm cell is a mix of what that individual inherited from each biological parent. This random assortment creates a unique person with risk factors and disease susceptibly inherited from the combination of the parents' genetic risk factors and susceptibility. Random assortment further ensures that siblings are not genetically identical (except for twins); they will inherit different combinations of their parents' DNA (see Box 21.1).

Structural Variation

Structural variation refers to changes in the genetic code that may be as large as an entire chromosome or as small as a single nucleotide (A-T or C-G pair) within a gene. These include genetic mutations and polymorphisms. Changes that are seen in less than 1% of the population typically are referred to as mutations. A *mutation* is a change to DNA that, depending on its location on the gene and the type of change, can impact the function of a protein encoded for by that gene. In some

---

Box 21.1 Patterns of Inheritance

Most traits and conditions have a genetic component that is inherited in one of a few common patterns. Identifying the pattern can inform diagnostic and counseling approaches about the risk of developing the trait or condition for the individual and their family members. Patterns of inheritance also can impact individuals' understanding of and experience with the condition.

Autosomal Dominant Inheritance

Autosomal dominant patterns of inheritance are indicated by conditions or traits for which having a mutation on one copy of the causative gene is sufficient to develop the phenotype. An individual with an autosomal dominant condition or trait often has a parent with the same condition. Each child of a carrier has a 50% chance of inheriting an autosomal dominant mutation, with males and females equally likely to be affected. Dominant traits usually are seen in multiple, successive generations in a family.

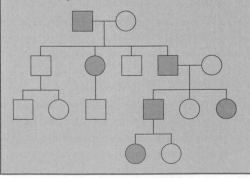

Autosomal Recessive Inheritance

Autosomal recessive patterns of inheritance are indicated by conditions that require both copies of the gene in question to carry mutations that prevent normal functioning. Individuals who have one working copy of a gene and one nonworking copy are called carriers and are at increased risk of having a child with the condition if the other parent is also a carrier. Males and females are equally likely to be affected by autosomal recessive conditions, and these conditions often are found in siblings. Affected individuals may have unaffected parents, and all offspring of an affected individual are carriers of the gene mutation. Each child of two carrier parents has a 25% chance of being affected.

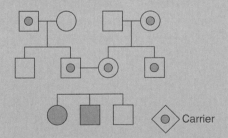

X-Linked Inheritance

X-linked patterns of inheritance are indicated by conditions or traits that are caused by changes in genes found on the X chromosome. The X and Y chromosomes determine an individual's sex; males have one X chromosome and one Y chromosome while females have two X chromosomes. This means that males have only one copy of each of the genes found on the X chromosome while females have two copies. As a result, females typically are less affected by X-linked conditions because they have one normal copy of the gene that may partially compensate for the missing or incorrect gene product. Because affected males transmit their only X chromosome to their daughters but not their sons (who inherit their Y chromosome instead), all daughters will become carriers while sons will not. Women who carry one normal copy and one mutated copy of a gene implicated in an X-linked disorder are called carriers. Each son has a 50% risk of inheriting the mutated version and thus, having the condition.

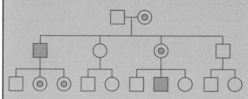

Multifactorial Inheritance

Multifactorial patterns of inheritance are implicated by conditions or traits with many contributing factors, including both genetic and environmental factors. These conditions or traits often occur in multiple family members due to shared environmental and genetic factors. Most commonly, chronic conditions such as heart disease and diabetes are multifactorial, as are many traits, including height and depression. Because multiple factors are involved in combination, some of which may not be easily identified, it is difficult to predict whether individuals will develop symptoms even if genetic testing for the known genetic factors is available.

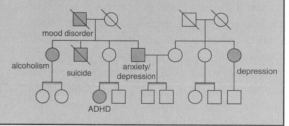

cases, a mutation can change the meaning of the DNA substantially, resulting in an ineffective or nonfunctional protein. In other cases, mutations do not disable to protein and are benign. Environmental conditions also influence the impact of a mutation. For example, a mutation in the gene that codes for hemoglobin B can result in sickle cell trait. This trait causes considerable damage and discomfort at high altitudes but has no impact at sea level.

Some genetic mutations have enabled adaptive responses to changing environments. For example, a small subset of people who are regularly exposed to human immunodeficiency virus (HIV) carry a specific mutation that prevents infection by denying the virus access to human cells. As far as we know, this mutation is not associated with any negative effects and may have other undiscovered properties, and most carriers are unlikely to know they have it. This mutation likely existed well before the HIV epidemic, but only with a changed

environment within which HIV exists did we become aware of its existence. Other beneficial mutations in our current environment include the ability to digest lactose and resistance to malaria infection in carriers of sickle cell trait.

Somatic mutations occur sporadically after birth. Although they may have a significant impact on the carrier, the carrier's children are not at risk of inheriting the mutation. Most types of cancer, for example, are due to genetic mutations in a single cell caused by exposure to environmental toxins. These mutations affect the individual but, because they are not present in the sex cells, cannot be passed onto the next generation. Only specific types of mutations, called *germline mutation*, are passed from one generation to the next in a family bloodline. Germline mutations are those that are present in the sex (egg and sperm) cells. A small subset of people who develop cancer carry a germline mutation, such as the *BRCA1* or *BRCA2* mutations, which predispose carriers to elevated risk of developing breast and ovarian cancer. In this subset of individuals, cancer develops only after exposure to an environmental toxin that causes an additional genetic mutation to occur. In this case, the germline mutation and the somatic mutation each act as an independent "strike" against the individual's resistance to cancer. Cancer in these individuals tends to occur at an earlier age because the mutation is present from birth.

Polymorphisms are changes in the DNA that are present in more than 1% of the population, making them genetically common. Many polymorphisms consist of a change to a single nucleotide (*single nucleotide polymorphism* or SNP). Although some polymorphisms are associated with moderate increases in risk for common diseases, not all polymorphisms are associated with disease risk. Examples of non–disease-related polymorphisms are those that contribute to eye and skin color.

Chromosomes provide the organizational structure for genes. Each chromosome contains hundreds of genes, and changes to the number or structure of the chromosome can have profound effects on the development of the individual. An extra chromosome 21 results in the constellation of health and cognitive issues known as Down syndrome. The presence of a single X chromosome with no other sex chromosome (each individual should have two sex chromosomes) causes Turner's syndrome in women, characterized by small stature, nonverbal learning disabilities, and fertility and other health concerns. Other disorders result from the deletion, duplication, or inversion of segments of specific chromosomes. Chromosomal abnormalities related to the number of chromosomes are thought to cause 50% to 60% of miscarriages because these changes are not compatible with supporting life.

New technology called *microarray* can identify deletions and duplications on chromosomes that are too small to have been detected by previous technologies. In most cases, microarrays are indicated for individuals who have significant developmental and health problems. Microarrays assess the entire genome rather than focusing in on detecting a specific mutation or condition. Because the technology is nonspecific, it has the potential to detect a genetic anomaly for a growing proportion of the affected population. Yet the use of this technology raises ethical and medical challenges. For one thing, microarrays identify changes in areas of the chromosomes that have not previously been associated with disease, so interpreting the results requires educated guesswork about the causative nature of the change and its impact on development. Also, analysis may identify risk information that is not connected to the concerns that initially led an individual or family to pursue genetic testing. For example, a deletion of a gene that is associated with an adult-onset disorder, such as amyotrophic lateral sclerosis (ALS, also known as Lou Gehrig's disease), could be identified in a child being worked up for developmental delay. Although these types of unanticipated results are not unique to genetics, they present a challenge to the introduction of new technologies, informed consent, and medical decision making.

GENE–ENVIRONMENT INTERACTION

A variety of models demonstrate current theoretical assumptions about the ways genes and environments interact. All diseases are caused by a combination of genetic and environmental factors. In some cases, disease occurs only after risk factors accumulate. It is similar to the threshold effect with exposure to environmental toxins—a certain amount of mercury is believed to be safe and tolerated by the body, but beyond that amount there is increased risk for health and cognitive problems. In the context of genetics, the presence of a mutation alone may not be sufficient to cause disease, but when environmental risk factors also are present (e.g., high-fat diet, smoking), the scales are tipped and the individual may meet the criteria for a clinical diagnosis. It is important to note that prior to having a clinical diagnosis, a person may have symptoms. For example, an individual may have relatively high blood pressure but not have clinical hypertension; an individual may have a persistent, relatively severe depressed mood (dysthymia) but never meet the diagnostic criteria for major depression. Early symptoms such as these also are due to a combination of genetic and environmental factors.

Some conditions occur only if specific environmental and genetic risk factors are both present. For example, people with a mutation in a gene responsible for breaking down certain components of alcohol, alcohol dehydrogenase, will develop facial flushing, heart palpitations, light-headedness, and nausea when consuming alcohol. Both alcohol consumption and this specific mutation are required for the effect to occur. Individuals with phenylketonuria (PKU) are missing an enzyme that breaks down one of the main components of protein, the amino acid phenylalanine, because of a genetic mutation. Phenylalanine is present in virtually all naturally occurring protein sources (e.g., beef, chicken, milk, pork). Individuals with PKU must eliminate phenylalanine from their diet or they will develop cognitive impairment over time. This specific genetic mutation is problematic only in a world where phenylalanine is an essential component of protein. In an environment that did not rely on phenylalanine, having the mutation would not affect a person's health or development. Because the disease is managed successfully if caught early, the United States Preventive Services Task Force (2009) recommends that all newborns be screened for PKU. As a result, all babies in the United States are tested for PKU right after they are born. In both examples, the genetic mutation has no impact unless specific environmental factors also are present.

Current research is focusing on understanding gene–environment interactions in more common diseases. For example, the interaction between genes that control pigment, such as melanin, and sunlight both are implicated in the development of skin cancer. Exposure to ultraviolet rays causes disease in combination with a genetic variant that produces insufficient pigment for protection. Similar interaction studies are being completed for other diseases, including diabetes and metabolic syndrome. Although more work is needed to fully elucidate the biology behind these disease processes, this type of investigation helps us better understand the way in which genetic and environmental risk factors impact disease risk.

Perhaps most exciting for social workers and others who seek to measure and modify environments to improve the health and mental health of individuals, families, and communities is the field of epigenetics. *Epigenetics* is the study of how environmental factors impact gene expression in individuals and groups. Although these changes are acquired during the course of an individual's life, that individual's children may inherit them. Epigenetic factors may impact the onset and expression of disease. For example, research on early breast cancer in African American women has linked social environments and hypervigilance to increased breast cancer risk for African American women on Chicago's South Side (Gehlert et al., 2008). Epigenetic research such as this has significant implications for social work interventions designed to identify environmental risk for and prevent health and mental health conditions before they occur. This research shows that living in an environment that requires heightened vigilance impacts hormone levels because of an increased need to modulate response to stress (McClintock, Conzen, Gehlert, Masi, & Olopade, 2005). Hormone levels impact breast cancer risk. Although this research is ongoing, initial findings from these studies suggest that changing the social environment may impact disease risk in the community. Epigenetic research demonstrates the important connection between animal and human research as well. Evidence from rat models links maternal care (licking) of infant pups to adult rat stress responses (Weaver et al., 2004). Here the environment influences the control of DNA processing by shaping how and when specific genes (stress response genes) are expressed later in life. Both of these epigenetic projects required collaboration across several disciplines.

Understanding Phenotypes

Phenotypes are the detectable end product of the interaction among genetic and environmental factors that contribute to a particular trait or disease process. They are the outcomes that we observe: physical traits, such as hair, skin and eye color, height, and weight, or disease processes, such as diabetes, heart disease, alcoholism, and depression. Yet one's phenotype is frequently too vague to direct effective interventions. Breaking down a broad phenotype into intermediate end points that correspond to each underlying pathway has clinical and social value. For example, heart disease can be caused by a variety of factors, of which poor food choice is only one pathway. For individuals living in minimally resourced environments, access to heart-healthy food choices are limited. For others, genetic factors impact their ability to metabolize cholesterol. For yet others, infections, such as rheumatic fever, or other disease processes, such as high blood pressure, can lead to heart disease. Different pathways may have specific indicators that are measurable before heart disease is diagnosed, such as cholesterol level, allowing for targeted intervention. Each of these pathways leads to heart disease in different ways, requiring targeted social and medical indicators and interventions. Dietary changes will not help to remediate heart disease linked to rheumatic fever.

Select phenotypes incur social stigma. Race, discussed later, is one. Cultural discourse links these phenotypes to patterns of trait or disease expression. For some, such as obesity, stigma grows from assumptions about the lack of self-control. Teasing apart the overarching phenotype, obesity, allows health and mental health professionals to identify the varied pathways leading to disease. From there social misconceptions can be addressed and individualized interventions designed. This section presents background on select phenotypes with which social workers are familiar.

Environment, Culture, and Evolution

Understanding the biological basis for differences among human populations requires understanding of genetic history and the impact of evolutionary pressures. Differences exist between populations for a number of reasons, including environmental conditions that create a selective advantage for a particular trait. For example, darker skin color for individuals living near the equator provides protection from the harmful effects of intense sunlight. Similarly, the ability to digest lactose is more prevalent in populations with a historically greater exposure to lactose-containing foods (i.e., dairy products). In both examples, the original population had some individuals with different forms of each trait (e.g., individuals with lighter and darker skin color near the equator and individuals with and without the ability to digest lactose in lands with cows). Over generations, individuals with the more advantageous trait for the environment were more likely to survive and have more children, thereby passing on that genetic variant and having it become more prevalent in that specific population. This phenomenon is called *natural selection* (Darwin, 1859) and can be seen over generations for many different types of traits and in all species.

Social and cultural pressures also may impact the type and prevalence of genetic attributes within a population. Groups descended largely from a relatively small founding population may have genetic disorders that were present among the founders. For example, the Old Order Amish population in the United States has cultural and social restrictions on marrying individuals outside the community. Consequently, the gene pool is relatively small, and there is a higher prevalence of certain predisposition to and incidence of genetic disorders than is seen in a larger population with more genetic variation. Specifically, the Old Order Amish have a higher prevalence of some rare, single-gene disorders as well as gene variants that convey risk for certain complex disorders including diabetes (McKusick, 1973; Pollin et al., 2008). The Ashkenazi Jewish population faces a different set of conditions because of what was present in the founding population and cultural mandates to marry within the group. Although more prevalent in these groups, these conditions can be seen in any population.

Race

Race is a powerful social construction in which phenotypic expression is linked to layers of sociopolitical history and cultural meaning. As genetic discovery enables differentiation of subgroups of the population, the genetics of race has been explored in a variety of politically and socially charged contexts. Hypotheses about links between genes and race are founded on assumed covariance between phenotype and other skills or attributes, such as intellectual prowess and athletic performance. An examination of social dialogue about genetics and race is beyond the scope of this chapter. Yet we would be remiss not to mention the ways genetics research has addressed the concept of race and the risks of using racial distinctions to categorize genetic variation. Of significant concern is genetics research that inadvertently (or deliberately) may promote essentialist thinking, where environmental conditions that lead to health and mental health disparities are obscured in favor of explanations that look to deterministic and "inevitable" genetic variation (Sankar, 2009). As social workers well know, understanding an individual's specific social, familial, and medical context rather than relying on assumptions based on a diagnosis or demographic information allows for the development of more effective approaches to practice.

In medical settings, race often serves as a heuristic, or cognitive shortcut, for the health professional to focus on certain disease risks based on the prevalence within that population (Satel, 2002). Although race is used as a categorical variable in research, it is difficult to operationalize since it is a social construct rather than a biological one (Bonham, Warshauer-Baker, & Collins, 2005; Dupre, 2008; Hunt & Megyesi, 2008). As a result, categorization of participants based on racial categories relies either on self-report or the researchers' perception based on visual cues. As a result, the term *race* may be used ambiguously, inconsistently, and without rigor (Hunt & Megyesi, 2008).

Furthermore, increased mobility and intermarriage have blurred the physical and social attributes that determine one's race. Although originally the observable genetic differences between races may have served as reliable marker of other unique characteristics of the population, such as beliefs or cultural heritage, which do not have a genetic basis, the mixing of populations and increasing globalization have made those markers much less useful. As race diminishes in its usefulness as a proxy for genetic background, this use has become less effective. Such an approach assumes race involves salient and innate differences, but this claim has not been substantiated in genetics research.

Genetic Contributions to Mental Illness

Psychiatric disorders tend to cluster in families; thus, interest in exploring genetic contributions to mental illness has grown since the inception of the Human Genome Project. Even with new technologies that make the entirety of the human genome more accessible, no strong single gene has been identified for any psychiatric disorder. State-of-the-art research suggests that mental illness develops like other complex disorders. That is, many genes, each associated with a small increase in risk, contribute to disease in combination with environmental factors (Dick, Rose, & Jaakko, 2006; Jaffee & Price, 2007; Wermter et al., 2010). For example, several researcher teams are investigating a gene–environment interaction in the development of depression in individuals exposed to stressful life events. A particular mutation in a gene that responds to a chemical (serotonin) released in the brain during stressful situations has been implicated in risk for developing depression. Some studies have found that having the mutation alone does not cause any problems. When the environmental factor (stress) is present, serotonin interacts with the altered protein and sets off a chain of events that increases risk for depression. Although other studies have not found the same interaction, the underlying disease pathway still is being considered and may help to clarify the specific mechanism (e.g., Caspi et al., 2003; Risch et al., 2009). A parallel body of research, *pharmacogenomics*, examines gene variants that impact the ability of individuals to metabolize drugs used to treat psychiatric conditions (Malhotra, Lencz, Correll, & Kane, 2007). The aim of this research is to optimize treatment by avoiding adverse effects and determining effective dosing efficiently. In combination, these bodies of research suggest a future role for personalized psychiatric–genetic medicine.

The mutation in the gene that responds to serotonin is implicated in elevating risk of depression and also has been tied to other mental health outcomes, including alcohol dependence. Depending on the research or clinical environment, explanations for addiction vacillate among genetic factors, adverse familial and social conditions, and personality or character deficits. Although addictions run in families, teasing apart how much of the clustering is due to genetic factors versus shared environmental factors, including exposure to addictive behaviors, is complicated (e.g., Crabbe, 2002). Twin, adoption, and family studies provide support for both genetic and environmental contributions (Agrawal & Lynskey, 2008). These studies suggest that the initiation of substance use is highly familial, yet not inherited. Shared genotypes within families may account for common behavioral responses to known environmental variants. Thus, some family members may be more sensitive to environmental determinants than others. Understanding the complex relationship of genes and environment in addiction may help elucidate other behavior pathways as well as help to target interventions.

TRANSDISCIPLINARY TEAMS IN PRACTICE AND RESEARCH

In many ways, genetics provides a unifying structure that brings specialists together to address different aspects of a single underlying disease. Listed in this section are the types of professionals most frequently involved in caring for an individual and family with a genetic condition. This list is likely to expand to include primary care providers, as additional genetic factors related to common disease are identified and as clinical testing becomes available. This list is not exhaustive. Specialists involved who can respond to specific concerns (e.g., endocrinologists, neurologists, dermatologists) will change based on the medical, psychosocial, and developmental needs of the affected individual and family. In general, the role of these specialists will be to diagnose, treat, and manage specific symptoms. Although genetics professionals typically will take the lead on patient care coordination, patient management is a shared responsibility among these professionals.

Who Is on the Team?

Clinical geneticists are physicians who have completed additional residency training in medical genetics. Clinical geneticists typically see patients for medical diagnosis and management. They help connect patients with the appropriate specialists to ensure current and anticipated medical issues associated with the underlying condition are addressed.

Genetic counselors are health-care professionals with combined graduate level training and expertise in medical genetics, patient education, and psychosocial counseling. Some genetic counselors are generalists while others may specialize exclusively in one area of medicine, such as cardiovascular or psychiatric genetics. In clinical settings, genetic counselors help individuals and families to understand and address genetic risks, make testing decisions, and adapt to genetic diagnoses, mainly on a short-term basis.

Nutritionists/dietitians work primarily with patients who have conditions that require their diets to be restricted, such as those with metabolic conditions such as PKU who cannot metabolize certain nutrients. Nutritionists/dietitians develop diet plans that ensure that individuals get the appropriate nutrients given their underlying condition and work with families to help them integrate changes in diet into their lives.

Physical, occupational, and speech therapists provide both short- and long-term support for individuals who have either delayed development of skills or experienced changes in skills due to a genetic condition. Patients affected at the beginning of life may benefit from these therapies by virtue of the help that they receive in meeting their developmental milestones. Adults who develop neurodegenerative conditions may lose abilities, including coordination, speech, and swallowing. Therapists sometimes can help to preserve and improve functioning.

Social workers, psychologists, and psychiatrists are part of the recommended care model for individuals experiencing infertility and considering predictive testing for adult-onset, neurodegenerative conditions such as Huntington disease. Their role in the testing process is to assess the individuals' baseline emotional state to determine the presence of risk factors associated with pregnancy. Social workers are trained to understand clients and families in their social and historical milieu by: eliciting family narratives of illness, caregiving, and loss; addressing outstanding emotional concerns; fostering active client participation in counseling and decision making; and bolstering client self-awareness. They may provide a variety of psychosocial services to individuals and families with genetic conditions, including: referrals; individual and family counseling; consultation; and ongoing support to individuals, families, and groups attempting to cope with genetic conditions. They also may facilitate family meetings about genetic testing and treatment, support medical decision making, and structure group interventions.

Research

Social workers currently are involved in genetics research of various types, and opportunities to be more involved are becoming more abundant. Social workers' training and perspective in assessing environmental conditions, dynamics, and development provide a needed perspective when considering the implications of genetic discoveries. Social workers have the skills to lead transdisciplinary teams to examine problems from a holistic perspective. To support social work leadership and participation in genetic research, in August 2010, the National Institutes of Health offered a week-long, intensive summer institute addressing the potential to integrate social work and genetic research. The program highlighted a number of opportunities and challenges to the interdisciplinary collaboration required to bridge professional boundaries successfully.

Opportunities

As the field of epigenetics expands, geneticists increasingly will need to partner with social scientists trained to: assess environments; hypothesize links between environmental strengths, constraints, and health outcomes; and design research to test these links. Social work strength in these partnerships lies in the profession's expertise in understanding the impact of familial and social conditions on human development throughout the life cycle and across diverse and dynamic environments. The rich history of innovative and applied research by social workers will facilitate ethical translation of genetic discovery into tangible products to support vulnerable and marginalized groups.

Challenges

Although complementary knowledge and skills across collaborators can potentiate research impact, disparate professional lexicons, beliefs about standard and rigorous research methodology, and perceptions about important targets of research and change may threaten collaboration. The use of discipline-specific terminology or different definitions of the same term can impede communication among team members. Laboratory research, common in genetics, may share little with participatory research, qualitative methods, intervention research, or self-report measures common in social work research (Padgett, 2008). Furthermore, meaningful outcomes may be defined differently by professional discipline. For example, polymorphisms (defined as "common" genetic variants) are those mutations present in at least 1% of the population. Understanding 1% of the variance in a population is

Box 21.2 Common Research Questions by Professional Discipline

Clinical geneticists investigate many aspects of the field, including molecular genetics, clinical application, and ethical and social questions about genetic testing. Common research questions include:

- How do we best define the phenotype and spectrum for a condition or trait?
- What are the distinct genetic contributions and gene–environment interactions for related phenotypes?
- What novel genetic variants are associated with common conditions or traits?
- What new therapies can be developed based on our understanding of genetic mechanisms?
- How do changes in gene expression impact the characteristics of disease?

Genetic counselors examine social science questions within the field of genetics and explore the process and outcomes of the profession. Common research questions include:

- How do patients respond psychologically to discovery of a deleterious trait?
- How can genetic counselors facilitate adaptation to a genetic condition?
- How does cultural or ethnic group identification affect patient educational and psychosocial needs?
- How do individuals share the results of genetic testing with family, friends, and partners?
- Does genetic counseling change compliance with medical recommendations?

Genetic epidemiologists examine the etiology, prevalence, and mechanisms of complex traits, focusing on the intersection of genes and environment in particular groups and populations. Common research questions include:

- Why is a certain trait or condition aggregating in a particular family or population?
- What are the prevalence, impact, and burden of a genetic variant in a population?

- What are the relative contributions of genes and environment for a given trait?
- What areas of the genome might yield the most information about particular conditions or traits (i.e., mutation hot spots)?

Population geneticists apply the techniques of molecular genetics to the study of human evolution and diversity. They typically have training in evolutionary biology or biological anthropology. Common research questions include:

- What genetic markers are associated with particular racial/ethnic admixture, linguistic group, or cultural/geographic heritage?
- What can we learn about human history and patterns of migration by tracing genetic markers?
- What factors influence population divergence or convergence?
- How have specific genetic variants moved through human populations and geography over time?

Social workers and other mental health and social science professionals examine the factors that influence the expression of and response to genetic information and testing for individuals, families, and groups. Common research questions include:

- How do environments shape the expression of conditions or traits?
- How do family legacies shape pursuit and interpretation of genetic testing results?
- How do shared understandings of disease shape medical decision making and management of genetic risk or conditions?
- How does health literacy impact interpretation of genetic test results?
- How do genetic variants contribute to mental illness risk behaviors, such as suicide and substance abuse?
- How can mental health providers best support decision making, family communication, and coping for patients engaged in genetic testing?

Source: Adapted from NCHPEG program Genetics for Social and Behavioral Science Researchers (in development).

meaningful from the perspective of a geneticist, but from a social science perspective, this may not constitute a meaningful finding.

Each member of the research team brings unique knowledge, research aims, and skills to collaborative endeavors (see Box 21.2). When these are congruent and complementary, transdisciplinary work is possible. However, cultural assumptions about what constitutes "good" science may thwart collaborative efforts if disparate understandings are not equally communicated, valued, or integrated into research plans.

GENETIC COUNSELING, EDUCATION, TESTING, AND REFERRAL

Genetic testing identifies changes in chromosomes, genes, or proteins. Unlike many other medical tests, the results of genetic tests largely do not change over time and are not influenced by the environment. Instead, tests identify genetic mutations that are a permanent part of a patient's DNA. Although test results are static, our understanding of how these results impact health and disease evolves as we learn more about genetic variation and environment interactions.

Different types of genetic testing are used to identify genetic contributions to disease in different contexts. The most common categories of and purposes for genetic tests are listed next.

- *Diagnostic testing* is used to identify an underlying diagnosis for individuals showing symptoms that indicate a genetic condition.
- *Carrier testing* is offered to asymptomatic individuals who are at risk of carrying a mutation for an X-linked or recessive condition due to family history or ethnic background. This type of testing is used most commonly to inform reproductive planning.
- *Predictive testing* is offered to (a) asymptomatic individuals who are at high risk

of adult-onset genetic disorders (such as Huntington disease) based on their family history and (b) individuals diagnosed with a disorder known to have a genetic component (such as certain cancers).

- *Prenatal testing* uses fetal DNA to test for certain single-gene and chromosomal disorders in fetuses at high risk due to family history, results of screening tests, or advanced maternal age.
- *Newborn screening* for a number of genetic conditions is performed on most newborns to identify those who would benefit from further testing, including diagnostic genetic tests, or treatment.
- *Susceptibility testing* is a relatively new category of genetic tests that provides information about risk to develop common and complex disorders. Results from this type of testing do not predict the onset of disease; they just indicate increased or decreased risk.

Referrals to Genetic Services

In general, genetics professionals use an individual's medical and family history to assess the genetic contribution to health and disease. Most often this assessment occurs when there is an increased risk for an underlying genetic condition, due to current health, family history, or background attributes (i.e., age, ethnicity). Increasingly, though, clinical tests are becoming available to test for genetic changes that increase risk for common, complex conditions. This means that a larger proportion of the population may be soon gaining knowledge about their genetic makeup.

Social workers frequently ask clients with physical and mental illness about family history and may, therefore, be in a good position to identify families that could benefit from genetic counseling. Before referrals are made, social workers should ask clients about interest in a referral. If the client is interested, referrals are appropriate when factors are present in the individual or family that suggest an increased risk for a genetic condition. For example, parents of children with multiple medical issues may benefit from a genetics referral to try to identify an underlying diagnosis. With the availability of new technologies that have been shown to be effective for multiple outcomes, genetic testing in the pediatric setting outside of genetic services is becoming increasingly common. Unfortunately, the interpretation of the genetic testing results can be complicated. Social workers can help to facilitate optimal care for their patients by assessing the needs of the individuals and their family and connecting them to the appropriate services.

Genetic services have long been integrated into standard prenatal care. Screening for a variety of common and preventable disorders, genetic and nongenetic, are offered routinely during pregnancy to identify fetuses that are at risk of being affected. Screening tests are not diagnostic, so prospective parents who screen positive are offered diagnostic testing for common chromosomal disorders. Follow-up genetic testing is provided for prospective parents to prepare for a child with special needs or to offer the possibility of termination if a condition is identified. Diagnostic testing also may be offered if there is a known genetic diagnosis in either parent's family or if either parent fits a specific risk profile, such as advanced maternal age or a specific ethnic background. The only genetic services incorporated into routine pediatric practice involve newborn screening for identifiable and treatable genetic disorders, yet the number and consistency of screening varies across state lines. Recent expansion of newborn screening recommendations includes conditions for which early detection will be beneficial, such as hearing loss (Berg et al., 2002). There is ongoing discussion and concern about the best approach to obtaining informed consent for newborn screening, since many parents are unaware that their children have been screened (Fernhoff, 2009).

Individuals, couples, and families often pursue genetic services after being diagnosed with or having a family history of a serious condition that may have an identifiable genetic component, such as adult-onset cancers or neurological diseases. Predictive testing raises psychosocial, and sometimes ethical, issues for patients and requires input from knowledgeable professionals, including social workers, to facilitate decision making that is congruent with patient values and priorities. Social workers should be prepared to provide reliable referrals and resources to clients interested in pursuing genetic consultation. This list of resources should include providers who specialize in genetic education and counseling in addition to online resources that can link clients to supportive and informative communities, particularly for rare genetic conditions. Because of the vast amount and variable quality of information available online, especially with respect to rare conditions, social workers also should be prepared to help patients interpret and assess the quality of information.

Although not routine, genetic services are increasingly available in other specialties, including oncology, cardiology, and neurology, to help facilitate assessment, testing, and treatment decisions. As genetic testing becomes more widely available for common, complex conditions and traits, there will be an increasing need for individuals to help both providers and patients understand and interpret the results.

The shortage of trained specialists, specifically genetic counselors and medical geneticists, who can deliver genetic services limits the availability of these tests through regulated channels, specifically in rural or underresourced environments. Genetic tests for common and rare diseases are more common now than they were a decade ago. Yet, as genetic testing moves from tightly controlled research settings with stringent procedures for informed consent to the primary care arena, in which a physician can order a test with little or no pretest or posttest counseling, informed consent may be compromised and the potential for misuse of testing increased (Resnik, 2003). In addition, some companies are marketing genetic tests directly to the consumer (DTC), enabling individuals and families to access them outside of medical settings. Although most DTC tests identify genetic variants that change only moderately an individual's risk for common conditions and traits, results could negatively impact patients, both medically and psychosocially (Gray et al., 2009). The validity and utility of these tests currently is being debated (e.g., Annes, Giovanni, & Murray, 2010; U.S. General Accountability Office, 2010; Waalen & Beutler, 2009). Whatever the fate of any one type of genetic testing, it is likely that without regulation, disparities will grow between those who have access to supportive care, genetic education, and counseling to manage test results and those who do not.

Access to genetic services is hindered further by widespread problems with health literacy, patient and provider lack of awareness about genetic tests and services, and difficulty negotiating complex health information and systems. In addition to limited access to genetic testing and quality risk management, marginalized groups have been less willing to engage in genetic research and testing to identify disease risk or traits than privileged groups (Halbert et al., 2006; Murphy, Wickramarante, & Weissman, 2009; Nanda et al., 2005). This may be due to skepticism about how results will be used and kept private and concern about whether results will be misinterpreted to exploit communities and groups. The legacy of the Tuskegee experiment and the recent biography of Henrietta Lacks (Skloot, 2010; see Chapter 3 for further discussion) support concerns that genetic testing may reinforce racism and that minority patients will be used as guinea pigs (Bussey-Jones et al., 2009).

Thus, access to genetic services is compromised not only by minimally resourced environments with few trained professionals and limited health proficiency, but also by the nation's centuries-old history of exploiting people of color for the benefit of privileged groups. Social workers must partner with community groups and advocates to enhance confidence in skeptical communities when quality services are available that can lead to early detection, treatment, and prevention of life-threatening disease. These partnerships provide valuable contexts for engaging vulnerable groups in cutting-edge research and practice while also protecting them from coercion or unfair burden.

As the demands for genetic services continue to increase beyond the capacity of genetic counselors and nurses to provide them, non-health-care providers may increasingly help patients to access, interpret, and adjust to genetic information. Social workers are in a unique position to promote access to resources, facilitate medical decision making, and provide emotional support over the dynamic and long-term adaptation to genetic information (Smets, van Zwieten & Michie, 2007).

Communicating and Interpreting Genetic Risk Information

Communicating genetic risk information to individuals and families is a complex and multilayered process. In addition to disease risk information, providers should be alert to the ways emotional reactions, perceptions of self-efficacy, social context (McCoyd, 2008), family loyalties, and medical histories (Kenen, Ardern-Jones, & Eeles, 2003; Werner-Lin, 2007) cloud comprehension and judgment. Evidence suggests the emotional and supportive parts of genetic services help patients understand risk information more than the educational or informational components (Edwards et al, 2008; Meiser & Halliday, 2002). Yet a recent literature review suggests that providers rely heavily on medical language while providing counseling and education (Meiser, Irle, Lobb, & Balrow-Stewart, 2008). Some providers may not be comfortable with the emotional tenor and intensity of genetic counseling and education and may retreat into the safety of neutral medical terminology. In such cases, social workers can provide support not only to patients, but also to providers, on how to manage countertransference reactions and seek collegial support to help providers to engage fully with distressed individuals and families. Providers must be coached to integrate the dual demands of sharing complex medical information and supporting the emotional experience of receiving that information.

Health Literacy and Numeracy

Health literacy is defined as the degree to which individuals are able to "obtain, process, and understand basic health information and services needed to make appropriate health decisions" (Ratzen & Parker, 2000). Health literacy is mediated by education, culture, and language proficiency and involves a variety of intellectual skills, including listening, speaking, writing, and reading. Approximately 90 million Americans, or half of all adults, have trouble understanding and using health information (Nielson-Bohlman, Panzer, & Kindig, 2010). Those most significantly impaired, and thus at risk of poor health outcomes, are elderly persons and individuals with limited education or English proficiency. A significant piece of health literacy involves *numeracy*, or the ability to find, understand, and use numerically based health information, such as probabilistic or risk information (Ancker & Kaufman, 2007). Genetic information is often expressed in numbers, including disease risk, penetrance (the proportion of mutation carriers who will manifest symptoms), mutation prevalence, inheritance patterns, and the benefits of risk reduction. Providers may assume individuals and families are able to interpret and use numerical information to make rational decisions, yet numerical risk estimates are hard to understand for the average patient. As a result, risk evaluations based on numerical data are overshadowed by vivid examples from the individual's family and social worlds (Hurley, Miller, Rubin, & Weinberg, 2006). Social workers should promote the use of basic health literacy screening tools to identify at-risk patients and to support their understanding and informed uptake of research, genetic testing, and treatment protocols.

Estimating Risk: Coping and Calculating

In genetic risk counseling, patients receive, and are presumed to integrate, objective risk information regarding their likelihood of developing disease, or of their child being born with a disease, based on the most up-to-date medical information available. Patients tend to interpret probabilistic information using a dichotomous, deterministic lens (Lippman-Hand & Fraser, 1979). This makes ambiguous information more manageable for them. Shifting risk estimated into absolutes (e.g., 1/0; yes/no; 100%/0%) prevents individuals from having to entertain the uncertainty (or multiple uncertainties) associated with genetic risk and its management. For example, if a fetus is diagnosed with an anomaly that is incompatible with life, women are much more likely to terminate. Although this certainty does not obviate the occurrence of significant and painful grief reactions, it facilitates decision making (McCoyd, 2008). When genetic testing information is more ambiguous, cognitive distortions may interfere with patients' ability to comprehend risk information accurately due to unique and complex family histories with the disease (Kenen et al., 2003; Werner-Lin, 2007), poor preexisting knowledge of genetic concepts, innumeracy, risk aversion, and defensive pessimism (Hurley et al., 2006). Interventions have been developed to improve patients' comprehension and ultimately to bring their "subjective" risk perception more closely in line with "objective" estimates through systematic analysis of evidence (e.g., Schwartz, 2001; Slovic, Finucane, Peters, & MacGregor, 2004). This formal risk analysis perspective tends to view affective responses as irrational. More recent scholarship argues that "rational" decision making requires an integration of both analytic and experiential (affective) systems. This perspective is congruent with the view that risk perception is "inevitably mediated through social and cultural processes and can never be known in isolation from these" (Lupton, 1999, p. 35).

For conditions with ambiguous penetrance, risk is difficult to quantify accurately (Sivell et al., 2008). *Defensively pessimistic* (Norem & Cantor, 1986) individuals may prepare for the worst by overestimating personal risk. Yet this may lead to drastic prevention measures that adversely impact health and quality of life (Braithwaite, Emery, Walter et al., 2004; Hallowell & Richards, 1997). *Protectively ignorant* (Yaniv, Benador, & Sagi, 2004) individuals may underestimate their own risk and thus avoid risk management or early detection protocols that could extend their lives while simultaneously maintaining their quality of life. As individuals "stage" closer to expected ages for disease onset, they may experience greater emotional distress and become averse to seeking information about genetic testing and risk management (Johnson, Case, Andrews, & Allard, 2010). In any case, attempts to correct mistaken beliefs may improve health outcomes. Social workers may partner with genetic counselors and other health professionals to help patients understand estimates as probabilistic rather than prophetic. Departure from deterministic understandings may increase anxiety but also will support informed medical decision making.

Reproductive Genetics and Infertility

Genetic information frequently becomes salient for individuals and couples considering pregnancy or anticipating the birth of a child. At these times, couples and providers focus on the health of the fetus and the risks that may impact a pregnancy or delivery. Because of the complexities of development, all pregnancies have a risk of miscarriage and birth defects, regardless of the genetic and environmental background of the biological parents. Most birth defects occur during the first trimester (www.acog.org/publications/patient _education/bp165.cfm), and some can be detected through ultrasound and blood tests. Others cannot, making it important to clarify the limitations of prenatal testing to the prospective parent(s).

Genetic services, specifically prenatal genetic counseling, often are incorporated into family planning and pregnancy care, because of the ability to detect certain types of genetic conditions prior to the birth, and in some cases the conception, of the child. Prenatal counseling discussions inherently evoke ethical and moral issues, because they involve decisions about an unborn fetus. Genetic counselors may be involved in providing information about the potential diagnosis and risks, as well as helping prospective parents with decision making that is compatible with their values and beliefs. Counselors are trained to facilitate these discussions in a nondirective way. Social workers also can be part of these discussions, especially with regard to exploring the couple's social and familial context and how certain decisions might affect their family system. Understanding the options available for testing may help to facilitate the decision-making process.

Social workers have long been involved in providing prenatal genetic services. Ongoing research examines the support needs of women carrying fetuses that have been diagnosed with genetic anomalies (McCoyd, 2008, 2010). This work suggests that one of the most critical factors in supporting women through genetic testing and decision making about pregnancy termination is a connection with empathic providers (McCoyd, 2010). This fact speaks to the need for social workers to support clients and educate physicians on how to provide compassionate and holistic care.

Prenatal Diagnosis

Genetic diagnosis of a fetus during pregnancy is done using a variety of methods. Screening tests do not test the fetus's blood directly but rather test pregnancy-associated proteins for the possibility of a genetic condition. These screening tests do not provide definitive diagnoses. Instead, they provide risk information that can help with making decisions about whether to seek further testing.

First-trimester screening involves a blood test and an ultrasound. These procedures can provide information about increased risk for certain chromosomal problems, including Down syndrome and trisomy 18 (having three copies of chromosome 18 rather than two). They allow the identification of Down syndrome in 82% to 87% of cases. Second-trimester screening for Down syndrome, trisomy 18, trisomy 13, and neural tube defects uses a blood test. If a woman has had a negative screen during the first trimester, she requires only one additional blood test, for neural tube defects, during her second trimester. Typically, a detailed ultrasound is performed at 18 to 20 weeks into a pregnancy to visualize the fetus and to screen for major structural abnormalities. Not all birth defects can be visualized, and some can develop after 20 weeks.

Women at high risk for having a child with detectable genetic disorders because of results from screening tests, ultrasound, family history, or advanced maternal age (greater than 35) may be offered prenatal testing of fetal cells. Chorionic villis sampling (CVS) and amniocentesis remove and isolate fetal cells that are then grown and examined for chromosomal anomalies. CVS can be done earlier in pregnancy (between 10 and 13 weeks) than amniocentesis (after 14 weeks). Both carry a risk for miscarriage in around 1% of cases. If there is a known single-gene disorder in the family, the fetal cells obtained through CVS or amniocentesis can be used to test for the presence of that known mutation. Social workers should be aware that although nearly all women receiving prenatal care receive an ultrasound, many low-income women cannot afford amniocentesis or CVS. Furthermore, any woman covered by a federal health insurance plan, such as through the military or a public program, will not be covered for pregnancy termination; federal law prohibits federal funds from being used for abortion under any circumstance.

In Vitro Fertilization and Preimplantation Genetic Diagnosis

In vitro fertilization (IVF) is a reproductive technology that enables some infertile couples to carry and give birth to a biologically related child. IVF first was used successfully nearly three decades ago and has become widely available around the United States. The procedure is expensive, and insurance coverage is not standard across plans. The procedure also is said to be emotionally exhausting, with multiple attempts often needed before a successful pregnancy is achieved. Male and female factors, or a combination of the two, contribute. Cultural mandates to procreate, fear of social judgment, and shame about infertility frequently push couples to keep their infertility

and IVF experiences secret, potentially depriving them of critical emotional support.

Preimplantation genetic diagnosis (PGD) was first developed in 1990 and by early 2005 had been used in over 3,000 IVF cycles, resulting in over 700 births (Klipstein, 2005). PGD is a technically complex and expensive procedure by which blastocysts (pre-embryo produced by cell division following fertilization) produced through IVF are examined for a specific genetic disorder before transfer. Only those embryos that are determined to be unaffected are transferred to the uterus. PGD allows couples at risk to begin a pregnancy with a blastocyst known to be free of the disorder in question. PGD commonly is used to detect chromosomal aneuploidies (an abnormal number of chromosomes) that produce disorders such as Down syndrome (trisomy 21) or Turner syndrome (monosomy X) and approximately 100 single-gene disorders. Currently, it is impossible to use a single PGD procedure to detect multiple conditions without compromising the viability of the blastocyst. Finally, IVF and PGD may both produce viable embryos that are never transferred to the uterus. Thus, initiating these procedures requires couples to consider what to do with unused embryos: to freeze them for potential future use, donate them for research, or destroy them.

PGD raises ethical and moral issues for both the couple and the population as a whole. Technically, PGD can be used to test embryos for a range of disorders, from those that are lethal in childhood, such as Tay-Sachs disease, to those that are adult onset and for which treatments are available, such as *BRCA1/2* associated breast and ovarian cancer. It also can be used to detect conditions such as deafness, for which there is disagreement about its consideration as a disease. Despite the issues it raises, PGD broadens the options for individuals who previously chose not to have children because they might pass on a genetic condition.

Carrier Screening

Couples who are planning a pregnancy and have a family history of genetic illness or who are among a high-risk group for a genetic illness may request carrier screening to identify genetic mutations or anomalies. Some of the disorders for which carrier screening is available are Tay-Sachs disease, sickle cell disease, and cystic fibrosis. If recessive genetic disorders are known to exist in a family, individuals may choose to know their carrier status for the disorder. Carrier screening may reveal that a person has an altered gene for the disorder. If the person's partner is also a carrier, the risk for a child with the condition is 25%. If only one person is a carrier, the couple's offspring will not be affected; thus, a single test may be all that the couple need. If a single member of the couple is a carrier, the couple may elect to replace that partner's germ cell (ovum or sperm) with donor ova or sperm to minimize risk. The use of donor material requires the use of assisted reproductive techniques. As a rule, donor sperm requires only intrauterine insemination while donor ovum requires a full IVF cycle for both the donor and the gestational mothers.

Ensuring that someone is not a carrier is difficult in some cases. For example, cystic fibrosis (CF) is an autosomal recessive condition caused by mutations in the *CFTR* gene. Although over 1,000 mutations are known to cause cystic fibrosis, the carrier screening panel is required to test for only 23 of them (Watson et al., 2004), because these 23 account for the vast majority of mutations found in the population with CF. Negative carrier screening using this panel will substantially decrease the chance that the individual is a carrier for CF but cannot eliminate the possibility entirely. In addition, the panel is optimized for the population that has the highest prevalence of people affected with CF, northern Europeans. Individuals in other populations may be more likely to have CF caused by mutations that do not occur on the standard carrier panel. Consequently, the detection rate is not the same across groups. This is true for other conditions as well. Therefore, couples must be counseled adequately about the limitations of testing as well as its benefits (see Box 21.3).

Genetic Testing for Adult-Onset Disorders

Genetic testing for adult-onset disorders identifies germline mutations in blood or tissue samples that are linked to specific patterns of disease risk. These illnesses typically present in adulthood, as is the case Huntington's disease and certain cancers. Individuals may present for genetic testing for a variety of reasons. If an abnormality is discovered, a patient or loved one is peridiagnostic, or if a family history indicates patterns of genetic inheritance, the individual may pursue genetic testing to inform treatment decisions. Individuals and couples frequently pursue genetic testing to inform family planning. Early population-based studies of interest in genetic testing for adult disorders predicted significant uptake, yet only a small percentage of individuals and families referred for genetic counseling complete that testing (Struewing, Lerman, & Kase, 1995). Individuals with family histories of disorders for which prevention and treatment remain elusive pursue genetic testing even less frequently than do individuals with disease for which effective treatment exists (e.g., Decruyenaere et al., 1997).

Genetic testing may provide individuals from families with extensive disease histories with a sense of increased control over inherited risk by minimizing uncertainty and opening avenues for advanced and targeted preventive medical care (Gooding, Organista, Burack, & Biesecker, 2006). If genetic testing reveals a genetic mutation, carriers must make crucial, and frequently distressing, decisions, about how to monitor their health (Erblich, Bovbjerg, & Valdimarsdottir, 2000; Schlich-Bakker, ten Kroode, & Ausems, 2006). Predominant models of health behavior suggest health decisions are "rational" when informed by a combination of a risk–benefit calculus, pressures from and modeling of important others, beliefs about control and mastery, and available resources (see Chapter 6, "Theories of Health Behavior"). Although socially focused models of health behavior and decision making exist, these models were conceptualized well before

Box 21.3 Essential Skills for Social Workers in Genetics

Social workers should develop skills to:

- Acquire a basic understanding about genetics as a science and a field of study, including its biological, psychosocial, ethical, and legal aspects.
- Gather relevant genetic family history information, including a multigenerational family history that includes parents, children, siblings, grandparents, aunts/uncles, and cousins.
- Identify clients who might benefit from a referral for genetic services.
- Properly communicate to clients the purpose of genetic services and the role of various genetic professionals.
- Provide culturally sensitive services to clients with or at risk of developing genetic conditions.
- Seek assistance from and refer to appropriate genetics experts and peer support resources.
- Explore with clients the possible range of emotional effects they and family members may experience as a result of receiving or refusing genetic information.
- Assist clients and their families in the genetic decision-making process and in adapting to genetic information throughout the life cycle.
- Discuss costs of genetic services and insurance benefits.

- Safeguard privacy and confidentiality of genetic information of clients to the extent possible.
- Facilitate the creation and maintenance of support resources for clients with genetic conditions.
- Obtain current genetic information from reliable sources, for self, clients, and colleagues.
- Educate clients, professionals, and the community about policy issues regarding genetics.
- Advocate for client-focused public policy in genetics.
- Assist clients in understanding the limitations and benefits of participating in genetics research and the importance of informed consent.
- Develop specialized knowledge and understanding about the history, traditions, values, and family systems of client groups as they relate to genetics.
- Participate in multidisciplinary teams that deliver comprehensive genetics services and conduct genetics research.
- Contribute to the development of research-based and practice-relevant knowledge of the psychosocial, cultural, economic, and ethical implications of genetics on individuals, families, and society.

Source: NASW Standards for Integrating Genetics into Social Work Practice by J. Weiss et al., 2003, Washington, DC: NASW Press.

the genetic revolution and may prove insufficient for the examination of individual and family experiences with hereditary disease. For example, these models do not take into account the importance of family histories in shaping cognitive representations of the illness experience long before the individual experiences a symptom or diagnosis, a scenario in which grief, self-concept, and relational dynamics are tied intimately to illness expectations and decision making.

Risk assessment and subsequent medical decision making often involve calculating genetically determined disease risk against other pressing psychosocial risks, such as the burden of a potential diagnosis on loved ones or anticipated decision regret from a specific course of action (or inaction). Psychosocial assessment of individuals pursuing genetic testing for adult-onset disorders must take into account the individual's dependencies, interdependencies, and obligations in family life. These obligations intersect with (anticipated) physical symptoms, affective factors that impact information processing and coping, and social contexts (Howard et al., 2009) to shape medical decision making about genetic testing, risk management, and prevention. For example, empirical findings suggest these factors shape the decision to complete risk-reducing mastectomy, salpingo-oophorectomy, or colectomy to minimize inherited cancer risk. In the absence of illness, some individuals may experience inertia in changing health behaviors. For others, anxiety and distress are consistent predictors of how they manage disease risk.

Genetic testing is available for some conditions for which no treatments exist. For disorders such as Huntington's disease and early-onset Alzheimer's disease, risk is not malleable via medical, surgical, or lifestyle intervention. Living with uncertainty about when and how a dormant genetic condition will become symptomatic may increase anticipatory mourning for a healthy identity and challenge adaptive coping to genetic testing results (Rolland, 2006).

Mapping Genetic Risk in Family Histories

Uncertainty about genetic testing results (e.g., many *BRCA* variants are not yet linked to concrete risk information), disease penetrance (not all gene mutation will lead to disease), illness onset and course (Alzheimer's disease onset varies tremendously), and outcomes (whether treatment will be effective in preventing or treating disease) shape coping and adaptation. Ambiguity challenges understandings of risk and makes advance planning difficult. Given that limited research addresses the variety of factors that scatter gene alteration carriers across spectrums of disease risk, clinicians continue to look at family histories as predictors of risk, as do individuals (Werner-Lin, 2007). Subjective perceptions of risk, couched in family histories with disease rather than statistical risk estimates, are powerful predictors of interest in and uptake of genetic testing and risk management choices for high-risk individuals and families.

A pedigree is a multigenerational representation of patterns of biological inheritance and disease expression that includes information about the family's geographic origins, births and deaths, medical problems, birth defects, and developmental delays (Bennett, 1999). Designed to identify patterns of genetic inheritance, a family pedigree focuses on biological families (Atkinson, Parsons, & Featherstone, 2001; Kenen & Peters, 2001) rather than the affective experiences and cognitive perceptions that guide health promotion and risk management behaviors around inherited risk (Patenaude, 2004). Early attempts to identify the genetic mutation for increased breast and ovarian cancer risk recruited families with multiple affected members within and across generations. In these studies, family history tools such as the pedigree were used extensively to identify patterns of illness expression and to suggest genetic markers for disease risk (e.g., Lynch & de la Chapelle, 2003).

Like the pedigree, a genogram maps multigenerational family patterns, helping to expand the family's scope of attention from the individual to the familial (Kenen & Peters, 2001; McDaniel, Rolland, Feetham, & Miller, 2006). A medically oriented genogram incorporates developmental, familial, community, and social factors that influence and are affected by disease expression and management as well as the emotional sequela (McGoldrick, Gerson, & Shellenberger, 1999). The process of creating a family genogram can bring to light shared and individual narratives and discourses around familial disease (Eunpu, 1997) and enable shifts in perceptions of disease risk (Werner-Lin & Gardner, 2009).

Mounting evidence supports the notion that individuals in families with ambiguous genetic testing interpret their risk based on patterns of illness expression in their families, family loyalties, and visual and personality characteristics (Werner-Lin, 2007). Reaching the age of a parent at their diagnosis and reactions to prior losses contribute to meaning attribution about genetic testing results (Gabriel, 1992; Werner-Lin, 2008). For example, significant illness milestones may increase anxiety or anticipatory loss. As illness experiences accumulate and recur over generations, as they frequently do with hereditary disease, they become family myths that include beliefs about who gets sick and why, how families care for ill members, appropriate modes of communication within the family and with outsiders, and illness outcomes. Those who test negative for genes linked to familial disease experience their own unique challenges in integrating genetic testing results, including survivor guilt, the need to alter trajectories so that they no longer make room for a future diagnosis, or disbelief at test results (Bakos et al., 2008; Sobel & Cowan, 2003).

Inherited Adult-Onset Disease Risk Across the Life Cycle

The timing of genetic testing in the life course plays a significant role in coping with and adaptation to testing results. Furthermore, coping and adaptation to genetic information changes over the life cycle, as salient developmental tasks shift.

Childhood. Children growing up in homes with parents affected by critical or terminal illness frequently grow up faster than peers because of responsibilities to maintain the household or to care for ill parents and younger siblings. Early parental loss drastically alters normative developmental trajectories and shapes perceptions of vulnerability to inherited disease in addition to coping and medical decision making.

Adolescence. Treatment has improved substantially for some genetic conditions (e.g., cystic fibrosis), and children with genetic conditions that previously were fatal now live well into adulthood. Providers are not necessarily prepared to address the concerns of adolescents aging out of pediatric care. Research is needed to identify the new challenges faced by adolescents as their disorders shift from fatal to chronic and as their care shifts from pediatric clinics with holistic resources to adult facilities that rely on patients to coordinate and manage their own care.

Young Adulthood. Individuals with inherited disease risk frequently pursue genetic testing during their reproductive years to inform marriage and family planning. Couples may promise to love each other in sickness and in health, yet the experience of creating a life plan that integrates the possibility of early illness and death is developmentally out of sync with normative developmental tasks of establishing intimate relationships and the start of family planning. Inherited disease risk may shape the qualities an individual seeks in a life partner (Werner-Lin, 2008) as well as a couple's hopes and fears about family planning. Genetic testing during this life stage informs: (a) life planning surrounding marriage, childbearing, and professional development (Hoskins, Roy, Peters, Loud, & Green, 2008); (b) the adult's capacity to remain healthy and vital to parent a child; and (c) the child's risk of developing the same condition as they reach adulthood. In some communities, such as Orthodox Jewish communities, genetic testing provides information about one's viability as a spouse. Parents may feel responsibility to protect children from genetic conditions or may experience guilt at potentially passing on genetic mutations to children.

NEGOTIATING COMMON ETHICAL CHALLENGES

Competent and skilled practice requires familiarity with common ethical challenges faced by health and mental health providers. Attempts to deal with ethical dilemmas must rely both on the National Association of Social Workers Code of Ethics and on major principles of bioethics, such as respect for autonomy, beneficence, and justice. This section of the chapter highlights some of the more challenging dilemmas confronting providers today, including informed consent, family communication and confidentiality, patient autonomy, and genetic testing of minors for adult-onset disorders.

Informed Consent

Originating in the doctrine of self-determination, informed consent is a process of communication between a provider and a patient, during which the risks and benefits associated with a procedure are explained, thus enabling the patient to make an educated and personal choice about whether to proceed. Individuals give informed consent when agreeing to any medical procedure. This consent should be voluntary and based on adequate and accurate information and understanding. A variety of issues challenge providers' ability to obtain informed consent across medical settings. For example, some have argued that informed consent procedures have suffered as prenatal genetic testing became integrated into standard prenatal care (McCoyd, 2010; Rapp, 1999). Although genetics is not the only medical discipline that has struggled with how to ensure informed consent, the nature of genetic research and treatment protocols present unique challenges. These protocols frequently involve complex and sophisticated explanations of diagnostic, treatment, and research procedures. That 90 million Americans have limited health literacy means that individuals across a variety of medical and community settings might agree to participate in protocols without sufficient understanding of the medical, social, psychological, economic, and legal risks they could incur.

Our ability to identify genetic vulnerability to a condition continues to outpace medicine's ability to treat it, marking a significant *therapeutic gap* (Holtzman & Watson, 1997) in genetic medicine. The information contained in informed consent documents presented at the time of genetic testing may be confusing and leave a person with unrealistic expectations or false assumptions about test results (Freedman, 1997). A person considering genetic testing or research participation in which genetic markers are used should engage voluntarily. There may be internal (anxiety, fear) or external pressures (family members or health-care providers) to engage in these activities. The question of how well individuals understand consent forms is subjective and is influenced by their emotional state at the time. Thus, the stress of genetic counseling and testing may limit the patient's or family's ability to attend sufficiently to the detailed explication of the risk and benefits of the procedure.

Currently, genetics research projects funded by the National Institutes of Health (NIH) are required to add genotype and phenotype data into a single, large database (dbGAP) that can be accessed by other NIH researchers. This is a protected database, and access is heavily regulated with specific attention to privacy and confidentiality. Pooling data among studies will increase the ability of researchers to investigate genetic contributions to both rare and common diseases, yet protocols using this database do not routinely query patients who have provided blood samples or tissue about informed consent that addresses confidentiality, the scope of future research, or the return of laboratory results (Ludman et al., 2010; Wolf, Bouley, & McCulloch, 2010).

Current protocols also have led to questions about the ownership of genetic material and about who should benefit from genetic discoveries. These issues are explored in the recent biography of Henrietta Lacks, who unknowingly "donated" the first human cells successfully cultured in a laboratory (Skloot, 2010). Although discoveries using her cells (called HeLa cells) led to significant breakthroughs in public health, her children and grandchildren remain impoverished and uninsured. Furthermore, they did not know that Ms. Lacks's cells had been obtained, cultured, or used for scientific research. Although new protections exist to prevent such situations, genetic research has identified significant gaps that remain in informed consent protocols for research.

Family Communication and Confidentiality

The familial implications of identifying genetic links to conditions and traits shifts the existing biomedical paradigm that focuses on the rights of the individual patient to a broader focus on the rights of family members. Although genetic testing information may be probabilistic, genetic testing of one family member for a condition may identify other family members at risk. This may motivate individuals to pursue testing, as in the case of a perimenopausal woman with a breast cancer diagnosis who pursues genetic testing not only to inform her own treatment decisions, but also to identify risk to her children. Patients may withhold genetic testing information from family members because they do not want to upset bereaved loved ones if they are estranged, if they perceive family members are unlikely to take action, or if they want to keep their risk information private (Offit, Groeger, Turner, Wadsworth & Weiser, 2004; Patenaude, 2004).

Genetic research using a family systems lens identified challenging family roles created by the possibility of genetic testing. The first individual in a family to pursue testing and to discuss risk with family members is the messenger of genetic information. Children testing positive for a recessive or X-linked genetic condition may identify parents as obligate carriers (Adelsward & Sachs, 2003, Dudokde Wit et al., 1997). Obligate carriers and others implicated by genetic testing in the bloodline may be unprepared to learn about or address their risk. Furthermore, perceptions of risk may be skewed, if risk information is communicated unclearly or inaccurately within families (Smith, Dancyger, Wallace, & Michie, 2010).

If genetic testing reveals risk information about an entire bloodline, the needs of the entire family must be considered. Providers may be challenged to help family members approach this question in a way that is respectful to everyone. Facilitating disclosure of genetic testing results in families includes attention to the rights of family members not to know. The concerns of individual family members unprepared to address and use genetic testing information reach beyond health risks; this information may impact mental health, individual development and family formation, relationship, and dynamics (Gilbar, 2007). Social work training includes skills that can be applied to support planned disclosure and to facilitate family discussion of genetic testing.

Because genetic testing reveals risk information for an entire family, individuals who do not know they may have inherited disease risk do not have the opportunity to engage in treatment or prevention. If treatments are available to prevent a fatal illness or improve quality of life and prevent suffering, are doctors obligated to share genetic information with other members of the bloodline? The Health Insurance Portability and Accountability Act requires physicians to breech confidentiality to "prevent or lessen a serious and immediate threat" (Department of Health and Human Services, www.hhs.gov/ocr/privacy/hipaa/understanding/summary/index.html). The Institute of Medicine concurs that when failure to communicate genetic information can result in serious, imminent harm or death, the physician may contact the family if the patient has not done so. Although some genetic diseases follow predictable patterns of expression, many inherited predispositions are ambiguous and uncertain, leaving significant gray area in interpreting federal policy and medical guidelines.

Patient Autonomy and Testing Minors

Children constitute an especially vulnerable group in terms of genetic screening, because they are dependent on adults (Knoppers, Avard, Cardinal, & Glass, 2002). When a genetic condition presents in childhood, genetic testing before the child is symptomatic, or as the child becomes symptomatic, may help physicians to manage the condition medically (Field, Shanley, & Kirk, 2007).

Genetic testing of minors is more ethically questionable for disorders that present later in life. These disorders vary widely, and families should be discouraged from genetic testing, unless children and teens can benefit from testing before they reach adulthood. The professional ethics of both geneticists and genetic counselors do not support testing children for adult onset disorders in most circumstances (e.g., the National Society of Genetic Counselors position statement, 1995). This is because they believe that children should have the right to decide about testing when they reach adulthood. Beyond the inability of a child to give informed consent, genetic testing in childhood presents a host of ethical and social concerns for children and families. Genetic testing in childhood removes children's right to know (or not know) their genetic status; opens them up to the possibility of discrimination in social, academic, and medical settings; and may impact their self-concept, self-esteem, and the ways they are parented (Ross & Fost, 2006). Although genetic testing at any stage of the life cycle informs family planning, testing during childhood removes reproductive confidentiality and may shape the messages children receive about becoming parents. Furthermore, the abstract nature of probabilistic risk information is hard for adults to comprehend; it is even more difficult for children to do so, as they have not yet developed the cognitive tools to understand abstractions or probability, or may be learning about their risk from parents with skewed perceptions or distinct motivations. Finally, as prenatal testing becomes more sophisticated, parents may be able to decide to pursue prenatal genetic testing for adult-onset conditions, whether to make decisions about pregnancy termination or to skirt recommendations against genetic testing in childhood. This means that a child may be born as a known carrier of a genetic condition that is unlikely to present for decades.

No legally definitive statement regulates the testing of minors for genetic conditions presenting in adulthood. In the absence of legal guidance, bioethicists and health and mental health professionals are left to debate what is in the best interests of the child. Who is in the best position to decide for or about the child? Although parents express considerable interest in genetic testing for adult-onset disorders during childhood, such testing is not recommended when no treatments exist for children. This is particularly evident when genetic testing may result in psychosocial harm (stigma, self-esteem) to the child and the family. Although parental anxiety may be reduced by genetic testing, families may have problems planning and adjusting expectations about the child's life and abilities. Parents may benefit from an explanation of why testing is not in the child's best interest. Children may be (unintentionally) coerced by parents or feel motivated by a parent's guilt and distress to pursue testing (Wilfond & Ross, 2009). Instead, children

should be informed about genetic testing after they reach adulthood (McConkie-Rosell & Spiridigliozzi, 2004).

POLICY DEVELOPMENTS

Health-care professionals and individuals, families, and groups pursuing genetic testing have been hindered by the concern that results might be used for discriminatory purposes. Of specific concern is the impact of genetic testing information on health insurance coverage and deductibles and other fees. In a few cases, employers inappropriately have required genetic testing of employees and then used results to make employment or promotion decisions. Although the civil rights of individuals with genetic conditions are protected under the Americans with Disabilities Act, protection from other types of discrimination does not exist. These concerns constitute a significant barrier to genetic services, particularly genetic testing.

After a 13-year process that culminated in May 2008, President George W. Bush signed the Genetic Information Nondiscrimination Act (GINA) into law (see Box 21.4). All aspects of the law were in effect as of November 2009. GINA was created to remove barriers to the appropriate use of genetic services. The legislation protects the public from the misuse of genetic information by health insurers and employers. GINA amended laws that do not apply to certain groups of individuals receiving federal benefits. Those excluded are members of the United States military, veterans obtaining health care through the Veterans Administration, individuals using the Indian Health Service, or federal employees enrolled in the Federal Employees Health Benefits program. However, the military and veterans' health-care systems have policies in place that provide protections similar to GINA. Federal employees likewise are protected by an executive order that was signed by President Clinton in 2000. Despite its limitations, GINA is landmark legislation that removes a significant barrier to genetic testing.

Box 21.4 Genetic Information Nondiscrimination Act

Genetic Information Nondiscrimination Act (GINA) states:

Under GINA, group and individual health insurers cannot:

- Use a person's genetic information to set eligibility requirements or establish premium or contribution amounts.
- Request or require that a person undergo a genetic test.

Under GINA, employers cannot:

- Use a person's genetic information in decisions about hiring, firing, job assignments, or promotions.
- Request, require, or purchase genetic information about an employee or family member.

GINA protects genetic information related to:

- Family medical history.
- Carrier testing: that is, cystic fibrosis, sickle cell anemia, spinal muscular atrophy, fragile X, and other conditions.

- Prenatal genetic testing: that is, amniocentesis, chorionic villus sampling, and other techniques.
- Susceptibility and predictive testing: for example, *BRCA* testing for risk of breast or ovarian cancer, testing for Huntington's disease, or HNPCC testing for risk of colon cancer.
- Analysis of tumors or other assessments of genes, mutations, or chromosomal changes.

GINA does not protect against or apply to:

- A condition that is already diagnosed and manifest, even if that condition is genetic.
- Life, disability, or long-term-care insurers (as of the date listed on this document).
- Information about current health status.
- Employers with fewer than 15 employees.

GINA does not protect certain groups of individuals.

Source: The Genetic Nondiscrimination Act (GINA), National Coalition of Health Professional Education in Genetics, 2010. Retrieved from www.nchpeg.org/index.php?option=com_content&view=article&id=97&Itemid=120

CONCLUSION

Genetic discovery may provide new interpretive frames for the meaning and cause of disease. The movement toward consumer-driven health care is challenged by the combination of limited health literacy and the beliefs about the promise of genetic discoveries that have yet to develop. Recognizing genetic, as well as environmental, factors that impact conditions and traits will allow social workers, in partnership with other health and mental health professionals, to develop interventions and resources that are targeted to educating and supporting the unique circumstances of individuals, families, and communities.

Adapting to and integrating genetic information into a life plan is an ongoing process, with fluctuating periods of tranquility and distress. For individuals from families with extensive disease histories, genetic explanations may increase distress and anticipatory loss by altering expectations about future health status. Alternatively, genetic mechanisms and the ability to test for the presence (or absence) of a disease-related mutation may enable patients to construct life plans that maximize healthy years. Whereas contact with genetic counselors and physicians is time limited, an underestimated strength of social work in genetics is social workers' ability to have ongoing contact with clients and their families (Weiss et al. 2003). The potential for prolonged contact with mental health services allows social workers to facilitate adaptation and coping over extended periods of time and throughout the life cycle as new concerns emerge and the meaning of risk shifts. Social workers are in a unique position to develop and implement relevant programs to provide ongoing support for families with educational and supportive services delivered at key points in the adaptation to genetic conditions (Taylor-Brown & Johnson, 1998).

SUGGESTED LEARNING EXERCISES

Read the exercises and discuss how you would help clients deal with their genetic concerns.

Learning Exercise 21.1

Tina and Jon are referred to a social worker after routine ultrasound identified multiple birth defects in their developing baby. The specific pattern of defects indicates their child has a rare, inherited genetic condition. After the initial diagnosis by the obstetrician, the couple met with a fetal-maternal specialist at a medical center who performed a high-resolution ultrasound and confirmed the findings. Because the couple is only eight weeks from the due date, pregnancy termination is not an option.

The couple was referred for genetic counseling after the diagnosis. The genetic counselor explored Tina and Jon's family medical histories and documented that no one has reported a stillbirth or neonatal death in three generations. Tina is 31 years old, and this is her first pregnancy. She has two older sisters and several nieces and nephews who are healthy. Jon is 38 years old and has two healthy school-age children from a previous marriage who stay with the couple on alternating weekends. The genetic counselor tells Tina and Jon that each of them carries a specific gene alteration and when they both pass the gene on to a child, the presence of the two altered genes will result in disruption of fetal development. There is no genetic test to confirm this diagnosis. Furthermore, each child they conceive has a 25% chance of inheriting both altered forms of the gene. Both appear to be too distracted and angry to absorb this risk information.

Tina and Jon are both distraught that so little is known about their baby's condition. Both are appropriately concerned and frightened. Jon is worried about Tina and how this

baby will impact her and their marriage. Tina is angry that she needs to wait and see what happens at delivery. When Jon is out of the room, she tells you she is jealous that Jon's other children are fine and worries about what she might have done to deserve this, to "ruin" her baby. Jon is not sleeping and is actively engaging Tina in discussions about a timeline and plans for conceiving the next baby.

1. Draw a genogram of this family, indicating both medical and family data.
2. What are the key pieces of information about the genetic condition? What is the mode of inheritance? Describe the risk to each future pregnancy.
3. You recognize that you need better information to counsel this couple. Find resources that will help you learn about this condition so that you can support them in their efforts at family planning.
4. What are the primary psychosocial concerns this couple might face after the child is born?
5. Prioritize these psychosocial concerns, and identify interventions and resources that will help support the family in your community.

Learning Exercise 21.2

Carolyn and Michael have been attempting to achieve a pregnancy since their wedding 8 months ago. Carolyn is 39 years old, and Michael is anxious about her fertility because of her age. Carolyn's mother was diagnosed with breast cancer at age 46 and died at age 51. Carolyn's maternal aunt and grandmother also died of breast cancer. After meeting Michael, Carolyn pursued genetic testing and was found to carry a *BRCA1* genetic mutation. Carolyn is eager to have children quickly given her age and her desire to complete risk-reducing mastectomy (surgical removal of breasts) and salpingo-oophorectomy (surgical removal of her ovaries and fallopian tubes) to minimize her chances of developing cancer.

For fertility reasons, Carolyn asks for a referral to a reproductive endocrinologist to discuss assisted reproduction. Michael and Carolyn come to the first appointment with questions in hand and a growing sense of urgency. Their consultation leads to several testing appointments with the good news that no obvious clinical condition appears to exist. During the discussion of what interventions might have the best success, the reproductive endocrinologist brings up the *BRCA1* mutation and introduces the possibility of pre-implantation genetic diagnosis (PGD) in combination with in vitro fertilization (IVF). PGD screens embryos from IVF for the *BRCA1* mutation, thus allowing only embryos without the mutation to be implanted. IVF is not guaranteed to achieve a successful pregnancy. The doctor advises the couple that there is no good data about the impact of IVF-associated hormone treatment on breast cancer risk for women with a *BRCA* mutation. The data for women at average risk for breast cancer show that there is no increased breast cancer risk associated with the hormone treatment. PGD is an additional cost on top of IVF, which is generally costly and not always covered by insurance.

Carolyn is interested in pursuing PGD. She discusses the procedure with her sisters, both physicians, and they agree that it is an attractive option. Michael is not interested in pursuing PGD. He is concerned about expense and the impact of the hormone treatments on Carolyn's cancer risk, especially given how close in age she is to when her mother was diagnosed initially. Carolyn and Michael meet with a genetic counselor who explains that, because of their age, there is a slightly greater than 1% chance that any fetus they conceive may have a chromosomal abnormality. Michael is very concerned about the risk and would like to conceive quickly. Carolyn feels differently; compared to her lifetime risk of developing cancer, her interpretation of chromosomal risk is more positive: a 99% chance that a conception at this age will not have any chromosomal abnormalities. She would like

to proceed immediately with PGD. Michael disagrees, stating they should not interfere with the natural process of creating a baby if no obvious fertility issue exists, since they have been trying to conceive for less than 12 months, and the baby may not inherit the mutation. Carolyn disagrees and feels very disappointed in Michael. She begins to experience severe anxiety, and they argue regularly. The couple is referred to you for counseling.

1. Draw a genogram of this family, indicating both medical and family data.
2. The couple has a number of competing pragmatic and emotional concerns. Describe these concerns and how they are related to perceptions of risk.
3. You recognize that you need better information to counsel this couple. Find resources that will help you learn about these conditions so that you can support them in their efforts at family planning.
4. Identify targets for change and appropriate interventions to support the couple.

SUGGESTED RESOURCES

American College for Medical Genetics—www.acmg.net

This site provides information about clinical geneticists and includes a search function to locate a clinical geneticist. The site also presents educational materials, including information about newborn screening and statements covering a variety of genetics issues.

Centre for Genetics Education—www.genetics.com.au/home.asp

The Centre for Genetics Education is dedicated to providing current and relevant genetics information to individuals and family members affected by genetic conditions and to professionals who work with them.

Duke Center for Human Genetics—www.chg.duke.edu/education/online.html

The mission of the Duke Center for Human Genetics is to discover genetic influences on human health, to characterize the relationship between genetic and environmental influences, and to foster the application of this knowledge to the practice of medicine. The site contains online educational programs for a variety of audiences as well as research resources.

Genetic Alliance—www.geneticalliance.org

Genetic Alliance was started by social workers to increase the ability of genetic advocacy groups to achieve their missions and leverage the voices of millions of individuals and families living with genetic conditions. The alliance has an annual conference, links to support groups for common and rare conditions, advocacy resources including specialty issue teams (e.g., access, disparities), a resource repository for educational materials and presentations, and news.

Genetic and Rare Conditions Site—www .kumc.edu/gec

The University of Kansas Medical Center has links to lay advocacy and support groups and information on genetic conditions/birth defects for professionals, educators, and individuals, national and international organizations.

Genetics and Public Policy Center—www .dnapolicy.org

The center helps policy leaders, decision makers, and the public better understand and respond to the challenges and opportunities arising from advances in genetics and their application to human health and well-being. The center's multidisciplinary team monitors advances in human genetics and their translation into clinical applications and conducts qualitative and quantitative social science and legal and policy analysis.

Genetics Science Learning Center—http:// learn.genetics.utah.edu/gslc/

The Genetics Science Learning Center is a science and health education program that aims to make biology and genetics concepts accessible. It provides educational materials and interactive programs on genetics for local and global audiences.

National Coalition of Health Professional Education in Genetics—www.nchpeg.org

NCHPEG promotes health professional education and access to information about advances in human genetics. NCHPEG draws on the collective experience and expertise of multiple organizations, professionals, and specialists to promote genetics education. The Web site offers free, online educational programs for a variety of audiences as well as biannual newsletters, core competencies in genetics, and information from the annual professional meetings.

National Human Genome Research Institute (NHGRI) at the National Institutes of Health—www.genome.gov

NHGRI is one of the 27 institutes and centers at National Institutes of Health. NHGRI led NIH's efforts toward the International Human Genome Project, which had as its primary goal the sequencing of the human genome. This project was completed successfully in April 2003. Now the NHGRI's mission has expanded to encompass a broad range of studies aimed at understanding the structure and function of the human genome and its role in health and disease. The Web site has informational and educational materials about all aspects of genetics.

National Society of Genetic Counselors— www.nsgc.org

This site provides information about genetic counseling and a search feature to assist people to find a genetic counselor. It also includes a list of resources for patients concerned about genetic discrimination.

REFERENCES

Adelsward, V., & Sachs, L. (2003). The messenger's dilemmas—Giving and getting information in genealogical mapping for hereditary cancer. *Health, Risk & Society, 5*(2), 125–138.

Agrawal, A., & Lynskey, M. T. (2008). Are there genetic influences on addiction: Evidence from family, adoption, and twin studies. *Addiction, 103*(7), 1069–1081.

Ancker, J. S., & Kaufman, D. (2007). Rethinking health numeracy: A multidisciplinary literature review. *Journal of the American Medical Informatics Association, 14*(6), 713–721.

Annes, J. P., Giovanni, M. A., Murray, M. F. (2010). Risks of presymptomatic direct-to-consumer genetic testing. *New England Journal of Medicine, 363*(12), 1100–1101.

Atkinson, P. A., Parsons, E., & Featherstone, K. (2001). Professional constructions of family and kinship in medical genetics. *New Genetics and Society, 20,* 6–24.

Bakos, A. D., Hutson, S. P., Loud, J. T., Peters, J. A., Giusti, R. M., & Greene, M. H. (2008). *BRCA* mutation-negative women from hereditary breast and ovarian cancer families: A qualitative study of the *BRCA*-negative experience. *Health Expectations, 11,* 220–231.

Bennett, R. (1999). *The practical guide to the genetic family history.* Indianapolis, IN: Wiley.

Berg, A. O., Allan, J. D., Homer, C. J., Johnson, M. S., Klein, J. D., Lieu, T. A.,...U.S. Preventive Service Task Force of the Agency for Healthcare Policy and Research (2002). Newborn hearing screening: Recommendations and rationale. *American Journal of Nursing, 102*(11), pp. 83–89.

Bonham, V. L., Warshauer-Baker, E., & Collins, F. (2005). Race and ethnicity in the Genome Era: The complexity of constructs. *American Psychologist, 60*(1), 9–15.

Braithwaite, D., Emery, J., Walter, F., Prevost, A. T., & Sutton, S. (2004). Psychological impact of genetic counseling for familial cancer: A systematic review and meta-analysis. *Journal of the National Cancer Institute, 96*(2), 122–133.

Bussey-Jones, J., Henderson, G., Garrett, J., Moloney, M., Blumenthal, C., & Corbie-Smith, G. (2009). Asking the right questions: Views on genetic variation research among Black and White research participants. *Journal of General Internal Medicine, 24*(3), 229–304.

Caspi, A., Sugden, K., Moffitt, T. E., Taylor, A., Craig, I. W., Harrington, H.,...Poulton, R. (2003). Influence of life stress on depression: Moderation by a polymorphism in the 5-HTT gene. *Science, 301*(5631), 386–389.

Crabbe, J. C. (2002). Genetic contributions of addiction. *Annual Review of Psychology, 53*(1), 435–462.

Darwin, C. (1859). *On the origin of species: By means of natural selection, or the preservation of favoured races in the struggle for life.* London, England: John Murray.

Decruyenaere, M., Evers-Kiebooms, G., Boogaerts, A., Cloostermans, T., Cassiman, J. J., Demyttenaere, R., & Van den Berghe, H. (1997). Non-participation in predictive testing for Huntington's disease: Individual decision making, personality and avoidant behavior in the family. *European Journal of Human Genetics, 5*(6), 351–363.

Department of Health and Human Services. (2005). Understanding HIPAA. Retrieved from www.hhs.gov /ocr/privacy/hipaa/understanding/summary/index.html

Dick, D. M., Rose, R., J., & Jaakko, K. (2006). The next challenge for psychiatric genetics: Characterizing the risk associated with identified genes. *Annals of Clinical Psychiatry, 18*(4), 223–231.

Dudokde Wit, A. C., Tibben, A., Frets, P. G., Meijers-Heijboer, E. J., Devilee, P., Klijn, J. G. M., ...Niermeijer, M. F. (1997). BRCA1 in the family: A case description of the psychological implications. *American Journal of Medical Genetics, 71,* 63–71.

Dupre, J. (2008). What genes are and why there are no genes for race. In B. A. Koenig, S. S. Lee, & S. Richardson (Eds.), *Revising race in the genomic age: Studies in medical anthropology* (pp. 39–55). Piscataway, NJ: Rutgers University Press.

Edwards, A., Gray, A., Clarke, A., Dundon, J., Elwyn, G., Gaff, C.,...Thornton, H. (2008). Interventions to improve risk communication in clinical genetics: Systematic review. *Patient Education & Counseling 71*(1), 4–25.

Erblich, J., Bovbjerg, D. H., & Valdimarsdottir, H. B. (2000). Looking forward and back: Distress among women at familial risk for breast cancer. *Annals of Behavioral Medicine, 22,* 53–59.

Eunpu, D. L. (1997). Generations lost: A cancer genetics case report commentary. *Journal of Genetic Counseling, 6,* 173–176.

Fernhoff, P. M. (2009). *Newborn screening for genetic disorders. Pediatric Clinics of North America, 56*(3), 505–513.

Field, M., Shanley, S., & Kirk, J. (2007). Inherited cancer susceptibility syndromes in paediatric practice. *Journal of Paediatrics and Child Health, 43*(4), 219–229.

Freedman, T. G. (1997). Genetic susceptibility testing: A therapeutic illusion? *Cancer, 79*(11), 2063–2065.

Gabriel, M. A. (1992). Anniversary reactions: Trauma revisited. *Clinical Social Work Journal, 20,* 179–191.

Gehlert, S. D., Sohmer, D., Sacks, T., Mininger, C., McClintock, M. & Olopade, O. (2008). Targeting health disparities: A model linking upstream determinants to downstream interventions. *Health Affairs, 27*(2), 339–349.

Gilbar, R. (2007). Communicating genetic information in the family: The familial relationship as the forgotten factor. *Journal of Medical Ethics: Journal of the Institute of Medical Ethics, 33*(7), 390–393.

Gooding, H. C., Organista, K., Burack, J., & Biesecker, B. B. (2006). Genetic susceptibility testing from a stress and coping perspective. *Social Science & Medicine, 62,* 1880–1890.

Gray, S. W., O'Grady, C., Karp, L., Smith, D., Schwartz, J. S., Hornik, R. C., & Armstrong, K. (2009). Risk information exposure and direct-to-consumer genetic testing for BRCA mutations among women with a personal or family history of breast or ovarian cancer. *Cancer Epidemiology, Biomarkers & Prevention, 18,* 1303–1311.

Halbert, C. H., Kessler, L., Wileyto, E. P., Weathers, B., Stopfer, J., Domchek, S.,…Brewster, K. (2006). Breast cancer screening behaviors among African American women with a strong family history of breast cancer. *Preventive Medicine: An International Journal Devoted to Practice and Theory, 43*(5), 385–388.

Hallowell, N., & Richards, M. P. M. (1997). Understanding life's lottery: An evaluation of studies of genetic risk awareness. *Journal of Health Psychology, 2*(1), 31–43.

Holtzman, N. A., & Watson, M. S. (1997). Promoting safe and effective genetic testing in the United States: Final report of the Task Force on Genetic Testing. Retrieved from www.genome.gov/10001733

Hoskins, L. M., Roy, K., Peters, J. A., Loud, J., & Greene, M. H. (2008). Disclosure of positive BRCA 1/2-mutation status in young couples: The journey from uncertainty to bonding through partner support. *Families, Systems & Health, 26,* 296–316.

Howard, A. F., Blaneaves, J. L., Bottorff, L. G., & Kim-Sing, C. (2009). Women's constructions of the "right time" to consider decisions about risk-reducing mastectomy and risk-reducing oophorectomy. *BMC Women's Health, 10,* 24.

Hunt, L. M., & Megyesi, M. S. (2008). Genes, race and research ethics. *Journal of Medical Ethics: Journal of the Institute of Medical Ethics, 34*(6), 495–500.

Hurley, K., Miller, S., Rubin, L., & Weinberg, D. (2006). The individual facing genetic issues: Information processing, decision making, perception, and health protective behaviors. In S. M. Miller, S. H. McDaniel, J. S. Rolland, & S. L. Feetham (Eds.), *Individuals, families, and the new era of genetics: Biopsychosocial perspectives* (pp. 79–117). New York, NY: Norton.

Jaffee, S. R., & Price, T. S. (2007). Gene-environment correlations: A review of the evidence and implications for prevention of mental illness. *Molecular Psychiatry, 12*(5), 432–442.

Johnson, J. D., Case, D. O., Andrews, J. E., & Allard, S. L. (2010). Genomics: The perfect information-seeking research problem. *Journal of Health Communication, 10*(4), 323–329.

Kenen, R., Ardern-Jones, A., & Eeles, R. (2003). Family stories and the use of heuristics: Women from suspected

hereditary breast and ovarian cancer (HBOC) families. *Sociology of Health & Illness, 25,* 838–865.

Kenen, R., & Peters, J. A. (2001). The colored, eco-genetic relationship map (CEGRM): A conceptual approach and tool for genetic counseling research. *Journal of Genetic Counseling, 10,* 289–309.

Kent, A. (2003). Consent and confidentiality in genetics: whose information is it anyway? *Journal of Medical Ethics: Journal of the Institute of Medical Ethics, 29*(1), 16–18.

Klipstein, S. (2005). Preimplantation genetic diagnosis: Technological promise and ethical perils. *Fertility and Sterility, 83,* 1347–1353.

Knoppers, B. M., Avard, D., Cardinal, G., & Glass, K. C. (2002). Science and society: Children and incompetent adults in genetic research: consent and safeguards. *Nature Reviews: Genetics, 3,* 221–225.

Lippman-Hand, A., & Fraser, F. C. (1979). Genetic counseling: provision and reception of information. *American Journal of Medical Genetics, 3*(2), 113–127.

Ludman E. J., Fullerton, S. M., Spangler, L., Trinidad, S. B., Fujii, M. M., Jarvik, G. P.,…Burke, W. (2010). Glad you asked: Participants' opinions of re-consent for dbGap data submission. *Journal of Empirical Research on Human Research Ethics, 5*(3), 9–16.

Lupton, D. L. (1999). *Risk.* London, UK: Routledge.

Lynch, H. T., & de la Chapelle, A. (2003). Hereditary colorectal cancer. *New England Journal of Medicine, 348,* 919–932.

Malhotra, A., Lencz, T., Correll, C. U., & Kane, J. (2007). Genomics and the future of pharmacotherapy in psychiatry. *International Review of Psychiatry, 19*(5), 523–530.

Manolio, T. A. (2009). Collaborative genome-wide association studies of diverse diseases: Programs of the NHGRI's office of population genetics. *Pharmacogenomics, 10*(2), 235–241.

McClintock, M. K., Conzen, S. D., Gehlert, S., Masi, C., & Olopade, F. (2005). Mammary cancer and social interactions: Identifying multiple environments that regulate gene expression throughout the life span. *Journals of Gerontology; 60B*(Spec. no. 1), 32–41.

McConkie-Rosell, A., & Spiridigliozzi, G. A. (2004). "Family matters": A conceptual framework for genetic testing in children. *Journal of Genetic Counseling, 13*(1), 9–29.

McCoyd, J. (2008). "I'm not a saint": Burden assessment as an unrecognized factor in prenatal decision making. *Qualitative Health Research, 18,* 1489–1500.

McCoyd, J. (2010). Authoritative knowledge, the technological imperative and women's responses to prenatal diagnostic technologies. *Culture, Medicine, and Psychiatry, 34,* 590–614.

McDaniel, S. H., Rolland, J. S., Feetham, S. K., & Miller, S. M. (2006). "It runs in the family": Family systems concepts and genetically linked disorders. In S. M. Miller, S. H. McDaniel, J. S. Rolland, & S. L. Feetham

(Eds.), *Individuals, families, and the new era of genetics: Biopsychosocial perspectives* (pp. 118–138). New York, NY: Norton.

McGoldrick, M., Gerson, R., & Shellenberger, S. (1999). *Genograms: Assessment and intervention.* New York, NY: Norton.

McKusick, V. A. (1973). Genetic studies in American inbred populations with particular reference to the Old Order Amish. *Israel Journal of Medical Science, 9*(9), 1276–1284.

Meiser, B., & Halliday, J. L. (2002). What is the impact of genetic counseling in women at increased risk of developing hereditary breast cancer? A meta-analytic review. *Social Science & Medicine, 54*(10), 1463–1470.

Meiser, B., Irle, J., Lobb, E., & Balrow-Stewart, K. (2008). Assessment of the process and content of genetic counseling: A critical review of empirical studies. *Journal of Genetic Counseling, 17*(5), 434–451.

Murphy, E. J., Wickramarante, P., & Weissman, M. M. (2009). Racial and ethnic differences in willingness to participate in psychiatric genetic research. *Psychiatric Genetics, 19*(4), 186–194.

Nanda, R., Schumm, L. P., Cummings, S., Fackenthal, J. D., Sveen, L., Ademuyiwa, F., . . . Olopade, O. I. (2005). Genetic testing in an ethnically diverse cohort of high-risk women: A comparative analysis of *BRCA1* and *BRCA2* mutations in American families of European and African ancestry. *JAMA, 294*(15), 1925–1933.

National Coalition of Health Professional Education in Genetics. (2010). The Genetic Nondiscrimination Act (GINA). Retrieved from www.nchpeg.org/index .php?option=com_content&view=article&id=97& Itemid=120

Nielson-Bohlman, L., Panzer, A. M., & Kindig, D. A. (Eds.). (2010). *Health literacy: A prescription to end confusion.* Washington, DC: National Academies Press.

Norem, J. K., & Cantor, N. (1986). Anticipatory and post hoc cushioning strategies: Optimism and defensive pessimism in "risky" situations. *Cognitive Therapy and Research, 10,* 347–362.

National Society of Genetic Counselors. (1995). Prenatal and childhood testing for adult-onset disorders [Position statement]. Retrieved from www.nsgc.org /Advocacy/PositionStatements/tabid/107/Default.aspx #PrenatalChildTestingAdultOnset

Offit, K., Groeger, E., Turner, S., Wadsworth, B., & Weiser, M. A. (2004). The "duty to warn" a patient's family members about hereditary disease risk. *JAMA, 292*(12), 1469–1473.

Padgett, D. K. (2008). *Qualitative methods in social work research* (2nd ed.). Thousand Oaks, CA: Sage.

Patenaude, A. (2004). *Genetic testing for cancer: Psychological approaches for helping patients and families.* Washington, DC: American Psychological Association Press.

Pollin, T. I., Damcott, C. M., Haiqing, S., Ott, S. H., Shelton, J., Horenstein, R. B., . . . Shuldiner, A. R. (2008). A null mutation in human APOC3 confers a favorable plasma lipid profile and apparent cardioprotection. *Science, 322*(5908), 1702–1705.

Rapp, R. (1999). *Testing women, testing the fetus: The social impact of amniocentesis in America.* New York, NY: Routledge.

Ratzen, S. C., & Parker, R. M. (2000). Introduction. In Z. Selden, M. Zorn, S. Ratzan, & R. Parker (Eds.), *National medicine current bibliographies in medicine: Health literacy* (pp. v–vi). Bethesda, MD: National Institutes of Health, U.S. Department of Health and Human Services.

Resnik, D. B. (2003). Genetic testing and primary care: A new ethic for a new setting. *New Genetics and Society, 22*(3), 245–256.

Risch, N., Herrell, R., Lehner, T., Liang, K., Eaves, L. Hoh, J., . . . Merikangas, K. R. (2009). Interaction between the serotonin transporter gene (5-HTTLPR), stressful life events, and risk of depression: A meta-analysis. *JAMA, 301*(23), 2462–2471.

Rolland, J. S. (2006). Living with anticipatory loss in the new era of genetics: A life cycle perspective. In S. M. Miller, S. H. McDaniel, J. S. Rolland, & S. L. Feetham (Eds.), *Individuals, families, and the new era of genetics: Biopsychosocial perspectives* (pp. 139–172). New York, NY: Norton.

Rose, R. J., & Kaprio, J. (2008). Genes, environments, and adolescent substance use: retrospect and prospect from the FinnTwin studies. *Acta Psychologica Sinica, 40*(10), 1017–1026.

Ross, L. F., & Fost, N. (2006). Ethical issues in pediatric genetics. In S. M. Miller, S. H. McDaniel, J. S. Rolland, & S. L. Feetham (Eds.), *Individuals, families, and the new era of genetics: Biopsychosocial perspectives* (pp. 486–505). New York, NY: Norton.

Sankar, P. (2009). Genetics research and race: Whither bioethics? In V. Ravitsky, A. Fiester, & A. L. Caplan (Eds.), *The Penn Center guide to bioethics* (pp. 391–402). New York, NY: Springer.

Satel, S. (2002, May 5). I am a racially profiling doctor. *New York Times.*

Schild, S. (1966). The challenging opportunity for social workers in genetics. *Social Work, 11,* 22–28.

Schild, S., & Black, R. B. (1984). *Social work and genetics: A guide for practice.* New York, NY: Haworth Press.

Schlich-Bakker, K. J., ten Kroode, H. F. J., & Ausems, M. G. (2006). A literature review of the psychological impact of genetic testing on breast cancer patients. *Patient Education and Counseling, 62,* 13–20.

Schultz, A. (1966). The impact of genetic disorders. *Social Work, 11,* 29–34.

Schwartz, L. R. (2001). Psychosocial interventions for women at increased risk for breast cancer. In A. Baum & B. L. Anderson (Eds.), *Psychosocial interventions for cancer* (vol. 19, pp. 287–304). Washington, DC: American Psychological Association.

Shih, R. A., Belmonte, P. L., & Zandi, P. (2004). A review of the evidence from family, twin and adoption studies for a genetic contribution to adult psychiatric disorders. *International Review of Psychiatry, 16*(4), 260–283.

Sivell, S., Elwyn, G., Gaff, C. L., Clarke, A., Iredale, R., Shaw, C.,...Edwards, A. (2008). How risk is perceived, constructed and interpreted by clients in clinical genetics, and the effects on decision making: Systematic review. *Journal of Genetic Counseling, 17*(1), 30–63.

Skloot, R. (2010). *The immortal life of Henrietta Lacks.* New York, NY: Crown.

Slovic, P., Finucane, M. L., Peters, E., & MacGregor, D. G. (2004). Risk as analysis and risk as feelings: Some thoughts about affect, reason, risk, and rationality. *Risk Analysis, 24*(2), 311–322.

Smets, E., van Zwieten, M., & Michie, S. (2007). Comparing genetic counseling with non-genetic health care interactions: Two of a kind? *Patient Education & Counseling, 68*(3), 225–234.

Smith, J. A., Dancyger, C., Wallace, M., & Michie, S. (2010). the development of a methodology for examining the process of family communication of genetic test results. *Journal of Genetic Counseling.* doi: 10.1007/s10897-010-9317-x.

Sobel, S., & Cowan, C. B. (2003). Ambiguous loss and disenfranchised grief: The impact of DNA predictive genetic testing on the family as a system. *Family Process, 42,* 47–57.

Struewing, J. P., Lerman, C., Kase, R. G., Giambarresi, T. R., & Tucker, M. A. (1995). Anticipated uptake and impact of genetic testing in hereditary breast and ovarian cancer families. *Cancer Epidemiology, Biomarkers & Prevention, 4*(2), 169–173.

Taylor-Brown, S., & Johnson, A. M. (1998). *Social work's role in genetic services.* Washington, DC: National Association of Social Workers Press.

U.S. General Accountability Office. (2010, July 22). Direct-to-consumer genetic tests: Misleading test results are further complicated by deceptive marketing and other questionable practices. Subcommittee on Oversight and Investigations, Committee on Energy and Commerce.

U.S. Preventive Services Task Force. (2009). Screening for phenylketonuria: Reaffirmation recommendation statement. *American Family Physician, 80*(12).

Waalen, J. & Beutler, E. (2009). Genetic screening for low-penetrance variants in protein-coding genes. *Annual Review Genomics and Human Genetics, 10,* 431–450.

Watson, M. S., Cutting, G. R., Desnick, R. J., Driscoll, D. A., Klinger, K., Mennuti, M.,...Grody, W. W. (2004). Cystic fibrosis population carrier screening: 2004 Revision of American College of Medical Genetics mutation panel. *Genetic Medicine, 6*(5), 387–391.

Weaver, I. C. G., Cervoni, N., Champagne, F. A., D'Alessio, A. C., Sharma, S., Seckl, J. R.,...Meaney, M. J. (2004). Epigenetic programming by maternal behavior. *Nature Neuroscience, 7,* 847–854.

Weiss, J., Black, P. N., Weissman, N., Oktay, J., Rodriguez, G., Johnson, A. M., & Whittemore, V. H. (2003). *NASW standards for integrating genetics into social work practice.* Washington, DC: NASW Press.

Wermter, A., Laucht, M., Schimmelmann, B. G., Banaschewski, T., Sonuga-Barke, E. J. S., Rietschel, M., & Becker, K. (2010). From nature to nurture, to gene x environment interaction in mental disorders. *European Child & Adolescent Psychiatry, 19*(3), 199–210.

Werner-Lin, A. (2007). Danger zones: Risk perceptions of young women from families with hereditary breast and ovarian cancer. *Family Process, 46,* 335–349.

Werner-Lin, A. (2008). Beating the biological clock: The compressed family life cycle of young women with BRCA mutations. *Journal of Health Social Work, 47*(4), 416–437.

Werner-Lin, A., & Gardner, D. S. (2009). Family illness narratives of inherited cancer risk: Continuity and transformation. *Families, Systems and Health, 27*(3), 201–212.

Wilfond, B., & Ross, L. F. (2009). From genetics to genomics: Ethics, policy, and parental decision-making. *Journal of Pediatric Psychology, 34*(6), 639–647

Wolf, L. E., Bouley, T. A., & McCulloch, C. E. (2010). Genetic research with stored biological materials. *IRB: Ethics and Human Research, 32*(2), 7–18.

Yaniv, I., Benador, D., & Sagi, M. (2004). On not wanting to know and not wanting to inform others: choices regarding predictive genetic testing. *Risk Decision and Policy, 9,* 317–336.

22

Pain Management and
Palliative Care

TERRY ALTILIO, SHIRLEY OTIS-GREEN, SUSAN HEDLUND, AND IRIS COHEN FINEBERG

The unique values that inform the purpose and perspective of social work practice are essential to the provision of quality palliative care and comprehensive pain management. Social workers historically have seen the alleviation of suffering as part of their mission, and this is reflected in a code of ethics that supports service, social justice, respect for the dignity and worth of the person, a belief in the central importance of human relationships, integrity, and competence (National Association of Social Workers [NASW], 1999). These ideals are woven through the fields of palliative care and pain management, yet social work has not been fully engaged in these areas of practice. In addition to shared values however, knowledge and expertise is essential if social work is to strengthen its voice in these practice arenas. In this chapter, we discuss the interface of values and knowledge and detail the richness of opportunity presented to social workers in the fields of palliative care and comprehensive pain management.

Chapter Objectives
- Define *palliative care*, including domains and guidelines established by the National Consensus Project for Quality Palliative Care and the preferred practices endorsed by the National Quality Forum.
- Define and distinguish *pain* and *symptom management* as both a focus of palliative care as well as an independent focus of social work practice.
- Confirm the unique opportunity and historical framework of palliative care that invites social work participation and leadership in this area of practice, and explore the obstacles to realizing the opportunity.
- Describe aspects of a biopsychosocial-spiritual assessment that inform a plan of care in palliative care and pain management.
- Define *interventions*, and illustrate their usefulness through patient narratives.
- Discuss ethical principles that relate to palliative care and the management of pain.
- Explore various models of team collaboration, sources of professional gratification and work-related stress, and opportunities for enhancing self-care.

PALLIATIVE CARE AND PAIN MANAGEMENT: AN OVERVIEW

The chapter first focuses on palliative care and its comprehensive approach to the care of patients with life-threatening illness. Although pain and symptom management are included as a core palliative care skill, a separate section discusses pain management as an independent subspecialty. Underlying both practice areas is a multidimensional focus encompassing biological, emotional, cognitive, socioeconomic, cultural, and spiritual aspects of the unique experience of patients and families. It is at this critical, yet nuanced, nexus that social work expertise is essential.

Palliative Care

According to the *American Heritage Dictionary*, palliate means "to alleviate without cure." The World Health Organization (WHO, n.d.) has adapted this basic definition to include that palliative care improves the quality of life of patients and families who are facing life-threatening illness through prevention and relief of suffering. Quality-of-life improvement might be achieved through the assessment and treatment of pain and other physical, psychosocial, and spiritual distress. Palliative care is important throughout the course of illness and may be integrated with disease-modifying therapies that are intended to prolong life. For example, palliative care may be incorporated with chemotherapy and radiation therapy in an oncology setting. In chronic renal disease, it may be provided along with dialysis. Interventions are adapted to the changing course of illnesses, such as when disease-modifying therapies lose their benefit or appropriateness. When this occurs, palliative care may become the primary focus of intervention. Palliative interventions affirm life and treat dying as a natural process. Clinicians generally work together as a team to assist patients and families, including children, to live as actively as possible with enhanced quality of life. Social workers help patients and members of their social support networks to cope during illness and their own bereavement. Palliative care interventions may include referral to a hospice program and a team-based program of care, support, and bereavement services for persons whose life expectancy is six months or fewer.

Pain and symptom management are essential components of palliative care, because uncontrolled pain and symptoms not only shape the lived experience of the patient, family, and staff but also influence bereavement and the legacy of the illness as it becomes integrated into the family narrative. Families describe this dynamic through comments such as "My mother suffered terrible pain; I cannot bear to think that my husband will suffer in the same way." The desire to create a family legacy of comfort and respect is one of the factors that drives the shared professional commitment to symptom assessment and intervention.

Pain Management

Although pain and symptom management are essential foci of palliative care, pain management as a specialty extends beyond life-limiting illness to chronic conditions such as migraine headaches, fibromyalgia, arthritis, and back pain. In 2006, the National Center for Health Statistics reported that more than 26% of Americans age 20 years and older had a pain problem during the last month that lasted for more than 24 hours. Thirty percent of adults age 45 to 64 years and 21% of persons age 65 years and older reported pain that lasted more than 24 hours. An estimated 9% of the U.S. adult population suffers from moderate to severe pain at any point in time (Roper Starch Worldwide, 1999). Although not necessarily life limiting, these conditions can force major life adaptation. As in palliative care, assessment and treatment ideally is based on a biopsychosocial-spiritual model. As a generic concept, *pain management* refers to both chronic and acute pain. The populations highlighted in this chapter include people who experience pain as a consequence of a life-limiting illness and those who are affected by chronic pain.

The International Association for the Study of Pain (2010) defines *pain* as

> an unpleasant sensory and emotional experience associated with actual or potential tissue damage, or described in terms of such damage. Although it is unquestionably a sensation in part or parts of the body, it is always unpleasant and, therefore, an emotional experience. (www.iasp-pain.org/AM /Template.cfm?Section=Pain_Defi%20.isplay .cfm&ContentID=1728#Pain)

It is clear from this definition that pain involves the physical and emotional self at a very basic level.

Acute pain differs from chronic pain in that it has a clear onset, follows an injury, and often but not always is accompanied by objective physical signs of autonomic nervous system activity, such as increased heart rate. It is self-limited, and its duration roughly parallels the healing of the injury. An example might be a fractured toe or a toothache. Chronic pain is largely defined temporally, and although it may begin as acute, it continues beyond the normal period of healing. Because pain may not be associated with observable tissue injury or sympathetic nervous system arousal, chronic pain may not be visible to others. This absence of objective signs often confounds inexperienced clinicians, who may conclude that patients' pain is not real and challenge their credibility (American Pain Society, 2003). This can be distressing for patients who may feel diminished by the experience.

A key characteristic of chronic pain from the patient's perspective is that it becomes like any other chronic illness. That is, as opposed to acute pain, the focus of care often shifts from searching for a cause and cure to managing the pain itself. Comprehensive assessment and interventions extend beyond the physical to psychological, social, cultural, and spiritual aspects of the patient's experience, comparable to the clinical assessment appropriate to palliative care patients and their families. Collaborative goals might include minimizing suffering and the negative impact of chronic pain and enhancing functioning and quality of life.

Challenges and Opportunities

Principles and values underlying palliative care and pain treatment have much in common with those of social work. In both, comprehensive quality assessment is individualized, patient and family centered, and multidimensional and includes biological, social, emotional, spiritual, and environmental factors that interact and contribute to an understanding of the patient and family experience. Underlying values that inform this process are a respect for the central importance of human relationships and an affirmation of the person-in-environment paradigm in all of its manifestations (Roy, 1981). Consideration of patient and family values, needs, beliefs, and goals is implicit in the principle of respect for the dignity and worth of the person. Historically, health social workers have championed the idea that context, community, and family are critical components of the illness experience of patients. Ida M. Cannon, who led the first social work department at Massachusetts General Hospital (see Chapter 1 in this book), saw the task of helping physicians understand the impact of the community and social context as essential to social work. This is a unique perspective that is a core element of both palliative care and pain management. The impact and potential of this role are enhanced by the plethora of interventions, ethical concerns, and policy issues that invite the participation of compassionate and competent social work clinicians to these two specialty areas of practice (Roff, 2001).

Rich opportunities exist concurrently with significant challenges for health social workers in palliative care and pain management. Although there are likely a myriad reasons for social work's lack of leadership in the two fields, lack of adequate training is perhaps the most salient. Increasing numbers of social workers are seeking mentorship in palliative and end-of-life care, yet many see pain and symptom management as outside their scope of practice. Very few social workers are exposed to pain management as a potential specialty practice. Schools of social work make difficult, complex decisions about curriculum content, and even though death is a universal experience, the topic typically is taught only as an elective course. Pain has been viewed largely as a physical problem, and the biopsychosocial-spiritual focus has come primarily from the fields of psychiatry and psychology. Few social workers practice in pain management programs in which their person-in-environment and strengths perspective can be well utilized. Many social workers in health-care settings struggle with the impact of shortened stays, competing priorities, and increasing caseloads. Counseling and pain management interventions may not seem sustainable in understaffed, managed care environments. (See Chapter 5 in this book for an explanation of managed care.) Historically, social workers have been less accountable for providing evidence-based interventions than their colleagues in nursing and medicine.

At the same time that the number of palliative care programs is increasing, these programs are expanding into settings such as extended-care facilities and home care. The

Center to Advance Palliative Care (2008) has defined doctors, nurses, and social workers as team members. In 2009, the NASW published *Standards for Social Work Practice in Palliative and End-of-Life Care* (NASW, 2009b), which included 12 standards that cover ethics and values, knowledge, assessment, intervention and treatment planning, attitude and self-awareness, empowerment and advocacy, documentation, interdisciplinary teamwork, cultural competence, continuing education and leadership, supervision, and training. NASW developed two Internet courses to further social workers' continuing education: *Understanding End-of-Life Care* and *Social Work's Role and Achieving Cultural Competence in Reducing Health Disparities in End-of-Life Care*. In 2008, the NASW and the National Hospice and Palliative Care Organization collaborated to develop a social work credential in hospice and palliative care (NASW, 2009a). Concurrently, accreditation agencies such as the Joint Commission (2010) include pain, palliative, and end-of-life care in their standards, creating opportunities for skilled social workers to participate in and lead institutional initiatives with the goal of both expanding their scope of service and improving patient care.

Social workers who work in any venue—including hospitals, public agencies, hospices, methadone maintenance programs, prisons, long-term care facilities, private practices, and government programs—have the opportunity to enhance the care of patients and the adaptation of patients and families affected by chronic or life-limiting illness. This broad range of practice settings creates a potential for quality care to be transferred from formal health-care institutions to the community. Although these settings may impose specific challenges, generic competencies and values underlie the social work approach. Understanding how community, culture, and institutional and family dynamics impact palliative care issues or pain experiences informs and guides intervention. For example, in a rural community in which pain often accompanies physical labor and thus is expected, it is important to recognize that a new pain may be ignored

or minimized until it interferes with work. In the prison population, tolerating pain may be a sign of strength and a defense against vulnerability. Expression of need or a request for care, even in cases of life-limiting illness, may be viewed by others as a sign of weakness. Inmates might avoid any medication that would impact their alertness and awareness of their surroundings. In a prison environment, coping skills that utilize internal processes such as relaxation, imagery, and focused breathing have the potential to restore some control and enhance internal comfort, thus minimizing suffering (Enders, 2004; Linder & Enders, 2011).

HISTORICAL PERSPECTIVE

Principles and behaviors that inform the work of palliative care and the treatment of pain have their roots in human antiquity and serve a vital social function. A historic tension exists between society's desire to flee from the ill, injured, or dead and our recognition that the vulnerable need assistance in order to survive. The need to flee is based on the fear that others' misfortune may befall us. At the same time, the desire to help the vulnerable and suffering is derived from an empathic understanding that we potentially need others for our own optimal survival. Caring for those who suffer reinforces important social bonds and the capacity to be empathic. Each society throughout history has evolved special ways of caring for its suffering, dying, and bereaved members. For example, shamans or healers proscribed behavior and offered guidance in times of crisis. Those who "know what to do" offer comfort, and such healers might be considered our earliest social work ancestors as they provided what might be thought of as early psychoeducational and spiritual support and expertise.

Until recently, limited interventions were available to influence the course of illness, so the alleviation of pain and suffering frequently was the most one could hope for. Palliative care was often the only means of medical intervention for those with serious illness. These earliest healers typically offered integrated spiritual, herbal, and behavioral interventions to normalize concerns and support the dying and their families. Compassionate support during illness or injury was the imperative, although the final outcome of illness or injury was understood to be outside of the healer's control. From the origin of human life until the development of widespread improvements in sanitation and public health and the advent of anesthesia, antibiotics, and other medical breakthroughs, people typically died relatively quickly after the onset of serious illness (Lynn, Schuster, & Kabcenell, 2000).

The origin of the words *hospice* and *hospital* date back to the fourth century. During the Middle Ages, hospices were established at key crossroads on the ways to religious shrines. These shelters helped pilgrims, many of whom were traveling to shrines in search of cures and many of whom died while on their pilgrimage. Returning crusaders, often ill or wounded, also died at these hospices, strengthening the association of hospices as places for the dying and destitute (Koppelman, 2003).

In addition to linguistic history, philosophical perspectives infused the evolution of medicine and the care of the sick. For example, the seventeenth-century lawyer and mathematician René Descartes popularized the dualistic-mechanistic model, which suggested that the body belonged to the realm of science and the spirit to the realm of religion (Koppelman, 2003). This set the stage for the "medicalizing" of dying, and by the mid-20th century, almost 80% of people in the United States died in a hospital or nursing home (Koppelman, 2003). This changing death trajectory coincided with the widespread use of antibiotics. The discovery of penicillin and other medical advances, such as improvements in anesthesia that made more daring surgeries possible, the medical field began to focus on expanding possibilities for cure. Attention to the traditional concerns of palliative care and pain management somewhat paradoxically became less important to the providers of mainstream medicine.

Prior to this time, pain medications typically had been herbal in nature, with reliance on alcohol and morphine as the most potent remedies for serious discomfort. In the mid-19th century, laudanum was widely available and became immensely popular. Easy access to these remedies allowed individuals to self-medicate, and addiction became a societal evil associated with stigma. Legislative regulations subsequently were enacted to protect the public. This fear of addiction to pain medications and the stigma associated with addiction and opioid medication use continues to influence professional behavior, patient and family perceptions of illness and its treatment, and public policy.

In London in the 1960s, Cicely Saunders, a physician previously trained as a nurse and social worker, developed the first modern hospice (Saunders, 1996). She pioneered the concept of "total pain," which recognized pain as a social, psychological, spiritual, and physical experience that required intervention provided by an interdisciplinary care team. She revolutionized the treatment of pain by scheduling around-the-clock use of opioids with the goal of managing persistent pain and minimizing its exacerbation. She was instrumental in encouraging patients to self-assess pain and incorporated the family into care (Forman, 1998; Saunders, 2001). In 1969, Elisabeth Kübler-Ross's book *On Death and Dying* set the stage in the United States for a revolution in the provision of end-of-life care, the development of palliative care as a medical specialty, and the renewal of interest in more sophisticated pain and symptom management strategies. More recently, pioneers like physician Jimmie Holland (Holland et al., 2010) have championed the development of psychooncology as a unique specialization that seeks to integrate the biopsychosocial-spiritual factors of illness. This model is exemplified by the decision of the National Comprehensive Cancer Network (Jacobsen, 2007) to encourage the use of "distress thermometers" as standardized screening tools to measure physical pain as well as psychological suffering in cancer patients.

Social workers often have failed to add their expertise to these developing specialties, leaving a vacuum that is being filled by psychologists, chaplains, nurses, and physicians sensitive to psychosocial issues. Although there have been recent efforts to highlight the contributions of social workers in these fields (Altilio & Otis-Green, 2011), there remains a need for social work leadership in palliative care and pain management across all aspects of care: policy, research, education, and clinical practice.

NATIONAL CONSENSUS PROJECT ON PALLIATIVE CARE

Palliative care programs are increasing in number at a rapid pace. In addition to the growing population of aging persons living with debilitating and life-limiting illnesses, reports such as the Institute of Medicine's *Approaching Death, When Children Die* (2003) and *Crossing the Quality Chasm* (2001) have called for improving access to palliative care during all stages of illness along the continuum of care. In 2004, the National Consensus Project for Quality Palliative Care (NCP) was established to formulate clinical practice guidelines to promote consistent and high-quality care and guide the development of palliative care services. The project's participants included professionals, health-care organizations, policy- and standard-setting bodies, consumers, and payers.

The consensus document *Clinical Practice Guidelines for Quality Palliative Care* that was originally published in 2004 by the NCP describes palliative care as consisting of interventions that may accompany life-prolonging treatments and be practiced at both the generalist and specialist levels. The implication that primary health-care providers integrate basic palliative care invites all health-care providers, including social workers, to learn core skills. The integration of palliative care into generalist practice has great potential to impact care for patients and families in various settings through the course of illness to the end of life.

In 2004, the NCP described the definition, scope, and goal of palliative care in this way:

The goal of palliative care is to prevent and relieve suffering and to support the best possible quality of life for patients and their families, regardless of the stage of the disease or the need for other therapies. Palliative care is both a philosophy of care and an organized, highly structured system for delivering care. Palliative care expands traditional disease-model medical treatments to include the goals of enhancing quality of life for patient and family, optimizing function, helping with decision making, and providing opportunities for personal growth. As such, it can be delivered concurrently with life-prolonging care or as the main focus of care. Palliative care is operationalized through effective management of pain and other distressing symptoms, while incorporating psychosocial and spiritual care with consideration of patient/family needs, preferences, values, beliefs, and culture. Evaluation and treatment should be comprehensive and patient-centered with a focus on the central role of the family unit in decision making. Palliative care affirms life by supporting the patient and family's goals for the future, including their hopes for cure or life-prolongation, as well as their hopes for peace and dignity throughout the course of illness, the dying process, and death. Palliative care aims to guide and assist the patient and family in making decisions that enable them to work toward their goals during whatever time they have remaining. Comprehensive palliative care services often require the expertise of various providers to adequately assess and treat the complex needs of seriously ill patients and their families . . . (2004, p. 6)

In 2009, this definition was reconfirmed, as were the eight domains of care. The clinical practice guidelines were expanded and are delineated in Box 22.1. The 2009 consensus document added justifications, supporting and clarifying statements, references, case examples, and suggested criteria for assessing outcomes, creating a rich and comprehensive tool for guiding generalist or specialist palliative care.

Box 22.1 NCP for Quality Palliative Care Domains and Guidelines

Domain 1: Structure and Processes of Care

Guideline 1.1. The timely plan of care is based on a comprehensive interdisciplinary assessment of the patient and family.

Guideline 1.2. The care plan is based on the identified and expressed preferences, values, goals, and needs of patient and family, and is developed with professional guidance and support for decision making.

Guideline 1.3. An interdisciplinary team provides services to the patient and family consistent with the care plan. In addition to nursing, medicine, and social work, other therapeutic disciplines with importance in the assessment of patients and families include physical therapists, occupational therapists, speech and language pathologists, nutritionists, psychologists, chaplains, and nursing assistants. For pediatrics, this should include child life specialists. Complementary and alternative therapies may be included.

Guideline 1.4. The use of appropriately trained and supervised volunteers on the team is strongly encouraged.

Guideline 1.5. Support for education and training is available to the interdisciplinary team.

Guideline 1.6. In its commitment to quality assessment and performance improvement, the palliative care program develops, implements, and maintains an ongoing data-driven process that reflects the complexity of the organization and focuses on palliative care outcomes.

Guideline 1.7. The palliative care program recognizes the emotional impact on the palliative care team of providing care to patients with life-threatening illnesses and their families.

Guideline 1.8. Palliative care programs should have a relationship with one or more hospices and other community resources in order to ensure continuity of the highest-quality palliative care across the illness trajectory.

Guideline 1.9. The physical environment in which care is provided should meet the preferences, needs, and circumstances of the patient and family to the extent possible.

Domain 2: Physical Aspects of Care

Guideline 2.1. Pain, other symptoms, and side effects are managed based upon the best available evidence, with attention to disease-specific pain and symptoms.

Domain 3: Psychological and Psychiatric Aspects of Care

Guideline 3.1. Psychological status is assessed and managed based upon the best available evidence, which is skillfully and systematically applied. When necessary, psychiatric issues are addressed and treated.

Guideline 3.2. A grief and bereavement program is available to patients and families, based upon the assessed need for services.

Domain 4: Social Aspects of Care

Guideline 4.1. Comprehensive interdisciplinary assessment identifies the social needs of patients and their families, and a care plan is developed to respond to these needs as effectively as possible.

Domain 5: Spiritual, Religious, and Existential Aspects of Care

Guideline 5.1. Spiritual and existential dimensions are assessed and responded to based upon the best available evidence, which is skillfully and systematically applied.

Domain 6: Cultural Aspects of Care

Guideline 6.1. The palliative care program assesses and attempts to meet the needs of the patient, family, and community in a culturally sensitive manner.

Domain 7: Care of the Imminently Dying Patient

Guideline 7.1. Signs and symptoms of impending death are recognized and communicated in developmentally appropriate language for children and patients with cognitive disabilities, with respect for family preferences. Care appropriate for this phase of illness is provided to patient and family.

Guideline 7.2. Postdeath care is delivered in a respectful manner. Cultural and religious practices peculiar to the postdeath period are assessed and documented. The body is cared for in a manner that is congruent with these practices, in accordance with both organizational practice and local law.

Guideline 7.3. A postdeath bereavement plan is activated. An interdisciplinary team member is assigned to the family in the postdeath period, to help with religious practices, funeral arrangements, and burial planning.

Domain 8: Ethical and Legal Aspects of Care

Guideline 8.1. The patient's goals, preferences, and choices are respected within the limits of applicable state and federal law, with current accepted standards of medical care, and form the basis for the plan of care.

Guideline 8.2. The palliative care program is aware of and addresses the complex ethical issues arising in the care of persons with life-threatening debilitating illness.

Guideline 8.3. The palliative care program is knowledgeable about legal and regulatory aspects of palliative care.

Source: Clinical Practice Guidelines for Quality Palliative Care, 2nd ed., by National Consensus Project for Quality Palliative Care, 2009, www .nationalconsensusproject.org

In 2006, the National Quality Forum (NQF) released *A National Framework and Preferred Practices for Palliative and Hospice Care Quality*. This document reflects the NQF's decision to accept and adopt the Clinical Practice Guidelines for Quality Palliative Care and provides 38 preferred practices on which measures for palliative care are to be developed. The NQF is recognized as the national leader in health-care quality improvement, representing a broad array of practice areas and topics. Consequently, the adoption of these guidelines both recognizes and legitimizes palliative care (NCP, 2009; NQF, 2006).

Although the NCP guidelines delineate shared aspects of practice responsibility for all disciplines, some areas seem to fall naturally into the domains of specific disciplines. For example, social aspects of care draw on the social work principle that highlights the importance of the person and their environment (Altilio, Otis-Green, & Dahlin, 2008). The domains, guidelines, and preferred practices are invitations for social workers to assert and enhance their expertise as essential to palliative care and reflect social work's respect for the individual experiences of patients and families. The next section discusses aspects of social work assessment to assist in elucidating the synergy of social work and palliative care.

BIOPSYCHOSOCIAL-SPIRITUAL ASSESSMENT

Comprehensive and ongoing biopsychosocial-spiritual assessment is a key function of social work in health-care settings and is the basis of effective treatment planning. As in any clinical situation, the scope of the assessment is modified according to context and immediate needs and goals. The assessment of an individual with chronic pain or a life-limiting illness involves gathering in-depth information about the physiological aspects of the symptoms and illness, addresses treatment, and complements competent medical management. A family history might include previous experiences with pain and illness, remote and immediate loss experiences, and pain- and illness-related behaviors as well as information about family roles, structure, functioning, communication and conflicts, social supports and resources, and cultural and spiritual values and networks.

Unique family factors and illness variables impact family function and response. Did the illness evolve over time or appear suddenly? Do the patient and family have a history with this specific disease or symptom? What is the role of the patient in the family? Is the family a cohesive unit? How adaptable and flexible are family members? Is extended family or social network support available? What life cycle issues are present? Is the family experiencing stressors, such as financial worries, preexisting conflicts, or illness? What might interfere with the family's ability to adapt, support each other, or use community resources?

Numerous needs and challenges arise when pain or life-limiting illness arises in the life of a family. Such needs and challenges may include: understanding the disease, its treatment, and potential prognosis; developing strategies to manage the impact of pain or illness; coping with and learning the language of professional caregivers and institutions; maintaining stability while restructuring to meet the changing individual needs of patient and family members; dealing with family responses as well as the individual emotions, grief, and adaptation of specific family members; planning for the continuation of family life through periods of change and uncertainty and possible death; and finding meaning as a family and as individuals.

People with chronic pain or chronic progressive diseases and the members of social support networks experience grief as they come to terms with the myriad losses associated with pain and illness. Many people living with chronic pain face similar loss experiences that are not related to life-limiting illness but similarly evoke grief and demand multiple levels of change and adaptation (MacDonald, 2000).

Illness-related behaviors and responses arise in the context of specific family, cultural, social, health care, and political systems that may influence the suffering component of the experience. *Suffering*, as defined by *Webster's Dictionary*, is "to submit to or be forced to endure, to tolerate as inevitable, to sustain loss or damage, to endure death, pain or distress." Suffering is a subjective experience viewed through the lens of an individual's life, values, perspectives, and priorities and is closely tied to a search for meaning. It may include pain but can exist in the absence of physical symptoms (Cassell, 1991). In the absence of meaning and a reframed vision of hope that extends beyond cure of a condition, suffering may continue despite excellent

management of pain and treatment of disease (Barkwell, 1991). Viktor Frankl, in his book *Man's Search for Meaning* (1984), develops "Logotherapy," a therapeutic concept based in the belief that finding meaning allows one to transcend loss and suffering. The construct is useful when working with people whose lives have been derailed by life-limiting illness or chronic pain. Clinicians can create a supportive space within which patients can gently and respectfully explore alternative sources of meaning and perhaps see the illness as an impetus for these discoveries (Lethborg, Aranda, Bloch, & Kissane, 2006; Otis-Green, Sherman, Perez, & Baird, 2002). Systematic psychosocial pain assessment (Otis-Green, 2006) can be a useful tool for identifying the unique impact of the multidimensional experience of pain on a patient and their families. Specialized spiritual assessment tools also are available for exploring patients' spiritual and cultural coping strategies and gathering insights into how they interpret their pain or illness experiences (Puchalski et al., 2009).

People with chronic illness may experience sadness and some symptoms of depression and anxiety. Symptoms may interfere with function and quality of life and be pervasive and persistent. Skilled assessment and treatment, including pharmacology and counseling, are essential to enhancing the quality of life of patients (Hultman, Reder, & Dahlin, 2008). Likewise, caregivers and other family members may become overwhelmed and exhausted over time and be at risk for physical and psychological effects (Schulz & Beach, 1999). In the palliative care model, the unit of care is the patient and those identified as family. Consequently, clinicians attend to the needs of caregivers and family as a necessary part of ongoing assessment and treatment. Comprehensive care of people with chronic pain also should involve those family members who are observers and often participants in the chronic pain experience (Glajchen, 2003). Caregiving over time has the potential to affect the emotional, physical, and financial well-being of the patient and family. Thus, vigilance, ongoing assessment, and advocacy are required to meet the current and anticipated needs of patients and their caregivers (Glajchen, 2011).

The perceptions, evaluation, and experiences of the patient, family, and health-care professional are unique. As a result, discrepancies in observations and assessment may occur, and these data become part of a comprehensive assessment. For example, the clinician's or family caregiver's appraisal of pain may not agree with that of the patient (Lobchuk & Degner, 2002; Miaskowski, Zimmer, Barrett, Dibble, & Wallhagen, 1997). Evidence suggests that clinicians underrate pain, especially when it is severe (Cleeland et al., 1994; Grossman, Sheidler, Swedeen, Mucenski, & Piantadosi, 1991; Von Roenn, Cleeland, Gonin, Hatfield, & Pandya, 1993). Appraisals are filtered through the experience, suffering, and cognitive and emotional distress of the appraiser; thus objective assessment is crucial to insure that appropriate interventions are directed to the right persons (Redinbaugh, Baum, DeMoss, Fello, & Arnold, 2002). For example, a family caregiver may perceive a loved one's pain to be out of control while the patient reports a reasonable level of comfort. The caregiver's perception may be affected by fatigue, fear, and feelings of helplessness. The appropriate intervention, therefore, might be for the social worker and team to reevaluate the plan of care and increase support through practical and psychological interventions rather than an increase in medication for the patient.

Individual and family attitudes and behaviors related to pain, illness, and death are infused with and enriched by cultural influences. Societal attitudes toward health, illness, and death have been influenced by a variety of ethical, political, religious, and philosophical beliefs in addition to changing medical practices through the 20th century. Although the standard medical approach to illness and health care in the United States is largely based on the Western bioethical model of autonomy, self-determination, and informed consent, the United States is a multicultural society in which beliefs and behaviors are informed by a range of values. The assumption that patients and families work from a

model of self-determination, accept the values implicit in advance directives, and become informed self-advocates may represent a clinician-driven focus that does not necessarily reflect the unique and individualized experiences of patients and their families. Psychosocial-spiritual assessment recognizes that cultural values and nuances inform patient and family understanding and adaptation to pain and symptoms, illness, and death and that care can be adapted accordingly (Crawley, Marshall, Lo, & Koenig, 2002; Im et al., 2007; Kagawa-Singer & Blackhall, 2001; Koenig & Gates-Williams, 1995; Koffman, Morgan, Edmonds, Speck, & Higginson, 2008). The next case example captures some of the complexity that is involved when the health-care team is faced with cultural beliefs that differ from the traditional Western bioethical model.

Case Example

Mrs. M is a 33-year-old Muslim woman from Nigeria diagnosed with ovarian cancer and hospitalized with symptoms of pain, nausea, and weakness. She speaks little English and communicates through her husband or through an AT&T language line interpreter. Although she has decision-making capacity, she requests that information be given to her husband, who will make the health-care decisions. This request is troubling to the health-care team who are more comfortable with the traditional Western model of informed, self-determined decision making. The social worker from the palliative care consult service asks the primary team to consider that one can retain autonomy while giving decision-making power to another individual. She acts as cultural mediator throughout the hospital stay. A discussion ensues about the harm that may result if staff's pressure to inform the patient of her prognosis is experienced as an assault on the beliefs and family structure that sustain the couple in times of crisis. The complexity is compounded with the suggestion of possible surgery, because the risk and benefits and nature of invasive surgery change the context and quality of the consent discussion. The patient, her husband, and the health-care team explore the interface of cultural, institutional, and legal issues and negotiate an agreement whereby the husband will consent with the patient assenting by marking an X on a witnessed consent form. The social worker also assists the team with these interventions and adaptations, which were required in order to provide respectful care to this couple:

- A visual pain assessment tool is combined with observation of nonverbal behaviors to help staff assess and manage Mrs. M's pain. Mr. M is reassured that when he is not available, his wife's pain can be assessed and managed in spite of the language difference.
- Issues related to prognosis, as per cultural and religious beliefs, are not discussed with the patient because both the husband and the AT&T interpreter report that discussing the possibility of death will be distressing, may

impact her adversely, and be interpreted by the patient and her husband as a challenge to the ultimate power and will of Allah.

- Postdeath needs and rituals are researched, discussed with an imam, and shared with nursing staff so that all will be prepared to provide respectful care during and after death.

The scope of a palliative care assessment (see Box 22.2) has much in common with a comprehensive pain assessment in that it can include physical, emotional, socioeconomic, cognitive, cultural, behavioral, spiritual or existential, and environmental realms. Quality palliative care also focuses on advance care planning and risk factors for complicated bereavement. A comprehensive assessment involves the individual as well as significant others and seeks to identify needs and any discrepancies in perceptions and understanding.

Box 22.2 Assessment in Palliative Care

Physical. Diagnosis and prognosis; history of disease or pain; symptoms; and impact on function, sleep, mood, and intimacy.

Emotional. Depression, anxiety, demoralization, fear, anger, grief, sadness, acceptance, guilt, shame, loss of control, helplessness, hopelessness; preexisting or comorbid psychiatric issues; coping skills; bereavement risk.

Socioeconomic. Sources and stability of income; access to care; entitlements; insurance issues; potential issues related to economic disadvantage or ethnic minority status; and impact and symbolic significance of disability status.

Cognitive. Attitudes, beliefs, and values; expectations that inform responses to pain and illness; internal dialogue and symbolic significance of pain, disease, and treatment; attributed meaning; impact on self-efficacy, self-image, and locus of control.

Cultural. Communication, gender, and language issues; degree of acculturation, assimilation, or generational differences;

beliefs related to illness, pain, decision making, truth telling, death; use of folk remedies and native healers.

Behavioral. Verbal and nonverbal communication; conscious and unconscious bodily responses such as grimacing, restlessness, or crying; regression, dependence, and acting out; problematic handling of medications and inability to cooperate with treatment plans.

Existential/Spiritual. Issues of meaning, despair, faith, and spiritual comfort; life review, hopes, and goals for the future; legacy-building opportunities; illness, pain, and suffering as related to beliefs such as redemption, endurance, and forgiveness; religious or spiritual beliefs that impact treatment decisions and peaceful dying.

Environmental. Emotional significance of the physical environment, including alterations that need to be made consequent to pain or disease-related issues, such as need for equipment, medical personnel at home; behaviors of staff, friends, or family that may increase distress.

INTERVENTIONS

For social work, the fields of pain management and palliative care present an emerging opportunity to apply skill sets that are a routine part of our training and to learn other skills to enhance the care and outcomes of patients and their families. Social work interventions may be focused in the arena of policy or public advocacy work or in the clinical realm of the patient's family experience.

Advocacy

Advocacy is an ongoing task; needs change, distress varies, and skills of self-advocacy may fade as the patient and family deal with protracted illness, symptoms such as pain and fatigue, and associated feelings of exhaustion, helplessness, and hopelessness. Unrecognized and unrelieved pain and symptoms and conflict and misunderstandings within families or with staff are examples of clinical situations that may require social work advocacy skills. Patients and families often need assistance in advocating for adequate discharge plans and negotiating with insurance companies. When patients and families are less distressed, advocacy skills can be taught with the goal of increasing self-efficacy (McCaffery & Pasero, 1999). In addition, there are multiple opportunities for promoting systems change within institutions as well as at a political and policy level.

Supportive Counseling Interventions

Supportive counseling interventions include techniques of clarifying, exploring, partializing, validating, and problem solving. Patients and family members often are faced with myriad illness-related issues, such as pain and crucial medical decision making. These interventions, along with intensive medical management of symptoms, establish a basis for trust while they explore immediate needs and concerns. They also have the potential to create a relationship environment within which the patient and family feel understood and validated.

Education and Anticipatory Guidance

Education is an essential part of helping people master circumstances. In the health-care environment, education often means exposure to the language of medicine in the setting of pain, illness, and anxiety. The health-care community is responsible for accommodating and adapting to the needs of patients and providing information in a way that supports patient and family understanding and competence. Health-care clinicians need to anticipate future challenges and offer preemptive education and support to patients and their loved ones, which may include exploring the use of advance directives.

Case Example

Maria introduces herself as the family's social worker by explaining that she is available to offer them support through Mr. S's upcoming hospitalization for cardiac surgery. In addition to asking about their immediate questions and needs, she provides a folder of information and suggests that they might find the material helpful as treatment evolves. She acknowledges that people have different ways of coping and discusses some of the resources, such as support groups and counseling opportunities, that others have found helpful. Maria closes by saying that she will be available to discuss a range of concerns, such as the impact of treatment on the family, its side effects, sexual functioning, finances, and spirituality.

The affective and cognitive components of pain described earlier in this chapter can be impacted by providing education and information about pain, management techniques, and strategies for coping. Many people are familiar with acute pain, and the transition to a chronic pain condition is often gradual and subtle. Consequently, the necessary emotional and cognitive adaptation to a chronic condition may be delayed. In the absence of clear education, expectation for cure may continue with the result that the patient and family have repeated experiences of failure and disappointment. Education helps patients and families distinguish between the preventive use of medications and addiction, physical dependence, and tolerance. Information should be customized to the needs of individual patients and families, because learning needs, language, and preferred learning styles differ.

Case Example

Mr. W is a 33-year-old unmarried male living at home with his parents who came to America from Trinidad. He hurt his back stocking shelves in the supermarket. He has been out of work for two years and, as a result of his ongoing struggle with worker's compensation insurance, he has become defensive and interprets pain-related assessment questions as a challenge to his credibility and the validity of his pain experience. His mother searched for curative treatment. When his pain continued, however, she began to wonder if he had a psychiatric as well as a physical problem. She sought a chronic pain program where, over time, educational interventions addressed these interrelated issues:

- Mr. W's pain experience includes physical, psychological, cultural, and systemic components. Multidimensional assessment of his pain is not intended to diminish his pain but rather to acknowledge him as a whole person, including but not limited to his physical self. Diagnostic and medical evaluation indicate that Mr. W's pain is no longer a signal that he is doing further harm to his body.
- His mother's behaviors, based in her culture and role, need to be refocused on supporting independence and recovery rather than "taking care of her son." His back pain is reframed from an acute to a chronic condition, requiring a caregiving approach that encourages efficacy and maximum functioning.
- Medications are prescribed to diminish his pain and also serve to validate symbolically the clinician's belief in his reports of pain.
- Mr. W is advised to consider participating in a vocational rehabilitation program rather than waiting for his pain to dissipate,

thus reframing the goal of care as being to maximize functioning rather than to ameliorate pain.

Cognitive-Behavioral Interventions

Cognitive-behavioral techniques recognize that the biological, cognitive, behavioral, and emotional aspects of experience are related and that interventions focused on any one aspect have the potential to modify the entire experience. The internal dialogue of the patient or family member becomes a source of rich diagnostic information, and the relationship of body, mind, and emotion becomes an avenue for helping to maximize feelings of control and self-efficacy and modify symptoms. Cognitive-behavioral interventions may be adjuncts to the medical management of symptoms. They often are used in combination and may be the primary interventions in chronic pain situations. They can be helpful to patients during procedures and diagnostic tests that often create distress and feelings of lack of control.

The strategies selected relate to the goals and condition of the patient and often tap into the patients' and families' interests and abilities. For those who are overwhelmed or physically or mentally exhausted, the clinician works to build a successful experience by selecting interventions that require less effort, such as those based in visual or auditory senses, such as audiotapes and music. These interventions can be taught to individuals and families or can be incorporated into group experiences. Education is often a basic component of these techniques. Normalizing aspects of cognitive-behavioral interventions helps patients and families integrate them more easily. To that end, comparing imagery to controlled daydreaming or distraction to being engaged in an exciting movie reinforces the familiar at the same time that new skills are being introduced. It can be helpful to introduce these techniques as an extension of natural abilities to distract from the painful stimuli, which does not mean that the pain is either nonexistent or psychological in origin (Altilio, 2004; Berlin, 2001; Devine, 2003; Jacobsen

& Hann, 1998; Loscalzo & Jacobsen, 1990). These techniques focus clinical attention on the relationship among body, mind, and emotion and provide options for interventions that reflect the multidimensional experiences of palliative care patients and individuals living with chronic pain (Kerr, 2000). The International Association for the Study of Pain (2009) and the National Cancer Institute (NCI, 2010) Web sites are important sources of information and references about how to integrate interventions into practice.

Cognitive Restructuring

Cognitive restructuring involves monitoring a person's interpretation of events in order to reduce feelings of distress, helplessness, and hopelessness. Exploring a patient's internal dialogue can help to identify thoughts and feelings that exacerbate pain, symptom intensity, and distress. The technique provides an opportunity both to explore fears and misconceptions and to reinterpret thoughts to enhance comfort and control (Bradley, 1996; Syrjala, Donaldson, Davis, Kippes, & Carr, 1995).

Case Example

Mr. K is a 51-year-old Latino married father of two adult children who was admitted to the hospital with back pain. Within a five-day period, he was diagnosed with lung cancer and informed that his cancer had metastasized to his liver and bones. His sister is an assertive, informed advocate who speaks English and is the primary spokesperson for the family with the health-care team. Mrs. K, whose primary language is Spanish, is frightened and tearful. It is an expected response, but one that is particularly distressing to Mr. K, who has seen himself as protector and provider. Mr. K's respiratory condition worsens precipitously, and before making a decision about resuscitation or appointing a health-care agent, he requires ventilator support and is therefore unable to communicate. Diagnostic work continues, and antibiotics are prescribed for his respiratory symptoms. The social worker and palliative care team continue to provide service to the patient and family to

maintain continuity throughout the crisis. Supportive counseling techniques are used to assist Mr. K and his family to integrate the quickly changing medical situation. They include education about diagnosis and treatment, validation of the range of emotions, concerns, and questions associated with the medical and family crises, and clarification of the intent and goals of the medical team. In family meetings, Mrs. K is determined to be the surrogate decision maker, although the process of decision making becomes one of family consensus. The social worker sees to it that Mrs. K has a staff interpreter to ensure that information is interpreted directly to her rather than through distressed family members and to validate the importance of her role and participation. In addition to current circumstances, the social worker and doctor explore the patient's prior articulated beliefs and values that might inform the decisions to be made on his behalf. This is especially important consequent to the family's perception that they would be "killing" Mr. K if they agreed to have the ventilator removed. The family indicates that Mr. K had shared his desire not to be sustained by machines. He also had told the team chaplain that he had a good life and that quality of life was more important to him than quantity. Using the technique of cognitive reframing, the family was asked to consider that discontinuing the ventilator reflects a respect for Mr. K's values and that, rather than "killing him," they were allowing death to occur, consistent with the guidance he had given. Family members allow the medical team to remove the ventilator. The social worker and physician provide anticipatory guidance to assist family members with their individual decisions to be present as the ventilator is removed, educating them about this unfamiliar process, using breathing and imagery techniques both to prepare them for Mr. K's death and to enhance coping with the actual experience.

Coping Statements

Coping statements are internal or spoken statements designed to distract, enhance coping, self-sooth, or diminish the threatening aspect of a situation or experience (International Association for the Study of Pain, 2009; McCaul & Malott, 1984; Syrjala et al., 1995). Catastrophic and defeating self-statements about pain can be replaced with internal dialogues that enhance coping, calm, and competence.

Distraction

Distraction involves refocusing attention to stimuli other than pain and to other aspects of self, which might include mental activity (internal) such as prayer, reading, or doing crossword puzzles, or physical activity (external), such as breathing, rhythm, or engaging in conversation (American Pain Society, 2005; Broome, Rehwaldt, & Fogg, 1998). Activities such as telling stories, music, life review, prayer, and reading silently or aloud can have therapeutic value while at the same time distracting from pain and other sources of distress (Altilio, 2002; McCaffrey & Pasero, 1999).

Self-Monitoring Techniques

Self-monitoring techniques such as diaries or journals externalize and objectify thoughts, behaviors, and feelings and create a personal history. The identification of attitudes, thoughts, and beliefs allows redefinition of the threatening aspects of experience toward the goal of decreasing distressing feelings and reactions. The techniques are adaptable to different personalities and goals, can be kept for a week or for months, can be written in telegram format or in paragraphs, and provide a link to the clinician (Altilio, 2004; American Pain Society, 2005). At times, diaries and audio recordings serve an additional purpose because they come to represent symbolically the therapeutic relationship, as in the concept of a transitional object, thereby extending the therapeutic benefit and comfort implicit in that relationship (Winnicott, 1971). Diaries can be useful in understanding the multidimensional aspects of illness and symptoms, including pain, insomnia, anxiety, and depression, and thereby guide interventions (Kelly & Clifford, 1997).

Case Example

The next journal entries were written over time by Ms. J, a 28-year-old woman with breast cancer that had metastasized to the bones, causing pain that impacted function, sleep, and mood.

11:00 am: I had a relatively good night's sleep. When I woke up, instead of turning on the TV, I tried to go back to sleep. I told myself that if I tried for 15 to 20 minutes to go to sleep, I could get up or watch TV. I fell back to sleep both times. [Coping statement integrated with sleep hygiene techniques empower and diminish helplessness related to sleeplessness.]

2:00 pm: Feeling very depressed because I was supposed to go out to dinner in the city, but I canceled because I feel so horrible. I'm also afraid that I'd be in miserable pain. That's why I canceled. But now I'm feeling depressed because I feel like this pain has control over my entire life. [Patient's catastrophic thinking and anticipation of pain controls behavior, exacerbating her helplessness and distress.]

4:30 pm: Feel really depressed about everything. The pain is making me feel like I'm dying [attributed meaning]. Not that it's that bad—it's not—it's actually pretty mild, but I just feel overwhelmed by everything; the decisions I have to make. [Patient differentiating pain, symbolic meaning of pain and feelings and distress generated by pending decisions.] (Altilio, 2004)

Relaxation Techniques

In the 1970s, a research cardiologist named Herbert Benson developed a simple relaxation technique that incorporates muscle relaxation and rhythmic breathing. Its goal is to elicit a relaxation response that counteracts fight or flight, the internal adaptive response to threat during which the body secretes catecholamines, or stress hormones, that prepare a person to fight or flee. This response is essential when facing acute threats and often becomes activated during medical procedures that may be frightening or threatening to patients, because the anticipated results, such as a diagnosis of cancer, will be life altering. The fight-or-flight response is not helpful when stress is chronic, as when the threat is an internal experience, such as pain or shortness of breath (Benson, 1975). It also often is disruptive during procedures that require patient attention or stillness. Learning the breathing technique that elicits a relaxation response may empower patients and families to cope with events, fears, and overwhelming thoughts, thus enhancing feelings of self-efficacy.

Many patients use breathing techniques with or without muscle relaxation to reverse their physiologic, emotional, and behavioral reactions to stress and pain. The choice of technique is based on a clinical evaluation. Most exercises combine repetition of a word, phrase, or breath, with or without imagery, and are enhanced by a quiet environment and a secure comfortable physical position. Clinicians often work with patients and families to practice techniques within the therapeutic relationship. Personalized relaxation and imagery exercises can be recorded for use by patients and families, thus creating the potential to extend their therapeutic benefit (Gallo-Silver & Pollack, 2000; Loscalzo & Jacobsen, 1990).

Imagery

Imagery is the use of mental representations to assist in the control of symptoms, to enhance relaxation and comfort, or to distance oneself from a problem and in so doing gain insight into it. Imagery often incorporates a relaxation exercise. Although visualization is the most common form, many exercises are enriched by involving the senses of taste, smell, hearing, and touch. Imagery can be used to mentally rehearse upcoming activities or feelings that are threatening (Eller, 1999; Graffam & Johnson, 1987; Luebbert, Dahme, & Hasenbring, 2001; Sheikh, 1983). Images elicited from the patient or family may represent personal memories or imaginary places and have the potential to enhance the therapeutic impact of intervention.

Hypnosis

Hypnosis is a technique for inducing a state of heightened awareness, increased suggestibility, and focused concentration that can be used to alter the perception of pain, reduce associated fear and anxiety, and sometimes control pain itself (Kirsch, Montgomery, & Saperstein, 1995; Montgomery, David, Winkel, Silverstein, & Bovbjerg, 2002). Autogenic self-hypnosis uses self-suggestions of warmth, heaviness, and relaxation in sequence throughout the body. It can be associated with decrease of pain and enhanced relaxation (Sternbach, 1987). Clinicians who choose to add hypnosis to their skill sets seek specialized training. The concept of suggestion, however, can be integrated easily into professional communication simply by attending to language. For example, the phrase "as you become more comfortable" implies both process and an expectation of positive outcome, a message significantly different from "when or if you become more comfortable."

Life Review and Legacy Building

The diagnosis of an advanced illness often is associated with an increased awareness that one is indeed mortal. Erikson (1963) speculated that those facing death attempted to resolve the conflict between "ego integrity" and "despair." Assisting patients with life review by focusing on generativity (continuing to be engaged in meaningful activities) offers a foundation for positive reflection at this vulnerable stage of life. New attention to existential "meaning of life" concerns may begin to take precedence as the individual considers the possibility of a limited life span or living with chronic pain. Social workers can assist during this period by normalizing these concerns, sharing time for review, and offering resources to assist in the life review process. Tools are available that offer guidance in recording life history on video- or audiotapes, in journals or scrapbooks, or through other artistic strategies (Babcock, 1997; McPhelimy, 1997; Otis-Green & Rutland, 2004). These efforts can be tremendously cathartic for the patient and of great value to loved ones as part of an intentional legacy-building exercise. With chronic pain, life review may happen as a natural part of integrating the impact of chronic pain as patients and families reflect on changes in their current lives, as well as their future hopes.

Case Example

Ms. T has been reluctant to come to the Detours group that meets monthly at the hospital. When her doctor tells her that it was for those with recurrent disease, she summons her courage and comes to a meeting. She is relieved to see so many others already grabbing snacks and finding seats. The social work facilitator invites the participants to share what "detours" life has thrown each of them. Ms. T finds herself relaxing as she listens to so many stories similar to her own. She has been feeling stuck and unsure of what to do since learning of the recurrence of her illness. The social worker encourages members of the group to think about what is most important to them and to consider how to ensure that what is most essential to them is not lost. Ms. T raises her hand to tell the group that her three children are what matters the most and asks the group for suggestions to help her "protect them from all of this." Later Ms. T tells her doctor that the group helped her to see that, although she might not be able to protect her children, she is thinking more clearly about how she can better prepare them for whatever they might have to face. In subsequent meetings, Ms. T develops a guardianship plan and works on recording and creating memories through videotape. She also prepares a book of reminiscences and memories for her children.

Integrative Strategies: The Use of the Expressive Arts

The expressive arts offer social workers enormous opportunities for culturally sensitive interactions with those they serve. Integrative interventions are especially useful as a distraction technique for those suffering pain. Although many pediatric units recognize the benefits of expressive art interventions, fewer adult units incorporate art, music, or play strategies into routine care. Health social workers are well positioned to recommend and coordinate integrative programs (Otis-Green, 2003). For example, hand or foot massage programs may fit well into a skilled nursing environment, the introduction of a music program may be appropriate for an intensive care setting, or the use of the visual arts may be incorporated into existing support groups. Developing a mind-set that looks for ways to integrate the expressive arts into conventional settings is a first step toward creating opportunities for the successful integration of these strategies.

Case Example

Mr. H is diagnosed with chronic renal disease and significant diabetic neuropathy, yet he comes regularly to the Hands on Harps concerts and workshops sponsored by the social work department. When asked what makes these meetings so important to him, he always beams and states that when listening to the music, all of his pain disappears and that although he lacks digital dexterity, "playing with the harp always sounds so sweet." When Mr. H becomes too ill to attend the workshops, his social worker arranges for the harpist to visit his hospital room. Mr. H's family later reports that they played harp music to him while they sat vigil awaiting his death and plan to play the CD at his funeral, since it always brought such comfort to him.

Child/Adolescent-Specific Interventions

In years past, children often were excluded from participation and interaction with the illness experiences of their family members. This well-meaning exclusion was intended to protect children from distress and confusion. It is now understood that providing children with age-appropriate information, and allowing them to participate as appropriate, can enhance their adjustment to a changed family experience and to the losses and adaptations that accompany chronic pain, progressive illness, and death (Harpham, 2004).

Most children are very perceptive but may lack both the cognitive and developmental abilities to understand what is happening in their family and may not have the language to talk about it. Although cultural variation may influence how families engage children and adolescents, clinicians can focus attention to child and adolescent coping by asking relevant questions as part of an overall assessment, not only of the immediate or nuclear family members, but also of grandchildren, nieces, and nephews who are emotionally connected to the patient. Age-appropriate information provided by significant adults can enhance understanding, dispel myths, fears, and anxieties, enhance trust, and help children to make sense of their own feelings as well as those of others. Many children worry that they have caused the pain or illness of loved ones, because of the magical thinking that may accompany their stage of development. They may have fears about their own health, overreact to comparable symptoms such as pain, and worry about how they will be cared for if income is lost or a parent becomes disabled or dies. Giving children permission to ask questions and express feelings and fears helps them feel secure and cared for. Techniques such as play therapy, art therapy, storytelling, and journaling can be especially helpful. Signs of regression or disinterest, while common for children, can be disconcerting for adults who may already be overwhelmed and misinterpret the behaviors of their children or adolescents. Education, reassurance, and maintenance of routine is often helpful (Heiney, Hermann, Bruss, & Fincannon, 2000).

Adolescents are at a particularly vulnerable stage of development that can be complicated when an adult is ill or affected by chronic pain. The need to be aligned with peers, to regulate uncertainty and anxiety, and the desire to achieve some degree of emancipation and independence may become more difficult when medical issues and role changes create additional anxiety and require the adolescent to limit peer activity and assume more responsibility at home. Resulting behaviors may include withdrawal, silence, or anger, and may reflect a myriad of feelings, such as embarrassment, sadness, guilt, depression, and anxiety. Social work interventions may include:

- Educating the family about adolescent-specific issues.
- Engaging and educating adolescents about medical situations in age-appropriate ways.
- Encouraging adults to continue to talk, even in monologue, about what is occurring, reinforcing stability as well as changes that may occur.
- Monitoring unobtrusively the teen's schoolwork and interactions with peers and significant adults.
- Assessing the pros and cons of alerting school personnel—teachers and counselors—about what is occurring in the family, ensuring that they respect the teen's confidentiality while offering additional support.
- Encouraging opportunities for contact with significant adults in the teen's life, such as aunts, uncles, and coaches.
- Evaluating for depression, anxiety, and changes in sleep and appetite.

Case Example

Mrs. L is a 42-year-old Latina married mother of two children—Paulino, age 9, and Pedro, age 5. She was diagnosed with a Stage 4 glioblastoma approximately four months ago. Despite limited response, she has continued to pursue treatments, including chemotherapy, and has chosen to participate in clinical trials. Mrs. L reports that when her husband is at work, the children act out. Paulino complains that his "summer is ruined," and Pedro talks back to his parents, does not adhere to set limits, and is beginning to regress, wetting his bed and soiling his garments. Mrs. L responds by apologizing and is overwhelmed by feelings of sadness, anger, and guilt. She is fatigued from treatments and paralyzed by the fear that she will die, leaving her children and husband. The social worker works with Mrs. and Mr. L to explore the potential benefits of a family meeting. They agree to a meeting of all family members to explore their understandings and to provide age-appropriate information for the children. During the meeting, the social worker reviews the meaning and etiology of fatigue and assists the children in reframing their understanding of Mrs. L's waning ability to participate physically in their lives. The age-appropriate needs of the children are acknowledged, and the family is encouraged to take advantage of their available supports. They identify family members, specifically an uncle and friends, who might assist in helping with the children. In addition to contributing to the lives of the children, allowing friends and family to participate will enable Mrs. L to focus her energy on meaningful activities with her sons, individually and together, creating memories. Friends and family are assigned tasks that allow them to realize their desire to help. They are grateful to know that they are contributing to the life of Mrs. L and her family. The social worker locates low-cost day camps in their area, providing the children with age-appropriate activities and allowing time for Mrs. L to rest. Mr. L is consistently engaged in planning, because it is essential that the children experience a relationship of trust and confidence in their father, who is likely to be the parent who raises them.

Family Meetings

Family meetings can be used as therapeutic tools for providing family-oriented clinical, palliative, and end-of-life care. They are forums for communication in which social workers have the potential to make tremendous contributions (Fineberg, 2010). In the hospital setting, such meetings, also called family conferences, may be defined as "a meeting which involves a number of family members, the patient, and hospital personnel in discussions concerning the patient's illness, treatment and plans for their discharge or their care outside the hospital" (Hansen, Cornish, & Kayser, 1998, p. 58). Family conferences are not the same as family therapy (Meyer, Schneid, & Craigie, 1989) because they focus on

immediate issues relating to health and care rather than longer-term improvements in family functioning. They can, however, enhance and enrich therapeutic work. Effective communication with families is particularly challenging, because family members are often the "hidden patients" in palliative care, both providing and needing care (Kristjanson & Aoun, 2004). This is especially true when family members, as defined by the patient, are chosen rather than related by biological or legal connections. By advancing a family systems theoretical perspective, family conferences bring a holistic approach that is emphasized in palliative and end-of-life care but largely absent in medical systems (Erstling & Devlin, 1989).

Family conferences have been shown to improve communication in palliative care (Hudson, Thomas, Quinn, & Aranda, 2009; Lautrette et al., 2007). Conferences often address emotionally intense topics, such as advance care planning, pain and symptom management, and ethical issues. They are important forums for decision making in hospitals, intensive care units, and clinics (Curtis et al., 2001; Hansen et al., 1998; Kushner, Meyer, & Hansen, 1989; Meyer et al., 1989). Conferences provide opportunities for collective patient, family, and health-care provider discussions (Ambuel, 2000; Liebman, Silbergleit, & Farber, 1975) that promote the inclusion of patients and families, invite family members to be active participants in care (Atkinson, Stewart, & Gardner, 1980), allow for collaborative dissemination of information and clarification of misinformation, and increase coordination of health-care providers to reduce the potential for patients and families to receive conflicting messages. Given the complexity of purpose implicit in family meetings, it is important to consider the involvement of both current providers and those who have a historical relationship with the patient and family. These providers often bring both emotional and clinical continuity as well as valuable information based on an ongoing relationship (Altilio et al., 2008). Although it is challenging to involve providers who may have worked with the patient in the past, technology such as Internet video conferencing now enables us to enlist participants who may be anywhere in the world. Social work advocacy for clinician continuity and participation may mitigate feelings of abandonment and honor prior discussions with patients and families related to their articulated values, goals, and decision-making processes.

Family conferences, while not normative in the care of persons with chronic pain, can serve as forums for educating and assisting families as they emotionally and cognitively struggle to move from an acute care model that anticipates that pain will dissipate to a recognition that pain may have become a chronic condition that requires adaptation and has a continuing impact on the life of the family. Varying combinations of patients, family members, and health-care providers may participate in family conferences, making these interventions adaptable for a broad range of family configurations and cultural traditions (Fineberg & Bauer, 2011).

SOME ETHICAL CONCEPTS RELATED TO PAIN AND PALLIATIVE CARE

Medical ethics was remarkably continuous and consistent from the time of Hippocrates until the mid-20th century. In recent years scientific, technological, and social developments have produced rapid changes in the many traditional conceptions of ethical practice and obligations in health-care practice. Medical care, living with chronic illness, and, in many instances, dying have become more complex than in previous generations as a result of our highly technical and disjointed systems of care. At times, it seems that our medical technology has surpassed the ability to make ethical decisions about its use.

Ethics is a branch of philosophy that seeks to determine how human actions may be judged right or wrong. The study of ethics implies that the human mind is the fundamental means by which actions can be judged (Beauchamp & Childress, 1989). Thus, ethics is not the same as moral theology or religious ethics since ethics uses reason alone and does not invoke religious beliefs as the source of its conclusions. Nor is ethics the same as the law. Although the law is largely concerned with the public good and the protection of individual rights, ethics goes further to look at the obligations of individuals to themselves as well as to others and to society.

In the practice of medicine, these obligations are intimately related to purpose. Pelligrino (1979) asserted that the purpose in medicine is a right and good healing action taken in the interest of a particular patient. Kass (1983) emphasized healing as the primary purpose of medicine while acknowledging that the pursuit of health, the prevention of death, and the alleviation of suffering were secondary to healing. Any dialogue that attempts to explore and expand these values and concepts should be based on a common understanding and acceptance of the language used. Palliative care, with an essential focus on serious illness, risk and benefits, goals of care, and decision making, requires that clinicians are familiar with common ethical principles and are sufficiently skilled to identify an ethical dilemma (see Chapter 3 for further discussion of ethics).

The four principles that underlie and guide ethical decision making are autonomy, beneficence, nonmaleficence, and justice. The following definitions establish a common language as a basis for collaboration and discussion.

Autonomy is derived from the Greek *autos* (self) and *nomos* (rule, governance, or law). Those who have autonomy "act intentionally, are informed and free from interference and control by others" (Lo, 2000, p. 11). In Western health-care systems, autonomy is promoted by providing information and assisting patients and surrogates to reach decisions. Closely tied to the principle of autonomy are the values of respect for persons, the right of self-determination, and informed consent. Cultural beliefs, values, and family dynamics often require thoughtful clinicians to adapt and negotiate in order to balance the principle of individual autonomy with unique patient and family circumstances. Respect for persons is based on the tacit belief in the value of each person; considers social, economic, and cultural variables; and includes the right to self-determination. Respect for persons supports the right of capacitated persons to determine the appropriate level, if any, of medical intervention and the right to change their decisions about treatment when their condition changes.

At its most basic, *beneficence* means no more than "do good." Similarly, the principle of *nonmaleficence* tells us to avoid doing harm. Ethical medical decision making is complex, and it is not always possible to know clearly what is "doing good" in the face of ambivalent and nonspecific potential outcomes. In addition, the concept of doing good may differ based on individual opinions, cultural and spiritual beliefs, and social preferences, as evidenced in the case example describing the care of Mrs. M.

Justice is an important ethical principle that involves provision of health care as related to the availability and distribution of goods and services. Some argue that society is expected to determine a just, or at least reasonable, distribution of the goods necessary to protect the dignity of the individual person. When we expand the construct of "distribution of goods" to include pain management skills and medications, it becomes a violation of the principle of justice as well as beneficence when vulnerable groups such as older persons, women, and minorities are not provided competent pain management equal to that provided to other groups (Bonham, 2001; Cleeland et al., 1994; Tarzian & Hoffman, 2004). Distribution is concerned with scarce resources. At times, demand outstrips supply, a reality that becomes particularly complex in the American health-care system, in which supply also is influenced by availability of services and access as determined by geography, finances, and socioeconomic status (see Chapters 5 and 7 for further discussion).

Ethicists have created specific guidelines to assist in deliberations of challenging ethical dilemmas wherein there may be conflict and confusion about actions that may have both benefits and harms. For example, the principle of double effect assists clinicians struggling with decisions related to interventions that may have intended positive effects at the same time as unintended, but foreseen, harmful effects. The concept of proportionality assists in the weighing of potential benefits and harms. The beliefs, values, and responsibilities of clinicians, patients and families, and institutions are infused with these profound and complex discussions. Social workers who are privileged to join in these deliberations have an important role in bringing their comprehensive assessment and understanding of patients and families to the process and assisting in ensuring that the process is respectful and informed and honors the participants as well as the complexity implicit in these discussions.

In addition to a working knowledge of autonomy, beneficence, nonmaleficence, justice, and double effect, social workers practicing in palliative care and pain settings require expertise in concepts such as euthanasia and physician-assisted death or assisted suicide. In the care of seriously ill patients, treatment of pain or shortness of breath often requires use of medications that may have the unintended side effect of sedation. Euthanasia, physician-assisted suicide, is not the same as withholding or withdrawing interventions that allow death to occur. Confusion about the intent of intensive symptom management, euthanasia, and assisted death on the part of the staff, patient, or family requires that social work clinicians, in consult with their nursing and physician colleagues, are knowledgeable, responsive, and vigilant in exploring observations and that they provide accurate information to dispel misinterpretation and perhaps alter the plan of care. Public discussion of these topics invites thoughtful and comprehensive social work analysis because they are reflective of profound and complex ethical and moral issues.

Euthanasia is the deliberate action by a physician or an individual other than the patient to end the patient's life for benevolent motives, such as the relief of suffering. The act is performed with the explicit consent of a competent adult who is the patient. The patient's death occurs consequent to the direct action of the medical provider. *Involuntary euthanasia* is the intentional administration of medications or other interventions to cause the death of a competent patient without the patient's explicit request and full informed consent. *Nonvoluntary euthanasia* is the intentional administration of medications or other interventions to cause the death of an incompetent patient who is incapable of explicitly requesting it (Emanuel & Emanuel, 1992). All forms of euthanasia are illegal in the United States.

Physician-assisted death is the provision by a physician of medications or advice that enables patients to end their lives. It is the ingestion of medications by a terminally ill, competent adult intended to hasten death. Patients take the medications themselves and are thus the direct agents of their own deaths. Two states currently allow physician-assisted suicide: Oregon (since 1998) and Washington (since 2008).

The Oregon Death with Dignity Act (ODDA) was structured around the three pillars of self-determination, professional immunity and integrity, and public accountability. Several unexpected outcomes have occurred over the decade during which ODDA has been in effect. Among them is the fact that relatively few persons have chosen to hasten death through this legislative vehicle. Before the act was implemented, opponents anticipated a demographic "surge" to Oregon of near-terminal patients. The empirical evidence does not bear this out. In 10 years, 541 Oregon residents have received prescriptions for lethal doses of medication to end their lives; of this number, 341 actually ingested the drugs. These figures are lower than those forecasted by those on both sides of the debate. Although those figures generally have risen each year, the deaths under ODDA are still a very small proportion of Oregon's total deaths. The principal concerns expressed by patients who choose to hasten their deaths is loss of autonomy, diminished quality of life, loss of dignity, and loss of control of bodily functions, all of which are aspects of care that are within the scope of social

work practice (Oregon Department of Health Services, 2008).

It appears that ODDA may have served as a catalyst for improving end-of-life care among Oregon practitioners, driving the increased use of hospice and palliative care and the improved management of pain. Ensuring death with dignity for all patients is a goal beyond the parameters of ODDA. It is influenced by improving the practice of all clinicians caring for seriously ill patients. Currently there is a move away from describing "death with dignity" and "physician-assisted suicide" toward language that describes the hastening of death by ingestion of medications provided by a physician as "assisted death." Of note, in Oregon, the cause of death on the death certificates of those who chose ODDA is the underlying terminal illness, thus not precluding provision of life insurance benefits.

Only a few states have offered initiatives to legalize assisted death, either through state legislatures or citizens themselves. Washington State has legalized its own death with dignity act, which was passed in November 2008. The first year's report is that 63 patients requested medication under the law, and of those 63, 36 people died after ingesting medication (Washington State Department of Health, 2009). These data are similar to data collected in Oregon, as are the top three reasons for pursuing assisted death among Washington patients: loss of autonomy, loss of dignity, and being less able to engage in activities that make life meaningful (Washington State Department of Health, 2009).

PAIN MANAGEMENT: AN OVERVIEW

In addition to the opportunity presented in palliative care, many people who live with chronic pain have needs that fall well within the purview of social work practice. In 2003, a national telephone survey of 1,004 adults revealed 57% of respondents to have reported chronic or recurring pain during the past year

(Hart, 2003). The survey considered chronic pain conditions such as back and knee pain, arthritis, headache, and migraine. Of those surveyed, 76% had experienced pain, either directly or through a connection to a family member or friend. Chronic pain had led to changes in employment, residence, personal freedom, or mobility. Steps taken to cope with pain included applying for disability and seeking help with activities of daily living. These findings reflect adaptation and experiences of loss that have the potential to affect self-esteem, identity, role function, and social and economic stability, both for the person living with pain and for close family members and friends. In addition to the personal and family impact, data from an American Productivity Audit in 2001 estimated that over half (52.7%) of the workforce reported pain conditions in the two weeks prior to the survey. In that two-week period, 12.7% of respondents lost productive time, with an average loss of 4.6 hours per week, at a cost of $61.2 billion a year (Stewart, Ricci, Chee, Morganstein, & Lipton, 2003). These findings point to a health and economic concern of major proportions.

Pain is necessary to survival and generally, but not always, signals physical injury or disease and alerts one to take some kind of action. Although pain arguably is a truly universal experience, at the same time, individuals, including clinicians, relate to pain through a kaleidoscope of cultural, familial, sociopolitical, and spiritual values. For example, pain can be viewed as a misfortune, as a weakness, a path to redemption, or a form of punishment. Some believe the appropriate response is to bear pain stoically while others view pain as a signal to seek medical attention and expect to receive help and care from family and friends. Although many expect to be healed through medical intervention, others believe that pain can best be controlled through prayer or psychological or integrative interventions (see Chapter 12 for further information). Patients with chronic pain that may or may not be associated with observable

tissue damage sometimes are accused of exaggerating pain and disability for secondary gain; yet many feel ashamed and or diminished by dependence on others and the need to apply for disability in a system that often challenges the integrity of applicants. Thus, we begin to see the complexity and importance of comprehensive clinical assessment and interventions to assist persons with pain that has the potential to impact profoundly their identity and the quality of their lives and the lives of their family and friends. This is true for chronic pain or for pain that accompanies incurable progressive illness.

Pain is also unique as a symptom, in that it is a subjective experience, and unlike other somatic experiences, such as high blood pressure, body temperature, or blood glucose levels, cannot be measured objectively (American Pain Society, 2003). Clinicians and family members must rely on the person's report of pain severity and its impact. Social work's emphasis on starting where the client is and assessing people in their environment serve as frames of reference that imply a respect for individuals' perceptions of their experiences and a valuing of the whole person, including but not limited to the body. In the management of pain, an analogous principle is to believe the report of pain; in palliative care, a comparable mandate is an understanding of the holistic experience including values, beliefs, and culture that inform the life of the patient and family. The task for social work clinicians is to complement values such as respect for the dignity and worth of the person with pain and palliative expertise that empower the profession to intervene on a clinical, institutional, policy, and research level.

Pain in Life-Limiting and Chronic Incurable Illness

In palliative care settings, the experience and management of pain is impacted by the multiple challenges presented by diseases such as cancer, multiple sclerosis, and acquired immunodeficiency syndrome (AIDS). These statistics provide a sampling of the diseases for which compassionate care demands that pain and palliative care needs are addressed.

Pain occurs in:

- 40% to 83% of patients with Parkinson's disease (Beiske, Loge, Ronningen, & Svennson, 2009; Ford, 1998; Goetz, Tanner, Levy, Wilson, & Garron, 1986)
- 42.9% of patients with multiple sclerosis (Solaro et al., 2004)
- 49% of pediatric cancer patients (Collins et al., 2000)
- 59% of cancer patients in active therapy (Van den Beulken-van Everdingen et al., 2007)
- 64% of cancer patients with advanced disease (Van den Beulken-van Everdingen et al., 2007)
- 88% of patients with AIDS (Frich & Borgbjerg, 2000)

Pain and symptoms such as shortness of breath, cognitive impairment, and anorexia present challenges to patients, their families, and caregivers that intensify the suffering and feelings of helplessness often associated with life-threatening and incurable progressive illnesses. The next narrative illustrates the impact of pain, fatigue, and cognitive impairment that extends beyond the direct experience of the patient.

Case Example

Mrs. D is a 65-year-old widowed African American woman diagnosed with chronic renal disease. She has been the emotional and administrative center of a large extended family and is becoming increasingly fatigued, spends more time in bed, and is less able to engage with, and direct, her family. Her pain is being managed intensively, and the medications prescribed have caused cognitive impairment. It is expected that as her body becomes tolerant to the medication, her cognition will improve. Her family is becoming increasingly distressed; wanting her to be more awake, physically active, and cognitively clear. They are angry with the palliative care doctor,

because they perceive his lack of expertise in prescribing as the reason for her cognitive impairment. Diagnostic assessment indicates that the symptom of fatigue reflects irreversible, progressive kidney failure. Social work interventions include:

- Reviewing the family's perception and understanding of the status of disease
- Exploring various factors that might inform the anger expressed at the physician, including a lack of understanding of the process of trialing and adjusting pain medications, racial tensions or misunderstandings, and fear that patient is being harmed rather than helped
- Exploring the symbolic significance and attributed meaning of the symptoms of pain and confusion to understand the impact on family of viewing their mother as confused and unavailable to them
- Assisting the family to integrate medical information by organizing a family meeting with the team, eliciting and exploring their own observations of the changes in the patient's condition
- Working with medical staff to prepare the family for the probability that Mrs. D will become increasingly sleepy and that, as she clears cognitively, they will need to value and maximize the time that she is awake and able to interact
- Acknowledging and exploring the individual and family response to this potential loss, and reinforcing community and spiritual supports that might be helpful to them
- Acknowledging the changing family structure as a loss experience, and assisting the family to consider how to move forward with roles and responsibilities

Mrs. D's narrative portrays how a multidimensional view of symptoms can be at the core of the assessment and intervention process. Each individual and family experiences symptoms in the context of either a chronic or potentially life-threatening illness and through their own unique history and family constellation. The next narrative takes the same symptoms—pain, fatigue, and cognitive impairment—but demonstrates how the etiology, impact, symbolic significance, and resulting interventions may differ.

Case Example

Mrs. J is a 35-year-old married mother of three children, ages 3 to 8. She has back pain that is often debilitating and interferes with her ability to parent, work, and participate in an intimate relationship with her husband. She is engaged in a multimodal treatment plan that includes medication trials, physical therapy, and cognitive-behavioral therapy. As directed by her doctor, she gradually has raised the dose of opioid medications and experiences increased side effects of fatigue, sleepiness, and cognitive slowing. Her husband and extended family worry that she is too impaired to care for her children, who appear to be increasingly "out of control." Her sister-in-law, who is not aware that she is receiving opioids for pain, interprets her behaviors as symptoms of drug addiction, and reports the family to child protective services.

In this context, Mrs. J's symptoms are medication side effects that precipitate an emergency situation stemming from her decreased ability to function. It compromises the safety of her family, and results in trauma and family conflict consequent to the charge of child endangerment. A proactive and preventive approach from the pain management team might have prevented the deleterious outcome. The social work plan included:

- Assessment of the relationship among the children's behaviors, Mrs. J's symptoms and side effects, and the increased family tensions
- Intervention with the family and child protective services to address the needs of the children and ensure the family's ability to provide support and supervision as medications are stabilized
- In consultation with Mrs. J, a meeting with family members, including the sister-in-law, to educate them about the differences among addiction, tolerance, and physical dependence, and behaviors related to medication side effects
- Engagement with family members as informed supports and participants in a plan of care that would involve multimodal treatments, including ongoing medication trials and titration of medications

VULNERABLE POPULATIONS AND DIVERSE SETTINGS

Undertreatment of pain is a multifaceted problem that involves educational, regulatory, and reimbursement barriers as well as beliefs, values, and behaviors that impact the individual's relationship to pain, medications, and health-care professionals. Poorly controlled pain causes unnecessary suffering for many, and particular groups have been identified as more vulnerable. The risk of undertreatment increases when assessment of pain becomes more of a challenge; for example, for those who have language or cultural differences and for infants, children, older persons, and people who are cognitively impaired or have mental illness (American Pain Society, 2003). Many of the barriers to pain management are psychosocial, political, spiritual, or cultural in nature and thus become appropriate foci for social work assessment and intervention (Altilio, 2004; Parker-Oliver, Wittenberg-Lyles, Washington, & Sehrawat, 2009).

Social work's heritage of service, commitment to justice, and advocacy for oppressed groups demands that we develop the ability to recognize and advocate for populations whose vulnerability and sense of impotence may be intensified by pain, illness, and the inherent continuing difficulty in accessing care from a health-care system that can be unresponsive (Mendenhall, 2003).

Geriatrics

Geriatric social work clinicians share responsibility for highlighting and solving the problem of unnecessary suffering in older persons caused by unrecognized and uncontrolled symptoms, including pain and depression (Beekman et al., 2002; Bernabei et al., 1998; Fox, Raina, & Jadad, 1999; Jerant, Azari, Nesbitt, & Meyers, 2004; Liao & Ferrell, 2000). Older people may experience multiple chronic illnesses over time that impact their quality of life as well as the lives of their family and caregivers. Uncontrolled pain can lead to depression and other mood disorders, agitation, social isolation, sleeplessness, decreased function, loss of appetite, and risk of falls (American Geriatric Society Panel on Persistent Pain in Older Persons, 2002; Stein, 2001; WHO, 2004). Older people often believe that pain is to be expected and, when asked, may not acknowledge "pain" but willingly affirm "aches" or "soreness." Additional barriers include myths and misunderstanding regarding addiction and worry about cost and side effects of medications. The focus of assessment often extends beyond physical pain to existential issues, such as the mortality of self and friends and the meaning and purpose of life. In this vulnerable population, cognitive impairment can complicate the expression, assessment, and management of pain and increase the clinical team's responsibility to adapt assessment and treatment for chronic conditions, such as osteoporosis, or for life-threatening illnesses (Sachs, Shega, & Cox-Hayley, 2004; Stein, 2001).

Palliative care and chronic pain interventions require accommodation of the particular needs of older people at the individual level by adapting assessment to functional limitations, such vision or hearing limitations. At the level of group, community, or society, social workers are charged to construct alternate palliative care models to respond to those who require care over the course of chronic, slowly progressing illnesses (Jerant et al., 2004).

Gender Issues

A person's experience with and response to pain is influenced by multiple factors, including gender. Men and women experience pain differently; research suggests that women are more likely to be inadequately treated both in chronic pain settings (Hoffman & Tarzian, 2001) and in the case of illnesses such as cancer and AIDS (Breitbart et al., 1995; Cleeland et al., 1994). The study of gender-based difference in pain includes consideration of such complex areas as:

- Biological factors, such as mechanisms related to opioid receptors, sympathetic nervous system function, and hormonal influence
- Psychological factors, such as cognitive appraisal and attributed meaning
- Behavioral responses, such as coping mechanisms; communication styles; and health-related activities, such as seeking care and taking medications
- Cultural and socialization factors that impact reactions, perceptions, thoughts, and behaviors on both the part of the patient and health-care practitioners (Unruh, 1996)

Although etiology and causation are not well understood, current research suggests that the pain reports of women are taken less seriously than those of men, that women's pain is more likely to be discounted as emotional or psychogenic, and that women receive less aggressive treatment (Fillingim, 2005; International Association for the Study of Pain, 2009). This disparity violates the ethical principles of justice and respect for the dignity and worth of the individual (Hoffman & Tarzian, 2001). Keefe and colleagues (2000) report significant differences in pain, pain behavior, and physical disability between men and women with osteoarthritis. Of note, when "catastrophizing" the experience was considered, the previously significant effect of gender disappeared. Gender differences in expression of pain were found in a classic early study in which males reported significantly less pain to female experimenters than they did to male experimenters (Levine & De Simone, 1991).

Minority Populations

In 2001, Bonham reviewed multiple studies documenting disparities in pain treatment by race, ethnicity, and socioeconomic status.

Although reports are somewhat inconsistent, substantial evidence exists to support the troubling conclusion that persons belonging to racial and ethnic minority groups are less likely to receive adequate treatment for acute and chronic pain (Anderson et al., 2000; Anderson, Green, & Payne, 2009; Bonham, 2001; Cleeland et al., 1994; Dannemiller Memorial Educational Foundation, 2004). Variables that underlie these disparities are multifactorial and may exist on the clinician, patient, family, or institutional level. They range from poor communication, mistrust, racism, and economic or educational disadvantage, to a health-care system that supports disengagement, lack of continuity of care, and fails to allow sufficient time in clinical encounters to bridge differences and enhance trust.

In addition, language differences can intensify misunderstanding and increase anxiety consequent to the patient's inability to comfortably communicate his or her needs to healthcare professionals. Evidence also suggests that inner-city pharmacies do not stock the opioids used to treat moderate to severe pain, creating an additional challenge for an already disadvantaged group. Informed social workers can assist their patients and colleagues to prevent crises by encouraging patients to contact their pharmacies to ensure that prescribed medications are available or to make alternate plans to secure them (Morrison, Wallenstein, Natale, Senzel, & Huang, 2000).

Substance Abuse

It is estimated that between 6% and 15% of the U.S. population has a substance use disorder that may involve the abuse of illicit drugs or misuse of prescription medications (Collier & Kopstein, 1991; Groerer & Brodsky, 1992; Zachny et al., 2003; see Chapter 17 for more information). Some medications used in the management of chronic pain and in palliative care are controlled substances. These and other classes of medications have the potential for abuse and diversion, creating a heightened vigilance when pain medications are prescribed for patients known to abuse drugs. Treatment

of patients with a current or remote history of addiction is impacted by clinical, social, regulatory, and policy challenges such as:

- Confusion and lack of understanding of these terms:
  - *Addiction.* A primary, chronic, neurobiological disease with genetic, psychosocial, and environmental factors influencing its development and manifestations. It is characterized by behaviors that include one or more of the following: impaired control over drug use, compulsive use, continued use despite harm, and craving. *Use despite harm* includes harm in the physical, emotional, or social arenas as well as harm to relationships, including relationships with providers. At times, behaviors suggestive of addiction are actually relief-seeking behaviors that dissipate after pain is managed.
  - *Physical dependence.* A state of adaptation that is manifested by a drug-class-specific withdrawal syndrome that can be produced by abrupt cessation, rapid dose reduction, decreasing blood level of the drug, or administration of an antagonist. Physical dependence may develop with chronic use of many classes of medications. These include beta-blockers, corticosteroids, antidepressants, and other medications that are not associated with addictive disorders.
  - *Tolerance.* A state of adaptation in which exposure to a drug induces changes that result in a diminution of one or more of the drug's effects over time. Tolerance may occur to both the desired and undesired effects of drugs and may develop at different rates for different effects. For example, in the case of opioids, tolerance usually develops more slowly to analgesia than to respiratory depression, and tolerance to the constipating effects may not occur at all. In many instances, this dynamic of diminishing effect is due to progression of disease rather than to tolerance to a medication.

- *Pseudoaddiction.* A term used to describe behaviors that may occur when pain is undertreated. Patients with unrelieved pain may become focused on obtaining medications, "clock watch," or request specific medications that they have found helpful in the past. Pseudoaddiction can be distinguished from true addiction in that the behaviors resolve when pain is treated effectively (www.ampainsoc.org/advocacy/opioids2.htm)
- Providers' fear of the processes and consequences of prescribing opioid analgesics, which has been referred to as opiophobia (Morgan, 1986; Shine & Demas, 1984).
- Fear of regulatory, law enforcement, and medical board scrutiny.
- Patient's, family's, and clinician's fears of causing relapse or activating a latent addictive disease.
- Worry about potential diversion.
- Lack of time, skill, and interdisciplinary support needed to assess, treat, and monitor the care of people with pain and problematic drug use behaviors.

Many people with the disease of addiction have multiple medical problems and consequently can be quite symptomatic. They often are marginalized and have few advocates (Otis-Green & Rutland, 2004). Those who used substances early in life may not have learned behaviors or skills that allow them to negotiate health-care systems. As a group, they may have no power base or political influence and often have alienated friends and family. They require expert and respectful treatment of their addiction or problematic drug-use behaviors as well as symptom management that maximizes benefit and diminishes harmful outcomes. Although experts in these dual fields of addiction and pain management are few, guidance is available through many resources that are easily accessible through the Internet. A treatment program requires expert assessment, structure, consistency, and psychosocial and psychological interventions to create a treatment plan that maximizes the opportunity for successful treatment of both pain and addictive disease and creates an environment of safety for patients, families, and prescribers. See Chapter 17 for a full discussion of substance use issues.

Policy Issues: Opportunity for Advocacy and Leadership

In 1998, the National Institutes of Health (NIH) estimated the financial impact of poorly treated pain to be in excess of $100 billion a year, including the costs of health care, compensation, and litigation. Above and beyond the multilevel impact of poorly treated pain on the quality of life of individuals and their families lie the financial implications of a public health problem of significant proportions.

For example, while the standard of care in both pain and palliative care is a multidimensional approach with a strong emphasis on psychosocial needs, reimbursement is insufficient to support this level of care. There is a need to collaborate with insurers and legislators to advocate for research funding and to document the potential impact of pain and palliative care interventions on the quality and cost of care for patients, families, and caregivers. This care often is provided at considerable physical, financial, and emotional cost to caregivers and ultimately to the heath-care system (Levine, 2004). Legislative efforts range from pain management bills that mandate professional education to those that recommend monitoring programs that require prescribers to submit patient prescription information to a central database. Although the goal is to decrease abuse and diversion of prescription medications, this program challenges core social work and human values, such as privacy, self-determination, autonomy, and confidentiality. These legislative efforts are rich areas for social work involvement. Whether as clinicians, advocates, community organizers, policy planners, or researchers, the need for a social work presence is critical.

Interdisciplinary and Transdisciplinary Team

An interdisciplinary team approach involving health-care providers from a number of professions is central to optimal palliative care practice (Lickiss, Turner, & Pollock, 2004; NCP, 2009; WHO, 1990) and is at the core of chronic pain care. In contrast to a multidisciplinary approach in which different professionals independently provide care, "interdisciplinary practice refers to people with distinct disciplinary training working together for a common purpose, as they make different, complementary contributions to patient-focused care" (McCallin, 2001, p. 419). A team addresses patients' and family members' needs—biological, psychological, emotional, social, and spiritual—by providing the dual benefit of specialized knowledge and skills from multiple professionals delivered in combination rather in isolation. Characterized by a collaborative effort that includes information exchange and coordinated care planning, it places the patient and family at the center of team deliberations and maximizes the unique contributions of each member (Connor, Egan, Kwilosz, Larson, & Reese, 2002; Loscalzo & Von Gunten, 2009). Intervention techniques, such as family conferences that include patients, family members, and health-care team members, promote such coordinated interdisciplinary practice (Fineberg, 2010).

Some highly coordinated palliative care teams may be using a transdisciplinary approach. The transdisciplinary team is characterized by substantial overlap in functions such that members share roles in addition to providing their discipline-specific contributions to the team. Although team professionals are not interchangeable, they share responsibilities for assessing and addressing patient and family care issues.

> In transdisciplinary work, roles of the individual team members are blurred as their professional functions overlap. Each team member must become sufficiently familiar with the concepts and approaches of his or her colleagues to be able to assume significant portions of the others' roles. (Hall & Weaver, 2001, p. 868)

The team approach requires professionals to act both as unique contributors and as team members. This dual role may be very challenging to health-care providers but offers a very powerful form of care. Team members, while readily able to verbalize and explain their roles both to other team members and to patients and families, are at the same time flexible in practicing their professional roles and careful not to compromise patient and family care due to overly guarded application of their professional "turf" (Otis-Green & Fineberg, 2010). Turf issues should be discussed openly so that they can be disarmed and minimized. In the setting of economic strains in health care, team members may be especially guarded about their turf in service of job security.

Teams that function well develop effective communication and mutual trust (Blacker & Deveau, 2010; Maddocks, 2006). Coordinated function is important for minimizing the conflicting and confusing transmission of information to patients and families, especially in the sensitive context of palliative and end-of-life care. Teams benefit when members engage in intentional team-building efforts, such as becoming more familiar with each other, acknowledging differences and similarities in perspectives, addressing conflict respectfully and openly, and developing nonhierarchical patterns of communication (Otis-Green & Fineberg, 2010). The latter activity is especially challenging in the health-care setting in which the biomedical model imposes a hierarchical perspective.

Self-Care

Practitioners working in the arena of palliative care and pain management often witness the anger, sadness, and suffering of those for whom they care, especially in situations in which patients are facing chronic pain or the end of life (Speck, 2006). In addition to clinical work with patients and families, institutional and setting-specific practices and perceptions and complex ethical dilemmas can be a source of stress, job dissatisfaction, and burnout (O'Donnell et al., 2008; Ulrich et al., 2007).

Social workers who remain with patients and their families throughout the course of treatment to the end of life can experience heavy emotional burdens, sometimes when disease-modifying treatments are continued and deemed to cause unnecessary suffering and at other times when the goal of care changes exclusively to intensive and compassionate comfort care. The emotional, existential, and spiritual depth of social work practice is characterized by the profession's use of self and the capacity to witness and "sit with" people's pain and suffering (Arnd-Caddigan & Pozzuto, 2009; Renzenbrink, 2004). This intensely personal and deep involvement on the part of clinicians demands conscious and candid attention to how they are preventing compassion fatigue, especially in the long term. Challenges for all practitioners include maintaining delicate professional boundaries in which investment and attachment to patients and family members is genuine, but not overly consuming. This balance of closeness and distance allows clinicians to provide sincere, meaningful, skilled care that is not so depleting that it causes practitioner burnout or compassion fatigue (Renzenbrink, 2004). Social workers who experience burnout and compassion fatigue typically report frustration with challenges within their environments of care and experiencing an unbalanced practice in the long term that has worn away their internal emotional resources to the point of apathy and inability to provide empathetic, dedicated care (Otis-Green, 2011).

Self-care requires maintaining balance between the personal and professional in the larger context of a social worker's life. Clinicians must develop and preserve boundaries between their professional and personal selves. This does not suggest an artificial separation, but rather a concerted effort to develop a rich personal life of relationships, interests, hobbies, and activities that are not related to work and an ability to enjoy one's personal time without having frequent intruding thoughts about work. Engagement in such a personal life, subtly full of life-affirming activities, becomes important for the rejuvenation of the self and the ability to continue practice over time.

CONCLUSION

The inclusion of palliative care and pain management in this book validates the emerging presence and potential influence of social work in these specialties. Palliative care has been a professional focus in England since the 1960s, as evidenced by the writings of Monroe (2004), Saunders (2001), and Sheldon (1999, 2000). In the United States, we see a burgeoning presence of social work in palliative care following in the footsteps of physicians and nurses. Social work presence in the specialty of pain management is limited and has yet to fully emerge.

The research of Sieppert (1996) and the work of Christ and Sormanti (1999) and Raymer and Csikai (2005) demonstrate the need for education, research, and leadership in both chronic pain and palliative care. The Social Work Summit on End-of-Life and Palliative Care, held in 2002 and 2005 (Altilio, Gardia, & Otis-Green, 2008), addresses the need for collaboration among practitioners, educators, and researchers.

The formalized curricula represented by Education of Physicians in End-of-Life Care and End-of-Life Nursing Education Consortium recently have been joined by the Social Work End-of-Life Curriculum Project (Raymer & Csikai, 2005), the ACE Project (Advocating for Clinical Excellence: Transdisciplinary Palliative Care Education), and the Promoting Excellence in Pain Management and Palliative Care for Social Workers courses (Otis-Green & Ferrell, 2010). In addition to the postgraduate certificate programs offered at the New York University Silver School of Social Work and Smith College School of Social Work, organizations such as Cancer Care, the National Association of Social Workers, and the Association of Oncology Social Workers have created additional comprehensive continuing education courses, many of which are available online. Since the 1970s, social work authors (Altilio, 2005, 2008; Glajchen, Blum, & Calder, 1995; Hudgens, 1977; Loscalzo & Amendola, 1990; Mendenhall, 2003; Roy, 1981; Subramanian & Rose, 1988) and advocates, including Yvette

Colón and Kristina Thomson, have championed and encouraged social work expertise in pain management. The Leadership Development Award, offered to social workers by the Soros Foundation Project on Death in America, focuses on end-of-life and palliative care and includes pain and symptom management as core skills for social work clinicians. The inclusion of these specialties in this *Handbook* further validates the role, responsibility, and opportunity for social work clinicians in these areas of practice.

Since its inception, social work has championed important values, including justice, commitment to the underserved and the vulnerable, and respect for the integrity and worth of all human beings. The fields of pain management and palliative care are like a tapestry in which these values are woven into every aspect of the work. People who are living with life-limiting illness and/or chronic pain interface with a health-care system that is struggling to repair fractures and bridge deep crevices. They are potentially vulnerable and often underserved. We hope that this chapter helps to alert social workers to the myriad of possibilities and opportunities to make a difference in the lives of these populations.

SUGGESTED LEARNING EXERCISES

Learning Exercise 22.1

Provide an example of how the skills and code of ethics every social worker learns can be translated to pain and palliative care social work practice.

Learning Exercise 22.2

Select a partner and conduct a role-play. One person takes the role of a patient in the hospital and the other of a hospital social worker called to assess why the patient is "so upset." The patient informs the social worker that she has just learned that the treatment seems to be no longer effective and that she is not going

to live more than three months. Using information from this chapter and your social work classes, conduct a social work assessment of this patient and create a social work treatment plan for intervention.

Learning Exercise 22.3

Identify a community social worker working in pain management or palliative care, and interview this person about his or her work. Questions might include:

* How did you select this line of work? How long have you worked in this area of health social work practice?
* What are some examples of ethical dilemmas that you have encountered working in this area of practice? How did you resolve them?
* How do you manage self-care and cope with challenging situations?
* What motivates you to do the work that you do?
* How do you work with other disciplinary professionals in your work setting or in the community?

REFERENCES

Altilio, T. (2002). Helping children, helping ourselves: An overview of children's literature. In J. Loewy & A. F. Hara (Eds.), *Caring for the caregiver: The use of music and music therapy in grief and trauma* (pp. 138–146). Baltimore, MD: American Music Therapy Association.

Altilio, T. (2004). Pain and symptom management: An essential role for social workers. In J. Berzoff & P. Silverman (Eds.), *Living with dying* (pp. 380–408). New York, NY: Columbia University Press.

Altilio, T. (2005). Social work. In M. Boswell & B. Cole (Eds.), *Weiner's pain management: A practical guide for clinicians* (7th ed., pp. 239–247). New York, NY: Taylor & Francis.

Altilio, T. (2008). Pain. In T. Mizrahi & L. E. David (Eds.), *Encyclopedia of social work,* 20th ed. (pp. 335–337). New York, NY: NASW Press/Oxford University Press.

Altilio, T., Gardia, G., & Otis-Green, S. (2008). The state of social work practice. In S. Blacker, G. Christ, & S. Lynch (Eds.), *Charting the course for the future of social work in end-of-life and palliative care: A report of the 2nd Social Work Summit on End-of-Life and Palliative Care* [Special report of the Social Work in Hospice and Palliative Care Network], pp. 10–14. Retrieved from www.swhpn.org/monograph.pdf

Altilio, T., & Otis-Green, S. (Eds.). (2011). *Textbook of palliative social work*. New York, NY: Oxford University Press.

Altilio, T., Otis-Green, S., & Dahlin, C. M. (2008). Applying the National Quality Forum Preferred Practices for Palliative and Hospice Care: A social work perspective. *Journal of Social Work in End-of-Life & Palliative Care, 4*(1), 3–16.

Ambuel, B. (2000). Conducting a family conference. *Principles and practice of supportive oncology updates, 3*(3), 1–12.

American Geriatric Society Panel on Persistent Pain in Older Persons. (2002). The management of persistent pain in older persons. *Journal of the American Geriatric Society, 50,* 1–20.

American Pain Society. (2003). *Principles of analgesic use in the treatment of acute and cancer pain* (5th ed.). Glenview, IL: Author.

American Pain Society. (2005). *Guideline for the management of cancer pain in adults and children*. Glenview, IL: Author.

Anderson, K. O., Green, C., & Payne, R. (2009). Racial and ethnic disparities in pain: Causes and consequences of unequal care. *Journal of Pain, 10*(12), 1187–1204.

Anderson, K. O., Mendoza, T. R., Valero, V., Richman, S. P., Russell, C., Hurley, J.,...Cleeland, C. S. (2000). Minority cancer patients and their providers: Pain management attitudes and practices. *Cancer, 88*(8), 1929–1938.

Arnd-Caddigan, M., & Pozzuto, R. (2009). The virtuous social worker: The role of "thirdness" in ethical decision making. *Families in Society, 90*(3), 323–328.

Atkinson, J. H., Jr., Stewart, N., & Gardner, D. (1980). The family meeting in critical care settings. *Journal of Trauma, 20*(1), 43–46.

Babcock, E. N. (1997). *When life becomes precious: A guide for loved ones and friends of cancer patients*. New York, NY: Bantam Books.

Barkwell, D. P. (1991). Ascribed meaning: A critical factor in coping and pain attenuation in patients with cancer related pain. *Journal of Palliative Care, 7,* 5–14.

Beauchamp, T., & Childress, J. (1989). *Principles of biomedical ethics*. New York, NY: Oxford University Press.

Beekman, A. T., Geerlings, S. W., Deeg, D. J., Smit, J. J., Schoevers, R. S., deBeurs, E.,...van Tilburg, W. (2002). The natural history of late life depression: A 6-year prospective study in the community. *Archives of General Psychiatry, 59,* 605–611.

Beiske, A. G., Loge, J. H., Ronningen, A., & Svennson, E. (2009). Pain in Parkinson's disease: Prevalence and characteristics. *Pain, 141*(1), 173–177.

Benson, H. (1975). *The relaxation response*. New York, NY: Avon.

Berlin, S. B. (2001). *Clinical social work: A cognitive-integrative perspective*. London, UK: Oxford University Press.

Bernabei, R., Gambassi, G., Lapane, K., Landi, F., Gatsonis, C., Dunlop, R.,...Mor, V. (1998). Management of pain in elderly patients with cancer. *JAMA, 279,* 1877–1882.

Blacker, S., & Deveau, C. (2010). Social work and interprofessional collaboration in palliative care. *Progress in Palliative Care, 18*(4), 237–246.

Bonham, V. L. (2001). Race, ethnicity and pain treatment: Striving to understand the causes and solutions to the disparities in pain treatment. *Journal of Law, Medicine, and Ethics, 29,* 52–68.

Bradley, L. A. (1996) Cognitive behavioral therapy for chronic pain. In R. Gatchel & D. C. Turk (Eds.), *Psychological approaches to pain management: A practitioners' handbook* (pp. 131–147). New York, NY: Guilford Press.

Breitbart, W., Rosenfeld, B. D., Passik, S. D., McDonald, M. V., Thaler, H., & Portenoy, R. (1995). The undertreatment of pain in ambulatory AIDS patients. *Pain, 65*(2/3), 243–249.

Broome, M. E., Rehwaldt, M., & Fogg, L. (1998). Relationship between cognitive behavioral techniques, temperament, observed distress and pain reports in children and adolescents during lumbar puncture. *Journal of Pediatric Nursing, 13*(1), 48–54.

Cassell, E. J. (1991). Recognizing suffering. *Hastings Center Report* (May/June), 24–31.

Center to Advance Palliative Care. (2008). *Palliative Care FAQ*. Retrieved from www.capc.org/reportcard/faq

Christ, G., & Sormanti, M. (1999). Advanced social work practice in end-of-life care. *Social Work in Health Care, 30*(2), 81–99.

Cleeland, C. S., Gonin, R., Harfield, A. K., Edmonson, J. H., Blum, R., Stewart, J. A., & Pandya, K. J. (1994). Pain and its treatment in outpatients with metastatic cancer. *New England Journal of Medicine, 330,* 592–596.

Collier, J. D., & Kopstein, A. N. (1991). Trends in cocaine abuse reflected in emergency room episodes reported to DAWN. *Public Health Report, 106,* 59–68.

Collins, J. J., Byrnes, M. E., Dunkel, I., Lapin, J., Nadel, T., Thaler, H. T. & Portenoy, R. K. (2000). The measurement of symptoms in children with cancer. *Journal of Pain and Symptom Management, 19*(5), 363–370.

Connor, S. R., Egan, K. A., Kwilosz, D. M., Larson, D. G., & Reese, D. J. (2002). Interdisciplinary approaches to assisting with end-of-life care and decision making. *American Behavioral Scientist, 46,* 340–356.

Crawley, L. V., Marshall, P. A., Lo, B., & Koenig, B. A. (2002). Strategies for culturally effective end of life care. *Annals of Internal Medicine, 136,* 673–679.

Curtis, J. R., Patrick, D. L., Shannon, S. E., Treece, P. D., Engelberg, R. A., & Rubenfeld, G. D. (2001). The family conference as a focus to improve communication about end-of-life care in the intensive care unit: Opportunities for improvement. *Critical Care Medicine, 29*(Suppl.), N26–N33.

Dannemiller Memorial Educational Foundation. (2004). The role of race, ethnicity and gender in the treatment of pain. *Pain Report, 7,* 9–11.

Devine, E. C. (2003). Meta-analysis of the effect of psychoeducational interventions on pain in adults with cancer. *Oncology Nursing Forum, 30*(1), 75–89.

Eller, L. S. (1999) Guided imagery interventions for symptom management. *Annual Review of Nursing Research, 17,* 57–84.

Emanuel, E. J., & Emanuel, L. L. (1992). Proxy decision making for incompetent patients: An ethical and empirical analysis. *JAMA, 267,* 2067–2071.

Enders, S. (2004). End of life care in the prison system: Implications for social work. In J. Berzoff & P. Silverman (Eds.), *Living with dying* (pp. 609–627). New York, NY: Columbia University Press.

Erikson, E. (1963). *Childhood and society.* New York, NY: Norton.

Erstling, S. S., & Devlin, J. (1989). The single-session family interview. *Journal of Family Practice, 28*(5), 556–560.

Fillingim, R. B. (2005). *Concise encyclopedia of pain psychology.* New York, NY: Haworth Press.

Fineberg, I. C. (2010). Social work perspectives on family communication and family conferences in palliative care. *Progress in Palliative Care,* 18(4), 213–220.

Fineberg, I. C., & Bauer, A. (2011). Families and family conferencing. In T. Altilio & S. Otis-Green (Eds.), *Textbook of palliative social work* (pp. 235–250). New York, NY: Oxford University Press.

Ford, B. (1998). Pain in Parkinson's disease. *Clinical Neuroscience, 5,* 63–72.

Forman, W. B. (1998). The evolution of hospice and palliative medicine. In A. Berger, R. Portenoy, & D. Weissman (Eds.), *Principles and practice of supportive oncology* (pp. 735–739). New York, NY: Lippincott-Raven.

Fox, P. L., Raina, P., & Jadad, A. R. (1999). Prevalence and treatment of pain in older adults in nursing homes and other long term care institutions: A systematic review. *Canadian Medical Association Journal, 160,* 329–333.

Frankl, V. E. (1984). *Man's search for meaning.* New York, NY: Simon & Schuster.

Frich, L. M., & Borgbjerg, F. M. (2000). Pain and pain treatment in AIDS patients: A longitudinal study. *Journal of Pain and Symptom Management, 19*(5), 339–347.

Gallo-Silver, L., & Pollack, B. (2000). Behavioral interventions for lung cancer-related breathlessness. *Cancer Practice, 8*(6), 268–273.

Glajchen, M. (2003). Role of family caregivers in cancer pain management. In E. Bruera & R. K. Portenoy (Eds.), *Cancer pain* (pp. 459–466). New York, NY: Cambridge University Press.

Glajchen, M. (2011). Caregivers in palliative care: Roles and responsibilities. In T. Altilio & S. Otis-Green (Eds.), *Textbook of palliative social work* (pp. 223–234). New York, NY: Oxford University Press.

Glajchen, M., Blum, D., & Calder, K. (1995). Cancer pain management and the role of social work: Barriers and interventions. *Health & Social Work, 20*(3), 200–206.

Goetz, C. G., Tanner, C. M., Levy, M., Wilson, R. S., & Garron, D. C. (1986). Pain in Parkinson's disease. *Movement Disorders, 1*(1), 45–49.

Graffam, S., & Johnson, A. (1987). A comparison of two relaxation strategies for the relief of pain and distress. *Journal of Pain and Symptom Management, 2,* 229–231.

Groerer, J., & Brodsky, M. (1992). The incidence of illicit substance use in the United States, 1962–1989. *British Journal of Addiction, 87,* 1345.

Grossman, S. A., Sheidler, V. R., Swedeen, K., Mucenski, J., & Piantadosi, S. (1991). Correlation of patient and caregiver rating of cancer pain. *Journal of Pain and Symptom Management, 6,* 53–57.

Hall, P., & Weaver, L. (2001). Interdisciplinary education and teamwork: A long and winding road. *Medical Education, 35,* 867–875.

Hansen, P., Cornish, P., & Kayser, K. (1998). Family conferences as forums for decision making in hospital settings. *Social Work in Health Care, 27*(3), 57–74.

Harpham, W. S. (2004). *When a parent has cancer: A guide to caring for your children.* New York, NY: HarperCollins.

Hart, P. D. (2003). *Americans Talk about Pain.* Available from Peter D. Hart Research Associates, retrieved from www.researchamerica.org/uploads/poll2003pain.pdf

Heiney, S., Hermann, J., Bruss, K., & Fincannon, J. (2000). *Cancer in the family: Helping children cope with a parent's illness.* Atlanta, GA: American Cancer Society.

Hoffman, D. E., & Tarzian, A. J. (2001). The girl who cried pain: A bias against women in the treatment of pain. *Journal of Law, Medicine and Ethics, 29,* 13–27.

Holland, J. C., Breitbart, W. S., Jacobsen, P. B., Lederberg, M. S., Loscalzo, M. J., & McCorkle, R. (2010). *Psycho-Oncology,* 2nd ed. New York, NY: Oxford University Press.

Hudgens, A. (1977). The social worker's role in a behavioral management approach to chronic pain. *Social Work in Health Care, 3,* 149–157.

Hudson, P., Thomas, T., Quinn, K., & Aranda, S. (2009). Family meetings in palliative care: Are they effective? *Palliative Medicine, 23*(2), 150–157.

Hultman, T., Reder, E. R., & Dahlin, C. (2008). Improving psychological and psychiatric aspects of palliative care: The National Consensus Project and the National Quality Forum Preferred Practices for Palliative and Hospice Care. *Omega-Journal of Death and Dying, 57*(4), 323–339.

Im, E., Chee, W., Guevara, E., Liu, Y., Lim, H., & Tsai, H.,... Shin, H. (2007). Gender and ethnic differences in cancer pain experience: A multiethnic study in the United States. *Nursing Research, 56*(5), 296–306.

Institute of Medicine. (2001). *Crossing the Quality Chasm*. Washington, DC: National Academies Press.

Institute of Medicine. (2003). *When Children Die: Improving Palliative and End-of-Life Care for Children and Their Families*. Washington, DC: National Academies Press.

International Association for the Study of Pain. (2009). *Psychosocial interventions for cancer pain*. Retrieved from www.iasp-pain.org/AM/Template.cfm?Section =Home&Template=/CM/ContentDisplay.cfm& ContentID=7193

International Association for the Study of Pain. (2010). *IASP pain terminology*. Retrieved from www.iasp-pain .org/AM/Template.cfm?Section=Pain_Defi.isplay .cfm&ContentID=1728#Pain

Jacobsen, P. (2007). Screening for psychological distress in cancer patients: Challenges and opportunities. *Journal of Clinical Oncology, 25*(29), 4526–4527.

Jacobsen, P., & Hann, D. M. (1998). Cognitive behavioral interventions in psycho-oncology. In J. Holland (Ed.), *Psycho-oncology* (pp. 717–729). New York, NY: Oxford University Press.

Jerant, A. F., Azari, R. S., Nesbitt, T. S., & Meyers, F. J. (2004). The TLC model of palliative care in the elderly: Preliminary application in the assisted living setting. *Annals of Family Medicine, 2,* 54–60.

Joint Commission. (2010). *Advancing effective communication, cultural competence, and patient-and family-centered care: A roadmap for hospitals*. Oakbrook Terrace, IL: Author.

Kagawa-Singer, M., & Blackhall, L. J. (2001). Negotiating cross cultural issues at the end of life "You got to go where he lives." *JAMA, 286*(23), 2993–3002.

Kass, L. (1983). Professing ethically: On the place of ethics in defining medicine. *JAMA, 249*(10), 1305–1310.

Keefe, F. J., Lefebvre, J. C., Egert, J. R., Affleck, G., Sullivan, M. J., & Caldwell, D. S. (2000). The relationship of gender to pain, pain behavior, and disability in osteoarthritis patients: The role of catastrophizing. *Pain, 87*(3), 325–334.

Kelly, P., & Clifford, P. (1997). Coping with chronic pain: Assessing narrative approaches. *Social Work, 42*(3), 266–277.

Kerr, K. (2000). Relaxation techniques: A critical review. *Critical Reviews in Physical and Rehabilitation Medicine, 121,* 51–89.

Kirsch, I., Montgomery, G., & Saperstein, G. (1995). Hypnosis as an adjunct to cognitive-behaviorial psychotherapy: A meta-analysis. *Journal of Consulting and Clinical Psychology, 63*(2), 214–220.

Koenig, B., & Gates-Williams, J. (1995). Understanding cultural differences in caring for dying patients. *Western Journal of Medicine, 163,* 244–249.

Koffman, J., Morgan, M., Edmonds, F., Speck, P., & Higginson, I. (2008). Cultural meanings of pain: A qualitative study of Black Caribbean and White British patients with advanced cancer. *Journal of Palliative Medicine, 22,* 350–359.

Koppelman, K. (2003). For those who stand and wait. In G. R. Cox, R. A. Bendiksen, & R. G. Stevenson (Eds.), *Making sense of death: Spiritual, pastoral, and personal aspects of death, dying and bereavement* (pp. 45–54). Amityville, NY: Baywood.

Kristjanson, L. J., & Aoun, S. (2004). Palliative care for families: Remembering the hidden patients. *Canadian Journal of Psychiatry, 49,* 359–365.

Kübler-Ross, E. (1969). *On death and dying*. New York, NY: Macmillan.

Kushner, K., Meyer, D., & Hansen, J. P. (1989). Patients' attitudes toward physician involvement in family conferences. *Journal of Family Practice, 28*(1), 73–78.

Lautrette, A., Darmon, M., Megarbane, B., Joly, L. M., Chevret, S., Adrie, C., & Azoulay, E. (2007). A communication strategy and brochure for relatives of patients dying in the ICU. *New England Journal of Medicine, 356,* 469–478.

Lethborg, C., Aranda, S., Bloch, S., & Kissane, D. (2006). The role of meaning in advanced cancer-integrating the constructs of assumptive world, sense-of-coherence and meaning based coping. *Journal of Psychosocial Oncology, 24*(1), 27–42.

Levine, C. (2004). *Always on call: When illness turns families into caregivers*. New York, NY: Vanderbilt University Press.

Levine, F. M., & De Simone, L. L. (1991). The effects of experimenter gender on pain report in male and female subjects. *Pain, 44*(1), 69–72.

Liao, S., & Ferrell, B. A. (2000). Fatigue in an older population. *Journal of American Geriatric Society, 49,* 426–430.

Lickiss, J. N., Turner, K. S., & Pollock, M. L. (2004). The interdisciplinary team. In D. Doyle, G. Hanks, N. I. Cherny, & K. Calman (Eds.), *Oxford textbook of palliative medicine* (3rd ed., pp. 42–46). New York, NY: Oxford University Press.

Liebman, A., Silbergleit, I.-L., & Farber, S. (1975). Family conference in the care of the cancer patient. *Journal of Family Practice, 2*(5), 343–345.

Linder, J. F., & Enders, S. R. (2011). Key role for social workers in correctional palliative care. In T. Altilio & S. Otis-Green (Eds.), *Textbook of palliative social work* (pp. 153–168). New York, NY: Oxford University Press.

Lo, B. (2000). *Resolving ethical dilemmas: A guide for clinicians*. New York, NY: Lippincott Williams & Wilkins.

Lobchuk, M. M., & Degner, L.F. (2002). Symptom experiences: Perceptual accuracy between advanced-stage cancer patients and family caregivers in the home care setting. *Journal of Clinical Oncology, 20*(16), 3495–3507.

Loscalzo, M., & Amendola, J. (1990). Psychosocial and behavioral management of cancer pain: The social work contribution. In K. M. Foley, J. J. Bonica, & V. Ventafridda (Eds.), *Advances in pain research and therapy* (Vol. 16, pp. 429–442). New York, NY: Raven Press.

Loscalzo, M., & Jacobsen, P. (1990). Practical behavioral approaches to the effective management of pain and distress. *Journal of Psychosocial Oncology, 8,* 139–169.

Loscalzo, M. J., & Von Gunten, C. F. (2009). Interdisciplinary teamwork in palliative care: Compassionate care for serious complex illness. In H. M. Chochinov & W. Breitbart (Eds.), *Handbook of psychiatry in palliative medicine* (2nd ed., pp. 172–185). New York, NY: Oxford University Press.

Luebbert, K., Dahme, B., & Hasenbring, M. (2001). The effectiveness of relaxation training in reducing treatment related symptoms and improving emotional adjustment in acute nonsurgical cancer treatment: A meta-analytical review. *Psycho-Oncology, 10*(6), 490–502.

Lynn, J., Schuster, J. L., & Kabcenell, A. (2000). *Improving care for the end of life: A sourcebook for healthcare managers and clinicians.* New York, NY: Oxford University Press.

MacDonald, J. E. (2000). A deconstructive turn in chronic pain treatment—A redefined role for social work. *Health & Social Work, 25*(1), 51–57.

Maddocks, I. (2006). Communication—an essential tool for team hygiene. In P. Speck (Ed.), *Teamwork in palliative care: fulfilling or frustrating?* (pp. 137–152). New York, NY: Oxford University Press.

McCaffery, M., & Pasero, C. (1999). *Pain: Clinical manual* (2nd ed.). New York, NY: Mosby.

McCallin, A. (2001). Interdisciplinary practice: A matter of teamwork—An integrated literature review. *Journal of Clinical Nursing, 10,* 419–428.

McCaul, K. D., & Malott, J. M. (1984). Distraction and coping with pain. *Psychology Bulletin, 95,* 516–533.

McPhelimy, L. (1997). *The checklist of life.* Rockfall, CT: AAIP.

Mendenhall, T. (2003). Psychosocial aspects of pain management: A conceptual framework for social workers in pain management teams. *Social Work in Health Care, 36*(4), 5–51.

Meyer, D. L., Schneid, J. A., & Craigie, F. C. (1989). Family conferences: Reasons, levels of involvement and perceived usefulness. *Journal of Family Practice, 29*(4), 401–405.

Miaskowski, C., Zimmer, E. F., Barrett, K. M., Dibble, S. L., & Wallhagen, M. (1997). Difference in patient and family caregivers' perceptions of the pain experience influence patient and caregiver outcomes. *Pain, 72,* 217–226.

Monroe, B. (2004). Social work in palliative medicine. In D. Doyle, G. W. C. Hanks, N. Cherny, & K. Calmen (Eds.), *Oxford textbook of palliative medicine* (3rd ed., pp. 1005–1017). New York, NY: Oxford University Press.

Montgomery, G. H., David, D., Winkel, G., Silverstein, J. H., & Bovbjerg, D. H. (2002). The effectiveness of adjunctive hypnosis with surgical patients: A meta-analysis. *Anesthesia and Analgesia, 94*(6), 1639–1645.

Morgan, J. P. (1986). *American opiophobia: Customary underutilization of opioid analgesia.* New York, NY: Hawthorne.

Morrison, R. S., Wallenstein, S., Natale, D. K., Senzel, R. S., & Huang, L. (2000). "We don't carry that": Failure of pharmacies in predominately nonwhite neighborhoods to stock opioid analgesics. *New England Journal of Medicine, 342,* 1023–1026.

National Association of Social Workers. (1999). *Code of ethics.* Retrieved from www.socialworkers.org/pubs /code.asp

National Association of Social Workers. (2009a). *Certified hospice and palliative social worker (CHP-SW) and advanced certified hospice and palliative social worker (ACHP-SW).* Retrieved from www.naswdc .org/credentials/credentials/chpsw.asp

National Association of Social Workers. (2009b). *NASW standards for practice in palliative and end-of-life care.* Retrieved from www.naswdc.org/practice/bereavement /standards/default.asp

National Cancer Institute. (2010) *Pain: Physical and psychosocial interventions.* Retrieved from www .cancer.gov/cancertopics/pdq/supportivecare/pain /HealthProfessional/page5

National Center for Health Statistics. (2006). *Health, United States, 2006.* Hyattsville, MD: U.S. Department of Health and Human Services.

National Consensus Project for Quality Palliative Care. (2004). *Clinical practice guidelines executive summary.* Retrieved from www.nationalconsensusproject.org

National Consensus Project for Quality Palliative Care. (2009). *Clinical practice guidelines for quality palliative care,* 2nd ed. Retrieved from http:// nationalconsensusproject.org

National Institutes of Health. (1998). *New directions in pain research (PA98–102).* Washington, DC: U.S. Government Printing Office. Available from www .painfoundation.org/page_fastfacts.asp

National Quality Forum. (2006). *A national framework and preferred practices for palliative and hospice care quality.* Washington, DC: Author.

O'Donnell, P., Farrar, A., Brintzenhofeszoc, K., Conrad, A.P., Danis, M., Grady, C., & Ullrich, C. M. (2008) Predictors of ethical stress, moral action and job dissatisfaction in health care social workers. *Social Work in Health Care, 46*(3) 29–51.

Oregon Department of Health Services. (2008). *Oregon Death with Dignity Act records & reports.* Retrieved from www.oregon.gov/DHS/ph/pas/

Otis-Green, S. (2003). Legacy building. *Smith Studies in Social Work, 73*(3), 395–404.

Otis-Green, S. (2006). Psychosocial pain assessment form. In K. Dow (Ed.), *Nursing care of women with cancer* (pp. 556–561). St. Louis, MO: Elsevier Mosby.

Otis-Green, S. (2011). Embracing the existential invitation to examine care at the end of Life. In S. H. Quall & J. Kasl-Godley (Eds.), *The Wiley Series in clinical geropsychology: End-of-life issues, grief and bereavement: What clinicians need to know* (pp. 239–311). Hoboken, NJ: Wiley.

Otis-Green, S., & Ferrell, B. R. (2010). Professional education in psychosocial oncology. In J. C. Holland, W. S. Breitbart, P. B. Jacobsen, M. S. Lederberg, M. J. Loscalzo, & R. McCorkle (Eds.), *Psycho-Oncology* (2nd ed., pp. 610–616). New York, NY: Oxford University Press.

Otis-Green, S., & Fineberg I. C. (2010). Enhancing team effectiveness. In B. Ferrell & N. Coyle (Eds.), *Oxford textbook of palliative nursing* (3rd ed., pp. 1225–1235). New York, NY: Oxford University Press.

Otis-Green, S., & Rutland, C. (2004). Marginalization at the end of life. In J. Berzoff & P. Silverman (Eds.), *Living with dying* (pp. 462–481). New York, NY: Columbia University Press.

Otis-Green, S., Sherman, R., Perez, M., & Baird, P. (2002). An integrated psychosocial-spiritual model for cancer pain management. *Cancer Practice, 10,* S58–S65.

Parker-Oliver, D., Wittenberg-Lyles, E., Washington, K., & Sehrawat, S. (2009). Social work role in hospice pain management: A national survey. *Journal of Social Work in End of Life and Palliative Care, 5*(1–2), 51–74.

Pelligrino, E. (1979). *Humanism and the physician.* Knoxville, TN: University of Tennessee Press.

Puchalski, C., Ferrell, B., Virani, R., Otis-Green, S., Baird, P., Bull, J., & Sulmasy, D. (2009). Special report: Improving the quality of spiritual care as a dimension of palliative care: The report of the consensus conference. *Journal of Palliative Medicine, 12*(10), 885–905.

Raymer, M., & Csikai, E. (2005). Social workers educational needs in end-of-life care. *Social Work in Health Care, 41*(1), 53–72.

Redinbaugh, E. M., Baum, A., DeMoss, C., Fello, M., & Arnold, R. (2002). Factors associated with the accuracy of family caregiver estimates of patient's pain. *Journal of Pain and Symptom Management, 23,* 31–38.

Renzenbrink, I. (2004). Relentless self-care. In J. Berzoff & P. R. Silverman (Eds.), *Living with dying* (pp. 848–867). New York, NY: Columbia University Press.

Roff, S. (2001). Analyzing end of life care legislation: A social work perspective. *Social Work in Health Care, 33*(1), 51–68.

Roper Starch Worldwide. (1999). *Chronic pain in America: Roadblocks to relief.* Retrieved 2010 from www.ampainsoc.org/links/roadblocks/

Roy, R. (1981). Social work and chronic pain. *Health & Social Work, 6*(3), 54–62.

Sachs, G. A., Shega, J. W., & Cox-Hayley, D. (2004). Barriers to excellent end of life care for patients with dementia. *Journal of General Internal Medicine, 19*(10), 1057–1063.

Saunders, C. (1996). Hospice. *Mortality, 1*(3), 317–322.

Saunders, C. (2001). Social work and palliative care, the early history. *British Journal of Social Work, 31,* 791–799.

Schulz, R., & Beach, S. R. (1999). Caregiving as a risk factor for mortality: The caregiver health effects study. *JAMA, 282*(23), 2215–2219.

Sheikh, A. A. (1983). *Imagery: Current theory, research and application.* New York, NY: Wiley.

Sheldon, F. M. (1999). Education for social workers. In D. Doyle, G. W. C. Hanks, & N. McDonald (Eds.), *Oxford textbook of palliative medicine* (pp. 1209–1212). New York, NY: Oxford University Press.

Sheldon, F. M. (2000). Dimensions of the role of the social worker in palliative care. *Palliative Medicine, 14,* 491–498.

Shine, D., & Demas, P. (1984). Knowledge of medical students, residents and attending physicians about opioid abuse. *Journal of Medical Education, 59,* 501–507.

Sieppert, J. D. (1996). Attitudes toward and knowledge of chronic pain—A survey of medical social workers. *Health & Social Work, 21*(2), 122–130.

Solaro, C., Brichetto, G., Amato, M. P., Cocco, E., Colombo, B., Daleo, G., …PaIMS Study Group. (2004). The prevalence of pain in multiple sclerosis: A multi-center cross sectional study. *Neurology, 63,* 919–921.

Speck, P. (2006). Maintaining a healthy team. In P. Speck (Ed.), *Teamwork in palliative care: Fulfilling or frustrating?* (pp. 95–115). New York, NY: Oxford University Press.

Stein, W. (2001). Assessment of symptoms in the cognitively impaired. In E. Bruera & R. K. Portenoy (Eds.), *Topics in palliative care* (Vol. 5, pp. 123–133). New York, NY: Oxford University Press.

Sternbach, R. A. (1987). *Mastering pain.* New York, NY: Putnam Books.

Stewart, W. F., Ricci, J. A., Chee, E., Morganstein, D., & Lipton, R. (2003). Lost productive time and cost due to pain conditions in the U.S. workforce. *JAMA, 290*(18), 2443–2454.

Subramanian, K., & Rose, S. D. (1988). Social work and the treatment of chronic pain. *Health & Social Work, 13*(1), 49–60.

Syrjala, K. L., Donaldson, G. W., Davis, M. W., Kippes, M. E., & Carr, J. E. (1995). Relaxation and imagery and cognitive-behavioral training reduce pain during cancer treatment: A controlled clinical trial. *Pain, 63*(2), 189–198.

Tarzian, A. J., & Hoffman, D. E. (2004). Barriers to managing pain in the nursing home: Findings from a statewide survey. *Journal of the American Medical Directors Association, 5*(2), 82–88.

Ulrich, C., O'Donnell, C., Taylor, C., Farrar, A., Danis, M., & Grady, C. (2007). Ethical climate, ethics stress and the job satisfaction of nurses and social workers in the United States. *Social Science and Medicine, 65,* 1708–1719.

Unruh, A. (1996). Gender variations in clinical pain experience. *Pain, 65,* 123–167.

Van den Beulken-van Everdingen, M. H. J., de Rijke, J. M., Kessels, A. G., Schouten, H. C., van Kleef, M., & Patijn, J. (2007). Prevalence of pain in patients with cancer: A systematic review of the past 40 years. *Annals of Oncology, 18*(9), 1437–1449.

Von Roenn, J. H., Cleeland, C. S., Gonin, R., Hatfield, A. K., & Pandya, K. J. (1993). Physician attitudes and practice in cancer pain management: A survey from the Eastern Cooperative Oncology Group. *Annals of Internal Medicine, 119,* 121–126.

Washington State Department of Health. (2009). *Washington State Death with Dignity Act.* Retrieved from www.doh.wa.gov/dwda/

Winnicott, D. W. (1971). *Objects and transitional phenomena in playing and reality.* Harmondsworth, Middlesex, UK: Penguin Books.

World Health Organization. (1990). *Cancer pain relief and palliative care (WHO Technical Report Series 804).* Geneva, Switzerland: Author.

World Health Organization. (2004). Aging, pain, and cancer: The role of geriatrics. *Oncology & Palliative Care, 17*(1/2), 1–12.

World Health Organization. (n.d.). *Definition of palliative care.* Retrieved from www.who.int/cancer/palliative/definition/en/

Zachny, J., Bigelow, G., Compton, P., Foley, K., Iguchi, M., & Sannerud, C. (2003). College on Problems of Drug Dependence Taskforce on prescription opioid non-medical use and abuse: Position statement. *Drug Alcohol Dependence, 69*(3), 215–232.

23

End-of-Life Care

YVETTE COLÓN

The purpose of this chapter is to provide basic knowledge about end-of-life social work practice. Social workers can have a profound impact on the experiences of individuals at the end of their lives and on their families, loved ones, and other health providers. Increasingly, however, social workers are challenged to provide services to the growing number of individuals who need end-of-life care—children and adults who are chronically ill or have life-threatening conditions—as well as those who care for them. Often they are not prepared for the myriad complex issues involved in end-of-life practice. Despite their increasing involvement in providing important psychosocial services to dying individuals, social workers do not receive relevant training in their undergraduate and graduate programs.

Chapter Objectives
- Define *end-of-life care*.
- Define *palliative care at the end of life*.
- Describe the roles that social workers can play in end-of-life care.
- Describe the importance of effective communication so that patient and family needs are expressed and appropriate end-of-life care is facilitated.
- Understand the process of end-of-life planning, including advance directives, to promote informed choices and help patients and families to clarify and communicate their preferences.
- Demonstrate an understanding of factors that influence the death and dying experience of cultural groups and disadvantaged persons at the end of life.

- Describe contemporary grief and loss theories.

The course of death and dying has changed tremendously in the past few decades because of social and technological advances. Increases in average life expectancy due to advances in medical science and technology (National Center for Health Statistics, 2010) have influenced our beliefs and attitudes about life and death. The course of illness and dying has changed; at one time, the onset of illness and subsequent death from certain illnesses was sudden and rapid, but now the typical death may be more prolonged. The place where death occurs has moved from the home or community to the hospital, nursing home, or institutional setting. These changes have posed enormous challenges in end-of-life and palliative care.

PALLIATIVE CARE

Palliative care is an interdisciplinary care model that focuses on the comprehensive management of physical, psychological, and existential distress. It is defined as "the active total care of patients whose disease is not responsive to curative treatment." Control of pain and other symptoms and psychological, social, and spiritual problems is paramount. "The goal of palliative care is the achievement of the best possible quality of life for patients and their families" (World Health Organization [WHO], 1990, p. 7). Palliative care aims to improve the patient's quality of life by identifying physical, psychosocial, and spiritual issues while managing pain and other distressing symptoms. Palliative care "affirms life and regards dying as a normal process; is applicable early in the course of illness, in conjunction with other therapies that are intended to prolong life, such as chemotherapy or radiation therapy, and uses a team approach to address the needs of patients and their families, including bereavement counselling, if indicated" (WHO, 2004, p. 3).

The palliative care model applies throughout the entire course of illness and attempts to address the physical, psychosocial, and spiritual concerns that affect both the quality of life and the quality of dying for patients with life-limiting illnesses at any phase of the disease. It includes interventions that are intended to maintain the quality of life of the patient and family. Although the focus intensifies at the end of life, the priority to provide comfort and attend to the patient's and family's psychosocial concerns remains important throughout the course of the illness. In the model's ideal implementation, patient and family values and decisions are respected, practical needs are addressed, psychosocial and spiritual distress are managed, and comfort care is provided as the individual nears the end of life.

Palliative medicine is the medical specialty dedicated to excellence in palliative care. Palliative care specialists, including social workers, typically work on teams and are involved when patients' disease is advanced, their life expectancy is limited, and medical and psychosocial concerns become complex and more urgent. In practice, these problems often are related to uncontrolled symptoms, conflicted or unclear goals of care, distress related to the process of dying, and increasing family burden. The social worker can educate the family about expected symptoms and their management, clarify information about medications and medical procedures, facilitate communications with the health-care team, help the family make decisions about practical and financial changes in the family structure, normalize their emotional experiences, and teach them effective coping skills.

HOSPICE

The emphasis of hospice care is on comfort at the end of life through control of pain and other symptoms. Rather than relying on curative interventions and technology, it returns the focus to natural approaches in the care of dying individuals. Hospice focuses on caring, not curing, and in many cases is provided in the patient's home. Hospice care also is provided in freestanding hospice centers, hospitals, and nursing homes and other long-term care facilities. Hospice services are available to patients of all ages, religions, races, and illnesses. Hospice care is covered under Medicare, Medicaid, most private insurance plans, health maintenance organizations, and other managed care organizations (National Hospice and Palliative Care Organization, 2010).

The hospice movement in the United States began in the 1960s when Dame Cicely Saunders, a British physician, introduced the concept of hospice at Yale University. She came to the United States to introduce the approach to symptom relief for dying individuals and discussed how St. Christopher's inpatient hospice, the first modern hospice, was established in London. Saunders presented the concepts of hospice to medical and nursing faculty and students at Yale. Florence Wald, dean of the Yale School of Nursing, created a multidisciplinary group at Yale-New Haven Hospital to look into changing the way that institution cared for dying patients, modeling their care after St. Christopher's approach. In 1975, the first hospice in the United States opened in Connecticut due to the work of this small group of individuals (Saunders, 1999).

Significant barriers to effective end-of-life care exist and include patients' and families' attitudes about death and dying, inconsistent communication between patients and the health-care team, insufficient training of health-care providers, physicians' inexperience with providing care, lack of access to care, and inconsistent reimbursement. The National Academies of Science, through its Institute of Medicine (IOM), produced an important report, "Approaching Death: Care at the End of Life" (Field & Cassell, 2002). Among its recommendations were these:

- Reliable and skillful supportive care should be provided to patients and families facing the end of life.
- Health-care professionals should know and use effective interventions to prevent and relieve pain and other symptoms.
- Palliative care should be recognized as a defined area of expertise, education, and research.
- The public should be educated about end-of-life care and advance care planning.
- Tools should be developed for improving patients' quality of life, and health-care organizations should be required to use them.
- Medical education should be modified to ensure that relevant attitudes, knowledge, and skills regarding end-of-life care are represented and included in teaching.
- Research should be undertaken to strengthen the knowledge base of end-of-life care.

Although efforts have been made to implement these recommendations to improve existing care at the end of life, progress has been slow.

ANTICIPATING THE END OF LIFE

Individuals at the end of life may experience many symptoms that can be distressing to them and their caregivers. Although the dying process is not consistent across individuals and families, some physical, physiological, and emotional changes can be predicted during the end of life. Advanced stage of illness can result in symptoms such as difficulty breathing, insomnia, loss of appetite, pain, nausea, and constipation. Patients also may experience heightened anxiety, depression, anger, or emotional withdrawal. Understanding the nature of the symptoms most frequently experienced by dying people and knowing how to help patients and their significant others cope

are critical to effective end-of-life social work practice. The social worker can take the opportunity to educate patients and families about the management of these physical symptoms and psychological responses.

During this important period of care, the social worker can act as a guide to help the patient and family prepare for the end of life. Knowing what to expect is important for social workers so they can help manage patient and family needs before, during, and after death. Social workers provide anticipatory guidance and expert psychosocial care to promote physical and psychological comfort for the dying person and for family members.

INTERDISCIPLINARY TEAMWORK

Individuals at the end of life often move between different health-care settings—from home to acute or long-term care facilities, outpatient or inpatient treatment (either curative or palliative), home health care, and hospice settings—as their disease progresses. They may receive care from several different physicians, nurses, and other health-care professionals during the course of their illness. Coordinating all necessary care during moves from one setting to another presents considerable challenges to patients, families, and health-care providers. Several different organizations and payment sources may be involved that may present barriers to optimal end-of-life care.

The involvement of an interdisciplinary palliative or hospice care team is an excellent solution to care coordination problems. These typically include:

- Patient
- Patient's family or caregiver
- Palliative care or hospice physician
- Patient's personal physician
- Nurses
- Social workers
- Clergy/pastoral counselors
- Pharmacists

- Home health aides
- Trained volunteers
- Physical, occupational, and speech therapists, if needed

Interdisciplinary teams are common in both hospice and inpatient palliative care settings. The team meets on a regular basis to discuss the patients in their care and to develop individualized care plans that focus on each patient's well-being and need for pain management and symptom control. To varying degrees, private and public insurance companies pay for end-of-life care services for patients who need them, such as medication and treatments, medical equipment and miscellaneous procedures, and tests necessary to provide comprehensive comfort care. Comprehensive care can include nursing, physician, and social work services along with homemaker (e.g., light housekeeping and meal preparation) and personal care (e.g., bathing and dressing) services.

COMMUNICATION: TALKING ABOUT DEATH AND DYING

Patients, families, and social workers may be influenced by misconceptions about death and dying. They may believe that it is depressing to talk about death or that dying patients and families want to talk only about positive things. They may think that talking about dying will make patients and families upset and angry, that individuals do not always know that they are dying, or that dying children do not know how to communicate their concerns and fears, for example. These myths and misconceptions often impede the ability to communicate effectively with patients and their significant others. To communicate clearly at the patient's end of life, social workers must focus on providing clinical care that supports the patient and underlying family values and meanings. Effective communication is critically important to understanding the experiences of others.

Social work traditionally has emphasized therapeutic communication with active listening. For effective communication with patients and caregivers facing the end of life, the first and most important skill that all social workers must develop is listening. Being fully "present" with another person is essential to effective communication. Asking questions or soliciting comments requires truly listening to responses. Listening involves paying attention not just to the words spoken but to all other verbal and nonverbal cues that are communicated simultaneously, no matter how subtle. Much information can be gained by listening to language content and style, choice of words, pauses, silences, body posture, mood, and facial expressions.

Open-ended questions are useful in gathering information from the patient and family. In contrast to closed-ended questions (which only allow yes, no, or another fixed response), asking open-ended questions provides an opening or invitation for patients and families to share information that is important to them. Gaining an understanding of the patient's concerns and style of communication enables social workers to provide the information the patient and family desire in a manner that they can understand (Byock, 1998). Rather than asking closed-ended questions, the social worker can ask questions that will elicit more information, such as "Can you tell me what you understand about the changes in your loved one's condition?" Reflective statements also help to clarify the social worker's and the patient's understanding. An example of a reflective statement is "What I heard you just say is _____. Is this correct? Is that what you intended?"

The ability to make empathic statements, demonstrating an awareness of and sensitivity to another's feelings, thoughts, and experiences (without having the same feelings, thoughts, and experiences of another), is easy for some and difficult for others, but it is a simple skill that can be learned and practiced. Listening to the patient and family, sharing reflective comments about the difficulty of the situation with them, acknowledging their fears and apprehensions, showing concern and looking into their eyes if appropriate are all simple actions that communicate understanding of the patient's experience. Additional techniques for gathering information can be found in Chapter 10 in this book.

Communicating with a child who is dying is a special challenge for families and health-care professionals. The death of a child is a unique tragedy, and adults, including social workers, may feel a profound need to protect and nurture the child and themselves against the loss, pain, and suffering inherent in the dying process. For these and many other reasons, communicating with dying children is difficult, and the resulting discomfort may prevent a social worker from exploring the important needs and concerns of children and their parents.

END-OF-LIFE CARE CONCERNS RELATED TO A DYING CHILD

Social workers are well equipped to help prepare parents and families to meet the emotional needs of a dying child. Parents and family members are faced with many issues, including concern that they may not be providing care as well as the health-care team in the hospital. They need to know that they are doing all that they can to care for the dying child.

It is important that the personal and professional challenges of the individual social worker are addressed in caring for terminally ill children and their families. When this is done, social workers are better able to offer support to other members of the health-care team. Health-care professionals, especially physicians, often find it extremely difficult to tell parents that there is no longer any effective cure-oriented treatment for their child. However, if parents are supported in discussing treatment focused on the end of cure with providers and the need to move to comfort (palliative) care, most end-of-life care providers may be better able to communicate more directly and effectively. The key for the social worker is to recognize the critical role of encouraging

and supporting parents in expressing their true feelings, concerns, and goals.

Children are never too young to be told that they or someone close to them is dying (Silverman, 1999). Dying children often know they are dying. Failing to acknowledge death creates a barrier between the child and the adults who are caring for her. Sick children have a common fantasy that they are responsible for their own illnesses; being sick can be interpreted as punishment. Many children who choose not to discuss painful feelings may be trying to protect their parents and siblings from further emotional pain. In the absence of honest discussion, silence only reinforces this and other misconceptions that the child and his or her siblings create. It isolates the child and limits the sharing needed for coping with overwhelmingly difficult experiences. Dying children experience feelings similar to dying adults: anxiety, fear, loneliness, and depression as well as hope and love. Children need to know that they are not responsible for their illnesses. Sharing information in a way that is cognitively and developmentally appropriate is essential.

Dying children of any age, as well as their siblings, have the capacity to communicate their concerns clearly. The ways children communicate depend on their age and developmental stage. Verbal language must be adapted to a conceptual level and vocabulary that the children can understand. Children may express their fears, worries, or concerns directly, indirectly, or symbolically. They can communicate in many ways other than direct conversation. Music, art/drawing, drama/storytelling, and play are some expressive therapies that can be used to foster effective communication with children.

SPIRITUALITY

Facing death often forces individuals to consider spiritual or existential issues that can be central to end-of-life care. Spirituality can be a profound resource for coping with the challenges of all aspects of life and death. Social workers in end-of-life practice must be sensitive to these concerns in their patients and be willing to assist with their spiritual explorations.

As defined by the *Merriam-Webster Dictionary* (2004), *religion* is "the service and worship of God or the supernatural," "a commitment or devotion to religious faith or observance" or a "personal set or institutionalized system of religious attitudes, beliefs, and practices." In contrast, *spirituality* is defined as a sensitivity or attachment to religious values, the quality or state of being spiritual. Spirituality is related to the human spirit as opposed to material or physical things. Definitions of religion and spirituality can be found in the literature discussing the integration of spirituality and mental health practices. Mauritzen (1988) defines *spirituality* as

> the human dimension that transcends the biological, psychological and social aspects of living. It is the "agent" for the integration a person's identity and integrity. In very general terms the spiritual dimension is the "agent" for an individual's existence as a person. (pp. 116–117)

Constructing a universal definition of spirituality, however, is difficult. It is important to be aware of the patient's and family's spiritual belief system; awareness and appreciation of a patient's spiritual orientation is essential to end-of-life care. Impending loss and the reality of death may shake people's spiritual beliefs and may leave them feeling angry or hopeless. For believers and nonbelievers, atheists or agnostics, the need to make sense of impending death is central to a person's struggles regarding meaning at the end of life.

Working in end-of-life care also may raise spiritual issues for the social worker. Witnessing the suffering of others or coping with the stress of working with dying individuals and their families may challenge the social worker's basic religious or spiritual beliefs. It may require the professional to deal with countertransference issues related to suffering and death (Katz & Johnson, 2006). Before social workers can help with these existential concerns, they must understand their own spirituality and religious beliefs and the influence of these beliefs on their professional and personal lives. When patients and caregivers express religious and spiritual concerns, the social worker's role is to listen so that she can help them find ways to address their needs.

DIVERSITY AND HEALTH DISPARITIES IN END-OF-LIFE CARE

All individuals' life experiences contribute greatly to the complexity and uniqueness of the end-of-life issues that we all face. These experiences, as much as anything, shape our desires and beliefs about health, illness, death, and dying. The Diversity Committee of the Last Acts Coalition (2001) advocates recognition, acceptance, and support of its recommendations concerning individuals' experiences with race; historical oppression; war and its aftermath; cultural, religious, and spiritual practices; affectional orientation; discrimination; and poverty. The true meaning of diversity (especially as it affects the end of life) is as much about these unique, view-shaping experiences as about the narrower yet more common concept that focuses on ethnicity or religion (Last Acts Coalition, 2001, p. 3). Death and dying among members of different racial or ethnic groups and disadvantaged persons can pose tremendous challenges to social workers. Cultural and economic factors play a significant part in health care, health-care decision making, and end-of-life experiences. Health care is less accessible to disadvantaged individuals, including people of color, immigrants, older individuals, children, women, the poor and uninsured, and those who are in institutions (i.e., nursing homes and prisons) (Smedley, Stith, & Nelson, 2002).

Because of group differences in health, the U.S. Congress requested a report from the IOM. Disparities consistently were found across disease areas, clinical services, and clinical settings (Smedley et al., 2002). The focus of the IOM report was on conscious and unconscious discrimination or bias and its effect on health-care delivery. The IOM's general recommendation was to increase awareness of disparities among the general public, key stakeholders, and health-care providers. The report provided specific recommendations for critical areas, including patient education and empowerment, cross-cultural education in health professions, legal, regulatory, and policy interventions, and health system interventions.

Communication between health-care provider and patient is vitally important to effective end-of-life care. A patient's understanding of his life-limiting illness will affect the course of his palliative care. Health-care professionals must be aware of subtle cultural variations in language, verbal and nonverbal communication, and expressions of distress (van Ryn & Burke, 2000). They must be able to comprehend the effects of ethnicity and spiritual beliefs on the daily lives of patients and families.

Culture influences what is considered a health problem, how symptoms are expressed and discussed, how health-care information is received, what type of care should be given, and how rights and protections are exercised (see Chapter 10 this book). In addition, health-care decision making is influenced by demographic factors, such as level of education, other socioeconomic status (SES) factors, geographic region (urban, rural), and time spent in the United States.

Kleinman (1988) proposed obtaining a patient's or caregiver's explanatory model of illness at any stage of the disease continuum by asking a series of questions designed to elicit their understanding of the situation (p. 42):

- What do you call the problem?
- What do you think caused the problem?
- Why do you think it started when it did?
- What do you think the sickness does? How does it work? How does it affect your body?
- How severe is the sickness? Will it have a long or short course?
- What care do you desire? What are the most important results you hope to get from your care?
- What are the chief problems the sickness has caused?
- What do you fear most about the sickness?

The need to provide culturally competent care has been emphasized in many arenas, that is, to respect and maintain sensitivity to issues related to an individual's culture, race, gender, sexual orientation, and SES while providing optimal end-of-life care. In 2001, the National Association of Social Workers (NASW) developed Standards for Cultural Competence in Social Work Practice. NASW defines cultural competence as

> the process by which individuals and systems respond respectfully and effectively to people of all cultures, languages, classes, races, ethnic backgrounds, religions, and other diversity factors in a manner that recognizes, affirms, and values the worth of individuals, families, and communities and protects and preserves the dignity of each. (p. 11)

The standards address these areas: ethics and values, self-awareness, cross-cultural knowledge, cross-cultural skills, service delivery, empowerment and advocacy, diverse workforce, professional education, language diversity, and cross-cultural leadership.

ADVANCE DIRECTIVES

Advance directives are written documents completed by an individual that specify treatment preferences for health-care decision making, particularly about end-of-life care and whether to use life-sustaining treatment. They provide an avenue for individuals to make known their wishes about end-of-life treatment. The most common advance directives are the health-care proxy (durable power of attorney for health care) and living will.

The Patient Self-Determination Act has done much to increase the use and awareness of advance directives. It was signed into law in November 1990 and became effective in December 1991 (*Federal Register*, 1991). The act is applicable in all 50 states. The law requires that all facilities receiving Medicare or Medicaid reimbursements ask newly admitted patients if they have health-care directives in place, provide a written explanation of the state's law on health-care directives, and provide an explanation of the hospital's policies in enforcing them. Health-care facilities also are required to record patients' health-care directives as part of their medical records. In addition, those facilities must educate staff and the community they serve about advance directives and ensure that patients are not discriminated against, whether they have an advance directive or not. Social workers can initiate direction and leadership in implementing this education.

A durable power of attorney for health care involves the legal appointment of an individual to speak for a person should that person become decisionally incapacitated. Multiple types of durable power of attorney are available, covering business, financial, or health-care decisions. The purpose of legally appointing a person as a health-care proxy is to ensure that an individual's wishes are followed in the event she is not able to make her own decisions. The person appointed as proxy acts to ensure that health-care providers know of those wishes and can advocate for their enforcement. The person named as an individual's health-care proxy should be someone the individual trusts and someone with whom she feels comfortable in discussing her wishes. The person appointed to oversee an individual's health-care wishes could be a spouse or partner, relative, or close friend. An individual serving as a proxy should be aware of state regulations or variations regarding advance directives. In addition, that person must be aware that he or she may have to fight to assert the patient's wishes in the event of a disagreement with the health-care team or with other family members.

A living will is a directive to a physician and health-care team that states a person's wishes about what life-prolonging treatment should be provided or withheld should he or she lose the ability to communicate those wishes. Life-prolonging therapies include mechanical ventilation, blood transfusions, dialysis, antibiotics, and artificially provided nutrition and hydration. A living will should be viewed as a way to guide a physician to provide medically appropriate care in keeping with the patient's wishes.

Any adult with decision-making capacity can complete an advance directive. Directives must be completed by the individual to whom the directive applies (i.e., a relative cannot complete an advance directive for the patient even though he or she may be the health-care proxy). Advance directives can be rescinded at any time for any reason. They should be properly signed and witnessed, but a lawyer is not required to complete or rescind a valid advance directive. The patient should retain copies of the directive and also provide copies to the designated proxy and to appropriate health-care providers. Advance directives are used more frequently by White, middle to upper SES individuals than by individuals from lower SES or ethnic or racial minorities. Social workers may need to be proactive in educating disadvantaged persons about the value of advance directives and help them with end-of-life care planning. Research suggests that many ethnic or racial minority groups in the United States fear being denied beneficial treatment at the end of life more than they fear receiving excessive therapy and therefore are less likely to complete an advance directive (Crawley, Marshall, Lo, & Koenig, 2002).

Social workers should discuss advance directives with each of their patients. They can help educate patients and families on the uses and benefits of advance directives and advocate for their choices. They can help patients complete an appointment of a health-care agent and a living will; ensure that this information is recorded in the patient's medical record; encourage the patient to inform the designated proxy of his wishes; and, if requested, help the patient discuss his wishes for end-of-life care with the designated proxy. A Consumer's Tool Kit for Health Care Advance Planning is available for downloading at the American Bar Association Web site (www.americanbar .org/groups/law_aging/resources/consumer_s _toolkit_for_health_care_advance_planning .html). Advance directives for each state and information about advance care planning also are available from the National Hospice and Palliative Care's Caring Connections Web site   (www.caringinfo.org/i4a/pages/index.cfm ?pageid=1).

UNDERSTANDING LOSS

Individuals and families facing end-of-life issues experience many kinds of loss besides impending death, including multiple losses (outlined next) as the person becomes more ill and withdrawn from prior life and activities. Understanding the common, natural responses to loss can facilitate a social worker's ability to prepare patients and families with anticipatory guidance and help them normalize the possible and often uncomfortable expressions of grief.

Loss often is thought of in relation to the death of a significant loved or valued person. This can include one's self, spouse or partner, siblings, children (including through abortion, miscarriage, or stillbirth), and other relatives. However, loss also can occur through:

- Separation or divorce
- Temporary or permanent placement in a nursing home, hospital, hospice facility, adoptive or foster home, or prison
- Geographic moves due to job relocation or assignment in the military
- Death of a pet
- Death of a close friend, coworker, business associate, colleague, or acquaintance
- Deaths of well-known personalities or celebrities (e.g., President John Kennedy, Princess Diana)

For the person who is dying, the end of life also brings the loss of part of the self, which includes physical, psychological, and social losses. Physical loss is the loss of body parts (e.g., amputations) and loss of functioning (e.g., lack of mobility, impaired bladder or bowel control, reduced sexual functioning). Psychological loss is also relevant for patients at the end of life and can include the loss of independence, dignity, self-esteem or self-concept, memory or mental acuity, and opportunity, goals, hopes, and dreams. Social loss includes loss of work or income and loss of social roles (i.e., role of partner/spouse or parent).

Each loss in a person's life is experienced uniquely because it is influenced by multiple factors, that is, characteristics of the individual, the nature of the relationship with the deceased person, how the loss occurred, and influences from the past.

Controversy has surrounded the concept of "stages" of loss, in part because it implies a linear movement through a grief process. More recent thinking discounts the notion that there is a homogeneous course through which everyone moves due to grief. Grief is a natural response to loss. It is not merely sadness or crying in response to a loss.

Different conceptual frameworks exist to explain the experience of grief. Rando (1984) conceptualized grief within three broad categories: avoidance, confrontation, and reestablishment. *Avoidance* includes "shock, denial, disbelief, emotional anesthesia, confusion, numbness, disorganization, and the intellectualized acceptance of the death." *Confrontation* is a "highly emotional state wherein the grief is most intense and the psychological reactions to loss are felt most acutely." *Reestablishment* is the "gradual decline of the grief and marks the beginning of an emotional and social reentry back into the everyday world" (pp. 28–29). The tasks of the griever are then to:

- Acknowledge, accept, and understand the reality of the loss.
- Experience the pain of the grief and react to the separation from that which was lost.
- Adapt to a new way of life.
- Reinvest in a new way of life.

There may be ambivalence about the appropriateness of expressing so many emotions and resistance to revealing those emotions to others. Grievers may feel overwhelmed by the intensity of their emotions and exhausted by the process. They may avoid or repress thoughts, feelings, or memories associated with the deceased person. They may protest or feel denial about the death or have feelings of unreality or depersonalization.

Factors that influence how individuals cope with loss include childhood, adolescence, and adult experiences of loss and how recently those losses occurred; successful or unsuccessful resolution of losses; previous mental health problems (i.e., depression); and any physical health problems, life crises, or life changes prior to the current loss. The relationship with the deceased person also plays a role in coping with the loss: the relationship (partner/spouse, child, parent), length of the relationship, role the deceased person occupied, strength of the attachment, and degree of dependency.

In addition, it is important to consider how the loss occurred. The circumstances surrounding the loss, preparation for bereavement (anticipatory grief), the griever's perception of preventability, perception of the deceased person's fulfillment in life, and any unfinished business that was present in the relationship with the deceased person all play a role in the grief process. These factors make grief a very personal and individual experience.

Grief counseling involves normalizing the grieving person's feelings and behavior and helping the griever identify and express her feelings, actualize the loss, facilitate her ability to live without the deceased person and to re-engage with life, and provide continuing support throughout the process. Social workers should be alert to symptoms of complicated or troubled grief while providing counseling to help patients and families normalize their often-difficult responses to grief. Uncomplicated grief is a grief reaction that, although painful, moves the survivor closer to acceptance of the loss and enhances the ability to carry on with life. In contrast, complicated grief is a grief reaction that includes difficulty acknowledging the death, intrusive thoughts about and yearning for the deceased person, and feelings of futility and purposelessness about the future.

ANTICIPATORY MOURNING

Grieving that begins before a death occurs is known as anticipatory mourning; the physical and emotional reactions involved are often the same as those experienced in normal grieving. Rando (2000) defined *anticipatory mourning* as

> The phenomenon encompassing seven generic operations grief and mourning, coping, interaction, psychosocial reorganization, planning, balancing conflicting demands, and facilitating an appropriate death that, within a context of adaptational demands caused by the experiences of loss and trauma, is stimulated in response to the awareness of life-threatening or terminal illness in oneself or a significant other and the recognition of associated losses in the past, present, and future. (p. 51)

Involving the whole family, as defined by the patient, in his care and treatment can decrease anxiety and allow for a sense of control, participation, and support. Meeting with the entire family as a group and establishing a personal relationship with each family member (if possible) is crucial. Within their ability, social workers can help families to express their anticipatory grief appropriately and develop or maintain open communication. Equally important is advising the family about the practical realities of illness and the death. Dying patients may be very concerned about these practical matters and do not want to burden their loved ones. Social workers can help patients and families plan for future care needs as well as preferences for burial and associated financial arrangements. These advance directives help people who are at the end of life feel some control and ensure that their wishes are honored.

COMPLICATED GRIEF

It is sometimes difficult to differentiate uncomplicated from complicated grief. Worden (2008) outlined four complicated grief reactions:

1. *Chronic grief* is grief that is prolonged, is excessive in duration, and never comes to a satisfactory conclusion.

2. *Delayed grief* is emotion that has been "inhibited, suppressed, or postponed." A subsequent loss may elicit an exaggerated reaction because the bereaved is grieving for two losses.

3. *Exaggerated grief* occurs when feelings of fear, hopelessness, depression, or other symptoms become so excessive that they interfere with the daily existence of the bereaved.

4. *Masked grief* includes symptoms and behaviors experienced by a person who does not recognize the fact that these are related to a loss.

One social work task is to recognize symptoms or responses that may indicate complicated grief, including an excessive degree of guilt, remorse, self-blame, a delay of up to six months in beginning the grief process, a prolonged grief process, hostility against the deceased person's caregivers, avoidance of the loss through overactivity, avoidance of emotional expression, severe depression or insomnia, or self-destructive behaviors (Worden, 2008).

DISENFRANCHISED GRIEF

Doka (2002) defined *disenfranchised grief* as the grief experienced in connection with a loss that is not socially acknowledged, publicly shared, or supported through usual rituals. Either the significance of the loss is not recognized or the relationship between the deceased person and the bereaved survivor is not socially sanctioned—the person suffering the loss is given little or no opportunity to mourn publicly. It is experienced when the relationship is not recognized (lovers, ex-spouses, same-sex partners, close friends), when the loss itself is not recognized (stillbirth, miscarriage, abortion, adoption, pet loss), or when the griever is not recognized (very young, very old, with developmental disabilities). The manner of death itself can be disenfranchising (murder, suicide, acquired immunodeficiency syndrome). When such deaths are treated as less than significant losses, the process of grieving becomes more difficult. Social workers who become close to patients who die also can be disenfranchised mourners. Their own grief experiences should be acknowledged and dealt with. Often social workers in the same area form support groups or hold brief ceremonies to recognize all of their patients who have died in a period of time.

SOCIAL WORK IN END-OF-LIFE CARE

Reese and Raymer (2004) provided evidence that social work involvement in hospice operations correlates significantly with reduced patient care costs. Their survey about social work involvement impacting hospice outcomes included social workers and hospice directors in 66 randomly selected hospices across the United States who completed questionnaires and reviewed 330 patient charts. The survey clearly indicated consistent benefits of social work involvement in all aspects of hospice care, to the patients and families as well as to the hospice administration itself. The qualifications of the social work staff and hospice staffing and budget policies were also important variables. Better outcomes were correlated with more experienced social workers, higher social work salaries, and higher social work staffing ratios. The authors recommended that social work participation take place from intake and assessment through continuing care to prevent crises, reduce the severity of anticipated problems, promote effective pain and symptom management, provide expert psychosocial interventions, and maximize the opportunities for patients and families to maintain a good quality of life at the end of life.

The Open Society Institute's Project on Death in America (PDIA) began the Social Work Leadership Development Awards Program to identify and support outstanding social work faculty and clinicians committed to improving the care of dying and bereaved people. The program promoted innovative research and training projects that reflected collaborations between schools of social work and practice sites that would advance the ongoing development of social work practice, education, and training in the care of the dying. These awards promoted the visibility and prestige of social workers committed to end-of-life care and enhanced their effectiveness as academic leaders, role models, and mentors for future generations of social workers. Between 2000 and 2004, 42 social workers were given the award. (For a list of PDIA social workers, please visit www.soros.org/resources/articles _publications/publications/pdia_20040101 /pdia_20040101.pdf.)

The first Social Work Summit on End-of-Life and Palliative Care took place in March 2002. Social work and end-of-life care experts met for a three-day summit to design a social work agenda to improve care for the dying and their families. The agenda called for organized professional leadership, standards of practice, and increased preparation at all levels of social work education. Leaders from national social work organizations, social work schools, hospices, hospitals, government agencies, and end-of-life care advocacy groups attended the meeting, representing more than 30 organizations. The summit was cosponsored by Last Acts, the Duke Institute on Care at the End of Life, and the Soros Foundation's Project on Death in America. The second Social Work Summit on End-of-Life and Palliative Care was held in June 2005; participants to this day continue their work through various projects and through many organizations.

As an outgrowth of the Social Work Summits, the National Association of Social Workers (NASW) began an initiative in 2003 to increase social workers' awareness of end-of-life issues; to create and advocate for more education and training opportunities in the field; and to promote the value of social work in palliative care, hospice care, and other end-of-life practice areas. NASW received a grant from the Project on Death in America to develop practice standards on palliative care, end-of-life care, and grief work to provide social workers with guidance for ethical and

effective practice (NASW, 2004) and to develop both a comprehensive policy statement on and a Web-based course on the standards with pre- and posttesting to document knowledge gains. This initiative complements other NASW policy statements on client self-determination in end-of-life decisions, health care, hospice care, long-term care, and managed care.

Recent significant efforts have been initiated to provide more formal transdisciplinary palliative care education to social workers and other professionals. The most notable of these was the Advocating for Clinical Excellence (ACE) project, a five-year National Cancer Institute–funded project held at the City of Hope National Medical Center, Duarte, California, and directed by principal investigator Shirley Otis-Green and coinvestigators Betty Ferrell and Marcia Grant. The objective of the ACE project was to improve the delivery of palliative care through an intensive advocacy and leadership training program for 300 competitively selected psycho-oncology professionals (i.e., social workers, psychologists, spiritual care professionals). The program sought to address the deficits in the delivery of quality palliative care and to provide the participants with strategies to empower them to become more effective role models and advocates for enhanced palliative, end-of-life, and bereavement care in their institutions and disciplines. More information about the program is available at www.cityofhope.org/education/health -professional-education/nursing-education /ace-project/Pages/default.aspx

COMPASSION FATIGUE

Social workers and other health-care professionals who work in end-of-life care experience a great deal of trauma of illness and death. Those who work in end-of-life care can experience short- and long-term effects that can be profoundly disruptive, both professionally and personally. Social workers develop and nurture a therapeutic alliance with patients and families; in that process, they can be seriously affected as a result of listening to stories of suffering and pain. Compassion fatigue, also referred to as secondary trauma, is the natural, predictable, treatable, and preventable stress resulting from helping a traumatized or suffering person (Figley, 1994).

Some professionals may be more vulnerable than others to compassion fatigue due to, for example, multiple losses, unresolved personal trauma, or insufficient recovery time. Social workers also grieve and need support. Each social worker has her own professional style and ways of coping that may mask symptoms and interfere with coping. All social workers need effective self-care strategies and stress management techniques to treat the symptoms of compassion fatigue. Strategies to prevent or cope with compassion fatigue include supervision, personal psychotherapy, grief support for staff, stress management, and maintaining a balance between personal and professional responsibilities (Katz & Johnson, 2006).

CONCLUSION

Many issues in end-of-life care are beyond the scope of this chapter: for example, pain management in palliative care and ethical issues, such as medical futility, withholding or withdrawing medical therapy, assisted suicide, euthanasia, and terminal sedation (for more details, see Chapters 3 and 22). It is difficult for social workers and health-care professionals to use their considerable skills in situations that ultimately will not change the final outcome of a life-limiting illness. Experience tells us that as patients and families approach the end of life, social workers often feel they no longer have a role to play. They may want to withdraw from the patient and family. One of the hardest tasks is to be emotionally present during moments when further curative medical treatment is not possible. Often all patients and families need is to have a social worker be a physical and emotional witness to their suffering. Accepting the limits of what we are able to do and sitting with a patient and family who are trying to cope with the end of life can be an important and meaningful experience,

for the patient and family as well as the social worker. Cultivating the ability to be present in the moment with patients and families and be a witness to their personal struggles at the end of life is one of the most difficult but important and rewarding skills a social worker can possess. Providing psychosocial support, teaching coping and communication skills, providing information and advocacy, collaborating with colleagues, and taking a leadership role within the transdisciplinary health-care team can equip a social worker to make a significant difference in the experiences of the end of life for patients and families.

SUGGESTED LEARNING EXERCISES

Learning Exercise 23.1

Maria is a Puerto Rican woman who was diagnosed with breast cancer at age 35. During the three and a half years that she lived after diagnosis, she received a variety of services from a cancer support organization, including weekly individual supportive counseling with a social worker and group therapy. At the time of her diagnosis, Maria had been married to Joseph for 13 years. They experienced fertility problems because of her cancer treatment. Maria reported to her social worker that this was a major source of conflict in the relationship and that she did not feel emotionally supported by Joseph.

Maria began working in a bank at age 17 and by age 30 had attained a middle management position. For two years after diagnosis, she worked full time while receiving chemotherapy every three weeks, refusing to take time off for her cancer treatments. She reported significant depression, anger, and apprehension about recurrence. Within six months of diagnosis, she had begun to reexperience previous losses, most significantly the loss of her mother to breast cancer when Maria was 10 years of age. She reported consistent faith that the chemotherapy would cure her mother and hopeless betrayal by God when her mother died. Her oncology social worker suggested a referral to a psychiatrist for Maria's worsening depression, which Maria declined, saying that she did not wish to take antidepressant medication.

Ultimately, Maria agreed to a stem cell transplant and left her job after a year of disability leave. She agreed to see a psychiatrist for a one-time consultation yet continued to decline antidepressant medication. The social worker reported that she became increasingly fatigued, depressed, and agoraphobic (e.g., she stopped going out alone secondary to panic attacks). Her cancer recurred after one year and she died 18 months later.

Answer these questions based on your interpretation of Maria's case:

1. How do you think that Maria defined good quality of life?

2. What do you see as the social worker's role in providing support to clients like Maria who would help them to achieve good quality of life as well as good quality of death?

3. Arthur Kleinman (1988) offers an explanatory model of illness that fosters a sensitive approach to helping clients like Maria. How might you have used his approach to elicit information from Maria to maximize your ability to help her? Recall that Kleinman suggested using these questions:

   • What do you call the problem?
   • What do you think caused the problem?
   • Why do you think it started when it did?
   • What do you think the sickness does? How does it work? How does it affect your body?
   • How severe is the sickness? Will it have a long or short course?
   • What care do you desire? What are the most important results you hope to get from your care?
   • What are the chief problems the sickness has caused?
   • What do you fear most about the sickness?

4. What do you consider to be the most pressing medical, psychosocial, and spiritual concerns that Maria faced? How would you prioritize these concerns in devising your approach to treatment?

5. How would you go about developing a plan of care for Maria that takes into account her cultural and spiritual perspectives and emphasizes her definition of good quality of life?

SUGGESTED RESOURCES

Web Sites

Aging with Dignity (Five Wishes)—www.agingwithdignity.org

The Aging with Dignity Web site contains the Five Wishes, a document that is an advance directive addressing the dying patient's holistic needs. It has been translated into a number of languages.

American Pain Foundation—www.painfoundation.org

The APF is a nonprofit information, advocacy, and support organization serving all people affected by pain. Its mission is to improve the quality of life of those affected by pain by providing practical information, raising public awareness and understanding of pain, and advocating against barriers to effective treatment.

Association for Death Education and Counseling—www.adec.org

ADEC is dedicated to improving the quality of death education; promoting the development and interchange of related theory and research; and providing support, stimulation, and encouragement to its members and those studying and working in death-related fields.

Cancer Care, Inc.—www.cancercare.org

Cancer Care is the largest national social service agency providing free emotional support, information, and practical assistance to people with cancer, their loved ones, and caregivers. Its Web site features a special section on end-of-life and bereavement concerns and includes educational information and resources for patients, caregivers, and professionals.

Center to Advance Palliative Care—www.capc.org

CAPC is a resource to hospitals and other health-care settings interested in developing palliative care programs.

End-of-Life/Palliative Education Resource Center—www.eperc.mcw.edu

This center shares educational resource material among the community of health professional educators involved in palliative care education.

Finding Our Way: Living with Dying in America— http://webpages.scu.edu/ftp/fow/

The Finding Our Way national public education initiative focuses on bringing practical information to the American public regarding end of life and its surrounding issues.

Growth House—www.growthhouse.org

Growth House is an international gateway to resources for life-threatening illness and end-of-life care. Its primary mission is to improve the quality of end-of-life care through public education and professional collaboration.

Hospice Foundation of America—www.hospicefoundation.org

HFA provides leadership in the development and application of hospice and its philosophy of care with the goal of enhancing the U.S. health-care system and the role of hospice within it. It provides end-of-life information for patients, families, and professionals.

National Hospice and Palliative Care Organization—www.nhpco.org

This is the largest nonprofit membership organization representing hospice and palliative care programs and professionals in the United States. The organization is committed to improving end-of-life care and expanding access to hospice care with the goal of profoundly enhancing quality of life for people dying in America and their loved ones.

Social Work Network in Palliative and End-of-Life Care Listserv—www.stoppain.org/for_professionals/content/information/listserv.asp

Hosted by the Beth Israel Department of Pain and Palliative Care, this listserv provides an opportunity for social workers in such fields as oncology, geriatrics, human immunodeficiency virus (HIV), hospice, nephrology, and pediatrics to network and discuss multidimensional aspects of palliative and end-of-life care.

Suggested Books

Berzoff, J., & Silverman, P. R. (2004). *Living with dying: A handbook for end-of-life healthcare practitioners.* New York, NY: Columbia University Press.

Bowlby, J. (1980). *Attachment and loss: Loss, sadness and depression.* New York, NY: Basic Books.

Doka, K. J. (Ed.). (2006). *Pain management at the end of life: Bridging the gap between knowledge & practice.* Washington, DC: Hospice Foundation of America.

Doka, K. J., & Davidson, J. (Eds.). (1998). *Living with grief: Who we are, how we grieve.* Philadelphia, PA: Taylor & Francis.

Fadiman, A. (1997). *The spirit catches you and you fall down: A Hmong child, her American doctors, and the collision of two cultures.* New York, NY: Farrar, Straus, and Giroux.

Field, M. J., & Behrman, R. (2003). *When children die: Improving palliative and end-of-life care for children and their families.* Washington, DC: National Academies Press.

Hilden, J. M., Tobin, D. R., & Lindsey, K. (2002). *Shelter from the storm: Caring for a child with a life-threatening condition.* Philadelphia, PA: Perseus.

Rando, T. A. (1991). *How to go on living when someone you love dies.* New York, NY: Bantam Books.

REFERENCES

Byock, I. (1998). *Dying well: Peace and possibilities at the end of life.* New York, NY: Riverhead Books.

Crawley, L. M., Marshall, P. A., Lo, B., & Koenig, B. A. (2002). Strategies for culturally effective end-of-life care. *Annals of Internal Medicine, 136*(9), 673–679.

Doka, K. J. (2002). *Disenfranchised grief: New directions, challenges, and strategies for practice.* Champaign, IL: Research Press.

Federal Register. (1991). Federal patient self-determination act 1990. Retrieved from http://euthanasia.procon.org /sourcefiles/patient_selfdetermination_act.pdf

Field, M. J., & Cassel, C. K. (1997). *Approaching Death: Improving Care at the End of Life.* Washington, D.C.: National Academy Press.

Figley, C. (1994). Compassion fatigue: Coping with secondary traumatic stress disorder in those who treat the traumatized. New York, NY: Brunner/Mazel.

Katz, R. S., & Johnson, T. A. (2006). When professionals weep: Emotional and countertransference responses in end-of-life care. New York, NY: Routledge.

Kleinman, A. (1988). The illness narratives: Suffering, healing and the human condition. New York, NY: Basic Books.

Last Acts Coalition. (2001). *Statement on diversity and end-of-life care.* Washington, DC: Author.

Mauritzen, J. (1988). Pastoral care for the dying and bereaved. *Death Studies, 12*(2), 111–122.

Merriam-Webster. (2004). *The Merriam-Webster English dictionary.* Springfield, MA: Author.

National Association of Social Workers. (2001). Standards for cultural competence in social work practice. Retrieved from www.socialworkers.org/practice /standards/NASWCulturalStandards.pdf

National Association of Social Workers. (2004). Standards for social work practice in palliative and end-of-life care. Retrieved from www.socialworkers.org/practice /bereavement/standards/default.asp

National Center for Health Statistics. (2010). Deaths: Final data for 2007. *National Vital Statistics Reports, 58*(19). Retrieved from www.cdc.gov/NCHS/data/nvsr /nvsr58/nvsr58_19.pdf

National Hospice and Palliative Care Organization. (2010). *What is hospice and palliative care?* Retrieved from www.nhpco.org/i4a/pages/index.cfm?pageid4648

Project on Death in America. (2001). *Report of activities: January 1998–December 2000.* New York, NY: Open Society Institute.

Rando, T. A. (1984). *Grief, dying, and death: Clinical interventions for caregivers.* Champaign, IL: Research Press.

Rando, T. A. (Ed.). (2000). *Clinical dimensions of anticipatory mourning.* Champaign, IL: Research Press.

Reese, D. J., & Raymer, M. (2004). Relationship between social work involvement and hospice outcomes: Results of the national hospice social work survey. *Social Work, 49*(3), 415–422.

Saunders, C. (1999). Origins: International perspectives, then and now. *Hospice Journal, 14*(3/4), 1–7.

Silverman, P. R. (1999). *Never too young to know: Death in children's lives.* New York, NY: Oxford University Press.

Smedley, B. D., Stith, A. Y., & Nelson, A. R. (Eds.). (2002). *Unequal treatment: Confronting racial and ethnic disparities in health care.* Washington, DC: Institute of Medicine.

van Ryn, M., & Burke, J. (2000). The effect of patient race and socio-economic status on physicians' perceptions of patients. *Social Science and Medicine, 50*(6), 813–828.

Worden, J. W. (2008). *Grief counseling and grief therapy: A handbook for the mental health practitioner* (4th ed.). New York, NY: Springer.

World Health Organization. (1990). *Cancer pain relief and palliative care: Report of a WHO expert committee* (WHO Technical Report Series, No 804). Geneva, Switzerland: Author.

World Health Organization. (2004). *The solid facts: Palliative care.* Geneva, Switzerland: Author.

Afterword

CANDYCE S. BERGER

Much has been written about the changes affecting the health-care arena. We are living in times that have been described as chaotic, tumultuous, and unstable (Berger, Robbins, Lewis, Mizrahi, & Fleit, 2003; Dombovy, 2002; Fairfield, Hunter, Mechanic, & Flemming, 1997; Ross, 1993). Many factors have contributed to this situation. The growing emphasis on fiscal restraint in health care, the technological explosion, ethical challenges, spiritual concerns, and consumer expectations all have had a significant effect on health-care service delivery. Although social work practice has been influenced by these changes, there is no evidence that we are being differentially impacted, experiencing a greater proportion of the negative consequences, such as downsizing and decentralization (Berger et al., 2003). Chapter 1 traces the 100-year history of social work involvement in health, and Chapter 2 explores the factors that have shaped the evolving roles of social workers. These chapters provide a context in which we can examine the environment for health social work today. We struggle more than ever with the challenge of defining social work roles in a health-care environment that responds to fiscal priorities, demands by payers for accountability, and consumerism. Today many health social work programs are harnessing their creativity and skills to expand social work roles and secure social work's position both in the present and for the future (Mizrahi & Berger, 2005).

Much of our unease is in response to a health-care system that is facing runaway costs without commensurate improvement in health outcomes. The United States has ranked poorly in international comparisons for all measures of health outcomes in spite of our constant ranking of number one for health-care costs. Health care currently consumes almost 16% of the U.S. gross domestic product, while health care in other industrialized countries accounts for 9% to 10% of their GDP. To explain this difference, some may argue that the tax burden of countries with universal health care, such as Sweden, Norway, and Denmark, accounts for their lower spending on health care. However, these countries consistently rank high in positive health outcomes while reporting the percentage of their GDP associated with health as ranging between 8% and 9% (http://csis.org). In addition, 50 million Americans are without health insurance, and many more struggle with intermittent or poor health-care coverage. The recession of 2009–2010 exacerbated this problem as many individuals fell into the ranks of the unemployed and lost their employer-based health coverage. According to the Centers for Disease Control and Prevention (CDC), 58.5 million Americans were uninsured at some point during 2009, and 38.5 million had been uninsured for more than one year prior to that date. The CDC estimated that about 25 million Americans are underinsured and find it difficult to afford the out-of-pocket medical expenses created by the gap in what their insurance will cover. Chapter 5 critically examines the financial, regulatory, and governance issues that shape health-care policy and the delivery of health-care services. Without radical changes to the nation's health-care policy and systems of care, we will continue to see health-care systems struggle to maintain fiscal viability through a variety of cost-containment strategies, including hospital closures, mergers, restructuring, and resizing initiatives and the push to community-based practice. All of these strategies will influence the staffing ratios in medical centers, service delivery, and social work roles (Berger et al., 2003; Globerman, Davies, & Walsh, 1996; Ross, 1993). Consequently, social workers in health care will continue to rely on clinical practice skills, but they also will need to expand their practice repertoires to incorporate community-based clinical interventions, macro-level practice skills that are essential to autonomous practice, and research techniques that enable them to use data to support their practices. A primary function of social workers will be to assist clients to overcome the barriers that inhibit access to high-quality health care services (Burg et al., 2010). Skills in advocacy will become even more critical to challenge policies and regulations that are driven by fiscal priorities that can compromise the quality of patient care.

MOVE TO THE COMMUNITY

While these changes promote feelings of fear and insecurity, new opportunities have been and will continue to emerge for social work. In the 20th century, acute care dominated health-care practice, moving the hospital to the central position within the health-care system. As we look to the 21st century, our emphasis is shifting to a new priority—the management of chronicity. This will promote expansion of community-based systems of care, where prevention strategies will assume a higher level of importance. Many scholars in the field of health social work believe, as in the past, that the future of the profession lies in our ability to work within the community, developing successful linkages across systems of care (Berkman, 1996; Davidson, 1990; Rehr, Rosenberg, & Blumenfield, 1998).

This book traces the changing roles for health-care social workers, balancing acute care with the movement to community-based models of practice. This shift to the community will require a greater understanding of interventions aimed at health promotion and disease prevention (Berkman, 1996; Davidson, 1990) with a greater awareness of the critical role of individual, family, and community behavior in shaping health status. Chapter 7 provides the theoretical foundations needed to understand health behavior so that effective, community-based strategies can be designed and implemented. Chapters devoted to community-based practice and public health augment this learning by examining the spectrum of issues shaping social work practice at the community level. These chapters are rich with theory, skills, and practical applications that will promote the development and expansion of social work community-based practice.

EXPANDED CLINICAL BASE

As we move from managing acute episodes of care to the management of chronicity, our focus will shift to the identification of at-risk populations whose health status is compromised by poor health behaviors, environmental challenges, and genetic predispositions. Systems of care for older individuals will be of paramount importance (Berkman, Gardner, Zodikoff, & Harootyan, 2006; Oliver & DeCoster, 2006). Another significant population at risk that will require more attention by health-care professionals is the growing number of immigrants who are entering our country through both legal and clandestine means. As the United States moves to tighten access along its borders, immigrants are being forced to turn to illegal means of gaining entry, often referred to as smuggling or trafficking. Victims of human trafficking face a variety of health risks associated with their pretrafficking condition (e.g., preexisting health condition associated with violence, poor access to health care, etc.), health risks associated with their journey (e.g., poor and dangerous traveling conditions, physical and sexual violence), and risks associated with their arrival in the United States (e.g., exploitation, poor working conditions, exposure to unfamiliar infectious diseases). Health-care providers, particularly at acute care access points, are likely to be immigrants' first point of contact. Effectively caring for this population will require assessment and intervention skills that take into account the dynamics of smuggling and trafficking as well as promote cultural sensitivity, an awareness of alternative methods of health care indigenous to the client's country of origin, and resources to assist clients who may be fleeing exploitation (Berger, 2010; Gushulak & MacPherson, 2000; Lusk & Lucas, 2009; Zimmerman, Hossain et al., 2006). The importance of taking patients' culture into account is reviewed in each chapter of this book and is examined in detail in Chapter 10.

Effective and efficient clinical interventions at the acute level will continue to be a priority for social work practitioners, but they will need to incorporate expanded clinical skills in such areas as brief assessments, short-term treatment, population-oriented care, case management, health promotion, and disease prevention. This expertise requires increased understanding of theories of health behavior and the influence of risk factors, such as socioeconomic status, the environment, mental health, substance abuse, ethnicity, culture, spirituality, family systems, and sexuality, all of which are effectively addressed in this book. Social work practice will be shaped by a growing emphasis on managing larger numbers of patients as their roles span the continuum of health care. This will call for social work practitioners who draw from a large repertoire of knowledge and skills and are able to broadly traverse larger systems devoted to service delivery. Parts II and III capture many of these issues, demonstrating the critical impact of biopsychosocial factors on health behavior and health outcomes. What kind of practitioner will be needed to face the challenges ahead?

There is little debate about the need for clinical skills in the future, but debate still rages as to the most effective approach: generalist versus specialist. A generalist approach utilizes fundamental skills of social work that are transferable across settings and populations served. Generalist approaches may be more effective with community-based models of care or in acute, general medical, surgical, or pediatric settings, where a broader understanding of illnesses, psychosocial implications of illness, and systems of care may be required. A generalist approach is particularly relevant to community-based practice, where a variety of skill sets are needed to effectively navigate a complex system of providers, payers, and clients (Ross, 1993). This does not mean that specialists will not also be needed.

Specialist models emerged in large, specialty hospitals where social workers were recognized and advanced professionally based on their expertise in a defined area of practice (e.g., disease or population expertise). To be successful, social workers needed to understand the details of specific diagnoses and their biopsychosocial ramifications for patients and families; they needed specific knowledge regarding the populations most likely to be affected and the resources and systems of care to be mobilized to address issues and problems related to the illness (Ross, 1993).

An interview with recognized health-care leaders ("How Are Hospitals Financing the Future?," 2004) discusses the importance of health-care systems delineating and promoting their unique competencies—they need to carve out their market niche. It was suggested that health-care systems should identify three to four service lines (e.g., cancer, cardiology, trauma) that will be priorities (i.e., Centers of Excellence) for the health-care system rather than equally distributing limited resources across all services. For social workers to be members of the health-care teams in these specialty centers, they will require specialized knowledge and skills to effectively and efficiently provide psychosocial services so that they can become an essential member of the team. Specialty content often is handled individually through scholarly articles or books that address a specific disease or population. Although a comprehensive analysis of all potential areas of specialization is not realistic within an overview book, the authors have done an outstanding job weaving in specialty content on key areas where a social worker is likely to be involved (see Part III).

AUTONOMOUS PRACTITIONER

As social workers broaden their knowledge and skills, they will need to be as adept at macro-level interventions as they are at clinical practice (Berger & Ai, 2000). Many health-care systems are moving away from silo organizational structures (i.e., centralized departments) to programmatic structures. Social workers may find themselves practicing in more autonomous, multidisciplinary settings where the leader may not be a social worker. Furthermore, as more seamless, comprehensive systems of care emerge, practitioners will need to rely on skills that span both micro and macro practice in order to navigate system complexity effectively.

These changes will require social workers to have greater knowledge of fiscal arrangements and processes and increased ability to assess organizational environments, as addressed in Part I. This knowledge needs to be combined with increased skills in decision making, conflict management, planning, community organizing, marketing, and program management. Political acumen will be essential to survival in an environment that is politically volatile due to constant change and limited access to health-care resources (e.g., money, staff, technology).

EMBRACING RESEARCH AS A PRACTICE NECESSITY

As health care expands over the continuum of care, practitioners will need to draw on skills in research techniques (Zlotnik & Galambos, 2004). Four factors shape the need to embrace research as an essential element of practice. First, population interventions are dependent on population-based research: epidemiology

(Berger & Ai, 2000; Berkman, 1996). This type of research will be essential to identifying populations at risk and to understanding the health-care needs of diverse populations by maintaining a cross-cultural perspective in all research endeavors. Second, the ability to assess and intervene effectively in health-care organizations and community systems will be dependent on accurate and timely data. Third, social work practitioners and educators in health cannot continue to ignore the mandates for evidence-based practice. Many of the health disciplines have already embraced this philosophy, and social work will need to move quickly in this direction to maintain or expand its role. Social work historically has relied on documenting the process of its interventions rather than the outcome. Social work will not survive as a provider unless it can harness available empirical information to design and support practice models and teach students the skills of evidence-based decision making. Doing this will require the introduction of reliable and valid tools to do assessments and to measure outcomes (Berger & Ai, 2000; Berkman, 1996). Finally, empirical research is an essential ingredient to effective advocacy. Although no single chapter in this book is devoted to research approaches, this content is woven throughout the book, emphasizing its importance in relation to specific settings, illnesses, and populations.

ROLE OF ADVOCACY

Advocacy is another theme that permeates throughout this book, acknowledging its importance as a priority for social workers in health care. Social workers must act to effect changes in policies and regulations as fiscal priorities threaten to compromise quality of care. We must embrace social work values, priorities, and ethics, recognizing when fiscal priorities compromise these professional tenets of practice. As health-care professionals, we must join forces with those most affected by the changes—patients and families—and develop coalitions with other health-care disciplines and advocacy groups to mobilize changes in health-related policies.

In conclusion, health care can be described as a tumultuous and often chaotic setting where change is the constant. Preparing social workers for this new environment borrows from the old as well as the new. To be successful in the future of health care, our practice must be grounded in theory and data. We need to be strategic, placing increased emphasis on documenting the results of our interventions. We need to free our creative energy to critically examine what we do and design and implement innovative strategies that span the continuum of health care. We need to be willing and able to take calculated risks, venturing into new arenas of care and incorporating new roles. According to Cowles and Lefcowitz (1995), "If we don't actively work to create the future, then we leave the future solely to chance" (p. 14). We must build a reputation as creative and innovative practitioners and assume responsibility for shaping our professional destiny as health-care practitioners.

The authors of this *Handbook* have put together an excellent resource to prepare social workers for the contemporary and future challenges of social work practice in health care. We need to be aware of our history, drawing strength from our longevity as practitioners in health care. Our historical emphasis on community-based interventions combined with our strengths perspective and sensitivity to cultural competency positions us to succeed in this changing health-care environment. We draw on a strong base of values and ethics that will support our professional goals and directions as we face new challenges and ethical dilemmas.

REFERENCES

Berger, C. S. (2010). Modern day slavery: Human trafficking and health. In W. J. Spitzer (Ed.), *Immigration: Issues in health care social work policy and practice* (7–12). Petersburg, VA: Dietz Press.

Berger, C. S., & Ai, A. (2000). Managed care and its implications for social work curricula reform: Policy and research initiatives. *Social Work in Health Care, 31*(3), 59–82.

Berger, C. S., Robbins, C., Lewis, M., Mizrahi, T., & Fleit, S. (2003). The impact of organizational change on social work staffing in a hospital study: A national, longitudinal study of social work in hospitals. *Social Work in Health Care, 37*(1), 1–18.

Berkman, B. (1996). The emerging health care world: Implication for social work practice and education. *Social Work, 41,* 541–551.

Berkman, B., Gardner, D., Zodikoff, B., & Harootyan, L. (2006). Social work and aging in the Emerging health care world. *Journal of Gerontological Social Work, 48*(1/2), 203–217.

Burg, M. A., Zebrack, B., Walsh, K., Maramaldi, P., Lin, J.-W., Smolinski, K. M., & Lawson, K. (2010). Barriers to accessing quality health care for cancer patients: A survey of members of the Association of Oncology Social Work. *Social Work in Health Care, 49*(1), 38–52.

Cowles, L. A., & Lefcowitz, M. J. (1995). Interdisciplinary expectation of the medical social worker in the hospital setting: Pt. 2. *Health & Social Work, 20*(4), 279–286.

Davidson, K. (1990). Role blurring and the hospital social worker's search for a clear domain. *Health and Social Work, 15*(3), 228–234.

Dombovy, M. L. (2002). U.S. health care in conflict: Pt. 1. The challenges of balancing cost, quality and access. *Physician Executive, 28*(4). Retrieved from InfoTrac.

Fairfield, G., Hunter, D. J., Mechanic, D., & Flemming, R. (1997). Implication of managed care for health systems, clinicians, and patients. *British Medical Journal, 314,* 1895.

Globerman, J., Davies, J. M., & Walsh, S. (1996). Social work in restructuring hospitals: Meeting the challenge. *Health and Social Work, 21*(3). Retrieved from InfoTrac.

Gushulak, B. D., & MacPherson, D. W. (2000). Health issues associated with smuggling and trafficking of migrants. *Journal of Immigrant Health, 2*(2), 67–78.

Health Insurance Coverage: Early Release of Estimates from the National Health Interview Survey, 2009. Retrieved from www.cdc.gov/nchs/data/nhis/earlyrelease/insur201006.htm

How are hospitals financing the future? Where the industry will go from here (Report 6: Executive summary). (2004). *Healthcare Financial Management, 58*(9). Retrieved from InfoTrac.

Lusk, M., & Lucas, F. (2009). The challenge of human trafficking and contemporary slavery. *Journal of Comparative Social Welfare, 25*(1), 49–57.

Mizrahi, T., & Berger, C. (2005). A longitudinal look at social work leadership in hospitals: The impact of a changing healthcare system on styles and strategies over time. *Health and Social Work, 30*(2), 155–165.

Oliver, D. P., & DeCoster, V. A. (2006). Health care needs of aging adults: Unprecedented opportunities for social work. *Health & Social Work, 31*(4), 243–245.

Rehr, H., Rosenberg, G., & Blumenfield, S. (1998). *Creative social work in health.* New York, NY: Springer.

Ross, J. W. (1993). Redefining hospital social work: An embattled professional domain [Editorial]. *Health and Social Work, 18*(4). Retrieved from InfoTrac.

Zimmerman, C., Hossain, M., Yun, K., Roche, B., Morison, L., & Watts, C. (2006). *Stolen smiles: A summary report on the physical and psychological health consequences of women and adolescents trafficked in Europe.* London, UK: London School of Hygiene & Tropical Medicine. Retrieved www.humantrafficking .org/uploads/publications/Stolen_Smiles_July_2006.pdf

Zlotnik, J. L., & Galambos, C. (2004). Evidence-based practices in health care: Social work possibilities. *Health & Social Work, 29*(4), 259–261.

About the Editors

Sarah Gehlert, PhD, is the E. Desmond Lee Professor in the George Warren Brown School of Social Work at Washington University, where she serves on the Faculty Advisory Council of the Institute for Public Health and the Executive Committee of the Institute of Clinical and Translational Sciences. Dr. Gehlert is the core leader of the Education and Training Core of the NCI-funded Program for the Elimination of Cancer Disparities at Washington University, and co-principal investigator of the NCI-funded Transdisciplinary Research in Energetics and Cancer Center. Dr. Gehlert directed the University of Chicago's Maternal and Child Health Training Program from 1992 to 1998 and was principal investigator on a NIMH-funded community-based study of rural and urban women's health and mental health from 1997 to 2001. She was the principal investigator and director of the University of Chicago's NIH-funded Center for Interdisciplinary Health Disparities Research and project leader of one of its four interdependent research projects from 2003 to 2010. She is a member of the Board of Scientific Counselors of the National Human Genome Research Institute at the National Institutes of Health. Dr. Gehlert is past president of the Society of Social Work and Research. She is a consulting editor of *Social Work Research* and is on the editorial boards of *Research on Social Work Practice, Health & Social Work,* and *Social Service Research.* In 2010, Dr. Gehlert was named a fellow of the American Academy of Social Work and Social Welfare. Dr. Gehlert worked for eight years as a health social worker.

Teri Browne, PhD, is the Health Social Work Services Research Assistant Professor at the University of South Carolina College of Social Work. Dr. Browne is a member of the National Institute of Diabetes and Digestive and Kidney Diseases' Dialysis Center Working Group of the National Institutes of Health, the National Kidney Foundation of South Carolina Medical Advisory Board, and the Southeastern Kidney Council Medical Review Board. She is the past national chairperson of the Executive Committee of the Council of Nephrology Social Workers of the National Kidney Foundation. Dr. Browne serves on the editorial boards for the *American Society of Nephrology Kidney News, Chronic Kidney Disease Update, American Society of Nephrology Kidney News,* and *Journal of Nephrology Social Work.* She is also a reviewer for several journals including *Social Work in Health Care, American Journal of Kidney Diseases,* and *American Journal of Public Health.* From 1998 to 2008, Dr. Browne was a nephrology social worker, working with hemodialysis patients and their families regarding assessment, counseling, crisis intervention, and case management.

Author Index